FIELDING'S THE WORLD'S MOST DANGEROUS PLACES®

Third Edition

Robert Young Pelton
with Coskun Aral & Wink Dulles

Fielding Worldwide, Inc.
308 South Catalina Avenue
Redondo Beach, California 90277 U.S.A.

Fielding's The World's Most Dangerous Places™
Published by Fielding Worldwide, Inc.
Text Copyright ©1998 Robert Young Pelton
Icons & Illustrations Copyright ©1998 FWI
Photo Copyrights ©1998 to Individual Photographers

FIELDING WORLDWIDE INC.

PUBLISHER AND CEO	Robert Young Pelton
GENERAL MANAGER	John Guillebeaux
OPERATIONS DIRECTOR	George Posanke
ELECTRONIC PUBLISHING DIRECTOR	Larry E. Hart
PUBLIC RELATIONS DIRECTOR	Beverly Riess
ACCOUNT SERVICES MANAGER	Cindy Henrichon
PROJECT MANAGER	Chris Snyder
MANAGING EDITOR	Amanda K. Knoles

CONTRIBUTING EDITORS

Jay Berman   O. Sam Mitani

COVER DESIGNED BY	Digital Artists, Inc.
COVER PHOTOGRAPHERS	Klaus Schönwiese
INSIDE PHOTOS	Robert Young Pelton, Coskun Aral, Jim Hooper, Anthony Morland, Roddy Scott, Peter J. Willems

BLACKSTAR: Sebastian Bolesch, Francois Charton, Charles Crowell, Caren Firouz, Cindy Karp, Erica Lanser, Vera Lentz, Malcolm Linton, Paul Miller, Debbi Morello, Christopher Morris, Rob Nelson, Rogerio Reis, Klaus Reisinger, Joseph Rodriguez, Robert Semeniuk, Joao Silva, Jay Ullal, Munesuke Yamamoto

NATIONAL GEOGRAPHIC: Rebecca Abrams, James P. Blair, Bruce Dale, James Stanfield

SIPA PRESS: Philippe Fabry, Albert Facelly, Patrick Frilet, Andy Hernandez, Armineh Johannes, Barbier A Kachgar, Francois Lehr, Richard Manin, John Mantel, Marc Simon, Bob Strong, Sergio Zalis

OTHER: Werner Funk, Franck Jolot

Inquiries should be addressed to: Fielding Worldwide, Inc., 308 South Catalina Ave., Redondo Beach, California 90277 U.S.A., Telephone *(310) 372-4474*, Facsimile *(310) 376-8064*, 8:30 a.m.–5:30 p.m. Pacific Standard Time.
Web site: http://www.fieldingtravel.com
e-mail: fielding@fieldingtravel.com

ISBN 1-56952-140-9

Printed in the United States of America

To Our Readers

Fielding's The World's Most Dangerous Places, or *DP*, has become Fielding's fastest-selling travel guide and the rallying point for a new type of traveler. A traveler who is a lot like the authors: curious, intelligent and skeptical of the sound-bite view of the world's least traveled places—people who trust other travel guides as much as we trust infomercials. The press (ever slow to discover trends that aren't pre-packaged as video press releases) has finally stumbled across *DP* and our readers. The media hype has begun. Of course most of our critics don't take the time to read the book, so we have been accused of being tour packagers to war zones, a handbook for adrenaline junkies and even the precursor of bus tours to hell. You, gentle reader, will determine the merits of *DP* on your own and like most of our readers will form your own opinion.

Many people ask how we do the things we do. The answer is simple. We just do it. We may not always be successful in our quest, but we always have a good time. The beat goes on, things change and the world turns, so drop us a letter if you have any comments or tips.

This edition marks the first time we have trimmed out some material, not because the world is less dangerous, but this book has grown to a size that may require a crane to simply lift it. Despite our frugality, the world is getting more complicated and dangerous each year. You'll also find new stories, rewritten chapters, new resources and a whole heap of web sites, unique contacts and phone numbers if you need to get the latest information after press time.

So to those oil workers in Algeria, mercenaries in Kinshasha, U.N. peacekeepers in Rwanda, reporters in Cambodia, horse wallahs in Kashmir, movie producers in Hollywood and journos in New York, keep wearing those Mr. DP shirts proudly, push those limits and keep your letters coming.

No walls, no barriers, no bull.

RYP

The Author

Robert Young Pelton

Pelton, 42, has led an adventurous life. His interest in adventure began at age ten when he became the youngest student ever to attend a Canadian survival school in Selkirk, Manitoba. The school was later closed down after the deaths of a number of students. Pelton went on to become a lumberjack, boundary cutter, tunneler, driller and blaster's assistant in addition to his more lucrative occupations as a business strategist and marketing expert. On his time off, his quest for knowledge and understanding have taken him through the remote and exotic areas of more than 60 countries.

Some of Pelton's adventures include breaking American citizens out of jail in Colombia, living with the Dogon people in the Sahel, thundering down forbidden rivers in leaky native canoes, plowing through East African swamps with the U.S. Camel Trophy team, hitchhiking through war-torn Central America, setting up the world's first video interview of the never before photographed *taliban* leaders in Afghanistan and completing the first circumnavigation of the island of Borneo by land as well as numerous visits to and through war zones. It is not surprising that his friends include shepherds, warlords, pengalus, mercenaries, nomads, terrorists, field researchers, sultans, missionaries, headhunters, smugglers and other colorful people.

Stories about Pelton or his adventures have been featured in publications as diverse as *Outside, Shift, Soldier of Fortune, Star, The New York Times, Los Angeles Times, Class, El Pais, The Sunday London Times, Der Stern, Die Welt, Washington Post, Outpost,* and hundreds of other newspapers around the world. He has also been featured and interviewed on a variety of networks including the BBC, NBC, CBS, ABC, ATV, Fox, RTL, CTV, CBC, and is a regular guest on CNN.

Not much slows Pelton down; he has survived car accidents, muggings, illness, attacks by the PKK, African killer bees and even a plane crash in the central highlands of Kalimantan. He attributes his numerous arrests and detainments to his hosts' need to get to know him better. Despite these minor setbacks, Pelton still faces each dangerous encounter with a sense of humor and an irreverent wit.

What makes Pelton's travels unusual is that they are his vacation. He wrote *DP* because he couldn't find an author who would.Unfortunately since he now devotes his time to writing and updating *DP*, he is fond of cursing and yelling "It's not an adventure, it's a job!" He doesn't quite know what he will do for his holidays now.

Pelton's approach to adventure can be quite humorous. Whether it's challenging former Iban headhunters to a chug-a-lug contest, calling the *taliban* a bunch of women to their face, loading expedition members' packs with rocks, indulging in a little target practice with Kurdish warlords in Turkey or filling up a hotel pool with stewardesses, waiters and furniture in Burundi during an all-night party, he brings a certain element of fun and excitement to dangerous places. As we go to press Pelton is off on a DP tour of duty in Algeria, Egypt, Pakistan, Afghanistan, Tajikistan, Kazakhstan, Myanmar and Papua New Guinea, winding up with a visit to the rebels on Bougainville. He freely admits that he will also visit England, Germany, Australia, New Zealand, Singapore, The Solomons and Tahiti; "just so I don't lose my perspective, or my tan."

Pelton is a Fellow of the Royal Geographical Society in London and author of *Fielding's Borneo,* and *The Indiana Jones Adventure and Survival Guide* for Fielding Worldwide. He lives in Los Angeles California.

The Co-Authors

Coskun Aral

Coskun Aral, 41, was thrust into the spotlight as a young photojournalist when he was caught aboard a Turkish 727 hijacked by terrorists in 1980. He risked his life to cover the hijacking from the inside. He survived the deadly shootout and his career was launched. Since then, Aral has made a living covering dangerous and forbidden places. His accomplishments range from being one of the few people who have photographed Mecca to being on first-name terms with a number of the major warlords. Aral has seen and done many things but has never lost his love for humanity.

His special relationships with some of the world's most dangerous people make him uniquely suited to contribute to this book. As a photojournalist, he has covered wars on the front lines in Afghanistan, Azerbaijan, Bosnia, Cambodia, Chad, Iran, Iraq, Kuwait, Liberia, Libya, the Philippines, Nicaragua, Northern Ireland, Panama, Romania, Sri Lanka, Bosnia and many other areas. He is also the only ten-time participant of the Camel Trophy and has participated in a number of scientific and endurance expeditions.

Aral was the only reporter in the world to interview the hijacker of the TWA plane in Beirut airport in 1985, and he spent more than 10 years covering the war in Lebanon. He covered the Gulf War from downtown Baghdad and has two *TIME* covers to his credit, as well as numerous magazine features. His adventures for *DP* as well as other topics are currently featured in his hour-long show, *Haberci* ("The Reporters,") on ATV in Turkey. He lives in Istanbul, Turkey.

Wink Dulles

Dulles covers the Far East for *DP* and for other Fielding books. He has spent hard time in Cambodia, Thailand and Vietnam, traveling by motorcycle. Dulles covered the elections in Cambodia and the subsequent breakdown of order in that besieged country, being in-country at a time when few foreigners dared. After the first edition of *DP* was published in 1995, he was "invited" back to Cambodia by the government to attend a personal tongue-lashing for his contribution to *DP*. Wink's other notable talents are being mistaken for Mel Gibson and playing a mean guitar. He even arranged the extraction of ABC journalist Ted Koppel from Cambodia. Articles on Wink's adventures have been published in *Newsday, National Geographic Traveler* and *Escape* magazines. In February 1996, Dulles guided the first American motorcycle tour of Vietnam and is still trying to ambush Khun Sa in Yangon for a foursome on the golf course. Dulles is the author of *Fielding's Vietnam, Fielding's Southern Vietnam on Two Wheels* and *Fielding's Thailand, Cambodia, Laos & Myanmar*. He lives in Bangkok, Thailand.

DP Contributors

The contributors to *DP* are in every way as, or more important, than the authors or co-authors. Despite the high profile publications on their resumes, our small band of brothers (we're always open to sisters) choose to travel to the world's most dangerous places on their own volition and then justify their foolhardiness by writing down their stories or selling their photos. Unlike big time news grunts who fly in on chartered planes complete with sat-tel links and expense accounts, *DP* contributors are a unique breed; real people doing real things in very real places.

Sedat Aral

Aral (coauthor Coskun's younger brother) has been a "hot spot" photojournalist for more than 12 years. He has covered Afghanistan, Azerbaijan, Bosnia, Chechnya, Georgia, Iran, Iraq, Lebanon, Malaysia, the Philippines and Syria, as well as news stories in his native Turkey. He has worked internationally for news agencies including Reuters and Sipa Press and works on assignment for *TIME*. Currently he is a special assignment reporter for the Sabah Media Group in Turkey. He can no longer enter Iran by official routes, having been deported twice for taking photographs. He has had his life threatened in Tunceli for photographing burnt Kurdish villages in the region closed to the press, and has been seriously beaten by police after photographing armed attacks on unarmed protesters. Aral lives in London, England.

Martin Gilmour

Gilmour was born in Scotland and served in the Royal Ordnance Corps of the British Army. A member of the French Foreign Legion for six years, he divided his time as a parachutist, sniper instructor, combat diver, and infantry corporal among other duties. He was also team leader for an International Rescue Committee in Rwanda. Gilmour is now a resident of New Zealand

Jim Hooper

Hooper is a freelance journalist based in the U.K. Wounded twice in Africa (obviously before he had a chance to read *DP*) Hooper is known for showing up where few other people dare. He is the coauthor of *Flashpoint! At the Frontline of Today's Wars* (with Ken Guest) and *Beneath the Visiting Moon*, a documentary account of his six months with a counterinsurgency unit in Namibia. During the war in Angola, Hooper accompanied UNITA forces on guerrilla operations against Soviet and Cuban-backed government forces. He also spent considerable time with the contract soldiers of Executive Outcomes in Sierra Leone. He has covered conflicts in Bosnia, Chad, Sudan, South Africa and Uganda. His meticulously detailed articles and way-too-close-for-comfort photos have appeared in a wide range of publications including *Jane's Intelligence Review*, *The Economist* and *The Sunday Telegraph* of London. Hooper lives in Hampshire, England.

Jack Kramer

Kramer has been sent to the world's most dangerous places on assignment for *TIME*, *Business Week* and *PBS*. He began his career by covering the civil rights movement in the Deep South during the mid-60s. In the late '60s, he went from covering the battles at home to experiencing and reporting on some of the bloodiest fighting of the Vietnam War, from Cam Lo to Khe Sanh. Later, his beat was the turbulent Middle East, including the Six-Day War, Sudan and Eritrea. He worked as a television producer for PBS on "Behind the Lines" and was *Business Week's* Cairo bureau chief, covering Saudi Arabia, the Gulf States and Iran. He covered Iran before, during and after the revolution and then restarted the defunct *Beirut Daily Star* in 1984. Kramer has covered Kenya, Rhodesia (Zimbabwe), Tanzania, Laos, Thailand, Tunisia, Turkey, Syria, South Africa and the Somalia crisis. He has traveled with the Innuit in northern Canada and with the Polisario guerrillas in Morocco. He is author of *Our French Connection in Africa*, a major investigative report published in *Foreign Policy*, and *Travels with the Celestial Dog*, a historical analysis of the 1960s. He lives in Washington, D.C., with his wife and their two children.

Rob Krott

Krott, 34 is a former officer and paratrooper who attended Harvard (anthropology). His military career has earned him various awards and decorations from ten foreign governments. Besides his anthropology pursuits (with Richard Leakey's Koobi Fora Project) he finds time to organize parachute jumps for ex-special forces and paratroopers around the world and cover conflicts as a correspondent. He is a rare blend of intellectual, soldier and adventurer. He has been on the ground in El Salvador, Guatemala, Sudan, Uganda, Somalia, Bosnia, Myanmar, Cambodia and Angola and continues to work in, or travel on assignment to, the world's most dangerous places. He has served with three foreign armies and lived with a number of rebel groups including the SPLA in Sudan, and the KNLA in Myanmar. He continues to spend a considerable amount of time in Asia, Africa, The Balkans and Latin America. He is a columnist for *Behind the Lines: The Journal of Military Special Operations* and is a senior foreign correspondent for *Soldier of Fortune*. He has been published in *Harpers, Explorers Journal and New African*. Krott has an affliction similar to Wink's. Rob is often mistaken for Chuck Norris in his travels. He is hoping some day to be confused with Robert Redford. He keeps *DP* honest with his multipage submissions o f corrections, illuminations and anecdotes. He lives in Olean, New York.

Anthony Morland

Morland was born in York, England, and grew up in London and Rome. He began his journalism career in Geneva and now works as an AFP correspondent for Agence France Presse in Abidjan, Ivory Coast. He resides in England.

Roddy Scott

Scott, 26, graduated from Edinburgh University and began his career as a journalist for a magazine in the Middle East. Scott says he went to one of those pseudo-military schools in his youth and thinks author bios are all bullshit anyway. His work speaks for itself. He seeks out the least visited or most dangerous spots and then manages to choose the world's most dangerous people to be his travel companions. He has traveled through Sierra Leone with the RUF rebels, The Bekaar valley with Hezbollah, Northern Iraq with the PKK, and other journos in gun-crazed Albania. He continues to write articles for a variety of newspapers and magazines including military and consumer publications on current affairs. He conducts radio interviews for *BBC World Service* and *Radio France International*. Scott lives in Ankara, Turkey.

Peter J. Willems

Peter J. Willems is a freelance journalist who spends much of his time in the Middle East and Central Asia.

Preface

Welcome to *DP3*, the third annual edition of *Fielding's The World's Most Dangerous Places*. In this edition you'll find contributions from enthusiastic adventurers who helped flesh out this ever growing tome. European based Roddy Scott and Jim Hooper covered Kurdistan, Albania, West Africa and the Horn of Africa. Their input makes this book a lot more interesting. *DP* contributors have had in-depth experiences that CNN would envy. I spent time in the south of Afghanistan and Pakistan being the first North American to meet with the *taliban*, while Coskun was in Kabul under siege chatting with Massoud. In Sierra Leone, Jim Hooper was riding in the gunships with the mercenaries of Executive Outcomes while Roddy Scott was the only outsider humping with the rebels in the rain forest below. Coskun Aral and Anthony Morland watched fighters dance in front of bullets in Monrovia while I was trying to track down Western hostages in Kashmir and Wink was examining the devastated Karen refugee camps in Myanmar. Later Hooper visited with the SPLA in Southern Sudan while Roddy was cooling his heels in an Ethiopian jail, fresh from his jaunt to Albania. We managed to cover most major wars and insurgencies firsthand. All in all it's been a busy year for everyone.

Loyal readers will be happy to know that we did lash ourselves to the mast and avoided the siren song of TV deals for reality shows (we were offered and passed on a half a million to do a blood and guts version of DP) and the saccharine "based on a true story" deals which will have to wait until I am longer in the tooth and can romanticize a little better.

Rest assured we stuck to our knitting and spent our time doing what we do best. We have been on the ground in Afghanistan, Algeria, Bosnia, Cambodia, Chechnya, Ethiopia, India, Indonesia, Iraq, Kashmir, Kurdistan, Laos, Lebanon, Liberia, Myanmar, Pakistan, the Philippines, Russia, Rwanda, Sierra Leone, Somalia, Sri Lanka, Syria, The Sudan, Thailand, Turkey, Vietnam and many other nasty and not so nasty places. We also have been doing our homework in the United States, in Los Angeles, Miami, New York and Washington, D.C.

Along the way, we have met with a lot of extraordinary people in fascinating places— old ladies that live in caves, gardeners that sell machine guns, snake charmers, skateboarders, spooks and other colorful people are part of our travels.

We have met with Nasrallah and Fadlalah of Hezbollah, Subcommandante Marcos of Mexico, Francis Ona of BRA, Abdullah Ocalan of the PKK, Massoud, Rabani, Dostum and the *taliban* of Afghanistan, the KDP and PUK of Kurdistan, the FIS of Algeria, and warlords in Liberia, Afghanistan,Turkey and Tajikistan as well, the Chechen, Albanian and Lezgi mafyia, the Moros in the Philippines, *mujahedin*, commandos, drug smugglers, police and a whole lot more people we really don't talk about.

When we weren't on the road, we hit the books, the Internet and made plenty of phone calls in our efforts to keep track of and make sense out of this crazy world.

As our loyal readers know, we hold no political affiliations or any political agenda sacred. That's why you won't see verbatim interviews, religious haranguing. pithy political comment or flatulent PC commentaries, and you definitely won't see any fair reporting. We aren't journalists. We aren't pundits. Hell, we're just passable writers.

Why?

I used to have a real job. My idea of a vacation was to spend two to six weeks under demanding physical and mental conditions to relax from my office job. When I returned I was refreshed, invigorated, educated and thankful to be back home. I now realize that I needed this high level of intensity to make me pay attention. I was completing my "education," albeit under bizarre circumstances, but nonetheless I would return with a smattering of a new language, an understanding of another byzantine political problem and a list of new friends who might range from farmers to nomads to warlords. As I continued to drop in and out of these places my friends and associates would suggest that I should put down the stories and tips on paper, so I began writing articles about my trips.

It might be disheartening or enlightening to learn that my first published piece was in *Four Wheeler Magazine* followed by a major article in *Soldier of Fortune*. So much for literary aspirations.

Then I wrote this book. I didn't mean to. I didn't want to. I just wrote an outline to show to other far more capable writers than I. All of them looked at me and politely explained that traveling to the world's most dangerous places just to write a travel guide was in a word, stupid.

So I kept writing, researching and traveling. Along the way I met an ever growing circle of adventurers in war zones and on expeditions. Finally I reached a point where the book sucked me in. I spent late hours, early mornings, long airplane flights and endless weekends polishing the keys on my PowerBook to create the first edition of *DP*. After two years, a lot of trips, and help from Coskun Aral and Jack Kramer, the first rambling edition of *DP* arrived.

When I proudly presented my *magnum opus* to booksellers, they coldly asked me, "Robert, why would anyone want to buy a book about places they don't want to go?" I had never really thought about *DP* in that light. Taken aback by the world's indifference to what I thought was an important book, I had to ask myself: Why would anyone explore the Lost World in Borneo when they could stay home and watch Spielberg's dinosaur version at the theater? Why would anyone risk their lives to meet Massoud or the *taliban* when they could watch Rambo defeat the Russians in 90 minutes from their BarcaLounger? Why would anybody want to do anything that was the slightest bit dangerous, uncomfortable, strenuous, or frightening? I was about to find out.

When *DP* first appeared, it sold out in two weeks. During the first year *DP* sold out four times and although we increased print runs dramatically for the second edition, we sold out three times leaving us an uncomfortable amount of time without a *DP* on the shelf. I knew that there were other people like me who knew exactly why this book was written and rejoiced in the pure sense of adventure for adventure's sake. More importantly, like-minded readers sent me dozens of tips, stories and comments that continue to shape and sharpen the book. So the next time you catch yourself wearing your Mr. DP shirt under your business suit, relax, you are not alone.

Who This Book Is For

Adventurers

This is a book for adventurers or those to want to understand what real adventure is about. What is an adventurer? I asked the same question when I read the results of an Aptitude and Interest test in high school. I had only qualified for three jobs: astronaut, advertising man and adventurer, and none of them were listed in the guidance counselor's office. I went into advertising and migrated into the adventure scene by default. I was in Kashmir when an old man explained to me that I was an astronaut because I go alone into places that nobody has been to. A rather cute but self-serving anecdote to show that adventurers are made not born. You don't need a Banana Republic correspondents vest ($95 by special order only) and a bullwhip to be an adventurer. You can be a regular guy or girl. Start small and work your way up. This book will give you enough background and information to help you decide whether you want to be Indiana Jones or East Hampton Hanna.

Adrenaline Junkies and Thrill Seekers

The people who practice sky surfing, bungy jumping and street luge can not truly claim to be adventurers but rather thrill seekers. Big wave surfers, mountain climbers and base jumpers seek a short jolt that affirms their need for thrills, but these sports are designed to create television commercials rather than meaningful accomplishments. They are out to scare themselves within their own perceptions of fear within a narrow, well-defined and statistical definition of danger.

There is also a hardcore group who, like Winston Churchill, feel that nothing beats the feeling of getting shot at and surviving. These are the hard core ex-SEALS, ex-Special Forces, ex-DEA, ex-Delta Force, undercover narcos, ex-Legionnaires. This book will provide some insight into the military and non-military world of adventure and introduce them to some positive outlets for their skills and energy. Like the group Spinal Tap, our amps go up to 11. But only if we can do something meaningful or illuminating.

Intelligence junkies

Those who have an unabashed curiosity about the world may be looking for a central source of information on dangerous places. This book can never compete with the files of the world's intelligence agencies (but *DP* has been called by one U.S. military trainer as "the best single source of nonclassified military information in the world") but it makes for good reading on a 20 hour plane trip, and reading will add a little color to your daily dose of CNN. We have no budget, are not journos and have no agenda. For now *DP* is nondenominational, fun and completely our view of the world.

Journalists

Journalists were once portrayed as hard-drinking, cynical idealists complete with dangling cigarette and battered notebook. Today, the people you see on TV are more likely hairsprayed, talking heads whose only scars are from plastic surgery. But there is also an unseen group of journalists out there. The shooters, stringers and Beta humpers who take the pictures, check the facts and interview the combatants. They don't make half a million a year, some don't even make $20,000 a year risking their lives only to have their work end up on the cutting room floor. They do it because it gives them an excuse to explore the outer limits of our world and hopefully make some sense of it. For them, this book will provide a leg up, give them a friend and maybe even stop a bullet if they stuff it in the front of their flak jacket.

Expats

Expats are those emaciated, short-sleeved, Iowa Sunday school families who seem to end up loaded on Marine helicopters every time a dangerous place falls apart. Hopefully, 15 minutes thumbing through *DP* can provide a little more insight into just what is really going on in that oil rich, skanky little cesspool you are being paid big bucks to move to. This book is also a good primer on where not to go hiking on weekends, how much you should really pay for that souvenir AK-47 and where not to bring that Barbie Doll. It'll even tell you where you can run your Toyota diesel on coconut oil.

The curious and easily amused

Anyone who wonders how to make an emergency I.V. out of a green coconut, or what kind of sneakers the PKK wear needs this book. You could stomp anyone at Trivial Pursuit (The Apocalypse Version) with all the esoteric trivia contained herein. More importantly, you can learn a whole heap more about the world and the people that live in it. For those who want to actually make the world a better place, we provide hundreds of resources and contacts that will let you do more good than just singing "We are the World" or even "I'd Like to Buy the World a Coke."

Hollywood and the Media

It seems that this book has a special place on the bookshelves of writers, film directors, TV producers and scriptwriters. Most are shocked to find that we are quite normal people, devoid of headbands, scars, cammo Hummers, steroid-sized muscles or even a publicist. We get about two calls a week from people who want to turn us into the next Rambo, Indiana Jones or Marlin Perkins. They suddenly realize what we see and do is far too cerebral and too real to sell Jenny Craig or Pontiacs. (Oh, you mean you actually go to these places?). When TV transcends The Grind, Jerry Springer or even EyeWitness News you will see *DP* on the box. But for now it's a book.

A Polite Discourse on Liability (Ours) and Gullibility (Yours)

If you decide to wax up your Discover card and actually go to some of the locations described in this book, please remember that visiting these places may likely get you killed or earn you the nickname Stumpy. On the other hand, since more people are injured in their homes than outside them, you may be safer traveling to some of the places in this book. So remember, this is a book about dangerous places, dangerous people and dangerous things. If you are one of those people who doesn't know the difference between phone sex and everlasting love, quickly put this book back on the shelf. Nothing in this book will get you out of a Somali jail and no one in Chechnya gives a damn if you really are a nice person and make a mean chocolate mousse. War zones reek of the smell of diesel, death, vomit and musty blown-up buildings. There is nothing photogenic, amusing or entertaining about other people's suffering. We do not (as we have been accused of in the *Sunday London Times*) endorse, encourage or approve of travel to dangerous areas unless you are there for a purpose and fully understand the risks involved.

Areas of conflict change daily, land mines are laid every night, and dictators move in and out of presidential mansions faster than summer replacement sitcoms. We've been taken to task by institutions like *Outside* magazine for our overly verbose disclaimer, but the bottom line in *DP* is about how to *avoid* danger.

Although we have traveled to (and continue to travel to) the regions in this book, much of the information is gathered from secondhand sources when we feel it is more accurate than our firsthand reports. War zones, Third World countries and nasty places are very mercurial places with no one really knowing what's going on at any one time. Situations change by the hour. We ask a lot of questions, and we write down the answers that make sense. We avoid recounting our interviews with politicians and zealots, and sometimes people tell us the wrong answer or, God forbid, just lie. We check out as much as we can, but we use a lot of common sense and street smarts in translating what we see and hear. So use this book and other sources as pieces of the puzzle. If you choose to travel to dangerous places, get your information updated by knowledgeable people before you go. Ask the embassy, police, locals, bus drivers and farmers what's going on. But remember, even if you think you have all the pieces, you're still part of a puzzle.

Our official disclaimer for people who didn't get the subtle point of the paragraph above: Due to the nature of this book and the unusual sources of information, we ask that you do not make any decisions based on the material presented here. In fact, this book is about places where you should not go (they *are* dangerous). This book is written by a group of people with help from correspondents, friends and contacts around the world. To protect many of our sources (we do have to, uh, break, or rather bend, some laws), we have not credited all of them. We cannot guarantee this information is accurate or reliable simply because by the time we get back and write it down, the situation could reverse. Do not use this book for the planning of any activity. We encourage you always to investigate thoroughly and use as many sources of information as you can find regarding areas where you wish to travel. Although we have an uncanny knack for predicting wars, massacres and kidnappings, Fielding and the authors cannot take responsibility for any misfortune, liability or inconvenience due to your interpretation, application or even understanding of the information in this book. Let's do it again in all caps now:

THE AUTHORS AND PUBLISHERS ASSUME NO LIABILITY NOR DO THEY ENCOURAGE YOU TO DO, SEE, VISIT OR TRY ANY OF THE ACTIVITIES OR ACTIONS DISCUSSED IN THIS BOOK. THIS BOOK IS INTENDED FOR BACKGROUND INFORMATION ONLY AND MAY NOT BE RELIABLE AFTER PRESS TIME.

The Modest Goal of the Authors: Unemployment

This book is not all doom and gloom. There are sections on how to "Make a Difference" and "Save the Planet." We show you how to actually connect with other people and organizations to effect change. It might be clearing land mines in Cambodia, finding the parents of Rwandan refugees, guarding food shipments in Sierra Leone, or even teaching people how to vote in Algeria. In all cases, I hope that this book encourages you to dig a little deeper into lesser-known regions and peoples of the world.

We do not support any cause, back any fight or endorse any activity that uses violence. But like spectators at a Brazilian soccer game we're not supposed to play but sometimes we get awfully close to the action. We can't afford to be partisan, but we encourage you to root and support your favorite cause. Don't be shy about contacting the resources listed to find out more.

So remember *DP*'s primitive formula: present knowledge in easy to understand packets, educate people to what is really going on, then show them how to fix it. Knowledge fights fear, builds hope, exposes cowards, supports the just and makes the world a better place.

Ten Questions, Ten Answers

These are the most commonly asked questions asked of us.

1) Who is Mr. DP?

Many people ask why we use the laughing skull as a mascot. Well, Mr. DP (as he is affectionately called) came into being because we needed something simple, memorable and small to give out as gifts to soldiers, freedom fighters and anyone who helps in our work. So I designed a mascot and printed a pile of stickers to slap on everything from AK-47s to APCs. Mr. *DP* is sort of Kilroy for the nineties. Either a not so subtle jab at the meaning of life or just another goofy sticker. Our T-shirts were created to provide memorable clothing that we could give out to our favorite people. They are XL, heavy duty and totally fashionable because we wear them. We just sell the extras because people think they are so cool. And of course some people just scratch their heads and wonder at it all.

2) Do you make personal appearances and talk about your adventures?

I once said that "neither I nor my coauthors have any interest in becoming celebrities or motivational speakers," but guess what we've become? Right now I appear in front of an average of 25 million people a month through articles and television appearances. We are surprised to find ourselves presented as pundits. Before Cambodia fell apart Wink was on CNN with his precise, condensed and deadly accurate prediction of the meltdown. Coskun and the ever-smiling Mr. *DP* has one of Turkey's top rated weekly shows (*Haberci* on ATV). So bear with us as we enjoy our 15 minutes of fame and if you do bump in to us make sure you buy us a beer and say hi. We always enjoy talking to people.

3) Do you visit every one of these places every year?

Between the three of us and our correspondents, we get to most of the interesting and most forbidden spots. We travel to places that are rarely covered or that we predict will change dramatically. Algeria, Bougainville, Sudan, Afghanistan,Tajikitan, Albania are just some of our stops. We use the phone a lot and take a lot of trips to find out exactly what is going on.

4) Why did you write the book?

This book exists because no one else would write it and I was surprised that there was no book on areas where travelers really need one. Once I started, I became enthused with the absolute coolness of wrapping up the big bad world within a thousand pages. I would compare the experience to doing a hard tour in the worst of the world's war zones and writing a doctoral thesis at the same time every year.

5) How can I write for DP?

Send in whatever you want. But we just don't have the budget to pay more than a T-shirt if we like what we read and publish it. We also seek out travel tips from the world's wild places. I didn't write this book for money or for fame so you shouldn't expect it either. We do it because we live it. Some readers have said they are "itching for action" and want to get in on what we do. We don't engage in any armed combat, we do not carry any firearms, and we do not harm, injure or kill people in our travels. We get shot at, abused, scammed, beaten, blown up, sick, bored and bashed, but we don't reciprocate. (Sounds like a bad "Kung Fu" episode.)

6) Who reads this book?

Judging from the letters I get and the people I meet, if you put all our readers together in one room it would be a great party. Surfers, combat photographers, graying intellectuals, politicians, soldiers, missionaries, grandmothers, young girls, Legionnaires, Trans sahara bikers, mountain climbers, mercenaries, embassy staff, movie stars, aid workers, college students, DEA trainees, spooks, security analysts and just regular folks who groove on adventure and discovery.

7) Do you encourage people to travel to the places in this book?

We are in the business of providing information, not promoting tourism. If any book could be criticized for discouraging travel, it is this one. The uniqueness of *DP* is that we rarely cover any attractions or provide any reasons to visit any of these countries. We only cover what is potentially dangerous and along the way open our readers' eyes. The underlying message of this book is to encourage people to better understand their world and not accept the traditional clichés. If that encourages you to brave the world's dangerous places, so be it.

8) How do you keep the book up-to-date?

We continually travel, research, check facts and interview people. We are truly information junkies, scanning thousands of documents every month. We are also completely unafraid to get on a plane or a camel and go directly into a hot spot to find out what is really going on.

9) Is *DP* a macho thing?

Some adventure magazines have tried to portray us as tough guys cruising the world looking for trouble. Magazines, newspapers, television and radio like to bestow titles like Dangerman, The Guru of Adventure Travel and The Real Thing. I can tell you that, from experience, trouble hurts and that tough is for leather and overdone steaks. I consider myself a seeker of knowledge, a far more cerebral occupation than "adventurer." We don't go looking for danger, we go looking for answers.

As for *DP* being a "guy" thing, sorry to disappoint you, over half the mail I get is from women and not one of them wants to be a guy. I like to say giving gender specific tips to war zones is like using alcohol swabs before lethal injection. It is politically correct but you're going to end up dead anyway. Women are as adventurous as men, but it seems they are restrained by their rather developed sense of self preservation and common sense. It would be fair to say that the male sex has a reputation of not being burdened with prudence or even common sense.

10) What is the most dangerous situation you have been in?

I truly can't answer this. There is no Dangermeter on my wrist and most people don't even know when they are in real danger. My pick for illustration purposes might be as mundane as surviving a plane crash in Borneo, Coskun hitting a land mine in Afghanistan or Wink riding his motorcycle through war-torn Cambodia. We really never set out to do anything overly dangerous. But we do pride ourselves on knowing how to handle ourselves in dangerous situations, and we have done a lot of fast talking at gunpoint. I have been described as "very lucky," Coskun as "charming" and Wink as "crazy," so that's as far as I can analyze it. So far, the gods have been smiling on us. We must be doing something right.

TABLE OF CONTENTS

WHAT IS DANGEROUS?

DANGEROUS PLACES

MR. DP'S LITTLE BLACK BOOK

LIST OF MAPS

WHAT IS
DANGEROUS?

What Is Dangerous?

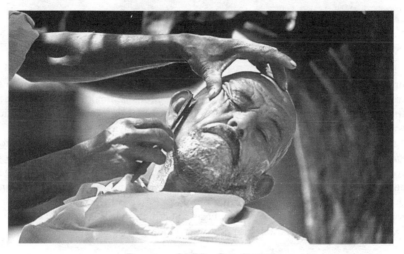

Danger Is My Business

Catchy heading, wrong message. The bizarre thing is that because I write a best-selling book about danger, it is quite fair to say that yes, danger is my business but this book is really about knowledge, safety, staying healthy, alive and happy. It is a book on how to make this world a better place by removing the perceptions, barriers and myths that keep people from truly understanding how the world works. So remember, safety is my business.

Fear

Fear: "a distressing emotion aroused by impending danger, evil, pain etc. whether the threat is real or imagined."

You need to conquer fear to understand danger. Fear is the tick, tick sound of sweat dripping from your chin onto a prison floor. Fear is the long ride down in a flaming airplane. Fear is the relentless onslaught of Lou Gehrig's disease. Fear is our perception of impending danger and misfortune even though it is usually irrational. Fear creates physical reactions that are designed to save us in an emergency. Rapid pulse, tightened muscles, adrenaline pumping and sharpened faculties. So when you feel fear, channel it into action. Fear is everything and fear is nothing. We all have fears, we all can sense danger and we all work hard to replace fear with knowledge. Fear is a natural reaction that can also be replaced by a calmness borne of acceptance and the comfort of a life well lived.

The fear of danger is a normal human reaction to the unknown. I used to have a fairly mundane job in a long dark 32-inch diameter mine shaft working with high explosives. It was mundane because I knew the dangers and was trained to avoid them—the difference is knowledge, training and mental preparation. Lots of people defuse land mines, jump out of planes, fight wars, dive under water and even rob banks for a living. They are all fairly comfortable with the risks involved and understand the consequences of not paying attention or screwing up. Every time I travel into an unknown area I don't feel fear; when I am in a dangerous situation I have learned to channel fear into action. But more importantly understand that ignorance breeds fear.

Danger

Danger: "liability or exposure to harm or injury."

Danger is not something you can measure, predict or prevent. The statistics fired at you by the government are for lab rats and grad students. In the real world, danger is an electric feeling in the air, a gutlike animal feeling that something bloody is about to happen. Danger is in the bloodshot eyes of a crack addict waiting for you to leave the hotel. Danger is in the fraying rudder cables on an aging Tupelov over Tajikistan. And danger is in the eyes of a crocodile waiting for you to brush your teeth along the stream bed. Danger is also in your mindless commute along the freeways, your drunken stumble across the coffee table to get another beer and the underdone quiche at Alfonso's. This book will help you understand what is and isn't dangerous and in the process help you become comfortable with the acceptance of danger as something that is overcome everyday. Danger is just knowing the odds and understanding the threat.

Adventure

Adventure: "An exciting or very unusual experience."

Adventure is the world's greatest teacher, and like all teachers will tell you the more attention you pay the more you learn. I believe that travel to the world's least visited places will not only make you pay attention but will teach you things you will never forget. Travel was my teacher. I learned Spanish from menus and smugglers in Central America, I learned about politics and strategy from warlords and I learned about humility and dedication from aid workers. I also learned a lot of bad things from people who were supposed to be good people.

Adventure and travel will teach you that people are the same and people are different. People are bad and people are good. Some places are safe and some places are dangerous. But the important thing is, you need to learn what is and isn't dangerous and when adventure is wise and when it is stupid.

What Is Really Dangerous?

There are three danger zones in life. First is making it through the first year of life. The second major hurdle is surviving until the ripe old age of 37 where accidental death is the grim reaper's best friend. Unintentional injuries are the fifth leading cause of death. The third stage is making it past the list of debilitating diseases that claim most people. It's important to understand the relative dangers of normal living to appreciate the numbers that you will read about in later chapters. The dangers that face you when you travel are infinitesimal when compared to just surviving the dangers you face in the nine to five grind, running to the fridge to get your eighth beer, or in the frenetic weekend activities that pass for relaxation.

All right, let's get to it. What is dangerous and what isn't? Since this is a book about dangerous travel, let's look at the odds. There's a one in 10 million chance of dying in a plane crash. Not bad. The odds of getting killed on a train are 10 times higher, about one in a million. Still good, but not great.

If you think that pilot error or cannibis-smoking railroad engineers are the cause of most accidents, try driving across the country. The chances of getting killed are one in 14,000—worse odds yet. That's dangerous, yet a full third of American drivers don't even bother to buckle up. The recent increase in American speed limits from 55 to 65 has jacked the accident fatality rate to a whopping 44 percent. But we are speeding ahead of ourselves. So what are the odds?

Time

The number one killer of men is that kindly looking fellow, Father Time. Although there is a statistical lengthening of human lives as standards of living, safety, nutrition and health care spreads to the lower incomes, we are all subject to deterioration of tissues. Most of us can expect to live to our mid-70s before getting nervous about getting our money's worth on a five-year carpet. In 1890, average life expectancy was 31.1 years. Today, it is up to 75.4 years. Joining the century club is completely possible for the next generation.

How does one cheat the grim reaper? First, don't let accidental causes get in the way. Second, exercise and eat right and maintain a positive mental attitude. How is that done? Travel, of course. People who live the longest seem to have an insatiable curiosity as well as a natural love for exploring the world. There are a lot of wiry octogenarians who seem perfectly healthy, have inquiring minds, travel a lot and are always looking for a good time. Some of them started reading Fielding guides when they were 30. They stay out of the house as much as possible, fully understanding that the home is the world's most dangerous place (see "Accidents") for people over the age of 75.

Accidental Death

OK, you bought a stack of travel guides and stretched your finances to buy that 'round the world cruise ticket. But how do you live long enough to enjoy all your acquired common sense? You have to get through four stages.

Young and Tender

This year, 35,000 children will not make it past the first year of life in the United States. If you make it out of the womb (half didn't) without a major congenital abnormality (7449 did), there's Sudden Infant Death Syndrome to deal with (4891). The next most dangerous incidents are choking (229), car crashes (160), ingesting a foreign object (103), burns or fires (98) and drowning (89).

Young and Reckless

Young male teenagers in cars seem to have a death wish. Eighteen may be a magic age for most people, but it is a very profitable target demographic for undertakers. Of every 100,000 18-year-olds, 55.5 will die in car crashes.

Middle-aged and Reckless

What is the number two accidental killer of people between the ages of 18 and 49 (after car accidents)? Dying to know the answer? It's accidental poisoning; a curious manner of death, with a rate highest for men aged 37. Most of this poisoning is the result of the deadly side effects of ingesting normal medicines.

Old and Clumsy

The next time you send Gramps downstairs to find his glasses, don't be surprised if he doesn't come back. Falls collect a number of victims in the age group above 75. Although the number pales in comparison to heart disease, it is worth remembering: 8336 people died from falls last year vs. 438,873 from heart disease.

Disease

OK, the ballet and meditation lessons are paying off. You are a now a graceful, cautious, levelheaded person; you drive real slow and tip your hat and smile at anyone who is carrying an automatic weapon. But there is an insidious killer that few of us have any control over. AIDS is spreading, at an alarming rate among young people, so if you are under 45, make sure you pack your leak-tested haz-mat suit with extra gaffers tape when you go to Club Med. HIV claimed 24,629 people between the ages of 25 and 44 and has become the number one killer for those 25–34.

When ya gotta go, ya gotta go	
1. Heart Disease	37.8%
2. Cancer	19.3%
3. Stroke	10.3%
4. Accidents (Non-Auto)	3.0%
5. Influenza (Pneumonia)	2.9%
6. Motor Vehicle Accidents	2.4%
7. Diabetes	1.9%
8. Liver Disease	1.7%
9. Arteriosclerosis	1.5%
10. Suicide	1.4%

When the numbers are totalled up, the leading cause of death caused by medical problems in America is heart disease (717,706 deaths). Cancer claimed 520,578 lives, strokes accounted for 143,769 fatalities and chronic obstructive pulmonary disease claimed 91,938 victims. It's a long way down to the next killer disease. Are there any trends to give us hope? The rates of stomach, uterus and liver cancer have dropped since 1930. But lung cancer and leukemia cases have climbed dramatically. So don't smoke, don't work in coal mines, don't have unprotected sex, and stay away from nuclear waste sites.

Granted, those numbers are great for the sedentary hordes that are content to watch "Wild Kingdom" reruns. So what about those wild-eyed adventurers slashing their way through the tropical jungle? We'd like to think we're all macho, but the reality is that the only guaranteed discomfort adventurers will experience is that mad dash to sit and ponder the world's great and varied selection of evacuation devices. (How come Rambo and Indiana Jones never have the runs?).

Dr. Richard Dawood put together an interesting chart in *Condé Nast Traveler* using info from the World Health Organization gleaned from a study by Professor Robert Steffen of the University of Zurich. The following table is the incidence of health problems experienced by travelers to tropical destinations (based on a sample of 100,000 people).

Health Problems Experienced (Per 100,000 Travelers)		
Experienced a health problem	55%	55,000
Felt Ill	25%	25,000
Consulted doctor	.08%	8000
Stayed in bed	.06%	6000
Unable to work upon return	.02%	2000
Hospitalized while abroad	.004%	400
Evacuated by air	.0006%	60
Died abroad	.00001%	1

Source: Conde´ Nast Traveler

Dawood mentions the results of a study done by the British Consumers Association among 15,972 members which revealed that 15 percent of their members had been sick on vacation. The results are not that surprising when you look at countries where travelers became sick:

When it comes to where you can get Montezuma's revenge, Tut's Trot or Delhi Belly, there are no surprises here. India (60%), Egypt (53%) and Mexico (40%) are the best places to get the runs. The most likely problem affecting travelers to tropical places are diarrhea or intestinal problems with about 25–40 percent of them being afflicted. Sunburn affects about 10 percent with the Caribbean and Mexico being the most likely place to get fried.

Malaria affected a minuscule number of travelers. Only about 1036 or about .0000345 percent of the 30 million U.S. residents who traveled abroad contracted the mosquito-borne parasite. About 3 percent of those cases were fatal.

Accident Facts

We weren't joking in saying that if you want to live longer, stay out of the house. But just don't leave too fast and don't take your car. People between the age of 70 and 90 are attracted to stairs like lemmings to cliffs. But even at younger ages, if you really want to live dangerously, stay at home. Most accidents happen at home. Any student of statistics will tell you that home is where people spend the majority of their time. Each year slippery tile floors, cheap ginsu knives and trendy glass coffee tables do more damage than all the world's terrorists.

When should you plan to spend a month in that seminary in solitary? Well the most dangerous month for accidents is August, with 9000 unintentional injuries versus a monthly incidence average of 7500. The safest month is February with only 5700. Curious to know the other most dangerous months?

Cause of Death	Most Dangerous Month	#	Least Dangerous Month	#	Avg
Car Accidents	August	4243	January	2869	3628
Falls	December	1145	February	959	1055
Drownings	July	886	November	147	385
Firearms	November	164	September	83	120
Fire	January	539	June	194	343
Poisoning	August	572	January	412	475

Source: National Center for Health Statistics and National Safety Council

Fly the Friendly Skies

From the moment you grasp your airline seat with sweaty palms to the minute your cab rolls to a stop at your front door, most travelers have a nervous feeling that their life has become more dangerous. The reality is quite the opposite. Remember we told you that fewer accidents happen to people when they travel than when they are at home. Why?

Well, think of who you trust your life to when you travel. For example, your takeoff. If you survive the cab ride you'll arrive in a well-designed, safe terminal complete with sprinklers, emergency exits and in many cases on-site medical staff. (Does your house have this?) When you board the plane, you enter a multimillion-dollar aircraft, the culmination of more than 100 years of aviation safety engineering. Every element and every part of the craft is regulated, inspected, maintained and replaced. Up front, you have two pilots who are the best of their kind. Many American pilots are Vietnam-era pilots who have flown in combat. All have racked up tens of thousands of hours in the air. Every pilot goes through intensive training and regular retraining to stay in top form. You are given flight safety procedures by individuals trained in emergency situations, first aid and other life saving procedures. Law mandates that there be a flight attendant for every 50 passengers. After you are aloft you are now under the control of a global traffic network that tracks all major aircraft and weather patterns using a network of computers and fail safe devices. When you finally arrive at your destination, tired but safe, you meet your driver/guide. Here, things may change. The fact that he is drunk, blind in one eye and drives what used to be a 1957 Chevy still can't take your mind off his gold tooth and missing fingers. So it's off to the rebel camp to meet the guerillas. "Oh, by the way," he says in his *aquadiente* -laced breath, "the *gobermente* overran the camp yesterday, but I think *el jefe* is still alive."

Regardless of your final destination, travel in the first world is pretty sedentary and predictable. Buses, trains and cars are subject to stringent safety laws in both construction and operation. Hotels have sophisticated sprinkler systems and emergency evacuation plans. Restaurants are inspected by health inspectors, and so on. You can even get your fare back if you are hijacked or killed. Remember that risk and travel are a sophisticated gamble. Nobody plays Russian roulette with six bullets or even two. The trick is to know when the odds are in your favor. Or in the words of Dirty Harry, "Do you feel lucky punk?"

What Danger Awaits the Weary Traveler?

The hordes of Tilley hatted ecotourists have not always been with us. In 1955 there were only 46 million people traveling from one country to another. Most of them were well-heeled folks "doing the continent" or "taking the sun." Ten years later there were 144 million and today there are half a billion. That's a lot of Samsonite. It also means you read a lot more about misfortune, illnesses and death. These travelers cleaned out their wallets to the tune of $315 billion. So what do those half a billion people worry about when they travel? A survey of vacationers in Europe came up with the following:

What me Worry?	Percent
Burglary of home while away	90%
Illness and accidents on holiday	40%
Family's safety	33%
Bad Accommodation	26%
Bad Weather	19%
Bad Food	18%
Work	6%

Americans tend to be a little diffident about the goings-on in other countries. Very few Americans list their own home towns as potentially dangerous places. You may be surprised to learn places Europeans regard as dangerous.

Europeans' most dangerous places	Percent
Florida	42%
North Africa	9%
Turkey	7%
California	7%
Kenya	7%

By the very definition of travel, you will be forced to choose some form of transportation. Planes are the safest means; cars are the most dangerous. In America, the death rate per miles traveled is comforting for those who fly but unsettling for the majority of people who like to drive:

9

Type of Passenger Transport	Death Rate (per billion passenger miles)	Passenger Miles (in billions)
Passenger Cars	.89	2393.2
Intercity Buses	.03	23.7
Transit Buses	.01	20.6
Trains	.02	13.5
Airplanes	.01	354.3

Expect danger every time you decide to get into a taxi; but expect death in a small minivan. You may prefer to travel by bus, cab, rickshaw, trishaw, *becek* or even rollerblades. These are official U.S. statistics—numbers that reflect one of the safest transportation systems in the world. But what about the more typical forms of transportation adventurers will be forced to use?

Minibuses

Imagine what happens when your body decelerates from 60–0 m.p.h. in two milliseconds. Now imagine a forest of rusty seat backs and a plate glass window in your way. Not pretty. Having been at the site of many bus crashes in my travels, I can best compare the scenes to putting a dozen mice in a coffee can along with glass and nails, slamming it against a wall and then shaking it for a few minutes more. Then spray the bloody contents across the path of oncoming traffic. That pretty much sums up the bloody and confused scene of a *matatu* accident.

The most dangerous form of travel in the world is the fabled minibus. These Third World creations are small Japanese-made transports with a drivetrain that was originally designed to haul a family of four, but ingenuity and greed prevails, and some will pack up to 16 passengers in one minibus.

The minibuses are used primarily for rush hour transportation of poor people to work. Unlike the large, regulated buses, minibuses are run by entrepreneurs who make their money by carrying as many people, as many times as they can. For example, in South Africa 60,000 accidents involving minibuses kill more than 900 people every year. In Peru, where they are called "killer combis," the death toll also includes nonpassengers trying to get out of the way of the weaving, speeding vans. The deadly driving style is a result of drivers who must make their money within the two hours of rush hour in order to make a profit on their rental owner's charge. Last year, 375 pedestrians were killed by the 30,000 or so minivans in Lima, Peru. The numbers are not available for most Third World countries. A rough estimate puts the chances of a fatality in a minibus, *matatu* or combi at about 30 times the normal U.S. accident rate. So the next time you plunk down between a quarter to fifty cents for one of these rides, consider how much you just sold your life for.

HOW TO SURVIVE MINIBUSES

There is a reason for the multitude of religious symbols, slogans and prayers painted on Third World buses. Once they cram their doors shut and the wobbly wheels start forward, your life is in the hands of a supreme being. If you travel via small buses, remember the following:

- **Don't travel at night. Most Third World minibuses make New York taxis seem tame.**

- **Avoid mountainous areas and/or winter conditions. Fly if necessary.**

- **Bring water and food with you, plan for the unexpected, delays and diversions.**

- **Ask whether the route goes through areas frequented by bandits or terrorist groups. You may be surprised to find out who controls the countryside.**

- **Sit near an exit or on top. At least make sure you are near an open window. Follow the DP rule: Be friends with everyone, your seat mate might be a rebel commander.**

- **There is a reason why you paid 83¢ to travel. You don't buy a lot of brake pads and clutches with that pocket change.**

- **Remember your rooftop luggage is prey for rummagers, slashers and thieves. Put your luggage in a standard trash bag, a canvas duffle or under everyone else's.**

- **Shirt slashers wait for you to doze off and slip out your money pouches. Put your money in your shoes if necessary.**

Taxis

Our esteemed founder was reputed to have once lost a libel case wherein he described a particular cab company as the biggest crooks in Italy. The cab company easily won the case because they proved, not that they were innocent, but that there were bigger criminal operations in Italy at the time.

When you get into a taxi driven by a stranger in a strange land, watch out. The odds for damage to your body, your sense of well being and your wallet sky rockets. Cabs in most countries have no seatbelts, no brakes, no license and no fare limits. In many countries such as Colombia, you may even get robbed in the bargain. Taxis can be controlled by telling the driver to drive slowly in his native language. I remember a friend of mine during one particularly terrifying cab ride, rummaging through his Greek phrase book yelling what he thought meant "slower" at the top of his lungs. As the driver divided his time between staring at us incredulously and trying to maintain control of his over-revved cab, we thought we were in the hands of a lunatic. At the end of our ride, the wide-eyed cab-driver was visibly relieved to see the last of us. Upon closer examination, we realized in our haste to translate, we had been requesting him to drive "faster, faster." To be fair, I also had a cab driver in Malaysia carry around stacks of expensive luggage well beyond any chance of recovery all day long for less than $20. Based on courtesy, cleanliness, knowledge and respect for human life, the world's best cab drivers are in London and the world's worst cabbies are in New York City.

HOW TO SURVIVE TAXIS

- Choose your cab rather than let them choose you.

- Never get into a taxi with another passenger already inside.

- Do not take gypsy cabs; ask the airline people how much it should cost to go to your city and then agree upon a fare before you get in.

- Keep your luggage in the back seat, not in the trunk.

- Memorize the local words for "no," "yes," "stop here" and "how much?"

- Have the hotel doorman or guide negotiate cab fares in advance.

- It is a global law that cabbies never carry change. Ask if the driver has change before you hand him a big bill.

- Many cabbies will rent themselves out for flat fees. Do not be afraid to negotiate the services of a trusted cabby as guide, chauffeur and protector of baggage.

- Do not tell cabbies where you are going, when you are leaving or any other particulars that could be of interest to bad people.

Automobiles

International accident rates for travel are clouded by lack of reporting by the large numbers of people who die in vehicle related accidents and don't have the courtesy to fill out the paperwork after they are dead. Countries like Mexico, Pakistan, Australia, India, Egypt and China have horrendous accident rates but do not figure prominently in studies. Countries like Afghanistan, Zaire, Sierra Leone and Liberia wish they had enough cars or roads to have accidents. Obviously, in the U.S., travel "down South" behind the wheel of a car can be nasty business. Here's what it's like outside the country:

International Vehicular Deaths (per 100,000 population)	
India	34.6
South Korea	30.4
Portugal	28.1
Brazil	22.7
Hungary	22.7
Greece	22.0
Venezuela	20.7

International Vehicular Deaths (per 100,000 population)	
Spain	20.5
Ecuador	20.0
New Zealand	19.5
Luxembourg	19.4
Poland	19.2
Belgium	18.4
United States	18.4

Sources: various, not all countries are included

How to get killed driving

If you have a death wish, find a 16-year-old to drive you around: Sixteen-year-olds are the most dangerous drivers in America, being involved in 1200 deadly accidents last year. But more driving-related fatalities involve the use of alcohol. A study by Ford Motor Company revealed that secondary roads have an accident rate nearly twice as high and a fatality rate more than double that of interstate highways. A nationwide organization of 25,000 sheriffs, deputy sheriffs and municipal, state and federal law enforcement officers were polled to find out what causes accidents:

Causes of Vehicular Accident	
Alcohol/Drugs influenced	90%
Speeding	83%
Running red traffic lights	78%
Not concentrating on driving	76%
Aggressive driving	68%
Tailgating	63%

Source: National Sheriff's Association

What are the chances you will be killed while driving or being driven overseas? The number of tourist deaths are insignificant compared to domestic death rates. The average death toll for Americans involved in traffic related accidents outside the U.S is 750 (with 25,000 injured in foreign accidents). If you compare that to the 42,000 who buy it stateside, it really isn't that a big deal. To give you an idea of the relative danger rates for those countries who bother to keep tabs on their vehicular carnage, we compare the higher U.S. rate with European regions. This time road deaths based on distance driven instead of population.

Deaths per 100 million kilometers driven			
Egypt	43.2	Bahrain	3.2
Kenya	36	New Zealand	2.2
South Korea	29	Israel	2.2
Turkey	22	Taiwan	2

Deaths per 100 million kilometers driven			
Morocco	21	France	2
Yemen	12.4	Germany	1.9
Austria	10.7	Japan	1.7
South Africa	10.4	Switzerland	1.6
Bulgaria	9.9	Ireland	1.5
Portugal	9	Denmark	1.5
Hungary	8	Finland	1.4
Macedonia	7.8	Thailand	1.3
Poland	6.3	Netherlands	1.3
Czech Republic	5.9	Norway	1.2
Spain	5.9	United States	1.1
Hong Kong	4.8	Sweden	1.1
Belgium	3.3	United Kingdom	1

Source: IRF, NSC, ASIRT, Others (various years)

The general rules of common sense apply in every country in the world. One strange danger is pedestrians who look the wrong way when they cross the street after disembarking the plane in London or other left-hand drive countries. If there is one general rule that can help save your life, it is to avoid driving or traveling by road at night. The night reduces visibility and is also the witching hour for drunks.

HOW TO SURVIVE AUTOMOBILES

There is little to be said that hasn't been said in every driver's education class. Speed, booze, bad roads, and other drivers kill. Driving in the Third World is not safe, so if possible check out the local Hertz Rent-A-Yak.

• Be familiar with local road warning signs and laws. For example, in Borneo there are signs telling you to stick to the left or right of the road to choreograph the intentions of oncoming logging trucks. In Europe, unless a road sign says otherwise, traffic to your right at any intersection has priority. In countries like Mexico you are considered at fault in any accident and will be hauled off to jail while your co-crashee staggers back to the cantina to finish his drink.

• Avoid driving yourself if possible. Nobody gets up in the morning and plans on having an accident. The fact that you are rubbernecking or checking maps while on the wrong side of the road dramatically increases your chances of an accident. Flying is safer than driving.

• Avoid driving in inclement weather conditions, night time or especially on weekends. Fog kills, rain kills, drunks kill, other tourists kill. It is estimated that after midnight on Friday and Saturday nights in rural America, three out of five drivers on the road have been drinking. That means if you are one of the sober ones, pray that the other sober driver is coming the other way.

- **Stay off the road in high-risk countries.** You may think the Italians, Portuguese and Spaniards display amazing bravado as they skid around winding mountain roads. The accident rate says they are just lousy drivers.

- **Reduce your speed.** To see the difference in impact at various speeds, try running as fast as you can into the nearest wall. Now walk slowly and do it again. See how much better that is?

- **Wear a seat belt,** rent bigger cars, drive during daylight, use freeways, carry a map and a good road guide, etc. You're not listening are you?

- **If you can hire a driver with car, do so.** Contact tour companies, embassy staff and hotel concierges. Many countries provide a driver when you rent a car, so make sure you feel comfortable with him. Try a one-day city tour first to see if the chemistry and his driving skills are to your tastes.

- **Don't drive tired or while suffering from jet lag.** Don't pull off to the side of the road to nap, don't leave possessions in plain sight, and try to park in lighted areas. I can see you're not listening, so just do whatever the hell you are going to do, but don't say I didn't warn you.

Boats

Row, Row, Row Your Boat may have a completely new meaning for you after you read this section. "Ro-Ro" is also short for "roll-on, roll-off" ferries that ply the frigid northern waters between Scandinavia, Russia, Europe and Great Britain. Ro-ros can also be found in Alaska, British Columbia, Washington and the Greek Isles and anywhere else cars are required to get to an island quickly and efficiently. There are about 2000 of these ferries worldwide. Since cars must drive through the ship's bow and then out the aft, the hulls feature large doors that yawn open. No problem when you are tied to a dock, but when heavy seas start pounding and water enters the ship, these mammoth vessels will flip like a waterlogged rubber ducky. The chances of anyone finding a lifeboat or even getting outside to jump overboard are slim to none. For example, 900 people perished in the *Estonia* disaster, The *Herald of Free Enterprise* sank in the English Channel killing 193. Not a trend but a warning. Since then maritime safety officials have demanded that bulkheads be installed to act as a second line of defense. Open deck ferries are safer since they allow water to run off.

Ferries in places like Bangladesh, Haiti, The Philippines and Hong Kong have had major disasters from capsizing due to overloading and collision. In roughly an eight-year period, there were more than 360 ferry boat accidents killing 11,350 people.

Those that fancy the life of Joseph Conrad should know that piracy is a major problem in Southeast Asia. There have been between 1000 and 1500 acts of piracy in the last ten years with an average of around 40 incidents a year. The vast majority are attacks against unarmed merchant vessels with ferries and private craft being the small minority. Most pirates are armed with submachine guns and use small speedboats to jump the slow moving vessels. They then commandeer the craft to a safe harbor where they unload the tons of cargo. The losses from piracy in the Pacific amount to over $100 million a year.

Cruise ships are much safer with the occasional engine room fire and food poisoning problem. However it doesn't provide much comfort to know that the *Achille Lauro*, (site of the terrorist takeover that ended in the execution of a wheelchair bound American Leon Klinghoffer), sank off the coast of Africa but is now being dredged up and refurbished for use as a luxury cruise liner.

HOW TO SURVIVE BOATS

It is hard to provide general safety tips considering the wide range of waterborne craft travelers can take. Large cruise ships have very different safety problems when compared to pirogues. Here is a starting list.

- **Know how to swim, or at least how to float. Panic kills.**

- **Wear or have quick access to a life preserver. Don't assume that the large chest labelled "Life Preservers" actually has usable life preservers in it. Look.**

- **Do not take overcrowded boats. Charter your own or ask when the boat will be less crowded. Overcrowding and rough seas are the number one reason for sinking of small and medium sized ships.**

- **Avoid travel in rough weather, during monsoon or hurricane season.**

- **Stay off the water in areas frequented by pirates. This is typically the strait of Malacca and the coastal areas of the Philippines, Thailand and Southern China.**

- **In cold weather remember where the covered life rafts are. Understand the effects and prevention of hypothermia.**

- **On large ships pay attention to safety and lifeboat briefings and practice going from your cabin to the lifeboat station with your eyes closed.**

- **Keep a small carry-on or backpack with your money, papers and minor survival gear (water, energy bars, hat, compass and map). Make it waterproof and a potential life preserver by using one or two garbage bags as a liner.**

- **Prepare and bring items to prevent seasickness, sunburn, glare and chapped skin.**

- **Bring binoculars, books, coastal maps, pens and a journal to pass away the time.**

Flying

North America is the safest place to fly. But that virtually implies that flying is generally dangerous. It isn't. Only 1187 people died in plane crashes in 1996. It is even more telling that among the top ten aircraft disasters most of them occurred when the planes were shot or blown out of the skies or while taxiing on the ground. So view any statistical journey into aircraft danger as proof of the relative safety of this modern marvel. One British study shows that flying is 176 times safer than walking, 15 times safer than car travel and 300 times safer than riding a motorcycle. Statistically if you were to take a flight every morning you would have to fly for 21,000 years before you would have a deadly crash. Australia has not had a fatal crash in 10 years. There are 12,000 (some say 9000) airliners in the sky making over 15 million flights carrying 1.3 billion passengers. With all that activity, there are only about 40 accidents involving major airlines (including cargo planes) every year. Still, the volume of air traffic and emerging travel boom in Asia has prompted Boeing to say that there will be a major air crash every week by the year 2010. A dramatic statement, but that still only means 12 more accidents a year at a time when there will be twice as many airliners in operation.

First World Roulette

If you fly any First World airline, your chances of being killed in a crash are one in 4.4 million, according to MIT. If you are on a U.S. carrier, flying coast to coast, the odds are even better, one in 11 million. About two-thirds of major airline crashes have been blamed on flight crew error. When you change from a big bird to a puddle-jumper you have just increased your chances of crashing by a factor of four. Commuter flights (flights with 30 or fewer seats) carry about 12 percent of all passengers. These small planes not only fly lower, take off and land more often, but are piloted by less experienced, more overworked pilots and are not subject to the same safety standards as large airliners.

Get on a smaller private plane or a charter and the odds multiply again. About 700 people die in small plane crashes each year in America. There are so many crashes that the small airplane industry has evaporated because of the resultant litigation. There are 650,000 private pilots in the U.S. and only 700 out of the 13,000 airfields have control towers. The accident rate for a small plane is about 11 for every 100,000 aircraft hours compared to 0.8 for commercial jets. There are two fatalities for every 100,000 hours of operation for small planes.

OK, that's the good news. Now I'll give you the bad news. Last year was the deadliest ever for deaths due to plane crashes. Well, that is if you eliminate the mileage covered by the typical plane flight and just look at the statistics by trip. Then cars are 12 times safer than airplanes. Want more? Well, maybe you should be sweating on take off and landing since 68 percent of accidents happen during the 6 percent of time spent getting off and back on terra firma.

Dangerous Trips	
Things look a little different when you eliminate the miles covered and focus on the accident rate based on the number of man-hours exposed to a form of transportation	
Motorcycle	300
Bicycle	60
Walking	20
Automobile	15
Airplane	15
Bus	6.6

Train	4.8
Bus	.1

Source: Royal Society for the Prevention of Accidents

Third World Roulette

You do need to know that 75 percent of air accidents happen in countries that account for only 12 percent of world air traffic. Also they happen in countries where travel by car is much more dangerous. Even U.S. puddle-jumpers are as safe as houses compared to Third World airlines. If you are flying anywhere in Africa, the chances of crashing are multiplied by 20—about the same odds as getting killed in an automobile accident in the States. Some experts calculate the odds of being killed in a plane crash are less than one in a million for North America, Canada and Western Europe versus one in 50,000 for the dark continent.

Latin America, the Middle East, Asia and Eastern Europe follow Africa as the most dangerous areas of the world. Some number crunchers say that Eastern Europe has the highest accident rate in the world to fly. Not surprising considering that poorer countries fly old aircraft usually purchased from major carriers who have already wrung every useful mile from their abused frames. In the U.S. the fatality rate can be expressed as 0.5 for every million miles flown, in Russia it is ten times higher (5.2) and twenty times higher in China (10).

Fatal Accidents per Hundred Thousand Flights	
Africa	21
Asia	13
South America	8
Central America	8
Europe	5
North America	2
Caribbean	2

Source: Flight Safety Foundation

The most dangerous places to fly are on local carriers in **China**, **North Korea**, **Colombia**, all countries in **Central Africa** and all countries in the **CIS**. In **Nigeria**, they had to ground all their planes when they found that one of the maintenance crews had stolen an important navigational computer. It is wise to avoid all flights inside **India** and throughout the **Andes**. But faced with taking a clapped-out bus over rugged mountains, most people choose clapped-out airplanes. China has the world's worst air piracy record, and Russian flight crews are known to accept bribes to overload planes with extra passengers, baggage and cargo.

Russian Roulette

If you consider that the space station MIR is the pinnacle of Russian aviation technology then the only safe thing about flying in Russia is that it's safe to be afraid. The U.S. State Department has instructed government employees to avoid using all Russian airlines unless absolutely necessary. Britain, Canada and other nations have issued similar warnings. The International Airline Passengers Association issued an unprecedented warning that flying anywhere in the former Soviet Union is unsafe. It's said that if the flight doesn't nail you, the food will. *DP* flew to Lake Baikal in Siberia where the passenger exit of a Tupelov had to be sealed with gaffer's tape before takeoff. We were on a commandeered military cargo flight and the only reason they taped the door shut was to make sure the door wouldn't fly open and suck the cargo out. Thoughtful touch. It's a good thing it was our gaffer's tape.

There are about 15,000 aircraft (major and minor) operating in Russia at any one time, most of them ready to be turned into frying pans. What's flying like in the CIS? Russian airports make inner city bus stations seem like Taj Mahals. Traffic controllers would have a hard time refereeing a volleyball game and the only time businessmen pick up stewardesses is when they fall over from drinking too much. Russian passengers think safety demonstrations are Macarena lessons and the only thing that falls down from the overhead panel during decompression will be your luggage.

Some sources put the odds of dying in a Russian crash at seven times the global average. Based on miles flown, ten times as many passengers died in Russian crashes than U.S. crashes. In one 18-month period, there were more than a dozen air crashes in the former Soviet Union, involving both commercial and military aircraft, killing more than 500 people. There are a number reasons to be afraid. Russia has a lot of nasty weather, bad runways, tough terrain, funky engines and slapped together aircraft. Safety inspectors make about $100 a month, making it easier to bribe them to keep the planes flying than actually doing the necessary maintenance work.

Before the Soviet breakup in 1991, Aeroflot was the largest airline in the world with more than 4000 planes. Carrying more than 100 million passengers annually, it maintained a safety record in line with the international average. Now the CIS has more than 300 separate carriers. To give you a taste of just how fun flying in Russia is, an Airbus A-310 crashed, killing all 75 people on board—apparently while the pilot was giving an impromptu flight lesson to his teenage son.

Things are looking up in Russia. Although almost half the Russian fleet was put into service during the Cold War, they are replacing their aircraft at the rate of about 150–300 a year. In many cases they are buying American. When Aeroflot looked to replace some creaky Tupolev 134's they bought Boeing 737's instead of a cheaper Russian repalcement. They even ordered Pratt & Whitney engines on a new score of Ilyushin-96's.

Colombian Roulette

In 1996, more than 550 people died in plane crashes in Latin America. In one crash, off the coast of the Dominican Republic, sharks beat the rescuers to the scene. Colombia has the worst air-safety record in the Americas, according to the International Airline Passengers Association, a consumer group based in Dallas. Citing aircraft accident rates, India and Colombia were declared the two most dangerous countries to fly in.

After deregulation in Colombia in 1990, the number of passenger and cargo airlines serving El Dorado Airport in Bogota surged from 24, three years ago, to 68 today. In the same four years, the volume of international passengers arriving in Colombia jumped by 55 percent. Last year El Dorado handled 170,000 takeoffs and landings. By comparison, Gatwick Airport in London registered 180,000 takeoffs and landings in 1992.

Chinese Roulette

There are about 40 different airlines flying in China. China is a leading contender for the title of the most dangerous place in the world to fly. The Flight Safety Foundation says that China accounts for 16 percent of all global flights but 70 percent of all accidents.

China's biggest problem is a shortage of pilots. Passenger air travel is expected to grow 20 percent annually until the year 2000. To keep up with demand, the country needs 600 new pilots a year. But China can only turn out less than half that number. Once a pilot is on the job, the workload is excruciating. Although Chinese regulations set the limit at 100 hours of flight time a month to avoid pilot fatigue, pilots average 280 hours. China's airspace is controlled by the military and civilian airlines must request use of it; then they are allotted narrow air corridors. There is a severe shortage of radar and ground equipment. Some parts of the country have no IFR controls, meaning that flying can be done only in good weather. In January of '97 the Chinese government said that the government owned airlines had flown 29 months without an accident.

Airlines on the *DP* "Thanks, I'll think I'll walk" list are Air Afrique, Nigerian Airways, Cubana, Indian Airlines, Garuda, Aeroflot and any airline that has a laughing goat as a logo.

HOW TO SURVIVE FLYING

Despite all the unnerving statistics, if you have a choice of transportation when traveling long distances, jump on a plane. This applies even in Russia, China or South America. Yes, it is dangerous but not as dangerous as enduring the kaleidoscope of misery and misfortune that awaits you on the ground.

- Stick to U.S.-based carriers with good safety records.

- Fly between major airports on nonstop flights.

- Avoid bad weather or flying at night.

- You can sit in the back if you want (the rear 10 rows are usually intact in case of ground impact but the passengers are dead) or above the wing (you may get thrown clear, seat and all) or near an exit (easier egress in case of fire or emergency landing) might be just as advisable.

- Avoid small charter aircraft, dirt strips and non-instrument fields.

- The smaller the plane the higher the risk. The poorer the country, same deal except when foreign carriers operate airplanes in Third World countries.

- Avoid national carriers that are not allowed to fly into the United States.

- Avoid military cargo flights, tagging along on combat missions, or flying over active combat or insurgence areas like Tajikistan and Afghanistan. (You paid $19.95 to be told this!)

- Avoid older Soviet or Chinese-made aircraft or helicopters.

- **Kroll puts out a monthly Airport and Airline Watch with enough hair-raising tales of smoke filled cabins, blown tires, near misses and hijackings to keep you glued firmly to the ground. $195 per year (703) 319-8050.**

- **After all this, remember that travel by airliner is the safest method of transportation and that your odds of surviving a plane crash are about 50 percent.**

- **If you are still terrified, remember you can buy flight insurance at 150 airports around the U.S. You can get half a million dollars of insurance for $16.65 or you can spend the same amount on four stiff drinks. We recommend the former, but usually end up doing the latter.**

Trains

Trains are supposed to be safe. After all they run on rails, are usually pointed in one direction and rumored to be immune to the inclement weather that dogs airplanes, buses and cars. There's a joke that conductors like to tell:"What is the last thing a bug sees when it hits the windshield of a train?" The answer: Its asshole. What that means is when trains do hit, they hit hard.

Trains tend to run into substantial objects like trucks stalled on crossings or other trains coming the other way. The fact that trains have limited mobility make them ideal targets for terrorists and bandits. Criminals enjoy the opportunities trains afford, as sleeping passengers present easy targets and a clean escape is available at the next rest stop.

Using the death rate per million miles as a guide, American trains are about twice as dangerous as flying, four times safer than driving and a lot safer than local buses. If they have a bar car you can quickly douse your fears as you watch the war-ravaged countryside zip by.

HOW TO SURVIVE TRAINS

- **Ask locals whether the train is a target for bandits (this is appropriate in Eastern Europe, Russia, Asia or Africa where terrorists, bandits and insurgents regularly target trains).**

- **Beware of Eastern European train routes where thieves are known to ride as passengers. Sleep with the window cracked open to avoid being gassed.**

- **Stash your valuables in secret spots making it more difficult for robbers to locate your belongings.**

- **The back of the train is traditionally the safest area in the event of a collision. Unless, of course, your train is rear ended.**

- **Keep your luggage with you at all times if possible. Be nice to the conductor and he will keep an eye out for you.**

- **Trains are preferable to buses or cars when traveling through mountainous areas, deserts and jungles.**

Natural Disasters

Have a nice day. Spoken like a true Californian. Out here we have earthquakes, mudslides, fires, drought and flood. And that's just the attractions at Universal Studios theme park. The reality is that about 11,000 people die worldwide from natural disasters. For example, in 1996 there were 600 major natural disasters. In one year there were 200 storms, 170 floods, 50 earthquakes, 30 volcanic eruptions and 150 landslides and forest fires. The bad news is that natural disasters are up 400 percent from three decades ago

An average 400 people are hit by lightning (about 90 die) every year in the U.S. The solution? Minimize contact with the ground and get down real low. Don't lie down. The most dangerous place to get hit by lightning according to the National Climactic Data Center are open fields and ball fields.

Making the Best of Nasty Situations

Or When Statistics Divided by Nobody=You

You should have the transportation thing down now. Everybody gets a little nervous when their body is accelerated or transported. You've also figured out why they don't have insurance machines in minibus terminals, and why bus drivers cover their entire windshield with religious fetishes. You also know the statistical equality between walking drunk and blindfolded down the middle of a freeway and driving your own car in Pakistan. So now we want to turn the danger meter up a few more notches. Let's do all these things in places where they have daily rocket reports instead of weather updates, and where nice rebels like filling up potholes every night with land mines. Welcome to travel in the world's nasty places.

Welcome to the Wars of the Innocents

Warfare is not a bad thing for tourists. It keeps them safe. Compared to today's complex and subterranean conflicts, wars in the first five decades of this century were geographically and politically concise affairs that ended with a winner and a loser. After a period of time, it was back to temple gawking and the normal business of tourism. Today warfare creates poisoned subways, blown up federal buildings, hijacked airplanes and smoking office towers in places where jaywalking is considered a crime. The old wars generated plenty of headlines to warn off bus tourists, plenty of State Department Warnings, and lots of photos of blown up people and cratered buildings to remind us just how dangerous it is over there.

But name a real war today. A war is where two sides have officially declared it and mobilized sharply uniformed armies. If you said Bosnia, Panama, Zaire (Congo), Sierra Leone, Somalia, or even Haiti, you're wrong. Those were just nasty places Uncle Sam sent soldiers to. If you said the Gulf War, The Cold War, The Iran-Iraq War or even The Vietnam War, you are way out of touch since those conflicts have been long resolved. Did you even know there are wars in Turkey, Cambodia, Papua New Guinea, Algeria and Colombia? Well, there are, only these countries don't like to use the "W" word because it scares away tourists and investors. The governments will tell you that they are "fighting criminal elements within their sovereign regions" or "prosecuting foreign elements within their borders." The truth is, there are no old fashioned wars today. Those who have officially declared wars like Syria and Israel do it more for the political effect than the ultimate military outcome. Wars in this decade are fought by the CIA (Sudan, Northern Iraq), mining companies (Sierra Leone), religious zealots (Afghanistan), wackos (Uganda), families (Somalia), drug smugglers (Colombia), puppets (Congo) and thugs (Albania). In most of these cases not one of the combatants has read the Geneva convention. Many don't even know where Geneva is. Think you're smart? When was the last time you visited the Somaliland, Republic of Bougainville, Pahktunistan, East Turkestan, Sanaag or Kurdistan? All these countries exist, but not on any western atlas. The truth is that there are thousands of people dying every year to defend or create these new countries.

So welcome to the War of the Innocents. According to the U.N., of the 82 or so armed conflicts that were fought in the past three years, only three were between nations. The rest were civil wars or insurgencies. Four million civilians have been killed in wars since 1990 and the death toll rises every minute. And, there is absolutely no guarantee that you might not be the next casualty.

It is difficult to define war today. No longer is it a series of well planned battles between two opposing armies. There are few uniforms, few battlefields and even fewer marching songs and flying colors. When they pick up bodies these days, they tend to be young girls in Algeria, old women in Afghanistan or teenage kids in Karachi. In the wars of the past, 90 percent of casualties consisted of soldiers; today, 90 percent of the casualties are civilians. This is the new face of war. The new battleground is the city and the suburbs.

In Algeria, Tajikistan, Turkey, Sri Lanka and East Timor, there is no formal war, yet the body count in each country exceeds the total number of Americans killed in Vietnam. Worse yet, armed groups in some of these countries are specifically targeting Westerners, other visitors or expats for kidnapping or execution. Is this a war or a turkey shoot?

Various liberation groups around the world are looking for a few good victims and that could be you. The total number of deaths from international terrorism declined from 314 to 165 in a one-year span, but the number of people wounded increased by a factor of 10—to 6291 people, according to the U.S. State Department. Of 440 terrorist attacks recently, Western Europe was the most popular venue with 272 attacks, the Middle East placed second, then Latin America. Ninety-nine terrorist attacks were directed at American interests. Since tourists don't visit these terrorist infested places, we force them to come to us. Civilized places where terrorism is a major problem are England, France, Spain, China, Turkey and the United States.

There are also nasty places that are never featured on the front page, such as Burundi, Russia, Sudan, South Africa and others.

Where are the hot spots? Usually in destitute countries where things fell apart a long time ago, countries making the rocky transition from dictatorships to democracy and countries that tried to stuff too many ethnic or religious groups into a happy second world state. According to the UN, Algeria, Afghanistan, Angola, Myanmar, Burundi, Egypt, Georgia, Haiti, Iraq, Liberia, Mexico, Mozambique, Nigeria, Sudan, Tajikistan, Rwanda and Zaire are nations in crisis and in danger of social disintegration. Some of these countries never had anything to disintegrate from.

There are many other civilized countries such as South Africa, Russia, Brazil, Pakistan and the U.S. where there is just old fashioned criminal mayhem taking place on a daily basis. There are about 30 wars where more than 1000 people are killed each year. Seven of those wars kill over 100,000 people a year.

Ever wonder why you don't see much on these places on your local newscast or even on CNN? First of all, the ratings and the PR strategies of low level conflicts suck. News crews need compliant officials and basic communications to cover stories. Many countries like Papua New Guinea, Sri Lanka and Turkey won't allow journos in for fear they will contest the "official" daily body count. A few folks like *DP* have to sneak in but we will never go prime time. And in the case of Sri Lanka, even the rebels won't let us in. So these places are assigned to eager, but poorly paid stringers who routinely send in casualty reports but never get the big picture. Also journalists aren't bulletproof anymore. According to the Reporters san Frontiere, an average of 60 journalists are killed each year and more than 125 are detained by local governments who objected to their reports.

Until more official wars start up (with official battlefield tours and air conditioned press offices), war correspondents will not make as much money as bleached blonde anchors and gossip columnists. Maybe that's why some of the better war correspondents have opted to embrace hair spray and reduce their fears to being punched out by Sean Penn. For now, the front-line witnesses of history will consist of a lot of scared civilians, ragged soldiers, gonzo stringers and *DP*'ers.

Watching War Waste

Believe it or not, until *DP* took out the calculator and pencil there was no single reliable "Chart of Wars That Can Kill Tourists Now." We are not going to provide any stirring editorials on the horrors or futilities of war, we just want you to know what's going on. There are lots of unofficial estimates, security service updates and state department warnings, but in our opinion there is no definitive list that reflects rebel, government and civilian casualties. The other thing you would expect is that these "kill" numbers would be changing at the rate of those national deficit billboards. I compared as many statistics as we could find, gave them a fudge factor (fibbing rebels and eager governments) and extrapolated them about two months down the road. Keep in mind that many of the high death tolls are the result of starvation being used directly as a tactic of war. Also many regions have no official reporting, so we rely on local folks to give us a feel for how busy the morgue is.

To show you just how much history you may be missing, *DP* has compiled the mother of all lists. In our futile attempt to makes sense of this list, we have used the term war to describe instances when police or military are actively campaigning. The grey bars denote areas recovering from warfare:

Country	Type	Cause	Since	With	Killed
ALGERIA	War	Religious, Political	1992	GIA vs. Gov.	80,000
AFGHANISTAN	War	Political	1989	Taliban vs. Tajiks	25,000

Country	Type	Cause	Since	With	Killed
ANGOLA	Banditry	Political Diamonds	1975	UNITA, FLEC	400,000+
ARMENIA	Ethnic	Religious, Ethnic	1988	Occupation of Azerbaijan	N/A
AZERBAIJAN	Ethnic	Occupation	1988	Nagorno Karabakh	40,000
BOUGAINVILLE	See Papua New Guinea				
BOSNIA-HERZEGOVINA	Ethnic	Occupation	1991	Serbs vs. Bosnian-Croats & Muslims	210,000
BURUNDI	Civil War	Ethnic	1988	Hutu vs. Tutsi	180,000
CAMBODIA	Civil War	Political	1970	Royalists/Khmer Rouge vs. Gov.	2,000,000+
CHINA	Occupation	Political	1950	Tibet	1,200,000
	Insurgency	Ethnic		Muslim Turks East Turkmenistan (Xiangang)	3000?
CONGO (BRAZZAVILLE)	Violence	Political	1995	Old Marxists vs. Gov.	10,000
CONGO (KINSHASHA)	Ethnic Political	Ethnic CIA	1997	Kabila vs. Mobutu supporters	200,000+
COLOMBIA	Drug War, Crime	Ethnic, Political, Ideological, Drugs	1986	FARC, ELN, EZLN	25,000
DJIBOUTI	Ethnic	Ethnic, Tribal	1991	Afar vs. Issa tribes	350
EGYPT	Fundamentalism	Religious	1992	The Islamic Group	700
GEORGIA	Ethnic	Ethnic	1992	Abkhazia	30,000
	Ethnic	Ethnic	1991	South Ossetia	N/A
	Ethnic	Political	1991	Mkhedrioni Horsemen militia	N/A
GHANA	Ethnic	Tribal	1994	Konkombas vs. Nunumba & Dagomba	6,000
GUATEMALA	Banditry	Economic	1968	Disbanded rebels	100,000
INDIA	War	Occupation	1989	Kashmir: Muslim vs. Hindu	25,000

Country	Type	Cause	Since	With	Killed
	Religious	Religious	1981	Punjab: Sikh vs. Hindu	14,000
	Insurgency	Tribal	1969	Andhra Pradesh: Maosist Naxalites: Peoples War Group vs Gov.	80
	Insurgency	Tribal Factional	1985	Assam: Bodos vs. Bengai Hindus NDFB vs. BLTF	5500
	Insurgency	Tribal	1954	Nagaland, Manipur: various tribal groups	N/A
INDONESIA	Insurgency	Occupation	1975	Timor: Timorese FRETELIN vs. Gov.	210,000
	Insurgency	Political	1989	North Sumatra: Aceh Merdaka (Freedom Aceh) vs. Gov.	2,500
	Insurgency	Occupation	1963	Irian Jaya: Papua Independent Organization (OPM) vs Gov.	150,000
IRAQ	War	Religious	1991	Southern Iraq Marsh Gov. Sunni vs. Marsh Arab Shi'a Muslim	250,000
	War	Ethnic	1981	Northern Iraq: Kurds vs. Gov.	180,000
ISRAEL	War	Occupation	1948	Jews vs Muslim	3500
KURDISTAN	See Turkey & Iraq			Kurds.vs Turks	30,000
LEBANON	War	Occupation	1982	South: Hezbollah vs. Israeli Defense Force	25,000
LIBERIA	Ethnic	Tribal	1989	Tribal warfare	150,000
MALI	Ethnic	Racial	1990	North: Arab Turag vs. Black	220
MEXICO	Ethnic, Drugs	Political Drugs	1994	South: Zapatistas, EPR	200
MOROCCO	Insurgency	Occupation	1973	Western Sahara: Polisario	2000?
MYANMAR	Ethnic	Ethnic	1992	Royhinga Muslims	N/A
	Ethnic	Ethnic	1948	Kachin Independence Army	N/A

Country	Type	Cause	Since	With	Killed
	War	Ethnic	1942	Karen National Union	N/A
	Ethnic Tension	Ethnic	1948	Karenni	N/A
	Ethnic Tension	Drugs	1948	Mong Tai	N/A
NIGER	Ethnic	Racial	1991	North: Arab Turaeg vs. black gov.	N/A
PAPUA NEW GUINEA	War	Mining Ethnic	1988	Bougainville Revolutionary Army (BRA) vs. Gov.	10,000
	Crime	Economic		"Rascals" vs. Police/ Army	N/A
PERU	Political Tension	Border Dispute	1942	Peru vs. Ecuador	30,000
	War	Ideological, Drugs	1980	Maoists groups	32,000
PHILIPPINES	Unrest	Political	1969	New Peoples Army	3,500
	War	Religious	1974	South: Abu Sayeff, MILF,	5000
RWANDA	Ethnic	Ethnic	1990	Huts vs. Tutsi	500,000
RUSSIA	Ethnic	Ethnic, Drugs	1994	Chechens	80,000
	War	Ethnic, Drugs	1991	Tajikistan	50,000
SENEGAL	Ethnic	Tribal	1983	Casamance (Dioula) vs. Senegalese (Wolof)	1000
SIERRA LEONE	War	Military Mining	1991	Coup leaders vs. ECOMOG (Nigeria)	30,000
SOMALIA	War	Clan	1978	Ogaden vs. Rahawaine clan	500,000
	War	Political	1991	breakaway Somaliland	350,000
SRI LANKA	War	Ethnic	1983	Tamil LTTE vs. Gov.	50,000
SUDAN	War	Ethnic,Oil Religious	1963	Muslim north vs. SPLA in South	500,000
TAJIKISTAN	(SEE RUSSIA)				
TURKEY	War	Ethnic	1984	Kurds vs. Gov.	30,000

Country	Type	Cause	Since	With	Killed
UGANDA	Insurgency	Religion	1979	North: Lord's Resistance Army	2000
	Insurgency	Religion	1995	West: Muslim West Nile Bank, ADF vs. Gov.	N/A
UNITED KINGDOM	Insurgency	Colonial Religious	1968	Northern Ireland IRA vs. Gov.	3200

SOURCE: DP, VARIOUS

History of War

18 million people have died because of warfare between 1945 and 1994

East Asia	10,371,000
Central/South Asia	2,857,000
Sub Saharan Africa	2,685,000
Latin America	447,000
Europe	186,000
North America	108,000

Source: IISS, London

The Killing Zones

You bought your flak jacket, got a great deal on a white hardskin Suzuki and swapped your expensive Leica M6s for disposable Nikons. You are on assignment thanks to an ambiguous commitment from a couple of weekly rags and a letter from a free counter-culture listing weekly. Your pack is stuffed with film, Power Bars, syringes and phrase books. Now all you have to do is figure out what the hell is going on.

War zones are pretty easy places to understand, as are their players. One side doesn't like the other side so it bums money from a rich uncle (which they will pay off in favorable trade deals and political favors). For example, Libya paid for Charles Taylor (Liberia) and Foday Sankoh (Sierra Leone) to raise hell. All the while the SPLA dances to the tune the CIA plays. Hey, those tanks and bullets cost money. Payback comes in lucrative oil and mineral deals once the rebels are in power.

There are front lines, kill zones and safe zones, but before you get to stumble around in these you need to get in. *DP* likes to travel without baggage, but if you are a photographer, producer or talking head you have to bring in tons of equipment, rent satellite links, order breakfasts, make appointments and do all that stuff you do back home, except at work there is no electricity, phone service, running water or civilization. You need to get permission. But not always from the guy whose picture is on their money.

Believe it or not, smart rebels usually open a press office in London, Paris or Washington while they have unlisted offices in Damascus, Tripoli or Khartoum.

To get in, you need permission either from the rebels (who usually are as extraordinarily inefficient, underfunded as they are helpful and incompetent) or the government (which is usually as slick and efficient as it is unhelpful). The rebels will give you a contact name, a place and time to show up, and a letter that just as likely will put you in jail (as *DP* discovered in Ethiopia) as into the middle of complete chaos. If you do it the official way, you need to be a bona fide journalist. Then the government (if it is looking for global brownie points) will load you up with official studies, contact names, military transportation in country and a tour of what may or may not be the front lines. Naturally, you see more bloodletting and violence at the front row of a Mike Tyson fight than on these tours which usually consist of more briefings, deserted rebel camps and captured prisoners.

Deadline	
Between 1987 and 1996, 474 journalists were killed. One hundred twenty-eight were killed in Europe and the Republics of the Former Soviet Union, 116 in the Americas, 94 in the Middle East and Africa, 85 in Asia and 51 in Sub-Saharan Africa. Reporters Sans Frontieres *says that 600 have been killed on duty and as a result of what they had written. In 1996 27 journalists were killed.*	
Algeria	60
Colombia	41
Philippines	30
Tajikistan	29
Russia	29
Croatia	26
Bosnia and Herzegovina	21
Turkey	20
Peru	19
India	17
United States	7

Sources: CPJ, RSF.

If you think you'll be the only journo in the thick of things, good luck. The CIA will not invite you to Northern Iraq or Southern Sudan to discuss long range planning any more than Kabila will invite you to Kinshasa to discuss his plans for Paris shopping trips. The world of war is a shadowy world of lies, propaganda and circumstantial evidence. Case in point, Turkey invited compliant journos to inspect the deserted PKK camp at Zap. *DP's* Roddy Scott goes in the back door, ends up being the only moron in Northern Turkey during the big Turkish offensive and is summarily tossed out by the KDP. Later the PKK's Ocalan wants to rant from his base in Syria (oops, we mean the Bekaa Valley) about how he actually abandoned the base on purpose and how he (very nobly, but tense sensitive) insists that "every Kurd will be a living bomber." Who the hell wants to risk their life to write articles about that? And what desk editor wants to figure it all out?

As for the bang-bang stuff, remember that traditional wars are fought like Red Rover, you run as fast as you can into the other side, lose a few people and then run back. Then it's the other side's turn. Whoever loses the most people or gains the most ground wins. Traditional warfare usually starts just before dawn and lasts until one side runs out of steam. Katushyas, artillery and tanks look good but not on the receiving end like *DP* experienced in Kabul. Gunships are really "in" because they can eliminate entire villages or rebel columns. Rocket pods and miniguns make nice puffs and direct the audience towards the target. Tanks and APC's are more for occupied areas because they are grenade-proof. Usually once the government gets the bill for all these pyrotechnics, it quickly figures out it's easier to negotiate a ceasefire while desperately trying to assassinate the rebel leaders. So get in quick, get out quick is the rule.

Today's low intensity wars are not the hand-to-hand stuff John Wayne popularized. Mortars and rocket launchers are big, usually forcing the other side back with shrapnel and the sight of eviscerated comrades. Wildly spraying the other side with bullets from behind corners and walls is popular. Night ambushes, bombs, mines and boobytraps are the meat and potatoes of smaller rebel groups. In most cases, the idea is to cause havoc, disrupt the normal flow of business and get governments where it hurts them the most; the pocketbook and the mind.

In all cases *DP* does not advise traveling in or to war zones because of the fluidity of the situation, the equal opportunity danger from gun ships and just the old fashioned danger involved. If you do find yourself in a war zone you might want to know how to live a little longer. Remember that a civilian or noncombatant is more likely to get killed than a soldier, and that usually means you.

HOW TO SURVIVE WAR ZONES

Remember that small wars are not a carefully planned or predictable activity. More importantly, land mines, shells, stray bullets and booby traps have no political affiliation or mercy. Keep the following in mind.

- Contact people who have returned or are currently in the hot zone. Do not trust the representations of rebel or government contacts. Check it out yourself.

- Avoid politics, do not challenge the beliefs of your host, be firm but not belligerent about getting what you need. Talking politics with soldiers is like reading Playboy with the Pope. It kills time, but is probably not a rewarding pastime.

- Do not engage in intrigue or meetings that are not in public view. They still shoot spies. Do accept any invitations for dinner, tea or social activities. Getting to know your hosts is important. Do not gossip or lie.

- Travel only under the permission of the controlling party. In many cases you will need multiple permission from officers, politicians and the regional commander.

- Remember that a letter of safe passage from a freedom group presented to an army check point could be your death warrant. Understand and learn the zones of control and protocol for changing sides during active hostilities.

- Carry plenty of identification, articles, letters of recommendation and character references. It may not keep you out of jail, but it may delay your captors long enough to effect an escape.

- Bring photographs of your family, friends, house, dog or car. Carry articles you have written or ones that mention you. A photo ID is important, but even a high school yearbook can provide more proof.

- Check in with the embassy, military intelligence, local businessmen and bartenders. Do not misrepresent yourself, exaggerate or tell white lies. Keep your story simple and consistent.

- Dress and act conservatively. Be quietly engaging, affable and listen a lot. Your actions will indicate your intentions as the locals weigh their interest in helping you. It may take a few days for the locals to check you out before they offer any assistance.

- Remember that it is very unusual for noncombatants to be wandering around areas of conflict. If you are traveling make sure you have the name of a person that you wish to see, an end destination and a reason for passing through.

- Understand where the front lines are, the general rules of engagement, meet with journalists and photographers (usually found at the hotel bar) to understand the local threats.

- Carry a lot of money hidden in various places, be ready to leave or evacuate at any time. This means traveling very light. Choose a place to sleep that would be survivable in case of a rocket or shell attack.

- Visit with the local Red Cross, UN, Embassy and other relief workers to understand the situation. They are an excellent source of health information and may be your only ticket out.

- If warranted buy and wear an armored vest or flak jacket (see the Save Yourself chapter). Carry your blood type and critical info (name, country, phone, local contact, allergies,) on a laminated card or written on your vest. Wear a Medic-Alert bracelet.

- Carry a first aid kit with syringes, antibiotics, IV needles, anesthetics and pain killers as well as the usual medication. It might be wise to use auto inject syringes. Discuss any prescriptions with your doctor in advance.

- Understand and learn the effect, range and consequences of guns, land mines, mortars, snipers and other machines of war.

- Get life and health (and KRE if relevant) insurance and don't lie. Tell them the specific country you will be traveling to. Also check with the emergency evacuation services to see if they can go into a war zone to pull you out.

- Carry a military style medical manual to aid in treating field wounds. Take a first aid class and understand the effects and treatment of bullet wounds and other major trauma.

TIPS FOR JOURNALISTS

- Remember that people in wartime are highly unstable emotionally. Many young fighters often can have a blood lust. They may not respond rationally. Be careful of revenge killings in areas where western mercenaries are found or in former European colonial regions.

- Journalists can be specifically targeted for execution. In former Soviet areas journos are considered spies (which they were). Areas of ethnic cleansing are very dangerous. Bosnia was a good example. Carry a detachable banner or sign with the local word for press printed on it. If a journalist is kidnapped contact the Red Cross Journalist Hotline, 19 Ave. De la Paix, CH-1202 Geneva Switzerland TEL: 41 22 734-6001, FAX 41 22 734-8280

- Carry and show your photos and articles. Do not show gory pictures or articles sympathetic to any side. Point to your name, show them your passport and help them understand your background.

- Travel with an open heart and do not criticize or judge. Do not lie or suggest any affiliation you don't have. In wartime people form alliances based on their gut feel and the look in your eyes. You will be checked out via computer or phone.

- **Try to use a simple notebook and write in your own handwriting as illegibly as possible. Use medium priced auto focus cameras that are not too painful to replace. Do not make drawings or maps. Ask permission or point to your camera and give a thumbs up.**

- **Keep a blank roll of film or tape handy. When soldiers demand your film or tape you can unload, make the switch and then reload the original.**

- **Snipers like to hone in on lights, bright colors and even decals. Things like cigarettes, head flashlights, video eye pieces, strobe ready lights and press decals can become targets.**

- **Arrive prepared for no electricity, food shortages, water shortages, no sheets, no laundry, no medicine and no banks.**

- **Contact the various journalist protection groups like CPJ (212) 279-3733, 465-1104 listed in the back of the book for more specific warnings and information on the region you will be traveling to.**

In the Land of The Yankee Pig

America is such a polyglot culture that it is impossible to stereotype a country of a quarter billion people who literally come from every country in the world (if you assume that the Indians came over the land bridge from Russia). Yet people from all over the world have an itch to walk straight up to you and yell, "Die American Pig!" or "Get out of Bosnia" or any other slogan of the week. It is questionable whether it is America or, for that matter, its power tool, the United Nations that aggravates or prolongs regional tensions when trying to relieve them. Do Russia and the United States have the right to military interference in foreign countries? Do aid programs actually create starvation and suffering by artificially shifting populations to refugee camps, and thereby increasing the birth rate and then creating total disaster when the supplies stop? America's biggest fault is that we instinctively rush in to save the world when the starving children and shattered bodies hit the headlines, but when we actually learn the real complexities and cost we recoil in horror and disappear.

Much of the anger toward Americans is a direct result of others' perception of our need to control foreign governments. If the government feels it lacks sufficient political clout in certain regions of the world, it brings out the checkbook. The U.S. bought peace in the Middle East by writing checks to both sides, thereby aggravating fanatics on both sides. We also support a wide variety of dictators, despots and other nondemocratically elected rulers because they are less antagonistic toward the U.S. The U.S. also wages financial, moral, covert (and not so covert) operations against enemies of the state, such as the Islamic fundamentalists, drug dealers, unfriendly dictators and gangsters. We do this by supporting (or sometimes creating) opposition forces with money, weapons and military training. This creates a lot of ill will towards "Americans" regardless of their beliefs or background.

You may find it surprising to see how obvious the U.S. "covert" presence is in Third World countries. Terrorist groups keep very good tabs on CIA and other government agents in their countries. And hey guess what? Spies look just like you.

The problem for the traveler is that in some areas, such as the Middle East, Southeast Asia, Central Africa and areas where Americans are rarely seen, you will be assumed to be working for or allied with American intelligence agencies. Although I'm Canadian, I have been accused on numerous occasions of being "CIA" in war zones simply because I had no plausible explanation as to why I was there.

If you look and act like an American you will be assumed to be gathering information. You'll run the risk of confrontation, kidnapping, detainment or harassment. Execution is rare, since Americans are worth more alive (financially and politically) than dead.

HOW TO SURVIVE BEING A YANKEE PIG

Whether you accept it or not, if you are of European extraction, or were raised on T-bones and Pepsis or even wear Eddie Bauer gear, you will be taken for a Yank in most of Russia, Asia, Australasia or Central and South America. Africans will probably mistake you for being German or French, and the Chinese have a tendency to think all Westerners and Europeans are the same.

Even the African-American traveler finds himself being simply a rich American when he looks for his roots in black Africa. In all cases, understand that along with your American Tourister luggage and Nikes, you carry a different kind of baggage. About 200 years of imperialism, covert action, warfare, occupation and political interference. Also a large part of the world just resents the fact that you are so damned affluent and healthy, and they're not. You may not have bombed Laos, smart-bombed innocent Iraqi children, overthrown every Latin America dictator, shot Moros in the Philippines or cut down the rain forests to grow cows for your Big Macs, but the chances are good you will be blamed for it.

- Dress conservatively, stay away from obvious American brands and logos and do not wear signs of wealth (gold watches, jewelry, expensive cameras, etc.).

- Learn or try to use the local language even if only to say "thank you" and "excuse me." Even learning the phrase, "I love your wonderful country," can get you a lot farther than, "Why the hell don't you wogs learn to speak American?"

- Call the local embassy to find out the do's and don'ts.

- Don't wear American flag pins, hand out Uncle Sam decals or argue foreign policy. Focus on learning rather than expostulating.

- Be compassionate, understanding and noncommittal about the current situation of the country. If you are a target of an anti-American diatribe, ask the person to tell you what he would do if he was President of the United States. He will probably be too shocked at your passive intellectual response to stay angry.

- Simple items like sunglasses, air-conditioned cars and lack of language skills can create barriers and misunderstanding.

- Say hello to everyone you meet on the street and in the course of your travels. Look people straight in the eye and smile. Be polite, patient and helpful.

Viva La Revolution!

Let's play out this scenario: A backward country emerges from decades under a totalitarian regime. Freedom is in the air. Tourist visas are as easy to get as Publisher's Clearinghouse entry forms. Hotels are hosed out and airlines change their names. You, being the adventurous type, are off in a heartbeat, eager to be the first to visit empty temples, scenic wonders, etc. One week later, tanks fill the streets, surly men in cheap uniforms are thumping innocent bystanders, you hear shots every night. One morning, someone kicks in your door, and it's not room service. You are officially an enemy of the people, and you will not be able to try out those bitchin' new Nike ACG's in the mountains after all. You are eating cockroach soup and watching your bruises turn ten shades of purple. What happened?

Students of history and readers of *DP* could tell you that you screwed up. You forgot that the countries most likely to be plunged into civil warfare are newly emerging democracies. Yes, you raving liberal, the most dangerous countries are the ones that still can't figure out how to operate a ballot box. One only has to look.

Once the iron hand is lifted, every crackpot faction has a voice and begins organizing. Since there is no effective way to compromise these well-meaning folks, they simply make their points more clearly by using rifles and shovels. Every colonial entry in Africa has gone through this turmoil. Some like Liberia and Angola just don't know when to stop. Other countries like Yugoslavia, Pakistan, Somalia, South Africa and India have no clue how to deal with their poverty-stricken masses. The most dangerous transition is from long term dictatorship to democracy as was experienced in the Soviet Union. Technically these are caused by special interest groups putting restraints on leaders and not allowing them to deal with minor uprisings. Division is the natural outcome, splitting the military, religious, regional and business elements into their tiniest elements. Ideally, they form their own spheres of influence creating the normal political structures found in first world countries. Unfortunately they adopt the brutal tactics of their former leaders and usually have the tanks and population fired up within weeks. Other groups like the Mafia, drug runners, terrorists and criminals make good use of the division and confusion to quickly establish wide ranging organizations and transportation corridors.

HOW TO SURVIVE REVOLUTIONARY PLACES

Although no one can predict a sudden change in government, there are some things that could keep you from appearing on CNN wearing a blindfold.

- **Check in with the embassy to understand the current situation and to facilitate your evacuation if needed. Remember that the local government will downplay the danger posed by revolutionary groups.**

- **Stay away from main squares, the main boulevards, government buildings, embassies, radio stations, military installations, the airport, harbor, banks and shopping centers. All are key targets during takeovers or coups.**

- **If trouble starts, call or have someone contact the embassy immediately with your location. Stay off the streets, and if necessary move only in daylight in groups. Stay in a large hotel with an inside room on the second or third floor. Convert foreign currency into Western currency if possible. Book a flight out.**

- **Understand the various methods of rapid departure. Collect flight schedules, train information and ask about private hires of cars and planes. Do not travel by land if possible.**

- **Do not discuss opinions about the former regime or the current one. Plead ignorance while you wait to see who wins.**

- **Keep your money in US dollars and demand to pay in U.S. currency. Do not depend on credit cards or travelers checks and don't be afraid to demand a discount since who knows what the old money will be worth.**

- **Do not trust the police or army. Remember that there will be many summary executions, beatings and arrests during the first few days of a coup or revolution.**

- **Hire a local driver/guide/interpreter to travel around town and or to go out at night. Don't be shy about hiring bodyguards for your residence or family.**

- **Listen (or have your guide listen) to the local radio station or TV station. Have him update you on any developments or street buzz. When the embassy has set up transport make your move with your bodyguards or guides.**

Fun-da-Mental Oases

There are many countries like Iran, Iraq, North Korea, Pakistan, Syria, and Afghanistan that would have Rush Limbaugh's head on a stick in less than fifteen minutes. These countries might have a Bill of Far Rights, but nothing that would protect your outspoken butt from a lifetime of incarceration or slow execution. They fall into two general categories. Fundamental and mental places. The first is usually a region where skateboarding, platform shoes and daytime talk shows will never see the light of day. These areas make the Puritans look like sex junket tourists to Bangkok. The second are places run by people, who with the aid of a pair of Ray Bans and no sense of humor, are simply the meanest baddest people that week. So lets start with surviving fundamentalist places—places like Afghanistan, Sudan and Iran and other dust-blown centers of religious zeal.

But before I chip in on a Patagonian time share with Salman Rushdie, I would be remiss to point out that not all fundamentalists are Islamic. We have our own religious hotheads Stateside, and even The Lord's Resistance Army in Uganda, makes the Ikwhan seem like a Berkeley political science class.

One billion of the world's inhabitants are Muslims and only 18 percent are found in the Arab world. Most live east of Karachi; 30 percent of Muslims are found on the Indian subcontinent, 20 percent in sub-Saharan Africa, 17 percent in Southeast Asia and 10 percent in the CIS and China. There are an estimated 5 million Muslims in the United States. Most Muslims will tell you that Jews, Christians and followers of their own faith are all "people of the Book" and that there is more to bind us than divide us. It just seems that the message doesn't reach the splinter groups who sign the checks for all those weapons, explosives and training camp supplies.

There is also a historic antagonism between Christianity and Islam with the line drawn through the Balkans and Transcaucasia and epicentering in Jerusalem. This primal distrust between infidel/crusader, jew/arab and west/east is still very much a part of world politics. This creates problems for Westerners when you travel to regions where the local media has inflamed people against the west.

We do a good job, too. There continues to be confusion and distrust generated by the media who are unable to understand the basic similarities between Islam and Christianity. Media focuses on the disparities, and usually the most extreme examples like the *taliban*, Moammar Qaddafi and Saddam Hussein. The presentation of Islamic fundamentalism as a religion rather than a political agenda is one example. The linking of the Koran with politics is another. When was the last time you saw footage of Bill Clinton praying at church intercut with his political speeches? Yet we are shown shots of Mecca intercut with AK-47 waving loonies on tanks or in the '80s it was pictures of Saudis praying with lines at gas pumps. Christian fundamentalism is just as dangerous and skewed as any other hard-core belief, but most Americans head into the Muslim world with a negative and dangerous image of Islam and its followers.

HOW TO SURVIVE FUNDAMENTALIST PLACES

When traveling to a fundamentalist-oriented, religiously zealous country, remember to smile, mind your own business, respect their customs and leave your personal opinions at home. Some religions tend to be a little more tolerant of loud-mouthed, boorish outsiders, but areas like the Middle East and Far East are very intolerant. It's touch and go if you are a heathen, risky to be a Jew and better to just be a Christian if you are asked.

- **Muslims are more conservative in rural areas and underdeveloped countries. Despite other guidebooks' warnings, Muslims understand that Christians have different customs and won't lop your head off the first time you make a *faux pas* by passing the falafel with your left hand.**

- **Be very careful in the area of sexual conduct, behavior at religious sites and deportment with women and religious objects. Sexually provocative clothes, obscene gestures, defiling the Koran, theft or insulting the prophet and women will get you in trouble.**

- **Do not proselytize, preach or conduct religious functions without permission of the local government. Do not wear religious symbols or use expressions that use the name of Christ, Allah, God or other religious entities.**

- **Read and understand the Koran and tenants of Islam. Most Muslims will be impressed that you have read the Koran and if you ask them questions about their religion.**

- **Feel free to admit that you are a Christian, but express your interest in knowing more about the Koran and Islamic way of life. Being a "student of all religions" is a good cop-out for the philosophically challenged. But beware that students and older men are very pleased to proselytize the word of Allah to a potential convert.**

- **If you are Jewish and traveling in a fundamental Islamic, your life may be at risk by identifying yourself as Jewish or discussing an opposing point of view. Also understand there are strong feelings between Shia and Sunni Muslim sects.**

- Do not squeeze hands when shaking, you may touch your chest after shaking hands in the traditional Muslim greeting. The left hand is considered unclean because, yes, rural Muslims wash their nether regions with that hand. Muslims also squat to urinate and find the Western habit of urinating with legs akimbo and penis pointing, far too theatrical for their tastes.

- Dress cleanly and conservatively, remove your shoes in mosques and temples. Do not point the soles of your feet to your host, use your right hand to eat, greet and pass objects around. Expect to be kissed on both cheeks by men. Friday is the holy day and anything else you need to know will be communicated to you by your hosts or friends.

- Ask permission before taking pictures, do not insist or sneak photos. Do not take photographs of women or the infirm or elderly. Don't blow your nose in public. Don't eat walking around. Don't admire objects in a host's home (he will feel obligated to give them to you). Gifts are expected when visiting homes. Do not show open affection. Do not show undue attention to women. The list goes on, but don't be paranoid, just respectful.

- Read up on the cultures of each region and ask permission when in doubt.

Jackboot Junkets

Now that you have a basic idea concerning religious countries, it's time to move on to those regions run by godless despots. The evil empires, the gold-braided braggarts who run vast chunks of Third World dung heaps—all those countries that have the oxymoronic title of Democratic Republic of Yadda Yadda. You won't even find much religion (let alone the Trinity Broadcasting channel) in these paranoid backwaters.

These folks allow tourists into their countries so their populace can see and recoil at the evils of a democratic government: the horrors of high caloric meals, freely elected governments and advanced education. Countries like Iraq, Iran, North Korea, Cuba, Myanmar, Congo, C.A.R, and other little cranky, tin pot countries are furiously pushing their domains back into the Stone Age and dragging their neighbors along with them.

Why visit these countries? Where else can you take a time machine back to the '50s, the '20s or even the turn of the century (we mean the 12th century)? Imagine meeting people who still herd sheep, break rocks, kill other people and even carve temples all for no regard for profit, without an education and while they're on the brink of starvation. These places are Robin Leach's worst nightmare. So why go?

The answer is simple. You have to go. Somebody has to show these people that there is a world out there full of Pop Tarts, Chevy Suburbans (without bullet-proofing), MTV, rotisserie barbecues, and fat happy people who actually die of natural causes.

If we don't go there, we will maintain our image of baby-eating sodomites who bayonet and barbecue old ladies for fun. It takes a lot of patience, a lot of money and a lot of *cojones* to travel through the last of the dark kingdoms. Strangely enough, most of these places are quite safe and once the police turn the corner, a lot of fun.

HOW TO SURVIVE BRUTAL DICTATORSHIPS

Ever want to see George Orwell's 1984 in real life? Visit North Korea. Want to see Killing Fields Part 2? How about the Congo. What about watching live executions on Friday Night Live? Go to Saudi Arabia or Nigeria. You haven't traveled until you've been to the world's last "It's my party and I'll rule if I want to" countries. Here are a few tips to keep you safe:

- Do not discuss politics with anyone. Usually they are no politics to discuss anyway. Do not continue conversations started by strangers, just smile and say "No compredo." Yes, you can be paranoid in these places.

- Try not to talk to locals, they will be questioned later or come under suspicion. Use your guide to select charming visitors to associate with. There really isn't much to talk about in these places anyway. If people stuff letters or postcards in to your hands, do not tell your guide or mail them in-country. They will expect you to mail them once outside the country.

- Most autocratic countries employ or encourage spying on foreigners. Do not be surprised if you are not only followed but your tails may even argue over who gets to follow you. At least you won't be mugged or pickpocketed.

- On the down side, expect to have your room and your luggage searched while you are out. Remember those letters people stuffed in your hand?

- Telephone and mail are subject to interception and/or monitoring. Be careful what you say. Make sure your room is very secure when you are in it.

- Any violation of the law (imagined or real) will result in severe penalties. There is very little your consulate, lawyer or senator can do for you since you are subject to the laws (or lack of laws) of the country you are in. Stay away from drugs.

- If you are a journalist, activist, eco-activist or infomercial host you will be considered a threat. Contact the freedom groups listed in the back of the book to understand what the risks are. The concept of rights, fair trial, or fair treatment are slim to none.

- If you are truly concerned about conditions in these countries, contact the Red Cross, Amnesty International or Reporters Without Frontiers to see what you can do to help. (See our reference section in the back.)

Gimmeyawalletland

Imagine a naked man walking down the street with $100 bills taped to his body. That's what the typical tourist looks like to the residents of nasty places.

The fact that you consider yourself the owner of your camera, wallet, luggage, watch and jewelry is not really a debating point with many of these folks. The concept that you might need to be killed to expedite the transfer of those goods is a really minor detail to some. You don't need to be robbed in these places to lose your money, the police and officials will simply ask for it with a smile.

In many war-ravaged, impoverished places such as Tajikistan, Cambodia, Somalia, Liberia, Zaire, Mozambique, or Sierra Leone, the only law is survival of the fittest or fastest. In countries like Nigeria, Bolivia, Russia and Colombia you will need criminals to protect you from the government. Criminal acts also pre-suppose that there is a criminal system to judge them as such. In most of these places—the border posts, checkpoints and police stations—you will lose your folding green to unpaid, corrupt, greedy and brutal officials. You are not alone because most of the residents of these unfortunate lands must endure the same treatment along with disease, starvation and brutality and no television. Many backpackers will get a quick education in danger as they try every strategy in the book to hold on to their dwindling resources. In case you wonder where the most honest countries in the world are they are Denmark, Finland, Sweden, New Zealand and Canada according to Transparancy International. Here are a few tips to at least stanch the flow and escape with your body parts intact.

HOW TO SURVIVE NASTY PLACES

Many tourists are surprised to find themselves victims of attack and extortion in "recovering" regions where tour prices are low and the crowds at the temples are slim. Be aware that banditry is a very real danger in areas like Kenya, Somalia, India, Cambodia, Pakistan, Afghanistan and Southern regions of Russia. Corruption (this assumes that there was a noncorrupt infrastructure to begin with) can range from ticket clerks mooching spare change to soldiers threatening to lift all of your possessions at military checkpoints.

- Understand that bribery is normal in many countries, but do not confuse this with theft. (See the chapter on Bribes.) Bluster, Negotiate, Smile, Gift or Ignore are the watchwords here. Cheap gifts (like Mr. DP stickers) can defuse many situations, smiling and talking gibberish can go a lot further than a "Fuck Off" and storming away.

- Understand that soldiers at checkpoints are often hungry, sick and impoverished. They will shoot if you don't stop. They can also work themselves into a frenzy if you piss them off. Be cool, smile and just keep talking.

- Meet with and discuss the situation with local embassy staff. Ask them specifically what to do if you are arrested, followed or hassled. Carry their card or at least number and address on you while in country. Ask them for names of military commanders, politicians or anybody important. Write it down. Who you know will help. A name on a piece of paper has more weight than just saying the name.

- Stay within well-defined tourist routes, lock all luggage and belongings in a secure place. Expect and prepare for everything you own to be stolen.

- Never travel in the country alone. Use a local guide to navigate check points and police. Always hire a driver recommended by someone you trust.

- Stay inside major cities at major hotels, eat at well-known, large restaurants. Never travel or go out late at night. Phone ahead to tell people you are coming over and call them again when you arrive home safely.

- Fly between cities and pre-arrange transportation from the airport to the hotel.

- Prepare for constant intimidation from police and military. Be firm about your innocence and try to lead them to your embassy or safe place. Find and remember to drop the name of a local bigwig if you are frog-marched at gunpoint.

- Remember that police will try to keep items removed during a search. So show them your wallet, watch for important papers but do not hand anything to them. If the soldier takes your passport into a bunker or building, walk with him (he will wave you back), but insist that you have important information for his superior.

- Keep abreast of the political and military situation. Keep in mind that kidnapping, extortion and murder are very real possibilities.

Impoverished Paradises

Not all countries are nasty, brutal or full of jabbering zealots. There are lots of places that are really nice–they just seem to have a lot of dead people on the side of the road in the morning. These places have a terminal funk to them. Hazy grey skies, the stench of things rotting, snotty-nosed kids with hands outstretched. These are the tough places, the hard countries that barely survive. Many of these places, like India, Egypt, Bangladesh, Kenya, Pakistan, Haiti, China and Indonesia, are like this because there are just too many people for the resources available. There are a lot of petty thefts, minor muggings, infectious diseases, scams and a few murders. But hey, is it ever cheap.

The trend in emerging dangerous places—normally underdeveloped nations—is that exploding population rates are creating tensions.

In 1950, 33 percent of the world's population lived in the developed, industrialized nations. Today, that share is approximately 23 percent. By the year 2025, it will fall to 16 percent; Africa then will have 19 percent of the world's inhabitants. Today, Western and Southeast Asia are home to more people than any other part of the world. The population of India will overtake that of China early in the next century. This area is also home to the most diverse mix of languages, religions and people in the world, many of whom have been feuding for centuries and who will continue to fight over land, religion and tribal disputes.

As populations grow and standards of living drop, people will live at ever-greater densities, creating more tension. *The World Bank's World Development Report* noted that only Bangladesh, South Korea, the Netherlands and the island of Java have population densities of more than 400 people per square kilometer. By the middle of the next century, one-third of the world's people will probably live at these density levels. Given the current trends, the population density of Bangladesh will rise to a hardly conceivable 1700 people per square kilometer. Population growth on such a large scale is intrinsically destabilizing. The wars in India show that even minor terrorist incidents can kill hundreds of people. Many of the world's most dangerous places will also be the most crowded and impoverished places.

Poorest People	% of Population in Poverty
Bangladesh	80
Ethiopia	60
Vietnam	55
Philippines	55
Brazil	50

Poorest People	% of Population in Poverty
India	40
Nigeria	40
Indonesia	25
China	10

On the African continent, 45 percent of the population is under the age of 15; in South America, it's 35 percent; in Asia, 32 percent. Only 21 percent of the population of the United States and 19 percent of Europe is under 15. Things are not going to get better in our lifetime.

The World Resources Institute reports that only three percent of the world's inhabitants lived in urban areas in the mid-18th century. By the 1950s, that proportion had risen to 29 percent. Today, it is more than 40 percent; by 2025, 60 percent of the world's people are expected to be living in or around cities. Almost all of that increase will be in what is now the Third World. The young people tend to migrate to major urban centers seeking Western-style jobs instead of back-breaking menial labor. Once in the city, they find that the competition for jobs is fierce and that petty crime against the more wealthy is the only source of income. But despite this, the cities continue to grow. Mexico City, which had 17 million inhabitants in 1985, will have 24 million by the end of the century; Sao Paulo will jump from 15 million to 24 million.

Waterworld?

Nearly 50 countries on four continents have more than three-quarters of their land in international river basins; 214 river basins are multinational, while 13 are shared by five or more countries. And nearly 40 percent of the world's population lives in an international river basin. The Jordan, the Ganges, the Nile and the Rio Grande Rivers have been at the center of international disputes. Because rivers in many areas serve as borderlines, water will continue to be a source of conflict. Europe needs more than 175 international treaties to regulate its four river basins shared by more than four countries. The Iraqis are busy draining their southern marches to displace people, while the Turks are busy building dams in east Turkey to flood out others.

Terrorist Places

There is no simple advice to give on how to avoid being the victim of a terrorist attack. Although terrorism is specifically designed to capture the world's attention, it poses a lesser threat than disease, car accidents, plane crashes and other afflictions that haunt the traveler. But having taken the lightly–booked anniversary flight of Pan Am flight 103, I can attest to the effectiveness of terrorism in deterring tourists.

Statistics are meaningless in understanding terrorism. Like a protoplasmic liquid, terrorism flows around the world and reshapes itself according to pressures mounted against it. In fact, like water, the harder you hit it, the more it hurts. Just when the experts figure they have it pegged, it assumes new, more frightening images–the World Trade Center, Oklahoma, Tokyo and Riyadh sagas—have overshadowed hijacking, embassy kidnapping, and airport bombing. In other words you might have to travel to Syria, Sudan, Libya, Iran and Israel to escape terrorism now.

The number of terrorist attacks increased to 440 from 322 in a one-year span; not an impressive figure in terms of the number of dangerous incidents compared to muggings. When you localize some of these activities though, it gets a little scarier.

The increase in terrorism was primarily due to activities of the Kurdistan Workers Party, or PKK, which launched hundreds of attacks, including indiscriminate bombings throughout Turkey, Western Europe and Germany. Fatalities from international terrorism worldwide resulted in 6291 people wounded in a one-year period. Of those, 5500 were injured in a gas attack on the Tokyo subway system, which was masterminded by the Japanese cult, Aum Shinrikyo. The unleashing of nerve gas in a heavily occupied public place sent a chilling message worldwide on the potential deadly effects of terrorism directed at people simply going about their daily activities. It also reminded us that even in a nonviolent country like Japan, terrorism exists.

You should be particularly careful in the following seven nations, currently designated as states that sponsor international terrorism: **Iran**, **Iraq**, **Libya**, **Syria**, **Sudan**, **Cuba** and **North Korea**. Although most European adventure travelers consider these countries quasi-safe for travel (except for the southern region of Sudan and the rougher parts of Cuba), the majority of Americans will never visit these regions.

There is an understandably high level of antagonism in Iraq, Iran and North Korea toward Americans, especially toward those who make it in—usually nuts or spooks. The fact that two Americans were slapped with eight year jail sentences for illegally entering Iraq should keep most travelers out. Read the chapter "Terrorism" for more info.

MAKING THE BEST OF
NASTY SITUATIONS

Business Travelers:
Professional Victims

There is a booming industry selling safety to business travelers. Companies like Pinkerton's, Jane's and Kroll will give you a blow by blow (every day if you like) of every maiming, kidnapping, bombing and attack. Almost all security services are targeted at businesses and businessmen (we're not being chauvinistic here, most victims are men). Yet when I give my talks on travel in dangerous places, I never meet any businessmen. Instead, I run into mostly gung-ho college students and graying, careful spinsters. I figure selling safety to business travelers is like offering sex education classes for monks. They don't see the need. After all, they are not really traveling. They get on a plane, have a couple of drinks, review the file and then meet the driver at the airport. They stay in a swank hotel, have dinner with the customer and then the driver takes them to the meeting the next day. Maybe they'll take in the risque show or just cruise the bars until closing time. Shower, buy a souvenir for the kid, a trinket for the wife and then back home in 10 hours. Hey no big deal, just another business trip.

The reality of business travel from the other side is a little different. By flashing that suit, Rolex President and Megaoil business card, you have become the enemy and the victim. You won't even have to pay the ransom out of your own pocket because they know you have a cash insurance policy for kidnapping.

Business travel is perhaps the most dangerous form of travel. The fact that you represent an American company can make you a target. You also lose the ability to discern about when and where to travel. Most tourists wouldn't consider flying into a Colombian war zone for a week. Yet folks from oil, computer, agricultural and food companies do it regularly. Most victims of terrorism tend to be working on a daily basis in a foreign country in areas where no sane traveler would go.

Finally, by doing business, you tend to frequent establishments and locations where thieves, terrorists and opportunists seek affluent victims—luxury hotels, expensive restaurants, expat compounds, airports, embassies, etc. As a businessperson, you cannot adopt the cloak of anonymity, since you will more than likely be wearing an expensive suit, staying in expensive hotels and have scads of luggage, cash and gifts. If you do business in places like Africa you may be surprised when you call the police for help and discover some don't have gas for their vehicles or bullets for their guns. In some countries like Sierra Leone, a diamond mining center, the police may even show up only to rob you (once they find gas and bullets).

Business travel exposes you to frequent car and air travel and other means of transportation. Many trips are also undertaken in bad weather conditions and at congested travel periods (i.e., Monday out, Friday back). You are fed very carefully through a chain of businesses that cater to businesspeople and become a high profile target for criminals who prey on business travelers. You make appointments well in advance with complete strangers and you have no idea of where you are going or where you are and you even tell strangers you are lost. I often shudder when I see oil field technicians, complete with cowboy hats, pointed boots and silver Halliburton briefcases, tossing beer-soaked profanities and Ben Franklins around the world's transit lounges. Can you think of a more inviting target?

Dangerous Places for Business Travel

Business travelers are by far the juiciest targets for terrorists and thugs alike. They make great kidnap victims as well as willing dispensers of cash for bribes. Any Third World country with oil should be considered dangerous.

Angola

Oil and diamonds shore up this shattered country. The country is looking for investors to help dig them out. However, impotent cease-fires are signed as frequently as bad checks and although the heavy fighting has wound down, the countryside is lawless.

Algeria

Algeria is dependent on foreign expertise and the most dangerous place in the world. Foreign companies are paying top dollar for oil workers.

Cambodia

Cheap labor and an eager government attract plenty of Chinese garment manufacturers to Cambodia. The land of the Khmers is essentially lawless except for a narrow strip around the temples of Phnom Penh and Siem Reap, thanks to the Khmer Rouge and banditry in rural areas. There is little business left to conduct in this post-election, war-torn country. Rising crime and armed carjackings in Phnom Penh are turning the capital into an anarchist's heaven.

Colombia

Colombia gets five stars for brutality, pervasiveness and ingenuity. The government wants businesses to absorb the cost of doing business in a war zone.

Nigeria

Nigeria is floating on oil but its people are dirt poor. I wonder where all that Shell money goes? For now, Nigerians could never be called lazy. They provide some of the best drug mules, scam artists, con men and extortion-based crime. If you get a fax from Nigeria asking for a meeting, run, do not walk to the nearest bunco squad.

Pakistan

Cheap, cheap, cheap is what draws Samsonite packing dealmakers to this promised land of profits. The government is considered corrupt. Political stability is tenuous and there is constant warfare and insurgencies.

The Philippines

The southern Philippines is where a host of motley terrorists-turned-brigands compete for hostages. They prefer to kidnap the children of rich Chinese but dabble with Westerners when they can.

Russia

Russia, specifically Moscow and St. Petersburg, is a quagmire for American businesspeople. It is faced with extortion, lawlessness and politically instability. There is growing disenchantment with the new Russian revolution. Many had a much better go at it with the communists. It's estimated that there will be more than 120 foreigners killed in Russia this year.

Business travelers in all Third World countries can expect to be hit up for tips, bribes, gifts and dinner checks.

Gangsters: The Businessman's Friend

Wherever there is money, there are gangsters. They have an amazing ability to ignore governments and streamline collection procedures. Do not be surprised if your business partner in Eastern Europe or Russia turns out to be a person of ill repute. Italian and Russian gangs are busy establishing links and are now working together in Germany to control a number of businesses: 17 percent of the 776 investigations into organized crime in Germany last year involved attempts to influence politics, big business or government administration. The main activities of organized crime were drug trafficking, weapons smuggling, money laundering and gambling. A while back, police uncovered profits from organized crime in those areas alone totalling US$438 million or 700 million Deutschemarks.

TIPS ON SURVIVING BUSINESS TRAVEL

- Con artists wait at airports, banks and tourist attractions. Be affable but do not go anywhere with your charming new friend.

- Enterprising desk clerks will sell your room key to equally enterprising prostitutes. Go straight downstairs until she is removed. If you stay to convince her to leave, she may yell rape and then you have the local cops to pay off as well as the desk clerk and the girl.

- Avoid restaurants frequented by expats and tourists. Don't make reservations in your own name. Do not sit outside.

- Dress in business attire or carry a briefcase only when necessary. Have your driver watch your back as you enter buildings or your hotel.

- Make copies of important papers, separate your credit cards in case you lose your wallet, keep the numbers, expiration dates and the phone numbers to order replacements.

- Do not show your name, country or hotel ID on luggage or clothing. When a clerk asks for your room number write it down for him.

- Do not discuss plans, accommodations, finances or politics with strangers.

- Wear a cheap watch (or just show the band outward). If driving, wear your watch on the arm inside the car. Leave jewelry at home or in the hotel safe.

- Get used to sitting near emergency exits, memorize fire escape routes in the dark, locking your doors and being aware at all times.

- Kidnappers need prior warning, routine schedules or tip-offs to do their dirty work. Vary your schedule, change walking routes and don't be shy about changing hotel rooms or assigned cabs.

- **Stay away from the front or back of the plane (terrorists use these areas to control the aircraft). Avoid aisle seats unless you want to volunteer for execution.**

- **Do not carry unmarked prescription drugs.**

- **Leave questionable reading material at home (i.e., *Playboy*, political materials, *DP* or magazines).**

- **Carry small gifts for customs, drivers and other people you meet.**

- **When you call with your plans assume someone is listening.**

- **Watch your drink being poured.**

- **Do not hang the "Make Up Room" sign on your hotel room door. Rather, use the "Do Not Disturb" sign. Keep the TV or radio on even when you leave. Contact housekeeping and tell them you don't want your room cleaned up.**

Business travel is not more or less dangerous, but people who travel on business tend to be preoccupied with appointments, directions and preparing for meetings. It also exposes travelers to areas where crimes are committed more often such as nightclubs, downtown areas, banks, ex pat restaurants and other high profile spots.

But cheer up, the chances of being kidnapped and returned home safe are the least of your worries. You could end up dead without even being kidnapped, extorted or waylaid. According to International SOS Assistance in Geneva, Switzerland—a company that specializes in health, security and insurance for travelers—a deadly traffic accident is the most likely reason you'll be flown home dead. Cardiac arrest is the second most likely reason. Tropical diseases are the third. Have fun.

Security Resources

Security is big business these days. Americans spend about $90 billion on security every year. We only spend $40 billion on police. In California there are four times as many private police as there are government police. In countries like Russia and South Africa people don't even bother calling for the police. Also see the "Save Yourself" chapter for more listings.

Control Risks Group Ltd.

One Penn Plaza, Suite 1710
New York, New York 10019
☎ *(212) 967-3955, FAX: (212) 967-3956*
http://www.crg.com
In the U.K.:

83 Victoria Street
London SW1H 0HW
☎ *[44] (171) 222-1552/388-1187, FAX: [44] (171) 222-2296/388-1189*

The Ackerman Group

1666 Kennedy Causeway
Miami Beach, Florida 33141
☎ *(305) 865-0072*
Ex-CIA agent turned security consultant, Mike Ackerman specializes in crisis resolution or hostage return through providing the financial and security resources required to resolve hostage situations safely. He speaks fluent Russian so it should be easy to figure out where he used to work for Uncle Sam.

Kroll Associates

900 Third Avenue
☎ *(800) 824-7502 (212) 833-3206,*
FAX (212) 750-8112
www.krollassociates.com
A security/investigative firm founded in 1972 by Jules Kroll and owned by Equifax (the credit info folks). In addition to gumshoeing on an international and corporate level, Kroll also offers a very useful service for business travelers. You can use your credit card to order a Travel Watch report for $9.95 each.

They also provide customer security services for business. Kroll has information on more than 300 cities worldwide that covers transportation to and from the city, emergency telephone numbers as well as health and safety concerns. They also have special reports on countries and regions. There are also new security tips on the Internet and computers, the airlines and in-depth country reports available.

Pinkerton Risk Assessment Services

200 North Glebe Road, Suite 1011
Arlington, Virginia 22203
☎ *(703) 525-6111, FAX (703) 525-2454*
fjohns@pinkertons.com

Pinkerton provides a wide variety of information and services for companies doing business in bad places. They also cover the USA and provide custom security services as well.

Kidnap, Rescue and Extraction

Seitlin & Company
2001 N.W. 107 Avenue Suite 200
Miami, Florida 33172
☎ *(305) 591-0090, FAX: (305) 593-6993*
e-mail: kandrguy@aol.com
http://www.icanect.net/seitlin/page2.htm
Seitlin is the largest insurance broker in Florida and is also known for the number of kidnap/ransom insurance policies it writes in Latin America. It can also cover you worldwide; it just costs a little more and might take a little more time to get you out. Seitlin can pick from all the top providers of KRE and is a good source of advice if you need to under-

stand just what you could be getting into. Luckily it only has to pay out about once or twice a year. Its clients include mostly wealthy Latin American families, corporations that do business south of the border and employees of multinational corporations. Other vendors of KRE are:

Chubb Insurance of Canada
http://masc-web.com/chubb/english/epd/kidnap.htm

Lloyd's of London:
http://www.cyberapp.com/kidnap.html

Black Fox International, Inc.
http://black-fox.com/kidnap.htm

Tourists:
Fodder for Fiends

We've tried to calm your fears, showing you that things are much hairier at home than on the road. There is one thing we should tell you. Given a choice between popping an 80-year-old peasant woman or a rotund 50-year-old Rotarian from Cleveland, the choice becomes easy. Tourists are fodder for fiends.

We are pickpocketed in the street when we bend over to give money to a blind old woman, our car window is smashed in and all our clothing is stolen when we are having an audience with the pope, our hotel is ransacked when we visit a village to help a sick child. We are scammed, lied to, beaten, shot, raped and in some cases murdered. Why? Well, look at it from the bad guy's perspective. He has a family to shelter, a vein to feed, a donkey payment, even an employer who will break his nose if he doesn't make the weekly number.

Examine the modern *touristicus domesticus*. They travel in predictably jabbering gaggles, following well-worn trails. Monolingual, they pay little attention to their environment since they are terrified of being left behind or having the bus leave without them. They are usually wearing outlandish colorful plumage. Gray walking shoes sprout cream of mushroom legs marbled with blue veins topped off by what could be spare tire or a bulging overstuffed money belt. The neck is usually tilted up with a rhythmic swivel bent slightly forward by the weight of their Sears Camcorder and SLR with zoom telephoto, binoculars and silkscreened vinyl camera bag. The right index finger is either pointed at the local attraction or pressing a shutter. The mouth is in a state of continual movement as they talk, not necessarily to each other, but to ensure that they are having a good time and seeing wonderful things. They usually arrive in shiny buses, descending like locusts as they strip souvenir stands clean and cluster in tight groups under the watchful eye of an overly pleasant multilingual guide holding an umbrella.

Tourists are not dumb or bad people, but they are the main source of sustenance for touts, louts and thugs. Some of these tourists do funny things. They sneak away from those bus tour hotels and migrate to seedy places to watch local women take their clothes off. They drink too much. They make friends too easily. They stay out too late. They stagger home at four in the morning singing German drinking songs and get lost. Not bad people, just trusting naive people in the wrong place at the wrong time.

There is a subspecies of the *touristicus domesticus*. It is the fabled *touristicus backpackensius*. Unlike the much derided domestic version, this species is more likely to be solitary, but most likely will be seen with a same-sex partner. The key indicators are hiking boots or Nike ACG's, hairy legs with knobby knees (often with scabs from mountain bike spills), T-shirts with politically correct slogans, hiking outerwear (with ski tags still attached), UV block sunglasses. The older members will have a gray pony tail. They like to think they are independent, even though they bunch up at the same youth hostels and flophouses each night. The key determinant is the right index finger jammed into the same page on their shoestring guides.

These folks are college educated, world wise and in their minds unlikely to be a victim of any criminal (after all they're not rich and obnoxious, like those other tourists). They are one with the earth and its cultures (they were into world music, waaaay before Sting or Gabriel), giving them a sense of love and harmony.

So what's to worry? Could it be that entire year's supply of money in their "secret" neck pouch? How about that new altimeter, stopwatch, chronometer watch? Those $120 boots are worth a quick $20. And the $400 backpack can fetch another quick $20. These travelers often enjoy entertainment and souvenirs of the narcotic kind, carry everything on their backs and wouldn't be noticed missing for at least a month. Good pickings for the charming bandito or even drug planting polizia.

The point of the two cheap shots above is to tell you that it doesn't matter who you think you are. You are a wealthy unarmed foreigner in a land that is not your own. If you are the victim of crime you will hotfoot to your nearest embassy or the next town. You will not be back to file charges or even see what happened to your favorite watch. So consider yourself the ideal victim. And unlike most books who tell you the same dumb stuff, *DP* is going to give you some tricks we don't want you to pass on to your friends.

The good news: The major purpose of crime against tourists is to quickly remove money and other valuables. The perpetrator does not want to hurt you or escalate your brief meeting into assault or murder since the *federales* will be more interested in finding him.

Rape is a function of social cultures clashing—usually a result of unaccompanied western women who travel in rural or sexually frustrated cultures. In a world where "Baywatch" and "The Young and the Restless" are the most syndicated shows in the world, one can do little but hope that they remake and syndicate "The Flying Nun" soon to balance things out.

In the case of homicide or brutal attacks, you have to look at the track record of the country you are going to visit. It is not uncommon for bandits to execute robbery victims simply because they won't get caught. Look for countries where they make tourist attractions out of skulls (Cambodia) or eat smoked monkeys (Congo) to give you a heads up.

DP Survival Course Five Things That Will Save Your Life

Be alert

Crooks need you to be distracted, lost, in need of assistance, or simply in the wrong place. Just adopting the habit of stopping and watching people around (and behind you) will arm you against crime.

Be sober

Alcohol, drugs, jetlag and having too good a time can fuzz your common sense, making you think for one unfortunate moment that you are with cool cats when you're really among wolves. Even pleasant encounters with the locals in bars can lead to ugly bruises and lost pesos if you don't stay in control. Scams begin when the perpetrator thinks he can overcome your better judgement. Bars and night-clubs are also where bad people hang out.

Use it or lose it

Preventing theft begins when you pack. If you are taking too many things or are forced to leave items in your car or hotel, you dramatically increase the chances of losing those things. Travel light, plan on giving away most of the items you bring and perhaps buying local clothes at your destination.

Insure and ensure

I know this is something Marlin Perkins would tell you, but it really does make a difference if your camera, clothes, health and even life are insured against loss when travelling. Travelers checks are a pain, but worth it for large blocks of cash. Also, credit cards let you do everything from chartering aircraft to buying blow-guns, and even medivac insurance ensures that you can be flown to your local hospital if you get hit by a poison dart.

Trust no one, suspect everyone

When you travel, you will meet hundreds of strangers with either pure or unpure thoughts. It all depends on the image you present. If you are interested in their kids, their health and their family, the chances of something evil happening to you decrease. At the same time understand that financial pressures in some countries might force these same people to finger you to a gang of thugs, or pick your pocket.

Stay away from tourists

Tourists attract petty criminals and con artists like dogs attract fleas. It goes without saying that crime occurs at youth hostels, tourist attractions, main plazas, red light districts and other popular spots.

Prevent opportunists

Crime generally occurs after you change $2000 at the Amex office or your wife hitches up her girdle to get $10 to pay the museum tickets. Zippers on back packs, luggage circling carrousels, papers sticking out of breast pockets, fat purses and bulging pockets are "Rob Me" signs. Places like trunks of rental cars, towels at beaches, and daytime hotel rooms are areas where cameras, money, and just about everything of any value should be expected to disappear.

Lock 'em, Fake 'em or Take 'em

Lock 'em Out

The best defense is preparation. By being careful you will avoid unfortunate incidents and wonder what all this fuss is about. Most hotel rooms can be flipped open by a 90-lb. maid, so it doesn't take much for a 200-lb. thug to enter your room at night. (That is where you keep all your worldly possessions isn't it?) Although this is not as pervasive as street robbery, hotel robbery is more serious. Use a wedge, motion detector or chair against the door when you go to sleep. During the day, leave a TV or radio on. Take the room key with you and keep your valuables in the hotel safe. In less developed countries, leave your valuables with the innkeeper or his family.

Use a retractable cable to tie your bags together even when in your hotel. Put locks on all openings, use twist ties on zippers to keep them together, etc. The harder you make it to steal your things the less chance they will be.

Fake 'em Out

If you find yourself being trailed by an unshaven man through the back streets of Malta, then it's time for Plan B. Strange as it seems, the act of throwing down your decoy pouch will defuse most situations. (Unless of course the swarthy man is just trying to catch up to you to return the camera you left at the restaurant.)

Assume that your attacker is just after your money. So give it to him, but not much of it. Carry a moneybelt, pouch, wallet and neck pouch with a little bit of money in each place. Protest a lot, and then run like hell in the opposite direction.

When you are being robbed, your attacker may have a weapon. The trick is to keep slowly shuffling backward as you fumble with your decoy pouch or wallet. If you think you can sprint into a safe place, do it. Most thugs will not chase you when other people are around. The attacker is as much of a coward as you. The difference is, he knows what he is doing and you don't.

If you feel mad as hell and decide you aren't going to take it anymore, try this trick I have used with complete success. Simply stick your hand in your shirt or waistband, turn around and start walking forcefully and directly towards your potential assailant. Never take your eyes off him. When he zigs, you zig and when he zags, you zag. In most cases (I repeat "most") he will think you are going to pull something on him and will quickly walk in another direction. Anyway it's more fun than waiting around, knees trembling, to find out what his real intentions are.

If you are forcibly restrained or bushwhacked, see the "Take 'em Out" section.

- Sew an inside pocket in your shirt under the arm, extend a pocket to the inside or add a panel to your boxers. Use velcro fasteners.

- The best place to hide money is within your various possessions: inside backpack tubes, shoe linings, on the back of telephoto lenses, sewn into pant cuffs, the lining of your luggage, in books, etc. You may lose some but you'll end up with something.

- Save your expired credit cards and unused *afghanis* to plump up a decoy wallet. Carry it in your inside front pocket. For you Bernard Goetz types, try one of my favorite surprises adapted from Iban headhunters; a one-sided razor blade tucked inside backpack pockets.

- Do not carry a purse. But if you must, don't carry any money in it since most thieves stay around only long enough to grab the purse and then run away.

- Gun magazines sell a number of concealable holsters, vests and attachments. They can also be used to carry money.

- Wear your watch on the arm that is inside a car and away from your window. It is better not to wear a watch at all since it is the first thing a thief (or customs inspector) looks at to judge your eligibility as a victim.

Take 'em Out

If you are attacked, your attacker will have the advantage. He will either sneak up behind you, walk up to you and then quickly turn, or he will hit you with a pipe or stick. Violent attacks often are performed by gangs. They will typically continue to kick and hit you while they tear off your possessions and empty your pockets. Quite honestly, you are better off shielding your head and stomach and helping them find what they are looking for. Keep in mind that if you choose to fight you are endangering your life. If you choose to fight back (you big bully) you must also be prepared to see this through until your attacker may become the victim. Not a comfortable thought for tourists out on the town for a night.

Any book that tells you how to be like Jackie Chan is, for lack of a better term, bullshit. People are all animals when attacked. When someone comes at you with an intent to hurt you, the last thing on your mind will be which smooth Kung Fu moves you will use to pulverize your opponent.

Typically the aggressor will have staked you out and followed you until you were in a place he wanted you to be. At this point everything you do must be reactive. By all means learn the basics of self-defense. Boxing, karate, knife fighting, SEAL training, are all fine. They will tell you which parts of the body really hurt when you jab them and a few nasty tricks that will leave your attacker sucking wind through broken teeth. You will only have this opportunity three or four times in a lifetime, and the downside is that if you do get a chance to be Bruce Lee, the locals will gather around and call you the bad guy.

- Do not carry a weapon. In many countries this will make you a criminal and subject to criminal charges, imprisonment and damages to your "victim." Instead, learn to use "soft weapons" like a pen, walking stick, Swiss army knife, flashlight, single edge razors etc. You can walk down the street at 4 a.m. with a sharp pen or a walking stick and feel fully armed.

- Be careful of items like pepper spray, mace, short non-folding knives and other offensive weapons. They can be used against you (many people who use pepper spray or mace often spray themselves or inhale the fumes) and will be considered offensive weapons.

- One of the best items is the kubotan (developed by Takayuki Kubota) who created a system of (believe it or not) pen fighting. The kubotan is a five-and-a-half inch long rod often attached to a set of keys. The basic principle behind the kubotan is to apply pressure and intense pain to your opponent.

- Learn to use a sharp object against the groin, upper neck, throat, eyes, and nose. All are useless unless your weapon is free and your arm is unrestrained. If you have never practiced these strikes, you will not make a significant impact. The proper thrust is a hard jab "through" the victim followed by as many blows as it takes to incapacitate the victim.

- If you are interested there are a number of books and courses on self defense. *DP* recommends Tai Kwon Do, karate, boxing and even Thai kickboxing. Even judo, aikido and jujitsu will make you comfortable with violence, reactive instincts and diversion of force. All are part of street survival and more importantly building self confidence. Once again consider the consequences of severely beating a stranger in a strange land. You may end up in jail.

The unarmed attack

Responses that are always successful in dealing out pain, regardless of relative size or strength are the heel of the hand under the nose, the bowling ball eyeball grip and the knee in the groin. Keep in mind that if your attacker wasn't pissed or violent before, he will be after you try any one of these attacks.

Any violent encounter has an emotional after-effect that may turn your trip into a nightmare. On one of my recent expeditions through Borneo, a female member was sleeping in a building on the end of a dock over 100 yards from shore. That night a person slit her sleeping bag, her underwear and began to feel her up. She was in the company of two other males who were sleeping. The next day she reported the incident and the police chief of the small fishing village trotted out the entire male population for her to make an ID. Terrified that she would identify the wrong person she hesitated. The police said if she did not identify the person, the entire village would be suspect. She identified one man and he was taken away. She was wrong. Fortunately, the villagers knew who it was and brought the guilty man forward.

It would be unfair to assume that there are specific forms of tourist crime and specific tips to prevent it. Just a quick glance at the clippings that pile up at DP and our firsthand experiences would scare anyone from wandering out their front door. But luckily crime is "relative." You stand a much better chance of being murdered or waylaid by a close acquaintance at home than a total stranger when you travel.

But nothing we can tell you can prepare you for the dangers out there. Safari tourists are robbed while on safari in the north of Kenya, while backpackers have sleeping gas injected in their sleeping compartments in Bulgaria. Most thefts on trains happen in stations, usually just before border crossings where thieves hop off before customs (but not before giving the conductor his cut).

Isn't Technology Great

The new counterfeit proof $100 bill is now busily being counterfeited in Russia, Lebanon and Syria.

In Colombia and Thailand, young lasses drop scopolamine into overpriced drinks, whores with hearts of gold instruct cab drivers to take you to their rendezvous, which is a back alley where only your wallet is emptied.

Shirt slashers in Venezuela snick through your shirt and grab your neck pouch; Mexicans spill beer on you while their compadre empties your pocket. Even cops will arrest you for phantom transgressions, and customs officials will tax you for imaginary activities.

Swarthy men will wave pistols at you urging you to pull over in Italy, Spain and Turkey. Colombian guerrillas, Chechen mafyia, Yemeni tribesmen, Afghan drug runners and Kashmiri mujahedin will kidnap you and maybe release you.

Out of work Khmer Rouge will kidnap and then clobber you with a hoe in front of your self-dug grave in Cambodia while crack heads in Miami will blast you right through your rental car window if you are too slow to find the electric window button.

Believe it or not, it gets worse. A busload of Greek tourists is machine-gunned to death because Egyptian terrorists think they are Israelis, a Palestinian man starts shooting at people at the top of the Empire State Building because he is "despondent." Afghan mujahedin behead a Norwegian tourist after they carve their group's name in his chest. It seems they were supposed to find expats or engineers, but found it was easier to kidnap a hiker. Next year who knows?

So before you weld your door locks shut and burn your passport, remember that despite all the efforts of the world's criminals to ruin your vacation, most tourists will complain about cold French Fries and lumpy mattresses. Oh, I almost forgot, the most common problems for travelers are diarrhea and sunburn. So, hey, let's be careful out there.

Dangerous Places for Tourists

Criminals know where, when and how to find tourists. And they know exactly what to say to them. They're nice. They'll ask you where you're from—and then jack you up for your wallet, camera and jewelry. You'll then have to leave town or spend all day in the police station filing a report. You'll have to rebook airline tickets and then hit the VISA or AMEX office to get new credit cards. Chances are you'll never be back to file a charge or testify.

Every year about half a billion people become official tourists. They leave behind about $423 billion in money on the official level. No one knows how much they contribute to the local thugs and con men. Tourists are robbed and beaten in most countries, but many never bother to report the incidents knowing full well the futility.

Tourists congregate in the same places. They drive in a state of rubbernecking ecstasy. And they are terrified of local law enforcement.

One of things that bad people want besides your money is your passport. The U.S. Embassy issued 1100 replacement passports to travelers last year, 1060 in Italy and 250 in Prague. The most common problem is pickpocketing (about 30 percent of crimes), followed by break-ins into cars. Nobody likes to be considered a tourist; we are travelers, cultural ambassadors yearning to soak up new experiences and sights. In America, few local people stray downtown after dark. Unfortunately, many tourists stay in business hotels built downtown and go for early morning jogs or late night strolls. Are they crazy? No, they're just tourists.

It seems odd, but the most dangerous places for tourists are where tourists hang out. In Europe, pickpockets and thieves like to hang out exactly where you will: the American Express offices (how did they know I just picked up a ton of cash?), popular tourist attractions, main squares and train stations.

Crowds are ideal areas for minor theft, getting on buses or trains, waiting in line for museums or even going to the bathroom. But the top spot to get ripped off is where the tourists are. It's the ideal place to meet con men, gypsy beggars, pickpockets and other minor ne'er do wells.

If you want to meet violent thugs and muggers you will have to wait until the sun goes down and hang around tourist bars. You know, those places where bus tourists sneak you away to down a few drinks and see the local lovelies without the benefit of clothing. Sometimes your new friend will drug your drink or will cause a scene with the bouncer resulting in your expulsion (minus your wallet). Your new drinking buddies may invite you to a swinging club which just happens to be in a deserted alley.

Trains

In Russia, China, Central and Southeast Asia, Georgia and Eastern Europe, trains are targets of organized thefts and abductions. In Central Asia and Eastern Europe thieves inject gas into sleeping cars. Pickpockets and petty thieves jump on at one stop, clean out cabins and then jump off at the next stop usually before a border.

Buses

Buses are prime targets of criminals and terrorists because they hold a lot of people in a confined area, have few exits and generally travel rural routes—also, the unarmed passengers are usually carrying most of their earthly belongings with them. Buses also follow regular routes along remote roads which allows the civilized bandit to pull off an 11:30 a.m. ambush and make it home for lunch. Checkpoints will shake you down for nonexistent drugs, unexpired visas, and lack of special permission for their area. Local thieves will jump aboard, rummage through the roof luggage and then jump off long before you notice your nice frameless pack missing.

Automobiles

Young kids will watch you park in the tourist attraction's parking lot and then swoop down to clean out your trunk. Junkies will smash every single car window along the beach in the Caribbean to find the wallets kept safe and dry inside. Skinny teenagers in cheap leather jackets will wait until you park your new rental car in Moscow before stealing it and hustling it off to Baku.

More Dangerous Places for Tourists

Here's a brief overview of where tourists are considered the daily sustenance for bad people.

North America/Mexico

The United States is plagued with inner-city crime. Guns are commonly used, and convenience store clerks should get combat pay. Tourists are under attack, often with more violent consequences than are found in many "uncivilized" countries. **Mexico** is still wild and woolly. Big, bad Mexican desperadoes still exist. Mexico's frontiers are rife with mean, dusty border towns where anything can be had for a price. Corrupt *federales,* will steal your money and sell you back your personal belongings. Cheap, dark bars still sell ammo, drugs and women. Convention hall-sized whorehouses feature nonstop knife fights. Petty crime flourishes in resort areas.

Jamaica mixes ganja, sun and reggae with a massive murder rate. Other Caribbean islands have their grubby little spots where tourists come to do bad things and end up thumped, robbed or killed.

South America

Mexico is Utah compared to **Colombia**. Kidnappers in **Peru**, **Bolivia** and **Brazil** await you. Pickpockets and thugs in Rio hope that tourism will pick up before the death squads kill them all.

Africa

In **Algeria,** Islamic fundamentalists are killing foreigners as fast as they can. Nobody even thinks of going to **Mauritania** unless they want to be kidnapped and sold off as a white slave. **Djibouti** still has rebel activity and **Ethiopia and Somalia** have the meanest bandits in the world. The **Sudan** has a very vicious war being waged in the South.

Sub-Saharan Africa

The Hutu and Tutsis in **Rwanda** and **Burundi** are still whacking each other with *pangas* and, if they by chance see a tourist, will stop fighting long enough to roll them. The mean deeds of folks in the **Congo**, **Central African Republic**, **South Africa**, and **Nigeria** would make a Russian gangster blush. Desperately poor urban thieves and roving bandits in **Tanzania**, **Kenya** and **Uganda** are stepping up crimes against tourists, and **Madagascar** requires a cautious approach as it slides into anarchy.

Adventure travel to the outlands and cities of **Sierra Leone**, **Liberia** and **Angola** are strictly for soldiers of fortune since even aid workers are fair game in these places.

Middle East/Mediterranean

Eastern Turkey is a mess: The Kurdish Workers Party, or PKK, has the tourist-terrorism thing down pat. The PKK issued a warning that effectively broadens their battleground to hotels, beaches and other tourist attractions. They take great pleasure in ensuring that the lives of all people visiting Turkey will be in danger. There are also nasty things being done by rival Kurdish factions, Armenian terrorists, the special ops groups, drug smugglers, Hezbollah and more in Northern Iraq.

Europe

Europe is supposed to be a safe haven for tourists, but petty crimes in the tourist areas and central cities are common. Skinheads are busy in **Germany,** bashing people with brown eyes and foreign accents. The Basque ETA in **Spain** likes to blow things up. **Paris** is crawling with gypsies and petty thieves. **Sicily** is still home to bandits who like to prey on tourists with *lupares* (sawed-off shotguns). Petty thievery runs rampant along the beach resorts of **Spain**, **France** and **Italy** during tourist season.

South/Central/Western Asia

The southern part of Russia is a seething mass of conflict with separatist, ethnic, mafia, drug and religious groups blasting each other into shreds. **Afghanistan** and **Tajikistan** are destitute, perpetual battlefield crisscrossed by drug smugglers. **Pakistan** has roving bandits and hot-headed killers that will rob policemen and armed convoys just for their bullets. Northern **Sri Lanka** is a bona fide war zone even though the beaches are full in the south.

Southeast Asia

Cambodia is a continual game of push-me pull-you as they play tug of war for control of the country. Meanwhile there are still enough land mines to put Doctor Scholl out of business. The north of **Myanmar** is still controlled by drug lords and hardwood timber smugglers. **Papua New Guinea** and **Irian Jaya** still have local tribal wars that break out around eco-trekkers. The sex tourism industry in **Thailand** and the **Philippines** along with prevalence of AIDS in Southeast Asia poses a different type of threat for the adventurous.

THE STING

When traveling through Asian countries you could be the victim of overzealous law enforcement agents. In India and Thailand, there have been reports of threats of arrest on drug charges unless you give officers money. In Thailand, police officers make a monthly salary of about US$200. Thai police officers and their informants can receive a reward of 10,000 baht per kg of pure heroin recovered. It has been stated that after refusing these demands some foreign travelers were booked and charged for using heroin.

Some travelers have paid US$150–200 to get these cops off their backs. If you are taken to court in Thailand, the odds are not good. No foreigner has been acquitted of an offense in more than 20 years. In India, there are 40 young Westerners serving lengthy jail sentences who claim they were sent to prison on bogus charges.

THE STING

Due to the severity of sentences and the low salaries of officers, Thailand, Malaysia and India can be considered the most dangerous destinations for backpacking youngsters. Indonesia, the Philippines and Latin America are also danger spots. The only solution is to avoid looking like a hippie, don't travel alone and try to get witnesses if you feel you are being pushed into an unethical transaction.

China/Far East

China is pushing its people to desperation and, despite more executions than there are daytime soap operas in Hollywood, crime is increasing.

Bribes

Crime Does Pay

Mordida, dash, spiffs, baksheesh, cadeaus, special fees, tea money, fines, gifts or whatever the term "bribe" is called is a regular part of travel in the Third World. In many cases, military, police and government officials will expect a gratuity to allow passage, as payment for minor infractions or to issue visas. In some cases, it may be your money or your life.

Paying Your Dues

Most travelers who are put in jail are involved in traffic- or drug-related offenses. Naturally, many countries have an unofficial method of dealing with these problems efficiently and profitably. It serves no purpose for small or poor countries to incarcerate you for lengthy periods of time. It also does not serve the purpose of policemen to spend their time filling out paperwork, when they can resolve the problem and teach you a lesson on the spot. From Minnesota to Malaysia to Mexico, I have been amazed at the solid financial education police officers have been given. (Which is better? $100 in your pocket or the policeman's pocket?) Be forewarned, there are many officers who do not accept or want bribes. The way to tell is simple. If an officer tries to resolve a problem rather than just write you up, handcuff you or arrest you, you are expected to begin the bribe process. If you feel an opening gambit has been made, then you are expected to explain to the officer your desire for a speedy amicable resolution of your problem. In most cases, the officer will shore your feelings of injustice about his having to take you all the way back to the station (always in the opposite direction you are traveling) to wait for the judge who is typically fishing or out until next week.

If he offers to take the fine back for you or to let you pay it on the spot, then bingo, the chiseling begins. Remember that bribes are a "cash-only" business and the amount you can pay will be limited to the amount of cash you have on you at that moment. Now that you have the rules of the game, please remember that offering any financial inducement to an officer, however innocently, is illegal and can put you in jail.

Delivering a Bribe

One must never discuss money or the amount or the reason for the gift. Typically, you will be presented with a "problem" that can be solved but will take time, money, or approval by a higher authority. You will naturally need to have this problem solved. You may ask if there is a fee that will expedite the solution of this problem, or if the local language fails you, you can point out your urgency and present a passport, ticket or papers with a single denomination of currency tucked inside.

DP's Guide to Bribes	
Minor traffic violation (speeding, imaginary stop signs, burned-out tail lights that magically work; usually levied on Fridays or Saturday afternoons).	**$5–$10**
Traffic violations (real stop signs, real speeding tickets).	**$10–$50**
Serious traffic violations (DUI, very serious speeding or racing).	**$50–$500**
Very serious traffic problem (accident with no fatalities).	**$500–$1000**
Accidents that involve fatalities require the application of funds to a judge, your lawyer, prosecutor and probably the police chief. Costs are usually in the $2000–$6000 range, and, yes, they will wait while your credit card clears. You will also be waiting in a jail.	**$2000–$6000**
If you are involved in something shady and need to correct the problem, it is wise to hire a lawyer. To make sure you get a lawyer who is sympathetic to the needs of the police, simply ask the police to recommend a good lawyer. The lawyer will negotiate fees for himself, the judge and the police.	**$10,000–$45,000**

The Price for Doing Bad Things

Bribes might not work if you are caught by the military, make the local papers or happen to be doing something the government is busy eradicating (usually with U.S. funds) at the time. Smuggling drugs, weapons or people requires the support of a large, covertly sanctioned organization. Freelancers are usually treated roughly with little opportunity to buy their way out. Depending on how big a fish they think you are, you can expect to pay about $12,000 to get out of a South or Central American jail. It is not uncommon to have to pay $30,000–$120,000 to beat a major drug rap.

If you are kidnapped by terrorists, you might feel lucky. They will typically hit up your government of origin or your family for your ransom. Americans fetch between $100,000 to $2 million, depending on who you work for. Many times guerrillas will attach political demands or have unrealistic demands like bumping Andy Rooney on "60 Minutes" to tell their side of the story. This lowers your chances of freedom dramatically since most governments have stated policies about negotiating with terrorists, though they are fairly helpful with kidnapping cases. The catch is that your government will expect you to pay them back.

Other reasons for bribes are to bring in cars, contraband, machine parts, business samples, cash or even a wife. In many countries the police derive their sustenance from local businesses. A recent article in *Newsweek* estimated that in Hong Kong, brothels provide $120–$600 a month. In Bangkok, the city's 1000 "entertainment houses" pay $600,000 a month to the local police. Strangely, these types of businesses can provide favors to travelers if you find yourself in a squeeze or need help approaching the police on a sensitive issue.

The best way to check out bribes is to contact the local embassy, expats who live in the area, local journalists (not foreign journalists) and local lawyers. It should be stated that in many cases a demand for a bribe can be talked down if you are doing nothing wrong. Many junior customs officials will spot first-timers and shake them down for everything from their *Playboys* to their underwear. Feel free to protest, but when the man with the big hat and gold stars agrees with the peon, it's time to start rolling off the twenties.

When It Is Better to Give Than to Receive

Many people view bribery as reprehensible and evil. These are usually the ones who have to pay the bribes. Others view the practice as a normal way to supplement meager government wages (you can guess who they are). All countries including America have this affliction. Africa is the worst place for bribery, followed by South America and Central America, with northern Europe being the most incorruptible place. Nigeria has the worst reputation for *dash* but you can expect any minor official in most poor African nations to ask for a *cadeau* in exchange for providing a higher level of service. Expats detest this practice because they have to go through customs and refuse to pay it. Tourists are more easily intimidated and usually have much more to lose if they miss a flight, connection or cruise because of unnecessary delays.

Remember that small bribes are used to facilitate services that can be withheld or denied. Usually tightwads will be processed, but at the back of the line. Obnoxious tightwads who like to make loud speeches about corruption may find themselves with insurmountable visa irregularities ("The stamp in your passport must be green ink for a fifteen-day visa").

A carton of cigarettes will ensure that you are speedily processed in most African countries. A bottle of Johnny Walker will not get you far in a Muslim country but will definitely expedite your exit visa in Colombia. Border crossings into most Central American countries can be made for a one hundred dollar bill, and you can drive as fast as you want in Mexico if you have a good supply of 20 dollar bills. With such gifts, you may not need a visa entering a country and the customs official may forgo even a cursory inspection of your vehicle.

If you need to be smuggled out of a country, it is a little more complicated. First, the "coyote" will demand about twice the normal fee for your departure and there is no guarantee that he will not turn you in for a reward. Secondly, the matter of securing an exit visa without the benefit of an entry visa will cost you between $100 and $200 dollars in most Asian and Latin American countries. Eastern European and CIS countries can be crossed for as little as $5, with no guarantee that you will not be finked on 10 miles down the road.

You don't have to be a criminal to pay bribes. Criminals take great pride in their ability to extract bribes or "protection money" from honest folks. Moscow has 12 major organized crime groups who've been known to extract up to 30 percent of monthly profits from businesses. So the best way to view bribes is as you would tipping. When a country lowers its wages to its police and officials below the poverty line, they look to you to make ends meet.

In summary, using bribery is like kissing in junior high school. Both parties must be willing, but you have to be given an opening before you make your move. If you are brash or unwise, you will be severely rebuked.

Dangerous Jobs

Danger Is My Business

Don't have time or money for a dangerous vacation? Why not get a dangerous job and make money too? In fact, the odds are that you could get your kicks by being splattered on Route 66. Highway deaths accounted for 20 percent of the 6588 fatal work injuries. According to the U.S. Department of Labor, truck drivers had more fatal injuries than any other occupation, with 762 deaths last year.

Homicide was the second leading cause of job-related deaths, accounting for 16 percent of the total. Robbery was the primary motive for workplace homicide. About half of the victims worked in retail establishments, such as grocery stores, restaurants and bars, where cash is readily available. (31,000 convenience store clerks are shot every year.) Taxicab drivers, police and security guards also had high numbers of worker homicides. Four-fifths of the victims were shot; others were stabbed, beaten or strangled.

Although highway accidents were the leading manner of death for male workers, homicide was the leading cause for female workers, accounting for 35 percent of their fatal work injuries.

Falls accounted for 10 percent of fatal work injuries. The construction industry, particularly special trade contractors such as roofing, painting and structural steel erection, accounted for almost half the falls. One-fifth of the falls were from or through roofs; falls from scaffolding and from ladders each accounted for about one-eighth. Nine percent of fatally injured workers were struck by various objects, a fourth of which were falling trees, tree limbs and logs. Other objects that struck workers included machines and vehicles slipping into gear or falling onto workers, and various building materials such as pipes, beams, metal plates and lumber. Electrocutions accounted for 5 percent of the worker deaths in a one-year span.

Occupations with large numbers of worker fatalities included truck drivers, farm workers, sales supervisors and proprietors, and construction laborers. Industry divisions with large numbers of fatalities included agriculture, forestry, fishing, construction, transportation and public utilities, and mining. Other high-risk occupations included airplane pilots, cashiers and firefighters.

The Most Dangerous Jobs in America, or Why Don't We See More Action/Adventure Shows Starring These Folks?

1. Truck driver	8. Taxicab driver
2. Farm worker	9. Timber cutter
3. Sales supervisor/proprietor	10. Cashier
4. Construction worker	11. Fisherman
5. Police detective	12. Metal worker
6. Airplane pilot	13. Roofer
7. Security guard	14. Firefighter

Source: U.S. Labor Department

California had the highest total fatalities on the job (601) with Texas finishing second with 497. Florida was a close third with 388. New York City led with the highest number of assaults and violent acts in the workplace (66). Apparently, something about the northeast provokes violence at work. The District of Columbia reported 76 violent acts and assaults on the job, and Rhode Island had 55. Hawaii had the highest number of work-related highway deaths with 60.

Victims of Violent Crime According to the U.S. Justice Department

Private company	61%
Government	30%
Self-employed	8%
Working without pay	1%

Source: U.S. Justice Department

Who's Out There?

The typical whacko who freaks out at work and starts banging away is typically a middle-aged male over 35, withdrawn, owner of a gun, has served in the military and probably drinks or snorts too much chemical substance.

The Locations Where These Crimes Took Place	
Other commercial sites	23%
On public property	22%
Office, factory or warehouse	14%
Restaurant, bar or nightclub	13%
Parking lot/garage	11%
On school property	9%
Other	8%

What's danger worth?

The U.S. Department of State thinks employees who work in dangerous places should receive an additional payment of 25 percent of their normal salary. French companies will pay up to double the standard rate to do business in remote or dangerous places. Americans are the preferred targets. Americans visiting or working in other countries are increasingly becoming targets of anti-U.S. attacks. Latin America is the most likely place for anti-American attacks, with the Middle East just behind.

Don't think that it matters to the private sector paymaster whether you are an American or a former Colombian sent to work in Colombia. You will get preferential treatment: 92 percent of U.S. companies pay the same incremental amount regardless of race or country of origin.

Dangerous Occupations

If you're seeking an adventurous career change and don't particularly like the idea of dodging bullets while you're selling Slurpies and cigarettes, here are a few other jobs you might consider:

Army Ranger

The Ranger course is 68 days and emphasizes patrolling and raiding. The course is being restricted, and very few noninfantry soldiers will be able to attend in the future. Troops from other branches can attend if they are being sent to jobs with a specific need for Ranger skills. The Ranger school is considered the toughest course in the army.

U.S. Army
2425 Wilson Boulevard
Arlington, VA 22210-3385
☎ *(703) 841-4300*

Bicycle Messenger

There are about 1500 bicycle messengers in New York City. Messengers are paid between $3 and $30 per trip. A good bike messenger should make about $125 a day. The faster you are, the more you can make, especially during rush hour. You have to supply your own bike (usually a $500 to $1200 mountain bike), safety gear and health insurance. The messenger company gives you a walkie-talkie and a big bag. Messengers work around the clock and break every rule in the book. Many practice "snatching" or grabbing onto a car or truck to speed up their trip. Contact individual messenger services in large cities for more information.

Blowout Control

If you like your work hot and dangerous, try containing oil blowouts. The most famous of these workers is, of course, Red Adair's group which inspired a movie starring John Wayne. Despite the dramatic footage of men covered in oil and being roasted, safety comes first. Red is retired, but the company lives on.

The general idea is that when oil wells catch on fire, or blow out, there is a lot of money being sprayed into the air. So these people have to work fast. Saddam Hussein overtaxed companies from eight countries when he set the Kuwaiti fields alight. There were 732 oil wells in need of capping, but not before US$60 billion worth of oil had disappeared.

Even though the companies can be paid up to a million dollars a job (mostly for equipment and expenses), a more realistic fee is between US$20,000 and US$200,000 to control a blowout. The members of the crew make about US$300 to US$1000 a day each plus room and board. The work requires a drilling background. It is tough, hard and dirty work. You also can't pick your customers, since blowouts happen anywhere, anytime.

Safety Boss
Red Deer,
Alberta, Canada
☎ *(403) 342-1310*

Boots & Coots
Houston, TX

☎ *(713) 931-8884*

Red Adair
Dallas, TX
☎ *(214) 462-4282*

Bodyguard

Not much danger here, but it sounds dangerous. Big and beefy works for the low level celebrity stuff, spry and deadly for the high level political jobs. You can make about $200–$300 a day (when you work) and if you think you'll be working on a yacht in Monte Carlo protecting bikini-clad rich gals, wake up and smell the B.O.

Most bodyguards work for businessmen. You can carry a gun but it'll just wear a hole in your nice dry cleaned shirts. If you're lucky you can get a full time gig where you also get to drive a car, open doors and other Step 'n Fetch-it stuff. Should something go down, you get to throw yourself in front of your employer and spend a few months in the hospital if you get shot. Ex's are the preferred folks here. ex-secret Service, ex-cops, ex military etc. *DP's* best bet for adventure (but not bucks) is to go south (Latin America) young man where bodyguarding is serious business. One of our buddies ended up being one of Vesco's bodyguards when he and a pal (ex-navy) were bumming around Costa Rica in the old days. They were hanging out in a bar and were enlisted to make a few sucres standing around looking tough.

International Bodyguard Association
458 West Kenwood
Brighton, Tennessee 38011
☎ *(901) 837-1915, FAX: (901) 837-4949*
The IBA is a professional association for bodyguards ($50 first year, $40 per year thereafter.) They also provide a skills course in firearms, bodyguarding.
P.O. Box 500
South Croydon, England CRZ 6ZD
☎ *[44] (181) 668 5190, FAX: [44] (181) 668 8745*

Asset Protection Team
10467 White Granite Drive, Suite 210
Oakton Virginia
☎ *(703) 385-6754*
APT is run by Chuck Vance, an ex Secret Service agent who married President Ford's daughter Susan.

Falcon Global Corporation
837 Washington Boulevard, Suite 2
Williamsport, Pennsylvania, 17701
☎ *(800) 326-9838*
Ex-Green Berets started Falcon Global to provide a little muscle during strikes.

Executive Protection Associates, Inc.
316 California Avenue
Reno, NV 89509
http://www.iapps.org/epaihm.html
Executive Protection Specialist Handbook

Varro Press
P.O. Box 8413 Shawnee Mission, Kansas 66208
☎ *(913) 432-5856*

Bounty Hunter

For those of you who can't hold a day job, you might consider bounty hunting. Since the romantic notion of men being brought in dead or alive for a price on their head is almost gone, you end up working for bail bondsmen, not the most romantic of employers. They will pay you a finder's fee so they don't have to cough up the entire amount of the court-imposed bail when their client doesn't show.

The job does not require much training or even much of anything except a pair of hand-cuffs and a little skip-tracing education. (Don't believe everything you see on "Rene-gade." It isn't necessary to have a Lorenzo Lamas physique, long hair or a Harley.) What you get for bringing in bad people is between 10 and 30 percent of the fugitives' bail from the grateful bondsmen. Their clients will not be happy to see you and, in most cases, will try to elude you, since you have neither an attractive uniform nor a big gun. If you have a permit to carry a gun, you are not always allowed to use it. You need a license to operate in Indiana and Nevada but in other states, you are essentially making a citizen's arrest, and if you end up with broken bones or holes in you, it's your problem. Some states don't like bounty hunters; you can't practice your business in Illinois, Kentucky or Oregon, for example.

There are about 2000 bounty hunters (50–100 are active) in the U.S. who return about 20,000 fugitives each year. It is estimated that about 35,000 folks jump bail (don't appear in court) and about 87 percent are brought back by bounty hunters. Most of these hunters don't make much money. The lower the bail, the less serious the crime, the less money they make, the easier the errant crooks or fugitives (don't forget they are innocent until proven guilty) are to find.

There is a market for high-end bounty hunters. There are many fugitive terrorists with very big prices on their heads. But you will need a working command of Arabic, Persian, French and some tribal dialects. You will need to be fully conversant with Islam and the Koran and be able to travel around Afghanistan and Pakistan. If you're caught, you will be lucky if you are shot. If you want to know more about bounty hunting or just hang out with the 1500 or so members of the NIBE contact the following:

National Institute of Bail Enforcement
P.O. Box 1170
Tombstone, AZ 85638
☎ *(520) 457-9360*

Western States Bail Enforcement Association
P.O. Box 352
Los Altos, CA 94023
e-mail: webmaster@bounty-hunter.org
http://www.bounty-hunter.org/

Cab Driver

Taxis were introduced in 1907 in New York City. Today, it is a job usually taken by recent immigrants. In New York City, there are 11,787 Yellow Cabs, 30,000 livery cars and between 5000 and 9000 illegal gypsy cabs. Cab drivers are usually independent contractors who lease their cabs from a cab company. In New York, a cabbie pays about $40 a day for the cab and maybe about $20 for gas. He gets to keep everything after that. The term for breaking even is "making the knot." There are no benefits, worker's comp or holidays. The hours are flexible, and you meet a lot of interesting people, albeit briefly. The Lexan dividers in some cabs have been credited with saving lives, but driving a cab is still a dangerous business.

In a recent one-year span in New York City, there were 40 murders of cabbies; most were drivers of livery or gypsy cabs. In a five-year period, 192 drivers were killed. There were 3892 robberies in that one-year period. The average amount of the theft was $100 in cash.

N.Y. Taxi Commission   ☎ (212) 302-8294, FAX: (212) 840-1607

CIA

The U.S. intelligence community is comprised of about 100,000 people who work for 28 different organizations. It takes eight agencies just to process and analyze the satellite images sent in by five different intelligence groups. It costs about $28 billion to find out what our friends and enemies are up to. The adventurous, spooky stuff is the Clandestine Service. You get to recruit foreign agents, pretend to be somebody else and then be air-lifted out by Marines or Navy SEALS when Uncle Sam screws up as they did in Northern Iraq. If you want to be a Clandestine Services case officer only mention your interest in your first interview. They need folks who have language skills and background in Africa, Central Asia (especially Former Soviet Republics) and of course they will wet themselves if you are a well placed North Korean or Iraqi. Entrance salary is between $31,459 to $48,222. Maximum age is 35 and you need to have a college degree. How do we know all this super spooky stuff. Well the CIA has taken to advertising in the *Economist*. For super secret jobs contact:

Chief Career Training Program
P.O. Box 1925
Washington, D.C. 20013
☎ *(703) 790-0345*

The job category that might attract MBAs/adventurers is what is known as *nonofficial cover*. Opportunity is knocking (or NOCing) for a few lucky business grads. Dissatisfied with the traditional foreign embassy bureaucrat or aid worker as a cover for its operatives, the CIA has decided to get creative. The CIA now recruits young executives through bogus companies usually based in northern Virginia. The ads appear in major periodicals and newspapers and seek recent business school grads who want to work overseas. The job pays well but requires training. The NOCs are not trained in Camp Peary nor do they ever appear on any CIA database to keep them safe from moles. Sounds like a great movie plot, so far.

The successful graduates are then posted with real companies overseas. Many large American corporations gladly accept these folks, since they get a real business grad who works long hours for free. Each NOC has a liaison person who must handle the intel that is provided by his charge. Many of these posi-

tions are with banks, import-export firms and other companies in such nasty places as North Korea, Iraq, Iran and Colombia. Although the CIA has to cut corners on its $28 billion dollar annual budget, NOCs cost more to train and support, but it's hoped they can provide hard information in countries where the embassy is a little light on cocktail party chatter.

If you are exposed or captured, you are officially a spy and not protected by a diplomatic passport.

CIA Employment Office
Career Trainee Division
P.O. Box A2002
Arlington, VA 22209-8727
☎ *(703) 613-8888, FAX: (703) 613-7871*

To join the Clandestine service branch of the CIA you need a bachelor's degree along with strong communication and interpersonal skills. Military experience helps. The CIA is keen on folks with backgrounds in Central Eurasian, East Asian and Middle Eastern languages (kind of tells you where the action is doesn't it?). You need to pass a medical, psychiatric and polygraph test. You must be a U.S. citizen and can't be over 35. The starting pay is $31,459 to $48,222. A lot of the training takes place at the

9000 acre Camp Peary, outside Williamsburg, Virginia. Here students spend a year at "the Farm" learning how to be spies.

Former CIA operatives can also sign up with any number of security consultants (See Save Yourself) or groups like CTC who provide the private sector with intelligence gathering and security.

Delta Force

The 1st SFOD-Delta (Delta Force) began in 1977 as Uncle Sam's sharp edge against terrorism. Today it is estimated to employ between 2500–8000 men (and females). Charlie Beckworth was given two years to create an anti-terrorism unit similar to European units like the SAS. There are three assault squadrons (A, B and C) made up of 75 people which are split into 4–6 man teams. When they need a lift they use the Air Force Special Operations Command and the Army 160th Aviation Regiment. It also has its own small air force made of civilian dressed aircraft which can be converted once in country. There is also the Funny Platoon, an intel group that uses female operatives.

A $75 million facility on old Range 19 (on Fort Bragg's McKellars road) at Fort Bragg is their home. Their specialty is storming buildings or planes and like the Navy SEALs; they may or may not have been used for a variety of rescue and black ops. The world knows about their botched attempts to rescue the hostages in Tehran and the casualties they suffered trying to take out Aidid in Mogadishu. Delta operatives have spent quite a bit of time cooling their hills in Cyprus trying to rescue hostages or Howard Air Force base in Panama.

Delta Force prides itself on being the world's best marksmen under all conditions. The latest thrill ride is being invited to sit in the middle of a Delta Force shooting house during CQB (Close Quarter Battle) and watch the team storm the buildings, kill all the paper terrorists without messing a single hair on the guests' head. Like the Navy SEALs (who often work in conjunction with the Delta Force), the Delta Force can go anywhere, anytime; they just leave the wet jobs to SEAL Team 6, the Navy's version of Delta Force. The FBI has a hostage team that handles domestic terrorist incidents. Delta Force operatives are recruited from the army. The average candidate is around 31 years old, has ten years of service, has an above average IQ. Candidates are by invitation only basis (usually recruited from Green Beret and Rangers) and must go through physical and psychological tests. There is an 18 day formal selection course that mimics the SAS course with the addition of rigorous mental tests after periods of physical hardship and sleep deprivation. If accepted the candidate then goes through a six month Operators Training Course. The course includes, shooting, air assaults, bodyguarding, high speed driving, mental sharpening and covert operations.

Explosives Expert

If Uncle Sam taught you how to blow things up, you might want to try demolishing buildings (no we don't mean Federal Buildings). The skill of imploding existing skyscrapers, apartment buildings and large factories has spawned companies that do nothing but take down buildings in a few seconds flat. Controlled Demolition Group holds the world record for blowing up buildings. Although not a dangerous job with the correct training (hell, even I used to work with explosives) it does demand a certain level of attention.

Controlled Demolition Group
Charlesworth House
Richardshaw Road
Leeds, England LS28 6QW

☎ *[44] (0113) 255-8455*
☎ *[44] (0113) 239-3191*
e-mail: *marketing@cdg5.discovery-net.co.uk*

Green Beret

The Green Berets are the outgrowth of the WWII "Jedburgh teams," special teams that were dropped behind enemy lines to link up with French partisans. They evolved into eight man Detachment Alpha or "A" teams. Each team member had multiple and overlapping skills. Later the teams would be expanded to 12 men. They were used to train other military or insurgent groups. Despite the shoot 'em John Wayne image, Green Berets are officially known as U.S. Army Special Forces, and they have always been linked with spook work and covert operations. They were created in 1953 by a veteran of the OSS (the precursor of the CIA) and the green beret wasn't officially endorsed until President Kennedy visited Fort Bragg in 1961. To get in, you have to already be a member of the Army and pass the three week selection course at Fort Bragg. Once accepted there is the Q course, a three to 12 month course that teaches the basic skills of counterinsurgency:

John F. Kennedy Special Warfare Center and School
Attention AMU-SP-R
Fort Bragg North Carolina 28307
☎ *(919) 432-1818*

101st Airborne Division
ATFN: RCRO-SM-SF-FC
Fort Campbell, Kentucky 42223
☎ *(502) 439-4390*

Mercenary

If someone paid you $40 million (some say $23 million), could you clean up a civil war? Well, that's what Executive Outcomes was reportedly paid to clean up things in Angola. They also cashed half of a $46 million fee to clean up Bougainville, but that gig was a fiasco. Nobody has a clean accounting on what they got in Sierra Leone but considering that one of last EO mercenaries left on the ground was an accountant, it should tell you "outsourcing your military needs" has become is a big business.

The curious thing about South African based EO is that it is part of a larger Canadian mining group that, along with killing rebels, also looks for gold in Uganda, explores in Ethiopia, and is busy in various mining operations in Lesotho, Botswana, Sierra Leone, South Africa, and a growing number of other African nations. They also have a large aviation division that can hustle up tired old Russian gunships as well as shiny business jets. The new mercenary business is convoluted and meant to be. Although EO is a security company, it is part of a group of 32 companies. If you are wondering what the folks working for EO make, it isn't much—about $1500 a month and all the land mines you can step on. Officers are in greater demand and can negotiate monthly salaries of $4500–$15,000. In-country shifts are eight weeks on and two weeks off. It helps to know a little Afrikaaner, since the officers use it as a code to confuse the bad guys. The mercs are typically black and recruited from the South Africa Defense Forces when they fought against the well-armed and highly trained mercenaries. The kill ratio is about 50 rebels to one mercenary. Yes, they do provide insurance coverage in case you get killed or injured. If you contact EO Mr. Pelser will politely ask you to send your CV (resume) but they typically only hire ex-SADF folks.

For those who want less action but more money. MPRI is owned and operated by former U.S. military officers and NCO's who provide training, equipping, force design and management, professional development, concepts and doctrine, organizational and operational requirements, simulation and wargaming operations, humanitarian assistance, quick reaction military contractual support, and democracy transition assistance programs for the military forces of emerging republics. Now entering its 10th year, MPRI has in excess of 350 employees. The 1996 volume of business exceeded $24,000,000. Other units like DSL provide a wide range of security services and manpower to the military, mining and oil businesses.

Defence Systems Limited
Eggington House
25-28 Buckingham Gate
London, England SW1E 6LD

☎ *(0171) 233-5611, FAX: (0171) 233-7434*
e-mail: DSL_London@dial.pipex.com

Executive Outcomes

P.O. Box 75255
Lynwood Ridge
Pretoria 0040, South Africa
☎ [27] (12) 473-789

GSG

Suite 11, Queensway House
St. Helior, Jersey JE4 81Y
Channel Islands, U.K.

☎ [44] (1534) 74-707

Military Professional Resources Inc.

1201 East Abingdon Drive, Suite 425
Alexandria, Virginia 22314
☎ (703) 684-0853, FAX: (703) 684-3528
e-mail info@mpri.com
http://www.mpri.com/

Minesweeper

Land mines kill or maim someone on this planet every hour. There is a big demand for former explosives and munitions experts to clean up these killers. Mine clearance personnel are paid about US$90,000 a year. There are about 20 companies that specialize in the detection and removal of land mines. Kuwait spent about US$1 billion to clean up the 7 million land mines sewn during the five-month occupation of Kuwait by Iraq; 83 mine clearance experts have been killed just in Kuwait. If you are looking for big money, be aware that local minesweepers in Angola make only US$70 a day.

Explosive Ordnance Disposal World Services

Fort Walton Beach, FL
☎ (904) 864-3454

Ronco

Berkeley, CA
☎ (510) 548-3922

Royal Ordnance

London, England
☎ [44] (81) 012-52-37-32-32

UXB

Chantilly, VA
☎ (703) 803-8904

Navy SEAL

Specialists in Naval Special Warfare, the SEALs (SEa Air, Land) evolved from the frogman of WWII. The SEALs have been glorified in films and books. Their most recent brush with fame was their less-than-secret invasion of Kuwait City, with the world's press watching and filming with high-powered camera lights. The SEALs were born on January 1, 1962 when they were created by President Kennedy along with the revitalized Green Berets.

In 1989 the SEALs were the first into Panama, using rebreathers and midget subs. In the Gulf War they even used custom-made dune buggies to operate behind enemy lines.

The SEALs go through 27 weeks of intense basic training, either in Coronado, which is near San Diego or on the East Coast. The training starts with a seven week exercise and swimming course just to get ready for basic training. Then there are nine weeks of extreme physical and mental abuse. The focus is on teamwork and surviving the constant harassment. The sixth week is "Hell Week," six days of misery and physical torture with little or no sleep. Then there is extensive classroom and underwater training in SCUBA (Self Contained Underwater Breathing Apparatus) diving. This phase ends with another serious physical challenge. The third and final phase is the UDT and above-water training on San Clemente Island. There is also a 6 month probation period.

SEAL teams must practice close-quarter battle drills by firing 300 or more rounds of 9-mm ammunition weekly. Each of the six-line SEAL teams is given 1.5 million rounds of ammunition annually to train its five 16-man platoons. According to the specs on their Beretta 92F pistols, this means they burn out one handgun a year. Their MP5 machine guns last a little longer. The symbol of a seal is the gold plated "Budweiser" pin, the eagle and a trident symbol. SEAL Team 6 specializes in anti-terrorist operations. They are controlled by NAVSPECWARCOMDEVGROUP out of Coronado, California.

If you just want to look like a SEAL you can shop at the same place SEALs shop. Be the first on your block to wear a shirt that says "Pain is just weakness leaving your body." **Bullshirts**, *1007 Orange Avenue, Coronado, CA 92118.*

U.S. Navy Human Resources
2531 Jefferson Davis Highway

Arlington, VA 22242-5161
☎ *(703) 607-3023*

Smoke Jumper

If the thought of being parachuted into a raging inferno and having to fight your way back until you can be airlifted out many sleepless nights later appeals to you, then you should try smoke jumping. Smoke jumpers are firefighters who must be in the air within 10 minutes and parachute into remote areas to fight fires. Dropped from small planes as low as 1500 feet in altitude, they quickly must hike to the scene of the fire, and instantly begin to chop and backburn areas to head off forest fires before they get too big. The work is all manual and requires strength, endurance and an ability to work around the clock if need be.

Most smoke jumpers are attracted by the danger and the camaraderie these jobs afford. They are known to be party animals, close friends and hard workers

Although the death of 14 firefighters in Glenwood Springs, Colorado, on July 6, 1994, reminded people that smoke jumping is dangerous, that there are only 387 smoke jumpers in the U.S. makes those deaths even more significant. The last time any smoke jumpers were killed actually fighting a fire was in 1949 during the Mann Gulch blaze in Montana. During this 45-year period of calm, one jumper pancaked into the ground due to chute failure and another hanged himself when he tried to get out of a tree where he had landed.

Like most dangerous jobs, the goal is to stay alive and healthy, and you definitely don't do it for the money. Pay for smoke jumpers starts at about $9 an hour, and there is additional pay during fires and with overtime. Most are part-time jumpers who earn the money during the hot summer fire season.

There are nine U.S. Forest Service and Bureau of Land Management regional jumper bases in the West. The supervisors react quickly to fires and send in anywhere from two or more jumpers, depending on the size of the fire. If a lightning strike starts a small blaze, fire jumpers can deal with it quickly and effectively before calling in the water bombers. Supplies can be parachuted in as soon as the jumpers are on the ground. Once done, the jumpers then get to hike out with their equipment or be picked up by helicopter.

Training requires federal certification to fell large trees and to be able to climb in and more likely, out of trees. They maintain their own chain saws and other equipment. Their protective Kevlar suits hold their equipment and protect them when landing in trees. Forest Service jumpers use round chutes and jump at 1500 feet BLM; smoke jumpers use the more modern rectangular chutes and exit at 3000 feet.

Aerial Fire Depot
Missoula, MT
☎ *(406) 329-3402 ext. 4893*

Payette Wildlife Center
McCall, ID
☎ *(208) 634-0700*

Northern California Service Center
Redding, CA
☎ *(916) 246-5467*

Redmond Air Center
Redmond, OR
☎ *(503) 548-5070*

U.N. Peacekeeper

Not many soldiers ask to be U.N. peacekeepers, and they usually find the idea of talking to a highly trained killer and making him Gandhi for a day even stranger. It's tough enough trying to figure out why someone is trying to kill his closest neighbor, or in our case, why we send pimply kids thousands of miles to whomp Third World revolutionaries.

Being a U.N. peacekeeper means wearing silly blue berets and driving around in white trucks. You can be shot at, but you can't shoot back. You can be insulted, but you can't insult back. In fact, you may find yourself actually helping people kill their enemy as you protect war criminals, maintain archaic political boundaries and provide security for execution squads. You will come under shell fire, and gun fire and have to keep up with deadly bureaucratic paperwork. In Bosnia, Canadians were told to return mines they dug up to the armies that planted them. Some scratched their initials on the casings and dug up the same mines weeks later. They must use photodegradable sandbags, and the rules of engagement are so Byzantine that it requires hours to get official clearances to shoot back when they come under fire.

United Nations   *New York, NY*
Field Operations Staffing   ☎ *(212) 963-1147*
42nd Street and First Avenue, Room
52280-D

Construction Specialists Wanted

For those who like the excitement of going into war zones with a slide rule, Brown and Root of Houston, Texas, may have a job for you. Not a military firm or even one that engages in any military activity, Brown and Root is an engineering firm owned by Halliburton. They specialize in infrastructure work, the mundane job of building sewers, pipelines and other necessary items required to restore shattered economies. The boss of this outfit is none other than Dick Cheney, former secretary of defense. Brown and Root does its work in places like Somalia, Haiti and The Balkans. For more information, call Brown and Root at ☎ (713) 676-4141.

The Wild Goose Chase

I found your book last Saturday in Pretoria, and I couldn't wait to write to you. I'm 28 years old, French and live in South Africa. I spent 4-1/2 years in the Naval Infantry as a sergeant, I resigned to join the Legion, but they didn't take me because I was short sighted. It was a shock because I never intended to be a civilian. I stayed in France got a diploma and became a fitness instructor in a gym. I missed the Army very much. I resigned to go to Bosnia to join HVO. I first went to Mostar where people were nice, but told me I had come a little late. I went to Zagreb where I tried to join the Croat Brigade. Unfortunately a law had been voted in which banned the hiring of foreigners. Two months later I was working as a fitness instructor for Club Med in Morocco.

A friend called and told me he could arrange for me to fight for the Karens in Burma (Myanmar). I quit to go back to France and meet the recruiter. He says he hasn't had any news from Burma for the last two months. "The Karens have lost Manerplaw so I prefer not to send you there now."

I became a security guard in Luxembourg, but it was too boring so I quit and left for South Africa. I tried to join Executive Outcomes but they only hire ex-SADF people. I ended up working for COIN security in the Comoros Islands. When I returned, some former EO people and I went to Kinshasa. We waited, but nothing happened. I was an interpreter and four members of the secret police stole $200 from me. We never got any money from the Zaireans. I was told that the contract was signed with Mobutu's government (it wasn't) that the money was on its way to South Africa (it never arrived) and that we would have all the equipment we needed (it never showed up either). I quit my job at COIN in expectation of going to Kinshasa but nothing ever came of it. Like you said the merc business is 99 percent bullshit and one percent reality. Long life to *DP* and best regards to the whole team.

—"B" a DP reader

Dangerous Diseases

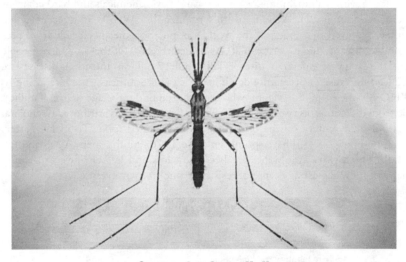

Souvenirs from Hell

Each time I stop in at my doctor's office (a tropical disease specialist with time in Vietnam), he asks me why the hell I do what I do. Yet, he takes great pains to describe the symptoms of the many tropical diseases that await me in the Third World. His lectures usually center around the lifelong pain and debilitation that can be inflicted on travelers who inadvertently ingest an amoeba, get bitten by a mosquito or become the host for a degenerative bug. I take his advice seriously, and I am as fastidious as I can be in adverse conditions. I am very careful about what I eat and how I sleep, and I follow the rules of common sense when it comes to avoiding infection. Despite this, I have spent nights shivering and delirious, lying in puddles of my own sweat on cement floors in the Sahara desert. I pay his bill gladly and trust to the cosmos and good common sense.

With this in mind, do not assume that this chapter is the be-all end-all reference source for tropical diseases. *Always confer with a specialist before taking any trip.* This way, you understand the odds and the penalties and can make an educated decision on the risks involved. Secondly, *always have full medical tests upon your return.* This means giving a little bit of yourself to the lab to run blood, stool and urine tests. Your doctor may ask you to come back again due to the long incubation time of some of these nasties. This is not hypochondria, but common sense. Early detection will increase your odds of successful treatment.

The odds of coming down with a bug are pretty good once you leave the antiseptic Western world. If you go off on an extended trip (one month or more) you have a 60–75 percent chance that you will develop some illness or problem, most likely diarrhea. Only about one percent of travelers will pick up an infectious disease. I once thought that the locals had built up resistance to the various bugs that strike down Westerners. But once in-country, you realize what a toll disease takes on the Third World. Not only are many people riddled with malaria, river blindness, intestinal infections, hepatitis, sexual diseases and more, but they are also faced with malnutrition, poor dental care, toxic chemicals and hard environmental conditions. The World Health Organization (WHO), in a recent global survey, reported that much of the world's population dies needlessly from preventable diseases due to a lack of access to health care. Of the 52 million people who die each year, infectious diseases kill about 17 million. Infectious diseases are the leading cause of premature death in Africa and Southeast Asia, according to WHO. Of the 11 million victims who are children under the age of five, 9 million die from infectious diseases. About 70 percent of the deaths attributed to cholera, typhoid or dysentery can be blamed on contaminated food. To make matters worse, 30 new diseases have sprung up since 1976, among them AIDS and the deadly Ebola virus. Antibiotics are becoming less and less effective in treating many of these diseases, because of resistance due to their overuse.

Ten Least Wanted	
The top ten killer diseases are primarily Third World, celebrity-free, low visibility killers of children.:	
Acute respiratory tract infections	4.4
Diarrheal diseases (cholera, typhoid, dysentery)	3.1
Tuberculosis	3.1
Hepatitis B	1.1
HIV/AIDS	1 million +
Measles	1 million +
Neonatal tetanus	460,000
Whooping cough	350,000
Intestinal worms	135,000

Source: World Health Organization

Malaria

Malaria is a very dangerous disease, affecting 500 million people worldwide and killing at least 2 million people every year. The mosquito-borne disease is found in 102 countries and threatens 40 percent of the world's population.

Over a million people in Africa are killed by malaria every year. Two million people die from it in a one-year period, according to WHO. More than 30,000 European and American travelers will come down with malaria this year.

The female *Anopheles* mosquito is small, pervasive and hungry for your blood, and likes to bite in the cool hours before and after sunset. As they seek out blood to nurture their own procreation, they leave the Plasmodium parasites in your blood system. The symptoms can start with a flulike attack, followed by fever and chills, then lead to failure of multiple organs and then death. In many cases, the symptoms of malaria do not start until the traveler has returned home and is in a nonmalarial zone. Remember that current chemoprophylaxis does not prevent malaria. Larium, Fansidar, and chloroquinine can lower the chances of getting malaria but do not provide any guarantee of being malaria-proof. Two of my fellow travelers (one in Africa and one in Borneo) did not realize they had malaria, because they believed that Larium would protect them from the disease. Luckily, they sought treatment in time.

Malaria is a very real and common danger in most tropical countries. Most malaria in Asian and African areas is quinine-resistant and requires multiple or more creative dosages to avoid the horrors often associated with the disease. The most vicious strain of malaria (*Plasmodium falciparum*) attacks your liver and red blood cells, creating massive fevers, coma, acute kidney failure, and eventually death. There are three other types of malaria in the world: *Plasmodium malariae, Plasmodium vivax* and *Plasmodium ovale* (found only in West Africa).

The *Anopheles* mosquito is the most dangerous insect in the world, and there are few contenders for its crown. Other biting insects that can cause you grief include the *Aedes aegypti* mosquito, which carries yellow fever. His kissing cousins, the *Culex, Haemogogus, Sabethes* and *Mansonia*, can give you filariasis, viral encephalitis, dengue and other great hemorrhagic fevers. Next on the list are tsetse flies, fleas, ticks, sandflies, mites and lice. We won't even bother to discuss wasps, horseflies, African killer bees, deerflies, or other clean biters.

These insects are an everyday part of life in tropical Third World countries. They infect major percentages of the local population, and it is only a matter of time and luck before you become a victim.

Prevention is rather simple but often ineffective. Protect yourself from insects by wearing long-sleeved shirts and long pants. Use insect repellent, sleep under a mosquito net, avoid swampy areas, use mosquito coils, don't sleep directly on the ground, check yourself for tick and insect bites daily and, last but not least, understand the symptoms and treatment of these diseases so that you can seek immediate treatment, no matter what part of the world you are in.

The Gift That Keeps On Giving	
Disease	**Annual Deaths**
Infected by malaria	500 million
Infected by HIV	20 million
Infected by AIDS	4.5 million
Acute respiratory infections	4.4 million
Diarrheal Diseases	3.1 million

The Gift That Keeps On Giving	
Disease	**Annual Deaths**
Tuberculosis	3 million
Malaria	2 million
AIDS	1 million

Worms

My least favorite are the helminthic infections, or diseases caused by intestinal worms. Unlike the more dramatic and deadly diseases, these parasites are easily caught through ingestion of bad water and food and cause long-term damage. Just to let you know what's out there, you can choose from angiostrongyliasis, herring worm, roundworm, schistsomiasis, capillariasis, pin worm, oriental liver fluke, fish tapeworm, guinea worm, cat liver fluke, tapeworm, trechinellosis and the ominous-sounding giant intestinal fluke (who's eating who here?). All these little buggers create havoc with your internal organs, and some will make the rest of your life miserable as well. Your digestive system will be shot and your organs under constant attack, and the treatment or removal of these nasties is downright depressing. All this can be prevented by maintaining absolutely rigid standards in what you throw or breathe into your body. Not easy since most male travelers find wearing a biohazard suit a major impediment to picking up chicks or doing the limbo.

Think of yourself as a sponge, your lungs as an air filter, and all the moist cavities of your body as ideal breeding grounds for tropical diseases. It is better to think like Howard Hughes than Pig Pen when it comes to personal hygiene.

The Fevers

The classic tropical diseases that incapacitated Stanley, Livingstone, Burton and Speke are the hemorrhagic fevers. Many of these diseases kill, but most make your life a living hell and then disappear. Some come back on a regular basis. It is surprising that most of the African explorers lived to a ripe old age. The hemorrhagic fevers are carried by mosquitoes, ticks, rats, feces or even airborne dust that gets into your bloodstream, and let you die a slow, demented death, as your blood turns so thin it trickles out your nose, gums, skin and eyes. Coma and death can occur in the second week. There are so many versions that they just name them after the places where you will stumble across them. Needless to say, these are not featured in any glossy brochures for the various regions. Assorted blood-thinning killers are called Chikungunya, Crimean, Congo, Omsk, Kyasanur Forest, Korean, Manchurian, Songo, Ebola, Argentinian, Hantaan, Lassa and yellow fever.

The recent outbreaks of the Hanta and Ebola viruses in the U.S. have proved that North America is not immune from these insect-, rodent- and airborne afflictions. So far, the Ebola Reston virus has only been found in monkeys sent by a Philippine supplier. All monkeys exposed to the virus were destroyed, and officials from the Centers for Disease Control reassured the public that Ebola Reston is a different virus from Ebola Zaire (now called the Democratic Republic of the Congo), the strain that killed 244 people in one outbreak. Still, experts warn that the Ebola Reston strain could mutate into a strain that is fatal to humans. The outbreak of plague in India also has travelers a little edgy about the whole concept of adventurous travel. There are real dangers in every part of the world and the more knowledgeable you are about them, the better your chances for surviving.

Sex (STDs)

The quest for sexual adventure was once a major part of the joy of travel. Today, the full range of sexual diseases available to the common traveler would fill an encyclopedia. Despite the continual global publicity on the dangers of AIDS, it continues to claim victims at an alarming rate. Whorehouses around the world are thriving, junkies still share needles, and dentists in many Third World countries still grind and yank away with improperly sterilized instruments. Diseases like HIV, Hepatitis A and B, the clap, syphilis, genital warts, herpes, crabs, lice, and others that Westerners blame on the Third World, and the Third World blames on the West, are very preventable and require parking your libido. Sexually transmitted diseases are a growing health hazard. According to WHO, 236 million people have trichomoniasis and 94 million new cases occur each year. Chlamydial infections affect 162 million people, with 97 million new cases annually. And these figures don't include the increasing millions with genital warts, gonorrhea, genital herpes and syphilis. The highest rates for sexually transmitted diseases are in the 20–24 age group, followed by 15–19 and 25–29. In many countries, more than 60 percent of all new HIV infections are among the 15–24 age group.

How do you avoid sexually transmitted diseases, some people ask? Well, keeping your romantic agenda on the platonic side is a good start. The use of condoms is the next best thing. Realistically the chances of catching AIDS through unprotected sex depends on frequency and type of contact. People infected by blood transfusions, prostitutes, frequent drug users, hemophiliacs, homosexuals, and the millions of people who will get HIV this year from heterosexual sex will continue to make HIV a growing danger.

Hepatitis A, B, C

Your chance of getting Hep B if you leave the U.S. is only 5 percent unless of course you go for a tattoo at the smack jabbers rusty needle convention in the Golden Triangle (and have unprotected sex afterwards with a Thai junkie hooker). All macho bullshit aside, men and women are at equal risk and health workers are at a very high risk when working in Third World countries. Carrier rates among the population in some undeveloped countries are as high as 20 percent of the total population. Many travelers get Hep B without engaging in any high risk activities because the virus can survive outside the body for prolonged periods. Infection can occur when any infected material comes in contact with mucous membranes or broken skin. Hepatitis A is a viral infection of the liver transmitted by the fecal, oral route through direct contact with infected people, from water, ice, shellfish, or uncooked food. Symptoms for Hep A include fever, loss of appetite, dark urine, jaundice, vomiting, aches and pains and light stools. You usually get Hep A in Third World countries with poor sanitation. It is easy to prevent with simple vaccination using one of the two vaccines available. For proper protection the vaccine requires an initial shot (good for three months) and then repeated doses to protect longer term.

DP fan and reader Dr. Susan Hou sent us a polite, but firm letter demanding that we expand information on this very easy to catch and very easy to prevent disease. We quote the good doctor (who has knocked around enough to earn a *DP* shirt):

"The majority of people with symptomatic Hepatitis B infection don't die, but spend a month wishing they would. One percent develop fulminate (Webster's: developing or progressing suddenly) disease and die of liver failure. (On the bright side, if you get back to the United States before getting sick, fulminate liver failure moves you to the top of the liver transplant list). Five to ten percent of people become chronic carriers which means they can infect other people. For women this includes 85 percent of the children they carry who don't get treated. Thirty percent of chronic carriers have ongoing liver disease (chronic active hepatitis). Many progress to cirrhosis and require liver transplants (but start out lower on the transplant list). People with chronic active hepatitis develop liver cancer at a rate of 3 percent per year. The bad news if you get a liver transplant, Hepatitis B is usually still in your body and infects the new liver."

The vaccine for Hepatitis B is 90 percent effective after three doses. See your doctor or a local health clinic for more information before you travel.

AIDS

Perhaps the most dangerous and publicized disease is AIDS. It strikes right at the heart of American phobia—pain for pleasure. AIDS is the terminal phase of HIV (Human Immunodeficiency Virus). HIV is usually the precursor to AIDS, and then the victim succumbs to death by cancer, pneumonia and other afflictions that attack the weakened human immune system. AIDS has roughly a nine-year incubation period.

Initially brushed aside as "the gay plague" or an "African disease," AIDS has in the last few years become the biggest killer of young American men and women. Washington, D.C. has the nation's highest AIDS rate, far higher than even New York or San Francisco, according to statistics released by the Centers for Disease Control and Prevention. The 1995 D.C. rate was 185.7 AIDS cases per 100,000 residents. Puerto Rico was second with a rate of 70.3 cases per 100,000, followed by New York, Florida and New Jersey. Nationwide, the rate of AIDS cases is 27.8 cases per 100,000. The CDC says that AIDS is spreading more among women and minorities now, while the epidemic among homosexual white men has slowed. Women accounted for 19 percent of all AIDS cases among adults and adolescents nationwide. A growing number of children are being orphaned by AIDS, which has become the leading cause of death among women of childbearing age in the United States, according to a study in the *Journal of the American Medical Association.* Experts project that about 144,000 children and young adults will have lost their mothers to AIDS by the year 2000. Blacks are six times more likely to have AIDS than whites and twice as likely to have AIDS as Hispanics.

As sobering as the U.S. statistics are, the rate of deaths caused by AIDS in other countries is alarming. The number of AIDS cases worldwide reported to the World Health Organization by governments reached 1,025,073 by January 1995. WHO said that chronic underreporting and underdiagnosis in developing countries means the actual figure is probably more than 4.5 million. More than

70 percent of the estimated cases were in Africa, 9 percent in the United States, 9 percent in the rest of the American hemisphere, 6 percent in Asia, and 4 percent in Europe. The statistics include only people with active cases of AIDS or those who have died from the disease.

An estimated one million Latin Americans could have AIDS by the turn of the century, according to the Pan American Health Organization. The group says HIV is increasing among women in the Caribbean and Central America and it is expected to increase rapidly, particularly in areas where injection drug use is prevalent. There are currently 2 million HIV-infected people in Latin America and the Caribbean. According to Italy's statistics institute, ISTAT, AIDS has become as big a killer in Italy as road accidents. An estimated 4370 Italians died from AIDS last year, compared to 6000 deaths on the roads. For young males between 18 and 29 in Italy, AIDS has overtaken drugs as the second leading cause of death. ISTAT estimates that the number of HIV-infected Italians is at least 100,000. AIDS is also on the increase in smaller countries. WHO estimates that at least 400,000 or one percent of Myanmar's citizens are infected with HIV. A high number of injection drug users, social tolerance of prostitution and large amounts of cross-border trade with nearby nations make Myanmar's populace more vulnerable. Condoms are also costly and rarely used in Myanmar, exacerbating the problem.

Ministry of Health statistics show that more than 100,000 residents of Zimbabwe have died of AIDS-related causes in the past decade. Another 100,000 or one percent of the country's population is expected to succumb to AIDS in the next year and a half. AIDS is expected to slow population growth, lower life expectancies and raise child mortality rates in many of the world's poorer countries over the next 25 years, according to a report by the U.S. Census Bureau.

By the year 2010, a Ugandan's life expectancy will decline by 45 percent to 32 years—down from 59 years projected before AIDS. A Haitian's life expectancy will fall to 44 years, also down from 59 years. Life expectancy in Thailand will drop from a projected 75 years to 45. By the year 2010, Thailand's child mortality rates are expected to increase from the current 20 deaths per 1000 children born to 110 deaths. In Uganda, the jump will be from 90 deaths to 175 deaths out of every 1000 children born. In Malawi, it will soar from 130 to 210 deaths per 1000. Overall, premature death rates in those countries will double by 2010 compared with 1985 levels.

In 16 countries—the African nations of Burkina Faso, Burundi, Central African Republic, Congo, Cote d'Ivoire, Kenya, Malawi, Rwanda, Tanzania, Uganda, Congo, Zambia and Zimbabwe, plus Brazil, Haiti and Thailand—AIDS will slow population growth rates so dramatically that by 2010, there will be 121 million fewer people than previously forecast. Thailand's population will actually fall by nearly one percent because of AIDS deaths.

DANGEROUS DISEASES

"Zoonosis"

According to journalists, AIDS first began near the Congo-Burundi border, but did it? A 1992 Rolling Stone article by AIDS activist Blaine Elswood places the blame on polio vaccines grown in primate kidney cells and then injected into humans in 1957 and 1958. Other researchers had injected malaria-tainted blood from chimpanzees and mangabeys into human volunteers. The first AIDS case was reportedly a British sailor (who had never been to Africa) who died in 1959. The case wasn't officially recognized by the Centers for Disease Control until 1981.

There are two types of human AIDS virus: HIV-1, the most common type, and HIV-2, originally found only in people from Guinea-Bissau in West Africa. HIV-2 is very close to SIV (Simian Immunodeficiency Virus) found in sooty mangabeys. Curiously, SIV is not found in the Asian macaques normally used for research. Sooty mangabeys are commonly eaten by villagers in Africa. There is no hard proof that AIDS came from monkeys or even from Africa, but the preponderance of evidence shows that AIDS may have originated in Central Africa within the past 50 years. AIDS continues to mutate as new strains continue to appear in West Africa and Asia.

Old-Fashioned Diseases

Many travelers are quite surprised to find themselves coming down with measles or mumps while traveling. Unlike the U.S., which has eradicated much of the childhood and preventable viruses through inoculation, the rest of the world is more concerned about feeding than vaccinating their children. The recent outbreak of plague in India is a good example of what you should watch out for. Whooping cough, mumps, measles, polio and tuberculosis are common in Third World countries. (Measles claimed the lives of 1.1 million in 1995.) Although some of the symptoms are minor, complications can lead to lifelong afflictions. Make sure you are vaccinated against these easily preventable diseases.

But don't just run off to be the next bubble boy and spend the rest of your life in a hermetically sealed dome. For travelers, these diseases are relatively rare and avoidable. To put the whole thing in perspective, the most common complaint tends to be diarrhea, followed by a cold (usually the result of lowered resistance caused by fatigue, dehydration, foreign microbes and stress). The important thing is to recognize when you are sick versus very sick. Tales of turn-of-the-century explorers struck down by a tiny mosquito bite are now legend. Malaria is still a very real and common threat. Just for fun, bring back a sample of local river water from your next trip and have the medical lab analyze it. You may never drink water of any kind again.

This is not to say that as soon as you get off the plane you will automatically be struck down with Ebola River fever and have blood oozing out from your eyes. You can travel bug-free and suffer no more than a cold caused by the air conditioning in your hotel room. But it is important to at least understand the relative risks and gravity of some diseases.

The diseases listed on the following pages are important, and you should be conversant with both symptoms and cures. Please do not assume that this is medical advice. It is designed to give you an overview of the various nasties that possibly await you.

Tropical countries are the most likely to cause you bacterial grief. Keep in mind that most of these diseases are a direct result of poor hygiene, travel in infected areas and contact with infected people. In other words, stay away from people if you want to stay healthy. Secondly, follow the common sense practice of having all food cooked freshly and properly. Many books tell you to wash fruit and then forget to mention that the water is probably more filled with bugs than the fruit. Peel all fruits and vegetables, and approach anything you stick in your body with a healthy level of skepticism and distrust. If you are completely paranoid, you can exist on freeze-dried foods, Maggi Mee (noodles), fresh fruit (peeled, remember) and tinned food.

It is considered wise to ask local experts about dangers that await. If you do not feel right for any reason, contact a local doctor. It is not advisable to enter a medical treatment program while in a developing country. There are greater chances of you catching worse afflictions once you are in the hospital. Ask for temporary medication and then get your butt back to North America or Europe.

Remember that the symptoms of many tropical diseases may not take effect until you are home and back into your regular schedule. It is highly advisable that you contact a tropical disease specialist and have full testing done (stool, urine, blood, physical) just to be sure. Very few American doctors are conversant with the many tropical diseases by virtue of their rarity. This is not their fault, since many tourists do not even realize that they have taken trips or cruises into endemic zones. People can catch malaria on a plane between London and New York from a stowaway mosquito that just came in from Bombay. Many people come in close contact with foreigners in buses and subways and on the street from Los Angeles to New York. Don't assume you have to be up to your neck in Laotian pig wallows to be at risk. Many labs do not do tests for some of the more exotic bugs. Symptoms can also be misleading. It is possible that you may be misdiagnosed or mistreated if you do not fully discuss the possible reasons for your medical condition. Now that we have scared the hell out of you, your first contact should be with the Centers for Disease Control in Atlanta.

Dr. Susan Hou recommends that readers leave behind (or take extra) medical supplies for clinics or doctors when they travel. It is a good rule never to give medication, pills or even first aid materials directly to sick people since most do not know the correct usage or are aware of side effects. She also suggested giving blood (you can bring your own 18 gauge needle), but don't give blood at high altitude.

A Rogue's Gallery of Diseases

This list is a simple and incomplete checklist of what to ask your doctor about when planning your trip. The best single source in the world for information on the various bugs and germs is the Center for Disease Control available on the web (http://www.cdc.gov), by phone ☎ *(404) 639-3311* or reprinted in book form. (See the Health/Security section at the back of the back of the book.) Always consult with a doctor before traveling to Third World countries, before taking medication and to ensure proper precautions are taken. If you are sick within a country, it is wise to have supplementary medical treatment and or evacuation insurance.

**African Sleeping Sickness
(African Trypanosomiasis)**
   Found: Tropical Africa.

Cause: A tiny protozoan parasite that emits a harmful toxin.

Carrier: Tsetse fly. Tsetse flies are large biting insects about the size of a horsefly found in East and West Africa.

Symptoms: Eastern trypanosomiasis: two–31 days after the bite recurrent episodes of fever, headaches and malaise. Can lead to death in two to six weeks.Western trypanosomiasis: produces a skin ulcer within five to 10 days after being bitten. The symptoms then disappear in two to three weeks. Symptoms reappear six months to five years after the initial infection, resulting in fevers, headaches, rapid heartbeat, swelling of the lymph glands located in the back of the neck, personality changes, tremors, a lackadaisical attitude, and then stupor leading eventually to death.

Treatment: Suramin (Bayer 205), pentamidine (Lomodine), melarasoprol (Mel B)

How to avoid: Do not travel to infested areas, use insect repellent, wear light-colored clothing, and cover skin areas.

AIDS (Acquired Immune Deficiency Syndrome)

Found: Worldwide.

Cause: Advanced stage of HIV (Human Immunodeficiency Syndrome), which causes destruction of the natural resistance of humans to infection and other diseases. Death by AIDS is usually a result of unrelated diseases which rapidly attack the victim. These ranges of diseases are called ARC (AIDS-related complex).

Carrier: Sexual intercourse with infected person, transfusion of infected blood, or even from infected mother through breast milk. There is no way to determine if someone has HIV, except by blood test. Male homosexuals, drug users and prostitutes are high-risk groups in major urban centers in the West. AIDS is less selective in developing countries, with Central and Eastern Africa being the areas of highest incidence.

Symptoms: Fever, weight loss, fatigue, night sweats, lymph node problems. Infection by other opportunistic elements such as Karposi's sarcoma and pneumonia are highly probable and will lead to death.

Treatment: There is no known cure.

How to avoid: Use condoms, refrain from sexual contact, and do not receive injections or transfusions in questionable areas. Avoid live vaccines such as gamma globulin and Hepatitis B in developing countries.

Amebiasis

Found: Worldwide.

Cause: A protozoan parasite carried in human fecal matter. Usually found in areas with poor sanitation.

Carrier: *Entamoeba histolyica* is passed by poor hygiene. Ingested orally in water, air or food that has come in contact with the parasite.

Symptoms: The infection will spread from the intestines and causes abscesses in other organs such as liver, lungs and brain.

Treatment: Metronidazole, iodoquinol, diloxanide furoate, paromomycin, tetracycline plus chloroquinine base.

How to avoid: Avoid uncooked foods, boil water, drink bottled liquids, be sure that food is cooked properly and peel fruits and vegetables.

Bartonellosis (Oroya Fever, Carrion's Disease)

Found: In valleys of Peru, Ecuador and Colombia.

Cause: *Bartonella bacilliformis*, a bacterium.

Carrier: Sandflies that bite at night.

Symptoms: Pain in muscles, joints and bones along with fever occurring within three weeks of being bitten. Oroya fever causes a febrile fever leading to possible death. *Verruga peruana* creates skin eruptions.

Treatment: Antibiotics with transfusion for symptoms of anemia.

DANGEROUS DISEASES

How to avoid: High boots, ground-sheets, hammocks and insect repellent.

Brucellosis (Undulant Fever)

Found: Worldwide.

Cause: Ingestion of infected dairy products.

Carrier: Untreated dairy products infected with the brucellosis bacteria.

Symptoms: Intermittent fever, sweating, jaundice, rash, depression, enlarged spleen and lymph nodes. The symptoms may disappear and go into permanent remission after three to six months.

Treatment: Tetracyclines, sulfonamides and streptomycin.

How to avoid: Drink pasteurized milk. Avoid infected livestock.

Chagas' Disease (American Trypanosomiasis)

Found: Central and South America.

Cause: Protozoan parasite carried in the feces of insects.

Carrier: Kissing or Assassin bugs (Triatoma insects or reduviid bugs). Commonly found in homes with thatched roofs. It can also be transmitted through blood transfusions, breast milk and in utero.

Symptoms: A papule and swelling at the location of the bite, fever, malaise, anorexia, rash, swelling of the limbs, gastrointestinal problems, heart irregularities and heart failure.

Treatment: Nifurtimox (Bayer 2502).

How to avoid: Do not stay in native villages; use bed netting and insect repellent.

Cholera

Found: Worldwide; primarily developing countries.

Cause: Intestinal infection caused by the toxin Vibrio Cholerae O group bacteria.

Carrier: Infected food and water contaminated by human and animal waste.

Symptoms: Watery diarrhea, abdominal cramps, nausea, vomiting and severe dehydration as a result of diarrhea. Can lead to death if fluids are not replaced.

Treatment: Tetracycline can hasten recovery. Replace fluids using an electrolyte solution.

How to avoid: Vaccinations before trip can diminish symptoms up to 50 percent for a period of three to six months. A threat in refugee camps or areas of poor sanitation. Use standard precautions with food and drink in developing countries.

Chikungunya Disease

Found: Sub-Saharan Africa, Southeast Asia, India, Philippines in sporadic outbreaks.

Cause: Alphavirus transmitted by mosquito bites.

Carrier: Mosquitoes who transmit the disease from the host (monkeys).

Symptoms: Joint pain with potential for hemorrhagic symptoms.

Treatment: None, but symptoms will disappear. If hemorrhagic, avoid aspirin.

How to avoid: Standard precautions to avoid mosquito bites: Use insect repellent and mosquito nets, and cover exposed skin areas.

Ciguatera Poisoning

Found: Tropical areas.

Cause: Ingestion of fish containing the toxin produced by the *dinoflagellate Gambierdiscus toxicus*.

Carrier: 425 species of tropical reef fish.

Symptoms: Up to six hours after eating, victims may experience nausea, watery diarrhea, abdominal cramps, vomiting, abnormal sensation in limbs and teeth, hot-cold flashes, joint pain, weakness, skin rashes and itching. In very severe cases victims may experience blind spells, low blood pressure and heart rate, paralysis and loss of coordination. Symptoms may appear years later.

Treatment: There is no specific medical treatment other than first aid. Induce vomiting.

How to avoid: Do not eat reef fish (including sea bass, barracuda, red snapper or grouper).

DANGEROUS DISEASES

Colorado Tick Fever

Found: North America.

Cause: Arbovirus transmitted by insect or infected blood.

Carrier: The wood tick *(Dermacentor andersoni);* also through transfusion of infected blood.

Symptoms: Aching of muscles in back and legs, chills, recurring fever, headaches, eye pain, fear of brightly lit area.

Treatment: Since symptoms only last about three weeks, medication or treatment is intended to relieve symptoms.

How to avoid: Ticks are picked up when walking through woods. Wear leggings, tall boots and insect repellent.

Dengue Fever (Breakbone Fever)

Found: South America, Africa, South Pacific, Asia, Mexico, Central America, Caribbean.

Cause: An arbovirus transmitted by mosquitoes.

Carrier: Mosquitoes in tropical areas, which usually bite during the daytime.

Symptoms: Two distinct periods. First period consists of severe muscle and joint aches and headaches combined with high fever (the origin of the term "break bone fever"). The second phase is sensitivity to light, diarrhea, vomiting, nausea, mental depression and enlarged lymph nodes.

Treatment: Designed to relieve symptoms. Aspirin should be avoided due to hemorrhagic complications.

How to avoid: Typical protection against daytime mosquito bites: using insect repellent with high DEET levels, wearing light-colored long-sleeve pants and shirts.

Diarrhea

Found: Worldwide.

Cause: There are many reasons for travelers to have the symptoms of diarrhea. It is important to remember that alien bacteria in the digestive tract is the main culprit. Most travelers to Africa, Mexico, South America and the Middle East will find themselves doubled up in pain, running for the nearest stinking toilet and wondering why the hell they ever left their comfortable home.

Carrier: Bacteria from food, the air, water or other people can be the cause. Dehydration from long airplane flights, strange diets, stress and high altitude can also cause diarrhea. It is doubtful you will ever get to know your intestinal bacteria on a first name basis, but *Aeromonas hydrophila*, Campylobacter, *jejuni Pleisiomonas*, salmonellae, shigellae, shielloides, *Vibrio cholerae* (non-01), *Vibrio parahaemolyticus, Yersinia enterocoliticia* and *Escherichia coli* are the most likely culprits. All these bugs would love to spend a week or two in your gut.

Symptoms: Loose stools, stomach pains, bloating, fever and malaise.

Treatment: First step is to stop eating and ingest plenty of fluids and salty foods; secondly, try Kaopectate or Pepto Bismol. If diarrhea persists after three to four days, seek medical advice.

How to avoid: Keep your fluid intake high when traveling. Follow common sense procedures when eating, drinking and ingesting any food or fluids. Remember to wash your hands carefully and frequently, since you can transmit a shocking number of germs from your hands to your mouth, eyes and nose.

Diphtheria

Found: Worldwide

Cause: The bacterium *Corynebacterium diptheriae*, a producer of harmful toxins that is usually a problem in populations that have not been immunized against diphtheria.

Carrier: Infected humans can spread the germs by sneezing, or contact.

Symptoms: Swollen diphtheritic membrane which may lead to serious congestion. Other symptoms are pallor, listlessness, weakness and increased heart rate. May cause death due to weakened heart or shock.

Treatment: Immunization with the DPT vaccine at an early age (three years) is the ideal prevention; treatment with antitoxin, if not.

How to avoid: Avoid close contact with populations or areas where there is little to no vaccination program for diphtheria.

Ebola River Fever

Found: Among local populations in Congo.

Cause: A very rare but much publicized affliction.

Carrier: Unknown, but highly contagious. In 1989 the virus was found in lab monkeys in Reston, Virginia. The monkeys were quickly destroyed. Outbreaks in the Congo and Central Africa are a risk.

Symptoms: The virus is described as melting people down, causing blood clotting, loss of consciousness and death.

Treatment: None.

How to avoid: Unknown.

Encephalitis

Found: Southeast Asia, Korea, Taiwan, Nepal, Eastern CIS countries and Eastern Europe.

Cause: A common viral infection carried by insects.

Carrier: The disease can be carried by the tick or mosquito. The risk is high during late summer and fall.The most dangerous strain is tickborne encephalitis transmitted by ticks in the summer in the colder climates of Russia, Scandinavia, Switzerland and France.

Symptoms: Fever, headache, muscle pain, malaise, runny nose and sore throat followed by lethargy, confusion, hallucination and seizures. About one-fifth of encephalitis infections have led to death.

Treatment: A vaccine is available.

How to avoid: Avoid areas known to be endemic. Avoid tick-infested areas such as forests, rice growing areas in Asia (mosquitoes) or areas that have large number of domestic pigs (tick carriers). Use insect repellent. Do not drink unpasteurized milk.

Filariasis (Lymphatic, River Blindness)

Found: Africa, Central America, Caribbean, South America, Asia.

Cause: A group of diseases caused by long, thin roundworms carried by mosquitoes.

Carrier: Mosquitoes and biting flies in tropical areas.

Symptoms: Lymphatic filariasis, onchocerciasis (river blindness), loiasis and mansonellasis all have similar and very unpleasant symptoms. Fevers, headaches, nausea, vomiting, sensitivity to light, inflammation in the legs including the abdomen and testicles, swelling of the abdomen, joints and scrotum, enlarged lymph nodes, abscesses, eye lesions that lead to blindness, rashes, itches and arthritis.

Treatment: Diethylcarbamazine (DEC, Hetrazan, Notezine) is the usual treatment.

How to avoid: Avoid bites by insects with usual protective measures and insect repellent.

Flukes

Found: Caribbean, South America, Africa, Asia.

Cause: The liver fluke *(Clonorchis sinensis)* and the lung fluke *(Paragonimus westermani)* which lead to paragonimasis.

Carrier: Carried in fish that has not been properly cooked.

Symptoms: Obstruction of the bile system, along with fever, pain, jaundice, gallstones, inflammation of the pancreas. There is further risk of cancer of the bile tract after infection.Paragonimasis affects the lungs and causes chest pains.

Treatment: Paragonimasis is treated with Prazanquantel. Obstruction of the bile system can require surgery.

How to avoid: To avoid liver flukes do not eat uncooked or improperly cooked fish—something most sushi fans will decry. Paragonimasis is found in uncooked shellfish, like freshwater crabs, crayfish and shrimp.

Giardiasis

Found: Worldwide.

Cause: A protozoa *Giardi lamblia* that causes diarrhea.

Carrier: Ingestion of food or water that is contaminated with fecal matter.

Symptoms: Very sudden diarrhea, severe flatulence, cramps, nausea, anorexia, weight loss and fever.

Treatment: Giardiasis can disappear without treatment, but Furazolidone, metronidizole, or quinacrine HCI are the usual treatments.

How to avoid: Cleanliness, drinking bottled water, and strict personal hygiene in eating and personal contact.

Guinea Worm Infection (Dracontiasis, Dracunculiasis)

Found: Tropical areas like the Caribbean, the Guianas, Africa, the Middle East and Asia.

Cause: Ingestion of waterborne nematode *Dracunculus medinensis.*

Carrier: Water systems that harbor *Dracunculus medinensis.*

Symptoms: Fever, itching, swelling around the eyes, wheezing, skin blisters and arthritis.

Treatment: Doses of niridazole, metronidazole or thiabendazole are the usual method. Surgery may be required to remove worms.

How to avoid: Drink only boiled or chemically treated water.

Hemorrhagic Fevers

Some of the more well-known hemorrhagic fevers are yellow fever, dengue, lassa fever and the horror movie–caliber Ebola fever. Outbreaks tend to be localized and subject to large populations of insects, or rats. Don't let the exotic-sounding names lull you into a false sense of security; there was a major outbreak in the American Southwest caused by rodents spreading the disease.

Found: Worldwide.

Cause: Intestinal worms carried by insects and rodents.

Carrier: Depending on the disease, it can be transmitted by mosquitoes, ticks and rodents (in urine and feces).

Symptoms: Headache, backache, muscle pain and conjunctivitis. Later on, the thinning of the blood will cause low blood pressure, bleeding from the gums and nose, vomiting and coughing up blood, blood in your stool, bleeding from the skin and hemorrhaging in the internal organs. Coma and death may occur in the second week.

Treatment: Consult a doctor or medical facility familiar with the local disease.

How to avoid: Avoid mosquitoes, ticks, and areas with high concentrations of mice and rats.

Hepatitis, A, B, Non-A, Non-B

Found: Worldwide.

Cause: A virus that attacks the liver. Hepatitis A, Non-B and Non-A can be brought on by poor hygiene; Hepatitis B is transmitted sexually or through infected blood.

Carrier: Hepatitis A is transmitted by oral-fecal route, person-to-person contact, or through contaminated food or water. Hepatitis B is transmitted by sexual activity or the transfer of bodily fluids. Hepatitis Non-A and Non-B are spread by contaminated water or from other people.

Symptoms: Muscle and joint pain, nausea, fatigue, sensitivity to light, sore throat, runny nose. Look for dark urine and clay-colored stools, jaundice along with liver pain and enlargement.

Treatment: Rest and a high-calorie diet. Immune Globulin is advised as a minor protection against Hepatitis A. You can be vaccinated against Hepatitis B.

How to avoid: Non-A and Non-B require avoiding infected foods. Hepatitis B requires avoiding unprotected sexual contact, unsterile needles, dental work and infusions. Hepatitis A requires proper hygiene and avoiding infected water and foods.

Hydatid Disease (Echinococcosis)

Found: Worldwide.

Cause: A tapeworm found in areas with high populations of pigs, cattle and sheep.

Carrier: Eggs of the echinococcosis.

Symptoms: Cysts form in organs in the liver, lungs, bone or brain.

Treatment: Surgery for removal of the infected cysts. Mebendazole and albendazole are used as well.

How to avoid: Boil water, cook foods properly and avoid infected areas.

Leishmaniasis

Found: Tropical and subtropical regions.

Cause: Protozoans of the genus Leishmania.

Carrier: Phlebotomine sandflies in tropical and subtropical regions.

Symptoms: Skin lesions, cutaneous ulcers, mucocutaneous ulcers in the mouth, nose and anus, as well as intermittent fever, anemia and enlarged spleen.

Treatment: Sodium stibogluconate, rifampin, and sodium antimony gluconate. Surgery is also used to remove cutaneous and mucocutaneous ulcers.

How to avoid: Use insect repellent, a ground cover when sleeping and bed nets, and cover arms and legs.

Leprosy (Hansen's Disease)

Found: Africa, India and elsewhere

Cause: The bacterium *Mycobacterium leprae* that infects the skin, eyes, nervous system and testicles.

Carrier: It is not known how leprosy is transmitted, but direct human contact is suspected.

Symptoms: Skin lesions, and nerve damage that progresses to loss of fingers and toes, blindness, difficulty breathing and nerve damage.

Treatment: Dapsone, rifampin and clofazimine.

How to avoid: Leprosy is a tropical disease, with over half the cases worldwide occurring in India and Africa. There is no known preventive method.

Loaisis

Found: West and Central Africa.

Cause: The loa loa parasite.

Carrier: Chrysops deer flies or tabanid flies in West and Central Africa.

Symptoms: Subcutaneous swellings that come and go, brain and heart inflammation.

Treatment: Diethylcarbamazine.

How to avoid: Deerflies are large, and their bites can be avoided by wearing full-sleeved shirts and thick pants. Hats and bandannas can protect head and neck areas.

Lyme Diseases

Found: Worldwide

Cause: A spirochete carried by ticks.

Carrier: The Ixodes tick, found worldwide and in great numbers during the summer. Ticks are found in rural areas and burrow into skin to suck blood.

Symptoms: A pronounced bite mark, flulike symptoms, severe headache, stiff neck, fever, chills, joint pain, malaise and fatigue.

Treatment: Tetracyclines, phenoxymethylpenicillin or erythromycin if caught early. Advanced cases may require intravenous penicillin.

How to avoid: Do not walk through wooded areas in the summer. Check for ticks frequently. Use leggings with insect repellent.

Malaria

Malaria is by far the most dangerous disease and the one most likely for travelers to pick up in Third World countries. Protection against this disease should be your first priority. As a rule, be leery of all riverine, swampy or tropical places. Areas such as logging camps, shantytowns, oases, campsites near slow moving water, and resorts near mangrove swamps are all very likely to be major areas of malarial infection. Consult with

DANGEROUS DISEASES

a local doctor to understand the various resistances and the prescribed treatment. Many foreign doctors are more knowledgeable about the cure and treatment of malaria than domestic doctors.

Found: Africa, Asia, Caribbean, Southeast Asia, the Middle East.

Cause: The Plasmodium parasite is injected into the victim while the mosquito draws blood.

Carrier: The female Anopheles mosquito.

Symptoms: Fever, chills, enlarged spleen in low-level versions; plasmodium falciparum, or cerebral malaria, can also cause convulsions, kidney failure and hypoglycemia.

Treatment: Chloroquinine, quinine, pyrimethamine, sulfadoxine and mefloquine. Note: Some people may have adverse reactions to all and any of these drugs.

How to avoid: Begin taking a malarial prophylaxis before your trip, as well as during and after (consult your doctor for a prescription). Avoid infected areas and protect yourself from mosquito bites (netting, insect repellent, mosquito coils, long-sleeve shirts and pants) especially during dusk and evening times.

Measles (Rubeola)

Found: Worldwide.

Cause: A common virus in unvaccinated areas.

Carrier: Sneezing, saliva and close contact with infected or unvaccinated humans.

Symptoms: Malaise, irritability, fever, conjunctivitis, swollen eyelids and hacking cough appear nine to 11 days after exposure. Fourteen days after exposure, the typical facial rash and spots appear.

Treatment: Measles will disappear, but complications can occur.

How to avoid: Vaccination or gamma globulin shots within five days of exposure.

Meliodosis

Found: Worldwide.

Cause: An animal disease (the bacillus *Pseudomonas pseudomallei*) that can be transferred to humans.

Carrier: Found in infected soil and water, and transmitted through skin wounds.

Symptoms: Various types, including fever, malaise, pneumonia, shortness of breath, headache, diarrhea, skin lesions, muscle pain and abscesses in organs.

Treatment: Antibiotics such as tetracyclines and sulfur drugs.

How to avoid: Clean and cover all wounds carefully.

Meningitis

Found: Africa, Saudi Arabia.

Cause: Bacteria: *Neisseria meningitis*, *Streptococcus pneumoniae* and *Haemophilus influenzae*. Children are at most risk. There are frequent outbreaks in Africa and Nepal.

Carrier: Inhaling infected droplets of nasal and throat secretions.

Symptoms: Fever, vomiting, headaches, confusion, lethargy and rash.

Treatment: Penicillin G.

How to avoid: Meningococcus polysaccharide vaccine. Do not travel to areas where outbreaks occur (the Sahel from Mali to Ethiopia) in the dry season.

Mumps

Found: Worldwide.

Cause: A virus found worldwide. Common in early spring and late winter and in unvaccinated areas.

Carrier: Infected saliva and urine.

Symptoms: Headache, anorexia, malaise, and pain when chewing or swallowing.

Treatment: Mumps is a self-inoculating disease. There can be complications which can lead to more serious lifetime afflictions.

How to avoid: Vaccination (MMR).

Plague

Found: India, Vietnam, Africa, South America, the Middle East, Russia.

Cause: A bacteria *(Yersinia pestis)* that infects rodents and the fleas they carry.

Carrier: Flea bites that transmit the bacteria to humans. Ticks, lice, corpses and human contact can also spread the disease.

Symptoms: Swollen lymph nodes, fever, abdominal pain, loss of appetite, nausea, vomiting diarrhea, and gangrene of the extremities.

Treatment: Antibiotics like streptomycin, tetracyclines and chloramphenicol can reduce the mortality rate.

How to avoid: Stay out of infected areas, and avoid contact.

Poliomyelitis (Polio)

Found: Worldwide.

Cause: A virus that destroys the central nervous system.

Carrier: Occurs through direct contact.

Symptoms: A mild febrile illness that may lead to paralysis. Polio can cause death in 5 to 10 percent of cases in children and 15 to 30 percent in adult cases.

Treatment: There is no treatment.

How to avoid: Vaccination during childhood with a booster before travel is recommended.

Rabies

Found: Worldwide.

Cause: A virus that affects the central nervous system.

Carrier: Rabies is transmitted through the saliva of an infected animal. Found in wild animals, although usually animals found in urban areas are most suspect: dogs, raccoons, cats, skunks, and bats. Although most people will automatically assume they are at risk for rabies, there are only about 16,000 cases reported worldwide. The risk is the deadly seriousness of rabies and the short time in which death occurs.

Symptoms: Abnormal sensations or muscle movement near the bite, followed by fever, headaches, malaise, muscle aches, tiredness, loss of appetite, nausea, vomiting, sore throat and cough. The advanced stages include excessive excitation, seizures and mental disturbances leading to profound nervous system dysfunction and paralysis. Death occurs in most cases four to 20 days after being bitten.

Treatment: Clean wound vigorously, injections of antirabies antiserum and antirabies vaccine. People who intend to come into regular contact with animals in high-risk areas can receive HDCV (human diploid cell rabies vaccine) shots.

How to avoid: Avoid confrontations with animals.

Relapsing Fever

Found: The louseborne version is found in poor rural areas where infestation by lice is common.

Cause: *Borrelia spirochetes.*

Carrier: Lice and ticks. Ticks are found in wooded areas and bite mainly at night.

Symptoms: The fever gets its name from the six days on and six days off of high fever. Other symptoms include headaches, muscle pains, weakness and loss of appetite.

Treatment: Antibiotics.

How to avoid: Avoid infected areas, and check for ticks.

Rift Valley Fever

Found: Egypt and East Africa.

Cause: A virus that affects humans and livestock.

Carrier: Mosquitoes, inhaling infected dust, contact with broken skin and ingesting infected animal blood or fluids.

Symptoms: Sudden one-time fever, severe headaches, muscle pain, weakness, sensitivity to light, eye pain, nausea, vomiting, diarrhea, eye redness and facial flushing. Blindness, meningitis, meningoencephalitis and retinitis may also occur.

Treatment: Seek medical treatment for supportive care.

How to avoid: Avoid contact with livestock in infected areas; protect yourself against mosquito bites.

River Blindness (Onchocerciais)

Found: Equatorial Africa, Yemen, the Sahara and parts of Central and South America.

Cause: The roundworm *Onchocerca volvulus.*

Carrier: Transmitted by blackflies found along rapidly flowing rivers.

Symptoms: Itching, skin atrophy, mottling, nodules, enlargement of the lymph nodes, particularily in the groin, and blindness.

Treatment: Invermectin or Diethylcarbamazine(DEC), followed by suramin, followed by DEC again.

How to avoid: Insect repellant, long-sleeve shirts and long pants. Avoid blackfly bites.

Rocky Mountain Spotted Fever

Found: Found only in the Western Hemisphere.

Cause: A bacterial disease transmitted by tick bites.

Carrier: Rickettsial bacteria are found in rodents and dogs. The ticks pass the bacteria by then biting humans.

Symptoms: Fever, headaches, chills, and rash (after fourth day) on the arms and legs. Final symptoms may include delirum, shock and kidney failure.

Treatment: Tetracyclines or chloramphenicol.

How to avoid: Ticks are found in wooded areas. Inspect your body after walks. Use insect repellent. Wear leggings or long socks or long pants.

Salmonellosis

Found: Worldwide.

Cause: A common bacterial infection; *Salmonella gastroenteritis* is commonly described as food poisoning.

Carrier: Found in fecally contaminated food, unpasteurized milk, raw foods and water.

Symptoms: Abdominal pain, diarrhea, vomiting, chills and fever usually within eight to 48 hours of ingesting infected food. *Salmonella* only kills about one percent of its victims, usually small children or the aged.

Treatment: Purge infected food, replace fluids. Complete recovery is within two to five days.

How to avoid: Consume only properly prepared foods.

Sandfly Fever (Three-day Fever)

Found: Africa, Mediterranean.

Cause: Phleboviruses injected by sandfly bites.

Carrier: Transmitted by sandflies, usually during the dry season.

Symptoms: Fever, headache, eye pain, chest muscle pains, vomiting, sensitivity to light, stiff neck, taste abnormality, rash and joint pain.

Treatment: There is no specific treatment. The symptoms can reoccur in about 15 percent of cases, but typically disappear.

How to avoid: Do not sleep directly on the ground. Sandflies usually bite at night.

Schistosomiasis (Bilharzia)

Bilharzia is one of the meanest bugs to pick up in your foreign travels. The idea of nasty little creatures actually burrowing through your skin and lodging themselves in your gut is menacing. If not treated, it can make your life a living hell with afternoon sweats, painful urination, weakness and other good stuff. There is little you can do to prevent infection, since the Schistosoma larva and flukes are found where people have fouled freshwater rivers and lakes. Get treatment immediately, since the affliction worsens as the eggs multiply and continue to infect more tissues. About 250 million people around the world are believed to be infected.

Found: Worldwide.

Cause: A group of parasitic Schistosoma flatworms (*Schistosoma mansoni, Schistosomajaponicum* and *Schistosoma haematobium*) found in slow moving, tropical freshwater.

Carrier: The larvae of Schistosoma are found in slow moving waterways in tropical areas around the world. They actually enter the body through the skin and then enter the lymph vessels and then migrate to the liver.

Symptoms: Look for a rash and itching at the entry site, followed by weakness, loss of appetite, night sweats, hivelike rashes, and afternoon fevers in about four to six weeks. Bloody, painful and frequent urination, diarrhea. Later victims become weaker and may be susceptible to further infections and diseases.

Treatment: Elimination of *S. mansoni* requires oxamniquine and praziquantel. *S. japonicum* responds to praziquantel alone, and *Schistosoma haematobium* is treated with praziquantel and metrifonate.

How to avoid: Stay out of slow moving freshwater in all tropical and semitropical areas. This also means wading or standing in water.

Syphilis

Found: Worldwide.

Cause: A spirochete *(Treponema pallidum)* causes this chronic venereal disease, which if left untreated progresses into three clinical stages.

Carrier: Syphilis is spread through sexual contact and can be passed on to infants congenitally.

Symptoms: After an incubation period of two to six weeks, a sore usually appears near the genitals, although some men and women may not experience any symptoms. Some men also experience a scanty discharge. A skin rash appears in the second stage, often on the soles of the feet and palms of the hands. It may be accompanied by a mild fever, sore throat and patchy hair loss. This rash generally appears about six weeks after the initial sore. The third phase of the disease may develop over several years if the disease is left untreated and may damage the brain and the heart or even cause death.

Treatment: Antibiotics are used to treat syphilis, and infected people should abstain from sex until treatment ends. Blood tests should be performed again in three months after the round of treatment. Sexual partners need to be tested and treated. Victims of syphilis should also be tested for other sexually transmitted diseases.

How to avoid: Abstain from sexual activities or use a latex condom.

Tainiasis (Tapeworms)

Found: Worldwide.

Cause: A tapeworm is usually discovered after being passed by the victim.

Carrier: Ingestion of poorly cooked meat infected with tapeworms.

Symptoms: In advanced cases, there will be diarrhea and stomach cramps. Sections of tapeworms can be seen in stools.

Treatment: Mebendazole, niclocsamide, paromomysi and praziqunatel are effective in killing the parasite.

How to avoid: Tapeworms come from eating meats infected with tapeworm or coming into contact with infected fecal matter.

Tetanus (Lockjaw)

Found: Worldwide.

Cause: A bacteria caused by the bacteria *Clostridiium tetani.*

Carrier: Found in soil and enters body through cuts or punctures.

Symptoms: Restlessness, irritability, headaches, jaw pain, back pain and stiffness, and difficulty in swallowing. Then within two to 56 days, stiffness increases with lockjaw and spasms. Death occurs in about half the cases, usually affecting children.

Treatment: If infected, human tetanus immune globulin is administered with nerve blockers for muscle relaxation.

How to avoid: Immunization is the best prevention, with a booster recommended before travel.

Trachoma

Found: Common in Africa, the Middle East and Asia.

Cause: A chlamydial infection of the eye, which is responsible for about 200 million cases of blindness.

Carrier: Flies, contact, wiping face or eye area with infected towels.

Symptoms: Constant inflammation under the eyelid that causes scarring of the eyelid, turned-in eyelashes and eventual scarring of the cornea and then blindness.

Treatment: Tetracyclines, erythromycin, sulfonamide, surgery to correct turned-in lashes.

How to avoid: It is spread primarily by flies. Proper hygiene and avoidance of fly-infested areas are recommended.

Trichinosis

Found: Worldwide.

Cause: Infection of the *Trichinella spiralis* worm.

Carrier: Pig meat (also bear and walrus) that contain cysts. The worm then infects the new hosts' tissues and intestines.

Symptoms: Diarrhea, abdominal pain, nausea, prostration and fever. As the worm infects tissues, fever, swelling around the eyes, conjunctivitis, eye hemorrhages, muscle pain, weakness, rash and splinter hemorrhages under the nails occur. Less than 10 percent of the cases result in death.

Treatment: Thiabendazole is effective in killing the parasite.

How to avoid: Proper preparation, storage and cooking of meat.

Tuberculosis

Found: Worldwide.

Cause: A disease of the lungs caused by the *Mycobacterium tuberculosis* bacteria or *Mycobacterium bovis*.

Carrier: By close contact with infected persons (sneezing, coughing) or, in the case of *Mycobacterium bovis*, contaminated or unpasteurized milk.

Symptoms: Weight loss, night sweats and a chronic cough usually with traces of blood. If left untreated, death results in about 60 percent of the cases after a period of two and a half years.

Treatment: Isoniazide and rifampin can control the disease.

How to avoid: Vaccination and isoniazid prophylaxis.

Tularaemia (Rabbit Fever)

Found: Worldwide.

Cause: A fairly rare disease (about 300 cases per year) caused by the bacteria *Francisella tularnesis* passed from animals to humans via insects.

Carrier: The bite of deerflies, ticks, mosquitoes and even cats can infect humans.

Symptoms: Fever, chills, headaches, muscle pain, malaise, enlarged liver and spleen, rash, skin ulcers and enlargement of the lymph nodes.

Treatment: Vaccination is used. Streptomycin primarily. Tetracycline and chloramphenicol are also effective.

How to avoid: Care when handling animal carcasses, removal of ticks and avoidance of insect bites.

Typhoid Fever

Found: Africa, Asia, Central America.

Cause: The bacterium *Salmonella typhi*.

Carrier: Transmitted by contaminated food and water in areas of poor hygiene.

Symptoms: Fever, headaches, abdominal tenderness, malaise, rash, enlarged spleen. Later symptoms include delirium, intestinal hemorrhage and perforation of the intestine.

Treatment: Chloramphenicol.

How to avoid: Vaccination is the primary protection, although the effectiveness is not high.

Typhus Fever

Found: Africa, South America, Southeast Asia, India.

Cause: Rickettsia.

Carrier: Transmitted by fleas, lice, mites and ticks found in mountainous areas around the world.

Symptoms: Fever, headache, rash and muscle pain. If untreated, death may occur in the second week due to kidney failure, coma and blockage of the arteries.

Treatment: Tetracyclines or chloramphenicol.

How to avoid: Check for ticks, avoid insect bites, attend to hygiene to prevent lice and avoid mountainous regions.

Yellow Fever

Found: Africa, South America.

Cause: A virus transmitted by mosquito bites.

Carrier: The tiny banded-legged *aedes aegpyti* is the source for urban yellow fever, and the haemogogus and sabethes mosquito carries the jungle version.

Symptoms: In the beginning, fever, headaches, backaches, muscle pain, nausea, conjunctivitis, albumin in the urine and slow heart rate. Followed by black vomit, no urination and delirium. Death affects only 5 to 10 percent of cases and occurs in the fourth to sixth day.

Treatment: Replace fluids and electrolytes.

How to avoid: Vaccination is mandatory when entering or leaving infected areas.

DANGEROUS DISEASES

Drugs

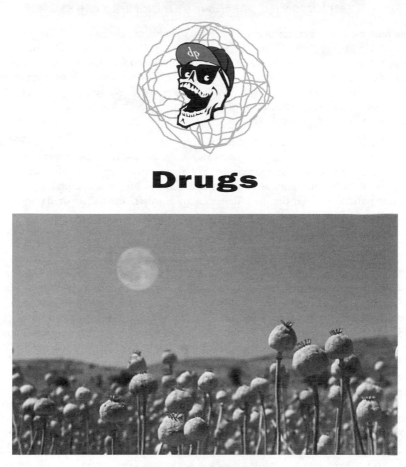

War's Bastard Son

Many Western travelers tend to view drugs as a furtive part of their youth or something that affects only inner cities, but the adventurous traveler quickly learns just how vital a role drugs play in the world's most dangerous places. In fact, in many places, danger is a prerequisite to ensure the smooth flow of illegal goods and profits the drug industry needs to escape interdiction. Whenever there is drug activity there is corruption, AIDS and organized crime. Here you'll enter a shadowy world where guests are unwelcome. Typically narco-regions are run by warlords, corrupt politicians, dirty cops or criminals, all of whom can be considered tourism-unfriendly. Mexico City's former police chief built a mansion styled after the Parthenon and stashed away between $1 to $3 billion of corrupt profits during his six year term. But this is only a small piece of the pie, especially when you consider the Cali cartel made $30 billion last year and the Gulf cartel profited $20 billion by government estimates.

With the increased presence of U.S. government agents and operatives the drug lords have become more careful and wary of unfamiliar faces—your life could be at risk if you are tagged as someone who should be removed. U.S. government sources spend millions unsuccessfully to try to solve the entire world's drug problems. But the problem also may be found within our own borders. The indisputable fact is that the Bolivian peasant who grows coca to feed his family, or Baluchi gunmen who are paid to protect a shipment are not the criminals because these folks are doing something accepted in their own world. We create the drug problem by demanding more and more hard drugs which keeps a hundred or so druglords around the world very wealthy.

DP spends much of its travel time in drug-infested regions hobnobbing with gunmen, warlords, smugglers, fighters and mafia hoods. In some of these regions there is no business other than drugs. We also notice that in the absence of an economy, bribes and guns are used to enslave peasants, couriers, politicians and entire nations to feed the drug demands of Europe, Russia, Australia and the Americas.

Heroin

The *Papaver somniferum*, or Eurasian poppy, was introduced to Asia from the Mediterranean by Arab traders in the 12th century and was cultivated for its medicinal properties. This innocent little flower has now grown up to become the half-brother of war. India, Myanmar, China, Pakistan, Laos, Thailand, Mexico, Uzbekistan and Afghanistan are the troubled homes of this gentle, unassuming weed that blows in the wind. Wars have been fought over opium since the 1839–1842 Opium War between Britain and China. Today, the battles are taking place on the streets of St. Louis, Miami, Los Angeles and small-town America. Crime experts say that as turf battles among druglords decline in the cities, America's small towns are becoming the fastest growing markets. A recent survey found that 47 percent of small town police chiefs consider drugs a serious problem and two-thirds say drug problems in their area have increased over the last five years. Millions of people are currently enslaved by the byproducts of the opium poppy. And heroin's slaves today aren't just junkies in backalleys. The media recently has had a field day exposing heroin addict movie stars and fashion models. Since the drug can now be snorted like cocaine or smoked rather than injected into veins, it has begun increasing in popularity.

Seventy percent of all illicit drugs in the U.S. are derived from heroin, originating in the land of Chinese druglords—the Golden Triangle of Southeast Asia. The current purity of heroin found on the street in the United States has jumped from an average 7 percent in 1984 to 36 percent today, a testament not only to its grip on a nation, but to the seemingly endless world supply of the narcotic. Heroin shipped into the U.S. comes from at least 11 different countries. The DEA estimates it stops 30 to 40 percent of drugs illegally entering the country.

Poppies can be grown in cool plateaus above 500 feet. The plants grow rapidly and propagate easily. Planted at the end of the wet season (in Asia in September and October), the poppy heads are later scraped after the petals fall off. The scraping creates an oozing sap that is removed from the plant and packed tightly into banana leaves. The crude opium is then transported out of the hills via pony or armed convoys to middlemen. For those who grow opium, few escape its enticing lure. Hilltribe growers swiftly become addicts themselves. Up to 30 percent of Southeast Asia's Hmong tribe is addicted to opium. Most of the income of northern Laos is dope money. In fact, small nickel bags, or *parakeets* as they are called locally, can be used as a form of currency.

The poppy is back big time and is often used in conjunction with cocaine to ease the crash. Purer forms can be smoked instead of injected. There are more than half a million heroin addicts in the U.S.

The Golden Triangle

The Golden Triangle has an estimated total potential opium production exceeding 4000 metric tons. While poppy cultivation increased in Myanmar and Laos, it has declined in China and Thailand. Myanmar is the world's largest opium producer, with an estimated 2340 metric tons, which can produce an estimated 234 metric tons of pure heroin, enough to satisfy much of the world's craving for the drug. In 1995, Laos, with an estimated 180 metric tons of potential opium production, edged out Pakistan and became the world's third largest potential producer of illegal opium after Myanmar and Afghanistan.

According to U.S. Government estimates, in 1995, growers in Myanmar, Laos, and Thailand cultivated an estimated 175,470 hectares of opium poppy, potentially yielding 2545 metric tons of opium gum. The fact that Myanmar was responsible for 154,070 hectares, with Laos kicking in a measly 19,650 hectares and Thailand filling in the rest, explodes the Golden Triangle concept. Myanmar is a narco economy just like Colombia and Peru. In fact, estimated opium poppy cultivation in Thailand decreased by approximately 17 percent to 1750 hectares from 2110 hectares.

Laos is the third largest producer of opium, with much of it going to its 42,000 opium addicts who consume 60 metric tons each year. Most poppy cultivation is in the Houaphan and Palavek regions. The smack that doesn't enter the arms of the Lao is smuggled out north to China via Luang Namtha and Phong Saly or to Thailand via Oudomsay province.

China is the other major Asia transportation route for heroin. Heading north from the Golden Triangle, most drugs are shipped from Yunnan through Guangxi and Guangdong provinces into Hong Kong for overseas shipments. A smaller amount is smuggled directly into Russia, and some heroin enters Guangxi province from Vietnam.

China has a minor opium crop primarily in the NW province of Ningxia. There is a conservative government estimate of 380,000 drug addicts in China but the real total is much higher. A six month crackdown just in Guangdong province netted 7500 drug dealers and 250 kgs of heroin. Most addicts are in Yunnan province which also has a skyrocketing AIDS problem due to syringe-needled junkies. Drugs are bad for your health in China. Most drug traffickers are executed by a single pistol shot to the back of the head immediately after trial.

Opium production in China's Yunnan Province is on the decline with a 36 percent drop in production.

Taiwan has more than 60,000 heroin addicts and is a transshipment point for Chinese heroin.

Vietnam has 9000 villages that produce 2300 hectares of opium under cultivation. The country also has more than 200,000 addicts (30,000 in Ho Chi Minh City) three quarters of who smoke opium while the other inject it. There are also about 3000 HIV positive persons, 80 percent of which are drug addicts.

Hong Kong (now part of China) continues to be a major money laundering center, and to a lesser amount, a shipment center.

Indonesia is a minor heroin transit point, primarily for Australia, Europe and the U.S.

Cambodia is a major smuggling center from Myanmar usually via speedboat to Thailand. This new export crop has attracted the attention of the local police and military.

The poppy is regionally cultivated in Third World countries with little or no political, military or police interference. Mexico, Lebanon and Turkey have faded from the scene, replaced by Afghanistan and Myanmar, both of which had bumper crops and governments who see no problem including drug sales to their personal GNP. Vietnam is the up and comer with 3150 hectares of opium poppy under cultivation (which would yield 25 metric tons of opium gum).

The Golden Crescent

Most of Europe's heroin comes straight from Afghanistan via the Balkan routes. Opium and heroin production are up under the *taliban*, and the transit lines are prospering from affluence in Europe and warfare in Central Asia. The northern branch of the Balkan Route is a heroin highway, servicing markets in the Czech Republic, Hungary, and other Eastern European countries.

The traditional route for Central Asian heroin has been the Balkans from Turkey to Austria. Increased demand in Europe, and open borders have expanded the route northward into Romania, Hungary, and the Czech and Slovak Republics, and southward through Croatia, Slovenia, the Former Yugoslav Republic of Macedonia, Greece and Albania. Slovakia is becoming a key conduit for smuggling Southwest Asian heroin to Western Europe.

Most of the drug trafficking through the Balkan route is under the protection of Kurdish groups like the PKK who have ready made distribution through immigrant networks in the major cities of Germany and the U.K.

Russia has become junkie central with high demand and short supply lines for not only heroin but also amphetamines. Russian authorities predict that drug use is now accelerating at a fifty percent increase per year and there are now over 2 million drug users in Russia. The Lezgi, Chechen and other Transcaucasia mafia groups control the drug trafficking and distribution in Transcaucasia, Central Asia and the Ukraine.

Tajikistan has become one of more lucrative areas for opium and hashish smuggling. A general lack of enforcement and a number of local warlords have made drug smuggling the only industry in Gorno Badakhstan. A kilo of opium can be bought locally between $100 and $120 and can be resold in Moscow 1800 miles away for between $5500–$6000. The presence of 25,000 underpaid Russian military with easy access to air transport to Moscow has made this the main drug highway between Afghanistan and Moscow. The 40,000 or so junkies in Tajikistan can barely get their hands on enough smack before it is whisked out of the country. Curiously, with all this temptation most drug seizures in Tajikistan are still made by Russian border guards who make about $36 a month. There is minor poppy cultivation near Dushanbe, the SE region of Khatlon, in the northern Leninabad region and increasingly in Gorno Badakhstan.

Ukraine has become a major conduit for drug smuggling from Central Asia and Turkey to Europe. It is also home to half a million addicts. The poppy growing regions of Central Asia (Kazakhstan, Krygyzstan, Tajikistan, and Uzbekistan) now are involved heavily in heroin trafficking between Southwest Asia and China into Russia and Europe. Tajikistan is a major opium and hashish thoroughfare between Afghanistan to Russia, the CIS, and Europe.

Kazakhstan is vast area is not only a major transshipment region from Tajikistan and China but is home to a woefully understated 17,000 drug users, 6000 of whom are addicts. It is also a major cannabis growing center (see Cannabis).

Krygyzstan has over 50,000 addicts and is a transit route from Afghanistan via Tajikistan.

Turkmenistan has a well established use of opium in its traditional foods and festivals. It also has a well-worn smuggling trail through the Kushka and to Mary. The Karakum desert provides a direct route from the north of Afghanistan to the Caspian sea and Russia. Most poppy cultivation is along the Iranian border in the Akhal Velayat.

Uzbekistan is used by the Azeria and Georgian mafia as a Central Asian hub to Russia through its main city of Tashkent. There are about 200,000 addicts and minor poppy cultivation in Samarkand and Syrhandarya. It is also a minor transshipment point from Afghanistan to Kazakhstan.

Afghanistan had a 33 percent increase in poppy cultivation in 1995 and continues to expand under the *taliban*. The *taliban* is against the consumption of drugs, but not the growing or exporting of drugs. Afghanistan grows most of the poppies and supplies much of the raw paste that becomes Europe's heroin. Poppy cultivation in Pakistan is down. Most transport is via Baluchi trafficking organizations operating out of Quetta, Pakistan. These groups place orders with the Afghani processors and arrange for shipment of the drugs from Afghanistan through Pakistan and to Iranian or Turkish buyers who move it through Iran and into international drug channels. Most Afghan opium is destined for processing into heroin in Turkey to be sold in the main cities of Western Europe.

Turkey is the terminus and major refining center of the Golden Crescent. Three quarters of Europe's heroin supply comes through or from Turkey. That's about 6 metric tons a month. Turkey's raw product comes from Afghanistan and Pakistan through the northern part of Iran. Drug labs are found primarily in the Southeast and in the Mamara region south of Istanbul. Istanbul is one of the world's centers for drug buying and selling. The major player is the PKK who use a network of Kurds as retail outlets to sell heroin in Europe. Turkish heroin goes for $6500 per kilo wholesale and when it gets to Germany or The Netherlands it jumps $35,000. If it gets to North America it can sell for up to $75,000. That's what the dealer pays.

The Americas: Heroin's Brave New World

Poppies can be grown anywhere in the world so it's surprising that it has taken this long for traditional coca producers to try opium poppies.

Colombia's attempt at diversifying into opium poppy cultivation is not going well. Colombia's 6540 hectares, assuming three crops per year, make it the largest potential opium producer in the hemisphere. For now they only have 1.5 percent of the world's production. They are trying to use their cocaine distribution and sales networks to sell an ultrapure form of heroin. Many druglords, like the Orejula brothers, run their empires from jail where it's probably safer.

Venezuela, not to be outdone, is busy putting in poppies in the Serrania de Perija frontier region. Mexican drug mafias are strongarming Huallaga Valley campesinos to plant poppies. The DEA claimed that South American heroin had the highest purity (average 59.3 percent) of any samples analyzed under its Domestic Monitor Program.

Mexico remains the second largest Latin American grower of opium poppy with approximately 5800 hectares under cultivation.

Cocaine

Crack is number one with a bullet in the U.S. Smoke it and you may get a groovy high or you may turn into a ruthless brute. Crack is big dollars, big profits and big trouble. Law enforcement credits much of the body count in the inner cities to gangs fighting over turf to sell the evil stuff. You only have about five years to wring every nickel out of the 2.1 million coke and crackheads until they die. Crack is cocaine you can smoke, but it is typically cut with anything that grandma left in the cupboard. Crack and cocaine enter the U.S. by the ton. A kilo of cocaine will sell wholesale for between $10,500 and $40,000.

The coca bush takes two years to mature at which point the leaves are picked and ground up. A hectare of mature coca bushes can yield around 2.7 metric tons of dry leaf, which in turn yields about 7.44 kilos of cocaine. It takes about 363 kilos of dry leaves to yield one kilo of cocaine. The amount of pure cocaine in the goods depends on the alkaloid level of the leaf. In the Chapare region of Bolivia they have a 0.72 percent alkaloid content. Cocaine goes for about $100 a gram on the street in the U.S. Do the math and figure out how much coca eradication equals how much cocaine not smuggled into the States. Unfortunately despite the valiant efforts of every law enforcement agency in the world, cocaine availability increases every year and prices are dropping.

Most addicts kick the habit by dropping dead. Unlike heroin which will give you 10 years of hell, cocaine and crack are more addictive and more destructive. It makes perfect sense that cocaine would be in such heavy demand in civilized countries. There are about 2 million crack or cokeheads in the U.S., enough to keep the cocaine trade booming.

Peru is the world's largest producer of coca with 115,000 hectares under cultivation. Although the government likes to blame their problem on the insurgent groups, several senior Peruvian Army officers are under investigation and one General was convicted. Drugs have also been found on Peruvian Navy ships and Air Force planes. Even the top security man and President Fujimori's strongman, Vladimir Montesinos has been fingered in this business. Peru ships its cocaine base to Mexico for processing. Smaller amounts are shipped by land into Chile and Ecuador.

The major markets for South American cocaine producers are the U.S. and Western Europe. The U.S. seizes an average of 100 metric tons every year, but admits that it has little impact on drug prices or reduced drug sales.

Colombia's coca production is up 23 percent, forcing local syndicate to expand distribution into Poland and the Czech Republic. To keep up their number two position, they also import coca base from neighboring Peru and Bolivia. Most Colombian cocaine is shipped in huge multi-ton sea cargo or eight ton shipments on old 727s to deliver to Mexico, Central America and the Caribbean where it is broken down into smaller shipments bound for the States or Europe. San Andres Island, an old stomping ground of *DP* is one of the major air transshipment points into Nicaragua and then to Mexico. About 62 percent of the cocaine and almost all the heroin nabbed in the U.S. comes from Colombia.

Bolivia is the number three producer of coca and cocaine and slipping in the ranking as Colombia takes over the Bolivian industry. Hectares of coca are grown in the Yungas, Apolo and Chapare regions. Processing centers are in Santa Cruz and Beni. Since coca is used as part of tea, for chewing and for traditional ceremonies, 12,000 hectares of cultivation is allowed legally. The best coca leaves come from Yungas, while almost all coca grown in the Chapare region is for illegal purposes.

Panama, even post-Manny, is still a major transportation center. And no, The Colon Free Zone is not a joke, but a major money laundering center.

Mexico has increased drug production so much that smugglers have switched from cargo planes to cargo ships to meet the demand. The cargo is picked up by high speed boats that meet them off the coast. Small planes are also used to drop drugs in country. The *contrabandistas* along the border are also eager to smuggle guns, dope or people if the price is right.

Nigeria is a major hub for smuggling by virtue of its corrupt customs and eagerness of mules who will carry cocaine either ingested internally in condoms or on their person. The Nigerians leave South America often via Rio then bring the cocaine to Nigeria for sales in South Africa.

The Caribbean island of Aruba, off the coast of Venezuela, is a major drug transshipment point. Shipments funnel in from Colombia, Venezuela and Suriname for transport to the U.S. and Europe. Also Vieques island (Puerto Rico) and U.S. Virgin Islands are popular delivery points from the islands of the Lesser Antilles. About 30 percent of the drugs that enter Britain come from the Caribbean. Drugs also flow from these islands into their home protectorates of France, and The Netherlands. Cocaine is shipped by sea from South America and then loaded onto aircraft and ships on the ABC Islands. Couriers are also used to transport drugs in 1–2 kilo amounts back to their home countries. They also launder drug proceeds in Aruba, Curaçao, St. Maarten and Bonaire. Antigua and Barbuda are major storage and transshipment points for Colombia, Venezuela, Trinidad and Jamaica. In general many of the island chains offer ideal smuggling and transfer points due to the large amount of shoreline, number of watercraft and lack of police in the area.

Suriname is the main gateway for cocaine into The Netherlands

The Dominican Republic is also a convenient stopping off point for Colombian drugs en route to America.

Brazil is a major air transit route for cocaine base from Peru to Colombia.

Cannabis

The weed is not really top priority with the DEA nor is it a major contributor to criminal activity. It is bulky, low margin and can be homegrown easily by cheapskate customers. In many countries, you will find marijuana plants growing wild in backyards, along roads and in fields. The benefits of the cannabis trade are the lack of expensive chemicals to create an end product and a laissez faire attitude towards personal consumption in many European and Asian countries.

Mexico weed production is down 35 percent to about 6900 hectares which can yield 3560 metric tons of end product. In Mexico coke is it. In 1995, there were 18,650 hectares of cannabis which produced over 5000 metric tons of weed.

Colombia is a bit player, but up and coming with about 5000 hectares under cultivation. Most weed is sent by sea to Mexico for land shipment into the U.S. Although gringos toke most of Colombia's sensimilla, they are increasing exports to Europe.

Jamaica may be the most visible consumer of ganja, which may contribute to its anemic 305 hectares or 206 metric tons of end product. Maybe there was too much sampling. The drug gangs have also started shipping cocaine.

The Bahamas is a major transshipment point for Jamaican weed and U.S.-bound coke from Colombia.

Guyana is a minor source for cannabis and is a transshipment point for cocaine from Colombia.

Cuba is a minor player with its North shore being a swapping point for Colombian drugs on their way to the States or Europe.

Trinidad and Tobago are major marijuana producing areas with an estimated 24 million marijuana plants found in the forested areas of north, east and south of Trinidad.

The Philippines is a big time producer and exporter of weed. Grown in Northern Luzon and Mindanao, its primary destination is Japan and Australia.

Central Asia is a major cannabis growing area with much of the product being turned into hashish.

Kazakhstan studies show that one out of every 14 people in the cities is a cannabis user. Every hippy's dream is the Chu valley where 138,000 acres of cannabis grow wild. There is an annual crop of 5000 metric tons per year. The primary regions for cannabis are the Taldy-Korgan, around the city of Almaty, Kzyl-orda and the south Zakakstan oblasts. There is also the ephreda plant which grows wild in the mountain ranges of the Zailyiski and Junggar and in the Talky-Korgan and Dzhambyl.

Major Drug Producers

Afghanistan

A common harvest of lawlessness is drugs. When the Soviets pulled out of Afghanistan, they left little government and less of an economy. So the gaps were filled in by industrious Afghans who raised poppies and sold them to the equally industrious Pakistanis. The Pakistanis jumped in when Iran's fundamentalist government got tough on drugs and Afghan routes to the west were interrupted by war. Today, Pakistan exports between 65 and 80 tons of heroin every year. Not much when you compare it to the 2630 tons from the Golden Triangle, but enough to generate US$1.5 billion in revenue.

- The major drug producing regions in Afghanistan are Helmand, Kandahor, Uruzgan and Nangarhar provinces. Less productive regions for poppies are the provinces of Badakhstan, Kunar, Farah and Nimroz. At first it was thought the anti-drug *taliban* would crack down (at least they told *DP* that they would shoot all drug smugglers) but it seemed that when the morality was balanced with the economics common sense prevailed and drugs are bigger than ever.

There are some fairly significant barriers for entrance into the drug business. First off you need to have access to very expensive, very controlled chemicals like ephedrine ($80,000 a ton), methaqualone, n-acetylanthranillic acid, acetic anhydride (for heroin). If you are in the coca to cocaine base business you need mountains of sulfuric acid, hydrochloric acid, sodium hydrochloride, and lime. The main areas for chemicals are India and China. Secondly, you need to control and protect cultivation areas and processing areas. This means gunmen, bribes and the occasional brutal murder. Finally you need transportation corridors and customers. This means staying on top of brutal and slippery alliances with terrorists, politicians, warlords, the military and organized crime. It is estimated the heroin business provides half a billion dollars a year to the Kurdistan Workers Party or PKK. Enough to pay for a television satellite to broadcast their very own MED/TV.

There are 38,740 hectares of poppy cultivation (yielding 1250 metric tons) in Afghanistan with about 85 percent coming from the provinces of Nangarhar and Helmand which is then refined to morphine or heroin base. Pakistanis then take delivery and refine the drug in Quetta and ship it by sea or land (across Iran) or northward through Central Asia by road.

Pakistan is a major refining and distribution area primarily in the Khyber region and Northwest Frontier Province (see Pakistan IADP) where 155 metric tons of opium was produced. There is also a significant addict population in Pakistan.

The northern provinces transship through Tajikistan and Central Asia.

Iran has a minor output of opium but is primarily a transshipment point for heroin from Afghanistan en route to Turkey in the north and from Baluchistan in the south.

The Haji Baig Organization

This is a Lahore, Pakistan-based group loosely modeled after the 1980s American S&L structure; in other words, most of the key players are currently in jail while making millions of dollars. This organization lacks the political halo and the tens of thousands of armed men the Myanmar groups possess, and they are paying the price.The leaders are all killing time in Pakistan on drug charges awaiting extradition to the States. Meanwhile, their organization relies on Haji Ayub Afridi to carry on business as usual. Afridi lives in Jalalabad, a half-hour outside Peshawar in a compound protected by antiaircraft guns and armed tribesmen. His responsibility is to keep the flow of heroin and hashish moving to local distribution and sales groups in New York, Newark, NJ, L.A. and San Francisco.

The Quetta Alliance

The DEA-named Quetta Alliance is a coalition of Afghan tribes (the Issa, Notezai and the Rigi) based along the Pakistan-Afghani border. The tribes control the output and shipment of processed opium (mostly morphine) to Turkey for further processing into heroin. The PKK and other terrorist groups in Turkey and Iran take care of security, and the final product is trucked from Istanbul to Europe for the last leg of the journey into America. The leader of the Notezai, Sakhi Dost Jan Notezai, is serving his third term in the provincial assembly, while concurrently serving time in prison on drug charges.

Drugs are also sent from Quetta to the Makran coast, where they are shipped via freighter to Marseilles and New York.

Crack

Crack has replaced heroin as the new "jones" that is dragging down the inner city. Not as addictive as heroin, it has an intense high that is psychologically addictive. In some American cities, three out of 100 first-graders are addicted to crack, thanks to their mothers. In 1995, 18 per 1000 live births were crack babies. Crack pushes users to violent criminal acts, sexual trading and other desperate measures to feed their habit. According to the Bureau of Justice Statistics, the typical crack user is low-income, white (49.9 percent) and desperate; 35.9 percent are black and 14.2 percent Latino.

The PKK

Although they are known as a Kurdish liberation group, these folks have enough dough to run a TV station in London, 30 radio stations and a host of newspapers and rent time on two satellites (for a reputed 2 billion English pounds). You don't get this kind of money selling "Free the Kurds" T-shirts. Dope is protected through east Turkey and into Cyprus and then shipped to sales networks in Europe and the U.S. These guys should sell stock!

The taliban

Although it cannot be said that the *taliban* are smuggling drugs, it can be said that regional governors who are set up by the *taliban* do allow the cultivation, sale, basic refining and transportation of drugs. Although initially they sent in armed groups to stop drug smuggling, it seems that the *taliban* forces routinely deduct their passage fee from drug caravans and the local governors profit from this activity as well. For now the *taliban* get either caustic or vague when you accuse them of condoning drugs but cultivation increases, chemicals continue to be smuggled in from Central Asia and shipments to Europe have increased.

Europe

Europe is a major consumer of illicit drugs. Amsterdam, Marseille and Baltic ports provide easy access for Asian and Central Asian purveyors.

Poland produces 20 percent of the amphetamines sold in Europe and is a major base for Chinese, Colombian and other drug groups looking for a safe central place to process drugs. There are about 200,000 drug users, and half of them are addicts.

England has an estimated 100,000 heroin addicts and is a major consumer of soft and hard drugs. Most of the heroin comes from Afghanistan via Pakistani organizations. Marijuana comes from Morocco. Cocaine comes directly from South America via Amsterdam.

Italy is home to three major criminal organizations: The Calabrian 'Ndrangheta, the Neapolitan Camorra and the Sicilian Mafia. All work directly with South American cartels to transport and sell cocaine in Europe. Most cocaine arrives by sea into mafia-controlled ports. There are around 150,000 addicts in Italy and 200,000 cocaine users.

Germany is the one place where cocaine costs more than the U.S. and use is up. Its ports of Hamburg, Bremen and Rostock are entry points for drugs and Frankfurt is the main air terminal used by Europe bound "mules" from Asia, Africa and Central Asia

Greece has 80,000 heroin users and is a major transshipment point into Europe from Turkey, by road, sea and air.

Bulgaria's lax airport security allows cocaine smugglers access to Europe. It also a main route into Europe from Turkey for West Asian drugs.

Cyprus is an important meeting ground and money laundering center for the Russian Mafyia. There are over 20,000 offshore companies, one tenth are Russian. Its central, neutral location and business infrastructure make it the ideal meeting place for drug deals, payoffs and discussions.

The Balkans

The well-maintained roads and compliant customs officials of the former Yugoslavia were the home leg of the long road from the poppy fields of Asia. The war messed up this convenient leg and now most heroin is smuggled through Albania, Macedonia and Bulgaria. About 70 percent of the heroin is smuggled under the direction of the Albanian mafia to customers in Germany and Switzerland. They are bosom buddies with the Italian mafia. The Albanian mafia is comprised primarily of the Kosovar clan. Heroin is also processed in Albania by the mafia to increase profits.

Albania is a mess with the mafia being a stronger force than the government itself. Criminals control most major ports and entry areas making it a free trade zone for drugs. Cannabis and poppies are also grown domestically. Albanians from the Kosova region are the main smugglers who deliver their wares to retailers in Italy, Turkey and along the Mediterranean

Trans-Caucasus

The rough and ready base of Europe is a natural conduit for anything coming from the foggy mountains of Chechnya, Georgia and other small states.

Chechnya paid for its revolution primarily with drug funds. The Russian military shipped heroin and hash using the Baku-Grozny-Rostov line. The Chechens raided over 559 trains in 1993 looting 4000 cars and stealing 11.5 billion rubles worth of legal cargo. It is not known how much drugs were taken. There is a nasty rumor that when Dudayev unsuccessfully demanded a higher cut of drug moneys from Defense Minister, Pavel Grachev he began to execute train conductors and confiscate all the drugs. Prompting Grachev to invade Chechnya.

Armenia is one stop for hashish and opium from Afghanistan on its way to Europe. There are also around 10,000 drug addicts.

Azerbaijan is another rest stop for smugglers from Central Asia, Iran and Afghanistan on their way to Russia or Europe. The drug trade is well entrenched with the main one being the route from Iran up to Russia and the Baltic states. There is a little side action smuggling drugs into Georgia.

Colombia

Colombia is the world's leading producer and distributor of cocaine, according to the DEA. It is the world's second largest producer of coca. They also are a major supplier of heroin and marijuana to the Mexican mafia. In the early '70s Colombia started out primarily as a grower of pot, with cocaine being a small part of the then $500 million a year export. Pot was mostly cultivated along the Atlantic coast. Today, it is estimated that Colombia's drug industry pockets about 3 billion a year in profits from the drug trade. They have a lock on 75 percent of the world's cocaine, and about 80 percent of the toot goes to Uncle Sam. To get an idea of what a narco government is, you have to understand that the entire gross domestic product of Colombia is only $5 billion.

Most coca is grown on 8–20 acre farms. The Colombian farmers get in 3–4 harvests a year. Some farmers are taking the next step and creating coca paste which sells for about $1100 per kilo. Most of the 135,000 acres of coca farms in Colombia are in the far south. It is estimated that there are 35,000 farmers in the business of growing coca and poppies. Only about 7000 families have switched to legal crops in the last two years.

Colombia has 50,900 hectares of coca, 2180 of opium poppy and 5000 hectares of marijuana under cultivation. Cocaine base is also flown into Colombia for processing via aircraft from Bolivia and Peru. Colombia's 80 metric tons of cocaine and 6.5 tons of heroin is then flown or shipped out to Mexico, Central America and the Caribbean. Ecuador, Venezuela, Paraguay and Haiti are also transshipment points and money laundering centers.

Thailand

Thailand's position in the Golden Triangle is more geographic than economic. It is a net importer of hard drugs and is a major transit route to Western countries. About 50 percent of the opium that enters Thailand from Myanmar heads for the U.S. The Thai opium crop is 25 metric tons and is under constant threat by government eradication programs and tough border controls with its northern bad boy neighbor Myanmar. Still the mule trains get through the rough terrain and insurgents keep the Thai soldiers from truly policing or sealing off the area.

Myanmar

Just under 70 percent of the world's heroin and 60 percent of heroin seized by U.S. law enforcement came from the Golden Triangle. The Golden Triangle is not really a geographic triangle but a loosely U.S. defined area that covers eastern Myanmar, northern Laos and scattered parts of northern Thailand. The common elements are remoteness and inaccessibility, lack of law enforcement and the right altitude and climate to permit the cultivation of poppies. It may be more accurate to describe the Golden Triangle as just Myanmar.

Visitors to this area will find the locals decidedly reserved and openly belligerent if pressed for details on their trade.The U.S. State Department estimates that Myanmar exports about 2300 tons of raw opium a year, primarily from the Kachin and north Shan states. Laos moves about 300 tons and Thailand about 30 tons. Currently there is no anti-drug program and even the most visible drug smuggler in the world, Khun Sa, has retired in luxury to Yangon. In fact the term warlord or drug czar has been replaced by the SLORC with a new title: Leader of National Races and include: U Sai Lin aka; Lin Ming-shing of the Eastern Shan State Army (ESSA); Yang Mao-liang, Peng Chia-sheng, and Liu Go-shi of the Myanmar National Democratic Alliance Army (MNDAA-Kokang Chinese); Pao Yuchiang, Li Tzu-ju, and Wei Hsueh-kang of the United Wa State Army (UWSA); and U Mahtu Naw of the Kachin Defense Army (KDA). All have been fingered by the U.S. government as the men who put the monkeys on the junkies.

For now the SLORCies are proud of the capture of a ridiculous 100 kgs of heroin as proof that they are "just saying no" to drugs in Myanmar.

The United Wa Army

Back in 1989, the SLORC Generals cracked down on Khun Sa. They overran his base in Ho Mong and subjected him to a list of horrors they felt Myanmar's smack daddy deserved: A mock trial, house arrest, no extradition, a job running the bus system, a nice house to stay arrested in, great medical care, around the clock bodyguards and only *one* round of golf on the Yangon links each week. Despite this cruel and unusual punishment and SLORC's clear message to all aspiring druglords, the heroin trade still continues in the north.

Today Khun Sa's Doi Land and Huay Makekahm heroin factories are humming along (they "crank" out 140 kg's of smack every month) under new ownership, the opium crop is up 10 percent and life is good for the United Wa Army.

The Wa Army is led by two men, former Commie Chao Nyi-Lai and Wei Hsueh-Kang, who operate out of the town of Pan Hsang in the easternmost corner of Myanmar. The Wei Siao brothers; Gang and Long are supposed to be the majordomos of drug dealing (Gang is wanted in the U.S. for drug trafficking) after Tei Kung MIng was offed in China. In any case the Wa boys and the United Wa State Army (an army of between 15,000 to 35,000 men) are in charge. They were trained well since they once provided raw opium to Khun Sa. The two leaders have political ambitions and claim that they want to shift the Wa people into legitimate crops once they have representation within the country of Myanmar. (Probably as soon as Joe Namath plays for the Jets again.) Opium production was up 10 percent in 1996 and instead of one big centralized high visibility operation (The big K's downfall) the opium business under the Wa is broken into smaller more numerous processors.

A third group led by Ai Hsiao-shih and Wei Hseuh-kang specializes in the transportation of raw and processed heroin into China and Thailand.

The Wa and the Shan—or more accurately the former Khun-Sa factions and Nyi-Lai/Hsueh-kang—account for 75 percent of the opium leaving the Golden Triangle. Most of Myanmar's opium is transported in pony caravans along simple trails into China's Yunnan province and eventually to the drug syndicates in Hong Kong, or it moves south through Chiang Mai in northern Thailand down to Bangkok. Once the pony caravans reach minor towns, the heroin is then trucked to major cities, from where it is shipped or flown to the United States or Mexico.

A third route is from Moulmein in southern Burma into Bangkok and, surprisingly, into Malaysia and Singapore. Malaysia and Singapore widely publicize their imposition of a mandatory death penalty for drug smuggling, while also serving as major centers for the export of drugs.

For now the Wa are big wheels in the opium trade. There are plans afoot to turn Khun Sa's big white house into a museum.

Bangladesh, with its harbors and airports, is a growing transshipment point. For now, they are trying to crack down on the use of phensidyl, a codeine based cough syrup in vogue with Bangladeshis.

India is a legal producer of opium (in the states of Madhya, Pradesh, Rajasthan and Uttar Pradesh) for medical purposes and is strategically situated between the Golden Crescent to the West and the Golden Triangle to the East. It also supplies processing chemicals to all major drug processing groups. The also produce methaqualone for sale in southern and eastern Africa.

The Hill Tribes

The real dirty work is taken care of by the region's poor but industrious hill tribes. Poppies in the Golden Triangle are grown and harvested by the Lahu, Lisu, Nfien and Hmong tribes, and cultivated among less odious but less profitable crops like maize. Since smart farmers maximize the use of their land and labor, it's not surprising that the annual opium production has tripled in Myanmar in the last 10 years. Depending on which druglord's auspices the farmer falls under, the raw product is sent to processing labs either along the Chinese border (Wa) or along the Thai border (Shan).

The Mong Tai Army

As broken as the surrounding topography, the Mong Tai (Shan State) Army, once led by the now retired Chang Chi Fu aka Khun Sa (Prince of Prosperity) disintegrated into factions in mid-1995 as the drug warlord cut a deal with Myanmar's ruling SLORC. Khun Sa, 63, now lives in Yangon in comfortable retirement. The USDEA were doing backflips when the K-Mart of heroin shut down. In August of 1996 street prices for heroin shot up 10 times their normal level as supplies disappeared down junkies' veins.For one brief shining moment it looked like the generals had been visited by the Do-Good fairy. The former headquarters at Ho Mong nine miles from the Thai border became a shell of its former glory with the population dwindling to less than 4000 compared to 18,000 in its heyday. But within the Wa, the new "Wa"-Mart of heroin filled Khun Sa's shoes.

Mexico

Mexico continues to be the financial and transshipment choice of South American drug cartels due to its lax banking laws, corrupt officials and its "don't ask, don't tell" policy of the military and government. The drug business in Mexico is sliced into three cartels; the Tijuana, Juarez and the Gulf. The Tijuana cartel under the Feliz brothers smuggles primarily heroin and majijuana, The Gulf cartel is the coca express and Amada Carrillo Fuentes' group (before he liposuctioned himself to death) used to cover trans border shipments from El Paso to Brownsville. In many cases, the cartels have cut out the beleaguered Colombian middle men and go right to the source for the coca paste.

Cocaine is smuggled in from South America in large multi-engine cargo jets and large cargo ships. Corrupt customs officials drive new Chevy Suburbans and the ruling class in Acapulco and Tijuana could outbid Bill Gates at any poker game. The downside is that Mexico's border population is coming down with a jones for their product and the U.S. government is losing patience with our biggest narco neighbor.

Belize, Costa Rica, El Salvador, Nicaragua, Guatemala and Honduras are major land, air and sea transshipment routes for Colombian drugs entering Mexico. Mexico snaps up about 50–70 percent of all cocaine from South America. Mexico's corrupt government and long border with the U.S. make it an ideal entry point for drugs and a major money laundering center.

Mexico produces about 80 percent of the marijuana, 20–30 percent of the heroin and a growing amount of methamphetamines.

Panama

The Darien region of Panama is a hot spot for coca cultivation for the Colombian drug czars. Local Indians are goaded into cultivating crops under the watchful protection of Colombian guerillas. Recently, officials destroyed more than five tons of cocaine, broke up six coca paste labs and burned down 200 acres of a coca plantation. Still, Panama retains its reputation as an ideal shipment point for drugs and is a major center for laundering drug money.

Peru

Coca is Peru's second largest crop (after maize) with 930 square miles under cultivation. The major areas are the Huallaya Valley and the Apurimac-Enc Valley east of Lima. The 115,300 hectares of coca leaf (60 percent of the world's total coca crop) under cultivation is worth 40–50¢ a kilo (down from $3 in 1994). The drugs are grown by peasants who sell to shippers and processors under the control of the Shining Path and oddly enough the Peruvian military.

Russia

Russia's geographical position makes it a major drug producing, shipping and consumption center. Its neighbors make good use of the corrupt and inefficient police and border guards. The Russians quickly motorized the business and Russian Generals made millions sending back drugs to Russia in lead lined coffins. The trade in Tajikistan sends Tajik agents bearing Russian military supplies; blankets, food, guns, shoes etc. into Afghanistan. An Afghan dealer swaps the material for drugs and then the Russian soldiers make a one million dollar ruble payment to the border guards. The soldiers then ship the drugs directly into Russia's major cities by military transport (air, rail or road) which is not subject to inspection. The favored route is from Tajikistan Krasnovodsk, Baku, Grozny to Rostov and then on to Europe through Estonia. Defense Minister Pachel Grachev is nicknamed Pasha Mercedes for his high lifestyle and his reputed income from drugs.

Drugs from the Golden Crescent (Pakistan, Afghanistan and Iran) are transported to major centers like Tashkent in Uzbekistan, or through the states of Chechnya, Tajikistan, Georgia and Azerbaijan. There are also major growing areas in southern Russia and the western Ukraine, as well as the states of Uzbekistan, Kazakhstan and Krygyzstan. The presence of foreign troops during the Balkan War has disrupted the once traditional smuggling routes into Europe, which are being replaced by Afghanistan to Tajikistan to St. Petersburg to Cyprus, and then out through ports on the Baltic Sea and Mediterranean.

Russian officials estimate there are about 5.7 million drug users in Russia, with hashish being the drug of choice. A U.N. report says there may be 100,000 opium poppy fields and more than 2.5 million acres of marijuana under cultivation within the country. Drug-related crime is up 15 percent and 23 tons of drugs were seized in raids last year. About 80 percent of drug dealers arrested in Moscow are Azerbaijanis; the rest are Chechens. Moscow banks are becoming popular with out of town drug dealers like the Sicilian mafia and the Colombian cartels to launder money. The total drug business adds up to an unimpressive US$25 million (compared to our US$500 billion narcotics industry). A kilo of hash in Russia goes for as little as US$15, compared to US$200 in Europe. Accordingly the profit savvy and brutal Russian gangs are also expanding into Europe and the United States.

Those drugs that don't end up in Moscow or St. Petersburg go through to the Baltics where eager Scandinavian and Lowlands customers await.

Africa

Africa is not a major consumer of drugs, but it is an important transshipment point. South Africa is a growing consumer of drugs.

Egypt has large opium and marijuana plantations in the remote valleys of the Sinai Peninsula. The government launched a military offensive to eliminate them in March of 1996. The flow of cash from the drug trade is supposed to have made the drug cartels' assets an estimated $15 to $60 billion. It is also a transshipment point for Asian heroin on its way to Europe and the U.S. Its control of the Suez Canal allow large cargo shipments from the Indian Ocean into the Mediterranean.

Morocco is a supplier to Europe with its 74,000 hectares of marijuana under cultivation.

Nigeria grows cannabis but is known primarily for its courier business. Nigerians supplies South American cocaine and Asian heroin to the U.S and Europe. Interpol considers Nigeria the third largest heroin smuggling area in the world. Nigerians also recruit non-Nigerians for the risky business as well. It costs about $5000 to get five keys of heroin past Nigerian customers inspectors.

South Africa is also a transshipment point for cocaine and heroin and is one of the largest producers of weed primarily for its own consumption.

East Africa ports and airports are a transit point for Pakistani couriers as well as sea and air shipments. Often Nigerian couriers will fly into Nairobi to pick up shipments then fly into Europe or the U.S. Kenya deals primarily in hashish from Pakistan and heroin from Asia. It is also the major producer of *khat* a mild narcotic favored by Yemenis and Somalis.

Yemen is a transit country for hard drugs and consumers of them.

Zambia is a major transit point for methaqualone destined for South Africa.

Zimbabwe grows and exports marijuana to Europe and transships cocaine from South America and methaqualone from India to South Africa.

The Drugstore

Opium

Opium has been used to kill pain, cure diarrhea and even as a social drug since 300 BC. Today, the legal use of opium is mainly to create morphine and codeine for medicinal purposes. Worldwide, there were an estimated 4000 metric tons of the stuff in 1995, double the amount produced in 1986.

Heroin

Heroin (from the Greek root, meaning "Hero") is the most refined byproduct of the opium poppy and causes a sense of power, creates a feeling of euphoria, relieves pain and induces sleep. Heroin has only been around since 1874 and was originally used for medicinal purposes without knowledge of its addictive properties. Today, 65 percent of the world's heroin supply comes from Myanmar, with Laos second. Northern Thailand barely hits the radar screen as a poppy grower. The U.S. government has vacillated between encouraging the production of heroin (as it did in its support of Laotian rebels during the Vietnam War) and condemning it (through its covert military ops in Thailand aimed at stemming the heroin tide washing up on the shores of New York City).

Even in its heavily cut street form (nickel bags diluted with sugar, starch, powdered milk or quinine to less than 10 percent purity), it is highly addictive, and its victims require larger and larger doses and more direct methods of ingestion to deliver a high. In New York City, the street price for a gram of 90 percent pure heroin is about $100, and a nickel bag goes for about $10; its dearth of purity means junkies can snort it instead of having to inject it. Some estimates tag the heroin trade as a US$4 to 10 billion a year business. There are about 600,000 users; half of them are concentrated in New York City. Heroin is becoming more popular; there was a 50 percent increase in heroin-induced overdoses as tracked by ER rooms in a half-year period in the U.S.

Methamphetamine

Meth, crank, or crystal was invented by the Japanese in 1893. The drug also contains ephedrine, found in over-the-counter cold prescriptions. Today it is a home-made drug popular with bikers, truckers and kids. Japan has 600,000 meth heads or tweakers. The Philippines is a transit point for crystal meth from China, Hong Kong and Taiwan on its way to local tweakers and into the U.S. via Guam and Hawaii. Ice, as it is commonly called, is cyrstallized, orderless and smokable. It first appeared in Hawaii in 1989 and came from South Korea, Taiwan and the Philippines. The symptoms are fast and intense euphoria with alertnesss for 8–24 hours. Coming down also includes paranoia, depression, convulsions, hallucinations, aggressive behavior and fatal kidney failure. It is not uncommon to meet serious tweakers in a zombie, sleepless state.

Primarily a cheap, working class drug, meth can be cooked up at home and can turn a twenty fold profit... if you don't blow yourself up in the process of cooking it.

Morphine

Morphine is bitter to the taste, darkens with age and is derived from opium (at a strength of between 4 and 21 percent). Most of its addicts are former soldiers who were treated with morphine as a pain killer after being wounded in combat.

Codeine

Codeine (0.7 to 2.5 percent concentration of opium) is an alkaloid byproduct of the poppy and is found in a variety of patent medicines around the world. In the U.S., codeine is only available in prescribed medications. However, these same medicines (i.e., Tylenol with Codeine) can be had over the counter in many countries, particularly in Central and South America and Southeast Asia.

Cocaine

Cocaine is a bitter crystalline alkaloid obtained from coca leaves. It creates a euphoric effect in users as well as a compulsive psychological need. It has limited medical applications as a local anesthetic agent. It is readily absorbed by the mucous membranes lining the nose and throat. Crack is a derivative of cocaine.

Marijuana

Mary Jane, grass, weed, or pot is a drug derived from *cannabis sativa*, a tall, leafy plant that is easily cultivated. The chemical that causes the high in pot is THC, or delta 9-tetrahydrocannabinol. More than 400 other chemicals are found in the cannabis plant. Marijuana is usually smoked in loosely rolled cigarettes and is considered a social drug consumed at parties or at home. There are many varieties, with the effects dependent on the amount of THC in the plant. Due to better strains of the plant being cultivated, the marijuana sold today is estimated to be 10 times stronger than the weed sold in the 1970s.

The effect of marijuana varies with the user, but typically results in a faster heart rate, bloodshot eyes and dry throat and mouth. Marijuana can cause acute panic, memory loss and a lack of motivation. Proponents of its use praise its medicinal effects, enhancement of mental powers and increased sensitivity, especially during sex. Others experience drowsiness, giddiness and stupor.

Hashish

Hash is derived from the resin of hemp plants. It is stronger than marijuana and can contain up to 50 percent pure THC. It is usually smoked in a pipe or smoked inserted into regular cigarettes. THC is a chemical that usually contains PCP.

PCP

PCP, phencyclidine, also called angel dust, was originally developed as an anesthetic in the 1950s. Today, it is illegal but it is easily manufactured. PCP acts as a stimulant and can stretch time, numb pain centers, and slow body movements. Some users have a sense of power and strength. Overdoses can create violent behavior, which may lead to rash acts when the victim feels invincible (jumping from high places, drownings, car accidents). Heavy users can develop symptoms of paranoia, fearfulness and anxiety.

LSD

LSD is manufactured from lysergic acid, which is a common fungus typically in grains or bread. LSD was discovered in 1938 and is odorless, tasteless and colorless. It is often in liquid or tab form. Hallucinogenics create a rush of unusual emotions, visions, experiences and sensations. They also increase heart rate, dilate pupils, and increase body temperature and blood pressure. Use of hallucinogens may unmask or exacerbate emotional problems. In some cases, LSD is cut with other drugs to change the high.

Mescaline

Mescaline comes from the peyote cactus, and its effects are similar to those of LSD, though less extreme. It is usually smoked or swallowed in pill form.

Psilocybin/Mushrooms

Psilocybin is a hallucinogen found in mushrooms. It is taken in its raw form (mushrooms) or in a powdered tablet.

"Khat's Fancy"

Although most countries outlaw the chewing of khat, a mildly stimulating drug, it is still legal in hot, dusty Yemen. It is estimated that half of Yemen's population is moderately drugged for at least part of the day. Khat, or qat, costs about US$3 for a day's hit and is chewed mostly by men. It is issued to soldiers to reduce tension and anxiety. It can also diminish sexual potency, as well as create loss of appetite or gastritis, inflammation of the gums, and quirky side effects. One of the side effects is the perception that the user can regale people with long speeches and stories. They seem inspirational and fascinating to the user, but sound ridiculous to the listener. Khat is a social drug, usually chewed in the afternoon or evening. It is not known to be addictive, but it may prevent users from falling asleep. The leaves of the plant are bitter and are left in the mouth like chewing tobacco and formed into a plug or ball.

DRUGS

Getting Arrested

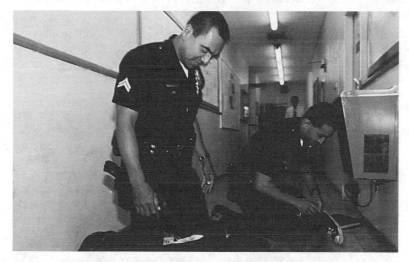

Oh Won't You Stay...Just a Little Bit Longer

You're catching some rays on the beach in Manzanillo. The low tangerine shafts of sunlight trickle across the purple Pacific as you wipe the piña colada foam from your lips. It's your last day. Monday, it's back behind the desk at Shrapnel-Wesson Bros., the brokerage people, in beautiful downtown Gary, Indiana. You lament the week ahead, as you notice the young Mexican kid approach your towel. Another souvenir or massage parlor tout. Jeez, they get these kids young, you think. Instead of balsawood dolphins, hammocks or whorehouse flyers, the kid pulls from his pocket a bag of weed. You do a double take. *Sensimilla*, the kid says. Twenty bucks. What the hell, you say. It's your last day. You're grabbed from behind. Someone's got your hair. Your face gets stuffed into the sand. Then a boot in the left ear. Christ, that hurt! Thirty minutes later, you're pissing against a stained cement wall. Your left eye has swollen over. You've signed a confession.

What the hell. It's your last day.

There are an average of 6000 Americans arrested in 90 different countries each year according to the State Department. About 1500 are doing time in foreign jails. The majority (about 70 percent) of the cases are drug-related. Mexico and

Jamaica are responsible for the bulk of the drug-related incarcerations, filing 72 percent of all drug charges against Americans traveling abroad.

The top five destinations for Americans seeking free room and board are Mexico, Germany, Canada, Jamaica and Great Britain. Last year, Mexico had 525 gringos on ice and had arrested 768 that year. Fifty-five of those weren't happy campers and filed complaints of mistreatment. The Mexican judicial system is based on Roman and Napoleonic law and presumes a person accused of a crime is guilty until proven innocent. There is no trial by jury. Trial under the Mexican system is a prolonged process based largely on documents examined on a fixed date in court by prosecution and defense counsel. Sentencing usually takes six to 10 months. Bail can be granted after sentencing if the sentence is less than five years. Pretrial bail exists but is never granted when the possible sentence is greater than five years.

Even those folks have it good. In places like Malaysia and Singapore, move dope and die. Zero tolerance. Deal dope and you'll get the rope. Getting beaten up in a Mexican jail may be inconvenient, but at least the *federales* are trying to teach you a lesson, one you might learn from in later life. In Southeast Asia, there is no later life.

Here are a few survival tips (at the risk of sounding like your mother) for those who don't want to die as a skinny, frazzled, psychotic wimp in a Pakistani jail:

Have nothing to do with drugs or the drug culture.

Those pleasant men in pressed uniforms are employed for a single purpose, to find your drugs. Once they've found them, make no mistake, you will be busted. Once you're tried (if you ever are), you will be going away for a long time. And then it will take a lot of money to get you out. A lot of it. And you'll look different, too. Not good.

Do not take anything illegal through customs, or anything that doesn't belong to you.

Do not be an unwitting mule and carry a package for a friend. Do not think you can sneak a few joints through. Customs officers live by two words: How much? How much is it going to cost you to get out of this mess? How much time are you going to do? How much will it cost to repatriate your remains?

Be careful with unmarked drugs.

Combining drugs or putting prescription drugs into reminder boxes may create questions of legality. Your personal appearance, the quantity of the drugs and the general demeanor of your inquisitor will determine if you are let off.

Avoid driving.

Car accidents are a great way to go to jail. In many countries, the Napoleonic code of justice is utilized. In other words, by law, you are guilty until proven innocent. For instance, if someone smacks into your car in Mexico, you'll go to jail. No witnesses and it may be a long time. Hire a driver and you're off the hook.

Be judicious in your enthusiasm to photograph military or government facilities.

Soldiers in Africa love camera equipment. If you want it back, you'll have to pay a fine. In most of the former Soviet republics, you will be arrested for taking pictures of army bases or airports. We have spent plenty of time fast-talking our way out of jail simply for carrying cameras in countries that demand you have national and regional permits to carry them.

Get the right kind of help.

The U.S. embassy will not lift a finger to get you out of jail. They may assist you, but if you have broken the law in that country, you are expected to do the time. Many countries will assume you are guilty and hold you until trial. It may take an extraordinary amount of time for your case to go to trial, and you may even be required to pay your room and board while in jail. Hire a local lawyer and explore all options for your release, including bribes and being smuggled out. Communicate your case to friends, and tell them to contact journalists in the local and national media. If you really did something stupid and you don't have any money, be prepared for the worst.

A Run For the Border: Northwestern Ethiopia, February 1997

From the air Assossa looks like a dismal and singularly uninteresting town, but typically African with its corrugated iron rooftops reflecting the sun's glare. The flight from Addis Ababa, the Ethiopian capital, has taken almost two and a half hours and is about to deposit me on the border with Sudan—where I am heading to join the Sudanese People's Liberation Army (SPLA) on their latest spring offensive against the Islamic government of Khartoum.

For the previous week in Addis Ababa I engaged in a series of meetings with the local representative of the SPLA to work out a series of rendezvous points along the border. Theoretically, providing I can slip past the Ethiopian army on the border, my crossing is all arranged. I will be meeting SPLA guerrillas at one of three places on the other side of the border. There is only one border, temporarily closed, to cross.

On landing, Assossa is as depressing on the ground as it looked from the air. There are no taxis, nor any other type of transport, a soldier informs me while eyeing me curiously. It is an inauspicious start. Plans A and B have automatically flown out the window. Only Plan C is left. I mull it over as I check into a hotel, only distracted momentarily when the reception takes one look at me and immediately doubles the price on the grounds that I am a foreigner. It is, I muse, a pity I can't give him something nice in return...like forged money which, with a bit of luck, would see him in prison for a few years (preferably after I am long gone). But then we can't have everything. And, aside from the lack of electricity and running water, the hotel is actually quite nice.

Sitting on the bed I pull out a military map of the border area and with a Silva compass begin to work out the bearings. Plan C is a night march across the border, which is roughly 25 km as the crow flies. I plan on being able to leave the town at 3 a.m. This would give me four hours until I have to find a spot where I can rest for the day before completing my march across the border the following night. In the meantime I wander around town: first to find out if there are any buses going to Addis the following morning. There is one at 7 a.m. and I'll have to pay on the bus, a helpful official at the rundown bus station informs me. I say I'll probably be on it unless I decide to fly or manage to hitch a lift, which is the fiction I maintain to anyone who asks how long I'll be in town, in the hope that nobody will miss me in the morning. If they do I can only hope that no one wants to take any responsibility for my disappearance.

For the remainder of the day I wander around town looking for the best place to leave in the morning and checking for any military observation posts in the near vicinity of the town. But despite the large number of soldiers who, for Africa at least, look at least semicompetent—never a good sign, there appears to be nothing, except most of the local population, that will hinder my progress. I troop back to the hotel to wait for darkness. Awakened by a knock on the door, I find the receptionist wanting my passport for the benefit of one of the local boys in blue. I refuse to surrender it and say he's already taken all my details.

A couple of hours later he returns and is more insistent. My passport, he promises, will be returned in a couple of hours. He swears on everything he can think of and like a fool I believe him.

My passport, when it eventually arrives the following morning, is accompanied by five rather scruffy individuals in military uniforms. One of them speaks understandable English and wants to ask me some questions. He tells me to pack my bags and come with them. Feeling somewhat resigned, I comply, and we all pile into a Russian-made military jeep. Heading out of town, we take the road that leads north to the Sudanese border and the town of Kurmuk, which had been my destination. I am momentarily cheerful at the prospect of getting closer to my destination, even if the chances of reaching it are rapidly receding. We pull off the road a few miles out of town into a military camp. As we drive through I notice nine 105 mm field guns and hundreds of boxes of shells—fairly normal stuff for a military camp on the border.

Coming to a stop we climb out and I am taken to a room that obviously serves as someone's sleeping quarters. I make myself comfortable on the mattress while the translator explains that they simply want to ask a few questions. The interpreter sits next to me while the trio sitting on ammunition boxes opposite do their best to imitate the Spanish Inquisition. Thankfully it's a poor imitation. Notes are taken on a scrap of paper—only after a pen that works can be found. For half an hour the questions come, anything but thick and fast. The most important questions inquire about my family tree. After giving my name I am asked for my father's name. I give it. Then comes the turn of my grandfather. "He's dead,"I say. The interpreter's English breaks down a little here and he passes on "hesdead," as my grandfather's name. "No, he is dead," I repeat. English is obviously not the translator's strongest point, as he now thinks I am correcting his pronunciation and repeats "hesdead" more clearly for the benefit of the three wise men opposite. "Listen you fucking moron, he's dead OK!" I repeat while drawing a finger across my throat. They want to know his name anyway and with a sigh of exasperation, I give it.

After much muttering it's time to pile into the jeep for another cruise around town. This time, however, it appears that they are looking for a more senior officer to deal with my case. He is found, eventually, in a local bar playing cards. He takes one look at me and declares that my presence, so close to the border, is illegal. I try to counter this by arguing, quite truthfully, that no one told me it was illegal and that if it was, why did the official state airlines, Ethiopian Airways, sell me a ticket. An infallible line of argument, I think.

He doesn't see my point of view.

After he issues a rapid string of instructions in Amharic to my escort, I soon find myself en route back to the military camp. I ask what's happening... "You'll be staying a while until your case is resolved," the interpreter informs me. Er, and how long will that be, I casually ask. "Maybe a month," comes the reply. How about a quick telephone call? "No, you're an illegal." Cigarettes? "OK." At least I've got cigarettes: the outlook could be worse.

Arriving back at the base the three wise men, whom I guess to be from military intelligence, a misnomer though it may be, scuttle into a building leaving me in the hands of a succession of different guards, some of whom speak English. I manage to bribe one to make a telephone call to a journalist I know in Addis Ababa. The second I palm the twenty dollars into his hand, (a good two weeks wages), he launches into a denunciation of the dishonesty of the Ethiopian army—no doubt in an attempt to make me confident I can rely upon his absolute integrity and reliability. I suddenly feel that I have almost certainly wasted my money. He is, as we Shakespeare scholars say, protesting a tad too much. With the return of the Three Wise Men I am driven to another part of the camp and installed in a small room with a bed in the corner. Taking out my penknife I carve a '1' into the wall and lie down on the bed.

Allowed to sit outside the following day I pass the hours listening to my walkman and watching the humdrum of the daily camp life. The camp has no perimeter fencing and to stave off utter boredom I make fictional escape plans. The few soldiers who try and talk to me are promptly told to get lost by my personal guard sitting ten yards away with an AK-47 in his lap.

The food the guard brings me is a disaster. I wake up at around 2 a.m. in the sure knowledge that I have about 30 seconds to get to the toilet before disaster strikes. Being locked up, I bang on the door to attract the guard's attention. There is no reply. In desperation I force open the wooden window shutters and poke my head through the window, peer into the darkness and try to scan the buildings around me for any sign of my guard. But he has obviously gone temporarily AWOL. It is, of course, a gross dereliction of duty—but I'm not complaining. As cautiously as I can, I climb out the window before sprinting to the toilet. It's overcast and moonless. No doubt if I was Rambo or Jean Claude van Damme, this would be the moment where I steal the jeep, race out of the camp throwing grenades—which would be handily available—at the few sentries who try to stop me and hightail it to the border and further adventures. But I'm not Rambo, there probably aren't any keys in the jeep, and quite frankly my concerns are more immediate. The toilet would be repulsive to a rat, but in my distressed state, I'm not a rat.

Back at my quarters I light a candle and smoke a cigarette. The light attracts the guard who should have been on duty, and within seconds there's a soldier shoving his face through the window almost shouting in Amharic. I understand the tone, if not the content, and he obviously wants to know what I think I'm doing dressed in the middle of the night, looking as if I am about to escape. Running anywhere (with the possible exception of the toilet) is the last thing on my mind—as I explain to the other soldiers when they promptly turn up at the sound of my guard's raised voice.

After three days my interpreter finally reappears with the Three Wise Men to inform me that my case is being "considered" and to take away a fairly standard map, which they find in my belongings. I have a mental image of a bare room somewhere with a telephone that doesn't work and a variety of officials scratching their heads, drinking tea and wondering what to do about me. There have been no more questions since my initial, somewhat half-hearted, interrogation.

Now, though, the restrictions around me seem to have been lifted, and my cell is the center of attraction with soldiers stopping to ask me what I am doing in the camp and offering me cigarettes. My guard has been changed and my new guard, Abdul, is young and talkative. At 21 he has been in the army since age 16 and somehow speaks better English than any of his superiors. "Don't worry," he re-assures me, "You have absolutely nothing to worry about, we are brothers." Nice though this is to hear, I can't quite see on what evidence he is able to base this optimistic judgment; and as for being brothers, well...he still has the AK-47, however kind he is. He does, however, let me exercise: and for five minutes in the morning and evening I am allowed to stretch my legs and jog the 20 yards or so between the barracks where I am being held, before being most cordially invited to resume my seat.

On the fourth day I get my answer while enjoying a late nap—there isn't much else to do. The Three Wise Men and an assortment of commanders crowd into my room, with smiles and grins all-around and inform me that I'm about to be released. After a hasty shave I'm driven to the grass runway and left to wait for the plane.

—**Roddy Scott**

GETTING ARRESTED

Guns

Boys and Their Toys

If you travel to dangerous places you will meet a lot of people with guns. You should know what guns can and cannot do. But you should never carry or use one in a war zone. Television is not a good role model for those who want to learn about guns. On TV, puny handguns fire off hundreds of rounds without reloading, and bullets seem lethally attracted to bad guys. In reality guns are rather simple and deadly. Imagine throwing a pea-size pebble at someone. Now imagine using a slingshot, projecting that pea-size objective at 1200 feet per second. Ouch. Bullets are just heavy projectiles that puncture flesh, bounce off and shatter bone and turn people into trauma cases more efficiently than a club.

There are more than 200 million guns in the United States. It is estimated that firearm injuries in the States cost about $20 billion in medical costs and lost wages. Firearms send almost 40,000 Americans to their graves each year (19,000 Americans use guns to commit suicide each year, another 18,500 are murdered with a gun, and at least 1500 more are accidentally shot to death). Gun-related homicides rose 18 percent in the last decade—30 percent among people ages 15 to 24.

The most dangerous handheld weapons are rifles. Handguns require short ranges and careful aim to be lethal. Handguns tend to be the weapons of choice for domestic violence and robberies. Most handguns lose any effectiveness after 25 yards. In fact, the Western movies where men bang away from across the street without hitting anyone are not too far from reality.

On the other hand, if someone is shooting a rifle at you, you will probably end up dead.

In the 1850s, rifles were called muskets. They were smooth bore, and long barreled (about 4–5 feet in length) and could kill a man at 100 meters. Loading slowed down the killing process to about eight shots a minute.

In 1855, the Crimean War introduced the rifled bullet, a major advance that pushed the killing range out to 600 yards. The French invention meant that armies could now battle without the standard volley, advance and hand-to-hand combat. Armies were slow to adapt the deadly new Minié ball, and the Civil War still saw armies facing each other 50 to 100 yards apart, firing at point-blank range and then charging.

The next big advances were in the late 1800s, when breech-loading weapons like the Mauser rifle and metal-cased bullets were introduced. The next step was the 1903 Springfield rifle and the later 1917 Enfield. These rifles were deadly out to 1200 yards and could be loaded and fired quickly.

WWI trenches were typically spaced 300 to 1200 feet apart and dictated rifle design. The ideal weapon was one that fired accurately, from rest with a minimum of maintenance and training. The focus was on careful killing of fleeting targets. When fighting got close, bayonets and pistols were the choice. Machine guns were heavy and water-cooled and used for withering fire during assaults or attacks. In 1917 came the introduction of the first semiautomatic weapon that could fire 20 rounds as fast as the trigger could be pulled. The simple Pedersen-device modification to the 1903 Springfield rifle was ordered too late to make a difference in the Great War but changed the use of rifles in warfare.

WWII introduced the idea of rapid-fire, portable weapons that could intimidate rather than kill. The M1 Garand (designed by John C. Garand) was a semiautomatic, gas-operated rifle that could fire 30.06 cartridges in eight-round clips. Later, it would be found that the number of rounds fired for every person actually killed was 15,000 rounds, even though the range of engagement closed to half WWI distances. Heavy bolt action rifles were still the infantry weapon of choice, but the Germans and Russians used machine guns and infantry attacks to good effect. The Germans were the first to create the Sturmgewehr (assault rifle), but the first successful version was the post-war Russian AK-47.

Assault weapons provide killing power out to about 600 meters, although battlefield results showed that 350 meters was the maximum practical range in combat. Most firefights occurred with opponents 200 to 300 yards apart.

Vietnam and a host of other dirty bush wars introduced the ambush concept of very high rates of fire, light ammunition and firepower. Ammunition had to be light, weapons cheap and easy to fix, and general tactics dictated spraying thousands of rounds during short firefights. The number of rounds per kill tripled from WWII levels to a staggering 50,000 rounds for each kill. In Vietnam, the light and deadly M-16 became the overwhelming choice of ground troops.

The future of rifle design is anyone's guess. Everything from all-plastic bullets to nonlethal ammunition is being developed. In the meantime, it seems to take a major war to change the face of battle and eventually the use of weapons.

Here's a quick primer on things that go bang:

Handguns

Small weapons with 2"–8" barrels designed for personal protection and intimidating people at close range. Typically, the number of bullets is five–20. Average is about eight–13. Lethal range is from up close to about 50 meters when fired at rest. In combat or tense, moving situations, they are deadly out to about 25 meters. Most people miss when they use handguns as a defensive weapon and hit people when they use them as offensive weapons. Consistent training, long barrel length and small caliber play a big part in attaining accuracy. Dale Towert gathers real life information that shows calibre and bullet selection make a bif difference. His tables show that .22's have a 21–34 percent chance of stopping people and 357 Magnums do a much better job at 68–98 percent. It all depends on your ammo, the range and most importantly where you shoot the perpetrator. Rifle calibres like .223 Remington and .308 Winchester deliver 93–100 percent. Twelve gauges hover at around 98 percent stopping power effectiveness. Remember the classic words of Robert Ruark. Use enough gun.

Rifles/Submachine Guns

Modern military rifles are usually fully automatic. They can be fired in single shots or on full automatic. Full automatic is the least accurate but most intimidating. If a soldier is careful when squeezing off single shots, he is probably trying to kill you. If soldiers are using full automatic (common at night and in attacks), it means you have scared the shit out of them. Sniper rifles are the world's most dangerous weapons, simply because they are only used to kill. Rifles are issued to most troops, however bullets are sometimes not issued to some African troops (or Iraqis). Submachine guns like the MAC-10 and Uzi were designed for spraying fast bursts of pistol-sized (9mm and smaller) bullets in close quarters. Assault rifles like the AK-47 and AK-74 have high burst rates but longer barrels and better accuracy. Most terrorist or liberation movements carry AK 47 assault rifles because they are cheap, easy to fix and accurate.

Most Asian and African soldiers tend to fire fast and aim high under stress. Middle Eastern and Central Asian countries like Afghanistan and Pakistan breed deadly shots, since they grow up using guns for hunting and engage in warfare at long distances. Jungle fighters like to spray bullets.

Machine guns hold about 20–70 bullets and go through them pretty quickly at full auto. An Uzi kicks out 600 rounds per minute but has a maximum clip of 40 rounds. About 10 bullets a second gives you exactly four seconds of looking good until you have to reload. Killing range can extend to 1400 meters (over a mile with tripod-mounted sniper rifles with scopes) and are effective between 400 and 600 meters. Assault rifles (the ones with large clips and short barrels) are designed to kill between 20 and 200 meters.

AK-47 (Avtomat Kalishnikova Obrazets 1947g)

If there is one visual symbol or prop that symbolizes the Soviet/revolutionary influence, it is the unmistakable profile of the AK-47. Once it was the hammer and sickle; now it is the banana-shaped clip and pointed barrel of the world's most dangerous rifle.

These weapons are cheap (between $50 and $350), available around the world, rock-hard reliable, and in use from Afghanistan to Zimbabwe. It is estimated that there are about 30 to 50 million copies of the rugged rifle in existence. They can pour out 600 rounds a minute and are designed to be manufactured and repaired in primitive conditions. They use a chromed barrel and the only major defect is the loud click when you change firing rate.

In 1941, the 23-year-old tank commander Mikhail T. Kalishnikov was wounded in the battle of Bryansk by the German invaders. While recuperating, he listened to the complaints of Russian soldiers about their archaic bolt-action rifles. Kalishnikov made use of his downtime to copy the current German machine pistol. His pistol never made it into the arsenal of the Russian army, but in 1943 it got him an entry to compete with other Russian gun designers to create the first Soviet assault rifle. An assault rifle is designed to be light, possess high rates of fire, and do double-duty as an accurate defensive rifle.

His design was chosen based on its durability and simplicity. The AK-47 and variants thereof have been manufactured in 12 countries from Bulgaria to Yugoslavia. The AK-47 and the AKM (a simpler-to-make variant) are sighted in to about 1000 meters, field-strip down to six parts, fire 30 rounds of the 7.62 X 39 mm cartridge and will deliver three-inch patterns at 25 meters. The rifle is accurate to about 200 meters when fired from the shoulder at rest, and accurate to about 50 yards fired from the hip. The newest version of the classic assault rifle is the AK-74 (adopted in 1974 by the Soviets), which uses a lighter but more accurate 5.45 X 39mm cartridge.

Kalishnikov was born in the Siberian town of Izhevsk, west of the Ural mountains. Today, Izhevsk is home to Izhmash, a former major arms manufacturing company that exports hunting rifles under the name, The Kalishnikov Joint Stock Co.

Kalishnikov still designs hunting rifles and has never received a royalty for his innovative design, though he has received many medals for it.

M-16

The M-16, or the civilian version called the AR-15, was introduced in 1965. By this time, the light and powerful AK-47 was the best weapon available. In Vietnam, the light and deadly M-16 suffered initially because of ammunition that caused fouling. And the lighter bullet was deflected by brush. After the problem was sorted out, it became the standard issue for all ground troops (replacing the M-14). The M-16 used a lighter (5.56) bullet compared to the Viet Cong 7.62 used in the AK-47. The M-16 round had just as much impact at 200 yards as the AK-47 round.

The M-16 lays down 700 rounds per minute with a muzzle velocity of 3250 feet per second. It comes with 20 or 30 round clips. With a weight of 6.6 pounds, it has been adopted by Asian armies as the weapon of choice.

The G3

Heckler & Koch are known for high-precision German weapons. A relative newcomer to the arms trade, they were formed in 1949 by three partners; Seidel is the modest one. Originally, the postwar German army used old M1 Garands and the FAL rifle. The G3 was adopted in 1959 and was the first entirely German designed and made rifle (based on the Spanish CETME). The G3 used the standard 7.62 X51 NATO cartridge, and its accuracy and durability led to it being adopted by more than 50 other countries. The basic rifle design was made in everything from sniper to.22 calibre versions.

The ultimate H&K version is the PSG1, a $5000 sniper version for military and police use.

The UZI

The UZI is the brainchild of Israeli designer Major Uziel Gal, borrowing heavily from Czech models 23 and 25. The Uzi is designed to spray a room with bullets or be used as an infantry weapon. The 9mm version has a rate of fire of 10 bullets per second. The magazine inserts through the pistol grip, and the UZI comes in 16"-long barrel or ultra-compact machine pistol size. The UZI is also a favorite of the U.S. Secret Service because of its small size and high rate of fire. Originally designed for 9mm NATO standard ammunition, the UZI was manufactured in a more powerful.45-calibre format for the U.S.

market. Magazines come in 20-, 25- and 32-round capacity (the.45-calibre version comes in a meager 16-round capacity).

Medium-Range Weapons

When bullets just won't communicate how much you hate people, the military can whip out some other gizmos. Mortars look like tubes with legs on three plates. They are designed to throw shells short distances in a high trajectory. The soldier drops the hand-sized missile down the tube and it fires. When it lands, it spreads shrapnel in a 20- to 60-yard perimeter, depending on the shell. The only good thing about mortars is that you can tell where they come from and they tend to target specific areas.

Artillery is another matter. Artillery sends medium to large shells screaming in waves. The shells are used either to demoralize troops or create havoc before an attack. Artillery kills more people than bullets. If you come under artillery attack, it is not a good sign. You should try to change your travel plans in a direction other than towards the guns.

Rockets (RPGs)

Those funny-looking green things on the end of long sticks are RPG, or Rocket Propelled Grenades. There are also LAW's or Light Anti-Tank Weapons. They don't actually blow up tanks like they do in the movies, but they might blow a track if you are within 25 meters. More than likely it will piss off the tank driver long enough to direct his gunner's attention towards the rather obvious backblast. Then expect to be vaporized by the shock wave from the tank's shell. LAWS and RPGs give significant range (for the classic guerilla hit and run attack) and cause widespread damage in crowded troop convoys or Sunday Schools. RPGs are very much in vogue in Afghanistan and West Africa because they were shipped in by the container and create mayhem for pennies. RPGs are used to attack small to medium-sized groups of men, trucks and sometimes armored vehicles. They usually signal the start of an attack and kill with concussion and shrapnel.

Machine Guns

Machine guns were put to good use in the trenches of World War I, where a team of two men with a Maxim could mow down hundreds of attacking troops. The only limitation was how much ammunition they had and if the gun would jam due to the barrel overheating. Travelers will only see the big machine guns at checkpoints and on top of tanks and bunkers. They are used to pin down or decimate large groups of attacking soldiers. They are also mounted on the back of trucks in places like Somalia. Machine guns fire belt-fed ammunition (great for wearing in bandoliers and posing for bad guy pictures) and require a tripod (unless you are Arnold Schwarzenegger) for accuracy. They are loud and require someone to make sure the bullets are feeding properly. They are deadly out to 2500 meters and can also fire armor-piercing bullets. If you are in an area that has a preponderance of these weapons, you can safely assume you are in an active war zone.

Long-Range Weapons

Those of you who were lucky enough to see our $5 million cruise missiles go streaking overhead understand why war sucks. Today, there are so many exotic weapons delivery systems that they fill their own Jane's book. Travelers won't come across too many of these weapons, unless they are on the wrong side of Uncle Sam. Some groups like to use Stinger surface to air missiles like the Chechens, the Afghans and the Hutus, but they are lethal and unexpected and there is no advice one can give on avoidance except take the train.

GUNS

Resources:

WARNING: Many of the companies do not deal with the public. Sales of weapons are regulated by state and federal law These are listings are for informational purposes.

Assault Rifles, Rifles, Combat Shotguns (including Sniping Rifles) by John A. Norris $29.95 (ISBN 1-85753-214-7) Brassey's

Eagle Industries
400 Biltmore Drive, Suite 530S
Fenton, Missouri 63026
☎ *(314) 343-7547*
Makers of Mr. DP's favorite pack, load-bearing vests and also other military, swat gear.

Knight's Armament Co.
7750 9th Street S.W.
Vero Beach, Florida 32968
Manufacturer and designer of weapons systems including suppressed 50cal. sniper rifles.

Jonathan Arthur Ciener, Inc.
8700 Commerce Street
Cape Canaveral, Florida 32920
☎ *(407) 868-2200*
Manufacturer of sound suppressed firearms and conversion kits.

Don AustinWagenKnecht
12400 Blue Ridge
Grandview Missouri 64030
☎ *(816) 765-2539*
Manufacturers of silencers.

AWC Systems Technology
P.O. Box 41938
Phoenix, Arizona 85080
http://www.awcsystech.com
Manufacturer of sniper rifles and silenced weapons.

Kent A. Lomont
R.R. 1

Salmon, Idaho 83467
☎ *(208) 756-6819*
Dealer in large caliber guns, mortars, old military weapons, even gatling guns.

Sight Unseen
5444 Corteen Place
North Hollywood, California 91607
☎ *(818) 759-8059, FAX (818) 763-4663*
Manufacturers of the remote video sighting system that lets you shoot around corners.

Cheaper Than Dirt
2536 NE Loop 820
Fort Worth, Texas 76106
☎ *(817) 625-7557*
Catalog of discounted sporting goods, ammo, holsters, night vision and even a cool night writing pen for $11.97.

Brigade Quartermaster
1025 Cobb International Boulevard
Kennesaw Georgia 30152
☎ *(770)428-1248*
www.actiongear.com
Safari, hunting shooting, and military wear.

TAPCO
P.O Box 2408
Kennesaw Georgia 30144
☎ *(800) 554-1445*
Hunting, military surplus, books and even bullet proof vests.

Training Courses

Gun Site Training Center
P.O. Box 700 Paulden, Arizona 86334
☎ *(520) 636-4565*

Tactical Firearms Training Team
16835 Algonquin Street, Suite 120
Huntington Beach, California 92649
☎ *(714) 846-8065*

Mas Ayoob's Lethal Force
P.O. Box 122 Concord, New Hampshire 03301
☎ *(603) 224-6814*

American Small Arms Academy
P.O. Box 12111
Prescott, Arizona 86304

Thunder Ranch
P.O. Box 53
Mountain Home, Texas 78058
☎ *(210) 640-3138, FAX (210) 640-3183*

H&K International Training Division
21480 Pacific Boulevard
Sterling, Virginia 20166
☎ *(703) 450-1900 #293*
Twenty Five different professional training are offered by Heckler & Koch.

Yavapai Firearms Academy, Ltd.
P.O. Box 27290
Prescott Valley, Arizona
☎ *(520) 772-8262*

Front Sight Firearms Training Institute,

P. O. Box 2619,
Aptos, California 95001
☎ *(800) 987-7719*
FAX: (408) 684-2137
http://www.frontsight.com/
One of the best training schools for shooters. For about $300 ($400 for 4 day) they offer 2 day handgun, shotgun or rifle courses that focus not only on skills but law, reactions (shoot or don't shoot), mental conditioning and how to deal with the aftermath of a shooting.

The Firearms Training Site

e-mail: aglock45@erols.com
http://www.erols.com/aglock45/
http://www.worldmedia.com:80/caq/

NRA home page

http://www.nra.org

The Second Amendment Foundation

http://www.saf.org/saf.org

The Citizens Committee for the Right to Keep and Bear Arms

http://www.ccrkba.org/ccrkba.org

The National Shooting Sports Foundation

http://www.wsa.com/ool/misc.files/
shootmain.html

Hunting and Firearms

http://www.wolfe.net/~hunter/

Right to Keep and Bear Arms page

http://www.teleport.com/~dputzolu/
rkba.html

National Survey of State Handgun Carry Laws

http://www.primenet.com/~kielsky/
states.txt

Electronic GunShop

http://www.xmission.com/~chad/egs/
egs.html

American Jousting Alliance

☎ *(805) 242-6904*

For those who have an aversion to guns, James Zoppe teaches 12th century style jousting, sword fighting and other totally archaic and nonmechanized forms of recreation.

Tomislavgrad, Bosnia: "Where They'll Give Any Idiot A Gun"

Another day in Tomislavgrad, much like any other. Two troops are standing at the bar in one of the numerous little Kaffee-Bar establishments and arguing loudly. One is bouncing an old U.S. Army "steel pot" helmet on the bar and shaking his head negatively while the other shakes his head positively and crosses his arms. Now a couple of their buddies are getting into it. Just when it looks like there is going to be *real trouble*, the guy with the crossed arms who's been nodding his head "yes, yes," decides to limber up a little by drawing his Tokarev. Uh-oh. Screw real trouble, this was a *situation*. But wait, amongst all the screaming in Croat, the drunks start to slam wads of dinars down on the bar. Translation: the guy with the Tokarev says the .30 caliber Tokarev pistol bullet will not penetrate his U.S. Army steel pot. Okay, I've seen discussions like this before...argue, make some bets, throw the helmet, flak jacket, etc. in the alley and fire it up. Come back inside. Have some more drinks. No problem. Standard scenario, I muse. More bets are made. Then the guy with the Tokarev cocks the pistol, grabs the helmet, *and plomps it on his head*, and...Oh Shit!...*Ka-Blam*! Redecorates the wall with his brains. Instant Jackson Pollock canvas.

If only he'd asked me, I could've told him.

Some of these Croat civilians, turned defenders of the homeland, have a strange attitude toward firearms. The fact that some of them are even carrying weapons scares the hell out of me. The Muslim and Serb yahoos are no different. Ignorant slivvovitz-swilling pig farmer gets automatic weapon. Yippee!

Ever wonder what became of the banjo boy in *Deliverance*? They gave him an AK and sent him to Bosnia.

One of the kids in Tomislavgrad had an uncle or third cousin six generations removed or some damn thing in New York, Chicago or Toronto (take your pick). Anyway he writes a letter begging for a bulletproof vest. So in the mail comes a Second Chance ballistic vest. Good quality stuff. Probably about $600 worth of Kevlar. He's so proud of his "bulletproof vest" that he wears it around town. Outside of his shirt. Shiny, bright white cover and all. But of course a few of the boys, jealous no doubt, have been making comments to the effect that it might not be as good as he thinks. This starts to gnaw at the sensibilities, limited as they may be, of our combat fashion victim. One day he's at home sitting in the kitchen showing off the vest to grandma. She thinks it's so nice that her boy Damir or Vlad or Stefan (take your pick) has this nice vest. So attractive too! He takes it off and says, "Here, grannie, you try it on." So the sweet little old 90-some pound Croatian *baka* tries on the vest. (Know where this is going, already, huh?) Grandson has a bright idea as grannie pirouettes, so he draws his Tokarev. *Bang! Bang! Bang!* Hits grannie three times—point blank. She lives. A couple of broken ribs... no problem. Grandson then shows the vest around town to all his buddies. Hey, it worked, and what the hell, the bullet holes weren't a problem. They were in the back.

Tom Myers and I roomed next door to each other for six months at Fort Benning in 1985. We were students in the same Infantry Officer Basic Course. After three years in the U.S. Army as a lieutenant he got out and joined the French Foreign Legion for a standard five year contract. When he was discharged he went to Bosnia and eventually ended up in Tomislavgrad, just after I'd left. There he met Dave, a Rhodesian war veteran, who had left after the political sell-out and went to South Africa where he served in the Recces. As Tom somewhat understatedly said, "He was a bit psycho." Probably because he used to play Russian roulette with a.357. You know, go into a bar, get everybody's attention, whip out a revolver, load one round, spin the cylinder, snap the weapon shut, put it to your head and then: Click! A real macho stunt. Mercenary theatre. Always a winner. Tough way to earn a free drink. According to Myers, "He finally *lost* one day, in a hotel in Split sitting there at the bar in front of God and everybody." Fred Verduin, another American "volunteer," occasionally hung out with the Russian roulette player who wanted Fred to try the game. Fred was tempted, he thought there had to be a trick to it. He found out this was not the case as he was sitting next to Dave that day in the bar in Split.

—Rob Krott

Kidnapping
You're in Good Hands

The kidnapping and occasional executions of travelers by such groups as the PKK in Turkey, Al-Faran in Kashmir, FARC in Colombia, the Khmer Rouge in Cambodia, make big headlines but don't reflect the real dangers of kidnapping. Even the recent kidnappings of nuns in Sierra Leone, oil workers in Yemen, researchers in Irian Jaya, journalists in Chechnya, or UN workers in Tajikistan don't properly convey the real threat of being kidnapped. The reality is that only one out of 10 kidnappings become public knowledge. Also, it generates extremely good business. If you happen to find yourself as one of the 200 foreigners who get kidnapped every year, there's little for you to do but hope that you'll be well treated.

Kidnapping is an ancient sport designed to generate cash, embarrass your enemies, find wives and/or force political action. Of the 8000 known kidnappings worldwide, 6500 were in Latin America with over half occurring in Colombia. There are, on average, ten people kidnapped in Colombia every day. The numbers increase dramatically when narco/terror groups like FARC kidnap an entire army garrison as they did last year. Some are multi-million dollar deals with nobody the wiser, and some are quick street abductions with $5000 payoffs the same-day profits.

The ideal victim of a kidnapping is a mid- to high-executive professional working for a multi-national corporation overseas. Foreign executives in Colombia will fetch $500,000–$2 million (depending on your point-man's negotiating skills), usually in a quick insurance-funded payoff. In Yemen over 100 foreigners have been kidnapped by tribesmen since 1993. Most are released safely. They target Italians tourists (over 1000 Italians visit Yemen every year) and businesspeople. Recently one tourist was shot and injured when a busload of 18 inconsiderate Italians ran a kidnapper's road block and were fired on.

Kidnappers can come in all shapes and demeanors. For example, Mexicans demand big ransoms, Peruvians and Brazilians like quick and easy grabs, Filipinos and Venezuelans prefer grabbing kids for cheap bucks, Colombians and Chechens go for convoluted, treacherous negotiations, Yemens and Tajiks treat you like visiting royalty but they are demanding political concessions not your wallet. There is an entire business category run by ex-spooks and ex-military intelligence folks that do nothing but return hostages, and most Americans, still putting their picture on a milk cartons, will get them back safely.

Give the Chechens a gold star for creativity during the war, commandeering buses, airplanes or even ferryboats. Now they snag just about anyone who has a logo on his hat. In the Philippines about 200 people are kidnapped each year. Around 10 percent of them are found dead even after the ransom has been paid.

Latin America is the most dangerous place in the world for kidnappings. More than 6000 people are kidnapped in Latin America every year. Colombia accounts for 4000 of those. Just under half of those kidnappings were carried out by FARC and ELN. The kidnapping business is estimated to be a $200 million a year, tax free business in Colombia. Brazil accounts for 800 kidnappings a year with 104 in Rio alone. In Mexico, there are as many as 2000 kidnappings a year where the average ransom is around $5000 for regular folks, but in the multi-million dollar range for bankers and businessmen. About 100 people are grabbed in Guatemala—mostly children of wealthy families and foreign workers. Ecuador and Venezuela each report around 200 kidnappings a year, and Peru estimates 100 hostages taken annually. In Honduras, primarily around the city of San Pedro Sula former Salvadoran guerillas have formed 10 gangs that kidnap about 120 people a year.

Keep in mind that all these statistics don't represent unreported snatches. Colombian groups are considered to be a major exporter of kidnapping to surrounding countries. Their twist is killing the families if they don't get the ransom. If kidnapping slows down they could always work for a credit card collection agency.

Although the media reports the big cases, most victims are ranchers and small businessmen. Foreign executives who work in the oil and energy industries are tops on most kidnappers' wish lists but aren't numerically high because of the security provided. The new trend is to snatch regular folks and then force their relatives to use their cash card to pay the ransom.

These days, Chubb, Fireman's Fund, AIG and Lloyds of London will write policies designed to make sure you come back alive if you get abducted. The premiums run from US$2500 to $100,000 a year, depending on where you plan to go and how long you plan to stay. Lloyds of London has experienced a 50 percent jump in policies written over the last five years, and more insurance companies are looking into offering the coverage. What do you get for your money? Actually quite a bit. Insurers will pay the ransom payment, medical treatment, interpreters and even your salary while you are involuntarily detained. The services of a security company to help spring you, (sorry no Rambo for Rent here) is included in the coverage.

Chubb has the best deal in town; annual payments total about US$1000 for every $10 million of ransom payments released. If you are deemed to be "high profile" or the target of previous kidnapping attempts, the premium skyrockets to US$25,000 a year. Kidnapping and ransom insurance for dangerous countries like Colombia cost around $20,000 a year for a million dollar policy, but expect to pay $60,000–$100,000 for a decent sized policy. Coverage is about half that for Brazil. In addition to insurance, armored cars and armed bodyguards are big in Latin America. Expect to pay between $60,000–$150,000 for an armor plated Suburban or Lincoln. Armed bodyguards should run you about $90–$250 a day depending on the country you're in. One alarming development is the increase in kidnapping of small children of wealthy victims. The only positive note is that the ransom for kidnapped children is a cheap $2000–$5000 with usually same day turnaround to avoid expensive diaper bills.

The World's Most Dangerous Places for White-Collar Expats

These 10 countries are the locations for 90 percent of all kidnappings

Colombia	Italy
India	Mexico
Pakistan	Peru
Philippines	Spain
Brazil	Venezuela

Expats who live in foreign countries are at most risk, while the casual tourist or in-and-out business visitor are almost risk free. Travelers who journey to remote regions in drug areas face a higher risk.

Kidnapping usually involves a group of men hustling you off the street into a car. They grabbed you because for some dumb reason you were profiled in the local paper as an "important executive and rising young star of Widget Exports." You also have a predictable routine for leaving work at the same time and walking the last few blocks from the train station. This makes it easy for the kidnappers to be ready with their car, engine running, gaffers tape at the ready.

You will most likely be blindfolded, gagged and bound. If you squirm or bite they'll thump you a few times to settle you down. Your first destination is a house or country hideout where you are kept in a room with no windows. To prove their point, they may photograph you with a Polaroid or record your voice on a cheap hand-held recorder. They may interrogate you to find out just how much you're worth. Then you will sit and wait, and wait and wait. If they don't get their initial demands, they may cause you pain or remove body parts (little fingers are popular) to get their point across. What will eventually happen? It depends.

According to Control Risks Group of London, about 40 percent of all hostages are released safely after the ransom is paid. Not very good odds. Having an insurance policy will make your chances of generating the necessary number of bucks a lot easier. But you won't have a choice should someone try to storm the joint in a rescue effort. About 34 percent of hostages are rescued from their captives before the ransom is paid. Being saved is perhaps a hostage's greatest threat. Let's say your right wing, NRA supporting, big game hunter boss (who voted for Ross Perot) says "Get my boy outta there now!" He sends in a highly trained team of hand picked ex-SEALS, kicked into action by a cigar smoking buzz cut. Oops, he just screwed up.

Approximately 79 percent of all hostages are killed during rescue attempts, according to Kroll Associates. Montesino's annihilation of the guerillas at the Japanese embassy without major casualties was extremely unusual.

So what if your wife won't return the kidnapper's calls and your boss figures he has really no need for you because the temp is generating twice the business you did. Nearly 11 percent of kidnapping victims are released without payment, either through negotiation or the abductors' realization that he or she will not be paid.

In Colombia a mere 3 percent of kidnappers are convicted compared to 95 percent in the U.S.

KIDNAPPING

How to Survive a Kidnapping

- Force yourself to be calm and compliant; there is little you can do by reacting violently.

- Do whatever your captors tell you to do without argument.

- Communicate with your captors to make them understand that you want to stay alive.

- Take control of your mental and physical state. Develop a routine that will include mental and physical exercise.

- If you think you can escape, do so, but stop if you are under threat of death or being shot.

- If you are being rescued by armed troops or police, stay flat on the ground. Make it difficult for your captors to drag you away, but do not resist. The greatest risk of death is during a rescue attempt.

Want to know how to avoid being kidnapped? Stay away form suspect places, vary your routine, keep a low profile, stay out of the local papers, avoid society bashes, live low key, use a driver/bodyguard and stay on top of the local threat assesment.

The most dangerous phases of a hijacking or hostage situation are the beginning and, if there is a rescue attempt, the end. At the outset, the terrorists typically are tense and high-strung and may behave irrationally. It is extremely important that you remain calm and alert and manage your own behavior.

Hostage Etiquette/Survival

- Avoid resistance and sudden or threatening movements. Do not struggle or try to escape, unless you are certain of being successful.

- Make a concerted effort to relax. Breathe deeply and prepare yourself mentally, physically and emotionally for the possibility of a long ordeal.

- Try to remain inconspicuous; avoid direct eye contact and the appearance of observing your captors' actions.

- Avoid alcoholic beverages. Consume little food and drink.

- Consciously put yourself in a mode of passive cooperation. Talk normally. Do not complain, avoid belligerency, and comply with all orders and instructions.

- If questioned, keep your answers short. Don't volunteer information or make unnecessary overtures.

- Don't try to be a hero, endangering yourself and others.

- Maintain your sense of personal dignity, and gradually increase your requests for personal comforts. Make these requests in a reasonable low-key manner.

- If you are involved in a lengthy, drawn-out situation, try to establish a rapport with your captors, avoiding political discussions or other confrontational subjects.

- Eat what they give you, even if it does not look or taste appetizing. A loss of appetite and weight is normal.

> • **Think positively; avoid a sense of despair. Rely on your inner resources. Remember that you are a valuable commodity to your captors. It is important to them to keep you alive and well.**

Kidnap, Rescue and Extortion Insurance

Who do you call when someone is kidnapped? Don't call Chuck Norris, Steven Seagal or Jackie Chan. You'll probably end up dead. Don't even call the police, they will jack up the ransom demand and be in cahoots with the kidnappers. You should call your insurance company followed by the embassy, and a professional hostage negotiator. *DP* advises that anyone in a hostage situation contact a professional in their home country before they contact the local police. Better yet, educate yourself about kidnapping before you find out the hard way.

A typical KRE policy with $1 million limit covers a family of 11 people. In Latin America, business is intertwined with extended family from grandparents down to grandchildren. An annual policy would cost between $7000 in Brazil up to a maximum of $26,000 in Colombia. When you cover a business family, you will always schedule each person. Corporations usually buy blanket policies that cover all employees.

In most countries except Mexico and Colombia unless you work for a large oil company, a $10 million policy for a Fortune 100 company will cost about $350,000 a year. Insurers like Seitlin also can write one shot, one month $1 million KRE policies for travelers and businesspeople for between $2500–$3000. Is it necessary? Well Seitlin believes you'd be crazy to do business south of Miami without $5–$10 million in KRE coverage. In Colombia a ransom less than a million is considered a joke.

Who you gonna call

Dying to know which security groups are called by insurance companies when you get kidnapped? Here is DP's insider list. If you can correctly guess which ex-affiliations these groups hold (Army, Air Force, CIA, Mossad, SAS etc.) we'll send you a free Mr. DP shirt.

Chubb uses the Ackerman Group

AIG uses Kroll Associates

Cassidy Davis Hiscox Consortium (Lloyds) uses Control Risks Group

Genesis (Lloyds) uses The Ackerman Group).

Cigna uses Pinkerton's

Some tips when you are invited to stay overnight.

• Try to avoid countries notorious for kidnapping: Colombia, Mexico, Chechnya, Yemen are just some. Americans doing business for Fortune 100 oil and mining companies in Colombia are at highest risk; low key backpackers and travelers are usually at low risk.

• Strange as it sounds, the odds of extracting you are better in areas where kidnapping is done in conjunction with the police. Brazil and Mexico are just two countries where kidnapping is a business conducted in conjunction with the local police. Areas where kidnapping is intertwined with Maoist or Marxist ideology are much harder.

- If someone you know is kidnapped, do not contact the police and do not talk to the press. Contact your embassy, the insurance company and/or a security consultancy to take the next steps. If you have a KRE policy, someone will be dispatched to act as a counselor within hours.

- Tape record or write down any messages and do not commit to anything until the counselor or security help arrives.

- Most security counselors will be ex-CIA, Mossad or other intelligence service pensioners. The British firms pull from their own pool of ex-SAS, Scotland Yard and MI-5 folks.

- Your security counselor will not make any decisions but he will facilitate the process and act as a coach, a mediator and a go between. They will usually setup a committee that analyze input and demands and then make decisions. Usually the decisions are: Pay the money, stall, or negotiate the ransom downwards. Not the best of jobs for amateurs.

- The fatality rate on security-consultant handled kidnappings is a reassuring 2 percent compared to 9 percent for homemade efforts. Part of the skew is because some kidnap deaths can occur at the attack—the victims may die of illness, heart attack, or they can be killed during rescue attempts.

Seitlin & Company

2001 N.W. 107 Avenue, Suite 200
Miami, Florida 33172
☎ *(305) 591-0090, FAX: (305) 593-6993*
e-mail: kandrguy@aol.com
Seitlin is the largest insurance broker in Florida that also does a ripping business in kidnap/ransom insurance. Luckily he only has to pay out about once or twice a year. Their clients include mostly wealthy Latin American families, corporations that do business south of the border and employees of multinational corporations. He can provide policies from all the major insurance brokers

Chubb Insurance of Canada

http://masc-web.com/chubb/english/
epd/kidnap.htm

Chubb offers Kidnap/Ransom/Extortion (KRE) coverage for busy executives with a healthy level of fear. Extortion can also cover computer hackers, contamination or even a computer virus.

Lloyds of London

1 Portsoken Street
London England, E1 8DF
☎ *(071) 480-4000, FAX: (071) 480-4170*
http://www.cyberapp.com/kidnap.html

Black Fox International, Inc.

P. O. Box 1187
205 Garvin Boulevard
Sharon Hill, Pennsylvania 19079
☎ *(800) 877-2445, (610) 461-6690,*
FAX: (610) 586-5467
e-mail: jc@black-fox.com e-mail
http://black-fox.com/kidnap.htm

Security Resources

Security is big business these days. Americans spend about 90 billion on security every year. We only spend $40 billion on public police. In California there are four times as many private police as there are government police. In countries like Russia and South Africa people don't even bother calling for the police. Areas affected by kidnapping also have a number of local firms that provide security and protection. Inquire at your local embassy or with other multinational companies.

Pinkerton Risk Assessment Services

1600 Wilson Boulevard, Suite 901
Arlington, Virginia 22209
☎ *(703) 525-6111, FAX: (703) 525-2454*

www.pinkertons.com
fjohns@pinkertons.com
Once on the trail of bank robbers in the Wild West, Pinkerton has gone global and high-tech. Today, you can get risk

assessments of over 200 countries online or in person. Pinkerton offers access to a database of more than 55,000 terrorist actions and daily updated reports on security threats. For the nonactive, you can order printed publications that range from daily risk assessment briefings to a monthly newsletter. Their services are not cheap, but how much is your life worth? Annual subscriptions to the on-line service start at about US$7000, and you can order various risk and advisory reports that run from US$200–$700 each. Pinkerton gets down and dirty with its counterterrorism programs, hostage negotiators, crisis management and travel security seminars.

The service is designed for companies who send their employees overseas or need to know what is going on in the terrorist world. Some reports are mildly macabre, with their annual businesslike graphs charting maimings, killings, assaults and assassinations. Others are truly enlightening. In any case, Pinkerton does an excellent job of bringing together the world's most unpleasant information and providing it to you in concise, intelligent packages.

Unlimited on-line access to their database on 230 countries will run you US$6000 a year. You will find the information spotty, with a preponderance of information on South and Central America. Many of the write-ups on everything from Kurds to the Islamic Jihad are written by young college students with little in-country experience. On the other hand, there are many holes that are filled by CIA country profiles (available at any library for free).

If you want to save a few bucks, for US$4000 a year (US$5000 overseas), you can get a full subscription of daily, weekly, quarterly and annual risk assessments, as well as analysts' commentaries, a world status map and a fax service that keeps you abreast of fast breaking events.

Cheapskates can opt for the US$2250 standard package, which eliminates the daily reports sent via fax, but provides you most of the other elements. If you want to order à la carte, expect services that range from a US$30 personalized trip package, to US$250 printouts of existing risk and travel advisories, to accessing the company's Country Data bank for US$1000 per country.

Control Risks Group, London

8200 Greensboro Drive, Suite 1010
McLean, Virginia 22102
☎ *(703) 893-0083, FAX: (703) 893-8611*
83 Victoria Street
London, England SW1H-OHW
☎ *[44] (171) 222-1552*

This international management consulting company specializes in political, business and security risk analysis and assessments, due diligence and fraud investigations, preventative security and asset protection, crisis management planning and training, crisis response and unique problem solving. With extensive experience in kidnapping, extortion and illegal detention resolution, they have handled more than 700 cases in 79 countries. Control Risks has 14 offices around the world including Washington, D.C., London, New York, Bogota, Mexico City, Bonn, Amsterdam, Manila, Melbourne, Moscow, Paris, Singapore, Sydney and Tokyo. Their international, political and security risk analysis research department is the largest of its kind in the private sector and has provided hundreds of companies with customized analyses of the political and security risks they may face doing business around the globe. An on-line Travel Security Guide addresses security issues in more than 100 countries.

Emergency Numbers for CRG:

LONDON: ☎ *(071) 222 1552 or (071)*
481 1851 (Nightline)
UNITED STATES: ☎ *(703) 893 0083*
AUSTRALIA: ☎ *(613) 416 1533*

Kroll Associates

900 Third Avenue, 7th Floor,
New York, New York 10022
800) 824-7502

☎ *(212) 833-3206, FAX: (212) 750-8112*
www.krollassociates.com

A security/investigative firm founded in 1972 by Jules Kroll and owned by Equifax (the credit info folks). In addition to gumshoeing on an international and corporate level, Kroll also offers a very useful service for business travelers. You can use your credit card to order a Travel Watch report for $9.95 each. They also provide customer security services for business. Kroll has information over 300 cities worldwide that covers transportation to and from the city, emergency telephone numbers as well as health and safety concerns. They also have special reports on countries an regions. There are also new security tips on the Internet and computers, the air-

lines and in depth country reports available

Ackerman Group

166 Kennedy Causeway, Suite 700
Miami Beach, Florida 33141
☎ *(305) 865-0072*
Mike Ackerman specializes in crisis resolution or hostage return through providing the financial and security resources required to resolve hostage situations safely.

TroubleShooters

USA: ☎ *(352) 343-2406, FAX: (352) 343-3864, Canada:* ☎ *(403) 885-5273*
Ex-US military folks who freelance for hostage situations and can provide aviation services for overseas extractions. They can provide assistance for executive protection, hostage retrieval and missing person searches.

Gizmos, Goons & Godsends

These are just a smattering of listings for folks who want to look further into this unfortunate growth business. Security firms can often prevent the problem from occurring. It is considered dumb to hire anyone to use force or violence to spring kidnap victims.

Target Communications Systems Gmbh

P.O. Box 730301, D-60505
Frankfurt, Germany
☎ *(069) 673551, FAX: 671030*
Offers a 100-page catalog of electronic security devices that one could misconstrue as being business eavesdropping equipment to give you a leg up on that next bid. Learn how to read envelopes without opening them, use pen sized transmitters and leave behind a sugar cube sized transmitter. Also info on tax havens, passports, and how to protect yourself from businessmen like yourself.

DAW

12400 Blue Ridge Boulevard
Grandview, Missouri 64030
☎ *(816) 765-2539*
Forget the old Tommy gun in the violin case. Be safe and persuasive with your very own Dignitary Protection Briefcase. It is a Halliburton equipped with a 32 round Mac11 machine gun complete with laser sight so you don't look stupid holding the briefcase up to your shoul-

der to scare off attackers. Around $2500 (silenced version is extra).

Inter American Security Products, IN.c

13605 SOuth Dixie Highway Suite 136-1
Miami, Florida 33176
☎ *(305) 256-0370, FAX: (305) 256-9587*
interarm@thenet.net
Concealable bullet proof vests starting at only $100. Also heavy duty flak jackets for around $500. Also see listings under "Save Yourself."

Executive Protection Associates

316 California Avenue
Reno, Nevada 8909
☎ *(408) 556-0430, (408) 244-4750*
epai-info@iapps.org
or
Kirchgasse 9
D-71154 Nefringen, Germany
☎ *[49] (0732) 9852 21,*
FAX: [49] (7032) 9852 22
Feeling paranoid? Why not hire EPA to find out who's bugging your phone, tailing your limo or planning your abduction.

Professional Bodyguard Association

P.O. Box 11493
London, N3 2TH England

xsas@msn.com

The e-mail address pretty much says it all. This group will also provide training for groups of up to four protectors in training. There is also a 800-page Bodyguard Training Manual available for study at home for 45 pounds (payable in Sterling only via bank draft). They are looking to train more Yanks so they have offered price reduction to offset the air fare costs. For more info, send five one-dollar bills (for postage), and they will send you a prospectus.

Falcon Global

1126 Washington Boulevard, Suite D
Williamsport, Pennsylvania 17701
☎ *(717) 321-6220, FAX: (717) 321-6222*

Falcon Global has elevated the goon business to a professionally managed level. They can provide security during labor disputes without provoking reruns of Matawa.

Yemen: A Matter of Honor

There are, would you believe, more guns per capita in Yemen than in any other country in the world. Yemen is one of the poorest countries in the world—with an average per capita earning of US $600 a year, but this does not hinder most of the male population from toting the latest version in automatic fire power. The other favorite, after guns, is *qat*—a leaf that when chewed in large quantities induces a mildly narcotic trance.

Wander anywhere in Yemen after lunch, government buildings (well, not there, they'll all have gone home), local markets or private houses and you'll find most of the male population chewing the proverbial cud, so to speak, with eyes in various states of glaziness. The whole male population goes into a collective trance. And if you want to join in about $4 will be enough to procure you enough *qat* for an afternoon's chewing.

I decide to visit the north, where Yemen shares a common border with neighboring Saudi Arabia, to the general discontent of both countries. Heading from the ancient capital, Sana'a, I take a taxi for the four hour ride to Sa'da, the provincial capital of the north, an area where tourists are more or less nonexistent.

A few kilometers outside Sa'da, a ten minute journey by car along the single asphalt road, I arrive at the *suq al silah*—the weapons market. It is in these markets that most of the tribal population buy the thousands of weapons sold each year in Yemen. It's an arms dealer's paradise; anything can be sold and everything *is* sold. I am offered an AK-47 for US$300, which I politely decline, (convinced I'm being ripped off). But from the wooden stalls, the dealers offer almost anything: alongside the AK's are American made M-16's, G-3's, (an expensive US $1000), Belgium FN's, Rocket Propelled Grenades, (RPG-7's—a mere US $500), warheads, night vision binoculars, fragmentation grenades, flares, pistols—Lugers, Walther PPK's, 9mm Brownings...take your pick, (starting price around US $15), military webbing...even the odd tank is up for grabs! It's everything you'll ever need to start a small war or equip your own private army; and in Yemen, the hundreds of different tribes are little less than private armies.

I watch as wild looking tribesmen stream into the suq to test weapons, although—God forbid—there is nothing as formal as a firing range. Guns are simply taken a small distance from the suq where, hopefully, nobody will be foolish enough to wander around. They're fired before being brought back for half an hour's bargaining over numerous cups of sweet tea. There is a refreshing informality to the scene. There is none of the pedantic questions of the modern western world involved in these happy transactions. No license necessary, no boring ID checks, none of the usual boring questions inquiring if you are of sound mind or are you barking mad to want a 12mm heavy machine gun. Are you a responsible adult? No, have you got a police record? No problem. (Visa cards, though, like American Express are not accepted).

Photographs, however, mine in particular, seem to present something of a problem. They are, I am abruptly told by a passing tribesman, *mamnua*—illegal. For a place where the boys in blue are just a little thin on the ground, (well, non-existent actually), the idea of something being illegal is intriguing. However, I am feeling distinctly confident about my right to do as I please. In my pocket, I have a permit from the local governor which states that I can go anywhere I like. With a triumphant, probably not very nice, grin, I tell the tribesman that if he has any problems he can complain to the governor. His reply wipes the smile off my face: "The governor," he says, "has no authority here...this is tribal territory." I look to my guide, Hamid, who is from the governor's office, for moral support. He is squirming with embarrassment, and does not contradict the tribesman. This may have something to do with the fact that Hamid is not carrying an AK-47. But for once I am not alone, and some tribesmen stick up for me, saying that photos are no problem. An argument ensues, and I take advantage of it to slink off in the search for fresh photos hoping that no one will notice that the subject of the argument has disappeared.

You might be wondering if there's a down side to so many weapons floating around: indeed there is, and it comes in the form of blood feuds, which Yemenis seem to covet as if they're going out of style. If you should accidentally kill a Yemeni, the best thing you can do is make a mad dash for the airport. Dialing the local equivalent of 911 will not do a lot of good—even if you can find a telephone. Otherwise, if you're lucky, you'll end up paying blood money to the family—how about $10,000 for the price of a human life? Although it does depend on whom you kill. If you're not so lucky you'll find the deceased's many brothers, uncles, cousins etc., paying a not-so-social call on you.

To gain a better insight into the world of blood feuds I dropped in on a prearranged *qat* chewing session with a local tribal sheikh, (family head). Removing my shoes, I join the other *qat* chewers in a long well-furnished room with cushions set around the edge. Set in each place is the general paraphernalia for *qat* chewing: lots of bottles of Coca-Cola and water pipes. Above each cushion there is a peg where chewers hang, not their coats, but their Kalashnikovs. It is only when I ask my host, Abdullah, about blood feuds that I learn that only a few months earlier his own brother was killed by a member of another tribe. He narrates the events that led to his brother's death with the detached dispassion of someone who has put his grief behind him.

I ask if he knows the identity of the killer. He does indeed, which bodes bad news for someone. "The man who killed my brother has left the area and headed south," he says—which sounds to me like acute common sense. So, what will happen next? He replies calmly and matter of factly: "When this man returns or whenever he is found, whatever is sooner, I will kill him," as if it is the most natural thing in the world—which it is—to personally avenge a brother. I ask, in a typically western manner, about the police. Might he not be arrested? He draws on his large and elegant water pipe before smiling gently, as if amused at the thought of the police doing anything, and says: "The police will do nothing; they will say it is a matter of honor, a tribal affair." And doubtless it will be.

—**Roddy Scott**

Land Mines

Boom Times

If there was ever a reason to pay attention in history class, land mines would be it. Why? Because travelers to dangerous places need to know more than the current situation; they must also know why and where wars were fought in the past. There may be peace in Mozambique, Eritrea, China, Jordan and the Ukraine, but there are plenty of souvenirs from past wars hiding in the ground. Someone is killed or injured by a land mine every 15 to 20 minutes.

The world has between 105 and 110 million land mines buried in 64 countries, according to the United Nations. Nobody actually knows exactly how many there are since the people who placed them never bothered to remember their exact location. Consequently, the people who find them remember for the rest of their lives—if they survive the blast.

Even though land mines maim and kill between 20,000 and 24,000 men, women and children every year, many governments claim they are not a threat to travelers. When the temples of Angkor Wat were mined and booby-trapped, the government was careful to put up little red signs. Even agencies like Greenpeace and the CDC contend the death toll is more like 9600. Mine clearance groups estimate that the number is 15,000, with about 80 percent being civilians and a third of those being young children. (Some anti-mine groups estimate 37,000 are killed every year.) The truth is there are few little red signs in the boonies and even fewer keeping count of the deaths and maimings. Death by land mine is nasty and lonely. Most victims bleed to death in remote places or are maimed for life. Being injured by a land mine is one of the most traumatic experiences, both mentally and physically, a human can live through.

Eighty-five percent of current mine-related casualties are in Afghanistan, Angola and Cambodia—all sites of past and present dirty little wars where land mines are the perfect weapon.

With so many mines, it only takes one false step to be killed or maimed for life. When *DP* was in Cambodia, we came across a young child dying from a land mine blast. He was walking behind a cow who stepped on the mine, but the shrapnel degutted the child like a fish. The cow's death at least had a benefit. When it comes to mines, all you get is angry, maimed or dead. There are movements afoot to ban land mines worldwide, but for now business is booming.

More Than You Ever Want to Know About Mines

The next time someone tells you that it is those crazy Russians and liberation groups that sprinkle the world's mines, you might want to check the receipts of the countries that are buying the land mines. According to *Janes Intelligence Review*, Iran, Israel, Cambodia, Thailand, Chile, El Salvador, Malaysia and Saudi Arabia top the list. Tsk, tsk, you say. Well, those folks have good reasons to buy those land mines: Iran has a nasty border with Iraq, Israel gets grief from Southern Lebanon, Cambodia has the Khmer Rouge to contend with, Thailand has drug runners, Chile has Paraguay, El Salvador has jungle insurgents, and Malaysia still has vivid memories of a nasty war with Indonesia back in the early '60s. Saudi Arabia figures land mines are cheaper than picket fences to mark its southern boundaries. We are sure there must have been good reasons for placing 400 million land mines after World War II. The scary problem is there are still between 65 and 110 million of those mines sitting under the ground. The real bad guys may be the people who cash in from making the grizzly leg poppers.

Who Makes 'em	
Country of Origin	**Places Used**
Belgium	Angola, Iraq (Kurdistan), Kuwait, Mozambique, Namibia, Somalia
Brazil	Nicaragua
Bulgaria	Cambodia
Canada	Iraq
Chile	Iraq (Kurdistan)
China	Afghanistan, Angola, Cambodia, Mozambique, Namibia, Somalia
Czech (ex)	Afghanistan, Angola, Cambodia, Mozambique, Namibia, Nicaragua, Somalia
Egypt	Afghanistan, Nicaragua, Iraq

Who Makes 'em	
Country of Origin	**Places Used**
France	*Iraq (Kurdistan), Iraq (Kuwait), Mozambique, Somalia*
Germany (former East)	*Angola, Cambodia, Mozambique Namibia, Somalia*
Hungary	*Cambodia*
Italy	*Angola, Iraq (Kurdistan), Iraq(Kuwait)*
Pakistan	*Somalia*
Romania	*Iraq (Kurdistan)*
Russia	*Afghanistan, Angola, Cambodia, Iraq (Kurdistan), Iraq (Kuwait), Mozambique, Namibia, Nicaragua, Somalia, Vietnam*
Singapore	*Iraq (Kuwait)*
South Africa	*Angola, Mozambique, Somalia*
Spain	*Iraq (Kuwait)*
United Kingdom	*Afghanistan, Mozambique, Somalia*
United States	*Angola, Cambodia, Iraq (Kurdistan), Mozambique, Nicaragua, Somalia*
Vietnam	*Cambodia*
Yugoslavia (ex)	*Afghanistan, Cambodia, Mozambique, Namibia, Zimbabwe*

Source: Janes Intelligence Review

Land mines are cheap and can be laid in relative safety, cripple economies, stall advances and create fear. The most industrious and creative producers of land mines are not the Cold War vassal states but the high tech Western countries who make such a big stink about all those little kids who get blown to bits. There are 100 different companies in 55 countries that make land mines. Of the 55 countries who design and manufacture antipersonnel mines (about 75 percent of all land mines), 36 of the countries allow them to be exported. Keep in mind that many mines are bought through shell companies who import them into "nice" countries and then export them to "nasty" countries. Even Switzerland makes and sells five models, while Iran, Cuba and Myanmar are able only to make one model of land mine.

The U.S. has taken steps to remove mines from its base in Guantanamo Bay in Cuba, but will leave them in the ground in Korea. They will destroy about $10 million worth of $2 antipersonnel mines and will use instead smart mines that destroy themselves or become inert when their batteries die. Here's a list of where you can shop for the 362 different models of land mines:

Stumps 'R Us: Who designs 'em	
Country	**# of Models Sold**
United States	37
Italy	36
Russia	31

Stumps 'R Us: Who designs 'em	
Country	# of Models Sold
Sweden	21
China	21
Germany	18
Vietnam	18
France	14
Bosnia Herzegovina	16
Austria	16

Source: Janes Intelligence Review

How Are They Used?

Land mines are supposed to be laid according to pre-agreed patterns. The area should be marked and maps kept to facilitate cleanup. Land mines are laid about six feet apart. One such NATO pattern is an A pattern with one antitank mine surrounded by three antipersonnel mines: one above and one on each side like a triangle with the antitank in the middle.

During hostilities, these mine fields are carefully marked with skull and cross-bones "Beware of mine" signs, backed up with accurate maps showing placement and layout. Once hostilities cease, the winning side then quickly and efficiently removes every single land mine, allowing people to live their lives free from fear. In your dreams!

That is wishful thinking, since the most effective way to sow land mines is to drop millions of small plastic mines by shell or from aircraft. Small bomblets, 247 to a pod, are dropped as part of cluster bombs. Most rebel groups will put mines in potholes, in detours, along walking paths and in fields; they'll even booby-trap intriguing items that villagers, soldiers or children will pick up. Guerillas don't follow patterns. Nobody knows how many mortar rounds, artillery shells and discarded ordnance will be discovered by curious children or diligent farmers. No one bothers to keep notes of where mines are planted as booby traps or nightly security perimeters.

The problem of land mines has become the largest single threat to the health of rural populations in countries that once suffered warfare. Mines can be part of a major defensive region, as in some parts of China, the Middle East and Europe. Mines are also used in combat operations to provide security and early warning or create surprises. Bosnia, Iraq and Kuwait are examples of countries that were heavily mined but stand a chance of being cleaned up. Other countries have actually become dumping grounds for millions of cheap mines laid down to terrorize the population. Most of the African countries, Afghanistan and Cambodia are full of land mine junkyards.

How Do They Work?

Most people picture the movie cliché of a careless GI hearing a soft click and then sweating buckets, while his buddy slides his knife under his boot to keep the detonator depressed. Not quite. Yes, mines are essentially dumb explosive devices that are detonated by pressure, but weapon specialists have learned a few tricks since those WWII movies.

First of all, a mine contains extremely explosive material that creates a wall of air and debris that expands outward at almost 7000 meters per second. Some mines add metal projectiles like ball bearings, sharp flechettes or even nails that puncture soft flesh and shred bone into a fine spray. The shock waves are so strong that many victims find their feet still in their boots and their bones turned into projectiles that kill other people.

If you don't die of blood loss, shock or as a result of being turned into Swiss cheese, infection is your worst enemy. The explosion will imbed bits of clothing, grass, mud, dirt and your trusty guide into the shredded mass of meat that used to be your legs. You will need to apply a tourniquet and get to a hospital (yeah, sure, there's probably one around the next sand dune) ASAP. Once you're under medical care, the mashed bits will be quickly amputated, you'll be punched with an IV and given enough morphine to kill a junkie.

Liquid Lunch in a Crunch

Many times victims of gunshot wounds, mine blasts and injuries caused by blood loss don't have to die. In order to create an IV solution to provide minimum nutrition and increase blood pressure, it is important to know how to administer an IV injection. If you do not have a sterile IV solution, one can be made by taking one liter of sterile freshwater (filtered, then boiled for five minutes and cooled while covered). Add 25 grams of glucose and 4.5 grams of table salt. In emergency cases, the juice from a green coconut can be used with just the salt added.

Other mines have cute names like Bouncing Betty, because they spring up and explode at eye level, releasing a lethal explosion of ball bearings, killing everything within 25 meters and wounding everyone else within 200 meters. Road mines are so large and powerful that there is a crater and little else left over. Enough scary stuff, let's get specific. Here are the basic types of land mines used today:

Scatter Mines

The Soviet-made PFM-1 butterfly-type mine delivers specialized deadly services. These small mines are sprinkled all over Afghanistan by Russians to injure, but not kill *mujahedin*. The idea is that a wounded person slows down two healthy people. That the Ruskies don't have the balls to go up into the mountains to plant them is another major attraction. These mines are dropped from helicopters and burrow into the ground using tiny wings. They explode when twisted or pressed firmly. The mines were a last-ditch effort by the Russians in Afghanistan, but now they mainly injure children since adults know not to pick them up. These mines have not found wide usage but are a disturbing use of lethal force. They do not always explode when first handled and can actually be kicked, dropped and twisted before they explode, leading some people to believe that the Russians designed them to kill curious children. There also are "smart" scatter mines that can arm themselves, detonate without direct pressure and self-detonate after a specified period. These smart mines are delivered by cannon, airplane or rocket.

DP's visit to Afghanistan proved that small scatter mines are still doing their deadly work, having seen many maimed children and young men missing their feet.

Antipersonnel, Small

Foot soldiers can't carry big heavy mines, so they make a lot of little plastic blast mines that can be sprinkled in villages, latrines and rice paddies. These mines are about the size of an oversized hockey puck and have a pressure-sensitive plate that the victim steps on. These mines are usually not buried but placed under brush, streams, wet potholes, rice paddies and mud. The mine takes very little pressure to set it off, and the victim will usually lose a foot and/or a leg up to the knee. These mines are not designed to kill but to create serious, incapacitating injury which effects the morale of the other side. No one feels gung ho when they see the results of a mine. Top sellers in this category are the Chinese Type 72, Italian TS-50 and US M14. These mines are very difficult to find, since many of them use plastic casings and cannot be readily picked up by normal metal detectors.

Antipersonnel, Large

These killer-blast mines usually pack about 200 grams of explosive (compared to 40 grams in the small category). The best-selling Soviet PMN likes to deliver leg-shattering wounds caused by small mines with higher explosive content. They are used to maim groups of soldiers, with severe wounds to groin and buttocks and loss of both legs common. These and their smaller cousins are the most popular mines in existence. They cost about US$3 each and can be found killing people in most Third World war zones. There are also large versions of these pressure mines that can kill entire platoons. These mines are typically buried just under the surface and can be easily found if they have metal parts.

Fragmentation Mines

Mines like the US M18A1 "Claymore" are designed to spray large areas with thousands of ball bearings. Other frag mines like the Russian POMZ-2 explode into thousands of sharp metal pieces. These mines are set up as booby traps (usually with trip wires) and are used to protect camp perimeters or ambush columns. There is a detonator pin that is attached to a wire. The mines are placed above ground, on trees, across narrow paths, inside buildings, along roads, or anywhere a group of soldiers would collect. One soldier trips over the wire, and instantly he and his buddies are killed. If the mines are never tripped, they sit waiting for the next victim.

There is also the Bouncing Betty type of fragmentation mines called "bounding" mines. They are designed to be buried in the ground in open areas, and when one of the whiskerlike sensors is triggered, the mine will project upwards and explode ball bearings or shrapnel in a lethal 360-degree radius. The Italian-made Valmara-69 is the most famous example of this mine. The explosion occurs at a three- to five-foot height maximizing the "kill ratio" (a popular term in all military sales films). Some mines have over 1000 individual pieces of shrapnel, so the chances of surviving by ducking or turning sideways are slim to none.

These mines are designed to be lethal and are left behind to slow down advancing armies, decimate charges and create maximum casualties.

Road Mines

The mines that do the most damage to wartime soldiers and peacetime mine clearance workers are the big plate-sized and plank-size tank killers. These are mines laid down in active war zones to kill and disable vehicles, kill the occupants and destroy the road. The British L9 and the Italian VS-22 are popular mines used in the Gulf War and in other combat zones. Road mines are also used in Somalia, Southern Lebanon and other active zones. Since these mines are easy to detect and placed around major transportation corridors, they are usually the first ones to be cleared up (or to be run over). Mines are almost always laid at night and rarely under paved roads. They are laid on dirt roads and along the side of the road.

LAND MINES

Other Mines and Hidden Dangers

If you really are kinky about mines, you can pick up a Jane's directory or send for brochures. There are many booby traps that are not technically mines. There are also extraordinary amounts of unexploded ordnance in the ground that may not jump up and bite you, but can be found displayed in villager's homes and souvenir shops.

What are your chances of finding one of these millions of mines? It simply depends on how far off the beaten path you travel and the military history of your country of choice. Off-roading in Angola would not be a good idea. Playing hide and seek around Cambodia is also not a good idea.

Where Are the Mines?

Eighteen African countries have between 18 and 30 million mines each; Angola has the most, between 9 and 20 million uncleared mines, and even the "lightly mined" countryside of Mozambique (with about 2 million) has turned many small roads into death traps and caused large game to vanish. Somalia has 1 million mines; Sudan has between 1 and 2 million (and growing); Zimbabwe and Ethiopia have major uncleared minefields (about half a million each). Bosnia Herzegovina, Cambodia and Croatia are the most mined countries in the world, with an average of between 92 and 142 land mines per square mile. This can be misleading, since the mines in Egypt are sitting in the remote northern deserts and the mines in Angola are in small towns and fields. All of East Asia has 15 to 23 million land mines. The Middle East has 17 to 24 million land mines, mainly in Iraq, Iran, Kuwait and the Israeli border. Saddam Hussein went a little overboard during his brief occupation of Kuwait and turned the entire country into a minefield, most of which has been cleaned up at great expense. Europe is home to 7 million mines, mostly along the former Soviet border. During World War I, seven countries fired nearly 1.5 billion shells. Ninety-five percent of them were conventional explosives; the rest were chemical shells. It is estimated that 30 percent of the chemical shells landed without ever exploding and have been sitting around since 1918. Most of the shells were used in Belgium. The Ukraine is home to over a million mines. Russia has both new minefields and WWII fields that were never cleared. Bosnia-Herzegovina has many uncleared fields, and new mines were being laid at a rate of 60,000 a week. At last count, there were 152 mines per square mile in this torn-up land.

Rank	Country	# of mines	Avg per sq mile	Area found
	The Land Mine Top 20			
1.	**Egypt**	23,000,000	59	*North toward border with Israel*
2.	**Iran**	16,000,000	25	*Along border with Iraq*
3.	**Angola**	15,000,000	31	*Rural areas*
4.	**Afghanistan**	10,000,000	40	*Scattered by air, also around Kabul*
5.	**Cambodia**	10,000,000	142	*Rural areas*
6.	**China**	10,000,000	3	*Along border with Russia*
7.	**Iraq**	10,000,000	60	*Along border with Iran*
8.	**Bosnia-Herzegovina**	3,000,000	152	*Throughout country*
9.	**Croatia**	2,000,000	92	*Throughout country*
10.	**Mozambique**	2,000,000	7	*Rural areas*
11.	**Eritrea**	1,000,000	28	*Along border with Ethiopia, rural*

Rank	Country	# of mines	Avg per sq mile	Area found
	The Land Mine Top 20			
12.	Somalia	1,000,000	4	*Along border with Ethiopia*
13.	Sudan	1,000,000	4	*Southern areas*
14.	Ukraine	1,000,000	4	*Old battle fields*
15.	Ethiopia	500,000	1	*Along border with Eritrea, Somalia*
16.	Yugoslavia	500,000	13	*Throughout country*
17.	Jordan	207,000	5	*Along border with Israel*
18.	Chad	100,000+	6	*Along northern border with Libya*
19.	Rwanda	100,000+	5	*Primarily in north*
20.	Vietnam	100,000+	8	*Southern areas, DMZ*

Source: U.S. Department of Humanitarian Affairs

Up to a million uncleared mines are left in South America. There are mines in Colombia, Chile and most areas of Nicaragua, Guatemala and even Cuba. Some areas of the Falklands are permanently off-limits because the British could not spare the men to clear the minefields. There is a lot of splattered mutton every week in the Falklands.

Most countries in Southern Africa have large mined areas, as do the entire Horn of Africa, all areas of Middle East conflict and most border areas from the Cold War. Although there are no mines in North America, we did send a few overseas. If you thought the U.S. didn't do those types of things, think again. Remember that Uncle Sam used to empty out our bomb loads over Laos, leaving millions of cluster bombs for little Laotians to discover. More than 300,000 tons of bombs were dropped on northern Laos during the Vietnam War. No one has any idea how much unexploded ordnance still lies in the jungles of Northern Vietnam. The overly cautious should understand that, along with cigarette butts, ammo containers and mixed-race children, land mines are just the litter of war.

A Thousand and One...a Thousand and Two...BOOM! Places Where They Haven't Counted All the Land Mines	
North, Central and South America	
Mexico	*Reports of land mine injuries, number unknown*
Guatemala	*Under 100,000*
Cuba	*Reports of land mine injuries, number unknown*
Honduras	*Under 100,000, along border with Nicaragua*
El Salvador	*Under 100,000, throughout country*
Costa Rica	*Under 100,000*
Colombia	*In remote areas, under 100,000*
Ecuador	*Along border with Peru*
Peru	*Along border with Ecuador*
Falkland Islands	*Throughout region*

A Thousand and One...a Thousand and Two...BOOM!
Places Where They Haven't Counted All the Land Mines

Africa

Libya	*Less than 100,000*
Uganda	*Along border areas, less than 100,000*
Burundi	*Newly laid mines, less than 100,000*
Zimbabwe	*Throughout country, more than 100,000*
Congo (Zaire)	*Less than 100,000*
Namibia	*Less than 100,000*
Western Sahara	*Less than 100,000*
Mauritania	*Less than 100,000*
Senegal	*Less than 100,000*
Guinea Bissau	*Less than 100,000*
Liberia	*Throughout country*
Sierra Leone	*Throughout country*
Tunisia	*Less than 100,000*

Middle East

Oman	*Throughout country, along borders*
Turkey	*Eastern areas, along eastern borders*
Lebanon	*Southern Lebanon, mined daily*
Syria	*Along border areas*
Cyprus	*Along Turkish/Greek division*
Yemen	*Along border areas*

Europe

Germany	*In former Eastern Germany, along border areas*
Slovenia	*More than 100,000*
Greece	*Less than 100,000*
Czech Republic	*Less than 100,000*
Denmark	*Less than 100,000*
Latvia	*Less than 100,000*

Asia

Belarus	*Throughout country*
Armenia	*Areas of conflict*
Azerbaijan	*Throughout country*
Tajikistan	*Border areas*
Myanmar (Burma)	*Throughout country*
Mongolia	*Border areas, less than 100,000*
Laos	*Throughout country, unexploded ordnance*

How Do You Get Rid of Land Mines?

There are movements by the UN, military and civilian groups (about 300 groups in total) to ban the manufacture and use of land mines. The chances are good of convincing First World countries of a ban, but the facts are that the most heavily mined countries are a result of dirty wars, not major conflicts. The majority of land mines have been planted in the last 20 years. Currently, 36 nations build land mines and most countries use them. These countries produce about 10 to 20 million units a year. About 2 million new land mines are laid each year depending on what conflicts are raging. The U.S. budgeted $89 million for land mine warfare in 1996.

The first task a newly stabilized country faces is cleaning up land mines. Traditional land mines are cleared in a variety of ways. In large open areas, tracked vehicles with flailing chains can clear most mines. In less accessible or poorer areas, the old-fashioned metal detector is used. Some new Scheibel-type models can detect many plastic versions. Some countries use the old-fashioned method of probing at a shallow angle with knives. Sniffing dogs can be used, along with a raft of new high-tech methods employing radar, sonar, thermal neutron, microwave, and even satellites. For now, most mines are detected and dug up the old-fashioned way, by hand or the painful way; by foot. Wildly speculative estimates on the costs to remove the world's land mines come in at about $33 billion.

In Cambodia, an on again/off again adventure travel destination, estimates hover around US$12 million annually for 10 years to remove the 10 million land mines left from the war. There are a few groups like HALO working in Cambodia, but they still have to put up with being kidnapped and harassed by roque Khmer Rouge bandits. There are 60,000 victims of land mines in Cambodia today, with every 237th Cambodian an amputee. But it is not the pain and disfigurement that ultimately kills. The reality is that unlike handicap-friendly America, losing a limb in the Third World is a fast ticket to poverty, begging, sickness and death.

Land mines can be found in Angola, Afghanistan, Bosnia-Herzegovina, Cambodia, Ethiopia, Eritrea, the Falklands, Iraq, Iran, Laos, Mozambique, Somalia, Thailand, Kuwait and Vietnam. In addition to carefully planted land mines, there is a significant amount of unexploded ordinance in Europe, Southeast Asia and the South Pacific. Don't get smug because you think you know your mines and your history. One mine clearance expert told us they are digging up British Land mines in Mozambique because Qaddafi had his folks dig them up in Libya and sell them to rebels. For those who need to know, there is an excellent book by Eddie Banks titled *Anti-Personnel Mines, A Recognition Guide* ($120, 512 pages, ISBN!-85753-228-7) sold by Brassey's ☎ *(800) 775-2518, FAX (703) 661-1501.*

One Small Step...

If you can't dig them up and you can't stop them from planting them, what can you do to help? First, write your local and federal politicians to make them aware that the U.S. and its allies manufacture these insidious killers. If you have experience in explosives or mine clearance, read the "Dangerous Jobs" section to contact a number of mine clearance companies. If you would like to donate money or time to help the innocent victims of mines, contact EMERGENCY, via Bagutta 12, 20121 Milan Italy (☎ 39-2-7600-1104, or FAX 39-2-7600-3719),

There were 7 million land mines laid in Iraq and Kuwait before and during the Gulf War. Kuwait spent $800 million clearing out land mines after the Gulf War.

It costs between $500 and $2000 per mine to remove them. A few years ago, 80,000 - 100,000 mines were removed around the world at a cost of $100 million. To remove all the mines in the world would cost $58 billion. Unfortunately, 2 to 5 million mines are put in the ground every year.

A *DP* reader who spends much of his time in mined areas while working for the U.N. Rapid Response Unit has sent in these tips:

Wheel of Misfortune: How to Avoid Land Mines

1. Never take a trip on a mined road before 9 or 10 a.m. Most mines are laid at night to surprise regular convoys or patrols. Try to follow heavy trucks. Keep at least 200 yards behind but do not lot lose sight of the truck.

2. Never take point. (Let others start walking or driving before you.) Keep a distance of at least 60-100 feet to avoid shrapnel. If someone is wounded by a mine, apply a tourniquet immediately to the damaged limbs to prevent death by blood loss.

3. When possible, follow local vehicles or stay on fresh tracks. If a mine goes off, **DO NOT RUN.** Stay where you are, and walk backwards in your own tracks.

4. Always stay on the pavement. In heavily mined areas, **NEVER** leave the pavement (even to take a leak). If you must turn your vehicle around, do so on the pavement.

5. If you have a flak jacket or bullet-proof vest, sit on it when driving.

6. Know the mining strategy of the combatants. Do they place mines in potholes (as in northeastern Somalia) or on the off-road tracks made by vehicles avoiding potholes (as in Rwanda, Burundi and Zaire)?

7. If you think you may have strayed into a mined area, go back on your tracks. Mines are usually planted at a shallow depth with their detonators requiring downward pressure. As a last resort, mines can be probed with a long knife or rod at a very shallow angle and a very gentle touch. Do not attempt to remove the mine, but mark it for later removal or detonation.

8. Never touch unusual or suspicious objects. They may be booby-trapped.

9. Travel with all windows open. Preferably with doors off or in the back of pickup trucks. This will release some of the blast if you hit a land mine.

10. If you have reason to believe that there has been mine activity (new digging, unusual tire tracks and footprints), mark the area with a skull and crossbones and the local or English word "MINES." Notify local and/or foreign authorities.

Land Mine Activist Wins Nobel Prize

Jody Williams, a 47-year-old Vermont woman was awarded the Nobel Peace Prize for her six year effort to ban land mines. Williams leads the International Campaign to Ban Land Mines and has succeeded in getting more than half of the world's nations to ban land mines. At presstime the United States, China, India and Pakistan had not agreed to sign the treaty.

Military and Paramilitary Organizations

How to Travel Free, Meet Interesting People and Then Kill Them

Why does a wholesome travel guide like *DP* dabble in the shadowy world of the military and contract soldiering?

Well first of all, a lot of our readers took their first big trip paid for by Uncle Sam. Secondly, for those who view signing up as a short cut to adventure, you should be informed that soldiering is probably the most glamorized but least adventurous profession out there. There is also the overly glamorized world of contract soldiering (also known as mercenaries) where people with military skills can work overseas protecting, training, and fighting.

There is a romantic side to contract soldiering, probably best typified by Rudyard Kipling's *The Man Who Would Be King*. It's a simple tale about ex-soldiers deciding to make themselves rulers in a remote northwest Indian backwater. The results are predictable, but the moral is timeless. The world is changed by men who step outside the boundaries of law and convention and take matters into their own hands. They force change. That is why you will find sedate countries both vilifying and hiring soldiers. Most people think mercenaries are cartoon characters or figments of scriptwriter's imaginations. The truth is Hollywood hires real mercenaries to consult on their action-packed feature films. Even Uncle Sam sells its expertise to Angola, Colombia and Uganda and other tin-pot countries to train local troops and indulge in close support on missions.

Adventure stirs deep in the loins of youth and there is little that a well-trained soldier can do in civilian life that matches the intensity and focus of combat. What else can well-trained adventurers do to make this world a better place and tell stories to their grandkids? In the old days, you could ride off to the Crusades, discover the New World or just raise hell in some wealthy potentate's army. Since then, there have been few noble wars to occupy the heroic and romantic. Between our great and not-so-great wars (when Uncle Sam made you volunteer), poets, thugs and the bloodthirsty have volunteered for a variety of romantic causes, from the Russian Revolution to the Spanish Civil War. Today, those who seek to make a difference by direct action can choose to join an army or group that is actively fighting for independence, freedom or any other cause. Keep in mind that you can lose your American citizenship if you choose to be a mercenary (although no U.S. contract soldier or mercenary has to date) and your chances of being summarily executed by the side of the road if captured are high. So let's start out with the PC version of military adventure The Army.

Happiness Is a Warm Gun: The Army/Navy/Air Force

Today's armed forces look pretty good to the hordes of young men and women who can't find jobs.

Despite the dire warnings of the State Department and foreign rumblings, there is little chance for an all-out good versus evil showdown in today's globo-cop environment. The world's businesses are just too tightly interwoven and politics too fractured to allow another Axis versus Allied confrontation. A quick look at where Uncle Sam gets to fire guns would result in firing blanks. Sure there is the quick dash to a Third World wasteland so our soldiers don't get rusty, but most of the current activity of the U.S. military consists of sitting on their behinds overseas or polishing their guns back home.

Sure, the U.S military has officially seen action in Bosnia, Korea, Vietnam, Lebanon, Iraq, Grenada, Panama, Libya, Somalia and Haiti; however, none of these have been official wars. Rather, they were primarily police actions or gun boat diplomacy. That said, there has been covert military action in Angola, Cuba, Cambodia, Laos, Nicaragua, Iran, El Salvador and numerous other areas, and training missions in Uganda, Colombia and dozens of other "which end does the bullet come out" armies we call allies. For the most part, you will see America's finest sitting on their duffs calculating their retirement income.

In the past, America had a big enemy to unleash its big army on. No more. Today's military is killing time instead of bad guys. In places like Bosnia, Lebanon and Somalia, America's finest are impotent, politically correct, overtrained and underpaid cops. With today's lack of clear objectives, simple villains or even positive role models, it is no surprise that the U.S. military is having trouble attracting the caliber of soldier it had with the draft. It's also not surprising that these gung ho soldiers want to do something meaningful with their skills when they get out. Meanwhile, our current all-volunteer army has lower scores, lower average IQ levels, and gender modified achievement levels as equipment and technology become more advanced and complicated. Just what would our well fed, by-the-book, bed-at-night, politically-correct, Geneva Convention style military do against barefoot *mujahedin* or female suicide bombers? Unlike the days of the Rough Riders when bar fighters, intellectuals, noblemen and cowboys joined up to fight the good fight, today's army attracts a totally different crowd. It could be said that today's military, with its Clintonesque desire to be PC, does about all it can do to take the adventure out of military service.

What can you expect if you sign up in today's army? The Army's nine-week basic training program at Fort Jackson, South Carolina, transforms civilians to soldiers 60 raw recruits at a time. At bases like Fort Jackson, 70,000 military personnel are trained annually, 3 million since the base's opening in 1917.

Upon arrival, you can expect to fill out horrendous amounts of paperwork. You spend the first six days at the Reception Battalion, where you pick up your uniforms, have your head shaved and are given 16-hour doses of KP, or kitchen patrol. The second week is filled with 12-hour days (with reveille at 4 a.m.), drill and ceremony movements, classroom work, land and navigation courses, bayonet assault training and an obstacle course centered around the Victory Tower.

The second month begins with basic rifle marksmanship. You will learn to understand and care for your M-16 like no other physical object you own. You will learn to fire at targets as far as 300 meters away. Based on your performance, you will be called a marksman, sharpshooter or expert. Toward the end of the second month, the weaponry gets serious, with the M-60 machine gun, AT4 antitank weapon and hand grenades. Instead of firing your weapon, you get a taste of what it will be like on the receiving end, as you learn how to move around under fire complete with barbwired obstacles, exploding dynamite and M-60 rounds being fired over your head as you crawl 300 meters on your belly.

The last week of training intensifies with PT testing and working with explosives. The climax is a three-day field exercise, where trainees get to play war by digging foxholes and taking eight-mile hikes with full packs. The last few days are spent cleaning barracks in preparation for the next cadets. How tough is it? New recruits will say very; the old salts will say not as tough as it used to be. Corporal punishment was banned in the mid-1970s, and sexual harassment has been added to the list of subjects taught. Minor punishment is confined to "smoke sessions," for the less than motivated. These semipunitive periods of intense physical training are designed to remind the errant soldier who is in charge. Soldiers are chewed out using the entire spectrum of profanity.

The front-leaning rest position (a push-up that is never completed) is also used as punishment. There is no form of entertainment, since there technically is no rest time. Television, newspapers and radios are taboo. Mail and occasional phone calls are allowed. Three washing machines and five showerheads are considered enough to keep 60 active men clean.

Once out of basic training, you can expect to be posted to an area in line with your specialty. The military is still using technology about 10–20 years behind what you find on the outside. The main focus in the military is changing from '40s style ground wars to '70s style rapid-deployment tactics. The Army provides lousy pay, good benefits, excellent training and a chance to pack in two careers in a lifetime. As for furthering a cause or making the world a better place, one only has to look at Lebanon, Kuwait, Somalia and Vietnam to see the results of gunboat diplomacy.

Beau Geste: The French Foreign Legion

The more romantic and politically insensitive might want to consider joining the Legion. The Legion is, more or less, France's colonial houseworker, oppressing minorities, liberating missionaries and generally keeping the natives from getting too restless. The Legion knows it does France's dirty work and recruits accordingly. They will take all comers, preferably foreigners and men who will not draw too big a funeral procession. The Legion is tough and disposable.

The best example of the Legion's mindset is the single most revered object in their possession—the wooden hand of Captain Jean Danjou on display in the museum in Aubagne. Danjou lost his hand when his musket misfired and blew up. He then died with the 59 worn-out survivors defending a hacienda on April 30,

1864, in a small hamlet called Camerone in Mexico. His men, exhausted after a long forced march to evade the 2000-strong Mexican army, decided to die rather than surrender. His wooden hand was found by the tardy relief column and enshrined to commemorate his courage. Over 10,000 legionnaires died at Dien Bien Phu in 1954 in a similar debacle. One unit suffered a 90 percent loss at Cao Bang, only to have 576 out of 700 killed four years later at Dien Bien Phu.

A normal army would frown upon the lack of reinforcement, bad strategies and resulting waste of manpower. The Legion (like all of French Military history) myopically elevates folly into legend and attracts thousands of eager recruits every year. The basic lesson is that with only 75 percent of the Legion being French, they are considered disposable.

Despite its notoriety, the Legion is still the army of choice when young men dream of adventure. The Legion is the tough guy's army, tailor-made for Hollywood film scripts, home for intellectuals, criminals and outcasts. It's a close-knit band of hardy, brutal men who are either escaping misguided pasts or seeking adventure in exotic places and doing heroic deeds. The lure of the Legion is communicated to us via simplistic movies like *Beau Geste,* or simplistic books that romanticize its violence and bloodshed. What they don't tell you is that the Legion has always been brutal and ill-equipped. But you get to learn to be a professional killer and chances are high that you will use those skills on other people.

The Legion was created in 1831 by King Louis Phillipe to assist in the conquest of Algeria. The king correctly assumed that paid mercenaries would not complain about the conditions or political correctness in carrying out his orders. Since then, the Legion has been used to fight France's dirty little wars in Algeria, Indochina, Africa and the Middle East. Although there have been many heroic battles fought in some of the world's most remote and hostile regions, you are better served by reading the multitudes of books about the Legion. The reality today is that the Legion has been downsized and specialized.

The Legion is one of the few action outfits (like the former Selous Scouts of Rhodesia or Oman's mostly British army) which offers the professional adventurer a steady diet of hardship broken up by short bursts of excitement and danger. This format has attracted many of the world's best-trained soldiers, like the SS after WWII or Special Forces vets from Vietnam. The world of adventure is shrinking, however. Today the French Foreign Legion is made up of 8500 officers and men from more than 100 countries. They no longer have any ongoing wars that require constant replacements. They now focus on picking and choosing from amongst the world's tough guys to enable them to field soldiers who are fluent in many languages and specialities without the religious, political or ethnic barriers that hamper other peacekeeping or expedition forces.

How to Get in

There are 16 Legion recruiting centers in France, the most popular being Fort de Nogent in Paris. Just ask at the police station for the *Legion Etrangere.* The more focused head straight for Aubagne, just outside of the dirty Mediterranean port of Marseille. You will be competing with over 8000 other eager Legionnaire wannabe's for the 1500 slots available. East Europeans make up about 50 percent of the eager candidates these days. Candidates are tested for their intelligence and physical fitness, and special skills are a definite plus. If you just murdered your wife's boyfriend the week before, be forewarned that all candidates are run through Interpol's data banks and the Legion cooperates with them to weed out murderers. If you just want to escape the IRS or alimony payments, the Legion could care less. After all, what better inducement is there to staying after your third year in Djibouti than the thought of spending that same time in jail Stateside.

You won't be required to bring an ID or proof of anything; when you sign up, you will be assigned a *nom de guerre* and a nationality. Being Canadian is popular, and calling yourself Rambo is definitely an old joke.

You must pass the same general standards as the French Army, but then the Legion takes over. You will learn to march like a mule in hell—long forced marches with heavy packs; jungle, mountain and desert training. You can bail out during the first four months of training, but from then on, you will speak the thick, crude French of the Legionnaire and learn to be completely self-sufficient in the world's worst regions.

There is basic training in Castelnaudary (between Carcassone and Toulouse, just off the A61), commando training in St. Louis near Andorra, and mountain training in Corsica. Four weeks into your training, you will be given the *Kepi blanc*, the white pillbox hat of the Legionnaire. Unlike the Navy SEALs or Western elite forces, the accommodations are simple and the discipline is swift, and other than special prostitutes who service the legion, there is little to look forward to in the mandatory five years of service. Legionnaires can get married after 10 years of service.

Once you pass basic training, you will be trained in a specialized category: mountain warfare, explosives or any number of trades that make you virtually unemployable upon discharge (except in another mercenary army). French citizens cannot serve, except as officers. Those French officers who sign on do so for a taste of adventure. In troubled times, the Legionnaires are always the first to be deployed to protect French citizens in uprisings or civil wars.

With this international makeup, it is not surprising that Legionnaires today find themselves as peacekeepers, stationed in the tattered shreds of the French empire or with the U.N. You may be assigned to protect the European space program in Kourou, in the steamy jungles of French Guiana, or to patrol the desert from Quartier Gaboce, in the hot baked salt pan of Djibouti. When it hits the fan as in Kolwezi or Chad, you can expect some excitement, a quick briefing, an air drop into a confused and bloody scene, followed by years of tedium, training and patrol.

Since the Legion attracts loners and misfits, and because many of them spend their time in godforsaken outposts, it is not hard to understand that the Legion becomes more than a job. In fact, the motto of the Legion is *"Legio Patria Nostra,"* or "The Legion Is Our Homeland," which describes the mindset and purpose. Many men serve out their full 20 years, since they are unable to find equally stimulating work on the outside.

When you get out, you don't get much other than a small pension, and the opportunity to become a Frenchman (Legionnaires are automatically granted French citizenship after five years). After a lifetime of adventure, and divorced from their homeland, the men of the Legion can look forward to retirement at Domaine Danjou, a château near Puyloubier (12 miles west of St. Maxim, north of the A7) in southern France, where close to 200 Legionnaires spend their last years. This is where the Legion looks after its own, its elderly, wounded and infirm. Here, the men have small jobs, ranging from bookbinding to working in the vineyards. Later, they will join their comrades in the stony ground of the country that never claimed them but for which they gave their lives. Remember, the Legion has always been disposable.

Humanitarian Combat Warrior

I joined the French Foreign Legion at Fort de Nogent on June 17, 1982. I joined for all the stereotypical reasons that young men do. Bored and dissatisfied in the British Army, I had read Simon Murray's book, *Legionnaire*, and decided I wanted to be the best—an elite soldier. Most of all, I wanted to fight. To a certain extent, I achieved that goal. Actually, I went AWOL from the British Army to join the Legion. The first thing my father knew about it was when the M.P.s turned up at his house and started chasing my little brother down the road thinking he was me. (My father was a civil servant, so the whole incident was very embarrassing to him and he was really angry with me, to put it mildly.)

I spent seven months in Beirut in 1983 and two years in Djibouti from 1986–1988. What I didn't realize when I signed up for the first five years was that 99.5 percent of the time I would be bored shitless, and 0.25 percent of the time I would be looking for clean underpants. My experiences in the Legion included work as a parachutist, sniper instructor, cold weather commando, long range reconnaissance patrol, combat diver, amphibious assault, unarmed combat and military skier. I completed my tour of duty as an infantry corporal in charge of nine infantry Legionnaires.

Life in the Legion was like a clip from a recruitment film. Everything I did was regimented. We marched at 66 paces a minute, singing marching songs in French and German. I worked from reveille until almost lights out five days a week and again most of the day on Saturday. Sunday was my day off unless I had guard duty, exercise duty, a course to study or had managed to land in prison. (Speaking of prison, the platoon commander can have you sent to prison for seven days for poor humor and if you're not smiling when you come out, you'll get another 15 days for a permanent bad attitude).

I wasn't permitted to wear civilian clothes for the first five years unless I had a leave pass for 72 hours or more. (I learned you don't get those unless you've spent a tour of four months or more abroad.) My salary in the Legion ranged from UK$2500 to UK$18,000 depending on risk/country. Most of the guys end up spending their wages on knives, cameras, booze, drugs and whores.

Fights are common, not only between Legionnaires but also between Legionnaires and NCOs. So, it's very much a case of survival of the fittest. (Only recently have deaths on Legion bases begun to be investigated). Rules are strictly enforced. It is not cool to drink a bottle of whisky, smoke an ounce of grass with your mates, then hit the town. It is definitely uncool to beat up a gendarme in

Marseille, throw his sidearm in the water and then run away. If he catches up with you and you're arrested, it can take years before you're free.

Life in the Legion is simple, brutal, and seems surprisingly normal because of the indoctrination recruits undergo. The Legion is a politician's dream; the indoctrination is such that, unlike a normal army, where it might be glorious to fall in combat, many Legionnaires think they are already dead. I only began to see it as abnormal after I left.

I left the Legion after my two year tour of Djibouti, moved to England and married the Ethiopian bar girl I had lived with in Djibouti. I had met her at the Hotel Menelek when I was a corporal in the Legion. (Some psychoanalysts might say that I was keeping the Legion with me after I left.) I may have left the Legion physically, but mentally I was, for all intents and purposes, still a Legionnaire. I was tough, arrogant, abrasive, sexist and violent. The first civilian job I took was as a shelf stocker in a supermarket. There was little demand for snipers in Southeastern England. Because I was uncompromising and ruthlessly efficient, I swiftly became shift manager. Most people who knew me before would admit to a grudging respect...but in reality they were frightened by something they could never comprehend.

My marriage broke up and my desire to "get away" led me to Mogadishu in 1993 where I worked for the Save the Children Fund. I ended up doing aid work because I was so desperate to get away from my Ethiopian wife and I thought I could manage logistics better than most (in a war zone!). There are many opportunities for ex-military guys both in the U.N. and in N.G.O.s. For the first time, I started to appreciate people for what and who they are. But I was still a "cowboy" at heart, death and risk were not cognitive thoughts for me.

I met my wife Isabella when she was a nurse working for the Save the Children Fund in Mogadishu. She's a Kiwi and I traveled to New Zealand with her on Christmas Day in 1993. It wasn't until I was racing around Rwanda as team leader for an international rescue committee in 1994, six years after leaving the Legion, that I thought about being killed and realized I had too much to live for. I didn't want to get killed in Rwanda because my wife was four months pregnant. I had finally broken away from the Legion. I was lucky and met the right person. We now have a daughter and live in New Zealand. I love them both very much. They have given me the sense of belonging that I was searching for when I joined the Legion. I'm a very private sort of a guy (as you'd expect from an ex-sniper), I have no close friends other than my wife and daughter. Maybe someday I'll write a novel about my experiences... I'll call it "the Humanitarian Combat Warrior."

—**Martin Gilmour**

Working Freelance

All right, you do your two, five or 20 years and you're out. Because McDonald's doesn't currently need any Green Berets or Navy SEALs to take down Burger Kings, just who is hiring military experts? Well technically, nobody. Although many countries like Brunei (which uses Ghurkas), the Vatican (which has about 100 Swiss guards) and Oman have armies staffed by paid foreigners (about 360 British officers were "seconded" to the Sultan to fight rebels), you will have to be hired out of an existing army (typically the British Army) to be considered. Many foreign armies are happy to enlist your services and the Canadian, British or Australian armed forces will even give you citizenship when you are finished. Times are tough, so there are plenty of people who like the idea of paid housing and training. You can expect stringent entry requirements and a thorough check of your background.

So now that you've realized that late night 7-Eleven clerks and bank tellers see more firefights than a U.S. Marine, just where can adventurers find some action?

Happiness Is a Dead Infidel: The *Mujahedin*

If the Legion seems a little too Euro or confining, you can try the next level down: an Afghan rebel. The qualifications are that you be a Muslim, don't mind being completely disposable and hate infidels more than the IRS. The most volunteering folks on this planet are the Afghans, or veterans of the war in Afghanistan against Russia. Being an Afghan means getting smack-dab in the middle of the Superbowl of religious wars: Jihad. There is always Jihad, or the Holy War, being exported by Iran against Russia, the Great Satan (us) and all its allies. Think of it as the Crusades of the 21st century.

Jihad started with Mohamed a century and a half ago and was really cooking during the crusades. It died down for five centuries, and then, an almost retro enthusiasm hit the big time twenty years ago. But the big J restarted in 1979, when the Soviets decided to install a puppet ruler backed by the Soviet Army. As with all foreign countries who decided to roll armies into Afghanistan, they forgot that the tribes of Afghanistan love a good fight. In fact, when there is no occupying power, they love to fight amongst themselves.

The "Afghans," or outsiders who fought in Afghanistan, are the direct effect of too much money, training and weapons being funneled into one of the world's poorest regions—Pakistan and Afghanistan. The U.S. decided this would be a great time to give the Russians a bloody nose, prompting them to send in massive amounts of money to support every tiny tribal religious or political group that hated the Russians. All the Afghan groups had to do was provide a head count, a list of weapons, an area of operations, and they were in business. Naturally, the real *mujahedin* looked upon the money from the infidels warily.

The result is that the U.S. and the Gulf States (through the CIA, through Pakistan) created a new "franchise" of warrior clans armed to the teeth with the common goal of causing the Russians grief. Simple gun-happy tribesmen were trained in everything from how to make explosives out of fertilizer to how to use Stinger missiles. The CIA not only provided more than enough money; they created an unholy network where these factions could swap war stories and business cards.

Over 10,000 volunteers traveled to Afghanistan to fight the Russians, most of them lured by money and a chance to poke the bear in the nose. Many more people, after hearing of the plight of the Afghan people, sent funds and were predisposed to the total annihilation of the Russian soldiers in Afghanistan. Recruits and funding were actively sought in 28 states in America, but the number of U.S. volunteers was minuscule.

The war in Afghanistan was the largest covert operation of the Reagan era. Over the course of the war, Western countries pumped in from $25 million to several billion dollars a year. The CIA, Saudi government and Gulf States signed most of the checks, with 70 percent of the U.S. aid going to training and arming the Islamic radicals. Pakistan was hired to provide training to the volunteers, and nobody ever thought about what these people were going to do after the war. The Russian people simply went bankrupt and flushed the Communist Party down the drain; the Russian army went into business for itself, renting and selling weapons to any social or political group that wanted them, and the well-trained and ideologically infused Afghans became terrorists for hire. Keep in mind that the term "Afghan" refers to fighters who traveled or were trained in Pakistan to fight Russians. They are typically young Muslim men (now in their thirties) turned on by clerical haranguing and with little financial incentive to remain in their home country. Their home countries are usually Muslim, have high birth rates, high unemployment and strong representation by Iranian-backed political and religious groups (usually from Egypt, Sudan, Algeria, Libya or Pakistan).

It is no coincidence that all the men arrested in the World Trade Center bombing were trained or involved in the war in Afghanistan.

It is no coincidence that all these men have links to Afghan Prime Minister Gulbuddin Hekmatyar, who was the most entrepreneurial and most dedicated anti-Soviet. He allegedly blew over $1 billion of U.S. aid during the war against the Soviets, but the truth is he squirreled away enough weapons to fight a civil war after the Russians left. That Hekmatyar hated the West didn't seem to bother Ronald Reagan. In the mid-'80s Hekmatyar set up an Afghan refugee center to coordinate and support the works of fundamentalist activities in America. The *taliban* recently told *DP* that when they took control of Hekmatyar's stockpile of arms, they acquired enough weapons and ammunition to fight a war for 20 years.

Most of the Afghan volunteers whom Hekmatyar recruited and trained did not come from America but ended up in America as refugees from Afghanistan. The CIA facilitated the handing out of visas and green cards, and many of these recent transplants can be found driving taxis in New York City. Using the funds supplied by the CIA, Hekmatyar set up a center in Brooklyn to raise funds for the *mujahedin* in Afghanistan and to send volunteers to fight in Afghanistan. The center also organized paramilitary training in the United States for Muslims.

Today *mujahedin* can be found in the refugee camps and mosques of Algeria, Morocco, France, Iran, Pakistan, Sudan, Egypt and other poor Muslim countries. There is not much paying work for the surplus of fighters, but they gladly accept infidels if they have special skills.

How to Get in

If you are a traditional Westerner, forget it. You are the enemy. If you accept Islam or want to provide training or skills, you may be considered. If you are from Sudan, Pakistan, India, Egypt, Turkey, Syria, The Philippines, Saudi Arabia or the Middle East, you stand a good chance. Currently there are mini Jihads in Algeria, The Philippines, Iraq, Iran, Azerbaijan, Georgia, Chechnya, Kashmir, China, Morocco, Egypt, Sudan, Yemen, Saudi Arabia, America, Lebanon, Turkey, and many more places. If you fought in the war against Russia and have contacts, you are in like Flynn. The problem is now finding an employer or a cause. Peshawar is still the major clearinghouse for Afghans. The *taliban* will take any Muslim willing to fight, and there are numerous insurgencies that will take volunteers.

Bosnia: Another War In Europe

"If there is ever another war in Europe, it will come out of some damn silly thing in the Balkans."

Prince Bismarck
1815–1898

September 1992

New to the war, we watched silently as the backhoe dug into the garbage dump. When the story began to appear, one journalist backed away in horror, then turned to retch. Eventually, almost 90 rotting corpses lay next to the pit. All Muslims or Croats and many in their eighties, their throats had been cut by Serbs. Had we done our homework properly, of course, we would have known it was a Balkan story already centuries old. Any of those shrunken faces could have been captioned with the same line from Joyce: "History is a nightmare from which I am trying to awake."

At a Serb checkpoint, I'm ordered out of the car by five drunken soldiers. One begins slapping me playfully while another burns holes in my jacket with his cigarette, all breaking into sly, superior smiles at my sudden efforts to brush out the embers. At their brigade headquarters a white Land Rover bearing the BBC logo and ëTV' in tall, black letters is proudly displayed as a war trophy. Resting on blocks, both doors mark the flight of the missile that tore the cameraman-driver to pieces. Serbs 1, media 0 on this front, though just one of the 78 journalists who would eventually die in the Balkans. Today the front lines are blanketed under freezing fog, the white opaqueness pierced with speculative bursts of automatic weapons fire. In a farmhouse-cellar-turned-bunker, the inevitable bottle of slivovitz appears and a tank commander asks if I will take a letter to a Croatian friend wounded on the other side. I agree and he writes quickly, translating as he goes along.

To Matĕ Jozaku:

Matĕ, I'm sending you this letter with wishes for a speedy recovery. When I heard you had been injured I took the news very hard. Your old friend, Jovan Jokanovic the shopkeeper, is writing this letter. Your driver's license is still with me; I hope I can personally return it eventually. Both your homes are intact, as are your brothers' homes. Please accept greetings from all your old friends on Vlasic.

Jovan Jokanovic

Outside old friends fire into the fog in hope of killing each other.

February 3, 1993

From the Muslim village a Serbian tank has been spotted 3 km to the west and the defenders race to position their state-of-the-art, anti-armor missile supplied by Iran with CIA connivance. I'm checking my cameras in the command bunker when three bearded soldiers enter and order me out. But these are not from the Muslim Bosnian army, they're mujahedin, avowed enemies of Serbs, Croats and the infidel West. In a nearby farmhouse eight expressionless faces regard me silently. A feeling of malevolence hangs in a room strung with Arabic banners.

Will I accept Allah? The Prophet, I answer carefully, said that those of the Book are exempt from forced conversion. An acne-scarred thug in the corner hisses to his fellow fanatics, "I want to kill him." Why? The thug speaks again, fingers fluttering as his eyes lift toward the ceiling. "So you can greet Allah." But the Prophet directed all good Muslims to protect the defenseless. He snaps the safety down. "I'm going to kill you now," he smiles. "Are you afraid to die?" Their Fundamentalism demands my humiliation, that I beg before the bullet in the head. Deeply frightened, I hold my executioner's eyes and whisper, "Inshallah." Frustrated, the leader grabs my cameras. "You are not welcome here. You will leave these and go." My secular Muslim guide, equally frightened, nods imperceptibly and we walk out alive.

Minutes later I hear the launch of a missile, then an explosion as the tank bursts into flames across the valley. There's an orange flash near the burning tank. I turn to my guide to see him diving for cover. I'm at the bottom of the frozen ditch with him when the Serb artillery shell lands short of us. Rising cautiously, we brush the snow off and step out again. There's a second flash. Back into the ditch. An hour later I'm in army headquarters in Turbe, relating what I've just been through. The Muslim commander pours us each a slivovitz. "Extremists," he shrugs helplessly. Outside, the Serbs are shelling the village. There's a lull and I run for the car just as a rocket slams into the road not more than 50 meters away. When I look up people are running, limping, crawling out of the smoke and dust. I think of the next one on its way. Fuck this for a job, I decide, jumping into Li'l Sue and screeching away in the opposite direction. (The next day the *mujahedin* kidnapped two British mercenaries serving as instructors in the Muslim army. They were taken to the same village, tortured and murdered. I'll never know why I lived and they died.)

February 1993

From an editor's ivory tower came the suggestion that a story might be found in Pale, the Bosnian Serb headquarters. When I mentioned it to the BBC, their first question was: "Soft-skinned or hardcar?" My sotto voice "Softskinned" drew sympathetic tsks from those whose hardcars carried a ton of protective steel and Kevlar. You'll have to run the airport and its Serb and Muslim snipers, they explained, then right at the end. Not left towards Sarajevo, because that's Sniper Alley, the most dangerous stretch of road in the world. I cross to the Serb side, where a soldier hitchhiking to Pale knows a way that misses the airport altogether. We turn onto a narrow country road, then a two-lane highway, where a Serb checkpoint sends us north to a mountain track that skirts Sarajevo. Story done, I retrace the route from Pale: rocky track, then the highway, where I look for the checkpoint. But heavy fighting earlier in the day has sent the Serb military policemen into their bunkers, and I miss the crucial turn.

Come round a curve where a 10 ton truck, tires flat, hulks across the road. I brake to a stop, sure that I've gone too far. Turn the tape player down and look around, seeing fresh debris from mortar shells. A careful six-point turn to avoid the mined shoulders and I'm heading back when a Serb leaps from his bunker, firing from the hip. Out of range and heart pounding, I stop at the first farmhouse to check the way. Straight back the way you came. Are you sure? The door closes. Body armor and helmet snugged, I slash through the gears, eyes switching from road to bunker and back again. No fire when I come abreast of the position, but immediately it's behind shots snap past. I duck my head and floor it, screaming around the truck blocking the road.

And things go from bad to very bad: steel barriers and anti-tank mines. Another AK opens up from the other side. Trapped, I slam to a stop and slowly step out, hands raised as stories of journalists executed by the Serbs flash through my mind. Fifty feet away a soldier curtly motions me forward while another stares down the sights of a Kalashnikov. Unable to think of a better opener than to suggest a solidarity against their enemy, I ask with unfeigned terror: "Where are the Muslims?" He jabs a thumb into his chest and growls, "We're the Muslims. I've just busted two front lines. Dokumenti!" He demands for my papers, and I pass them over reluctantly, for nestled opposite my UN press card is—oh joy, oh joy—my Serbian accreditation. I'm soon surrounded by scowling combatants who, when I finally explain that I'm lost, think it's the funniest thing they've heard all day. All save one, whose slivovitz breath curls my nostril hairs as he wails, "But I almost killed you!" Meanwhile, my Suzuki jeep, Li'l Sue, is idling happily in the middle of the road, Nat King Cole crooning 'Unforgettable' on the tape deck. I'm sent out to move her, but "keep low" they motion, pointing across the road and saying, "sniper, sniper." A sprint and dive through the open door and whip into the side road, skirting another line of mines, then into Sarajevo and a four hour interrogation as a possible Serb spy.

Awake in the freezing Holiday Inn to Serb artillery. In the dining room the warries from the world's heavies are gathering for breakfast. Long silences when shells land close enough to rattle coffee cups. Two Spanish journalists say they're driving out in a few minutes. Please, can I follow? "Si, but you must go very fast." I'm right behind you, amigo. Wrapped in flak jackets and helmets, we blast out of the underground carpark in tandem, squealing up the winding drive and racing flat out through the city, cutting across pavements where the road is blocked by rubble, hammer shifts on the corners to the sound of incoming fire. Skid into the sandbagged UN compound and tag on to the end of a French armored patrol to the Serb lines. A crumbling wall bears WELCOME TO HELL in angry brush strokes, and then it's down Sniper Alley, waiting for the sudden hole in the windshield and praying that if it happens someone will come back for me. Arrive at last Serb checkpoint, hold breath until across, then on to Kiseljak and the BBC, telling yesterday's story between gulps of scalding tea.

You're one lucky bloke. Day you went over a French photographer was hit in the throat and a Reuters chap in the foot as they were crossing the airport in soft-skins. Yesterday a French soldier was killed and three wounded by an RPG. I wonder suddenly at my luck in missing the airport, of going through an active front under fire from both sides, of facing the mujahedin in Bijelo Bucje. And the times under tank, mortar, rocket or artillery fire and not a scratch. How much luck are we given? Anyone know the situation between here and Travnik? Pretty nasty because of fighting between Muslims and Croats. Dutch aid driver wounded this morning, and a French TV crew took some hits, but hardcar, so no-one hurt. I try to ignore that sixth sense whispering "Don't do it," and head for Travnik.

Pass through successive checkpoints, Muslim, Croat, Muslim again. At each hastily rigged blockade fingers slip inside trigger guards and muzzles swing towards me. Approach each slowly, hoping they can see PRESS on the hood. Through the last one and the empty road winds along a narrow valley where gutted farmhouses still smolder. I pass a freshly burned out VW. Five minutes later an Opel, windows starred by bullets, blocks half the road. Below the open door something darker than the gray asphalt is congealing in the cold air. My knuckles whiten at the sound of a shot. At me? At someone else? What the fuck am I doing here? Outside Kacuni a British light tank blocks the narrow bridge. What's the situation ahead? Some automatic stuff, and there's a sniper just over there. Firing starts beyond the bridge and the hatch slams shut. Go on, or turn back? Open Li'l Sue's door and rap it twice to hear the tinny ring. She's brought me through 10,000 miles in this lunatic asylum. Probably take me 10,000 more. But not today, and I pull back.

March 1993

From the dark hills a tracer streaks over the snow-covered road and burns into the gathering dusk. Below its path more than a thousand Muslims stagger under the weight of suitcases and bags, the last of a lifetime's possessions. A father draws a small sled, his crippled daughter and her crutches balanced atop what they have been allowed to keep. A second tracer splits the air. It's a reminder of the Serbs' promise to mortar the road if their unarmed victims have not completed the three mile journey by nightfall.

Land Rovers move up and down the road collecting those who have begun collapsing in the snow. In the back of Li'l Sue five people clutch suitcases. In front an old man holds his grandson, a son and daughter-in-law sit on the hood as I edge past a British light tank and its 30mm cannon aimed toward the Serb lines. At the edge of Turbe my passengers step back into the snow. "Where will we go?" one old woman sobs. Another tracer flashes above us, scoring its way into the dark. A convoy of British army trucks looms out of the night to begin collecting the hundreds of refugees still struggling towards safety. Li'l Sue and I are no longer needed. I nose through the mass of dazed and bewildered people, surprised by my tears of anger and relief. My last story, I keep thinking, my last story from this madhouse. I'm alive and I'm going home.

—Jim Hooper

Happiness Is a Hired Gun: Mercenaries

So you did your time in the army and can field strip everything from a Makarov to a Chinese nuclear missile, you can fly an Apache helo or an F117 blindfolded, you could parachute directly into Saddam Hussein's Jacuzzi without tripping the disco light alarms and can speak 145 languages (including tribal dialects) and swear in 89 of them. You have been trained to kill a man just by twitching your ears, can make explosives out of Rice Krispies and list every LIC and Tango group by acronym alphabetically in Russian. You're under 40, fit and ready to go private. Congratulations, you can now work at Home Depot in the plumbing department or seek employment as a mercenary.

Well, we may be getting a little carried away but the bottom line is it won't take long before you start discovering that international security companies are fork ing over $10,000–$15,000 a month for high level contract soldiering these days. You only have one problem. Uncle Sam would rather see you work as a Burger King manager than sell your precious skills to the highest bidder. Yes, there are U.S. groups like MPRI and DSL who have dull-as-dishwater brochures and who do equally dull things like train foreign armies or write operational manuals in Serbo Croatian.

Any U.S. citizen entering a foreign army without prior approval (in writing) from both the Secretary of State and the Secretary of Defense will forfeit U.S. citizenship, although Congress has ruled that enlistment in a foreign army is not a clear enough declaration of intent to voluntarily renounce citizenship.

The Hague 1907 Convention banned operation on the territory of neutral states of offices for recruitment of soldiers (volunteers or mercenaries) to fight in a country at war. In 1977, part of a supplementary protocol to the 1949 Geneva Convention on the Protection of Civilian Population in Time of War made freelancers liable to court trial as criminals if they are taken POW. If found guilty, they can be simply shot on the spot as criminals.

The U.N. General Assembly reached a consensus in 1989 on recruiting, training, use and financing of mercenaries. If you are interested in volunteering, make sure you understand the laws and penalties that will suddenly apply to you. If you think fighting for money will make you popular and chicks will dig you, think again. On the other hand, if Uncle Sam has spent five years and about half a million dollars turning you into all that you can be, there are employment choices other than flipping burgers or working at Jiffy Lube.

Americans have not always been the ideal volunteers. In fact, the last two great wars showed that the majority of Americans held back until they were pushed into it, But once they were in it, they finished the job. There are two major developments you have to come to terms with.

¿Gringos? No me gustan.

First, most foreign armies don't want American volunteers. Americans have an image of wanting too much money, complaining too much, and creating too many political overtones when captured or killed. Recently, American mercenaries have fought in Angola, Rhodesia, Guatemala, El Salvador, Nicaragua, Sierra Leone, Myanmar, the Congo, Lebanon, Bosnia and Russia. Many are motivated by religion (black Muslims in the Middle East), background (Croats in Yugoslavia), money (Central America) or a misguided sense of adventure (Angola). The U.S. is not adverse to hiring or supplying mercenaries, starting back when Benjamin Franklin hired the Prussian officer Friedrich von Steuben to instill discipline into the Continental Army, or when Claire Chennault was hired to give China grief with his Flying Tigers. And Americans are not adverse to being mercenaries (we are capitalists after all). In modern times U.S.-hired mercenaries have been as diverse as the Ray-Banned pilots that flew for Air America, the advisors who trained Nung or Montagnard tribes in Vietnam or the doomed Contras in Nicaragua. There have been Americans in the Congo, Sierra Leone, Rhodesia, Myanmar, Israel and as far back as fliers in WWI, advisors to Haile Selaisse in Ethiopia and dozens that fought and died in the Spanish Civil War.

Mercenaries continue to do *our* dirty, or covert work, but our government does not like the idea of *you* running off to fight in other people's wars.

The second development is the creation of the International Security Firm. Companies like MPRI, Sandlines and EO are doing a lot of the clean and dirty work countries can't or won't do themselves. For example, Executive Outcomes brochure promises:

- To provide a highly professional and confidential Military Advisory Service to legitimate governments.
- To provide sound military and strategic advice.
- To provide the most professional military training packages currently available to Armed Forces, covering aspects related to sea, air and land warfare.
- To provide advice to Armed Forces on weapon and weapon platform selection.
- To provide a total a-political service based on confidentiality, professionalism and dedication.

Today, those who wish to be wild geese or soldiers of fortune will find few clear career paths. You will need the minimum service and training provided by a Western military power. Special forces members, explosives experts, pilots, and officers with training experience and other specialized skills are in demand.

Although the need for foreign volunteers cannot be predicted, there are certain starting points for employment. The main centers for recruitment of mercenaries (almost always ex-soldiers) are Pretoria, Johannesburg, Istanbul, Bangkok, London, Brussels, Marseille, Washington and Beirut. High level security employers have offices in Washington, New York, Pretoria, London or Paris. They supply men to train troops, provide security and generally do what the local military can't or won't do. Make sure you have a contract and remember even the best laid plans go awry as they did for EO in PNG.

Employment with a Difference

Getting a job in the merc world is a long way from the "Employment with a difference" classified ad placed by Mike Hoare in South Africa when he set out to recruit mercenaries to fight in the Belgian Congo. Having neither the budget nor the time to train men, he put together what he called his "Wild Geese," the name of an ancient Irish band of soldiers for hire. He managed to defeat the Simbas, rescue white women and embarrass the UN. And, he received a book and movie deal later.

Remember, if you find a recruiter in a bar who is looking for "a few good men," they are usually filling grunt and junior-officer levels only for second tier gigs. The players have already cut their deal up at the top, and they need to fill in the holes to get paid. Top level giggers like Executive Outcomes got $20 million for supplying 2000 soldiers and another $20 million for arms and supplies. Not bad, but don't forget they still paid their ground pounders about $2000 a month.

There are also horror stories about hucksters preying on the gullible, as in Angola in the '70s. The U.S. government paid to hire mercenaries out of London in their bid to oust the Cuban supported MPLA. Four groups of 185 men were sent in to fight with the FNLA. It was a disaster from the start. Psychotic officers (like 25-year-old Costas Georgiou, aka "Colonel Callan") executed their own people, few skirmishes were won and when it was over, 13 mercenaries were put on trial and four were executed by a firing squad (one had to propped up on his stretcher to be shot properly). The high hopes, empty talk and wasted time continue today (see IADP: *The Wild Goose Chase*). Even if you do find someone who has a gig for you, remember that they get paid by the head count, and once in that country you can be turned down, arrested or sent into action on your first day without training, weapons, gear or ammo. The reality is that most experienced mercenaries either use the old boy network or simply fly to the capital city of an emerging war zone and offer their services directly to the military advisors for whichever side they feel is the most desperate. Their services usually include rounding up cannon fodder like you.

There are also a lot of home-grown soldiering that usually leads nowhere. Some like the Falangists and Chamounists in Beirut in the '80s brought in eager French Falangist Party students, but most look for trained, hardened professionals with special skills. Your paycheck is an occasional bad meal and a place in heaven for fighting the good fight. Young Kashmiris are given a few weeks training and humped off across the mountains to Indian Kashmir to raise hell and end up dead in shootouts.There seems to be no age limit. In Africa young Ugandan school boys are rounded up and used as porters for rebel groups, kidnapped young girls become part time pillows and cooks. Isn't war fun?

Death From Behind a Desk

Because of the old-boy network and need for inside contacts, many soldiers of fortune do not make their money fighting on the ground, but make themselves available for higher level training and transportation contracts. They might source leased aircraft, arrange weapons transfers, organize rescue attempts, or train eager recruits to shoot guns and blow things up. All the while living in air-conditioned comfort complete with CNN.

Today's mercenary is not a cigar-chomping, muscle-bound adventurer with a bandolier of 50mm bullets and grenades hung like Christmas ornaments. He is more likely to be an unemployed soldier 30–35 who can't find work with his specialized skills. The pay is good when you have skills and tepid if you don't (mercenaries make between $2000 and $15,500 a month, depending on skills, rank and type of job, and the benefits), EO takes great pains to provide medivac, health and life insurance as well as long term treatment for wounded. And the chances of getting killed depend on which side you pick. If you are fighting a bush war, your enemy will take great pleasure in torturing you and parading you around like a three headed goat. Americans can also lose their passport or citizenship if they fight in the service of a foreign army. Others will most definitely be jailed and tried for war crimes. Mercs are not accorded prisoner of war status under the Geneva Conventions.

Are there any loopholes? If you are hired to invade another country, destroy property, kill or hurt people, or even to destabilize a democratic or undemocratic government, you are breaking the law. If you do not live in the attacked country, have a foreign citizenship, are on a mission to rescue someone, or you're just hanging around a war zone, you can be shot as a spy or foreign agent. If you are in a country that has declared a state of war, remember it is much easier and cheaper to shoot questionable characters than to fill out the paperwork.

If you want to truly be a volunteer like the German Steiner (the Sudan) or Argentinian Che Guevara (Uganda, Cuba, Bolivia), remember that Steiner was tried, imprisoned and tortured, and Guevera was ventilated by CIA operatives and dumped in a hastily dug Bolivian grave.

There are some gray areas that afford some (but little) protection. Make sure you enlist in a recognized foreign army. Join a foreign legion like the French Foreign Legion; have a civilian work contract for a recognized government. You could fight with a recognized army in a foreign territory (like our army in the Gulf or Vietnam) that is not technically at war but helping someone else win a war.

The skinniest loophole is offering your services for a higher pay rate in a foreign army where you are seconded to another army. Technically, you can join as a regular service member if there are no local troops with comparable experience. Will that stop the opposing side from parading you around like a zoo animal, then doing a flamenco dance on your testicles? No.

Soldiers of Misfortune

Be warned that there are plenty of cheap movies and bad books attempting to add the luster of righteousness and adventure to the mercenary life. These books tend to be short on facts and long on gun talk. They provide hard-to-find tips like "never handle explosives carelessly" (from the *Mercenary's Tactical Handbook* by Sid Campbell) to "take no unnecessary risks" (from the *African Merc Combat Manual* from Paladin Press).

There are some good books on this nasty business, most long out of print: *The Brother's War* by John St. Jorre, *Legionnaire* by Simon Murray, *Mercenary* by Mike Hoare, *The Last Adventurer* by Rolf Steiner, *Mercenary Commander* by Jerry Puren, and probably the most accurate, well-written and depressing of the bunch, the *Whores of War, Mercenaries Today* by Wilfred Burchett and Derek Roebuck. *Whores*, published in 1977, chronicles the misfortunes of 13 American and British mercs in Angola who were captured, tried and executed or imprisoned. Sobering stuff for wannabe's.

Movies like the *Dogs of War* and *The Wild Geese*, and TV shows like *Soldier of Fortune* have some credible origins in real events, and real mercenaries were used as resources to create the scripts as well advise the filmmakers on location. But somehow once the cameras rolled, it all turned into pure gun love complete with sweat, bulging muscles, babes, hand held machine guns and chomping cigars.

Some would-be mercs and real mercs read *Soldier of Fortune* magazine. To be fair, writers, like yours truly and *DP* contributors Rob Krott, Jim Hooper and Roddy Scott, have been published in *SOF*. But in our opinion, *SOF* adds a little too much macho gun-love salsa to what are typically skanky, sweaty low budget guerilla tours with complicated political backgrounds. So what separates the "pass the cigars and keep feeding me ammo" publications from the real thing? Well we at *DP* like to think that the real litmus test of a publication's readership is always the quality of the ads. Yes, *SOF* is read religiously by a large military readership but there are those ads that make you wonder just who is *really* reading this adventure mag. Here, the terminally tough can order "Combat Babe" posters for

$10, buy military medals they never won, learn how to be a private eye and even correspond with "gorgeous" and obviously lonely Russian, Asian and Latin ladies. For those who can read without the need for large pictures, there are articles on "Screw the Bitch, Divorce Tactics," secrets on how to hit a man 11 times in one second or less, or help on where to buy steroids. If you're less of a lover and more of a handyman you can learn how to convert your SKS to full auto or buy a Ferret armored vehicle.

The bottom line is the merc business is about 99 percent bullshit and one percent reality, and the reality part usually sucks. Despite having to buy your own beret, cigars and big knife, you will end up spending time in the most godawful parts of the world, and if a land mine doesn't get you, then the bugs will. If the bugs don't get you, the long arm of the law will.

Any time you leave the apron strings of Uncle Sam's army, you are on your own, and even if you are not in violation of any laws, you will be accused of being a criminal (actually, a criminal has rights—you won't) without any rights and dealt with accordingly.

To be fair, we should inject a little romance and adventure into this much maligned avocation. The true movers and shakers in the mercenary world are the classic megalomaniacs; vicious self-promoters and verbose ex-soldiers who see their role beyond that of a short-term gun toter—as a potential ruler of faraway kingdoms. So our advice, if you are going to get into this nasty business (the retirement program sucks), is to think big, don't take any checks and make sure you remember your hat size when you order your crown.

The Men Who Would Be King Club

The Kingdom-making business has been around for a long time. Men like Englishman (and eventually Rajah) Brooke of Sarawak bought a fast ship with a few naval guns. He used them to chase off pirates in exchange for giant chunks of Borneo. William Walker and a bunch of ne'er do wells ran Nicaragua with a Gatling gun and a few Colt Navy pistols. Hell, even I was offered in on a deal to take over a Caribbean island, so there still must be opportunities for adventurers out there.

The late '60s and early '70s were the glory years for mercenaries like "Mad" Mike Hoare, "Black" Jacques Schramme, and Bob Denard. They weren't bright or avaricious enough to grab the main bedroom in the royal palace instead of the barracks the first time around, but it didn't take them long to figure things out. Why support a tin pot ruler so they could continue to loot the national treasury to shop in Paris when you could loot the treasury and go shopping in Paris yourself? So if you want to join "The men who would be king club," here is a short list of the folks who thought big:

The Comoros 1978

One of the more successful attempts was made by Bordeaux native Bob Denard who actually managed to run the Comoros Islands between 1978 and 1989. The Comoros are an Indian Ocean island group just northwest of Madagascar. The major export of the long forgotten islands is *ylang-ylang*, a rare flower used in the production of aromatic oils. On May 13, 1978, 49-year-old Denard landed with 46 men in a converted trawler named the *Massiwa*. He had sailed from Europe with his black uniformed crew to claim ownership of this tiny but idyllic group of islands.

Denard had been here before to train the soldiers of Marxist ruler Ali Soilih. Soilih was busy kicking out Ahmed Abdallah. Abdallah fled to Paris and later, short on funds but high on ambition, offered to cut Denard in on the deal if he would return him to power. The deal was rumored to be worth $6 million. Denard enjoyed his new role as "man who would be king." Soilih was a young despot who appointed a 15 year old to run the police department, burnt all government records, and after a witch doctor told him he would be killed by a white man with a black dog, he killed every black dog on the island. Abdallah took all the political heat as his puppet. Denard, a former vacuum cleaner salesman and policeman, had seen what a few trained soldiers could do in his various adventures as a mercenary in Katanga, Yemen and Benin. This time he was in charge. He landed quietly at night and proceeded to the palace to find Soilih in bed with three girls watching a pornographic movie. He shot him, and the next morning drove through town with Soilih's body draped over the hood. Denard had with him a black Alsatian. The crowds cheered and Denard became an able leader of the Comoros for 11 years with 12 other white mercenaries. He took a Comoran wife, bought a villa, converted to Islam and became Said Mustapha Madjoub.

During his reign, South Africa used the Comoros to ship arms to Iraq and monitor ANC training camps in Tanzania, the French used his islands to ship arms to the right wing Renamo guerillas. Finally after he (or someone else) shot the puppet ruler Abdallah in a heated argument, the tide turned against Denard. His presence angered the other African states to such a degree that the French arranged for Denard's resignation in 1989. Denard, disappointed and back in South Africa, spent his evenings planning his return to paradise. Sounds like a great premise for a sequel (See "The Man Who Would Be King Part V.")

Equatorial Guinea 1972

The Dogs of War, by Frederick Forsyth, was published in 1974. Forsyth is said to have modeled the lead character in the book after Denard. In the book and in the film, a group of white mercenaries are hired to take over a West African country on behalf of an industrialist who finds it cheaper to take over the country rather than pay for its mineral resources. The movie ends with the mercenaries suddenly having a change of heart and installing an idealistic and honest leader. Naturally, the book and the film are fiction. Well, not completely, said an investigative report by London's *Sunday Times*. They claimed that *The Dogs of War* was based on a real incident instigated by the author. The *Times* claimed that in 1972 Forsyth allegedly put up just under a quarter of a million dollars ($240,000) to overthrow President Francisco Macias Nguema of Equatorial Guinea. Forsyth was no stranger to the murky world of mercenaries, since he had spent considerable time in Nigeria covering the Biafran civil war. While he was there, he met a Scottish mercenary named Alexander Ramsay Gay. Gay was only too happy to train and equip a small group of men who would set up a homeland for the defeated Biafrans. It is reputed that Gay was able to purchase automatic weapons, bazookas and mortars from a Hamburg arms dealer, then hire 13 other mercenaries along with 50 black soldiers from Biafra. They then purchased a ship called the *Albatross* out of the Spanish port of Fuengirola. The plot was blown when one of the

British mercs shot himself after a gunfight with London police. The mercenaries were denied an export permit for their weapons and ammunition, and the ship and crew were arrested in the Canary Islands en route to their target.

Forsyth denies the story or any participation in the plot and admits to nothing more than writing a solidly researched book.

The Seychelles 1981

Dublin-born "Mad" Mike Hoare was hired by persons unknown (most say former premier Mancham in cahoots with South Africa) to take over the Seychelles, a nation of 92 islands 1000 miles off East Africa. Hoare served in the Royal Armored Corps in World War II and left with the rank of Major. He emigrated to South Africa after the war and made ends meet by being a safari guide, car dealer and accountant, until he was hired by Moise Tshombe in 1964 to help him defeat rebels. Hoare put together about 200 male white mercenaries and led probably the last efficient use of a mercenary army in Africa—to save lives and put down a revolt in the Belgian Congo.

Hoare's last big gig (Major Hoare does not work too often due to his high price tag) was a Keystone cops affair that would seem to be the result of a bad scriptwriter rather than real political intrigue. They were supposed to overthrow the socialist government of President Albert Rene of the Seychelles and to take control of the idyllic Indian Ocean archipelago. In December of 1981 their plan of flying in as a visiting rugby team quickly unraveled when customs inspectors found heavy weapons in the bottom of their gym bags. A brief shoot-out between the 52 raiders and police ensued on the tarmac with the mercenaries' transportation being quickly hijacked and flown back to safety in South Africa. It was not known for whom or why this was done, but suspicion falls on the South African government. Some analysts believe that Hoare backers were South African businessmen looking for a tax haven. A Durban newspaper charged that several of the mercenaries were South African policemen.

The leniency with which the mercenaries were treated back in South Africa adds to that suspicion. The 44 mercenaries who made it back were put on trial (wearing beach shirts and khakis) not for hijacking the Air India aircraft, which would have meant a mandatory five to 30 years in jail; they were charged with kidnapping which requires no mandatory penalty.

The South African Cabinet also approved the freeing on bail of 39 of the 44 mercenaries on the condition they keep a low profile and not discuss the coup attempt. Five mercenaries were arrested in the Seychelles and it is assumed that three others are dead or hiding in the hills.

Others blame ousted Seychelles President James Mancham, who was exiled after Rene's successful 1977 coup. Although Mancham denied the accusation, one of the captured mercenaries had a tape recording of Mancham's victory speech intended for broadcast after the coup. Oops. The soldiers for hire were paid $1000 each and were promised $10,000 if the coup was successful.

The Sudan 1975

Rolf Steiner was a member of Hitler's Youth (Hitler Jugend). He joined the French Foreign Legion at the age of 17 in 1950. He fought at Dien Bien Phu and in Algeria and made the mistake of joining the anti-De Gaulle OAS—finding himself a drummed out corporal chief and a civilian.

In the fall of 1967, Biafra was busy spending oil money and French secret service funds on hiring mercenaries from Swedish pilot Count von Rosen (pilots were paid between $8000 and $10,000 per month in cash to fly in supplies) and paying Swiss public relations firms to publicize their plight. Money flowed freely; grisly battle-scarred veterans like Roger Faulques were paid 100,000 British pounds to hire 100 men for six months but only delivered 49. He was asked to leave, but Steiner, one of the mercenaries he had hired, chose to stay.

In July of 1968 Steiner asked for and was given a group of commando-style soldiers and had great successes against the Russian-backed Nigerians. He was later given the rank of colonel and given command of thousands of soldiers. This created an instant Napoleon complex and Steiner experienced a series of military defeats and routs. He was reigned in by removal of his Steiner Commando Division and after an angry confrontation with the Biafran leader, Sandhurst-educated General Emeka Ojukwa, he was shipped out of the country in handcuffs.

Steiner then showed up in the Southern Sudan among the Anya Na fighting the Islamic North. He taught agriculture, defense, education and other essential civic skills to the animist tribes. For a brief shining moment, he was their de facto leader, until he was captured by the Ugandans and put on trial in Sudan in the mid-'70s. He was released after spending three years in a Sudanese prison where he was tortured and beaten. His captors' favorite tortures were hanging Steiner by his feet and stuffing peppers up (down?) his anus. Some say he was a crazed megalomanic; other say he tried to apply his skills to aid a tiny struggling nation. He died in South Africa of a kidney ailment.

The Comoros 1995

They say sequels are never as interesting as the originals, and, in this case, they're right. Remember Bob Denard (see "The Man Who Would be King: Part I"). It seems that staring out the window got to be too much for him, so at the crusty old age of 66, Denard decided to give it one more go. On October 4, 1995, Denard and a group of 33 mercenaries (mostly French) rented a creaking fishing trawler and sailed back to the Comoros to recapture his little Garden of Eden where he had been King (actually, head of the Presidential Guard, watching over a puppet ruler) from 1978–1989.

They landed at night and quickly sprung their old buddies out of the islands' main jail; then they captured the two airports, the radio station and the barracks. After that, they rousted the doddering, 80-something Said Mohamed Djohar out of bed. By morning, Denard was on top and Djohar was a criminal charged with misrule and stealing government funds.

Two days later, the French government landed 600 troops and after a brief but halfhearted fight, the mercenaries were rounded up and Denard was shipped to France where he will be tried and jailed to keep him from island hopping again.

Papua New Guinea 1996

Papua New Guinea has had a dirty little bush war (as they are called in the trade) festering on the island on Bougainville. A large copper mine owned by Rio Tinto now called (RTZ-CRA) provided 45 percent of PNG's income, and now it was in the hand of a rag tag group of rebels who had the gall to just shut it down. The PNG Defense Force has been trained by the Aussies and the U.S. Special Forces since 1975. Enter Colonel (retired) Tim Spicer, the CEO of Sandlines, a U.K.

based security, and Executive Outcomes (run by Chairman Nick van der Berg). Now it seems that EO had invented the equivalent of a Visa card for cash-strapped Third World countries that had rebel problems. He would take your collateral and get a piece of the mining action (or be paid by the mining company direct) in exchange for training and liberation services. In PNG's case about $46 million worth. Now, PNG would have been placed in a dire predicament if the rebels had captured a university or public broadcasting radio station, but luckily they grabbed a gold and copper mine instead that could be put back into business in a jiffy.

Well, this didn't sit well with the PNG military commander who was having a hard time getting bullets and uniforms for his men, let alone fair haired mercenaries complete with Russian gunships. He was a little riled that all this newly found dough was being spent on military tourists and proceeded to lock up the EO mercs and even invited fair haired Colonel Tim to stay behind to answer a few questions. Hell, EO was even going to fly their wounded to Brisbane, Australia, for medical care while the PNG ground pounders had to make do with local quacks. To make a long story short somebody cashed the 50 percent deposit, all the killer boys went back to SA and the rebels on Bougainville had a whoop up to celebrate the easiest victory they ever won. It seems the government figured it might be cheaper to sign a peace deal instead of killing all the islanders with high priced mercenaries. Well, good *DP* reader, was this a triple layer black op with a positive political spin or a Keystone Kontract Killer escapade? To find out contact:

Sandline International	**LTC Tim S. Spicer**
525 Kings Road	*Cavalry and Guards Club*
Plaza 107	*127 Piccadilly*
London, England SW 10 062	*London, W.1 England*

The Players

These days, the old Dogs of War business is drying up like blood on a Kinshasa backstreet. Gone are the skull and cross bones patches of Steiner, gone are the nicknames like Black Jack and Mad Mike. The Che Guevaras, Abu Nidals' and Carlos the Jackals are now nothing but memories. The last attempt at putting together an old fashioned merc army was with 300 or so drunken army of Serbs and Europeans shipped in to fight off Kabila. The French put together a motley crew of 300 South Africans, Brits, French, Serbs, Angolans and other nationalities. The new merc scene (or should we say the international security scene) is taking advantage of thousands of laid off, well trained soldiers and the need of oil and mining companies to keep things flowing in Colombia, Angola, the Sudan, Congo, Papua New Guinea and other unstable regions. For those who like their action raw and gritty there is no shortage of unpaid volunteer work in Afghanistan, the southern Philippines and Latin America. For now, it seems the job opportunities for scarred, tattooed mercenaries looking through the classified section for "Make Big Money Killing Insurgents" ads are over.

But wait. If you are a trained security consultant, there is hope. Believe it or not, you can see many of the major recruiters listed under "Corporate Security" in phone books in Joburg, London, Washington, Miami and Paris. You'll find these euphemistically or acronymicly named companies in any big mining or oil center towns. These are really the only places where ex- (and current) soldiers are actively recruited for "security" and "training" work overseas. Some times you actually will end up staring at a video monitor in an air conditioned trailer at an African oil refinery or teaching 18 year olds how to clean a Makarov. With the right credentials, the right background and the right questions you'll get work. Even if you do plug into this world there are no shortage of experienced people.

Other groups, such as the Ghurkas, the Swiss Guards, and the French Foreign Legions, are not your classic "Dogs of War" type of mercenaries but vanishing anachronisms. Small but oil rich countries like Oman, Brunei need outside help to keep things quiet, but usually with the Queen's troops army on hire, the Ghurkas and SAS. Even the Pope hires mercenaries to keep the Holy See nice and safe. The good news is that right now, stinking rich, but "security asset" poor, flyspeck states are eager employers but usually by contract through their biggest mineral resource company (which of course is blessed by the appropriate ex-colonial country). Other countries like Myanmar, Angola, Croatia, Namibia, Guatemala, El Salvador, Afghanistan and other war-torn regions use foreign advisors (with spooky assistance) supplied by other countries like Iran, Cuba, Libya, Syria, Pakistan, Britain and of course the U.S. to keep their army trained. But in the days of rapid-reaction forces, the U.N., and political correctness, the days of the Wild Geese are long gone. These days a mercenary is more likely to be hired by a oil company than a slobbering dictator.

For now, South Africa is the major supplier of mercenaries for work around Africa. By the year 2000, it is estimated that the South African government will lay off 60,000 soldiers. Here's just a peek at some of the players.

Executive Outcomes

Nick van der Bergh and Eeben Barlow run Executive Outcomes, based in Pretoria, South Africa. Executive Outcomes was founded in 1989 by the 17-year veteran and former long-range recon soldier from South Africa's 32nd battalion. They began the new trend for corporate mercenaries in March, 1993 when UNITA captured a oil storage area in Soya owned by Heritage Oil and Sonangol. The Forcas Armadas Angolanas (FAA) didn't quite know how to oust the rebels without blowing up the precious oil and drilling equipment. The State owned oil company approached Barlow, who despite the impressive sounding name, was a one man band training the South African army and advising a mining company on security. He put together a group of 50 men and ousted the rebels. When UNITA screamed that white mercenaries were fighting in Angola, the oil company mentioned they were just security guards. UNITA had no idea they were actually white and black ex-South African Defense Force men who had fought *for* UNITA during the 1976-1988 war in Angola. Money changes everything in the merc business.

The oil company's representations that EO's men were security guards was curious considering that the men who were securing the oil facility were the UNITA rebels.

EO's men attacked with 600 FAA troops and only ended up with three South Africans wounded. The facility was retaken and as soon as EO's men left UNITA retook the facility back. It was an important event because it showed that outside "security" forces could be used because they were politically sterile and provided military skills without jeopardizing the stability of tottering regimes.

A $140,000 contract in September of 1993 was to protect a diamond mine in Canfunfo in Lunda Norte, Angola. EO considers themselves a security service that stabilize mining operations allowing governments to write checks based on the smooth flow of raw resources. For example, Angola's diamond fields generate $350–$450 million dollars a month. Estimates put EO's former Angola contract at $40 million (about half for soldiers and half for equipment and supplies). Soldiers of UNITA (National Union for the Total Independence of Angola) finally overran the mine, leaving 36 people dead, most of them from the security firm. The men were provided as military trainers but were allowed to carry out preemptive strikes against UNITA if they felt they or the mine were threatened. Since things have quieted down in Angola, they are training MPLA soldiers to handle the upcoming peace.

EO's strength is "using enough gun," creating detailed plans, acquiring and coordinating air support and paying close attention to the real sources of money: the mine owners and not the Ray-Banned dictators.

After their success in Angola, Barlow made a sales call with his unusual wares in March of 1995 to the beleaguered Valentine Strasser and got busy shortly thereafter. The deal is supposedly worth between $500,000 and $1.5 million a month. It could be the latter figure, since the payment was based on EO securing the diamond fields from the rebels and part of the payment was made by giving Branch Energy the concession to the Koidu diamond field (the Sierra Leone government still holds a 60 percent ownership). Branch Energy is owned by Strategic Resources Group, a British company based in the Bahamas, that in turn owns Executive Outcomes. True to form, EO captured the Kono diamond district from the rebels in two days, instead of the nine they estimated. Other reports say that Bahamas-based but British-owned Heritage Oil and Gas (part of the same group that owns EO) financed the EO intervention in exchange for diamond concessions and that the fee was 1.5 million pounds per month. Branch Energy is reputed to be the largest shareholder in Heritage (which also owns Branch Mining) to develop the diamond fields (worth an estimated 180 million pounds). Because of the sale of EO parent company, Dogs of War Inc., is now Canadian owned, which puts an entirely new light on any contracts they sign.

It gets even more confusing when the alleged links of the Heritage Board of Directors are explored, revealing vague but interesting connections to British liberal newspapers and a former Liberal leader. There are also direct connections between South African military intelligence officers and officers of Heritage Oil and Gas. Far too shady for *DP*, but a good story for "60 Minutes."

Troops were in-country by April, and they quickly managed to push back the rebels from 36 km to 126 km from the capital in just nine days. They then pushed the rebels out of the Kono diamonds fields (about 216 km east of Freetown) in just two days using helicopter gunships. Shortly after leaving Sierra Leone, about 3000 rebels were invited back in to Freetown by coup leader Johnny Koroma.

EO says they are supplying men and expertise to seven countries in Africa, among them Kenya, Angola and Uganda. They are discussing deals with customers in Malawi, Mozambique, Sudan, and even a client in Southeast Asia.

It seems that Executive Outcomes is just one of 80 companies. For example, the company that owns EO is **Strategic Resources**, based in Pretoria. ☎ *[27] 12 3-481-352.* That company owns a percentage of Branch Mining, which has been given mining concessions as partial payment for EO providing security in Sierra Leone. Now this is either a great yarn, a fantastic movie plot or an indication of how wars may be fought in the future. You decide. De Beers the giant diamond consortium has called EO "a bunch of bandits." As for founder Barlow he says "as long as our clients are happy with our work…we will continue doing our work as best we can."

Executive Outcomes
P.O. Box 75255
Lynwood Ridge

Pretoria, 0040 South Africa
☎ *(27) 12 473 789*

Gurkha Security Guards (GSG)

Reputedly, GSG is a front for the British Government set up to facilitate sending Ghurkas to Sierra Leone to defend the diamond mines. Nick Bell, a former officer in the Gurkha regiment of the British army managed to provide a few good men. The salary is as high as $8000 a month. Not bad for the wages of war.

GSG mainly consist of Brits who have had service with Her Majesty's Forces or other security work. Obviously, they lean toward hiring men from Nick's old outfit. His last client was the government of Sierra Leone, which was fighting an all-out war against RUF, a rebel faction. Nick does his recruiting out of hotel rooms in places like Banbury, Oxfordshire, according to the *New African.*

Job security is a little dicey since the leader of the GSG contingent in Sierra Leone, American Bob MacKenzie, was killed in the Malal Hills in February of 1995. He was also reportedly eaten by the rebels. After MacKenzie was killed, the Ghurkas returned to Nepal. There are a number of companies that provide security to outside countries based in St. Helior like Frank E. Basil Inc. and Allmakes (Jersey) Ltd.

GSG

Suite 11, Queensway House
St. Helior, Jersey JE4 81Y
Channel Islands, U.K.
☎ *[44] (1) 534-74-707*

Military Professional Resources, Inc.

There is an option for those with a little silver around the temples and a spare tire around the middle. Billed as the "greatest corporate assemblage or Military Expertise in the World," Military Professional Resources, Inc. (MPRI) is a group of former military professionals who train armies and do what retired generals do. They are based in Alexandria, Virginia, and claim to pull in about $12 million a year in assignments. Not bad for an eight-year-old company with 160 employees and about 2000 top kicks on call. Although their brochure copy would not get them much ink in *Soldier of Fortune*, their terminology sounds ominously like the doublespeak of Executive Outcomes. What does MPRI offer their well-heeled but disorganized customers? Their brochure offers Doctrine Development, Military Training, War Game Support, and even Democracy Transition. *DP* could not find Advanced Medal Polishing, Golf 101 or Cocktail Party Banter in the list, so we are somewhat suspect of their credentials. However, they are credited with training the Croat army who smacked the bejeezuz out of the Serbs in Krajina province back in August of '95. If you are tired of wearing your medals at home contact:

Military Professional Resources Inc.

1201 East Abingdon Drive, Suite 425
Alexandria, Virginia 22314
☎ *(703) 684-0853*
FAX: (703) 684-3528
e-mail info@mpri.com
http://www.mpri.com/

WARNING

Joining any military or paramilitary organization and/or fighting with a foreign army may subject you to prosecution, imprisonment or execution by other countries. If you are a U.S. citizen, you can lose your citizenship and be liable for international crimes. Association or contact with mercenary recruiters and groups can make you subject to investigation by U.S. and international law enforcement agencies.

Military/Adventure Resources

Books International

69B Lynchford Road
Farnborough
Hampshire, England GU14 6EJ
☎ *(01252) 376564*
FAX (01252) 370181

Books International specializes in military reference books for the modeler, collector, researcher or curious. You won't find too many cerebral products here but plenty of hard-to-find illustrated books on past wars, equipment, history and military reference works. Where else would you find an illustrated reference guide to Polish military helicopters or a real life photo book of the Navy SEALS?

Brassey's Inc.

8000 Westpark Drive
First Floor
McLean, Virginia 22102
☎ *(703) 442-4535*
FAX: (703) 790-9063

Brassey's is the publisher of choice when British military men want to fill their mahogany bookcases. They are known for their annual *Defence* yearbook that keeps the Brits up to date on the rest of the world. Each issue has essays and intros on the leading political and military topics. If you want to be the model of a modern major general, you should look into their books on biological, nuclear, naval, historical and military warfare. Their annual update of *The World in Conflict* is a must-read for professional adventurers. There are drier books on ammunition, land force logistics and radar and other technical reference manuals. It is no surprise that their U.S. rep is based in McLean, Virginia.

Covert Action

1500 Massachusetts Ave., N.W., #732
Washington, D.C. 20005
☎ *(202) 331-9763*
FAX: (202) 331-9751

A magazine written by some ex-company folks who have no qualms about telling it like it is. Plenty of facts, numbers, dates, photos and other material to back their statements up.

For Your Eyes Only

Tiger Publications
Post Office Box 8759
Amarillo, Texas 79114
☎ *(805) 655-2009*

Billed as an open intelligence summary of current military affairs. Editor Stephan Cole puts together the biweekly eight-page newsletter to provide an excellent update on military, political and diplomatic events around the world. Somewhat right-wing and hardware-oriented, it still provides a balanced global view of breaking events. An annual subscription costs $65 (26 issues). Sample copies are $3 each. Back issues are available for $1.25–$2, depending on how many you order. FYEO is also available on NewsNet, ☎ *(800) 952-0122* or *(215) 527-8030*.

Jane's Information Group

1340 Braddock
Suite 300
Alexandra Virginia 22314
☎ *(703) 683-3700*
FAX: (703) 836-1593

Jane's is the undisputed leader in military intelligence for the world's armies. About a quarter of a million people subscribe to their annual guide on aircraft, but only about 11,000 need to know what's new in nuclear, biological and chemical protection clothing. Just as teenagers await the new car catalogs in the fall, the world's generals eagerly await the new Jane's reports on weapon systems, aircraft, ships, avionics, strategic weapons and other hardware. Esoteric fans thumb through their yearbooks on "Electro-optics, Image Intensifier Systems" (not to be confused with their guide to thermal imaging systems) or Air Launched Weapons. Arms dealers never travel without their *World Markets for Armoured and Military Logistics Vehicles*. Prices for the books or CD-ROMS run between $400 and $9000. If you are buying an update of an existing book or CD-ROM, the price drops about 25 percent. For your money, you get one annual guide, 11 monthly updates and a summary report. Jane's also publishes a monthly intelligence review, *Jane's Intelligence Review,* that provides background on global conflicts, terrorist groups and arsenals.

Jane's Security and Counterintelligence Equipment Yearbook

A new service is *Jane's Sentinel,* a series of regional security assessments with monthly updates and a broadcast fax service. *Sentinel* breaks down the world into six regions and provides reports on physical features, infrastructure, defense and security, as well as general information like maps and graphs.

In case the world is smitten with a bad case of peacefulness, Jane's also dabbles in the mundane. They have guides to airports, the container business and railways.

If you have ever have been torn between buying a Vigiland Surveillance Robot or a Magnavox Thermal Sniper Scope, Jane's makes it as easy as shopping at Victoria's Secret. The book contains an overview and listing of all major equipment used by security, antiterrorist and civil defence organizations.

The New Press

450 West 41st Street
New York, New York 10036
☎ *(212) 629-8802*
FAX: (212) 268-6349
This publisher of "serious books" can be counted on for interesting new books. Their titles include *Civil Wars: From L.A. to Bosnia* by Hans Magnus Enzensberger, a book that helps readers understand the new forces that shape conflicts, and two books by Gabriel Kolko—*Century of War*, a new view of wars since 1914 with some excellent insights to war after WWII, and *Anatomy of a War*, the story of the Vietnam conflict from the Vietnamese, U.S. and Communist Party viewpoints.

Paladin Books

Post Office Box 1307
Boulder, Colorado 80306

Your best source for militaria, gung-ho adventure books and such classics as *Advanced Weapons Tactics for Hostage Rescue Teams.* Send for a listing or catalog. Much of the material is flatulent diction, tough guy fantasies from military manuals or bizarre "get even" tomes. But there are some gems among the stones.

Soldier of Fortune

5735 Arapahoe Avenue
Boulder, Colorado 80303
☎ *(800) 877-5207 (subscriptions)*
☎ *(303) 449-3750 (editorial)*
The political left imagines the SOF reader as a gun-polishing, beer-drinking closet Rambo who actually cleaned latrines in Nam. Well, they are probably half right. It's the other half of the readership and content that is impressive. For every three articles on self-defense, gun control or new fighting knives, there is a good firsthand description of one of the world's dirty little wars. SOF does provide some very interesting on-the-ground reporting from countries undergoing Third World turmoil. Their editorial position is somewhat to the right of Ronald Reagan and Wyatt Earp, but the magazine is still an important source for information on weapons and little-known conflicts. Subscriptions are $28 a year with newsstand issues going for $4.75

Soldier of Fortune Expo

P.O. Box 693
Boulder, Colorado 80306
☎ *(303) 449-3750*
☎ *(800) 800-7630*
Alone in your room, dreaming of foreign adventure and glory? Why not get those army surplus fatigues cleaned and pressed, get a suitable buzz cut, suck in your gut, and hang out with thousands of other "military/survivalist" enthusiasts? Every Fall this Expo is more than just row after row of guns and survival equipment; it's also a chance to see real men fire off real machine guns. You get to see things blow up and watch real men fight with pugil sticks; worship real mercenaries, tough guys and heroes up

close, as you strut around the convention center terrified that people might think you are actually a wimp; hear speakers tell you why our government can't be trusted and learn what you can do to maintain your God-given right to own metal tubes that propel projectiles.

The Stockholm International Peace Research Institute

FAX: [46] (8) 655-97-33

This group publishes an 870-page annual on the world's military expenditures, arms production and trade.

Behind the Lines

P.O. Box 456 Festus Missouri 63028
☎ *(314) 937-7204*

The journal of U.S. Military Special Operations is a bimonthly, 80 page magazine featuring articles on theory, history, development and first hand accounts of actual missions. $24 per year.

Play That Funky Music White Mercenary Boy

In an effort to give the men of Executive Outcomes a kinder, gentler image, they put together a country music video called "And They Call Us the Dogs of War." The video shows EO staff distributing Bibles and working on do-gooder projects like building water purification plants in Angola. It has not hit MTV yet.

MILITARY AND PARAMILITARY
ORGANIZATIONS

Terrorism

I Hear You Knocking, But You Can't Come In

Terrorism can be easily defined as "premeditated, politically motivated violence perpetrated against noncombatant targets by subnational groups or clandestine agents usually intended to influence an audience" as it is by United States Code Section 2656(d). This definition is obviously the work of leaders of established and recognized countries, most with democratic political processes. It should be remembered that the United States of America, Russia, China, France and Israel, along with numerous other now respectable countries, began their road to independence using terrorist methods and actions against their past leaders.

Today, few can argue that terrorism is a legitimate and sadly productive method to gain international attention, demand concessions and eventually establish legitimate states and political parties. Despite what the world governments espouse, there are few minority groups that can use the existing political process to gain their independence or freedom without resorting to outrageous tactics.

The less potent the group is as a political force and the thinner the support base, the more likely the group will resort to more dramatic methods to secure world attention. The leaders of these groups tend to be from the upper classes, college educated, creative, egotistical and flamboyant almost to the point of ridiculousness. Che Guevara, Yasir Arafat, Abdullah Ocalan, Carlos the Jackal, Abu Nidal, and Rafael Sebastin Guillen Vicente, a.k.a. Subcommandante Marcos, the pipe-smoking, wisecracking son of a furniture salesman are not the exception but the rule.

The real bad men are the dark silent politicians, theocrats and businessmen who write checks for these groups or provide safe haven. Iran, Libya, Sudan, Syria (and its vassal state Lebanon) Pakistan and Afghanistan are where you will see the roots of evil. The State Department estimates that about 21 percent of world terror is directed against the U.S. The number of Americans killed hovers between a couple and a dozen. Of course, the State Department turns a blind eye towards Oklahoma.

There are various proven methods of gaining the world's attention. The first is to execute or kidnap Americans while they are abroad. This will guarantee at least two to five minutes on CNN, with 30-minute repeats every half-hour until the situation is resolved. The next most common method is usually hijacking; the third and most frequent is bombing, the last and possibly least effective are attacks on military or police forces. Sending a well-written political proposal with workable, fair solutions to the ruling party won't even get you a return phone call. You gotta have a gimmick, and fear among the populace will definitely get you attention.

There is another level of terrorism activity that doesn't make the headlines but is necessary for the ongoing support of organizations and activities. If terrorist groups are not funded by a government (such as Iran, Iraq, Libya or private sources), they must resort to extortion (demanding money in exchange for lack of violent attacks), robbery (theft of money or possessions by force or threat of force), kidnapping (abducting people who then are released in exchange for negotiated amounts of money) or drug or weapons smuggling (payment for safe transport of illegal goods). Other groups are for hire and will conduct assassinations, kidnappings, warfare, bombings or other criminal attacks for a fee. Many times these acts are carried out under the name of a terrorist group but are simply criminal acts. There are various freelance terrorists like Abu Nidal and the now forcibly retired Carlos. They would provide spectacular sound bites and video clips for a fee and/or a piece of the action. All that was missing was a director and a producer.

It is important to note that terrorists would like to attack at the heart of the intended enemies' strongholds but are neither strong, wily or powerful enough. Worse yet, there are few terrorist groups who can handle the ideologically numbing bureaucracy it would take to pick up the trash and clean out parking meters. Just look at the poor Palestinians who are now faced with beating their own people to quell rioting and protect Israelis. So most groups content themselves with chipping away at the public confidence, gaining a hollow importance but taking no real steps toward bettering the plight of the people they represent. Some groups like Hezbollah and Hamas are strong political entities with equally strong military arms. Other groups like the Kurdish independence groups are caught in a Catch-22, with their political structures banned forcing them to continue as terrorist organizations.

Understand that terrorism is the smallest threat to travelers. In fact more people are killed by lightening than terrorists. Most victims are innocent people who live within the victim country. Once in a while we are treated to splattered tourists in Tel Aviv or kidnapped trekkers in Kashmir. Once again this has now become the exception, not the rule.

The reality is that terrorism is successful by its ability to create terror. The fact that every major and minor airport in the world has metal detectors, security guards and X-ray machines is testament to the terrorists' effectiveness—as is the fact that Americans can rattle off two or three well-known terrorist groups but couldn't possibly tell you the legal political parties in Israel, Cambodia or Colombia.

Follow the Leader

The writing may be on the wall for the old terrorist groups of the past 20 years. The demise of Marxist-style terrorism may crumble under the weight of paperwork and the fundamental inability of these groups to grasp success. The IRA ran out of patience to outtalk the verbose Brits, the PLO still can't manage its own people, and Fidel has started to wear natty Western business suits while stumping for investors. Terrorism requires polite attacks to avoid alienating future investors.

While the PLO is figuring how to write parking tickets and the IRA is busy beating drug dealers to death with hammers, other groups ponder the benefit of actually getting what they want. They know that sooner or later their actions will force compromise and integration. Freedom fighters, from the Kurds to the Afghans to the Sudanese, are dividing into smaller warring factions. If the truth be known, these folks are happiest channeling eons of subjugation and oppression into some pretty spectacular and brutal events but have little stomach for politicking.

Some of the most dramatic terrorist acts have been the bombing of the Marine Barracks in Beirut, the bombing of the World Trade Center in New York, the downing of Pan Am 107 over Lockerbie, Scotland, the total destruction of the William P. Murrah building in Oklahoma City, and the world's first large-scale chemical gas attack on five Tokyo subway trains. It is important to note that in each one of these cases, the perpetrators were either apprehended, identified or killed in the act. Crime does not pay and wages of fear suck.

Terrorism: No Longer a Growth Industry

Terrorism is running out of money, and, with the rash of suicide bombings in Sri Lanka and Israel, terrorist groups may be running out of recruits. The former and current supporters of terrorism against the West find themselves banished from the world marketplace and proudly trying to pretend they never needed all that Western money anyway. Libya, Iraq and Iran all make hollow speeches, while privately their emissaries desperately try to get invited back into the real world's economic cocktail party. When you make it big in the terrorism network, you are guaranteed to have a short career. When Carlos was an embarrassment to the terror network, he was shuffled between Libya, Iraq, Jordan, Syria and Yemen and finally ended up in the Sudan before he was then served up to the French to entice the U.S. to lift sanctions. The FBI and CIA have tracked down Pakistani and Egyptian terrorists right to their hideouts in Pakistan and Afghanistan by offering rewards that are in the millions. How did they catch them? There are some very wealthy Afghan and Pakistani bodyguards today.

The thought that should give Westerners pause is that these folks are emulating the early actions that led to the nations of China, France, Israel and the U.S.

Terror Mutates

The pure ideology of '70s terrorism is slowly evolving into a cash-based, self centered ideology better suited for the '80s (we never said terrorists are up on trends—after all, they do spend a lot time in hiding). Despite the lack of big-time sponsors, terrorism will continue to be a threat to all Western travelers. Westerners are high-profile pawns in the publicity game. The savvy traveler needs to understand the difference between the Algerian terrorist (who will cut your throat without even rifling through your pockets), a Mexican terrorist (who has no reason to harm an American tourist), a Filipino terrorist (who will trade you like a used car salesman), a Kurdish terrorist (who will use you as a political pawn and usually release you unharmed and well fed), a rogue Khmer Rouge gunmen (who wants his $10,000 or you get whacked) or a plain ol' thug who may have been fighting for some funky acronymic rabble, but just likes the Rolex you have and can't be bothered asking you politely for it. Terrorism may also be faceless in the case of bombings in Paris, Tel Aviv, Karachi and other urban centers. So keep in mind that carrying around a copy of Mao's little red book or Qaddafi's green book or even Carlos' black book won't get you as far as carrying a Gold card. Money is the primary goal of most terrorism groups in the Third World, publicity is second, and achievement of political objectives is a distant third. From Colombia to Kashmir, bad guys are taking the money and running.

For those who want to understand more about the aims of various political, terrorist or freedom groups, they can be contacted at the addresses at the end of this chapter. Keep in mind that any contact with this group may put you under the direct scrutiny of U.S., European and Israeli intelligence agencies and lead to criminal charges being filed if any collusion or support is proven.

Group	Leader/Goals	Cause	Location	Size	Began
Hezbollah	Nasrallah and Fadlallah lead a religious/political party with military and information wings. Funded and controlled by Iran	Anti-Israel, Shia Islamic Fundamentalistics	Mekteb-1 Hezbollah, South Suburb, Bir-al Abed, Beirut, Lebanon. Operates out of Bekaa Valley with cels in Argentina, U.S. and Europe	Thousands	1982
PKK	Pro Kurd alleged to be funded by extortion of Kurdish businesses in Europe and drug transshipment	Kurdish Homeland in SE Turkey	Mekte-Bi Amele-1 Kurdistan Barelias-Chotura West Bekaa, Lebanon Military base is Zap, Northern Iraq	10,000–15,000	1974
Abu Nidal	Freelance group under Sabri al-Banmna	Anti Israel/PLO offshoot	Now living in Libya, Sudan and Bekaa Valley		1974
Abu Sayeef	Abdurajik Abu Bakar Janjalani		Jolo & Basilan in southern Philippines	200	1991
ETA	Basque separatists supported by Libya and the IRA	Basque homeland	Border areas in Northern Spain and SW France	Hundreds	1959

Group	Leader/Goals	Cause	Location	Size	Began
Sendero Luminoso	Maoist meanies who babysit coca trade	Maoist Drug Production	Peru	300	1967
Tupac Amaru	Rag tag remnants		Peru	200	1983
Alex Boncayaso Brigade	Communist group seeking overthrow of government	Communist	Manila, Philippines	?	1985
GIA	Loose groups of armed men backed by Iran, Sudan and France based Algerian expats	Islamic Fundamentalistics	Algeria	1500	1992
Dev Sol (DHKP/C	Marxist Kurdish fighters	Kurdish Independence Anti U.S, anti NATO	Turkey	500	1978
Islamic Group	Iran and Sudan supported and trained fighters. Blind Sheik Al Rahman (in prison in the U.S.) is spiritual leader	Islamic Fundamentalistics	Egypt	Al Minya area	1975
Hamas	Palestine political party with military wing backed by Saudis, Sudanese Iran and expats	Islamic/ Anti Israel	West Bank, Gaza Strip	Thousands	1987
Harakat ul-Ansar	Islamic group supported by Pakistan that seeks independence of Kashmir	Islamic/Anti India	Muzaffarabad, Pakistan	300	1980?
IRA	Irish Separatist supported by Libya, Irish expats. Military wing of SinnFien.	Anti U.K.	Belfast, Ireland	Hundreds	1969
Kahane Chai	Supported by U.S and European Jews. Founded by Binyamin Kahane.	Anti Palestinian	Jerusalem	?	1993
Kach	Founded by Rabbi Meir Khanane	Anti Palestinian	Jerusalem	?	1993
Tamil Tigers		Tamil homeland in Sri Lanka		10000	1983
Mujahedin-e Khalq Organization	Supported by expat Iranians, seeks to overthrow current Iranian government	Anti Iran	Iraq	Thousands	1965?
National Liberation Army	Maoist-Marxist -Leninist group seeking to overthrow government but gets funding from kidnapping and drugs	Anti government	rural parts of Colombia	3000	1963
PFLP-GC	Pro Palestinian	Anti Israel	Lebanon, Syria	?	1968
PLF	Pro Palestinian	Anti Israel	Lebanon, Syria	50	
PFLP	Pro Palestinian	Anti Israel	Lebanon, Syria	8000	
DFLP	Pro Palestinian	Anti Israel	Lebanon, Syria		
PLJ	Pro Palestinian	Anti Israel	Lebanon, Syria	?	1972
FARC	Communist rebel group, controls most drug shipments in Colombia.	Anti U.S, anti government	Colombia and border areas	7000	1966

Freedom Fighters

It would be very easy to list a number of groups under terrorists that are actually fighting for political change. Fighters in Timor, Bougainville, Mexico, Israel, Turkey, Iraq, Iran, and to a certain extent America, are fighting for political determination. On the minuscule islands of Bougainville, Timor and the Comoros, there are pocket sized insurgencies that may or may not lead to political independence. In countries like Iraq, Turkey and Tajikistan, there are massive areas under the control of rebel factions or warlords who don't see eye to eye with the official government.

Some groups like FARC, ELN, the PKK and The Wa Army cloak themselves in a Marxist or liberation dogma but are essentially making a living by protecting massive amounts of drug shipments within their are of control.

In areas like Algeria, Israel and Sri Lanka, it is hard to figure out who is trying to liberate who from who as hundreds of innocent bystanders are killed in the process.

Afghan Aftereffects

There are some 14,000 foreign veterans of the Russian/Afghan war. This network of experienced veterans are members of hard-line Islamic groups in Algeria, Egypt, Jorgan, Palestine, Pakistan, China and even The Philippines. (Nearly 3000 Algerians, 2000 Egyptians and 10,000 Arabs fought in Afghanistan.) These fighters make up the core group of most Islamic fundamentalist struggles.

Only 100 full time U.S. spooks and diplomats actually controlled "Operation Cyclone" from Pakistan and Washington from 1986 to 1989. Massive amounts of weapons and supplies were shipped in to the resistance fighters. The U.S. spent half a billion dollars a year while the Saudis kicked in $240 million a year. The operation not only dumped containers and storage yards worth of weapons in Afghanistan but also created a generation of out of work fighters, many of whom continue to train or actually fight in Algeria, China, Chechnya, Tajikistan, Egypt, Sudan, The Philippines, Afghanistan, Morocco, Kashmir and other jihads where muslims fight against secular or non Muslim governments.

The major training center for *mujahedin* used to be Peshawar, Pakistan on the border with Afghanistan. Now terrorists can find sanctuary in Iran, Sudan, Libya, Pakistan, Afghanistan, Cuba, Iraq, Lebanon and North Korea. In many cases, the leaders of those countries utilize the services of terrorist groups.

The U.S. State Department puts out rewards of up to 4 million dollars to find over 30 leading terrorists and international criminals. Drug dealers like Khun Sa (who lives in luxury in Yangon), terrorists like Dursun Karatas, the leader of Dev Sol, or even the two Libyan intelligence agents, Lamen Khalifa Fhimah and Abdel Basset Ali Megrahi, the two men accused of masterminding the destruction of Pan Am Flight 103 over Lockerbie, are all worth serious cash to Uncle Sam.

Terrorism in Europe

There are about 5 million non-European immigrants living in Germany, of which about 45,000 are known to be members of extremist groups. About half of this latter group are considered to be prepared for violence.

The total numbers are not impressive, but the support they provide to terrorism groups is. Europe provides a much more lucrative and unsuspecting field of battle for groups from the PKK of Turkey to the GIA of Algeria. A rough estimate of expats from countries with potential sympathies to terrorist groups include 70,000 Tamils and Sikhs, 30,000 Afghans, 300,000 Kurds (3500 are known members of PKK), 650,000 Yugoslavs, 70,000 Palestinians and 85,000 Iranians. The disenchantment of these recent immigrants and the intolerance shown by their host countries (some with insurmountable citizenship laws) have created fertile ground for groups like Hezbollah and the PKK.

The PKK has a network that covers 26 cities in Western Europe. The PFLP is estimated to have 50–60 terrorists in Europe; al-Fatah has 1700 supporters in West Germany; the PFLP-GC has 30 expert terrorists in West Germany. A sleeper network of Abu Nidal was exposed in Portugal, and the ranks are growing, not shrinking, despite a get-tough attitude by Germany, Spain and France.

Qaddafi was an ardent supporter of the IRA, training Irish Republican soldiers and providing explosives and arms. Libya also supports the Basque ETA, and the early struggles of Charles Taylor in Liberia and Foday Sankoh RUF in Sierra Leone.

The Bad Boys Club

The U.S. has a list of "rogue" nations. They are countries who won't play ball with the rest of the world and more importantly give Uncle Sam the finger every time we try to spank them. In an adolescent sort of way you have to give these guys credit for being just like America was two hundred years ago. For now these regions are the playground of the CIA and consume the lion's share of our fly over, covert action, satellite photography and covert messing around budgets.

Iraq

Boy does America hate this country. We hate them so much that we always call their leader by his first name. Oooh, that smarts. This guy had the nerve to try to take our oil. So "Saddam" is in the dog house, big time. It's important to remember that we don't do much about it since we did leave him with enough weapons, soldiers and ammo to keep Iran occupied. He babysits the Mujahedin-e Khalq (MEK), an army of pissed off Iranians that waits for the green light to invade Iran from their base in Iraq.

So I guess its OK if he offs members of Iraqi National Congress (INC), gasses Kurds, kills family members and even lets his son beat and torture their own national soccer team.

We let him charge rent to the Abu Nidal organization (ANO), the Kurdistan Workers' Party (PKK), the Arab Liberation Front (ALF), and the former head of the long shut down 15 May Organization, Abu Ibrahim. All in all what eats Uncle Sam the most about Saddam is that he is actually smarter, meaner and badder than us.

Iran

The land the Ayatollah built remains the most ardent sponsor of sanctioned terrorism and the greatest source of concern. You have to give Iran credit for thinking big. Just like we send forth Coca Cola and McDonalds to spread capitalism and the American Way, they franchise Hezbollah to spread fundamentalism to the masses.

Iran's surrogate political and military arm, Hezbollah, was responsible for the bombing of the Israeli Embassy in Buenos Aires in early 1992 and remains the leading suspect in the July 1994 bombing of the Argentine-Israel Mutual Association in Buenos Aires that killed 96 people. Iran opposes the Middle East peace process and arms and funds rejectionist groups who espouse violence.

They also bankroll Hamas, Palestine Islamic Jihad and many other Muslim or anti Israeli groups. Iran also likes to zap dissidents even when they move away. Offing members of the Mujahedin-e Khalq (MEK), the Kurdish Democratic Party of Iran (KDPI), former members of SAVAK and the Shah's buddies get you serious brownie points here.

You don't want to get a bad book review because they still have a hard on for Salman Rushdie, even though they never actually read the book. They still have a $2 million dollar bounty on Rushdie's balding pate. Despite vocal condemnation it seems like the eraser on the mullah's *fatwa* pen is broken. Now we do have a warm spot for Iran, but only because we hate them less than Iraq and they did drastically reduce the population and military strength during their long drawn out war.

Cuba

We'd have to say Cuba is bad boy number three (after Iraq and Iran) just because it is so damn close. It is odd that the U.S. is powerless when it comes to Uncle Fidel. We thumped Panama, Grenada, Nicaragua and every other banana republic that gets in our way, but when it comes to Fidel, we just sit and wait. Fidel is out of the terrorism business but still is buddy-buddy with Colombian groups like FARC and the ELN. However, drug transshipments may play a bigger part in his enthusiasm rather than left wing ideology. Havana still provides safe haven to several terrorists who sought sanctuary several years ago. A number of Basque Fatherland and Liberty (ETA) terrorists live on the island, along with some Latin American terrorists and a few U.S. fugitives. When Fidel goes, it is expected that Cuba will come back into the right wing fold, but drugs and the bad guys won't automatically go away.

Libya

The colonel's ties with terrorists and insurgents reached their peak in the '80s but are ongoing. Despite the continual pleading by Qaddafi to be allowed back into the political and financial playpen of the world market, he continues to harbor those responsible in placing the bomb on Pan Am flight 103 in 1988. And the French want to chat with him regarding the bombing of UTA flight 772. United Nations Security Council Resolution 883 froze selected Libyan assets and banned the sale of many categories of oil-industry equipment. Qaddafi has made a series of silly demands in exchange for the suspected terrorists but has yet to show any good faith. He does have a snazzy set of outfits though when he makes those pleas. Despite his sad game face, he does back once insurgents and now *el jefes* in West and Central Africa (Foday Sankoh and Charles Taylor). Libya writes allowance checks (or cashes rent checks) to the Abu Nidal organization (ANO), the Palestine Islamic Jihad (PIJ), and Ahmed Jabril's Popular Front for the Liberation of Palestine–General Command (PFLP-GC). Abu Nidal has his headquarters in sunny Libya, and Abu Nidal (real name: Sabri al-Banna) calls Tripoli home.

Qaddafi has also been busy building a subterranean factory to manufacture chemical weapons. Seems he knows how to get in on the ground floor on what may be a big business.

North Korea

North Korea has been out of the terrorism business since 1987. Today it is busy bumming food from the people they used to blow up. They are held responsible for the bombing of KAL flight 858 and are home to the aging Yodo-go chapter of the Japanese Red Army. Plus this country is so damn strange its probably better off if they just keep to themselves. Right now, the xenophobic North Koreans are just coming into the '40s let alone the '90s.

Syria

Syria continues to play pocket politics against Turkey (stealing water from the Euphrates) and Israel (for stealing the Golan Heights). Assad support groups are currently carrying out terrorist attacks against its stronger neighbors. Assad is a slick dude since he doesn't actually push the button on any terrorist acts, he just makes them happen. Part of his style is to allow groups to live in Damascus and to allow "stuff" to happen in the Bekaa Valley and Southern Lebanon. Ahmed Jibril's PFLP-GC and the Palestine Islamic Jihad (PIJ) are headquartered near Damascus. Lebanon's Bekaa Valley is training-camp central to HAMAS, the PFLP-GC, the PIJ, and the Japanese Red Army (JRA). The Kurdistan Workers' Party (PKK) continues to train in Syria-controlled areas of Lebanon, and its leader, Abdullah Ocalan, resides at least part-time in Damascus.

Reach Out and Stop Someone

When I visited Syria, I tried to find a phone book to look up terrorist groups. I was never actually shown a phone book but was told that if I give the operator the name of the persons or groups I wanted, they would look it up. When I gave them the names and organizations of the folks we were looking for the operator replied (without missing a beat), "Those people don't live here, they live somewhere else."

Later, I went to make an unannounced visit to Assad in his massive hill-top house. I just smiled and waved at the first checkpoint, where the guards were too stunned to react. At the second checkpoint, one soldier leapt on the hood of my battered VW bug while it was still moving. He shoved his machine gun through my window with one hand and held on to the car with the other. I still get a chuckle when I think of him staring at me bugeyed and terrified with his face pressed against the windshield. After I stopped to help him off my hood, I told him I was just going up to see Assad. He said "This is not allowed." When I asked why, he just repeated "This is not allowed." Despite my eloquent protestations he kept looking and nodding down at his aimed machine gun as if I didn't get the point. He had a pained smile on his face all the while trying to remember how to deal with smiling jabbering tourists that just won't go away. Finally feeling sorry for him (and being surrounded by nervous armed soldiers), I decided to come back another day.

When I turned around to go down the hill the guard remembered to say, "Have a nice time in Syria." A comment that is used by all the military and secret police to ensure that everyone keeps smiling. -RYP

Sudan

This embattled country has provided safe haven to a number of international terrorist groups. They are cozy with their neighbor, Iran, and turf out terrorist groups like pawns in a chess game. They coughed up Carlos the Jackal a while back hoping that it would get them some gold stars. No luck. Being caught red handed in the attempted assassination of Hosni Mubarek and being behind the assassination of Anwar Sadat won't make them many friends soon. Sudan's support of terrorist groups includes providing bases for paramilitary training, indoctrination, money, travel documentation, safe passage and refuge in Sudan. Several Iranian-backed terrorist groups use Sudan as a transit point and meeting place. Naturally the CIA is busy helping the SPLA in the south.

Terrorists tend to strike countries where there is the potential for the greatest amount of economic damage. Tourists and tourism facilities are prime targets, because crippled tourism cuts off vital foreign hard currency. Following the 1985 hijacking of TWA flight 847 enroute to Athens, the Greek government estimated that the subsequent tourism damage topped out at more than US$100 million.

Does terrorism work? In April of '96, nineteen Greek tourists were gunned down in Cairo by Egyptian fundamentalists, killing with them half the tourism receipts from the previous year. Why? Because Egypt groups retaliated for Israel de shelling a refugee camp in Southern Lebanon, killing nearly 200 innocent victims. Why? Because Hezbollah had killed innocent Israeli citizens in rocket attacks. Why? because Israel occupies Lebanon to create a buffer zone against terrorist attacks. Why? Because the U.S. financially supports and stands behind an occupying nation jammed right smack in the middle of the Arab World. Why? Because we support countries who believe in peace and freedom.

How does Iran, Syria and the rest of Arab world fight back against the U.S. and support the Palestinians? By supporting terrorist groups.

Yes, as you can see, terrorism works, but for all the wrong reasons.

Terrorism and Counter Terrorism

You won't find much of interest when it comes to terrorism related pages. It's not as if terrorists get gabby with government information agencies about their activities, bases and members. Also remember that word terrorism is a Western term used to imply criminality on the part of the "terrorist" organization. Outside the U.S. you will hear the word terrorism used to describe some of our covert and overt activities when we prop up corrupt and non elected governments. So make your own decision.

Resource

The World in Conflict
> by Dr. John Laffin $39.95 (ISBN 1-85753-216-3) Brassey's
> A round up of the world's wars, the combatants tactics and background.

Low Intensity Conflicts
> by CSM James J. Gallagher, $14.95 (ISBN 0-8117-2552-9) Stackpoole ☎ (800) 732-3669
> A good manual for soldiers or journalists who want to understand various attack formations, ambushes, peacekeeping operations and even how checkpoints are set up.

Patterns of Global Terrorism
> http://www.usis.usemb.se/terror/index.html
> Annual report on global terrorism.

Terrorism
> http://www.terrorism.com/

Terrorism Research Center
> http://www.infowar.com/
> ☎ (813) 393.6600
> FAX: (813) 393.6361
> EMAIL: infowar@infowar.com
> Links to info on privacy, espionage, terrorism and much more.

FEMA Fact Sheet:
> http://www.fema.gov/fema/terrorf.html
> Terrorism Help & Tips from FEMA.

Hate groups, terrorists, & radicals
> http://www.xensei.com/users/hubcom/hate.htm

Terrorist weapons
> http://www.onestep.com/milnet/tweaps.htm

Terrorist use of chemical weapons
> http://groucho.la.asu.edu/~godber/research/cwpaper.html

Counter Terrorism
> http://www.counterterrorism.com/

Terrorist Profile Weekly—The Terrorist Fanzine.
> http://gopher.well.sf.ca.us:70/1/Publications/online_zines/Terror

Terrorism & Counterterrorism
> http://www.spystuff.com/listsites.html

Bureau Of Diplomatic Security: Reward info for criminals
> http://www.heroes.net/content.html

Terrorist's Handbook
> http://pilot.msu.edu/user/snooktyl/

Pyrotechnics, Fireworks, explosives
> http://www.amazing1.com/fire.htm

JollyRoger's CookBook
> http://www.voicenet.com/%7Ewizkid/jr.html

The Big Book of Mischief
> http://www.cybercity.hko.net/berlin/solon/bigbook/MAIN.html

Revenge Page
> http://www.cs.uit.no/~paalde/Revenge/

Defense, Aircraft and Counter-terrorism Page
> http://crisny.org/users/siegelm/defense.html

Virtual World of Spies and Intelligence

> http://www.dreamscape.com/frankvad/
> counter.html

Terrorism Research Center

> http://www.geocities.com/CapitolHill/
> 2468/tc2.html

Virtual World of Spies and Intelligence

> http://www.dreamscape.com/frankvad/
> terrorism.html

Counter-Terrorism Page

> http://www.emergency.com/cntr-
> terr.htm

Terrorist Profiles

> http://vislab-www.nps.navy.mil/
> %7Egmgoncal/tgp2.htm

Domestic Terrorism

> http://enhtech.com/veterans/vjv1n4/
> vj2.html

Most Wanted

> http://www.MostWanted.com/

Cyber Muslim

> http://www.uoknor.edu/cybermuslim/
> cy_jihad.html

Center for Terrorism in India

> http://rbhatnagar.csm.uc.edu:8080/
> india_terrorism.html

Perilous Times—Terrorist Page

> http://www.teleport.com/~jstar/ter-
> ror.html

Terrorist Profile Weekly Archives

> http://www.site.gmu.edu/~cdibona/
> tpw.html

Intelligence Web

> http://www.awpi.com/IntelWeb

Index Terrorist Groups

> http://www.site.gmu.edu/~cdibona/
> grpindex.html

Society of Competitive Intelligence Professional Homepage

> http://www.scip.org

All Intelligence and Counter Intelligence Agencies

> http://www.kimsoft.com/kim-spy.htm

Other People, Other Voices

These are not terrorist sites but rather communication tools used to circumvent the barriers the traditional media puts up. Not many Eyewitness News shows cover the uprising in Bougainville, even fewer know where it is.

Television

Two groups have television stations that we know of: The PKK has MED-TV a satellite station that conveniently goes on the blink every once in a while.

MED-TV

> The Linen Hall, 162-168 Regent Street,
> London W1R 5AT
> ☎ [44] (0) 171-4942523
> FAX [44] (0)171-494-2528
> e-mail: med@med-tv.be

MED-TV is the world's only satellite channel that broadcast Kurdish programming to receivers in Europe, North Africa and the Middle East.

Radio

Most rebel groups have radio stations or transmitters. Whether it's Foday Sankoh of the RUF (Sierra Leone) who used to broadcast from a transmitter in his hotel suite in the Abuja Sheraton, or Charles Taylor's hip-hop KISS-FM in Monrovia, radio has been used to send boring pap (VOA), transmit bullshit (Marxist drivel), whip up people to a frenzy (Milles Collines, Burundi) and to play music with revolutionary themes.

Clandesite Radio Stations

> http://up4c03.gwdg.de/~kuhl/cla

Websites

A few caveats about these websites. First, don't assume you are sending e-mails directly to the rebel leader's tent. Most of these websites are put together by well meaning college students and supportive left wingers. Other sites are outlets for suit-and-tie pressure groups that use the website to send out boring press releases on national struggles. Keep in mind that some of these sites hop around like fleas on a dog's back and, in the case of terrorist groups, a government can take the position that you are consorting with wanted felons. All e-mail is monitored to these sites so don't think you are having an intimate tete-a-tete. Send us an e-mail if the site disappears or new ones appear.

TERRORISM

Colombia

ELN (Colombia)

http://www.voces.org

FARC (Colombia)

*http://burn.ucsd.edu/%7Earchive/ats-l/
1996.Jun/0008.html*

**FARC-EP—Fuerzas Armadas Revolucionarios
de Columbia—Ejercito del Pueblo (Colombia)**

*http://sociology.adm.binghamton.edu/
pages/farc/*

Indonesia

East Timor

http://www.ozemail.com.au/~ekeberg/

Iran

Iranian KAR

*http://www.geocities.com/CapitolHill/
7148/*

Iranian People's Fadaii

http://www.fadaii-minority.org/

Arm The Spirit

*P.O. Box 6326, Stn. A
Toronto, Ontario
M5W 1P7 Canada
http://burn.ucsd.edu/~ats/*

Communist Party of Iran

*http://www.pi.se/webpage/commu-
nist.party.of.iran/index.html*

The Constitutionalist Movement of Iran

http://www.irancmi.org/index2.htm "

Organisation of Iranian People's Fedaian

*http://193.80.248.16/
iran.kar.fadai.aksariyat/*

Organisation of Iranian People's Fedaian

http://www.fadaii-minority.org/

Organisation of Iranian People's Mojahedin

*http://www.iran-e-azad.org/farsi/
index.html*

Tudeh Party of Iran

*http://www.demon.co.uk/mardom/
tudeh.htm*

Workers-Communist Party of Iran

http://www.wpiran.org/index.html

Iraqi National Congress

http://www.inc.org.uk/

People's Libration Party-Front (DHKC)

http://www.ozgurluk.org/dhkc

Iraq

Iraqi National Congress

*9 Pall Mall Deposit
124 -128 Barlby Road, London, England
W10 6 BL*
☎ *(0181) 960-4007,
FAX: (0181) 960 4001
In Sulaymania Iraq,* ☎ *[873] (68) 234-
6239 FAX [873] (68) 234-6240*

http://www.inc.org.uk

Patriotic Union of Kurdistan

☎ *011-44-181-642-4518
Att: Latif Rashid
http://www.puk.org*

Ireland

**Irish National Liberation Army &
Irish Republican Socialist Committee (USA)**

http://irsm.pair.com/irscna/irscna.htm

Irish Republican Socialist Committee—IRSC

http://irsm.pair.com/irscna/irscna.htm

Irish Republican Army—IRA

*http://www.tc.umn.edu/nlhome/
m058/soko0009/*

Sinn Féin

*http://www.irlnet.com/sinnfein/
index.html
Sinn Féin,
51/55 Falls Road,
Belfast, Ireland*
☎ *[44] (1232) 624421
FAX: [44] (1232) 622112*

Sinn Féin

*44 Parnell Square,
Dublin 1, Ireland*
☎ *[353] (1) 8726100,
[353] (1) 8726839
FAX: [353] (1) 8733074*

Kurdistan

PKK (Kurdish Workers Party)

*Mekte-Bi Amele-1 Kurdistan
Barelias-Chotura
West Bekaa, Lebanon*

Kurdistan Information Centre

*10 Glasshouse Yard
London EC1A4JN
United Kingdom*
☎ *[01144] (171) 250-1315
Att: Mizgin Sen*

Kurdistan Workers Association

☎ *011-44-181-809-0743*

Kurdistan Solidarity Committee

☎ *[01144] (171) 586-5892
Att: Estella Schmidt*

Kurdistan (Turkey, Iraq, Iran)

*http://www.humanrights.de:80/~kurd-
web/humright/hrrep_e.html*

Kurds (Turkey)

http;//www.kurdistan.org/

American Kurdish Information Network

*2623 Connecticut Avenue NW #1
Washington, D.C. 20008 1522*
☎ *(202) 483-6444, FAX: (202) 483-
6476
http://www.kurdistan.org
e-mail: akin@kurdish.org*

A not very informational information group that is a front for the PKK. They post press releases about the PKK and Kurdish items. We had a rather humorous and obtuse conversation about how much money the PKK sends them. They also have an office in London that is a little easier to deal with and less paranoid. (Also try the Kurdistan Solidarity Committee.)

Kurdistan Democratic Party

2025 I Street N.W.
Suite 1108
Washington, D.C. 20006
☎ *(202) 331-9505*
FAX: 331-9506
http://www.kdp.pp.se/
http://home1.swipnet.se/~w-11534/

Patriotic Union of Kurdistan

☎ *011-44-181-642-4518*
Att: Latif Rashid
U.S. ☎ *(703) 345-3056/*
England ☎ *[44] (181) 993-2196*
France ☎ *[33] (1) 3916 0473*
Turkey ☎ *[90312] 4402199*
Germany ☎ *[49] (30) 344 8738*
http://www.puk.org

Lebanon

Al Manar—The Tower

http://www.almanar.com.lb/
Hezbollah's Beirut-based television station.

Hezbollah's Islamic Resistance Aid Committee

http://www.moqawama.org/
EMAIL: moqawama@cyberia.net.lb.
Moqawama is the word for resistance in Arabic.

Mexico

El Insurgente—EPR & PDPR

http://www.xs4all.nl/-insurg/

Zapatista Army of National Liberation—EZLN

http://www.ezln.org/

Zapatistas

http://www.peak.org/~justin/ezln/ezln.html

Palestine

Info on Palestine

http://darkwing.uregon.edu

Papua New Guinea

Bougainville Freedom Movement

Sasha Baer or Vikki John
P.O. Box 134, Erskineville NSW 2043,
Australia
http://www.magna.com.au/~sashab/BFM.htm

Bougainville Interim Government—Australia

Moses Havini, Australian Representative
34 Darvall Road, Eastwood 2122 NSW,
Australia
☎ */FAX: [61] (02) 804-7602*

Rosemarie Gillespie, Overseas Research Officer

24 Garling Street, Lyneham ACT 2602
Australia
☎ *[61] (6) 257-1298*

Bougainville Interim Government—Solomon Islands

Martin Miriori
Netherlands
☎ *[31] (55) 577-99-60*
FAX: [31] (55) 577-99-39
C\O Robin Sluyk
e-mail: unponl@antenna.nl

Peru

Voz Rebelde Internacional—MRTA

http://www.cybercity.dk/users/ccc17427

Committee to Support Revolution in Peru—CRSP

http://www.csrp.org/index.html

Committee Sol Peru

http://www.etext.org/Politics/Committee.Sol.Peru/

El Diario Internacional

http://www.netizen.org/peru/

Tupac Amaru—MRTA

http://users.cybercity.dk/~ccc17427/

MRTA Rebel Voice

http://burn.ucsd.edu/~ats/mrta.htm

Peru's People's Movement

http://www.blythe.org/peru-pcp/

The Philippines

Communist Party of the Philippines

http://www.geocities.com/~cpp-ndf

NPA - New People's Army

National Democratic Front
NDF International Office
P.O. Box 19195
3501 DD Utrecht
The Netherlands
☎ *[31] (30) 23.10.431*
FAX: [31] (30) 23.22.989
EMAIL: ndfp@hkstar.com
http://www.geocities.com/~cpp-ndf/npa.htm
Filipino site links to National Democratic Front and the Communist Party of the Philippines.

Spain

Euskal Herria Journal—ETA Euskadi Ta Askatasuna

http://www.igc.apc.org/ehj/

Internet zine from the Basques (ETA)

Sri Lanka

Tamil Tigers

> Eelam House.
> 202 Long Lane
> London SE1 4QB, UK
> ☎ (0171) 403-4554
> FAX: (0171) 403-1653
> http://eelam.com:80/freedom_struggle/

TamilNet

> http://www.tamilnet.com/"

Ilankai Tamil Sangam—USA.

> http://www.randomc.com/~rajan/"

Tamil Information Centrum—Sweden

> http://home1.swipnet.se/%7Ew-11270/
> tamil/index.htm

Turkey

Revolutionary People's Liberation Party-Front— DHKP-C

> http://www.xs4all.nl/~ozgurluk/
> dhkc1.html

Other

Al Hayat

> www.sitecopy.com/alhayat/

Arab language newspaper with direct and sympathetic connections to the Islamic struggles around the world.

Adventure Calls

Think adventure is a calling for nut cases? Well, you can blame your thirst for adventure on your parents. A study published in *Nature Genetics* reported that people who are prone to be exploratory and excitable have a longer version of a gene called D4DR found on chromosome 11. The gene helps regulate dopamine which controls pleasure and emotion in the brain. Although the research is not conclusive, the researchers believe that finding this gene may help identify thrill-seekers.

If you indeed possess that extra gene, you will find that there is no one perfect source for information on travel or adventuring to far-flung places. This is only a sampler of what is out there. We encourage readers to send in any sources they have come across to expand our list and to report on the experience.

Everybody has a different idea of adventure. It could be bird-watching or it could be parachuting into jungles to fight with rebels. So don't assume that there is only one flavor of adventure.

A few things to keep in mind when dealing with folks who offer adventurous travel: Tell them why you are calling. Ask them for more information. Ask them to describe the typical member, client etc., and then ask for references. Do not take brochures or PR material at face value.

There is no one way to join or organize an expedition. By definition, all you have to do is walk out your door. Most expeditions have goals, structure, deadlines, budgets, and so forth, and require more planning than execution. Most are scientific in nature. Many are adventurous or exploratory, with little of the painstaking information recording required of expeditions in the old days.

Expeditions

Expeditions are simply formalized trips. Like any great endeavor, they should have an objective, a unique sense of purpose and maybe a dash of insanity. A lot of people dream about doing great things and being lauded for their superhuman status.

An expedition is a way to say "Here is what we said we would do, and here is what we did." There is little to no reward for climbing Mt. Everest blindfolded or swimming the Atlantic while towing a barge. There is far more reward in being an actor portraying the adventurer. Sigourney Weaver (as Dian Fossey) and Patrick Bergen (as Sir Richard Burton) put more in the bank than their real-life counterparts ever made in a lifetime—a sobering thought. Fame does await the bold. And after that fame comes an endless procession of rubber chicken dinners and out-door store openings. The more literate of them will write a book that will grace remainder lists for years to come. So consider an expedition as a good use of your skills and talents, with the only reward being the satisfaction of fellowship, a job well done and a better understanding of our world. Along the way, you will enter an elite club of men and women who have tested themselves and found them-selves to be comfortably mortal.

Now a warning to the adventurous who view expeditions as an interesting way to see the world. All expeditions have some hardship involved. In fact, more and more of them seem to feature physical discomfort. Rannulph Fiennes' jaunt to the pole on skis is an example of this craziness. He could have flown, but he want-ed to do something that had never been done before. Other expeditions like the recent attempt to climb Mt. Kinabalu in Borneo the hard way turned into a fiasco because a group of men decided to do whatever they felt like and got lost. They were found later, close to starvation on a mountain that is routinely climbed by schoolchildren. Expeditions are usually led by tough, experienced men who think there is nothing unusual about forcing physical and mental discomfort on others. So it is not surprising than many expeditions tend to be run either by emotion-less, sadomasochistic, raving egomaniacs—men who were dressed as girls when they were young or questionable characters with overstated credentials—who are forced by their lack of job skills to make their living in godforsaken places.

If you can combine all these characteristics into one person, then you stand the chance of mounting a successful expedition. Why would someone want to walk to the North Pole, bake in the Sahara or pick ticks out of their private parts, you may well ask? The answer is always unsatisfactory. Most expedition junkies are always testing themselves, proving other people wrong and seeking to top themselves in their next hare-brained adventure.

Why do I sound so cynical here? Maybe because I have watched various expedi-tion leaders lose it and seen many of my well-trained friends throw their hands up in disgust. The biggest single enemy of the expedition is bad chemistry, usually caused by the fearless leader's inability to lead men by example rather than brute force.

My more pleasurable expeditions have always seemed leaderless, where the group reacted in unison allowing creative interpretation of directions, deadlines and goals. Also, you must truly know your fellow expedition members. Men and women react very strangely under stress. Some revert to childish whining, others become combative, and still others simply lose it both mentally and physically.

The best way to see if you have picked the right partners in an expedition is to have a dry run that includes at least 48 hours without sleep, in adverse conditions. Sleep deprivation, combined with some mental and physical abuse at the 36-hour stage, will show a person's real mettle. Strangely enough, in my experience, white-collar workers, physical fitness nuts, city dwellers, businessmen, triathletes and sportsmen do very poorly in the ill-defined noncompetitive expedition envi-ronment. People with military experience, medical personnel, aboriginals, pho-tographers, blue-collar laborers, and folks with rural backgrounds do very well.

The attributes to look for are experience in hard conditions, physical fitness, a sense of humor, a levelheaded approach to stress, pain and discomfort, and a gen-uine desire for knowledge and fellowship.

Expedition members should be chosen for specific knowledge, such as medical, language or bushlore; always get references. Members should never be chosen for prestige, ability to provide funding, or university credentials, and absolutely stay away from taking on journalists, relatives of backers and good-looking members of the opposite sex.

How to Launch an Expedition

1. Pick a region or topic that is newsworthy or beneficial to sponsors.

2. Select a specific task that you will accomplish, and one that will make the world a better place or create publicity.

3. State specifically how you will generate publicity (book, speeches, press releases, photographs, magazine articles).

4. Write a one-page query letter that states your purpose, method of execution and perceived result. Ask for a written show of support (do not ask for money) and other people who should be made aware of your expedition.

5. Gather letters of support from high-profile politicians, community members and scientists, and include them in your proposal.

6. Write an expedition plan (much like a business plan), and explain the benefits to the backers and sponsors.

7. Create a sponsorship program. Tell and show the primary sponsor what they will get, secondary sponsor and so on. As a rule of thumb, ask for twice as much money as you predict you will need, and come up with something to present to a recognized nonprofit charity at the end of your expedition.

8. Once you have your expedition goal figured out and raison d'etre, send a one-page press release and your outline to all news organizations, telling them your intentions and you need sponsors. It is important to set a date to let sponsors know that you are going with or without their funds.

9. Gather lists of potential sponsors, and then phone to get the owner, president or founder's name. Send in your pitch, along with any early PR you generated. If the president or owner likes it, they will delegate it downward. If you send it in blind, most companies will put you in the talk-to-our-PR-company-who-then-promise-to-talk-to-the-client loop.

10. Follow up with a request for a meeting (money is never pledged over the phone), and thrill them with your enthusiasm and vision.

11. Send a thank-you letter with a specific follow-up and/or commitment date. Promise to follow up with a phone call on a certain date and time.

Do this thousands of times, and you will have enough money to do any hare-brained thing you want.

Just as Columbus had to sweet-talk Isabella after the banks turned him down, you have to be creative and ever hopeful. Remember, everyone interested wishes they could go with you, and their investment is just a way of saying I am part of this adventure.

The best sources for tough expeditions are the Royal Geographical Society in London and the National Geographic Society in Washington. Local newspapers will carry features on "brave young men and women" who are setting out to do whatever has not been done. In most cases, they will be looking for money (always an automatic entree into an expedition) or someone with multiple skills (doctor, cook, masseuse) to fill out the team. Be careful, since it all comes down to personality fit. Many people have never spent more than a weekend in close proximity to their spouse, let alone a total stranger; shakedown cruises are well advised, and go with your first impression. Things usually only get worse.

The up side is that you can be the first person on your block to pogo-stick to the North Pole, balloon across the Sahara or kayak Lake Baikal. Fame and fortune may await. You will need lots of money, time and the enthusiasm of a Baptist preacher. Remember that 99 percent of your time will be spent raising funds and planning. The best single source in the world is the Expedition Advisory Centre of the Royal Geographical Society in London.

Expeditions are usually funded by universities or governments, and there are no real grapevines other than reading scientific journals, staying in touch with universities or talking to expeditioners and outfitters. Most participants will be scientists and will often bring interns (for a fee) to help defray costs. The best way to find out what is happening is to contact a university directly to see if any expeditions are being mounted.

Expedition Planning

The National Geographic Society

The august and venerable National Geographic Society has become the best and most popular means for the world to understand itself. Back in 1888, it was simply a group of philanthropists who wanted to increase and diffuse geographical knowledge. Since then, they have funded almost 5000 expeditions and educated and entertained hundreds of millions, and today are the largest geographic group of any kind on this planet. They manage to maintain a rough edge and an accessible front. Unlike the tiny, musty adventurer's clubs, the National Geographic Society has gone global. You can sit in your own musty den and travel to more countries, experience more expeditions and learn more about our world, thanks to their efforts.

Many adventurers were weaned on their yellow tomes. A generation further back was titillated by sights of unclothed natives and exotic locales. If any magazine could be called adventurous, it would be good old *National Geo.*

National Geographic Society has 9.7 million members in almost 200 countries. Over 44 million people read each issue of the magazine, 40 million watch their documentaries on PBS and 15 mil-

lion watch "On Assignment" each month. Though not exactly an elite group, being featured in or by a National Geographic publication thrusts you into the mainstream of adventure/ entertainment. If you are written up or have an article in the *National Geographic Magazine,* you can work the rubber chicken circuit for the next decade. If you are featured on any of their television specials, like Jacques-Yves Cousteau ("The Voyages of the Calypso") or Bob Ballard ("The Search for the Titanic"), you can contemplate licensing and even starting your own TV series.

Despite being Valhalla for adventurers, the National Geographic does its bit to generate content. In 1992, the Society awarded 240 grants for field research and exploration. The Nat Geo is also on a mission to create higher awareness of geography among students, because they would have little product to sell if people didn't know the difference between Bahrain and the Bahamas. If you are young and a whiz at geography, you can try to join the 6 million people who take part in the National Geographic Bee.

The National Geographic is probably the biggest and best source for just about any information about the world and adventure. They offer a staggering range of books on everything from the Amazon to Zaire. They now offer *World*, a kids magazine with three million readers a month, *Traveler Magazine* with another three million and "National Geographic Explorer" (8 million viewers a month), a radio station (a million listeners a day) and home videos with 5.4 million viewers a year. You wouldn't think there was enough adventure, geography and science info out there, but Nat Geo just keeps on churning it out with CD-ROMs, Geoguides, popup action books, news features, on-line services, globes, atlases, a museum and more. How do they do it? For starters, they pull in about half a billion dollars in tax-free income. Just call ☎ *(800) 638-4077* for a catalog of what interests you and join today.

National Geographic Research & Exploration Quarterly
1145 17th Street North West
Washington, D.C. 20036
☎ *(800) 638-4077*
A quarterly journal with a definitely scientific bent. Better laid out and illustrated than other dry journals.

National Geographic Magazine
1145 17th Street North West
Washington, D.C. 20036
☎ *(800) 638-4077*
The old standard (requires membership) at $21 a year is still a great bargain. Editorial stance is getting tougher. More articles on pollution, politics and natural threats, in addition to the standard "purdy" pictures. The magazine has launched a small but well-traveled group

of photographers who capture the world for a handsome fee.

The Royal Geographical Society
1 Kensington Gore
London, England SW7 2AR
☎ *[44] (71) 589 5466*
The fabled exploration society that still requires nomination by an existing member to join. When in London, non-members can visit the Map Room in their creaky Victorian headquarters on Hyde Park near Albert Hall. They also have an impressive photo archives and reference book selection.

The Royal Geographical Society Magazine
Stephenson House, 1st Floor
Bletchley, Milton Keynes
MK2 2EW
☎ *(0908) 371981*
A monthly magazine that is a lot drier and a lot less pretty than a *Nat Geo* publication but much tougher and smarter in its editorial focus. Covers expeditions, environment, travel, adventure—all with a scientific bent.

RGS Expedition Advisory Centre
1 Kensington Gore
London, England SW7 2AR
☎ *[44] (71) 5812057*
Contact the Expedition Advisory Centre. Don't be shy about calling or ordering any one of their excellent (but very British) books on expedition planning. They have an incredible selection of how-to books, and you can also get listings of past expeditions, contact other people interested in expeditions and get in touch with experts who have been to your area of interest. They do not sponsor expeditions but have a handbook on how to raise money.

All Inclusive Expeditions

The line between soft and hard adventure is the word "expedition." Experienced rafters, climbers, canoeists, hikers and divers usually seek out the small category of hard-core trips that may or may not provide any touristic benefit but push them to the limit. The common goal is to do something first, more intensely or just better than anyone has done before.

Mountain Travel/Sobek Inc.
6420 Fairmont Avenue
El Cerrito, California 94530
☎ *(800) 227-2384*

MTS is always trying to open up new areas or try new rivers. Usually trips are offered as part of their catalog, or if you call them directly they might have the same idea you have and help you put together a run (at a cost, of course). MTS does the old-fashioned type of expediting and running expeditions.

The Sports Advisory Bureau

Sports Council
16 Upper Woburn Place
London, England WC1H 0PQ
☎ *[44] (71) 388 1277*

They can put you in touch with the major specialist sport and adventure groups in the UK. From there, you can ask around as to who's climbing what mountain or running what river.

Expedition Organizers

If you would like to do more than wander around a country, try joining an expedition. Americans haven't quite caught on to this method of travel, but Europeans and the Japanese are crazy about it. Accordingly, they offer a lot more variety than some of their Stateside counterparts.

Brathay Exploration Group

Brathay Hall
Ambleside
Cumbria, England LA22 0HP
☎ *[44] (53) 9433942*

The Brathay Group has launched more than 550 expeditions since 1947. Every year about 125 young people (15–25 years old) in groups of about 20 set off on a variety of scientific trips. There are sponsors for the financially disadvantaged and most members contribute toward the cost of each expedition.

Trekforce Expeditions

134 Buckingham Palace Road
London, England SW1W 9SA
☎ *[44] (71) 824 8890, FAX: [44] (71) 824 8892*

Trekforce has six-week expeditions to Indonesia between June and November. Trips include four days of jungle training and require the ability to work side by side with scientists at a variety of scientific sites. Some of the projects have included Sumatran Rhino surveys, trips to the Baliem valley in Irian Jaya, grasshopper studies and even restoring a British fort in Sumatra. You must be over 18 years old and are expected to raise the $4000 or however much it takes for airfare and your expenses.

Environmental Careers Organization

68 Harrison Avenue
Boston Massachusetts 02111
☎ *(617) 426-4783*

Helps find paid, short-term positions for college students and graduates.

Earthwork

The Student Conservation Association
Post Office Box 550
Charlestown, New Hampshire 03603
☎ *(603) 543-1700*

Provides lists of internships for students in the natural resources area.

Green Corps

Field School for Environmental Organizing
3507 Lancaster Avenue
Philadelphia, Pennsylvania 19104
☎ *(215) 879-1760*

Selected applicants can join annual training programs in environmental studies and campaign organizing.

University Research Expeditions Program

University of California
Berkeley, California 94720
☎ *(510) 642-6586*

Local and worldwide field research programs are available throughout the University of California network.

Oceanic Society Expeditions

Fort Mason Center
Building "E", Suite 230
San Francisco, California 94123-1394
☎ *(415) 441-1106*

OSE manages research projects around the world and promotes the collection and analysis of scientific evidence that can be used in the protection of marine and terrestrial natural habitats. Natural history and volunteer-assisted research expeditions are guided by OSE naturalists and use local guides when possible. Encounter the legendary pink dolphins of the Amazon River, help a research team document bottleneck dolphins in Belize, get up close to Costa Rican humpback whales, or study sea turtles in Suriname. More than 30 unique expeditions are offered each year.

Wexas International

45 Brompton Road
London, England SW3 1DE
☎ [44] (71) 589 3315, FAX: [44] (71) 589 8418

A British travel club with members in 130 countries. Its *Traveller* magazine is a good source for finding expedition members, discounts or travel partners. You can also find deals on airfares, insurance, car rental and hotels.

World Challenge Expeditions

Soane House
305-315 Latimer Road
London, England W10 6RA

☎ [44] (81) 964 1331, FAX: [44] (81) 964 5298

World Challenge Expeditions puts together young people in groups of 12–16 members, and sends them off to foreign lands to conduct an environmental field project. These are not real scientific projects but tasks designed to build leadership skills and self reliance. Each member of the team has a chance to lead at least once during the month-long expedition.

Applicants must be between 16 and 20 years old, and the cost runs about $3000. Applications should be in before February.

Resources:

Australian New Zealand Scientific Expedition Society

http://www.vicnet.net.au/~anzses/

ANZSES

P.O. Box 174
Albert Park 3206
Victoria, Australia
☎ [61] (3) 9866-8699, FAX: [61] (3) 9866-8044

A non-profit organization which launches scientific expeditions into wilderness areas of Australia.

Cordell Expeditions

4295 Walnut Boulevard
Walnut Creek, CA 94596 USA
☎/FAX: (510) 934-3735
http://www.ccnet.com/~cordell/

A tax-exempt, nonprofit research association founded in 1977 that principally explores offshore submerged marine sites that support extensive biological communities.

Earthwatch

680 Mt. Auburn Street
P.O. Box 403,
Watertown, Massachusetts 02272;
☎ (800) 776-0188, FAX: (617) 926-8532
EMAIL: info@earthwatch.org
http://gaia.earthwatch.org/

An international nonprofit organization which offers its members the opportunity to work side by side with field scientists. Since its founding in 1972, Earthwatch has mobilized over 2,030 projects in 118 countries and 36 states.

More than 48,400 EarthCorps volunteers have contributed over $34 million and 5,635,300 hours.

Expedition Society

Richard Pierce
P.O. Box 506
West Boxford, Massachusetts 01885
☎ (508) 352-6902
Email:RAP38@aol.com or
http://www.conveyor.com/expeditions/

Planet Earth Expedition

http://www.shasta-co.k12.ca.us/www/ telementors/test.html
A pretend scientific web site for 6th grade adventurers.

Scientific Exploration Society

Expedition Base
Motcombe, Dorset, SP7 9PB
Membership & FULCRUM
☎ (01747) 853353,
FAX: (01747) 851351
http://www.wessex.co.uk/ses/
Colonel John Blashford-Snell's organization that mounts scientific expeditions that paying members join for about $3000–$5000 plus air. Four meetings are held each year in London where members and their guests are welcomed to illustrated talks and lectures given by explorers, conservationists and scientists.

South American Explorers Club

126 Indian Creek Road
Ithaca, New York 14850
☎ (607) 277-0488

http://www.solutions.net/rec-travel/
south_america/s_am_explorers_club.html
The non-profit South American Explorers Club is a source of travel information about South and/or Central America. With Clubhouses in Lima, Peru; Quito, Ecuador, and Ithaca, New York.

Royal Geographical Society of Australasia, SA Branch

c/o State Library of South Australia
North Terrace
Adelaide, South Australia 5000
Postal Address:
GPO Box 419
Adelaide, South Australia 5001
☎ (08) 207-7265/207-7266,
FAX: (08) 207-7247
http://www.asap.unimelb.edu.au/asa/
directory/data/301.htm

The Coral Reef Alliance

CORAL
64 Shattuck Square, Suite 220
Berkeley, CA 94704
☎ (510) 848-0110, FAX: (510) 848-3720
e-mail: CORALmail@aol.com

http://www.coral.org:80/Home.html
CORAL is an independent, non-profit membership organization that works to address the worldwide problem of coral reef destruction. They provide links to expeditions and works that look for volunteers.

2111 Foundation for Exploration

http://twenty-one-11.org/exp-link.html
P.O. Box 338
Mountain View, California 94042-0338
☎ (888) 843-2111
e-mail: foundation@twentyone-11.org
Provides links to ongoing expeditions and expedition organizers.

Scientific Expeditions

http://wk122.nas.nasa.gov/NAS/
FAST/FASTtreks/index.html
An online, interactive exploration into data. FAST Expeditions allow FAST users to load datasets and scripts into FAST from the World Wide Web. Comes with instructions.

Commercial Expedition Organizers

The Association for Tropical Lepidoptera

P. O. Box 141210
Gainesville, Florida 32614-1210,
FAX/☎ (352) 373-3249)
http://www.troplep.org/
A nonprofit scientific society and educational membership organization, founded in 1989 to promote the study and conservation of Lepidoptera worldwide, especially in the tropical regions of the world. They also organize expeditions to places like Taiwan, Chile and Brazil.

Odyssey Expeditions

1239 Biltmore Drive
Fort Myers, Florida 33901-8707
☎ (803) 670-8767
http://falcon.jmu.edu/~cabrercm/
A nonprofit organization offering tropical marine biology voyages in the British Virgin Islands to high school and college students. Students can learn marine science, advanced diver training, and practical seamanship skills aboard Beneteau yachts equipped as complete research and dive platforms on three week voyages of discovery. Scholarships

and academic credit are available. Cost is between $3000–$3500.

K & J Slavin (Quest) Ltd.

Cow Pasture Farm, Louth Road
Hainton
Lincolnshire, England LN3 6LX
☎ (0507) 313401, FAX: (0507) 313609
e-mail: kjslavin@btb.com
http://www.btb.com/kjslavin/
A family business operating from the rural countryside of Lincolnshire in England since 1979. Ken Slavin supplies Land Rovers, spares and accessories to areas outside Europe where no existing Land Rover dealer operates and also customize vehicles for aid groups and expeditions

Expedition Research

Expedition Research
PO Box 1961
Snohomish, WA 98290
☎ (360) 668-6179, FAX: (360) 668-7137
http://www.expeditionresearch.org
A non-profit membership organization incorporated in Washington State, U.S.A.

Oceanwide Expeditions

Badhuisstraat 148-150,

4382 AP Vlissingen, Netherlands
FAX: (31) 118-418584.
http://www.ocnwide.com/

Travel aboard old Dutch sailing ships or
Russian research ships (icebreakers).

Running with the Bulls

Have you ever dreamed of being one of the corredores in the annual encierro of Pamplona? Probably not, but many of us have dreamed of running with the bulls ever since we read Hemingway's account of it in the Sun Also Rises. Little did he know that he would elevate the running of the bulls in the medieval city of Pamplona to the level of the Holy Grail for adventurers. Twelve people have been killed in the run. No one bothers to keep track of the trampled, tripped and torn. The consumption of alcohol is considered to be mandatory, and the cost and scarcity of hotel rooms means that sleeping is completely on a "when available/as needed basis."

The running of the bulls is part of the Festival of San Fermin, July 6-14, every year in the Spanish province of Navarre. As if it matters anymore, Saint Fermin was martyred in the third century.

The bulls are let loose from a corral about 800 meters away from the bull ring, and they run through the barricaded streets on their way to it.

A rocket is fired off to start the run on Calle Santo Domingo at 7 a.m. on the seventh day of the seventh month. Don't eat breakfast first, since it is customary to celebrate afterwards with hot chocolate and deep-fried churros, essentially a long Spanish donut. Get there early. The students from the local university tend to be the most enthusiastic members of the crowd. Foreigners are usually too damn serious. The course is a lot shorter and tighter than most people expect it to be. Novices (or Los Valientes, the Brave Ones) get about a five-minute head start on the bulls but are quickly overtaken. The most dangerous part of the course is the tight turn onto Estafeta Street. Here, bulls and corredores discover that two objects can't occupy the same place at the same time. The lack of space is aggravated by lines of policemen who prevent the more timid from bolting over the barricades. The bulls are prodded on by the less valiant (those running behind or spectating) who smack them with rolled-up newspapers. Once bulls and runners stream into the bull ring, free-form amateur bullfighting breaks out. Once you get bored, head into the old quarter for breakfast or to the cafes to continue your celebrating. If you end up feeling like a Union 76 ball on a car antenna, the Red Cross is nearby to attend to any minor injuries.

If for some strange reason you do not spend the evening drinking and carousing, the best accommodations are to be found in the nearby town of Olite, about 40 kilometers away.

In July of 1995 an American from Chicago was gored in the chest and thrown 23 feet in the air, becoming the first fatality in over 20 years.

Sounds like a great concept for a Reebok commercial.

Volunteer Vacations

For those of you who flunked science but still want to do something meaningful with your time, consider volunteering in a foreign region. You can do anything from writing pamphlets to cleaning toilets. In most cases, there will be a "goal" and you will help in "achieving that goal." You, of course, will pay for all the expenses involved and will have to make a donation as well. Once on site, you will be working with motivated people who are trying to change whatever it is that causes problems in the local region. It can be lonely, frustrating and ultimately depressing. On the other hand, there is no better way to understand the world's problems. There are thousands upon thousands of opportunities for people who want to give of their time and skills. There are even more opportunities for people who don't mind paying to volunteer. In some cases, state agencies have replaced paid workers with paying volunteers for maintenance of trails, parks, and so forth. Archaeological digs are popular, as are works projects in Third World countries. The list and choice of volunteer vacations is so extensive that there are over 40 books and directories currently in print on the subject. There are enough of these opportunities to ensure that you will end up in the dangerous place of your choice, whether it's digging ditches in Sierra Leone, working on a Kibbutz in areas occupied by Israel or counting trout in the good old U.S.A. You can choose from mild to wild. If you want to work overseas and get paid contact: Fischer Report, *P.O Box 2770 Laguna Hills California 92654* (one year subscription is $400).

An excellent resource is *Volunteer Vacations*, by Bill McMillon, and published by the Chicago Review Press, Another more cerebral source is:

Directory of Lay Volunteer Opportunities
St. Vincent Palloti Center for Apostolic Development
Box 893 Cardinal Station
Washington, D.C. 20064
☎ *(202) 529-3330, FAX: (202) 529 0911*
Let's start off the listings with a higher moral tone. You can work with a number of religious organizations like the MaryKnolls missionaries and other groups around the world.

Archaeological Institute of America
675 Commonwealth Avenue
Boston, Massachusetts 02215
☎ *(800) 338-5578, (617) 353-9361,*
FAX: (617) 353-6560
Call to order their annual listings of digs around the world that are looking for volunteers.

Council on International Educational Exchange
205 East 42nd Street
New York, New York 10017
☎ *(212) 661-1414*
Field programs and summer academic programs in Latin and South America.

Earthwatch
680 Mt. Auburn Street

Box 403N
Watertown, Massachusetts 02272
☎ *(800) 776-0188, (617) 926-8200,*
FAX: (617) 926-8532
Offers working vacations on 155 field research expeditions around the world. Document the decay in the coral reef off Maui, excavate Mayan sites in Guatemala, or help scientists in Siberia study active volcanoes.

GAP Activity Projects Limited
44 Queen's Road
Reading, Berkshire, England RG1 4BB
☎ *[44] (734) 594914, FAX: [44] (734) 576634*
The "gap" is a British term to describe the year between grade school and college. The GAP places young people in a variety of work situations in Russia, Hungary, Japan, China and Poland. Positions include business, medical, adventure training, conservation and teaching.

Institute for International Cooperation and Development
Post Office Box 103-F

Williamstown, Massachusetts 01267
☎ (413) 458-9828
Semester-long programs worldwide that combine cultural and educational experiences.

Raleigh International
Raleigh House
27 Parsons Green Lane
London, SW6 4HZ England
☎ [44] (71) 371 8585,
FAX: [44] (71) 371 5116
Can you swim 500 meters? Can you speak English? Good, you're on. Raleigh International sends eager young (17–25 years old) volunteers to the far corners of the world. The goal is to work on community, research and conservation projects while having a bit of adventure. The charity likes to challenge young people and develop their leadership skills and self-confidence.

UNIPAL (Universities' Education Fund for Palestinian Refugees)
33A Islington Park Street
London, England N1 1QB
☎ [44] (71) 2267997,
FAX: [44] (71) 2260880
UNIPAL provides teaching and social services to the Palestinians in Israel and Jordan.

Volunteers for Israel
330 West 42nd Street, Suite 1318
New York, New York
☎ (212) 643-4848

Those who want to work on kibbutzim, Israel Defense Fund bases or in hospitals can expect to pay between $500 and $1000 for the privilege. Age is no object, other than you must be more than 18; over 15,000 people have signed up with this 13-year-old agency.

Volunteers for Peace
43 Tiffany Road
Belmont, Vermont 05730
☎ (802) 259-2759
A work camp–type environment with placement worldwide.

Volunteers in Technical Assistance
1815 North Lynn Street, Suite 200
Arlington, Virginia 22209
☎ (703) 276-1800
If you have a specific technical skill that you would like to share or apply with others, contact this group. They prefer to communicate by mail and will ask you some specific questions before referring you to one of the many volunteer groups in their listings.

Volunteer, The National Center
1111 North 19th Street, Suite 500
Arlington, Virginia 22209
☎ (703) 276-0542
If you want to narrow down your choices, make this group your first stop. They will simply refer you to a group of organizations they think will match your interests.

Volunteer Resources

Alliance of European Voluntary Service Organizations
http://www.astro.rug.nl/~grijs/aevso.html
American Friends Service Committee
http://www.afsc.org/
British Trust for Conservation Volunteers
http://www.demon.co.uk/dobx/btcv/inter.html
Earthwatch
http://www.earthwatch.org
Earth Pledge Foundation
http://www.earthpledge.org
EarthWise Research Expeditions
http://www.teleport.com/~earthwyz/volunt.htm

Global Volunteers
http://www.globalvlntrs.org
InterAction
http://www.interaction.org/ia/
International Community Service Resources
http://www.contact.org/comserve.htm
Remote Area Medical
http://www.usit.net/hp/ram/help.html
Trans-Cultural Study Guide
http://www.moon.com/trans.cultural/trans.cultural.html
United Nations Volunteers
http://suna.unv.ch/
Volunteer Opportunities
http://www.gorp.com/gorp/nonprof/main.htm

Volunteer Organizations-Bernd Wechner's list
http://www.aitec.edu.au/~bwechner/Documents/Travel/Lists/Volunteer-Orgs.html

Volunteers For Peace
http://www.vermontel.com/~vfp/home.htm

Volunteers in Asia
http://www.moon.com/staying.healthy/travel.health/volunteers.html

Academy of Leisure Sciences
http://www.geog.ualberta.ca/als/als1.html

adventure.online
http://www.adventureonline.com

Alliance for Off Campus Programs
http://www.sound.net/~learn

American Institute For Foreign Study (AIFS, Inc.)
http://www.aifs.org/

AmeriSpan - Spanish immersion programs
http://www.amerispan.com

Australia Internship Programs
http://205.214.89.2:80/internships/

Bennett School of Travel
http://bwtravel.com/overview.html

Centre For Tourism
http://www.scu.edu.au/ressci/tourism/

Council on International Educational Exchange
http://www.ciee.org/ciee.htm

Cruise Ship Employment
http://www.cruisekat.com

Earthwatch
http://gaia.earthwatch.org

Educational and Cultural Exchanges
http://www.usia.gov/usiahome/educatio.html

Explorations In Travel, Inc.
http://www.xensei.com:80/users/explore/

French language and cultural workshop
http://www.greendolphin.com

The Graduate Tourism Program Home Page
http://www.monash.edu.au/ncas/tourism/tourism.htm

Hospitality Net
http://www.xxlink.nl/hospitalitynet/job

Hospitality Training Management
http://qb.island.net/~htm/index.html

ISTC
http://www.istc.org/default.htm

International Institute Of Tourism Studies
http://www.microstate.com/pub/micros/gwu/

Internships
http://www.advc.com/internships

James Cook University
http://www.jcu.edu.au/dept/Tourism/tourpage.html

Joint Language Training Center
http://www.cc.utah.edu/~coj6886/jltc.html

Laboratory For Leisure, Tourism Sport
http://yoda.ucc.uconn.edu/users/yiannakisa/mylab.html

MayaQuest Learning Adventure
http://mayaquest.mecc.com/

National Center For Educational Travel
http://www2.ios.com/~ncet/

Outdoor Recreation Research
http://sfbox.vt.edu:10021/Y/yfleung/recres.html

Peace Corps
http://www.clark.net/pub/peace/PeaceCorps.html

Programs for Americans Going Abroad
http://www.cdsintl.org:80/fromus.html

Recreation and Leisure Studies
http://www.geog.ualberta.ca/als/rlsres.html

Servas Association
http://www.crs4.it/~gavino/SERVAS/

South Florida Travel Academy, Inc.
http://www.netrunner.net/~academy/

Smoky Mountain Field School
http://web.ce.utk.edu/departments/noncredit/smoky/smoky.html

Stanford University Overseas Studies Program
http://www-osp.stanford.edu

Study abroad
http://www.studyabroad.com

Summer Study at Oxford University
http://www.ostavizn.com/site/Oxford1.html

U.S. National Park Service Employment
http://www.nps.gov/personnel/index.html

University of Surrey, UK, Department of Management Studies
http://www.surrey.ac.uk/DOMS/wwwdom1.html

Working Overseas

Working overseas is a lot more romantic than it is financially rewarding. My stepfather pulled down a mediocre wage looking for oil in Canada but managed to get a six-figure tax-free salary with a simple idea. He figured he would find the thing of most value to the wealthiest people in the world. What's that, you ask. Water and the Saudis, of course. Most jobs overseas require training and lengthy job searches. There are some shortcuts: The military, the diplomatic corp, multinational corporations, airline stewards, aircraft ferry pilots, even foreign correspondents all will guarantee you frequent flier miles and broken marriages. On the other hand, the world will be your playground, and you will develop an understanding and enjoyment of the world few people will ever appreciate.

Vacation Work Publications
9 Park End Street
Oxford, England OX1 1HJ
☎ *[44] (865) 241978,*
FAX: [44] (865) 790885
A British source for publications on summer jobs, volunteer positions and other new ways of travel. If you cover the postage, they will send you their latest catalog about books and specific publications on subjects that cover teaching or living and working in various countries around the world. A small sampling of publications can show you how to teach English in Japan, work on a kibbutz in Israel, choose an adventure holiday, get au pair and nanny jobs, find summer employment in France and much more.

EcoNet and PeaceNet
18 De Boom Street
San Francisco, California 94107
☎ *(415) 442-0220*
An on-line group that can link you up with like-minded conservationists and possibly a job.

Foundation for Field Research Programs
Post Office Box 2010
Alpine, California 91903
☎ *(619) 445-9264*
A comprehensive directory of Field Research Programs around the world.

Archaeology Abroad
31-34 Gordon Square
London, WC1H 0PY England
AA puts out three bulletins a year advertising overseas excavations that need volunteers and staff. They are primarily looking for people with excavation experience (grave digging and gardening don't necessarily qualify you).

The Astrid Trust
Training Ship Astrid
9 Trinity Street
Weymont, DT4 8TW England
☎ *[44] (305) 761916*
Every year the square rigger *Astrid* offers two 3-month, transatlantic voyages for 26 young people. The seven-week trip heads to the Caribbean from Weymouth in September and from St. Lucia to Weymouth in mid-May. There are also short summer cruises while in England, where the crew can learn to sail and scuba dive and take part in expeditions onshore.

Transitions Abroad
Box 3000
Denville, New Jersey 07834
☎ *(413) 256-3414, FAX: (413) 256-0373*
This bimonthly magazine is targeted for people who want to live and work in a foreign country. It includes a directory of international volunteer positions and lists job opportunities including teaching and technical positions. $38 for 12 issues.

Web Resources:

Overseas Jobs Express
Premier House, Shoreham Airport
Sussex BN43 5FF
☎ *[44] (1273) 440220,*
FAX. [44] (1273) 440229
email: OJE-books@overseasjobs.com
http://www.overseasjobs.com

Job Search Overseas
P.O. Box 35, Falmouth
Cornwall, TR11 3UB

☎ *(0872) 870070, FAX. (0872) 870071*
A monthly paper which collects international job ads from other sources for the working traveller.

Overseas Employment Newsletter

A newsletter published by Overseas Employment Services, every two weeks, in which they "describe in detail at least 300 currently available jobs for a broad range of skills, careers and positions in many developing nations and industrialized countries around the world." The same group also publish a variety of useful books on the same topic.

Overseas Employment Services

P.O. Box 460,
Town of Mount Royal,
Quebec H3P 3C7 CANADA
☎ *(514) 739-1108, FAX: (514) 739-0795*

Web Travel Resources: Clever ways to travel for free or little cost

http://www.prairienet.org/~dbrown/
travel.html

AESU

http://www.charm.net/~aesu/
Low Cost Airfares Tours to Europe.

AYH Regional (ENEC)

http://www.tiac.net/users/hienec/

AYH National Office

http://gnn.com/gnn/bus/ayh/
index.html

Campus Travel

http://www.campustravel.co.uk

College Travel International

http://www.prairienet.org/rec/travel/
homepage.html

Council Travel

http://www.ciee.org/cts/ctshome.htm

Hello America

http://www.helloamerica.com/cat-bin/
signon/HelloAmerica

ISTC

http://www.istc.org/

INational Center for Educational Travel

http://www2.ios.com:80/~ncet/

STA Travel

http://www.sta-travel.com/

Student and Budget Travel Guide

http://asa.ugl.lib.umich.edu/chdocs/
travel/travel-guide.html

T@P Travel

http://www.taponline.com/tap/
travel.html

Travelhouse

http://www.cymfony.com/travelhouse

USIA

http://www.usia.gov/homepage.html
Educational and Cultural Exchanges.

Travel Agents and Cheap Airfares

Access Travel (Quality Travel Services)

http://www.accesstravel.com

Air Consolidators—TravelScope

http://www.worldhotel.com/buttons/
cheapfares/consolidator.html

Consolidators—FAQ

http://www.digimark.net/rec-travel/air-
travel/consolidators

Discounted Air Fares Worldwide On-Line

http://www.etn.nl/discount.htm

Air Brokers Int'l - ('round the world)

http://www.aimnet.com/~airbrokr

AESU Flights—Low-Cost Airfares to Europe

http://www.charm.net:80/~aesu/

Around-the-World Airfares Adventures

http://www.highadv.com/

Avanti Destinations

http://www.teleport.com/~avanti/
index.html

Budget Travellers World

http://minyos.xx.rmit.edu.au/~tbmlc/
travel/cworld/index.html

Cost Busters Travel

http://www.newmall.com/cbmain.html

Cyber Air Broker

Http://www.airdiscounter.com

DIA Travel and Tours

http://www.diatravel.com/

Diethelm Travel, Thailand

http://www.mnsinc.com/cicm/thai-
land/diethelm.html

European Travel Inc... online

http://www.european.com/~eurofile/
home.html

Global Internet Travel
   http://www.globaltravel.com/

MK Ways
   http://www.siam.net/mkways

OSky Plus Travel
   http://netmar.com/~yoak/

Travel Avenue-A Rebate
   http://www.interaccess.com/travlav/
   trav_web/trav.htm

Travel Bargains Website
   http://www.Real-TravelBargains.com/
   index.html

Travel Discounters
   http://www.tagsys.com/Ads/NetSale/
   index.html

Travel Discounts page
   http://www.traveldiscounts.com/dis
   count/index.html

Travel Information Service
   http://www.tiss.com/

Travel Travel
   http://www.mindspring.com/~travtrav/
   travel.html

TravelWise Travel Specials
   http://www.shore.net/olm/Travel-
   Wise.specials.html

Travel World
   http://www.omnitravel.com/

Traveler's Net (rebates)
   http://www.travelersnet.com

UniTravel Online
   http://www.unitravel.com/

Web-ers Travel Service
   http://www.transport.com/~rose/web-
   ers/

Wholesale Travel Centre
   http://www.dgsys.com/~airfare/
   index.html

**The World Wide Wanderer Cyberian
Bucket Shop Guide**
   http://www.dcwww.com/wanderer/
   WWWanderer_home_page.html

1 Travel
   http://www.1travel.com

Campus Travel Web Site
   http://www.campustravel.co.uk

Rules of Politically Correct Travel

• *Try to learn and use the local language.*

• *Dress conservatively.*

• *Try to use nonpolluting conveyances (bike, hike, canoe).*

• *Use public transport (bus, train, plane) to save fuel.*

• *Stay to marked paths; do not litter.*

• *Respect local cultures.*

• *Try to choose locally run establishments (restaurants, hotels, tour guides) rather than
chains.*

• *Hire a local guide to add to your knowledge and exchanges with locals.*

Destination: Adventure

For the less organized and mildly impetuous, we offer straight shots into the unknown. We all yearn to stuff a few things into a faded knapsack and hit the road. For those who look a little farther down the road, it means a dirt-cheap ticket from a bucket shop and a bunch of needles and expensive pills. Where do you want to go? We have put together a smattering of rough-and-tumble places that will get you started. For those who like a baby-sitter to keep them out of trouble, I have included the addresses of tour packagers and outfitters.

For those who like trendy style, color coordinated yuppie sports check out:

Extreme Sports

http://www.extreme-sports.com/

The Radzone

http://www.radzone.com/

Say "Cheese!"

A plane ride is a plane ride, but when they crack open those aluminum doors and the heat and smell clobber you like a hammer, you know you have arrived. Outside, the heat rises in waves and the reddish-brown earth tells you that you have come a long way. On one such trip, I had to take a picture of the UTA DC-10 on the broken and potholed tarmac. I had to capture the silver bird crowned by a single monstrous cumulus cloud incongruously surrounded by soldiers with faded green uniforms. No sooner had I raised my camera to my eye than I was arrested by two scowling soldiers. Stupid, I should have known better than to take a picture in a West African airport. Thinking quickly as they grabbed for my Leica, I waved toward the cockpit. The soldiers balked, trying to figure out who I was waving to. Why, of course, I was taking a picture of the pilot. I explained quickly to the French ground crews to tell the pilot that I had taken a picture of him, not the airplane. The guards frog-marched me up the ladder, and, to my relief, the pilots played along. The soldiers let me go and explained how lucky I was that I wasn't taking pictures of the airport. There was no law as far as they knew against taking pictures of the pilots. –RYP

Arctic/Antarctic

We used to say the Arctic was a great place to live if you were a Popsicle. Having been born in Edmonton, Alberta, and having participated in snowshoe marathons in my youth, all I can say is the frozen food section in the grocery store is about as close as I want to get to the colder climes these days. But don't let me stop you if your idea of fun is trying to unstick your private parts from your zipper after relieving yourself in a blizzard.

For cold-weather travelers, the most popular place is Antarctica, where legions of red survival–suited tourists create more photos of penguins and icebergs than ever could be viewed by their warmer relatives; second is Alaska and then the Northwest Territories. Siberia and Kamchatka are a distant fourth, but ripe for development. People who venture to the poles have to be a little crazy, since there is essentially nothing to see. The folks who pay a minimum of 10 grand to get to the North Pole are really sitting over a mass of water. Weather permitting, you get a few hours before you are bundled back on the plane for the long return flight. April is really the only hospitable month that the Pole can be visited with some certainty. There is some awe-inspiring and desolate scenery along the way, and you will be sick of flying as you must first get to Yellowknife, then Resolute, then a weather station on the edge of Ellesmere Island. From there, you wait until the weather clears and off you go. Make sure you know there is a geographic North Pole and a magnetic North Pole. The Magnetic North Pole wanders around like a bedouin looking for an oasis. A visit to the geographic North Pole may be all in good fun, but a visit to the South Pole is a different story. As bad as the weather is up north, it is much worse in the south. The vibes are very different as well. Scientists want nothing to do with the variety of adventurers, tourists and nuts who want to do everything from ski to motorcycle to the South Pole. Most of these people require very expensive and difficult extraction once they come face to face with the harsh realities of Antarctica. Cruise ships are considered a major evil, with their disturbance of animal populations, litter and general disruption of this pristine area.

Is it dangerous in the colder climes? Well, what do you think? You can start with the cold. Hypothermia, exposure, frostbite and plain old freezing to death are the constants. Falling through thin ice, predatory polar bears, crevasses, fires caused by unattended heaters and the list goes on. Being an old hand in the north, I won't bore you with long descriptions of 100-m.p.h. winds, helicopter crashes, drilling through blood blisters with pocket knives to relieve the pain, how flesh sticks to metal, why engines have to be run 24 hours a day and what frostbite can do to your toes. If you want all the gory details, contact the following:

Adventure Canada

1159 West Broadway
Vancouver, British Columbia, Canada
V6H 1G1
☎ *(604) 736-7447*

OK, you've been there, done that, visited all 235-some-odd countries. What is left to impress your friends? How about a round of golf on the North Pole? You can also claim to visit Greenland, Russia, Canada and the U.S.A. as you whack your ball around the four international zones that meet at the North Pole. The trip costs $10,200 and golf clubs are provided.

Adventure Network International

200-1676 Dranleau Street
Vancouver, British Columbia, Canada
V6H 3S5
☎ *(604) 683-8033, FAX: (604) 689-7646*

Nothing to do in late November or early December? Then the Antarctic is the place to be. Pat Morrow and those crazy adventurers at ANI (founded in 1985 by a group of expedition guides) have put together a two-week ski and snowmobile trip, where an intrepid few can stay at Patriot Hills base camp (the only private base camp in the Antarctic) and then visit the surrounding area on skis or via snowmobile. Flights are available to overfly Mt. Vinson and the Ellsworth mountains. Campers can participate in the two-week ski trip that includes outside camping. If that sounds too tame, how about flying down to the South Pole and driving some *Ski-Doos* back to the base camp? All you need is $50,000 (that's not a typo) for the three-week stint. If this seems cheap, then get in line for a month-long trip that crosses the

Ross Ice Shelf to Cape Evans, where you will be met by an expedition ship. The ticket is $100,000 per person. That's a lifetime of Club Meds for most folks.

Arctic Experience

29 Nork Way
Banstead, England SM7 1PB
☎ *[44] (737) 362321*

A small outfit specializing in putting together European-based Arctic expeditions for small groups.

Borton Overseas

5516 Lyndale Avenue South
Minneapolis, Minnesota 55419
☎ *(800) 843-0602, FAX: (612) 827-1544*

Every spring Borton runs eight-day tours of Greenland that include two days of dog sledding. Participants can visit a remote Inuit village as well as tour Ammasalik and Sarfagajik Fjord.

Ecosummer Expeditions

1516 Duranleau Street
Vancouver, British Columbia, Canada
V6H 3S4
☎ *(604) 669-7741*

A neighbor of ANI on picturesque Granville Island, this group is the best kayak outfitter in North America. They will send you to both warm and cold climates to get eye level with the world. Their trips to Ellesmere Island are not strenuous and cover only about five to 20 miles a day, leaving plenty of time to get to see the wide variety of wildlife that becomes visible in the summer.

Special Odysseys

3430 Evergreen Point Road
Post Office Box 37A
Medina, Washington 98039
☎ *(206) 455-1960*

If you really want to get to the North Pole, it will cost you about eight days and 10 grand just to land, walk around and then get back in the plane the same day. The trip leaves every April, and I am sure can provide you with some type of sporting event other than golf.

Arctic Adventure Aps
Aaboulevarden 37, DK-1960
Frederiksberg, Copenhagen, Denmark
☎ *[45] (1) 37 12 33*
The experts on the massive island of Greenland. They can get you there just about any time you want to go.

Quark Expeditions
980 Post Road

Darien, Connecticut 06820
☎ *(800) 356-5699 or (203) 656-0499*

Eighteen grand will put you in a nuclear-powered Russian icebreaker with a bunch of prefab living quarters bolted on. The 500-ft. Sovetskiy Soyuz puts its 75,000 horses into crushing through up to 16 feet of ice. Quark puts an ecospin on this trip, so expect to be educated by scientists and come back knowing more about the Arctic than you ever wanted to know. The Soyuz will cut a hole right on up to the geographic North Pole (the magnetic Pole is too flaky).

Adventure Trips

For those who have no particular method of transportation in mind, you might want to contact these groups:

Above The Clouds Trekking
P.O. Box 398E
Worchester, Massachusetts 01602
☎ *(800) 233-4499*
If you're seeking in-depth exploration of remote lands and exotic cultures, this travel outfit provides expert guides and average group size of eight. Destinations include Bhutan, Pakistan, Tibet, Madagascar, Nepal, Norway, France, UK, Costa Rica and Hawaii. Call for a free brochure.

Adventure Center
1311 EP 63rd Street
Emeryville, California 94608
☎ *(510) 654-1879, (800) 227-8747*
Since 1976, Adventure Center has offered more than 160 affordable adventure programs worldwide. Programs include hiking, trekking, wildlife, natural history, sea treks, river journeys and cultural adventures. Discover ancient Mayan sites, sail Turkey's Aegean coast, experience the rain forests of Costa Rica.

MIR Corporation
85 S. Washington Street, Suite 210
Seattle, Washington 98104
☎ *(800) 424-7289*
Discover off-the-beaten-path Russia, Czech Republic, Uzbekistan, Mongolia, Hungary, Ukraine, Poland and China, including Trans-Siberia rail journeys and Central Asian explorations.

Turtle Tours
5924 East Gunsight Road
Cave Creek, Arizona 85331
☎ *(602) 488-3688, FAX: (602) 488-3406*
Post Office Box 1147
Carefree, Arizona 85377
For 11 years Irma Turtle has specialized in introducing small groups of travelers to the world's dwindling nomadic and tribal peoples. Starting with trips to the Sahara to visit the Turegs, she has expanded her offerings to cover South America, the Middle East and Asia. If you want to experience the Wodaabe gerewol festival in Niger, the Pushkar camel fair in Rajashtan in India or the Asmats of Irian Jaya, she can provide an existing itinerary or put together a custom trip. Turtle offers a good selection of destinations for groups as small as two. Choose from Trans Sahara, The Empty Quarter, Northern Kenya, Namibia, Ethiopia—all designed to add an element of contact with culture, and peoples that other operators don't offer. Ground costs, per person for group tours run about $3500 for 14 to 18 day trips.

Discovery Expeditions
Expedition Base

Motcombe, near Shaftesbury
Dorset, England SP7 9PB
☎ *[4] (747) 54456*
Colonel John Blashford-Snell runs a variety of very adventurous and rewarding trips for "active mature adults." There are no age limits or special requirements, but they do ask that prospective team members get together at a briefing weekend (in England) to deter-

mine their compatibility and for a briefing on the realities that await them. Blashford-Snell's reputation as a "famous explorer" truly has the credentials to make any expedition interesting and worthwhile.

Other adventure-minded agencies include the following:

Backroads
> *1516 5th Street*
> *Berkeley, California 94710*
> ☎ *(800) G0 ACTIVE, FAX: (510) 527-1444*

Explore Worldwide
> *Aldershot, England GU11 1LQ*
> ☎ *[44] (252) 344161 (24 hr)*

Foundation for Field Research
> *P.O. Box 2010*
> *Alpine, California*
> ☎ *(619) 445-9264*

InnerAsia
> ☎ *(800) 777-8183*

Bolder Adventures
> *P.O. Box 1279*
> *Boulder, Colorado 80306*
> ☎ *(800) 642-ASIA*

Ecotour Expeditions
> *Post Office Box 1066*
> *Cambridge, Massachusetts 02238*
> ☎ *(800) 688-1822, (617) 876-5817*

Natural Habitat Wildlife Adventures
> *1 Sussex Station*
> *Sussex, New Jersey 07461*
> ☎ *(800) 543-8917, (201) 702-1525*

The Nature Conservancy
> *International Trips Program*
> *1815 North Lynn Street*
> *Arlington, Virginia 22209*
> ☎ *(703) 841-4880*

Tread Lightly
> *1 Titus Road*
> *Washington Depot, Connecticut 06794*
> ☎ *(203) 868-1710*

Wilderness Southeast
> *711-J Sandtown Road*
> *Savannah, Georgia 31410*
> ☎ *(912) 897-5108*

Twickers World
> *20/22 Church Street*
> *Twickenham, England TW1 3NW*
> ☎ *[44] (81) 892 7851,*
> *FAX: (081) 892 8061*

Karakoram Experience
> *32 Lake Road*
> *Keswick, Cumbria C12 5DQ*
> ☎ *(07687) 73966, FAX: (07687) 74693*

Brathay Exploration Group
> *Brathay Hall*
> *Ambleside, Cumbria LA22 OHP*
> ☎ *(05394) 33942*

Butterfield and Robinson
> ☎ *(800) 678-1147*

Adventure Center
> *1311-E 63rd Street*
> *Everyville, California 94608*
> ☎ *(800) 227-8747*

International Expeditions
> *1 Environs Park*
> *Helena, Alabama 35080*
> ☎ *(800) 633-4734*

National Audubon Society
> *700 Broadway*
> *New York, New York 10003*
> ☎ *(212) 979-3066*

Sierra Club Outings
> *730 Polk Street*
> *San Francisco, California 94109*
> ☎ *(415) 923-5630*

University Research Expeditions
> *University of California*
> *Berkeley, California 94720*
> ☎ *(510) 642-6586*

World Wildlife Fund Travel Program
> *1250 24th Street, N.W.*
> *Washington D.C. 20037*
> ☎ *(202) 293-4800*

Overseas Adventure Travel

349 Broadway
Cambridge, Massachusetts 02139
☎ *(800) 221-0814*

Ballooning, Hang Gliding and Flying

Balloons are not really a method of travel, unless you are Richard Branson. Balloons are expensive, vicarious, and sometimes deadly as a method of long-distance travel. As a vehicle for short, breathtaking ascents, they are a blast. Zeppelins have fallen out of favor (and out of the sky), so for now any desire to float through the sky is limited to balloon tour operations, hang gliding and soaring (glider flight). The newest adventure twist is bungy jumping from balloons.

Balloons travel with the prevailing wind, so you can't really determine your path. A variety of balloon safaris are available in Africa. For example, a balloon ride with champagne breakfast in the Masai Mara in Kenya will set you back about $250 per person for the four-hour event. If you are really nutso about starting every day with a balloon ride, then give one of these folks a call. If you are more interested in emulating Tom Cruise in *Top Gun*, you can sign up to fly a fighter plane at Air Combat USA.

Adventure Balloons

3 Queens Terrace
Hanwell
London, England W7 3TS
☎ *[44] (81) 840-0108*
A specialist in balloon holidays in Great Britain, France and Ireland.

Air Escargot

Remigny, France 71150
☎ *[33] (85) 87-1230*
Balloon trips in the Burgundy area with evenings at fine restaurants. Expect to pay about $300 a day per person and stay in luxury accommodations complete with daily balloon rides.

Bombard Balloon Adventures

6727 Curran Street
McLean, Virginia 22101
☎ *(800) 862-8537, (703) 883-0985*
Where would you like to go? Bombard is the world's largest balloon tour operator and can take you just about anywhere you want to go. They claim to have sent more than 14,000 people on trips over the last 18 years.

Air Combat USA

230 Dale Place
Fullerton, California 92833
☎ *(800) 522-7590 or 714-522-7592*
If you're dying to use a nickname like "Iceman" or "Maverick" and have always salivated over fighter planes, this is the place for you...if you have the guts and enough big bucks. For $695, you can man the controls of a tactical fighter

trainer and engage in simulated aerial dogfighting with other *Top Gun* wannabes. For your money, you get a one-hour ground course, one-hour of flight time, a videotape of your experience and a one-hour debriefing afterwards. No flying experience is required. An instructor sits next to you the entire time, but even novices get to take the controls. Flights are conducted daily and reservations are needed.

Fly a MIG

Incredible Adventures
6604 Midnight Pass Road
Sarasota, Florida 34242
☎ *(800) 644-7382*
http://www.mig29.com/mig29/
Just think the Russians spent all this money so that well-heeled dentists and plastic surgeons can fly a real MiG. The rather steep fee includes flying to Russia, lots of training and warning and your choice of a MiG-21, 25 or 29. For a few extra bucks ask them if you can drop bombs on Chechen or Tajik rebels (just kidding).

Military Parachuting Tours

P.O. Box 1573
Olean, New York 14760
DP and SOF contributor Rob Krott puts together parachuting tours around the world with various elite military groups. You get to earn a jump badge from each country and you can into a lit-

tle of the hot stuff if you pick the right tour. Sort of a Merc-Lite tour. Recommended for ex-special operations soldiers and other para groups. Training and qualification available for non-parachutists.

Vanuatu Land Diving

Vanuatu National Tourism Office
☎ *(408) 685-8901*
Kiwis claim bungy jumping started in New Zealand, but natives of Vanuatu say they started it all. On southern Pentecost Island, you can take a leap with jungle vines wrapped around your ankles. Vine lengths are custom-cut to fit each diver, and your hair will just barely brush the grass before you are hurtled back into the air. Unfortunately, one unlucky vine clinger bit the dust while land diving for the Queen.

Four-Wheel Drive

Adventure Racing

Racing originated with the marathon, based on the distance a messenger ran from the battlefields of Marathon to Athens. (He died of course). The concept of pushing oneself past the limits has evolved from polite joggers to Triathlons and Ironman competitions where swimming and biking is integrated so that the competitors could tan and have an excuse to buy a $2000 bike to ride through the park on weekends. It seems that when TV and sponsors become involved these simple tests of personal best became more akin to the events held at the coliseum of ancient Rome. Now people who desperately fear aging or being a wimp can travel to exotic lands and do silly things for the benefit of cameras and sponsors. The Camel Trophy (which sells off road vehicles, clothing and subliminally cigarettes), The Raid Gauloise (which sells those nasty Francophone cancer sticks) and the Eco Challenge (which sells anything you want to wear logos for) are the new breed of adventure racing. Of course there is also the Olympics with mountain biking, pentathlon and other rugged sports. The only major difference is that you have to beat out 1. 6 million people to be part of the Camel Trophy and the rest requires a checkbook and a disclaimer.

Adventure Racing News

P.O. Box 15095
Boston, Massachusetts 02215-0002
☎ *(617) 266-5637, FAX: (617) 266-7680*
http://www.tempestco.com
A web site dedicated to adventure racing

Beyond Adventure Sports

P.O. Box 270862
Fort Collins, Colorado 80527
☎ */FAX: (970) 484-7485*
email: BeyondAS@ix.netcom.com

The World's Toughest Cigarette Commercial

The Camel Trophy is the major marketing effort of Land Rover and World Brands, Inc. (WBI), a fully owned subsidiary of RJR Nabisco, the makers of Camel cigarettes and Oreo cookies. No longer directly flogging Camel cigarettes, the Camel Trophy is an event designed to create the imagery that sells about $400 million a year in licensed watches and about 80 different styles of boots. Pretty sneaky. This is an ideal way to push imagery (sans cigarette) in countries that don't allow overt cigarette advertising. WBI does not release budgets for the Camel Trophy, but DP estimates the total marketing cost worldwide at between $20 and 30 million, with each division kicking in funds from their advertising budgets. They fly in 120 journalists from around the world to cover not only the main event but also the qualifications trials usually held in a European location. Simple math would tell even the most gullible that licensing revenue (typically 5–15 percent of the gross) from $400 million sales would barely cover the event cost, let alone the corporate and advertising campaign. There is also a "coincidental fascination" with countries that are open to this macho brand image. You don't see a lot of Camel Trophies in North America or Europe. In fact, there have been none. Asia, South America and Africa are the venues of choice. There is also a growing disaffection by journalists who find the increased emphasis on yuppie sports, macho posturing, unabashed posing for the PR cameras and RJR's denial of tobacco hype to be a little too much.

Many yearn for the bad old days when it was a group of young men trying to get from Point A to Point B in their Land Rovers. The fact that a cigarette company paid the tab to sell more smokes in Europe and the Third World was fine since it was no secret. Now team members come from countries where the people smoke a lot of cigarettes but don't buy a lot of adventure wear. For example, why do the Canary Islands (I never knew RJR could confer sovereignty on areas), Russia and Poland compete when Canada and Mexico do not? It obviously has to do with the presence of RJR cigarette entities, not potential clothing purchasers. Now things are a little too posey and murky, and the journos I talk to don't like it. U.S. journalists who want to participate should contact Glenn Campbell, public relations representative for Land Rover North America, (818) 799-0877 FAX: (818) 799-0878, or Mark Shirmer at Land Rover North America, (301) 731-9041.

The actual event can range from comical to magical to pathetic, as the organizers try to create as much havoc and "toughness" as possible. I enjoy the camaraderie and exotic locations of the event, but the overall mindset of the organizers should be questioned once in a while. My claim to fame in Africa was having a knife pulled on me by event leader Ian Chapman, who was terrified that I would throw him in the swimming pool with his pretty little kilt on.

The Camel Trophy does afford the regular Joe an opportunity to compete for and get a spot in a world-class competition that pits him against the best that other countries have to offer. Rather than compete, the participants are united by adversity, and winning the team spirit award can provide a lot more weight than the actual trophy. The team spirit award is voted on by the competitors, while the overall trophy is decided by some voodoo method only the organizers understand.

What kind of people make the cut? Triathletes, joggers, weight lifters and racers shouldn't even waste the postage. The key is teamwork, a sense of humor and the stamina to go through a lot of crap and keep smiling. Hard-core athletes rarely have the team spirit or stamina required for a two-week event. Musclemen and racers couldn't handle the bad days, when two to three miles seem like a long way. Finally, who makes it? Stable, good-humored people, who can endure being squeezed in a vehicle with three other people for two weeks. Professional racers are disqualified automatically, and females are welcome.

The World's Toughest Cigarette Commercial

The initial cut is based on experience—can you drive off-road, pitch a tent, read a map or change a tire? Once accepted, you will spend a miserable frozen weekend in Grand Junction, Colorado, with team organizer Tom Collins. You will be run through the standard officer candidate tests, silly things like sliding people through rope webs, balancing on a log, even winching vehicles places they should never fit into. Forty-eight hours later, sleepless, bagged and tired, you will find out if you made the first cut. If you make it, you get to go to the finals, usually held in Europe. Here, they mess with your mind and run you through junior commando school, fun things like dragging a Land Rover half a mile with its wheels locked the wrong way (it can be done), building bridges, getting dumped in freezing cold water and playing the Flying Wallendas while crossing high wires—all posed for the cameras and designed to generate a sinking feeling of self-doubt for the real event.

The real event is quite different. A convoy of yellow vehicles will snake its way across some fetid hellhole. There are few roads and fewer reasons why trucks should pass here. The event is usually run in the wet season so that there are plenty of opportunities to use your winch or slide down hills. The competitions are great fun and deadly serious. High-speed driving is not a factor in any of this. Rally driving is being phased out in favor of more ecosensitive events like building research facilities. You are graded on how well you perform in these tasks as well as how you perform as an overall team member.

Few people can claim the honor of having been on the Trophy, and most people would never want to. But, hey, that's adventure.

The Camel Trophy
Tom Collins
U.S. Camel Trophy Team Coordinator
Snowmass, Colorado
FAX: (303) 927-9308
www.landrover.com

Eco Challenge
9899 Santa Monica Boulevard
Los Angeles, CA 90212
☎ (310) 553-8855, FAX: (310) 553-7497
www.ecochallenge.com

The Eco-Challenge is sort of a Raid Gauloise-Lite. Designed to appeal to American Yuppies who buy a lot of brightly colored gear and created by Mark Burnett, the event is a direct, unashamed attempt to sell sponsorship and provide a TV show load of pathos and agony by people who actually pay for the experience. Burnett got the idea after he took part in three Raid Gauloises and despite some rather disastrous setbacks he decided that Americans would pay to be lost in the woods and grimace a lot. Like any new venture the Eco Challenge had its financial setbacks, screw ups, outraged environmentalists and tenuous existence. But now the Eco Challenge has graduated from MTV and has a multimillion dollar deal with Discovery Channel so it should hit the big time soon. You know things are getting a little too Yuppified when you have team names like Team Land Rover, Team Rolex, Team Nike and Team Reebok.

Here's the scoop. You must go from point A to B, a distance of around 350 miles. You must enter as a team of five people with at least one person being certifiably female, (women buy yuppie gear too you know). It costs about $15,000–$40,000 to compete, $10 grand for the entry fee and the rest for travel, gear and training outings. Between points A and B contestants must utlilize a virtual sporting goods store of conveyances: canoes, horses, rafts, mountain bikes and climbing gear. It is expected that about half of the logo-festooned teams will drop out. (If one of your team flakes, you're out.) The race is usually won by Europeans who have been doing these things for years.

In Utah, it took the winning team 7 days, 16 hours and 12 minutes to win. Not bad considering they had a 35-mile horseback ride and run, 25-mile hike/ swim through a canyon, a 60-mile desert hike, 30-mile mountain bike ride and a 75-mile raft trip (23-miles of it whitewater), a 24-mile hike through the mountains, a 1200-foot vertical ascent, a 14-mile hike through a canyon, and a final 52-mile canoe trip.

Burnett figures it costs $2.5 million to stage the event and with about 75 teams competing, it should be around for a while.

Marlboro Adventure Team

☎ (800) MARLBORO

A newcomer and somewhat panty-waisted event asks that team members have expertise in four wheeling, dirtbiking, whitewater rafting and horseback riding. An 11-day adventure that covers 600 miles in the American Southwest, the Adventure team event is beautifully photographed be Pete Turner and amply promoted complete with Adventure Gear and plenty of print advertising. This event is open to anyone who can fill out a form and pass the initial knowledge tests.

Applications can be had by calling:

☎ (800) MARLBORO. (Closing date is around April 22 each year.)

Raid Gauloise

470 Waverly Drive
Beverly Hills, California, 90211
☎ (310) 271-8335
www.raid-gauloises.com
Created in 1988 by a French journalist who felt that the Camel Trophy was too easy. Gerard Fusil put together a 300 mile, 10 day torture test that attracts masochists from around the world. Unlike the Camel Trophy which is free, participants in the Raid Gauloise must pay their own way plus the $13,000 entry fee for the privilege of walking,

climbing, riding, rafting, parachuting and canoeing themselves to exhaustion. There is no cash prize, little fame and a lot of camaraderie. The event takes place in a different exotic location each year.

Alies Kar, The Adventure Company, Inc.

8855 Appian Way
Los Angeles, California 90046
☎ (213) 848-8685
Everything's clear to this outfitter that can take you on four-wheel-drive tours around Southern California and Baja.

Borneo Safari

P.O. Box 171 888 68
Kota Kinabalu, Sabah, Malaysia
FAX: [088] 426-180
An event that's been around for 6 years winds and grinds through Northern Borneo (Sabah). *DP* always has a blast but if you don't like mud, very large insects, not sleeping and noodles, forget it. Open to competitors, participants and journalists.

Bush Trek 4WD Services

44 Tulloch Avenue
Maryland, New South Wales 2287
☎ (049) 515815
Garry Walthers will yank you out of a tight spot, train you not to get into a tight spot or set up four-wheel-drive tours.

Four-Wheel Drive

Cape York Guides
Post Office Box 908
Atherton, Queensland 4883
☎ (070) 911978, FAX: (070)912545
Four-wheel drive trips through the top end of Australia. You can bring your own or rent one of theirs. Travelers can rely on good cooking and expert guidance.

Land Rover Adventure Outfitters

McVeigh Associates, 7 12th Street
Garden City, New York 11530
☎ (800) 726-5655
FAX: (516) 742-9103
Land Rover organizes off-road expeditions worldwide with itineraries including a seven-day safari in North Africa, eight days in Colorado's Rocky Mountains, five days on the pioneer trail in the Red Rock canyons of Moab, Utah, a 10

day safari through the dunes and wadis of Oman, nine days in Australia's Outback, and more. Accommodations are ultradeluxe, and the tab isn't cheap, but what price can you put on unforgettable experiences?

The Lost Patrol

Suite 172
11919 North Jantzen Avenue
Portland, Oregon 97217
☎ *(503) 731-3030*
Billed as the longest, coldest, toughest winter rally in the world, The Lost Patrol is a quick run up the Alcan highway in the dead of winter. Using standard TSD rally methods, the idea is to have the most accurate and consistent times. Sometimes this means driving as fast as the law of gravity and friction will allow and sometimes crawling to make up time. The Rally leaves Seattle at the beginning of February with about 30 entries and ends up in the Arctic about a week later.

The winner might pick up about a grand (depending on who donates the purse) and side bets are encouraged. Economically, the entry fee of $2500 doesn't make this a paying proposition, but what better things could you be doing in the dead of winter?

Richard Petty Driving Experience

6022 Victory Lane
Harrisburg, North Carolina, 28075
☎ *(800) BE PETTY*
Talk slow, spit far and drive fast in a real Winston Cup stock car. There are five courses to choose from and three locations (Las Vegas, Atlanta and Charlotte). Does not include oversized hat or sunglasses.

Southern Traverse

P.O. Box 410
Queenstown, New Zealand
☎ *[64] (3) 442-3660,*
FAX: [64] (3) 442-3667
www.southerntraverse.com
The grand daddy of them all, The New Zealand race was the forerunner in covering long distances in short periods and then tossing in mountains, roaring rivers and no sleep to make it interesting. Entry fee for a five member team is NZ$2,750. They also offer a rental and accommodation package. Entries are limited to the first 50 teams.

Jungle Trekking

Many people would never think of going to a tropical jungle with a tour operator while others wouldn't think of going without one. Keep in mind that most of these folks will hook you up with local ground operators, so expect to find the same trips offered by many agencies. Top jungle destinations are Irian Jaya, Papua New Guinea, Borneo, Sumatra, Vietnam and the Amazon; the most popular are Costa Rica and Belize.

Adventure Center

1311 63rd Street
Suite 200
Emeryville, California 95608
☎ *(800) 227-8747, (510) 654-1879*
A lower-cost alternative.

Custom Wilderness Adventures

P.O Box 941
Punta Gorda, Florida 33951
☎ *(941) 637-4935*
Runs La Selva Project expeditions into the Peruvian Amazon. Travel by dugout canoe and learn survival skills from the Indians. Must be physically fit.

Ecosummer Expeditions

1516 Duranleau Street
Vancouver, British Columbia, Canada
V6H 3S4
☎ *(604) 669-7741*
I know you are getting sick of "sea"ing this company in here, but it just so happens that they are one of the best packagers to Papua, New Guinea.

Journeys/Wildland Adventures

4011 Jackson Road
Ann Arbor, Michigan 48103
☎ *(800) 255-8735*
An excellent choice for trips to Madagascar, Brazil and Venezuela.

Mountain Travel/Sobek Inc.

6420 Fairmont Avenue
El Cerrito, California 94530
☎ *(800) 227-2384*

Although they are primarily a rafting company, they have developed good contacts and a good nose for exotic tours.

SafariCenter

3201 North Sepulveda Boulevard

Manhattan Beach, California 90266

☎ *(800) 223-6046, in California (800) 624-5342*

An excellent selection of adventure and jungle tours.

Kayaks

The Shotover in New Zealand, the Sun Khosi in Nepal, the Rogue River in Oregon and the Cheat, the Upper Yough, the Gauley and the Tygart in the Allegheny mountains in West Virginia are some of the top spots. West Virginia probably offers the widest selection of Class IV to V runs on the continent. Rafters can conquer these rivers with impunity, but kayakers need a healthy dose of Class IV skills before venturing out. Kayakers need look no further than Ecosummers located in Vancouver for the widest selection of kayak trips.

Ecosummer Expeditions

1516 Duranleau Street

Vancouver, British Columbia, Canada

V6H 3S4

☎ *(604) 669-7741*

Ask for their annual catalog of trips along the West Coast of North America as well as some intriguing Arctic and foreign destinations.

Motorcycle

Motorcycle touring comes in four flavors: the classic Harley/Gold Wing big-butt road riders; the leather-clad, bug-splattered BMW crowd; the brightly colored and over-revved sport Tourers, and the sunburnt, trans-Sahara off-road crowd. All can be considered adventurous and dangerous, but the choice is ultimately yours. There is a law of diminishing returns if you are crossing Mali dehydrated, stricken with dysentery and nursing a broken ankle. You will probably dream of cruising the Grand Tetons adjusting the air suspension and the radio on your Gold Wing. There are happy mediums. Usually BMWs are found in scenic places like New Zealand, California and the Alps. If you want to ship your own bike, expect to pay between $1500 and $3000 for the roundtrip. You might want to look into BMWs European delivery plan, where you will pay about what the discounted price is in the States. You then pick up your bike in Munich, drive all over Europe and bring it back to Munich where they will pay for the crating, shipping and taxes. You can also look into buy-back deals, where you sell the bike back at the end of the trip. Stateside, you can arrange rentals through Von Thielman or Western States Motorcycle Tours. Bikes rent for about $500–$800 per week, with insurance extra. If you are interested in touring Vietnam, I should plug Wink Dulles' book *Vietnam on 2 Wheels*, the best (and only) guide to motorcycling through South Vietnam. Call ☎ *(310) 372-4474* to order your copy.

Do it on a Hog

While recently researching Fielding's America West, I pulled into a famous roadside diner along Route 66. A row of gleaming custom Harleys were lined up outside. Inside were burly leather-clad bikers...who spoke only German. Yes this is America and one of the hottest trends (it was over 110 degrees outside) is to dress up like a reject from the Village People, rent a Harley and see America. Interested? You will need a motorcycle, drivers license, have credit cards that can handle a stiff $2000 security deposit, and be 25 or older.

Average cost is $70–$150 a day (insurance runs another $26 a day), and you are allowed 150 free miles. You can arrange one way rentals within each state or pay extra to have it shipped back from another location. Here are some outfits that rent Harleys.

California Cruisers in Los Angeles and San Francisco (310) 777-8337.

Do it on a Hog

American Road Collection in Miami ☎ *(305) 736-8433, Ft. Lauderdale* ☎ *(954) 359-3599. There are also renters in Aspen, New York, Key West, Boston and Martha's Vineyard.*

You can choose from a wide selection of new models. Fat Boys, Softtails, Wide Glides and Dyna Glides, Road Cruisers, Sportster and some custom models. The most popular time is winter and Germans are the main customers. Is it worth it? According to a survey done by ARC, 98 percent of customers loved it.

You can also "hog it" abroad. Or, if you're into more sedate bikes, that's an option, too. The first step is to contact the companies that strike your fancy and then start packing your leathers:

Alaska Motorcycle Tours
Post Office Box 622
Bothell, Washington 98041
☎ *(800) 642-6877, (206) 487-3219*
Timothy McDonnel runs shiny new Honda Gold Wings through the summer wilds of Alaska. The tour covers about 1600 miles over seven days. Figure on about $250 a day; that includes your gas, high-end hotels and the bike rental. You pay for your own food.

Adventure Center
1311 63rd Street, Suite 200
Emeryville, California 95608
☎ *(800) 227-8747, (510) 654-1879*
The Center reps the Australian Motorcycle Touring ☎ *(011 61) 3 233-8891*, where owner Geoff Coat runs eight- and 10-day trips beginning in Melbourne. You can expect a well-serviced BMW R80 and twin share accommodations. Tours run about $120 a day, and watch out for those kangaroos.

Baja Off Road Tours
25108 Marguerite Parkway
Suite B-126
Mission Viejo, California
☎ *(714) 830-6569*
A former Team-Honda dirt-bike racer will put you on a Honda 250 or 600cc dirt bike and send you off to La Paz (seven days) or San Felipe (four days). You will experience one of the primo desert riding and scenic runs in Mexico. The all-inclusive trips will cost you about $300–$400 a day. You pay the airfare to Southern California.

Beach's Motorcycle Tours
2763 West River Parkway
Grand Island, New York 14072
☎ *(716) 773-4960, FAX: (716) 773-5227*

http://bma.buffnet.net/
Why not buy your bike overseas? Beach's will set you up on a rental or your very own BMW as you tour the Alps. They have trips to New Zealand, Great Britain and Australia as well. Tours to Europe run $3800 for rider (with a $300 single supplement) or $3000 for a rider. Two week trips in New Zealand will sent you back $2800, ($200 single supplement) or add a passenger for $2050. You can also ship your own bike for the ride. Beach's will handle the crating, shipping and customs involved. Expect to pay about $800–$1800 each way to Europe; New Zealand is about 30 percent more. Tours are longer than most (16–22 days) but are great deals and highly recommended. Costs are about $200 a day, plus about $50 a day for the rental of the bike.

Desmond Adventures
1280 South Williams Street
Denver, Colorado 80210
☎ *(303) 733-9248, FAX: (303) 733-9601*
One of the best ways to see the Alps is on a 16-day Alpentour devised by the Desmonds. You can choose from East or West. Expect to pay about $4000 per rider and about $500 less for the passenger. It includes roundtrip airfare from New York, meals, bike rental and insurance. The trip is van-supported, so bring lots of camera gear and luggage. You can also choose your weapon, from mighty CBR 1100cc sport bikes to nimble Honda Trans Alps (Beemers, Trans Alps, CBR's Katanas sport bikes or Kawasaki Concours).

Edelweiss Bike Travel

Armonk Travel
146 Bedford Road
Armonk, New York 10504
☎ *(800)255-7451, (914) 273-8880*

The U.S. agents for Edelweiss Bike Travel *(Steinreichweg 1, A6414 Meiming, Austria)* can send you just about anywhere, including the CIS. Its homegrown 12-day Alpine ride is one of the most popular (and the best deal) for mountain rippers. They like to stick you on BMW 750s, the rideable but standard for many bike rentals, but larger bikes are available for 10–20 percent more. Edelweiss provides support vans.

Explo-Tours

Arnulfstasse 134
8000 Munich 19, Germany
☎ *[49] (89) 160-789, FAX: [49] (89) 161-716*

Africa nuts who like chipped teeth and sandblasted eyeballs will love the offerings of Explo-Tours. They arrange tours across the Sahara, through Central Africa and into South Africa on spartan but reliable Yamaha XT350s. Naturally, only Germans are crazy enough to keep this company in business, but most Germans speak English. This is some serious riding, so participants must be physically fit and ready to ride thousands of miles in sweltering heat. The trips are great bargains at about $150 a day, including bike rental. There is a support van if you or your bike conk out, and when you return, you'll know more than a plasterer about mud and sand.

Great Motorcycle Adventures

8241 Heartfield Lane
Beaumont, Texas 77706
☎ *(800) 642-3933, (409) 866-7891*

If you are looking for a little danger, how about a mix of Mexican roads and fast bikes? Well, OK, how about offroading on slow bikes? GMA organizes off-road trips to Copper Canyon, the Yucatan and the Sierra Madre mountains on dual-purpose bikes. Tour costs include food, lodging, tours, gas and insurance. Trips are about $160 a day, not including bike rental (dual-pur-

pose bikes are only $500 a week). If you really want to do it on a fast road-bike, then expect to pay another $600 a week.

MHS Motorradtouren GmbH.

Donnersbergerstrasse 32
D-8000, Munich, Germany
☎ *[49] (89) 168-4888*
FAX: [49] (89) 166-5549

MHS offers a wide array of bike tours (including Southern California). You can choose from their popular week in southern Italy tour or any one of the other tours, including northern Italy, Kenya, Sicily, Tunisia, Hungary, the U.S.A. and South Africa. European tours run about $150 a day, with bike rentals (BMWs or Suzukis) costing about $900 a week. A cool idea for *Easy Rider*-wannabes is the one-way Drive U.S.A. program, where riders can pick up a bike at either coast and drop it off on the other.

Motorrad-Reisen

Jean Fish
Post Office Box 591
Oconomowoc, Wisconsin 53066
☎ *(414) 567-7548*

The U.S agent for Motorrad-Reisen, *Postfach 44 01 48, D-8000, Munich 44, Germany,* ☎ *(011 49) 89 34 48 32*, can send you on a motorcycle adventure (we don't use the word "holiday") to Kenya, southern France, the Alps, Italy or Russia. As with most German companies, it offers less expensive tours with less frills. You can also purchase a new BMW, ride it on your trip and ship it back home.

Villa Moto-Tours

9437 E.B. Taulbee
El Paso, Texas
☎ *(800) 233-0564, (915)757-3032*

One of the few companies that can stick you on a Harley. As you guessed from the name, Pancho Villa specializes in tours through Mexico down to the Yucatan Peninsula. They also can take you through Costa Rica, Baja, the Sierra Madre central coast and the Southwest U.S. Harleys and the Southwest—what a combo. The prices are fair, about $110 a day, with bike rental running about $50–100 a day extra.

Rocky Mountain Moto Tours Ltd.
Post Office Box 7152
Station E
Calgary, Alberta T3C 3M1
☎ *(403) 244-6939, FAX: (403) 229-2788*
Touring the dramatic countryside of Alberta and British Columbia may be a good second choice to the Alps. Using Honda 600cc dual-purpose machines, RMMT takes you on the remote back-country routes. Their rates of about $120 a day, including bike rental, are downright cheap. Choose from seven-day tours of the Bugaboos and 10-day trips through Big Sky country.

Western States Motorcycle Tours
1823 East Seldon Lane
Phoenix, Arizona 85021
☎ *(602) 943-9030*
Western states will put a fire-breathing Harley between your legs and point you in the right direction. You can arrange a buy-back deal if you plan on being gone a long time, or you can rent everything from a Gold Wing to a Harley for about $100 a day.

Von Thielman Tours
Post Office Box 87764
San Diego, California 92138
☎ *(619) 463-7788, FAX: (619) 234-1558*
If you are a jaded biker and view the Alps and New Zealand as commonplace, then Von Thielman has the antidote. This company has been around long enough to put together tours that bring the jaded back. How about Southern California, Thailand, China, Argentina or even Jamaica? The company has really got its act together. They can send you out alone, help you buy a new bike, ship yours or give you a wide selection of dual-purpose and touring bikes.

Mountaineering

There is little argument that the Hindu Kush in Nepal is the *ne plus ultra* of peaks and trekking. Only about 40 years ago, the ascent of a major peak would put you on the rubber chicken circuit until you grew old. Now, even Mount Vinson in the Antarctica has had 130 successful summit trips. Up and coming places include the peaks of Alaska, Argentina and Pakistan, with the Alps looking like a drive-through window at McDonald's. The Holy Grail is to conquer the seven summits or climb the highest mountain on each continent. Many guides will require that you have proof of your skills before taking you along.

The international UIAGM or the local AMGA provides certification and standards for guides. See the listings under schools in the "Save Yourself" chapter, or to find out more about schools, guides and programs, contact the following:

American Mountain Guides Association
Post Office Box 2129
Estes Park, Colorado 80517
☎ *(303) 586-0571*

Canadian Mountain Guide Association
Post Office Box 1537
Banff, Alberta, T0L 0C0, Canada
(403) 678-4662

Himalayan Kingdoms
20 The Mall
Clifton
Bristol, BS8 4DR, England
☎ *[44] (272) 237163, FAX: [44] (272) 744993*
One of the leaders in expedition and advanced quality climbs.

Summits
Post Office Box 214
Mount Rainier, Washington 98304
☎ *(206) 569-2992, FAX: (206) 569-2993*

The World's Most Dangerous Mountain

K2 is called the killer mountain, simply because on average it kills every second person who tries to conquer the summit. The 50 percent fatality rate makes Everest's 25–30 percent fatality rate seem almost safe.

The World's Most Dangerous Mountain

Mount Everest has been climbed more than 650 times, and to date about 100 people have died in the attempt. The 45˚ slopes are fairly easy to negotiate, so Everest's notoriety as the world's highest mountain continues to attract thrillseekers and climbers. Tens of thousands have made the trek to the 17,500-foot-elevation base camp. A permit costs $10,000. K2 is 236 meters lower, but it is considered the world's most dangerous mountain to climb. Only 100 people have reached the 8611-meter summit of K2, and more than 45 people have died trying. The slopes of K2 average about 60˚ and the storms are so violent that no one managed to conquer the mountain between 1986 and 1991. Avalanches are frequent, and the most dangerous segment involves passing through a bottleneck area prone to avalanches.

In 1993, 40 people reached the summit of Everest the same day, and in May of 1996, eight out of 30 climbers died on Everest when a storm hit. There were 11 different groups trying to make it to the top at the same time. Over a million people followed the disaster online.

The odds are one in three climbers will die attempting to reach Mt. Everest's summit. The total cost to risk your life on Everest or K2 is between $30,000 and $100,000, depending on what your guide thinks his life is worth.

Overlanding

Although not technically four-wheel driving, you will be sitting in a four- or six-wheel-drive Bedford as you bump and lurch across Africa. Any old African hand knows that you use a Bedford to pull out a Land Rover and you will need a tank to pull out a Bedford.

Overlanding became all the rage in the early seventies when companies could take you all the way from London to South Africa for only $1200 bucks. Today, prices are up around $5000, and the conditions and roads have since worsened. Most overlanding is done on a communal basis. Cooking and other camp chores are usually shared. Most only invite young people along. You can imagine the social dynamics of young people usually on their first or second major trip away from home. Cliques emerge, rebellions soon form, people leave and seats, toilet paper and girlfriends are fought over. In the end, everyone departs firm friends.

Himalayan Travel, Inc.

Post Office Box 481
Greenwich, Connecticut 06836
☎ *(800) 225-2380, (203) 622-6777*
The agent or Tracks Africa can send you on a 15-week overland trip from Fez in Morocco to Dar es Salaam in Tanzania. The route changes or the trip is cancelled, depending on who's killing who along the way. If things are relatively quiet, expect to pay about $4000 per person.

Dragoman c/o Adventure Center

1311 63rd Street, Suite 200
Emeryville, California 95608
☎ *(800) 227-8747, (510) 654-1879*
Contact the Adventure Center if you want more punishment than Tracks Africa delivers. If you want to do 19 weeks, Trans-Africa will weave you through West Africa as well as hit most countries in Central and East Africa.

Dragoman is a British company that uses Mercedes trucks. The 20-year-old company can also take you on a seven-week tour down the spine of South America.

Forum Travel International

91 Gregory Lane, Suite 21
Pleasant Hill, California 94523
☎ *(510) 671-2900, FAX: (510) 946-1500*
If you want to travel 5000 miles from the headlands of the Amazon to the tip of Patagonia, then mark five months off your calendar and call Forum Travel. Probably a little too much of South America for anyone, so you can bail on any one of the 11 sections, each lasting about 12 days. The cost is $1800 per stage, but do you really want to spend $20,000 bouncing around in a modified Mercedes troop truck?

Trans Continental Safaris

James Road
Clare, South Australia 5453
☎ *[61] (88) 423-469, FAX: [61] (88)*
422-586

The continent of Australia may look small, but it is very big from the windshield of a Toyota Land Cruiser about to run out of gas. Although there are many operators who will run you around in a four-wheel-drive truck for the day, it is best to stick with a pro who puts together long-distance safaris. TCS will provide one- to 37-day tours of Australia's outback, complete with driver/cooks/guides who know how to fix the air conditioning and also tell you enough dirty jokes to make the long distances bearable. They supply all the camping equipment you will need; all *you* need is the stamina.

World Expeditions

Suite 747, 920 Yonge Street
Toronto, Ontario Canada M4W 3C7
☎ *(800) 387-1483*

World Expeditions will show you the most remote sections of the Australian outback on a 15-day trip from Marlin Coast to Cape York. Starting and returning in Cairns, they will introduce you to the aborigines, the Australian rain forest and the rugged scenery of northern Australia.

Diving

Scuba (Self Contained Underwater Breathing Apparatus) was invented by Jacque-Yves Cousteau and a partner back in the 1940s. Since then, SCUBA tourism has taken Americans to some of the most beautiful places on the planet.

The highest percentage of underwater species is found around the island of Borneo, decreasing as you get farther away. The U.S. has only about 250 species, Hawaii about 450, Indonesia about 2500. There is much talk about where the best dive sites are. There is always a hard-core crowd that will invariably travel to the next best place. I was on Sipadan in Sabah, Malaysia, during the early years, and it was spectacular. At that time, they were busy creating a new dive site in Indonesian Borneo—Kalimantan. Now that Sipadan is known worldwide, there are many more dive sites waiting to be discovered in Indonesia. The best dive sites in the world for pure color and variety are in Indonesia, followed by Thailand, Malaysia and then the South Pacific and the Red Sea. The adventurous will choose the Sea of Cortez for its amazing proliferation of large fish; others prefer wreck diving in Truk or even the frigid waters of the Inside Passage in British Columbia. Having dived from the Seychelles to Hawaii, my personal preferences are the island of Sipadan and live-aboards in the remote Nusa Tenggara islands of Indonesia. The more adventurous claim that Papua New Guinea has much to be explored and that the Galapagos is the next big place. The top dive sites are Indonesia, Micronesia, Truk, Bajal, Australia, Hawaii and Papua New Guinea.

As you probably already know, you need to be certified to dive (although I was on a dive trip where Mexican dive masters certified the rookies with about 90 seconds of boat-side instruction). Most dive tour companies will link you up with the dive site of your choice. Don't hold high hopes for luxury or gourmet food.

Many people can't decide whether to bring all their shiny new gear or to rent. If you just spent $3000 on all the gear, then you are more than likely going for one reason, so bring the whole kit. Many airlines offer extended luggage or weight allowances if one of your bags is dive gear. If you are going to bring your gear, take a small tool kit, including spare O-rings, straps and batteries.

My experience is that, at a minimum, it is best to bring your mask along with octopus, regulator and gauges. The next level would be booties and BC. Pack your dive knife, tanks, flippers and wet suit for warm water dives. Photographers will want to bring their certification card, logbook, camera, film, flash, batteries and maintenance pack.

There is a caveat. I ran out of air at 90 feet below in the clear waters of the Cayman Islands. The reason? The vibration from the plane flight had loosened my regulator, and, I went through 3000 psi of air in about eight minutes. Speaking of close calls, there is also divers insurance that will make sure you get repatriated or flown to the nearest decompression center. Contact **Divers Alert Network**, ☎ *(800) 446-2671*, or **Divers Security Insurance**, ☎ *(800) 288-4810*. Remember to wait that extra day to fly home after diving. To start planning your next great dive trip, contact the following:

Avalon Aquatics

615 Crescent Avenue
Avalon, California 90704
☎ *(800) MR-SHARK, (310) 510-1225*
All types of diving adventures are offered here, from introductory to instructor level. An all-day shark diving adventure costs $250 per person, which includes transportation, tanks and food.

HydroSphere

860 de Lima Paz, Suite D3
Pacific Palisades, California 90272
☎ *(310) 230-3334*
This company offers intense shark diving experiences in the world's largest cage, plus the opportunity to assist university researchers with a shark tagging program. Day and night shark tagging and research expeditions are offered, with student prices from $79, adults $99 and special rates for groups. The expeditions to see kelp forests, sea lions and sharks are led by former Cousteau Society team member and documentary film producer, Yehuda Goldman. Programs are also offered for children, snorkelers, nondivers and even nonswimmers.

Innerspace Adventures

13393 Sorrento Drive
Key Largo, Florida 34644
☎ *(800) 833-SEAS, FAX: (813) 596-3891*
A 20-plus year old dive travel agency that can get you deals as well as great dive sites. Micronesia is a specialty.

Island Dreams Travel

7887 Katy Freeway, Suite 105
Houston, Texas 77024
☎ *(800) 346-6116*
Specialists in the Western Caribbean.

San Diego Shark Diving

P.O. Box 881037
San Diego, California 92168-1037
☎ *(800) 888-SD-SHARK,*
(619) 299-8560

If you've seen *Blue Water, White Death* or *Jaws*, it might interest you to know that you can dive with live sharks and experience the same feeling as a worm on the end of a hook. The place is called Sharksville, and it's about 20 miles off the coast of San Diego, California. After a rolling, choppy boat ride, you get to sit in a 16' x 8' shark cage about 10 feet below the surface while they throw chum in to attract sharks. The chances are good you will see blue sharks ranging in size from five to eight feet. You may also see mako sharks and albacore tuna. The water is cold, so bring a wet suit. Tough guys get to go outside the cage for more adventurous escorted shark dives. Those with a more scientific bent can take part in a blue shark tagging program. The San Diego dive master also has a chain mail arm that he lets the sharks chew on while you get some great photos.

Sea Safaris Travel, Inc.

3770 Highland Avenue, Suite 102
Manhattan Beach, California 90266
☎ *(800) 821-6670, in California (800) 262-6670*
An agency staffed by divers that can set you up in Asia, the Caribbean, the South Pacific and the Middle East.

See & Sea Travel Service, Inc.

50 Francisco Street, Suite 205
San Francisco, California 94133
☎ *(800) 348-9778, (415) 434-3400*
A good choice for more exotic and far-flung dive trips. See & Sea has an excellent selection of live-aboards.

Safaris

Arguably, safaris were the first adventure or ecotour. Back then, travelers would save wildlife by collecting samples for museums by shooting and mounting them. Now, all you hear is the clicking of cameras and whirring of videotapes. Most safaris in Africa today are nothing more than small tours conducted via zebra-striped buses carrying tourists in floppy bush hats brandishing new auto-everything cameras.

Masai Mara and Krueger Parks are glorified zoos without bars. The sight is still spectacular, and the photographs make everyone feel like they were the first one to set eyes on a lion kill or multihued African sunset. Despite the rampant commercialism, there is still a primitive joy in drinking a bloody Mary while watching the sun go down in Africa. I also enjoy the raw fear of camping without a tent in hunting areas of Tanzania and listening to the lions coughing and roaring at the intruders.

It is quite easy to fly directly to Nairobi or Dar es Salaam and book your own safari. You can also rent your own four-wheel-drive vehicle and stay at the various game parks or campsites. In fact, *Fielding's Guide to Kenya*, the most complete guide to homestays, game lodges and campsites, will show you how easy it is.

The best safaris in the world are private tented safaris to the lesser-visited areas of Africa's parks. In terms of wildlife, South Africa has an overabundance of it, along with clean, efficient facilities. Kenya has the creaky colonial ambience many people expect, and Tanzania is the stronger and more realistic of the two. My personal favorite is the rugged and remote Ruaha in Tanzania.

If you want to get your money's worth, the best way to get around is by air. That way, you can hit as many regions as you want and get a good grounding in geography as you bump and shudder through the hot African sky. Masai Mara has the most wildlife per square foot but has an equal number of tourists. Northern Kenya is plagued with bandits but has more dramatic scenery. Tanzania can be tedious (Selous) or dramatic (Ngorongoro Crater) but is what most people expect Kenya to look like. The Okavongo Delta and Namibia are becoming ideal second safari areas, and regions in Uganda, once the most beautiful country in Africa, are supposed to be coming back slowly. If you want to set up a safari in Africa, we recommend these groups:

Abercrombie & Kent

1520 Kensington Road,
Oak Brook, Illinois 60521
☎ *(800) 323-7308, (708) 954-2944*
The most famous African Safari and adventure tour operator does tours on the "cushy side" but the Kents run a first-class show. They also can put together custom expeditions, since they know most of the major ground operators on every continent.

American Museum of Natural History Discovery Tours

Central Park West at 79th Street
New York, New York 10024
☎ *(800) 462-8687, (212) 769-5700*
One of the best sources for high-end natural history tours. Although the tours are set up using a variety of ground operators, the museum provides stimulating guides and guest lecturers.

Borton Overseas

5516 Lyndale Avenue South
Minneapolis, Minnesota 55419
☎ *(800) 843-0602, (612) 824-4415*
A ground operator who specializes in Tanzania.

Ker, Downey, Selby

Box 41822
Nairobi, Kenya
☎ *(254) 2 556466*
The classic tented safari is the specialty of this group of independent outfitters and former big-game hunters.

Global Adventures

8762 South Morning Dove Lane
Highlands Ranch, Colorado 80126
☎ *(303) 791-9959*
http://www.globaladventures.com
Here's a company that can arrange Ranger Training, Motorcycle tours from

Capetown to Cairo, white water rafting and more.

Tamu Safaris
Post Office Box 247
West Chesterfield, New Hampshire 03466

☎ *(800) 766-9199)*

Wildland Adventures
3516 Northeast 155th
Seattle, Washington, 98155
☎ *(800) 345-4453*

Walking/Trekking

This is the most laid-back method of travel. You will meet people, get healthy and presumably do most of your travel in the world's most beautiful places. There is some danger of kidnapping and robbery as well as the usual penalties caused by tripping, falling and general wear and tear. Most trekkers hire porters and spend the evenings in small huts or villages. Trekking does not have to be set up from home, since most countries that are known for trekking supply the manpower for tour packagers overseas. Make sure, however, that you bring all the camping do-dads and clothing you will need.

The most popular trekking sites are Annapurna in Nepal, Zanskar in Ladakh, Bernese Oberland in the Alps, the Milford Track in New Zealand and Chiang Mai in Northern Thailand.

L.L. Bean Outdoor Discovery Schools
☎ *(800) 341-4341 ext. 6666*
Hands-on instruction and wilderness trips for beginners and experienced outdoor enthusiasts. Good preparation before you tackle more adventurous treks outside the United States.

The Ramblers Association
1-5 Wandsworth Road
London, SW8 2XX, England
A group that can advise you on where to hike in Britain and set you up with the resources you might need for a European walking holiday. As you may have guessed from the name of this group, their members are not triathletes or mountain climbers. For actual tours, contact Rambler's Holidays below.

Mountain Travel-Sobek
6420 Fairmount Avenue
El Cerrito, California 94530

☎ *(800) 227-2384*
The IBM and GM of adventure tours can send you anywhere that's worth trekking to. Although their expertise is really rafting and climbing, their trekking expeditions make use of many of the same contacts and guides.

Rambler's Holidays
P.O. Box 43
Welwyn Garden City, England AL8 6PQ
☎ *[44] (707) 331133*
A British group that can set up walking tours in Europe and Britain.

The Sierra Club
730 Polk Street
San Francisco, California 94109
☎ *(415) 776-2211*
One of the better sources for trekking, hiking or climbing trips around the United States and the world.

White-Water Rafting

Rafting has captured the imagination of Americans. In fact, when you ask most people what adventure is, they will reply, "a rafting trip on the Colorado." The truth is that rafting is among the safer aquatic sports. Bobbing like a cork on thundering white water, large flexible rafts carry thousands of people a year down the nation's major rafting rivers. As a method of travel, rafts, canoes and kayaks are a pain. They must be trucked in to the river and trucked out, and you are always wet and soggy and cold. But rafts and canoes provide the best way to see a lot of the primitive world. I have traveled by canoe in Africa, North America and Asia and found that the purity and simplicity cannot be beaten for communing with nature. I also have despised the primitive method of transportation after carrying a water-logged six-man canoe across the nine-mile Grand Portage.

The top domestic rivers for white-water rafting are the Tatshenshini in Alaska, the Colorado in Arizona, the Chiclo/Chicoltin in British Columbia, Canada, and the Upper Youghiogheny in West Virginia. Internationally, there are many rivers yet to be run, among them the upper reaches of the Mahakam in Borneo, the Bio Bio in Chile, the Obihingoú in the CIS and the Zambesi in Zimbabwe.

To find out where you can eat H_2O, contact U.S.A. Whitewater at ☎ *(800) USA-RAFT* for a selection of outfitters in the U.S.

In this country, these two international outfitters stand head and shoulders above the rest:

Mountain Travel/Sobek Inc.

6420 Fairmont Avenue
El Cerrito, California 94530
☎ *(800) 227-2384*
The granddaddy of adventure tour companies, Sobek joined Mountain Travel to create the Thomas Cooks of ecotourism. I once stayed with a remote tribe in Borneo who used the word "sobek" to ask for money. They explained that an American rafting expedition had been through and when the natives said the word "sobek," the rafters gave them

money. Such is ecotourism. MTS has specialized in Asia and Africa and are really the only sources for reliable rafting trips in Papua New Guinea, Ethiopia and Borneo.

Steve Curry Expeditions Inc.

Post Office Box 1574
Provo, Utah 84603
☎ *(801) 224-6797*
The master of the Yangtze in China, Curry also provides expertise in Latin America and the Soviet Union.

Adventure Travel Publications

Business Traveler International

51 East 42nd Street
New York, New York 10017
☎ *(212) 697-1700, FAX: (212) 697-1005*
Geoffrey H. Perry has about 40,000 avid readers who need to know facts, not gushy descriptions of the world's regions. The magazine can be counted on to provide on-the-ground information, comparative charts and travel tips that are always useful. A year's subscription is $29.97. Single copies are $3.

EcoTraveler

9560 S.W. Nimbus Avenue
Beaverton, Oregon 97008
☎ *(800) 285-5951*
Definitely on the fluffy side, an adventure magazine in the genre of: "Oh Muffy, won't we look so butch in hiking boots!" This is the latest in the wave of new ecozines that channels college guilt into politically correct travel experiences. This bimonthly lacks the veracity of *Escape* but does cover faraway regions. I can't help feeling like I'm being scolded on proper etiquette for scuba divers ("Get involved in local environmental issues"). There are lots of "I was there and this is what I did" articles for the politically correct and eco-

logically aware. On the positive side, there are lots of local getaways, plenty of pictures and, of course, lots of ads. A subscription to *EcoTraveler* costs $11.97 for a year (six issues), or you can buy it off the rack for $3.95.

The Educated Traveler

P.O. Box 220822
Chantilly, Virginia 22022
☎ *(800) 648-5168*
A newsletter that covers museum-sponsored tours, learning vacations, cultural tourism and more for $65 a year. A little stuffy but a good source for unusual travel opportunities.

Escape Magazine

3205 Ocean Park
Santa Monica, California 90405
☎ *(800) 738-5571*
An outdoor/adventure/world music pub that features a good mix of Third World adventure stories with practical info. The editor/founder, Joe Robinson, has a good eye and ear for real adventure and you never know what will crop up in this quarterly magazine. *Escape* also covers world music and sociopolitical issues in between stories about blisters and leeches. Good stuff

and available at major bookstores or by subscription.

Great Expeditions

5915 West Boulevard
Vancouver, British Columbia
☎ *(604) 257-2040*
A magazine that gets down and dirty with firsthand information on trips by its readers to exotic places. The magazine is tough to find but worth it for the up-close info it provides.

Maplink

25 E. Mason
Santa Barbara, California 93101
☎ *(805) 965-4402*
One of the best sources for maps from around the world. Call for a free catalog.

Outside Magazine

400 Market Street
Santa Fe, New Mexico 87501
☎ *(505) 989-7100, (800) 678-1131*
Created by Jann Wenner who founded *Rolling Stone*, *Outside* is now published in New Mexico by Mariah Media, Inc. The monthly magazine includes colorful features on destinations and activities for outdoor-loving travelers. Off-the-beaten-path places are spotlighted, along with profiles of adventurers. Departments include travel tips, environmental news, sports reports, and consumer reviews of travel gear, including apparel, camping gear, mountain bikes, etc. A yearly subscription is $14.97.

South American Explorers Club

Lima Clubhouse
Avenida Portugal 146
Brena District
Lima, Peru
Mailing address:

Casilla 3714
Lima 100, Peru
U.S. Associate address:

126 Indian Creek Road
Ithaca, New York 14650
☎ *(607) 277-0488*
Books, maps, trip reports, rain-forest advice. The main clubhouse in Peru has an excellent library of maps and other helpful publications. Membership is open to all and includes their magazine: *The South American Explorer.*

Travel Guides

Travel guides are an odd source of travel information, more for what they don't tell you than what you can find inside. Most travel writers write champagne tour guides on beer budgets. Budget guides tend to stick to inner cities, known hiking trails or tourist ruts (even though they profess not to), simply because they avail themselves of the local tourism industry to get around. The other problem is that the data can be horribly outdated or wrong. Check the copyright in the front of the book, get to know the writer, and get at least a couple of opinions before you go.

Fielding Worldwide, Inc.

308 South Catalina Avenue
Redondo Beach, California 90277
☎ *(800) FW -2 GUIDE,*
FAX: *(310) 376-8064*
Internet: http://www.fieldingtravel.com
Temple Fielding got his start writing disinformation pamphlets for Tito while in the employ of the OSS in World War II. After that auspicious beginning, he also wrote one of the wittiest, right-on travel guides to Europe back in 1947. Carrying on that tradition, Fielding guides continue to focus on the unusual, the unknown and the unique. Our web site features the entire text of *Worldwide Cruises* and *The World's Most Dangerous Places*, as well as the largest travel links on the web.

Lonely Planet Publications

Embarcadero West,
112 Linden Street,
Oakland, California 94607
☎ *(415) 893-8555*
Web site: http://www.lonelyplanet.com
The '70s and '80s bible of adventure travelers and expats. Plenty of good practical info served up with a sense of juvenile naiveté. The books are worth it for the maps alone. Most of the 190-plus books are updated on a two- or

three-year cycle, so check the copyright date. Tony and Maureen Wheeler built Lonely Planet from the kitchen table to a $12 million publishing business. Their recent shot at guides to civilized countries falls well short of the standard they set for Third World countries. Their web site contains book excerpts ideal for getting an overview of a country and some old but useful updates from readers.

Moon Publications
722 Wall Street
Chico California 95938
☎ *(800) 345-5473, (916) 345-5473*
Web site: http://www.moon.com
A company launched by their flagship book on Indonesia by founder Bill Dalton. Moon is quietly building a following and slowly building a library of good, comprehensive, intelligent books on the world. Well researched, well written and very practical, they cover domestic locations very well and are updated when needed. Web site features Road Trip USA.

Rough Guides
1 Mercer Street
London WC3H 9QJ
☎ *[44] (71) 379-3329*
Web site: http://www.wired.com
A new in the U.S. but over in Europe, Rough Guides have out–lonely planeted Lonely Planet by emphasizing detail, attitude and opinions as well as facts. They tend to dwell on places you have no intention of going, and their information is lacking on anything above backpacker budgets. Better written than most books. Their web site features an ever expanding offering of book content and a few links.

Footprint Handbooks
6 Riverside Court
Lower Bristol Road
Bath BA2 3DZ
☎ *[44] (225) 469141, FAX: [44] (225) 469461*
www.footprint-handbooks.co.uk
Among the most compact and well-researched travel guides to the world's remote regions. These tiny, expensive travel bibles contain phone numbers, maps, sidebars, intros and just about everything needed for reference. They are thin on accommodation reviews. They began at the turn of the century with their South America guide and have expanded into Asia, the Caribbean and Africa.Not much on their web site other than a slow loading catalog.

Travel Publishers on the Web
Fielding Worldwide
http://www.fieldingtravel.com
Fodors Travel Publications
http://www.fodors.com
Footprint Handbooks
www.footprint-handbooks.co.uk
Gault Millau Travel Guides
http://www.gayot.com
Globe Pequot
http://www.globe-pequot.com
Hayit
http://www.hayit.com
Insider's Guides
http://www.insiders.com/explore/
Moon Handbooks
http://www.moon.com
Lonely Planet
http://www.lonelyplanet.com.au/
Macmillan Reference
http://www.mcp.com/
Rough Guides
http://roughguides.com
Karen Brown's Guides
http://www.karenbrown.com
Let's Go
http://www.letsgo.com
Traveler's Tales
http://192.190.21.10/gnn/bus/oratt/index.html
Rick Steves
http://www.ricksteves.com
Travel Magazines
Condé Nast Traveler
http://www.epicurious.com
Travel & Leisure
ttp://pathfinder.com/Travel/TL/index.html

Travel Holiday

http://www.dc.enews.com/magazines/
travel_h/

Monk

http://www.neo.com:80/Monk/

Travel Books Review

http://members.aol.com/travbkrev/
tbrintro.html

Travel Weekly

http://www.traveler.net/two

Vagabond Monthly

http://www2.globaldialog.com/~tpat-
maho/index.html

Other Publications

New Internationalist/Third World Guide

Post Office Box 1143
Lewiston, New York 14092
☎ *(905) 946-0407, FAX: (905) 946-0410*
Founded in 1970, the *New Internation-alist* "exists to report on the issues of world poverty and inequality: to focus attention on the unjust relationship between the powerful and powerless in both rich and poor nations...." Well, you get the point. This rather biased magazine does provide a good second look at the world's people and has some interesting things to add to any cocktail political discussion. A good source for folks looking for information to make their case against the world's military/industrial complex. Subscriptions are $35.98 per year, with corporations being dunned $60 (as you would expect from these folks).

Third World Guide

New Internationalist
55 Rectory Road
Oxford OX4 1BW
☎ *(0865) 728 181, FAX: (0865) 793 152*
If the *New Internationalist* magazine is a little too strident in its bashing of the U.N., big business and First World countries, at least you should own its most illuminating product, a fascinating annual called *Third World Guide*. This unusual guide covers 173 countries, is put together by researchers, journalists and academics in Third World countries and provides information on arms, housing, aid, refugees, food and country profiles on newly formed nations. The 630-page '93/'94 issue covers 30 emerging nations and has 55 maps, 780 diagrams and 6800 references. The full-sized book will set you back a hefty $38.95, plus $3.95 shipping and handling. Now in its ninth edition. Stick this hefty guide next to your CIA handbooks and you have a fairly balanced portrait of the world.

World Press Review

200 Madison Avenue
New York, New York 10016
☎ *(212) 889-5155*
The *World Press Review* consists of material excerpted from the press outside the United States. *WPR* is a nonprofit organization/educational service and seeks to foster the international exchange of information. The magazine does a good job of providing updates on news from various countries but, more importantly, showing the variety of responses on global affairs, whether it is the U.S. invasion of Haiti or what the rest of the world thinks of Saddam Hussein. Their choice of news sources is quite good and varied. The leaning of the publication is noted before the clip (pro-government, centrist, liberal, conservative business, etc.). The *Review* also makes good use of political cartoons from around the world. Subscriptions are $24.97 for 12 issues.

The Economist

111 West 57th Street
New York, New York 10019
☎ *(212) 541-5730, (800) 456-6086,*
FAX: (212) 541-9378
The granddaddy of world mags is devoid of the cheesy stereo ads of the *New York Times* or the "grow new hair" ads found in *Time* and *Newsweek*. Their readers just don't have time to read the ads. In fact, the *Economist* probably has the most time-starved

readership of all the news magazines—a blue-chip collection of world leaders, policy makers, big business, etc. If they get something wrong, chances are the person that they are writing about will contact them to correct it. Their lofty and somewhat ludicrous goal is to "take part in a severe contest between intelligence which presses forward, and an unworthy, timid ignorance obstructing our progress." I suppose they mean that their subscription drives are hampered by stupid people who don't see the value of paying $125 a year (for 51 issues) to bone up on global and financial news. The magazine's easy-to-use format and impressive attention to facts before opinions make this a must-have for globally aware readers. Their special sections are packed full of first generation information, and they even throw in charts, graphs and other helpful graphics. If you can't get enough, the *Economist* also puts out quarterly indexes and some very impressive year-end wrap-ups in book form.

Geographical

Post Office Box 425
Woking GU21 1GP
☎ (0483) 724122, FAX: (0483) 776573
A surprisingly intelligent magazine that explores adventure, science, politics and geography. A monthly published for the Royal Geographic Society. Very little posturing, long on facts, with maps and research; the magazine provides coverage other magazines can't deliver. Definitely a recommended publication for adventurers. $57 for an annual subscription or $5.50 on the newsstands.

United Nations Publications

Sales Sections
2 United Nations Plaza
Room DC2-853, Department 403
New York, New York 10017
FAX: (212) 963-3489
The United Nations provides an enormous amount of important information on the world and its people. The first step is to send away for their catalog of publications. Their rather dry but informative publications cover narcotics, disasters, agriculture, economics, hunger, poverty, war and just about anything else of interest. They range from thrilling books like *ESCAP Atlas of Stratigraphy IX: Triassic Biostratigraphy and Paleography of Asia—Mineral Resources Development Series and Stratigraphic Correlation Between Sedimentary Basins of the ESCAP Region* to *Urban Crime Global Trends and Policies.*

Travel Book Stores

Adventurous Traveler Bookstore

P.O. Box 577
Hinesburg, Vermont 05461
☎ (800) 282-3963
http://www.gorp.com/atbook.htm
More than 3000 books and maps for hiking, biking, kayaking, snorkeling, fly-fishing, trekking and general travel worldwide. Call for a free catalog or find it on the World Wide Web.

AAA

600 S.W. Market Street
Portland, OR 97201
☎ (503) 222-6720

Stanfords

12-14 Long Acre
London, England WC2E 9LP
☎ [44] (71) 836 1321,
FAX: [44] (71) 836 0189
Also at

156 Regent Street
London, England W1R 5TA
Billed as the world's largest map and travel book shop, this is a great source for hard-to-find maps and books.

Adventure 16 (chain)

4620 Alvarado Canyon Road
San Diego, CA 92120
☎ (619) 283-2374

California Map Center
   3211 Pico Boulevard
   Santa Monica, CA 90405
   ☎ *(310) 829-6277*

Rand McNally (chain)
   8255 Central Park Avenue
   Skokie, IL 60076
   ☎ *(708) 329-8100*

Travel Emporium
   20010 Ventura Boulevard
   Woodland Hills, CA 91364
   ☎ *(818) 313-9452*

Traveler's Choice Bookstore Inc.
   111 Green Street
   New York, NY 10012
   ☎ *(212) 941-1535*

Distant Lands
   56 South Raymond Avenue
   Pasadena, California 91105
   ☎ *(626) 449-3220*
   email: Distant☆deltanet.com

Complete Traveller
   199 Madison Avenue
   New York, NY 10016
   ☎ *(212) 685-9007*

Travel Books & Language Center
   4931 Cordell Avenue
   Bethesda, MD 20814
   ☎ *(301) 951-8533*

Travelfest Superstores
   1214 W. 6th Street
   Austin, TX 78703
   ☎ *(512) 479-6131*

Voyager's Travel Store
   19009 Preston Road #300
   Dallas, TX 75252
   ☎ *(972) 732-9373*

Nations
   502 Pier Avenue
   Hermosa Beach, California 90254
   ☎ *(310) 318-9915*

We recommend buying travel guides from travel specialty stores because they actually use and read the books. Don't be shy about calling the publishers direct if you have more specific questions. Borders and Barnes & Noble carry a good inventory but shy away from the esoteric titles. Amazon.com is a good tool for searching (www.amazon.com).

Internet Travel Sites

If you spend much time with your computer on the Information Superhighway, otherwise known as Cyberspace, you may want to check out some of the travel information sources listed here. As the World Wide Web grows, more and more companies are creating their own Web Pages. You can access information ranging from State Department Consular Information Sheets and Travel Warnings to foreign exchange rates and which immunizations you need for traveling to New Guinea or any other destination in the world. To access these sources, you'll need a computer, modem and communications software and membership with an on-line service like **America Online**, ☎ *(800) 827-6364.*

Adventurous Traveler Bookstore
   http://www.discribe.ca/other/bluep.htm
   This on-line warehouse of adventure titles will have you considering travel to countries you never knew existed. The catalog of 2200 titles can be accessed through keywords and handy indexes. You can order choices, access phone numbers or download an order form on-line. A hot list includes new titles and additions added weekly.

City.Net
   http://www.city.net

Tourism and cultural information on cities worldwide.

Fielding Worldwide
   http://www.fieldingtravel.com
   If you're enjoying this book, you'll want to check out Fielding's catalog of other travel guides. The Fielding Web Site includes excerpts from bestselling travel guides, such as *Fielding's Guide To Worldwide Cruises, DP*, sample maps, photos and charts, plus news on upcoming travel guides and itineraries for adventure-oriented travelers.

Foreign Exchange Rates

Internet: http://www.dna.lth.se/cgi-bin/ kurt/rates/

This site lists current exchange rates and helps you do the math to find out how much your dollar will buy in countries around the world.

Foreign Languages for Travelers

Internet: http://insti.physics.sunysb.edu/ mmartin/languages.html

How do you say "Where is the bathroom?" in St. Petersburg? This site helps travelers learn rudimentary phrases in French, Italian, German, Spanish, Russian, Portuguese, Dutch and Polish. The site includes basic phrases and links to dictionaries and sound.

International Travel and Health

Internet: http://www.who.ch/Travelandhealth/home.html

The World Health Organizations's Web site issues bulletins on malaria, vaccination requirements and other health topics grouped by region.

Magellan Basic Maps

CompuServe: gomagellan

This collection of on-line maps shows 500 regions. You must read the licensing agreement before accessing the maps, but if you accept the agreement, you can download the world.

Perry-Castaneda Library Map Collection

Internet:http://www.lib.utexas.edu/ Libs/PCL/Map-Collection/

This huge map collection includes satellite maps of the planet, islands, oceans, countries, national parks and a variety of other topics.

Round The World Travel Guide

Internet:http://www.digimark.net/rectravel/rtw/html/faq.html

Along with general information on a plethora of places, this guide offers information on offbeat travel options, such as freighters that book passengers. Topics such as Transportation, People, Money Matters, Communications and Major Decisions help on-line travelers plan the perfect trip.

Time Zone Converter

Internet:http://hibp.ecse.rpi.edu/cgibin/tzconvert

Type in a date, time and two cities, and get back the time for each. This site can be very helpful for planning trips, booking flights and scheduling long-distance phone calls.

Traveler's Corner and Traveler's Edge

America Online: keyword travel, traveler's corner

Weissman Travel Reports hosts forums and provides short summaries of national and international destinations. Helpful information includes safety tips, restaurants, hotels and costs.

Yahoo Travel Links

Internet: http://www.yahoo.com/Recreation/Travel/

You can book a plane or train ticket, check rental car rates or find a bed-and-breakfast in England at this site. If travel information exists, you're likely to find it here.

A word of caution: Unless a web site is developed by a known provider of content, be somewhat skeptical of the veracity or purpose of the content. Also, there is more change than Las Vegas odds in the web business, so don't be surprised if some of these folks vaporize.

Adventure Clubs

So you feel a little strange at cocktail parties. Your friends jabber on about mutual funds, car leases and football games. You, on the other hand, want to discuss the pros and cons of female circumcision, the relative merits of Chinese- vs. Bulgarian-made AK-47s, the quality of polo played at Chitral vs. Gilgit, or even the archaeological merits of Nemrut Dagi. Your friends think you are talking about a new rock group and then slowly fade to the opposite corner. Seems like you need to find the right social circle. Well, take heart. There are actually clubs for adventurers. Obviously, these groups have their share of toupee-wearing, bring-'em-back-alive bullshitters, but you can probably find someone who can engage you in a spirited discussion about which side of the Rift Valley their ancestors came from in Swahili.

Adventurers are lone wolves, social misfits or even outcasts. Misunderstood by their friends and inept in their mundane existence, they tend to travel alone, romanticize the esoteric and only later realize that they are trendsetters. Occasionally, by choice or by circumstance, we find ourselves in the company of other adventurers, huddled in bomb shelters, squeezed into native huts or killing time in Central American jails. For a brief shining moment, we have found an equal, only to be dumped back into the real world, where most people think we're crazy.

The reality is that danger creates a special fellowship. You'll find instant camaraderie whether you are sitting around a small fire drinking bad cognac and discussing politics as the sun rises in an Asian jungle, or shivering in a mountain hut in Pakistan while arguing about the firing rates of automatic weapons. These serendipitous friendships under adversity create bonds and memories. It is not surprising that these adventurers would seek to re-create the boisterous warm feelings that many of them had around foreign campfires. Back in the real world, we do long for those clear, crisp moments when minds met and the world made sense.

Keep in mind that I believe in the words of Marx (Groucho, that is): "I would never join a club that would have me as member." But if you like wildlife and animals of the social kind, you may want to check out an adventure club in your neighborhood. There tends to be a liberal sprinkling of windy Baron Munchausen's complete with pencil mustaches and Faustian guts, as well as honest-to-goodness adventurers. In any case, the clubs can be an excellent way to learn about the world of adventure and the quixotic people that make it tick.

Be forewarned that each club has a unique personality. Many of the clubs demand that you earn your spurs before joining, some have a prepubescent abhorrence of females, and others are more businesslike and adopt the patina of adventure only as a decorating trend. Obviously, geographic proximity will dictate your choice, so it is up to you to inspect and decide. My personal favorites? I prefer the less arthritic and gravitate toward the scientific. The Royal Geographical Society is probably the best blend of historical and dynamic. There is a constant list of presentations and events that lean toward the scientific. If you prefer hanging out with aging astronauts or port-soaked big-game hunters, the American clubs may appeal to you. If you would like to cultivate a wider social circle, the foreign clubs may be ideal. If you would like to trade witticisms à la Oscar Wilde, then maybe the Savage Club is for you. In any case, here are descriptions of clubs designed for fellowship among the adventurous.

The Adventurer's Clubs

These are clubs where kindred souls can gather to swap tall tales and compare adventures. The Adventurer's Club originated in New York in 1912 and was the brainchild of a group of 34 men, among whom were soldiers, sailors, hunters, trappers, explorers, travelers, journalists, authors and scientists. Their goal was to promote the exchange and dissemination of knowledge in the areas of exploration, geography and natural history, as well as provide a social center for adventurous types. Today, these antique clubs have a hard time attracting the new breed of ecosensitive, bungy-jumping rock and rollers. The average age is 50 plus, but some young people are still attracted by the club's aura of history and tradition.

The concept of manly men surrounded by dusty trophies in creaky surroundings has kept these clubs alive and active. Within their confines, you can make such butch toasts as "To every lost trail, lost cause and lost comrade" or "To adventure, the shadow of every red-blooded man" without fear of ridicule. The original New York club spawned similar clubs in Chicago (1913), Los Angeles (1921), Copenhagen (1937) and Honolulu (1955). Although the Chicago club will boast they predate the New York club, they are essentially cut from the same cloth—superannuated boys clubs where members can proudly display their trophies and tell tales of adventures past.

Here, members can attend or give weekly presentations of their most recent exploits. Presentations cannot cover subjects that are controversial, religious or political in nature. (That puts *DP* fans out of the running.) If you have just come out of the jungle and are looking for a little female companionship, you are definitely in the wrong place. The club is very politically incorrect in its very male membership but does hold Ladies Nights "occasionally."

To be eligible for active membership, you must prove you are a real adventurer, not just someone with tattoos and a devil-may-care smirk. You must show "competent proof" of having:

- had outstanding adventure in travels off the beaten trail, hunting, mountaineering, aviation, sailing, diving, sports or similar activities;
- held responsible positions in official expeditions and explorations, the results of which have been published;

- taken calculated risks above and beyond the call of duty in military or public service;
- achieved distinguished and outstanding success and recognition for your research and explorations in the fields of geography, geology, archaeology, anthropology, natural history and kindred arts and sciences.

The clubs generally offer active memberships, associate memberships and consular memberships, with fees based on how much money you are willing to contribute.

Membership to any level provides for visiting membership in the other Adventurer Clubs as well as the Savage Club in London and the Explorers Club of New York.

The Adventurer's Club of Chicago

300 West Grand Avenue, Suite 270
Chicago, Illinois 60610
☎ *(312) 822-0991*
The Chicago club was started by journalist (Major) W. Robert Foran. He and a group of adventurers, big-game hunters and military men used to meet informally until 1911, when during a boozy meeting they decided to form a club and even came up with the motto "a hearth and home for those who have left the beaten path and made for adventure." It might have something to do with Foran having just returned from one of Teddy Roosevelt's big-game expeditions in Africa and feeling like he needed a permanent watering hole. In any case, the strangely nomadic club has occupied eight locations in its 83-year history. A real bitch, considering what a pain it is to move those shrunken heads, mounted trophies, stuffed bears, weapons, photos and other bric-a-brac that adorn the club.

Only 200 adventurous posteriors can be warmed by the clubhouse's fire at any one time. Both men and women (since 1989) are invited to an "exploratory visit." Membership is open to men and women. You simply write a letter to the president or drop off your application at the club.

The Chicago club prides itself on not having relaxed its membership standards and provides a rough but incomplete list of what they consider adventurous activities.

The list of adventurous pursuits that would qualify one for membership starts with "travel to remote areas not readily accessible by tour guides" and continues with hunting, fishing, photography (in remote areas) white-water rafting, ballooning, underwater activities, extended stays in remote areas and environmental testing, and winds up with archaeologists, treasure hunters and astronauts.

The board of directors will look for the element of risk to life and limb and prefers that your adventure be far from home and off the beaten path. They are open to new interpretations of adventure, so those four days you spent blindfolded, drunk, condomless and in heat in a Thai whorehouse may possibly qualify you for membership.

Once you have been initiated, you get to do silly, adventurous, manly things like "worship Wahoo," the household god, by donating to the baksheesh bowl (a charitable fund used for members in need), carry club flags to far-off places and then bring them back, and enjoy the hospitality of the Long Table, the lubricated fellowship at the "sign of the whale bar," and the general adventurous ambience of swapping yarns amongst the formaldehyde, rust and dust of an adventurer's club.

The Adventurer's Club of Los Angeles

2433 North Broadway
Los Angeles, CA 90086-2541
☎ *(213) 223-3948*
The Adventurer's Club of Los Angeles meets in downtown L.A. every Thurs-

day evening. The spacious club boasts trophies that would dignify many museums. Members and guests gather at 6 p.m. in the club's dining room and engage in sprightly conversations over dinner. At 8 p.m. they convene in the central meeting hall where a featured speaker recalls his exploits in adventure, exploration, arts and science. Most of the presentations contain "off-the-record" and "behind-the-scenes" stories not covered in commercial presentations. Controversial and religious subjects are not presented in the weekly assemblies, and the "manly men" deign to hold Ladies Nights about six times a year. The hand of good fellowship is extended to visiting members of the Savage Club of London, the Explorer's Club of New York, the Adventurer's Club of Chicago, the Adventurer's Club of Copenhagen, the Adventurer's Club of Moscow and the Adventurer's Club of Honolulu.

Los Angeles Explorers Club

706 West Pico Boulevard
Los Angeles, California 90015
A somewhat aging male-only and nomadic club of 200 male members, who recently voted down accepting women members 95 to 5. Unlike the grand New York Adventurer's Club, the L.A. club has kept its trophies and bric-a-brac in storage for years. The membership is diverse, and the meetings have included entertaining presentations by interesting people, such as Will Rogers, who spoke on the eve of his departure on his round-the-world journey. He died two weeks later, when the plane he was riding in, piloted by Wiley Post, crashed in Alaska. Dues are $150 per year; members pay for their meals.

The Explorer's Club of New York

46 East 70th Street
New York, NY 10021
☎ *(212) 628-8383, FAX: (212) 288-4449*
This club is 90 years old and a popular hangout for media types. The Explorer's Club was formed in 1904 by Henry Collins Walsh, when he invited a group of buds to create a club "to encourage

explorers in their work by evincing interest and sympathy and especially by bringing them in the bonds of good fellowship."

The nonprofit club began in 1905, and the founding members consisted of an Indian fighter, museum curator, Arctic explorer, mountaineer, archaeologist, war correspondent and hunter.

What makes the Explorer's Club a must is the fascinating decor created by 90 years of collecting trophies and junk from around the world. The six-story 1910 town house with its magnificent library is an "in" site for parties in New York.

For those who do not live in New York, there are 27 regional chapters, seven of them in other countries (Australia, Britain, India, Norway, Poland and Western Europe).

The club likes to lend out numbered flags, so that you can take them to some godforsaken place on some harebrained quest, and then throw a party when you return the dilapidated piece of cloth.

They sponsor some expeditions, award medals (the Explorer's Medal) and provide local support to scientific and educational programs, all based on merit. The club publishes a quarterly journal and a newsletter and offers a 25,000-item library, a 500-item map room and historical archives.

Membership includes 3000 men and women, with 500 of them outside the New York area.

As with most of these clubs, to join the Explorers Club of New York, you have to have some type of experience in being "adventurous." Driving a cab in Harlem probably won't impress them, nor will big-game hunting trips, extensive travel without a scientific purpose or photography in remote parts of the world. But if you provide sponsoring letters, fill out the application form and fork over the hefty membership fee, your chances are good.

You can be a "fellow" if your exploits are published, or try for regular membership if you are modest about your exploits. In any case, it will depend on what the membership committee and the Board of Directors say.

Also available are student memberships (16–24 years of age, over 24 if you are pursuing a graduate degree), and corporate memberships.

Savage Club

1 Whitehall Place
London, England SW1A 2HD
☎ *(071) 930 8118*
The Savage Club is one of the more unusual clubs for adventurers. It was founded in 1857 by a group of "merry fellows" at the Crown Tavern. Their quaint logo features a Plains Indian, but the club members do not know how the club and the members became known as "Savages." Some say it was a dead poet or a poverty-stricken journalist; others say it was a sick joke since the club consists mostly of men of the arts. The Savages are writers, doctors, lawyers, actors, musicians and artists. They welcome "solitary men or irrelevant characters, kind or quirky ones" and those who have "packed their accolades (but not their psyches) in their knapsacks and pursued in common cause the Savage fellowship."

The club has rules which must be obeyed. No guests may buy drinks, no one may enter the bar with an overcoat (the penalty is a round for all present), tipping is forbidden, and any member is encouraged to expostulate at the drop of a hat. The accent here is on being somewhat eccentric and entertaining.

The posh Savage Club is famous for holding on to two cases of bourbon requested by writer Samuel Clemens (Mark Twain). When asked if he wanted to take the liquor with him, Clemens requested that the club hold on to it until his return. When a prewar visitor informed them that Clemens had been dead for quite some time, they said they were bound by duty to honor his wishes

and to hold on to it until his return. The clubhouse and Clemens' liquor were destroyed during a WWII air raid, ending what could have been a long running joke. Why is the Savage Club a great adventurer's club? Well, there is a bald-pated dullness when surrounded by people of the same persuasion. How many big-game-hunting stories or eating-grubs-with-the-pygmy stories can you endure? The mix of intellectuals at the Savage Club encourages lively discourse and a chance to find an appreciative audience.

Joining is not as difficult as it may seem. The club welcomes applications from "gentlemen over 18 connected professionally with literature, art, music, drama, science or law in their creative and interpretive aspects, and to such other gentlemen as are deemed to have contributed to one or more of these disciplines." Attainment in hobbies, pursuits and other interests go a long way to impress the qualifications subcommittee. Two sponsors (both must be "Savages") are required to nominate a candidate. They must write a lengthy letter explaining why the candidate will make a great Savage. A resume, or curriculum vitae, along with a month-long probationary period are required.

The Royal Geographical Society

1 Kensington Gore
London SW7 2AR
☎ *(011 71) 581 2057,*
FAX: (011 71) 584-4447
Not technically a "club" but a vital social and scientific institution. The RGS was founded in 1830, with the goal of advancing geographical science and the "improvement and diffusion of geographical knowledge." The London-based society takes its mandate seriously, and although most Americans will remember the great expeditions of Sir Richard Burton and John Hanning Speke to discover the source of the Nile, few may know that they continue to send adventurous men to the far corners of the world.

Their focus today is a little more politically correct, centering on a range of environmental issues. The RGS welcomes any member regardless of nationality, etc. The only trick is you have to be nominated by other members and seconded by another if you wish to be a Fellow. The 12,000 or so members typically have academic qualifications or expedition experience or are widely traveled. It is somewhat difficult to be nominated as a Fellow (30 pounds per year—most are graduates and work in geographical professions), but there are also Associate Members (24 pounds), Educational Corporate Members (60 pounds) and Corporate Members (200 pounds).

Once you are a member, you can subscribe to the 164-year-old *Geographical Journal*, the largest circulation of any British academic journal. The rather staid and colorless journal is published three times a year and contains original research papers and important articles on geography. The monthly *Geographical Magazine* is more colorful and deals with more contemporary issues. There is also a newsletter that keeps members aware of upcoming events and activities in the RGS.

The RGS is headquartered in Lowther Lodge, a Victorian-era brick building across the street from Hyde Park and close to major museums. From the outside, statues of Shackleton and Livingstone peer around the corner from their niches in the walls. Inside, you find the exact kind of casual bric-a-brac you would expect to find in a house that has been storing other people's stuff for more than 150 years. Stuffed penguins are crammed in stairwells, portraits of the great explorers glare down on you, and there are more maps and books than you could possibly read in a lifetime. The library holds more than 150,000 books, periodicals and reference materials; the Map Room is stacked floor to ceiling with over 850,000 maps, globes and atlases. The Picture library has an excellent but somewhat confused selection of period photographs. The Archives holds the crown jewels of the RGS, the personal papers, diaries and observations of the world's great explorers. The RGS continues to sponsor expeditions and organize major field research programs.

There is also an excellent Expedition Advisory Center that is invaluable for anyone considering traveling the hard way or desiring to meet up with other like-minded people. The 15-year-old EAC is open to all and has assisted more than 500 expeditionary teams in providing training and advice to primarily university-level groups. Their impressive publications assist adventurers with tips on everything from the fund raising phase to gaining a publication contract for expeditions.

On the social side, activities surround the ongoing lecture program. RGS holds regular lectures on subjects as diverse as screening adventure films to nuts-and-bolts presentations on geomorphology. There is daily lunch, cocktails are served before and after lectures, and events can be held at the Society's headquarters.

The Expedition Advisory Centre

Royal Geographical Society
1 Kensington Gore
London SW7 2AR
☎ *(011 71) 581 2057,*
FAX: (011 71) 584-4447
Not a club or even a place where more than five people can sit down at one time. The EAC's home is in a crowded set of offices about the Royal Geographic Society's headquarters in London. They do a yeoman's job of singlehandedly running the only support group for expedition planning.

The Centre provides information, training and, most importantly, encouragement for anyone planning an expedition overseas. Their cumulative knowledge and vast contacts can help you decide what type of flashlight works best underwater, the best place to buy snake venom antidote, or even if there are other equally eager folks who want to join on. Nobody at the center writes checks for great ideas or does any work for you, but they can point you in the right direction and show you how and why expeditions are funded.

There is an annual program of meetings that brings seasoned pros together with fresh-faced explorers. In November there is an expedition planning seminar that generates enough enthusiasm to send anyone to the North Pole. For Americans the major source of help is the list of publications that pack years of solid experience into a bookshelf of manuals.

The Centre keeps a list of people who are interested in joining expeditions (people with medical and multidisci-plinary scientific skills are most in demand; photographers and folks who just are looking for something to keep them busy are the least in demand).

If you would like to get the latest prices and listings, just send a fax to the address above and request a list of publi-cations (you can use your credit card and there is a discount of 10 percent if you order more than 3 to 9 copies of the same publication, 25 percent if you order more than 10 of the same one).

There are books on fund-raising for expeditions, joining an expedition, writ-ing expedition reports, reference sources, expedition field techniques on collecting and studying everything from meteors to reptiles to people and hand-books on expeditions to polar, tropical, desert, underwater, underground and rain forest sites, and their expedition yearbooks detail the various expeditions the EAC has assisted or kept track of.

Maliau: The Lost World

Seeking out the last wild places for this book was not as easy as simply picking a green spot on the map. I spent a long time looking for areas in Borneo that could be future ecological and cultural highlights. Our goal was to publicize threatened and significant areas in Borneo that are important not only to the region, but to the world. One area needed no discussion: a perfectly balanced environment, untouched by man, home to a diverse array of species and biosystems... and in danger of becoming a coal mine.

"Ever heard of the Maliau?" Jon Rees asked. "No." "The Lost World, the last wild place in Borneo." "Really? Tell me more." The phone line between Malaysia and Los Angeles gave its characteristic echo as our voices sped up to satellites and down again, bridging the thousands of miles between us.

"There have only been four expeditions into the Maliau, three scientific and one I did just for the hell of it. Now a surveyor is there mapping coal seams. I think it's the right time for the world to find out about the Maliau Basin."

We talked at length about what was needed to get in and out of the basin. On my topographical aviation map, the Maliau looks like a giant volcanic basin. It is not. The Maliau Basin is a sedimentary formation of eroded sandstone and mudstone. The steep cliffs surrounding the basin, one of the features that has earned it the name, "Lost World," make it almost inaccessible. The only way in, at the lower end, is guarded by a series of impressive waterfalls and gorges.

The Maliau Basin is unique in that it is an area that has lain unvisited and untouched since the dawn of time. Now the area is getting serious attention from logging companies, coal mining and oil drilling interests.

Maliau means "murky" in the Murut language which is a good description of its past and possibly of its future.

Expeditions Into the Maliau

In 1947, a pilot flying from the west coast of British North Borneo to Tawau experienced a rude shock when he narrowly avoided colliding with a wall of steep cliffs emerging from the misty jungle. This minor incident is the first recorded mention of the Maliau Basin. The "Lost World" was recorded in the *Borneo Bulletin*—and then quietly slipped back into obscurity.

The nearest Dusun villagers lived only four days away, but their belief that a fierce dragon inhabited Lake Limunsut at the base of the cliffs didn't encourage exploration. Muruts along Sungai Sapulut were known to have reached the lower basin, calling it the "Mountain of Stairs" in reference to the many waterfalls and limestone ledges.

The first Western attempt to enter the "Lost World" was in 1976 during a forest service expedition to Lake Limunsut. They tried in vain to scale the escarpment but were forced to turn back just forty feet from the upper edge.

Four years later, the Sabah Museum mounted an expedition to penetrate this remote area. The expedition ran out of supplies, was felled by malaria, and had to give up before they could conquer the escarpment.

In 1982, they managed a brief reconnaissance by helicopter, landing on a gravel bar near the falls. This preliminary mission was designed to lay the groundwork for a more intensive expedition a year later. They were greeted by animals that had never seen man before: a docile 22 foot, 400 pound python, mildly curious bearded pigs and a *kijang*, deer. In all, this brief foray into the wilderness posed more questions than it answered.

Finally, in April-May of 1988, a 43 man expedition spent three weeks in the Maliau unlocking its secrets. What they found was impressive. The 390 square ki lometer basin covers an area of 25 kilometers across and is protected by an encircling escarpment that climbs up to 1500 meters. The highest point is Gunung Lotung, estimated to be 1900 meters high, but it has yet to be properly surveyed.

This expedition identified 47 species of mammals, including rhino, proboscis monkey and clouded leopard; 175 species of birds, including the Bulwer's Pheasant (once thought extinct in Sabah); and 450 species of plants, many of them rare species. Their scientific finds and increased understanding of this absolutely untouched region led them to declare it a conservation area. But, along with the numerous rare plants and unusual ecosystems, the expedition also discovered significant coal seams.

There had also been a more adventurous and less scientific foray into the Maliau. Jon Rees walked in from Sapulut with three other Americans, a New Zealander and a Brit. They had heard there was a place no one had ever been, so they hiked through solid jungle from Sapulut for three days, plunged down into the Maliau River, walked along the ridge trail for five days, spent time in the central area and then devised a curious way to exit the basin. They had carried in canisters of two chemicals, used in boat building to create a buoyant foam. They also carried in two presewn plastic socks sewn in the shape of a Hobie cat.

The group tried to create hulls by hanging the socks in a tree, mixing the chemicals and pouring the chemical mixture into the socks. However, instead of a light, crisp vessel, they got two soggy bananas. The foam did not expand to its full volume, due either to altitude, heat, humidity or to all three. Nonetheless, they made a platform with roughly hewn crossbars and an old tennis net, tied sticks to the sawed-off blades of paddles, and proceeded to float down the Kuamut for 10 days to get out.

Their total time in the country was 27 days longer than any other outsider before them. During their foray they came across all the major mammals of Borneo except the rhino, and discovered "Jalan Babi," the curious highway used by pigs to enter the Maliau. The profusion of coniferous and oak trees attracts the pigs in impressive numbers every year.

Because of the area's inaccessibility, various expeditions had passed the Maliau Basin by, or skirted its perimeter. The Maliau has a curious history of being discovered and then undiscovered. The purpose of our trip was to bring this area to the attention of the world and by so doing provide incentive for the government of Sabah and Malaysia to preserve the touristic and environmental importance of this region.

Into the Maliau

Mention the Maliau in Sabah, and the name Tony Lamb always seems to come up. Tony is a dedicated scientist, whose fascination and experience with the Maliau Basin made him the perfect choice for our expedition. Tony was in charge of the Tenom Research Center, now retired, and his special interest is in the identification, propagation, and domestication of tropical fruits. He also has a vast knowledge of local insects, birds and mammals. His knowledge of the orchids and plants is encyclopedic. Only accurate identification of the multitude of trees prompts him to defer to a tree expert.

Tony was born in Ceylon, (now Sri Lanka) and grew up on a tea plantation during the British colonial period. Being educated in England and spending many years in Malaysia, another former British colony, may explain his genteel and pleasant nature.

The helicopter descended: white, clean and gleaming. We waited; brown, muddirty and disheveled, from our previous adventure in Batu Punggul. Once on board and aloft, the complexities of the jungle intermingled into a rich, green blanket. The heavy heat became an icy coolness as the Bell 206 gained altitude.

From above the miles and miles of jungle carpet, the ground was unbroken, except by a few large rivers that had cut the dirt right down to the sandstone. Here, there was diversity, but also a monotony of endless green: a carpet of color every few miles from a flowering tree, subtle shades of green, blending from dark brownish green to light green and even yellowish green. If the helicopter went down in this canopy, we would never be found.

Off in the distance we saw the crisp shape of a continent rising above an ocean of mist. The sharp outline of the steep cliffs cut an exact shoreline in this cloud as if it were an island.

We asked the pilot to take us higher to get a better idea of the shape of this vast island within an island. It looked like an elephant track in hard dirt that has been washed by rain. The basin also could be described as a crown shape that rises in the north to a tiara-like configuration and slopes down on each side to where rivers have cut a series of jagged canyons through which they spill like wax from a candle. The Maliau is an important drainage basin that creates the Sungai Maliau, which tumbles down to create the Maliau Falls, then drains into the Kuamut, which links up with the Kinabatangan.

The area is so vast that we flew long and hard before we found the chain of rapids and waterfalls spilling out of the basin seen by so few people. The drainage of the entire 25 kilometer-wide basin made a most impressive showing. As the pilot dived and maneuvered between the steep cliffs, the ground turned from a smooth carpet to individual giants. What had looked like strewn pebbles were house-sized boulders. What had looked like rapids, were 20-30 foot waterfalls that cascaded into basin after basin. An extraordinary sight.

We were thankful that we did not have to walk in. The only ground access in is a full day hike from the nearest timber camp on the Tawau Keningau timber road. The downside to this method is a very steep and dangerous cliff ascent late in the day or early the next morning. For those pressed for time, a helicopter can be chartered from KK or Sandakan. It will not be cheap.

We decided to drop our gear at a helipad first, then have the pilot drop us off at the highest helipad. We would then walk down to the base camp from where we would explore the basin. The first day would be an ambitious, but easy, walk of about 8 kilometers through dense jungle. That was our plan. Things did not quite turn out that way. We were in the "Lost World," subject to its whims and desires.

The pilot tapped his gauge, alerting us to his low fuel. We broke out of our aerial reverie and began to search for the helipad. Crude helipads had been hacked out of the dense jungle to let the research and survey teams in. Our goal was to pick the most remote site and then walk along the ridge to the confluence of the two good sized rivers.

The helicopter touched down. We leaped out and immediately sank up to our chests in moss. Shocked by the lack of solid footing, we realized that the firm peat forest floor was an illusion. The stumps of the trees poked through three to four feet of moss and leaf litter before rooting in the thin hard bedrock.

We labored like horses in deep snow to get the gear away from the rotor wash. As the chopper lifted back into the bright sunlight, we had a chance to record our first impressions of the Maliau Basin.

It was cool near the rim. The altitude and humidity created an agreeable atmosphere. There was moss everywhere. The curious lack of soil and depth of the moss was typical of a peat forest. The trees were not the typical lowland dipterocarps. Here, there were conifers. Big conifers.

It was a discomforting feeling to descend from the clear, piercing blue sky into the dark grasps of the jungle. The trees towered above us. The contours of the basin, which had seemed gentle and caressing, were now wickedly steep and forbidding. Instead of seeing clearly in 360 degrees, we were now confined to staring at patches of sky through 60-100 foot trees.

Our weight restrictions and the distance we needed to fly to get to the Maliau dictated that we make two trips. Our solution was to send Jon back with the pilot to help find the helipad.

We flew into helipad four and set up camp at the base of the hill, lugging our gear and crashing through the dense brush like drunk elephants.

We were just five minutes down the trail and suddenly Tony asked us to stop. It appeared he had already made a discovery. He pointed to a thimble-sized plant that closely resembled a cross between an alien spaceship and a Victorian light standard. He collected the second finding ever of a small saprophytic plant; *Thysmia aescananthus*. The tiny plant is nestled under the roots of a tree and would have been easily crushed. Tony mentioned in a casual manner that the first time this plant was found was in exactly this same spot on an earlier expedition. The uniqueness and fragility of this area began to sink in.

Tony explained that we were in unique coniferous forest dominated by huge Agathus (related to the New Zealand cowrie pines), dacridiums and podocarpus trees, mixed with oaks and casserinas as it mixes with the lower hill dipterocarp forest.

This was truly pristine forest. There was no evidence of fire. There have been no natural calamities. There are no people to disturb the forest and there is no wind. Nothing to disturb the test tube-like conditions for creating new species. The only major trauma is the life cycle of the giant trees as they grow, die, and then crash into the forest, unheard and unseen, creating a gaping hole in the canopy for their offspring to fill.

Night on the Edge of the World

We began our trek to the rim and then down along the edge to our rendezvous at a preagreed base camp. For navigation we had a compass and a crude map.

The size of the Maliau is overwhelming. Like most wilderness areas, there is a mixture of monotony and surprise: smooth skinned gum trees, disrobed and red in the normally green jungle; streams that run with tea-colored water; pitcher plants that festoon trees like Christmas decorations. As we increased in altitude the trees became stunted, the moss became thicker and the forest wetter.

We could tell when we were close to the rim because we hit a green wall of moss. There is a distinct rim forest that lives in the constant wash of the mist and fog that pours over the rim. The trees are twisted and gnarled with their roots raised as if to keep their feet dry. The moss is constantly wet. Walking through the almost impenetrable maze of roots and branches drenches you as they squish their burden of water. It is chilly. It is also silent. There does not appear to be any life along the rim.

Another surprise was that the spectacular view we thought would greet us, did not exist. The dense growth at the rim blocked any chance to get a clear view of the surrounding jungle. We were floating in a "sea of mist" that stretched as far as the eye could see. "Sea" is an appropriate description because the mist bobs and ebbs like an ocean. It hits the cliffs, curls up and then floats above the trees, spraying a fine cool mist over the trees and moss.

I pushed out to get a view over the ledge and had a gut wrenching revelation. When the mist cleared for a few seconds, I saw below me over a thousand feet of sheer cliff. More correctly, "behind" me was over a thousand feet of sheer cliff. I had learned another intriguing fact about the rim forest. The roots of the trees grew far out over the cliffs. Covered with moss and detritus and being continually moist, the roots support more plants and trees, encouraging the process to repeat itself. I should have learned my lesson when we leaped off the helicopter into a mossy trap. Wiser, I gently returned to the safety of the cliff five feet behind me.

Tony and I, realizing that the day was getting late and that we had a long hike ahead of us, made haste along the rim. From the air, the rim looks like a smooth, clean edge sloping softly to a basin. Toiling antlike on the ground, it is a wonderland of ravines, cliffs, gullies and inaccessible smaller cliffs. In some places, water too impatient to flow into the central basin, has sliced through the edge of the precipice, creating a magical series of waterfalls and ledges ending in one last leap of escarpment. The water never hits the ground, dissipating into mist and drops of moisture.

We made our way through alleys of 20 feet high, five feet wide and 60 feet long slabs of sandstone. We clambered up the root-bound cliffs and slid down the other side. We passed the remains of a camp. This was the first evidence of man after the helipad—further evidence of the search for coal. In the coming days we would come upon holes dug to measure the depth of soft black coal. They had picked a most impressive spot: water had carved a notch in the cliff face providing a picture window view of the top of the mist sea.

Soon the path flattened out. Instead of the steep climbing and tumbling, we were dodging, ducking and twisting around the chaotic moss forest. I couldn't help but think of British Columbia or the Olympic National Park in Washington. It was cool, green and refreshing when we were moving at a clip. We took a short breather. As soon as we stopped, the chill attacked.

We pressed on. Tony vaguely remembered there is a quicker route further down the rim. I chose to travel along the rim in my quest for a photograph that would capture the congested wet moss forest and the ocean of fog that gave us tantalizing peeks, but never the full picture.

The game path was now marked with survey sticks and occasionally flagging tape. We had been walking for a full day without food or water. Luckily, we were travelling light and the cool wet rim had made water abundantly unnecessary.

Tony's muttering, normally an ongoing description of plant life and other information, turned to concern. He didn't remember that ridge. We should be higher up. It was getting rather late.

Our crude maps showed we were still quite a long way from the helipad and eventual base camp where our gear was stored. Looking back, I could see the profile of the cliff that matched the map. The problem was, I was looking up at the ridge and it was behind me.

We continued. We were losing altitude at an alarming rate. It was getting darker. Now Tony and I were sure something was wrong. The map showed a smaller plateau below the cliff edge. We had been mindlessly following a game trail that we assumed would follow the ridge. Instead, we had found a way out of the basin and down the cliff.

We discussed our situation. We could turn back, but we didn't know exactly where we went off the ridge and down onto this lower plateau. Since the path winds and curves tree by tree there would be no sure way of knowing where the path diverged, if it diverged at all. Plus, it was getting dark. Being lost in unexplored jungle at night with sheer cliffs was not a welcome feeling.

We decided to go forward because it would take us closer to our rendezvous. We would then cut in towards the cliff face as we got to the end of this minor plateau. There might be a way up, similar to the way we were fooled into coming down.

We continued losing height until we were in the depths of a black swamp. Trees blocked the light as our feet were sucked into the dark ooze. We were tired. It was late and the swamp was a depressing place to spend the night. Noxious gases were released as we struggled to pull our feet free. A blue oily film floated on the surface of the mosquito infested slime.

We decided that the swamp was the last place we wanted to spend our first evening in the Maliau. We could see the cliffs looming above us. We made a bold decision. We would push up the cliffs since the path we were taking went deeper and deeper into the lowland jungle.

Tony was tired. He had been helicoptered in from his comfortable desk job and he was now sitting in a dark swamp, about to cliff climb with a stranger, at night, in one of the most remote jungles in the world.

I was concerned about him. He had twenty years on me, but he was the one who suggested that we haul ourselves up the cliff. All he asked was that we have a good rest before we attempted the ascent. I gave him what little water I had, knowing it would be the last of our water for some time.

The sun had set, but there was still a dull light that illuminated our climb. The first section up was through tight brush and razor-sharp roatan. It was demanding, but doable.

We hit the first ledge. Using cracks in the rock, we pulled ourselves up. We hit our second ledge. Once again there were enough crevices to gain a purchase. Then we hit the wall—sheer cliff that ended in a green cornice of tangled, moss-covered roots. Momentarily set back, we explored the base of the cliff for a way up. We were drenched by the constant fall of water from the moss forest high above us. We had followed a narrow game trail along the base. We could spend the night here in the overhang below the face, but the sight of our quest, after working so hard, drove us on.

We had no ropes, no climbing gear, so it would be tough going. Office building-size chunks of cliff had fallen off and blocked our way on the side. Occasionally there was a collapsed section but they ended up in sheer overhangs. Finally, we found what we were looking for: a section of the cliff that had fallen away leaving a crack that enabled us to get tantalizingly close to the green overhang—more importantly, a large tree root that gave us something that would allow us to hike up the clean, cliff face.

I climbed up to see if it was possible. I pointed out to Tony that once we were over, we could not come back down. We could find another cliff face just as high, if not higher, beyond this climb. Tony told me to go first. We could barely see in the dusk. We were soaked with sweat, hungry and thirsty after our climb. We didn't know if we had the energy to make this climb.

I began to climb. I fell back, a handful of moss and dirt clutched in each hand. I burrowed my hands to find something solid. I began to climb slowly and nervously. A slight tug or pressure could bring down tons of rock and trees on top of me.

As I gained in height, the chance of going back down seemed dimmer and dimmer, making each upward move that much more desperate. My muscles were shaking with exertion as I reached the cornice. What looked like a green ledge was now a four foot overhang covered in slippery moss and elastic roots. For awhile I was baffled. I could not get a grip on anything to move myself back and then over. I could not go down, sideways or up. My muscles were turning weak and my mouth was dry. I locked my legs around the dangling roots and jammed my hand into the deep moss. Still nothing to hold onto. If there was nothing to hold onto, maybe I could use that to my advantage. Desperately, I began to burrow through the roots and moss with my bare hands. I almost laughed with the sight I must have presented as I broke through the dirt and moss to finally find a tangle of solid roots above. My strength was drained as I wedged my arm in like a stick and threw my leg up to avoid falling back to the rocks below.

Catching my breath, I found myself in the cloud forest of the rim. I crawled the remaining fifty feet under roots and over moss to discover that we were back on the rim.

Covered in dirt and my clothes dripping, I weakly made my way to the ridge. I yelled to Tony we had made it. I searched for a creeper or vine to help Tony up.

I tore off a creeper and dangled it down for Tony to tie his pack to. Tony said, "Don't worry. I'll come up with my pack." He began to climb using the vine for support. When he reached the green wall that I had to burrow through, he used the vine to crawl over. As he tried to lift his leg up for the final push, he paused, looked at me and then fell back down. It all happened in slow motion. I almost laughed as Tony calmly looked at me as he slowly shrank in size and fell to the rocks below. When he hit, back first, I don't think he even blinked. No screams, yells, or grunts. He just lay there calmly, eyes wide open. I assumed he was dead.

Now I was faced with a decision. Go down and apply first aid (or last rites) or climb up and go for help to carry him to the helipad. Thankfully, before I had time to decide which action to take, Tony quietly said, "I think I hurt myself." Surprised he was alive, I asked if he needed assistance.

"No, just let me lie here awhile."

He had fallen a sickening distance. Later we discovered what had saved his life. He had fallen in the crevice of two large moss covered rocks. In the crevice, the moss was almost three feet thick. Twelve inches either way, he would have had only two inches of moss to cushion the impact.

He rested for quite a while. This time, I hauled his pack up and then used the vine to take him all the way up. It was dark now. We shivered with cold as the temperature dropped and the sweat from our exertion chilled us. It looked like rain.

I found a hollow tree large enough to hold two people in moderate comfort. Lining it with fern fronds, it made a passable bivouac for the night. Tony's pack held a cornucopia of treasures: a tin of sardines, one can of orange juice, newspaper, plastic bags—and eureka!—a pack of matches.

After planting Tony in his fern bower, I set about building a fire to dry our clothes and to provide some heat. It was not easy to create fire with wood that has been continuously wet.

After a few false starts and with the last of the dry newspaper, the fire reluctantly smoked to life. It is almost perverse to say we spent quite an enjoyable evening with a roaring fire on the edge of the cliff inside a fern-lined hollow tree. It is hard to describe the pleasures of relative existence. I say "relative" because we might have had to spend the night in the swamp. We might have had no matches, no food, and Tony could be dead.

The rain came down in polite periods, allowing us to dry out in front of the fire. Each onset was heralded by gentle showers before the deluge.

Tony became consumed by thirst, so I set off to find water, using the large plastic bags Tony brought to collect plant samples. At night the confused tangle of trees turned into a nightmare of dead ends, pits, and the ever present cliff face.

I tried walking down to where the water eventually gathers in small streams before joining the rivers that flow everywhere in the Maliau Basin. In the blackness I realized that by going down and then coming back up, it would be impossible to know if I should go left or right to return to our camp, despite the light from the roaring fire, which disappeared within 20 feet. I yelled to see if sound travels. The thick moss absorbed all sound. I wisely decided to follow the edge.

I walked for about a mile in the dark along the rim in search of water and almost fell into an open pit. Open is not a good description because it was full of brown water. I kneeled down and drank my fill from the gritty stagnant water. I kindly did not tell Tony where I found the water.

The morning dawned cold and wet. The fire was still smoldering. The sun skittered across the top of the mist, creating a strange sunrise. I climbed out on an overhanging limb to take a picture. The trees grew out and over still blocking a clear view of the golden ocean below. I still couldn't capture the sense of being on the edge of a lost world. I was barred in by the jungle.

As we warmed up in the sunlight, Tony took stock of his damage. His leg had been twisted in the fall. His back had been bruised by landing on his pack. He could walk, but in great pain. We made our way slowly to the base camp. At every steep descent or ascent, Tony's condition worsened. But he still stopped to point out rare plants and unusual species. We also passed signs of people—traps set by the logging camp workers for deer, pigs and rhino. A single rhino horn can be worth a year's wages. Poachers dig large pits near the wallows and come back once a month to check on their luck.

We met up later that day with Coskun and Jon. They had spent a cold and wet night listening to civets fighting with rats. They looked tired and haggard.

In my pack, I had the foresight to bring a bottle of cognac. After our first meal and a celebratory toast, we set up camp for the next week. We spent the following days exploring the basin and the highways of water that led down to the great waterfalls below. Walking in the cool water on the flat sandstone bottom was pleasant.

The rivers run reddish brown from the tannin that leaches from the podsol, or heath forest. Podsol (a Russian word) forests have poor acidic soils and leaves full of tannin. The constant percolation of the water creates the tea-colored stain in it.

The foam in the water is caused by saponins in the leaf matter. This creates the impression that the water is dirty and full of detergents. The truth is, this is pure water collected from rain, which drains into the Kuamut river. If coal mining is allowed to affect the natural water retention and drainage, not only would there be flash floods, but sulphur from the coal would pollute the water downriver.

The Future of the Maliau

There is a considerable amount of coal in the Maliau Basin. Borneo is cursed with low sulphur coal and oil; the finest available. It runs in shallow seams about four to seven feet thick, close to the surface. Initial estimates of income to be derived from this coal are significant. The unknown factor is that coal sells very cheaply in the Third World and the discovery in Kalimantan of the world's purest coal casts a shadow over the feasibility of the Maliau being an efficient source of coal.

Thankfully, the Maliau is identified by the Sabah Foundation, the state owned timber concession, as an area for preservation. Scientists like Tony Lamb and others have identified many rare species in the unique eco and biosystem of the Maliau. Also, the world famous international expedition, the Camel Trophy, will attempt to walk into the Maliau Basin, focusing much needed attention on the area.

One morning the Iban workers and the surveyor from the coal company stopped by our base camp. We were aware of their presence but had never run into them before. They were surveying the area's coal seams, and the orange flagging tape was sprouting like wild flowers. We carried the scars on our shins from hitting the punji-like stakes they leave when they clear the survey trails, or *rentuses*.

We chatted with Tony Voon, the head surveyor. He is a pleasant Chinese man who is an old hand in the Maliau. He has worked on and off surveying coal for the Kuching-based Broken Hill Coal Company for the last six years. He has surveyed the 40 kilometer rim path and most of the basin. Like the few people who have made it into the "Lost World," he has come to love the Maliau, despite the long term implications of his work. The poignancy of this dilemma was highlighted when he came by one morning with a bright magenta orchid; a rare Dendrobium Aegle. His find was the second known plant of its type on earth. The delicate plant he held in his hand had been found only once before and that was in Borneo. The man who had discovered the first of its species was Tony Lamb, who found it first in Gunung Alab in 1991.

I found it hard to understand how two people with such dissimilar goals could share in such a similar joy of discovery. If the Maliau is not protected soon, it will surely become the "Lost World."

—**RYP**

DANGEROUS PLACES

A word about *DP's* ratings.

When I set out to take on the task on ranking the relative dangers of the world's hot spots, I discovered very quickly that there is no single source of safety, deaths, casualties, or misfortunes. In areas like Afghanistan, Algeria, and Somalia there aren't a whole lot of bureaucrats with clipboards keeping count of rapes, muggings, car accidents or pickpockets. Other countries like the U.S., India and Egypt spend an inordinate time filling out paperwork but mange to skew a lot of data to shift blame. The U.S has a very comprehensive system of travel warnings but conveniently overlooks the dangers within its own borders. India will be generous in counting Pakistan casualties in Kashmir but be stiff lipped about its own dead. Even tourists killed in army rescues are considered casualties by terrorist actions.

So we essentially threw all the official statistics in the dumpster and used our own research. How do we rank these places? First of all we travel without a protective shield, we have the ability to compare disparate places within narrow time periods and we grind through massive piles of documents to determine just what is going on around the world. So with this caveat in mind, here is how you can interpret our ratings:

★★★★★   **Hells on Earth**

A place where the longer you stay, the shorter your existence on this planet will be. These places combine warfare, banditry, disease, landmines and violence in a terminal adventure ride.

★★★★   **Very Nasty Places**

Danger here is regional, definable and avoidable, but the odds are that the unwary traveler will be coming home as cargo.

★★★   **Dodgey Place**

Three stars designates places with very specific problems, usually avoidable. Danger may also be sporadic, seasonal or local.

★★   **Heads Up Places**

Danger lurks in these places, but usually the violence is very contained or is easily identifiable.

★   **Bad-rep Lands**

Places that are not really dangerous but have a bad rap for isolated incidences. If you work hard enough, you could get waylaid or interred.

Warning (and a few tips)

The world is constantly changing, and the places that we feature do so at a lightning-quick rate. Many of the people, alive when we went to press, may have since bit the dust, and many of the places we covered may now go by a different name. Keep in mind that the relative danger of a place can rapidly increase or decrease as this paper yellows and the rebels of this world plot. Want a few tips? Most major offensives occur in the dry season (tropics), towards the autumn (temperate), before peace accords (to gain land) and, of course, while you are sitting in the town square thinking you are watching a military parade.

Always check out the local sources we provide and go online to check out local news. Use Fielding's LinkFinder on our web site www.fieldingtravel.com to find local information sources before you go.

Dangerous Places
(Short and Sweet)

We have been noticing that a lot of people never actually read the entire copy of *DP*. They prefer to keep it propped on their coffee table or carefully positioned on their office bookshelf. In recognition of this, we have created a very short, highly opinionated, condensed version of the book that will keep you swimming with free drinks and companionship while you slowly work your way through to the back of the book.

Afghanistan	Civil war between northern Tajik fundamentalists and back-country Pahktun fundamentalists. The only country where religious students know how to drive tanks.
Algeria	Muslim fundamentalists are mad because they were cheated out of a 1992 election victory. Slaughtered villagers and heads on sticks make this the Jihadsicle capital of the world.
Angola	A civil war between pouting egos (that is really about who controls diamond mines) leads the MPLA to cry "Savimbi come home" (and bring your diamonds).
Armenia	The Armenians want it all, and they want it now (see Azerbaijan).
Azerbaijan	Squabbling with Armenia about a little 'ole chunk of land (about 20 percent of their country) that used to be theirs (see Armenia).
Bangladesh	The home of Shanti Bahini, Chakma and 200,000 Royhinga refugees. Where's George Harrison when you need him? These folks are very nervous about tidal waves because they don't surf.
Bolivia	Coca, Tupac (not the late Shakur) Katari and grinding poverty. Peasants still get more money for that white powder than those Alpaca blankets.
Bosnia-Herzegovina	"Hunted" war criminals who have popular TV shows. Death camps but no bad guys; ethnic cleansing with no messy residue. Who says you can't learn from history? All this is just a train ride and 50 years from Nazi Germany.
Bougainville	Fuzzy-haired rebels with rusty shotguns fighting for a fly-speck-size island. Mercenaries spanked and turfed. Odds are they'll actually win as long as the copper flows again.
Burundi	Rwanda, the sequel. Same story, different location. Nobody cares.

Cambodia	Hidden land mines, Khmer Rouge stragglers, plagues of Vietnamese whores, raped temples, a lonely dictator and a sad king in exile. But hey who cares? Strap on your backpack cause its cheap, cheap, cheap.
Colombia	The nastiest place in the Western Hemisphere: drugs, kidnapping, murder, terrorism, ecotourism and great beaches.
Congo	Nasty large central African hellhole run by Marxist ex-terrorist (not to be confused with the other Congo below).
Congo	Nasty small central African hellhole run by whoever has the most ammunition (not to be confused with the other Congo above).
China	Human rights, sweat shops, occupation of Tibet, the border with Bhutan and oppression of the Muslims in the northwest. Big place, big problems, still under a firm communist grip, which means Americans can still get free "Made in China" toys in their next Happy Meal.
Corsica	Swarthy men who want to have their own country of swarthy men. Unfortunately, the Legion likes Corsica (its base) and killing insurgents (their job). Tourists are guaranteed to have a blast.
Cyprus	Turks versus Greeks separated by a thin blue line. The oldest U.N. mission that keeps on going and going and going....
Djibouti	The hottest, lowest place in Africa doesn't seem like it would be worth fighting over, but the Afars and the French Foreign Legion do.
Egypt	Fundamentalists like to hide in the weeds along the Nile and take pot shots at tourists. Could this be an exciting new theme park ride?
Haiti	Decades of brutal dictatorship, crime and corruption briefly interrupted by some good old-fashioned gunboat diplomacy.
India	Seven revolts, hundreds of languages, countless religions and manufacturing more people daily than China in half the space. Great restaurants, lousy weather, nice people.
Indonesia	Half of East Timor used to be a Portuguese colony. Some folks in Aceh and Irian Jaya are not happy that one man owns the entire country. Great surfing, lousy politics.
Iran	The big bad wolf of our times. Bankroller for most of the major Middle East terrorist groups. New boss wants to cozy up to Uncle Sam, seems like we're still sitting on a few of their assets.
Iraq	A punch-drunk dictator who doesn't know when to retire to Miami Beach (he must like sand) and write his memoirs. A starving impoverished country that picks fights with the wrong people (U.S., Iran, Kuwait, Kurds, Shiites and the dictator's own family).
Israel	An occupying force that doesn't get along with the former landlords. Plenty of nasty neighbors and oppressed Palestinians to keep shopping and bus trips exciting.
Kenya	The northern border is a nasty place, thanks to Somali gangs. The beach towns are getting ugly (and we don't mean middle-aged European women in bikinis). Lots of crime, poverty, corruption, conflict, but it doesn't stop the tourists.

Laos	Too poor to really have a good knockdown insurgency since the U.S. carpet-bombed it. Warlords still have Chao Fah rebels and a running feud with Thailand over the border.
Lebanon	Northern Lebanon welcomes tourists, NASA wishes they had the rocket budget southern Lebanon has. The north has great beaches, great food. The south has fireworks. Hey, was that a rocket attack or is it a national holiday? Home of Hezbollah.
Liberia	An escaped federal felon with a warrant for his arrest gets to run Uncle Sam's little experiment in democracy. Don't pack those AK's away yet.
Malaysia	Clean modern place surrounded by vicious seaborne pirates.
Mexico	Low budget, party kind of place teetering between the Third and First World. Nice rebels, nice beaches, nasty criminals.
Morocco	Despite the lack of news, the Polisario still conduct sand wars.
Mozambique	More land mines than people. All sold out of "watch your step" signs.
Myanmar	More Generals than a GMC truck dealer. Ecotourism and rainforest lodges built with slave labor on evicted homelands. Everybody's happy except most of the people who live here.
Northern Ireland	Keep your fingers crossed, and kiss your four leaf clover. Let's hope shopping in London doesn't get exciting again.
Pakistan	Fierce mountain tribes in the northwest. Fierce desert tribes in the south. Fierce Muslim tribes in the northeast. You get the picture.
Papua New Guinea	Remote jungle island terrorized by "Rascals," kidnappers and thugs. Also about to lose Bougainville to home spun rebel group.
Philippines	In the South, Muslims vs. Christians. Didn't we figure this stuff out during the Crusades? In the North, it's communists vs. government. Didn't we figure this out in the Eighties?
Peru	Tupac and Sendoro are fading into history. Who's worse (or who moves more drugs), the government or the rebels?
Russia	Discos, limousines, drugs, gangsters, gunfights... where's Coppola and De Palma?
Rwanda	Quiet for now because there is no one left to kill anybody. They'll need about 10 years to build up enough people to start panga whacking again.
Sardinia	Swarthy gangsters import drugs, kill people, make money. See Chechnya and Corsica and Russia and....
Senegal	*Casamance* is still hiding in the swamps.
Sierra Leone	A prez named Johnny hooks up with a rebel leader named Foday. Is this half of a new doo-wop group?
Somalia	The land of Mad Max or "My Toyota can whip your Toyota". The only country run by an AWOL marine from Orange County, California.
Spain	The Basques want to be free. Free to do what? Herd sheep?
Sri Lanka	Suicide frogmen, self evaporation and cyanide pendants are popular here.

Sudan	A two-decade war where starvation is a weapon. Black vs. Arab, Christian vs. Muslim. Nasty war, no end in sight.
Suriname	Rebels in the jungle, crime, corruption. Business as usual in the south Caribbean.
South Africa	Joburg is the most dangerous place outside a war zone. Rape and murder capital of the world. Good wine, great surfing and game parks.
Tajikistan	Cold bleak Russian military outposts surrounded by mujahedin and drug smugglers. Afghanistan for the 90's.
Turkey	The Kurds want their own country; Turkey says quit whining. The PKK like to kill people, blow things up and shoot schoolteachers. For now, come visit our sunny land (the west part at least).
Uganda	Muslim rebels, a wacko that wants to run the country using the Ten Commandments and kills people for riding bikes. Great fishing.
United States	Land of the Reality Show and Baywatch. Over 70 people killed a day and over 200 million guns ready to party. Do you feel lucky, punk?
Western Sahara/ Morocco	This sand ain't your sand, this sand is my sand. No, this isn't Coney Island on a long weekend.

Afghanistan
★★★★

White Dawn

The *taliban* religious students (seeker of truth) started as a loose collection of 30-something mullahs and volunteers from Kandahar. The *taliban* (as they called themselves) now have to learn how to run a country. Devoid of press agents or even graphic designers, they have raised their white flag across most of Afghanistan leaving two pockets in the north. *DP's* buddy Ahmed Shah Massoud holds the area north of the Salang pass (his old stomping ground against the Russkies) and the drug happy region of Mazar-i-Sharif (controlled by roly poly Uzbek warlord Dostum). His second banana, Malik Pahalawan, did a quick fake out in June of '97 and turned against Dostum and invited about 3000 of the Sunday School army in. Dostum turned the tables in September and Malik had to catch the next place out. The Tajiks and the Uzbeks soon got a taste of *taliban* fun (none) and were told to turn over their guns. A concept symbolic to asking the NRA to voluntarily hand their guns over to the Democratic Party.

Being denied badly-dubbed Rambo movies and Danielle Steele novels was bad enough, but not having guns was unacceptable. So the local folks turned their beloved guns on their new guests, killing about 800 fighters and creating the first

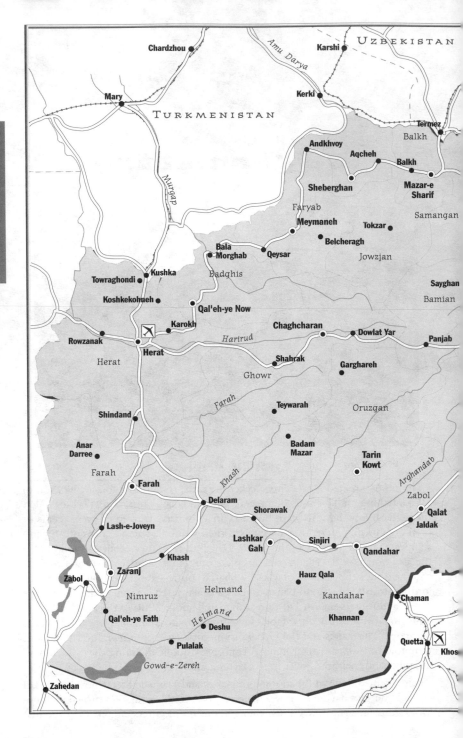

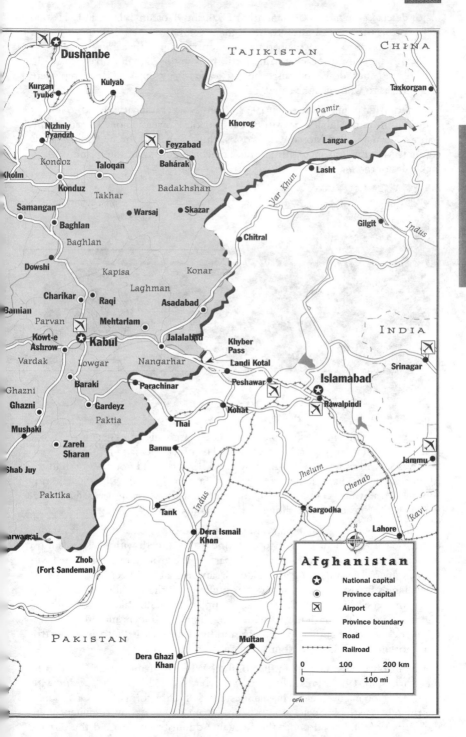

AFGHANISTAN

Afghanistan

⊛ National capital
⊙ Province capital
☒ Airport
     Province boundary
     Road
+-+-+-+ Railroad

| 0 | 100 | 200 km |

| 0 | 100 mi |

©FWI

major defeat in the *taliban*'s 18 months of fighting. Dostum is back and Massoud still controls the north. I guess those Afghans can be wiley after all. For now the determination as to who actually runs the country is up in the air just like the Katushyas that arc towards each warring faction. Even the Afghan embassy in Washington was shut down because the pro-*taliban* and pro Alliance rep were bickering as to who runs the show.

Modern Afghan misery began in 1978, when Noor Taraki attempted to import communism into Afghanistan with the aid of the Soviet Union. His successor, Babrak Karmal, asked Moscow for troops, thus, signaling the beginning of the conflict. Marxism was met with mortars, machine guns, and the primitive flintlock rifles of the *mujahedin*, or holy warriors.

Eighty-five thousand Soviet soldiers invaded Afghanistan. Their pretext was that the puppet ruler, Karmal, needed help. The official demand for this intervention was sent from Kabul and signed by Karmal, who could not have been in the Afghan capital at the time because he was riding into Kabul with a Soviet army convoy. Meanwhile, Gulbuddin Hekmatyar spent the Russian war safely in Peshawar while Massoud was fighting in the mountains.

The conservative Muslim *mujahedin* put up an unexpected and bitter resistance to the new government. Soviet troops, armed to the teeth with Moscow's most modern materials of doom, were picked apart on the ground by elusive rebel *mujahedin* guerrillas, employing antiquated weapons that had been state of the art when Jane's first started publishing their guide to all the world's blunderbusses. Later, the rebels, backed by the CIA and supplied through Pakistan, began picking Soviet gunships out of the sky with U.S.-supplied Stingers and other surface-to-air rockets. The fighting was bloody, and both sides settled into a war of attrition, not unlike the U.S. effort in Vietnam a decade earlier.

How involved was the CIA in the conflict? When Afghanistan was invaded by the Soviets in 1979, President Jimmy Carter provided the *mujahedin* with US$30 million in covert aid. This manifested itself in the form of the CIA supplying the rebels with old Soviet arms procured from Egypt. As covert military aid to the *mujahedin* increased under the Reagan Administration, so did the carnage and the number of refugees. By 1985, the Afghan rebels were receiving US$250 million a year in covert assistance to battle the by now 120,000 Soviet troops. This figure was double 1984's amount. The annual amount received by the guerrillas reached a whopping US$700 million by 1988. In all, the Soviets lost with 14,453 dead. Probably the most expensive funerals the U.S. ever created. Even after the Soviets withdrew from Afghanistan, the spook bucks kept flowing. In 1991, anywhere from US$180 million to US$300 million was funneled into Afghanistan by the CIA. In all, the CIA spent about US$3.3 billion in rebel aid over the course of the war. The aid was not democratically parceled out to all Afghan tribes and states, but deftly flowed only to the tribal and political leaders who were friendly with Pakistan. Under these conditions, the *taliban* emerged.

An initial agreement to end outside aid was signed in April 1988 by Afghanistan, the U.S.S.R., the U.S. and Pakistan. The accords were signed on the condition that the U.S.S.R. pull out its troops by the end of the year. The Soviets' withdrawal occurred in February 1989. Another agreement, signed between the Soviet Union and the U.S. in September 1991, also sought to arrange the end of meddling into Afghanistan's affairs by the two superpowers. By the middle of April 1992, *mujahedin* guerrillas and other Islamic rebels moved in on Kabul and ousted President Najibullah. A 50-member ruling council comprised of guerrilla, religious and intellectual leaders was quickly established to create an Islamic republic.

The *taliban* swept like a *khamsin* from the south all the way to the outskirts of Mazar i Sharif. Not used to treachery or suicide attacks, they have come very close but they stay out of the steep mountain passes or areas where they have no local support. Their power-base is in the Durrani Pushtun provinces of southern Afghanistan. The center of Pakhtun culture and coincidently the home of the monarchy. The Pakhtun or Pathans are a group of 15–17 million people of which 10 million live in Afghanistan and the rest in Pakistan.

The Pakhtuns have not forgotten that it was from Kandahar in 1747 that Ahmad shah Durrani created the Pushtun tribal confederacy that became what we call Afghanistan today. Since that time, a Pakhtun has always ruled Afghanistan except for a brief period in 1929 when the Tajik, Habibullah called the shots. This was truly to be a grass roots uprising and a true jihad.

The *taliban* was started in the Maiwand district of Southern Afghanistan by a group of 30 former religious students who had studied together in the provincial madrassahs from Kandahar and Helmand province. Their leader was one-eyed 35-year-old Mullah Mohammad Omar. Most of the students were veterans of the war against the Russians and were unhappy with the power vested in a few warlords by their control of U.S.-supplied weapons. The uprising began when they attacked the highway checkpoints manned by their followers—extortion, robbery and rape were daily occurrences. These atrocities not only angered the common people but they cut into the business of influential traders based in Quetta in Pakistan and in Kandahar. These traders financed the initial campaigns of the *taliban* to clear Kandahar of the warlords.

They also had support from the madrassahs in the refugee camps of Baluchistan and Peshawar where thousands of Afghan refugee youth were studying. The Pakistani madrassahs in the south were supported by businessmen and religious leaders who had connections with the Pakistani religious party Jamiat-i-Ulema Islami, led by a member of Bhutto's government; Fazlur Rahman. Their brand of Islam is the strict, old fashioned Sunni Deoband school—so strict that the leaders forbade their pictures from being taken.

The first area the *taliban* captured was the border town of Spin Baldak in October 1994. It didn't take long, about two to three hours. In two days the entire city of Kandahar fell to the *taliban* after weak resistance. In November and December, the provinces of Uruzgan to the north and Zabol were taken by troops riding in the back of pickup trucks waving the Koran.

In January, the *taliban* took over Afghanistan's major opium growing center; Helmand, without a single shot fired. In late January and February, Ghazni and Maidanshahr came under *taliban* control, erasing Hekmatyar's supply line to his position at his base of Charasyab south of Kabul and in Logar province. On February 14, Hekmatyar fled Charasyab. All this was accomplished with an army of less than 3000 ill-equipped, ill-trained men.

The *taliban* fights in small groups called *lashkars*. This is the Afghan name for a tribal war party. Estimates put the *taliban* army at 10,000–15,000 men and their holdings at about 80–90 percent of the country—the largest unified area since the Soviets occupied the country. The first setback for the *taliban* came in May of '97 when Dostum assassinated Abdur Rehman Haqqani, a close ally of his number two General Malik Pahlawan because he wanted to negotiate a settlement with the *taliban*. Malik turned on Dostum and formed an alliance with the *taliban* allowing them into Mazar-i-Sharif. When the *taliban* began to disarm the Shia's in their most holiest of cities (the prophet Ali is buried in Mazar-i-Sharif and the *taliban* are Sunnis who view the Shia's as a cult). A battle ensued forcing the *taliban* to retreat and creating the first major setback in their 18 month history. For now Mazar-i-Sharif continues to be the only city the *taliban* do not control.

The *taliban* is in control of the majority of the third poorest country in the world. Even though these religious students have the Koran down pat, they need to cram Politics for Beginners and Economics 101 if they want to get a degree in Political Correctness. Their down home Pakhtun brand of Islam is a little rough for the more sophisticated northern Tajiks, big city dwellers and Uzbeks. Still their frontier justice has brought relief from two decades of warfare and oppression. The battle still rages in the north as Massoud defends his home turf from yet another enemy. The country will be as safe or unsafe as it always has been for the near future: Pocket warlords, roving brigrands, shifting politics, bored occupying forces, Soviet land mines and more checkpoints than Starbucks in Seattle make this the Final Frontier for hardcore adventurers.

The *taliban*

The black-turbaned *taliban* are a PR agent's worst nightmare. They come to press conferences with Noriega-style Ray Bans, scruffy beards, armed bodyguards and an attitude that makes Farakahn seem like an ambassadorial candidate to South Africa. The *taliban* are not bad guys, they're just a little rough around the edges. They burst on the scene in the first week of October 1994 from their base in Kandahar. Their leaders are primarily selected from the Durrani tribes hailing from the backwater southern provinces of Helmand and Uruzgan. They are considered a simple, pure people led by very religious but culturally isolated mullahs who've had enough of the oppression of '80s era warlords.

The *taliban* began in Kandahar where trucks driving towards Kabul were forced to pay a toll of 2 million Afghanis (about US$250–300) to cross the checkpoint. Charging tolls is generally accepted in Afghanistan, but other, more repulsive things happen that could not be ignored. The gunmen would force young boys, who have the misfortune to pass through the checkpoints, to undergo a mock public marriage and then sodomize them repeatedly. Outraged by the treatment the warlord dealt to his own people, the local *taliban* took action. Religious leader Maulavi Mohammed told his spiritual leader that he had a dream to create a new Afghanistan, free of the cruel men created by outside interference. Omar then got together a group of 50 men and hung them from their tank barrels as a warning and a message that things were going to change.

The highest decision-making body in the *taliban* is the *Shura*, which reportedly numbers 30 but has grown to include leaders from areas that have come under the *taliban's* influence. The inner core of the Shura is limited to eight members, of which a group of four leaders, all from Kandahar: one-eyed Maulvis Umar, Mohammad Rabbani, Mohammad Abbas and Borjan are considered the brains behind the *taliban*.

The *Taliban* Can and Can't List

Confused by dress codes? Baffled by protocol? Now the taliban *have made it easy for social klutzes to follow the rules.*

No dancing	*Can't do the Lambada naked*
No movies	*Debbie can't do Kandahar*
No book reading	*Can't read DP to find out what you can't do*
No soccer	*Watch the Jihad Allstars play buzkashi*
No magazines	*Can't check out Martha Stewart's new 1001 ways to Kabob your Goat.*
No drinking	*No Colt 45 unless it really is a Colt 45*
No paper bags	*No sneaking Colt 45s in a bag*
No flying kites	*No Afghani Space Program*
No photography	*Rides on Xerox machines are definitely out*
No videos	*Debbie can't do Herat either*
No foreigners with Afghan women	*It's a guy thing*
No recycling the Koran	*See paper bags*
No white socks for females	*No coed cheerleading either*
No jobs for females	*No Oprah or Days of Our Lives either*
No schooling for females	*No books, no magazines, you get the picture by now*
Men must wear head coverings and grow beards	*Bic is out of business*

Source: Radio Shariat, Kabul

In *taliban* areas, soccer, volleyball and even chess have been banned because they cause youths to miss some of their five daily prayers. Women must wear the *burqa*, a baggy veil that covers the entire body and men must have short hair and long beards. Western pleasures like books, movies and beer are all forbidden.

The most grisly change is the practice of public executions where the victim's relatives get to execute the killer with a machine gun or knife. In some cases the killer's father must do the killing and buy the bullets used to end his son's life. Public amputations of thieves hands are common and are performed by doctors who administer a pain killer first.

DP spent some time with these focused folks. Much of the press likes to present the *taliban* as uneducated thugs and point out isolated incidents as examples of cruelty and barbarism. The truth is that the *taliban* is probably the least Westernized government to emerge in Asia and has few if any members who could be called professional politicians.

Their goal is to clean out the outside-supported factions and establish an Islamic government that would make Iran look like Fire Island on a holiday weekend. They have banned education for females. They are not wild about Shias, football, cocktail parties and women's lib. They are led by Maulana Mohammed Umar and a group of 22 Imman who have created a *shura*, or parliament, to run the country. The two principal military leaders are Maulan Mohammed Rabbani (no relationship to President Burhanuddin Rabbani), based in Logar, and Maula Mashar, in Wardak. The fighters of the *taliban* are recruited from religious schools and refugees in Afghanistan and Pakistan and look exactly as you would expect a grass roots militia to look; they possess neither uniforms nor training, and are completely devoted to their cause. The Iranians (predominately Shia) are hardly friendly with the hard-core Sunni *taliban*. The group currently operates a tiny radio station in Kandahar and, once in power, promises to permit the broadcasting of radio and television programs, as long as all media is devoted to spreading the word of Allah.

Direct telephone numbers to contact the *taliban*:

Lahore: ☎ *042-669087* (Dari spoken) *taliban* office, Lahore

Quetta: ☎ *081-822422* (Pushtu spoken) *taliban* HQ, Kandahar

Mullah Mohammad Omar

One-eyed Mullah Omar is Commander of the Faithful, top dog and head cheese of the *taliban* and of Afghanistan. Omar is not so much the political leader of the *taliban* as he is the poster boy and religious diviner. He is Afghanistan in a microcosm. War hero, politician, religious leader and visionary shaper of the new Afghanistan. Omar was born the son of a poor farmer in 1962 in Uruzgan or the Mewand district in SW Afghanistan. He wanted to study the Koran, but the jihad against the Russians interrupted his studies. He was wounded four times in one firefight, losing his left eye. His friends say he was a pretty good shot with an RPG. He then ascended the ranks to be the Chief Commander in the Harakat-i-Inqilab-i Islami party of Mohammad Nabi Mohammad. April 3, 1996, over 1000 Muslim clergymen chose Mullah Omar to be the "Amirul-Mumineen" (Supreme Leader of the Muslims). He can usually be found in the newly undecorated governor's mansion in Kandahar holding court.

In the main mosque in Kandahar, Omar brought out the holy cloth from the Prophet Mohammed (a rare occurrence and one that only happens in times of need) and used it to enthrall the cheering *taliban* fighters. It is said that this is why Kabul fell so easily (actually Massoud had held Kabul under siege from the hills surrounding it and left to defend his home mountainous turf of the Panshir valley).

Ahmed Shah Massoud

The "Lion of Panshir" is credited with being the main reason the Russians high-tailed it out of Afghanistan. Rabbani's defense minister, Commander Ahmed Shah Massoud, is an old friend of *DP's* and controls a well-trained 6000-man Tajik army and has been fighting for 18 years. He is holding out in the Panjshir valley, but may never have the same control as he had with Rabbani in Kabul. Don't be surprised if the Northern Tajiks try to break away from the Southern Pahktuns. A split pretty much on par with the city born Yankees and the rural Southerners in the civil war.

This is not a romantic war of tribal warriors on horseback. Massoud is currently getting aircraft and pilots from India, ammunition from Russia and military training advisors from Iran. He even has about 20 SCUD-Bs stashed in the Panshir valley. His soldiers make around 15,000 Afghanis a month (and a 56-kg wheat ration). His strong hold (and home) has been Jebel Seraj about 80 km north of Kabul along the Salang Pass. This one-time bitter enemy of Russia is now the recipient of massive shipments of weapons and ammunition from his former foe, Rabbani, who is still recognized as the president of Aghanistan by Iran and receives moral if not financial support from their Tajik brothers in Tajikistan. Massoud wants to fight the *taliban* on as many fronts as possible but attributes the *taliban's* success to support by the Pakistan Secret Police (ISI). Something he knows first hand since he was originally trained by the ISI when he was a student in Peshawar. Massoud is the third of six sons of a well off Tajik army officer. He was raised in Kabul and attended the French Lycée Istiqlal secondary school. He studies at the Poly-technic college where he also met Rabbani (see below). He joined groups that worked to overthrow the leftist Afghan president Mohammed Daoud, and fled to Peshawar after the government cracked down on student rebels.

He along with other Afghan refugees were trained by the ISI in the Cherat Army camp near Peshawar. Here he met Hekmatyar, who was the most dominant figure in the Afghan student group.

Massoud was sent into Afghanistan in July of '75 with 30 other Afghans, resulting in half of his comrades being arrested or killed. Two months later, Massoud formed an alliance with Rabbani, who led the Jamiat-i-Islami (Islamic Society), and Hekmatyar to form the hard-line Hezbi Islami group.

Pakistan backed Hekmatyar and turned against Rabbani resulting in arrests and torture and murder of some of Massoud's friends. He never forgave Hekmatyar and the Paki-stanis for their treachery.

Daoud was killed in a military coup that brought the Communists to power in 1978 and Massoud returned to the Panjshir in '79 to join the growing revolt. Within a year Mas-soud became the leader of the Pansjir. When the Russians invaded to prop up the Com-munist government, they tried unsuccessfully to wrest the strategic valley from the rebels. Hekmatyar was the main recipient of the CIA and the ISI's largesse and Massoud fought alone with his minor resources. After the fall of the Russians, a civil war broke out with Pakistani-backed Hekmatyar and Rabbani. For now Massoud takes the long-term view hoping that Afghanistan will be run by its own people and that the outside meddling of Russia, the U.S. or Pakistan will slowly bleed themselves to death.

Those who want to contact Massoud can try to reach him through his younger brother Ahmad Walid Massoud at the Afghan embassy in London ☎ *(0171) 589 8891.* Wally will provide assistance only to mainstream and credentialed journalists, aid workers etc.

Embassy of the Islamic State of Afghanistan (UK)
31 Prince Gate London SW7 1QQ
☎ *(0171) 589 8891, FAX: (0171) 581 3452*

Jamiat-i-Islami (Islamic Society)
Jamiat-i-Islami (Islamic Society) is influenced by the thinking of Pakistani theologian Abul Ala Maududi and Egyptian thinker Sayyid Qutb. Afghan Islam began on the cam-pus of Kabul University in the mid-1960s as a reaction to the Marxist trend among the

students. The professor trained at Cairo's Al-Azhar University, Burhanuddin Rabbani, attracting students of science, engineering and medicine. Hekmatyar (Kabul University) and Massoud (Kabul Polytechnic) were both engineering students who began their political careers on Kabul campuses. The party of Rabbani and Massoud pushes a revolutionary but modern form of Islam.

Gulbuddin Hekmatyar

Hekmatyar is the late 40-something leader of the Hezbi Islami and came to prominence as the most favored of the 12 Afghan rebel factions nurtured by the CIA. He is originally from Baghlan and is the head and founder of the Hezbi Islami group. He first studied at the Afghan military academy, then switched to the engineering department of Kabul University in 1968. Some of his friends call him "Engineer Hekmatyar" but he never graduated from Kabul University. Hekmatyar spent four years in the communist PDPA (People's Democratic Party of Afghanistan), which was made up of both Parchami and Khalqi groups. In 1972, Hekmatyar was jailed for killing a Maoist student, but then fled to Peshawar, Pakistan, where he founded Hezbi Islami. He has changed alliances and benefited greatly in his position as leader of the Pashtuns until recently when the *taliban* became the major Pashtun group. Hekmatyar was once Rabbani's prime minister, but broke away and began a yearlong siege of Kabul. His army was trashed in March 1995 by the *taliban*, but now he's back in Kabul. Detractors point out that Hekmatyar spent the Russian war safely in Peshawar stockpiling CIA-supplied weapons and money while Massoud was fighting in the mountains with weapons stolen from dead Russians. His forces were the major beneficiary of weapons from Pakistan and once bragged that he could fight a war for 25 years without ever needing supplies. His arms cachés are now in the hands of the *taliban*. Be careful before you trash talk about Hekmatyar because he still has a lot of fans in Pakistan; in fact, one of them tried to off the *taliban* mullahs while *DP* was there. For now Hekmatyar is looking for a sugar daddy to replace the billions of dollars of arms he lost to the *taliban*. For a list of unemployed warlords see Rashid Dostum.

President Burhanuddin Rabbani

Rabbani is a former theology professor from Kabul and the former official political leader of Afghanistan (although his term has legally expired), but one wonders what he has been leading. A highly educated man and former professor, Rabbani made an attempt to build a bridge between opposing forces when he named Hekmatyar prime minister in 1993 and again in 1996. But there is little room for compromise in this fundamentalist country. He is backed mainly by the Tajiks in the north (3.5 million people or about 25 percent of Afghanistan's population) and maintained his power only with the military might of Massoud. His Jemiaate Islami party is the only non-Pathan party in Afghanistan.

General Rashid Dostum

Roly-poly Rashid got caught up in his own web of intrigue when his second in command defected to the *taliban* in May of '97. Rashid is an old time commie warlord who is propped up by Uzbekistan and drug transportation from the hash and poppy rich fields around Mazar-i-Sharif. He packed his bags, family and flunkies and flew out to Ankara, Turkey, where he bravely proclaimed "The war is not over." He promised to return "when the conditions are right." The conditions were right when on September 12, Dostum blasted his way into Mazar and sent Malik packing.

Dostum, the former military commander under Najibullah, is now looking after the Uzbeki's interest in northern Afghanistan. The sight of his boss swinging in the breeze has not made him a fan of the taliban.

The taliban are learning to spin, they have changed the Department for Promoting Virtue and Preventing Vice to the Religious Police. The problem is they arrested a high ranking UN official and Christiana Amanpour in Kabul for taping at a women's hospital. When they are not arresting CNN/UN celebs the religious police make sure that all men have enough beard to protrude out of fist when grasped at the base and that women are completely covered by their burqas.

Mujahedin, Pathans and the "Afghans"

The Wiley Pathans (called Pakhtuns in their own language) are not a generic group of evil looking, bearded men waiting perpetually in ambush along Afghanistan mountain passes. The Pathans are a group of tribes that make up 40 percent of Afghanistan's populace and 13 percent of Pakistan's. They are primarily rural, clan based and aligned in major ethnic or geographic alliances. Their love for freedom, guns and adventure are probably their most publicized traits but they are also loyal, honest and moral.

Years of war and over 3 billion in covert U.S. aid have created three new warrior castes in Afghanistan. The older generation of Afghani *mujahedin* are Tajiks and Pathans who spent their young lives in nomadic columns killing Russians in the early '80s. The second group are the infamous "Afghans"—the people the CIA (through the Pakistani secret service) hired and trained to fight the Russians. They are called "Afghans" because they are not Afghani. (Stay with me, this stuff is complicated). These "Afghans," estimated to be around 5000 in total, were primarily Baluchis, Algerians, Egyptians, Saudis, Filipinos and Palestinians. Most of these men have returned to their home countries and are wreaking havoc everywhere from Zamboango, Philippines (Abu Sayeff) to Algiers, Algeria (GIA) and Manhattan, New York (World Trade Center bombing).

Both these groups were well trained, impoverished and savvy in the arts of deception, marksmanship, explosives and terror, and they have been in great demand in other parts of the world by Iran and Sudan for their absolute devotion to *jihad.*

The third group or new generation of *mujahedin* are youngsters who grew up in the squalid, mud-walled refugee camps of Peshawar and Quetta. These are the young men who grew up under the brutality of the warlords and are heeding the call of the *taliban.* The new *mujahedin* view the liberation of their country and the absolute dictate of Islam as their mission and for now these fighters have no interest in global politics or foreign intrigue. They just want a country to call their own.

Osama Bin Laden

Sort of the Ross Perot of the Middle East. Laden is a right-wing billionaire who combines industrial activity with political activism. Although Laden's chances of creating a hard line Saudi government are about the same as Perot's Presidential bid, it still makes for an interesting story. The 45-year-old Laden found a friend in the *taliban* and intends to stay in Jalalabad with about 50 of his family members and bodyguards. The U.S. State Department considers Laden one of the world's most significant sponsors of militant Islamic activities. Laden sponsored and led a number of Arabs in their fight in Afghanistan against the Russians in the '80s. He has been living in the Sudan for the last five years. In 1994, he was stripped of his Saudi citizenship after Algeria, Saudi Arabia and Yemen accused him of supporting subversive groups. He has also been fingered in the 1996 bombing of the U.S. barracks in Dhahran.

Pakistan

If you look on most maps, you will see a distinct border between Afghanistan and Pakistan. T'ain't so. Anyone with a pony or a pair of Reeboks can skip over the border and back. (Just don't try this at the official border crossings. Also, watch out for those land mines.) Even though the Durand line was created as an official demarcation between the two countries, it is not recognized by both Afghanistan and the Pathan tribes whose homeland it divides. Pakistan has absorbed most of the refugees created by the fighting in Afghanistan and keeps warm ties to whoever is in power. During the time Uncle Sam was supporting the *mujahedin,* Pakistan diverted arms to the mullahs rather than the various tribal chiefs, who were less religious but equally warlike. More specifically, the Pakistani government of General Zia—killed in a plane crash on July 18, 1988—supported the Ghilzai tribe from eastern Afghanistan, where most *mujahedin* leaders came from. The southern Durranis still support the Afghani royal family of former king Zahir Shah. There is also an intense desire for statehood among the Pathans for "Pahktunistan," with a bent toward Afghanistan that might remove most of the NWFP and the tribal areas from the map of Pakistan.

The 'Afghans'

After DP's recent tour of Afghanistan, we were amazed that everywhere we went—the coffee shops, the stalls, everywhere—we saw nothing but guys about 30 years of age sitting around. They were all veterans of the war against the Soviet Union. Killers with hard, deeply-lined faces. None had jobs. They were just sitting around, waiting. Imagine if you trained a bunch of steel workers in Pittsburgh to kill—and then took away their jobs.

Virtually every male in Afghanistan old enough to lift a rifle fought against the Russians. But Afghanis weren't the only ones. The other "Afghans" included more than 3000 Algerians who fought in Afghanistan, as well as 2000 Egyptians. Hundreds, if not thousands, of others arrived from Yemen, Sudan, Pakistan, Syria and other Muslim states.

In all, according to some estimates, 10,000 Arabs received training and combat experience in Afghanistan—of whom nearly half were Saudis. A big chunk of the financial backing for the Afghan warlords came—and continues to come—from the fundamentalist Wahhabi sect in Saudi Arabia.

The war in Afghanistan graduated a lot of students, and many are continuing their education in places as far away as Bosnia, the Philippines and the U.S. In fact, fighters trained in Afghanistan have surfaced in at least a dozen different struggles, including conflicts in China, Kashmir, Chechnya and Algeria. More than 1000 veterans of the war in Afghanistan fought in Bosnia. Abu Sayyaf, a radical new Islamic group comprised of "Afghanis," has emerged as the principal Muslim guerrilla movement in the Philippines. Ramzi Ahmed Yousef, the mastermind behind the 1993 bombing of the World Trade Center in New York City, is an Iraqi who was trained in Afghanistan. In Algeria, the last two leaders of the radical Armed Islamic Group (GIA) were Afghan veterans.

And wherever the 'Afghans' go, the conflicts become bloodier, and Islamic "justice" becomes unjust. Whereas nine journalists were killed in Algeria by Islamic extremists in 1993, more than 50 were assassinated in 1994–95. In the Philippines, Abu Sayyaf staged one of the most brutal attacks in the country's two decades of Muslim separatism when, in April 1995, 200 heavily armed Islamic guerrillas attacked the southern town of Ipil, killing 50 and razing the city. Yousef himself was involved in a plot to assassinate Pope John Paul II and was linked to the bombing of a Philippines Airlines plane in December 1994.

When Afghanistan's taliban *have finished their task of uniting the country, one can only wonder what the 20,000 unemployed* taliban *will do. Revolution anyone?*

Boy, if you hate crowded hiking trails and booked hotels, have we got a place for you. Although the U.S. State department says don't go, the Afghans don't mind if you visit. There is no U.S. Embassy at the moment (hell, there's no anything at the moment). *DP* hooked up with the Turkish embassy in Kabul and all we did was count new rocket craters for entertainment. But things will slowly get back to normal, which means extreme wild west conditions with an early morning rocket attack advisory. Yes, you can get a tourist visa for three months for US$30 per visa application, with security of swiss cheese. Please note that the embassy in Washington is officially shut down at press time since the two honchos (one *taliban* the other Alliance) kept bickering over who ran the country.

Embassy of the Islamic State of Afghanistan

2341 Wyoming Avenue, N.W.
Washington, D.C. 20008
☎ *(202) 234-3770/1, FAX: (202) 328-3516*

The *taliban* won't win too many design awards with their new flag. It is pure white and is a symbol of peace. They told us they might get around to designing a flag (send any ideas to the embassy) but for now white is cheap, easy to see and, with their latest setbacks in the north, it could come in handy if they need to surrender.

Journos and scribes are officially banned by the *taliban* and the north is having a hard time keeping the thrice daily UN flights from Peshawar arriving safely. Although *DP* was one of the first people to visit with the *taliban*, the folks that followed us pissed them off big time with all that negative spin. The *taliban* put up with dozens of interviews with agitated bleached blonde female correspondents seeking to expose their lack of enlightenment, and a raft of wanna be adventurers writing for men's magazines. These folks don't actually cover the war, document the suffering or even say anything positive about the *taliban*.

Back when journos were allowed in, *DP* called the embassy to get the latest tourism trends. Apparently, Afghanistan is where all the journos were headed to earn their spurs. When asked who is going to Afghanistan, our contact replied, "Lots of journalists." The embassy needs $60, a couple of photos and a letter from your company saying why you want to be Afghanistan bound. Pleasure tourists may find their visa request turned down unless they are truly persuasive.

The *taliban*-friendly U.S embassy (locked in their usual time warp) told us that Massoud was getting support from "Russia and the Soviet Union" and when pressed for advice on how to stay safe, they came up with "Don't steal anything." Any other advice? "Well you might have to grow a beard, or if you are a woman you might have to wear the chador, well no, now that I think of it, I guess Diane Sawyer didn't have to." We assume he meant the chador not the beard.

The London Afghan Embassy is run by Massoud's brother Wali. He can get you a visa for the north but can't do much about arranging a flight in. You can take a bus into Mazar-i-Sharif from Dushanbe but getting into Tajikistan is its own nightmare (see the *Tajikistan* chapter).

All border crossings are technically open, but the embassy recommends that travelers use the crossings from Pakistan, Iran and Tajikistan only. Our latest forays in-country reveal that although border crossing security is in evidence at major roads and mountain passes, entry into Afghanistan is very easy. In fact, the hardest part is selecting your entry point from the many offers you will receive from willing guides. The best way in is from Pakistan. Don't do it in the winter because of the bitter cold—and snow has a way of hiding the land mines. The intrepid can stroll into Afghanistan over the many mountain trails that connect the two countries in the north. Since these are usually drug smuggling routes, all travelers will be suspect. The DEA (via the Pakistani agency) is actually offering tribesmen a bounty on any gringos caught buying drugs so be "vewy, vewy cawfuwl" as Elmer Fudd would say.

Afghans are quite hospitable and will offer food and whatever lodging they have. You are expected to reciprocate with some type of gift or remembrance. Photos of your family are great icebreakers and gifts like flashlights, medicine or even clothes are received well. Make sure you pick the right guide, one on good terms with the tribes who control the regions you will be passing through. You will probably be the only tourist in Afghanistan. Camels can be rented to carry heavy gear for US$10 dollars a day, and guides go for about US$20 a day, plus *baksheesh* (a tip). Travelers would be ill-advised to go gem hunting or arms collecting in the hills at this time due to the prevalence of land mines—still the number-one killer and maimer of humans and other living things—and the propensity of Afghans to kidnap foreigners for a few quick dollars.

Most of the country to the south and west of Kabul is in the hands of the *taliban*, who also control the entry and movement of all outsiders.The northwest is in the hands of the Tajiks and the Wahkan corridor is a no mans land under any conditions due to the mountainous terrain and drug smuggling. Those who want to meet the *taliban* can also contact them in Pakistan:

Taliban

> Post Office 868
> Peshawar University
> North West Frontier Province, Pakistan
> Quetta ☎ *(081) 447300 (fax and phone)*
> Peshawar ☎ *(0521)*

Peshawar

> ☎ *(0521) 42645; contact Abdul Ghafoor Afghani.*

Quetta (fax/phone)

> ☎ *(081) 447300. Contact: Mohammed Masoom Afghani*

Currently, the *taliban* "extend an open hand to all peace-loving nations of the world," and hold no animosity toward Americans, even though the Yanks are responsible for much of the chasm that Afghanistan fell into after the war with the Russians. Those who would like to do something about the poverty should contact CARE in Peshawar ☎ *[92] (521) 40328/40614* or in Atlanta ☎ *(800) 521-CARE.*

Afghanistan was sort of an AdventureLand for journalists until the *taliban* told them to go home. Although they told me I was the first North American the *taliban* had talked to two years ago, I am sure the thrill has long worn off as everyone from *National Geographic* to *Dateline* does their prerequisite Afghan adventure story. Travel outside of any city is dangerous, and you will be stopped by roadblocks. Not all are guaranteed to be friendly. The Afghan embassy's *chargé d'affaires* in the States, either has a problem with English or total command of the language when he advises *DP* readers: "Tourists must have caution and be more careful where not to go [sic] and where not to go." The favored modes of travel are by minibus (cheap and available in all small towns), private car (not as available) and pack animals, which are slow and a great way to see what land mines can do. There is no law inside Afghanistan other than the *taliban*'s industrial strength version of *sharia*, usually mixed in with a little local tribal law.

It is helpful if Westerners adapt some elements of Afghan dress and have a basic understanding of the Pakhtun (Pathan) language. If you are too successful you may be roughed up by an enthusiastic *taliban* who thinks you are one of those Tajik city slickers who refused to pray 5 times a day. *DP's* advice is to wear plain khakis, keep your cameras packed away until you use them and always ask permission, we repeat, always ask permission before taking pictures. Even CNN's Christian Ammanpour was arrested in Kabul. Taking photographs can create trouble, as the *taliban* abide by a law that forbids the re-creation of images of people. We were told to get decent jobs and stop insulting Allah when taking pictures of wounded Afghans and avoided being shot by having the wounded take our pictures. They had never seen a camera before.

Most important is knowledge of the customs of Islam. The *taliban* and most Afghans are absolutely fundamentalist in their beliefs of Islam. Currently, there is little animosity toward Westerners, but you will be lectured continuously on Islam and considered an oddity for not embracing what is essentially the only religion in Afghanistan. Any major affront to Islam could result in severe punishment or execution.

Most people traveling in Afghanistan are soldiers and truck drivers who are either transporting food stuffs and basic goods (tires, cotton, fuel) or smuggling heroin, hashish, electronics or arms between the Gulf states, Iran, the CIS states, Pakistan and China. Many of the goods are sold in Pakistan or shipped out of Karachi. Hitchhiking is easy but we recommend using the mini buses.

Embassy Location

Because there is no U.S. embassy in Afghanistan and no country represents U.S. interests here, the United States government is unable to provide normal protective services to U.S. citizens in Afghanistan. The nearest U.S. embassies and consulates are in Pakistan and Tajikistan. The telephone number for the U.S. embassy in Islamabad, Pakistan, is ☎ *[92] (51) 826-161/ 179*. There is little they can do for you once you are in Afghanistan.

U.S. Consulate in Peshawar, Pakistan
   ☎ *[92] (521) 279-801/2/3*

U.S. Embassy in Tashkent, Uzbekistan
   ☎ *[7] (3712) 771-407/771-081*

U.S. Embassy in Dushanbe, Tajikistan
   ☎ *[7] (3772) 21-0356/-0360/-0457*

U.S. Embassy in New Delhi, India
   ☎ *[91] (11) 600-651*

The bus system still operates and airlines are flying in and out the southern cities. The airport at Kabul is expected to be reopened soon. The North is jammed with refugees trying to escape the fighting and they were charging locals as much as $500 for exit visas.

Everywhere

The Russians took great pains to make Afghanistan a dangerous place for years to come. There were about 12 million land mines scattered by air and buried in the ground throughout Afghanistan. You will see many people with their leg (or legs) amputated just below the knee. Much of the maiming of children is caused by small, green plastic butterfly mines that were scattered from Soviet planes and helicopters. Designed to blow only the foot off the unfortunate, the mines are hard to spot and continue to injure indiscriminately for decades to come. (See Land Mines)

The Borders

Despite the anti-drug stance of the *taliban*, Afghanistan is still a major drug-trafficking country. Large armed convoys guard the transport of opium to Pakistan, Tajikistan and Uzbekistan and Iran within Afghanistan. When Russia stopped patrolling its Afghani border, the country became the second major conduit of opium and heroin (the Golden Triangle in Southeast Asia is the number-one source and conduit of poppy-based drugs) but Afghanistan is the largest exporter of hashish in the world. Up to 14 metric tons of hashish have been seized by the border states of Uzbekistan, Turkmenistan, Kyrgystan, Tajikistan and Kazakastan. Badakhshan borders Russia's Tajikistan, where Russia has deployed 25,000 troops to help fight antigovernment Islamic guerrillas believed to have bases in Afghanistan. The border with Tajikistan is frequently bombed by Russian planes. The border with Iran is very tense due to the distrust by the Iranian Shiites for the Sunni *taliban*. The North is still held by Massoud and is an active battle zone.

The Khyber Pass/Tribal Areas

The Khyber Pass is still controlled by tribal chiefs (one of who is keen on his son marrying both of my daughters) who make a living by shipping drugs, shaving a few rupees from truck drivers and kidnapping travelers that ply this historic route. Robbery, murder, extortion and/or kidnapping are an everyday occurrence for the unwary, and it has only been the lack of foreigners that have kept this region out of the headlines.

Tribes

Most people are unaware that Afghanistan is still a land of tribal chiefs and feudal kingdoms. This is the land of *badal*, where every Afghan man must avenge a wrong, no matter how slight and how long it takes. Every major tribal home in Afghanistan is a small stone-and-mud fortress, and each person must stand watch in the tower. Tribes have been keeping score over how many of each other they have whacked, with a rivalry that approaches USC-UCLA fervor. They also take their tribal codes and Islam seriously. When *DP* was cruising through one tribal area, we were told a tribe member had seen a young woman and a man from another tribe kissing on a hillside. The father of the girl captured a cousin of the object of her affection, tied them both to a tree and pumped 75 bullets into them.

Guns

When it comes to gun love, the Afghanis have no equal. Afghanistan has more guns per capita than anywhere else on earth. England allowed the Pathans to manufacture their own guns 200 years ago, and the CIA delivered enough weapons to keep Afghanistan swimming in weaponry for years to come. But this was all dwarfed by the stockpiles of weapons the Russians abandoned or lost in the 10 years of warfare. One Afghan gunman philosophically pointed out to *DP* the unique relationship Afghanis have with their ballistic toys when he said, "You have your cameras, and we have our guns."

If the containers and warehouses full of pristine weapons aren't enough, the Affridi tribe of Afghanistan and Pakistan still pumps out about 900 to 1200 copies of modern weapons a day in its gun factories in Darra Adam Khel.

Happiness is a Worn Gun

The laws of supply and demand are very much in effect in Afghanistan. Used and new guns are cheap and available on a level that would make a sporting goods buyer at Wal-Mart envious.

The common macho decoration in the tribal areas is not an earring but a well-worn AK-47 or Kalashnikov, carried for the same purpose an Englishman carries an umbrella: The one time you leave it at home is the one time you need it. Travelers do not need guns, since there are plenty of gunmen for hire in Afghanistan (about US$20 a day each). Buying guns (or drugs) is not illegal in tribal areas, because there are no laws in tribal areas. The moment you leave these areas, though, you are in trouble, since you are now a bonafide terrorist/criminal; so we do not advise purchasing dope and arms or consorting with drug or gun dealers.

Happiness is a Worn Gun

For those who can't resist a bargain, the best place to buy guns is actually just outside Afghanistan in Pakistan. Take along an Afghan guide and go visit the Smugglers Bazaar (20 minutes east of Peshawar) in Darra (about 40 minutes south of Peshawar). DP did a little pre-Christmas shopping (peace on earth, goodwill to all men) to discover that you can buy a worn but serviceable AK-47 for 6000 rupees (US$200). Pros know to buy the short Chinese-made assault versions, since their barrels don't heat up as much and they can be concealed under your shwalwar qamiz. These go for about 12,000-30,000 rupees (US$375-1000). Chinese- and Russian-made pistols are between 300 and 1200 rupees with the Afghan-made knockoffs at the low end of the price spectrum.

Rambos can pick up Chinese and Russian rocket launchers for 30,000 rupees (just under a grand), and rockets by the case for 400 rupees (US$125) each. Grenades are a bargain at 100 rupees (US$3) each. Other items for sales at bargain basement prices include land mines, anti-aircraft guns, bazookas, Stalin Organ-style rocket launchers (the self-propelled kind) and even lovely used Russian tanks.

Wannabes who simply appreciate the smell of cordite and advanced hearing loss can arrange to fire automatic weapons. One banana clip of 30 bullets will set you back 200-300 rupees, about 10 bucks. Cheap even by Coney Island standards. The hottest-selling items are still the pen guns that fire a single bullet and can be used to write ransom notes. They are a measly 200 rupees, or six dollars. Naturally, you will need a complete Soviet era–uniform, bayonets, combat gear, watches, boxes of uncirculated rubles (wrapped and still in serial number order) and medals to complete your cold war GI Joe play kit.

Kidnapping

The Afghans are among the most hospitable people in the world. In fact, some may invite you to stay with them for a long, long time, unless you or your relatives can cough up the ransom. Kidnapping is actually a tribal tradition that goes back before recorded time. It is an easy way to get a wife, get your goats back or make some extra money in lean years. Recently, kidnapping has been a means to bring attention to tribal disputes or grievances. Locals, expats and tourists are routinely kidnapped in Afghanistan and near the border with Pakistan. Ransoms run from US$2000 up to US$50,000 and more for foreign workers. The positive side to this is that if you're traveling under the protection of one tribe and are kidnapped by another, your host tribe has an obligation to free you. The people in the greatest danger are foreign workers who travel in a predetermined route or stay in a fixed place.

Mines

The Russians buried and dropped (see Land Mine Chapter) about 12 million mines in the ground. Some say at the current removal rate it will take 20,000 years to remove all the mines, more than 50 different kinds and not just Russian made. There are RAP-2's from Zimbabwe and even NR-127's made in Belgium. According to the UN, 162 of Afghanistan's 356 districts are affected by mines. The UN had a list of 2353 minefields back in '94. The most dangerous areas for mines are Helmand with 5 major fields, Kandahar with 47, Paktia with 118, Logar with 53 and Herat with 86. The areas affected are grazing land, irrigation systems, agricultural land and cities.

Don't assume these mines are all on the ground. There are a lot of high tension lines and electrical plants that are mined. The ideas is to booby trap the infrastructure to kill the Pakistani phone and electrical people who are helping the *taliban* restore power and phone service. Although much work had been done to clear land mines, consider all areas of Afghanistan (including cities) deadly. In 1996 in Kabul, one person an hour was killed by landmines and unexploded ordinance. Kabul is only the third most mined area in Afghanistan and only in a desperate, last-minute attempt to keep the *taliban* at bay.

Between 2000 and 4000 people die from land mines every year in Afghanistan with many deaths going unreported. Refugees returning to their homes are at greatest risk. Many of the deaths are attributed to children who collect the mines and shells to sell as scrap. In many towns, children actually play with defused disc shaped mines. The infamous butterfly mine has one wing full of liquid explosives that explodes when twisted or bent. Back in '95 the UN figured there were 530 square miles of areas filled with land mines and UXO (unexploded ordnance). Afghanistan currently has the world's largest demining program and in seven years has destroyed over 200,000 devices, but has cleared only 80 square kilometers. The most heavily mined areas are security zones around the major cities along the Iranian and Pakistani borders. (Herat, Kandahar, Jalalabad and Khost).

Places to find mines in Afghanistan

Unused footpaths

Verges of tracks and roadways

Vehicle turn-around points

Near culverts and bridge abutments

Along damaged building walls

In doorways

In deserted homes

In and around wells

Follow the basic rules and you will survive: Do not wander off of the hard surface (even when taking a leak). Learn to squat at the edge of the road to urinate like the locals do. Do not travel in snow. Land mines were laid in strength along mountain passes and can be more sensitive with ice and snow cover. Do not turn over or pick up any items, do not inspect abandoned military vehicles, do not run up a hill to get a better vantage point, the list goes on.

I Guess I Should Have Stayed at Home Department

What were people in Afghanistan doing when they were killed or injured by a land mine.

Fetching water	*20 percent*
Traveling	*15 percent*
Fighting	*13 percent*
Playing with a mine	*8 percent*
Demining	*4 percent*

Drugs

Afghanistan is essentially a smuggling and transportation economy. Drugs represent the largest single hard-currency earner. Poppies and *sensimilla* products are easily grown and are in wide propagation. The best hashish in the world comes from Mazar-i-Sharif in the north, a major destination for Western drug smugglers before the Russians rolled in. The

Russian army picked up the nasty habit of smoking opium and mainlining heroin while they were here (a practice that continues to this day in needle-strewn streets from Grozny to Moscow). Haji Ayub Afridi controls most of the traffic in heroin and hash from Afghanistan into Pakistan. His massive house in Landi Kotal is famous for its opulence. Instead of jockeys on the lawn, he has opted for anti-aircraft guns. I was offered a job as one of his gunmen, but figured that 2000 Pakistani rupees a month (about $65) and a new Kalashnikov were not an upward career move. Ayub has about 100 gunmen and was forced to move to Jalalabad from Landi Kotal after the U.S. pressured Pakistan to "clean up the drug trade."

Most drugs are trucked directly through Peshawar and Quetta with the complicity of border guards and police. Other tribes like to pack the brown stuff the hard way (overland by mule through Iran and Turkey). Other middlemen use human mules. Freelance smugglers and stupid tourists still buy hashish and heroin in the smuggler's bazaar in Peshawar, Pakistan, and discover when it's too late that the government offers a 5000 rupee reward for turning in dope heads (your guide gets to keep your dope money). Other smugglers (usually Nigerians, Afghans and Pakistanis) end up losing their heads when caught flying through Saudi Arabia with dope poorly concealed in various luggage and orifices.

Stingers for Sale

Want a quick $55 million? Just round up the 300 or so aging Stinger missiles given to the Afghan rebels in the mid-1980s and send them back to Uncle Sam. The U.S. government has a standing offer to buy back the handheld, heat-seeking, antiaircraft weapons not because they need them for defense purposes, but because of the threat they pose to commercial aviation in the Middle East. The Stingers make the perfect gift for armchair terrorists craving to take a commercial jetliner out of the sky on a Sunday afternoon. The most recent commercial victim of this effective weapon was a Tupolev Tu-154 in Georgia.

The bad news is that tribal chiefs who are trafficking in opium were outbidding the CIA for the leftover Stinger missiles now in the hands of Afghan mujahedin commanders. Recently, one tribal chief bought 105 Stingers in the Towr Kham region. Other bidders are fundamentalist groups, as well as Iranian and North Korean intelligence services. Keep in mind that stingers are heatseekers and are only efficient at altitude where planes are landing or taking off. You're safe at 35,000 feet.

Even though things are settling down, medical care never has been Afghanistan's strong point. Health care is available in the major cities but a traveler with a serious condition should seek help in Pakistan or Iran. Better yet take the next flight home or to London. Even the most basic medical care is limited or nonexistent, with extreme shortages of most basic medicines. Malaria (primarily the benign vivax form) is present below 2000 meters (6562 ft.) between May and November in the southern area and falciparcium strain occurs in the warmer south. Chloroquine-resistant falciparcium has been reported. Rabies, tick-borne relapsing fever and Cutaneous leishmaniasis are present.

AFGHANISTAN

Electricity (when you can find it) is 220v/50Hz. The official languages are Pashtu (mostly in the south and east) and Dari Persian (in the North and West). Many people speak English and some Russian. The money is the Afghani and the black market is the only real place you can exchange notes. The money changers are fair since this is how all people change money. Try not to use pre 1990 U.S. $100 bills since many money changers won't take them. Afghanistan has very little infrastructure, but since its major business is smuggling, it has always been possible to travel throughout the country by bus or taxi. It is common for the driver to pay a tax at each roadblock and you will find many roadblocks. There is little in the way of hotels or restaurants, but travelers will stay in simple roofed accommodations and eat at stalls. The phone system is unreliable and in many areas non-existent. Although the government is the *taliban*, it is left to each governor to decide the fate of wrongdoers and other judicial matters. The *taliban* has shut down most night life. When shops are open they start at 8 a.m. and close between noon and 1 p.m. and then reopen until 4:30 p.m. Some shops are closed Wednesday and Friday. Traffic drives on the right and the normally paved roads are full of potholes from shells and disrepair. Jalalabad is the main smuggling area for cars, electronic goods and drugs into Pakistan, so be judicious when asking questions or taking photographs.

If you need assistance, contact the embassies in Washington and London.

Embassy of the Islamic State of Afghanistan (USA)

2341 Wyoming Avenue NW
Washington, D.C. 20008
☎ (202) 234-3770, FAX (202) 328 3516
Currently shutdown.

Web Sites

www.netiran.com
www.afghan-web.com
www.commercenetindia.com
www.igc.org
www.citynet.com

www.fieldingtravel.com
http://www.incore.ulst.ac.uk
http://www.bekkoame.or.jp.
http://www.einet.net
http://menic.utexas.edu
http://www.accessasia.com
http://www1.gazette.com
http://www.afghani.com
http://www.geocities.com
http://www.netlink.co.uk
http://frankenstein.worldweb.net

9/12/1997	Dostum returns to Mazar-i-Sharif after heaving fighting and looting.
5/28/1997	*Taliban* forces retreat from Mazar-i-Sharif after losing 100 men in 18 hours of fighting. This marks the first retreat in the *taliban*'s history.
5/24/1997	General Malik Pahlawan turns against warlord Rashid Dostum opening the city to the *taliban*. The Uzbeks and Tajiks revolt when the *taliban* tries to disarm them.
9/27/1996	The *taliban* drive Massoud, Rabbiani and Hekmatyar out of Kabul exactly one year after their founding
619/96	Pakhtun leader Hekmatyar signs a peace pact with former enemy Rabbani becoming Prime Minister in Kabul.

10/17/1995	Thousands of the inhabitants of the capital fled the city in the wake of a *taliban* militia attack. The fierce fighting between *taliban* and Rabbani forces around Kabul compelled hundreds of families to leave the city. Families shifted from Kabul to Jalalabad, capital of Nangahar province, and stayed in camps. Many refugees headed towards Pakistan.
09/0619/95	The Pakistani embassy was set on fire in four places. At least 5000 Afghans marched on the embassy in protest of alleged Pakistani support for the Islamic *taliban* militia.
919/94	The *taliban* emerges from the southern province of Kandahar.
1/119/94	Hekmatyar lay siege to Massoud and Rabbani in Kabul turning the city into rubble.
04/15/1992	Najibullah leaves. Rebels beginning battle of Kabul as factions war for control.
2/15/1997	The last Soviet soldier leaves Afghanistan.
1988	Gorbachev announces Soviet withdrawal from Afghanistan.
1986	Soviets install Najibullah as the 100,000 Soviet soldiers fight against seven U.S. backed rebel factions.
12/1979	Moscow turfs the socialist government and installs Babrak Karmal Soviet troops enter Afghanistan to prop up Karmal.
1978	Socialists under Hafizullah Amin tage a coup in Kabul. Moscow begins to send aid.
1973	King Zahir Shah is overthrown

AFGHANISTAN

December 1996: Sex, Drugs & Rock'n'Roll

I was unloading my luggage from a Flying Coach after pulling into Kabul when I heard a call to prayer coming from a mosque across the street. I flagged down a taxi and was still loading my luggage when three Toyota 4x4s came screaming around the corner, slamming on the brakes in front of me. Half a dozen *taliban* soldiers jumped out of each truck and ran toward the mosque. They started beating, kicking and dragging men who were missing prayer into the mosque. I pulled out my camera and started shooting what was going on. Suddenly, four of the soldiers saw what I was doing, turned, and ran toward me with sticks and AK-47s held in the air. I bolted to the taxi, dove into the back seat, and heard sticks pounding the rear of the car as we pulled away.

The *taliban* militia made a promise to bring law and order to Afghanistan by establishing an Islamic state running on strict Islamic law. It appears to me that their promise has been carried out. The crime rate in Kabul has dropped to almost nil. But not only are the laws coming out of the *taliban* mullahs' interpretation of Islamic law, but the rules for enforcing the laws are decided by the *taliban* soldiers themselves. They have their own set of rules and they change sporadically, usually on a whim.

I was walking through the Farshga bazaar when I saw a boy at the top of a traffic tower with a bruised and swollen face that was painted black. While the *taliban* soldiers surrounding him were laughing hysterically, he was beating an empty gas can with a stick and crying: "The one who does something like me will be punished worse than what is happening to me." Another witness told me later the real meaning: "They only beat *me*; if they catch *you* they will cut off your hand." He was taken to a "police station" where the soldiers could punish and keep him in jail as long as they wanted to. He was caught stealing a jar of purified butter.

I started moving away from the tower when I heard a big explosion in the center of the bazaar. I ran to where the terrorist bomb went off, believed to be planted by *mujahedin*, and found dead bodies and many people injured among bits and pieces of carts, boxes, meat, and sheepskins scattered across the open market. Within a flash, *taliban* soldiers came running in, swinging clubs and firing their AK-47s in the air to chase people away from the scene. They were beating people, trying to help the wounded and desperate vendors who were bleeding from where they caught shrapnel, but trying to collect their goods in a hurry to evacuate. Those who were in the bazaar were attacked by a terrorist bomb set by the *mujahedin*; they were then attacked by the *taliban* soldiers who had promised to bring safety and protect the innocent.

Another afternoon when I was getting a briefing at the UN office on their mine clearing operations, Dostum's planes came in and dropped several bombs two blocks away from the office. I scrambled to my feet after being blown to the ground and ran to the bomb site. I started taking pictures of people being dragged from what used to be houses when an AK-47 struck me across my back with full force. I stumbled forward and another *taliban* soldier grabbed my camera, threw it on the ground and kicked it. I saw soldiers all around hitting, pushing, and kicking me like I was a hacky-sack. Luckily, one threw me in the direction of where my camera was sitting. I scooped it up, saw an opening, and ran from the turban thugs. What a fool I was thinking that the *taliban* soldiers would assume that a journalist taking pictures of innocent victims would help prove their enemy is evil to the bone—which is what they believe about Dostum. Instead, it was attack the journalist for no particular reason.

On my way to the front-line north of Kabul, I was stopped four times at checkpoints. After I was ordered back to the city each time, I would get out of the car and talk to the soldiers about their recent success and what would be the results if they took the whole country. That earned me a cup of tea and freedom to move on to the front. Near the front I stopped to chat with soldiers sitting on a Russian T-52 tank. We got along well, and they invited me to get into the tank and take a look inside. As I was peering down the barrel through one of the "windows," I heard someone yelling as he was climbing up the side of the turret. I poked my head out of the hole and saw an AK-47 four inches from my nose. I crawled down the side of the tank cautiously and passively and listened to my translator standing near the tank interpret what the soldier was screaming while his gun was still trying to impale me. "If you come back here again, I will kill you!" As we drove away I was a bit thankful because an AFP veteran, Terrence White, told me what happened to him when a *taliban* soldier didn't like what he was covering. The soldier said in all seriousness: "If you come here again, I will fuck you, *then* I will kill you!"

If I was betting on what the *taliban* soldiers would do next, I would be broke in a day. They have little compunction to enforce law and order. But the topsy-turvy make-up of Afghanistan gets even better when you're in *mujahedin* territory, and the stakes get higher.

I was in the trenches surrounded by *mujahedin* soldiers at Dar Alaman frontline in August, 1996 just before the *taliban* rolled into the capital. We were drinking tea, but shells came whistling in sporadically that sent me to the dirt. I soon noticed that the soldiers kept moving in to get closer and closer to where I was sitting. They were pointing at my camera and my hair, whispering and smiling at each other. I quickly realized that I had to do something fast because I had suddenly become a target of the *mujahedin*, not the *taliban* artillery. I jumped up quickly to put them offguard. I raised my camera, made movements to get them to pose for a portrait, and climbed out of the trench to position myself as far away as possible to take the picture. Right after I took it, I waved and smiled to say "thank you," turned and ran to the last checkpoint.

My interpreter looked excited as he ran up to greet me. "You're back! You're back!" he yelled.

"You're right, I didn't get hit," I said, assuming that's what he meant.

"Sir, I didn't expect you to get injured by the *taliban* shelling. I didn't go with you because the *mujahedin* have no laws. They could have taken your camera, your money, and used you to please them. Then they would have used you for target practice. Nobody would have cared."

After we left the front and I was eating lunch at the Kamdeesh restaurant in Shar-i-Nau, one of the few areas in Kabul that was not leveled during the civil war, an aged Afghan sitting next to me told me an ugly story. "One night *mujahedin* soldiers came to my neighbor's house in a jeep. My neighbor has a beautiful fifteen-year-old daughter," he said tears rolling down his face. "The soldiers burst into the house, took my neighbor's daughter and turned her over to the commanders at their command post. They kept her and used her for one week. Finally, the commanders let her go and the soldiers left her on the doorstep. She and her family were shamed for life."

In December, after I moved into the *mujahedin* areas in the north, I had an interest in the Baglan province. An Ismailia warlord, fighting with the *mujahedin*, is the leader of the region and is famous for having bizarre quirks while keeping his forces intact and keeping his factories, power stations, and mines working, which is a rarity in Afghanistan. During the four hour drive from Dostum's stronghold to Puli Xamri, the Baglan stronghold, we were stopped a dozen times. The *mujahedin* demanded a payment for us to continue. My interpreter, Idrees, who learned the ropes by traveling with journalists in the past, told the soldiers that I was a foreign diplomat. After looking me up and down, they waved us on.

But at the last "checkpoint," the *mujahedin* dragged us out of the car, held us at gun point, and ordered a strip search. I couldn't even find the first button on my shirt to undo, while Idrees, acting very relaxed, sighed and started talking while unzipping his pants. "General Said Jaffer will be really angry when we don't show up for our appointment with him in Puli Xamri. As you know, he will throw a fit and send out a search party." I was standing there only in my pants near the Hindu Kush in the dead of winter freezing to death while the soldiers gathered in a huddle to decide what to do. They came back and growled at us to collect our clothes and get out of their sight.

Said Jaffer Nadiri, the Commander and Governor of the Baglan province, was educated in England and the United States. His father was in prison while the Afghani government backed by the Soviet Union was in control. Less than ten minutes after the interview started in his living room, the 32-year-old leader held up his hand to stop me asking another question and demanded in fluid English, "What do you drink? Vodka? Whisky?" He caught me offguard. "Well? Tonight we should have a drinking-fest in my guest house."

He led me from his living room to a guest house the size of a high school gym. There was a swimming pool, heated in the winter, with pool and ping-pong tables, a sauna, and a bar we were headed for. As we walked into the bar, I was jettisoned out of Central Asia. There were Bon Jovi, AC/DC, and bikini posters on the walls, a full bar on one end and a Sony stereo system on the other. "Sex, Drugs, and Rock & Roll!" he barked and laughed as he poured us our first drink. He ordered one of his servants to put on Pink Floyd and started reminiscing. "I watched *The Wall* ten times when I got a copy. Excellent movie! But when I asked one of my men to copy the video for a friend of mine, he accidentally erased it. Ha! Ha! I had him strip, lay down on the floor face down, and beat him with a horse whip until I was satisfied."

After our third drink, three commanders came in for a nightcap, After they had taken a few shots of vodka, the tall, bulky commander next to me jumped up, picked me up and screamed in broken English, "You spy! You spy!" The other two ran over and pinned me against Bon Jovi a foot off the ground while the first one frisked me (looking for a tape recorder). Said Jaffer came to my rescue and ordered the commanders to leave after one more shot. As they were leaving, a servant came in with a large chunk of hash that looked like a cow paddy on a silver tray. Said Jaffer pinched off a small piece and held it out for me saying, "Anyway, it's hash time! Sex, Drugs, and Rock & Roll!"

—**Peter J. Willems**

Afghanistan, March, 1983: In the Lion's Lair

An expedition into war-torn Afghanistan has developed in Paris. Three French doctors from Médecins sans Frontières decide to go to the Panshir Valley head-quarters of the Afghan resistance. In addition to myself, two other journalists will join us: Philippe Flandrin, a Frenchman, and the Iranian-born photographer Reza Deghati. Deghati wants to go to east Kabul to meet the monarchists of leader Mahaze Melli. Flandrin will continue to Baktia outside Kabul to locate the Hezbe-Islami and their leaders, Yunus Khales and Abdul Haq.

We fly to Peshawar to meet the *mujahedin* organization. The Hezbe-Islami propose to bring us into Panshir, but we prefer to trust the people from Jemiaate-Islami, because this time they control the Panshir region. The leader of this organization is Muchai Barzali. The trek will cover about 450 kilometers and is ex-pected to last one month.

The three doctors will bring in food and medicine, and the guerrillas will pro-vide protection. We wait until March for the snow to start melting. We will climb the 4500-meter-high mountain of Hindi Kuch. On the other side, we are expect-ing jeeps to be waiting to provide us with transit to Peshawar. But after the long, grueling trek, we will find no jeeps.

The trip begins on March 10, 1983. We dress like Afghans because we are cross-ing tribal country. I bring along three cameras. Flat-footed and out of shape, I am always behind. Our convoy moves at night to avoid the Russian helicopters. De-spite our stealth and our altitude, the group is often attacked by Soviet gunships. I have brought along some dry fruit to supplement the meager rice rations. As our food supply dwindles, I discover there is nothing in the countryside with which to replenish our supplies. Once in a while, we come across a small tea shop in the villages.

In my fatigue and hunger, I make the mistake of taking a leak while standing up. An Afghan spots me and the alarm goes out. Muslims always squat to urinate. The group decides that I'm a Russian spy and that I am to be shot. Our body-guards come to my rescue and argue that Turkish Muslims always stand to piss, and that I am a true Muslim. The argument rages on; our explanation finally prevails. It is a close call. One of our convoy is not so lucky. A young man is shot to death in the backyard of a village house because the hairs on his arms are not pointing in the correct direction. If he had been cleaning himself five times a day in preparation for prayer, the hairs on his arms would have been pointing toward his hands. The sentence is passed by the leader of our column, and he is shot out of sight of the others.

It is frigid in the mountains. Sometimes we have to cross ice-cold rivers fully clothed. I am amazed that I do not freeze to death. I am starving. I dream of greasy hamburgers and crisp french fries.

On the last leg of the journey to the Panshir Valley, we ride in a truck. The truck hits a land mine and rolls over, launching a piece of a metallic ladder into my jaw and knocking out three of my teeth. I lose a lot of blood, but managed to survive solely because of the doctors.

We finally reach the Panshir Valley and set up a makeshift hospital. Wounded rebels are carried in, some from two to three days away. There is no anesthetic; bullet wounds are washed out with tea. During Ramadan, a Muslim fast lasting 40 days, the Afghans would not give blood, so I and the doctors give blood, depending on the blood type necessary.

The man named Massoud, "The Lion of Panshir," is the reason for our trip. The rebel leader has asked for medical help and the doctors come at great personal risk. Massoud and I became friends. Massoud was educated in the Lycée Istiqlal (a French high school) in Kabul. Now a resistance leader, he was considered to be very clever and was always on the move. He needed medical help because his men were dying slow, agonizing deaths from gunshot and shrapnel wounds. The doctor Gilles will accompany us. We take the injured back to Pakistan in a convoy. Since I am the least injured member of the group, I will be the leader. As a token of the rebels' appreciation, I am given a horse. I use it to help transport the wounded. When we arrive back in Pakistan, we are detained because we carry no identification papers. Finally, we are permitted entry.

I traveled back to Afghanistan two more times to cover the *mujahedin*. Gilles returned to Paris, and shortly afterwards committed suicide.

—Coskun Aral

Note: Also see "Pakistan: In A Dangerous Place" to read about *DP's* interview of the *taliban*. (Although TIME magazine incorrectly claims they were the first to interview the *taliban* and specifically Mullah Omar, *DP* beat them by five months and CNN by two weeks.)

AFGHANISTAN

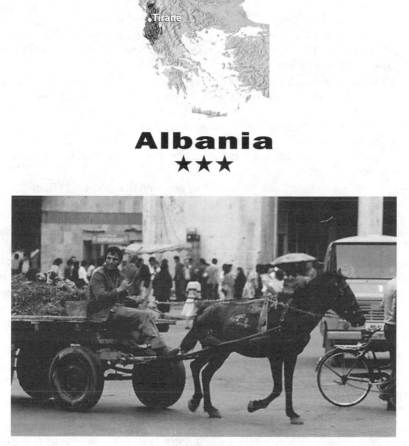

Albania
★★★

Albaniacs

The fun began in January 1997, when the inevitable end of pyramid investment schemes vaporized more than half of the Albanian population's savings. Having no one to blame except their own greed and gullibility, the people quickly blamed the government. Soon the riots and the looting escalated into full scale anarchy. The "Albaniacs" were born.

Thousands of repressed, newly impoverished people attacked, looted and burned banks, jails, museums, government buildings and armories until all were picked clean or destroyed. Soon, even President Sali Berisha's 25-year-old son and 18-year-old daughter joined the thousands of frightened Albanians who escaped for Italy. Foreign military helicopters came in to help evacuate 500 of the 2000 or so foreigners in the country, but curtailed their operations after dodging heavy groundfire from trigger-happy Albaniacs. Fortunately, they were too drunk to hit any of the choppers. Hey, is this a fun place or what?

After Albanians looted the armory 25 miles north of Tirana, they couldn't quite figure out what to do with their newfound toys. Kids swapped grenades, shells and bullets of various calibers like baseball cards while those looking for bargains on a slightly used AK were paying US$5–$20 bucks to become one of the hundreds of wannabe Jesse James, firing their weapons at no particular target. Upscale embassy vehicles were the first to disappear, the more enterprising grabbed gunboats and fired on the coastal ports just for fun. Someone even snagged a fleet of MiG fighters in the pandemonium.

When the mobs took over in March 1997, thousands of the young and old dragged off as many weapons and tools of destruction they could carry. Soon cheap guns were for sale as far away as Bulgaria. Most were buried or hidden. The more industrious Albaniacs were using newly acquired tanks to smash down walls and rob banks. One group used an APC to drag a bank safe out of Gjirokastra and off into the woods. In Saranda, thugs stole oxygen bottles to use on their welding equipment to open bank safes.

Even the government took advantage of the confusion to bomb ethnic Greek villagers in Gjirokastra, 125 miles south of Tirana. In Korca, rival mobsters had a shootout for control of the town (a popular shipment point for shipping drugs into Europe) leaving more than 25 people dead in the streets. Payback and gun love are big in Albania. Drunk Albaniacs sent thousands of tracers arcing into the night sky just for the cheap light show. Newtonian physics then came into play, as dozens of innocent villagers were killed when the bullets came whistling back to earth.

The post-Communist paranoia started at the top when charismatic President Sali Berisha, a former cardiologist and one of the founders of the student-led anti-Communist Democratic Party in Tirana in 1990, proclaimed that the unrest was caused by a Communist rebellion backed by foreign intelligence agencies. Nobody was listening. Albaniacs were convinced the government was behind the pyramid investment schemes collapse. When things escalated from protests to violence, the government threw in the towel rather than be lynched.

It's okay to be paranoid in Albania. It used to be illegal to name your kid Alexander, Christos or even Nick. Greeks were not popular there even though they make up a large portion of the population. Revenge is big in Albania too. Pro-Berisha journalists were attacked, threatened and beaten once anarchy reigned. The Greeks in the south saw a crack in the wall and shoved both fists into it. The mafia beat them to it, blowing each other away under the guise of establishing "citizen defense" groups.

Word got around that if you were going to rob and pillage, disguises were *de rigueur* in case of later reprisals. Wigs, band-aids, tape, masks, medical gauze, even paper bags with eyeholes became the latest Albanian fashion statement at ad hoc checkpoints. The Energizer Bunny look was especially popular, as the legs of extra-large pantyhose masks doubled as floppy, shriveled bunny ears.

The normal tension between Greeks and Albanians, and the war against the drug mafia, became the least of Albania's worries. Greek terrorists were nothing compared to well-armed and very drunk home-bred thugs dressed like flat-nosed, pink rabbits.

Vlora was the nexus of the southern revolt led by the Socialists, the new improved name of the old Communist party that kept Albania in the Middle Ages for so long. The only semblance of a political agenda was evidenced by the posters tacked to the city walls: "Berisha go away. You are crazy. People will win

ALBANIA

BOSNIA-
HERZEGOVINA

SERBIA

Valbonë

Han i Hotit

2

Bajram
Curri

Drin

Bajzë

1

Laq i
Koman

Koplik

Lake
Scutari

Ligeni i
Fierzës

Shkodër

Laq i të
Dejës

Pukë

4

Kukës

Drin i zi

3

Shëngjin

Lezhë

Rrëshen

Zall-Reç

6

Buenë

Adriatic
Sea

Milot

Rubik

7

Peshkopi

Laç

Burrel

5

8

9

Klos

Krujë

Shijak

10

Mat

Tiranë

11

MACEDONIA

Durrës

Kavajë

12

Librazhd

Rrogozhinë

Elbasan

Shkumbin

Lake
Ohrid

Cërrik

13

Lushnjë

Gramsh

Pogradec

Lake
Prespa

Seman

Qyteti
Stalin
(Kuçovë)

16

Devoll

Fier

14

Berat

15

Maliq

18

Korçë

Vyosë

Ballësh

Osum

19

Selenicë

Çorovodë

Strait of
Otranto

N

Vlorë

Mavrovë

21

2

Ersekë

25

Këlcyrë

22

Tepelenë

Përmet

24

Albania

Gjirokastër

National Capital

Region Capital

Secondary City

Primary Road

Railroad

Administrative Border

Delvinë

GREECE

0   25 km

0   25 mi

Sarandë

23

©FWt

**Disricts (rreth)
of Albanii**

1. Shkodër
2. Tropojë
3. Kukës
4. Pukë
5. Krujë
6. Mirditë
7. Mat
8. Dibrë
9. Durrës
10. Tiranë
11. Librazhd
12. Elbasan
13. Lushnje
14. Fier
15. Berat
16. Gramsh
17. Pogradec
18. Korçë
19. Skrapar
20. Përmet
21. Tepelenë
22. Vlorë
23. Sarandë
24. Gjirokastër
25. Kolonjë

against you." Tiny gangster-run fiefdoms like the port of Saranda tried to disarm everyone under 18 and stay out of the mafia and socialist tainted anarchy. Rebel groups from eight towns met in Gjirokastra to form the "National Front for the Salvation of the People." They demanded the resignation of Berisha and a role in any new political structure in Tirana. Thankfully, Berisha finally resigned and was spared the meathook. (He has since returned to post-meathook Albania.) He got the message when the army base in his stronghold of Bajram Curri, 135 miles north of Tirana, was looted. Troops melted away when angry crowds appeared.

When the government ordered all foreigners and journalists out of the country, *DP* took a quick boat ride from Corfu into Albania and soon discovered that Albania is definitely not "The Next Place" for a Mediterranean vacation. The best shopping bargains in Albania were blank Albanian passports (US$100) and slightly damaged Kalashnikovs for US$20–$50. Young, 10-something Albaniacs had smashed the wooden stocks off AKs to make them easier for their little hands to handle.

More than 360 people were killed in Albania's latest violence and some 3400 injured. Things will have calmed down by the time our gentle readers get a chance to visit low-budget, thrill-a-minute, post-democratic Albania. For now there are plenty of guns buried in backyards. Stay tuned for The Return of the Albaniacs.

Albania is one of the poorest countries in Europe and has vacillated between communism, democracy and anarchy since it proclaimed independence on November 28, 1912 after a history of Roman, Byzantine and Turkish domination. Order totally disintegrated in Albania in early March 1997, when rage over collapsing investment schemes—in which half the population lost their entire life savings—plunged Albania into anarchy. Albanians pillaged hundreds of thousands of weapons from government armories during the chaos. Most of these weapons remain in the hands of private citizens. Much of the southern portion of Albania remains under the control of insurgents, including Vlora. A multinational force of 6000 troops from Europe was sent into Albania in April 1997 to restore order. President Sali Berisha conceded power (however, retaining the presidency) to a caretaker government led by Berisha's socialist rivals and scheduled new elections for June 29, 1997.

President Sali Berisha

Even God would get dissed if he defaulted on a pyramid scheme and left half His followers penniless. Charismatic Berisha played hard ball during the unrest but finally gave in to demands that he set up an interim government until new elections could be held. He's a lucky guy. On June 4, 1997, someone chucked a grenade at Berisha during a campaign appearance. The assailant's aim was perfect, but he forgot to pull the pin—or, in the Albaniac tradition of weapons proficiency, perhaps didn't realize there was a pin that needed to be pulled. For now he's back in charge thank's to peacekeeping forces but *DP* has a sneaking suspicion he still keeps his bags packed.

Criminal Gangs

Local mafias and criminal gangs took over the southern half of Albania in March 1997. Highly organized and heavily armed bandits, gangsters, looters, mobsters and hell-raisers took over from fleeing cops and were ignored by the police when they came back. Cops who have returned to their jobs in Saranda, for instance, do nothing as heavily armed bandidos cruise by them in stolen luxury cars. Gangs of armed, drunken thugs roam the southern countryside, looting, killing, raping and pillaging. In Gjirokastra, 20 men gang-raped a college student. Fighting between two criminal gangs in Korca has left at least 26 people dead. When a team from the British embassy, including the ambassador, went to Durres—25 miles from Tirana—to supervise an evacuation, a gang stole all 18 of their cars, forcing the embassy staffers to join the evacuees. Bon Voyage.

The Italian Army

Spearheaded by the Italian military, 6000 peacekeepers have been sent to Albania to restore order and patrol the borders. The largest foreign contingent, the Italians, comprises a third of the troops now in-country. France has 1000 troops in Albania. Greece and Turkey sent 700 each; there are 400 from Romania, 325 from Spain, 120 from Austria and 100 from Denmark.

The Albanian government no longer requires visas of U.S. citizens for stays up to 30 days. A passport is required. A US$10 airport fee must be paid to Albanian customs officials upon departure. Things will be rather fluid for a while with foreigners being suspect for the next few months. Adventurers can just charter a speed boat from Corfu. For specific entry/exit requirements, travelers can contact the following:

Embassy of the Republic of Albania

1150 18th Street, N.W.
Washington, D.C. 20005
☎ (202) 223-4942
FAX (202) 628-7342

Albania used to have a low rate of crime. However, crimes against tourists (robbery, mugging and pickpocketing) are waiting to happen, especially on city streets after dark. Credit cards, personal checks and traveler's checks are rarely accepted in Albania. In addition, hotel accommodations outside Tirana are very limited, and even confirmed reservations are sometimes not honored.

Transportation is rudimentary and, in a word, sucks. Hotels are either upscale or cockroach motels. Most folks stay with the locals.

U.S. Embassy

Rruga E Elbasanit 103
Tirana, Albania
☎ (355-42) 32875.

Banks

Two banks were robbed three different times early in the unrest in the city of Gjirokastra. During one robbery, 30 men attached a steel cable to the bank's vault and used an armored personnel carrier to drag it out of the bank and into the woods.

Rebel Roadblocks

Good for either a laugh or a bullethole, rebels manning hundreds of rebel checkpoints in Albania dress up in wigs, ski masks or like clowns so as not to be recognized. Many of the "guards" are drunk to the point of incoherency. Rape and robbery is the order of the day. Expect nothing less than being separated from your valuables, and perhaps a lot more, should you be stopped at one.

Pyramid Schemes

Imagine hundreds of thousands of drunken, armed Americans terrorizing the streets of Washington after Tupperware and Amway go bankrupt. Well, that's what's going on in Albania. Some of the Albanian investment schemes involved the mafia laundering the proceeds of smuggled oil from Libya and Iraq to Serbia via Montenegro. Pyramid schemes were used to launder the dirty oil money, which was then unloaded into the Albanian national bank. This got the government involved, as the boys in office borrowed the cash to help pay off its massive national debt. Liking what they saw, the Albanian people started getting into the pyramid game by investing their life savings in the schemes. When the smaller pyramids—such as Gjallica, Sudja, and Populli—started going broke, investors wanted their money back. Oops. Meanwhile, the larger schemes saw what was happening and pooled their resources in an attempt to get a license as a private bank. Mafia cash is the suspected reason why pyramid companies such as Vefa survive.

Camera Crews and...

Armed bandits have held up at least six different foreign television networks, relieving the crews of their equipment, vehicles and money. On March 2, 1997, several television crews and reporters were beaten silly outside the parliament building.

...Being a Journalist

Albanian journalists fled the country when parliament declared a state of emergency in March 1997, at least those critical of the government. But journos loyal to President Sali Berisha were deprived of the last laugh when left-wing extremists started putting together black lists of government-loyal publications and sentencing their publishers and writers to death. Regardless of their leanings, journalists face peril in Albania. The Tirana offices of Koha Jone, a leading independent daily usually critical of the government, were razed in March 1997. Reporters for the paper fled into the countryside, moving each night so they wouldn't be discovered. Others were beaten by the police. One Koha Jone reporter on the lam, Martin Leka, hid in a farmhouse for a week. When he started going stir crazy, he dressed up as a woman and went out for a walk.

Glow Worms

In April 1997, the director of the Albanian army's chemistry unit, Col. Asllan Bushati, appealed to some folks who unwittingly stole radioactive materials and lethal chemicals from four military bases to return the hazardous material, including cobalt and strontium, to the authorities. The bandits were also implored not to abandon the material in a field, as the radiation could enter the human food chain.

There is one doctor for every 574 people in this country of 3.3 million inhabitants. The official language here is Albanian, and the currency is the New Lek.

Condé Nast Traveler naively touted Albania as "The Next Place," and it may be if you make your vacation plans 12 years out. In the meantime, the country will have some growing pains to ride out.

The government estimates that 652,000 weapons and 3600 tons of explosives were looted from over 1200 army depots. So far only 25,000 have been returned.

Vulnerable to earthquakes and riots, lowly Albania lies at the southeastern end of the Adriatic Sea. It gained its independence from Turkey in 1913 and became a Stalinist communist state in 1944. Its first multi-party elections were held in 1991. But it's been pretty rough sailing since. The country possesses Europe's least developed transportation system. In fact, private cars were prohibited until 1991. And, today, the horse and cart remains a normal means of transportation.

Muslims comprise about 70 percent of the population, while Greek Orthodox account for 20 percent and Roman Catholics 10 percent. Ninety-eight percent of the population is ethnic Albanian, officially, although ethnic Greeks in Albania contend their own group makes up about 10 percent of Albania's population.

Albania receives fewer than 100,000 visitors every year. Crime is on the rise and tourists are frequently targeted. Marijuana is widely grown in Albania.

04/11/1997	Foreign troops arrive in Albania for the first time since World War II.
03/02/1997	Parliament declares a state of emergency
11/06/1994	Voters reject draft constitution favored by Berisha in a referendum.
02/1992	Communists routed in elections
02/1991	First elections since World War II
4/11/1985	Enver Hoxha, Albania's communist ruler for four decades, dies.

The War Against the Sky, March 1997

At least the taxi mafia are having a good time of it. The hordes of foreign journalists flooding into Southern Albania, as the country descends into chaos and anarchy, are being charged as much as $300 a day for the privilege of being chauffeured around, the equivalent of several months wages for the average Albanian. Equally swift to rise to the challenge are the speedboat mafia. For those journalists wanting to slip into the south of the country via the Greek island of Corfu, the 30 minute ride is a mere $500.

And it is by speedboat that I make my entry to the southern port of Sarande a week or so after furious mobs had stormed military armories for weapons and taken control of the city. The collapse of a series of pyramid investment schemes with government connections and the loss of most people's life savings left civilians in the south in a state of incoherent anger. With one other foreign hack, I climb into the small speedboat that has arrived in the harbor of Kassiopi, in the north-east of Corfu, under the watchful eyes of Greek commandos there to ensure that the Albanians bring none of their usual trading wares across with them on their way to pick up journalists, illegal refugees, guns, drugs etc., the normal everyday exports from Albania.

For half an hour or so we bump our way across the sea, hitting troughs that almost throw me out of the boat, until we reach the calm of the coastline which we hug until drawing into Sarande. Given the TV reports that have been coming out of Sarande the town is quiet—with only the occasional burst of gunfire coming from a distant quarter. After a quick coffee we decide to travel up to Gjrokaster, a 45 minute drive and the most recent town to fall into the hands of the so-called 'rebels'—in reality little more than mobs of enraged civilians. Confronted with this anger, the police and army would generally just pack their bags and head for home.

Leaving the town, we pass the wreckage of a car in which only days earlier a hapless policeman was burned alive. Two old Soviet T-55 tanks form part of the roadblock which signals the end of the town and leaves us free to continue on our journey. Apart from the sporadic roadblocks that have been set up by a variety of local village militias, the dominant feature of the Albanian countryside are the thousands of concrete bunkers and machine gun positions that were erected by the Stalinist dictator Enver Hoxha, for the day that Albania would be invaded.

Gjirokaster, when we arrive, is alive with the sound of gunfire. The din is deafening as pistols, AK-47s and 12mm machine guns release bullets into the air in what has been termed 'Albania's war against the sky.' I decide that there is little to do but wander around and take a few pictures. The town itself is pleasant and old with its typically Balkan cobbled streets. I discover the unpleasant side to the town almost immediately. Walking down one of the gently inclining streets, I notice a man approaching.

From 30 yards away, it is more than obvious that he is almost—but unfortunately not quite—paralytically drunk. He is also in charge of an AK-47, which he is firing into the air. On seeing me he staggers in my general direction, and to my dismay, decides to stop firing in the air and point his gun straight at me. I give him the kind of smile that any dentist would recognize straight off, while my legs go weak at the knees. It's a pity, I can't help thinking as I watch him lurch towards me with glazed eyes and his finger on the trigger, that there aren't any manuals about dealing with drunks in charge of an AK-47—I could use one. On reaching me, he drunkenly reaches up to try and take my watch from my left hand, and it is only then that I realize that I have raised both my hands above my head, although I can't remember doing so. Since he is much smaller than me I quickly lower my arm to let him have easy access to my watch and hope he doesn't get the bright idea to take my cameras as well. My wallet is in my back pocket, and I wonder if I can persuade him to accept Visa or MasterCard in lieu of cash, if only because credit cards are useless in southern Albania and without cash, I am sunk. I suspect he might prefer cash.

Somewhat to my relief, however, two other locals arrive on the scene and gently take the drunk—he still hasn't managed to get my watch off—and lead him away from me. I watch nervously, silently cheering every step they take him; but drunkenness has a determination all of its own. The weapon taken from him, he makes his way back to where I am standing; and instead of wanting my watch decides to hug me while muttering in Albanian. He eventually leaves and stumbles back to his friends while I smile blandly and hope that, with a bit of luck, he might manage to blow his own head off by the end of the day.

Twenty minutes later I reach the town center. It is full of armed and often masked civilians milling around enjoying the freedom that the lack of any state authority brings— gleefully emptying weapons into the air as spent casings rain onto the street. I wonder what the chances are of my eardrums surviving in tact— probably quite slim. Of slightly greater concern, however, is exactly where the spent bullets will end up. None of the gun-toting mob seem to be able to grasp one of the most elementary laws of physics: what goes up must come down. The results are often tragic. More people die from falling bullets than anything else.

I pick up a taxi and it's a Mercedes, probably one of a batch that has been stolen from Greece and given a quick change in color and number plates. The driver offers me a bottle of whisky and I gratefully sit back, take a swig and begin to feel slightly more relaxed as we cruise around town before beginning the search for a hotel.

The hotel is a vast Stalinist concrete monster and for US$10 I procure one of its many freezing rooms. I meet a group of Greek journalists from Skai TV and, after an unsuccessful search for restaurants and food, share a tinned meal with them washed down with some imported vodka. We swap information and chat about the situation generally agreeing that it is one of the crazier places dominating current affairs. The so-called rebels have no coordination or leadership; there are simply vast numbers of angry people with weapons—all of whom want the Albanian President, Salih Berisha, to resign for his association with the disastrous pyramid schemes. I ask if I can share transport costs with them for a while and they readily agree.

We head out of town early in the morning at around 6 a.m.; our destination is Erseke, a small town a couple of hours' drive through the southern mountains which is still under government control. We stop, however, a few miles outside of town. A few cars are coming through the mountain passes and we stop them to inquire about the situation in town. Nothing is happening, we are told. The town is still under the control of the police. But in one of the cars a young man tells us he is the local civilian leader—and informs us that he is going to a small town we had passed through to garner help from outside to lead a rebellion in Erseke. If we go into the town and wait for a couple of hours, he says, he will be back with outside help to eject the police. We cruise the few miles until we reach the edge of town. Four distinctly unhappy looking policemen man a roadblock. I don't have an official visa to be in the country, but the policemen don't ask and wave us through. People mill around in the streets as we drive by, a few make V-signs. We eventually go to a cafe, drink some arak and wait. Looking out the cafe window, I notice that the streets are quieter, there are fewer people, and a solitary policeman drives a police van up and down the streets before disappearing from view. It is as if the whole town is collectively holding it's breath and, like us, waiting.

Cruising back to the original police block at the entrance to town we find it abandoned. The police, rather sensibly, have obviously decided that going off duty might just enable them to collect their pensions—if the government has any money. Not much more than fifteen minutes later, as we sit in the car smoking and waiting, the sound of automatic fire resonates throughout the town. From the far end of town an army truck comes tearing down the main street: there are no soldiers, however, only armed civilians who have come to "liberate" the town.

Within minutes the streets are jam-packed as people crowd around the few guns available to take turns at firing—as usual—in the air. But unlike in the movies, ammunition has an irritating habit of running out and it is not long before some-one has the bright idea of looting the local armory that the police have aban-doned. En masse the mob heads for the armory and soon carry out everything from boots to boxes of ammunition. To increase the general merriment, some-one decides that the whole place would definitely be brightened up somewhat with a touch of pyrotechnics, and smoke is soon billowing from the buildings. It's a complete free-for-all as everyone takes whatever they can carry and smashes any-thing that is too awkward to pick up. An army jeep is overturned by a jeering mob, after which a man empties his AK-47 into it, causing sparks to fly but, alas, no explosion. With the jeep safely out of commission, the mob turns to a police van. It is quickly overturned and within minutes blazing away. To add to the gen-eral ambience, anyone with a gun empties clips of ammunition into the air to cel-ebrate the town's newfound "freedom."

With nothing else left to burn or loot, the rebels have a brief discussion about what to do next and, infused with confidence, decide it would be a capital idea to liberate the next village from the clutches of the government. Piling onto the back of the military truck, they roar off down the road, with us in hot pursuit. But after no more than two minutes of driving, the truck stops on a bend. About 300 meters further down the road I can see an ambulance stuck in a small ditch. "Po-lice," comes the explanation. It seems we have caught up with some of the police-men who left the town earlier, but who must have been cursing their luck at being caught by civilians intent upon spreading the anti-authority revolt. To my amazement, no one seems to know what to do: The 30 or so armed men in the truck (who not so long ago had been firing bullets into the air and shouting anti-government slogans) seem to go into a collective paralysis.

There cannot be more than four or five policemen in the ambulance—which is revving desperately in an attempt to get out of the ditch—yet nobody seems to want to go any farther. Only two or three jump down and sensibly make for the high ground, using the cover of the trees and bushes to approach the van. But even they do not venture too far. The revolutionary fervor has dissipated somewhat.

For the policemen, though, the level of revolutionary fervor may be somewhat academic. Faced with 30 armed, albeit not particularly determined, men with AK-47s they do what any sensible (and more than likely disenchanted) and unwilling wearer of an uniform would do under the circumstances: they surrender. At the sight of a policeman standing beside the ambulance with his arms raised high, a great cheer rises from the mob as they race forward.

On reaching the ambulance, they find only one policeman. He is quickly surrounded by the angry mob. While some try to punch and kick him, others try to protect him, and it is not long before he is bundled into the back of the ambulance. This brief brush with authority seems to have something of a sobering affect on the mob, and the plans for the liberation of the next village are abandoned.

The following day, however, we return. The next village, we are told, revolted without assistance the previous day. Driving on for 40 minutes or so we eventually arrive, but the villagers are in the process of looting the extensive military armory that has been so irresponsibly abandoned by the police and soldiers. The road to the armory is so bad that we are forced to walk. Already there are numerous civilians returning from the armory, trooping along the wooded road, carrying a vast and varied number of weapons. Over the brow of a hill, I can see plumes of smoke rising.

Approaching the camp, we meet more civilians leaving, all carrying what they can. Up ahead a building is blazing with flames billowing out of a top story window. The scene, once we are inside the perimeter of the camp, is chaotic. There are weapons of almost every conceivable type lying littered around: RPG-7's with warheads, boxes of hand-grenades, rifles, gasmasks, uniforms, even anti-personnel mines.

I watch as young children, no more than ten or eleven, try to load weapons, unaware of how to fit magazines into the rifles, ignorant of where the safety catch can be found. Other children roam around the ammunition dump picking up what they can, supremely ignorant of the weapons they are carrying, and unsupervised by adults. As usual those who don't understand their weapons are firing them continuously into the air without, at least, having to worry about ammunition shortages.

Another group is busy tearing the covers from 20 or so four-barrelled anti-aircraft guns. Outside the camp perimeters heavy machine guns are being belt fed and trained on a concrete bunker placed on an opposite hilltop. Other locals are still in the process of familiarizing themselves with the obviously unfamiliar weapons. "We are here because we are sick of being lied to," a man says. "We want real change in Albania, real democracy." Behind him flames engulf the barracks.

—Roddy Scott

ALBANIA

Algeria
★★★★★

Rock the Casbah

Ever since one of the 20 companions of Hercules founded a trading center here, Algeria has been rocked by rebellion and warfare. The Romans, Vandals, Hafsids, Merenids, pirates (the famous home base of Barbarossa, aka Red Beard and the Barbary pirates), Spanish, Arabs, Turks and French all pillaged, abused and destroyed the former breadbasket of the Roman Empire. The current killing is gaining rapidly on the 250,000 body count racked up by the French in their eight-year "Vietnam" from 1954–1962. Today the war is a sick soap opera where the former terrorists (FLN) and current leaders let the new rebels (GIA) destroy their own people and future political legitimacy. There is also firm suspicion that the body count is helped by right wing killers who play tit for tat.

Most of the killing takes place just outside Algiers and in Algeria's Mitidja Plain. This fertile, and now dirt cheap and deadly farmland, stretches southward from the outskirts of Algiers, and is now called the Triangle of Death. An apt name for what may well be the most deadly real estate since Cambodia's Killing Fields. This is the stomping grounds of the insurgent Armed Islamic Group (GIA), the

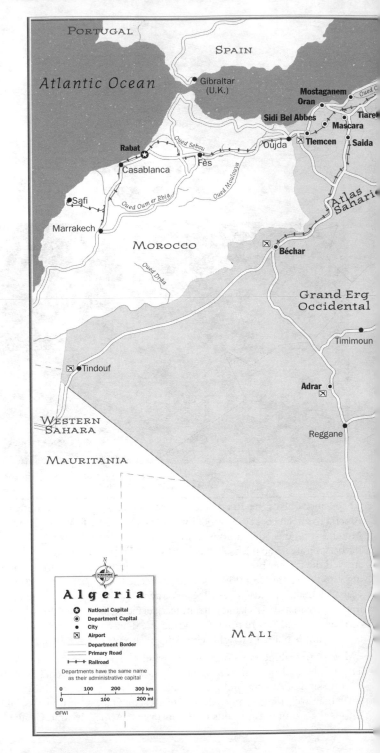

ALGERIA

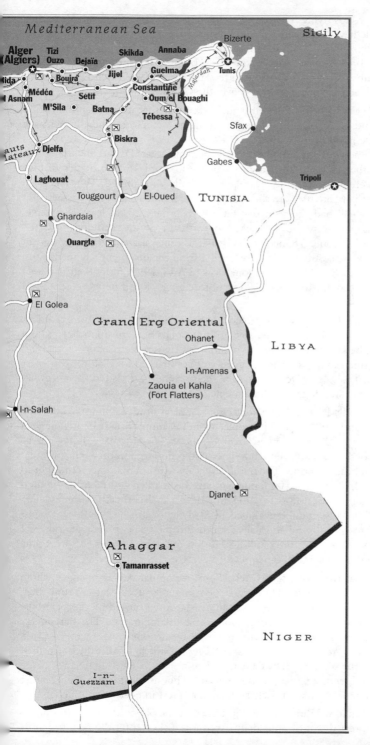

radical rebel groups trying to oust the presidency of Liamine Zeroual. More than 80,000 people have died (with 400,000 displaced), many of them fertilizing this valley with their blood. Here, the most common item can become an executioner's weapon: rusty knives, axes, home-made bombs, hoes, grenades fashioned from Coke cans and rakes. All are used to slaughter old men, school girls, farm boys, teachers and anyone else who gets in the GIA's way.

In February 1997, the GIA said it would "slash the throats of all apostates and their allies" and set "explosions in the very heart of Algiers and Blida." They have certainly made good on their threats. On May 14, 1997, more than 30 villagers were slaughtered by the rebels in the sleepy hamlet Douar Daoud, including two infants, 15 other children and seven women. On April 16, the bodies of four young girls were found outside the village of Chaib Mohammed. They had been raped before their throats were slit. On April 12, 22 villagers were massacred in Douar Menaa—all had their throats cut. On February 23, at least 18 people, mostly young men, were shot or hacked to death at a phony roadblock near Saida. On June 24, some 18 people had their throats slashed in the village of Mouzaia. More than 300 people were killed during the insurgent's Ramadan run of terror in early 1997. During only one week in April 1997, more than 140 people were slaughtered. More than 100 were foreigners, killed between 1992 and 1996.

The GIA sends *DP* crudely assembled and energetically written faxes claiming that all singers, artists, journalists, soldiers and policemen are nonbelievers, and that they will be killed. There was no mention of lawyers, boxing promoters and used-car salesmen, but take it for granted you are marked for death if you enter Algiers or the Triangle of Death. (Despite the warnings, *DP* visited Algiers to see these rabid dumpster dogs and share the negative vibes.)

Since the cancelled 1992 Algerian elections, radical fundamentalists have murdered more than 13,000 innocent people, including more than 100 foreigners, in an effort to topple the government. Among the victims are playwrights, artists, journalists, politicians, and even schoolgirls who refuse to don the *hejab*, or traditional Muslim head covering. The number of slain Muslim militants is thought to be over 20,000. More than 100 foreigners have been killed and 23 others injured in Algeria by terrorist groups. In 1994 and 1995, Algerian security forces killed 5029 guerrillas; Muslim militants killed 1400 civilians, of which 500 were women. The victims include 52 journalists killed during the two-year period, 372 union activists, 184 magistrates and 84 Muslim religious workers. At press time 65,000 were dead and 50–200 people died every night.

They brag that they have sent Cheb Hasni (a popular Algerian singer whom they shot to death) to hell. They kidnapped singer Lounes Matoub, but then, after having second thoughts, released him. Matoub's (an ethnic Berber) only crime was recording a satirical song about the fundamentalists. The Berbers are the country's largest ethnic minority and a group no one wishes to mess with. The communique to *DP* went on to say, "Now we will start with the journalists, the poets and the soldiers. Belly dancing is a prayer to Satan. When Satan's messengers give a direction to people, they dance." They ask that if you dance, please stay out of Algeria. Not an entirely surprising request in post-disco Algeria.

The fundamentalists' threats are not just the rhetoric of bored bullies. Journalists are under a direct threat of immediate execution if they enter the country; more than 70 have been killed and 700 have fled. Wearing glasses, Western clothes or even looking educated can make you a target. It is estimated that the entire wealth of this country of 28 million is in the hands of only about 5000 people.

Algeria is no stranger to hatred and death. Eight years of cruel warfare with the French started back in 1954. During this tenure, a quarter of a million people were killed and more than a million *pied noirs* (black feet), or white colonists, were forced out. Despite the messy divorce, Algeria's 133-year marriage to France has made it more French than Arabic.

France has always had a love-hate relationship with Algeria, due more to its geographical proximity than to its cultural dissimilarities. In Algeria, Russia has found a major customer for its military hardware and expertise, and Italy makes sure Algeria continues to pump out the oil and gas it needs to keep those Fiats and Ferarris topped off.

Algerian militants are training at military bases in Sudan, and financially supported by Iran. Most of the trainees were veterans of the Afghan war and traveled to Sudan via Iran. These militants are trained to add to the core of the underground Islamic fundamentalist movement held responsible for the killing of more than 210 members of Algeria's security forces. For now the world pretends that Algeria doesn't exist.

If you call the Algerian embassy in the U.S (as *DP* did) and ask about dangers in Algeria, they'll reply, "What danger?" We figure any "safe" country where the U.S. State Department advises travelers "to have substantial armed protection" must be a hell of a safe thrill ride. In a mere six years, Algeria's Islamic insurgency has taken more lives than were lost by the U.S. during the Vietnam War, yet we get little exposure of the 80,000 lives lost. Something evil and dark is happening in Algeria, but because few journalists will enter the country, it remains a silent distant butchery.

Simply put, Algeria is the world's most dangerous place for travelers. It's a country where whacked-out fundamentalists and burned-out Algerian veterans of Afghanistan's war with Russia like to cut the throats of farmers and brown-eyed schoolgirls, not to mention shooting expats who might be still writhing after a bomb attack.

Even the main rebel groups have taken to blowing each other away. In January 1996 alone, more than 50 radicals were killed when the FIS and GIA decided to take out each other. Meanwhile, foreigners working in the calmer, but still tense southern portion of Algeria, live in armed isolation waiting for a transfer to safer places like Somalia and Southern Lebanon. You know when CBS News calls *DP* to send in our vacation tapes from our trip to Algeria that this is a dangerous place.

President Liamine Zeroual and the FLN

The old guard revolutionaries (Zeroual was an officer in the Algerian army against France) who kicked the French out in 1962 are now the ones who have to go. The current FLN party held on to power by simply cancelling or manipulating elections that the newer and more vital Islamic Salvation Front would have won fair and square. The FLN tried everything, from adding seats in their strongholds and arresting FIS members to cancelling the elections altogether. The military is directly in control of the High Security Council, with General Khaled Nezar, the leader of the Algerian military, pulling the strings. The former General, former ambassador to Romania and hardliner, has softened recently. Zaroual has sprung FIS leaders, pushed for power sharing. Maybe someone who has seen political power overthrown understands how easy it is. He also has the foresight to understand the new domino theory of North African states becoming hardline around him.

Islamic Salvation Front, Front Islamique du Salut (FIS)

The Islamic fundamentalist FIS, founded in March 1989 was once a strong political party that should have been in power, but was banned by the Algerian government after the 1992 elections were voided. The FIS signed a peace agreement on September 24, 1997 to essentially show that the GIA is conducting the grisly killings.

FIS leader Shaykh Abassi Madani and his hawkish deputy, Ali Belhadj, were released from jail and transferred to a cushy villa under house arrest in an effort to strike a compromise with the fundamentalists, but put back in jail after the government refused to meet the leaders' demands. But in another conciliatory gesture to the rebels, Madani was freed on parole in July 1997, although his influence over the rebels has waned. Most consider Abdelkader Hachani the FIS leader. Hachani was sentenced in July 1997 to five years in prison, but was then freed by authorities. Ali Belhadj (b. 1955) was a former teacher and Imam of a mosque. He was imprisoned twice before for anti-government views.

The government's policy of attacking and jailing FIS leaders has had the same effect Hercules had on the Hydra. Instead of one unified Islamic group, they now had dozens of smaller groups each with a different agenda and approach. The GIA, MIA, AIS are just some of these younger, more implacable groups. And even the GIA has splintered into smaller factions. The FIS may not be able to bring these new groups under the sway of the Majlilis Echoura, the high council of the FIS.

About 400 members of the FIS were sent to the Bekáa Valley in Lebanon for training in 1990. FIS members have also been trained in the Sudan by Hezbollah. The party is still a grass roots political and religious movement that originally attracted the dispossessed. The party has grown to involve the support of the majority of the country, including intellectuals and professionals.

Armed Islamic Group, Groupe Islamic Armee, el-Djama'a el-islamia el Mosalaha (GIA)

The GIA, numbering between 20,000 and 25,000 fighters are organized into tiny, unrelated and sometimes warring divisions. Some say their headquarters is in the Hatatba mountains 50 miles south of Algiers. At its core are some of the most heartless and cruel men on earth: Algerian veterans of the Afghan war, or *mujahedin*. They're hard, brutal religious zealots trained in Sudan, battle tested in Afghanistan and bankrolled by Iran.

Formed by Djamel Zitouni, alias Abou Aberrahmane Amine, the GIA split away from the FIS, disagreeing violently with its softer position. Zitouni was killed on July 16, 1996 during infighting that led to the split of the GIA into three factions. The "mainstream" GIA is now led by Miloud Hebbi, Slimane Mehrezi, or depending on who you talk to. The faction which followed Zitouni is led by the late Antar Zouarbri (aka Abu Talha), and was considered the most brutal. It was rumored he was killed in a July '97 shootout by the army. It probably doesn't matter since the GIA has lost eight leaders in five years. Realistically no one knows the actual structure or leadership of this phantom organization.

There is another group led by Mustafa Kertali, that performs its massacres under the banner of the Islamic Movement for Preaching and Jihad (MIPJ). Kertali is believed responsible for whacking Zitouni. When politicians and academics are in the news for being dead, MIPJ is most likely to have written the headlines. Other leaders included El Mansouri El Miliani, Abdullah Qalek, Abdel-Haq Ayadia and Djafar El Afghani.

Few if any journalists have dared meet with the GIA because of its hatred toward Westerners and its lack of clear focus or agenda. Some journos believe that the cut throats and cold-blooded massacres of rural peasants has more to do with a major land grab than politics. Much the same way the PKK terrorizes small villages that might interfere with its lucrative heroin routes. The GIA has razed some 1000 schools and executed at least 200 teachers. Of the 100-plus foreigners killed by militants in Algeria since 1992, most were victims of the GIA. The current leaders of Algeria are under a death sentence decreed in a fatwa by Sheik Abedel-Haq el Ayadia, one of the founders of the GIA. The fatwa is all encompassing and includes the people who support the government, including foreign workers and journalists.

The Italian mafia in Sicily and Naples are rumored to be the main hardware suppliers of the GIA arsenal. The law of the GIA is the Hadith el Quran (Koran) much like the *taliban*'s countrified version of *sharia* or Koranic law. The fighters can be found in the Algiers region and in the twisting backstreets of Algiers. One minor lifesaving point: The GIA is said to steer clear of Americans or Germans because their countries granted asylum to their leaders.

The GIA's alleged mouthpiece is the Saudi newspaper Al Hayat, published in London, Paris and Beirut. They also have a web site which flickers on and off. Al Hayat is not to be confused with a popular downtown Damascus hotel. The newspaper's web site is:

Al Hayat

http://www.alhayat.com

The Army and the Death Squads

Groups of five to 10 men in plain clothes work the inner city, while 35,000 troops man an "infernal arc" in the Mitidja between Algeria, Blida, Laarba and Medea. Out in the countryside, small groups of soldiers travel in helicopters and armored personnel vehicles to track down fundamentalists. It's clobbering time in Algeria. The annual U.S. report on human rights said there was "convincing evidence" of systematic torture and executions of suspected GIA and FIS insurgents. The right wing groups are called "eradicators" or ninjas.

Hamas

A popular moderate Islamic party and a good starting point to find the FIS or GIA.

The Cops

Police and security forces in Algeria consist of three organizations: (1) the national police (DGSN); (2) an agency of the ministry of the interior, Gendarmerie (MOD); and (3) the communal guards, similar to village or small town police with limited training and equipment. There is an ongoing problem with the terrorists infiltrating the ranks of all three. In addition, the terrorists have obtained hundreds of police uniforms and badges and have masqueraded as police to carry out terrorist and criminal operations. Some of these operations have included assassinations of GOA officials by terrorists operating fake police checkpoints. Throughout the war, terrorists have targeted GOA officials, journalists, foreigners and randomly selected Algerian citizens. But the cops and security forces have borne a large proportion of the targeting and, as such, suffered numerous casualties. The large number of deaths within the police forces, coupled with the uncertainty about fellow officers' loyalties, have resulted in low morale in the police ranks.

Algeria is a dash-in/dash-out place for journos and a no-go place for tourists. Algeria does not issue visas to persons whose passports indicate previous travel to Israel or South Africa. Both "tourist" and business visas cost US$30. There isn't a predetermined length of stay. Instead, you must request the length of and reason for stay on the visa application. Visas permit entry into Algeria at authorized checkpoints by air, land or sea. At press time, Americans and other foreigners were permitted entry into Algeria from Libya, Mali, Tunisia, Niger and Mauritania. There is no entry into Algeria from Morocco. *DP* went in as a tourist denying ourselves the luxury of an armed escort.

From the U.S., the best way to get to Algeria is to fly through France to Algiers or Oran. However, there have been periodic interruptions of Air Algérie's service between Paris and Algiers due to a dispute between the airline and the Paris Airport Authority. Therefore, when departing from Paris, you may need to either fly or take the train (TGV) to Lilles, Lyon or Marseilles. From these cities, you can catch flights to Algeria.

Journalists should definitely transit through Paris because the city is a hub of numerous contacts of all political leanings within the Algerian expat/exile community. Among these folks are a number of Algerian journalists who can be contacted through French journalists. Journalists need six photos, your CV, two completed forms, a $32 money order made payable to the Embassy of Algeria, and you must tell them if you have been to Algeria before and wait two to three weeks.

On our way to Algeria for the blood soaked local elections in October '97, the foreign news desk of CBS called to see if we could send some of our footage back. When we told him that RYP was going as a tourist and not as a heavily guarded journo he quickly hung up.

For more information concerning entry requirements, crazy travelers may contact Mr. Kamel Hadri at the following:

Embassy of the Democratic and Popular Republic of Algeria

> *2137 Wyoming Avenue NW,*
> *Washington, D.C. 20008*
> ☎ *(202) 265-2800, FAX: (202) 265-1978*
> *e-mail: embalgus@ cais.com*

Tourists may be restricted in their movements and either monitored or escorted by the military. Theoretically, tourists are permitted in Algiers, the highway leading to Oran, as well as Oran itself and other towns along the coast, including Tlemcen. The border area northeast of Nefta on the Tunisian border may also be accessible, as well. Restricted areas include a huge swath of real estate in the Grand Erg Occidental with El Golea as the nucleus.

If a journalist wants to visit another area of the country other than Algiers, travel is restricted to air (via the domestic carrier, Inter-Air Services), and the itinerary must be cleared by authorities beforehand. In all likelihood, travel outside Algiers will be with a police or military escort. Even with an armed escort, travel in the Algerian countryside is hazardous. Journalists are not permitted to freely report on the civil war. For journalists, the best advice is to conduct business in your hotel, and have your interview subjects visit you at the hotel. Journalists are monitored and are usually assigned police or military escorts. It is illegal to move outside Algiers without them. Permission for independent travel is rarely granted. Those who slip away from their escorts and travel outside Algiers will be deported.

The government has rigorously enforced a late-night curfew in the central region around Algiers. Roadblocks are located at most of the major intersections and many others. The government isn't the only one setting up the blocks. Fake roadblocks are also set up by the GIA and others for the purposes of robbery and murder. There has been a slew of robbery and assault incidents involving foreigners, especially in the far southern region of Algeria near the border with Niger. Algeria south of Tamanrasset is particularly dangerous.

The two routes south across the Sahara are closed (there is an alternate route through Mauritania to Senegal). Foreign oil workers in the south bypass the north altogether, flying directly into their installations and living in highly-secured compounds. Control Risks Group, a business consultant to companies doing business in foreign countries, rates Algeria as the most dangerous place in the world to do business. About 2000 French citizens, mostly businessmen and diplomatic staff, remain in the country.

DP's Tips on Surviving Algeria

1. The government of Algeria is not wild about tourists. Even accredited journalists will be allowed entry only after approval from Algiers.

2. All accredited journalists are met on arrival by a protection team supplied without charge by the government.

3. In Algiers, journos can only stay at the Hotel al-Jezzair ☎ *[213] (2) 59-10-00* or the Hotel Aurassi ☎ *[213] (2) 64-82-52*. Both are guarded 24 hours a day.

4. During your stay, you will be escorted at all times by the "ninjas," black-uniformed security police. You will be driven to meetings and escorted back to your hotel. The teams only operate in Algiers. For trips outside the city, taxis can be hired for about $60 a day from your hotel.

5. Those who want to wander around town will be given walkie-talkies. Do not wear these conspicuously. Do not stay in one place any longer than 10 minutes (the typical time it takes locals to alert GIA gunmen).

6. You will be allowed to walk around town unescorted or to leave Algiers only if you sign a disclaimer.

7. The most dangerous place in Algiers is the Kasbah. One Western journalist went there unprotected and was shot within five minutes.

8. If you are in Algiers, say hello to the U.S embassy staff—major consumers of *DP* T-shirts and stickers, as well as all around good sports.

9. Police emergency is ☎ *17*, ambulance is ☎ *62-33-33*.

With terrorists in the north and bandits in the south, most of Algeria is dangerous. The Zabarbar forest, Blida mountains and the Jijel region are frequently napalmed by the government in their quest to rid themselves of fundamentalist pockets. MiG-23s regularly drop napalm on remote regions used by the terrorists for their bases of operations.

Algiers

A global study conducted by an international business group, Corporate Resources Group, rated Algiers the worst city in the world. The group based its findings on criteria such as quality of life, security, public services, mental and physical care and facilities, and political and social stability. They could have saved their money. Every night an average of 50 people are killed in the city of Algiers. There are also frequent bomb attacks in crowded public areas such as markets and mosques.

Schools

In addition to journalists, teachers are a favorite target of Muslim militants. It's not unusual for two a week to be whacked in Algiers, and, as of mid-1996, some 700 schools have been razed by fire or sabotaged.

Bandits

As if the terrorists weren't enough, there are also numerous incidents of banditry and assault involving foreigners that have been reported in the far southern region of Algeria near the border with Niger. Bandits have robbed, assaulted, kidnapped and killed travelers in Algeria south of Tamanrasset.

Being a Journalist

At least 70 journalists have died in Algeria since 1993. Foreign journalists are forbidden to leave their hotels in Algiers without an armed escort for protection against attack. That's the government line. More than likely, it's also to keep them from having a chat with the bad guys. Journos caught sneaking out without their babysitters are deported and not let in again.

You must understand that it isn't completely your skin they are trying to save. Since outside hacks have such high PR value when dead, the GIA gets all dreamy eyed and weak in the knees thinking of your recently butchered carcass on the cover of *Newsweek*. If they have to take out an entire post office, office building or nursery school to get you, that's OK, too.

Being a Kid

The GIA likes bombing youth centers and slicing the throats of pop singers and youth idols. The GIA believes that schooling for kids is an "obstacle to the Holy War in Algeria." The youth of Algeria have only two choices in life: join the GIA or join the Algerian military regime. Most just want to find a decent disco.

Criminals

As if getting your throat slit wasn't bad enough, the threat of theft is increasing in Algeria. The most frequent crimes involve the theft of auto parts from parked cars. Car windows and trunk locks are frequently broken in the hope that the thief will find something of value within. Home burglary is an increasingly serious problem, and most residences of foreigners are protected by alarm systems, watch dogs and/or guards. Experienced expatriate residents should venture out into the city with only a minimum amount of cash carried in a carefully concealed location. Vehicles are not generally parked in unguarded locations because of theft and vandalism.

Booby Traps

Booby traps proliferate in the country. One of the less ingenious, but still surprisingly effective modes, is the old "booby trap in the corpse trick." A while back, the booby-trapped corpse of a slain security force member exploded when it was picked up by two security force members, killing them both.

Hospitals and clinics in Algeria are available, but limited in quality. Your best bet is to ask to be taken to the Ain Naadja Military hospital in the suburbs of Algiers. If you have the choice or the time, ask to be taken to a military hospital instead of the closest public one. You may find a hand grenade in your bed pan. If you are seriously wounded, you stand a better chance by being flown out to nearby France, Britain or Germany. Medicines can be difficult to get and expensive. Don't expect much outside of the major cities. A 24-hour chemist is at *19 rue Abane Ramdone,* ☎ *63-36-31* or *2 rue Didouche Mourad,* ☎ *63-47-43.* There is a civilian hospital; Hôpital Mustopha near *place de Mer,* ☎ *66-33-33* (ambulance also available at this number).

Algeria, with a population of just under 29 million people, is the size of Europe with a climate that varies from arid to semi-arid. The coast gets wet winters and hot summers. Cold winters characterize the high plateau. Sunni Muslims make up 99 percent of the population; virtually all are of Arab-Berber descent.

The currency is the Algerian dinar. Change your money at the hotel (you don't just walk around and get change here). Electrical current is 137/240V with the European two-pin plug. Phone and fax service is available from major hotels and businesses but you may have to wait for a free overseas line. Most people speak French and Arabic. English is spoken only in the main cities and in big hotels and businesses.

The work-week in Algeria is Saturday through Wednesday, at least for those who work; 84 percent of Algerians between the ages of 15 and 30 are jobless, and inflation is at 55 percent. Factories are functioning at 50 percent capacity. In addition, Algeria has the lowest farm yield of any Mediterranean country, forcing it to import two-thirds of its food.

Traveler's checks and credit cards are acceptable in only a few establishments in urban areas. Currently, the government of Algeria requires all foreigners entering the country to exchange US$200 into local currency. Documentary proof of legal exchange of currency is needed when (or if) you leave Algeria.

Embassy Location

U.S. Embassy

4 Chemin Cheikh Bachir El-Ibrahimi
B.P. 549 (Alger-Gare) 16000, Algiers
☎ *[213] (2) 69-11-86, 69-18-54,*
69-38-75, 69-14-25.

Government Agencies

Office of the President

Presidence de la Republique
El Mouradia
Algiers, Algeria
☎ *[213] (2) 60-03-60*

Office of the Prime Minister

Palais du Governement
Algiers, Algeria
☎ *[213] (2) 63-23-40*

Ministry of Defense

Avenue des Tagarins
Algiers, Algeria
☎ *[213] (2) 61-15-15*

Ministry of Foreign Affairs

6 Rue 16n Batran
El Mouradia
Algiers, Algeria
☎ *[213] (2) 60-47-44*

Press Agencies and Newspapers

Reuters

6 Boulevard Mohamed Khemisti
Algiers, Algeria
☎ [213] (2) 64-46-77

Associated Press (AP)

4 Avenue Pasteur, BP 769
Algiers, Algeria
☎ [213] (2) 63-59-41

Agence France Presse (AFP)

6 Rue Khettabi
Algiers, Algeria
☎ [213] (2) 63-37-02

Selima Ghezali or Djamal Labidi

La Nation
33B Rue Larbi Ben M'Hidi
Algiers, Algeria
☎ [213] (2) 61-94-03

Mohamed Allouache

El-Houria
33 Rue Larbi Ben M'Hidi
Algiers, Algeria
☎ [213] (2) 61-58-14

Le Matin

1 Rue Bechir Attar
Hussein-Dey
Algiers, Algeria
☎ [213] (2) 66-30-13/14

Omar Belhouchet

Director
El Watan
1 Rue Bechir Attar
Algiers, Algeria
☎ [213] (2) 66-26-41/42/44

Athman Senadjki

Editor-in-chief
El Khabar
1 Rue Bechir Attar
Algiers, Algeria
☎ [213] (2) 66-19-31/32

Algerian Press Service (APS)

20 Rue Zouieche
Kouba
Algiers, Algeria
☎ [213] (2) 68-05-30

06/05/1997	President Liamine Zeroual's government is re-elected; the FIS is banned from participating in the polls.
05/05/1995	Islamic extremists kill five foreigners working at a pipe mill at an industrial zone in the Ghardaia region of northern Algeria. The victims were identified as two Frenchmen, a Canadian, a Brit and a Tunisian.
12/1991	The first parliamentary elections ever held in Algeria are won by Muslim fundamentalists. The elections were nulled by the government, tossing Algeria into civil war.
04/20/1980	Berber spring. Berber ethnic protests are held in Tizi Ouzou.
08/20/1955	Algerian independence fighters launch their first armed offensive against French forces in eastern Algeria.
11/08/1942	U.S. and British forces land in North Africa.

ALGERIA

Bougainville
★★★
Jungle Boogie

The island of Bougainville is really part of the North Solomons, a name that is more indicative of its true geographic and ethnic alignment than its current position as an Eastern outpost of Papua New Guinea (PNG). True, PNG is an autonomous country, but Australia business interests call the shots and cash the checks here. There is a lot of potential wealth in PNG, but it needs big cash to punch the big holes it takes to pull out the buried mineral wealth Something the T-shirt, flip flop wearing natives don't have a lot of.

Western history of the islands started when Louis Antoine de Bougainville generously gave his name to the big island (and the colorful thorny flowering bush that comes from the region.). When he approached the smaller island to the north he was greeted by cheers of "buka buka" which loosely translated means "what? what?" He promptly named the island Buka.

The lush islands were traded like baseball cards between the French, British, Germans, Japanese and Australians without anyone bothering to ask the locals their opinion until, in 1964, copper was discovered in Panguna.

Overnight, Bougainville copper created an instant metropolis and the money flowed—flowing out of Bougainville and into Australian and PNG pockets. Laborers and technicians were flown in to work the mine, but only one in five of the 4000 laborers was a foreigner. Although a few folks benefited, the quality of life for the people actually decreased as pollution from the mine began to destroy their pristine homeland.

In 1987, the Panguna Landowners Association led by Pepetua Sereo and Francis Ona was formed and they wanted their slice: $10 billion dollars and back payment of mine profits. A year later after they were rebuked, the Bougainville Revolutionary Army was formed and the mine began to experience a number of shut downs due to demonstrations, attacks and sabotages.

The mine was shut down in 1989 and the army was sent in to clear things up. Large numbers of people were rounded up and moved to 40 "Care Centers" or concentration camps. The press was kept out to make sure the word "civil war" didn't hit the papers. A recent sprinkling of gonzo journos have snuck into the south to tell the real story.

So far it is estimated that 7000–10,000 citizens and soldiers have been killed in this conflict with neither side offering an accurate body count. The blockade caused the expected suffering and deaths among the 12,000 non-combatant population as well. In 1997, the situation came to a head as London-based Sandlines brought in the mining companies' best friend: mercenaries from Executive Outcomes (fresh from their successful handiwork in Sierra Leone) to do a little surgical killing.

The tables turned when the Army locked them up and mutinied. They were incensed that the government would spend $34 million on a contract for 40 South African mercenaries complete with infrared equipped helicopter gunships instead of on equipment for them. For now things have become more conciliatory between PNG and BRA, and the military blockade has been lifted.

Bougainville could be considered the ultimate tropical getaway: No crowded hotels, no beach vendors and the thrill ride of a lifetime as you cross open water dodging gunships and machine gun equipped speedboats. The mine used to provide 45 percent of PNG's folding green but for now it's just a big hole in the ground as homespun rebels keep the army at bay.

Bougainville Revolutionary Army (BRA)

Former truck driver Francis Ona and his BRA are a rag-tag group of determined rebels who are forcing concessions from the main government in PNG. The Bougainville Interim Government (BIG), affiliated to the BRA, declared independence in May of 1990. The PNG Government reacted by imposing a complete economic and communications blockade. For now the rebels are fighting a bush war without any outside help. The island of Bukato is under government control as are many areas of the island of Bougainville, but the BRA still controls areas in the south and center of the island. At last count 67,300 Bougainvilleans are currently living in 49 government-run Care Centres in Bougainville. The BRA have taken hostages (usually Government defence soldiers) and have been accused of executions.

Francis Ona

The top banana is former surveyor for BCL, Francis Ona. He has come up in the world if you consider the $200,000 bounty on his head. You can find him in Guava (a local word for big hole) near the mine and about 30 miles from Akampos. Guava is now the headquarters for the new "Republic of Bougainville."

Papua New Guinea Defence Force (PNGDF)

There are about 750 soldiers on the island of Bougainville. Forcibly retired General Jerry Singirok, who led the expulsion of Executive Outcomes mercenaries, believes they can whup the BRA mano-a-mano, but won't get the chance now that he has resigned.

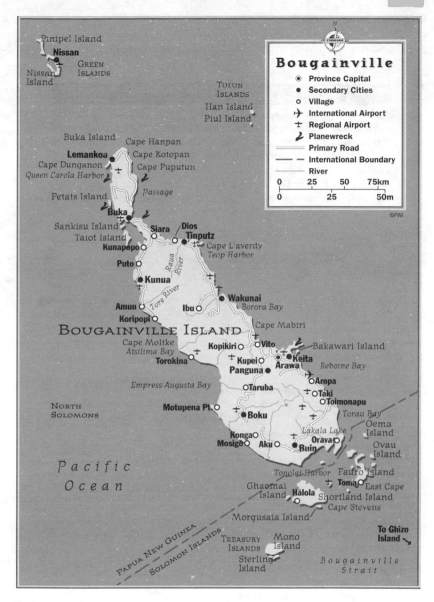

The Panguna Mine

The Bougainville Copper Mine (BCL) in Panguna sits high in the clouds. This huge open pit mine is jointly owned by the PNG Government and the Australian mining company CRA (Conzinc Rio Tinto). In November 1988, the BRA blew up power pylons and other installations forcing operations to shut down. When the BRA began to attack government offices and non-Bougainvilleans, PNG Riot Squad Police were deployed in December, 1988, followed by three companies of regular PNGDF troops which arrived in March 1989.

The Aussies

Dr. P. van Rooyen sent a polite letter on to a Cairns hospital on behalf of Sandlines a contractor with the PNG Government he said he was "constructing a medical scheme" for its employees.

Jap Crap

If you do make the trip to Bougainville you might want to visit a piece of history. Near the village of Aku (24 kms before Buin) about an hour walk from the road, lies the wreckage of Japanese Admiral Yamamoto's Betty Bomber. He was shot down April 18, 1943 by U.S. P-38's. All around the island are other relics of WWII. Buin is full of Japanese equipment and fortifications. A downed and very dead American pilot was found in his Corsair in 1968 just half a kilometer from Buin-Kangu Hill road. The mangrove swamps on Sohano island near the Buka passage to the north are also full of old equipment including a Japanese fighter. Green Island was a dumping ground for U.S. equipment after the war.

Although Papua New Guinea is half of the second largest island in the world, you won't be visiting PNG. You, my adventurous friend, have to sneak in from the Solomons to the south which is a British protectorate where all you need is the usual passport, onward/return ticket, proof of sufficient funds, yadda yadda, yadda. You can get a visitor's permit for a two months stay in one-year period. For more information, consult the British Embassy.

The army has run PR tours for compliant journos in the north island of Buka. About half a dozen journalists have snuck in from the south to see the situation firsthand but the PNG government would love to get their hands on them and make the OJ trial look like a summer re-run. Most infiltrators start on the island of Ghizo in the New Georgia Islands (part of the Western Province of the Solomons). In the town of Gizo (a town of about 5000 people) there is a church and a hospital. Both are critical, the Bishop at the church to get in and the hospital if you have to come out fast. The rebels bring their wounded to Gizo, get supplies and hang out. The church also has a powerful radio to contact the rebels. Here you will be six hours from Bougainville. It doesn't really get hairy until you clear the island of Vella and enter PNG waters.

For more information on the Solomons contact the nearest British Consulate General: CA ☎ *(310) 477-3322*, GA ☎ *(404) 524-5856*, IL ☎ *(312) 346-1810*, MA ☎ *(617) 437-7160*, NY ☎ *(212) 752-8400*, OH ☎ *(216) 621-7674* or TX ☎ *(713) 659-6210*.

British Embassy

19 Observatory Circle, N.W.,
Washington, D.C. 20008, ☎ *(202) 986-0205.*

If you visit the rebels, you go in by boat and come out by boat. On the island, you walk or hitch a ride on the coconut oil powered Toyotas. (You need about ten coconuts to equal one liter of diesel). There is a good road around the west side of the island but when the rains hit, you have to ford the rivers. Bring as much as you can in for gifts or sustenance unless you really like bananas, tapioca and yams.

BOUGAINVILLE

Like we said, you go in by boat and you go out by boat. It isn't any safer running the blockade in or out.

The South Island

Although the PNG government has eased off a bit, it doesn't mean they might get aggressive again. The BRA are hit and run specialists, but the Aussie mercenary pilots can lay down a hell of wallop with their gunships. The rebel headquarters are in Guava, a mountainous village in the center of the island.

Port Moresby, PNG

As if it matters, there is a major crime problem with "rascals" or thugs in the main cities of PNG. There is also rape, robbery, car jacking, theft, mugging and the usual symptoms of primitive society forced to deal with Batman T-shirts and the Spice Girls. If you want more background call the Embassy Duty Officer at ☎ *(675) 321-1455, FAX: (675) 321-1593*, If you get thumped or waylaid call ☎ *(675) 693-8799* for help.

Our hard working embassy in-country tells us not to patronize disreputable bars, proposition women, stay out after midnight or visit cemeteries, dead end streets or the remote bush. If you would like this in the crystal clear language of our government: "PNG is experiencing incomplete transition from subsistence agriculture" in a country that has "unifying elements that are counterbalanced by social strains." Thanks guys.

Being a Buka

An average of three islanders die every day from starvation, sickness or warfare. It is said that the Bukas are the darkest skinned people in the world.

Have guns will travel

Executive Outcomes or EO flashes a card almost identical to TV's Paladin or a knight chess piece. The company's form of security for mining operations is part of a new trend in "outsourcing security services to stabilize entire countries as evidenced in Angola and Sierra Leone. When PNG PM Julius Chan brought in the hired guns he neglected to tell folks that he actually owned a piece of a mining security firm that took care of some nasty business in PNG. Well enough dirt, what do you get for $36 million (up from the original fixed price of $32 million) these days? Well, first you get an ever so euphemistic proposal with statements like: "This operation is highly sensitive and needs to be carried out with a precision that will completely disable the enemy command structure with minimum collateral damage in order to make it acceptable to the Government and people of PNG and to world opinion."

Have guns will travel

Nicely put but how exactly do you snuff out the fuzzy haired little buggers so the big boys can cash their checks?

"To achieve this, the military imperative is the ability to gather high-grade, specific intelligence about the location, capacity and intentions of the enemy force, particularly their C3I assets and match that intelligence with a strike capability, the key ingredients of which are: firepower, mobility, precision, speed and surprise." What this means is that EO's air wing will bring in one fixed wing aircraft carrying $4 million worth of electronic eavesdropping and sensing gizmos to take pictures and record sounds and then send in troops and helicopter gunships to wax the leaders. Soldiers would be paid around $13,000 a month and get full medical and insurance benefits and rapid evacuation via EO's jet aircraft to Australian hospitals.

The PNG Government had to pony up all logistic support including fuel, accommodation, food and medical support for all personnel. It also included three secret trips by team leader and now jailbird Tim Spicer.

The deposit of $15 million was cashed. The mercs are all back here killing time instead of islanders.

Hey, you're on a tropical island with no sanitation and no doctors. What could go wrong? It might be illuminating to know that of the 80,000 Japanese troops on these islands during WWII, 23,000 were taken prisoner, 20,000 were killed, but a staggering 37,000 died of starvation and disease. Malaria is a major problem. If you need help there is a tiny clinic in Akampos, but you best get off the island to Gizo for anything more than a Band-Aid.

There are no nuts or bolts. You bring everything in, you eat disgusting food, you hope you get out alive. There is no electricity unless provided by generator. As in the great words from *Gilligan's Island;* no phones, no lights no motor cars, not a single luxury. Even money is a curiosity. Bougainville is 200 km long and an average of 80 km wide, yet there are 19 different languages spoken. Thankfully, a pidgin form of English is one of them. It is only 20 km from the Solomons but is connected politically to PNG. It is mountainous terrain covered with tropical jungle, complete with misty mountains and steaming vents. The highest point is actually an active volcano. which adds a bit of drama to the whole affair. Most of the 156,000 residents live along the coast with about 12,000 people living in the embargoed area of south Bougainville.

Embassy/Contacts

The Solomons are a British protectorate. Passport, onward/return ticket and proof of sufficient funds required. Visitors permit issued on arrival for stay up to two months in one-year period. For further information, consult the British Embassy at:

☎ *(202) 986-0205*

Papua New Guinea Embassy

3rd Floor, 1615 New Hampshire Avenue, NW, Washington, D.C. 20009
☎ *(202) 745-3680, FAX: (202) 745-3679.*

Embassy of the United States of America

P.O. Box 1492
Port Moresby, Papua New Guinea
☎ 321-1455, FAX: 321-3423.

Papua New Guinea Consulate

Suite 2700, 145 King Street West
Toronto, Ontario M5H 1J8
☎ (416) 865-0470,
FAX: (416) 865-9636.tan

Bougainville Freedom Movement

Sasha Baer or Vikki John
P.O. Box 134, Erskineville NSW 2043,
Australia
http://www.magna.com.au/~sashab/
BFM.htm

Bougainville Interim Government—Australia

Moses Havini, Australian Representative

34 Darvall Road Eastwood 2122
NSW, Australia
☎/FAX: [61] (02) 804 7602

Rosemarie Gillespie, Overseas Research Officer

24 Garling Street
Lyneham ACT 2602 Australia
☎ [61] (6) 257-1298

Bougainville Interim Government—Solomon Islands

Martin Miriori
Netherlands
☎ [31] (55) 577-99-60,
FAX: [31] (55) 577-99-39
C\O Robin Sluyk e-mail:
unponl@antenna.nl

4/15/1997	Day that Executive Outcomes would be ready to swing into action.
1/30/1996	Rebel leaders and their delegation are ambushed returning by boat to Bougainville from the Cairns peace talks.
4/17/1990	The Republic of Bougainville declares its independence.

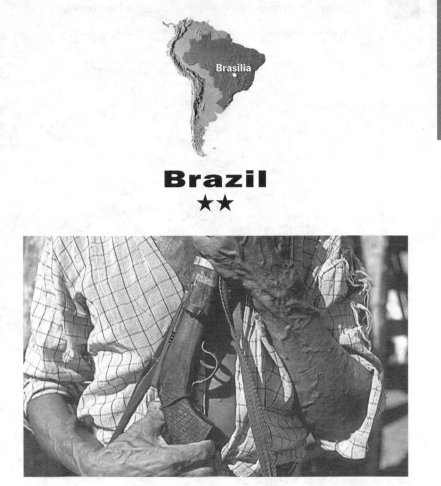

Brasilia

Brazil
★ ★

Street Kids Named Desire

Imagine a country where the most dangerous criminals are those that are supposed to protect you; a place where you are always the prisoner. Could it be Hell?
Close. It's Brazil, where the most dangerous people are cops, anyone who ever
was a cop, and anyone who's ever thought of becoming a cop—not to mention
all off-duty cops. Four policemen and the brother-in-law of one of the officers
were arrested in August 1994 for the murders of eight young boys (the youngest
was eight) outside the Candelaria Church, a popular Rio tourist attraction. In
April 1997, 17 cops went on trial for the massacre of 21 residents of a shantytown
in Rio. The victims' crime? Living in a neighborhood where some police officers
were killed.

Rio de Janeiro is a continuing source of petty crimes committed by street kids
barely out of pajamas. Shopkeepers pay the cops to pick off the toddler thieves
like coyotes on a Wyoming sheep farm. About five children are murdered a day,
according to the University of São Paulo. Treated like vermin, most street urchins
have a short life span. Many work for drug dealers; they sniff glue and gasoline to

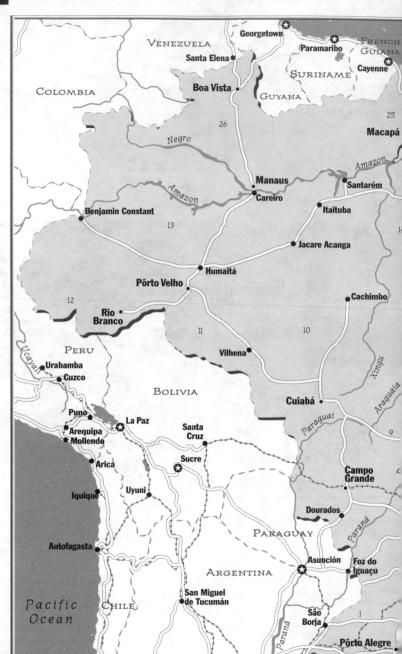

Atlantic Ocean

Brazil

- ✪ National Capital
- ⊙ State Capital
- ● Secondary City
- — State Border
- ═══ Primary Road
- ═══ Secondary Road
- ┣━┣━┣ Railroad

0   250   500   750 km
0   250   500 mi

©FWI

Belém
São Luís
Santa Inês
24
Fortaleza
Teresina
Pôrto Franco
22
Picos
21
Natal
20
João Pessoa
Miracema do Norte
23
19
Recife
Juázeiro
18
17
Maceió
Tocantins
15
Barreiras
16
Aracaju
rupi
Ibotirama
São Francisco
Salvador
Brasília
Vitória de Conquista
oiânia
Pirapora
Montes Claros
Pôrto Seguro
berlândia
8
7
Belo Horizonte
Vitória
5
Volta Redonda
o Paulo
Niterói
Rio de Janeiro
ritiba
Santos
Florianópolis
io

States of Brazil

1. Rio Grande do Sul
2. Santa Catarina
3. Paraná
4. Mato Grosso do Sul
5. São Paulo
6. Rio de Janeiro
7. Espírito Santo
8. Minas Gerais
9. Goiás
10. Mato Grosso
11. Rondônia
12. Acre
13. Amazonas
14. Pará
15. Tocantins
16. Bahia
17. Sergipe
18. Alagoas
19. Pernambuco
20. Paraíba
21. Rio Grande do Norte
22. Ceara
23. Piauí
24. Marnahão
25. Amapa
26. Roraima

Note: Brasília is surrounded by a federal district

kill their hunger pangs. There is little sympathy on behalf of Rio's citizenry for these prepubescent dope peddlers, and it's unlikely that the police, who knock them off on a regular basis, will be convicted for what is generally viewed as a socially beneficial act.

Is is estimated that there are 7 million kids living on the streets in Brazil. Hunted by death squads like rats in a sewer, they subsist by begging, stealing and deionizing themselves on petrol-based solvents. Are they a threat? You bet.

Other criminals in Brazil fall under the umbrella of nebulous quasi-terrorists. One street gang, with visions of sugarplums and Abu Nidal, menacingly calls itself the Commando Vermelho (Red Command). This "terrorist" group strikes in a sporadic fashion, but its actions are essentially criminal activities. In fact, the Red Command may be no more than a gang operating under a *nom de guerre*. And the absence of any identifiable pattern in the crimes suggests most are the work of individuals rather than any organized group.

There's a huge difference in living standards between the developed south of Brazil and the northeast. Consequently, there has been massive migration to Rio's and São Paulo's slums. This has caused a sharp increase in urban violence. A group of neo-Nazi nasties called *Carecas do Brasil* (Skinheads of Brazil) operate with two other extremist clubs out of São Paulo and specialize in brutally beating *Nordestinos* (northeasterners) along with Jews, blacks and gays, not to mention murdering street kids.

The poverty-stricken lower classes have essentially seen zero benefits from the past growth of the economy. About half of all Brazilians are black, and they make, on average, about half of what the whites make. In Brazil, nearly one-fifth of the population is illiterate. The country also has one of the world's most disparate income distributions: 60 percent of the national wealth is possessed by one percent of the population, with maybe 50 percent of the population living in poverty. Since World War II, the purchasing power of Brazil's minimum wage has been cut in half. Because of widespread inefficiency and corruption, only eight percent of the government's social spending reaches the poorest of the population. In Rio, poor families have become squatters on empty lots and in abandoned and partially completed housing complexes. Brazil's underbelly is also being corroded by the spread of drug abuse and such diseases as AIDS, bubonic plague and cholera—a few good reasons for a lot of crime.

You might expect a little mayhem in a country where 20 percent of the population lives in extreme poverty and another 20 percent is said the be "barely surviving." In one nine-month period, there were 6012 murders in Rio alone—a 10-percent rise over the same period the previous year. On the city's "Day of Peace" in November 1995, there were 24 murders in greater Rio, a city of 6 million—which equals one murder an hour. About 90 percent of all the violent crimes in the city are committed against or by minors. Most of the violence can be linked to drugs and theft. Teenage drug bosses have set up their narco shops in the *favelas*, the slums in Rio's surrounding hillsides, and loaf around in sandals toting automatic rifles. In February 1997, police found a gang of street kids in possession of an anti-tank rocket launcher, anti-tank rockets and machine guns. Eeks! Such weaponry might help explain the ease Brazilians enjoy stealing cars. Auto thefts average a staggering 3000 per month in Rio. Banks are also a target. Since 1995, more than 770 banks in Rio have been robbed—of more than US$40 million.

The street kids, or "street urchins," are often themselves the target of death squads. In the first five months of 1997, 239 children between the ages of 7 and 16 were murdered in São Paulo, a huge jump over 1996. During all of that year, 337 kids were whacked. About 80 percent of the kids murdered in Brazil live in squalor, and more than 90 percent are connected to the cocaine trade. In Rio, the scene is even uglier. Between 1987 and 1997, some 6000 street kids were murdered by death squads.

Between 1990 and 1995, there were 568 kidnappings in Rio, something prepubescent dope peddlers like to do when cash and stash run low. Although it is improving in both efficiency and honesty, Rio's 18,000-man police force is so corrupt that the families of kidnap victims rarely report the crime and privately pay off the ransoms themselves. Have fun at Carnival!

Try, Try Again

A mathematics teacher, down on his luck, attempted suicide July 9, 1997 by detonating a bomb he was carrying aboard a TAM airliner. The blast killed another passenger, who was sucked out of the aircraft, but not the bomber himself. Not pegged as the culprit, the man was set free, only to wind up in a São Paulo hospital the next day–still quite alive–after being run down by a bus in another suicide attempt.

Hit Squads

Despite their reputation for tardiness and diffidence in daytime law enforcement, the Military Police are famous for off-hours overzealousness. Human rights groups estimate there are two police-committed killings a day on average in Brazil. About 200 police officers are fired every year for their participation in organized kidnapping, corruption and death squads. The Vigario Geral shantytown massacre on August 30, 1994 is probably the most famous example of their devotion to cleaning up the streets. That night 21 men, women and children were murdered by at least 30 masked gunmen believed to be police officers acting in vengeance for four officers killed two days earlier in the shanty town.

But while the Policia Militar (usually retired or off-duty police officers) spend their off-hours in hit squads eliminating street kids, the hit squads are being hunted by other less violent but equally eager hit squads. Brazil has created a force to police the police force, a federal police unit tasked with investigating and eliminating death squads all over the country. Death squads and drug traffickers are considered major contributors to Rio's murder rate of more than 60 per every 100,000 people.

Rather then retaining attorneys to handle legal matters, Brazilians prefer hit men. The tab reads like a restaurant menu. Want to off an impoverished peasant? This week's special is only US$70. But if you want to take out a prominent politician, expect to pay for the caviar: about US$20,000. About half of the 12 killings a day in São Paulo are contract snuffings.

Teenage Drug Gangs

Prepubescent drug gangs in Rio are involved in an estimated 90 percent of all the city's violent crimes. Hundreds of drug dealers operate in the hillside slums ringing the city. A popular activity for the teens these days is setting street people on fire. During a two-month period in 1997, street kids set at least four people ablaze, killing all of them.

A passport and visa are required. Tourist visas are valid for 90 days, must be obtained in advance, and are free of charge (although there is a US$20 processing fee levied on Americans). Minors (under 18) traveling alone, with one parent or with a third party, must present written authorization by the absent parent(s) or legal guardian, specifically granting permission to travel alone, with one parent or a third party. This authorization must be notarized, authenticated by the Brazilian embassy or consulate, and translated into Portuguese. If you are caught entering illegally, you must leave the country voluntarily within three to eight days. The Ministry of Justice can hold you for 90 days before deporting you.

For current information concerning entry and customs requirements for Brazil, travelers can contact the following:

Brazilian Embassy

3006 Massachusetts Avenue N.W.
Washington, D.C. 20008
☎ *(202) 745-2700*
FAX (202) 745-2827

Brazil also has consulates in Los Angeles, San Francisco, Houston, Miami, New York, Chicago and San Juan.

DANGEROUS PLACES

Rio

Rio likes to party, so it's no surprise that the areas surrounding beaches, discos, bars, nightclubs and other similar establishments are dangerous, especially at dusk and during the evening hours. Prime targets in Rio are the popular beaches and neighborhoods of Copacabana and Leme.

São Paulo

There were 4500 murders in São Paulo in 1996, giving the city a murder rate of 6.9 homicides for every 100,000 people. However, crimes of opportunity—such as larceny, purse snatching, armed street robbery, car theft and carjackings—pose the greatest threat to foreign visitors in São Paulo. Most foreign visitors dress differently and do not speak the local language, increasing their chance of being recognized as a foreigner and, therefore, perceived as an easier target for criminals.

Recife

A crime wave has broken out in this northwestern city, the capital of Pernambuco state. Goons and bullies have started boldly stopping cars on Recife's main streets and robbing motorists. Pedestrians are being assaulted and shops broken into. Armed thugs have been machine-gunning ATMs. Much of it's due to continuing police strikes.

Ciudad del Este, Paraguay

This smugglers' boomtown is technically in Paraguay along the border with Brazil and Argentina, but may as well be in Brazil. This is a major base for drug traffickers smuggling Bolivian cocaine via hidden landing strips cut out of the jungle. More than US$12 billion moves through here a year. As the Brazilian drug lords have been pushed out of the shantytowns of Rio, they've found a convenient base in Ciudad del Este. In fact, this place has it all—murder, mayhem and even Islamic fundamentalist guerrillas, who are suspected of using the city to launch bombing attacks against Israeli and Jewish targets in Argentina. There are about 200 murders a year in this city of 100,000, most of the executions identical in appearance with Brazilian gangland slayings. It costs US$500 to bribe a customs official in Ciudad del Este, and a bogus passport can be had for US$5000. The city is also a channel for smuggled electronics goods and computers from Miami and stolen cars from Brazil. It's estimated that half the cars on Paraguay's roads were stolen in Brazil.

Ciudad del Este is a tax-free center and popular with Paraguayans for its bargains on consumer goods. The 400-yard bridge is usually packed with trucks and passenger cars stuffed with brand-new goods bought in Brazil. It is also a great place to pick up bogus U.S. dollars, antiaircraft guns, rare and endangered animals, weapons, and drugs. The area is also called the "Triangle"—the frontier area between Argentina, Brazil and Paraguay—a South American Barbary Coast rough-and-ready area with a Shia Muslim community of about 6000 people. Lebanese, Syrians and Iranians came here in the early 1980s and brought with them a New World cell of Hezbollah. Hezbollah trains local recruits in the jungles around the main city of Foz do Iguacu and gets its support from both the local merchants and Iran.

Brazil's Roads

Brazil possesses the world's worst highway safety record. More than 50,000 people are killed and another 350,000 injured every year on Brazil's roadways. To put things in perspective, the U.S. has 10 times as many vehicles as Brazil—198 million to Brazil's 20 million—but only about 41,000 traffic deaths each year. At least a third of Brazil's 50 million motorists don't have a drivers license. How bad is it? At an Indy-car Grand Prix in Rio a few years ago, Brazilian veteran race driver Emerson Fittipaldi took a helicopter to the track.

Kidnapping

Kidnapping in Rio and São Paulo has become a pastime in the last few years. And it's as easy as stealing an apple off a produce cart. Reported kidnappings doubled annually in the mid-90s. Authorities believe the actual number was far greater. Many in Brazil have no faith in the police to handle kidnapping situations competently and successfully. It's part of a vicious cycle, giving kidnappers the confidence for carrying out their activities.

Police Strikes

In 1997, police strikes spread to 15 of Brazil's 27 states. Police, more than 30,000 of them, have been demanding higher wages, which typically start at below the poverty level. And it seems that everyone is taking advantage of the picketing policemen. Robbers hit eight banks in Recife in one day. Motorists have been parking in restricted zones and barrelling the wrong way down one-way streets. Police in Brazil make between $74 and $384 a month. This has not only attracted less desirable candidates for the country's forces, but also increased corruption. The flunky flatfoots have been clashing with army troops sent in to replace them.

Organized Crime

Some 65 mafia leaders from the Cosa Nostra, Camorra, N'Drangheta and La Sacra Corona Unita mobs have bases of operations in Brazil. Most of the mobsters make Rio their headquarters. Sixteen mob bosses have been jailed in the past four years in Brazil;

12 were arrested in Rio. The crooks have been taking advantage of Brazil's chaotic three year economic program and the lack of legislation against organized crime. The Italians aren't the only boys in town. Gangsters from Russia, Korea, Japan and Nigeria have also set up shop in Brazil.

Land Disputes

During 1995 and 1996, 1.3 million people were involved in 1304 violent incidents over land disputes in Brazil, 750 in 1996 alone. That's the highest number since 1985. More than 112 people have been killed since 1995, and 976 have died between 1985 and 1996. This isn't difficult to imagine in a country where one-fifth of the population owns 90 percent of the land.

Body Parts

The business of murder for body parts is thriving in Brazil. Even public health hospitals have been allegedly running body parts businesses. Homeless street kids are abducted and slain for kidneys, livers and other viscera that hasn't rotted from glue.

Medical care varies in quality, particularly in remote areas. Cholera has been reported in the Amazon Basin region and northeastern Brazil. Some cholera outbreaks have also been reported in major cities. However, visitors who follow proper precautions about food and drink are not usually at risk.

Brazil has a population of 155 million and possesses the world's largest rainforests. The population is 80 percent Roman Catholic and speaks Portuguese, Spanish, English and French. The climate ranges from tropical to semitropical with a temperate zone in the far south. The literacy rate is about 81 percent.

Air service runs efficiently throughout the country, as does railroad service. The telephone system is adequate, particularly in the major cities, including Rio, Brasilia, São Paulo, Recife and Salvador. Taxis abound in most urban areas. Tipping isn't necessary. Taxis are best hired from your hotel. Radio taxis are more reliable, and trustworthy, than meter taxis. When tipping in restaurants, 5 percent is usually considered appropriate.

Don't wear the colors of green and yellow, the colors of Brazil's flag. You'll be instantly pegged as a tourist. Taking the Metro isn't advised. Credit cards are widely accepted except for the remote boonies. The currency is the real, which is roughly equal to the U.S. dollar (1 real=US$1.08). The electrical current is 126V throughout most of the country and 22V in Brasilia. The local time is 3 hours behind GMT.

Emergency Numbers

Local "911-type" police numbers include the following:

Rio tourist police
☎ 511-5112

Fire
☎ 193

Military police (patrol)
☎ 190

Civil police (investigations)
☎ 147

The U.S. embassy is located in Brasilia:
Avenida das Nacoes, Lote 3
☎ [55] (61) 321-7272

There are consulates in the following:

Rio de Janeiro

Avenida Presidente Wilson 147
☎ *[55] (21) 292-7117*

São Paulo

Rua Padre Joao Manoel 933
☎ *[55] (11) 881-6511*

Porto Alegre

Rua Coronel Genuino 421 (9th floor)
☎ *[55] (51) 226-4288*

Recife

Rua Goncalves Maia 163
☎ *[55] (81) 221-1412*

There are also consular agencies in the following:

Belem

Avenida Oswaldo Cruz 165
☎ *[55] (91) 223-0800/0413*

Salvador de Bahia

Avenida Antonio Carlos Magalhaes S/N
Edificio Cidadella Center, Suite 410
Candeal
☎ *[55] (71) 358-9195*

Manaus

Rua Recife 1010, Adrianopolis
☎ *[55] (92) 234-4546*

Fortaleza

Instituto Brasil-Estados Unidos (IBEU)
Rua Nogueira Acioly, 891
Aldeota
☎ *[55] (85) 252-1539.*

Burundi
★★★★★

The Problem

Each day at nightfall in Burundi's capital of Bujumbura, the streets are empty. Grenade blasts (grenades can be had for a mere US$7) and machine-gun fire from both the city and the surrounding hills shatter the night silence. Occasionally, there is screaming and crying. The impression is that you're suddenly being caught in the middle of an invasion. Then, in the morning, it is calm. You're surprised to discover that corpses do not litter the streets. There is little, if any, evidence of fighting. When inquiring among locals about the cause of the evening's disturbance, you will be answered with two words: "Burundi's problem." It would seem "the Switzerland of Africa" has a bit of a problem. A problem that has existed for over 30 years.

It wasn't always like this. The Twa pygmies used to live in peace under the triple canopy rain forest. The pastoral Bantu Hutus migrated into this fertile region and were followed by the tall nomadic Tutsis. The Tutsi immediately showed the less warlike folks how things should be run and gained the favor of the colonial masters.

Burundi endured one of Africa's worst tribal wars in 1972. War is not the right word. Genocide fits better. It all happened after King Ntaré V returned in April of that year. Usually, when the president of the country promises safe conduct to a returning monarch, the chances are pretty good the red carpet will be rolled out. Well, that wasn't exactly what Burundi President Michel Micombero had in mind for the return of the man he overthrew. Not even a party. No sooner had Ntaré V stepped off the plane than he was judged and executed by Micombero. Hell of a homecoming. What happened afterward defies explanation.

Thousands of invading exiled Hutus attending Ntare V's return to Burundi were slaughtered by the rival Tutsis. But the Tutsis didn't stop there. Over the next eight weeks, nearly a quarter of a million native Burundi Hutus were massacred by the Tutsis. The genocide was followed by coup after coup after coup, until Burundi's first democratically elected leader, Melchior Ndadaye, a Hutu, assumed the presidency in June 1993. All's well that ends well? Hardly.

Tutsi paratroops assassinated Ndadaye on October 21, 1993, abruptly ending the four-month experiment with democracy in the central African state. The pre-dawn coup was led by Army Chief of Staff Colonel Jean Bikomagu and former President Jean Baptiste Bagaza, who was himself overthrown in 1987. The paratroops arrested Ndadaye and detained him at the Muha barracks on the outskirts of Bujumbura before executing him. The coup was the fifth since the country's independence in 1962, and led to unprecedented violence and death. More than 200,000 deaths were caused by the unrest, equaling if not exceeding the casualties that occurred in the 1972 genocide that swept the country. Tribal massacres drove nearly a million Burundians into neighboring countries to escape the slaughter.

The coup collapsed, but it hardly made any difference. Burundi itself had already collapsed. Ethnic fighting between the Hutus and the minority Tutsis, who controlled the military and have dominated politics since Burundi's independence from Belgium in 1962, continued to ravage the country. Pictures revealed hundreds of bodies, devastated towns, destroyed farms and a countryside that had been set on fire. Corpses littered the landscape, after the army stood by and watched as Tutsis and Hutus slaughtered each other. Thousands of Burundians marched through the streets of Bujumbura, urging the remnants of Ndadaye's government to emerge from hiding and lead the country from the chaos caused by the military revolt. As many as 500,000 refugees had fled to Rwanda alone.

The Trash War

The morning was foggy, and we had driven up the slippery slopes from Tanzania. When we camped for the night, we saw no one. Now we were surrounded by a circular wall of people. They pressed in slowly, curious to see what these visitors might have. They began to touch at first, and then grab. Fighting back, we chased them off. As they ran and tripped, they grabbed anything they could pry loose—empty water bottles, scraps of paper. As the bolder ones tried to grab and run back into the crowd, they were immediately pounced upon by other Hutus, who ripped and tore whatever meager trophy they had retrieved until they possessed minuscule scraps in their hands. The Hutus were stealing trash, fighting for trash. As we quickly jumped in our vehicles and drove off, we watched them continue to beat and fight each other for trash until, finally, the battle was lost in the fog.

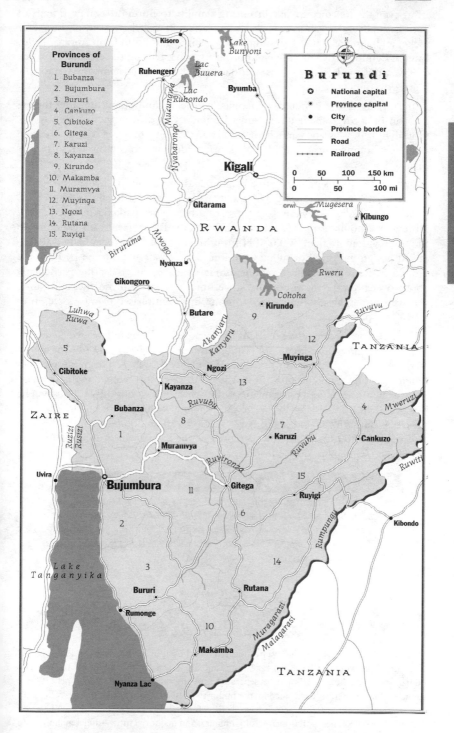

Provinces of Burundi

1. Bubanza
2. Bujumbura
3. Bururi
4. Cankuzo
5. Cibitoke
6. Gitega
7. Karuzi
8. Kayanza
9. Kirundo
10. Makamba
11. Muramvya
12. Muyinga
13. Ngozi
14. Rutana
15. Ruyigi

Burundi

⊕ National capital
⊛ Province capital
● City
Province border
Road
Railroad

0   50   100   150 km
0   50   100 mi

©FWI

But even the foiled coup failed to bring stability to Burundi. The presidents of both Burundi and Rwanda were aboard a plane that was blasted out of the sky by rocket and gun fire as it was landing at Kigali airport in Rwanda on April 6, 1994. Intense fighting broke out in neighboring Rwanda. During the ensuing 14-week civil war in Rwanda, Tutsi rebels swept across the country, decimating the mainly Hutu government.

On April 29, 1994, hundreds of people fled shelling in Bujumbura, after the expiration of a government ultimatum to militants to turn in their weapons. Although Burundi escaped much of the 1995 fighting between the two ethnic groups, Hutu militants of the "People's Army" declined to comply and surrender their weapons.

Violence, perhaps a precursor to a total breakdown in Burundi, again broke out in January 1996, as Burundi government troops attacked a Rwandan Hutu refugee camp and killed 20, wounding scores of others. This sparked a mass exodus of more than 14,000 terrified Hutus who beat tail for Tanzania, already crammed to the brim with more than 700,000 Hutu refugees from both Burundi and Rwanda. Although the Burundi ruling coalition has been sternly warned by both the United Nations and the U.S. about ethnic violence, and the army particularly about overthrowing the precarious government, the raid in northeast Burundi was seen as a highly choreographed attempt in a multiphased plan to force Hutu rebels into permanent exile.

Pierre Buyoya became the president of Burundi in a Tutsi military-backed coup in July '96. Former president and Hutu, Sylvestre Ntibantunganya, hot-footed it to the American ambassador's home, a place we remember well from our pleasant lunch. He didn't emerge until June 1997. Another coincidence is that we also met the new prez (and former major in the army) at a whoop-up in '91 when he was president from 1987–1993. The only change we found was an embargo imposed by Burundi's neighbors. Buyoya's army of some 20,000 men will be busy fighting the 3500 Hutu rebels who represent the 85 percent of Burundians who are Hutu. Gentlemen, sharpen your machetes.

The 1:30 to Paris

Our arrival was not an important event, but reason enough for lunch at the embassy. After a brief tour, including meeting the grizzled marine security officer, we had lunch high up in the hills overlooking Bujumbura. In between polite conversation, a silence would fall as an airliner took off from the airport. Without looking, our hosts would rattle off the flight and carrier, as if repeating a religious chant.

It was much easier when only Twa pygmies lived in the virgin forests. The invasion of Hutus and then Tutsi would make Hitler take notes and force Darwin to rethink his theory. The human species in Burundi should be separated into the quick and the dead. This majority agrarian Hutu nation has been ruled by the minority Tutsis since independence from Belgium in 1962. More than 180,000 people have died in Burundi since 1993 in civil wars between Tutsis, who control the 18,000-man-strong military, and majority Hutus—and a million more made refugees. (According to some estimates, some half a million people are reported to have been killed—mostly Tutsis—in 1994 alone.) Burundi's president, Pierre Buyoya, has been struggling to maintain peace since he was chosen by the military in July 1996 to step back into office after successive Hutu-controlled governments—the last one led by Hutu President Sylvestre Ntibantunganya—failed to restore order in this carnival of massacres. Buyoya first seized power in a 1987 coup and led Burundi to free elections in 1993. Hutu Melchior Ndadaye was elected president but assassinated by Tutsi paratroopers four months later. Then the carnage began.

As part of Buyoya's security plan and in a move reminiscent of South Vietnam's "Strategic Hamlet" program of the 1960s, more than 600,000 people—Hutus and minority Tutsis—have been rounded up by the government and placed in some 200 camps dotting the countryside, to the outrage of the U.S. and the subdued disapproval of the U.N. The Hutus, encamped by force, live a more cramped existence than their fellow Tutsis, who mostly come to the camps by free will in fear of Hutu rebel attacks. For their part, the Hutu rebels that formed the army of the Ndadaye government (and the ex-armed forces of Rwanda and Zaire) are returning to Burundi from their camps and bases in Congo and Tanzani for their revenge. Buyoya is in no mood for compromise, though. He hasn't committed himself to new elections nor one day sharing power with the rebels. Rather, he'd been busy beefing up his 20,000-man army for more bloodshed.

The Hutus

Hutus, Bantu race, comprise about 85 percent of Burundi's population and were the victims of a Tutsi-led mass genocide campaign in 1972. After President Ndadaye was overthrown and executed in an abandoned coup effort in October 1993, the Hutus went on a stampede. When it was over, nearly a quarter million corpses were left in the wake. The leader of the Hutu rebels, the National Council for the Defense of Democracy (CNDD)—its armed wing is called Forces for the Defense of Democracy—is Leonard Nyangoma, a former interior minister.

The Tutsis

The Tutsis are originally Nilotic herdsmen from the north. The Tutsi-led military junta purged the military and bureaucracy of Hutus from 1964–1972. In 1972, a large-scale revolt by the Hutus killed several thousand Tutsis. The Tutsi machine followed with the mass extermination of selected and unselected Hutus. Any Hutu with an education, a decent job or any degree of wealth was arrested and murdered, most in a horrifying fashion. More than 200,000 Hutus were slaughtered in the ensuing three months. The Tutsi army's makeshift trucks could be seen in the streets packed with the mutilated corpses of Hutu victims.

Party for the Reconciliation of the People (PRP)

Led by Mathias Hitimana, now under house arrest, the Hutu dissident group opposes the oppression of the Hutu people by the government. The group, a champion of Hutu dissidents, is a frequent instigator of street clashes with government security forces.

National Liberation Front (NLF)

The armed wing of the Hutu Party of Liberation of the Hutu people is based and prevalent in the northwestern province of Cibitoke. They are hostile to foreigners, especially white expats, and killed three Swiss Red Cross workers when they ambushed and machine gunned a clearly marked Red Cross vehicle in June of '96.

You can get into Burundi by air, road or lake ferry. Keep in mind the airport in Bujumbura opens and closes like an L.A. rave club. By land from Rwanda, you can get in from Butare as well as Bujumbura. Expect to have your belongings searched on both sides of the border. From Zaire, you can get into Burundi from Bakavu via Uvira. You can also get to Bujumbura from Bakavu via Cyangugu in Rwanda. On Lake Tanganyika, you can get in from Tanzania. (Few travelers stay long in Burundi. Most are in transit between Tanzania and Rwanda.) However, at press time, all land crossings were closed to foreigners.

A passport and a visa are required. Only those travelers who reside in countries where there is no Burundian embassy are eligible for entry stamps, without a visa, at the airport upon arrival. These entry stamps are not a substitute for a visa, which must subsequently be obtained from the immigration service within 24 hours of arrival. Visas cost from US$30 to US$60, depending on anticipated length of stay. Travelers who have failed to obtain a visa will not be permitted to leave the country. Multiple entry visas valid for three months are available in Burundian embassies abroad for US$11. Evidence of yellow fever immunization must be presented. Also, visitors are required to show proof of vaccination against meningococcal meningitis. Additional information may be obtained from the following:

Embassy of the Republic of Burundi

2233 Wisconsin Avenue, N.W., Suite 212
Washington, D.C. 20007
☎ *(202) 342-2574*

Permanent Mission of Burundi to the United Nations in New York

☎ *(212) 687-1180*

Burundi has a good network of roads between the major towns and border posts. Travel on other roads is hazardous, particularly in the rainy season. Public transportation to border points is often difficult and frequently unavailable, but it is improving. There has been a proliferation of modern Japanese-made minibuses in recent years. They're usually not terribly crowded and are far less expensive than taxis. These buses leave terminals *(gare routière)* in every town in the early morning through the early afternoon, and depart when they are full. They display their destinations on the windshield. The government-owned OTRACO buses are mainly found in and around the capital of Bujumbura. Total road miles are 3666; 249 of them are paved. There are six airfields in the country, only one with a permanent surface.

The border with Zaire is closed temporarily to prevent Hutu rebels from crossing into Burundi. Route One, the main highway linking Bujumbura with the rest of the country, is frequently closed because of land mines placed by Hutu rebels, usually northeast of the capital. The road is also the site of frequent ambushes. More than 125 people, mostly civilians, were killed in more than 20 ambushes early in 1996.

There is an eight-mile *cordon sanitaire*, or clean line, around the city of Bujumbura as well as a 9 p.m. curfew. Life may go on as normal during the day, but the killing begins at night. As many as 100 people die every week in Burundi, mostly because of attacks by Hutu insurgents who have their bases in the refugee camps in Zaire and because of Army reprisals against local Hutus.

Bujumbura

Sporadic violence remains a problem in the capital, Bujumbura—better known to locals as "Tutsiville," as the Tutsis have slaughtered most of the city's Hutus or sent them fleeing into the hills—as well as in the interior, where large numbers of displaced persons are encamped or in hiding. Renewed warfare in neighboring Rwanda has caused thousands of Rwandans to flee to Burundi and other countries in the region. The U.S. embassy has reiterated the importance of using extreme caution, with no travel to the troubled neighborhoods of the capital and none but essential travel in the city after dark. Armed Tutsi thugs and army soldiers comb the streets after dark, preying on the remaining Hutu militiamen. The Hutus, for the most part, have fled into the surrounding hills and each morning stream down into the capital to go to the market or do other chores before heading back to the hills before dark—to keep from being shot. As one journalist notes: "At 8 p.m., a Burundian must already be where he plans to spend the night." Burundi periodically has closed its land borders without notice and suspended air travel and telephone service in response to political disturbances.

The Border with Tanzania

At least 1500 Hutu rebels surged across the border from their base camps in Tanzania in March and April 1997, and are engaging government forces in the southern provinces of Bururi and Makamba.

Route 7

Strategic Route 7, which snakes southeast from Bujumbura, is closed, due to continued rebel attacks, effectively cutting off the entire south of the country.

Crime

Street crime and muggings in Burundi poses a high risk for visitors. As *DP* knows first hand. Crime involves muggings, purse snatching, pickpocketing, burglary and auto break-ins. Criminals operate individually or in small groups. There have been reports of muggings of persons jogging or walking alone in all sections of Bujumbura, especially on public roads bordering Lake Tanganyika.

Bujumbura U.S. embassy sources report that dangerous areas for criminal activity in Bujumbura are the downtown section, the vicinity of the Novotel and the Source du Nil hotels, and along the shore of Lake Tanganyika. The majority of the criminal incidents in the Burundian capital consist of muggings, purse snatchings, and auto break-ins (to steal the contents).

Mines

Land mines are becoming a very popular way of killing people. They are freshly laid on a nightly basis.

Street Demonstrations and Clashes

Minority Tutsi youths regularly engage with the military and police in street protests in Bujumbura. Although the protests are not anti-U.S. in nature and Americans and other foreigners are rarely targeted, stay off the streets during any public rally. Relatively peaceful demonstrations can turn violent.

Northern Burundi is in the throes of one of the biggest typhus outbreaks since World War II, mostly due to overcrowded camps and unhygienic conditions. The reported cases have surged to more than 20,000 since October 1996, when the outbreak was first observed.

There are 14 hospital beds and 0.5 doctors for every 10,000 people. Yellow fever and cholera immunizations are required. Inoculations for tetanus, typhoid and polio are also recommended, as are gamma globulin shots and malaria suppressants. Doctors and hospitals often expect immediate cash payment for health care services. U.S. medical insurance is not always valid outside the United States. Supplemental medical insurance with specific overseas coverage, including medical evacuation coverage, has proved to be useful. The Center for Disease Control recommends that travelers to Burundi receive the meningococcal polysaccharide vaccine before traveling to the area.

A per-capita annual income of around US$150 makes the country perhaps the poorest in Africa, even more impoverished than neighboring Rwanda. Despite Burundi's tiny size (six and a half million people in 10,747 square miles, the country is divided into 15 provinces, each administered by a civilian governor. The provinces are subdivided into 114 communes, with elected councils in charge of local affairs.

Burundi's climate varies from hot and humid in the area of Lake Tanganyika, with temperatures around 86° F, to cool in the mountainous north, about 68° F. The long rainy season runs from October through May.

Hutus comprise about 85 percent of the population. About 14 percent are Tutsi. Kirundi and French are the official languages; Swahili is also spoken; English is rare. Indigenous religions are held by 34 percent of the population; Roman Catholics make up 61 percent of the population; Protestants account for 5 percent. The literacy rate is about 50 percent.

The currency in Burundi is the Burundi franc (BFr). The electrical current is 220/240V.

Embassy Locations

U.S. Embassy in Burundi
Ave des Etats-Unis
B.P. 34, 1720, Bujumbura
☎ *[257] (2) 22-34-54*
FAX: [257] (2) 22-29-26

Burundian Embassy in United States
2233 Wisconsin Avenue, N.W., Suite 212
Washington, D.C. 20007
☎ *(202) 342-2574*

Burundian Embassy in Canada
151 Slater Street, Suite 800
Ottawa, Ontario, Canada K1P 5H3
☎ *(613) 741-7458*
Telex: (369) 053-3393
FAX: (613) 741-2424

07/25/1996	Pierre Buyoya succeeds Sylvestre Ntibantunganya in a bloodless coup.
04/25/1994	A military coup in Burundi fails when soldiers, fearing the triggering of a tribal bloodbath similar to the one in neighboring Rwanda, refuse to participate in the military mutiny.
04/06/1994	A plane carrying the presidents of both Rwanda and Burundi is shot out of the sky as it attempts to land in Rwanda.
10/28/1993	Evacuations to Bujumbura. Foreigners in Burundi are evacuated to Bujumbura, as concern over tribal violence associated with a failed military coup grows.
10/28/1993	Six government ministers are confirmed murdered during a failed coup in Burundi.
10/21/1993	Paratroops overthrew President Melchior Ndadaye and execute him.
06/02/1993	Melchior Ndadaye becomes Burundi's first democratically elected president.
11/06/1976	Lieutenant Colonel Jean Baptiste Bagaye leads a coup and assumes the presidency, suspending Burundi's constitution.
04/19/1972	Natré V returns to Burundi and is executed by President Micombero, sparking one of the bloodiest wars in African history.

BURUNDI

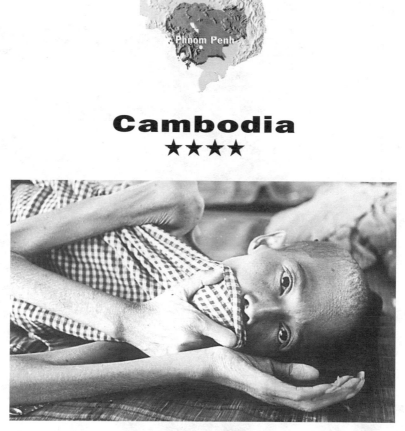

Cambodia
★★★★

Into the Void

It's no longer the Khmer Rouge who are postured for murder, abductions and maiming—but the legitimate political parties locked in a power struggle where anything goes and everything does. Since the UN-supervised elections of 1993, Cambodia has been sinking into a dangerous political free-for-all and a constitutional free-fall. Co-Premiers Hun Sen's and Prince Norodom Ranariddh's respective parties, the formerly communist Cambodian People's Party (CPP) and Funcinpec, have gone to the lowest depths to extort, shame, slander, defile and kill each other as they line up their ducks for elections in '98.

The shit finally hit the fan over the weekend of July 5, 1997, when Hun Sen bitch-slapped Ranariddh and seized sole power of the shredded government in a bloody coup d'etat which killed at least 60 people and caused $76 million in damage to the frail economy. The Phnom Penh airport was once again riddled with bullet holes and mortar blasts. The move cost Cambodia admission into the powerful Asian trade bloc ASEAN and the world a helluva lot more: the $3 billion UN effort in 1993 to bring peace to Cambodia. Pol Pot and the Khmer Rouge

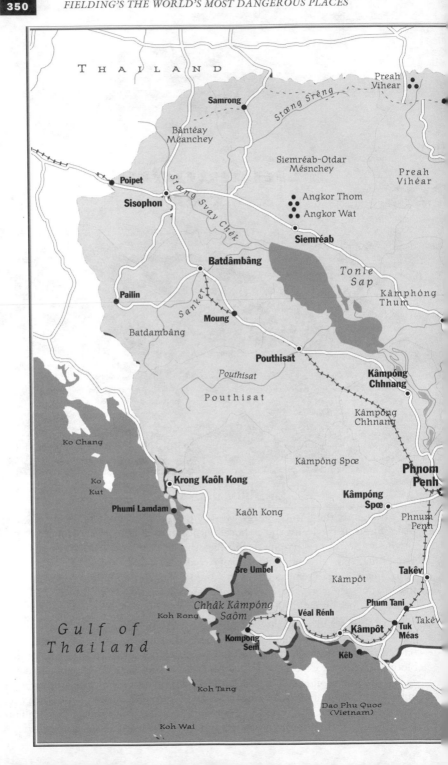

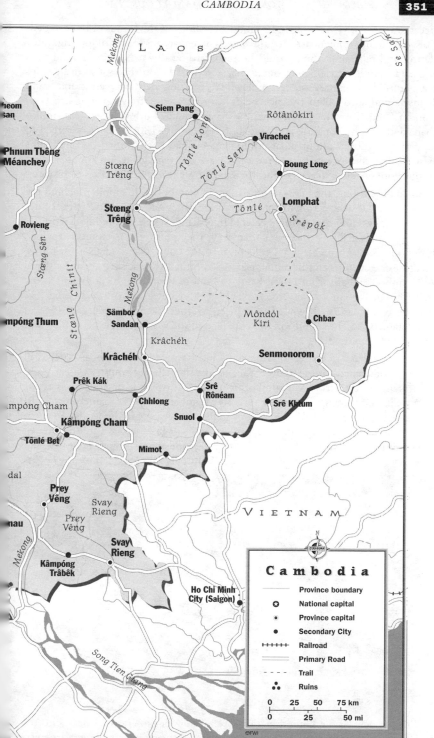

LAOS

Siem Pang

Rôtânôkiri

Virachei

Tônlé Kong

Tônlé San

Boung Long

Stœng Trêng

Lomphat

Tônlé

Srêpôk

Phnum Tbêng Méanchey

Rovieng

Stœng Trêng

Stœng Sên

Stœng Chinit

Mekong

Sämbor

Môndól Kiri

Chbar

mpóng Thum

Sandan

Krâchéh

Senmonorom

Krâchéh

Prêk Kák

Srê Rônéam

Chhlong

Srê Khtum

mpóng Cham

Snuol

Kâmpóng Cham

Mimot

Tônlé Bet

dal

Prey Vêng

Svay Rieng

nau

Prey Vêng

VIETNAM

Svay Rieng

Mekong

Kâmpóng Trâbêk

Ho Chi Minh City (Saigon)

Song Tien Giang

Cambodia

— Province boundary
⊛ National capital
• Province capital
● Secondary City
+++++ Railroad
— Primary Road
- - - Trail
⁚ Ruins

| 0 | 25 | 50 | 75 km |
| 0 | | 25 | 50 mi |

©FWI

became a sideshow, first time in Cambodian politics, as thousands of Phnom Pen-hoise, including soldiers, took to the streets in a covetous frenzy of looting, mur-dering and pillaging. Tanks could be seen rattling down Norodom Boulevard packed to turret with stolen refrigerators, stereos and motorbikes. Car dealerships were gutted as military officers hot-wired spanking new Mercedes and Land Cruisers and sped off to the rice fields. Corpses were strewn in the streets of Phnom Penh. Terrorized tourists and expats hightailed it for the Hotel Cambo-diana and, finally, Bangkok and Singapore. Aboard C-130s, they were forced to land at an airport without radar equipment—it had been swiped by Hun Sen's best. Bullets and rockets ricocheted off the ancient temples at Angkor as soldiers of both sides sought solace behind the fabled bulkheads of 900 years of history.

Greed has become the new face of danger in Cambodia. It's hidden behind the fancy and bombastic acronyms of its political parties and the sound bytes of de-mocracy spewed by corruption's elected guardians. When the middle-aged little boys in Windsor knots don't get their way, they pull out their guns, in which Cambodia is awash. Just a few weeks prior to the coup, Cambodia's most prom-inent businessman, Teng Boonma, got pissed off with the service aboard a Royal Air Cambodge flight from Hong Kong to Phnom Penh. Did he complain at the ticket counter upon arrival? No. Instead, he shot out a tire of the Boeing 737 with his bodyguard's AK while the Pratt & Whitneys were still spinning. He was not detained. So Hun Sen took the cue, flipped the world the bird and blew out the tires of democracy.

Anywhere that a hundred of Interpol's most wanted fugitives can safely call home is somewhere you wouldn't want to live. Perhaps no country on earth has so brutally suffered from as many forms of conflict over the past 35 years as has Cambodia. Civil wars, border wars, massive bombardment via a superpower's B-52s, a deforestation rate considered unparalleled anywhere in the world, an auto-genicide unprecedented in its savagery—effectively eliminating a full quarter of the country's population—and, now, a failed, blood-soaked experiment with de-mocracy have ravaged this once proud and culturally influential empire.

With the help of the United Nations, Cambodia began crawling back into the world on its knees in 1993, literally, as so many of the country's citizens are missing limbs after accidental encounters with one of the perhaps 6–10 million land mines still buried beneath the countryside's topsoil. And those not missing arms or legs are most assuredly missing relatives, victims of Pol Pot's murderous Khmer Rouge regime of the mid- and late 1970s. The Khmer Rouge was responsible for perhaps two million deaths between 1975 and 1979. Many of Pol Pot's victims who survived the genocide today roam Phnom Penh's trash-laden boulevards like zombies out of a George Romero film. Some are hideously disfigured; nearly all are penniless and they follow Western tourists like gulls behind a shrimper, begging for handouts.

In many areas across the lush Khmer countryside, bones spring from the earth like desert cacti, still shrouded with the tattered garments their owners were clothed in on the day they were slaughtered—a testament to Pol Pot's demonic wrath. Red signs depicting skulls and crossbones are tacked to trees, sharing the bark with bullet holes, warning of land mines. Orange tracers raining back and forth between warring factions in the night sky, streaking in a large arc across the Asian twilight, appear to be a display of grand fireworks that simply aren't functioning properly, some sort of defused celebration—which is in fact what Cambodia is.

Rebel Etiquette

In 1992, UNTAC issued a pamphlet to its soldiers and workers listing helpful Khmer phrases for use in the event of being detained or robbed by the KR. Translated, a couple read:

• *That's a very nice gun, sir. I'd be honored to give you the gift of my truck.*

• *My watch is very expensive; that's why it makes me very happy to present it to you as a gift.*

The Khmer Rouge, shredded and factionalized by the backroom politicking and pork-barrelling of Hun Sen and Ranariddh, started walking out of the jungle in 1996 after promises by the two leaders of amnesty, wristwatches, army commissions, a couple of hundred bucks and free white chicks. What's left of the rebels are hardliners who've been squeezed into the remote northwestern countryside along the Thai border, where, along with the tattered remnants of Ranariddh's followers, they are pumping last gasps from the magazines of their AKs at Hun Sen's overpowering forces. In the latest violence, the KR, astoundingly, seemed to simply melt away. Pol Pot, the coveted final chess piece on Cambodia's blighted board only a few days before the coup, became simply a withering old man being toted around the jungle with IV tubes dangling from his bony arms. A non-player, a footnote, a cigar butt. He was paraded about the KR headquarters and sentenced to "life imprisonment" by the guerrillas in July 1997—and seen by the outside world for the first time since 1979. A miserable man dying a miserable death in a miserable country led by other miserable men.

In September 1993, the world paid for a democratically elected coalition government took office in Cambodia, following a two-year, $3 billion United Nations peacekeeping program. Bickering and sniping between Cambodia's two ruling parties, Funcinpec and the CPP, escalated into violence and finally a violent coup in July 1997 in which Hun Sen deposed Norodom

Ranariddh and sent him squealing to the UN—and anyone else who would listen—for help. Do you think the UN could get their money back? Foreign investors are packing their bags and the package tours are being canceled like a Stone Temple Pilots concert. No matter what happens politically here, there will be little incentive to return. Cambodia lives true to its Wild West legacy, on a knife edge.

Passenger Justice

Halfway into town after arriving at Phnom Penh's Pochentong Airport, my taxi driver stopped. A police motorcycle carrying two of Phnom Penh's finest had pulled onto Pochentong Boulevard from a side street directly in front of a small Toyota, which slammed into the rear of the bike. The bike was eaten by the sedan's grille and lay crumpled beneath the undercarriage. One of the cops staggered away in shock. The small Toyota was packed with perhaps eight Khmer passengers. The other cop bolted to his feet and raced to the right front door of the car. He opened it, dragged out a young, shock-stricken Cambodian man and began kicking the crap out of the poor soul, pummeling his rib cage with his military boots. It seemed to make no difference that the steering wheel of the Toyota was on the left-hand side, the actual driver of the car grimacing in either the realization of imminent pain and arrest or in the delight that his car had been stolen and smuggled into Cambodia from Vietnam (where they drive on the right side of the road) and not Thailand (where they drive on the left).

Ta Mok

The man with Star Wars sounding name is probably the most brutal rebel leader alive. The one-legged Mok runs what is left of the Khmer Rouge out of Anlong Veng and is known for scores of atrocities and cold blooded murders of his own people and Western tourists. Ta Mok was the one that carried out Pol Pots execution plans. For now he pays the rent by selling timber to Thailand. He controls the 3800 Khmer Rouge that are hunkered down in Anlong Veng.

The Khmer Rouge, or NADK (National Army of Democratic Kampuchea)

The Khmer Rouge, like the Afghans, is another CIA Frankenstein. CIA puppet Lon Nol was installed as Cambodia's leader in 1971, the Maoist Khmer Rouge are believed responsible for some two million deaths during their vicious, extreme and xenophobic experiment in radical collective agrarianism between 1975 and 1979 in a genocide unparalleled in modern times. Perhaps a quarter of the Khmer population perished from executions, torture, disease, starvation and exhaustion in only four years at the hands of the KR. The KR and leader Pol Pot were ousted from power in January 1979 by the Vietnamese and retreated to Cambodia's western jungles, where they've been—despite mass defections—fighting a war of attrition against the government, slaughtering ethnic Vietnamese and abducting foreign tourists ever since. Since August 1996, some 15,000 guerrillas have defected to the government side, reducing the KR to a has-been. The defecting rebels were played like cards by Hun Sen and Ranariddh before the July 1997 coup. In the days leading up to the coup, the KR completely disintegrated as the last remaining holdouts—including the four top KR leaders: Pol Pot, Khieu Samphan, Ta Mok and Son Sen—scrambled to cut deals to save their asses. Khieu Samphan, Pol Pot's former spokesman and nominal leader of the Khmer Rouge, had closed a deal with Ranariddh—granting the KR henchman amnesty and a significant role in a Funcinpec political alliance—just hours before the putsch began. Son Sen was reportedly shot dead by Pol Pot. As for

Pol Pot himself, he was put on a show trial by the remaining KR forces in July 1997 and sentenced to life under "house arrest." The KR announced it was renaming itself the National Solidarity Party and would work for change peacefully. Unlikely. Their objective hasn't changed: the ouster of Hun Sen. That is also unlikely—unless it's by force.

Unlike some other insurgencies across the globe, the Khmer Rouge has not built a web site, but a Yale research team has put together a biographical database for the web containing about 6000 biographies of Khmer Rouge leaders and their victims. More are being added. There is also a geographical database of maps of the killing fields and mass graves, as well as an archive of more than 6000 photos of KR victims after their arrest. Check out:

Yale Research Database
http://www.yale.edu/cgp

Hun Sen

Cambodia's second premier, Hun Sen, is a turncoat Khmer Rouge who was installed as Cambodia's puppet president by the Vietnamese after their defeat of the Khmer Rouge in 1979. He is shrewd, power hungry and paranoid, and disdains the press. He ruled alone until the 1993 elections but was named co-premier despite losing the elections to Prince Norodom Ranariddh. Hun Sen grew up the son of a peasant near the Vietnamese border, though he's better known these days as a son of a bitch for staging the violent July 1997 coup which ousted First Premier Ranariddh. During calmer times, he enjoys an occasional cigarette—48 a day—lobbing grenades at opposition figures and naming schools after himself. Not known for his subtlety he was busy executing Ranariddh during his coup and doesn't quite know what all the fuss is all about. Just politics as usual in Cambodia.

Prince Norodom Ranariddh

Ranariddh is technically Cambodia's first prime minister despite being deposed by Hun Sen on July 5, 1997. The king's son and born with a silver spoon, Ranariddh—before the coup—ran the country as if he were hosting a dinner party. Although painted as the good guy during the crisis of '97, Ranariddh's hands are dirty with his courting of the Khmer Rouge. To buy votes for the 1998 elections, Ranariddh's olive branch to the KR were offers of wristwatches, money, new legs and senior positions in the Cambodian military. He struck deals with KR monsters such as Ieng Sary and Khieu Samphan. Sary's punishment for the death of 2 million Cambodians was his own little fiefdom in western Cambodia and all the nice little gems and hardwood forests that came with it.

Ieng Sary

Former KR big shot Ieng Sary—Brother Number Two, foreign minister in Pol Pot's '75–'79 regime and a butcher in his own right—initiated the mass KR defections in August 1996 and was rewarded by the government with a royal pardon for his genocide crimes and the leadership of the former KR headquarters of Pailin, which Sary rules with virtual autonomy from Phnom Penh. Sary and his boys have swapped shoulder patches, but that's about all.

King Norodom Sihanouk

In 1941, the French made Prince Sihanouk king of Cambodia, believing they had installed another loyal puppet on the throne who'd do anything they asked of him for the price of a lavish existence. Instead, King Sihanouk moved in the direction of Cambodian independence. In 1953, he declared martial law and dissolved the parliament. On November 9, he proclaimed Cambodia an independent state. But internal divisions continued to hamper the solidarity among the nation's leaders. In 1955, Sihanouk abdicated the throne in favor of politics. Politically, Sihanouk has vacillated between the right and the left throughout his career (intermittently supporting the Khmer Rouge and its foes alike). Known for bending with the wind, he is nonetheless still worshipped by the core of the Cambodian people. Ill with cancer, he resides primarily in Beijing and Pyongyang, North Korea. His relationship with the late North Korean leader Kim Il Sung was deep and lasted for decades. In the name of national reconciliation, he pardoned Khmer Rouge henchman Ieng Sary in 1996. He has remained noncommittal regarding the coup which ousted his son. Sihanouk these days spends most of his time being sick in Beijing and quashing reports he is considering abdicating and again entering politics because of the deep rifts in the present coalition.

Sam Rainsy

In October 1994, the government performed a major housecleaning of its cabinet, including the firing of popular finance minister Sam Rainsy, a brilliant, French-educated free market reformer, outspoken government critic and ardent anti-corruptionist who became a darling of Western diplomats. Rainsy was subsequently stripped of his MP position in parliament and expelled from Funcinpec in May 1995. On November 9, 1995, Rainsy launched a new political party in Cambodia called the Khmer Nation Party (KNP). The party was immediately declared illegal by the government, although no direct action was taken to dismantle it or throw its leaders in jail. Rainsy formed an alliance with Ranariddh in the run-up to the '98 elections, and it's been bloody. On March 30, 1997, three or four grenades were tossed into a demonstration he was leading in front of the parliament building, killing 19 and wounding 120.

Pol Pot

Poor old Pot. Now 70 and on his last legs, he was trotted out in front of his former comrades and a couple of invited journos to take his licking. There was to be no smack on the back of his head with a hoe, or having his head squashed under the tires of a truck for this former history teacher. No Pol (or is it Pot?) was brought to tears by the tongue lashing his former buddies gave him. The man responsible for the deaths of between 1 and 2 million innocent Cambodians in a four year period and the recent brutal murders of his close aides finally got what he deserved.

It looks like Pol Pot will be banished to live in his own house in Anlong Veng with the company of his ex-ammo porter wife and two kids. He will be kept alive with IV treatments for his cerebral malaria and will not be allowed to watch Jerry Springer reruns. Where's Amnesty International when you need them?

His real name is Saltoh Sar. He was born to well off rice farmers, went to Paris on a scholarship to study electronics and became a Communist. Back home he taught history and geography. He helped to organize the Khmer Rouge in '63 and his little cadre took off during the Vietnam War when U.S. bombers carpetbombed their homes. In 1975 about 70,000 KR's overthrew Lon Nol and Year Zero began. The pogrom began in earnest and only stopped when the Vietnamese army invaded in 1979. China was the main supporter of the Khmer Rouge and had no problem supplying money, weapons and advisors for the three decades of the KR's existence. The murderous regime with Pol Pot hung out around the Thai border area as the Khmer Rouge slowly shrank from losses or defected under Pot's brother in law Ieng Sary.

A passport is required. An airport visa valid for a 30-day stay is available upon arrival at Phnom Penh's Pochentong Airport from the Ministry of National Security for US$20. As we go to press, the airport is full of bullet and mortar holes and the crash of a Vietnamese Tupolov didn't make visitors feel good about the future of air safety in Cambodia. You can also apply to:

General Direction of Tourism

Chief of Tour Service Office
3 Monivong Street

Phnom Penh
☎ 855-23-24607 or 23607
FAX: 855-23-26164 or 23-26140.

You will need to send the following: full name, passport number, photocopy of the front section of your passport, date and place of birth, arrival and departure dates and itinerary. They will confirm receipt of application. Visas will then be issued on arrival at Pochentong Airport. You will need two passport-sized photos. Visas are good for stays up to 30 days.

That's the official line. But try to get to Bangkok first for the latest dope on getting over the border. Most travel agents there will say you've got to cough up anything from US$80 to US$120 and wait three days for your visa. But you can also try simply getting on a plane, as I have done, and pay US$20 cash at Pochentong for a 30-day visa.

Visa extensions can be applied for, but not necessarily granted, in Phnom Penh at the following:

Foreign Ministry

240 Street and Samdech Sothearos Boulevard
Phnom Penh, Cambodia
☎ 24641 or 24441

General Direction of Tourism

3 Monivong Street

Phnom Penh, Cambodia
☎ 855-23-723607
FAX: 855-23-426164 or 426140

Phnom Penh Tourism

313 Samdech Sothearos Boulevard
Phnom Penh, Cambodia
☎ 723949, 725349, or 724059
FAX: 885-23-426043

You can also arrange for visas in Vietnam. Allow three to five days for issue. Various Saigon tour operators run boats up the Mekong River from Vietnam to Phnom Penh. However, most of these excursions have been curtailed due to lawlessness and bandit attacks on river-going vessels. Entry by land from Thailand is illegal, however an increasing number of travelers are reporting success entering Cambodia by sea from Trat, Thailand. Although this is illegal, it is expected by both Thai and Cambodian border authorities that this method of departing Thailand and entering Cambodia will soon be permitted for foreigners. In this anticipation, or for a bribe, they may stamp your passport.

Through Vietnam

Crossing into Cambodia from Vietnam is very popular with budget travelers. There are several border checkpoints, but at the time of this writing, only one is usable by foreigners, the Moc Bai-Bavet checkpoint on Route 1. A bus leaves at dawn daily except Sundays from both Phnom Penh and Saigon; it's a hellishly crowded affair, and very slow with frequent stops. Once the bus reaches the border there is a wait of several hours while the authorities on each side pour over travel papers, visas, and every box and basket on the bus in search of contraband. Total travel time is about 12 to 13 hours, if the bus doesn't break down. Verdict: not recommended.

A better way is to catch a "share taxi" to the border from either side; from Phnom Penh the fare can be as low as US$5 per person if the car is full. Upon arrival at the border, simply walk to the other side and stick your thumb out for the next taxi or private car willing to ferry you the rest of the way. This cuts a good four hours off the bus trip, and is usually much more comfortable. Be sure the price is agreed upon before getting into the car.

Through Thailand

There was a time several years ago, when the UN was in town, when travelers could cross into Cambodia at the Klong Leuk checkpoint in Aranyaprathet. Then it was simply a matter of finding a taxi in Poipet and gritting your teeth for the 12 hours of "lambada road" to Phnom Penh ahead.

Not anymore. Foreigners are currently prohibited from crossing the Thai checkpoints due to security reasons. Don't even think of getting off the road and sneaking across unless you want to be called "Stubby;" the Thai-Khmer border is one of the heaviest mined areas in the world, and claims new victims nearly every day.

In 1996, people were still crossing into Koh Kong province from south of Trat town in Thailand. A few hundred baht was paid to the soldiers at the border, a speed boat taken to Kompong Som, and the traveler was home free. This is illegal, but was feasible at the time as the Cambodian authorities rarely checked visas. Of course, the same route must be taken when leaving the country. Ask around in the Trat guesthouses before attempting this.

From Cambodia into Thailand is not as easy. The Thai police are wise to this trick, and if they catch you in the country (most likely to happen in Trat town or the vicinity) without a properly stamped visa, you could win a free vacation in the Bangkok immigration jail. Best not to try this.

From Laos

To date, no one knows of any tourist who has made the crossing into Cambodia from Laos. This is probably because the northeast of Cambodia is mostly thick jungle with little population. Theoretically it should be possible, but again you would be entering illegally if your visa (assuming you had one in advance) was not stamped. If you must do it legally, the best route would be along the Mekong River, as there is sure to be a checkpoint for the locals, or along a well-traveled logging road.

Intercity buses and trains are out of the question for foreigners, due to the high probability of banditry and guerrilla attacks in the countryside. Intercity buses are officially off limits to foreigners and trains are often restricted to Cambodian citizens. Officially, travel in Khmer Rouge-controlled areas is restricted. By road, Siem Reap can be reached from Phnom Penh by road via share taxis, which take National Route 5 to Battambang and then swing east around the Tonlé Sap Lake. The trip is long and arduous, however, and security on the Battambang-Siem Reap leg is chancy. National Route 6, the most direct road from Phnom Penh, is still highly insecure between Kompong Thom and Siem Reap.

By air, Royal Air Cambodge (owned by Malaysian Air Service) flies new Boeing jets and ATR turboprops to Siem Reap from Phnom Penh several times daily and several times weekly to Sihanoukville, Battambang, Ko Kong and Rattanakiri.

There are now several companies running a speedboat service to Siem Reap via the Tonlé Sap River. The trip takes about five hours from Phnom Penh; foreigners pay US$25, Khmers 50,000 riel one-way. Two types of boats make the run: long, enclosed boats bought second-hand from Malaysia, and comparatively new, smaller speedboats with twin outboard engines run by a Chinese company. The long boats are the more comfortable, with aircraft-like interiors, air conditioning, and real (if tiny) toilets. Be sure to bring toilet paper, as none is provided. Earplugs are also a good idea, as the drone of the engine competes with Chinese video dubbed in Khmer and played at top volume. The smaller speedboats are supposedly a bit faster, but the double-row bench seats get uncomfortable after an hour, and the "toilet" is a roofless box at the stern. Both boats depart every day at 7 a.m. from the Psar Toit area north of the Japanese Bridge. A free shuttle to the pier leaves about 6:30 a.m. from the Capitol Hotel.

Travel to Siem Reap is also possible on the slow cargo boats, which depart Phnom Penh regularly and take a full 24 hours. The boat anchors in the middle of the river for the night; travelers must bring their own sleeping gear. Price is about 3500 riel one way.

The Entire Country

Southeast Cambodia has seen an upsurge in banditry, lawlessness and military activity due to renewed civil war. Several other areas, such as parts of Battambang Province, are also insecure due to factional fighting. The temples at Angkor should be safe to visit, but first check with the U.S. embassy in Phnom Penh. They were certainly not safe to visit during the summer of 1997. Travel in other areas of Siem Reap province can be highly dangerous, as bandits prey upon large parcels of the province. Visitors traveling outside urban areas are urged by Western embassies to exercise caution and restrict travel to daylight hours and only in vehicle convoys to enhance security. Crime, including armed vehicle theft, is a serious problem in areas including the capital city, Phnom Penh. Travelers can register and obtain updated security information from the U.S. embassy upon their arrival in Phnom Penh.

Phnom Penh

Although things have returned to normal after the July 1997 coup, "normal" in Phnom Penh is daily occurrences of armed robbery, banditry and murder. Armed bandits dressed as soldiers prey on foreigners. An American tourist was robbed and shot dead just prior to the July uprisings. A Canadian was also killed photographing looting in the city. Soldiers will have no scruples about shooting you should you end up in the wrong place at the wrong time. Stay off the streets after dark.

Banteay Srei

One American—Susan Hadden, 50—was killed and another was wounded by bandits on January 15, 1995, in the vicinity of Banteay Srei Temple, a little-visited site approximately 30 kilometers northeast of Siem Reap and Angkor Wat. The area surrounding Banteay Srei Temple continues to be unsettled and dangerous. Since January 16, 1995, the Cambodian government has prohibited travel to that temple.

Rattanakiri

Due to its sheer remoteness in the northeast of Cambodia, and because of a lack of infrastructure and a nonexistent security apparatus, travel here should be done very cautiously. In April 1997, three foreign aid workers—two American women and a Frenchman—had their NGO 4-wheel-drive vehicle shot at and halted in the province by heavily armed men in military uniforms. They were robbed and their vehicle was set ablaze and destroyed.

Land Mines

U.N. officials and demining experts estimate that between 6 and 10 million mines are scattered around the country. The Russian PMN2 antipersonnel mine is most common in Cambodia. Between 150 and 300 people are killed or maimed every month. It is estimated that one person in 236 in Cambodia is an amputee because of an injury from land mines. The government says it needs US$80 million over the next five years to clear them. The most heavily mined areas are Kampong Thom, Siem Reap, Kampong Chang, Kampong Speu, Koh Kong, Oddar Meanchey, Batneay Meanchey, Battambang and Pursat. As of February 1997, the Cambodian Mine Action Center had only cleared 5 percent of the old minefields in Cambodia. Only 50 square miles of the 1160 square miles of mined areas have been cleared.

Clearing Mines

While *DP* was in Cambodia, a group of 29 mine disposal workers was attacked by the Khmer Rouge in Siem Reap province. The Mines Advisory Group was accused by the KR of laying mines. The 10 gunmen made off with an English mine clearer—Christopher Howe—and his interpreter. A man who was arrested later said he was paid US$20 to show the KR where the mine clearers would be working that day. A group of three women who went to negotiate the Brit's release were themselves taken hostage, and all five were taken to Anlong Veng, a KR camp run by General Ta Mok. Howe and his interpreter have not been heard from since.

Crime

There are frequent armed thefts of vehicles, armed extortion attempts and numerous incidents of petty crimes, such as those from hotel rooms and purse snatching. Automatic weapons abound in Cambodia, and are possessed and used by numerous citizens, even within Phnom Penh. The Khmer Rouge does not have a retirement plan, so many former KRs are roaming the country with their weapons looking for spare change.

Hooligan Haven

The Interpol representative office in Cambodia believes that at least 100 of Interpol's most wanted criminals are hiding in Cambodia. The fugitives are said to be taking advantage of Cambodia's relatively lax legal system and the present inability of Royal Cambodian Government (RCG) law enforcement agencies to meaningfully fight crime. Interpol was further reported to be concerned that the apparent influx of criminals may signal a rise in organized crime activities in Cambodia—a country which has already seen an upsurge in international drug trafficking attributable to deficient law enforcement abilities.

In addition, police have launched a major investigation into the operations of a Phnom Penh-based company linked to Yoshimi Tanaka, a Japanese Red Army member, on charges of using counterfeit U.S. dollars. Police in Phnom Penh believe that Kodama International Trading (KIT), run by Tang Cheang Tong, a Japanese citizen of Khmer-Chinese origin, helped Tanaka launder fake U.S. currency through its export-import operations. Tanaka was arrested on the Cambodia-Vietnam border on March 24, 1996, by Cambodian police, Interpol officials and U.S. federal agents after being accused of disposing of counterfeit dollars in the southeastern Thai resort of Pattaya. Cambodian customs officials and police were at various times offered up to US$40,000 in bribes to let him cross the border. Notorious as one of Japan's best-known fugitives, Tanaka was also wanted for his role in the 1970 hijacking of a Japanese airliner to Pyongyang, North Korea.

Car and Motorbike Jackings

There's been a surge in armed carjackings and forcible rip-offs of motorbikes in Phnom Penh. Even the police are not immune to becoming victims. In many instances, the victims are shot.

Trains

Western tourists traveling by railroad have a better chance of being robbed and/or abducted than not. The Cambodian railway system may be the most lethal stretch of tracks in the world. In addition to the Westerners who have been abducted off trains by the Khmer Rouge, the guerrillas often target ethnic Vietnamese as well as other Cambodians. On New Year's Day in 1995, KR guerrillas ambushed a train 60 km northwest of Phnom Penh, killing eight and injuring 36. Among the dead were four women. The rebels stopped the train by blowing up the tracks in front of it and then spraying the railway cars with machine-gun fire and B-40 rockets. Now that the KR is mostly gone, bandits have risen to the opportunity and taken their place.

Buses

Due to the high incidence of banditry, Western tourists are prohibited from traveling aboard local buses. Only the bus to Saigon is open to foreigners.

Farmers

Yes, even you have a price on your head. And some rice farmer with a sickle may cash in on it. Police arrested three farmers on charges of conspiring to abduct or kill foreigners for cash rewards from the Khmer Rouge. The Khmer Rouge tells us that Americans are worth $10,000. The three were arrested in the northwestern city of Battambang and charged with offenses under legislation passed in 1994 to outlaw the Khmer Rouge. The farmers were planning to abduct or kill foreigners who were exercising in the town along the river. Khmer Rouge rebels had told the sodbusters they would pay US$1600 for each foreigner abducted and US$800 for each one killed. Life's cheap. Nice to be wanted.

Timber

The Khmer Rouge made about US$10 million a month in timber sales to Thailand before their ranks were decimated by defections, according to Global Witness. And it would be fair to say that someone has taken their place. The government of Cambodia has authorized soldiers to open fire on logging trucks or boats taking lumber out of Cambodia.

Outside of the major cities, you are out of luck here. It would be best to fly to Singapore for treatment of serious wounds or diseases. You can expect malaria and other tropical bugs endemic to Southeast Asia. There is one doctor for every 27,000 people in Cambodia.

Update all your shots and take the usual precautions for malaria and other tropical diseases. There are many virulent strains of malaria that are resistant to all prophylactics. Inoculations are not required unless you're arriving from an endemic area.

Dr. Gavin Scott is Phnom Penh's senior Western doctor and the only native English speaker. He can be contacted at the **Tropical & Travelers Medical Clinic** (*No. 88 Street 108,* ☎ *366802*).

There is no truly modern hospital facility in the country. You will need to buy your own drugs (usually expired). Best to stock up in Bangkok, where many useful preparations can be had over the counter. Dangerous snakes include vipers, cobras and king cobras, hanumans and banded kraits.

Hospitals in Phnom Penh

SOS International Medical Center
83 Issarak Boulevard; ☎ *015-912-765, 364127.*
Emergency medical care, up to limited Western standards.

Calmette Hospital
Monivong Boulevard; ☎ *723173.*
This is the best facility in the country, although it's hardly up to Western standards.

Access Medical Services
203 63rd Street; ☎ *015-913-358.*
Australian nurse; vaccinations.

European Dental Clinic
195A Norodom Boulevard; ☎ *62656, 018-812-055.*

Clinique Borei Keila
172 Tehcoslavaquie; ☎ *360207.*

Kantha Bopha-II
Pediatrics Hospital, Vithei Oknha Chun.

Maternite Somphop Panya
  282 St. Kampuchea Krom; ☎ *366046.*

Polyclinic and Maternity Angkor
  75 St. Oknha Pich; ☎ *018-811237.*

Polyclinic and Maternity Psar Chas
  38-40 110 Street; ☎ *426948, 360436.*

Polyclinique Aurore
  58-60 113 Street; ☎ *018-810339.*

Raffles Medical Center
  Sofitel Cambodiana, 313 Sisovath Boulevard Office 3, Ground Floor. ☎ *017-204088, 426299 (ext. 631/7).*

Visalok Polyclinic
  80 Monireth Boulevard; ☎ *427069, 365160.*

Americans can register at the U.S. embassy in Phnom Penh and obtain updated information on travel and security within Cambodia. *Fielding's Thailand, Cambodia, Laos and Myanmar* and *Fielding's Vietnam Including Cambodia & Laos* provide up-to-the-minute coverage of travel in Cambodia.

Embassy Locations

U.S. Embassy
  No. 20, Mongkol Iem Street (Street 228)
  Phnom Penh, Cambodia
  ☎ *[855] (23) 26436 or (23) 26438; cellular: 018-810465; FAX: 855-23-27637*
  The consular entrance to the U.S. embassy is located at *16 Street 228*

(between Street 51 and Street 63). The embassy is able to offer essential consular services.

Cambodian U.N. Section
  866 U.N. Plaza, Suite 420
  New York, New York 10017
  ☎ *(212) 421-7626*

07/05/1997	Hun Sen ousts Norodom Ranariddh in a coup which kills more than 50 people.
03/30/1997	A grenade blast rips through a demonstration organized by the Khmer Nation Party, killing 19 and wounding 120 others, including an American political consultant.
06/18/1996	Ieng Sary, a top Khmer Rouge leader, defects to the government, bringing with him 1000 KR guerrillas, their weapons and 20 tanks.
01/15/1995	American Susan Hadden is killed by the Khmer Rouge near Banteay Srey temple.
07/26/1994	Three Western tourists bound for Sihanoukville by train are taken hostage by the Khmer Rouge and subsequently executed.
04/11/1994	Three Westerners are taken hostage along Route 4 in southern Cambodia by the Khmer Rouge and subsequently executed.
01/07/1979	Vietnamese take Phnom Penh and install Hun Sen as prime minister of Cambodia.
04/17/1975	Pol Pot and Khmer Rouge roll into Phnom Penh and seize control of Cambodia.

CAMBODIA

10/09/1970	Cambodian monarchy abolished. The country subsequently is named the Khmer Republic.
11/09/1953	Independence Day.
06/19/1951	Army-people solidarity day celebrates the founding of the Cambodian People's Armed Forces.
02/03/1930	Founding of the ICP, the Indochinese Communist Party.
05/19/1928	The birthdate of Pol Pot, the leader of the Khmer Rouge.
05/24/ 563 B.C.	Birth of Buddha.

CAMBODIA

Over the Line

We went to Cambodia on a lark. These days, Cambodia is not necessarily the most dangerous place in the world, or even a nasty place, but it is an exotic, very inexpensive stop that every traveler to Asia should make. Is it safe? Well, if you stay inside the tourist ruts (literally), don't venture outside the ill-defined "safety" zone and watch where you step, Cambodia can be safe. Cambodia can also be brutal if you pass through the invisible safety barrier and end up in the hands of the Khmer Rouge. Just remember the advice of your first grade teacher, "Don't color outside the lines."

Cambodia has provided a safe corridor for tourists wanting to visit the great temple complexes around Angkor Wat. Depending on who you talk to, the Khmer Rouge is either a mighty Chinese-backed juggernaut, complete with tanks, foot soldiers and tacit support from the Thai generals along the border, or a rag-tag band of starving anachronisms who have resorted to banditry just to eat. The truth is somewhere in the middle and at both ends of the spectrum.

One tourist can fly into Phnom Penh and Siem Reap on a modern jet, stay in a five-star hotel, and see the temple complex, complete with cold Pepsis, an air-conditioned car and a good meal, followed by an ice-cold beer at one of the many nightclubs the U.N. soldiers used to frequent. Another tourist can find himself kneeling at the edge of a shallow, hastily dug grave, waiting for the rifle butt that will slam into his cortex, ending his brief but adventurous life. The difference between the two scenarios might be 10 km or lingering a few too many minutes along the road.

Despite the kidnapping, execution, injuring and shooting of a number of tourists over the last few years, the government of Cambodia considers its country safe...within certain limits. Those ellipses can be the difference between life and death here.

####

When we buy tickets, the Malaysian-trained ticket agent for Royal Air Cambodge, a joint venture between Malaysian Airlines and the Cambodian government, is cordial and efficient. We ask whether many tourists come to Cambodia. He thinks we must be very stupid spies and points to the lack of tourists in the check-in area.

We ask, "Is it dangerous in Cambodia?" He looks up and says, "I would say it is a lot safer than Los Angeles," referring to the shooting of Haing Ngor, the Cambodian doctor turned actor who starred in *The Killing Fields*. He had managed to survive Cambodia, only to die on the mean streets of Los Angeles. He was killed for a gold locket (that contained a picture of his dead wife) by a member of the Lazy Boys, a street gang made up of Chinese kids. That gold locket was what carried him through the horrors of captivity and his escape; it also killed him. Haing Ngor thought he had crossed over the line, but he never made it.

On the flight in, my sober thoughts about Cambodia are confirmed by the sight of the hard brown country below us. A visual shock after flying over the endless green carpets of Malaysia and Thailand. Cambodia has long been denuded and carved into a patchwork for wet season rice cultivation, interrupted by movie-prop-style sugar palms in random patterns.

When the monsoon arrives, the countryside floods, roads are impassable and the rice fields turn rich green. Food becomes plentiful. There is hope and happiness in the wet season. The dry season is a time of hardship and killing.

The dry season is when the government launches its tank and infantry attacks against the Khmer Rouge, who then retreat into their strongholds near Thailand and their jungle and hilltop hideouts. Slipping away like children chasing pigeons, the KR wait for the rainy season to regroup and infiltrate back to the south. The dry season is the most dangerous time for tourists. It is when food and supplies are at their scarcest for the wandering bands of KR and bandits. It is when the Khmer Rouge must rob and kidnap to raise money to buy supplies or just eat. Many say that members of the KR army simply take off their uniforms and dissolve into the general populace.

The wet season is the most dangerous time for the locals. This is when the KR enters villages to press-gang farmers, kids, anyone who can carry a gun. Should the young people not be there, the KR promise to come back and kill the entire family if they do not supply a raw recruit. They also carry off rice, building materials and any possessions the villagers have not buried. The wet season is when it is easy to plant land mines and booby traps, which become invisible in the dry season. The villagers are constantly maimed and killed as they go out to work their fields and paddies during the wet season.

Our flight is full of fat, middle-aged Chinese businessmen with bad haircuts who immediately start gambling and drinking as soon as the seat belt sign goes off. We ask why they are going to Phnom Penh. They all have clothing factories there, we are told. "Cambodia is just like Thailand was ten years ago. Cheap, very cheap."

As the plane comes in for the final approach, I notice the rows of rusty tanks and APCs below. Studying the parched ground interrupted by wispy brown bushes and meandering vein-like footpaths, I can't help thinking that Cambodia looks like the skull of someone recovering from heavy chemotherapy.

Upon landing, formalities are brief—$20 in U.S. currency and a visa. The line, the crush of tourists, and the exotic-looking posters of Angkor Wat on the walls make me feel like I am paying to get into a theme park. Another sick irony makes me laugh—it costs $38 to get into EPCOT, and there are a whole lot less land mines there. On the simple forms we fill out, it seems the government wants to know if we are bringing in any gold bars, ammunition or firearms.

Pushing through the usual Third World crush of touts and taxi drivers, we pause again; these people are only asking for two and three dollars to drive us into town. Obviously, the supply is a lot higher than the demand here. Driving into town, the bullet holes, grass-filled craters and fading scorch marks have all been cleaned up. Phnom Penh is bustling, not a Bangkok bustle, but still busy for a city that once looked like a scene from *Full Metal Jacket*. As if to provide a counterpoint to the death and destruction all around, our driver slows down as he passes a row of small shops with Vietnamese women sitting outside. He points, smiles and simply says, "fucking." This is obviously the tourist route into town.

There is still something missing, though. There are very few, if any, people over the age of 45. More than one million people, some say more, were killed here by Pol Pot and the Khmer Rouge in their attempt to re-engineer society. Today, like Saigon, the post-war generation is gregarious and eager to meet Westerners. The men above 30 are more reticent. Around town, there are men and boys who have been maimed by land mines. They beg, politely repeating, "*Bapa Yam*" (or "please, sir, rice"). I also notice that there are no flowers in Cambodia. The tattered army uniforms and shiny plastic limbs make me think back to Afghanistan.

A few months earlier when we were at the headquarters of the *taliban*, their stairwells and courtyard were full of maimed fighters. The difference is that the tiny Russian mines only took off the foot at the ankle. Here, the legs are gone up to the knee and sometimes higher. Here, the men have prosthetic limbs; in Afghanistan, they gave the wounded a stick to walk with. Here, there has been a different kind of horror. In Afghanistan, the fighters and old men proudly wear their DP stickers and T-shirts. In Cambodia, if a soldier or civilian has been through the holocaust, he is more likely to politely hand back the image of the grinning skull of Mr. DP. There are far too many images of real skulls here. I notice something else. There are no birds in Cambodia.

Walking down the main drag in Phnom Penh, we are followed by a Ray-Banned man in a yellow shirt and string tie. He doesn't do his job well, since we repeatedly sneak up behind him and give him a start. Paranoia and post-traumatic stress are just below the surface here.

As all good tourists must, we visit the killing fields as well as the police detention and torture center. It is hard to understand the methodical nature of the Khmer Rouges' killing, as we view black-and-white photos of every victim seated in a posing stool, their paperwork filled out in triplicate.

There are so many skulls, they make murals, maps, monuments and whatever else they can think of. They try to be educational with their macabre building materials, but once again I can't help think what a great pavilion and "audio-animahorrific" ride this would make. There are still hundreds of thousands of skulls left in the ground to make displays, office buildings or even entire pavilions.

More than 20,000 U.N. soldiers used to keep the lid on this country, but today just about the only remnants are the white Land Cruisers and Toyota pickup trucks of the U.N., repainted with various aid logos. You can see these vehicles parked outside the other remnants of the U.N.'s efforts. Upscale restaurants, air-conditioned massage parlors, cheap whorehouses and surprisingly high-end discos keep Phnom Penh and Siem Reap hopping late into the night. For a Westerner, a massage costs $5, a night of Cambodian passion, $25. In the bigger dance halls and restaurants, cheap beer is sold by attentive uniformed women who represent and get a commission from their sponsoring brewery. You can't slowly savor a beer here, as your glass is filled past the meniscus level by chatty beer ladies or impatient "go dancing" girls.

We hire a driver to tour the countryside, The hotel we stay in is run by a woman who has hired her ex-husband's old army buddies. Not a difficult thing to do, since most Cambodian men are either in the army or have served in it. We ask the ex-army buddies who hang around the hotel if Cambodia is dangerous. They glibly reply, "Not so much anymore." We ask again, not happy with this pat answer. They pause and say it depends where you go. We ask our driver, who responds: "As long as you visit the temples, it is fine; if you go beyond..." His explanation trailing off, he points to the hills and countryside.

Wink tells him of his trip north of Siem Reap. The driver thinks we are asking if this trip would be dangerous. He replies, shaking his head and laughing at our folly, "No, you cannot do that." Wink explains that he has already done it. The driver says, "Then you are very lucky to be alive."

The manager of a Thai-owned bank where we stop to change money is equally impressed and amused as he overhears Wink jabbering away in Thai. He has been here for three months. He cautions us that it is dangerous here. He says, "Do not go out after dark. There are many guns. Men dress up like police and stop foreigners at roadblocks. Do not drive outside of the city. It is dangerous." We ask if anyone has been robbed. He says, "Yes, many people." He warns us to be extra careful. The recent division between the two rulers sharing power is heating up, and he tells us that "the word is out on the street that there may be a coup soon." Aware that three foreigners were sprayed with machine-gun fire when they were mistaken for "white mercenaries," we thank him for the tip.

We ask around town if we can rent motorcycles to ride up to Siem Reap. Not possible, we are told, for the simple reason that at best you are guaranteed to run into Khmer Rouge roadblocks and be abducted, worst case is you will be shot and robbed. No cab drivers will take us. We book a flight instead.

Arriving in Siem Reap, we hire a driver and tell him we want to retrace the route of the American tourist who was injured in a rocket and machine-gun attack just north of the Angkor temple complex. He does not think that is a good idea. "It is too dangerous." He refuses to take us there, so we content ourselves with visiting the temples in the company of reappearing chattering clusters of Japanese, Germans and Thai tourists.

Cambodia politicians are happy. The package tourists are finally coming back; the temples used to be silent with the occasional backpacker, expat or aid worker carefully avoiding the smaller paths and out-of-the-way complexes. Soon there will be a major development just outside the temples as well as in the nearby city of Siem Reap. This former battle zone is sprouting giant five-star hotels with room capacities in the hundreds, more appropriate for Las Vegas than this tiny country. The red skull signs that signaled areas still full of land mines are mostly gone. The soldiers no longer carry AK-47s (it scares the tourists, they tell us). When we ask where the machine guns are, we are told don't worry—there are plenty at the army base. For now, Cambodia is one of the cheapest places to visit. A beer costs $2, a meal in a restaurant goes for about $3—steep, considering we are paying $3 a night for two people in a room. We get our laundry done for a buck. And all of this in U.S. greenbacks.

Hanging around the great man-made lake that surrounds Angkor Wat, we watch the sunset turn the temples' towers to a fiery red. It is hard to believe that the sun has been turning the temples this color for the last 700 years. There are a few bullet holes from where the Vietnamese army once camped out here. All the major statues have been stolen, destroyed or removed by Europeans, the Khmer Rouge or vandals, but there is still an awesome power of solemnity that holds visitors in its sway. The slightly bemused expressions of the great faces of the Bayon

are a perfect contrast to the bloodthirsty scenes carved on the friezes that decorate the temple walls. This is not the first nor last time these walls have marked a
dangerous place.

I strike up a conversation with a member of military intelligence for the Siem
Reap provinces. He tells us that two Khmer Rouge generals have defected with
military plans. One apparently wanted a Range Rover as part of his retirement
package.

That same day, a British minesweeper and his interpreter are kidnapped by the
Khmer Rouge a short distance from here. Surprisingly enough, our friend is quite
pleased, since one of the goodies one of the generals dropped off at their office
was a plan to kidnap a foreigner. The only snag is they had to make do with a Brit
instead of a Yank.

Americans are the most favored kidnap victims, followed by British and then
French. Yanks bring in an automatic US$10,000 and provide the necessary pub-
licity to give the government grief. We ask him how safe it is. He says, in town, at
the temples and in daylight, there is no problem. But 20 km away, there is a battle
raging. We also tell him about *DP's* trip by motorcycle around the countryside.
He also thinks we are talking in the future tense. He says that would not be a very
good idea. We say, no, we already took the trip. He also says Wink was very lucky.

That night back in Siem Reap we go to a nightclub. The sign outside says "no
guns or explosives." The music is pure sing-song Khmer played at ear-damaging
levels. The Khmers respond to the music in a circular line dance reminiscent of
that on a bad TNN show. Wink decides to get up and jam with the band. The audience is dumbstruck and stares open-mouthed for two songs. The dance floor
clears out, and the Cambodians don't know if they should clap or cover their ears.
Wink finishes up to a round of applause. After Wink sits down, it seems not everyone is thrilled with his impromptu jam session. We are challenged to a fight in
a less than sensitive manner. An elbow not once, not twice, but three times in the
back—hard. We decide to split. This would not be a John Wayne punch 'em up,
but probably a good ole' sloppy burst of gunfire. As we change venues, the group
of surly Cambodian men follows us out into the street. We face off, neither side
wanting to be the first to start hostilities. Luckily, our driver pulls up and we drive
off.

We stop at another place with the same bad music, same knife-edge tension.
Wink sums it up by saying these people are very fucked up. The more genteel
would say they suffer from post-traumatic stress, though they aren't even aware
of the term here. There has been a lot of killing here. There is still a lot of rage
and sadness. He echoes a sentiment a Malaysian friend expresses to me on hearing
that I would be going to Cambodia: The people here are very quiet and angry—
they have seen too much.

We sit with three Cambodian girls, or rather three girls make a hurried grab for
the empty chairs at our table. Westerners are big game for these bar girls. Wink
chats with them in Vietnamese. In Cambodia, most working girls are divided into
"go dancing" girls, women who sit, talk and dance with and maybe sleep with
you on request, and "taxi girls," who are simply sex girls. There are also houses
where the function of intercourse is emotionally and financially comparable to the
drive-through window at McDonald's. Most of the girls are Vietnamese, but
these girls are Cambodian. To prove it, they mimic the ancient hand movements

and music of the *apsara*, the temptresses seen on the temples at Angkor. Wink is surprised, since most girls who were trained dancers were killed by the Khmer Rouge. Aspiring to more intellectual entertainment, we teach one of the girls a few English words at her request. She tells us that if she learns English, she will get a better job. We find out that what she means is that she can sleep with more Westerners and therefore make more money. She tells us with some pride that one Japanese man actually paid her $40 for the whole night. A curious career ambition.

Sitting outside to avoid the chilling air conditioning and deafening noise inside, we are interrupted as a Cambodian cop comes flying out of the glass entry doors, followed by shouting, punching and kicking patrons. The girls sitting with us immediately react, jump up, and drag us around the corner and down an alley. They plead with us to "Go, go, run! Please, before you are shot!" Not quite knowing what they are talking about, we walk back to the front to watch the fight, but the girls push us back, pleading with us to run away.

We push past them and are in time to watch the cop being kicked and beaten and then slammed unconscious into the back of a pickup truck. The girls explain that we are lucky (a term we are hearing a lot here). Usually, there is gunfire. They mimic the action of someone firing a machine gun. They tell us that this week "a man fell down, went to sleep." I laugh. The expression on the girl's face tells me that she is not trying to be cute; she is trying to avoid saying the word "died." She halfheartedly repeats the machine-gun pantomime and tries to make me understand. The sad look in her eyes tells me that I am being far too casual about a very real threat. With a sense of resignation, she says, "This is a dangerous place. You should not be here."

—RYP

Postscript: Fifteen months later, Prince Norodom Ranariddh is ousted in a bloody coup by Hun Sen which killed more than 50 people, including three foreigners.

Chechnya
(Ichkeria)
★★★

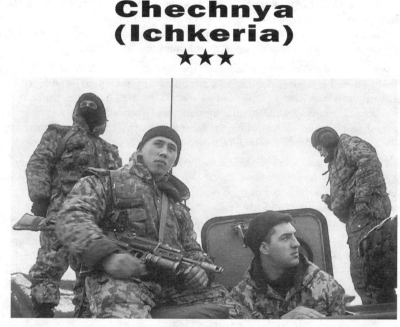

Howling Wolf

It seemed only a matter of time before the fiercely independent Chechen people would rise up against "Mother Moscow." Banished to northern Kazakhstan (along with the Tartars) by Stalin for being German collaborators, the Chechens have a mean streak as wide as the mountainous border that divides their country.

After they were repatriated, the Chechens, hardened and without any means of earning a living, set about forming the largest criminal gangs in the former Soviet Union. They were as far from the socialist, there-is-no-God, one-size-fits all Soviet model as one could be. First, Chechens are Muslim; second, they are more entrepreneurial than Donald Trump, and their loyalties are to one of the more than 100 *teips,* or clans, that constitute Chechen society. The Chechens thought and acted just like the lone wolf that has become their symbol.

For centuries, they have been considered by Russians as the toughest, baddest people in the former Soviet Union. Their image certainly isn't enhanced by the Chechen tendency to raise money through hijacking airliners, hospitals and school buses and then hot-footing it back to Chechnya to hide out in their inaccessible mountain villages. Some folks might even call them hillbillies, and Ned Beatty wouldn't be alive long enough to squeal like a pig if he went eco-touristing through Chechnya, now renamed Ichkeria.

DP thought it was strange that the news media were quick to recast the ornery Chechens as the heroic-defenders-of-their-homeland underdogs in the West. Outnumbered by five (some say 10) to one, the Chechen irregulars, along with volunteers and mercenaries (some brag they get paid the equivalent of $2000 a day, but the reality is about one-tenth of that), resigned themselves to waging a guerrilla war from the mountains. The Russians seemed happy to oblige, as their forces hid in their newly built forts along the major highways. In Grozny, nervous Russian troops stopped and checked papers endlessly and regularly arrested any male Chechens they found hiding in their homes just to be sure.

It was a story the Western media loved—peasants armed with sticks and shovels defiantly dancing around bonfires in central Grozny, seemingly holding off the entire might of the Russian army and air force. Chechen fighters, unshaven and dirty, waving their flag while strafing fighters soar overhead and turn their parliament into Swiss cheese. Meanwhile, the most feared army in the world turned out to be shivering, underfed, stoned, confused and mostly prepubescent.

Just prior to Russia's intercession into the rebellion, Russian Defense Minister Pavel S. Grachev bombastically boasted that a single paratroop regiment would need only a couple of hours to wipe out the rebellion. Boy, was he wrong. Two months later, Russia could say it had taken the rubble that once had been Grozny—but there was little of which to be proud.

Although the vastly superior Russian forces eventually took the Chechen capital in February 1995, they faced a low-budget Afghanistan army for the next 20 months. The Chechen insurgents—many of them former Soviet soldiers trained in mountain guerrilla fighting—dug into the hills and waged a long and fierce battle of attrition against an undisciplined, under-aged band of Boris' best. And, in true Afghanistan form, the Russian army set up a puppet government, while the rebels regrouped in the hills.

Between 1500 and 3000 Chechen fighters in three groups fought this pocket *gazavat*, or Holy War. Dazhokhar Dudayev ran his tiny rebel army from his "secret" base in Roshni-Chu, about 45 minutes south of Grozny until he was hit by a Russian missile, which finally homed in on his satellite phone in a clearing 20 miles southeast of Grozny in April 1996. Reportedly, he was smuggled out through Azerbaijan via Turkey and hidden in a NATO hospital in southern Germany.

In February 1995, the Russian army needed 38,000 troops just to keep the lid on Chechnya, and the Interior Ministry had deployed an additional 15,500. But an aggressive drive by the Chechen fighters on August 6, 1996, (Yeltsin's inauguration day) reversed the war, driving thousands of Russian troops and civilians out of Grozny. When Alexander Lebed was sent in by Yeltsin to work out a ceasefire, he found Russian soldiers had become demoralized, vanquished and lice-ridden weaklings. After the ceasefire went into effect, sporadic firing continued and Chechen refugees were bombed by the Russians as they fled the city. The Chechens want nothing short of outright independence while the Russians would like

them to accept autonomy within the Russian Federation much like that negotiated with Tatarstan.

Chechnya's political status is still in dispute. Chechnya still proclaims its independence, and Moscow still considers it part of the Russian Federation. Meanwhile, Grozny is a city of blackened ruins, and the Chechens don't seem in any hurry to rebuild it. Instead, they're busy with kidnapping journalists and others. Four Russian journalists were abducted in March 1997. Nine days earlier, an Italian photographer was snatched. By mid-1997, seven journalists were being held by kidnappers in Chechnya. Although there has been little fighting since the war ended after peace accords in August 1996 and again in May 1997, a number of armed groups not under the control of democratically elected Chechen President Aslan Maskhadov remain active. The Economist figures Chechen warlords made $8 million from ransoms last year. It seems that the film *Prisoner of the Mountain* has turned into an infomercial. Today things look tough in Chechnya. Grozny is a wasteland, people live hand to mouth, and kidnapping journalists may be the only source of hard currency left.

Belligerent Chechnya, only a thousand miles south of Moscow, gave Russia the ultimate headache: another Afghanistan. Chechnya proclaimed its independence in 1991. Boris let'em alone for a while (not a bad idea, considering the Chechen *mafyia* seem to have a tight grip on Moscow) but sent in the heat in December 1994. The death toll in the 21-month war was, according to varying estimates, between 18,000 and 100,000 people—90 percent of them civilians. A third of the surviving 1 million Chechens were left homeless. The Russians list 1200 soldiers as missing, while the Chechens report 1447 of their own bravehearts astray of the flock.

The conflict was ignited by a big oil deal struck by Azerbaijan, which needed to export the oil through Russian pipelines that pass through Chechnya. Both Grozny and Moscow wanted a piece of the action. It seems that, now, tens of thousands of deaths later, both sides will get what they wanted. A July 1997 agreement permits Russia to send oil through a pipeline across Chechnya linking Baku, Azerbaijan's capital, with Russia's Novorossiisk terminal. The pact also permits Chechnya to sell its oil directly to foreign buyers.

Boris Yeltsin

Boris was mad as hell, and he wasn't going to take it anymore. Boris forgot that the massive army of Stalin and Breshnev is long gone. When Boris pushed the button, all he got was a bunch of sparks and fizzles. Finally, when he sent in the few generals who would obey him, the entire world saw the ineptitude and deceit on television every night. An early 1995 poll gleaned that 72 percent of the Russian people do not trust Boris Yeltsin, although his popularity has increased dramatically since. The Chechens celebrated his inauguration by defeating the Russian army in Grozny and killing more than 2000 people.

Alexander Lebed

When Lebed ran for president in 1996, one of his campaign promises was that he could bring the war in Chechnya to an end. He demanded that Yeltsin fire Interior Minister

Anatoli Kulikov, whom he blamed for the disaster that returned Grozny to rebel control. After Lebed lost, he was surprised when Yeltsin appointed him special representative to find a settlement to the Chechnya mess. Lebed is described by government colleagues as a bull let loose in the Kremlin corridors, but if he can find a way for Russia to save face in the war that cost it $5 billion, he stands to become a formidable political figure at a time when Yeltsin's health is declining. Lebed negotiated the August 31, 1996, ceasefire with Aslan Maskhadov, calling for Russian troops to be withdrawn for "humanitarian reasons," and bullied Yeltsin into giving him authority over all armed forces and intelligence services in Chechnya. Although he was sacked soon afterward, in October 1996, Lebed is quickly racking up points with the Russians and the Chechens. He is poised to become Russia's next leader. A recent poll by the Russian Independent Institute for Social and National Issues revealed Lebed to be, by a long-shot, Russia's most trusted politician.

The Chechens

Mountain-bred and mean as polecats, the Chechens are an unaligned assortment of 30 major clans that are constantly fighting for influence and shifting alliances with other clans. Each clan is led by a spiritual mystic. They adhere to a Sufi mysticism branch of Sunni Islam called Muridism. This branch of Islam divides its followers into sects led by local feudal leaders. They are united only in their opposition of domination by Christians. In fact, they break all the fundamentalist Islamic laws. The men smoke and booze it up, while the women do not cover their heads, as they're required to do in stricter branches of the religion. Instead of praying five times a day, Chechens may pray only once or twice a day.

During the war, the Chechens' military chain of command was like a pickup basketball game. If units of irregulars met up with each other, it was purely by happenstance. They go out and fight, then come back to eat and sleep. They're about as coordinated as a demolition derby, but equally as destructive and resourceful. Chechen troops made flak jackets out of spent magazines from their AKs. They unearthed and replanted Russian land mines and fashioned rockets from downed Russian choppers into surface-to-air missiles which were fired through crude pipes.

Russia has supported the Terkhhu Clan, which is usually in power, for almost a century. The Nadterechny faction of the Terkhhu Clan still receives direct aid (in the form of tanks and weapons) to fight the Myalkhi Hill Clan.

Chechen Republic of Ichkeria Homepage
http://www.chechnya.org

Shamil Basayev

Computer salesman-turned-mountain guerrilla, Shamil Basayev, is the man really in charge of Chechnya. Of the three main Chechen factions, Basayev and his Lone Wolf are the most powerful. During the war, Basayev—a kidnapper and hijacker who orchestrated the guerrilla raid on the Russian town of Budyonnovsk, resulting in hundreds of deaths, in 1995—operated from mountainous southern Chechnya and still wears a silver ring with the lone wolf symbol of the country. He fared well enough in the January 1997 elections that Chechen President Aslan Maskhadov made Basayev his deputy prime minister. Although Basayev is still considered a terrorist by Moscow for his past savagery, it was probably a wise move by Maskhadov.

Aslan Maskhadov

Maskhadov became Chechnya's president as a result of the January 1997 elections. Known as a moderate and perhaps the man best suited to restore some semblance of order to Chechnya, Maskhadov was grudgingly endorsed by Moscow as the lesser of a dozen evils, and perhaps even helped into his latest role by the Kremlin. He is revered by Chechens as a fighter and the man who won the Chechen war, and equally as a diplomat who ended it. Maskhadov is a brilliant military strategist but has the personality of a piece of cardboard.

The General Representative of the President of the Chechen Republic— Ichkeria First Deputy Prime Minister
Khoj-Akhmed Nukhayev
The coordinator
Zulay Khamidova
☎ *([0] (212) 257-68-15*
FAX: [90] (212) 257-68-17
e-mail: dbolat@dominet.com.tr

Ambassador at Large of the Chechen Republic
Prince Charles Tchkotoua
☎ *[44] (171) 352-3597*
FAX: [44](171) 352-8968
Caucasian-Chechen Information Committee
Ankara, Inkilap sok. No. 15/8
☎ */FAX: [90] (312) 431-5115*

Salman Raduyev

Raduyev is the extreme Chechen. In January 1996, he led a Lone Wolf team in taking 3000 hostages at a hospital in the Dagestan town of Kizlyar. Russian forces surrounded the village and pounded the rebels and hostages for several days before suffering the ultimate humiliation. Raduyev broke through the Russian perimeter with his fighters and 100 of the hostages and made a successful run for the Chechen town of Pervomaiskaya. Although the Russians claimed one of its snipers killed him in March 1996, Raduyev returned to Chechnya in July and claimed responsibility for a series of trolley blasts in Moscow. Reporters noticed that Raduyev had lost his left eye in the March attack and had gotten his mug rearranged by plastic surgeons in Europe after recuperating in the Middle East. Raduyev and his boys are the most radical of the Chechen separatists and don't recognize the legitimacy of Maskhadov's government. Raduyev continues to stir up trouble in the Chechen countryside and just like *DP* believes that Dudayev (and Elvis) is still alive. Raduyev can be found in his headquarters in Grozny.

Tartars

Not the stuff the dentist scrapes off your teeth, but a group of about 180,000 people who were shipped off along with the Chechens by Stalin. The Tartars fought alongside Chechen rebels against the Russian government. Of the current community of 6 million Tartars, 250,000 are found in the Crimea, but their sympathies lie with the Chechens.

Dzhokhar Dudayev

Dead or alive? Dudayev was wounded and left for dead but he was rumored to have been smuggled out of the country to a German hospital to recuperate in April 1996. Looking and acting surprisingly like Boris Badenov of "Rocky & Bullwinkle" fame, Dzhokhar (pronounced Jokar) Dudayev is a Muslim and a former general in the Soviet air force. He was a member of the Myalkhi Hill Clan, a very unpopular clan amongst other Chechens. The Myalkhir Hill Clan is poor, feisty and treacherous, sort of the Chechen equivalent of our white trash without the mobile homes.

Dudayev delivered on his promise of a *gazavat*, or Holy War, when Moscow invaded his tiny gangster kingdom. Dudayev hated Russians (who weren't too fond of him, either— even those opposed to the war and Boris Yeltsin alike).

Dudayev's men were veterans of the war in Abkhazia, where they are mildly related and supportive of the 20-odd clans that are fighting the Russians there. Dudayev's son was killed during the Russian assault on Grozny.

Dead or In Bed

DP was told that Dudayev is in a NATO hospital in southern Germany. Supposedly he was seriously wounded by a Russian rocket attack on April 20, 1996, and then smuggled by Russian OMON troops through Azerbaijan, then Turkey and by plane to the NATO base. The vacation was supposed to have been arranged by Uncle Sam, Turkey and Moscow to let Yeltsin get his job again.

Iman Shamil did the same Jesus act back in the 19th century when he fought off the Russians. This would all be conjecture had not Salman Raduyev suddenly appeared from the dead and also said Dudayev is alive. Raduyev was shot in the face by a Russian sniper and was assumed dead. Raduyev underwent plastic surgery and reappeared on July 18. Talk about comebacks. Raduyev has survived four assassination attempts since his plastic surgery.

Zelimkhan Yanderbiyev

After the Russian Army decided to reach out and touch Dudayev with a guided missile while he was making a satellite call, *DP* scrambled to get some background on his replacement. Within a day of Dudayev getting his April 21 airmail present from Yeltsin, a bogus story placed by the Russian puppet government said Yanderbiyev had been shot dead in a quarrel.

Yanderbiyev is a former writer and had been Dudayev's vice president since 1993. He was the founder of the Vainakh Democratic Party in 1990. He helped form the Congress of the Chechen movement that brought Dudayev to power in 1991.

He went to Moscow to sign a peace treaty, but Yeltsin actually sneaked off to Yanderbiyev's turf and did a surprise inspection of the troops in Chechnya. The idea was that Yeltsin wouldn't return a package from the Chechens while he held their leader hostage in Moscow. Sneaky guys, these Russians. Within hours of the peace treaty being signed, Chechen rebels were blasting away at Russian soldiers. Yanderbiyev may have kept to the shadows while Dudayev was boss, but he is actually the main ideologist behind the Chechens' move for freedom.

The Russian Army

The Russian army, since the czarist era and through the Soviet period, has always relied on brute force and sheer numbers to win wars—which they haven't been doing a lot of recently. Tactically deficient and technologically marginal, the army has always relied on overpowering numbers of untrained troops to take home battlefield trophies. Even during the Soviet era, there was little need to train elite commando units, as there weren't any uprisings for them to put down. As one observer stated: "They have probably a far greater willingness to use massive force than surgical force."

By the time the Russian army was booted out of Grozny, its soldiers were lice-ridden and begging for food in the capital. To get through their roadblocks, all it took was a loaf of bread. If you threw in some Camel cigarettes or vodka, they'd roll out a red carpet and give you an armed escort (big deal). Unpaid, hungry and hung over, the soldiers were known to sell their weapons on the street to the highest bidder.

Chechnya is currently a state within Russia. The official line is that there has been a peace accord, but that doesn't stop both sides from killing each other or you. A passport and Russian visa are required for all U.S. citizens traveling to or transiting through Russia by any means of transportation, including train, car or airplane. While under certain circumstances travelers who hold valid visas to some countries of the former Soviet Union may not need a visa to transit Russia, such exceptions are inconsistently applied. Travelers who arrive without an entry visa may be subject to large fines, days of processing requirements by Russian officials, and/or immediate departure by route of entry (at the traveler's expense). Carrying a photocopy of your passport and visas will facilitate replacement should either be stolen. Foreign journalists were expelled from Chechnya in March 1997 during a wave of kidnappings. Reporters are allowed to work in the country only on trips organized by the Chechen Interior Ministry.

All Russian visas, except transit visas, are issued on the basis of support from a Russian individual or organization, known as the sponsor. It is important to know who your sponsor is and how they can be contacted, as Russian law requires that your sponsor apply on your behalf for replacement and extension of and changes to your visa. The U.S. embassy cannot act as your sponsor. Tourists should contact, in advance, their tour company or hotel for information on visa sponsorship.

For current information on visa requirements, U.S. citizens can contact the Russian consulates in New York, San Francisco or Seattle, or the Russian embassy in Washington D.C.:

Russian Embassy
> *Consular Division*
> *1825 Phelps Place N.W.*
> *Washington, D.C. 20008*
> ☎ *(202) 939-8918, 939-8907, or 939-8913*

All foreigners must have an exit visa to depart Russia. For short stays, the exit visa is issued together with the entry visa; for longer stays, the exit visa must be obtained by the sponsor after the traveler's arrival. Russian law requires that all travelers who spend more than three days in Russia register their visas through their hotel or sponsor. Visitors who stay in Russia for a period of weeks may be prevented from leaving if they have not registered their visas. Errors in the dates or other information on the visa can occur, and it is helpful to have someone who reads Russian check the visa before departing the United States.

The southern borders are not manned, and checkpoints are only on main roads. Most soldiers can be bribed due to their low pay and acceptance of side income. Do not expect any assistance if you are detained. A well-known American aid worker was executed by the Chechens when Russians incorrectly leaked information that he was a spy.

Entry into Chechnya should only be attempted by journalists or aid groups. Journalists must get permission from the Chechen Interior Ministry. During the war, journalists could enter Chechnya on the ground with the Russian army after flying from Moscow to Ordzonikidze. Journalists covering the conflict from the rebel side could either contact Chechen elements in Moscow or fly from Moscow to Kizljar in Dagestan and make their way to the mountains near Gudermes to make contact with the insurgents. *DP* arranged for the Chechen Mafia to transport us into Grozny. It included a meeting in Istanbul with a Chechen representative, a flight to Moscow to meet with the Chechen Mafia and then a long flight into Dagestan. From there we were met by fighters and hiked into the area around Grozny. (See "In a Dangerous Place .")

Today, journalists seeking entry into Chechnya or other information should contact one of the following representatives. In New York:

Anthony Pell
> ☎ *(212) 888-3273*
> *FAX: (212) 223-4997*
> *e-mail: pell@moveworld.com*

Joseph Michenfelder
> ☎ *(212) 807-1557*
> *FAX: (212) 807-1564*
> *e-mail: pancomm@tiac.net*
> *Hoashamed Nouhaev*

First Deputy Prime Minister
> *Grozny,* ☎ *[7] (867) 363-40-03*

For inquiries to the Istanbul office, try getting hold of:

Mansour Jachimczyk (Chief Advisor on Foreign Affairs)
> ☎ *90-212-257-3616 or 90-212-257--6815, cell phone: 90-212-532-27147177*
> *FAX: 90-212-257-3286*
> Also what's an emerging republic without a web site? Start with
>
> *http://www.chechnya.org*

There is no way to safely get around Chechnya. The only mechanized means of getting around the republic are via military convoys and occasionally by passenger cars. The countryside is still highly unsettled, with roving bands of armed men. Journalists can only travel in Chechnya on escorted junkets.

The Entire Country

Although the Russians have pulled out, there remain thousands of armed insurgents who are not directly under the control of the Chechen government. Any remaining military activity would be confined to the southwest. Most of the 400 villages are heavily armed and very jumpy. The area is under martial law. For those who like political subtlety, the area north of the Terek river is pro-Russian and does not grumble, the lowland middle of Chechnya is under heavy occupation, and the mountainous southwest is still happy fighting the war that was supposed to have been ended by the peace agreement.

Grozny

The Chechens control Grozny and the battered Russians have pulled out. Grozny would make a great film set, since only Kabul in Afghanistan has been more obliterated in recent years. A Turkish company has been awarded a US$284 million contract to rebuild downtown Grozny. We wonder if they can find enough Chechens to inhabit it.

Being a Chechen Civilian

More than 80,000 civilians have been killed or are missing. Another 450,000 or so are refugees. Either Russian pilots are bad shots or they feel the odds are better at snuffing unarmed civilians. Markets (bazaars), medical facilities and civilian cars on the roadways—some sites hit multiple times—were the Russians' favorite targets. The Russians even attacked a funeral procession in Samashki, killing three.

Being a Russian Civilian

Chechen terrorists took 255 hostages aboard a ferry in the Black Sea in January 1996. Chechen fighters also took a Russian hospital in Budyonnovsk in June 1995 and another one in Kizlyar in January 1996. Russian forces killed perhaps hundreds in their efforts to win them back.

Looking after Chechen Citizens

Six Western aid workers—five women and a man—were shot and killed December 17, 1996, by Chechen separatists in the worst premeditated attack in the 134-year-old history of the International Committee of the Red Cross. The NGO pulled all of its remaining workers out of the country and suspended all aid to Chechnya.

Kidnapping

Taking their cue from Colombia and the Philippines, radical Chechen separatists have turned to kidnapping to boost their coffers. Targets most in desire by Chechen extremists not under the wing of Maskhadov's government are journalists, specifically Russian journalists. Seven Russian journos were in captivity as of mid-1997.

Not much to speak of here. Chechnya is a fairly healthy place, but with very limited medical resources and facilities.

Chechnya is a self-proclaimed republic in Russia with a population of 950,000 people lying just to the east of the principal road crossing the central Caucasus, ranging from the plains and foothills into the alpine highlands. Its neighbors are Dagestan to the east, the Turkic-speaking Kumyk people of Russia to the north, the Inguish to the west and the southern Ossetians and Georgians to the south. Grozny is the largest city and capital with an official population of about 400,000 depending on how severely it's getting pounded at any given moment. It was generally depopulated as a result of the Russian bombing and folks have been coming back in trickles since the Russians left.

Chechen is the principal language, spoken by some 97 percent of the population. Inguish is a closely related language understood by most Chechens. Most Chechens, as well, can speak Russian. Chechens and the Inguish are almost entirely Sunni Muslims of the Hanafi school. Religion is the central component of Chechen culture.

The currency is the Russian ruble with an exchange rate of about 5000RUR to US$1. The electricity is 220V/50Hz.

01/1997	Maskhadov elected president of the Chechen Republic.
08/31/1996	Lebed and Maskhadov sign peace treaty ending the war in Chechnya.
08/06/1996	Chechen fighters reverse the war, driving Russian troops out of Grozny.
03/31/1996	Yeltsin announces peace plan and says all Russian military operations will be suspended.
01/16–19/1996	Pro-Chechen commandos hijack a Black Sea ferry at the Turkish port of Trabzon, taking 150 hostages, most Russian tourists. Hostages are later released after the hijackers claim their aim of drawing worldwide attention to Russian atrocities in Chechnya is achieved.
01/17/1996	Russian troops attack Chechen fighters and their hostages dig in the village of Pervomaiskaya on the Chechnya/Dagestan border. Eighteen hostages are reported missing by Moscow, which also claims killing 153 Chechens and taking 28 prisoner.
01/09–24/1996	Chechen commandos, led by Salman Raduyev, take 2000 people hostage at a hospital in Kizliar in the republic of Dagestan.

06/14–20/ 1995	Chechen fighters take the southern Russian town of Budyonnovsk and 1500 hostages in a hospital. Russian forces free 200 people on the 17th, but at least 150 are killed. Talks were held between Chernomyrdin and the Chechen leader of the hostage-taking, Shamyl Basayev. Agreement reached freeing the remaining hostages in return for a halt in fighting in Chechnya and negotiations for the withdrawal of Russian troops in Chechnya.
02/09/1995	Former Soviet leader Mikhail Gorbachev describes the campaign as a huge mistake that would cost the country dearly.
04–08/1994	Kidnappers from Chechnya carry out a series of hostage seizures of civilians in southern Russia. Russia blames Dudayev, and call on Chechens to topple him.
06/1992	Chechnya and Ingushetia split, Ingushetia remaining in the Russian Federation.
11/1991	Yeltsin declares a state of emergency in Checheno-Ingushetia and sends troops to Grozny. Troops are blocked at the airport, parliament overrules his declaration, and Yeltsin pulls them out after three days.
10/1991	Dudayev launches a campaign to topple Moscow's temporary administration, attacking government offices and holding mass rallies. He wins 80 percent backing in presidential polls and unilaterally declares Chechnya independent.
09/05/1991	The government of Checheno-Ingushetia, which supports the August hard-line coup against Mikhail Gorbachev, resign, Soviet Air Force General Dzhokhar Dudayev leaves Estonia and is installed as national leader.
1944	Hundreds of thousands of Chechens are deported by Soviet dictator Josef Stalin with other Caucasus peoples to Soviet Central Asia. Many die during the journey or in exile. After Stalin's death, they are allowed to return home in 1957.
1934	Chechnya merges with neighboring Ingushetia in Checheno-Ingushetia.
1921	Chechnya became part of Russia's Mountain Republic, which is formally incorporated into the Soviet Union in 1924.
1859	Chechnya is incorporated into Russia.
1817–1864	Imperial Russia fights a 40-year war to conquer mountainous lands between itself and newly acquired Georgia, defeating the Chechens and other Muslim peoples.

CHECHNYA (ICHKERIA)

Chechnya, 1995: Front Row Seats

One can never lead a normal life as a war photographer. As soon as the words "hostilities have broken out in..." are heard on CNN, it is expected that there will be a flow of videotapes and photographs that cover and explain the conflict. Most journalists are dispatched in a hurry and get in-country before the borders are closed. Others must make their way in by whatever means necessary. *DP* is part of the latter.

The large networks and news gathering organizations pay extraordinary amounts of money not only to send in news teams but also to charter airplanes, couriers and even military planes to get their dispatches out of the country. Satellite telephones and transmitters make it easy to send reports now, but the units are expensive and heavy to pack.

When Russia sent its troops into Grozny, there were plenty of journalists and reporters. As the situation became embarrassing, the Russians began to simply round up and send journalists out of the country. Previously, Dudayev had expelled all Russian reporters because of their inflammatory articles. When the Russian and Western press began to highlight the Russian incompetence and division, the Russians rounded up the Western press. Unlike major conflicts where the press are carefully clothed, fed, housed and "spun" by briefings, press releases and carefully prepared interviews, Chechnya was the opposite. Russian troops couldn't care less if they shot at the glint of a camera lens or a sniper's telescopic sight. Mortars, bombs and shells dropped by the Russians cared even less.

We wanted to see for ourselves, so we sent in a correspondent to try to understand the situation firsthand. The story of just what it takes to get into a war zone like Chechnya will give you some idea of the new face of reporting war.

We made our preliminary arrangements before leaving Istanbul with the "Caucasus Peoples Federation," a group that was supporting Dudayev's fight in Chechnya, or Chechenstan as it is locally known. The plan was to allow us to go in with a group of "volunteers," or mercenaries, via Baku in Azerbaijan through Dagestan and then on to Grozny. Although they could provide some forms of transportation to the border, from Hasalyurt we would have to walk for about three days through the mountains in the middle of winter to reach Grozny. Although we were being sent in under the protection of the Chechen forces, there was no guarantee who would be in charge once we arrived.

We set off the day before Christmas with minimal survival gear: our cameras, a stove, some tins of fish and warm clothing. We fly to Baku, in Azerbaijan, to meet the people who will take us into Grozny. The "friends" turn out to be members of the Lezgi Mafia, one of the toughest groups in Russia and the Transcaucasus region. The Lezgi number about 1.5 million and live in the north of Azerbaijan and in south and central Dagestan. Our goal is to fly 1800 km east to Baku and then travel 400 km north along the Caspian Sea through Dagestan and then west 50 km over the border into Grozny.

These entrepreneurial bandits have decided that since things are heating up (and as they don't know the difference between *DP* and NBC), they will need a $5000 transportation fee. Now normally when you make a business transaction in any country, you have some basic understanding of the value of money, and the intentions and general cost of a service. When you are dealing with the Mafia in Azerbaijan, however, there is no guarantee that you will not end up a frozen cadaver with a slit throat two miles out of Baku.

Seeing how we have a plan "B," we have nothing to lose by negotiating this fee down to a paltry $1000 which included transportation, food, lodging but no cable TV.

Plan "B" was the official Russian tour of Chechnya. Most Westerners are not aware of Moscow's new entrepreneurial spirit. Journalists who are accepted can arrange a $4000 junket into Chechnya from Moscow via military transport. We opt for the lower-priced, more adventurous ground operator version via the locals.

We make our deal over tea and cigarettes, and, once accepted, we are as good as kinfolk with these tough characters. Although we are kissing cousins, we also agree to pay our fee once we are over the border in Hasalyurt. The man who is to take us there tells us we will have company. He is bringing in 10 mercenaries and volunteers from Iran, Uzbekistan and Tadjikistan who will be joining us 10 km short of the Azerbaijan-Dagestan border. Oh, he mentions casually, a load of antitank missiles as well. We don't ask him how much money this one trip will clear but it is obvious that war is good for business in these parts.

One of his men drives us two hours north to Quba in a Lada, complete with reflective tinted windows. The Mafia may have money, but they sure don't have taste. We stay at an old Russian farmhouse surrounded by apple orchards as far as the eye can see. Now abandoned, it was a way station and safe house for the Lezgi Mafia. In the courtyard are two tractors with the antitank rockets. The men are packing oranges, apples, flour and other agrarian items to camouflage the clearly labeled crates.

We are awakened early the next morning and set off north toward Qusar, a town about 25 km short of the Dagestan border. We are now traveling in three groups. The first group consists of two Lezgi, who would travel ahead of us to meet with the local officials, grease the border guards, and ensure our safe passage into Dagestan. Behind us come the volunteers, now happy farmers bringing in foodstuffs. The border is officially closed, but the guards just stare dispassionately at us and never bother to even wave us down or check our passports. We thought the mirrored windows were bad taste; now we know their function. Inside Dagestan, we stay in the car until we reach an old Lenin Pioneer Camp, a relic of the Russian regime, where primary and high school kids learned the ways of the revolution. It is the Soviet version of our Boy Scout camps.

That night we have a typical Azeri meal—smoked meat and smoked fish, washed down with homemade vodka strong enough to remove paint. Tonight will be cold, but the fire from the vodka will warm us up.

After our feast, we set off down a small side road that leads to the official checkpoint at the border. The cart track is used by the local farmers and is too bumpy to allow large trucks. There is little reason for a 24-hour border patrol, and, by "coincidence," there is no border patrol that night. As we travel along the gray

Caspian sea into Derbent, we learn some unsettling news. Moscow has replaced the local police and border guards with special security team members known as "Omon." This is indeed a bad "omen." Security is tight because one of Dudayev's assistants has made a visit to Turkey and asked for the Turks to send assistance to Chechnya via Azerbaijan. The sudden heavy presence of the Russian military is to cut off any aid coming to the embattled capital of Grozny.

We are told this by a Lezgi mafia customs official. The fellow who holds this oxymoronic post advises us that in order for us to continue through Dagestan, we will need to become citizens of the Dagestan Autonomous Region.

That night, a man from the local police force brings two blank passports and we become Dagestanis for $300 each. It is a busy night as we fill out forms and complete the passports. Before dawn the next morning, it seems that our new status is to be rewarded. Our transport is a brand-new BMW bought (or stolen) in Germany. We leave our old passports behind as partial payment and to avoid being searched and arrested as spies. Dagestan is a war zone with a penalty of two years in jail for crossing the border illegally. The Russian soldiers are also empowered to detain and/or execute people whom they suspect as volunteers or spies.

I wonder who Sefail Musayev is, but I carry his passport thankfully. The fact that we cannot speak a word of Russian makes every border crossing a gut wrencher. The Russians are not in any mood for levity, but our Azeri driver/guide manages to chat and joke our way through a total of seven checkpoints. At each tense checkpoint my hair turns a little grayer, the lines on my face are etched deeper and I wonder what the hell I am doing here. When we reach the bustling city of Mohachkale (or Makhachkala), we finally can breathe. From here it is 170 km to the border of Chechnya. From this point on, our driver knows nothing of the conditions ahead.

We drive on in our beautiful new BMW, feeling like royalty, although we are the last people the Russians want in this area. We come to Kizlar, and our driver stops to talk with a Chechen contact family, who works as a link between the Chechen Mafia and the Lezgi. We ask about the Reuters journalists who are based in Hasalyurt. We have made an earlier deal to use their transmitter and satellite phone. The news is not good. The day before, the Russians severely bombed the Hasalyurt-Grozny road, knocking out a number of bridges. The journalists who were staying in the local sports stadium and using it as a base for their forays into Grozny were rounded up and sent back to Moscow.

After coming this far we have no way to send out our information and no one to take us across the border; all that lies ahead of us is a bombed-out wasteland.

After much discussion with the Chechen family, we learn there is one chance. If we can make it to Babayurt, another border town, we can try to contact a group of Chechen volunteers who are to cross the border soon. They mention that we will be safer in Chechnya, since the Russians are increasing their crackdown on foreigners and volunteers in Dagestan daily.

Kizlar is about 40 km north of Hasalyurt, and Babayurt is halfway in between. One of the refugees from Kizlar staying in the house offers to come with us to help us get into Chechnya and to ease our way past the checkpoints that await us. Our luck holds, because the Russians have concentrated their Omon special forces south of Hasalyurt and the checkpoints to the north are manned by local Dagestanis. We meet up with a group of 20–30 Chechen volunteers who are preparing to cross the border that night. We discuss the various ways into the country. Most agree that to try to walk over the mountains into Grozny is futile since the snow is now 4 to 5 meters deep. The 130-km trip will take at least a full week, with an excellent chance of being attacked by jets or helicopters during the day.

We decide to tag along with the heavily armed volunteers. We begin our trip in a convoy of cars and cross the empty border post. Around midnight, the drivers of the cars drop us off and return. We will continue on foot. We walk for six or seven hours, covering 20 km of frozen lowland impeded only by a slight snow cover. We let the main group of armed volunteers go on ahead of us. Our group was not armed, but if they meet up with the Russians, we are close enough to hear the sound of gunfire before we stumble into the same trap.

The cold is numbing, and we plod on through the night like zombies. The wind whips and slaps our faces, making icicles on my mustache. The moon is our only light. After a while, we come upon a dirt track that leads to the village ahead. The wind not only brings cold and pain; it now brings the sound of heavy gunfire, alternately fading and building. Our temperatures begin to rise, as we go through the fields leading down to the village. Rockets and automatic weapons crack and thump in the crystal-clear night. As we crunch our way down to the village, the light of the dull blue sky begins to rise like a curtain at the start of a movie. The sound of the Russian helicopters increases from a muted drumroll to a thunderous chorus.

My cold hands reach for my frozen cameras in anticipation. This is the play for which we have come, the drama to which we have fought so hard for admission. Now on with the show.

—**Sedat Aral**

CHECHNYA (ICHKERIA)

Bogotá

Colombia
★ ★ ★ ★ ★

Coca Loco Land

In February 1997, full-page ads appeared in major U.S. daily newspapers proclaiming: "We're Well On The Way To Making The Drug Traffickers Suffer As Much As The People They Supply." The expensive ads weren't placed by the Policeman's Benevolence Association, nor by the National Ad Council—but instead by the Colombian government in a highly unusual and surprisingly disarming effort to win public support for the country's recertification as a U.S. ally in the war against drugs. Perhaps more than the gains made by the Colombian government in combatting drugs, the ads revealed the desperation of this troubled land.

Each hour someone is killed in Bogota, the capital city of Colombia. The 8600 cadavers that pass through the morgue pile up every year at an average of 24 a day. Violent death is so ingrained in Colombian life that the health department has listed violence as the leading cause of death for individuals over 10 years old. To date, there isn't a known vaccine for a bullet to the head.

The victims fit a neat pattern: male—one or more bullet holes—61.2 percent are under 34. Firearms account for nearly 37 percent of the deaths (traffic accidents account for 14 percent and 30 percent are from "unknown causes"). For those who like to play the odds in this beautiful land, your insurance company will tell you that there are four kidnappings and 73 murders every day. A car is stolen every 24 minutes, and 142 houses are broken into every day. At least Russian roulette gives you better odds.

The only saving grace in these morbid stats is that 75 percent of the 26,642 murder victims in Colombia in 1996 were classified as "common criminals." Colombia has a murder rate of 81 per 100,000 inhabitants (nine times higher than the U.S. average), making it among the most violent countries in the world for murders.

These National Statistics Office figures do little to reveal the entire story of what is happening in Colombia. Colombia is turning into a lawless nation that functions on the edge, barely keeping the lid on anarchy. Colombia's wealthy citizens, not to mention its intellectuals, have fled to escape kidnapping, extortion and murder threats. The drug lords, criminals, revolutionaries and terrorists not only wage war against the government and infrastructure but among themselves.

In all, the price of the guerrilla war in Colombia since 1990 has cost a staggering US$20 billion, or 4 percent of the GDP yearly. Extortion, kidnapping, oil pipeline attacks and murders inflicted by a 10,000–15,000-rebel-strong force (there were a mere 215 insurgents in 1964) have cost the state oil company, Ecopetrol, US$550 million—through lost royalties, pipeline attacks, repair and security costs, and ransoms. Private-sector oil companies consider the loss of US$430 million—due to death, destruction and mayhem—as the cost of doing business here.

In Colombia, crisis management teams outnumber pipeline teams. Negotiations consultants are hired, not to strike deals on leveraged buyouts and drilling concessions from the government, but to procure the release of hostages. More than 800 people are being held captive in Colombia as this ink dries. One Colombian study estimates that, including extortion and drug trafficking, rebel income between 1991 and 1994 reached US$1.8 billion, providing the guerrillas an annual per-capita income of US$45,000, compared with Colombia's GNP per-capita income of US$1401.

Of all the folks killed here since 1990, more than half of them were innocent bystanders. Colombia has spent $3.4 billion to fight rebels since 1990. One pipeline near the Venezuelan border was blown up 229 times during a 260-week period. That's almost as regular as the fireworks every night at DisneyWorld.

Although the government has extended an olive branch to Colombia's insurgents and promised the Colombian people they would make peace with the rebels, only one faction has stepped forward so far—the 250 guerrillas of the Jaime Bateman Cayon group, a breakaway coterie of the now-defunct M-19 insurgents. Those talks subsequently broke down.

Colombia may well be the butthole of South America. Don't believe us? You can actually receive updated security information about Colombia from the State Department by dialing ☎ 202-647-5225, and then enter the following letters: C-O-L-O-N.

Caribbean Sea

Guajira

Santa Marta
Ríohacha
Barranquilla
Atlántico
Ciénaga
Valledupar
Cartagena
Maracaibo
Magdalena
César
Tolú
Sincelejo
Montería
Sucre
Turbo
Córdoba
Bolívar
Norte de
Santander
Cúcuta
Pamplona
Bucaramanga
Santander
Barbosa
Paz de Río
Medellín
Antioquia
Arauca
Arauca
Casanare
Meta
Puerto
Carreño
Quibdó
Boyacá
Tunja
Yopal
Chocó
Pereira
Manizales
Vichada
Valle
del
Cauca
Armenia
Bogotá
Ibagué
Girardot
Puerto López
Villavicencio
Puerto Inírida
Buenaventura
Cali
Meta
Guaviare
Cauca
Neiva
Guainía
Popayán
Huila
San José del
Guaviare
Guainía
San Felipe
Tumaco
Florencia
Guaviare
Vaupés
Mitú
Pasto
Mocoa
Nariño
Putumayo
Caquetá
Vaupés
Quito
ECUADOR
Amazonas
BRAZIL
Caquetá
Putumayo
Amazon
PERU
Amazon
Iquitos
Leticia
Javari

PANAMA

Pacific
Ocean

VENEZUELA

Atrato

Cauca

Pan American Highway

Magdalena

Colombia

- ⊛ National Capital
- ⊙ Department Capital
- ● Secondary City
- ⊠ Airport
- ↧ Port
- Province Border
- Road
- ╈╈╈ Railroad

| 0 | 100 | 200 km |
| 0 | | 100 mi |

©FWI

Central Provinces
1. Risaralda
2. Caldas
3. Cundinamarca
4. Quindío
5. Tolima
6. Districto Especial

Colombia is currently the most dangerous place in the Western Hemisphere, and perhaps the world because it is not considered a war zone. Latin America's longest running insurgency—lasting some 30 years—has taken the lives of more than 20,000 Colombians and foreigners in the last 10 years, 56 percent of them civilians. (Some estimates say 18,000 were killed between 1990 and 1994 alone.) It is a war of proxy. Of those killed, only five percent died with a gun in their hands. Some 180,000 people were displaced from their homes in 1996 alone. Things are not looking up 462 FARC, 348 ELN, 60 EPL, 133 police, 360 soldiers and thousands of civilians died in 1996.

The country's rebel groups are at the zenith of their power. They control half of Colombia. Numbering between 10,000 and 15,000, guerrillas are operating in 60 percent of Colombia's 1100 municipalities. Their coffers have been pumped up lately by the proceeds from kidnapping, drug trafficking and extortion payoffs. The rebels lack the means and numbers to achieve any real political clout, but are looking to strengthen their hand in any future peace talks by escalating the level of violence in 1997. Colombians fear there won't be any peace until there first occurs a major escalation of the conflict. Although the Colombian military is 120,000-troops strong, only about 17 percent of the soldiers are professionally trained.

If you travel to Colombia, you will be the target of thieves, kidnappers and murderers. In 1996, there were 1337 terrorist crimes committed. Civilians and soldiers are routinely stopped at roadblocks, dragged out of their cars and summarily executed in Antioquia Department. Tourists are drugged in bars and discos, then robbed and murdered. Expats, missionaries and other foreigners are favorite targets of terrorist groups, who kidnap them for outrageous ransom amounts that climb into the millions of dollars.

Should you be victimized or seek revenge due to a misfortune, expect little comfort or sympathy from the police, military, and judicial or diplomatic folks; they're busy covering their own asses from the threat of terrorism, drug cartels and crime lords. Since 1990, more than 4620 police officers have been killed. Only 12 percent of the crimes committed in Colombia ever reach the judicial system.

Any good news? Some. The death squads have forced many drug traffickers to move into neighboring Brazil for "health" reasons. But the bottom line here, as one journalist commented, is this: "As many drug-trafficking countries fret about becoming another Colombia, with narcotics-dominated politics, Colombians worry that their country will become another Somalia, run by warlords."

Ernesto Samper & the Government

Liberal Ernesto Samper Pizano squeaked into power June 19, 1993 in a dead heat with Conservative Andres Pastrana Arango. Considering that only one of every three Colombians voted, it doesn't seem to make any difference who runs the country. Samper has been accused as being a stooge of the Cali drug cartel, despite his public calls for the extermination of Colombia's drug problem. A recent investigation into his alleged ties with druglords concluded that he was offered backing but didn't accept it. Meanwhile, Samper has all but given up hope on making peace with the rebs. Colombia's military budget is being jacked up to 10 percent of the government's total spending—the highest level in Latin America.

Alfonso Valdivieso

As the government's chief prosecutor, Valdivieso, a highly popular anti-corruption and anti-drug champion, presided over the jailing (or killing) of all of Colombia's billionaire drug lords. He was the force behind the investigation into Samper's election campaign that almost resulted in Samper's dismissal from the presidency on corruption charges. The chief prosecutor's job is considered the second most powerful in the country behind the presidency, which Valdivieso wants. He stepped down in May 1997 to run for Samper's job. Betting men have pesos saying he'll get capped first.

Bolivarian Movement for a New Colombia, Revolutionary Armed Forces of Colombia or Fuerzas Armadas Revolucionarias de Colombia (FARC)

FARC was founded in 1964 and is currently estimated to have between 12,000 and 17,000 members (propped up by 4500 to 5500 armed combatants). Led by 60-something Manuel "Sureshot" Marulanda, their stock in trade is kidnapping, extortion and protection of rural drug operations across Colombia. FARC is the largest and oldest rebel group operating in Colombia. The Patriotic Union (UP) is FARC's political arm, seeking change through old-fashioned rhetoric and arm twisting.

The group specializes in armed attacks against Colombian targets, bombings of U.S. businesses, kidnappings of Colombians and foreigners for ransom, and assassinations. During the first six months of 1997, the group had already kidnapped more than 60 civilians. Their funding comes from extortion (ransom payments) and income from the trafficking of drugs (predominantly cocaine). FARC has well-documented ties to drug traffickers and Cuba. The dope bucks provide much needed hard currency for Cuba, whose economy has been in tatters since the collapse of the Soviet Union.

FARC is the largest, best-trained, best-equipped, and most effective insurgent organization in Latin America—the one Western terrorist group voted "most likely to succeed" by U.S. intelligence services. Many consider FARC to be the "military" arm of the Communist Party of Colombia (PCC). The leadership of FARC is composed largely of disaffected middle- and upper-class intellectuals, although it recruits from the peasant population in an effort to maintain a popular base. FARC also draws support from traditional left-wingers, workers, students and radical priests. The popularity of FARC has been undermined by the questionable practice of kidnapping peasants and murdering them as "collaborators" and "traitors" if they're not cooperative.

FARC is the principal force behind National Simon Bolivar Guerrilla Coordinator (SBGC), which includes all major Colombian insurgent groups. FARC was able to muster this coalition due to its closer ties with Colombian narcotics traffickers than the other insurgent groups. The relationship appears to be the strongest in those areas where coca cultivation and production and FARC operational strongholds overlap. In exchange for FARC protection of narcotics interests, the guerrillas have received money to purchase weapons and supplies. There is evidence that various FARC fronts have actually been involved in processing cocaine.

On June 15, 1997, FARC, in a major publicity coup, released 70 Colombian soldiers, some of whom had been held for more than nine months. (Media attention, in fact, is one of the group's biggest goals. They've set up press offices in Mexico and Costa Rica and regularly e-mail to the media their accounts of battles with government troops. You can check out their web site listed below.) However, hopes for a possible path toward peace were dashed shortly afterward when FARC resumed full-scale offensive operations. FARC has been maintaining close contact with the ELN, suggesting that the two groups are planning joint operations.

Revolutionary Armed Forces of Colombia
http://members.tripod.com/~farc

National Liberation Army (NLA), or Ejercito de Liberacion Nacional (ELN)

A rural-based, anti-U.S., Maoist-Marxist-Leninist guerrilla group formed in July 1964, the ELN raises funds by kidnapping foreign employees of large corporations and holding them for lofty ransom payments. The ELN conducts extortion and bombing operations against U.S. and other foreign businesses in Colombia, particularly the deep-pocketed petroleum industry. The group has inflicted major damage on oil pipelines since 1986.

They boast up to 2000 members, many of whom have been trained and armed by Nicaragua and Cuba. The ELN seeks "...the conquest of power for the popular classes..." along with nationalizations, expropriations, and agrarian reform. ELN leader Ike de Jesus Vergara was arrested in Bogota in March 1997 and number-four Diego Antonio Prieto was gunned down by Bogota police in June 1997. But the losses haven't slowed the ELN down.

The ELN is a political-military organization that draws its support from among students, intellectuals, peasants and, surprisingly, the middle-class workers of Colombia. Operations include the kidnapping of wealthy ranchers and industrialists, assassinations of military officers, offing of labor leaders and peasants, multiple armed robberies, various bombings, raids on isolated villages, weapons grabs on police posts and army patrols, and occupations of radio stations and newspaper offices. The ELN is currently perfecting attacks on petroleum pipelines and facilities, seeking to damage Colombia's economic infrastructure and investment climate. But the group still targets the military. On July 6, 1997 it took down a military chopper, killing 20 soldiers and one civilian, over a section of pipeline it had earlier blown up. The Cano-Limon Covenas pipeline, the largest in Colombia, was attacked no fewer than 40 times during the first half of 1997. The ELN has sabotaged the pipeline hundreds of times over the last decade, causing more than US$1 billion in damage. When operating normally, the pipeline ships 175,000 barrels of oil a day, about 45 percent of Colombian oil exports.

National Liberation Army
http://www.voces.org

Popular Liberation Army (EPL/D)

This dissident former affiliate of the Popular Liberation Army based primarily in Uraba can't seem to get ahead. The PLA signed a peace treaty several years ago with the government but these Maoist EPL/D sad sacks won't quit. The EPL/D leaders are followed and arrested on a regular basis (probably due to informants from the PLA). The 2800 armed troops demobilized in 1991 and the group changed its name to Esperanza, Paz y Libertad (Hope, Peace and Freedom), retaining the initials EPL. As the new group/party has had political success in the polls since making peace with the government, members have become favorite targets of disgruntled and jealous FARC fanatics, who moved into the areas the EPL abandoned The Colombian government announced that they had wiped out the last remaining members of the EPL in 1996.

Dignity for Colombia Movement (DCM)

This player on the scene seems to have a fairly simple agenda. Kill every member of the 165-member House of Representatives who votes to clear President Ernesto Samper of drug charges. A refreshingly direct change from our own political pressure groups.

Jame Bateman Front

This is a group of about 200–250 fighters who split from the M-19 group when it became a political group. They are based outside of Bogota and are active again after peace talks with the government stalled last year. Bateman guerrillas kidnapped British diplomat Timothy Cowley in August 1995. He was released four months later after, what police claim, was a sensational rescue operation. However, it's more likely the rebels received a ransom before police arrived, released Cowley, and headed back into the hills. The group's political leader, Jorge Eliecer Zapata, was arrested in July 1997 in Cali.

The U.S. Military

The U.S. government has unofficially declared war on the drug trade in Colombia and, therefore, FARC. Currently, there are officially nine U.S. advisors in Colombia training troops; 62 military technicians are installing radar bases; 32 members of a navy construction battalion in Meta province are building a military base on the Meta River, a heavily used artery for drug transport; 156 U.S. Army engineers northwest of Cali are building a school, clinic and road. Although covert U.S. involvement in Colombia is low-key presently, further disintegration of Colombia's infrastructure would undoubtedly lead to an increased presence.

Right Wing Death Squads

The most dangerous group is the Peasant Self Defence group of Cordoba and Uraba (ACCU). This group executes peasants of course. How do you get to be so lucky? Well according to leader Carlos Castano, the ACCU must receive three independent accusations, which are reviewed by a secret tribunal and then you get to be one of the 100 or so corpses left lying in the street.

More than a hundred groups of teams made up of five to 10 members each are paid by wealthy and influential Colombians to kill former and current left-wingers and communists on an ongoing basis, and to act as a more effective deterrent to kidnapping, murder and extortion than the police or military. The death squads are primarily active in Medellin and Bogota, Uraba and around Meta and Antioquia Departments. Another principal player is the Macetos paramilitary group, which is centered in the San Martin municipality. This group has performed numerous massacres against leftist guerrilla groups and their sympathizers. A group called the Hoods operates out of Cartagena and is believed responsible for some 30 deaths since 1985. These so-called "self-defense groups" are not illegal under Colombian law and, despite UN urging to outlaw them, continue to find both government and military support. As one Colombian colonel phrased it: "The army sees the enemy of its enemy as its friend."

The Orejuela Brothers and the Cali Cartel

How powerful is the drug business in Colombia? Gilberto and Miguel Rodriguez Orejuela, brothers who head the notorious Cali cartel and considered the most infamous drug traffickers in Colombia's history, were each sentenced to a mere 10 years in prison in January 1997 for smuggling hundreds of tons of cocaine into the U.S. They could get off in five and have been busy running their operations unabated from the slammer.

Fidel and Carlos Castano

Controlled by the drug lords, the Castanos run the northern seven of Uraba's 11 counties. They founded "The People Persecuted by Pablo Escobar," a group instrumental in the capture and death of the notorious leader of the Medellin cartel. Now they run a land-grabbing fiefdom in northern Colombia, executing any antagonistic peasants who get in the way.

Eastern Plains Cartel

This fledgling, little-known cartel, based in southeastern Guaviare Department, has the distinction of boasting Colombia's largest cocaine lab ever discovered by authorities. The 1.5-square-mile complex was capable of processing 1.5 tons of raw cocaine per day before it was raided in January 1997. That would be half the amount of cocaine shipped daily to the U.S. by Colombian drug traffickers. The lab had its own airstrip and employee housing quarters and was protected by FARC guerrillas.

COLOMBIA

The "Extradictables"

Letters from a group called the "Extradictables" are being received by news organizations warning that editors and journalists will be killed if Colombia reinstitutes an extradition law with the U.S. Colombia's extradition treaty with the U.S. was declared unconstitutional in 1991, but it's been back on the agenda. Journalist Gerardo Bedoya, who urged a return of the law, was gunned down in March 1997.

A passport and a return/onward ticket are required for stays up to three months. Minors (under 18) traveling alone, with one parent, or with a third party must present written authorization from the absent parent(s) or legal guardian, specifically granting permission to travel alone, with one parent or with a third party. This authorization must be notarized, authenticated by a Colombian embassy or consulate, and translated into Spanish. Visas are not required for citizens of the United States, Canada or Great Britain for stays up to 90 days.

For up-to-the-minute information regarding entry and customs requirements for Colombia, contact the nearest consulate in Los Angeles, Miami, Chicago, New Orleans, New York, Houston or San Juan, or the embassy in Washington D.C.: **Colombian Embassy** *2118 Leroy Place NW, Washington, D.C. 20008,* ☎ *(202) 387-8338.*

An onward ticket is not always requested at land crossings but you may be asked to prove that you have at least US$20 for each day of your stay in Colombia. Thirty-day extensions can be applied for at the DAS (security police) office in any city.

Entering Colombia by land usually presents no problems at the frontiers. But note that when leaving Colombia by land, you'll need to have an exit stamp from the DAS. You may not be able to get this stamp at the smaller frontier towns. Get the stamp in a city. Otherwise, you may be detained.

Cities within Colombia are served by Avianca, Aces, SAM, Intercontinental, Satena and Aires airlines. The bigger cities are reached on a daily basis, the smaller ones less frequently, sometimes once a week. By air, Avianca and American Airlines fly regularly to Bogota from the U.S., Cali and Barranquilla. There is an airport tax of US$18. Prices are higher in the high season (June–August, December). Purchase intra-Colombia tickets inside the country.

Buses are a great way to get around, but incidents of thefts are increasing. The air-conditioned buses are often quite frigid when the air conditioning is working. When it isn't, they're hot, since the windows don't open. Bring your own food, as rest stops are infrequent. Additionally, expect the bus to be periodically stopped and boarded by police. Your identity will most likely be checked. Occasionally, a photocopy of your passport will be sufficient. Make one and have it notarized. Buses leave according to schedule, rather than when they are full. Colombia's VELOTAX minibuses are efficient. However, other buses experience frequent breakdowns (see "Dangerous Things").

Taxis are plentiful. Take only metered taxis. But if one cannot be found, negotiate and set a fixed price before you enter the taxi. Women should not take taxis alone at night (see "Dangerous Things").

The roads in Colombia are often dilapidated and unmarked. Avoid driving at night; Colombian drivers are careless and often reckless.

Santa Marta

The north end of town and the Rodadero Beach areas are extremely dangerous. Do not travel alone into these areas. Daylight armed robberies of tourists are commonplace. Thieves will often relieve their victims of their clothes as well as all other valuables.

The Darien

Pressed against the Panama border, Uraba is the murder capital of Colombia—more than 700 people were killed in Uraba by leftist guerrillas in 1996. The country's richest banana-growing region, it's also home to myriad drug runners, leftist guerrillas and para-military outfits. Uraba's annual murder rate of 254 per 100,000 people is the highest in Colombia. On February 14, 1996, guerrillas massacred 10 banana farmers—and 10 more people were mowed down by AK-47 and R-15 gunfire in a billiards hall on April 4. How bad is Uraba? Local officials are pleading for U.N. intervention and for a peacekeeping force to be installed. The area around the Darien Peninsula is a major transit point for contraband goods and a center for drug processing. The FARC group provides protection for the drug labs. Two Austrian and two Swiss tourists were kidnapped while they went to visit a nature preserve in March of '97. Their kidnappers demanded $15 million and FARC wasn't going to use that cash to save the rainforest. Two of the victims were killed in the government rescue attempt.

Cartagena

Professional pickpockets abound, especially at the beaches. They especially like to strike in crowded areas. Cameras are a favorite trophy for thieves here. Scams in Cartagena are numerous. Other crooks pose as tour guides. Some of them can be rather touchy if you turn down their expensive excursion offers. If you're offered a job on a ship bound for the U.S. or other parts of South America, don't believe it because this is most assuredly a con.

Medellin

Despite being a major drug traffickers' center and the new murder capital of Colombia, the city is a remarkably friendly place. Medillin had 5245 murders last year. That's only one murder every two hours. However, it's not the druglords you should be afraid of here. Rather, it's petty thieves and street thugs. Medellin has been experiencing a rash of bombings, most attacks being carried out by the FARC. On one day alone in June 1997, FARC bombed the union offices of a lingerie maker, two private homes in Caicedo neighborhood, five city buses and, for the *piece de resistance*, guerrillas booby-trapped a FARC flag, which exploded when a man tried to remove it at Antioquia University.

Valle Department

Everywhere off the main roads in Valle Department is extremely unsafe due to guerrilla activities. Beware particularly of Cauca Department E off the Pan-American Highway. Tourists should avoid this area entirely. Areas of Cra 6 are also extremely dangerous, including Parque Bolivar and the market. There has also been guerrilla activity in the Purace National Park area, particularly near the Popayan-La Plata Road. In Inza, women should not be on the streets unaccompanied.

Other Guerrilla Areas

The Departments of Boyaca, Norte de Santander, Casanare, Caqueta, Huila, Putumayo, Cesar, Guajira, Arauka, Meta, as well as the Turbo/Uraba region.

The Upper Magdalena

You'll constantly encounter riffraff here, touting everything from drugs, gold and emeralds to pre-Columbian art. The items are always fake, except for the drugs.

Bogota

Narco-traffickers/guerrillas have threatened and carried out terrorist attacks against Colombian officials, foreign embassies, and other targets. Expect to travel in fear of violent crime, particularly in the south of Bogota. Tourist areas are infested with thieves, pickpockets and opportunists. The richer, northern suburbs of Bogota have experienced a rash of car bombings. If you survive the 7.5-mile ride into Bogota from the airport, be forewarned that crime is prevalent in the vicinity of hotels and airports. Large hotels, travel agencies, corporate headquarters and other institutions that display U.S. corporate IDs are targeted by terrorists for bombing attacks.

Colombia East of the Andes

This area can be hazardous to your health, with the exception of the city of Leticia in the Amazonas Department and adjacent tourist areas in Amazonas.

North Coast/Barranquilla/Isla San Andres

Cali is the home of two of the major drug cartels. Expect plenty of fighting between the two rival groups. The island of San Andres is a major drug shipment area. Cartagena is considered somewhat safe, due to the increased presence of police protecting the lucrative tourist trade. Expect tourist crime.

Barranquilla is the site of guerilla attacks on businesses and government centers. The busy port is a major center for drug traffickers. Guerrillas like to regularly attack the Navy base near the airport at night. Outside the city limits is the domain of bad people, particularly at night.

Cali and Valle de Cauca Department

During the first five months of 1997, 721 murders and 18 kidnappings were committed in Cali and Valle de Cauca Department. It's hard to believe, but these figures represent a 27-percent downward trend in murder and kidnapping in the area, that's if the figures can be believed. 1997 was an election year. Rarely does the crime rate go down while unemployment is rising, as it is in Cali. Wanna get a job here? Good luck; the unemployment rate is 17 percent. In 70 percent of the crimes committed in Cali, either the perpetrator or the victim is under 17 years old. In 1995, 1243 minors were arrested for crimes ranging from robbery to murder.

Cali-Buenaventura Highway

The highway between these two cities has become prime pickings for guerrillas and common thugs. Kidnappings have increased markedly on the highway, most performed by FARC rebels and bandits. The road is also the venue for a surge in truck-jackings by "land pirates."

U.S. Companies

Several terrorist or guerrilla groups are active in Colombia; U.S. interests are among their targets. Kidnapping for ransom or political purposes, including U.S. citizens, is increasingly common in Colombia. In early 1994, bombs destroyed a Mormon temple in Medellin, damaged another in Bucaramanga, and damaged a Coca-Cola bottling plant in Bucaramanga. Additionally, two American missionaries were kidnapped for political reasons by guerrillas.

Kidnapping

Remember the last time you asked your boss how much you were really worth? Well, you may find out on your next trip to Colombia. In 1996, there were a reported 1439 cases of kidnapping, a 35-percent increase over 1995. About a third of the abductions were carried out by rebel groups, while common criminals attached to kidnapping gangs snatched 885 victims. More than 200 children were kidnapped in 1996. Of all those abducted in Colombia in 1996, 39 percent are still in the custody of their kidnappers, 30 percent were released after a ransom was paid, nine percent were killed by their abductors and 15 percent freed during government raids. Seven percent escaped.

Kidnapping has become a US$350 million industry in Colombia. In 1997, an average of four people were kidnapped a day. In 1996, at least 45 foreigners were abducted and more than US$160 million paid to kidnappers in Colombia. A Briton was killed in August of '95, while an American was released after being held for 11 months. It seems his captors just gave up on ever getting the $5 million they were asking for. In February 1997, an American geologist was found shot dead 11 weeks after he was abducted. Three American missionaries abducted in 1993 remain missing.

Fewer than one in 30 kidnappers are ever caught and sentenced. Fewer than half the kidnappings that actually take place are ever reported. Luckily, Colombians make up the bulk of the victims. Most never report the abductions, fearing it would just advertise their culpability. There were believed to be 10 Americans being held captive in Colombia as of February 1995. A splinter group of the Popular Liberation Army (EPL) took responsibility for the January 1995 abduction of Edward Gravowsky. Although the EPL was disbanded in March 1991, a group of about 150 diehards remains. Gravowski was the fourth foreigner kidnapped by Colombian guerrillas in a four-month period. In the past few years, only one in 10 of the reported victims has been rescued by security forces. Many others are murdered by the kidnappers, who often demand large ransoms and then return a corpse.

Murder

Think the U.S. is the murder capital of the world? Think again. Colombia has the highest murder rate in the world with Johannesburg and Washington D.C. not far behind. For every 100,000 people, 81 are offed. That's about nine times the rate in the U.S. Although guerrilla groups do have some hand in the slayings, a full 75 percent of the country's murders are committed by common criminals. In 1996, 26,642 people were murdered in Colombia, and average of 73 per day. Midway through 1997, there was an average of 68 murders a day. Violence, not natural causes, is the leading cause of death in Colombia.

Massacres

In addition to kidnapping and murder, Colombia keeps statistics on massacres like sportswriters report baseball box scores. In the first quarter of 1997, 164 people were killed in massacres in Colombia, compared to 72 people in the first quarter of 1996, a 128-percent increase. Acts of terrorism (mostly bombings) rose 46 percent during the same period. Colombia's rate of violent crime is unequaled anywhere else in the world. Normally playing down the significance of such grisly statistics, one government official disarmingly admitted in April 1997: "In Colombia, the notion of the value of human life has largely been lost."

Being Mayor

More than 50 Colombian town mayors were murdered during the first six months of 1997 alone, making Colombian politics little more than campaign trails of blood. It seems FARC and ELN have actually banned campaigning in the south while in the north right wing death squads have banned leftist parties.

"Sicarios"

Sicarios are Medellin's teenage assassins. Police claim that as many as 2000 of these prepubescent killers—typically hired by drug dealers, the Medellin cartel, businessmen and even police to off their rivals—are on the streets of Medellin. Independent sources say that between 5000 and 7000 young people in the city have committed murder for pay at least once.

Oil Pipelines

There are 40 foreign oil producing companies in Colombia. Occidental Petroleum (Oxy) is the country's largest. The Cano-Limon oil field (along the border of Venezuela and Colombia) yields Colombia's largest oil deposits. The 470-mile pipeline cost over a billion dollars and is the focal point for guerilla activity. Nasty men have blown up the pipeline over 400 times since it came on line in 1985. In 1988, an Oxy engineer was kidnapped and sprung for an impressive US$6 million dollars. To make things fair, the government of Colombia took responsibility for the repair of the pipeline every time the bad guys punched a hole in it. It takes about 36 hours to repair the bomb blasts. About 190,000 barrels of crude oil flow through the pipeline every day. The joke is that the rebels claim that the pipeline is robbing the Colombians of their natural resources. The real criminal seems to be the Colombian government, which skims 85 percent of every dollar generated by the oil. There is a $1.20 a barrel "war tax" to help fight the guerillas and a tax of 12 percent of all profits taken out of the country. Occidental Petroleum has shut down its Camo Limon oil field because of continual attacks by rebels. They say it costs them $100,000 each day they are shut down. Some 11,000 Colombian soldiers are guarding oil installations. The Casanare field run by Oxy has reserves estimated to be $40 billion, with the potential daily output of half a million barrels a day,.

Heroin

With the U.S. appetite for cocaine at a relative nasal trickle, the Colombian cartels have turned to heroin. Of the heroin hauls seized in the U.S. in 1993, only 15 percent came from Colombia. The figure more than doubled to 32 percent the following year, and doubled again to 62 percent in 1995. Colombian traffickers have tapped their Asian, Italian and Afghan contacts for the expertise in growing poppies and refining opium in the Andes. In 1997, sample purchases of street heroin by DEA agents sold in the northeast indicates that 90 percent of America's heroin may now be coming from Colombia. As many as 600,000 Americans now use heroin as their drug of choice. Since 1990, the incidents of emergency room admissions for smack ODs more than doubled, from 36,000 to 76,000 (1995). The Colombian government has spent $985 million on drug eradication programs, $40 million of which has come from Uncle Sam.

Scopolamine

Scopolamine (or Burundanga, as it is called locally) is a drug Colombian thugs use to incapacitate tourists in order to rob them. It's spiked into drinks in bars, and into cigarettes in taxis. The drug renders victims unconscious and causes serious medical problems. Colombian doctors report that hospitals receive an estimated 2000 Scopolamine victims every month in Bogota. One out of every three patients in the emergency room has been intoxicated with the drug. The druggings occur in all areas of the city throughout the day, but with more frequency at night. The most effective way to administer Scopolamine is in a liquid form, which can incapacitate the victim in two to three seconds. However, research has revealed that street tactics can involve the drug being utilized in a spray, dust or smoke form as well. Most drugging incidents take place in bars and discotheques. Some incidents occur when the server brings you a drink. On the way to the table, he/she will drug the drink or bottle. This usually occurs toward the end of the night, when most people are less observant. After being drugged, the server helps you to the door, where an accomplice is waiting.

Power Blackouts

When the lights go out, make sure you are nowhere to be found by street criminals. Common street crime increases exponentially during blackouts in major cities.

Picking Bananas

Banana growers have been targeted by both ELN and FARC guerrillas for their alleged support of right-wing death squads. Since 1989, more than 3000 banana workers have been whacked in rebel attacks. A large number of banana workers in the country are members of the Hope, Peace & Liberty political party, a former radical leftist guerrilla group which gave up its armed struggle in 1990. Many of the slayings are in revenge for the movement giving up the fight.

Phony Cops

A common scam is to approach an obvious tourist as an alleged "policeman," saying that he is checking for counterfeit U.S. dollars and wants to "check" the foreigner's money. The person gives the criminal his/her money, receives a receipt, and the "policeman" disappears. Others request that the victim accompany him "downtown." You have just been kidnapped. In Bogota, gangs of phony cops have been targeting houses for robbery whose occupants are out and tricking domestic staff and nannies to gain entrance.

Strolling Through the Country

You may want to save the rain forests, but coca growers and processing labs would prefer that you stay at the beach. Two French tourists were snatched by FARC in the La Macarena nature preserve south of Bogota. The countryside is effectively controlled by rebel groups who view you as a source of income.

Bombs

Bombs don't drop from the sky here. They usually drive up to you. Car bombs are deliberately detonated in crowded central locations. Buses are bombed, as well as oil pipelines, refineries, hotels and office buildings. Bombing is a deliberate attempt to capture publicity and strike fear into the populace. The victims are incidental.

Driving

Colombia's roads are in poor condition. Many routes aren't marked. Avoid driving at night. Many vehicles have dim headlights, if any at all. Other drivers are reckless. Cattle are unwitting, as they pause to pee in the middle of the road at midnight.

Taxis

Women should never travel alone at night in taxis. Both sexes are subject to popular scams where the driver feigns a mechanical breakdown. The passenger is asked to get out of the car and help push the taxi to a "jump-start," which separates passengers from their luggage. The driver will then start the car and drive off. Use only well-marked taxis; do not share a ride or enter a cab with more than one person, even though many cabdrivers will tell you that your travel mate is for protection—remember, you only need to be wrong once. Lock the doors, and be prepared to have Scopolamine sprayed in your face by keeping alert and a window cracked (not enough to let people reach in).

Buses

Bus travel in the south of Colombia can be hazardous. Thieves haunt buses in this area waiting for passengers to fall asleep. Then, guess what they do? Buses between Bogota and Ipiales and between San Augustin and Popayan are frequented by scam artists/thieves who offer doped chewing gum, cigarettes, food and sweets before taking everything you've got. Theft, druggings, extortion and kidnapping occur frequently on buses in both the city and rural areas.

Hotel Rooms

Hotel rooms of foreigners are infrequently raided by the police looking for drugs. Having a witness around may prevent them from planting drugs in the room. But, then again, it may not.

Planes

In Colombia, many radar and ground tracking stations are damaged by rebels and drug smugglers to protect illegal drug shipments. More than 1000 people have died in Colombian air accidents since 1986.

Drugs

Despite what we said about the few criminals that get to justice in Colombia, if you get arrested for any drug-related crime, expect threats of lifelong incarceration and spending a few thousand bucks bribing your way out of jail. The government will do little to help, as they hold the belief that gringos are the root of Colombia's drug ills (and they're right). Any foreigner who wants to cut out the middlemen and go into competition with the Colombian drug dealers should watch the movie *Scarface* a few times. Strangely enough, every year some yahoo ends up in a Colombian jail for doing exactly that.

Hassles with Police

Many police officers and soldiers will shake you down for doing everything from taking pictures to walking on the beach at night. The best bluff is to demand to see their supervisor and walk quickly in the direction that takes you farthest away from them. If the police really do arrest you, get on the horn to the consulate ASAP. They can't do much if you really screwed up, but they're all you've got.

Medical care is adequate in major cities, but varies in quality elsewhere. Health problems in Colombia include the presence of cholera, though cholera is found largely in areas outside the cities and usual tourist areas. Visitors who follow proper precautions regarding food and drink are not generally at risk. Doctors and hospitals often expect immediate cash payment for health services. U.S. medical insurance is not always valid outside the United States. In some cases, supplemental medical insurance with specific overseas coverage is considered useful. If you are the victim of a Scopolamine attack, remember to seek medical assistance immediately. Scopolamine is usually mixed with other narcotics and can cause brain damage.

Spanish is the official language. English is common in major cities and tourist centers. The Colombians like to party, so expect massive crowds and price hikes during local holidays. Electricity is 110V/60hz. Local time is the same as New York. The local currency is the peso, about 837 to the U.S. dollar at press time.

Temperatures are fairly high throughout the year. It gets cooler and wetter the higher you go. Seaside areas are muggy. Heavy rain falls between April and October.

Business hours are from 8 a.m.–noon and from 2–6 p.m, Monday–Friday. Bank hours in Bogata are from 9 a.m.–3 p.m. Monday–Thursday, and from 9 a.m.–3:30 p.m. on Fridays, except the last Friday of the month, when they close at noon. In other major cities, they're open from 8 a.m.–11:30 a.m. and from 24 p.m. Monday–Thursday. On Friday, they're open until 4:30 p.m., except the last Friday of the month, when they close at 11:30 a.m.

Embassy Location/Registration

Upon arrival, U.S. citizens are urged to obtain updated information on travel and security within Colombia an to register with the following:

Consular Section, U.S. Embassy
Calle 38 No. 8–61
Bogota, Colombia
☎ *[57] (1) 320-1300*

U.S. Consulate
Calle 77, Carrera 68
Centro Comercial Mayorista
Barranquilla, Colombia
☎ *[57] (58) 45-8480 or 45-9067*

Anniversaries are bad days for a stroll in the country or shopping downtown in Colombia. Rebel groups like to remind people by blowing things up.

10/08/1987	The Simon Bolivar Guerrilla Coordinating Board (CNG) is an umbrella organization, under which the Revolutionary Armed Forces of Colombia (FARC), the National Liberation Army (ELN) and a dissident faction of the Popular Liberation Army (EPL) coordinate political positions and organize joint terrorist operations. It was founded on this date.
08/28/1985	April 19 movement (M-19) originated; leader Ivan Marino Ospina was killed in a clash with government troops.
11/20/1983	Legalization of the M-19. The April 19 movement (M-19), a leftist terrorist organization, was legalized by an amnesty law after the group had made peace with the government. The M-19 is now a legitimate political party.
04/29/1967	Founding of the EPL (Popular Liberation Army).
08/15/1964	The National Liberation Army (ELN) began its armed struggle.
05/27/1964	When government troops attacked the "independent republic" that communist peasant groups had set up at Marquetalia, Caldas Department.
11/11/1957	The Popular Liberation Army (EPL), a leftist terrorist organization, has since made peace with the government and become a legitimate political party. However, a dissident faction continues the armed struggle against the government.
07/17/1930	Communist Party founded.
08/07/1819	Battle Of Boyacas.
07/20/1810	Independence Day.

Colombia: Un Favorito, Por Favor

I had agreed to go out with the official's daughter. She was coming into San Andreas tomorrow from Cali for Holy Week. To decline the social request would not be a wise idea. I watched in amazement, as this distinguished gentleman was able to piss in the sink at the same time he was washing his hands. We were in his hotel suite, which served as his full-time home. He was a very high level government official on the island. Instead of wallpaper, he had cases of Mumm's champagne stacked up from floor to ceiling, creating a pleasing but somewhat industrial pattern. His choice of music was limited to the one or two AM radio stations on the island—he used a state-of-the-art quadraphonic stereo system to blast out Julio Iglesias. Like most of his possessions, they were "gifts" or leftovers from customs inspections of travelers.

He explained how he makes his money. He has a group of three to five "beach boys" who sell coconut oil on the beach to tourists. Along with the golden fragrant oil in old beer bottles, they offer hash or marijuana to unsuspecting tourists. As the sun goes down, they turn in the money they've made and carefully point out each and every person who bought drugs that day. During the night, the doors of the surprised victims are crashed down and they're trotted off to jail at gunpoint. They then pay the judge, the lawyer, the DAS, the F2 and, of course, the Aduana dearly for their freedom. In fact, they even have to pay for meals while they are in jail. As he adjusted his evening clothes and carefully combed his hair, I thought he looked rather dashing...for a thug.

—**RYP**

Congo (Zaire)
★★★★

Heart of Désiré

It's hardly surprising that Laurent Désiré Kabila and the late Mobutu Sese Seko (born Joseph Désiré Mobutu) share the same middle name. Leaders of the former Zaire since the 19th century—all despots—have, through personal desire, raped this lush, mineral-rich country with impunity, turning what is potentially the richest African nation into a stinking cesspool of squalor and greed.

Like a child born prematurely, Zaire became the Democratic Republic of Congo on May 16, 1997, after a seven-month pregnancy. The "pregnancy" in this case was brutal, short-term insurgency led by veteran guerrilla Kabila, who swept his ragtag rebel army westward to Kinshasa and toppled long-time dictator Mobutu in a mere seven months. For Mobutu, the end was not a pretty picture. He suffered from a wicked case of prostate cancer (and some say AIDS). But the real cancer that killed Joe Mobutu was borne of 32 years of greed, corruption, brutality, ethnic hatred and chaos. CIA-installed Mobutu, a one-time key U.S.

403

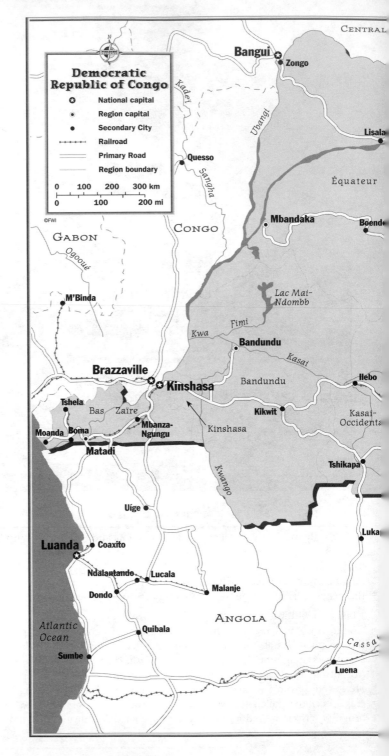

Democratic Republic of Congo

⊗ National capital
⊙ Region capital
● Secondary City
+++ Railroad
── Primary Road
── Region boundary

0   100   200   300 km
0   100   200 mi

©FWI

ally, plunged the former Zaire into despair and unimaginable poverty during his three-decade rule, amassing for his own coffer of a fortune in diamonds (US$4 billion) to make him one of the richest people in the world.

The Democratic Republic of Congo should be the envy of Africa. Twice the size of Texas, it is the African continent's third-largest country, after Sudan and Algeria. It boasts fertile soil, vast mineral wealth and the world's eighth longest river. This natural force is powerful enough to provide electricity for the entire African continent. Instead, its 44 million people are among the poorest in the world, and among the world's most likely to hack each other to pieces.

There is no other country on the continent that more typifies the deep, tormented core of darkest Africa. The Portuguese first poked around the area in the 15th century, but it was the Belgians that began the plunder in earnest. Belgian King Leopold colonized Congo in the 19th century and duped his stronger European rivals into thinking his sortie into Africa was simply an honorable humanitarian mission. Instead, he made the Belgian Congo his personal treasure chest, amassing a fortune in diamonds and rubber plantations. His employees were slaves, whose hands and feet he had cut off as punishment for not meeting quotas. One interesting twist is that Leopold made the Congo his own personal property. Likewise, Congo's natural resources and a healthy dose of Western aid made Mobutu one of the world's richest men. Kabila will be sorely tempted. Joseph Conrad based his famous tale of depravity and corruption on this dying, diseased land when it was called the Belgian Congo. It is hot, violent and dark. Congo is everyone's favorite hellhole—corrupt, fetid, dangerous and deadly. Whether it's the bloodshot-red eyes of your first customs inspector or the apocalyptic way the earth reclaims the symbols of civilization, you will always remember your first trip to the dark heart of Africa: abandoned bulldozers, wooden houses, even 150,000 missing Hutu refugees. So into this history or greed, depravity and corruption comes Marxist, former terrorist and Tutsi-backed Laurent Kabila. When 1.2 million Hutu refugees streamed into northeastern Congo (then Zaire), they joined a substantial number of former Rwandan Hutu soldiers and government officials already there. From their makeshift camps in Congo they began staging raids against the then Tutsi Patriotic Front which controlled Rwanda. In July 1996, the killing of Tutsis spread from Rwanda to Congo.

This was when Paul Kagame (see "Rwanda Players") put together and trained 2000 Tutsi fighters from Zaire and sent them back into their homeland to resist the Zairean attempt to oust all Tutsis from Zaire.

Instead of a bloodbath, the Zairean soldiers fled, leaving a curious power vacuum in Kivu provinces. Realizing that he could not just take over Zaire, the Rwandan Kagame dialed up Uganda leader Yoweri Museveni (who had supported Kagame's fight to oust the anti-Tutsi government in Rwanda in the early '90s). Museveni suggested that his old bushfighter pal, Kabila, would be an ideal next-door neighbor for Rwanda and Uganda. So Kagame faded away and, in two weeks, Kabila—a low budget rebel who was visited (and dumped) by Che Guevara in the 1960s but who couldn't get arrested for jaywalking in Kinshasa—now was the leader of a revolution, thanks to Kagame, Museveni and, of course, the CIA.

The Name Game

Many people are confused by the names given to this festering region. In 1483, Portuguese Admiral Diago Cao arrived at the mouth of a large river. He asked the locals who said "Ndazi" (river) which the Portuguese misheard as Zaire. Since the Portuguese had named the river Zaire they automatically called anything upriver or in the basin Zaire. In Nov. of 1908, the Belgian parliament changed the name to the Belgian Congo as a warning to other colonial predators. Half a century later in 1960, independence brought the name Republic of Congo, when the politicians had enough time to come with a constitution and create 21 autonomous provinces. In 1964, it was renamed the Democratic Republic of the Congo. The fact that there was another country peopled by the Bakonga tribe didn't matter. It was called Congo (Brazzaville) vs. Congo (Kinshasa). Mobutu not only changed his name but decided to create the Republic of Zaire to shift the focus off of the Bakonga tribe. After all they just lived around the mouth of the river. Meanwhile, commie Kabila kept fighting for the "Democratic" Republic of the Congo even though he had no intention of holding democratic elections and was not a Bakonga by birth.

Museveni makes sure that Kabila keeps it nice and orderly so he and Kagame don't have to look over their shoulders. Canadian and U.S. mining companies have returned to work on Mobutu's personal gold mine, a 32,000 square-mile private mine in Kilo-moto possessing at least 100 tons of gold yet to be dug up by the new boss of Congo.

The world is waiting to see. Kabila has promised elections for 1999. Mobutu also promised elections back in 1990. They weren't held. The closest thing to an election in Congo, since the country's independence from Belgium in 1960 occurred in 1980 when Mobutu was re-elected—but he was the only candidate; it was a landslide. Not exactly a litmus test of democracy. Kabila—who has an unsettling resemblance to Idi Amin—is going to need some heavy-duty willpower to keeps his fingers out of Congo's cookie jar. For now, the area is still a central African hellhole run by kids toting rusty machine guns.

Laurent-Désiré Kabila

Born in Kalemi, Kabila is not from any major ethnic tribe in the Congo. With his seven-month KO of Joey Mobutu, this guy's either the George Foreman or Idi Amin of modern Africa. Kabila, in his late 50s, has finally achieved his dream of taking over an area the size of Western Europe. His job now is to figure out how to govern more than 250 tribes and rebuild an economy that has been sliding over the abyss. If he does it the right way, Congo could become an affluent country with its copper (Shaba), diamond (Kasai) and gold mines. Kabila is a down-home, old-line Marxist who has been battling Mobutu for three decades. Camped out in the cool jungles around Lake Tanganyika, he never made much headway but did convince the Soviet Union, Cuba and China to send his rebels lunch money. Back then, his group had the snappier sounding name of the People's Revolutionary Party and the name he had for his country to be was the Democratic Republic of the Congo.

In his days as a jungle fighter (Kabila hosted Ché Guevara in the 1960s before Ché decided Désiré's boys made better detox patients than revolutionaries), Kabila got to know Yoweri Museveni, now leader of Uganda. It paid off big time when Paul Kagame was looking for a front man to cover his back. When it became apparent in early 1997 that Kabila's march to Kinshasa would hit little flak, Kabila doffed his military fatigues in favor of business attire, ready to cut deals rather than throats. It seems he won't have to dabble in gold and ivory trading to pay the rent—now he'll have a whole country to barter with. A mining firm has already given Kabila's government US$50 million as down payment to dig for copper and cobalt as well as a private jet. Meanwhile, Kabila has banned all political parties and essentially created a military dictatorship run by Tutsis. Kabila's been quoted as saying: "If I can't do better than Mobutu, then our rebellion will have been a failure." With such high standards, it's little wonder that Ché split. Stay tuned for the Kingdom of Greater Hima, a Tutsi-controlled region where Tutsis talk and Hutus walk.

Alliance of Democratic Forces for the Liberation of Congo-Zaire (ADFL)

The new wind blowing may be just as stench-filled as the old wind. The ADFL was formed October 18, 1996, in Lemera, South Kivu, but is an outgrowth of Kabila's old Marxist group, the Parti de la Revolution Populaire founded in the '60s. The Rebel Alliance, as it's popularly called—whose official seal is Disney's Lion King—is an ever-expanding army of rubber-booted soldiers who trudged some 1700 kilometers on foot through the jungles and mountains to reach Kinshasa in only seven months. These guys should've been sponsored by Timberland. To help fund their drive to the capital, the rebels taxed foreign journalists. Visiting a rebel-held area cost journos nearly US$600. At arrival in Goma, correspondents paid a US$70 fee, US$60 for press credentials, US$65 for a safe passage pass and another US$8 as an arrival fee. With eastern Zaire lacking an international telephone system, reporters had to bring in their own satellite phones, which the rebels taxed US$350 a pop. When leaving, there was a US$20 departure tax and another US$11 in "airport fees." If you thought Congo's rebellion wasn't given enough media coverage, now you know why.

Mobutu Sese Seko Kuku Ngbenda wa za Banga (formerly Joseph Désiré Mobutu)

Joe Mobutu's an ex-player, but it would be unfair to not at least keep him in just for yuks. The late self-proclaimed and former "Redeemer," "Liberator," "Helmsman," "Messiah," "Guide" and the "cock who will jump on anything" (we are not making this up) isn't doing a lot of redeeming, liberating, steering or guiding anymore. Most of his estimated US$4–$8 billion in ill-gotten wealth is safely out of the country and tucked into his family's Swiss banks. The Swiss froze a US$2.75 million villa on Lake Geneva, but the former dictator had 24 other houses around the world to choose from.

How did he get so rich? Well, for example, when the German company OTRAG was looking for a place to test satellite rocket launchers, Mobutu gave them a chunk of his country as big as Belgium. The fee was $50 million dollars which Joe simply deposited in his personal account. He managed to siphon off aid money coming in and sales of raw resources going out. When that wasn't enough, he would simply write himself a check from the main mining concessionaire. In 1978, he made Gecamines write him a check for the entire year's export sales ($1.2 billion). That's a lot of villas. Most foreign aid loans or projects benefited him directly and nobody every wanted to repossess Zaire. He would siphon CIA money destined for UNITA (who were fighting the MPLA) in Angola to the south and any money sent to the government to fight communism (aka Kabila) went straight into his pockets.

At the end, his wealth didn't help nor did he have any friends. He died in Morocco surrounded by about 40 hangers-on and his immediate family. He was 66. Considering that most Congolese don't live to see their 60th birthday, Mobutu Sese Seko did pretty well for the son of a maid from Gbadolite. His Israeli bodyguard, leopard skin cap, harlequin outfits and ivory cane became fashion statements among dictator wannabes and fans of Eddie Murphy. Not a man with an eclectic taste in women, Mobutu's mistress was his wife's twin sister. For now his multiple offspring will live well on the boulevards of Paris.

Etienne Tshikidi

Safari-jacketed, 64-year-old "Tshi-Tshi"— as he is affectionately called—is a former university chancellor and leader of the Union for Democracy and Social Progress. He appears to be the only educated, nonviolent potential leader in Congo, which is probably why he'll do very poorly with Kabila. Tshi-Tshi was democratically elected as prime minister in 1992 and was exiled by Mobutu to his birthplace of Mbuji-Mayi in Kasai Oriental region of Congo after he was booted out of office in 1994. He hopes to run for president if elections are held. Good luck, Tshi-Tshi.

Maji-Maji Ingilima

These young folks (also called *mai mai*) make warfare in Africa fun. They would feel right at home in Compton. The *mai mai* are ganja-stoked, witchcraft-practicing teenage street-fighters who wear faucets, rosary beads and garden hoses as jewelry and worship water. They wear a cool grass headdress that makes them invisible in battle. Their name means "powerful water," a super-duper magic potion they whip up that protects them from bullets (although the headdress and magic potion do not come with a money-back guarantee). They are just local kids letting off a little steam and aren't quite up on the political situation. They have fought on both sides of the war and, of course, been killed in large numbers by both sides. The *mai mai* also make for great party hosts; they practice cannibalism and have attacked Hutu settlements. They are primarily from the Hunde, Nande and Nglima tribes near Goma. The main goal of the *mai mai* is to protect their villages around Bunia. Don't forget to lock up your gardening tools.

Banyamulenge

Ethnic Tutsis who live in the Mulenge mountains of South Kivu province started the ball rolling. Although they have lived in Zaire for hundreds of years, their incentive to rebel against Mobutu's forces was only triggered after being ordered by Zairean soldiers in September of 1996 to move to Rwanda along with the Rwandan Tutsi refugees or face being hunted down and killed. Bad move. The ethnic Tutsis in Zaire were denied citizenship in 1981 and things have been tense ever since. Muller Ruhimbika is one of the top kicks here but Kagame calls the shots. Their party name is Alliance Democratique des Peuples (ADP) and their leader is Douglas Bugera from Rotshuru. The Banyamulenge are the dominant force in Kabila's army.

Interahamwe

The Hutu militiamen who led the genocide in Rwanda have lived in the Zairean refugee camps and prevented the more than one million refugees from returning home to Rwanda. The refugees began to return only when the Zairean army brutally attacked Hutu camp dwellers and forced them back home, also sparking the well-planned revolt.

Gorillas

Not guerillas, which have gone legit, but the two-thirds of the world's remaining silverbacks that forage through the mist-covered highlands of eastern Congo. There are estimated to be only 600 of these gorillas left in Rwanda; no one knows exactly how many survive in Congo. Other than the adventurous trips on the dilapidated river boats that ply the Congo River, this is the only thing that most Westerners connect the former Zaire with. Dian Fossey is long gone, but there are still guards and gorillas in the 3200 square-mile Virunga National Park. Many guards were killed, trees were cut for firewood and some gorillas were poached during the confusion, but it is expected to resume operations.

The Virunga National Park is open for business after only losing 18 mountain gorillas to poachers since 1995. There are about 350 gorillas left in the park a little bit over half of the 610 remaining mountain gorillas left on the planet. The entry fee will be $120. The park used to pull in about $140,000 a month. Don't forget to add in tips, today's park rangers make about 50 cents a day when they are paid.

The Tutsis

The Nilotic Tutsis tend to be the educated and wealthier of the ethnic groups in eastern Congo. The Tutsis originally migrated south from the Rift valley as cattle herders 400 years ago and eventually settled with and intermarried with the agrarian Hutus. They created the two countries of Rwanda and Burundi (where they make up about 15 percent of the population) and are also found in eastern Congo and southwest Uganda. The Tutsi ruled the Hutus as serfs in Rwanda, whereas in Burundi a tribe called the Ganwa (unrelated to either the Hutu or Tutsis) ruled both. Later the colonial rulers favored Tutsis in selected governmental posts and even though missionaries would educate Hutus, there always remained both an imbalance and an integration. This odd symbiotic and volatile relationship is the reason why it is difficult to make clear ethnic or political distinctions in the killing and violence that will continue to affect the area.

A passport, visa and vaccination certificate showing valid yellow fever and cholera immunizations are required for entry into Congo. Before Mobutu's fall, visas were not issued to nationals of countries practicing "discriminatory" visa policies toward the Congolese. Although the government did not name the countries to which this edict was applied, U.S citizens did have difficulty obtaining tourist visas. *DP* talked with the new brass at the Congo embassy in Washington and was told "no problem" regarding the availability of tourist visas. Keep in mind that some travelers have been obliged to transit Brazzaville in neighboring Republic of the Congo to reach Kinshasa, which means a Congo (Brazzaville) visa may also be necessary. U.S. citizens should apply at the Congo embassy in Washington, D.C., well in advance of any planned trip. Visa fees range from US$45 for a transit visa to US$360 for a six-month multiple-entry visa. Most visitors will opt for the one-entry, one-month visa for US$75, or US$120 for multiple entries for the same period.

You will need a valid passport, proof of inoculation against yellow fever, a copy of your return ticket as well as application forms and two passport photos. If you show up in person, it takes 48 hours for a visa to be issued or 24 hours if you are a diplomat.

For more information, the traveler may contact the following:

Embassy of the Democratic Republic of Congo
1800 New Hampshire Avenue NW
Washington, D.C. 20009
☎ *(202) 234-7690/91*

Congo's Permanent Mission to the U.N.
2 Henry Avenue
North Caldwell, NJ 07006
☎ *(201) 812-1636.*

Border Crossings

A special exit permit from Congo's immigration department and a visa from an embassy of the Congo are required to cross the Congo River from Kinshasa to Brazzaville, in the Congo. Unofficially expect to see a special visa price be invented on the spot and don't be surprised if your money disappears quickly into the same official's pocket.

There are three ferry crossing points for overland traffic between Congo and the Central African Republic. They are located at Bangui, Mobaye and Bangassou.

Of the 146,500 km of local roads, only 2800 km are paved. Most intercity roads are difficult or impassable in the rainy season. When driving in cities, individuals often keep windows rolled up and doors locked. At roadblocks or checkpoints, documents are displayed through closed windows. A government "mining permit" may be required to travel to large areas of the country, regardless of the visitor's purpose in going there. This permit must be obtained before entering the "mining zone." Requests for *cadeaus* or bribes are the norm. If you bring a camera you will absolutely need a permit that says you are a journalist. The cost is whatever you get dunned after they arrest you for not having a permit.

The Entire Country

Although there are several flights each week between Kinshasa and European cities, schedules are often disrupted by security problems in Kinshasa or when the soldiers in neighboring Brazzaville start shooting it up. There have been instances of bullets and shell fragments falling on Kinshasa from fighting in Brazzaville. Civil disturbances, including looting and the possibility of physical harm, can occur without warning in all urban areas of Congo. Kabila's army has shown respect for law and order but it's still honeymoon time in Congo. Congolese security personnel are suspicious of foreigners (French nationals are *tres outre*) and sometimes stop travelers on the street for proof of immigration status or can charge you with mythical infractions. The hiring of brutal, drunken Serbian mercenaries by Mobutu in his final days did not create a lot of good will toward visiting Westerners. Border control personnel scrutinize passports, visas, and vaccination certificates for any possible irregularity and sometimes seek bribes to perform their official functions. Travelers are urged to be cautious and polite if confronted with these situations.

Crime

In a country where there is little law, where underpaid police and soldiers are often criminals, you have to park your moral indignation when visiting. Morality, legality and right-or-wrong issues have to be sidelined in the interest of survival. Customs officials have an unwritten law of extracting about US$100 from all Western travelers who enter Congo. All border officials will hit you up for some type of *cadeau*, or gift. Once inside, you may wish you were being jacked up by a uniformed border guard rather than the street criminals who will continually hit on you. There is plenty of armed street crime, especially in Kinshasa, where violent crime is commonplace. Vehicle thefts, including hijackings at gunpoint, are on the rise.

Congo is quickly reverting to an agrarian, or barter, economy. Congo has also become a predatory environment where the use of deadly weapons has led to the deaths or serious injury of several expatriate citizens. As the economy continues to collapse, crimes such as armed robbery, vehicle theft and house break-ins increase accordingly, with the foreign community and travelers expected to become more frequent targets. If you look to the police for help, you may find yourself being taken for even more.

Taking Photos

Photography of public buildings and military installations is forbidden, as is photography of the banks of the Congo River. Offenders can expect to be arrested, held for a minimum of several hours and fined. You need a special permit if you are a photojournalist. In the tradition of West and Central Africa, most folks carrying professional looking cameras are arrested on a regular basis. If you don't know how these infractions are resolved read the chapter on "Bribes."

Carrying Money

While U.S. dollars and traveler's checks can, in theory, be exchanged for local currency (the Congolese franc) at banks in Kinshasa, banks often do not have sufficient cash on hand to make transactions. Visitors may be given an unfavorable rate of exchange and can be very time consuming. Participating in the unofficial, "parallel" money exchanges that flourish in some areas is illegal. Some foreigners have been picked up for infractions of this type and their money has been confiscated. Credit cards are accepted at a few major hotels and restaurants. It is illegal to take Congolese francs out of the country. Don't fall for the "we're plainclothes police and we need to see your money" scam.

The Police

Cops make a maximum of about US$50 a month, if and when they get paid. There's no back pay if the accountants miss a pay day. That's where you come in. If you are stopped by the police for whatever reason, you will be considered a necessary part of the foreign economic investment in their country. You don't have to give them anything but to wriggle away takes time and bluster. Tourists are rarely beaten or actually charged with crimes (unless they get uppity) so smile, jabber and smile. If you are waylaid by a real criminal don't bother reporting it. The police and government soldiers have been traditionally responsible for much of the crime in Congo, especially violent crime. There's little cause to believe the modus operandi will change much with the new government.

It is almost pointless listing the various health problems in Central Africa since most of them originate here. Getting sick in Congo is as inevitable as it is debilitating. This is the home of Ebola and a future incubator of some of the world's nastiest diseases. If you come down with anything, try to get on the next plane out to Joburg or Europe. Medical facilities are extremely limited and unsanitary. Any long-term visitor should purchase medical insurance that pays for Medevac costs to Europe or the U.S. See the "Diseases" chapter.

Congo is big (905,365 square miles), diverse (more than 250 tribes) and dirt poor. The infrastructure has crumbled. More than 80 percent of the population is unemployed and most portable resources are smuggled out of the country. Most of the country's gold and over half of the diamonds are smuggled out to avoid lining the government's pockets. The rest of the gold, copper, oil, coffee, diamonds and other natural resources that are officially produced are quickly vacuumed out of the ground and shipped off to the UK, Canada, Japan and America. One thing to keep in mind is that the region's former alignment with France has radically changed to a U.S./U.K. alignment under Kabila. The French are not unwelcome, but things could be a little tense if you light up a Gauloise.

DP reader Chris Toliver, a photographer who covered the revolution says the Hotel Membling or Hotel Intercontinental is your best bet but expensive ($200 a night, $30 for dinner) There is the C.A.P. protestant mission for $35 a night with meals included. They will also set you up with drivers, interpreters and cars. The inflation rate in Congo, at 2870 percent (during *DP's* March 1997 visit), was the highest in the world; the GNP is actually lower than it was 30 years ago and the word "industry" is an oxymoronic term used to describe Congo's anemic 10 percent of capacity output. The U.S dollar (bring 5's and 10's) is now the real currency for visitors. The Congolese Franc is the new currency. The Congo is a country sitting on top of 70 percent of the world's cobalt, one that produces nine tons of gleaming gold every year. So things may get better with Mobutu gone.

The official language is French; the local tongue is called Lingala. Most Congolese are Christian. The population is about 44 million.

Embassy Location

U.S. Embassy in Congo
310 Avenue des Aviateurs, Unit 31550
APO 09828
☎ *[243] (12) 21532/21628*

09/08/1997	Death of Mobutu
05/16/1997	Mobutu gives up presidential powers and flees the country. Kabila renames Zaire as the Democratic Republic of Congo.
05/04/1997	Mobutu-Kabila peace talks break down.
01/08/1997	The Republic of Congo becomes the Democratic Republic of the Congo.
10/26/1996	Tutsi soldiers slaughter Hutu refugees in Zaire. Hutus use refugee camps as bases for attacks on Tutsis in Burundi.
09/1996	In eastern Zaire, Tutsis revolt after officials try to banish them. Kabila takes the helm of the rebellion and attacks refugee camps to snuff former Rwandan Hutu soldiers. Kabila begins sweep across eastern Zaire.
07/1996	Mobutu leaves for cancer treatment in Switzerland.
10/27/1971	Democratic Republic of the Congo is renamed the Republic of Zaire.
11/24/1965	Revolution Day commemorates the establishment of the Second Congolese Republic by General Joseph Mobutu (now Mobutu Sese Seko) following his seizure of control of the government on this date.
05/25/1963	The Organization of African Unity (OAU) was founded on this date. The day is celebrated as Africa Freedom Day. The OAU was organized to promote unity and cooperation among African states.
06/30/1960	Independence Day. The Belgian Congo becomes the Republic of the Congo
10/14/1930	Birthday of former President Mobutu.

Kinshasa, 1997

The rebels had just taken over the capital and were dealing out a little street justice (as my driver called it). I had arrived there early and happened to catch an execution of some of Mobutu's DSP (aka the bad guys). Within an hour of the murders about a dozen members of the press corp arrived. I could name names but what's the point. *Reuters, Sigma, Time, CNN, ITN,* even *Vanity Fair* was looking for some bang bang. Hearing about the great photo-op they missed, the journalists decided to stay until there was another execution. They waited from about 9:30 a.m. until 2 in the afternoon. My ride wanted to wait around for an execution so I sat on a four foot high pile of discarded uniforms in the hot sun. Bored, I decided to make some friends. I bumped into the "generals" who were running the detention camp. They proceeded to get me rip roaring drunk on local Primus Malt liquor and occupy the time until my ride figured it was time to go. Travel tips? Well, the French are all pretending to be Canadian, it's harder to buy your way out of trouble with Kabila's folks, and it's still the 16-years-olds with AK-47's running the show.

—**Chris Toliver**

India
★★★

Kashmir Sweat

It is a miracle that India even exists. Being a powerhouse nation of so many ethnicities and religions, it should have ripped itself into a bunch of dinky fiefdoms long ago, each with hundreds of years of history, separate religions, dialects and customs. Instead, 866 million Indians and their government hobble painfully forward—burdened not only with poverty, skin-and-bones hunger and sickness, but also with an alarming birthrate and a potential nuclear conflict with neighboring Pakistan.

Like a terminally ill patient, India deals with the ugliest boils and rashes first. Its big problems are in the extreme south with the Tamil Tigers, and in the north with Sikh, Muslim and tribal separatists. Every time a bomb goes off (and they go off a lot), the suspects include Indians, Pakistani agents, Kashmiri separatists, Sikh terrorists, Maoist tribal rebels, Tamil Eelam guerrillas, Muslim militants, drug traffickers and even gangsters. Mother Teresa was the only one exempt from suspicion.

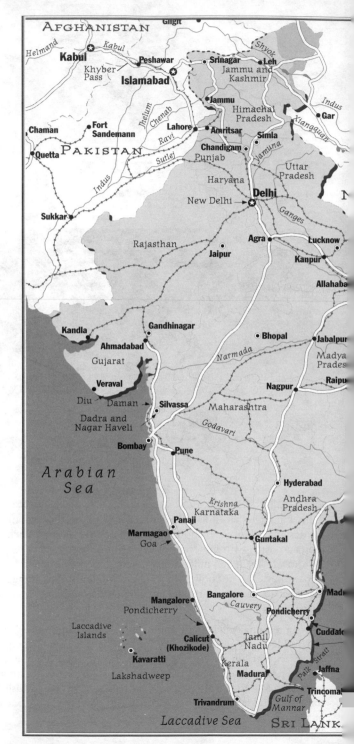

India bristles at its colonial made borders. Although the core of India has the gray industrious bustling of a Third World country, its borders are very much warring outposts complete with bunkers, artillery duels, terrorists raids and MiG-21's.

One of the ugliest scenarios on the horizon could be India's nuke race with Pakistan. While the world ignores the global consequences of what is perceived as a Hatfield-and-McCoy stick-fight in the boonies, the CIA quietly announced recently that Pakistan and India are two of the planet's top choices for potential serious instability. It is a war kept out of headlines as the two sides face off in high altitude bunkers and have firefights on glaciers.

India has the capability of lobbing a nuclear warhead within 1000 feet of a target 150 miles away, striking most major Pakistani cities within five minutes after launch. In this part of the world, that's close enough. In January 1996, a mosque in the Pakistani-held portion of Kashmir was turned into mush by a conventional rocket; it killed 20 worshipers. Each side blamed the other, and an artillery and small arms squash match ensued.

India and Pakistan, in their relatively embryonic relationship, have already fought three wars. Pakistan has gone home crying each time. In between official wars both countries recruit, train and field separatist extremists—Pakistan funds the nasties in the Indian-controlled region of Kashmir, while India fans the flames of hatred in Pakistan's Sind area.

In the tortured Northeast, tribal groups based deep in jungle hideouts fight for freedom and to keep settlers from drowning them out. Bombings, kidnappings, riots and assassinations are the general tone.

Not one to miss out on a gang banging, China is also part of India's multi-front diplomatic fray. Just to keep China honest, India fought a brief border war with the Sinos back in 1962. Since then, though, the two countries' relations have improved—if for no other reason than their mutual respect for the size of each others' populations, and the realization that a conventional ground war might take a few hundred years to fight, and still leave each country with populations the size of the U.S.

India is a relatively safe country with some nasty exceptions. Breathing, driving, and hiking can quickly end your life here. Long famous for being one of the dirtiest most overcrowded countries in the world, travelers now visit the far flung and scenic regions of Kashmir or the Northeast to escape the troubles.

The kidnapping of Westerners and the beheading of a Norwegian tourist in Kashmir sent chills up and down the spines of Patagonia-clad yuppie trekkers worldwide. After two-plus years, the hostages still haven't been found—dead or alive—despite a U.S. reward of US$2 million (and an Indian bounty of US$28,500) for information regarding their whereabouts. In the northeast, rebel groups bomb trains and raise havoc. Luckily there are few tourists. Those who see the traditional sites should be forewarned by the roadside spectacle of mangled buses, lorries and people. India has the most dangerous road system in the world.

INDIA

The Government and the Indian Army

Prime Minister Inder Kumar Gujra has about 400,000 soldiers, border troops and police at his service to keep the peace in Kashmir. It is the largest force India has ever fielded against a secessionist rebellion. The Indian government subscribes to the Domino Theory: If Kashmir is allowed to break away from India, other parts of the country with separatist groups would follow and India would exist no longer. To battle its numerous insurgencies, the government will be establishing a counter-insurgency force of 60,000 troops, the largest of its kind in the world. The move comes after India has reassessed its security threats determining (finally) that its most dangerous enemies are not Pakistan and China—but domestic rebels.

The Honourable Inder Kumar Gujra
Prime Minister of India
South Block
New Delhi, India 100 001
FAX: (91) 11-301-0700

Pakistan's Inter Services Intelligence (ISI)

This is Pakistan's slightly more militarized and crudely transparent version of the CIA. They are no less obvious in their activities than our corn-fed, tow-headed operatives in short sleeved checkered shirts from J.C. Penney. At least we think of creative covers when we send our fair-haired, blue-eyed boys into Kurdistan, the Sudan and Pakistan by creating plausible deniability. (Spooks? We're here to improve agriculture output!) The ISI doesn't seem to work up much of a cover as it sends legions of thin mustachioed (ex?) military Punjabis to train young press-ganged Kashmiris in how to liberate their homeland. If you want to know more, just ask any dark skinned New York cabbie with a Muslim last name; they'll tell you about what is going on in their homeland. The ISI coordinates and bankrolls the training and deployment of a number of rebel groups operating in India's northeastern states. The ISI has reputedly also set up training camps and bases in India's neighbors, including Nepal, Bhutan and Bangladesh. Besides being accused of also supplying money and arms to the *taliban* in Afghanistan, it is looking for parts for Pakistan's nuclear program.

Kashmir

The Jammu and Kashmir Liberation Front (JKLF)

The leader of the local JKLF is Halil Hyder, and its headquarters is in Anantnag, 44 miles from Srinagar. It has been fighting since 1990. Founded in 1977 and led by President Yasin Malik, the JKLF wants to make Muslim Kashmir independent from Hindu India. The ball got rolling in 1988 when one of the leaders, Amanullah Khan, got together with the Srinagar-based Islamic Students League. They typically plant bombs and engage in antigovernment activities.

Amanullah Khan

Jammu Kashmir Liberation Front
Lower Plate
Muzafferabad
Azad Kashmir, Pakistan
FAX (92) 058-2504
e-mail jklf@isb.comsats.net.pk

Kashmir Liberation Cell

Domel Road
Muzafferabad
Azad Kashmir, Pakistan
☎ (92) 058-2065

Al-Faran

Nobody that *DP* has talked to in Kashmir or Pakistan had ever heard of Al-Faran (the mountain people who some say they took their name after a mountain in Saudi Arabia near Mecca), but they quickly became famous. On July 4, 1995, two Brits and two Yanks were nabbed by Al-Faran, reputedly a shadowy Kashmiri separatist group but actually Afghan mercenaries hired to spring captured fighters out of jail. One of the Americans escaped, and the remaining hostages were joined with a German and a Norwegian seized in a separate incident. The Norwegian, Hans Christian Ostro, was beheaded and left in the village of Seer with the words "Al-Faran" carved on his back. The group demanded the release of 15 Afghan fighters in exchange for the hostages, but quickly was forced to disperse, and many members were gunned down in raids and standoffs. The hostages are seen sporadically (see *IADP Kashmir*) and the families search for them continues. Al-Faran is thought to be a front group for Pakistan-based Harkat-ul-Ansar (HUA see below), which lost four leaders in shoot-outs in a mere four months. The HUA appealed for the release of the hostages and insists this was a rogue act. The truth is, that Al-Faran was sent in to capture high level Western expats (engineers or embassy folks) and screwed up. They snagged the picnicking tourists out of impatience. The Turkish, Afghan and Pakistani *mujahedin* were long on meanness but short on smarts. They panicked when nobody budged. They offed the Norwegian, dumped the remaining hostages with local groups and then some ran back to Pakistan after a major shoot-out in Dec '96. The alleged mastermind of the hostage-taking—Harkat-ul-Ansar leader Sanaullah—was gunned down in June 1997 by cops who had stopped him for questioning. Two other members of HUA (see below) were shot or beaten to death by police. There are now four fewer guys the hostages' families can get answers from.

Harkat-ul-Ansar (HUA)

HUA chief Parvez Ahmad Gazi was popped by Border Security Force troopers in May, as was new HUA head Peer Baba. And Sanaullah's predecessor, HUA "Supreme Commander" Arif Hussain Sheikh, was whacked in a crossfire between police and separatists on March 17, 1997. HUA is the union of Harakat ul-Jihad and Harakat ul-Mujahedin. The leader is Maulana Saadatullah Khan (until of course he gets popped). HUA is the main recruiter and trainer (with help from the Pakistani Secret Service) of young Kashmiri's and out of work *mujahedin* from Pakistan. If you are looking for *mujahedin* time to add to your resume, they will train you for five weeks in the dark arts of light weapons, land mines, booby traps and covert operations and then send you marching over the mountains to raise havoc in Indian-occupied Kashmir. The group is also known for sending eager fighters into Bosnia (all gone home now), Tajikistan (Tajik resistance), Myanmar (training Muslim rebels in the Arakan mountains) and other Muslim holy wars. They have become sort of a Burger King jihad around the world. They also provide much needed medical, food and other relief besides military.

Hizbul Mujahedin (Fighters for the Party of God)

The new players and leaders of Kashmir's struggle for independence are now the largest military force against the Indian government.

Syeed Salahuddin, whose real name is Syeed Mohammed Yusuf Shah, is the commander of the Hizbul Mujahedin. It receives financial backing and support from Pakistan. Pakistan's Prime Minister Benazir Bhutto wants the Muslim majority states of Jammu and Kashmir out of Hindu-dominated India and aligned with Pakistan. The rebels claim they are fighting for *azad* Kashmir, or free Kashmir. Currently, there are about 15,000 active rebel fighters with several subfactions among them. The rebels operate in small hit-and-run groups in cities like Srinagar, or from remote bases in Kashmir. Pakistan has fought two out of three of its last wars over Kashmir, and the situation is expected to remain tense for years to come. The geopolitical volleyball started when Britain sliced up India and Pakistan in 1947, based on geographic divisions rather than religious ones. At the time, India promised to hold a plebiscite among all Kashmiris to determine whether the territory should be part of India or Pakistan. It backed down, and the conflict has been going on ever since.

All-Party Hurriyat (Freedom) Conference

This is an alliance formed by the numerous guerrillas who use secession from India as a common rallying point. Omar Farooq is the leader of the All-Party Hurriyat Conference, the umbrella group formed of 32 rebel organizations. Farooq is also the hereditary Mir Waiz of Kashmir, the religious leader of the region's Muslims. The losers seem to be the Hindus of the region. At last count, there were about 400,000 Hindu refugees from the Kashmir Valley in refugee camps around the state's winter capital of Jammu.

Jamiat ul-Mujahedin (JUM)

The JUM is a pro-Pakistan Muslim separatist group known for its bombings in Jammu and Kashmir states in northeastern India. Its leader, "Supreme Commander" Ghulam Rasool Shah, was arrested in June 1997. The JUM takes its directions from Pakistan's Inter Service Intelligence (ISI), claim Indian officials. New Delhi accuses Pakistan of fighting a proxy war against India by arming and training separatist groups such as the JUM, charges the U.S. State Department generally concurs with.

Karachi

Muthiida National Movement (MNM)

The bustling port of Karachi is a war zone, thanks to the MNM. The name means Refugees National Movement and is led by Altaf Hussain (who conveniently lives in sedate London). The Urdu-speaking Mohajirs feel they are discriminated against (which they are) by the Sinhis. There is also a lot of banditry, drug feuds and Sunni/Shiite violence that is blamed on the MNM. There is even a splinter group called the MNM Haqiqi—or the real MNM.

Every day this dirty, sprawling metropolis of 13 million people tosses five or six bodies into the back of a police van for ID. In 1995 there were 2100 people killed in Karachi, strikes crippled the economy, and people feared for their lives. Now only a couple of hundred die each year. The government's reaction was to declare open season on the MNM. In many cases suspects are rounded up (many with a price on their head) and simply shot later. There is a new law that allows cops to shoot to kill if they even think you are about to commit a terrorist act. If they don't hit you they have to arrest you. Terrorists can get seven years just for being suspected of stirring up sectarian hatred.

There is also a ping-pong series of killings between minority Shiites and majority Sunnis that keep the morgue busy.

The North East

Naxalites

The Maoist Peoples War Group (PWG) and the Maoist Communist Center (MCC) are just some of the hard line Maoist groups that raise hell in and around Bihar. They want the Indian government to take land from the rich and distribute it to the poor. Obviously they didn't pay attention in history class.

The various radical communist groups all are descended from the armed peasants who operated in the 1960s under the banner of "Naxalites." They take their name from the Naxalbari, or "chicken neck," the strategic 20-km stretch alley of land running between Nepal and Bangladesh. Guerrillas of the PWG concentrate their attacks in Andhra Pradesh, targeting cops and government officials, using homemade, remote-controlled land mines. The group also operates throughout the Dandakaranya region straddling four states: Orissa, Maharashtra, Madhya Pradesh and Andhra Pradesh.

United Liberation Front of Assam (ULFA)

Assam supplies half of India's oil and 15 percent of the world's tea, but its people have nothing to show for it. The ULFA, drawn from the ranks of those who call themselves Asamese, was supposed to cede its fight for a socialist state in Assam when it signed a peace deal with the government in January 1992. The hard-liners said "screw that" and began a campaign of kidnapping and extortion against the rich tea growers. The Indian Tea Association quickly put together a 7000-man private army to protect itself from ULFA thugs.

There have been reports of large-scale extortion and attacks on police stations through-out Assam by both ULFA and the National Democratic Front of Bodoland (NDFB), for-merly called the Bodo Security Force. Security forces have stepped up their operations against the militants and rounded up large numbers of both suspects and weapons. Assam state officials, however, are hoping that the government in New Delhi will send in a para-military force to end the rebels' kidnappings. For now, Assam is an especially dangerous place if you grow tea. Crumpets, anyone?

The Bodos

The Bodos comprise some 800,000 people out of Assam's 25 million inhabitants. Bodo tribals living in northwest Assam between the north bank of the Brahmaputra River and the foothills of the Himalayas for 30 years have been duking it out with the Bengali Hin-dus and the Indian government for a homeland that would split the state in two. The Bodos are pissed at the swarms of Bengalis immigrants that have settled on their tradi-tional tribal lands over the past 20 years, as well as the wholesale raping of the environ-ment by illegal loggers. They like to chop up Bengali villagers and blow things up (trains, bridges, etc.). The struggle became truly violent, however, only after 1985. The Bodos claim some 1200 of their people were slaughtered by Indian security forces before the 1993 autonomy agreement. The pact was never carried out by the government and the Bodos renounced it in 1996. However, the Bodos are divided by factionalism. The National Democratic Front of Bodoland (NDFB) and the Bodoland Liberation Tiger Force (BLTF) have been hacking each up each other with as much fervor as with immi-grants and government security forces. Some 5500 people have been killed in the insur-gency since 1987.

The Nagas

The radical Naga movement is considered the godfather of India's rebel factions and includes groups such as the National Socialist Council of Nagaland (NSCN), known for its massacres of civilians, namely ethnic Kukis. Naga militants are fighting for a separate homeland composed of Nagaland (in the northeast) and areas in adjacent states where Nagas have settled. Nagas in both Nagaland and adjacent Manipur charge that ethnic Kukis have settled on ancestral Naga land. The bloodbath in the northeast continues unabated.

Punjab

The Sikhs

The Sikhs want their own turf, and India doesn't want them to have it. They are led by Sohan Singh, a 78-year-old doctor who was captured by the Indian government in November of 1993. Typically proud and bellicose, a small segment of Sikhs wants to establish an independent homeland called Khalistan, or Land of the Pure. The Sikhs tar-get security forces and other government symbols in their bomb attacks. The problem is that the bombs, although they may lean left or right, don't have political affiliations—and kill a lot of innocent people. Sikhs comprise only 2 percent of India's population, but they are a majority in Punjab state. The center of the Sikh terrorist movement is in the capital of Punjab, Chandigarh. Pakistan is sympathetic to the Sikh movement. Although the

Indian government claims that the movement has been shrinking since its leader was captured, there are still a lot of angry bad boys in turbans with the last name of Singh (all Sikhs carry the name Singh, meaning "lion").

Khalistan Affairs Center
851 National Press Bldg.
Washington, D.C. 20045
☎ *(202) 637-9210, FAX: (202) 6379211*
e-mail: kac@cyberspace.org
web site: khanda.unl.edu:80/~sikhism/kac

Police Chief Kunwar Pal Singh Gill

What was India's answer to putting down the Sikh rebellion? They hired a poet. But you won't find Gill giving readings at a gay encounter session in the East Village any time soon. Gill's the kinda guy who loves the smell of napalm in the morning. The Indian government gave him carte blanche for whacking rebel Sikhs in the '80s, and he cashed in. He turned a force of nervous flatfoots into a death machine. He handed out promotions and cash prizes for corpses without asking for evidence of guilt. Gill has retired, but the lawlessness he created in Punjab hasn't. Gill is still active, though, accusing Amnesty International of being a pro-separatist front.

A passport and visa (which must be obtained in advance) are required for entry into India for tourism or business. Visas range from 15 days to six months and can be had in single-entry or multi-entry versions. The only visa extendable is the six-month version. Evidence of yellow fever immunization is needed if the traveler is arriving from an infected area. Convicted drug offenders in India can expect a minimum jail sentence of 10 years and heavy fines. Indian customs authorities strictly enforce the laws and regulations governing the declaration, importation or possession of gold and gold objects. Travelers have sometimes been detained for possession of undeclared gold objects. For further entry information, the traveler can contact the following:

Embassy of India

2536 Massachusetts Avenue, NW
Washington, D.C. 20008
☎ *(202) 939-7000, 939-9849 or (202) 939-9806*
Or contact the Indian consulates in Chicago, New York and San Francisco.

Bombay International Airport is a 45- to 60-minute car ride from Bombay and about 23 miles northwest of the city. There is a departure tax of US$10 for international flights, US$3 for Southwest Asian flights.

Between India and Nepal, border crossings are open at Biranj-Raxaul, Kakarbhitta-Siliguri and Sunauli-Gorakhpur. Sunauli is the best entry point if coming from Kathmandu to Delhi or elsewhere in northwestern India. Overland travel between Dhaka and Calcutta is possible. The only border checkpoint open with Pakistan is Lahore-Amritsar. This crossing can also be made by train.

The major airports in India are at Bombay (Mumbai) and Delhi. Other international flights arrive at Madras and Calcutta. A taxi from the airport to the center of New Delhi runs about Rs150. In Bombay it will cost you Rs170 and takes about an hour; in Calcutta, about Rs120. You can prepay in New Delhi and Bombay, but drivers will haggle a fixed price with tourists.

Indian Airlines has an extensive network inside India. In addition to the four international airports, 115 other airports serve domestic routes. The international carrier, Air India, also runs some domestic flights. These folks are facing some competition these days from upstarts Jet Airways and Sahara Indian Airlines.

The size of the railway network was estimated at approximately 63,900 km (37,850 miles) in 1990. India's railway network is the largest in Asia and the second largest in the world. The rail system is the lifeblood of the Indian people. There are a number of different classes of trains—and the reservation system can be confusing for all classes. Foreign visitors can take advantage of the tourist quota allotment. Train passengers have been subjected to robberies and schedule disruptions due to protest actions. There are six classes of bus service—from ordinary to deluxe sleeper. The private buses tend to be faster and more comfortable than the state buses. Travel by road after dark is not recommended.

Restricted Areas

Permission from the Indian government (from Indian diplomatic missions abroad, or in some cases, from the Ministry of Home Affairs) is required to visit the states of Mizoram, Manipur, Nagaland, Meghalaya, Assam, Tripura, Arunachal Pradesh, Sikkim, parts of Kulu district and Spiti district of Himachal Pradesh, border areas of Jammu and Kashmir, areas of Uttar Pradesh, the area west of National Highway 15 running from Ganganagar to Sanchar in Rajasthan, the Andaman and Nicobar islands and the Union Territory of the Laccadive Islands. All are considered dangerous areas except the Andamans and Islands where the government tries to preserve the indigenous peoples way of life from the Nikon-equipped, eco-yuppies. Oh, before the Andamans were pacified sailors, they ate anyone who washed ashore.

Kashmir

In 1989, the Muslims became violent in opposing Indian rule. There are 6 million people in Kashmir; 4 million of them are Muslim. Since 1989, about 25,000 people, mostly Muslims, have been killed. Half the toll has been civilians. Most of the casualties have been in the Kashmir Valley area around Srinagar. Kashmir is currently divided, with some parts under the control of Pakistan rebels and others under the auspices of the Indian army.

The Kashmir Valley drew 500,000 to 700,000 tourists a year in the 1980s. No more. Now, each week about 50 people lose their lives in Kashmir due to violence. It is even more frightening to know that the executed Norwegian tourist, Hans Ostro, contacted three Indian government tourist offices to inquire about the danger and was told that there were no risks. Terrorist activities and violent civil disturbances continue in the Kashmir Valley in the states of Jammu and Kashmir. There have been incidents in which terrorists have threatened and kidnapped foreigners.Undoubtedly, though, Pakistan is the biggest influence on India's foreign relations. India and Pakistan have duked it out on the battlefield three times since World War II—in 1947, 1965 and 1971. Today, it is very much a hot insurgency fought in a cold place.

Relations between the two became less strained only after Rajiv Gandhi replaced his mother as India's prime minister. In December 1985, Rajiv Gandhi and Pakistan President Mohammed Zia ul-Haq each pledged not to throw the first punch, particularly jabs aimed at the nations' nuke sites. The hot spot is the overlapping area that is known as the line of control. Both India and Pakistan claim an area of the Karakoram mountain range that includes a well armed 50 mile front along the 21,000 foot high Siachen glacier region. The two countries have established military outposts in the region and armed clashes have occurred. The UN has one of its oldest and smallest field missions here (UNMOGIP). Forty four South Koreans sit here to monitor how many times the combatants break the 1949 cease fire agreement. Because of this situation, adventurers traveling to or climbing peaks anywhere in the disputed area face significant risk of injury and death. The disputed area includes the following peaks: Rimo Peak, Apsarasas I, II and III, Tegam Kangri I, II, and III, Suingri Kangri, Ghaint I and II, Indira Col and Sia Kangri.

Increased violence in Kashmir, the one Indian state where Muslims comprise a majority, has brought about a greater likelihood that the two countries will again go to war. India claims that Pakistan is fueling the flames by encouraging and supporting Kashmir secession from India. Of course, rather than Kashmir becoming an independent entity, Pakistan would like to be the sponge that absorbs it. The Indian governor of Kashmir charged Pakistan in January 1994 with hiring more than 10,000 Afghan mercenaries to help Kashmiri rebels in their efforts against the government. Although media attention has been found on the kidnapping and executing of only a group of Western hostages, there have been over 2000 kidnappings since 1991. Half of them survive.

Assam and India's Northeast

India's northeast is treated like a rich mother-in-law by New Delhi—hit up for its riches but never invited to dinner. Connected to the rest of India only by a thread, but exploited like a pipeline, India's northeast has been racked by a half-century of separatist insurrection, tribal wars, massacres, terrorism and guerrilla warfare. Little wonder—some 200 aboriginal groups comprise the northeast's population. Every day, someone is killed due to strife in one of the seven northeast states, at least five of which are suffering from violent insurgencies, mostly tribal-based. AIDS and drug smuggling are rampant. The states have been stripped of their oil and tea and have received little in return, spawning separatist groups like the All Tripura Tiger Force, ULFA, The Bodo Liberation Tigers and the National Democratic Front of Bodoland. However, India's "chicken neck"—as the 20-km wide strip of Indian land separating Nepal and Bangladesh is called—doesn't necessarily divide the good guys and the bad guys. The Bodos have been in a slugfest with the Asamese—to protect their language and culture—and even with each other. Meanwhile, Manipur, with a 2000-year history as a colorful kingdom with a constitution dating from 1180, is better known these days as just another deadly stop along the heroin funnel from Burma. More than 60 people were killed during a single two-week period in July 1997. Most of the killing here is related to the Naga's fight for independence (more than 1500 people have died in Nagaland alone), the battle for control of Burma's drug smuggling routes and good 'ole Hatfield & McCoy shoot-outs. Separatist guerrillas have started enforcing their own anti-drugs policy: narcotics users are shot in the head after three warnings. In Assam tea plantation owners are raising private army of 7000–8000 retired soldiers to guard the plantations. The 200 tea estates will also continue to pay protection money to the insurgents.

Punjab and Uttar Pradesh

Separatist violence continues in the Punjab and nearby regions outside Punjab state. Gangs have kidnapped and held for ransom foreign company executives. Militants and robber gangs operate in the area in and around Jim Corbett National Park and Dudhwa National Park, as well as on roads leading to Hardwar, Rishikesh, Dehra Dun and Mussoorie. The most active and violent have been Sikh militants, who stepped up their attacks in 1997 on thickly populated targets, including transportation depots and marketplaces. The Sikhs are fighting for an independent homeland in Punjab, Khalistan (Land of the Pure). On July 8, 1997, 33 people were killed and 66 injured after a bomb exploded aboard a passenger train in southwestern Punjab state. Since 1984, when Prime Minister Indira Gandhi was blown away by her Sikh bodyguards, more than 25,000 people have been killed in the conflict in Punjab.

The cops, in their effort to put down the rebellion, have been as ruthless as the secessionists. More than 70 police officers have been charged with murdering alleged separatists.

Shiite Muslims have been raising havoc in Uttar Pradesh state, particularly since the June 1997 arrest of Shiite leader Maulana Kalbe Jawwad.

Delhi

In Delhi, several bombings have resulted in casualties and property damage. The targets are areas of public access, such as public transportation facilities, bazaars and shopping areas, and restaurants. In the states of Jammu and Kashmir, and Punjab in northern India, the terrorist threat is considerably higher. Bombings, kidnappings and assassinations are common occurrences in these regions. The State Department is advising American citizens not to travel to Kashmir and to avoid nonessential travel to Punjab.

Foreign residents throughout India usually employ *chawkidars* (residential guards) outside their homes. Police assistance throughout northern India can be requested by dialing 100 from any public phone; 100 connects to the nearest police control room, which can usually dispatch a patrol vehicle.

Bombay (Mumbai)

There has been an increase in the number of organized criminal gangs operating in Bombay, and police confirm that the problem exists throughout Maharashtra state. Drug gangs have proliferated in the larger cities, and police report these gangs have moved into some of the most affluent areas of Bombay. In 1994, there were three drive-by shootings in the Malabar hill area of Bombay. Home burglary still remains the most prevalent crime in Bombay, often committed by servants or other persons with easy access to the residence involved.

Calcutta

Insurgent activities, including killings and kidnappings by the United Liberation Front of Assam (ULFA) continue in the northeast. Despite army intervention, violent dissidence continues in parts of Assam. Local ULFA militants have carried out coordinated kidnappings throughout the state. A Russian mining engineer was killed and a number of Indian hostages taken, including several high-ranking officials. Political clashes occur sporadically in different parts of west Bengal and Bihar. Americans who are members of the Ananda Marg have been victims of mob violence in some areas of west Bengal and Bihar states (especially Calcutta and Purulia district) and are not welcome by state government authorities, who, upon locating such individuals, usually detain and deport them.

The crime situation in west Bengal and Orissa relates to petty thefts, etc. However, in Bihar, there have been killings and other violence stemming from caste and tribal differences. Travel by road after dark is not recommended, and train passengers have been subjected to robberies and schedule disruptions due to protest actions.

The South

Sri Lanka is a thorn in India's side because of the ethnic conflict between Sri Lanka's Sinhalese majority and the island's Tamil minority.

In May 1991, Prime Minister Rajiv Gandhi was killed in Tamil Nadu by a suicide bomber. Members of the Sri Lankan Tamil terrorist group, Liberation Tigers of Tamil Eelam (LTTE), commit acts of terrorism and violence throughout southern India.

Insurgents and Separatists

More than 100 rebel factions, with 10 being militarily significant, and about 60 inter-group clashes a year. Thousands of Kashmiri youths have received rudimentary training in Afghanistan and Azad Kashmir that takes two weeks to three months. Although there are plenty of weapons supplied by Pakistan, there is little organized fighting. Typically a mine will be laid across a road and a military convoy will be under attack by small-arms fire from a group of 5 to 10 insurgents. The insurgents then run away and do not press their advantage. The ratio of deaths for insurgents to military is about five to one. There are also about 1000 volunteers, primarily from Afghanistan (500), Saudi Arabia (80) and Sudan (200) fighting in Kashmir.

Being Kidnapped

About 500 people are kidnapped in Kashmir each year, including Westerners. Over 2000 people have been kidnapped in Kashmir since 1990. Less than half of them survived the ordeal.

Prithvi Rockets

The name "Prithvi" means Earth. The latest models of these nuke-capable projectiles, first tested in January 1996, have a range of 150 miles and can strike most major Pakistani cities within only a few minutes after launch. The short-range version can carry a 1000-kilogram payload. Although the Indians have some fine tuning to do on their accuracy, these little puppies are quite capable of mass death and destruction. It simply remains a matter of on whom and what they fall.

The Roads

According to the National Transportation Research Centre in Trivendrum, Indian roads are the most dangerous in the world. With one percent of the total vehicles in the world, India accounts for 6 percent of total road accidents and has the highest accident rate in the world at 34.6 per 100,000 people. In October 1989 there were about 2 million km of roads in India, 33,112 km of which were National Highway. While this constitutes only 2 percent of total road length, it carries around 35 percent of the traffic.

Bus & Train Stations

Bus depots and train stations—particularly in the north, including Delhi, and the north-east—have become favorite targets of separatists, who employ remote-detonated bombs in their ongoing campaigns of murder and terror. Almost daily attacks typically kill and injure dozens of people.

Political Rallies

Various separatist groups love to blow up politicians using suicide bombers. These bombs usually contain way too much explosive material and nasty things like ball bearings. Needless to say, they bury what's left of the politician in a sandwich bag and a lot of people die. Political rallies in India are much safer on TV.

Police Crackdowns

The army likes to talk to folks early in the morning. Between 3 and 4 a.m. they will seal an area off, roust folks from their beds and take them to a open area. They are divided into young, middle-aged and old. Women are allowed to return to their homes. Then the men are paraded in front of "cats," hooded informers who point out Kashmir insurgents. (The term "cats" comes from Concealed Apprehension Technique.) Anyone who looks like a bad guy is taken away for further interrogation. Some of the men never return home.

While the male population plays "What's My Line," soldiers go through the houses, searching for weapons. In many cases, the unprotected women have been raped and the homes looted.

The Indian Army is known for their violent and poorly planned hostage rescue attempts, village shootouts and brutal interrogations of prisoners. Although we don't expect many *DP* readers to become prisoners, it is not uncommon to stumble in on a village shootout as we did in Kashmir. As for being rescued by the military if you are a hostage, you have a 50/50 chance of surviving... if you duck.

AIDS

There are 3.8 million Indians with HIV and 200,000 with AIDS. India is predicted to have the highest incidence of AIDS in the world by the year 2000.

Press Releases

On July 8, 1996, Muslim guerrilla Ikwhan Jammu kidnapped 19 journalists for 10 hours. It was a year after the kidnapping of German Dirk Hasert. The journalists were on their way to a press conference held by the Muslim Mujahedin in Achabal (40 miles from Srinagar), another guerilla group. Ikwhan held the journalists because their editors refused to stop publication of their newspapers after they refused to publish one of the group's press releases.

Malaria

Calcutta, West Bengal and northeastern India are once again suffering from serious outbreaks of malaria. Calcutta is reported to be the worst hit of the country's major metropolitan cities. Reports suggest that this is a continuation of a longer trend of higher incidences of malaria in general and of malignant and chloroquine-resistant strains in particular.

Yanni

Five Indian farmers threatened to set themselves ablaze in protest to a March 1997 concert in front of the Taj Mahal by Greek-born New Age musician Yanni. The farmers claimed that some 250 acres of crops were destroyed to make way for a stage for the concert. Crops aside, the sodbusters may have mistaken "easy listening" for "easy glistening" in the publicity announcements.

Delhi Belly is a bitch here. The chances of seeing India without frequent side trips to the john are slim. More serious intestinal problems include typhoid, cholera, Hepatitis A and parasites. Don't be shy about consulting an Indian doctor. They know their stuff and they are reasonable. Adequate medical care is available in the major population centers but limited in rural areas of the country. The key is to take preventive measures against malaria, hepatitis, meningitis and Japanese encephalitis which also includes taking precautions to avoiding getting bit by mosquitoes. Dengue and Japanese encephalitis are mosquito borne viral diseases that pose a danger in rural areas during the rainy season. Travelers arriving from countries where outbreaks of yellow fever have occurred will be required to furnish a certificate for yellow fever vaccination. Cholera and gastroenteritis occur during the summer monsoon months, mostly in the poorer areas of India. The best protection includes eating only at better-quality restaurants or hotels, drinking only boiled or bottled mineral water and avoiding ice. Take along medication for intestinal problems and read up on the free information provided by the CDC.

India has three main regions: the mountainous Himalayas in the north; the Indo-Gangetic Plain, a flat, hot plain south of the Himalayas; and the Peninsular Shield in the south, where India's neighbors Sri Lanka and the Maldives are located. The coldest months are January and February, with sweltering heat between March and May. The southwestern monsoon season is from June to September. The post monsoon, or northeast monsoon, in the southern peninsula occurs from October to December.

India is hot, dirty and humid throughout most of the year. The North is cool in the highlands and alpine above that. If you are looking to latch onto some bacteria, Southern India is the place to do it. Bombay may be the dirtiest city on earth and there will be plenty of people to pass on germs to you. The hottest months are April to July, the wettest months from June to August.

There are more than 900 million people crammed into India's 3.3 million square kilometers (1.3 million square miles). About 40 percent of India's people live below the poverty line, defined as the resources needed to provide 2100 to 2400 calories per person per day. About 70 percent of the population lives in the countryside. The official language is Hindi, but English is the second language and is widely spoken. All official documents are in English. In keeping with India's diverse makeup, 18 languages are recognized for official use in regional areas, of which the most widely spoken are Telugu, Bengali, Marathi, Tamil, Urdu and Gujarati, each with its own script. Hindus do not eat beef. Muslims avoid pork. Sikhs do not smoke. Strict Hindus are also vegetarian and do not drink.

Banking hours: 10:30 a.m.–2:30 p.m., Monday to Friday; 10:30 a.m.–12:30 p.m., Saturday. Business hours: 9 a.m.–noon, 1–5 p.m., Monday to Friday. Stores are open 9:30 a.m.–6 p.m., Monday to Saturday. The workweek is Monday through Friday.

The rupee (about 31 to the U.S. dollar) is the currency and should be changed only through banks and authorized money changers. Electricity is 230–240v/50hz.

Embassy Location

U.S. Embassy
Shanti Path, Chanakyapuri 110 021
New Delhi
☎ *[91] (11) 600651*

U.S. Consulates General

In Bombay:
U.S. Consulate General
Lincoln House
78 Bhulabhai Desai Road, Bombay 400026
☎ *[91] (22) 363-3611*

In Calcutta:
U.S. Consulate General
5/1 Ho Chi Minh Sarani, Calcutta 700071
☎ *[91] (33) 242-3611, 242-2336, 242-2337*

In Madras:
U.S. Consulate General
220 Mount Road, Madras 600006
☎ *[91] (44) 827-3040, 827-7542*

Other Useful Numbers

Ministry of Communications
Sanchar Bhawan, New Delhi 110 003
☎ *383600*

Ministry of Tourism and Civil Aviation
Parivahan Bhavan, Sansad Marg, New Delhi 100 001
☎ *351700*

Ministry of External Affairs
South Block, New Delhi 110 011
☎ *301-1813*

Web Resources

The Times of India
http://www.timesofindia.com/

Oneworld Online
http://www.oneworld.org/news/asia/india.html

SAPRA (Security & Political Risk Analysis India)
http://www.subcontinent.com/sapra/sapra_3.html

The Hindu
http://www.webpage.com/index.h tml

IndiaExpress
http://www.indiaexpress.com/news/

The Hindustan Times
http://www.hindustantimes.com/

Deccan Chronicle
http://www.deccan.com/

India Abroad
http://www.indiaabroad.com/

News India
http://www.newsindia-times.com/

The Afternoon Dispatch and Courier
http://www.afternoondc.com/index1.htm

Deccan Herald
http://www.deccanherald.com/

The Ministry of External Affairs of the Indian Government
http://www.meadev.gov.in/

The Consortium Of Indian Military Websites
http://www.bharat- rakshak.com/

Press Information Bureau of the Government of India
http://www.nic.in/India- Image/PIB/

U.S. State Department Human Rights Report on India
http://www.usis.usemb.se/human/india.html

U.S. AID's Country Health Statistics Profile
http://www.info.usaid.gov/countrie s/in/india.txt

U.S. State Department Consular Information Sheets
http://travel.state.gov/india.html

The Ethnologue
http://www.sil.org/ethnolo gue/countries/Inda.html

11/12/1996	Mid-air crash of a Saudi 747 and a Kazakh cargo plane kills 349 people in the world's worst mid-air disaster.
08/13/1995	Norwegian Hans Christian Ostro is found beheaded near Anantnag, 37 miles from Srinagar.
07/04/1995	Al-Faran guerrillas kidnap two Britons, and two Americans near Pahalgam, 55 miles from Srinagar.
10/1994	Rebel leader Shabir Shah released from prison.
06/1994	Two Brits are kidnapped and released unharmed 17 days later.
03/1993	Three hostages are swapped for seven guerrillas.
12/06/1992	Hindu extremists destroyed the 16th-century Muslim mosque at Ayodhya in India's Uttar Pradesh state. The subsequent rioting and Muslim-Hindu clashes that engulfed India, Pakistan, Bangladesh and other nations resulted in over 1000 deaths. Hindus claim the mosque was built on the birth site of the Hindu god Rama, a claim disputed by Muslims.

08/1992	Two army engineers are kidnapped and killed after the government refuses to release 17 jailed rebels
02/1992	India plants mines along border with Pakistan to stop traffic of insurgents between countries.
11/1991	The manager of the state-run radio station is kidnapped and exchanged for a guerrilla.
09/1991	A former Kashmiri minister and her husband are kidnapped and freed in a raid one month later. The brother-in-law of an Indian minister, a policeman, an insurance worker, and a bank employee are kidnapped the same month. They are exchanged for rebels but not until a hostage's severed thumb is sent as proof.
07/1991	Four government officers are kidnapped and executed three months later.
06/1991	Eight Israeli tourists are kidnapped. Six escape and one dies in the attempt. An oil executive is kidnapped and released 53 days later.
05/21/1991	Former Prime Minister Rajiv Gandhi is assassinated during a campaign rally in Tamil Nadu state.
03/1991	Two Swedish engineers as well as a daughter and wife are kidnapped. The wife and child are released but the men are not released until 97 days later.
02/1991	A pregnant 29-year-old is kidnapped and swapped for five rebels.
03/1990	Kashmiri political leader Mir Ghulum Mustafa is kidnapped and killed.
12/1990	Indian army fires on demonstrators, killing 38 in Srinagar. Separatists begin a military campaign for independence.
12/1989	Guerrillas kidnap daughter of Indian home minister and swap her for five insurgents.
01/06/1989	Two of Prime Minister Indira Gandhi's Sikh bodyguards are hanged for her assassination on October 31, 1984.
01/03/1989	Muslim Kashmiri militants begin their campaign for independence from India.
07/06/1987	Seventy-two Hindus are killed in an attack by Sikh militants on a bus in the Punjab.
04/29/1986	Sikh militants seize the Golden Temple of Amritsar in Punjab and declare the independent state of Khalistan. Expelled by government of India forces the next day.
06/23/1985	A bomb explodes on an Air India flight over the North Atlantic following its departure from Canada, killing all 329 passengers on board. A second bomb explodes at Narita airport in Japan, killing two people. Sikh extremists claim responsibility for both bombings.
12/03/1984	A chemical leak at Union Carbide's Bhopal plant results in 2000 deaths and nearly 150,000 injuries.
10/31/1984	Indian Prime Minister Indira Gandhi is assassinated by her Sikh bodyguards. Anti-Sikh rioting following the assassination resulted in thousands of Sikh deaths throughout India.

INDIA

INDIA

08/09/1984	The head of the Indian security forces that stormed the Sikh golden temple of Amritsar is assassinated by Sikh terrorists.
06/06/1984	Indian troops stormed the golden temple of Amritsar, killing 300 Sikhs.
02/11/1984	Maqbool Butt, founder of the Jammu-Kashmir Liberation Front, was hanged in a New Delhi jail for the 1965 murder of an Indian intelligence agent in Kashmir. Militant Muslims have marked the anniversary of his death with sometimes violent demonstrations in Jammu and Kashmir.
01/26/1950	India's constitution is promulgated and India becomes a republic within the Commonwealth. (Republic Day is also called Constitution Day.)
01/30/1948	Mahatma Gandhi is assassinated.
08/15/1947	Independence Day.
04/13/1699	Sikh religion was founded by Guru Gobind Singh.
07/13	Martyr's day in Kashmir. It commemorates the deaths of Kashmiri nationalists during the British raj.

Kashmir 1996: Kashmir Sweat

Some say the blonde-haired, suntanned head of Hans Christian Ostro was balanced between his legs for effect while others say the head was found 40 meters away. Some say that the words "Al-Faran" were carved with a knife on his back, while others say they were on his chest. All agree that the Norwegian tourist was beheaded while still alive. This is not what Kashmir claims happens to its tourists. And this crude method of death is supposed to be reserved for those in Third World countries where human behavior is still in a primitive, barbaric state—not for Westerners who are simply visiting what has been called among the most "beautiful and historic parts of Asia." But it happened.

News of trouble piled up quickly at first: One American escapes, a Norwegian is killed, the others are sick, and rescue attempts fail. There are conflicting reports of shootouts, executions, sightings and burials. And then silence. The families search desperately in vain. The world's best intelligence groups search in vain. Over half a million Indian troops search in vain. Then, as dramatically as the story appears, it disappears. Not surprising since the Westerners were about one percent of the 548 people kidnapped in Kashmir in that same year. Over 2000 people have been kidnapped in Kashmir since 1990, less than half of them survived the ordeal. Something evil is happening in northwestern India.

Kashmir is a tourist destination and it is a war zone. A quarter of a million Indian soldiers, long-range artillery duels, grenade and mine attacks have resulted in a death toll that climbs like a rocket heading into space. So far there have been more than 25,000 people killed with a burn rate of about 50 deaths a week. I decided there is only one way to find out what is going on in Northwest India—I put Kashmir on my list of places to visit.

My first stop, Delhi. You drive into town from the airport and then begin an inescapable spin into the city center. The British built Delhi in the shape of a wheel, with the hub being a group of colonial white three-story buildings the same color as a faded linen suit. New Delhi is a sprawling city built more like a sewer with a central drain. Foreign tourists arriving from the airport serve as Delhi's main source of hard cash, therefore, compliant cab drivers funnel new arrivals to "official tourist offices" even in the wee hours of the morning.

It's 5:30 a.m., the air is still cool and thick—the best time of the day. But already the dirt and smoke hang low over the trees and people hurry about dressed in clean clothes. Soon the heat and dust will descend upon this bustling country and India will fade to quivering pastels.

Four hundred rupees gets me into town in an aging black Ambassador taxi. A '50s anachronism (still made in India), the Ambassador is a genetic mixture of Austin A-55, Morris Minor and bad Indian craftsmanship. (This Third World luxury on wheels can be yours for $US8500.) The early morning is also when the street cleaners poke supine men sprawled along the streets and gutters to see if they are dead or just hung over. One man is carted off, dead.

The cities of India consist of overflowing rivers of people running between buildings like an unstoppable torrent. Walking, crawling, riding, or running they are surprisingly quite efficient, forming huge mobile masses that rarely collide. Even the animals display a sense of order, so to speak, as the macaques in narrow alleys are creative enough to run along the tangled electrical wiring overhead and somnambulate cows sit calmly on traffic medians surrounded by oceans of smoke-belching vehicles.

Much of India is not dangerous. It is a refreshingly energetic, polite and industrious country. Some visitors may be mildly amused by the Indian habit of adopting the worst elements from various cultures whether they be '50s cars and motorcycles from the British, '70s weapons from the Russians, home decor from China, or '60s musicals from the Americans. American culture is transcendent here. India's Hollywood, or rather "Bollywood," now cranks out musicals that are reminiscent of "West Side Story," only it sounds like the songs are performed by Alvin and the Chipmunks on speed. You can't help but wonder if the youth of India, faced with carrying on centuries of complex culture and religions, just said "Fuck it, let's watch MTV."

Ticket to Ride

I take my driver up on his offer and visit not one but a dozen "tourist" offices. I walk in and find calm, friendly people behind the smudged dark glass of the counter windows of the air-conditioned office. Wherever I want to go, the answer is always: "No problem, sir. When would you like to go?"

I then inquire about kidnapping, murders, a rather large insurgency and the upcoming election with its resultant mayhem. Their smiles get wider, "No problem, sir. When would you like to go?"

They recommend the "Golden Triangle tour," a three-day excursion that takes travelers to Agra for the Taj Mahal, Jaipur and then back to Delhi. Having experienced the three-day journey previously, flanked by apocalyptic bus and car crashes (about one every 10–20 km), I wonder if this is actually more dangerous than going to Kashmir.

At one office, a Kashmiri man asks me darkly what I know about the hostages. He closes his office door as he sends the errand boy out for tea. We engage in a serious discussion about what is happening in Srinagar. We keep the conversation light but I sense he knows my purpose. I decide that I will return here to buy my tickets.

The next order of business is to wander around Delhi, engage in small talk, and hopefully get some bits of advice on Kashmir. Indians speak of Kashmir in the same manner and tone as a father would when discussing an unruly child. One man says "India has been patient and polite, but soon there will be a war—a 30-minute war, and this time we won't hand Pakistan back to the Muslims." Tough talk, but a good betting man's position since Pakistan has been thumped in wars over Kashmir three times before in 1948, 1965 and 1971.

The Valley of War

Kashmir is just one of India's ethnic, tribal, religious and financial conflicts. Kashmiris are independent, nonpolitical people living in a proverbial garden of Eden. When Britain divided India, the local mughals who ruled predominately Muslim Kashmir threw their lot in with Hindu India. Confronted by the idea of a Muslim majority being pledged to India, Pakistan and a large number of Kashmiris voiced disapproval and the problems started. Pakistan is not the gateway to Kashmir, nor do India's tourists want to vacation in a foreign, Muslim country. Kashmir was the most visited region in India until the late '80s and the gateway to the region has always been through Delhi and the South. Today it is not a war of Kashmiris vs. Indians. Any Kashmiri cab driver in New York will tell you that they would rather be pushing a hack rather than being press-ganged and forced to fight India. Kashmir is a war that Pakistan and India want, not the Kashmiris.

The tug-of-war for Kashmir is understandable. It's not some desolate Afghan desert or steamy uncharted jungle, rather a major tourist area immersed with history. Some people believe it to be the Bible's Promised Land, the place where Moses wandered to and was buried; one of the places where Jesus spent his youth and where he ultimately returned and died. There are many such legends about Kashmir and what's more, it is a beautiful, fragrant land inhabited by kind, handsome, creative and generous people. It is a land once blessed with peace, but when you hear a MiG-21 scream through the valleys, you realize that Kashmir is also a war zone.

Today, the border between Pakistan and India is an ill-defined series of armed border camps featuring daily firefights on scenic glaciers and artillery duels with cannons that can lob shells more than 20 miles. The Line of Control was determined in 1972, after the last war, and continues to be contested daily. Skirmishes are common and the resulting deaths are never featured in any newspapers There is also an active insurgency within Kashmir instigated and supported by Pakistan under the direction of its secret police, the ISI—the same folks that were the middlemen between the *mujahedin* in Afghanistan and the CIA back in the '80s.

On any given week, there are more than a quarter of a million Indian soldiers stationed in this tiny valley and in the mountains that surround it. Pipe-shaped MiG-21's fly hourly sorties as they thunder and echo through the valley. Every corner and crossroad is protected by soldiers hidden inside sandbagged, wire-fenced fortifications. There is no place where you cannot see at least 20 to 50 soldiers at any one time. Inside and outside the major cities and towns there are firefights, dozens of mine or grenade attacks, the odd village burning and massive sweeps for *mujahedin* every day. When asked about these specifics the tourist folks say that Kashmir is a great place to do a little trekking among fields of fragrant saffron and deodar. Yes, they admit, there are problems but nothing to worry about.

Before embarking on my date with fragrant saffron and deodar, I decide to play tourist and see what our officials have to say. I call the U.S. Embassy in Delhi to ask for advice on traveling to Kashmir. A bumbling, apologetic staffer offers a stern warning but cannot provide details, after all, they have a MIA somewhere in the cedar forests. Then I'm connected to an unnamed embassy liaison who sounds like an airline reservation recording. He tells me they are advising against all travel to Kashmir particularly because of the election. I ask for specifics. He has none. I ask him where he gets his information. He gets it from the press. Has he been there? No. I ask him where the hostages are and if they are dead or alive. He doesn't know. When I ask about the whereabouts of the Delta Force team, the German GS-9 and British SAS teams sent to Kashmir to help in the hostage recovery effort, the staffer finally shows a little emotion. "I can't tell you that," he barks. I get the same warning and lack of hard info from the Canadian embassy as well. It may be chilling to note that some of the kidnap victims also made calls be-fore traveling to Kashmir, but they were told no problem. Well, now there is a problem, but no one seems to want to tell me what it is.

No one blinks when I buy a ticket from Delhi to Srinagar. I change a few crisp US$100 bills into a dirty brick of rupees. The two-inch wad is bundled with in-dustrial-sized staples. I am given the secret on peeling the money: twist back and forth and don't worry about the rust spots or gaping holes where the bills were stapled. At 35.8 rupees to the dollar, that means I must carry bricks to pay for large items.

Kashmir is jammed up tight against the Hindu Kush, a name that appropriately translates to "Killer of Hindus." This region is also squeezed in by Pakistan, China and India. From the air Kashmir does look like Shangri La — a completely self-sufficient, isolated garden of Eden with no real connection to any of its neighbors.

I am intrigued by the irregular curved patches made by the stepped and irrigat-ed yellow rice fields. Medieval European-style houses with steep, pitched tin roofs create jumbled intersections with no straight roads. Each village is softened by a ring of golden sycamore trees with leaves turning gold. In this medieval jumble of well-worn brick homes there is a sense of the English countryside.

Snow-capped peaks frame the rice fields and orchards that grow in the cool mountain temperatures and clean air. It is this scenery and mountain air that has attracted visitors from the hot arid flatlands to the south. Oddly, it doesn't look like a war from 30,000 feet. As we land, the hard scream of the engines warns me that reality awaits down below. We are landing at a speed that would be more ap-propriate for takeoff—a technique similar to carrier flights where maximum air speed is needed in case of abort or evasion.

The plane slams down in Srinagar, and I notice rows of bunkers on each side of the runway as we whiz past. Russian-made MiG-21's and large camouflage trans-port planes stand ready to take off. The thrust reversers and hard brakes push against the seats and the belts. As I disembark, there are 20 soldiers ringing our plane, guns at the ready. My fellow travelers, who I thought were businessmen or returning locals, turn out to be journalists here to cover the election. A handful of anemic looking hippies in their early '20s look curiously out of place. It seems they are trying to recapture the love and drugs that brought thousands of their parents here in the early '70s before the Russians invaded Afghanistan and before *jihad,* or holy war, was in the news.

My plan is to stay at Adhoo's, a well known hotel for journalists and then head into the countryside. My cabdriver has other ideas. He extols the beauty of houseboats, the joys of trekking and the ecstasy that awaits me in the trout streams high up in the mountains. Because he has a polite and unnerving habit of looking directly at me from the front seat when he drives, I say that's nice, but for now please shut up, turn around and drive.

The convoluted and crowed road into town is overseen by a massive military presence. My newfound guide advises me sotto voce when to not take pictures by saying "military" as we approach each sandbagged bunker. I make him very ner-vous by taking pictures of the checkpoints as well as the scenic spots. The blast marks and nervous state of patrolling soldiers indicate that when my guide speaks of the various attacks that have occurred here, it is not a history lesson but something immediate and real.

Hundreds of skinny, mustached soldiers with ill-fitting uniforms stand guard every 50 meters as we enter Srinagar. Each corner is controlled by a 20' x 20' bunker crudely built of sandbags and covered with plastic mesh to deflect hand grenades. From within these bunkers peer the white eyes of dark skinned, helmeted soldiers with just the tips of their machine guns protruding.

Each intersection is clogged with soldiers on guard and roving groups of Jammu Kashmir Police outside the bunkers directing the chaotic traffic. They work in groups of four with short sticks and whistles. They argue, cajole, yell and threaten to keep things moving. They never quite agree on their diverse directions to each motorist as they wave their two-foot sticks and bang on the hoods of the cars. Meanwhile the jumbled traffic completely ignores them. As we sit stuck in traffic at the battle-worn traffic circles, my guide continues to rattle off a list of recent attacks at each bunker. I can visualize how one grenade thrown at the bunker would roll down into the stalled traffic and shred dozens of innocent bystanders. Any machine gun fire from the slit bunkers would add to the death toll. For now I am just stuck in traffic with about five-to-eight soldiers banging and yelling under the watchful eye of very nervous troops.

The journalists have missed the traffic jam and have beat me to the hotel. Much to my chagrin, there are no vacant rooms. All the other hotels in town are occupied by the military. What to do? Well, the houseboat doesn't sound too bad now. My driver seems quite pleased since he happens to have a cousin who owns a houseboat.

The British began the custom of residing in houseboats because they could not own land. The ornately carved boats became de rigueur in the '70s for marijuana-smoking tourists who could indulge themselves in the local weed safe in isolation from the police on land. Dal Lake is lined by empty houseboats, all 980 with romantic or foreign sounding names.

The houseboats of Srinagar are long, gently curved rectangular barges with a porch at the entrance and bedrooms toward the back. There is also a large sitting room, dining room and extra bedrooms. Most are ornately carved and fashioned out of the fragrant cedar that grows in the mountains.

There is nothing wrong with staying on a houseboat on Lake Dal but I didn't want to be a sitting duck. After I visit the boat, it seems to be a smarter place to be than the frequently attacked hotels with their great iron gates and barbed wire. The lake makes the gunfire and shouting echo at night, making it seem more like an amusement park complete with fireworks rather than a fully-active war zone.

The owner of a particularly fine houseboat next door to the one I choose to stay at tells me it took eight people working for five years to create his 20' x 80' masterpiece. It curves gently upwards at each end and is built of fragrant deodar, a local pine that comes from the mountains. As I talk to my neighbor, it becomes evident that the investment of so much money during a time where there are no tourists was not the wisest thing. But he was never in it to make any money to recoup his investment. All he has is pride in the beautiful craftsmanship. Someday when the tourists return, he will have enough money to furnish it. As I get in a shikara or small canoe to visit his house, my host, who is returning from the opposite shore, assumes that I am jumping ship for his neighbor's boat and screams, "Wait, wait, I am coming, I am coming!"

It's not too profitable to lose track of your tourists around here.

I decide to go for a walk in the old town as the sun sets over the deep blue mountains. The owner of my houseboat, nervous about my visiting his neighbor, offers to come along. Or rather insists.

I like the cool crisp colonial feel of Srinagar. The solidly built British style mansions that overlook the lake give the city the feel of being in an upscale resort, which of course it once was. These homes are now occupied by Kashmiris who sell carpets, rice and wool.

Along the narrow streets are shops where carvers, weavers and craftsmen create the intricate handicrafts and goods the area is known for. The Kashmiris are excellent craftsmen and the long winters and lack of professional jobs give them plenty of time to create meticulously ornate carpets, paper maché, and needlework. Most of them work by the golden glow of a single fly-specked light bulb. Almost all families in the towns work the looms or carve during the winter to earn money. Their goods are usually sold by local co-ops which once provided an important supplement to the summer tourism income. Now there is no summer tourism income and India does not allow wholesale exportation of these goods. Therefore, tourists must come to India to buy these goods, but the problem is, there are no tourists.

As if to add drama to my bucolic stroll, in front of me, a large brown eagle swoops down and repeatedly attacks a chicken who is walking mindlessly down the street. The eagle flies down the narrow lanes, claws spread and repeatedly attacks the terrified bird. The chicken finally runs under the house and the eagle calmly waits on a telephone pole for its prey to reemerge. An omen or a warning?

There is little evidence of the nightly tension here as the sun sets. True, the walls and streets are decorated with green scrawls of graffiti—"JK-LF" for Jammu Kashmir-Liberation Front or "AZ-JK" for Azad Jammu Kashmir. But children play, women cook and men smoke as if it is just another day. When I mention to my guide, Ahmad, that I have seen this graffiti in Pakistan, he is surprised that I know what this means. I explain to him that a few months ago, I was on the other side of the border where the Harkut and other groups are very visible with big offices complete with neon signs. When I say the word "liberation" for the second time he uncharacteristically says "That is all bullshit."

I ask him what he means.

"They do not want liberation, they are just using us," he answers.

This is the first indication that my guide has opinions about what is going on.

Although both the people of Srinagar and their dwellings have suffered from the war, the buildings have fared better. The old town bears the damage from bombs, fire and bullets. In the blue dusk and warm light from the shops, I feel as if I am in a medieval village complete with rambling lanes and quaint cottages.

I stop to talk to the locals who introduce some of their friends as freedom fighters. A joke or a test? They are testing my sympathies. There have been three years of war in this town. Threatened by *mujahedin* and by the Indian military, there is no safe political or moral ground for these people—survival is foremost. I notice the soldiers on patrol are now wearing bulletproof vests and helmets instead of their crisp uniforms.

My guide, who is Muslim, asks me if I like Muslims. I say yes. He asks me what I think of the *taliban*, whom I visited a few months earlier in Afghanistan. He asks in the same manner someone would ask you about a football team. He is uncomfortable with the image Muslims have in this Hindu-dominated region. It is portrayed as Muslim against Hindu, but in reality it is the Muslim Kashmiris who are dying.

He apologizes, then asks me if he can take me to a carpet shop; he gets a three percent commission and I don't have to buy, just look and have some tea. Inside the carpet shop, there is a Japanese businessman intent on negotiating down the price of the carpets. I listen to the pitch, examine the merchandise and learn that a carpet costs US$5000–US$8000 here. A large sized carpet with fine knots takes two years to make and is made by hand with each fiber hand knotted and tightened. The photo album of satisfied customers is a popular sales tool here. The pictures all date back to the late '80s. The Kashmiris will weave any design you would like these days. They need the money.

Walking back to the houseboat in the dark I find myself in the middle of a night patrol; 12 men are spaced 20 meters apart (in case of grenade or mine attack), carrying sub machine guns at the ready. There is no curfew tonight, but anyone out on the streets at 8:30 at night better have a good reason. The night is when the *mujahedin* attack and the soldiers make it clear from the looks they give me that they don't like my presence.

The Next Day

Only five people were killed yesterday. But today is a special day. The new government will be sworn in and the *mujahedin* have called for a general strike. This means shops must be closed, no one is to work and truck drivers and cab drivers are to stay home. Along the road there are soldiers every 20–50 feet. There is no civilian traffic allowed, only armored military vehicles. Naturally, this is the day I have chosen to take a drive in the country.

Ahmad greets me by saying, "Please hurry, our cab driver is afraid." Hyperventilating would be a better term. The driver says hello and flashes me a pained smile. He rattles off his warnings: the ministers are being sworn in today; the *mujahedin* will strike; the roads are closed; there is a general strike. He asks in a pleading tone if we can skip the Tomb of Yusaf, a tomb that is said by some to be the tomb of Christ. It is right next to the mosque and things are buzzing right now. I tell him that today I will go to Gulmarg, a popular trekking area on the unofficial Pakistani /Kashmiri border. We are going on a holiday jaunt to the front lines.

To protect us, the driver has created a homemade "PRESS" sign, and with the characteristic Kashmiri artistic flair, has used three different colors of ink in an intricate design. I ask him why he just doesn't put a bullseye on the passenger door. He smiles that pained smile again.

As we drive out of the city and toward the mountains, my guide points to certain spots and intersections. All that can be seen are bunkers with blast marks from previous attacks. Pointing out recent grenade attacks instead of scenic wonders seems to be the standard patter of cab drivers. We pass through the town of Gumpti. Ahmad says "We are afraid of this place." I ask him if there is a way to tell the *mujahedin* from the local people. He says, "The fighters are taller, like Afghans, and, like Afghans, they love to fight."

We pass through yellow rice fields on roads bordered by poplars and sycamores turning gold in the autumn weather. The blue snow-covered mountains in the distance are clean and pure against the trees and fields. The only reminder that we are in a hot zone is the constant presence of passing armored troop carriers, road patrols along the roads and various checkpoints.

My driver and my guide continually scan the roadside for anything unusual. To break the suspense, I decide to talk about cars. I am fascinated by our antique '50s Austin-like HM Ambassador, a car that is still made in India. I ask Ahmad what the HM means. He nervously says Hizbul *mujahedin*. I point to the "HM" sign on the dash, and he corrects himself, "Oh that, Hindustan Motors."

The guide and the driver chat nervously. Someone has too much interest in our passage. Ahmad warns, "That man was watching us." They both look over their shoulders to see if it was a curious local or a *mujahedin* writing down the license number for summary retribution. It's amazing how much driving gets done here even though the driver is looking over his shoulder instead of out the front windshield.

The scenery of the countryside is spectacular so I have to get some photos. I get out and walk through the rice paddies, now dry and mature. Men and women from the villages squat on their haunches, and using a small sickle, they snick off handfuls of rice stalks that are left to dry in the sun. Later the stalks will be threshed over a rock or wooden bench. The warm sun on my back, the crunch of the sickles and the beehive shaped mounds of rice stalks make for a very bucolic setting.

Wrapped up in photographing this rural scene, I unknowingly step right into a concealed machine gun nest and almost trip over the barrel of a.50 caliber gun. The two camouflaged soldiers are polite, but urgently direct me away from their post.

Getting back into the car I begin to wonder just how much I think I see and how much I don't see. We enter a village called Magam, about halfway to Gulmarg. Just before we reach Magam we pull off the road to let a convoy of dark colored troop trucks and armored personnel carriers rush by at high speed. Just behind the roof of each truck is a machine gunner squinting grimly behind large ski goggles.

There is something going on up ahead.

As we clatter towards Magam, the scene becomes less pastoral and more ominous. The soldiers we are seeing are not the anemic recruits we saw back in Srinagar. The cropped mustaches, tight bandannas and well-oiled weapons…they've come from where the fighting is.

We arrive in Magam shortly after the main excitement — a shootout, followed by a military sweep and then another fight to the death by *mujahedin* holed up in the basement of a house. The soldiers are busy questioning the locals and searching homes. They don't seem to pay much attention to me.

There is an odd, evocative scene amongst the chaos. It's hard to tell if the crowds are looking at us, watching the soldiers or under arrest. I don't quite know who is who. Who is *mujahedin* and who is villager? Who is under arrest and who is informer? Who is spy and who is an innocent bystander? The people that don't fit in this scene are the Hindu and Ghurka soldiers who look nervous and twitchy.

Off in the distance another tableau is laid out. I watch a squad of soldiers coming in from patrol through the rice fields. They do not stick to paths between the paddies and are nervously making their way to the village. I remember seeing this scene on television back home a long time ago, except the setting was Southern Vietnam. This is India's Vietnam. The foe is within and without.

There are hundreds of soldiers now, lining the villagers up and checking papers. Some just stand around while others search. The soldiers are friendly and I hand out Mr. DP stickers that feature our laughing skull mascot. Soon the Indian Army officers come over for stickers. I ask them about the hostages. With some conviction they say the hostages were here but now they are gone. They say the hostages are south in Jammu. They won't come up this high this winter.

We continue our trip to the front lines. Our taxi clatters up the mountain toward the border. As we sign in at the military checkpoint guarded by Ghurkas I notice in the logbook that two Taiwanese tourists have passed through here the day before. A few miles later the road disappears. It has been taken away by a landslide. There are horsemen, or pony wallahs, waiting here. The horses formerly carried tourists around the hills, but the horsemen say they have been sitting where the road is washed out for ten days without seeing tourists. The Taiwanese never made it this far so they must have turned back at the checkpoint or given up when they saw the road was washed out.

Gulmarg is the site of an 18-hole golf course (the world's highest) and a rather impressive ski lift built by a Swiss company surrounded by rustic chalets. Now the hotels are empty and falling apart, the ski lift is in pieces. The golf course is kept well cropped by grazing goats and today there is one family sitting peacefully on an abandoned putting green enjoying the scenery.

I hire small mountain ponies to take us up to the vale of Khilanmarg and then the mountain of Apharwat.

My anemic horse, Peter, keeps tripping over my legs, which I have to hold up to keep from dragging on the ground. My pony wallah says that Peter is small because he had little to eat when growing up. I offer to switch and carry Peter up the mountain and the horseman laughs.

We ride through Gulmarg and up into the mountains. I ask Ahmad if there are *mujahedin* here. He says occasionally the guides see groups of 20–40 armed men in the forest, but it is best to turn in the opposite direction. Has anybody seen the hostages here? No, but there is a rumor that they were spotted walking towards Jammu in the Kishtawar area. Kishtawar is beyond the southeasternmost point of Kashmir and we are on its northerwesternmost point. There have been many sightings and rumors of sightings of the hostages, but this one makes sense, as it is impossible to survive high in the mountains. Even the shepherds go down in the winter.

The October sun is warm, but the temperature in the shade is ten degrees cooler. At these altitudes it gets bitterly cold at night. The only shelter are seasonal herders' huts and abandoned villages. Up here there is no food, no communications, no transportation other than by foot or pony. The kidnappers would have to rely upon villagers for food, clothing and concealment. But there are no villagers here. People will later ask me if I was afraid of being kidnapped. The answer is no because, quite frankly, the thought does not enter your mind when you are surrounded by the solitude and beauty of the mountains.

In the valleys below, the snow covers some areas. There is no undergrowth and the grass has been trimmed by grazing animals. Despite sporadic snow cover, we can travel unimpeded in any direction in the valley. The downside is that there is no natural cover, no place to hide. We can spot shepherds two to three miles away. The air is so clear that we can see the 8000-meter high Nanga Parbat (The Naked Mountain) off in the distance. Ten miles away we can see soldiers on patrol are visible in the form of tiny bobbing dots. Kashmir would be a very difficult place to travel through undetected.

If I thought I could come here and learn all there is to know about the hostage situation without any probing, I would have been very disappointed. And, as I expected, the locals are hesitant to discuss anything; the military has no idea where they are, at the same time they say they know where they are.

The rumors I am chasing down seem to be ill-founded. In truth I didn't come here to find the hostages—it would take great conceit to assume that I can learn something that the relatives, FBI, CIA, SAS, GS-9 and other intelligence and military special operations groups have not—but rather to understand the lay of the land and background of the conflict in Kashmir. The five abducted Westerners are not the first hostages to be taken here and they will not be the last. Sometimes knowledge requires studying the obvious and circumstantial. More importantly, I am trying to understand how every traveler's nightmare occurred in the hopes that others will not have to enter the same dark underworld.

I want to see how close we can get to the border. The horses cannot walk in the steep, deep snow, so we climb until the snow drifts becomes too high. It is cold now and I am not dressed for alpine exploration. A military camp looms on the summit above. My guide says going further is ill-advised. "From this point two things will happen, either we will be shot at by the military or we will freeze to death." Realizing that the Pakistani military is not looking for overnight patrons and that we have 4–5 hours to return, I turn back.

Back down below the snow line we rest by a natural spring next to the destroyed ski lift. Two MiGs streak over us, sending those now familiar thundering echoes through the mountain valley. By now passing MiG's serve as a reminder to look at my watch. It must be tea time.

As we descend we chat with some shepherds who are laying in winter feed for their animals. A small calf bleats. The shepherd says it has been born too late and will not make it through the winter. They will kill it and head down in a week or so. Have they seen anything? The old shepherd's tan and weathered face tells me he has not lived this long by chatting about such things to strangers. He just smiles and poses for pictures with his daughter.

Driving down the winding mountain road, we are waved off the road by soldiers. From up the hill comes a convoy of Indian Army trucks. In the middle of the convoy is a Mahindra jeep with big red letters spelling out COMMANDING OFFICER complete with stars at each end. Inside is a portly, campaign bar decorated man and his driver. Not the secretive choice of transportation in a war zone. On the way back through Magam, troops are still mopping up. The villagers still stand passively watching them and then at us. I notice a group of young, well-muscled soldiers wearing black bandannas around their heads and carrying short assault weapons. They also wear special ops gear and soft-soled shoes. The war has come here.

That night back at my houseboat, I talk to an 80-year-old who was once a travel guide in the '30s and '40s, who casually puffs away on his "hubbly bubbly" as the British used to call hookahs, and reflects on the state of his country. He speaks in the same archaic form of colonial British. He talked of how his country used to be "damned cheap" and how "he was a jolly chap" in his youth. He remembers walking 14 miles to school. He recounts the joy of tourists when he showed them his country and how much he loves fly fishing, hiking and camping. But with the war, not to mention his bad legs and old age, all that is over. But it is still his country. This is a statement that the *mujahedin* and Indian army cannot make yet.

He has lived through the three wars with Pakistan but the past year has been the worst in his life. He says he wishes he could trade eyes with me so that I could see what he has seen. He doesn't speak the horrors and I do not ask him to. He points to his silver hair and to his heart and blames the deteriorating condition of both on the war. He says things are getting better now. He hears through the grapevine that there are now about 100–400 tourists a week and he hopes the new government will work out the problems. The prime minister is a good man, he says. But I don't think he cares anymore who runs the country.

Changing the subject, I ask him about the tomb of Yusaf and his eyes light up. "You know about this?" he asks excitedly.

I tell him what I have read and heard: Jesus' Hebrew name is Yazu. That Jesus wandered as far as India in his youth between the ages of 12 and 25 and returned to his beloved Kashmir after his staged crucifixion is a belief shared by many. He was also rumored to have traveled back to England with Joseph or even walked across the New World. According to local legend, Jesus was known as Saint Yuz Asaf, a man who performed miracles and preached in the first century A.D.

Some Kashmiris believe that their valley is the true promised land and some believe they are descended from one of the lost tribes of Israel. It sounded like the usual Chariot of the Gods stuff but worth exploring.

I ask him what he knows about the tomb. He says the tomb contains the body of Yusaf.

"He is your prophet and he is our prophet. Yusaf is all around us," he says.

I ask him when Yusaf was buried there.

"Four thousand years ago, before there was history," the old man says.

Who is Yusaf?

"Yusaf is everywhere, everything. When you breathe in and out that is Yusaf. Everything around you is Yusaf."

So much for accurate historical recall.

Not knowing quite where to go with this outburst of religious enthusiasm, I ask if the man in the tomb is Jesus Christ? He says quite frankly that he doesn't know.

As I go to bed my guide says, "Make sure you make yourself very clean tomorrow." He even tells me how to wipe the dust off my hiking boots. "We must be very clean for Yusaf tomorrow."

The next day we head for the Tomb of Yusaf. It is in a very nondescript building near the famous wooden mosque of Srinagar. The mosque was originally built in 1385 and has been burned and rebuilt five times since. Constructed with wood shingles and 300 cedar trunks the mosque retains its medieval look and also seems to retain its inflammatory character as the mullahs whip up hatred against the Indian army. The mosque is the flashpoint for most demonstrations and resultant violence in Srinagar.

All traffic is prohibited from entering this area, but we cajole the police into letting us pass. Large blue APCs with turret gunners roar up and down the street around the mosque. People gather to make their prayers at the mosque. My guide prays and kisses the ornaments as we enter.

Inside is a glass container and within that is a faded, dusty, shroud-covered tomb. A cement block inset with a pair of unauthentic looking footprints sit nearby. Otherwise there is nothing. Outside are demonstrations and troops. Inside, my guide is praying quietly. Is this the tomb of Christ? Does it matter? Is there a reason why he has chosen this beautiful but troubled land? Why would a prophet be in a Muslim country run by Hindus surrounded by Buddhists? I wonder if he or anyone can hear my guide's Muslim prayers. Like the hostages, this is an enigma whose need for a solution is overshadowed by the harsh reality of survival. But my trip to this tomb taught me that it is important to understand that the Kashmiris can accept these enigmas without facts or resolution. I think I have found my answer. The hostages are here and they are not here. Kashmir is a war zone and it is a tourist haven. It is whatever it must be for people to survive.

Things are heating up outside and my guide says it is time for me to leave. I think he is concerned I will miss my flight until he points to the angry crowds outside. I realize the quiet tomb has made me forget where I am. I head for the airport. We go through five identical in-depth searches on our way to the airport. Every single item from film canisters to food bars is opened. My batteries are taken out of every single battery powered device I have and are confiscated. A box of matches is taken and stuck in a soldier's pocket. He shrugs as if to say better in his pocket than in the trash. My guide is pressed against the fence by the crush of people. He asks me to think about him at Christmas and send his family something. He says Kashmir is dying. I thank him and wonder why he has chosen a Christian holiday to ask for something for his Muslim family.

The airport is packed with soldiers. I sit next to a Sikh army captain just back from the front. He says the war is fairly routine now. "They fire 500 rounds; we fire 1000 rounds back." There are casualties on both sides. I tell him of my trip into the mountains and he looks at me rather incredulously. When I give him the details he nods his head gently.

"The west is very dangerous," he says. "You never know who your enemy is. Is he *mujahedin* or Kashmiri or both?"

I ask him about the hostages and pull out a map. He pushes the map back in my hand and says, "Please, do not show me anything. I am not supposed to talk to you."

I realize that we are being watched by a number of officers in the waiting lounge. I ask him about the hostages and if the rumors that they were recaptured and held on an Indian military base are true. "That is silly" he says.

I ask him if the army knew where the hostages were.

"Don't you think that if we knew where they were, we would go in and get them?" he asked insulted.

I ask if they really did kill the leader of Al-Faran and if the hostages were wounded in the resultant fire fight.

"That is something I cannot talk about."

He gives me some tips. The spring is the most dangerous time, when the snow melts and the terrorists (as he calls them) can move freely without leaving tracks. The winter is much safer and there are fewer attacks. The militants like to use big road mines that they set off under the troop trucks. He has been here a year and a half and is tired of the fear and killing. He pulls out the army campaign ribbons he has for Kashmir and then quickly tucks them away.

He tells me he is bringing back dead soldiers to their families in India. His job is to explain to the bereaved families what must be done, the paperwork, how to file for benefits and how to conduct the funerals of their children. He is not too emotional about his job since he brings out a lot of dead soldiers. One thing he is happy about is the Army accepting his resignation. He plans to emigrate to Toronto to set up a trucking company with his brother. He says he is in love with Canada. But there are problems there. His brother has been forced to cut his hair and abandon his turban because of all the locals calling him "Paki." He is afraid that he too will have to cut his hair and beard. "Paki" is an odd insult to a Sikh from India fighting a war with Muslim Pakistanis in Kashmir.

On the other side of me is a young Canadian couple returning from backpacking through India. They were told it would be safe, something utterly believable for them because "there sure is a lot of security." I tell them that 45 people died this week and that the man on the other side of me is paying excess baggage fines on stiffs. They laugh, thinking I am kidding. I notice they clutch a well-worn Lonely Planet guide to India. They said they had heard that there was a war here but that it is much better now. They are right; there is officially no war here. The government even bans books that reveal the disputed border between Kashmir and Pakistan instead of the official version. And in a way my touristic friends were right. They went hiking, had a good time and are heading home tanned and happy. They are surprised to hear there were some other tourists who came here for the same thing but never even made it to the hiking part, let alone the airport.

Back in Delhi, I have dinner at the home of a Kashmiri who has moved his business from Srinagar to Delhi. During my initial fact-finding stay in Delhi he was fascinated by my desire to seek out what is really going on, and wanted to talk to me when I got back. He has a curious habit of calling me "My Dear" or "Dear," but I'm not dissuaded since I am getting accustomed to their humorous use of the colonial British tongue. I meet him at his house to have dinner with his family.

He owns three houseboats and a small hotel in Srinagar. Many families have handed down tourist businesses since the 1930s. He wishes I could have met his father since he loved to fish and hike. He also has a fondness for the mountains, something that every Kashmiri seems to take great pride in. He is essentially a refugee, albeit better off than most, from the war. He says the fighting is between Pakistani *mujahedin* and the Indian army. He doesn't believe Kashmiris have taken up the fight. "Why would you risk your family and your little ones?" he asks. "If Kashmiris were to fight, it would be for independence, not to be part of India or Pakistan. It is not worth dying for India or Pakistan."

When I ask him about the hostages, he gives me the same reply virtually every other Kashmiri had given me, "What do you know about the hostages?"

I tell him that I think the Al-Faran have gone back to Pakistan and that the hostages have either been moved south or are dead by now. One thing is for sure: the hostages are the last thing the Kashmiris have to worry about. He agrees, as if to help me understand that the hostage situation is not the work of Kashmiris. "The Kashmiris only have two enemies; India and Pakistan," he says. "We do not know why India needs or wants Kashmir, or why Pakistan needs or wants Kashmir."

The hostages have become a riddle, an enigma and a mystery. And like religion, the weather and the future, it is something Kashmiris are very comfortable accepting.

"We are not a fierce warring tribe, but a people who love our cool mountains and who exist by showing others our beautiful country," my host says. "We just want our own way of life and not be forced to live in the heat and squalor of Delhi. Why do we sweat in this heat when we could be in our beloved mountains with our families? "

But for now the Kashmiris sweat.

Back in America, I talk to James Bowman, the campaign director in England. He is sure that the hostages are still alive. It helps that Terry Waite, former envoy for the Anglican Church, and once a hostage himself, is involved. The families return regularly to put a fire under the government and check with their own group of Kashmiri investigators. They have met with the prime minister of India and have begged him to warn tourists of the dangers in Kashmir. He won't. But he encouraged the relatives to do what they can to warn off other unsuspecting tourists. As for the two-year-old question: "Are they dead or are they still alive," the families firmly believe they are alive. Some journalists and governments say they were executed on Dec 13 or 15 last year. No one has proof and no one has produced a hard bit of evidence other than the eyewitness testimony of villagers who say they have seen the hostages.

Kashmir is a dangerous place. And for the hostages it will forever change their view of Westerners being able to ignore minor politics in search of adventure or relaxation. Westerners are an ideal negotiating tool and once they lose that status their existence becomes a liability. The long confinement of other hostages like Terry Waite and Terry Anderson have shown that time may be on their side. For now the families work, wait and wonder.

For now they sweat.

—**RYP**

Note: The hostages were last seen by a number of villagers in May of 1996 in the village of Kuzuz. In the Kishtawar area of Kashmir. There is a reward of US$30,000 for information leading to the retrieval of the hostages. Any one with information or who wishes to assist the families in their ongoing search for their loved ones should contact:

James Bowman
Director
The Hostages in Kashmir Campaign
Independent House
112 Borough Road
Middlesbrough, England TS1 2ES
☎ *[44] (1642) 339090, FAX: [44] (1642) 339191*
Web: www.hostagesinkashmir, e-mail: jbowman@itl.net

Iran

Ayatollah Not to Come

Ronald Reagan had it easy. When he thought the world was being overrun by zealots, controlled by subversives, bullied by foreign-controlled thugs or just getting too full of fanatics, lunatics, heretics, zombies, crazed clerics, guerrillas, psychotics and brainwashed bandits, all he had to do was call up Moscow and threaten to push the button—drop the "big one" or send in the Marines. Back then, the Soviet Union policy of "guns for butter" demanded that lackeys like Libya, Cuba, Bulgaria and East Germany export death and fear to feed their people. Today, there is a new "Evil Empire" that asks all Muslims to strike at the heart of the Great Satan, and not in exchange for a paycheck.

Their M.O. is surprisingly similar to the old-fashioned brand of communism: Find the oppressed, teach them to respect themselves, give them pride, and then give them a gun. The commies screwed up by tossing out religion. The Iranians know that adding their interpretation of the Koran to this classic revolutionary format is like adding nitro to gasoline. It burns brighter and goes faster.

447

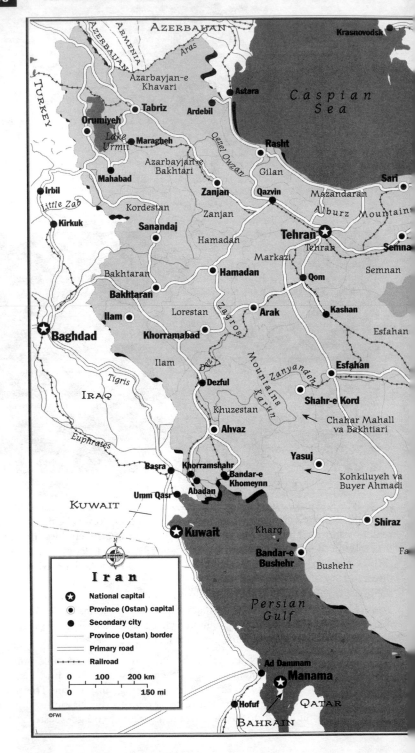

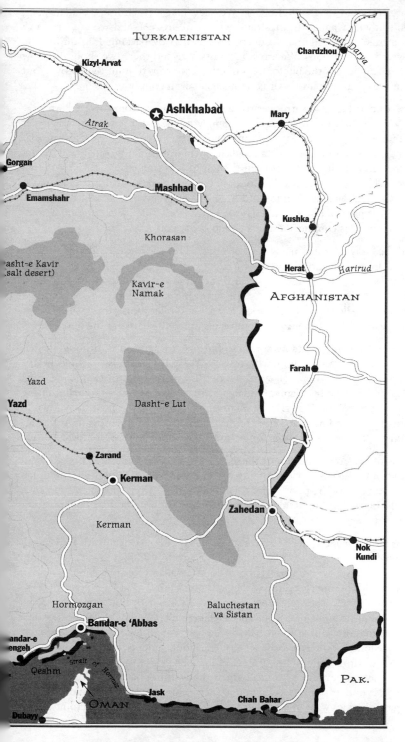

How can the Great Satan fight back? We can't nuke it (then Iraq would invade), we can't buy it (what with, the Iranian assets we froze?), and we can't pay our worst enemies to bleed Iran to death (as we tried by backing Iraq during the eight-year war with Iran). We arrest terrorists here and there, we shoot one now and then, and we pay the bill for a lot of other countries to hunt them down, but you can't use a gun against a virus. Fundamentalism continues to spread.

We scream at Libya to turn over the alleged destroyers from the Lockerbie disaster, only to find out that they were simply filling out an evil purchase order from Iran to pay us back for downing one of *their* flights. We snatch one evil henchman from his bed in Pakistan and charge him with the World Trade Center bombing, only to find out that even though he was trained by Iran, it was Iraq who actually wrote the check. We fork out billions for peace in Israel only to discover that Hezbollah is an Iran- and Syria-backed franchise operation. We dare not even get involved in Sudan, Algeria, Egypt, the Philippines, Bosnia, Turkey and India. Jihad is coming soon to a country near you.

Jihad, or Holy War, has many eager recruits. The poor, war-hardened Muslim teenagers from the dusty cities of the Middle and Far East see jihad as their great war. They sign up with the same fervor that cleared out the iron mines and dead-end towns in World War I. It was not surprising in December of '94 when it slipped out that Iran had spent more than US$10 billion on weapons just in the last five years—all that money and not one B1 or ICBM among the purchases.

Pity poor Bill Clinton and his southern Judeo-Christian roots. Although he has a red phone, he doesn't know who to call. Worse yet, this just may be the big one—truly the war to end all wars. From New York City to Zamboanga, the world is under siege by Islamic fundamentalists. Bill may be at the helm during the apocalypse, World War III, the 21st-century crusade, the final showdown in the land of Gog and Magog, home of the Antichrist, the fomentors of Armageddon. Whew, this was a lot easier when it was just commies or dominoes.

Who is to blame for the rise of this fanatical empire? Is our addiction to fossil fuels to blame? Like a junkie spending his rent money, are we pouring too much hard currency into dirt-poor Third World countries? Are we financing our own downfall? Or is there something about Islam and the Middle East we just don't understand.

In our (and Europe's) need to have stable oil supplies, we dealt with Iran like an overprotective parent. We put in the shah of Iran and told him to keep pumping. We continue to support a tribal clan in Saudi Arabia, and we are willing to send in one less Stealth bomber, because we actually don't mind Mad Dog Hussein barking at Iran's western border. What we received for our trouble was close to the second coming. Khomeini, a dour and intelligent cleric, made the Pope look like Rodney Dangerfield. Iran for the first time had a charismatic, devout leader. It didn't take long for the *fatwas*, or religious pronouncements, to start shooting off like missiles. More importantly, Iran used the new power vacuum created by the loss of Soviet money and began to harness the seething hatred of Western "corruption" beyond its borders. (Oh, you mean they don't want a nation of drunken video game junkies who think religion is a TV channel next to the Home Shopping Network?)

Muslims, once content with being misunderstood but never bellicose, were told to strike down the Great Satan. Some of us laughed at Khomeini's return to the biblical era. But when jihad began appearing on CNN, we stopped laughing.

Iran was the principal supporter of Somali warlord Mohammad Farah Aidid. Iran sent 10,000 troops into Azerbaijan against the Armenians. Iran sent 60 tons of weapons and 400 Revolutionary Guards into Bosnia. Iran supports fundamentalist insurgent groups in Algeria, the Philippines, the U.S., Afghanistan and Egypt. Iran caused the Yemeni civil war by creating the fundamentalist party in northern Yemen that unbalanced the ruling coalition. Iran supplies 19,000 barrels of oil a day to North Korea and receives Scud missiles and weapons in exchange, which they exchange with all the above for their souls. Iran has disputes over no fewer than three islands—Abu Musa and the Greater and Lesser Tumb islands. Iran is the ultimate player in the big jihad. And they don't want no stinkin' Mickey D franchises.

The list of killings, subversive activities, insurrection and general mayhem attributed to Iran is impressive. Intelligence agencies keep monstrous dossiers on the convoluted connections between the religious leaders in Iran and the skinny, unshaven men who pull the trigger. The problem is that the religious leaders are not politicians, and wield absolute control over their military and political leaders. The Koran spells out very clearly what is right and what is wrong. If Western leaders do so much as affront the Iranian view of Islam, it won't take much more than a brief discussion and a nod of the head for the next terrorist attack to be launched. They will go so far as to issue a *fatwa*, identifying someone as an enemy of Islam, to make him a target for life. Salman Rushdie has switched to children's tales, but there is no court of appeals for him.

Like showbiz agents from hell, the Iranians orchestrate the creation and success of some very scary groups. To cover its tracks, Tehran backs a variety of terrorist cells, covertly training and arming them at bases inside Iran itself and various satellite sites in other Third World cesspools.

You got the wrong one baby, uh huh

In January 1995, the Ayatollah Ali Khamenei issued a religious decree apparently banning the consumption of both Coca-Cola and Pepsi, American soft drinks that had recently been reintroduced into Iran. Khamenei was asked by a local paper, "Assuming drinking Coca-Cola and Pepsi politically strengthens world arrogance and financially helps Zionist circles, what would the Islamic decree on the issue be?" Khamenei replied: "Anything that strengthens world arrogance and Zionist circles in itself is forbidden." Only time will tell which real thing Iranians consume, Islamic dogma or the right one, baby. You probably won't be surprised to learn that satellite dishes are also banned.

Iranian relations with other Islamic countries have gone to hell in a handbasket because of well-founded allegations that Iran is supporting Islamic terrorists. In March 1993, Algeria broke diplomatic relations with Iran, citing Tehran's aid to over-the-edge fundamentalist rebels. (In 1997, Iran said the equally fundamentalist—but Sunni—*taliban* are not really in power in Afghanistan.) This has forced Iran to seek closer ties with more xenophobic Islamic states, although it periodically makes conciliatory overtures to the West, especially concerning the reform of its economy. Iran is also sticking its nose in the new breakaway Islamic

IRAN

states that helped comprise the former Soviet Union in Central Asia. Iran has offered to aid Azerbaijan in its conflict with Armenia over the Nagorno-Karabakh enclave. Even though Iran has criticized Russia for helping Tajikistan battle Islamic fundamentalist insurgents, no reactionary Third World country in its right mind puts too much distance between itself and the "Moscow Machine Gun & Missile Market's" weekly specials. In March 1993, Iran and Russia reached an agreement for economic and military cooperation.

What does the future hold for better relations between Magog (the home of the biblical Antichrist) and the Great Satan (me and you)? Iran doesn't like our opposition to the established fundamentalist states, especially those backed by Iran. We haven't got a hope in hell of infiltrating them or buying them off, so we'll just have to chase them around the world like international Keystone Kops for the foreseeable future. For now, the government wants tourists and once they lure them inside, they'll track them like child molesters. So if you want to discover a place with no tourists, no crime, and no fun. This is it.

Iran has two demands of The Great Satan: 1) gimme back our frozen assets, and 2) mind your own business. Hey what's their beef? Uncle Sam only spent $20 million trying to overthrow their Uncle Ayatollah. That's less than we spend on daily cruise missile-grams to their neighbor Saddam. Americans are still obsessed with blindfolded U.S. embassy staffers being paraded around Tehran's streets decorated with blazing Uncle Sam piñatas. It's nearly 20 years later and now we're the ones with blindfolds. Iran has elected a moderate (well in Iran, he's a moderate) cleric by the name of Mohammad Khatami who actually wears a suit instead of bed sheets. The voter turnout was the highest in Iran since the mullahs came to power in 1979. Americans can travel freely in this country if they don't mind being shadowed like North Korean agents at a used plutonium sale. For now Iran is open, the gals are loading up on the Revlon (under the chadors of course) and "Baywatch" via satellite dish is slowly eroding the old Iran we've come to hate. Oh, don't forget that hard-liner Ayatollah Ali Khamenei still tosses the lightning bolts in this nation of very heavily clothed people.

Ayatollah Mohammed Ali Khamenei

"Ayatollah" means "sign of god," and this ayatollah is Iran's spiritual leader and big cheese. A hard-liner and a fundamentalist to the max, he still holds most of the power after the May 1997 election of Khatami to president.

The Revolutionary Guards

This group of 120,000 well trained, politically indoctrinated soldiers were originally a bearded rabble of zealots run by ad hoc neighborhood groups or *Komitehs*. The man in charge is Yahya Rahim Safavi who was appointed by hardliner Ayatollah Ali Khameni. So if you ever wonder who is large and in charge, it is not the nice moderate President.

President Mohammad Khatami

Moderate Khatami overwhelmingly defeated rival Ali Akbar Nateq-Nuri—by a margin of 20 million votes over Nuri's 9.7 million votes—in the presidential elections of May 1997.

Khatami is being hailed as "Ayatollah Gorbachev," but it remains to be seen what kind of reforming he can do. But this guy's no Jack Kennedy. Khatami was born in 1943 to a fundamentalist cleric and highly vocal critic of Shah Mohammed Reza Pahlavi. Khatami followed in his dad's footsteps, being assigned to Hamburg, Germany, in 1978 to head an Islamic center dedicated to political change in Iran. He returned to Tehran after the shah fled Iran and Khomeini returned to Tehran from exile in Paris. He was Iran's Minister of Culture and Islamic Guidance in the 1980s, where he gained his reputation as a "cautious liberal." During his tenure at that post, Khatami allowed Western newspapers and magazines into Iran. He also lifted a ban on women singing in public, although the audiences were required to be all-female. Hey, it's a start. If Khatami moves at all with reforms, it will be gradually. He was ousted from ministerial power in the early 1990s during a backlash to lipstick and nail polish being worn by women. Sorta shows you what he's up against.

Mujahedin Khalq Organization (MKO)

The MKO is a Marxist Islamist group founded by the college educated children of wealthy Iranians. Their original fought against the Shah. Backed by wealthy expat Iranians they are the largest anti-government group. They like to attack Iranian embassies abroad and have killed U.S. military personnel when the Shah was in power. Their big stick is the NLA, a standing army complete with tanks, women fighters and jets that sit in Iraq waiting for the word. The MKO is officially branded a terrorist group by the U.S. government and its claims to be the Iranian government in exile are disputed. The Muslim Iranian Student's Society is the fund raising front. In September of '97 the Iranians delivered some "thinking of you" messages via bomber and rockets. The group continues to launch attacks against Iran.

Khomeini Money

In 1989 the Iranian government used its official government currency presses to print the first of about $10 billion in counterfeit U.S. currency. The U.S. bills of 100-dollar denominations were originally used to finance terrorists in the Bekaa valley. There were little if any clues to the bills' origin (some say the zeroes have flattened tops).

The U.S. government estimates that there is around $400 billion in U.S. currency outside of the country. The paper used is the same paper used by the U.S. mint, and, in many cases, the bills cannot be detected even by optical scanners. The bills continue to appear, and have been spotted most recently in North Korea. In dangerous places where U.S. currency is the standard, DP has taken to carrying only $20s and not accepting any $100 bills printed in the '80s. The new $100 bill should solve this problem for now.

Ali Akbar Nateq-Nuri

Ali Akbar Nateq-Nuri may have lost to Khatami, but he's not going to go away. Many in Iran believe Ali Akbar Nateq-Nuri lost the May 1997 polls solely because it was thought he, as president, would have decreed that women in public wear the long, hooded traditional chador, a one-piece garment about as popular in Iran as "Satanic Verses." The real fabric of Iran may have been evidenced by the high turnout at the polls. Nateq-Nuri still leads the ultra-conservative parliament and remains Khatami's nemesis.

Former President Ali Akbar Hashemi Rafsanjani

You may remember him as the patient towel headed guy who politely endured Mike Wallace's dumb questions on "60 Minutes" as he tried to show that Iran wants to be buddies and Mike wanted to spank him for something that happened twenty years ago. What Mike didn't know was that Rafsanjani was the good guy. During his term he attended to the economy and repaired the damage left by the war with Iraq. He worked to get Iran reacquainted with the international community by expanding world ties and by arranging the release of hostages held by terrorist groups with ties to Iran. Rafsanjani had tougher problems than being grilled by Mike. He has narrowly escaped seven assassination attempts. Rafsanjani is credited with persuading Khomeini to finally agree to a cease-fire in the war with Iraq in August 1988.

Ali Mohammed Besharati

He's the influential interior minister. A former Revolutionary Guard, Besharati was one of the students who seized the American embassy in 1979. His latest action was to unsuccessfully ban Iran's embarrassingly popular satellite dishes—which he views as instruments of Western filth—when he learned that "Star Trek" and "Baywatch" were getting better ratings than "Muslim Mullahs! Live From Mahabad!" and "Good Morning, Tehran—with Ali Mohammed Besharati."

The Mujahedin-e-Khalq

Founded in 1980, this is an armed group based in Iraq. Its ideology is a combination of Islam and Marxist babbling. The group is headed by Masud Rajavi. The Iranian government insists that the *mujahedin* is supported by England and France. The government may be looking for an excuse to conduct a full-scale attack on *mujahedin* forces in Iraq, where the time seems appropriate for Saddam Hussein to look the other way. Iran's top judge accused the Mujahedin-e-Khalq of conducting a campaign of bombings and assassinations aimed at igniting sectarian tensions. Although government repression has significantly curtailed the effectiveness of the Mujahedin-e-Khalq, the guerrillas still conduct operations inside Iran and remain vocal in the opposition to the government of Iran. The organization was 50,000 strong after the Islamic revolution, with nearly half a million supporters. About 5000 activists have been executed in the government's crackdown, and more than 25,000 imprisoned. After the cease-fire in the Iran-Iraq war, the *mujahedin* invaded Iran but were crushed by the Iranian armed forces.

Did Bob Hope Get the Film Rights?

During the spring of 1997, the Iranian army staged war games called "The Road to Jerusalem." The government said the military exercise by more than 200,000 troops and militia was a "message of peace and friendship."

Maryam Rajavi and the National Liberation Army of Iran

The NLA is the military wing of the National Council of Resistance (NCR) and is a 30,000-strong Iranian resistance force based in Iraq. But unlike other liberation groups, some 35 percent of the group's soldiers are women, as are nearly three-quarters of its officers. Training at Al-Ashraf Camp inside Iraq just out of the reach of Iran's howitzers, the fully-armed NLA doesn't collect paychecks and bestows near-deity status to its female leader, Maryam Rajavi, whom the rebel group hopes to install as Iran's next president. The NLA claims to have launched at least 100 sorties into Iranian territory since it was formed in 1988. Have these folks got a chance against the mullahs? NLA troops have taken a vow of celibacy until Iran's government is toppled, so we know they're at least motivated. The NLA is one of the few armored liberation groups. The NLA can field 160 T-54/55 tanks and dozens of rocket launchers, APCs, towed howitzers and even attack helicopters. Even so, these guys and gals are more talk than action.

Not only is it legal to travel to Iran, but the country is planning to open its first tourist office in the U.S. in New York City. The staffers at Iran's U.N. mission in New York got a little giddy and loosened their guard with *DP* after the elections. "Iran is very safe!" he proclaimed. "We love Americans! Many Iranians want to be just like Americans. Tell me when you're coming. I will tell you how to leave the airport (without being followed)!"

U.S. passports are valid for travel to Iran. However, U.S./Iranian dual nationals have often had their U.S. passports confiscated upon arrival and have been denied permission to depart the country documented as U.S. citizens. To prevent the confiscation of U.S. passports, the Department of State suggests that Americans leave their U.S. passports at a U.S. embassy or consulate overseas for safekeeping before entering Iran. To facilitate their travel in the event of the confiscation of a U.S. passport, dual nationals may obtain in their Iranian passports the necessary visas for countries that they will transit on their return to the U.S., and where they may apply for a new U.S. passport. Dual nationals must enter and leave the United States on U.S. passports.

The U.S. government does not have diplomatic or consular relations with the Islamic Republic of Iran. The Swiss government, acting through its embassy in Tehran, serves as the protecting power for U.S. interests in Iran and provides only very limited consular services. Neither U.S. passports nor visas to the U.S. are issued in Tehran.

Visa and passport are required. The Iranian government maintains an interests section through the Pakistan Embassy in Washington, D.C.:

Embassy of Pakistan

> *2209 Wisconsin Avenue, N.W.*
> *Washington, D.C. 20007*
> ☎ *(202) 965-4990*

Mehrabad International Airport is seven miles west of Tehran, about a 30-minute drive. Airport facilities include a 24-hour bank, 24-hour post office, 24-hour restaurant, snack bar, 24-hour duty-free shop, gift shops, 24-hour tourist information and first aid/vaccination facilities. Airline buses are available to the city for a fare of RL10 (travel time: 30 minutes). Taxis also are available to the city center for approximately RL1200–1500. There is a departure tax of RL1500. Transiting passengers remaining in the airport are exempt from the departure tax.

Once inside Iran, transportation by private car (with driver) or with a guide (who will be assigned to keep tabs on you) is recommended.

Nowhere/Everywhere

Forget about crime. A pickpocket would have two strikes and then he could audition for Flipper sequels. The problem in Iran is everyone wants to know what you're doing here. U.S. citizens traveling in Iran have been detained without charge, arrested and harassed by Iranian authorities. Persons in Iran who violate Iranian laws, including Islamic laws may face penalties that can be severe.

The eastern and southern portions of Iran are major weapons and drug smuggling routes from Pakistan and Afghanistan. Drug and arms smuggling convoys may include columns with tanks, armored personnel carriers and heavily armed soldiers. Right now, Iran is a brave new world for U.S. travelers. Most of the country can be considered safe (that's the good news), but it's still very much a police state (the bad news).

Uncle Sam

The Iranians (or at least those that haven't immigrated to America) have been foaming at the mouth about "Raygun," "Boosh" and now "Cleentun" for so long that they forgot we are fairly decent folks. You won't find outright hostility but you may be hard-pressed to keep up if you get into a "did not! did too!" argument.

Drugs

Three pieces of advice: Don't do 'em, don't bring 'em in, and don't take 'em out. Iran has executed well over 1000 people since 1989, when it made possession of 30 grams (slightly over an ounce) of heroin or five kg (11 lbs.) of opium a capital crime. Read that as death. The Golden Crescent—Pakistan and Afghanistan—has become the world's second-biggest source of heroin after the Golden Triangle of Southeast Asia. Opium is grown mostly in Afghanistan, processed in the tribal areas of Pakistan where Pakistani law doesn't reach, and smuggled to Iran for shipment to the West. About 10 percent of the drugs that enter Iran are destined for consumption in Iran and the rest for other world destinations, including London, Paris and New York. There are approximately one million addicts among Iran's 60 million people.

Imported Goods

On May 6, 1995, President Clinton signed an executive order prohibiting exporting goods or services to Iran, re-exporting certain goods to Iran, new investments in Iran or in property owned or controlled by the government of Iran and brokering or other transactions involving goods or services of Iranian origin or owned or controlled by the government of Iran. These restrictions have been added to those already contained in the Iranian Transactions Regulations that prohibited unauthorized importation of Iranian-origin goods or services into the United States. For information regarding the issuance of licenses, contact the Licensing Division, The Treasury Department's Office of Foreign Assets Control at ☎ *(202) 622-2480).*

FAC issues licenses only for goods that were located outside of Iran prior to imposition of these sanctions on October 29, 1987. Goods in Iran after that do not qualify for authorization from Customs criteria for authorization. Iranian-origin goods, including those that were in Iran after October 29, 1987, may enter the United States if they qualify for entry under the following provisions administered solely by Customs:

(1) gifts valued at US$100 or less,

(2) goods for personal use contained in the accompanied baggage of persons traveling from Iran valued at US$400 or less, or

(3) goods qualifying for duty-free treatment as "household goods" or "personal effects" (as defined by U.S. law and subject to quantity limitations).

Inquiries about these provisions should be directed to Customs in the U.S. port where the goods would arrive.

A yellow fever vaccination is required for travelers over the age of one year coming from infected areas. Arthropod-borne diseases and Hepatitis B are endemic. Malaria is a risk in some provinces from March through November. Food- and water-borne diseases, including cholera, are common, as is trachoma. (Snakes and rabid animals can also pose a threat.) Basic medical care and medicines are available in the principal cities of Iran, but may not be available in outlying areas. There are three doctors and 14 hospital beds for every 10,000 people. The international travelers' hotline at the Centers for Disease Control, ☎ *(404) 332-4559*, has additional useful health information.

Iran is hurting because of the long drop in world oil prices. The *rial* fluctuates on the free market as much as 15 percent a day. About 3000 rials are equal to US$1. Inflation is between 60–100 percent a year, and a thriving black market takes advantage of outrageous official rates. Government employees make the equivalent of US$60 a month, and many Iranians are forced to take two jobs to get by. Iran is home to more refugees than any other country in the world. There are an estimated 2.2 million Afghans, 1.2 million Iraqis and 1.2 million others who have fled the strife in Pakistan, Azerbaijan and Tajikistan. The country is held together by a wide net of informers. But give Iran credit, like most exporters of terror, it's a peaceful country.

About three times the size of Arizona, Iran is a constitutional Islamic Republic, governed by executive and legislative branches that derive national leadership primarily through the Muslim clergy. Shia Islam is the official religion of Iran, and Islamic law is the basis of the authority of the state. Islamic ideals and beliefs provide the conservative foundation of the country's customs, laws and practices. Shiites comprise about 95 percent of the country. Sunnis make up about 4 percent. The literacy rate is at about 75 percent. Iran is a developing country.

The workweek in Iran is Sunday through Thursday. Electricity is 220V/50hz. Languages are Farsi, Turkish, Kurdish Arabic and scattered English. Only about half of Iran's population speaks Farsi.

Temperatures for Tehran can be very hot in the summer and just above freezing in the winter. The northern part of the country can experience quite bitter winters. Iran has a mostly desert climate with unusual extremes in temperature. Temperatures exceeding 130° F occasionally occur in the summer, while in the winter the high elevation of most of the country often results in temperatures of zero° F and lower.

There is no U.S. embassy or consulate in Iran. The U.S. does have an interests section at the Swiss embassy in Tehran:

Swiss Embassy, U.S. Interests Section
Bucharest Avenue
Argentine Square
17th street, No. 5
Tehran
☎ *[98] (21) 625-223/224 and 626-906.*

Web Resources:

Hey there's a party going on. But you won't find these parties in Iran. For now you can find them on the web.

Communist Party of Iran
http://www.pi.se/webpage/commu-nist.party.of.iran/index.html

Constitutionalist Movement of Iran, The
http://www.irancmi.org/index2.htm

Organization of Iranian People's Fedaian
http://193.80.248.16/iran.kar.fadai.aksariyat/

Organization of Iranian People's Fedaian
http://www.fadaii-minority.org/

Organization of Iranian People's Mujahedin
http://www.iran-e-azad.org/farsi/index.html

Tudeh Party of Iran
http://www.demon.co.uk/mardom/tudeh.htm

Workers-Communist Party of Iran
http://www.wpiran.org/index.html

Iraqi National Congress
http://www.inc.org.uk/

05/24/1997	Khatami, a moderate, is elected president.
07/03/1989	The Ayatollah Khomeini dies.
02/14/1989	Khomeini announces a death decree on *Satanic Verses* author Salman Rushdie, an Indian national, resident in the United Kingdom.
07/03/1988	The U.S.S. *Vincennes* mistakenly shoots down an Iranian Airbus airliner over the Persian Gulf.
12/04/1984	Four Islamic Jihad terrorists hijack a Kuwaiti airliner bound for Pakistan from Kuwait and order it flown to Tehran. Two U.S. aid personnel are killed during the hijacking, while two others, another U.S. aid official and an American businessman, are tortured during the ordeal. Iranian troops storm the aircraft on December 9, retaking it from the hijackers.
06/28/1981	The prime minister and 74 others are killed in the bombing of the legislature.
01/20/1981	U.S. embassy hostages released. Fifty-two American hostages are freed after 444 days in captivity, following an agreement between the U.S. and Iran arranged by Algeria.
09/19/1980	Iran-Iraq war begins.
07/27/1980	Death of the shah of Iran.
04/25/1980	The day operations to rescue American hostages fails in the desert of Iran, due to operational shortfalls and an aircraft accident.
11/04/1979	The U.S. embassy is seized and 63 people are taken hostage.
04/01/1979	Islamic Republic Day commemorating riots by Islamic fundamentalists in Isfahan.
03/10/1979	Death of Kurdish leader Mullah Mustafa Barzani. (Kurdish regions.)
02/11/1979	Revolution Day. Celebration of the victory of the Islamic revolution.

IRAN

02/04/1979	Iranian revolution begins. Iran's Shiite clerics start their takeover of the government.
02/01/1979	Khomeini returns from exile and calls the start of the "Ten Days of Dawn," commemorating the 10 days of unrest, ending with Khomeini taking power on February 11 (the "Day of Victory").
01/16/1979	The shah departs Iran.
11/04/1978	Student uprising against the shah.
09/09/1978	The shah's troops open fire on protesters in Tehran, killing several hundred demonstrators.
11/04/1964	The Ayatollah Khomeini is exiled to Turkey.
06/05/1963	The arrest of the Ayatollah Khomeini by the shah's police. Also the Day of Mourning and Revolution Day.
01/22/1946	Kurdish Republic Day.
02/07/1902	Birth date of the Ayatollah Ruhollah Khomeini.
06/28	Revolutionary Guard's Day.
03/21	Persian New Year. Kurdish New Year celebrated.

Islam

Islam is the religion of more than a billion people on this planet. Long viewed as the Arab religion, it is just as likely that a Muslim is Indonesian, Chinese, Russian, Filipino or even an African American today.

Islam is based on some very simple premises. It could be said it is a shade more intolerant (towards Jews and nonbelievers) and a shade more merciful (in charity toward orphans and widows) than Christianity. Muslims have dietary and health laws (no pork or alcohol), have a period of fasting (the ninth Muslim month of Ramadan) and are encouraged to make a pilgrimage to Mecca at least once in their lifetime (the hajj).

Muslims' adherence to the Koran (a holy book revealed to Mohammed by God) and the tenets of Islam range from tolerant to fanatic—just like Christianity and Judaism. The two main sects of Islam are the mostly Arab Sunnis (85 percent) and the mostly Persian Shi'ites (15 percent). The Iranian Shi'ites are the more evangelistic of the two branches. Sunni is considered the pure form of Islam by the Iranians. Shiite is considered an offshoot, due to its worship of Ali, much like Christianity—with its devotion to Jesus Christ—is considered a branch, or offshoot of Judaism.

Are there really any major differences between Christianity and Islam? First, Muslims believe that both Christians and Jews have it all wrong since they worship untrue gods. Second, Muslims see decadence as a sign of Westerners being immoral infidels.

Islam

Terrorism has been linked with Islam–an unfair connection since Christian anti-abortion groups are just as reprehensible in this practice as Islamic fundamentalists from a legal sense. There is no denying that Iran has encouraged the development and activities of fundamentalist groups around the world, just as Russia and the U.S. have advanced their own causes in Asia and Central America respectively. The one area where Islam scares Westerners is that there is no promise of material happiness or personal gain from terrorist activities. More important, Islam has not lost a war since the Crusades. The real enemy of Islam is factionalism. Warring Islamic groups in Afghanistan, Iraq, Turkey and Iran show that any ideology loses its momentum once a common enemy is removed.

Iran: Hijacked

In October of 1980, I was 23 and a beginning war correspondent. I was returning from my first trip to Iran, where Iraq had just launched what was to be a long, deadly war of attrition. I went to the front, but my film was developed and the best shots confiscated by Iranian censors. I was left with useless shots of people, smiling soldiers and not much else. After I checked in with SIPA, my photo agency in Paris, I was told to try the other side—Iraq. On my way, I decided to cover the military maneuvers of the Turkish army near Diyarbakir in the southeast of Turkey. First, I would stop in at Ankara to get my visa for Iraq.

Our Turkish Airlines *Boeing 727* takes off as scheduled around 5:30 p.m. for its 35-minute-long flight. But one hour later we still have not landed. The other passengers and I start feeling uneasy. I wonder if the wheels of the plane are blocked. Suddenly, the voice of the pilot breaks through the tension: "Ladies and gentlemen, we might be obliged to land in Diyarbakir. Otherwise, we will head toward Iran. I now give the microphone to a Muslim brother." Instantly, the entire plane knows we have been hijacked.

Yilmaz Yalciner, the leader of the hijackers, carries on with his statement, given in the most imperative intonation:

"Islam takes over the plane. Long live the Divine Ayatollah Ruhollah Khomeini…. *Shariat*, the unique sure way to bring happiness to the entire human race, is the name of our mission. We are changing the route of this plane so as to go to Tehran, the cradle of the Islamic Revolution. Then, my three Muslim brothers and I will proceed to Afghanistan, where we will fight alongside the brothers who are leading the jihad [Holy War] against the Russian atheists. For this reason, I am now going to pass around the hat. Whatever you give, make sure to give with your heart."

The passengers, in a state of shock after this announcement, search their pockets for some money. The collection begins. The passengers, afraid of the reprisals, give as much as they can to the militant who is passing a bag. Yilmaz Yalciner counts the money and gets back to the microphone: "Eighty-nine Turkish Lira [US$100]," he says, "it's really too little for people like you, but thanks anyway. Don't forget that we are going to fight with this money against the atheist Soviets."

For the passengers, the unbearable wait starts.

Nobody moves anymore; there is little to talk about, and everyone knows the gravity of the situation. All of us are probably thinking the same thing—fanatics are unpredictable. All we can do is wait anxiously for their next move. Once more, the voice of the hijacker breaks the heavy silence: "All women onboard must cover their hair—it is a rule of Islam. And Islam only constrains you to do good things." The 28 female passengers quickly cover their hair with whatever is available, including the white cotton cloth of the headrests of their seats. Some women, short of anything looking like a *chador*, shroud themselves under their husband's jackets.

Being a photojournalist first and a terrified passenger second, I pull out my camera and start taking photos. I am more concerned about running out of film since I do not know how long the ordeal will last. I find myself elated that I am at the center of what will be an international story, but scared out of my wits that the usual *laissez passer* accorded to the press will not be observed by the Muslim fanatics. The hijackers seem just as terrified as the passengers but apparently find comfort in carrying out this simpleminded and dangerous act.

At first, I photograph the passengers clandestinely, but this is not the story. Then I have an idea. I inform my friend Osman, a radio journalist, sitting next to me about my intentions to talk to the hijackers and ask their permission to take photos of the whole event. He quickly dismisses the idea as insane and advises me to adopt a low profile instead, so as not to attract their attention.

My hunch is that the hijackers are Iranian. I figure that if I show them the recent stamps in my passport and some of the recent Iranian photos I have with me they might allow me to document the hijacking. I head toward the first-class compartment where three of the militants have gathered, and tell them I am a journalist and ask permission to take photos. One of them, Omer Yorulmaz (I learned his name later), calmly tells me to wait and he will check with the leader in the cockpit. In the meantime, I go back to my seat to get my cameras. He comes out and tells me I can enter. I am elated.

As I quickly take photos of the crowded cockpit, I notice the contrast between the tense but efficient crew, and the theatrical laughter of the hijacker (Yilmaz Yalciner) as he holds a gun close to the right temple of someone sitting behind the pilot. I am even more elated with the fact that this is the first time a hijacking has ever been photographed in the air.

Suddenly, Yalciner commands me to stop. I realize his smile is a natural schoolboy's reaction to the camera and not indicative of the tension in the cockpit. Ignoring me, he resumes his negotiations with the pilot. I am being watched carefully by another hijacker. The pilot, Ilhan Akdeniz, is trying to convince Yalciner once and for all: "It is impossible," he says, "to violate Iran's airspace. There is a war going on! They are going to shoot us down with missiles! They won't want to know whether we've been hijacked."

Yalciner's answer surprises everyone, "Don't worry, the Muslim world knows me very well. Khomeini knows me too. Stop worrying—we'll make it to Tehran."

The pilot explains there would not be enough fuel. He asks if the plane can land in Diyarbakir to refuel. The hijackers, convinced, agree. That issue resolved, the lead hijacker seems to relax and resume his casual demeanor.

He turns toward me and tells me abruptly, "I am not a mean terrorist. I am a good terrorist. So you're a journalist? So am I, and the three brothers, too," he explains. "You can take more pictures of me, you know, but I must admit, I don't know how to pose," he adds before bursting out laughing.

They are all working for a banned publication called *Shariat*. Hence, the name of the "mission" they are undertaking. They are religious terrorists belonging to the "Akincilar group" (independent Sunni Muslims linked with the National Salvation Party).

I resume taking pictures of the scene, and of the passengers. The passengers still have no idea what fate has in store for them. These hijackers appear unusually calm. They are obviously fanatics to the point of candidness; they seem to be absolutely confident that they are going to get to Tehran. But I can feel their tension. I lie to them pretending I understand their motivation and want to provide them oodles of publicity. They are quite willing to talk. I ask them how they managed to smuggle their guns onto the Boeing in spite of the tight security control. Yalciner pulls out a book, which he opens to show me that it had been hollowed to make room for a pistol. He laughs heartily about the clever trick he has played on the security guards. Another shows me an attaché case filled with Turkish lires so that they can survive in their new country, Iran. It is hard to tell whether I am in the presence of childish stupidity or enormous confidence.

We make small talk until the plane lands at Diyarbakir. The passengers don't know what city or country they are landing in. Most passengers know that bad things start to happen once hijacked planes touch down.

I become self-conscious realizing that I am the only one who does not seem afraid. The passengers look at me with hatred and fear. Am I a hijacker? The confusion makes them suspicious. I find myself in a no man's land between the passengers and the terrorists. Because of my decision to document this criminal act, the terrorists have made me part of their drama. By not intervening against the hijackers, I have become a co-conspirator in the minds of the passengers. The camera has given me a special passport.

The hijackers also treat the cowering passengers differently. The burning light in the hijackers' eyes looks nothing but ominous.

We wait on the ground. The stewardesses attend to the people quietly and efficiently. The air in the plane is hot and stale. There is no more water or food. The plane feels like a tomb or a submarine that had sunk to the bottom of the ocean. Outside our plastic windows the ground crews, the vehicles and the world seem a thousand miles away. Time is irrelevant.

It is not hard to figure out what is going through the minds of the 148 people aboard. The hijackers are also getting tense, and I sense it is time to stop taking pictures.

It is now 8:30 p.m. We have only been on the plane for three hours, but no one aboard would forget this day. Given the time for reflection, I remember why I am going to Diyarbakir in the first place. I realize that the hijackers have made a fatal mistake: They have landed in the center of a major military base and smack in the middle of preparations for showy military maneuvers. I was supposed to cover the strength and power of the Turkish Army. I was about to be center stage. To make matters worse, the Turkish and European press are there in full force. Faced with the tedious coverage of a nonevent, they were delighted to be at the scene of a hijacking. The worst part is that the new hard-liner president of Turkey himself, Kevan Evren, is at the airport and has taken charge of the event. He declares, "No concessions."

The negotiations between the hijackers and the Airport Authority are going on with no apparent progress. The hijackers make a concession—they will free the women and the children. But it really doesn't matter what they agree to, since their fate is being decided for them in the smoke-filled meeting rooms inside the airport.

At 10 p.m., 19 *Celik Kuvvet* (Steel Force) commandos take off from Ankara and Adana. Their planes land at Diyarbakir at 11 p.m. At midnight the airport is blacked out and the plane is by itself on the tarmac. The fear aboard is palpable.

It is now Tuesday. We have lived another day. At 1 a.m., electronic listening devices are installed on the body of the plane to locate the hijackers. Four more hours are necessary to prepare the rescue operation. Inside the grounded plane the passengers are aware of, and can see, nothing.

At 5 a.m., the commandos split into two groups. One group silently cuts open the rear door, while the front group creates a minor diversion near the cockpit. The commandos burst through the back of the plane, yelling, "Lie down, everybody," followed by a shoot-out. The sound of the firefight in the small enclosed space is deafening.

The passenger I photographed in the cockpit is wounded and later dies in the hospital. I duck under my seat, afraid that my camera might be mistaken for a gun. I regret not taking pictures, but realistically I know I would be killed instantly.

Crowded below the seat, I have just enough time to hide some film in my underwear and to give some rolls to Osman, the radio journalist sitting next to me. The three surviving hijackers surrender quite easily as if all was in good fun.

The passengers are asked to lie down on the tarmac and later we will be driven to army barracks. I am pointed out by some of the passengers as one of the hijackers. In fact, the news wire reports include me in the list of hijackers arrested in the assault. I am taken into custody for interrogation.

After some minutes, most of the passengers are freed and brought to the barracks. Five passengers and I are kept behind. The three hijackers are taken away in a truck. Then the police throw the six of us in a second truck, which follows the first one. My cameras have been confiscated. I still feel confident that the whole situation will soon be clarified.

There are six of us crammed into the same jail cell. We are tired, dirty and thirsty from the 12-hour ordeal. Two engineers, one Italian and two Turkish customs officers who usually control the passports on board, Osman, the radio-journalist, and myself are detained. The police suspect the customs officers of complicity. They want to confirm the identities of the foreign engineers. Osman is detained because he is a journalist, and I, because I am a suspected terrorist. The hijackers are put in another cell not far from ours.

My interrogation is a lot tougher than I anticipated. I am bullied by the policemen when they discover that I work for SIPA Press (SIPA means donkey in Turkish). When I tell them that I was born in Siirt, they realize that I am a Kurd. They find my story hard to believe—that I would simply ask permission to take photos because it is my job. They do not believe I am only a journalist, and I am sent back to my cell. During the entire night, we can't sleep very much, as we are disturbed by the comings and goings of our jailkeepers accompanying the hijackers to their interrogations. We can hear a lot of their yells. We are very uneasy about all this. We can also hear the news on a radio set. I gather that everybody believes I am the fifth terrorist and I therefore should not expect any mercy.

The next day, Osman is freed and I have time to give him some more film to take to SIPA. I am left alone in the cell. Later on, the terrorists and I are sent to another jail well known as a torture center for prisoners captured by the military.

Luckily, this time my interrogation is shorter. I am told I will be released because they checked my identity and they understand I have told the truth. It seems also that some people (journalists and politicians) have vouched for me. Never underestimate the usefulness of political contacts.

I am very surprised and elated when I am finally released. I rush back to SIPA's headquarters in Istanbul, just in time to learn that only a handful of my photos have been published in Turkey as well as around the world. Most of them had been lost due to Osman's mishandling of the developing process. But there were more rolls of film that I had hidden under the aircraft seats that had still not been recovered.

IRAN

1985: Hijacking No. 2

Five years later (1985) I was involved in another hijacking. This time I am not inside the plane, flight 847 a TWA *Boeing 727*, but on the tarmac in Beirut.

The plane is coming from Athens, Greece, and going to Rome, Italy. Two Shiite Lebanese order the pilot to divert the flight to Beirut. Other hijackers join them at Beirut. They demand the discharge of more than 700 Shiite prisoners and others detained in Israel. One passenger, a Navy hardhat diver (not a U.S. Navy SEAL as some people believe) is killed by Mohammed Ali Hamadei. Between June 14 and 26, 111 passengers are released, as well as five crewmen. The 36 other passengers and three other crewmen are detained until June 30. The plane is prevented from leaving Beirut by the Lebanese authorities.

So it becomes a long wait with pictures few and far between.

The hijacking is a comic opera. The hijackers are able to roam about outside the plane and even go back home to sleep at night, thanks to the complicity of the AMAL militia. I am a little wiser, tougher, and cynical. I decide to leave the dull, monotony of the airport and cover the more saleable action in town. I negotiate a deal with one of the hijackers for him to cover the event from inside the plane. The hijacker agrees and I give him an automatic camera. The reward for my ingenuity is that I am run over by an armored vehicle, which crushes one of my legs. I assume the hijacker showed up with the film to get his payment, but he didn't know that I was in the hospital with an injured leg. So I could not get the photos. *C'est la guerre.*

—**Coskun Aral**

Iraq

Bad Boys Club

In March 1997, Saddam Hussein sued a French magazine for defamation for referring to the Iraqi dictator as an "executioner," a "murderer," a "monster" and "a perfect cretin." It's unlikely he'll get Kuwait back in damages. Kuwait, for its part, has sued Saddam for equally inflammatory remarks and for damages stemming from Iraq's attacks on Kuwaiti oil fields. Somebody call Johnny Cochrane.

Iraq is the newest member of Uncle Sam's ostracized Bad Boys Club. Saddam now joins Fidel, Muammar and Kim Jong in the foursome Bill won't play golf with. What are the membership privileges? Well, first off, you won't be able to do business with the States, and, on top of that, you get your home leveled by an F-15. Best of all, though, is that you get to run a country that has frustrated and embarrassed every effort of the world's only superpower to suppress you.

After Saddam's recent efforts to turn the Persian Gulf deserts into Mr. Boffo's hell, people were surprised to learn that not only did Saddam still have an army, he was willing to use it and lose it. Saddam doesn't have a whole lot of options

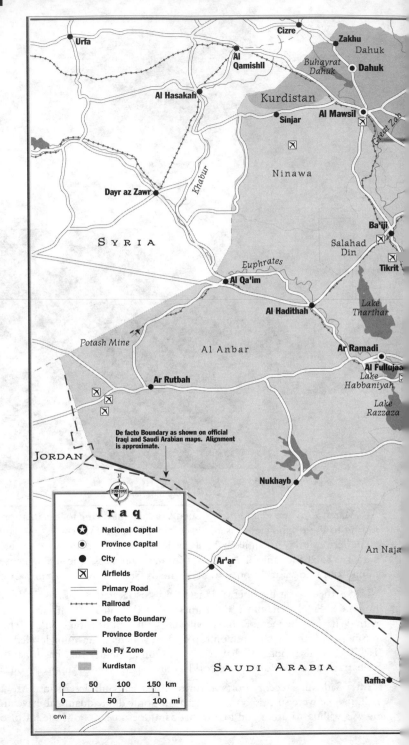

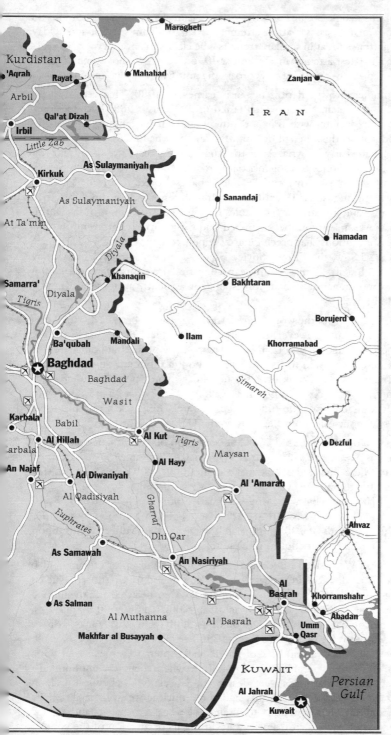

these days. His people are hungry, the country is in shambles, and he is still the target of one or two assassination attempts a year. Saddam's eldest son, Uday, continues getting shot at in similar attempts—he claims to have survived 13 or 14 himself. In the latest attempt in December 1996, Uday was shot some 10 times and is believed to be sporting a new prosthetic unit where his leg once was.

Iraq's plummet into the depths began in earnest in 1980. That year, Saddam launched the war against Iran, which lasted until August 1988. Iraq had long-standing border disputes with Iran and Kuwait, and a fierce animosity toward Israel. In addition to this, the ruling Iraqi Ba'ath Party had a 20-year rivalry with the ruling Ba'ath Party of Syria. After the August 1988 cease-fire with Iran, Iraq supplied arms and money to the Christian forces in Lebanon to relaunch the war there against the Syrian army and Islamic Lebanese forces. It invaded and annexed Kuwait in August 1990, with the apparent intention of seizing funds from Kuwait's banks and investment companies for the reconstruction of Iraq. During the Iran-Iraq war, many countries supplied Iraq with arms in contravention of international conventions that preclude arms supply to countries at war. Suppliers included the U.S.A., the former Soviet Union, France, Germany, U.K., Italy, China, Chile, Brazil and East European countries. Iraq was accused of using chemical weapons against Iranian forces and subsequently against the Kurds in northern Iraq.

For now, Iraq is one of the world's great travel bargains. You'd have a hard time finding things to buy, however, no matter what budget you're on. But if you want to top your tank off, you're in luck. The collapse of the Iraqi dinar from its official rate at about $3.20 to its real rate of about a thousand times less means that when you buy a full tank of gas using dinars, you pay less than an Uncle Sam's penny. Gasoline costs.0009 cents a gallon, or 0.07 dinars a liter. But if you make other transactions at the official rate, beware. Don't reach out and touch someone; telephone calls from Baghdad to the U.S. can cost $158 a minute.

The embargo on Iraq imposed after Iraq's invasion of Kuwait, and a scarcity of U.S. dollars, is pulling the value of Iraq's currency to the value of used Charmin. In a country where educated people make about 2000–3000 dinars a month ($2–3!), there is little to buy and even less to buy it with. Just imagine a country where a crisp U.S. 100-dollar bill will bring you nearly 5000 25-dinar notes. It's positively retro! The currency is worth so little that people pay for goods, where they can find them, in wads of 100 25-dinar bills wrapped with rubber bands. Shopkeepers don't even bother counting the notes.

After the Gulf War, Allied forces had destroyed, neutralized or captured 41 of the 42 Iraqi army divisions in the war zone of Kuwait and southern Iraq. The coalition estimated the number of Iraqi prisoners of war at 175,000 and the number of Iraqi casualties at 85,000–100,000, out of an estimated 500,000 soldiers positioned in the combat area. Iraq lost 3700 of its 5500 main battle tanks, 1857 of its 7500 armored vehicles and 2140 of its 3500 artillery pieces. Ninety-seven of Iraq's 689 combat aircraft and six of its 489 helicopters were destroyed. One-hundred-sixty combat aircraft were flown to Iran, where they were impounded as war reparations. Nine airfields were destroyed, as well as 16 chemical weapons plants, 10 biological weapons plants and three nuclear weapons facilities. Yet Baghdad continues holding onto thousands of pieces of civilian and military equipment that it had stolen from Kuwait during its occupation of the country.

Iraq currently possesses approximately 9000 pieces of military equipment, including trucks, jeeps, armored personnel carriers and missiles, as well as perhaps 6000 civilian items. These items were supposed to have been returned under the 1991 U.N. Security Council Resolution.

Iraq has rebuilt much of its infrastructure, including the phone system, electrical plants, government buildings and bridges. The Iraqi people have shown themselves to be a very resilient people. Saddam's is not the first dictatorship they have endured, and it won't be the last. Economic embargoes tend to have greater ramifications on innocent citizens than on the dictators who led them into it. Despots rarely go hungry. They're occasionally assassinated, but usually with full stomachs. Saddam still sports that tire around his waist, while his people are being starved to death by the West. Just a single well-aimed cruise missile could dramatically change things for the better in what used to be the cradle of civilization.

Saddam's effectiveness in eliminating successors and the West's fear of a more belligerent successor are the main reasons he is still in power. He seems to be somewhat confident of a long reign, despite the U.S.'s claim that its embargo will ensure his demise. Why do we know he is confident? Well, since the Gulf War, he has spent $1.2 billion building or rebuilding more than 40 palaces in Iraq. In April 1997, Saddam threw himself a lavish 60th birthday bash, complete with a Tigris River procession of 60 Turkish yachts, to remind everyone he was still alive. Meanwhile, things keep getting worse for the common folk.

The U.N. reports that most of Iraq's population is experiencing mass deprivation, chronic hunger and endemic malnutrition, along with the collapse of personal incomes and a rapidly increasing number of destitute, jobless and homeless people. Sounds like a great place for a bargain vacation. For now the Iraqis can sell oil for food.

In 1996, President Clinton sent a Labor Day present to Saddam in response to his sending the Republican Guard north. (About 44 cruise missiles, half from B-52's from Guam and half from the navy.) The goal was to take out radar and air defense installations in the south. Those destroyed were rebuilt and operational two months later, making the attack merely a very expensive pre-election Labor Day fireworks show. C'mon, Bill; we sent you a copy of *DP*. You should have known how it would play out.

The UN oil-for-food program has begun. It was resisted for months because of Iraqi concerns about losing its sovereignty. The UN plan allows Iraq to sell $2 billion worth of oil over a six-month period but it must use the revenues to buy food and medicine for its people. Publicly Saddam may be squawking, but his accountants are having some new deposit slips printed up. Iraq's economy is expected to grow some 30 percent in 1997 because of the limited oil exports.

Meanwhile, the Iraqi dinar continues to plunge. About 1100 dinars fetch a buck these days. And the dinar won't catch up any time soon. U.S. Secretary of State Madeleine Albright declared in March 1997 that economic sanctions against Iraq would remain as long as Saddam stays in power. The sanctions have decimated the Iraqi people. More than 180,000 Iraqi children under five years old suffer from malnutrition.

Considering that Baghdad is now the Garden of Needin', and once breadbasket of the ancient world and part of the fertile crescent, the boys from Baghdad have done a good job of screwing it up—despite having enough oil to make Saudi Arabia look like a dry sump in Lubbock. Instead of basking in its riches, Iraq is poor, the consequence of Saddam's maniacal insistence on becoming the superpower of the Middle East. The Gulf War was a laughable attempt by Hussein to shun international diplomacy and snatch back oil-rich Kuwait. Either Saddam didn't pay attention during history class or he just likes expensive fireworks, because he qualified his country for the Third World Club in a mere three months. Among the guests invited were terrorist Abu Nidal, who recently relocated his Fatah Revolutionary Council to Iraq.

President Saddam Hussein al-Tikriti

Saddam the president, supreme commander, head of the National Command Council and self styled Hero of al-Qadisiay, Knight of the Arab Nation, descendent of the prophet, son Iman ALi Ibn Abi Talib, is still the man. He had an early start at being a bastard. He was born out of wedlock on April 28, 1937 in the village of al-Ouja an hour drive north of Baghdad. The man who sired him died before he was born. He got the name Saddam or "the stubborn one" because his mother tried to unsuccessfully abort him by strenuous labor. He was raised by an uncle, Khairallah Talfah, an Iraqi army officer who was jailed for a botched coup attempt against King Feisal II. He moved with his uncle to Baghdad in 1955 and grew up in the Tekarte area. He was considered bright, cruel and violent. In his youth, he entertained himself and his friends by torturing and killing dogs and cats by sticking a red hot steel rod up their anuses and in their eyes. He is said to have killed his first victim (a relative named Saadi) in his 20's. He joined the Ba'ath Party (Party of Arab Renewal) in 1957 and participated in an assassination attempt on Iraq's General Kassem on October 17, 1959. The attempt failed, Saddam was injured and fled to Syria for six months. He then went to study law in Egypt in 1962 and returned to Iraq after Kassem was deposed and executed in public.

Saddam married his cousin Sajida Talfah (the oldest daughter of Khairallah Talfah, the man who raised Saddam) in an arranged marriage in 1963. She bore two sons: Uday was born in 1964 and his second son, Qusay was born in 1966. To show how close fruit falls from the tree in Iraq, he made his wife's brother, Adnan, defense minister and his wife's father, governor of Baghdad. You should also know he had Adnan killed.

The tables turned when Marshall Arif took power and arrested and jailed Ba'ath party members including Saddam. Saddam escaped and finally returned when Kassem was deposed in 1968. This time Saddam became the ruling Ba'ath party's Deputy Secretary General and chief inquisitor under President al-Bakr. Saddam kept busy executing hundreds of citizens, cozying up to the Russians and handing out jobs to fell Tikritis. On May 16, 1979, al-Bakr died from heart failure. His heart stopped because he was poisoned. The "stubborn one" had come from being a bastard to becoming the head bastard by the age 43.

IRAQ

Saddam was famous for launching the 20th century's longest official war. The war with Iran that killed a million Iraqis lasted eight years. His big claim to fame was the invasion and rape of Kuwait. Under direct orders from Saddam, Iraq soldiers are said to have removed more than 10,000 luxury vehicles (sold at public auction in Bagdad for $125 million), 3216 bars of gold, 63 tons of gold coins and anything else of cultural or economic value, and had it shipped back to Iraq.

Saddam's banker is half brother and former head of the Mukhabarat, Barzan al-Tikriti who lives in Geneva (Uday is married to his daughter and stays with him when in Geneva). He is officially the UN rep for Iraq, but he spends most of his time stashing away Saddam's bucks and buying weapons including nukes.

Despite questionable and ill-fated foreign policy moves that have caused the impoverishment of his country, not to mention the deaths of more than 100,000 Iraqis in the Gulf War, he still retains a respectable following. He is president and chairman of the Revolutionary Command Council (RCC), regional secretary of the ruling Ba'ath Party and head of the 100,000-strong Popular Militia. When he needs help running the country, he hires home boys from his hometown of Tikrit, north of Baghdad. The Tikritis are known as a minor league mafia who have graduated to running Iraq.

Hussein's absolute rule rests with his status in the RCC. The chairman of the RCC is, ex-officio, president of the republic. The president appoints ministers and judges, and laws are enacted by presidential decree. Routine governing of the country is carried out by an appointed council of ministers.

Saddam is swiftly using up his nine lives. He survived a failed military coup in May 1991, and he offed 18 senior army officers just to make sure he could get a good night's sleep. In 1984, one of his stand-ins was assassinated by the Shiite Dawas (see "The South"). His current body double is Faoas al-Emari, a man who has a hard time getting an insurance policy. It isn't known how many times the U.S. tried to take him out during the Gulf War. In June 1991, he fired 1500 senior army officers and 180 senior police officers as a reward for following his orders during the Gulf War.

Assassination attempts are the biggest concern for Saddam. After one attempt, more than 200 current and former officers and civilians were arrested, including the commander of the Republican Guard's tank battalion, Brig Sufiyan al-Ghurairi, and former parliamentarian Jasser al-Tikriti. All the plotters hailed from Saddam's hometown of Tikrit, as well as from Mosul and Ramadi. The attempt appears to have been the first in which members of the Tikrit clan played an important role in trying to remove their favorite son.

Saddam also leans on the loyalty of his security services and the Republican Guard divisions of the army to put down any uprisings. One coup leader was chopped into pieces and delivered back to his family. The Republican Guard suppressed the Shiite uprising in the south of the country and the Kurdish rebellion in the north. Saddam's paranoia is well-founded. He is surrounded by very brutal supporters like Ali Hassan al Majid (nicknamed Chemical Ali and the man who personally emptied his gun into the head of the prodigal Hussein Kamal). Saddam has developed a not-too-paranoid fear of being poisoned by shaking someone's hand. So if you happen to run into him, no soul shakes and definitely no tongue. His favorite song? The subtle and melodic; *Saddam, Oh Saddam, You Great and Powerful One.*" In October of 1995, he held a plebiscite to see if Iraqi's wanted him, and surprise! He received 99.9 percent of the vote. It is assumed that the 45 people who voted against him in Baghdad were either blind or shot as they were exiting the polls.

Saddam is one hell of a guy. In fact, he's like Qaddafi with *cojones*, or an Assad with more bluster and a guy who regularly takes on the entire Western world, his own people, his relatives and just about anybody who isn't him. Whatever you believe, one thing for sure is Saddam Hussein still calls the shots in Iraq.

The Bad Boys Club: Current & Recent Past

What do all these guys have in common? They like uniforms; they're on a first-name basis with editorial cartoonists; and they're all current or former targets of CIA plots.

Dues-Paying Members	
Fidel Castro	Cuba
Muammar Qaddafi	Libya
Saddam Hussein	Iraq
Kim Jong II	North Korea
Emeritus	
Manuel Noriega	Panama
Ayatollah Khomeini	Iran
Daniel Ortega	Nicaragua

Uday Saddam Hussein al-Tikriti

If you think Saddam is bad, wait till his son gets to run Iraq. Uday is the classic Ferrari-driving, gun-toting bad-boy son of a dictator. Tall, good looking and with a heart as black as Satan, Uday takes great pleasure in raping, murdering, gambling, partying and generally doing just about anything he wants to do including killing one of his father's best friends at a high level dinner party. He was born June 18, 1964 and has a brother Qusay who runs the Mukhabarat (Iraqi secret service). Uday is known for motivating the members of the Iraqi soccer team by torturing them and is known as a hair trigger sadist. Accordingly, there were few tears when on December 12, 1996, he got a taste of his own medicine. Uday was speeding to Baghdad's al-Masur Club when six men sprayed his supposedly bullet-proof Porsche with machine gun fire. Uday was hit 14 times by bullets through the windshield. Uday had a hard time finding anyone who would treat him until Fidel Castro's personal doctor arrived. His left leg is useless and it remains to be seen how well he will recover. The men who shot him is a Tikriti whose father had his tongue cut and was executed on the orders of Saddam. Those who want an inside look at sadism to the limit should pick up the fascinating book, *I was Saddam's Son*, by Latif Yahih and Karl Wendl.

Chemical Ali

Interior Minister and cousin Ali Hassan al Majid makes Saddam and Uday look like Mother Teresa. Ali is called Chemical Ali because he was convinced the best way to get rid of the Kurds was to gas them. He orchestrated the gassing of Kurdish villages carried out by low flying helicopters intended to kill every living thing in the area, including plants and wildlife. In March of 1988, in the village of Halabja, 5000 Kurds died writhing in agony and ten thousand were seriously affected. Even Saddam thought that this, perhaps, went a bit too far.

Ali blew away the husband of one of Saddam's daughters, Hussein Kamel, when he was lured back with the promise of a full pardon by Saddam.

The North: The Kurds

According to Saddam, the Kurds are just puppets of Iran, the U.S. and Israel. Only a few days after the Gulf War ended, major insurrections broke out in both the south of Iran and particularly in Kurdistan, where Kurd rebels seized large areas of territory by the first week of March 1991. Iraq's "elite" Republican Guards used repugnant brutality in suppressing the Kurd rebellion. Kurd refugees fleeing the wrath of the Republican Guard numbered 2 million or more along the Iraqi borders with both Turkey and Iran. The U.S. and Great Britain dispatched troops to northern Iraq on a short-lived effort to entice the Kurds to return home.

When the Iraqi army pulled out of the north they left a political vacuum. The U.S.-controlled area is now called Kurdistan. Of the 19.2 million people in Iraq, 21.6 percent are Kurds (73.5 percent are Arabs). There is a legitimate argument for the state of Kurdistan since the Kurds were left out of any postcolonial country-carving. The Iraqi army has been doing bad things to the Kurds while away from the scrutiny of the world. They have used a variety of methods to exterminate the Kurds, including bombing, starvation and even employing chemical weapons. Hussein is less interested in being nasty to the Kurdish people than he is in keeping the oil their new country would sit on—especially the oil fields in the Kirkuk area. (See "Kurdistan.")

The CIA

In perhaps the biggest botch that ever happened, perhaps 300 Iraqis died in 1996 in a failed CIA attempt to overthrow Saddam Hussein. The blundering, that cost the U.S. northern Iraq, was one of the agency's biggest failures in its 50-year history. The attempt to oust Saddam was spawned by the CIA's belief that Saddam was ripe for a downfall after the defection of his son-in-law Lt. Gen. Hussein Kamil in 1995. In early 1996, President Bill Clinton approved $6 million for a covert ops group set up by the CIA called the Iraqi National Accord. Drafted from the ranks of former Iraqi officers, its mission was to implement terror in Baghdad through bombing attacks. Saddam got hip to the plan and had an Iraqi intelligence official telephone the CIA officer in charge of the coup plot in Amman, Jordan, and recite details of the plot. Saddam responded by having his tanks roll through Arbil in Iraqi Kurdistan. Thousands of Iraqis and Kurds on the CIA payroll had to be evacuated out of Iraq through Turkey and Guam to the U.S., where, we presume, more than a handful had their faces and fingertips changed. The CIA has spent some $100 million since 1991 in an effort to bag Saddam Hussein.

The South Marsh Arabs (the Ma'dan) and the Shiite Dawa Party

This area between the Tigris and the Euphrates has been home to the Ma'dan for over 5000 years. Today, the people live in rural simplicity and survive by raising water buffalo and sheep, growing rice, and selling reeds which are used to make mats. The people live on islands and travel using ancient dugout canoes. Many of their villages are actually man-made floating islands. There is also a group of about 10,000 insurgents who fight against the government of Iraq. Although the people allude to it as the Garden of Eden, it is a hot, humid place infested with mosquitoes, fleas and ticks. Winters are cold, with gales coming from the mountains of Kurdistan to the north or Iran to the east.

It seems every country makes fun of whomever lives in the south—Spain, Italy, the U.S. Russia and even Iraq have their hillbillies and country folk who just want to be left alone. In Iraq, there are about 50,000 Shiites living in the areas once considered to be the Garden of Eden. Some are Sabeans who predate Islam. The government of Hussein is Sunni, even though 55 percent of Iraq are Shiites. The Shiites in the south are supported by Shiite Iran. The Dawa is a group founded by Ayatollah Baqir al-Sadr who played host to Ayatollah Khomeini when he was on the run. Because of a deal struck by Saddam with the shah in 1978, Khomeini was physically tossed out of the holy city of Najaf, Iraq and split for Paris. Chemical Ali personally strangled Ayatollah Baqir al-Sadr and had his two sisters hung. The Dawa party was banned and is now covertly headquartered in Basra.

For now, Saddam is building dams, draining the marshes and pouring poison into the rivers (he loves to play with chemicals, doesn't he?) in an effort to simply eliminate every living thing in the marshes. When he gets bored of poisoning the people, crops and animals, he has his army pound on them with artillery, strafe them with gunships and drop large bombs on them. If things are a little slow, he has his soldiers burn hundreds of acres of weeds just to give them something to do.

Uncle Sam, The Allies and Armageddon

It is hard to say whether we wanted to flatten Iraq or just drop off a lot of old ordinance. They didn't let many journos in on the Mother of All Battles. Even Saddam parked the Journos until he could find enough dead babies to photograph. We fought a war, managed to shoot more of our own people than the enemy did, and then handed everything back to everyone and went home. It's no wonder that Saddam announced he had won the war because in fact, he did. He stripped Kuwait faster than Uday can get a transvestite naked and then left the smoking bits for us to fix. He even got so bored he did the spank-the-kid, kick-the-dog routine by Scudding Israel just so he'd have a live version of Space Invader to watch from his bunker.

Despite the fact that we dropped 227,000 bombs (of which only 8000 were "smart") we only killed 3000 civilians. It seems you could kill that number of people just by dropping rocks or pennies out of B-52's. We didn't take out "the Stubborn One" and we didn't even mess up those nice pictures of him all over Baghdad. However, we did bomb a civilian shelter and yes, Iraq has a bad habit of camouflaging their military installations to look like suburbs, but all in all, we didn't do a very good job.

We left about 400,000 soldiers, 2200 tanks, 2500 APCs, and 1650 artillery pieces. We dropped over 120 million pounds of explosives in just under a month, and we didn't even make one of those big craters that people like to visit after the war. And God forbid we mention how much those cruise missiles cost and how many people each one didn't kill.

There are about 300 combat aircraft left that are hampered by the two no-fly zones monitored by the West. Why didn't we leave Saddam with a slingshot and two rocks? Well, seems that George Bush was more worried about Iran, so he whittled Saddam's toys down to Third World size. We think we got all of his Scuds, but the CIA still insists he's hiding a few. Who cares? We're not going back there again.

It seems next time, we should step aside and let the GIA, Hezbollah, Syria, Tutsis, Hutus and whoever else has a blood lust for Saddam have at it. We could have bought a trillion machetes on credit (at about $2 each) and let loose the entire nations of Rwanda and

Burundi into Iraq. Then, when they're done, go in and suck all the oil out. Now that would scare Saddam.

Supreme Council of the Islamic Resistance in Iraq (SCIRI)

There were about 40,000 rebels in southern Iraq under an umbrella called the Supreme Council for the Islamic Revolution in Iraq. Most have regrouped in the north. Many were killed in 1991 by Saddam Hussein during the aborted uprising. They have joined with the Iraqi National Congress (INS) and are based in Sulaymania (Kurdistan)

Iraqi National Congress

The CIA bankrolled the INC in the SAS hotel in Vienna, Austria, in 1992. The tab was $15 million and the idea was to combine all the anti-Saddam groups under one organization. Ahmed Chalabi, a Jordanian based Shiite Iraqi and former banker, was picked to run the INC. (See Kurdistan.)

Iraqi National Congress
9 Pall Mall Deposit
124 -128 Barlby Road, London, England W10 6 BL
TEL: (0181) 960 4007 FAX (0181) 960 4001 PR: (0171) 233 9034
In Sulaymania Iraq, (873) 68 234 6239 FAX (873) 68 234 6240
http://www.inc.org.uk

Iraqi National Accord

The Saudis and the CIA bankrolled this group as an alternative to the INC. Led by Ayad Alawi, an Iraqi doctor from Baghdad, it is headquartered in Amman, Jordan. The CIA kicked in $10 million to get things going, but used the INC to raise hell in Kurdistan. (See Kurdistan.)

Iran

Saddam hates Shiite Iran and wasted a million Iraqis in a bizarre WWI-style retro war of trenches and artillery duels. He kicked things off on September 22, 1980 when 400,000 Iraqis invaded Iran across an 800 mile front. Eight years later, the war ended with no winner. The only good news is that Saddam is still alive because the U.S. figures that having Iraq in one big nasty piece keeps Iran out of Baghdad.

Potatoes for diesel

Despite the embargo on Iraq, when DP visited northern Iraq in October of 1994 during Hussein's military feint to the south, we passed a line of trucks three kms long and in rows of three waiting to bring in basic foodstuffs. The truck drivers were rewarded for their three-day waits by filling homemade rusty tanks bolted below the trucks full of crude diesel fuel, which would later sell in Turkish gas stations for around 10,000 Turkish lira a liter.

Travel Warning

The Department of State warns all U.S. citizens against traveling to Iraq. Conditions within the country remain unsettled and dangerous. The United States does not maintain diplomatic relations with Iraq and cannot provide normal consular protective services to U.S. citizens.

The Iraqi embassy considers Iraq safe for travel, and they are probably about 80 percent right. It's the 20 percent you have to worry about. Border crossings between Jordan and Iraq are closed; all others are open. Crossings from Turkey are backed up but are orderly and efficient.

You must be a reporter or use a foreign passport. Passports and visas are required. On February 8, 1991, U.S. passports ceased to be valid for travel to, in or through Iraq and may not be used for that purpose unless a special validation has been obtained. Without the requisite validation, use of a U.S. passport for travel to, in or through Iraq may constitute a violation of 18 U.S.C. 1544, and may be punishable by a fine and/or imprisonment. An exemption to the above restriction is granted to Americans residing in Iraq as of February 8, 1991, who continue to reside there, and to American professional reporters or journalists on assignment there.

In addition, the Department of the Treasury prohibits all travel-related transactions by U.S. persons intending to visit Iraq, unless specifically licensed by the Office of Foreign Assets Control. The only exceptions to this licensing requirement are for journalistic activity or for U.S. government or United Nations business. The categories of individuals eligible for consideration for a special passport validation are set forth in 22 C.F.R. 51.74. Passport validation requests for Iraq should be forwarded in writing to either of the following addresses:

Iraqi Embassy

> *1801 P Street, N.W.*
> *Washington, D.C. 20036*
> ☎ *(202) 483-7500*

Deputy Assistant Secretary for Passport Services

> *U.S. Department of State*
> *1111 19th Street, N.W., Suite 260*
> *Washington, D.C. 20522-1705*
> *Attn: Office of Passport Policy and Advisory Services*
> ☎ *(202) 955-0231 or 955-0232; FAX (202) 955-0230.*

The request must be accompanied by supporting documentation according to the category under which validation is sought. Currently, the four categories of persons specified in 22 C.F.R. 51.74 as being eligible for consideration for passport validation are as follows:

[1] Professional reporters: Includes full-time members of the reporting or writing staff of a newspaper, magazine or broadcasting network whose purpose for travel is to gather information about Iraq for dissemination to the general public.

[2] American Red Cross: Applicant establishes that he or she is a representative of the American Red Cross or International Red Cross traveling pursuant to an officially sponsored Red Cross mission.

[3] Humanitarian considerations: Applicant must establish that his or her trip is justified by compelling humanitarian considerations or for family unification. At this time, "compelling humanitarian considerations" include situations where the applicant can document that an immediate family member is critically ill in Iraq. Documentation concerning family illness must include the name and address of the relative, and be from that relative's physician attesting to the nature and gravity of the illness. "Family unification" situations may include cases in which spouses or minor children are residing in Iraq, with and dependent on, an Iraqi national spouse or parent for their support.

[4] National interest: The applicant's request is otherwise found to be in the national interest.

In all requests for passport validation for travel to Iraq, the name, date and place of birth for all concerned persons must be given, as well as the U.S. passport numbers. Documentation as outlined above should accompany all requests. Additional information may be obtained by writing to the above addresses or by calling the Office of Passport Policy and Advisory Services at ☎ *(202) 326-0231 or 955-0232.*

U.S. Treasury Restrictions

In August 1990 President Bush issued Executive Orders 12722 and 12724, imposing economic sanctions against Iraq, including a complete trade embargo. The U.S. Treasury Department's Office of Foreign Assets Control administers the regulations related to these sanctions, which include restrictions on all financial transactions related to travel to Iraq. These regulations prohibit all travel-related transactions, except as specifically licensed. The only exceptions to this licensing requirement are for persons engaged in journalism or in official U.S. government or U.N. business. Questions concerning these restrictions should be directed to:

Chief of Licensing Section, Office of Foreign Assets Control
U.S. Department of the Treasury
Washington, D.C. 20220
☎ *(202) 622-2480*
FAX (202) 622-1657

In the past year, most foreigners detained at the Kuwait-Iraq border, regardless of nationality, have been sentenced to jail terms of seven to 10 years for illegally entering Iraq.

During 1992 and 1993, Iraq detained nine Westerners—three Swedes, three Britons, a U.S. national, a German and a Frenchman—on charges of illegally entering Iraq. They were released by late 1993 after much diplomatic energy. In March 1995, two Americans were held and sentenced to eight years in prison. Tom Jerrold and an ABC news crew were also detained, but were released after the U.N. intervened. Brent Sadler, who interviewed the two Americans in the Iraq jail, was asked for his written permission to be in the jail, even when accompanied by a Polish diplomat negotiating the release on behalf of the U.S. State department!

There have been attacks against foreigners, and antagonism is still high in the Western world. Many Egyptians and other Arab expatriates were killed by disgruntled, unemployed Iraqi ex-soldiers. Don't forget that expats were held hostage by Hussein from mid- to late 1990 during the Mexican standoff between Iraqi and Allied forces over the Iraqi annexation of Kuwait. All travelers and foreigners in Iraq run the risk of being detained, harassed and questioned, particularly in the south near the Kuwaiti border. The Iraqi embassy referred us to Mr. Ganji at Babylon Travel, ☎ *(312) 478-9000*, for readers who want more details about travel to Iraq.

AIDS Test

Iraqi government officials have seemingly watched so many soap operas and pay-per-view dirty movies while out of the country that they think all Westerners are sex-crazed adulterers, fornicators and deviants.

Therefore, all visitors over age 12 and under 65 who plan to stay in Iraq for longer than five days (official visitors have 15 days) must call on the Central Public Health Laboratory in Al Tayhariyat al Fennia Square between 8 a.m. and 2 p.m. to either present HIV and syphilis (VDRL) certificates or arrange for a local test at a cost of ID100. HIV and VDRL certificates valid for Iraq may be obtained in the U.K. by arranging a blood test with a general practitioner. The sample should then be tested by a Public Health Laboratory Service listed on the blank certificate and attested by the Foreign Office and the Iraqi embassy in London. Failing to comply with these requirements carries a fine of ID500 or six months imprisonment. A yellow fever vaccination certificate is required for all visitors arriving from an infected area.

Iraq has 38,402 km of paved roads. Expressway No. 1—a 1200-km, six-lane freeway—connects Baghdad to Kuwait in the south and runs to Jordan and Syria in the west. A 630-km freeway (Expressway No. 2) runs north from Baghdad to the Turkish border, where it links up with the modern freeway connecting southeast Turkey to Ankara and Istanbul. Another Baghdad-Basra route is planned via Kut and Amarah and will be known as Expressway No. 3.

There are 2032 km of rail network, including the 461-km Baghdad-Kirkuk-Arbil line, the 528-km Baghdad-Mosul-Yurubiyah standard line and the 582-km Baghdad-Maaqal-Umm

Qasr standard line. The 516-km line between Baghdad and al-Qaim and Qusaybah on the Syrian border was opened last year. The 252-km northern line between Kirkuk, Baiji and Haditha, which connects the Baiji oil refinery with the al-Qaim fertilizer plant, was opened in 1988.

Iraq's main port of Basra is inoperative, because of the closure of the Shatt al-Arab waterway during the war with Iran. Several Iraqi naval vessels were sunk in the waterway during the Gulf War.

Iraq has an international airport at Bamerni, 17 km south of Baghdad. Another international airport was planned for Mosul, with a 4000-meter runway capable of handling 30 landings and takeoffs a day. Domestic regional airports at Arbil (3000-meter runway), Amara and Najaf (for small 50-seater aircraft) were also planned. Iraqi Airways has a fleet of four Boeing 747s, two Boeing 737s, six Boeing 727s and two Boeing 707s.

You can rent a car from the airport. You will need both national and international driving licenses. You can also take the bus service for the 17-km trip from the city center to the airport. In Baghdad, the double-decker buses are cheap and can take you just about anywhere you want to go; don't forget to buy your tickets at the kiosks first. There are also private minibuses and shared taxis. A train service operates three times a day from Baghdad to Basra; don't plan on comfort or air conditioning unless you're lucky. You can choose from three class services with sleeping accommodations, restaurant cars and air conditioning. You can take the train between most of Iraq's major centers (Baghdad-Mosul, Baghdad-Arbil and Baghdad-Basra).There is also regular bus service from Baghdad to other major cities and regular flights between Baghdad, Basra and Mosul. Domestic airports are at Mosul, Kirkuk and Basra, as well as Baghdad.

Taxis must be negotiated in advance. During the war, *DP* paid $1200 to get out of Baghdad to Turkey (but we didn't have to tip). Taxis have meters, but it is legal to charge twice the amount shown on the meter. After 10 p.m. there is a surcharge.

Baghdad

Baghdad is the location for periodic bombings against state targets and occasional unsuccessful coup attempts against the regime of Saddam Hussein. Passersby occasionally sustain injuries in such incidents.

The Kuwaiti Border

The Iraqis are sore losers. U.S. citizens and other foreigners working near the Kuwait-Iraq border have been detained by Iraqi authorities for lengthy periods under harsh conditions. Travelers to that area, whether in Kuwait or not, are in immediate jeopardy of detention by Iraqi security personnel. Journalists and oil workers have been detained. And there are untold numbers of land mines waiting to be unearthed.

Everywhere Else

Hostilities in the Gulf region ceased on February 27, 1991. United Nations Security Council Resolution 687, adopted on April 3, 1991, set terms for a permanent cease-fire, but conditions in Iraq remain unsettled. Travel in Iraq is extremely hazardous for U.S. citizens. Iraq is crawling with informants who report any movements of foreigners and dealings with locals. Because of Iraq's "Big Brother" environment, do not try to bribe police or military personnel.

Soccer Games

Monday night's a great night for football! In July 1996, in a soccer game in Libya involving a team sponsored by Libyan leader Muammar Qaddafi's eldest son, murder and mayhem broke out after the referee made a call against Saadi Qaddafi's team. Junior's players began beating up the ruffled ref and players on the opposing team. When fans started to heckle Saadi and his team, Saadi's bodyguards responded by spraying the stands with bullets. Spectators shot back. When the cordite finally settled, the body count stacked up to as high as 50. Not to be outdone, Saddam's eldest son and head of the Iraqi soccer federation, Uday—the Middle East's master of half-time speeches—had members of the Iraqi national team tortured after they were eliminated from World Cup qualifying contention with a couple of losses to lowly Kazakhstan on June 29, 1997. After the final loss, Uday ordered the team to a military base where the players were caned on the soles of their feet and beaten on their backs. They were tortured and had their hair and mustaches shaved off. We'll probably see a lot of rookies in training camp next summer.

The diseases you should be vaccinated against are typhoid, cholera and hepatitis. Tap water should be sterilized before drinking, and visitors should avoid consuming ice. Milk is unpasteurized and should be boiled. Comprehensive medical insurance covering repatriation is essential, unless you want to get even sicker in an Iraqi hospital. Health and sanitary conditions weren't too good before the war, and they are worse now in all the major cities. Water, refuse and sanitation services are nonexistent, especially in the south, where outbreaks of typhoid, hepatitis, meningitis and gastroenteritis had reached epidemic proportions by late 1993. An outbreak of cholera was contained. Hospitals and other medical facilities were also damaged during the war and vital electricity supplies disrupted. Many expatriate doctors and hospital staff left the country. Stocks of pharmaceuticals have been depleted, and there are severe shortages of even nonprescription drugs. Essential drugs are almost nonexistent. If you need or think you may need medication or drugs, bring plenty with you. You can always donate or sell what you don't need on your way out.

Iraq has a population of 21.5 million. Although 53.5 percent of the population are Shia Muslims, the minority Sunni Muslims (41.5 percent) are politically dominant.

The Iraqi currency, for what little it's worth, is the Iraqi dinar (ID). One ID=1000 files. Banks are generally open from 8 a.m.–12 noon. Government offices are generally open 8:30 a.m.–2:30 p.m. Businesses are open 8 a.m.–2 p.m. Shops, when they have anything to sell, don't follow the clock, opening at dawn, closing for lunch when the sun is high, and reopening when the day cools off around 4 p.m. Small shops tend to open very early, close during the middle of the day, and then reopen from around 4 p.m. till 7 p.m. or later. Food markets open around 9 a.m. and close at midday, or when supplies are exhausted. The Islamic year contains 354 or 355 days, meaning that Muslim feasts advance by 10 to 12 days against the Gregorian calendar each year. Dates of feasts vary according to the sighting of the new moon, so they cannot be forecast precisely.

There is a neutral zone between Iraq and Saudi Arabia, administered jointly by the two countries, with Iraq's portion covering 3522 square km. The country's most fertile area is the centuries-old flood plain of the Tigris and Euphrates rivers, from Turkey and Syria to the Gulf. The northeast of Iraq is mountainous, while the large western desert area is sparsely populated and undeveloped. The northern mountainous region experiences severe winters, but the southern plains have warm winters with little rain and very hot, dry summers. The temperatures in Baghdad are between 40°F and 60°F in January, and between 75°F and 90°F in July and August. The average annual rainfall is 28 mm.

Alcohol is available only in international hotels. During the Ramadan fasting month, both smoking and drinking in public are forbidden.

Money Hassles

The Iraqi dinar is virtually worthless (3.2 to the U.S. dollar officially; 1000 to the dollar semi-officially and 3000 dinars to the buck on the black market). The shortage of foreign currency has created a thriving black market, although the penalties for its use are severe, with heavy fines and possible imprisonment. The difference in exchange rates is vast between the black market and the official rates. You must declare your funds on entry, but few people do. It is legal to bring only ID25 into Iraq and take out ID5. Any amount of hard currency may be imported, but this must be declared on entry, and receipts must be obtained for any expenditure in Iraq. The balance and receipts must be shown upon leaving the country. Credit cards are not generally accepted, and traveler's checks are virtually useless. Iraqis traveling abroad may take out ID100.

Embassy Location

There is no U.S. embassy or consulate in Iraq. The U.S. government is not in a position to accord normal consular protective services to U.S. citizens who are in Iraq. U.S. government interests are represented by the government of Poland, which, as a protecting power, is able to provide only limited emergency services to U.S. citizens. The U.S. interests section of the embassy of Poland is located opposite the Foreign Ministry Club (Masbah Quarter):

U.S. Interests Section, Embassy of Poland
P.O. Box 2447 Alwiyah
Baghdad, Iraq
☎ *(964-1) 719-6138, 719-6139, 719-3791, 718-1840*

05/1996	Iraq is permitted to sell $2 billion worth of oil over six months to buy food and medicine.
04/16/1991	U.S. President George Bush announces that U.S. Troops would enter northern Iraq to create a safe haven for displaced Kurds around Zakhu.
03/02/1991	Iraq signs a cease-fire agreement with allied forces ending the Persian Gulf War.
02/27/1991	Allied forces in Kuwait and Iraq suspend military operations against Iraq.
02/24/1991	Allied forces launch the ground assault against Iraqi forces occupying Kuwait.

01/30/1991	Iraqi and multinational force elements have their first combat engagement in Khafji in the Persian Gulf War.
01/17/1991	The start of hostilities between the multinational forces and Iraqi forces. The beginning of Operation Desert Storm.
08/02/1990	Iraqi forces invade Kuwait and seize control of the country.
08/15/1986	Turkish troops raid Kurdish rebel camps in Iraq.
11/26/1984	Relations with the U.S. restored.
06/07/1981	Israeli warplanes attack an Iraqi nuclear power plant near Baghdad.
09/19/1980	Iran-Iraq war begins.
03/10/1979	Death of Kurdish leader Mullah Mustafa Barzani (Kurdish regions).
06/01/1976	During this month, Syria enters the civil war in Lebanon on the side of the Christian Phalange and against the Palestinians and their Muslim allies. In response, Abu Nidal renames his terrorist group then based in Iraq the Black June Organization and begins attacking Syrian targets.
07/17/1968	Ba'ath Party seizes power.
02/08/1963	Revolution Day.
02/03/1963	The Ba'ath Party takes power in a popular revolt.
07/14/1958	Republic Day. Celebrates the coup by General Abdul Karim Qasim during which King Faysal II and Prime Minister Nuri as-Said are killed.
04/08/1947	Iraqi Ba'ath Party founded.
01/22/1946	Kurdish Republic Day.
04/28/1937	Saddam Hussein's birthday.
03/21	Kurdish New Year celebrated.

Northern Iraq: Things Go Better With Coke

"Welcome to Iraqi Kurdistan," says the sign. Immediately below the words a picture of the legendary Kurdish leader, Mullah Mustafa Barzani, beams reassuringly—as if to discourage any negative thoughts that you might have upon entering one of the world's more troubled regions. But if journalists and aid workers are welcomed with open arms in Kurdistan, most of the local population have a somewhat different perspective on their *de facto* Kurdish state. Six years of autonomous Kurdish rule in northern Iraq have left many not so much with a vague desire to leave, but a desperate urge to get out any way they can. But then, as a general rule of thumb, wherever the press pack heads en masse can only spell bad news for the local populance. If it's not a natural disaster, it's famine and war that have journalists flocking to such places, like so may bees around a honey pot. In the case of northern Iraq it's generally war—Kurd versus Kurd, although the specter of massive food shortages occasionally raises its ugly head, and, of course, from time to time Saddam Hussein makes an appearance for good measure—just to keep the international community on its toes.

Just one month prior to my arrival, Saddam had made a rare appearance—to the joy of the international media circus—and had helped the faction headed by Massoud Barzani to oust the rival faction of Jalal Talabani from the region. Even by Byzantine and Machiavellian standards of Kurdish politics, this was cynicism in the extreme. You could almost be forgiven for forgetting that Saddam has spent most of his spare time lobbing chemical weapons at Kurdish villages in northern Iraq—no doubt maintaining that it was all to do with population control, which is such a worry in so many parts of the Third World. Well, it was certainly population control, no error, to the tune of somewhere in the region of 250,000 Kurds. (It was otherwise called genocide.)

From the northern Iraqi town of Zakho I set out for the self-declared capital of Kurdistan, Erbil. For $15, I manage to procure a taxi for the five hour journey, although after six years of sanctions, most cars are little more than battered old wrecks—rusty, unpainted and more importantly barely able to go more 20 kph. I'm drinking the local equivalent to whisky and watching the news on television when a message is thrust into my hands. "Urgent Appeal" the paper is titled. I read on with growing interest:

"It is for three days that our country and people are subjugated to the most aggressive foreign invasion in the border areas adjacent to Iran in the Governorate of Sulaimaniya.

"Iran is carrying out this attack with the cooperation of Jalal Talabani. We call upon all the countries throughout the world to help our people against this barbaric invasion."

It is signed, "Massoud Barzani." The next morning I dash straight for the local public relations office to see what's happening and to ask to go to the front line. Eventually, though, I hitch a lift with other newly arrived hacks. All is relatively calm, a group of peshmerga inform us. Clustered around a Toyota pick-up with a 12mm Dshk loaded on the back, they fire off a brief burst somewhere in the vague direction of the other side. We take advantage of the "calm" to pay a visit to the rival faction—but not before someone produces a white T-shirt to tie to the car's aerial.

As we cruise through no-man's land, it is not long before we see tiny figures on the distant mountain tops, and as we pull round a bend, the first checkpoint becomes visible. Slowing to a stop, a curious group of peshmerga gather around us to find out who we are. "Sahafya," or press, we say in our best Arabic. We are waved on with due decorum.

Koi Sanjaq, our first port of call, would hardly qualify for a town in the west. Its dusty alleyways and two main roads resemble a large village, but it is a typical Kurdish town with the inevitable street stalls selling everything from the tasteless locally made Aspen cigarettes, at about 15 dinars (50 cents) a packet, to ammunition webs. It is also the birthplace of Jalal Talabani. Today, however, it is crowded with Talabani's victorious militia, who have just retaken the town. The streets are jammed with hundreds of peshmerga, wearing green ribbons around their foreheads, and with Kalashnikov assault rifles slung over their shoulders. Children are shouting excitedly and waving green flags at the passing vehicles full of fighters.

We are led to the local headquarters where we meet the commander. He is none other than Kossrat Rassul, the former prime minister of Kurdistan (from happier and calmer days). He is dressed in traditional Kurdish clothing which is adorned only with a pistol at his hip. "It is," he says with a mischievous smile, "good to be a peshmerga again...politics was so boring." We ask if it will be possible to interview Mr.Talabani, and he promises to arrange it. There is, we notice, a rather substantial quantity of brand new assault rifles. Where, we muse, have these come from? "We bought them from the market," says Mr.Rassul, with an enigmatic grin, making the origins of these new weapons as clear as mud. He is not lying, (surely he wouldn't deceive the press?) and is doubtless referring to the Iranian market. We mutter sardonically *sotto voce* amongst ourselves. Otherwise, though, we have carte blanche to go where we like.

But first we are packed into Toyota Landcruisers, one for us and two for our "escort," to be driven to Jalal Talabani's mountainous camp of Zahle on the Iranian border. The drive is like a Camel Trophy race as we cruise up the massive mountainous peaks and along hairpin bends that make me shudder just looking down into the ravines far below. "So are we in Iraq or Iran?" I ask our driver. "Half-half," he replies, laughing. Talabani, when we eventually reach him, is hospitality itself as we are invited into his tent for a roast kabob supper. His manner only changes when we do the formal interview and he venomously denounces his rival, Massoud Barzani, as traitor to the Kurdish people for inviting Saddam into the region.

We head back immediately. We have to get our film back to our respective agencies as fast as possible, returning to Koi Sanjaq in the early hours without breaking down. The journey through the high mountain passes that make up Kurdistan is broken only when we stop for the periodic roadblocks. Manned by Kurdish militia, locally called peshmerga, they dress in the traditional costume: baggy trousers, waistcoats, cumberbunds, ammunition webs and AK-47s. The roads, in places, are littered with ammunition casings and the occasional burned out car or tank. From time to time I ask the driver to pull over in a village to buy a can of the universally available Coca-Cola. Sanctions there may be, but it seems that alongside weapons, Coke will always get through wherever you are. Before Erbil, however, I stop at the mountainous town of Salahudin, home to Massoud Barzani and the HQ of the Kurdistan Democratic Party. The region is in one of its sporadic peaceful lulls. I have my doubts, however, as to how long it will last.

Twenty-four hours is the answer. It is my first night in Salahudin. I am drinking *arak* and spending an unpleasant few hours in the local hotel Grotsville. But at dawn we manage to persuade a taxi driver to take us across the front line. This time, however, we are not so lucky. Our taxi driver is plainly barking mad: he drives towards the first check point as if it is the final lap of the Grand Prix. And we pay the price: the peshmerga at the check point open up on us with their AKs, although the first indication I have of this is the sight of bullets ricocheting off the tarmac around us—the sound came later. It is time for cool, calm, collected thought and fluent clear use of the local language, so I scream "Stop" as loudly as I can, as if the driver wasn't sitting right next to me, but miles away. But the bullets, to my relief, are wide, merely warning shots, and once we establish our bona fides at the check point we are waved through. No harm done, except to nerves.

It is only on arrival in the self-declared 'capital' of Iraqi Kurdistan, Erbil, that we learn that fierce fighting is taking place near the town of Dhokan. We dump our film and are almost immediately on the road again. An hour's journey and we are mingling with long columns of peshmerga marching haphazardly down the road; others are trooping up into the mountains, from where there is already the chatter of heavy machine guns. On the roadside there are two open-topped jeeps with small katusha rockets mounted on the back. Beside the jeeps the operators are peering through binoculars and range finders, muttering like mad professors. The depression of a remote control switch sends a red streak into the sky amidst eardrum shattering noise. As I watch the white mushrooms sprout on the opposite side of the valley I am foolish enough to be mildly pleased not to be on the receiving end. But, as usual, the other side are not to be outdone. A minor tit for tat ensues, the slight hiccup being that we are on the receiving end of accurate field artillery, a trifle more powerful than the katushas.

Before long the constant whistle and then scream of the shells begins to reap a grim harvest. It's the human equivalent of nine pin bowling, as the wounded are rushed off the battlefield; I decide prudence is the better part of valor. Unfortunately so do most of the fighters, and the jeep I am trying to climb into is full. But if the fighters think that retreat is an option their commanders have other ideas and promptly order them all to dismount. Even not being able to understand Kurdish the gist is clear enough: "stay and fight, it's what you're paid to do," is obviously the rather unwelcome message they are getting.

The situation soon begins to degenerate into something resembling a black comedy. From my new vantage point—a safe(ish) distance from the shelling—I watch as one group of fighters start setting up roadblocks to prevent their colleagues from retreating. But soon the men at the roadblocks are outnumbered and outgunned by those retreating. I am transfixed with admiration at the speedy way they change tack and let their colleagues through.

On my walk back to my taxi I meet a commander. He has no doubt as to what the problem is, "It is all the fault of the British government," he declares. "I see," seems to be the best response to this rather outlandish statement. "Yes," he continues, "the British, for their own perfidious reasons—old imperialist habits die hard—are supporting the other side." I promise to take the issue up with John Major, in the unlikely event of ever meeting him, before I head back for an evening's drinking at the hotel to prepare myself for the next day.

—**Roddy Scott**

IRAQ

Israel

★★

Eye For an Eye

On November 4, 1995, the blood spilled from the top of the ladder. Israeli Prime Minister Yitzhak Rabin was gunned down at point-blank range by an unrepentant 25-year-old Jewish extremist, Yigal Amir. The Jewish-Palestinian struggle came full circle, as Israel discovered the biggest threat to the peace accord may not be Hamas, the Palestinian terrorist group bent on Israel's destruction, but from right-wing Jewish extremists within its own precarious borders.

The leader of Shin Bet (the General Security Service, or GSS—Israel's secret service apparatus), known only as "K" under Israeli law, resigned after taking responsibility for a dearth of GSS precautions in preventing the assassination of Rabin. But it's interesting to note that "K" was long aware of the kinetic dangers posed by the enemy within; his college master's-degree thesis had been on the need of Israel's security forces to be prepared not only for the Palestinian threat, but also that from Israel's own hard-core religious right.

Reach Out and Kill Someone

Israel paid a Gaza businessman one million dollars and a false passport to deliver the booby-trapped cellphone to 30-year-old Yehiya Ayash in the Gaza Strip. The phone was a loaner while Ayash's phone was being repaired. Yehiya Ayash was from the West Bank and is credited with the string of suicide attacks and bombings. He did not know that the phone had high explosives in the earpiece set up to be detonated by audio signal. The security people made a call to Ayash and then triggered the explosion. It is not known whether the call made to Ayash was collect or not. The businessman is suspected to be in hiding in the States where his son lives.

Despite the Israelis' need and demand for a homeland, their Arab brethren refuse to see things eye to eye; it's more like eye for an eye. Despite the peace agreement reached with the PLO, the trading of eyes and teeth between Israel and its numerous enemies continues at unprecedented levels. The increase in terrorist threats against Israel, particularly in the wake of the historic Israeli-Palestinian pact, has turned out to be more than merely the holy smoke of bored car bombers. Although the number of anti-Israeli terrorist incidents instigated by Palestinians dropped to 14 in 1996 (compared to 33 in 1995), Palestinian extremists opposed to peace with Israel conducted four massive suicide bombings in Tel Aviv and Jerusalem in early 1996, killing 65 civilians.

America's checkbook diplomacy convinced Israel and the Palestine Liberation Organization (PLO) to recognize each other's right to exist on September 9, 1994, with the historic signing of a Declaration of Principles by Rabin and PLO Chairman Yasir Arafat. It would be fair to say that the increase in attacks, deaths and political violence is escalating due to the intense opposition to the agreement by extremist Palestinian groups such as Hamas and right-wing Jewish groups.

While most of the world has lauded the pact as the most significant peace agreement in decades, enemies of Israel and Israeli settlers in the Occupied Territories, believing they'd been bought out by the U.S.—which essentially they were— have nothing but revenge in mind for Arafat. These "enemies" include some heavy hitters. Both Abu Nidal of the Fatah Revolutionary Council and Ahmed Jibril, leader of the Popular Front for the Liberation of Palestine–General Command (PFLP-GC), have threatened to assassinate Arafat for treason. George Habash, head of the Damascus-based Popular Front for the Liberation of Palestine (PFLP), said the agreement would, ironically, increase *intifada*, the uprising on the West Bank and the Gaza Strip. He was right. Right-wing Jewish settlers and Hamas alike have launched terrorist attacks in an attempt to discredit and dissolve the agreement.

Earlier that year, on May 4, 1994, Rabin and Arafat signed a long-awaited pact allowing Palestinians limited self-rule in the Gaza Strip and Jericho. Under the agreement, Israeli forces were withdrawn from designated areas, turning enforcement over to a Palestinian police force. A week later, the first contingent of nearly 150 Palestinian police officers entered the Gaza Strip from Egypt. (The agreement calls for an eventual force of 9000 officers to police what is to become Palestine.) The new cops were greeted with flowers by inhabitants in the Strip. Not so by Hamas and other radical factions.

While I was doing a radio interview, one listener phoned in and was surprised to hear me include Israel in *DP's* list of war zones. Then, on April 10, 1996, Israel

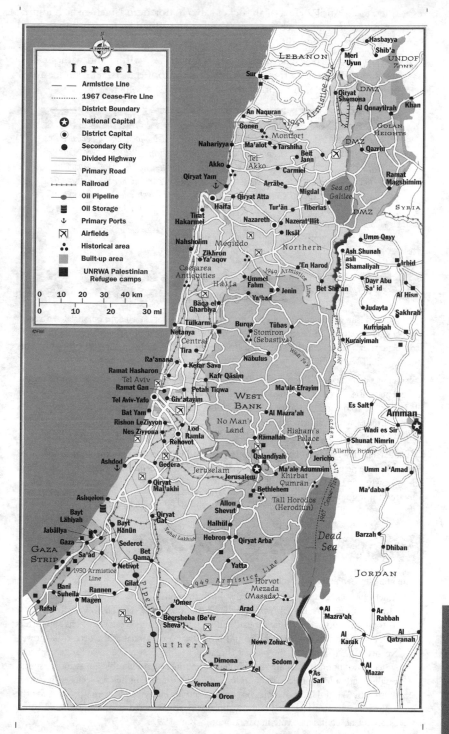

responded to an April 9 Hezbollah rocket salvo in northern Israel—which injured 40 people—by invading Lebanon. Hezbollah continued to launch hundreds of Katyusha rockets into northern Israel despite the invasion.

Despite the recent peace accords, Israel is still at war within and without. The assassination of Rabin by a right-wing Jew is sad proof that Israel is under attack by even its own people, in addition to Hamas and Hezbollah.

Gee, I wonder why they're so mad...

It seems that their friends, the Israelis, like to make life miserable for their former landlords. Palestinians must carry ID cards. Sixty thousand in Gaza and the West Bank need magnetic-striped ID cards to cross into Israel. There are literally hundreds of Israeli checkpoints that range from minor ID checks to complete strip searches. More than 25,000 Palestinians in Gaza must go through checkpoints every day to their jobs in Israel. Electric fences are being built, license plates are color-coded, and life is generally miserable for these folks concentrated in the areas forcibly occupied by Israel.

In Hebron, the word has been out for months: "Clashes start at 10 a.m. on Shalaleh Street." Rubber bullets, stones and firebombs are the order of the day in the West Bank and the Gaza Strip. And so it's been since the Middle East peace process has been all but derailed by smooth-talking "Bibi" Netanyahu.

Israel was carved out of Palestine by the British after World War II to provide a home for the Jews. The Arabs who had inhabited the region for hundreds of years were not happy. Not at all. Like most colonial border carvings, both sides are still arguing about it. What complicates the situation is that Jerusalem is a holy site for Christians, Jews and Muslims. It's a stew pot, filled with just the right spices and garnishes for one helluva long war.

The Israelis' land grabs in Egypt, Jordan, Syria and Lebanon have not made them very popular with their neighbors. Peace agreements with their once bellicose neighbors have cooled things down, but Hamas, Hezbollah and their hometown supporters of Iran, Syria and Lebanon aren't just going to forgive and forget.

Prime Minister Benjamin Netanyahu

American packaged to the max, Netanyahu is the consummate baby-kissing politician—apple pie style with a kosher twist. Maybe a little too kosher. His Likud Party leans so far to the right, soon the Mediterranean will be lapping at the West Bank. His supporters include ultra-orthodox Jews who would blow away Yasir Arafat at the drop of his towel. Netanyahu may represent the biggest threat to Middle East peace since Saddam's Scuds rained down upon Jerusalem. The problem is he's just such a likeable guy—and he speaks English with a McDonald's accent. Consequently, everything he says seems as if it were written by White House staffers, or scriptwriters in Hollywood penning a pilot for the night soap, "Golan Heights." Netanyahu was nearly indicted for corruption and barely escaped a no-confidence vote in parliament in June 1997.

The Israeli Military

Without the Israeli army, Israel would cease to exist. A tiny nation with a reputation for striking first, Israel has been on the offensive rather than the defensive for most of its short life. The armed forces total 141,000 personnel including 110,000 conscripts. The army consists of 104,000 personnel, including 88,000 conscripts and 598,000 reservists. The navy has 9000 personnel, including 3000 conscripts and 300 naval commandos and a further 10,000 reservists. Naval bases are at Haifa, Ashdod and Eilat. The air force totals 28,000, including 19,000 conscripts and a further 37,000 reservists.

The Israelis spend about 20 percent of their budget on defense. Uncle Sam kicks in another $1.8 billion a year. Troops are stationed in the occupied zones, throughout the country and along the border with Lebanon, where a security zone is controlled by the South Lebanese Army (SLA), a militia funded by Israel. The military is a big part of any Israeli's life in Israel. Military service is four years for officers, three years for men and two years for unmarried women. Annual compulsory reserve duty continues up to the age of 54 for men, 24 for single women. Because of the Palestinian *intifada*, or uprising, annual compulsory reserve duty was increased to 62 days from 42 days in 1988. Jewish and Druze citizens are conscripted, but Christian, Circassian and Muslim citizens are exempt. However, they're permitted to volunteer.

The military budget was $6.9 billion in 1994, $4.7 billion in 1990 and $4.3 billion in 1989. This includes an allocation to cover the Palestinian *intifada* in the Occupied Territories. Of Israel's 5.8 million people, more than one-sixth are Arabs. Troops are also stationed along the border with Lebanon, where a security zone is controlled by the South Lebanese Army. The security zone is designed to prevent guerrilla attacks on the country. In addition, troops are stationed on the Golan Heights. The navy patrols the eastern Mediterranean and the Red Sea. Israel has a strategic cooperation agreement with the U.S., signed in 1982.

The fear of an Arab chemical or missile attack has prompted the Israeli government to research and develop increasingly sophisticated weapons. It was the largest foreign participant in the U.S.'s Strategic Defense Initiative (SDI). The U.S. paid 80 percent of the cost of the Arrow antimissile system, which Israel can use for its own defense. In addition, the navy is developing an interceptor system capable of destroying missiles, ships and aircraft within a 12-km range. An intelligence gathering satellite is being developed. Its aim is to reduce dependence on U.S. intelligence sources. Although it has never been confirmed, Israel is believed to have the capacity to manufacture nuclear weapons.

Hezbollah

The most dangerous thorn in Israel's side is Hezbollah, the Iranian-backed Shia group that continually battles Israel on its northern border. Under the religious guidance of Sheikh Fadlallah, the most senior cleric in Lebanon, Hezbollah members are typically Shiites recruited from the various Palestinian refugee camps. The Israelis conduct numerous retaliatory attacks against these camps in revenge for Hezbollah's shelling and rocketing of Israel.

Shortly after the revolution in Iran, the country began recruiting the most fanatical Shiites to set up its first major military base outside Iran, at Zabadani in Syria. The Iranians sent in about 5000 Pasadaran to Lebanon to help the fight against Israel. A thousand of these troops fought the Israelis in the Shouf mountains. After the fighting ended, 500 Iranians stayed behind in the Bekaa (or Biqáa) Valley under the protection of Syrian forces. The Baalbak area became something of a Silicon Valley for terrorism, where a number of special-interest groups lived and trained, from Abu Nidal's headhunters to the Libyans. The Bekaa Valley became the world headquarters for terrorism in 1982. Supplied from Damascus and supported by Iran, these Iranians quickly consolidated their dominance of

Hezbollah. Soon, Hezbollah would become a federation of 13 Islamic terrorist movements (11 Shiite and two Sunni). Decisions are made by a religious council. Although Sheikh Sayyid Muhammad Hussein Fadlallah says he is not the movement's leader, it's known that his authority is absolute, even if not secured with a title. He was born in 1943 or 1944 in Najaf, Iraq, to a family originally from Lebanon. He rose to prominence after the Iranian revolution. He is an author of two books on Islam: "*Islam and the Concept of Power*" and "*Dialogue in the Koran.*" His religious preachings and his political beliefs are one and the same: Jihad is absolute and all encompassing and the war must be fought by whatever means necessary.

Hezbollah's Sayyid Abbas al-Mussawi has vowed that the terrorist group will continue its struggle until the city of Quds (Jerusalem) is liberated. Israel invaded Lebanon in April 1996 in an attempt to oust Hezbollah, who continued to pound northern Israel with rockets. The recent spat with Lebanon displaced 10 percent of the population of Lebanon, destroyed 200 homes and caused $600,000 in damage. Israel fired 11,000 shells and launched 1000 aircraft sorties. Despite the cultural and scenic attractions of the Holy Land, you could end your vacation as a puff of holy smoke. You stand a better chance of being caught in a terrorist attack in Tel Aviv than in most cities of the world.

For more information, see "The Players" section in the Southern Lebanon chapter.

Islamic Jihad

Islamic Jihad sprang from the Muslim Brotherhood in Cairo. It was founded by Dr. Fathi Shakaki, a medical student from Gaza when he felt that the Brotherhood would not take direct action against Israel. He inspired the *intifada* in December of 1987, pulling in the support of the Brotherhood, which then formed Hamas, to become a militant arm. The headquarters of the movement is in Damascus, Syria.

Shakaki was assassinated in Malta in October 1995 by Israel's covert agency, the Mossad. The new leader is Ramadan Abadallah Shallah, a British-educated teacher who has been living in hiding since the mid-'80s. His last job was teaching Islamic studies in Tampa, Florida.

Harakat al-Muqaama al-Islamiya (HAMAS)

Hamas was formed in August 1988 in the West Bank by Sheik Ahmad Yassine as competition to al-Fatah (Arafat's group) for political leadership of the 1.8 million Palestinians in the occupied zones. Yassine was a refugee in 1948 and is well connected to the Ikwhan or The Muslim Brotherhood in Egypt. He controlled all the Muslim organizations in Gaza as a holy man. When the *intifada* began he created HAMAS to lend support and provide an alternative to the PLO. In May of '89 he was charged with manslaughter and sentenced to 15 years in prison. The nearly blind, paraplegic, 61 year old Sheik Ahmed Yassine was released in October of '97 to kick start the peace process. Yassine was one of 11 children, remains poor despite the fact he handled millions of dollars in funds and lived in a three room flat in the Sabra area of Gaza City. He was jailed in 1989 and was released either because the Israelis did not want him to die in prison or as a token gesture for a botched Mossad hit on another Hamas leader.

Currently, the group is supported by about 30 percent of the Palestinians in the Gaza Strip and is the second most powerful organization behind Fatah, the PLO's military wing. The *intifada* (which began in the summer of 1988) hardened Hamas into the most ardent and powerful group defending the Palestinians' perceived right to not only self-determination, but to the destruction of Israel. Part of their success strategy is a decentralized structure based on the Muslim Brotherhood, a popular Islamic fundamentalist group. Hamas has been having its lunch handed to it by Shin Bet (the Israeli Secret Police). In August of '95, Shin Bet held a news conference to gloat over the capture of Abdel Nasser Issa, 27, and his apprentice, considered to be the head bomb-maker for

Hamas. Both men credited Yehiya Ayash—aka "The Engineer"—as the man who taught them their bomb-making skills in the Gaza Strip. Issa is accused of recruiting and transporting suicide bombers. The arrest also confirmed that the group's spiritual mentor, Sheik Izzadine Khalil, is now in Damascus. Khalil was deported from Israel in 1992.

But in a turn of events for Hamas, Ayash was assassinated by Shin Bet in January 1996 in a daring cellular phone explosion in Gaza City. Most Israelis rejoiced, while others pondered how many Palestinians Ayash had taught his trade to and how many of those would employ their new skills to avenge their mentor's death.

For now, there are plenty of angry 14- to 20-year-olds to toss rocks, pull triggers and vaporize themselves for Hamas. The only university these kids have a chance of attending is the ultra-radical Islamic University of Gaza.

Hamas is short for *Harakat al-Muqaama al-Islamiya* (Islamic Resistance Movement), but also means zeal or enthusiasm in Arabic. Hamas members are not the well-trained military terrorists of al-Fatah but a youthful cadre of young Palestinians mostly enlisted from the poorest parts of the Occupied Territories. Most believe that they will find salvation and martyrdom by destroying Israel. Every member is sworn to destroy Israel and to create a new Islamic state based on the Koran. Initially, their campaign of rock throwing turned to stabbing Israeli citizens, including teenage schoolchildren. After Hamas killed five Israeli Defense Force members, 415 Hamas members were exiled to southern Lebanon by the Israelis, provoking an international outcry. In the seven years of *intifada*, Israelis have killed more than 2000 Palestinians. Hamas has slain more than 575 collaborators and more than 160 Israelis. The attacks have escalated in their frequency and nature, including the recent bombing of a Tel Aviv bus. Hamas is expected to continue to terrorize Israelis into the foreseeable future, and Yasir Arafat and his Palestinian police will be expected to control Hamas, thereby pitting Muslim against Muslim to maintain peace with the Jews. The Jordanian chapter seems to be the most hawkish of the bunch and was credited with the July 1995 bombing in Ramat Gan.

Hamas is loosing its support among the Palestinians and looking to mend fences with the PLO. They have an office in Tehran where they get financial support and receive military training from Hezbollah.

Izz ad-Din al Qassam Brigade

The military wing of Hamas is the smallest section of the group, numbering only a few hundred young men. But the group's political followers number in the tens of thousands. Hamas, like Hezbollah, has created schools, clinics, mosques and financial support systems for the poor, widows and orphans. The group even sponsors a soccer team.

It is important to note that the Qassam Brigade and militant Palestinians will continue to attack, murder and terrorize Israelis while the political structuring continues. Volunteers to the Qassam Brigade are trained in Sudanese camps and in Southern Lebanon by Hezbollah. The Iranians provide more than US$30 million a year, including use of a radio station in southern Lebanon that broadcasts messages of revolution into Israel. The Hamas base of power is in the West Bank and Gaza Strip. They have managed to create an alliance of the 10 Palestinian groups including the PLFP and the DFLP. The leadership of Hamas is young and highly educated. Hamas runs information offices out of Amman, Jordan (Ibrahim Ghosha and Mohammed Nazzal); Tehran; Lebanon (Mustapha Kanua), and Khartoum, Sudan(Mohammed Siam). Their U.S. rep (Moussa Abu Marzouk) operates out of Damascus, Syria.

Because of Hamas' political strength and the support it receives from Palestinians, it finds a ready source of financing from Muslim and non-Muslim wallets alike. America is an important source of funding for Hamas. It is alleged by the Israelis that the leadership and central control of Hamas is actually in the United States, an accusation once dismissed by the FBI but now being studied very seriously.

Organizations considered supportive of Hamas in the U.S. are the following:

The United Association for Studies and Research in Springfield, Virginia
The Islamic Association for Palestine in Dallas, Texas
The Monitor and the Al-Zaituni (Olive Tree in Arabic)
The Islamic Committee for Palestine
Muslim Youth League
Mostazafan Foundation in New York
Muslim Students' Association in U.S. and Canada
Al-Da'wa (the Call)

Yasir Arafat and the PLO (Palestine Liberation Organization)

The PLO began in 1964 as a Palestinian nationalist umbrella organization dedicated to the establishment of an independent Palestinian state. After the 1967 Arab-Israeli war, control of the PLO went to the most dominant of the various *fedayeen* militia groups, Yasir Arafat's al-Fatah. In 1969, Arafat became chairman of the PLO's executive committee, a position he still holds. In the early 1980s, the PLO became fragmented into several contending groups but remains the preeminent Palestinian organization. The United States considers the Palestine Liberation Organization to be an umbrella organization that includes several constituent groups and individuals holding differing views on terrorism. At the same time, U.S. policy accepts that elements of the PLO have advocated, carried out, or accepted responsibility for acts of terrorism. PLO chairman Arafat publicly renounced terrorism in December 1988 on behalf of the PLO. The United States considers that all PLO groups, including al-Fatah, Force 17, Hawari Group, PLF and the PFLP, are bound by Arafat's renunciation of terrorism. The U.S.-PLO dialogue was suspended after the PLO failed to condemn the May 30, 1990, PLF attack on Israeli beaches. PLF head Abu Abbas left the PLO executive committee in September 1991; his seat was filled by another PLF member.

In the early 1970s, several groups affiliated with the PLO carried out numerous international terrorist attacks. By the mid-1970s, under international pressure, the PLO claimed it would restrict attacks to Israel and the Occupied Territories. Several terrorist attacks were later performed by groups affiliated with the PLO/al-Fatah—including the Hawari group, the Palestine Liberation Front (PLF) and Force 17—against targets inside and outside of Israel.

Formerly the No. 1 bad boy of terrorism, Yasir Arafat and his fashion-conscious wife have gone mainstream. It remains to be seen whether he can be as powerful in peace as he was in war. Arafat's administrative skills are primitive at best, and his handling of economic issues in the autonomous zones of Jericho and the Gaza Strip have come under fire—the protests fueled by Arafat's own assertions that the peace accords would bring greater prosperity to Palestinians. Skeptical investors are staying away from the Gaza Strip, at least until the former terrorist charts an economic course for the newly liberated Palestine.

Arafat's group al-Fatah trained more terrorists and freedom fighters than any other group in the 1960s and 1970s. Running the government of the West Bank, Gaza and Jericho may be more of a challenge than the terrorist battle he fought to get to this position. As Israel withdraws its occupying troops, it will be up to Arafat's group to provide security and management of these impoverished, undeveloped and primitive areas. More importantly, he will be expected to protect the Jewish settlers (or occupiers, from the Palestinian point of view) from Hamas.

Perhaps wishful thinking, but Arafat feels that economic aid will undermine the Hamas' zeal and build a lasting peace. He doesn't have much choice; a forceful attempt to restrain Hamas would plunge Gaza and Jericho into civil war. Now he must battle two enemies instead of one. In the meantime, Arafat continues to tiptoe around continued Hamas bus bombings in Tel Aviv and Shin Bet assassinations of Palestinians in his own new backyard.

Bit Players

Anu Nidal

Nidal (real name: Sabry al-Banna) was born in Jaffato a wealthy family (like all good terrorists), His dad had 13 wives and he was one of 24 kids. No wonder he had to raise a little hell to get attention. He worked in Saudi Arabia where he joined the Baathist Party. He got involved with Arafat's al-Fatah group when it was formed in Kuwait in 1959. He was sent to open a PLO office in Khartoum in 1969 and was tossed out for recruiting Palestinian students to the cause. He then tried the same thing in Baghdad for the PLO and did better. The Iraqis thought that Arafat was a wussy and that big bad Nidal should be the PLO chief so they supported his efforts to run the Iraqi PLO, which included a radio station, newspaper and student scholarships. He became a tool of the Iraqis and a thorn in Arafat's side as he invented Hollywood like cover names (Black September, Black June, Al Aqab, etc.). He split from Arafat (who was happy to have a little bit of Palestine instead of demanding total expulsion of the Jews) in 1973 and actually tried to assassinate Arafat with death squads. His attempt to kill the Israeli ambassador in London triggered the Israeli invasion of Lebanon in the early '80s which triggered a long civil war. Nidal is semi-retired now, but is an example of how much damage nations can do with a classic bad boy terrorist toy.

Popular Front for the Liberation of Palestine (PFLP)

This group of about 800 Palestinians follows a Marxist-Leninist doctrine and disagrees with Arafat's deal with the Israelis. The PFLP lost a lot of steam when Wadi-Haddad was taken out in 1978. Qaddafi and Assad provide most of the folding green for this hard-line group who is based in Syria and Lebanon. For more information, see "The Players" section in the Lebanon chapter.

Popular Front for the Liberation of Palestine-General Command (PFLP-GC)

PFLP-GC's leader Ahmad Jabril regarded, and still does, Habash's PFLP as a bunch of wimps, so he and his men split in 1968 to focus on killing and maiming, while Habash employed just a little less violence to achieve his ends. Because Jabril was a captain in the Syrian army when Assad was minister of defense at the time Israel took the Golan Heights, it's understandable why the PFLP-GC is tighter with Syria than latex on an aerobics instructor. The PFLP-GC is headquartered in Damascus. Iran chips in when they run short of funds.

The group's sensationalist suicide attacks, employing everything from hang gliders to hot-air balloons, has given its "airline" the fewest number of members of any frequent flyer program found in Palestine. Although not as large as the vanilla-flavored PFLP, the PFLP-GC is still a major threat to Israelis. For more information, see "The Players" section in the Lebanon chapter.

Palestine Liberation Front (PLF)

This is a break-away faction of the PFLP-GC (which is a break-away faction of the PFLP, which is a break-away faction of the PLO). If this sounds like a scene from Monty Python's "*Life of Brian*," you're not far off. The PLF is led by Abu Abbas, or Muhammad Abbas, who usually hangs out in Libya with his buddy Qaddafi or in the Bekaa Valley. Abbas' group is tiny, possibly nonexistent. Their most famous job was the attack on the *Achille Lauro* and the less than admirable killing of wheelchair-bound Leon Klinghoffer. They are estimated to have 50 members. For more information, see "The Players" section in the Southern Lebanon chapter.

The Palestine Islamic Jihad (PIJ)

A small group founded in the '70s that seeks the creation of a Islamic Palestinian State. Based in Syria, backed by Iran they carry out suicide attacks against Israelis in the West Bank, Gaza Strip and Israel. They have threatened to attack U.S. interests in Jordan.

Democratic Front for the Liberation of Palestine (DFLP)

The Hawatmeh faction does not go along with the Arafat-brokered peace and continues its opportunistic attacks and raids. For more information, see "The Players" section in the Lebanon chapter.

Right Wing Groups: Kach/Kahane Chai

Kach was founded by rabbi Meir Kahane and Kahane Chai (Kahane Lives) was founded by his son Binyamin Kahane. These groups are considered terrorist groups by the Israeli government. There are random incidents of far right-wing Israelis and external Jewish groups such as the Kahane Chai and Kach, as well as individuals striking against Palestinians and moderate Jews. These groups present little danger to Americans.

JDL

The JDL consists of about 150 hotheads who were implicated in a number of bombings in the U.S. back in the early '80s and late '70s.

Ben Gurion International Airport is 20 km from the center of Tel Aviv. Taxis are common and a bus service runs every 15 minutes. A passport, an onward or return ticket and proof of sufficient funds are required. A three-month visa may be issued for no charge upon arrival and may be renewed. Anyone who has been refused entry or experienced difficulties with his/her visa status during a previous visit can obtain information from the Israeli embassy or nearest consulate regarding the advisability of attempting to return to Israel. Arab-Americans who have overstayed their tourist visas during previous visits to Israel or in the Occupied Territories can expect, at a minimum, delays at ports of entry (including Ben Gurion Airport) and the possibility of being denied entry. To avoid these problems, such persons may apply for permission to enter at the nearest Israeli embassy or consulate before traveling. For further entry information, travelers may contact the following:

Embassy of Israel

3514 International Drive, N.W.
Washington, D.C. 20008
☎ *(202) 364-5500*

Or contact the nearest Israeli consulate general in Los Angeles, San Francisco, Miami, Atlanta, Chicago, New Orleans, Boston, New York, Philadelphia or Houston.

The major airport is Ben Gurion International Airport with a smaller civilian airport in Tel Aviv. There are also airports in Jerusalem, Haifa, Eilat, Herzlya, Mahanayim and Sodom. A new airport at Eilat is under construction and will replace the old one. National airline El Al operates international flights to Europe, North America and some African countries.

Israel has a modern road system, although it abounds with crazy drivers. Road accidents have been on the increase in the last decade, due mainly to deteriorating road conditions. There are approximately three fatalities for every 100 million km traveled. Emergency rule has been lifted in Batman, Bingol and Bitlis provinces.

Hassles with Police

Israel has strict security measures that will piss off visitors. Prolonged questioning and detailed searches take place at the time of entry and/or departure at all points of entry to Israel or the Occupied Territories. American citizens with Arab surnames can expect extra-close scrutiny at Ben Gurion Airport and the Allenby Bridge from Jordan. Cameras or video equipment are always suspect and items commonly carried by travelers—even toothpaste, shaving cream and cosmetics—may be confiscated or destroyed for security reasons, especially at the Allenby Bridge. During searches and questioning, access may be denied to U.S. consular officers, lawyers or family members. Should questions arise at the Allenby Bridge, U.S. citizens can telephone the U.S. Consulate General in Jerusalem for assistance at ☎ *[972] (02) 253-288*. If questions arise at Ben Gurion Airport, U.S. citizens can phone the U.S. embassy in Tel Aviv at ☎ *[972] (03) 517-4338*.

Broadcasting and the Press

Journalists are required to submit all relevant items to the censor's office for approval before transmitting them abroad or issuing them in the local media. The occupied territories are officially open to media coverage, but local commanders may close specific areas for a limited period "for operational reasons." Since the *intifada* began in the occupied West Bank and Gaza Strip in 1988, censorship, closures, arrests, detentions and distribution restrictions have muzzled Palestinian newspapers; those that can still publish are virtually unable to use original material. Various measures were also enforced on newspapers in Israel and on foreign media correspondents, most of whom are Israeli citizens. The army has sometimes imposed news blackouts. The media has regularly complained about security forces personnel impersonating journalists in order to obtain information about the Palestinian *intifada*, and putting journalists' lives at risk.

Israel Television and Israel Radio are owned by the government and run by the Israel Broadcasting Authority (IBA). Its central committee members oversee programming. Israel TV broadcasts on one national channel in Hebrew and Arabic, funded by viewer license fees and, more recently, by commercial sponsorship.

The Occupied Territories

Following the killings of Palestinians in Hebron on February 25, 1994, the Israeli government closed the West Bank and Gaza Strip. The West Bank has since been partially reopened. Travel restrictions may be reimposed with little or no advance notification, and curfews placed on cities or towns in the Occupied Territories may be extended or, if lifted, reimposed. Palestinian demonstrations in the West Bank and the Gaza Strip have led to violent confrontations between the demonstrators and Israeli authorities, resulting in the wounding or death of some participants. Demonstrations and similar incidents can occur without warning. Stone-throwing and other forms of protest can escalate. Violent incidents such as stabbings have occurred. Vehicles are regularly damaged.

Northern Israel

See "Southern Lebanon."

East Jerusalem

Although the Department of State had warned all U.S. citizens against traveling to East Jerusalem, the West Bank and Gaza, the consular section of the U.S. consulate general at *27 Nablus Road, East Jerusalem*, remains open. Traveling by public or private transportation in parts of East Jerusalem less frequented by tourists, however, remains dangerous. If persons must travel to other areas of East Jerusalem, including the Old City, or to the West Bank, they may consult with the U.S. consulate general in Jerusalem, and in the case of travel to the Gaza Strip, with the U.S. embassy in Tel Aviv, for current information on the advisability of such travel.

Suicide Bombers' homes

Two months after "The Engineer" was cellphone-whacked by the Israelis, the Israeli army blew up his family home in the West Bank village of Rafat in March 1996, sending a clear message to suicide bombers and other Hamas volunteers that anyone considering blowing their own viscera into the heavens in the name of Allah may want to consider the fate of their families before pulling the pin. Would-be jihad martyrs, take note: After you kiss your own good-bye, the Mossad will make quite certain your kids, mom and pop, and other relatives quickly join you in Mohammed's tent in the sky. Or at least the Israelis will blow up their houses.

Buses

One and a half million Israelis use the bus every day, almost 25 percent of the population. There have been nine suicide attacks on buses since April 1994, resulting in 67 people killed. Injuries run at two to three times the death rate. One American tourist was among the dead. Violent incidents also involved bus stops. The U.S. embassy is advising its employees and American citizens in Israel to avoid use of public transportation, especially buses and bus stops. This restriction does not apply to tour buses. Although Israelis must take the bus, only thrill seekers and cheapskates need expose themselves to what is Israel's most dangerous form of transportation.

Driving

Traffic fatalities increased from 387 in 1985 to 415 in 1986 and to about 500 in 1987. In 1986 there were 1.5 motor vehicles involved in road accidents per 1 million km traveled. There are 3.2 fatalities for every 100 million km traveled.

Rocket Attacks

Rocket attacks from Hezbollah positions in Lebanese territory can occur without warning close to the northern border of Israel.

Land Mines

In the Golan Heights, land mines in many areas have not been clearly marked or fenced. Walk only on established roads or trails.

Being arrested in the West Bank and Gaza Strip

U.S. citizens arrested or detained in the West Bank or Gaza Strip on suspicion of security offenses often are not permitted to communicate with consular officials, lawyers or family members in a timely manner during the interrogation period of their case. Youths who are over the age of 14 have been detained and tried as adults. The U.S. embassy is not normally notified of the arrests of Americans in the West Bank by Israeli authorities, and access to detainees is frequently delayed.

Medical care and facilities throughout Israel are generally excellent. In 1987, there were 153 hospitals, including 60 private hospitals, with 27,500 beds. Israel has one of the highest doctor-patient ratios in the world, about one doctor for every 339 patients. Travelers can find information in English about emergency medical facilities and after-hours pharmacies in the *Jerusalem Post* newspaper. Water is normally safe to drink, but bottled water is a better choice for the cautious. Tap water outside the main towns is not safe for drinking.

Israel is a small country, about 20,700 square km (7992 square mi.), that forcibly occupies the Golan Heights (annexed from Syria in 1981; 1150 square km, 444 square mi.), the West Bank (annexed from Jordan; 5878 square km, 2270 square mi.) and the Gaza Strip (363 square km, 140 square mi.). The territories currently occupied and administered by Israel are the West Bank, Gaza Strip, Golan Heights and East Jerusalem. The Israeli Ministry of Defense administers the Occupied Territories of the West Bank and Gaza Strip.

The population includes 635,000 Muslims, 105,000 Christians (almost all Arabs) and 78,000 Druze. Although Israel claims Jerusalem as its capital, the claim—especially to East Jerusalem, annexed in 1967—is disputed by most countries. The currency is the new *shekel* (IS), with 100 *agorot* to the *shekel*. The weather is arid, warm and mild most of the year with hot days and cool evenings. Because of its higher elevation, Jerusalem is quite cool, and even cold in the winter. In Tel Aviv and along the coast, the weather is more humid with warmer nights.

The Jewish Sabbath, from Friday dusk until Saturday dusk, is rigorously observed. Stores close on Friday by 2 p.m. and do not open again until Sunday morning. Most cinemas and restaurants are closed on Friday night. In most cities during the Sabbath there is no public transport (except for taxis), postal service or banking service. It is considered a violation of the Sabbath (Saturdays) to smoke in public places, such as restaurants and hotels. The same is true on the six main Jewish religious holidays.

Jewish religious laws *(Kashrut)* prohibit the mixing of milk products and meat at the same meal. Kashrut is strictly enforced in hotels. Because of this, some restaurants serve only fish and dairy dishes while others serve only meat dishes. Pork is banned under religious laws, but some restaurants serve it, listing it euphemistically as white steak.

Banks are open from 8:30 a.m. to 12:30 p.m., and from 2 p.m. to 6:30 p.m. on Sunday, Tuesday and Thursday, and from 8:30 a.m. to 12:30 p.m. on Monday, Wednesday and Friday. Businesses are open from 8:30 a.m. to 7:30 p.m. Sunday to Thursday; some are open 8:30 a.m. to 2:30 p.m. on Fridays. Government offices are open from 7:30 a.m. to 4 p.m. Sunday through Thursday.

Embassy and Consulate Locations

U.S. Embassy

71 Hayarkon Street
Tel Aviv, Israel

U.S. mailing address
PSC 98, Box 100
APO AE 09830
☎ *[972] (3) 517-4338*

U.S. Consulate General

27 Nablus Road
Jerusalem

U.S. mailing address
PSC 98, Box 100
APO AE 09830
☎ *[972] (2) 253-288 (via Israel)*
☎ *[972] (2) 253-201 (after hours)*

Useful Addresses

Ministry of Communications

P.O. Box 29515
Tel Aviv
☎ *[972] (3) 5198247*
FAX [972] (2) 5198109

Ministry of Tourism

24 King George Street
P.O. Box 1018
Jerusalem 91000
☎ *[972] (2) 754811*
FAX [972] (2) 253407 or (2) 250890

07/30/1997	Fifteen people are killed in two suicide bomb blasts in Jerusalem.
04/10/1996	Israel invades Hamas positions and cities within Lebanon after a Hezbollah rocket attack on northern Israel injures 40 people.
11/04/1996	Prime Minister Yitzhak Rabin assassinated by right-wing extremist.
10/11/1994	The Palestine Liberation Organization (PLO) Central Council approves Chairman Yasir Arafat's peace deal with Israel by a vote of 63 to eight, with 11 members abstaining or absent.
09/23	Yom Kippur.
09/13/1994	Israel and the Palestine Liberation Organization sign a peace agreement in Washington, D.C., outlining a plan for Palestinian self-rule in the Israeli Occupied Territories.
09/09/1993	The PLO and Israel sign a mutual recognition agreement.
12/17/1992	More than 400 suspected members of Hamas are forcibly expelled from Israel into Lebanon, following the kidnap-murder of an Israeli border policeman. The expellees are refused entry into Lebanon and forced to camp in the Israeli-controlled security zone in south Lebanon.
12/16/1991	The United Nations General Assembly repeals the 1975 resolution which said Zionism is a form of racism.
05/15/1991	Palestinian Struggle Day.
01/15/1991	Abu Iyad, the second-ranking PLO leader, and two other high-ranking PLO officials are assassinated by a guard suspected of working for the Abu Nidal Organization (ANO).
10/08/1990	Eighteen Arabs died during clashes with police at the Temple Mount religious site.

ISRAEL

05/20/1990	A lone Israeli gunman kills eight Arab laborers in Rishon le Ziyyon, south of Tel Aviv. Nine workers are injured. The gunman was identified as a discharged Israeli soldier.
07/28/1989	Israeli commandos seize Shaykh Obeid from a village in southern Lebanon and detain him in Israel on allegations of involvement in terrorist activity on behalf of Hezbollah.
12/09/1987	Date used to mark the beginning of the *intifada*, or uprising on the West Bank and the Gaza Strip.
10/01/1985	The Israeli Air Force bombs the headquarters of the Palestine Liberation Organization (PLO) in Tunis.
05/17/1983	Israel signs an accord with Lebanon for the withdrawal of Israeli troops from most of south Lebanon.
06/06/1982	Israel invades Lebanon.
06/04/1982	Israeli planes bomb Beirut.
03/26/1979	Egyptian-Israeli peace treaty.
09/17/1978	Camp David accords signed.
03/16/1978	Israeli forces invade Lebanon.
07/04/1976	The Israeli raid on Entebbe airport in Uganda freeing 103 hostages from a hijacked Israeli airliner.
10/06/1973	The Yom Kippur War begins.
09/06/1972	Palestinian Black September terrorists massacre Israeli athletes at the Munich Olympics.
05/30/1972	Members of the Japanese Red Army (JRA) kill 26 people in a massacre at Lod Airport.
02/21/1970	Suspected members of the PFLP-GC place a bomb on a Swissair passenger jet enroute from Zurich to Tel Aviv, resulting in the death of all 47 passengers.
07/22/1968	Members of the Popular Front for the Liberation of Palestine (PFLP) hijacked an El Al flight enroute to Tel Aviv and forced it to land in Algiers. The attack marks the first aircraft hijacking by a Palestinian group. The hijackers are said to have believed Israeli General Ariel Sharon was on the flight. The passengers and crew are detained by Algeria for six weeks.
06/05/1967	The Six Day War ends.
05/31/1967	Israeli troops capture East Jerusalem in the Six Day War.
01/01/1964	Fatah Day. The Palestine Liberation Organization (PLO) is founded at a meeting in Jerusalem.
04/14/1949	Holocaust Memorial Day.
03/21/1949	Palestinian Solidarity Day. Arab solidarity day with the Palestinian people against Israel.
05/14/1948	Israel is proclaimed a state, as the British mandate in Palestine expires. Arab armies launch attacks on Israel immediately following the proclamation.

05/14/1948   The first Arab-Israeli war begins shortly after the State of Israel was proclaimed.

05/07/1948   Israeli Independence Day, as observed by Arabs in the Occupied Territories.

11/02/1917   Anniversary of the Balfour Declaration, which promised a Jewish homeland in Palestine. Demonstrations in the Occupied Territories and the Gaza Strip area have occurred on this date.

Kurdistan
★★★★

Blowing Your Kurds Away

Kurdistan is not a country, but not because it shouldn't be. When the Ottoman Empire disbanded at the end of World War I, the Western Allies created the country of Kurdistan in 1920 with the Treaty of Sevres. They changed their minds in 1923, when they decided it was more expedient to suck up to Turkey and make it an anti-communist buffer zone against Russia. However, the 1923 treaty of Lausanne did provide for basic recognition and rights, but this has been largely ignored by Turkey and Iraq.

As many as 12 to 15 million Kurds live in Turkey (a third of Turkey's members of parliament and foreign ministers have a Kurdish background), 5 to 7 million live in Iran, 1.5 million live in Syria and 4 million live in Iraq. There are approximately a million Kurds in Russia. There are also Kurds in the Caucasus region. The Kurds are aligned along tribal loyalties with the KDP being led by the Barzani tribe under Massud Barzani. His grandfather Ahmad Barzani led the initial uprising against Iraq in 1931, which was continued by his son Mustafa Barzani in 1961. In 1992, after the U.S. created a safe haven in northern Iraq, the two opposing Kurdish parties finished in a dead heat, creating the constant tit-for-tat

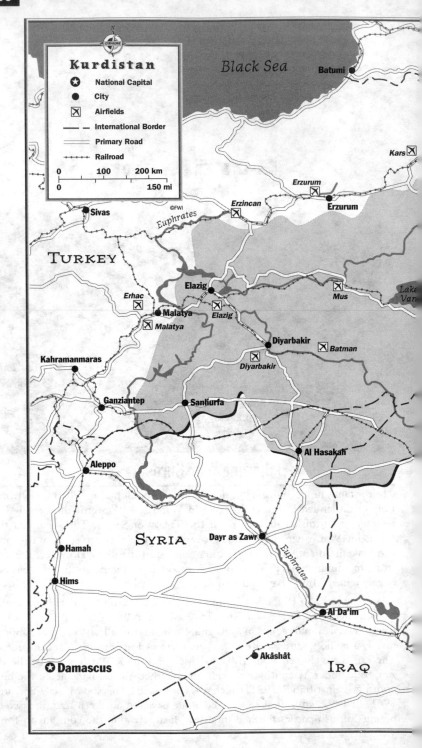

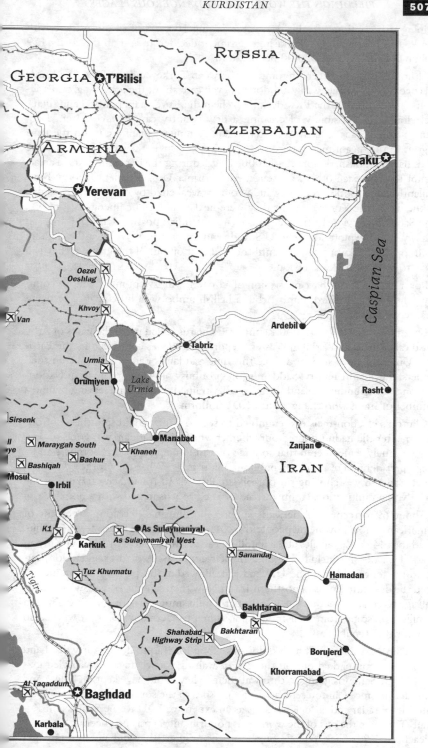

sniping that continues to this day. After waging 10 years of all-out warfare with the PKK, someone in the Turkish government decided to add up the cost: $179 billion dollars and over 22,000 people dead.

Although there has been ongoing war between Turkey and the PKK, the Kurds as a people do not necessarily condone or even care about the terrorist group's actions. The actions of the PKK do little to help the Kurds gain political and financial clout. The possibility of creating a new country carved out of Iran, Iraq, Turkey and Syria is as likely as Saddam taking a military planning job at the Pentagon. In the meantime, warfare and fear grip eastern Turkey. The army and the PKK have demolished more than 2000 villages during the last eight years in an attempt to erase each other's presence. After former U.S. President George Bush gallantly came to the aid of Kuwait, a country weakened by too many late nights at the disco, the Kurds thought they were next in line to be liberated from big, bad Saddam. Obviously, the Iraqi Kurds never studied postwar Eastern European history or oil exploration. The U.S. did send them bread. We save the military stuff for rich backward people; until they get that oil out of the ground, they will have to be poor backward people.

For now, the Kurds have possession of a frozen, windswept mountainous country. The capital of Kurdistan is Arbil, a hellish limbo with little chance of being granted independence.

On August 31, 1996, 40,000 Republican Guards rolled up to the gates of Arbil (also called Irbel and Erbil in Western reports). Arbil was controlled by the Patriotic Union of Kurdistan, and since this time Saddam's elite soldiers were issued bullets, they left in a hurry. Saddam's folks got busy blowing up the Iraqi National Congress, rounding up and shooting CIA-trained flunkies and leaving behind a number of Iraqis who changed into KDP uniforms.

Clinton's election-meisters scrambled to see how they could spin this confrontation, after Bill hadn't figured out whether whomping Saddam was good or bad. They vaguely remembered that footage of cruise missiles, stealth bombers and a stern president were good for public opinion polls. What they forgot was back then, Saddam was choking off our oil supply and Bush had Schwarzkopf in the field with a multinational army instead of Dick Morris in bed with a hooker.

About 69 percent of Americans supported Clinton's decision; 0 percent of Americans know how many people the cost of a cruise missile can feed. (*DP* figured that 44 cruise missiles at $1.5 million each translates to $113.20 per Kurd in Iraq. That doesn't include building or delivery costs. A mild exaggeration, but appropriate, considering the UN had just allowed a $50-per-Kurd allowance to feed the destitute Kurds in northern Iraq.) Now they can sell Tomahawk parts for salvage to scrape together the $3500 per family smugglers are charging Kurdish families to escape from their mountainous hell to Germany. Darn, it worked so well for the Republicans.

Saddam wasn't fazed a bit. It didn't take long for Iraq to do the dirty deed and they were soon parked out on the desert, waiting for whatever newfangled gizmos Uncle Sam was going to throw at them. They could have kept on killing and plundering since Clinton sent his cruise missiles to the south, knocking out unrelated Iraqi radar and air defense sites as an expensive IOU to the Saudis and Kuwait. This time the rest of the world was not drinking Pepsi and cheering from the bleachers. With Slick Willie's finger on the trigger, they did not want to get caught in the crossfire (political or military)—so most European, Asian and Arab neighbors publicly dissed Bill while checking to make sure their Swiss bank accounts were OK. Meanwhile, the U.S. spent a lot of taxpayers' money by launching B-52s from Louisiana to Guam and then to the Persian Gulf to launch 13 cruise missiles. Those salvos nearly matched another 14 Tomahawks from U.S. warships in the Persian Gulf. The next day, the military used the bizarre term of "mopping up" to justify the launching of another 17 Tomahawks to take out the 15 air defense centers in the south.

The U.S. did not do anything to protect the Kurds or to defend the "safe haven" they created for Kurds after the Gulf War. A few days later, Saddam and his new Kurdish buddies captured the rest of Kurdistan.

The intrigue came to light when the papers revealed that Saddam had wiped out a 6-year, $20 million CIA operation to back Barzani and his KDP. The goal was to support a grass-roots uprising against Saddam run by a handful of CIA agents with dozens of trained (yes, you guessed it) terrorists to overthrow or assassinate Saddam. Barzani decided to ditch Uncle Sam and called in Uncle Saddam instead, with much more effective results.

The outlook for the Kurds is dim since their demands for a new homeland would not only remove a major chunk of Turkey but a major portion of Iran, Iraq and Syria as well. They also run up against Turkey's goal of uniting the various peoples within its border and the call for peaceful and political settlements to rights, but they maintain a hard line on secessionist groups. Even if Turkey were to be conciliatory, many people forget that the PKK is waging a battle on four fronts (not including its terrorist activities in Europe) and has little chance of convincing the hard-line governments of Iraq, Iran and Syria to give them concessions.

The PKK targets the local population and is on the run from the Turkish Special Ops teams. The PKK controls the countryside at night, and the government controls the major cities. There is continual warfare on a daily basis, as the Turkish government seeks to annihilate the 10,000 or so ground troops the PKK has in the country. The PKK shows no quarter to Kurds they think are sympathizers, yet are surprisingly lenient with foreigners they kidnap. Of the 20 or so foreigners they kidnap in a year, all are released without harm.

In 1993, the Kurds began a sporadic bombing campaign in Istanbul and Antalya designed to scare off Western tourists. In Europe in 1993, the Kurds created global publicity when they executed a series of terrorist activities against Turkish embassies and businesses (airline offices, banks and travel agents). Germany, with a Turkish community of more than 2 million (a quarter of them Kurds), was understandably nervous about becoming a battleground and quickly banned 36 Kurdish political organizations.

France also banned two Kurdish political groups, and Great Britain is trying to figure out how to stop the regular extortion of Turkish emigrants and/or their businesses by the Kurds.

Their efforts have been successful in creating sympathy for a people deposed. In our own humble opinion, one of the most powerful opinion shapers was Coskun's photos of the Kurdish refugees fighting for bread featured in news magazines around the world, including *Time*. The problem is that there is little even a sympathetic person can do to help the Kurds.

While the U.S. turns a blind eye to the PKK atrocities in Turkey, it is actively using the Kurds to help destabilize Hussein in Iraq. "Kurdistan" was effectively created when the U.S and Turkish military (Operation Provide Comfort) created a safe zone for the 1.5 million Kurds displaced by Hussein's attempt to eliminate the Kurds. During the three-year military occupation by the Americans, they managed to form two major political parties from the diverse group of Kurds. There were actually democratic elections held among the area's 3.5 million residents in 1992. The area is essentially divided into east and west. The west is controlled by the Kurdish Democratic Party (KDP) and the east by the Patriotic Union of Kurdistan (PUK), led by Jalal Talabani, with the center being the regional capital of Arbil.

In May of 1994, fighting broke out between the two parties after a PUK leader was assassinated. The two parties then decided to settle their differences without the aid of a ballot box. Using anti-aircraft guns and other heavy weaponry, they duked it out in the central mountain town of Shaqlawa. About 200 people have been killed in a war that was conducted while the leader of the PUK was in Damascus.

In Iran, the Kurds are found in the area known as Kordestan. Their language is banned and teaching of Kurdish history and culture is forbidden. After World War II, their bid for a homeland was put down and the leader was executed. After Khomeini came to power, the ayatollah bombed their villages and camps, creating a lasting insurgency that is active to this day. There are about 200,000 soldiers keeping the lid on Kordestan today, and Kurdistan Democratic party (KDPI) guerillas attack military centers on a regular basis. Iranian government agents have assassinated KDPI leaders in Austria and Germany. The leader of the KDPI is Mustafa Hejri, who is based in Iraqi Kurdistan and seems to get some support from Baghdad.

There is also a left-wing group, the Komala, which is supported by the government of Iraq.

Kurdistan is a mish-mash of political and tribal angers whose guerrillas tuck themselves in remote pockets of someone else's country between hit-and-run attacks on the Turkish army and on each other. Iraqi Kurds established a de facto state of Kurdistan in northern Iraq after the Gulf War but don't send away for any stamps just yet. Some 28,000 people have died since the PKK began its war for autonomy in southeast Turkey in 1984. Hundreds continue to die as rival Kurdish factions battle it out with each other and the governments whose land they sit on.

The United States/CIA/Iraqi National Congress

Bill Clinton OK'd a $20 million in covert action to overthrow Saddam from the north. The actual figure ended up being $200 million. Small change compared to a stealth program but at least you get titanium scrap if you buy a an airplane. All Uncle Sam got was a black eye and a lot of well meaning Iraqis killed. Saddam outfoxed Slick Willie and killed or captured most of the U.S. Kurdish operatives in his September 1996 raid on Arbil. Kurdistan's biggest chance is if Uncle Sam officially muscles a big chunk of Saddam's real estate for the Kurds. The problem is you have civil war the second the rival groups scramble for domination.

The CIA started the INC in the SAS hotel in Vienna, Austria in 1992 with a $15 million contribution. The idea was to combine all the anti Saddam groups under one organization. Ahmed Chalabi, a Jordanian Shiite and former Iraqi banker, was picked to run the INC.

Two dozen CIA agents set up offices in Arbil on Ain-Kawa street working under the cover of coordinating aid for "Operation Provide Comfort." They got to work and hire over 800 Iraqis, set up radio and television stations and created an entire ops center with the ability to monitor all radio and television communications in Iraq. Soon there were 40 agents running the program. Agents were sent throughout Iraq to plant bombs and raise havoc. The CIA had set up insiders (some say Hussein Kamal) to plant a bomb inside Saddam's palace. The problem is that the CIA are amateurs compared to the shady dealings of the Husseins. Saddam's youngest son Qusay had planted agents in the Iraqi deserters that were recruited by the INC/CIA. They knew every detail of the "covert" operation. (See KDP) before it happened. The CIA somehow didn't even know that Barzani's son had met with Saddam Hussein and his two sons in one of his lush palaces on August 25, six months before Saddam's tanks rolled into Arbil. The deal would be to get all the guns and help they needed in exchange for the elimination of the CIA and INC operation.

On August 31, Saddam blew the INC headquarters and four years of CIA to bits. The CIA had bugged out the day before by driving across the border. Unfortunately they left the names and addresses of their well intention Iraqi and Kurdish operatives. All the expensive equipment was boxed up and send to Baghdad. Ninety six people were executed and up to 300 INC people were arrested. Hundreds of undercover operatives, sleepers, and officers were killed. Saddam executed 120 officers along with two members of his general staff.

Iraqi National Congress
9 Pall Mall Deposit
124–128 Barlby Road, London, England W10 6 BL
☎ *[44] (181) 960 4007, FAX [44] (181) 960-4001, PR: [44] (171) 233-9034*
In Sulaimaniya Iraq, [873] (68) 234-6239, FAX [873] (68) 234-6240
http://www.inc.org.uk

Jalal Talbani and the Patriotic Union of Kurdistan (PUK)
Led by Jalal Talbani, who lives in Damascus, Syria, and supported by the Turkish Army and Iran, the PUK is reputed to have 20,000 armed men. In September of 1996, Iran sent in troops and weapons to support the KPP against the PUK in Northern Iraq.

The PUK got F*K'd; that would be a concise way of describing what Slick Willie, Uncle Saddam and the West did to them in August of '96. The PUK represents the vast majority (70 percent) of the 3.2 million Kurds in Iraqi Kurdistan. They have been forced to align themselves with the Iranians who make both the U.S. and Iraq see red. This time they took it out on the yellow, the official color of the PUK party (red is the color of the KDP). Their headquarters in Sulaimaniya was overrun in September 1996 and their followers fled toward Iran.

Patriotic Union of Kurdistan
☎ *[44] (181) 642-4518*
Att: Latif Rashid
USA ☎ (703) 345-3056/
UK ☎ [44] (181) 993-2196
France ☎ [33] (1) 3916 0473

Turkey ☎ *[90312] 4402199*
Germany ☎ *[49] (30) 344 8738*
http://www.puk.org

Nassud Barzani and the Kurdistan Democratic Party (KDP)

The KDP is led by Massud Barzani and backed by Iraq, because they consider him the lesser of two evils. The KDP considers Talbani to be a pawn of the CIA, which he was until the summer of 1996 when he began getting arms and funds from both the CIA, Turkey and Iraq's Estikhbarat, the military intelligence arm run by Saddam's son Qusay. The KDP has stronger support among the rural Kurds.

Barzani, (b. 1945) is the son of KDP founder Mulla Mustafa Barzani and makes a living controlling the main border crossing at Zakhu (see "In a Dangerous Place: Turkey"), the only lifeline the north has with the Western world. Barzani also monopolizes the revenue from the drug trade and other illegal trade between Iraq and Turkey. The KDP charges a tax for the *masot*, or crude fuel oil, that is trucked across in rusty tanks. Barzani's long-term goal is the establishment of Kurdish authority within a Kurdish state in northern Iraq, which would be part of a federation with the rest of Iraq. Barzani has the support of about 30percent of the Kurds inside Iraq. He was supported by the U.S. and a group of CIA people who worked out of Sulaimaniya until the Republican Guard came to call. He now considers Saddam his ally. His see-saw alliances are simply short-term tactics to get the upper hand on the PUK. The KDP is aligned with the Turkish army to help exterminate the PKK from their bases in Northern Iraq. The PKK bases are ideal for defense since they include caves in steep mountainous areas.

Kurdistan Democratic Party

2025 I Street N.W., Suite 1108
Washington, D.C. 20006
☎ *(202) 331-9505, FAX: 331-9506*
http://www.kdp.pp.se/
http://home1.swipnet.se/~w-11534/

Necherwan Barzani

A low budget version of Saddam's son Uday. Necherwan owns the only Ferrari in Kurdistan and is the next generation for the Kurds struggle. Unfortunately he likes fancy suits, fast cars, loose women and owns restaurants and hotels where he puts on lavish parties. His father and son, Necherwan, live off the "customs fees" they collect from trade between Turkey and Iraq.

The Turkish Military and Police Forces

The presence of more than 160,000 military and police has turned eastern Turkey into a war zone, and travel is strictly controlled. The 750,000-member Turkish military has staged three coups since 1960 in the fear of Muslim fundamentalism upsetting Turkey's secular traditions. Turkish Prime Minister Necmettin Erbakan and his Islamic-led government resigned in June 1997 before he became the victim of the fourth coup. The rebels might want to note that the Turkish military considers the influence of Muslims in the government a bigger threat than Kurd separatists.

The Kurds

Kurdistan became part of the Ottoman Empire about a thousand years ago. It was a feudalistic system holding together a mixture of mountain people. Today, Kurdistan is a poor region, backward, difficult to reach, and underdeveloped by Turkey for fear its neighbors, the former Soviet Union, would annex the region.

The Kurds were considered bandits (*eksiya* in Turkish). Stubborn, backward people, they refused to fit into the societies that had built countries around them. For years police and military dealt harshly with the Kurds, who not only rebelled against outside authority but continually warred among themselves.

Ataturk

In 1928, Mustafa Kemal, or Ataturk (Father of the Turks), began the process of unifying Turkey. As with many strong nationalistic movements, his attempt required the assimilation and subjugation of the many political and ethnic groups into one stronger group. Ataturk chose to align Turkey with the West rather than the East. The changes meant going so far as to change the written language from the Arabic form to the Latin, and even banning the fez. Although the seat of the government is in Ankara and the major focus of the Turks is Istanbul, it did not address the needs of the 20 million or so Kurds who inhabit the poorer east. Kurds also are the major minority in southeastern Turkey as well as in the bordering areas of Iraq, Iran and Syria. Turkey's new love affair with the West meant that they found themselves with their Kurdish language banned and their customs under siege because of the need to Westernize all aspects of Turkish life.

The Kurdish Worker's Party (PKK)

Formed on November 27, 1978, in Siverek and led by Abdullah Ocalan who runs the operation out of a comfortable house in Damascus, Syria, and the Bekaa Valley. Ocalan, who was put in the slammer in 1971 and 1975 for his commie tendencies, has moderated his early visions of a separate Kurdish state and has said that "independence within existing borders is more realistic." But his is still very much a socialist agenda, even if half his fighters have never heard of Marx. In December 1995, he renounced the old Soviet-style ways and the Soviet symbols were removed from the PKK flag. Ocalan's priorities include eliminating rival Kurdish groups. His strongest ally has been Syria's Hafez al Assad. Although Syria withdrew support for the PKK in 1988, it was in rhetoric only. He simply had the PKK bases inside Syria moved to Lebanon's Bekaa Valley. PKK guerrillas or *Pesh Merga* (those who face death) are recruited from the villages of eastern Turkey and the refugee camps in northern Iraq. They are trained in terrorist training camps in Lebanon and Iraq. One of the main PKK bases is in Zaleh near the Iranian border with Turkey. The other is Zap in northern Iraq.

Politically, the Kurds found themselves a long way down in the pecking order when it came to representation, financial aid and clout, since the Turkish government has been loathe to develop the east because of the threat of invasion from the former Soviet Union, Iran and Iraq.

To fight for their rights, the Marxist Kurdish Worker's Party, or PKK, was formed to create an independent Kurdistan. Initially, the PKK pursued its demands through political actions. There were various Kurdish political parties but none that demanded absolute autonomy to the party and carried out acts of murder and intimidation like the PKK. The PKK was outlawed in 1980 for its terrorist activities against the government. Although there had been terrorist incidents since the '70s, full-scale warfare erupted in 1984, starting in Siverek (see "In a Dangerous Place: Eastern Turkey") and has continued uninterrupted now for 14 years.

In 1987, Turkey essentially declared war on the PKK and locked down the entire eastern provinces. As of this writing, there are major military operations against the Kurds in northern Iraq, maneuvers Turkish troops conduct with every break in the weather.

Before and after the Gulf War, Iraq carried out a campaign of genocide to effectively push the Kurds out of Iraq and into Turkey. In 1989, Turkey accepted 150,000–300,000 Iraqi Kurds who were fleeing extermination by Saddam Hussein. It is estimated that Hussein's brutal campaign pushed 1.5 million Kurdish refugees into northern Iraq and southeastern Turkey, where many live in makeshift camps.

Iran supports the Kurds since they create conflict in one of the more Westernized and liberal Muslim nations.

The greatest damage the Kurds do to Turkey is to realign this wealthy and sophisticated country with its more backward but equally fractured Eastern neighbors. The chances of Turkey joining the EC are slim, and the increasing force that the local and national governments use against the PKK is reinforcing the brutal genocidal image the Armenians have projected.

On the other hand, the PKK has broken the cardinal rule of terrorist groups in alienating the Western press and governments. There is little sentiment for the PKK's extortion tactics against its own people. The PKK is a revolution run by an absentee landlord. They have effectively removed any constructive voice for change by being banned as a political party in Turkey. They are ineffective in providing normal fund-raising or publicity by being banned in Europe. They cannot form a workable government to take care of their own people, forcing the U.S. and U.N. to effectively run Kurdistan as an aid station in northern Iraq. This does not give them a solid footing in the international community. The atrocities committed against unarmed schoolteachers, Kurdish women, children and old men are publicized by the Turkish government and media. Maybe to clean up its image as a bunch of unshaven terrorists, the PKK has been using women suicide bombers in attacks against police stations and military installations. Talk about blonde bombshells.

PKK (Kurdish Workers Party)
Mekte-Bi Amele-1 Kurdistan
Barelias-Chotura
West Bekaa, Lebanon

Kurdish Information Center
10 Glasshouse Yard
London ECI
☎ *[44] (171) 250-1315, FAX: [44] (171) 250-1317*
http://www.kurdistan.org

American Kurdish Information Network (AKIN)
2623 Connecticut Ave., N.W.
Washington, DC 20008-1522
☎ *(202) 483-6444, FAX: (202) 483-6476*
e-mail: akin@kurdish.org
Web Site: http://burn.ucsd.edu/~akin

These folks are the U.S. mouthpiece for the PKK. Give them a call if you plan a trip to the area, but don't expect a lot of useful travel tips. An AKIN rep told *DP:* "We are against all forms of violence. But we support the struggle for freedom of all oppressed people."

MED-TV

MED-TV, the broadcast voice of the Kurd rebel movement, launched in March 30, 1995. Uplinked from London, taped in Brussels, Berlin and Stockholm, the station (named after the Medes, the ancient name for kurds) is beamed to West Asia, including Turkey and Kurdistan, and has drawn the ire of the Turkish government. For millions of Kurds, the TV station has defined them culturally and realized their dream of sovereignty. But it's really nothing more than a spout piece for the PKK. But as one booster proclaimed: "For the first time in history, the Kurdish people can now see their own lives, their own reality, reflected on television screens across the world." How is this reality portrayed? Through reruns of Robinson Crusoe, Madame Bovary, Gulliver in Lilliput and dubbed Charlie Chaplin films. The latter must have been a true Kurdish feat: Charlie Chaplin films are silent. Who pays the multi-million dollar tab? Private citizens and the Kurdish Foundation Trust.

MED Broadcasting Ltd.
The Linen Hall
162-168 Regent Street
London W1R 5AT
☎ *[44] (171) 494-2523*
FAX: [44] (171) 494-2528
e-mail: med@med-tv.be
Web Site: http://www.ibibe/med/www/intro.htm
MED-TV is broadcast on Intelsat and Eutelsat (ESC II F2 transponder 25, 10 degrees east; downlink frequency 10971.667 MHz [P-V] polarization vertical) between 1400 and 2300 GMT.

To enter Turkey, American citizens need a valid passport good for at least six months. A visa is required for U.S. nationals. Visas for a three-month stay are available for $20 and can be had at Turkish Consulate General offices or at the port of entry into Turkey. (See the "Getting In" info in the Turkey chapter.) Without some covert contact in the area known as Kurdistan, entry into the region, especially northern Iraq, is next to impossible. Even *DP* staffers have a hard time. Jim Hooper was tossed out in 1997. Journalists seeking entry into Turkish Kurdistan should direct all inquiries to:

General Directorate of Press and Information
Office of the Prime Minister
56 Konur Sokak
Ankara, Turkey
☎ *(312) 417-6311*

All three major Kurd rebel groups are warring with each other in addition to the Turkish army, making travel by foreigners through and around Kurdistan extremely hazardous, if travel is even possible. You better enjoy the company of a pack mule and escorts with rifles slung on their shoulders. Mules don't come with assigned seating, air conditioning nor a snack and beverage service.

Rezerv Yor Seet Noww!

The following is a sampling of the regulations on a passenger ticket for Turkish domestic carrier Bodrum Airlines. Their use of English is impeccable, wouldn't you say?

1) You cannot give back your ticket, but if you annonce us before 24 hours your depart that you cannot fly you can use your ticket with in one year. After passing one year, you can not fly with your ticket.

2) You have to get in touch with contuar befe 30 mitutes of the departure, atherwine you don't get on the board and you don't have any rights for justice.

3) If someone gets ticket by doing tricky, Bodrum Airlines has rezerved the rights that there is no must to give a permation that passenger gets on the board.

4) Bodrum Airlines is not able to carry out flight schadule if an unusual thinks take place like bed weather, NOTAM, float, fire, eath queke, war, gone of elefricity, natural disaster, etc.

5) Do not allawe to drink alcaol and smoke cigarets on board.

Northern Iraq

In May 1997, Turkey sent more than 25,000 troops into northern Iraq to blast out bases the PKK has been using to launch attacks on Turkey. Some 3000 PKK guerrillas were killed in the offensive. After Turkish forces pulled out of Iraq in June, rebel leader Abdullah Ocalan declared that the PKK controlled the entirety of northern Iraq. Saddam chuckled at the news. The Turkish army has claimed it pushed 4000 rebels across the border into Iraq in 1996.

Southeastern Turkey

Diyarbakir has become relatively safe during 1997. People have even started going back to the discos. But there's no dancing in the streets in Ovacik, Nazimye, Tatvan, Tuncele, Cemisgezek, Mutki, Eruh, Sylvan, Dugan Mountain, Pasinler, Semdenli and Cukurca—where fighting still rages between rebels and government forces.

Murder

Since hostilities with the PKK began in 1984, there have been more than 3000 unsolved murders in Turkey, most in the eastern provinces. Turkish security forces are suspected behind the great majority of them. Corpses are usually dismissed by authorities as the work of the PKK. Relatives of victims who bring charges against military personnel stand an excellent chance of becoming victims themselves.

Guarding Villages

To root out remaining pockets of rebel resistance in eastern Turkey, the government relocated some 3000 subsistence farmers who were thought to be PKK sympathizers. Those with the brains to keep their political sympathies to themselves—about 70,000 folks considered loyal to the government—were rewarded with a gun and $200 a month in cash and instructed to defend their villages, hardly night watchman's pay in eastern Turkey. But instead of cozying up with "I Love Lucy" reruns and Taco Bell Value Meals in a warm shack, these guys have become target practice for hungry soldiers and rebels alike. The army tends to burn entire villages to the ground for a few loaves of bread, while the PKK simply kill the village guards and take the community's food. An average of 10 village guards a month are killed.

Medical care in the area known as Kurdistan is rudimentary and far below Western standards. The only care of any value is given by NGOs operating in the area. Diyarbakir in eastern Turkey provides the best medical services in the region. For serious illnesses or injuries, this is where you'll want to start. Then get your ass to Istanbul.

"Kurdistan" is a self-styled "homeland" that rebels are making an effort to carve from four countries: Turkey, Iraq, Iran and Syria. Kurdistan covers an area of 74,000 square miles and is mountainous with fertile valleys. There are 25 to 28 million Kurds in the world, who claim to be the world's largest ethnicity without a country to call their own.

The Kurds are mostly Sunni Muslims and are descended from the Medes. Their language is a form of Persian, but centuries of isolation have created many dialects and tribal schisms. Rebel Kurds cannot claim a capital. Strongholds at both Iraq's Arbil and eastern Turkey's Diyarbakir have been largely recovered by the Iraqis and Turks respectively. Culturally, most Kurds—although known for their gaudy attire—have assimilated successfully into Turkish society.

Business hours in eastern Turkey are much the same as in the rest of the country, from 8:30 a.m.–noon and 1:30 p.m.–5/5:30 p.m. Monday through Friday. Turkish post offices are recognized by the black PTT letters on a yellow background. In the smaller towns in eastern Turkey, they maintain the same hours as regular businesses, but are open from 9 a.m.–midnight in the major cities. Northern Iraq has no such luxuries.

Local time is GMT+3 hours April-September and GMT+2 hours October-March. Electricity, where it's available, is 220V/50Hz. Tap water is chlorinated in Turkey, but bottled water is recommended. Inside Iraq, drink only bottled water. The currency in Turkey is the Turkish lira (100,000TL=US$1.30). The Iraqi dinar is virtually worthless (3.2 to the U.S. dollar officially; 1000ID to the dollar semi-officially and 3000 dinars to the buck on the black market).

Web Resources:

Komala
http://www.pi.se/webpage/communist.party.of.iran/Komala/Komala.html

Kurdish Parliament in Exile, The
http://www.ariga.com/peacebiz/peacelnk/kurd.htm

Kurdistan Democratic Party
http://www.kdp.pp.se/

KDP
http://home1.swipnet.se/~w-11534/

Kurdistan Workers' Party,
http://www.uni-passau.de/~lindeman/kurdd.htm"

National Liberation Front of Kurdistan, ERNK (Political Wing of the PKK<
http://www.megabaud.fi/~ernk/

Patriotic Union of Kurdistan PUK
http://www.puk.org

People's Liberation Party-Front (DHKC)
http://www.ozgurluk.org/dhkc

KURDISTAN

DANGEROUS DAYS

05/14/1997	Turkey sends some 50,000 troops into northern Iraq to destroy PKK bases. An estimated 3000 people are killed.
08/31/1996	40,000 Republican Guards take Arbil.
03/30/1995	MED-TV begins broadcasting.
04/16/1991	U.S. President George Bush announces that U.S. Troops would enter northern Iraq to create a safe haven for displaced Kurds around Zakhu.
03/02/1991	Iraq signs a cease-fire agreement with allied forces ending the Persian Gulf War.
02/27/1991	Allied forces in Kuwait and Iraq suspend military operations against Iraq.
01/17/1991	The start of hostilities between the multinational forces and Iraqi forces. The beginning of Operation Desert Storm.
08/02/1990	Iraqi forces invade Kuwait and seize control of the country.
08/15/1986	Turkish troops raid Kurdish rebel camps in Iraq.
09/19/1980	Iran-Iraq war begins.
03/10/1979	Death of Kurdish leader Mullah Mustafa Barzani (Kurdish regions).
06/01/1976	Workers' Party of Kurdistan formed.
01/22/1946	Kurdish Republic Day.
04/28/1937	Saddam Hussein's birthday.
03/21	Kurdish New Year celebrated.

Lebanon
★★★★

Hell's Boot Camp

If God created a training ground for the Armageddon, Southern Lebanon would be the stage. Once called the Paris of the Mediterranean, it is more like bullet-riddled plaster of Paris. No longer vibrant but tired, the shattered ruins of Western development and Eastern tradition stand broken, sad and dead.

The realities of Beirut would challenge even the most creative scriptwriter. Religion, drugs, war, love and death all have interacted in this biblical epic of destruction. Southern Lebanon has been incinerated by the heat of Judeo-Arabic hate. The one true god has surfaced and has remained unshakable: the U.S. dollar, now the formal currency of this land. Beirut is trying to shake itself off and evolve from its 12th-century feudalism into the 20th century. Someone, though, needs to inform the fanatics.

For 15 years, from 1975 to 1990, Lebanon was plunged into a civil war that violently divided the country into regions controlled by religious and ethnic factions, including Sunni, Shiite and Druse Muslims and Maronite Christians. A central government in Lebanon was onc in name only.

The war was fueled by the belief that the 1943 National Pact, which had determined the distribution of power between Christians and Muslims and among the different Muslim sects, no longer reflected the nation's ethnic and religious demographics.

Introduced by Muslim leaders and Syrian officials and approved by the surviving members of the legislature, the 1989 Taif Agreement reestablished a central and legitimate government in Lebanon. The larger Muslim population was reflected in an increased number of seats in the National Assembly. De-facto leader General Michel Aoun, however, refused to accept the Taif Agreement and remained in power until he was ousted by factional Lebanese Army units and Syrian forces in October 1990.

Although a number of Maronite Christians boycotted the polls, Lebanon conducted its first legislative elections in 20 years in the fall of 1992. The assembly has 128 members. The Taif agreement stipulated that half the membership of the

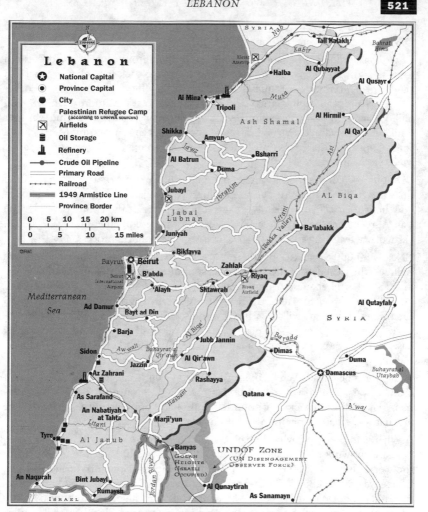

National Assembly chamber should be Muslim and the other half Christian, altering the 5:6 ratio that had existed previously.

The majority of Lebanon's political parties have traditionally been based on ethnic and denominational differences, mainly because seats in the National Assembly are distributed on the basis of religion as opposed to politics. The AMAL (Movement of the Deprived) is a Shiite party that was at vicious odds with left-wing Palestinian forces during the civil war. It now spends a good portion of its time protecting the position of Shiite Muslims forced out of their homes by fighting among rival pro-Palestinian forces and between those forces and Israeli-backed forces in the south. And Hizb al-Ahrar al-Watani—Parti National Liberal (NLP, or National Liberal Party)—refuses to join with any Muslim groups that are linked to Palestinians or Palestinian independence. Of course, the militant Shiite group, al Jihad al-Islami (Islamic Jihad, or Holy War—a.k.a. Hezbollah) has claimed responsibility for a number of kidnappings of foreigners in Lebanon, as well as other terrorist acts, including the 1983 Beirut bombings in which 300 U.S. Marines and French troops were killed.

Beirut, as is much of Lebanon, is again reaching out to the world—and Western tourists and businesspeople are beginning to trickle back in. Lebanon's rebirth can be evidenced by the requests made to tourist offices in London and other Western European capital cities. Some estimates reveal that more than US$400 million has been raised by billionaire businessman and Lebanese Prime Minister Rafik Hariri to rebuild central Beirut. Major hotel chains, including Marriott and Inter-Continental, are running hotels in Beirut. Things looked as sunny as the Mediterranean sky.

Despite the continuing gloom, Lebanon has made progress toward rebuilding since the civil war. In Beirut, armed militias are gone and the dreaded Hezbollah now limit their activities mainly to the southern part of the country. Under the Taif Agreement, the Lebanese have created a more equitable political scheme, particularly by giving Muslims a greater say in the political process.

Nearly 30,000 Syrian troops still refuse to move from Beirut. Damascus says this is due to the weakness of the LAF. Israel continues to support a proxy militia, the SLA (Southern Lebanese Army), near its border. About 1000 Israeli soldiers and 3000 SLA militiamen patrol the 15-km-wide security zone established in 1985 against anti-Israeli guerrillas, as Israel withdrew the bulk of its 1982 Lebanon invasion force. But they're still playing rocket volleyball in the south on a weekly basis. Syrian troops are based principally in Beirut, North Lebanon and the Bekaa Valley.

The fright began all over again in April 1996 when Israel, in response to what it claimed was an unprovoked Hezbollah rocket attack on northern Israeli settlements that killed 40, viciously pounded both Beirut and the southern city of Tyre in what was called "Operation Grapes of Wrath."

What is important is what Lebanon could be and probably will be. The Lebanese are known for being, along with the Chinese and Indians, the merchants of the world. Between 500,000 and 800,000 people left Lebanon during the war. Which war you might ask. The war that destroyed $15 billion worth of infrastructure and countless futures. Today the people who remain baby-sit about 640,000 registered refugees who are not allowed to work at professional or skilled jobs. They have an occupied southern area that is an active war zone, and they have bully neighbors to the east (Syria and Iran) who use Lebanon in the finest of puppet traditions to smack Israel so that they don't get smacked back. Lebanon always loses. Israeli planes do not streak into Tehran or Damascus but into the shell-shocked refugee camps to deal out punishment.

Back before "the war," tourism used to be 20 percent of Lebanon's gross national product. Hezbollah is running tours and even providing security for historic areas. But there is a dark side, there are continual covert attempts by Israel to assassinate Hezbollah leaders. In most cases commando raids have resulted in disasters leading some to think that there is a high placed mole in the Israeli military. intelligence system. In September of '97 Nasrallah's son was killed by Israelis. Today, folks in Beirut ignore the fact that the airport is guarded with antiaircraft guns and that the south is a free fire zone and look forward to the big tourism boom. The anti aircraft guns are not decoration. Israel conducts about two air raids a week into Lebanon. The fact that the States is known as the Great

Satan might have something to do with the anemic tourism figures. The only boom they get in Lebanon is the sound of incoming artillery shells from Israeli troops. The most popular poster boy is not Mickey Mouse but the Ayatollah Khomeini. The ruins at Baalbeck are also famous for being the main headquarters of Hezbollah, a university and training center for terrorists, the place where the U.S. hostages were kept and the future site of a music festival. For now, Lebanon rebuilds and awaits its tourists to deliver it from the Stone Age. In 1996, nineteen SLA militiamen, 27 Israeli soldiers, 54 guerillas and 155 civilians were killed in this "peace keeping" zone.

Lebanon is an occupied country trying to emerge from the rubble of civil war, which has seriously damaged the economy and the social fabric. Lebanon is amazingly resistant considering Syria controls the military and political fate of it, while Israel illegally occupies the south. The population is composed of both Christians and Muslims from a variety of sects. Hezbollah still controls the south, while the north is still safe. The 12-year ban on travel to Lebanon has been lifted by the State Department (although 10,000 Yanks already lived and worked in Lebanon), but it hasn't changed things in the south.

Although the north is getting busy building hotels and office buildings, the south is still biblical style fire and brimstone. The Israelis occupied Southern Lebanon in direct violation of UN resolutions and international laws back in the early '80s so Hezbollah is their punishment.

In April 1996, Israel, in retaliation to Hezbollah rocket attacks on northern Israeli settlements, pounded Beirut and the southern city of Tyre in "Operation Grapes of Wrath." The world saw images of an Israeli helicopter gunship take out an ambulance in Amiriyya in Southern Lebanon near Tyre, killing four children and two women. More than 400,000 civilians fled Southern Lebanon in a scene of biblical connotations; most of them ended up as refugees in Beirut with nowhere to go. Hezbollah continued to hurl Katyusha rockets at northern Israel like a fireworks display from hell. History has never been kind to Lebanon, a country that has been conquered, sacked, pillaged, rebuilt, demolished and then rebuilt by everyone from the French to the Babylonians.

Few playwrights could create a cast of characters and dramas as dark and complex as the terrorist groups in Lebanon. Forged by desperation, nurtured by Syria and Iran, supported by oil money and hardened by Israeli intolerance, the terrorist factions in Lebanon have worldwide reach and are responsible for much of the pain, death and suffering since the early '80s.

Syria

Lebanon is a vassal state of Syria. Syria entered Lebanon in 1976 to support the Christians in the civil war and never went home. Just as Assad plays policy by proxy with Turkey via the PKK, he enjoys tweaking Israel through his support of Hezbollah (along with Iran). Most people forget that Syria is officially at war with Israel. Syria still has between 40,000–20,000 troops (the U.S. says 25,000) deployed in eastern Lebanon. Syria uses Hezbollah to carry out its dirty work against Israel: a charge that Israel has always echoed. That's why Israel considers Lebanon to be merely a buffer zone between itself and Syria.

Syria is still angered that the Israelis stole the strategically important Golan Heights from them during the 1967 Arab-Israeli war.

The Father, Son and the Holy Ghost

Travelers to the Middle East take a while to get used to the giant posters of photogenic folks like Saddam Hussein, Khomeini and Assad. In Assad's case he has a problem. Not only does he feature his ever-smiling image, but he began to add polo-playing, Ray-Banned, super-macho son, Basil, to his image. The only problem is that Basil convinced his driver to let him drive to the airport in Damascus. Basil wiped out the Ferrari when the long straight road turned right into the airport. Basil died on that foggy day and his driver actually shot himself before the ambulance arrived. Luckily Assad has another son, Bashar. Unfortunately he's a weak-chinned dentist who doesn't come close to that Syrian macho look required for maximum poster impact. So for now, they are slowly adding the shy awkward looking Bashar to stickers, flags and posters, but Basil still remains.

Hezbollah (Party of God)

Hezbollah was founded after the invasion of Lebanon in 1982 by the Israelis. Hezbollah means Party of God. The name comes from the torture and murder of a young mullah in Qom, Iran, in 1973. His last words were "that there is only one party, the party of God." Hezbollah is an Iranian-backed organization that polarizes the plight of Muslims into Muslim versus the Great Satan. The Great Satan can be Israel or America, depending on expediency. Hezbollah is a political machine as well as a terrorist organization. Their mission statement doesn't leave a lot of room for interpretation. Simply stated, their goal is the complete annihilation of Israel. After that, they plan to "return the Jewish occupiers back to where they came."

So its probably understandable that Israel and Hezbollah don't get along. The fact that Iran writes the checks and Syria provides the real estate complicates things, but there are enough downtrodden Palestinian refugees to wage jihad against Israel for years.

This group has been responsible for some of the most well known acts of terrorism in the last 15 years, including the bombing of the U.S. Marine barracks in 1983, the hijacking of the TWA flights, the kidnapping of Western hostages in Beirut and the car bombing of the Israeli embassy in Buenos Aires, Argentina, in 1992 that killed 56 people.

Hezbollah is a political, social and military organization that seeks to achieve in Lebanon what the Muslims achieved in Iran. It espouses an intense hatred of any influence that does not support its views of Shi'a ideology. The movement was born from the merger of Sheikh Husayn Musawi's Islamic Amal and the Lebanese branch of the Da'wa party in 1982–'83. It should be noted that Sheikh Musawi was killed in early 1992 in Southern Lebanon in an Israeli attack on his motorcade. Three area councils—Beirut, the Bekáa Valley, and Southern Lebanon—oversee activities in their respective regions. A series of functional committees play roles in policy recommendation and execution. A consultative council *(shura)* functions as the principal governing body on day-to-day matters but actually exists to advise Iran on the unique situation of the Islamic movement in Lebanon. Hezbollah elements receive training in the Bekáa Valley of eastern Lebanon. Through this connection, Iranian revolutionary guardsmen provide political indoctrination, financing and material support. The Hezbollah and the revolutionary guards work together on terrorist operations. The group itself seldom claims responsibility for specific acts, but does so under a variety of aliases.

Hezbollah has grown to be the most dangerous and committed liberation organization in the world. Under the direct control of Tehran, Hezbollah, the group seems to be the most successful in following in the steps of Mohammed by combining religious, political and military fanaticism to spread the cause of fundamentalist Islamic belief. If Iran continues to cozy up to the U.S. it may reduce the support and force Hezbollah to look else where for funds.

Today, Hezbollah conducts its most visible campaign of terror in the very southern part of Lebanon. But recent events in Brazil and Argentina and recruitment drives among Algerians in Europe indicate that they are expanding their activities toward a more global scale reducing the risk of direct retaliation.

Hezbollah has been involved in numerous anti-U.S. terrorist attacks, including the suicide truck bombing of the U.S. Marine barracks in Beirut in October 1983 and the U.S. embassy annex in September 1984. Elements of the group are responsible for the kidnapping of most, if not all,U.S. and other Western hostages in Lebanon. The military wing is estimated to have 5000 members.

Hezbollah operates in the Bekáa Valley, the southern suburbs of Beirut and in southern Lebanon and has established cells in Western Europe, Africa and elsewhere. The group has claimed responsibility for attacks as far afield as Argentina. It receives substantial amounts of training, financial aid, weapons and explosives, as well as political, diplomatic and organizational assistance from the Islamic Republic of Iran. Iran provides an estimated $50 to $100 million to Hezbollah every year. It also furnishes funds to Hamas, Islamic Jihad and the PFLP-GC. Libya kicks in some dollars and safe haven, and Sudan provides training bases and freedom from arrest.

They want to establish a revolutionary Shi'a state in Lebanon, modeled after Iran, eliminate non-Islamic influences, force Western interests out of the region and, of course, become Lebanon's principal Islamic movement with close ties to Iran.

Hamas (Islamic Resistance Movement)

Hamas was formed in late 1987 as an outgrowth of the Palestinian branch of the Muslim Brotherhood and has become Fatah's principal political rival in the Occupied Territories. Various elements of Hamas have used both political and violent means, including terrorism, to pursue the goal of establishing an Islamic Palestinian state in place of Israel. Hamas is loosely structured, with some elements working openly through mosques and social service institutions to recruit members, raise money, organize activities and distribute propaganda. Other elements, operating clandestinely, have advocated and used violence to advance their goals. Hamas' strength is concentrated in the Gaza Strip and in a few areas of the West Bank. It has also engaged in peaceful political activity, such as running candidates in West Bank chamber of commerce elections.

Hamas activists—especially those in the Izz Al-Din Al-Qassam forces—have conducted many attacks against Israeli military and civilian targets, suspected Palestinian collaborators and Fatah rivals. During 1992, elements of Hamas were responsible for several prominent anti-Israeli attacks, including ambushes of military units in the West Bank and the murder of a member of the Israeli border police in December 1992. Hamas increasingly uses lethal weapons and tactics—such as firearms, roadside explosive charges and car bombs—in their operations.

It is estimated that there are tens of thousands of supporters and sympathizers. Funding is received from Palestinian expatriates, Iran and private benefactors in Saudi Arabia and other moderate Arab states. Some fund-raising and propaganda activity takes place in Western Europe and North America.

Harakat Al-Muqawama Al-Islamiya, Islamic Resistance Movement, (HAMAS)

AKA: Abdallah Azzam Units (operational cell units of Qassam, formerly known as Azzedine al-Kassam Units, reorganized after 12/92 deportations; active in and around Napulse, Jenin, and Tulkarem in the northern occupied territories)

The Islamic Association for Palestine is a religious association based in Dallas, Texas, and associated with HAMAS. They published the group's charter in English and distribute the communiqués, Al-Zaytuna, and other publications. Dallas is also home to the Holy Land Foundation for Relief and Development a charity organization. The United Association for Studies and Research based in Springfield, Virginia is also linked to HAMAS.

HAMAS was formed in December 14, 1987 and is headquartered in the Sheikh Radwan district of Gaza City. They have a training camp at a farm outside of Khartoum in the Sudan. They also have offices in Amman, Jordan and support groups in Britain and the U.S. with offices in Chicago, New Jersey, and Virginia, Washington DC, Detroit, and Kansas City.

They believe that there is no solution to the Palestinian problem except through Jihad. There are at least 15–20 special operatives active in Gaza (HAMAS claims 28) and 20 in the West Bank and between 750 and 1200 active fighters. Their most famous member was Yehiya (Yaki) Ayyash aka 'the Engineer' or 'the man with seven souls' an explosives expert who was behind a number of bombings in Tel Aviv.

HAMAS' budget is about $30 million a year about with about a third coming from the U.S. and Europe. The rest comes from Iran, Jordan, Sudan, and the Gulf States. They publish Al-Thabat (Perseverance) and Al-Zaytuna, the pro-HAMAS publication published in the United States.

Palestine Liberation Front (PLF)

The PLF is a terrorist group that broke away from the Popular Front for the Liberation of Palestine–General Command (PFLP-GC), in the mid-1970s. It later split again into three factions: one pro-PLO, another pro-Syrian, and the last pro-Libyan. The pro-PLO faction is led by Mohammed Abbas (Abu Abbas), who became a member of the PLO executive committee in 1984, but left the executive committee in 1991.

The PLF was established under Mohammed Abu al Abbas in opposition to PFLP-GC leader Ahmed Jibril's support for the Syrian incursion into Lebanon in June 1976. After unsuccessfully attempting to gain control of the PFLP-GC in September 1976, the PLF was split from the PFLP-GC officially by PLO chairman Yasir Arafat in April 1977. The PLF was established with Iraqi support, and its existence as an independent group was recognized when it obtained seats on the Palestine National Council in 1981 with its headquarters in Damascus. Near the end of 1983, the PLF itself split into factions, when Abu Abbas felt that his organization had become too close to Syria. Leaving Damascus, along with many supporters, Abu Abbas went to Tunis to align himself with Arafat and the mainstream Fatah organization. Following the *Achille Lauro* incident, the Abu Abbas faction relocated to Baghdad at the request of the government of Tunisia. The parts of the PLF remaining in Damascus were further split in January 1984, when Abd al-Fatah Ghanem attempted a takeover of the PLF offices and held Tal'at Yaqub, secretary general of the PLF, hostage. Through Syrian intervention, Yaqub was released and Ghanem formed his own faction with ties to Libya. Yaqub's faction joined the Palestine National Salvation Front and is generally aligned with Syria. Operationally, the Abu Abbas faction of the PLF has demonstrated creativity and technical acumen. The group has employed hot-air balloons and hang gliders for airborne operations, and a civilian passenger ship for mounting a seaborne infiltration operation. The *Achille Lauro* hijacking in October 1985—followed by the murder of an elderly American citizen, Leon Klinghoffer—contributed to the international condemnation of Abu Abbas and the PLF. In 1988, the PLF and Yasir Arafat feuded over the PLO's moderating stance on Israel and on the use of terror against Israel. The differences appear to have been overcome when the PLO refused to condemn an attempted attack by the PLF on a Tel Aviv beach.

The Abu Abbas faction of the PLF carried out an abortive seaborne attack staged from Libya against Israel on May 30, 1990. The same group was also responsible for the October 1985 attack on the cruise ship *Achille Lauro*. A warrant for the arrest of Abu Abbas is outstanding in Italy. The PLF openly supported Iraq during the Persian Gulf War.

There are at least 50 members within the Abu Abbas faction. The other two factions have between 200–250 members. They receive logistic and military support mainly from the PLO, but also from Libya and Iraq. They are working to destroy Israel.

Popular Front for the Liberation of Palestine–General Command (PFLP-GC)

The PFLP-GC receives logistic and military support from Syria and Iran as well as financial support from Libya. The group is given safe haven in Syria and has a base in Na'ameh, just south of Beirut.

Ahmed Jibril formed the Popular Front for the Liberation of Palestine-General Command in 1968 when he became disenchanted with George Habash's leadership of the Popular Front for the Liberation of Palestine (PFLP). An officer in the Syrian army, Jibril was initially interested in developing conventional military capabilities to complement PFLP-GC terrorist activities. As a result, the PFLP-GC has always been known for its military expertise. In addition to ground infiltration capabilities, the PFLP-GC has worked toward developing air and naval striking capabilities as well. PFLP-GC terrorist activities have included the use of letter bombs and conducting major cross-border operations directed at Israeli targets. The PFLP-GC has also shared its terrorist expertise with other international terrorist groups, such as the Armenian Secret Army for the Liberation of Armenia (ASALA), as well as European groups that have sent members to Lebanon for training. The PFLP-GC arsenal includes sophisticated weaponry, such as Soviet SA-7 antiaircraft missiles, heavy artillery and light aircraft, such as motorized hang gliders and ultralights. The Communist Bloc countries provided small arms, such as Kalashnikov assault rifles and RPG-7 antitank rockets, but Syria and Libya may have served as conduits for such support. The PFLP-GC actively participated in the Lebanese conflict, including sniping attacks that injured U.S. marines who were members of the peacekeeping forces in Beirut in 1982–83. In addition, the group attacked Israeli citizens and interests through operations launched from Lebanon. The PFLP-GC has also occasionally recruited West Bank Palestinians to conduct terrorist operations inside Israel.

The group specializes in suicide operations and has carried out numerous cross-border attacks into Israel, using unusual means, such as hot-air balloons and motorized hang gliders. It is not known how many current members there are, but the more radical factions tend to attract young volunteers at a greater rate than the more moderate.

Popular Front for the Liberation of Palestine (PFLP)

Marxist-Leninist group that was a member of the Palestine Liberation Organization (PLO). Founded in 1967 by George Habash. After Fatah, the PFLP is the most important political and military organization in the Palestinian movement. The PFLP has spawned several dangerous terrorist groups.

The group committed numerous acts of international terrorism between 1970 and 1977. Since the death in 1978 of Wadi Haddad, the PFLP's operational planner of terrorism, the group has carried out less frequent but continued attacks against Israeli and moderate Arab targets.

The group of about 800 men receives most of its financial and military aid from Syria and Libya. The PFLP is trying to create a Palestine in the manner of a Marxist-Leninist revolution. The PFLP was formed after the Arab defeat in the 1967 Arab-Israeli war. George Habash created the PFLP as a merger of three formerly autonomous groups—the Arab Nationalist Movement's Heroes of the Return, the National Front for the Liberation of Palestine and the Independent Palestine Liberation Front (to be distinguished from the present Palestine Liberation Front—PLF). Referred to by his followers as *al-Hakim* ("The Wise One" or "The Physician"), Habash has remained consistent in his position towards solving the Palestinian problem—the total liberation of Palestine.The PFLP established itself early as one of the most violent Palestinian terrorist groups. It concurrently sought to establish strong ties to other Marxist revolutionary organizations. Those links facilitated PFLP operations in Europe, which gave the group much of its notoriety. Habash strongly favors well-publicized attacks on civilian targets, and the PFLP reputation for ruthlessness was built on that strategy. As a result of ideological inflexibility, internal disputes and personality conflicts, the PFLP has spawned several splinter groups, including the PFLP–General Command (PFLP-GC) and the Democratic Front for the Liberation of Palestine (DFLP). The PFLP was one of the most active terrorist organizations in the early 1970s. As a result of publicity that attracted condemnation even from Communist Bloc countries, the PFLP curtailed international operations and concentrated on developing conventional and guerrilla forces for use against targets in Israel.

South Lebanese Army (SLA)

The SLA has been Israel's early warning system since 1978. After the Israelis were pushed out of the country by Syrian- and Iranian-backed militia in 1985, they left behind a little pocket protected by Lebanese General Antoine Lahd.

The SLA controls about 8 percent of Lebanese territory. Although no one believes that the moniker Lebanese is correct, these are occupation forces paid for and trained and supported by Israel. The SLA is about 2500 strong and manned by Christians and Shiites. They also have backup from about a thousand Israeli Defence Forces (IDF). The SLA occupies a string of hilltop bunkers that parallel the Israeli-Lebanese border. They are well armed but no match for the hardened Hezbollah fighters who control the region. Many of the SLA soldiers are inducted without their consent and the constant boredom and stress have taken their toll on discipline. There are about 160,000 Palestinian refugees in Southern Lebanon. They provide a fertile recruiting ground for Hezbollah. The various Palestinian groups, such as the PFLP, PRLP-PC, DFLP and Abu Nidal's FRC, also recruit from these camps. True to Middle East politics though, the refugee camps have their own small cliques and groups that often create violent confrontations without outside agitation. Hezbollah's main source of support comes from the Bekáa valley and squalid camps in southern Beirut.

The United Nations Peacekeeping Mission (UNIFIL)

The United Nations Interim Force in Lebanon is kept away from the border, so its 4500-person task force gets to twiddle its thumbs in Naquoura on the coast. They operate checkpoints inland from Tyre and throughout the area. They can only try to keep carloads of machine gun– toting Palestinians from wiping each other out. They also create a human barrier that Israel has to think about if they roll tanks back into Lebanon.

The Lebanese Army

The Lebanese army prefers to let the Israelis and Palestinians duke it out while they look the other way. Since the Lebanese army is under the direct influence of Syria, they are not about to fire on Islamic elements to please their bellicose neighbor to the south. On the other hand, they feel a slight obligation to bring some law and order to the south, but so far there is little indication that they will replace the SLA or the United Nations.

The Israelis

Israel is still at war with Hezbollah, which is backed and directed by Iran with the assistance of Syria. Israel is not foolish enough to take on Syria or Iran directly, therefore each side has created its pawns to judge the strength and commitment of the other without resorting to total warfare. Israel has the SLA, and Syria has Hezbollah. Israel may decide to invade Lebanon again to push back Hezbollah fighters and clear out the Palestinian refugee camps, but each side remembers the lingering and vicious war that was triggered by Israel's invasion of Lebanon in June of 1982, which has lasted in various forms to this day. There are about 1200 Israeli troops in Lebanon.

For now, Israel is content to wage an eye for an eye war. When Hezbollah sends shells and rockets into Israeli outposts, the Israelis are content to send in their Cobra gunships and take out preannounced villages, cars or buildings.

A passport and visa are required. Send a SASE for an application form. To get a visa in advance you should send; a cover letter specified length of stay and purpose of trip, two 2" by 2" notarized photos. The cost is $20 for a single entry visa and $40 for a multiple entry and a return SASE envelope.

You can't enter from Israel but you can enter from other neighboring countries. Cost for a visa issued at the border is $33. The Lebanese embassy wondered what we were talking about when we asked about the dangers of travel in South Lebanon. When we asked if there were travel restrictions in Southern Lebanon, the official answered, in a Sphinx-like tone, "Is it not part of Lebanon?" When we asked about dark dubious goings on in the Bekaa Valley, true to form he answered with a question, "Where did you hear this?" Finally when asked how a visitor would know whether one is in a dangerous area or not the man replied, you can play it "by the ear." We would assume that he meant that any traveler in South Lebanon knows the difference between incoming and outgoing Katyushas, artillery and jet fighters.

The phone attendant neglected to remind us that Lebanon is home to Hezbollah who (along with its string-puller Iran) still considers America the Great Satan.

Our state department is a little more blunt: "The expiration of the passport restriction should not in any way be construed as a determination by the Department of State that it is safe for Americans to travel to Lebanon. U.S. citizens who travel to Lebanon despite this warning, should exercise extreme caution and avoid traveling in the southern suburbs of Beirut, the Bekaa Valley, and southern Lebanon." It's also important to know the U.S. embassy in Beirut is still in siege-mentality, and access to the Consular Section is not possible unless prior arrangements have been made. If you want to register with the U.S. Embassy, you should do it by phone, fax, or by mail. The phone numbers for the U.S. Embassy in Lebanon are ☎ *[961] (1) 417 774, 415-802, 415-803, 402-184, 402-200, 403-300,* and *FAX: 407-112.*

Australians, Americans, Canadians and most European nationals can get a visa issued at the border.

Embassy of Lebanon

2560 28th Street, N.W., Washington, D.C., 20524, ☎ *(202) 939-6300*

Consulate generals of Lebanon, located at

7060 Hollywood Boulevard, Suite 510, Los Angeles, California 90028, ☎ *(213) 467-1253;*
1959 E. Jefferson, Suite 4A, Detroit, Michigan 48207, ☎ *(313) 567-0233; and*
9 East 76th Street, New York, New York 10021, ☎ *(212) 744-7905.*

Getting in to Lebanon is fairly simple these days...unless you think you are going south. A visa is required and don't be surprised by the number of road blocks, Syrian soldiers and armed people smiling at you. *DP* considers this region one of the most friendly and interesting places as long as you know where you are going.

Renting a car is probably the best way to see Lebanon. The two areas you need to know about are the Bekaa Valley, a major militarized area used by terrorist groups for training and safe haven, and Southern Lebanon, an armed buffer zone that has daily rocket and mine attacks as well as sporadic firefights.

Southern Lebanon

Southern Lebanon was the base for the PLO in the early '70s, and now it is Hezbollah and SLA territory. It is a no man's land, 850 kilometers square, that protects Israel's border. The area south of the Awwali River is known as Southern Lebanon. To the east is Mount Hermon and the Syrian-Lebanese border and to the west are the ancient cities of Tyre and Sidon. The landscape is rough, with small villages and wadis connected by poorly maintained roads. The area has predominately Shiite Muslims, who eke out a living growing oranges and olives.

The best way to find out what the hot zone of the day is, listen to Voice of the South Radio operated by the SLA, which will broadcast areas to be attacked by Israeli jets or helicopters.

The entire area is under curfew at night and few SLA or IDF soldiers venture out after dark. It is at night that Hezbollah will mine the roads with remote-control bombs. The terrorists will also use rockets against bases and missiles, usually Saggers or SA-7s, against helicopters. Hezbollah strongholds are at Mlita, Jebel Safi, Ain Busswar, Mach Gara and Saghbine.

The Bekaa Valley

Not technically dangerous to travelers, but a place from which danger comes. The Bekaa is home to training camps for everybody from the PKK to Hezbollah. It is also the home of the "supernote," the counterfeit US$100 bill that can not be detected as such. Shiite Muslims, under the direct control of Iranian Intelligence agents, have been producing three times as many US$100 notes here than we have back home. Don't feel singled out though they also run off German and Saudi bills too.

The Airport

The State Department has a warning about BIA: The FAA has not certified Beirut International Airport (BIA) as secure for U.S. carriers. U.S. carriers may not fly into Beirut, and the Lebanese national carrier, Middle East Airlines, is prohibited from flying into the United States. All U.S. citizens working at the U.S. Embassy do not normally use Beirut International Airport due to the concern about security of passengers and aircraft. The Department of Transportation continues to have restrictions on the sale of airline tickets to Lebanon. Information on the restrictions can be obtained from the Department of Transportation at ☎ (202) 366-4000.

Prisons

Israeli controlled prisons in Lebanon are notorious for torture and brutality. A young Lebanese prisoner, held for 10 years without a trial, died in January 1995 of torture. He was the third prisoner from the Khiam Detention Camp in Israel's Southern Lebanon occupation zone to die in less than two months. Israel and the Southern Lebanese Army have refused to allow prisoners' families to visit them, as well as refusing international humanitarian agencies access. Perhaps 250 Lebanese and 100 Palestinians are held at Khiam. One human rights agency estimates that 80 percent of the inmate population has heart, pulmonary or nervous disorders due to the extreme dampness of their cells. It is also believed the prisoners are allowed outside only once every three days.

In Beirut and the surrounding areas, basic modern medical care and medicines are widely available. Such facilities are not always available in outlying areas.

And You Thought "Cops" and "Rescue 911" Were Reality TV

*What is the hottest TV station in Lebanon (well, actually number four in the ratings)? If you are a fan of reality shows, you might want to check out **al Manar** (the Beacon), the new TV station sponsored by your local purveyor of fine terrorist activities and mayhem: Hezbollah.*

Al Manar is probably the strangest of the 50 odd new TV stations in Lebanon. They feature live action shots of rocket attacks against Israelis and other bang-bang news reports. Just so things don't get too exciting, there is also daily news dished out by glum-looking, chador-wrapped female newscasters. And the long (and we mean long) three- to four-hour interviews with the leaders of Hezbollah are guaranteed to make sure you sleep right through retaliatory raids by the Israelis. DP did an interview with Hezbollah leader Sheikh Hassan Nasrallah and Fadlallah; they make the Unabomber's 30,000-page manifesto seem absolutely terse and well organized.

Al Manar is owned by well-heeled Shia Muslims, and programming content has to be "blessed" by a senior cleric who OKs what is selected by a committee. No Showgirls NC17 programming here. The station broadcasts movies, sports and documentaries. But you won't see a lot of women in strong roles—i.e., cussing and drinking. Those who wish to reach this militant demographic can buy 30-second spots for as little as US$400.

Useful Addresses

www.lebanon.com

Good source for news, links, travel and local information

Embassy Locations

U.S. Embassy

P.O. Box 70-840, Beirut, Lebanon.
☎ [961] (1) 402-200, 416-502, 426-183,
417-774, FAX: 407-112.

Embassy of Lebanon

2560 28th Street, NW
Washington, D.C. 20008
☎ (202) 939-6300

Hezbollah

Mekteb-1 Hezbollah
South Suburb
Bir-al Abed
Beirut, Lebanon

PKK (Kurdish Workers Party)

Mekte-Bi Amele-1 Kurdistan
Barelias-Chotura
West Bekaa, Lebanon

04/10/1996	In retaliation to what it claimed was an unprovoked Hezbollah rocket attack on northern Israeli settlements that injured 40 after Passover week, Israel viciously pounded both Beirut and the southern city of Tyre in what was called "Operation Grapes of Wrath."
04/20/1993	Russia and the United States issued invitations to Israel, Lebanon, Jordan, Syria and the Palestinians to meet in Washington, D.C., to resume peace talks stalled by the Israeli's expulsion of 400 suspected Hamas activists to Lebanon.
12/17/1992	The government of Israel deported more than 400 suspected members of Hamas; however, the government of Lebanon refused to allow the deportees to enter and they were sent "camping" in the Israeli "security zone" in Southern Lebanon.
02/16/1992	General Secretary Abbas Musawi was killed in an Israeli helicopter ambush near the village of Jibsheet in southern Lebanon.
10/30/1991	The first round of Arab-Israeli peace talks began in Madrid, Spain.
07/28/1989	Israeli commandos seized Shaykh Obeid from a village in Southern Lebanon and detained him in Israel on allegations of involvement in terrorist activity on behalf of Hezbollah.
02/28/1987	Georges Ibrahim Abdallah, a principal figure in the Lebanese Armed Revolutionary Faction, was sentenced to life in prison for murder.
01/28/1987	U.S. bans travel to Lebanon.
06/14/1985	TWA flight 847 was hijacked from Athens to Lebanon. One of the hijackers, Mohammed Ali Hamadi shoots and kills U.S. Navy diver Robert Stetham in Beirut on June 16 and dispersed the remaining passengers throughout the city. Thirty-nine American citizens were released on June 30 in Damascus, Syria.
09/20/1984	Fourteen people were killed and 70 were wounded when a van loaded with 400 pounds of explosives drove past the checkpoint in front of the U.S. Embassy annex in Awkar and exploded. The driver of the van was shot and killed by British security guards. Islamic Jihad claimed responsibility for the bombing in a call to the media.

02/06/1984	West Beirut fell to Muslim militias.
10/23/1983	Islamic Jihad (read that as Hezbollah) bombings in Beirut killed more than 200 U.S. Marines and more than 50 French paratroopers.
04/18/1983	A car bomb exploded in front of the U.S. embassy in Beirut, killing 63 people, including 17 Americans. More than 100 others were wounded. Islamic Jihad claimed responsibility, calling the bombing "part of the Islamic Revolution." Iran subsequently denied having any role in the attack.
09/15/1982	Israel invaded West Beirut.
09/15/1982	Lebanese Christian Phalangists killed hundreds of Palestinian refugees in a camp near Beirut.
09/14/1982	President-elect Bashir Gemayel was assassinated.
07/19/1982	David Dodge, president of the American University of Beirut, was kidnapped. He was subsequently released on July 19, 1983.
06/06/1982	Israel invaded Lebanon.
06/04/1982	Israeli planes bombed Beirut.
03/16/1978	Invasion by Israeli forces.
06/01/1976	During this month, Syria entered the civil war in Lebanon on the side of the Christian Phalange and against the Palestinians and their Muslim allies. In response, Abu Nidal renamed his terrorist group, then based in Iraq, the Black June Organization and began attacking Syrian targets.
04/13/1975	Phalangist militiamen attacked Shia Muslim targets, sparking the first round of fighting in the Lebanese civil war.
04/11/1968	The Popular Front for the Liberation of Palestine (PFLP-GC) split from the PFLP under the leadership of Ahmad Jabril.
07/15/1958	U.S. Marines were sent to Lebanon in order to thwart the overthrow of the government.
11/22/1943	Independence Day.
05/06/1915	Martyr's Day.

LEBANON

Lebanon, 1980–1986: Living with Death

For more than 15 years, the war in Lebanon was the compulsory and compulsive topic of headlines and television news throughout the world—a hopeless quagmire of death and destruction. A place where we could never figure out who was killing who or why.

With its 17 different religious communities and an obsolete political system, Lebanon was, and still is, the ideal battlefield for warlords who have wanted control of this ancient region. Lebanon also became the best place for marketing and testing weaponry coming from all corners of the planet.

The war began in Ayn er-Remmane (a suburb east of Beirut), on April 13, 1975, with a massacre: During the inauguration of a church, by the leader of the Katayeb party, four people were shot dead from an unidentified car. The retaliation was immediate. A few hours later, in the same place, Christian militants machine-gunned a coach transporting Palestinians from the camp of Sabra to the one at Tall ez-Zatar. Twenty-seven people died in this coach and three more in the crowd. The answer was prompt: One hundred Christians were killed the very next day. Massacres and revenge had become a common feature of this war.

Unlike the wars that make good movies or backdrops for spy novels, Lebanon was not black and white, good and bad. Lebanon was and still is a nest of wars. It is a civil war between several of the 17 religious communities. It is a national war in which Lebanese fight Palestinians, Lebanese (or at least some of them) fight against Syrians, Lebanese (or the majority of them) fight against Israelis. It is a religious war between Christians—the majority group when the state was created in 1920. It is a war of sects between Sunnites and Shiites, the latter of whom constituted the majority, and within the Shiite community, between Amal, pro-Syrian, and Hezbollah, pro-Iranian. It is a war between militias of all factions, but more particularly, from the Christian group. It is a social war pitching the poor (Christians and Muslims) against the rich (Christians and Muslims).

What made this new medieval hierarchy so bizarre was that a few months prior, Lebanon was called the Switzerland of the East. With an affluent population of just under 3 million in 1975, it was a comfortable, tolerant, harmonious and beautiful place, and was an important seaport, banking center and holiday resort.

The war in Lebanon was my "home" for many years. I became acquainted with a lot of different people, learned about their difficulties, saw many of them wounded or dead. I saw history firsthand. The new war of terror was fraught with booby-trapped vehicles, suicide commandos, kidnappings, and so on. I would like to think that in later years, people will look at my photos, examine the faces of the people who fought this war, and try to understand why humans can do these things. I flew in and out, depending on the level of activity at the time. Like drifting in and out of a bad dream, there are certain incidents that capture the war in Lebanon and will explain the unique people, places and activities that have shaped this turbulent region.

1980—Popples and Missiles

The history of Lebanon is best left to scholars and philosophers, since, like the rest of the Middle East, it is like a mass of knots that once untied, bears no resemblance to the original structure. When I first came to Lebanon, the war had been raging for five years. Eager to earn my spurs as a war correspondent, I went to visit the Druses, an ancient heretic sect born in Egypt around the year A.D. 986, and later classified as Muslim. I was there on a short assignment to take photos of SAM-106 missiles being secretly deployed in the Bekáa Valley by the Syrians who (at that time) backed and actually controlled the Druses. Along the road, I saw hashish plantations that kept the militiamen loyal and well paid. Drugs were an important source of income for all the militiamen controlled by the Syrians.

It is not surprising that in a war-torn country with a dismembered economy, the people try to make the quickest profits possible. The missiles were there all right, amidst the hashish fields.

1982—A View to a Kill

I flew into Cyprus (the Greek side) from Paris because the airport in Lebanon was closed. We then waited for two days before taking a cargo boat transporting wood to the Lebanese port of Jounieh. The Israelis had crossed their common frontier with Lebanon and were moving forward toward West Beirut. Their ultimate target was to be the headquarters of the Feddayins of the Palestinian Liberation Organization (PLO), led by the ever elusive Yasir Arafat, and other Palestinian groups. Around the same time, the Israeli Air Force launched heavy bombing raids using American-made fighters and Israeli-made *Kfirs*.

It is hot and sunny out, but the black smoke has turned everything to grey. From time to time, I can hear small explosions accompanied by bursts of flames.

The journalists are all staying at the Hotel Commodore off Hamra Street. This is where the journalists usually gather to watch the war. Today, I have decided to set up my observation from the terrace of the Hotel Carlton, a cheaper place but affording an equally cinematic vista of Beirut under the bombs. The Carlton Hotel is situated in the residential quarter of West Beirut in Raoucheh, by the coast. I spend time with an Algerian journalist named Sadri. The streets below are empty. Everybody is seeking refuge underground. For the first time in my life, I am watching the heavy bombing of a modern city. We stare in amazement at the jets hurling down dangerously close to the ground (100 to 200 meters). At the same time, warships launch their shells from the Mediterranean Sea, shooting missiles of 150- to 240mm caliber. The noise and destruction are overwhelming—30,000 people die during those terrible days, most of them civilians buried in the rubble of collapsing and burning buildings. I am struck by the Israelis deliberately killing innocent people—people who are not attacking them, but who are easy to kill. I do not know whether to be angry or appalled.

We decide to climb down from our "watchtower," on the 13th story's terrace, to take pictures of the destruction. There are two armed men ahead of us. Suddenly, the two of them turn toward Sadri and myself, abruptly asking us to hand over our cameras. I think at first they are going to take all the cameras, but I soon understand that they only want mine because I have got the latest Nikons whereas Sadri has only old Leicas. Our two aggressors then shoot around our feet and start shouting at us to freeze. Then they frantically run away, holding our cameras tightly in their hands. A young Palestinian man, wearing a *keffieh* and a sash, who has been watching from a nearby balcony, comes down to the street and asks us for details, then starts making a call on his walkie-talkie. Soon men in jeeps and military vehicles arrive on the scene. They ask us, "Where did the thieves run?" After indicating the way, I am told that direction leads to the headquarters of the Panarab party, the Mourabitoun, which follows Nasser's ideology.

The bombing is still going on, but the Palestinians seem to ignore it; they surround the Mourabitoun building, and one of them, using a megaphone, requests the cameras as well as the surrender of the thieves. Their answer does not come in words but in bullets. The Palestinians reply in kind. During the shoot-out we take cover under a car. The car explodes from a grenade thrown by a Mourabitoun, and we are dragged out by a Palestinian fighter. The shoot-out lasts about 30 minutes. Finally, the men inside the building send out our cameras. The cost for their return has been three men killed and 10 people wounded.

1982—Through a Glass Darkly

I knew a young man, a Christian Maronite, during those turbulent days in Lebanon. He had told me about his education at the Sorbonne (he spoke perfect French) and revealed his refined taste for arts and culture. He was involved in a shoot-out against another faction, and I was there to cover the event, confident in my friend's desire to protect me from harm. But under fire, the blood lust comes. He becomes another person, shouting, firing, demonstrating his joy at killing people. In the massacre that ensues, it is obvious that he is deriving great pleasure at cutting off the heads and ears of his victims. He even tries to kill me, after having declared his friendship the very day before, when he sees me taking pictures of what he is doing.

####

I had planned to go to Khalde, near the front, with my friend Reza, an Iranian photographer working, like me, for SIPA, a photo agency. We decide to leave in the very early morning and on foot, since nobody wants to take the risk of driving us there due to the intense gunfire. We want to see for ourselves how far the Israelis have advanced and to take some pictures.

Khalde is a small town facing the Mediterranean Sea about 10 kilometers away from Beirut and about eight kilometers from Baabda, the inland town where the Lebanese presidential palace stands. The Israelis had been progressing very quickly over the past few days, using the coastal highway across Israel and Lebanon. Baabda is about to fall, and soon afterwards so will Beirut.

We walk in the rising heat toward the white smoke in the distance and listen to the sound of the gunnery; we are also aware of the brisk clattering noise made by the bursts of machine guns and the isolated shots of automatic weapons. We come across two soldiers walking slowly in the heat. One is helping the other, who is obviously terminally wounded. They do not utter a word as we pass them and do not even acknowledge our presence when I take their picture.

Nothing unusual perhaps, but enough to force us to breathe a little faster and to feel a little edgy.

The tension and mounting fear get to us, and Reza stops and says he will not go any further because it is too trying to do anything in such adverse conditions.

For some reason, I decide to carry on alone, and there I am walking and getting tired when I see a group of people near a petrol station. It is on the front. I am stopped by one of them who is carrying a Kalashnikov. He asks who I am, listening carefully to my answer. Then he tells me that he and his friends belong to the SAIKA, a pro-Syrian organization fighting against the Israelis. As soon as he understands I am Turkish and I speak a little Arabic, he befriends me, telling me his name, Saleh, and offering me some tea and sandwiches.

We all sit around an improvised table made from an oil drum. I take some pictures of him. One photo is still my favorite, a portrait in classic warrior pose; he's ready to shoot on sight, looking through the hole left by a shell in the inner wall of an abandoned house. All the while, the bombardment is going on around us.

Then it happens: First a giant flash of white light, followed by a shock... around me everything seems to be rocking, and I lose consciousness for a minute.... When I wake-up again, I can see nothing but dust. I think that it must have been the explosion of a shell. Everything is so silent that I think I have lost my sense of hearing.

The dust settles and I realize that I am surrounded by the pieces of hacked bodies. I panic. The next thing I remember is that I can hear again; people are shouting and running in every direction. Around me nothing is the same anymore: tables upturned, glass broken, dust, rubble...blood, torn limbs...and so on. I look at myself frantically. I have been lucky. I am complete, without even a bruise, but I am trembling. Then I see them: Saleh's eyes, wide open, transfixed, staring at me. The explosion had instantly killed most of the people who were drinking tea around us. Only Saleh, the Syrians and I have been spared.

All of a sudden, a man comes to the scene from the burning petrol station, brandishing his Kalashnikov. He starts yelling that I am a spy, responsible for the bombings, and that I ought to die. He shoots in my direction. For a second, I am petrified. Saleh understands the danger faster than I, and he shouts at me to run away to a safer place. Thanks to his intervention, I realize that my life is at stake and I start running away as fast as I can, leaving the burning petrol station behind me.

Nobody has followed me. I shut myself in a bath cabin. And I cry and cry and cry....

I stay in the bath cabin for a few hours, till the end of the bombardment. In the evening, I go out and walk back to Beirut. I am still in a state of shock when I meet a fellow photographer, Patrick Chauvel, who works for Sygma.

As I tell him my story, I realize that in the panic, I have left all my cameras behind near the petrol station. Chauvel cheers me up and tells me not to worry. His words cannot calm me, since I realize that without my cameras I am just an idiot wandering through a war zone.

The next morning, I start asking everybody how I can go back to Khalde to fetch my cameras.

I find an Italian nurse working, like Saleh, for the SAIKA organization. She drives me in her ambulance to look for the leaders of the SAIKA. We find them just as the bombardment is resuming.

We go inside a grocery store to feel the illusory but comforting presence of a ceiling above our heads. The gunnery is intense. We have nothing to do but wait anxiously. I feel useless without my cameras. Suddenly, as if answering my silent prayers, one of the combatants comes smiling like a politician, proudly handing me a video camera. I explain to him that it is not mine since I only work with still cameras; he says I can have that one as a replacement. I agree to take it anyway to prevent an argument. I can tell by the stickers that it belongs to the CBC (Canadian Broadcasting Company) who are staying at the same hotel as I am.

Back at the hotel, I return the videocamera to the Canadian television crew who had lost it the day before.

I feel anguished not to be able to take pictures. Luckily, Robin Moyer, a *Time* correspondent, lets me borrow one of his cameras.

Two days later, the Italian nurse comes to tell me that my cameras have been found among the corpses of Palestinians in the morgue of Sabra in West Beirut. One of my cameras is broken, but the other one is still usable. I am happy to retrieve them but sad to do so on corpses. I cannot help thinking that a piece of these people is inside my bashed cameras, along with their joy when they took pictures of each other with my cameras and how their happiness had been halted so stupidly and so suddenly.

SIPA covers only half of my expenses while I am in Lebanon. To stay one night in Beirut costs as much as US$400 in a big hotel, so I decide to stay in a hotel inside a refugee camp opposite the Hotel Commodore. The other journalists can afford to be driven around in armored vehicles and stay in the Commodore. A Palestinian named Mahmud has become my driver, and he provides me with all sorts of information and help.

I take an interesting shot, in East Beirut, of a woman carrying a child in her arms running away from the explosions. She is surrounded by soldiers carrying machine guns who seem to protect her amidst cars and rubble and smoke. One can see how the people had to move from house to house during the bombing in order to avoid getting killed. This picture has been taken with a broken camera (that's why it is blurry) because of the bombings.

The other journalists cannot go out of their hotel. I manage to snap this shot and others, because I am close to the action. But it is impossible to send my film out because of the siege. The American television crews organize "shippings," but the print journalists who want to use this system have to pay $10,000 per package. I only have $100, but my friend Reza proposes to put my film with his own in an envelope to be given to the American newspapermen.

I am most surprised when I get a telegram of congratulations a few days later. The pictures had reached Paris via New York, and I am told that one of my pictures had been chosen to become the cover of *Time* magazine, *Paris Match, VSD* (French) and other magazines around the world.

Being a war correspondent, I can say that I was there when it happened. My photos are silent witnesses to war. Most people see these scenes on TV during their evening meal, are very moved for a short while, and then flip the channel to something else. But a magazine photo can haunt you for a long time.

I am in a street not far from the Hotel Commodore, the general headquarters for the Red Cross, when a booby-trapped car explodes. Usually journalists arrive with the police and the military too late to capture anything but the confusion and wet blood.

For once, I am there right on time and I have the reflexes to take photos during the panic scene which follows the explosion. Everybody is running, desperately looking for shelter or just to get away.

I notice a young man start running who is wearing only a white singlet and carrying his pajama-clad son. He is followed by his wife. He is holding a silver pistol in his right hand. I start taking pictures of the three, rapidly running along with them as they rush in my direction. I am quite excited with my eye glued to the viewfinder, and so the pictures will come out a little blurry. I see him leveling his pistol at me, taking aim and shooting, but I don't connect his actions with reality. And he keeps shooting as he runs by me. All around me, everyone is screaming and yelling. The explosion has blown out all the windowpanes around us, and the noise of the glass crunching and shattering under the feet of the passersby adds to the cacophony. Then the sirens take over, first those of the ambulances, very quickly and on the spot, as usual in Beirut, then those of the vehicles of the civil protection.

After the scene has calmed down I walk back to my hotel, and it is only then, in the lobby, that I realize what had happened. The hotel attendants and the clients are all watching me with a look half disgusted, half concerned. I looked at my clothes, trying to understand what is wrong; then I put my hand on my head. When I remove my hand, I see that it is smeared with blood. The man's bullet had grazed my scalp.

1985—The Show Must Go On

In Beirut, a massacre always follows another massacre. The chain is impeccable and implacable. This time, it is the Druzes who are responsible for the deaths of some 300 Christian combatants of the Kataeb party and of the Lebanese forces. The Druzes have lived for centuries in the mountains of the Shuf and been considered to be ferocious warriors. Their leader is Wallid Jumblatt (the son of Kamal Jumblatt, founder of the PSP, Progressive Socialist Party).

The Druzes have just finished a merciless battle in the mountains overlooking Beirut, in the southeast of the city, which they won against the Phalangists. Once their victory was assured, they immediately perpetrated a massacre in order to avenge another massacre perpetrated against them (so they claim) by the Christian Phalangists.

I go to Bhamdoun, about 20 kilometers southeast of Beirut with two other journalists to visit Wallid Jumblatt and see the situation. The two other journalists are Samy Ketz of the AFP (*Agence France Presse*, French Press Agency) and David Hirst of the *Guardian*. We have been blindfolded to prevent us from seeing the exact location of the headquarters.

We meet with Wallid Jumblatt; then we go to see firsthand the extent of the damage inflicted upon Bhamdoun and its defenders. Although we are forbidden from taking pictures, we are not blindfolded and I am able to take some photos with an autofocus camera. I count approximately 300 dead. Most of them had been killed, after having been captured, hanged with electrical wires, and dragged through the streets, where they were abandoned like trash. It is hard to understand how killing, and killing cruelly can be such a joyful activity.

I am able to photograph the gaiety of the Muslim combatants after they have massacred their enemies. Some of them had discovered some mannequins in a shop and amused themselves with one of these, transporting it to the street in front of me, and then hanging it with a cable. A placard was attached under its strangled neck on which they hastily wrote the name: Amin Gemaye (the Christian president of Lebanon). One of the Muslim militia kisses a dummy dressed in a grey flannel three-piece suit. The whole scene is surrealistic. They do it because they are aware I am recording their actions. It is not much different from what soccer supporters do after a match or what happens during a carnival. The camera is a tease.

####

The Muslim militiamen of the AMAL movement had asked some photojournalists to accompany them. The sky, usually bright blue, is evenly grey-white, very shiny, and quite disturbing for the eyes—not very good for pictures either. The militants want us to come to the vicinity of an ancient well situated 10 kilometers north of Sidon. It's in a region that was recently under the control of the Lebanese forces and has fallen into the hands of the Shiites of the AMAL movement and the Druses of Wallid Jumblatt's PSP. They had just made a horrible discovery.

Hunters had signaled to the militiamen the presence of corpses in the bottom of an ancient well. The militiamen had to go down wearing gas masks. When we arrive, they show us the decomposed bodies of Muslim militants killed a year before on a beach near Sidon during a massacre by the Christians.

Later, I learn that there is some doubt about the identity of the corpses I had photographed near Sidon. Some people claim that they are not Shiite Muslims but perhaps even Christians. A small voice awakens in my head:

> *Like a bullet, I pride myself on my lack of alignment or cause, but I am becoming a tool for killers, a weapon to be used by whomever wants to create damage.*

####

Some time later, I take a photo-souvenir of a very special sort. It is in Jieh, a Christian village set along the road to Sidon. This village has been besieged by Wallid Jumblatt forces. They eventually managed to break the resistance of the villagers, and on their victory, they allowed the photographers to take pictures of their rejoicing. They look like the famous hunters of the safari days in the African savanna, proudly posing with one foot on the slaughtered lion. The difference is that the lion has been replaced this time by an unlucky and very dead enemy soldier.

The men are proudly posing, lifting their weapons high above their heads in a victory gesture, while stepping joyfully on the corpse of their enemy, as if they were walking on a carpet.

Without this picture, the world might seem saner, cleaner and fairer, but now that this picture is recorded, people will know how low humanity can sink.

####

Weapons and soldiers. That's what the war is about, no? I have taken countless shots of both. It is always a surprise for me to see how the soldier identifies himself with his weapon. Everybody knows that there is something sensual about holding a weapon. In the case of men holding a gun or a machine gun, it also has something to do with male pride. I have never encountered a soldier who refused to be photographed, and in every case the rifle or gun is raised upward like an erection.

In Lebanon, stereotypes are falling apart. There is a clash of cultures and images. In past wars, soldiers were like football players. One red, one green. One good, one bad. Here, everyone is evil, everyone is righteous. There is no regular army to speak of. The militiamen are usually dressed in a hodgepodge of half-civilian, half-military clothing. They choose freely the fashion they want to follow after their favorite mythology, revealing an incredible mixture of Western and Oriental influences. Some of these men wear big cowboy hats, or T-shirts with the picture of Ayatollah Ruhollah Khomeini on them, or hairbands and ammunition bands crossed on their chest like Mexican revolutionaries in Zapata's time.

All the world's a stage and we are just actors upon it.

These past days, I have accompanied the Druses militia close to the demarcation line in the Shuf mountains in southeast Beirut. They are fighting against the Christian Phalangists, using Soviet-built tanks that they received from their Syrian allies. With these weapons, the fight will be fierce and not likely to last very long. I manage to get close to what is happening. I always have to remember that I only have a still camera, not a movie camera. I have to take shots with continuity, so as to make my "story" understandable. Sometimes I wish I could just watch and direct what is happening to tell the story. I am allowed 36 pictures for each camera I carry; then I must reload.

I try to capture the essential moments even though I have no idea of the outcome of each battle. The dust flying, the oblique light of the sun contrasting with the silhouettes of the soldiers, the sudden movement of a tank, the bursting of a shell, the assault of the infantry, the last moments of a soldier brought on a stretcher to an ambulance. I am able to take these pictures because I follow the militiamen everywhere instead of staying in a downtown hotel with the rest of the journalists.

I am becoming biased because I am learning too much.

1986—I Am the Piano Player

Snipers get their kicks shooting at isolated and unarmed people. Many snipers are mercenaries hiding out in apartments on top of buildings.

I meet a sniper today, a Frenchman, who uses a rifle specially designed for his line of work, made in the U.S.A. He would shoot people, then play the piano, mostly Mozart, then resume his watch, waiting for the next target to come along. He killed children or old ladies without remorse or hesitation. Dozens of deaths have been attributed to him, but he has never expressed the slightest regret because, as he explained to me, he was on the demarcation line, the line that separates Beirut into two parts, East and West, and it was not to be crossed. Therefore, he had every right to do what he did.

Special rifles are available for conscientious snipers. For example, the American M-16 with a field glass and the Soviet-made Brejnev. I took many pictures of people trying to pass the demarcation line; very few of them made it.

My advice concerning snipers is to never be number three. The first one across the street has a 90 percent chance, the second has a 50 percent chance, but the third has no chance at all, because the sniper has had ample time to adjust his aim and tracking.

I am beginning to remember rules that should never be needed.

The main contradiction of a war is its perpetual vacillating between lawlessness and obeyance to strict and strange rules. To kill at random whatever comes in front of your rifle does not mean there are no situations where some sort of rules are followed. In the past, for example, the soldiers were not supposed to go about killing each other during certain periods of the day, at night, and on Sundays.

In Beirut, there is an unwritten tradition, somewhat bizarre, probably inherited from the Middle Ages, and respected by all parties: Shoot from 5 a.m. till 8 a.m., then stop for breakfast, and resume shooting up to lunch time, stop again for lunch and a siesta, and resume shooting until sundown.

1986

The influence of Muslim fundamentalism is felt more and more in Lebanon. It comes from Iran whose leaders have always said they wanted to export their Islamic Revolution to all the Arab countries first and then to the rest of the world.

As Islam is the second most important religion in Lebanon, it was normal that the new ideology would provoke a tremor in the diverse Muslim communities. Things would have been complicated enough that way, but the Iranians infiltrated the country and trained the people to the new ideas so that many turned to Iran as a model to follow. A movement was born that was soon going to be well known throughout the world for the expediency of its methods and for its extremism. This movement is the Hezbollah, the Party of God.

The Shiites have been influenced by the Khomeini-like AMAL militia. I have taken many photos that show the extent of the personality cult to which the famous Ayatollah is subjected in the various Muslim communities and factions.

Fanaticism is an indispensable feature of many wars, especially those fought for religious reasons. Everybody remembers the kamikaze of the Second World War who gladly gave their lives for their Emperor-God. The same thing happened in Iran during its eight-year-long war against Iraq, and in Lebanon. Sana, the young Palestinian girl who blew herself up in the explosion of a truck she had loaded with explosives, was a modern kamikaze. She took the time to explain her gesture to journalists (including myself) and had taped a message that was distributed to the press after the success of the operation.

Looting and robbing became very commonplace in Lebanon. People actually went shopping with a weapon.

I come across the body of an old man who has been murdered for the plastic bags full of goods he had just bought in Beirut.

I can imagine him, just moments before, walking peacefully under the bright blue sky, feeling the warm sun on his back and the heat bouncing off the hot road. The shining light is difficult to bear, so he lowers his head. Suddenly, everything seems to blur, the world around him stops, the light diminishes, and a pain digs into his belly. He has dropped his bags; blood is gushing out of his bowels. He dies wondering what he has done to deserve such an ending....

Why am I taking a picture of this?

I have heard that the young Lebanese militants have taken up Russian roulette as a badge of courage. I introduce myself to a group of militants averaging 19 years of age. I gain their trust slowly, and I eventually ask them how they feel about the war and how they cope with anxiety, fear of death, and the like. I also talk to them about my own fear of death; then I switch from this topic to war being a big lottery, and what do they think of games, gambling, etc. At last, I am able to ask them about Russian roulette, saying only that I have been told it is common practice for the militants but that I have never seen proof.

They remain mute for a while; then one of them nods in a silent acquiescence. He explains to me that almost all the militants, whatever the party, play this game, that he himself has played it often and that it is quite an enthralling experience, quite addictive in fact. I then ask him to permit me to photograph them during a game, but they quickly reply that it is not possible because all this is done clandestinely and that if their chiefs hear about it they will be punished. I eventually manage to photograph them, but due to my subjects' suspicion of being jinxed I am barred from taking pictures of the real game of death.

The table is set with a white tablecloth. The bets have already been taken. The game is for money and for the thrill. The rules of the game are simple and well known. Everybody bets on the chances of the shooter surviving and the game starts. The game must be played with a six-shot revolver, usually a small Smith & Wesson or Colt Detective. One bullet is loaded into the chamber, and the cylinder is spun around. Without looking, the player must hold the pistol to his temple and pull the trigger.

If he survives, the gun is passed, the barrel spun and the trigger pulled again.

The game can stop at any time or start anew. In Lebanon, some men have taken to playing this game alone.

This nihilistic game is perfect for Lebanon, where life is worth little and drugs and death provide the entertainment. In the beginning of the war, they were content with smoking hashish or marijuana to pass the time. Now it is cocaine and heroin. Death is the ultimate high.

The young bearded man has put a gun on his right temple. He is now facing his possible imminent death. The others watch him in awe. For a brief moment, he is a superior being, a true hero; in a second he might become a true zero....Like a powerful drug, every drop of adrenaline surges to his brain, he pulls the trigger slowly, his testicles tighten, and then...click. Today he is lucky—after all, it was but a mock game.

Two days after having posed for these photos, he tried his luck once more, with a loaded pistol this time (the very one in my pictures), and died. There was no click.

How can young men kill themselves for no reason? Russians invented this game when they were bored on the battlefield. These photos were taken 10 years after the beginning of the war. These young men have known nothing but war, death and violence during the crucial years of their adolescence.

I have heard that sound before. Click is the sound my shutter makes when I push the button. With that click comes the same rush of adrenaline, the feeling of omnipotence. As long as I click that shutter, I am immortal, free from death, separated from the horror on the other side of my lens. But someday I will not hear the click.

####

The incident happened during Terry Waite's press conference at the Hotel Commodore, the headquarters for the French press. An Anglican minister from England, Waite had come to Beirut to help find a solution to free the hostages and ended up kidnapped and remaining as a hostage for more than three years himself.

A car with three passengers inside is the target of a shoot-out probably just aimed at scaring Terry Waite. When the car stops in the middle of the street, I realize that the driver has been hit by a bullet. I rush to help the driver, forgetting about taking pictures, and try pulling him out. An American journalist (working for *U.S. News*) comes to our rescue, but we both arrive too late. The driver of the car is dead.

Later on, the driver is considered a hero by the militiamen and other witnesses of the simple violent event. The shooting is filmed by the cameramen who have come for the press conference and is shown around the world by the TV networks.

Just another death, no pictures, another nameless victim.

####

I am traveling in and out of the main Palestinian camps of Beirut, Sabra and Chatila and Borj el Barajneh. They are all situated in the south of Beirut, not far from the City of Sports. The war is more violent than ever. The leader of Shiite militia AMAL, Nabih Berri, who is also the minister of state for South Lebanon and who proclaimed himself minister of national resistance to fight against the Israelis, receives his orders from Syria and has the camps attacked.

The AMAL and the Lebanese forces militiamen can be organized like search-and-destroy teams and go from one house to the other to accomplish their task, or they surround a quarter and wait patiently for the end, cutting all the roads and blockading the supply of food and water. The people inside are starving, and some have already died of hunger and thirst. Those who are daring enough to get out are killed instantly by the militiamen standing outside.

The women and the children are, of course, suffering more than the men, because they cannot fight and must wait anxiously for the outcome of all this. They already know by instinct that the worst is always guaranteed. I also try to record their suffering for their history. Sometimes the women come to me, begging me to stop this nightmare, as if I can do something about it. My so-called "neutral position" makes everybody believe I can be a go-between.

Some Palestinians manage to sneak out of the camps, but the militiamen are waiting outside, and whenever they have a doubt about the identity of one person or another, they apply what is known around here as the "tomato test." It consists of asking the person caught to pronounce the Arabic word for "tomato." A Palestinian will denounce himself immediately by pronouncing this word as *panadora* instead of *ponadora*, which is the way the other Arabs pronounce it around here. Once a Palestinian is found, he is usually taken aside and executed. Hundreds of people have already died that way, or another, since the reawakening of intercommunal feuds.

####

Today, I follow and photograph a child who has probably become half-crazy because of the bombings. He is hanging around in the camp of Sabra, wearing only his underwear and a pair of grotesque pink slippers, far too big for him. As soon as he sees me, he starts behaving like a clown, dancing, chanting, making faces amidst the rubble and the ruins of the camp. I take many pictures of him, because he seems to me the epitome of what has happened to the people here. Being very young, he represents the future of this world without a future. His hopeless behavior reminds us of the hopeless world that humankind is proposing for the young generation of this country who were born with the war. Next to him is a young man wearing a funny straw hat, his face covered by a yellow handkerchief like a bandit set out to attack the stagecoach in the western movies, but this one has given it a personal touch—he has poked three holes in his mask in order to breathe and see. This young man was following the kid; he is probably his brother or a relative. I found the contrast between the two very weird.

####

I did something unusual, even for me, a few days ago. Something which has left a bitter taste in my mouth. Photojournalists are sometimes like vultures hovering above and around those who are going to die or who have already met their demise, in the vulgar expectation of a spectacular shot.

The light is bright as usual in this "blessed" country, but the sky is uniformly white. I go to a Palestinian camp near Sidon during a heavy attack. The camp has been bombed nonstop for many days. The shells keep exploding around us, damaging only the walls of the houses, until one, guided by I don't know which force, bursts out very close to a group of people. A child happens to be there....badly injured in the chest and belly, he dies almost immediately.

I then see his father, a man in his late twenties, coming to his side, in a very dignified way. He covers the frail dead body, still dripping blood, with a white sheet in the false hope to stop the draining and to resuscitate his son.

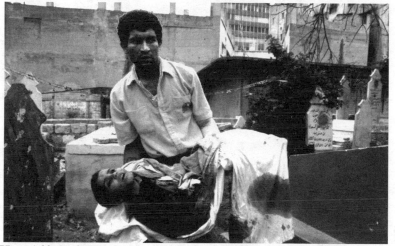

He quickly understands that the task is beyond his limited powers and he lifts his child in his arms, unaware of his weight, and directs his steps toward the cemetery. I decide to follow him. We are alone. No one else has come. I am taking photos all the while. I will never forget the gaze in his eyes.

In a universal gesture of love, devotion and pity, he is looking for the proper place to bury his child.

There are still human feelings in Lebanon. I am thankful I still have mine.

—**Coskun Aral**

LEBANON

Monrovia

Liberia
★★★

Chuck Taylor and his All Stars

Where would one go to see a cast of outrageously wild characters dressed in odd-but-uniform military gear and going by names that would make a sailor blush? At the premiere of Oliver Stone's next flick? Nope. Try Monrovia, Liberia, where Libya-backed, self-proclaimed criminal Charles Taylor has surrounded himself with the finest military men (all so competent that they were promoted directly from volunteer to General) Liberia could muster. General No-Mother-No-Father, General Housebreaker, General Fuck-Me-Quick and the gregarious General Butt Naked were just some of the colorful and oft-defeated warriors. General Butt Naked was particularly visible since he fought battles in his prime-evil buff—his only uniform was a pair of scuffed tennis shoes and his only armor the protective stench of stale liquor no bullet would dare penetrate. Around him chanted young children brandishing sticks and swearing like diseased sailors. They are just the finest examples of a century and a half of civilization in darkest Africa.

LIBERIA

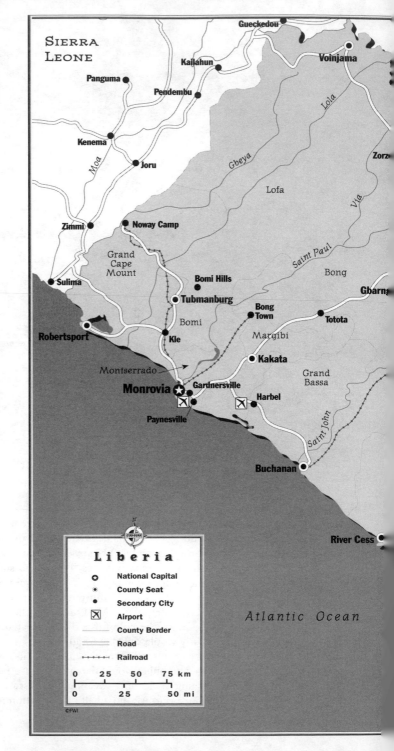

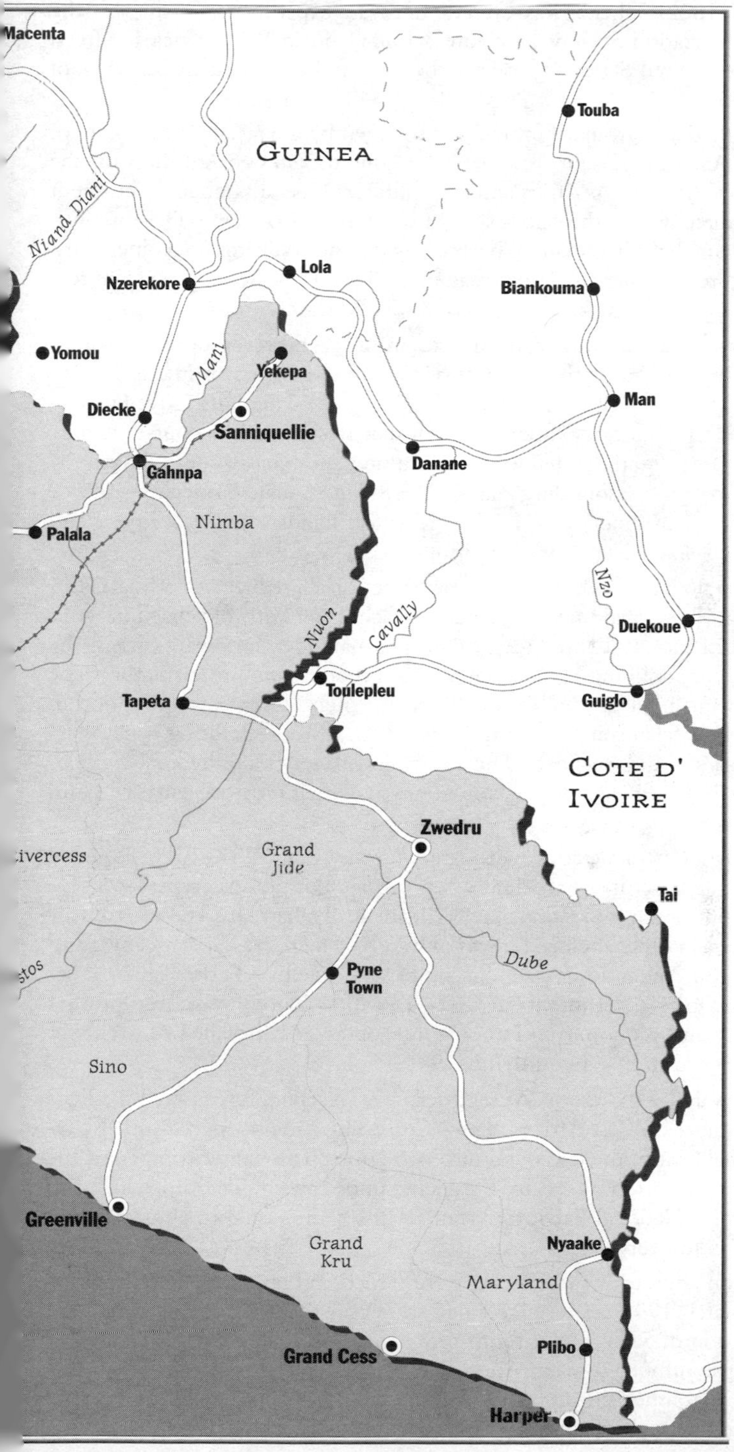
Macenta
Guinea
Touba
Niand Diani
Lola
Nzerekore
Biankouma
Yomou
Mani
Yekepa
Diecke
Sanniquellie
Man
Gahnpa
Danane
Nimba
Palala
Nzo
Nuon
Cavally
Duekoue
Toulepleu
Tapeta
Guiglo
Cote d' Ivoire
Zwedru
Grand Jide
Tai
Dube
Pyne Town
Sino
Greenville
Grand Kru
Nyaake
Maryland
Grand Cess
Plibo
Harper

Founded in 1822, Liberia was an attempt—an experiment, really—by the American Colonization Society to create a homeland in West Africa for freed slaves from the United States. It became the Free and Independent Republic of Liberia in 1847.

It's interesting that a group of individuals so jaded by the racial strata system of 19th-century America chose to re-create the United States constitution on the other side of the Atlantic. As Africa's first "republic," Liberia's debut government was modeled directly after the one it sought to escape. With names like Joseph J. Roberts, William V.S. Tubman, Charles Taylor and William R. Tolbert, Jr., prominent figures in Liberian history read more like a Palm Beach polo team roster than a struggling ragtag community of displaced slaves.

The attempt at creating a duplicate America in Africa, however, never came full-circle, namely because more than a century's worth of efforts at bringing the aboriginal population onto the same "playing field" as the emigrants proved unsuccessful. Instead of democracy, liberty and all that stuff, Liberia's course became marred by factional fighting, civil war, partitioning and bloody coups led not by men with sinister, nasty-sounding names like Stalin, Arafat, Noriega, Hitler or Amin, but with such innocuous, landed-gentryish handles as Doe, Taylor and Johnson. Sounds like a New York law firm.

Instead of freedom for all, Liberia became a free-for-all, reduced to primal clashes among rival clans, randomly slaughtering each other with old machine guns from the back of ancient, dented jeeps. Bands of marauders cut swaths across the rain forest plateau, donning Halloween masks and bolt-action rifles, as they rape and pillage in small villages before finally razing them. Calling the situation in modern Liberia a "civil war" is giving it too much status—crediting it with too much organization and purpose. The reality is villagers slaughtered by tribal-based militias that mark, like dogs pissing on a tree, their territory with the skulls of their victims.

One of the few Liberian leaders with any longevity was William V.S. Tubman, who was in his sixth term as president when he died during surgery in 1971. He was replaced by his longtime associate, William R. Tolbert, Jr. Tolbert actually lasted nine years in office, before he was ousted by a mere master sergeant, Samuel Doe, in 1980. Yet another coup attempt was borne by Charles Taylor, a senior official in Doe's government, in 1989. Leaving a bloody wake in capturing most of the nation's economic and population centers, Taylor failed by a whisker to wrestle power from Doe by mid-July 1990.

Shortly afterwards, a six-nation West African peacekeeping force called the Economic Community of West African States Cease-Fire Monitoring Group (ECOMOG) essentially partitioned Liberia into two zones. The first encompassed the capital of Monrovia and was led by President Amos Sawyer. The other half, run by Taylor and his National Patriotic Front (NPFL), amounted to about 95 percent of Liberian territory.

Reconciliation and peace agreements were signed and ignored like journalists' bar tabs. A March 1991 conference failed to get anything accomplished except for the reelection of Sawyer as interim president. Despite a peace agreement in 1991, fighting continued to flare. Another peace agreement and cease-fire in July 1993, which established an interim government and set up general democratic elections, crumbled a short time later in November.

Gambia, Nigeria, Mali, Ivory Coast, Switzerland and Benin are among the venues that have hosted Liberian peace talks since Taylor launched the civil war the day before Christmas in 1989. Some ended with agreements hailed at the time as historic. All proved to be failures.

The 12th agreement, signed in Benin with U.N. guarantees, seemed the most likely to succeed. It ended up in tatters. Only 3000 of Liberia's estimated 60,000 fighters—many of them teenagers addicted to drugs along with killing and raping civilians—were disarmed.

At least a third of Liberia's prewar population of 2.5 million fled the country after fighting broke out on December 24, 1989, when Taylor invaded Liberia from the Ivory Coast. In 1993, the U.N. estimated 150,000 had died, but stopped counting after that. (As of mid-1997, most estimates put the death toll at nearly 200,000.) It became nearly impossible for relief workers to operate in rebel-controlled areas. A peace accord signed in August 1995 called for country-wide ECOMOG deployment and disarmament of factional fighters, but 10 months later neither of these processes had gotten off the ground.

In April 1996, Monrovia was again launched into lawlessness. Fighting resumed in earnest between the rival factions. In only three days, Monrovia toppled into anarchy. Thousands fled the capital city in panic. As many as 20,000 Liberians descended upon the residential annex of the U.S. Embassy. U.S. military commandos evacuated about 2000 frightened American citizens and other foreigners by chopper to the Sierra Leone capital of Freetown, starting in the middle of the night on April 8, as Monrovia's airport was destroyed in the fighting. Evacuations continued for at least two months.

Yet a disarmament program, part of an ambitious transition program (and the war's 14th peace agreement) developed by the Economic Community of West African States (ECOWAS)—designed to dissolve Liberia's armed factions—became tremendously successful only nine months after Monrovia's anarchy. By February 1997, more than 10,000 fighters had been demobilized and 5000 arms recovered.

Up until July 24, 1997 Liberia was run by a six-member interim Council of State, led by charismatic chairwoman Ruth Perry who replaced Taylor stooge Wilton Sankawulo in this, Liberia's 14th, peace accord since 1989.

Before the Perry-led Council of State, the country was terrorized by up to 60,000 young (sometimes under 15), brutal, drunken and armed thugs who dressed up in masks, wigs and ballroom gowns and wielded rusty guns and vicious tempers to steal food, rape and butcher people. Bandits and terrorists continue to wax and dismember each other in the countryside, although the overall level of violence has dropped considerably.

In July of 1997, Charles Taylor was elected with an impressive margin (even though earlier he swore he wouldn't run for office and go into business). Things are eerily calm in Monrovia and his countrymen and many enemies are waiting to see what Chuck and his All-Stars will do.

LIBERIA

Fly the Friendly Flag

Ever notice that small type that follows those cool cruise ads? It usually says Liberian Registry. Yes, you read right, Liberia, the country without a postal system, phone network or even a government, sells a lot of flags and registrations. Over 1600 ships totalling 59.8 million gross tons fly the Liberian flag. In fact, the $50 million in fees paid to the Liberian government comprises 90 percent of the revenue to the government in tough times. It is called a flag of convenience, and shipping lines escape many of the taxes and restrictions imposed by more sedate countries. Liberia maintains that it spends 10 percent of its earnings training ship inspectors and says they are second to none in safety. The government of Liberia is run by a six-member council that includes tribal chiefs, warlords and politicians. Charles Taylor, a former civil servant and now lead member in the council who started the civil war in 1989, now says that none of the funds is used for the military but instead go towards schools, travel and payroll.

The checks are cashed by an American company called International Trust Company, which manages the registration business for the government of Liberia. The International Maritime Organization is permanently based in London, England.

The second most popular country to register ships? Why the conflict-, crime- and drug-free country of Panama, of course.

Liberia was once the most Americanized country in Africa. And, in a way, maybe it still is: violent, treacherous and floating calmly (for the moment) in a violent backwater eddy of outside agitation, tribal hatred and old fashioned greed. This is a country created by former slaves who brought American surnames and American-style politics to Africa. And, it appears, racism, guns, and crime. Liberia now barely functions as a country. The prolonged civil war has reduced the country to a subsistence economy. More than 150,000 were killed in the civil war between 1989 and 1997. The most recent peace agreement (the country's 14th since 1989) signed in August 1996 has been relatively effective in disarming the various factions. Chuck Taylor took the July 1997 elections and quickly put his brother and sister-in-law into his cabinet and left some seats open for his former warlord enemies. Things are calm now and it remains to be seen whether ethnic tensions and the mess with Sierra Leone will force Chuck Taylor to put his All-Stars back on the field again.

Charles Taylor and the National Patriotic Front of Liberia (NPFL)

Chuckie has pulled off the big one. He's now the prez. Not bad for a guy who's still wanted in Boston for a 1985 jail break. Charles Taylor, in his late 40s started the miserable war in Liberia back in 1989. He has an interesting resume for a politician. In 1984, he was accused of embezzling $900,000 from the Liberian coffers and then fled to the U.S., where he was captured for extradition back to Liberia. He bragged about how he sawed through the bars of the laundry room after bribing his jailors with $30,000. He went to live in the Ivory Coast, where he assembled an army (actually about 150 people) with the help of the Ivorian president, whose brother-in-law, William Tolbert, was executed by Samuel Doe. He gathered together another 4000 soldiers from the Gio and Mano tribes from eastern Liberia and began his "rebellion" in 1989. What he actually did was knock Liberia's delicate infrastructure into the toilet for the next 50 years at least. Oh, did we also tell you that Chuckie is a stooge of Qaddafi along with Foday Sankoh, the leader of the RUF in Sierra Leone?

Chuck has taken to wearing suits instead of military fatigues. Taylor is a descendant of freed American slaves, and his enemy is the Krahn tribe (about 2 percent of the population) led by warlord Roosevelt Johnson. Taylor unsuccessfully tried to take Monrovia in 1990 and 1992. When politics did what bullets couldn't, Taylor was made part of a ruling committee, but he overstepped his authority when he tried to arrest Johnson. All hell broke loose, and the U.S. had to send in the marines to evacuate the embassy and foreigners stuck in the crossfire. Taylor's choice of media is the KISS-FM radio station in Monrovia. His troops were ill-equipped and were famous for his groups of teenage soldiers, one of which is called the Butt Naked Brigade, a group of brutal young kids who fight wearing only tennis shoes.

As one of Chuck's new tourism ideas, he has ordered all expat Liberians to return home to get new passports. Uh huh. Meanwhile the ULIMO-K factions are building their strength in nearby Sierra Leone.

Diamonds Are Forever

When Charles Taylor married his girlfriend on January 28, 1997, he promised her he would not run for president, but would instead open a business. He lied.

Mu'ammar Qaddafi

Ole Mu'ammar has been stirring things up here and in Sierra Leone for a while now. Seems like if he can't have these countries, he will at least make them unavailable for others. His main man is Blaise Compaore, the president of Burkina Faso, who funnels arms from Libya to Taylor in Liberia and Sankoh in Sierra Leone.

Alhaji Kromah, Roosevelt Johnson and the
United Liberation Movement of Liberia for Democracy (ULIMO)

Warlord Kromah leads one wing of the ethnically divided United Liberation Movement (ULIMO), and was a member of the six-member collective presidency called the Interim Council of State. His boys are at relative peace with the other two main factions—the Liberian Peace Council and the NPFL—and control the western portion of the country. The ULIMO-J faction, led by Chief of Staff Roosevelt Johnson, likes to war with the ULIMO Mandingos when things get slow. Johnson usually wins. But Johnson can't see the forest for the trees and is now content to trade lead with ECOMOG and the forces of Charles Taylor over a diamond mining concession dispute. He certainly wasn't happy with his former cabinet post of minister of rural development. To show his countrymen and the world how seriously he took his job, he kept his hacker bush boys fed by hijacking food aid convoys moving through his territory on their way to the thousands of displaced Liberians and refugees from Sierra Leone's smouldering civil war in the north. He was seemingly out of the peace process and the inner circle of Liberian political power until Taylor tried to have him arrested in April 1996. The fighting lasted two weeks between the rival factions, and Johnson negotiated directly with the U.S. government for a cease-fire.

Samuel Doe and the United Liberation Movement of Liberia for Democracy (ULIMO) and
Armed Forces of Liberia (AFL)

The now dead Doe, a Krahn, was a 28-year-old master sergeant who put an end to the line of wealthy coffee-colored descendants of freed black slaves from America when he overthrew and executed Tolbert and 13 ministers. That he televised their executions didn't bode well for Liberia's future. When a coup was attempted, Doe's soldiers drove around Monrovia, publicly displaying the offenders' severed testicles. Doe persecuted the Gio and Mano tribes along with anyone else he didn't like and laid the groundwork for

Taylor's emergence. Charles Taylor, then head of the new government's procurement, first came to prominence when he pocketed almost a million dollars and fled to the U.S. When he was not busy killing and torturing people for fun, Sam Doe was applying his newfound financial genius. He managed to plunge the country deeper into debt by printing new money to pay the bills, while bumming millions of dollars in foreign aid. He did manage to cut all government workers' salaries by $10.

He was offered safe passage out of Liberia by the U.S. government but turned it down. Probably because Doe lived in luxury on the fifth floor of the Executive Mansion, with his two pet lions (which he fed with his many victims) and protected by his Israeli-trained bodyguards. Until one day in September of 1990, when he went to visit the ECOWAS headquarters. (See "Prince Johnson"). His memory lives on with the Krahn tribe and the high falutin-sounding ULIMO group who control small pockets near the Sierra Leone border (from their base in Freetown) and Tubmanburg. The Armed Forces of Liberia (AFL) is a splinter group loyal to the dead Doe and responsible for the slaughter of hundreds of people at Harbel in 1994.

Prince Yormie Johnson and the Independant Patriotic Front (IPF)

Johnson originally was allied to Taylor when he first attacked Doe in 1989. He then broke away with 1000 of his better-trained troops from the Gio tribe, leaving Taylor with the larger but less effective Mano tribal troops. In 1990, when Taylor controlled the countryside, Johnson controlled most of Monrovia, killing and torturing at random. About 200 of Johnson's men captured Doe when he went to the ECOWAS headquarters. They later cut off his ears and tortured him to death while videotaping the festivities. His dismembered body was paraded around Monrovia. Johnson and Taylor both claimed the presidency and set off another round of bloodshed. The fighting lasted seven weeks between the rival factions and as it raged Johnson was flown by U.S. marines to Accra, Ghana to attend peace talks. None of the other warlords showed up and Johnson complained bitterly when both the Americans and ECOMOG refused to take him back to Monrovia.

Armed Forces of Liberia (AFL)

The AFL was formerly the national army under the Doe regime, and largely comprising ethnic Krahns—Doe was a Krahn. By 1992, as a result of the civil war, the AFL maintained only limited authority and most of its equipment had been destroyed or rendered useless. The army these days is essentially just another faction.

During the April and May 1996 clashes in the capital, Krahn fighters loyal to Johnson were based in an AFL barracks downtown. Although its high command said the AFL was not involved in the conflict, many of its soldiers were thought to be fighting alongside fellow Krahns loyal to Johnson and Boley against the forces of Charles Taylor and Alhaji Kromah. Two men claim to be the AFL's chief of staff. Abraham Kromah was "appointed" to the position by the virulently anti-Krahn NPFL while Brigadier General Phillip Karmah inherited it when his predecessor was killed early on in the spring clashes in the capital.

Economic Community of West African States Cease-Fire Monitoring Group (ECOMOG)

The six-nation peacekeeping force sent in by the Economic Community of West African States (ECOWAS) was tasked with keeping Liberia cool and calm but spent most of its time hiding in camps during the '96 flare-up. Then-leader General John Mark Inienger bravely returned to tour the looted capital and pledged "to do everything possible to protect the city" and, we are sure, his hide. Their most shining moment was back in 1990 when Sam Doe went to negotiate at ECOWAS headquarters; Prince Johnson's troops broke in, shot him and cut his ears off while the peacekeeping troops sat and watched.

"General" Butt Naked

The Krahn fighter who led the Butt Naked Brigade, which, as you might expect, goes into battle in their birthday suits as a sign of defiance and invincibility. Now a celebrity in Monrovia, young boys cheered the amply endowed "general" when he "swung" through the capital on his motorbike. For now *DP* readers want to start a fan club for General Naked but we can't find him. Anyone out there know what Butt Naked is doing these days?

Political Parties

Founded in 1878, the True Whig Party ran the country until the 1980 coup, after which it was banned. It was revived in 1991. The National Patriotic Party (NPP), formed in December 1991, is the political wing of the National Patriotic Front of Liberia. The Independent Democratic Party was created as the political branch of the breakaway Independent National Patriotic Front of Liberia (INPFL) in 1991. Also formed in 1991, the United Liberation Movement of Liberia for Democracy (ULIMO) was organized by supporters of the late President Samuel Doe. It split into two factions in November 1992, one being based in Tubmanburg, Liberia, and the other in Freetown, Sierra Leone. Former members of the pan-African Movement for Justice in Africa founded the Liberian People's Party (LPP), a significant factor prior to the 1980 coup that brought Doe to power. The party's leader is former interim President Amos Sawyer. The Unity Party is spearheaded by Ellen Johnson.

Rubber, Timber and Iron

There is little left in Liberia, except for rubber plantations, the rain forest and the iron rusting the ground. The Firestone company owns the largest rubber plantation in the world, about one million acres that it originally leased for 6 cents an acre back in 1926. The world's largest rubber estate, about 30 miles east of the capital, is now better known as a former battlefield. It is assumed that Chuck will begin to line his pockets with the proceeds from Liberia's raw resources.

The roads leading from Monrovia are passable for limited pre-approved travel, but they can be dangerous. Liberia is accessible by road from Danane, Ivory Coast. This road leads to NPFL stronghold Gbarnga, from there is a road to Monrovia. U.S. embassy employees are not allowed to travel outside Monrovia, except for official business. Roberts International Airport outside of Monrovia is closed. Spriggs Payne International Airport reopened in June, 1996. West Coast Airlines, WESWUA and Air Ivoire have resumed Monrovia service. Overland routes to other West African countries are open but touch and go. Travelers who plan a trip to Liberia are required to have a passport and a visa prior to arrival. Additionally, in order to be granted a visa, you must present to a Liberian embassy a letter stating the purpose of your visit and another from a doctor confirming you have no communicable diseases. Evidence of yellow fever vaccination is required. An exit permit must be obtained from Liberian immigration authorities upon arrival. There is no charge for a tourist visa.

If you are caught entering illegally, you will be arrested and tried, at which point you will be imprisoned or deported.

Further information on entry requirements for Liberia can be obtained from the following:

Embassy of the Republic of Liberia

5201 16th Street, N.W.
Washington, D.C. 20011
☎ *(202) 723-0437 to 723-0440*
This building is currently closed because of fire. The temporary address is the following:

5303 Colorado Avenue, N.W.
Washington, D.C. 20011

When traveling by road in Liberia, extreme caution is urged even when roads are open. Motorists are frequently hassled at checkpoints manned by stoned, hungry, unpaid and impoverished soldiers. Cigarette rolling papers, indeed any kind of paper to make joints with, will increase your popularity immensely, as will booze, cigarettes, etc. But not a good idea to travel by road without someone who has done so before, and who knows how to deal with the fighters. As far as payoffs go, there is no rule of thumb—as little as you can get away with. Flashy watches, jewelry, sunglasses, etc....should be kept well out of sight and will be asked for as presents. Try to show your papers without actually handing them to the guard.

Roads leading out from Monrovia are passable but dangerous, more so at night. Travelers to the interior of Liberia may be in danger of being detained, harassed, delayed, injured or killed to use the usual jargon. The embassy tells us that the only area traditionally considered "safe" is inside the capital of Monrovia, since the Liberian Council of State does not control many areas outside of town.

If you think they won't steal your watch or car remember that during the April clashes, the U.N. had 489 vehicles stolen (worth $8.3 million). Only 11 have been returned.

Monrovia

Although a dusk-to-dawn curfew has been lifted in the capital city, Monrovia's crime rate is high, regardless of the level of tensions. Foreigners are targets of street criminals. Residential break-ins are common. The police are largely incapable of providing effective protection.

In April 1996, Monrovia plunged into seven weeks of fierce factional fighting after Charles Taylor tried to arrest rebel leader Roosevelt Johnson. The streets were littered with some 1500 corpses and the American government ordered the evacuation of the Embassy—nearly 2000 people in all, including other foreigners. It is important to check in with your embassy if you want a chopper ride out if things go to hell again.

Anywhere Outside of Monrovia

The situation in Liberia can change daily. Although a very scant security buffer exists around Monrovia, tensions remain high in much of the country. There have been incidents of violence against civilians by partisans of Liberia's several factions.

Are We Having Fun Yet?

I remember the look of disgust on the war photographer's face at an all-night party in Paris. He would start to tell stories of what he had seen in Liberia and then stop himself and change the subject. His photographs of the atrocities had been published around the world, yet these photos paled when compared to the horror of the others in his private collection. In the last few years the stories coming out of Liberia strain the credulity of even the most seasoned reporters. A typical day with Sam Doe was sleeping in, drinking American beer and then jumping in jeeps wearing Halloween costumes. People would be shot for fun from the speeding jeeps, and some hapless victims were dragged back to the Executive Mansion to be tortured to death and then fed to Doe's two pet lions. Rapes and torture were common. Not too many journalists were sad when Doe was tortured to death on video tape.

Peace Accords

There have been no fewer than 14 peace accords in Liberia since 1989, each of them brutally shattered before even the ink could dry. The current agreement was signed in August.

Costumes

In Liberia, if you see anyone dressed in a wig, a Batman mask or a ballgown—run like hell. In a macabre twist to the killing and maiming, tribal militiamen don the clothing of clowns and women while razing villages and slaughtering and raping their inhabitants. The costumes provide protection from bullets.

Embassy Locations and Useful Telephone numbers

U.S Embassy

111 United Nations Drive
P.O. Box 10-0098
Monrovia
☎ *(231) 226370/226154*

Liberian National Police Force
☎ *225825 or 222113*

Victoria Reffell

Information Minister and good place to start if seeking Charles Taylor
☎ *(231) 227007, FAX 227006*

Maddison Weon

Ulimo-J deputy chairman. Good contact for Ulimo-J leader Roosevelt Johnson
☎ *(231) 226763/8 or 225804*

ECOMOG HQ

Freezone, P.O. Box 10-9033, 100 Monrovia
☎ */FAX (231) 226244*

Emergency
☎ *115 (Don't hold your breath!)*

All visitors more than one year old must have a yellow fever vaccination certificate. Malaria and Hepatitis B are widespread, and such arthropod-borne diseases as river blindness and sleeping sickness can also be a hazard. There are 15 hospital beds and one doctor for every 10,000 people.

Liberia, 37,743 square miles, is situated on the west coast (Ivory Coast) of Africa, bounded by Guinea and Sierra Leone on the north and Cote d'Ivoire on the east. Monrovia, with a population of about half a million, is the capital. Liberia's total population is estimated at 2,839,000, with about half the inhabitants living in urban areas. Currency is the Liberian dollar. Officially there is parity between the U.S. and Liberian dollars but ubiquitous money changers will give around 50 Liberian dollars to the greenback. (Take a bag instead of a wallet—the notes only come in five dollar denominations.)

Liberia has a tropical climate, with temperatures ranging from 65°F to 120°F. The rainy period extends from May through November and is characterized by frequent, prolonged and often torrential rainfall. Humidity is high, usually between 70 and 80 percent.

LIBERIA

Indigenous Africans (including Kpelle, Bassa, Gio, Kru, Grebo, Mano, Krahn, Gola, Gbandi, Loma, Kissi, Vai and Bella) make up 95 percent of the population; Americo-Liberians (descendants of black American settlers) account for 5 percent. Liberia is officially a Christian state, although indigenous beliefs are held by 70 percent of the population. Muslims comprise 20 percent and Christians only 10 percent of the population. English is the official language. There are close to 20 local languages derived from the Niger-Congo language. About 20 percent of the population uses English. Illiteracy stands at about 60 percent.

Lodging, water, electricity, fuel, transportation, and telephone and postal services continue to be uneven in Monrovia. Such services are nonexistent or severely limited in rural areas. All electrical power is supplied by generators. Mail delivery is erratic. Parcel delivery service is available to Monrovia. Courier mail services are available in Monrovia.

U.S. citizens who register at the U.S. embassy in Monrovia may obtain updated information on travel and security in Liberia. Don't be surprised if you meet them at the departure lounge at the airport.

Embassy Locations

U.S. Embassy (in the capital of Monrovia)
111 United Nations Drive, Mamba Point
☎ *[231] (2) 222-991 through 222-994*
FAX [231] (2) 223-710
The U.S. embassy's mailing address:

P.O. Box 10-0098
Mamba Point, Monrovia
or APO AE 09813
or P.O. Box 98.

Liberian Consulate (in Canada)
1080 Beaver Hall Hill, Suite 1720
Montreal, Quebec, Canada H2Z 158
☎ *(514) 871-4741*
FAX (514) 397-0816

04/06–5/26/ 1996	Monrovia and Liberia again were plunged into civil war. Corpses littered the capital's streets, and perhaps 2000 Americans and other foreigners were airlifted from the American Embassy.
12/14/1989	Charles Taylor launches his rebellion from neighboring Ivory Coast.
01/06/1986	New constitution inaugurated.
04/12/1980	President William Tolbert was overthrown in a coup led by Staff Sergeant Samuel K. Doe, who subsequently suspended the constitution and imposed martial law.
05/25/1963	OAU—Africa Freedom Day.
07/26/1847	Independence Day.
02/11	Armed Forces Day.

LIBERIA

Liberia: Theme Park of the Macabre

Getting into Monrovia is cheap, getting out is not. The Russian Hind ferried journalists into the war zone at no charge (we find out later that it costs $5000 to get 11 people out). When we arrive we find out that the new economy is driven by journalists, $12 for french fries, $4 for a beer or a half a gallon of water. We take a ride with the U.S. Marines who are evacuating terrified expats and civilians. Considering that we are being dropped into a confused fire fight, we find it funny that they explain how our life jacket works and give us ear plugs to avoid hearing loss.

The Sea Knights fly in a group of three, it seems to be overkill against the freaked out kids with broken rifles and sticks below. Shots are fired up at us from the ground. The Marines respond with devastating firepower from all three helicopters. The choppers land in the huge compound in the U.S. Embassy. We sign a release form absolving the Americans from any blame. A strange formality after watching the machine guns blast away at the fighters on the ground. This is a land with no laws, no higher court and nobody to protect us. It is truly the law of the jungle. As the throbbing Sea Knights lift off we are keenly aware that there is no way out know. We have arrived in Hell without a return ticket.

The size of the compound is roughly ten football fields and there are about 2000 Liberians camped out. At one end is the loot market. Here everything from escargot to computers are for sale. All the material has been looted and there is a definite shortage of buyers.

We stay at a Lebanese run hotel. It is supposedly safe here because the two Lebanese brothers (who fought with the Falangists in Lebanon) pay off the warring groups. It has the curious distinction of being used by the factions as the marker for the end of the fighting since it is about 200 meters from the well-protected U.S. embassy. It costs $200 a night but they fulfill the two main needs of all combat journalists: a satellite phone and a bar.

The fighting rages on at night but it is quiet in the morning. We walk out and meet with Roosevelt's group, the Krahns. It looks like a nursery school, children as young as 6 or 7 are among the fighters. I guess it's not much different than playing G.I. Joe except this is the real thing and you get killed when you lose instead of crying to your mother. The morning is the time when the soldiers scrounge for food and booze, clean their weapons and play a little football. They also smoke weed which grows wild here. As the drugs and alcohol take over, the insults will begin and the fighting will begin.

We decide to see what the government forces are up to. It's a long walk, since there are few private cars and only scrounged gas. To use a silly but appropriate cliche, it is hot as hell.

The fighters like journalists. They think they will be famous if we take their picture. In fact many will do things they would not normally do because they think they might be on the cover of *Time*. Beheadings and mutilations are offered but refused. It is almost a design your own atrocity place for the "bang-bang" folks.

The situation is understandably confused. Roosevelt's troops control the suburbs and Taylor's troops control the center. It is important to keep in mind that Taylor's forces are not thrilled with the idea of journalists documenting their activities. The peacekeepers called ECOMOG are rarely keeping the peace. For now Taylor's forces have rockets and mortars and usually win any pitched battle. The battles start with a charge. One side (usually Roosevelt's) will break and run, drawing Taylor's troops deeper into the suburbs and unfamiliar areas. Then the Roosevelt troops will circle around and attack the attackers from behind and the sides. The government troops will break and run to the safety of their lines. Along the way a few people are left dead or dying. The dead ones are the lucky ones since now the blood lust and adrenaline take over and the atrocities begin. The fighters invite us to watch what will happen. We put our cameras away.

We go to visit the hospital. All they have is prayer. There is about one doctor for 10,000 people here. As we leave the hospital we bump into a tough group of Roosevelt's men. These fighters have been trained and carry AK-47s. They are surrounded by children who carry anything that even looks like a gun. They wear bizarre items like wigs and life jackets that they say protect them from the bullets. They are here for the thrill, the smell of blood and the exhilaration of escaping death. They dance, sing songs, yell insults and wiggle their private parts at the opposing side to incite a battle. One kid fires his rifle in time to the music playing on his Walkman. It is common to see a small child beat an older person senseless with his rifle just for fun. The leaders give the children drugs making them even more savage.

The one place that no one trifles with is the U.S. Embassy. Snipers shoot to kill and they don't miss. Marines with machine guns have no qualms about wiping out any foolhardy warriors who shoot at them. The dead are like a macabre theme park. Each side uses a totem or fetish to show their territory. Monrovia is decorated with severed heads put on tables as warnings, children with deep knife wounds and bloated corpses. I get some other journalists to help me drag an old man who is wounded in the face by shrapnel to the hospital. It seems to be a trivial symbol of decency in this godforsaken place. We know that he will not make it, but we feel better for helping him.

Running low on money and getting weary of the brutality, we buy places on one of the Hind helicopters back to Freetown in Sierra Leone. There is a huge fuel tank and a large Coca Cola sign inside the worn Russian helicopter. Like the end of a bad nihilistic science fiction movie, we are leaving a social experiment gone badly wrong and can't wait for the lights to come up and the darkness to end.

—**Coskun Aral**

Monrovia, May 1996: My First War Zone

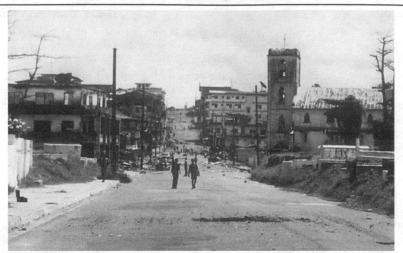

At least the dogs had a good time of it. From the balcony of the Mamba Point Hotel I could see a small pack of mongrels, perhaps half a dozen, gathered on a beach where huge Atlantic rollers crashed incessantly, ignorant of the mayhem that had brought these shores to international headlines. Food had become very scarce so I was surprised to see the dogs gorging themselves, tails wagging contentedly. Most people could hardly afford the inflated cost of feeding themselves, so it seemed unlikely anyone would think of the welfare of animals.

They hadn't. A convenient telescope revealed the largest and fiercest of the dogs chewing on something I couldn't quite make out. A slight adjustment brought into focus five swollen brown figures, then an arm, then my first ever human corpse.

"Welcome to Monrovia," said a war-junkie photographer, handing me a beer.

I arrived in the Liberian capital in early May, three weeks after the city exploded into an orgy of factional clashes and violent looting. U.S. Marines were still evacuating American citizens and other "friendly nationals," a massive operation that promoted this hitherto neglected corner of West Africa to the number one media event across the globe.

Back in April, ashen-faced evacuees landing in Freetown—the capital of neighboring Sierra Leone—had spoken of being robbed in their homes at gunpoint, often by children carrying automatic weapons as tall as themselves. Hundreds of fighters, many making their first visit to the capital after battling in the bush since civil war broke out in December 1989, roamed the streets of Monrovia, exhilarated by the freedom to help themselves with impunity. Little of the cash generated by Liberia's rich resources of diamonds, timber, and scrap metal had gone much further than the faction leaders during the war. Pay day for the foot soldiers had arrived at last.

The West African peacekeeping force, known as ECOMOG, sent to Liberia in 1990, and in charge of security in the "safe haven" of Monrovia, seemed powerless to prevent either the looting or the battles raging downtown. Some witnesses saw ECOMOG troops joining in the pillage.

The first journalists to land at the U.S. embassy, courtesy of the Marine Corps, were greeted by an exasperated Ambassador William Milam.

"What the hell do you want to come here for? Everyone else is trying to leave!"

Liberian civilians certainly were not having a good time of it. The million residents of a capital whose population had doubled since the start of the war because of its "safe haven" status did not get much airtime on the networks. A few thousand, however, were granted their fifteen minutes of fame by virtue of being crushed for ten days into a leaky, rusting Nigerian freighter with little food or water, let alone sanitary facilities, as Liberia's West African neighbors, one after the other, refused to let it dock.

Did the hundreds of paid-up wanna-be Bulk Challenge passengers left behind in Monrovia's port feel lucky to have been spared such a nightmare odyssey? No. Living in freight containers neatly arranged in rows on the port's football pitch, sometimes more than a dozen to a container, their unanimous sentiment was: "We've had enough. We want to leave now."

If Monrovia was a mess before the spring clashes—with no power lines, little running water and that tired look of a city in dire need of several thousand gallons of fresh paint—by the time the fighters had made their mark, with rockets, bullets, spray paint and a burglar's disregard for the personally sacred, downtown areas of the capital became uninhabitable. Most of the time the city was deserted by all except a few uniformed and armed peacekeepers and Lebanese traders busy welding closed the steel shutters of their supermarkets and electrical goods stores. Occasionally, when calm broke out, civilians would venture out in search of water, food, and lost relatives. Sticking close to the side of buildings, they would snake in single file only to scatter in seconds when gunfire erupted.

The streets were strewn with a bewildering variety of refuse. Rubble from shelled houses, rotting corpses, ragged clothes, passports (boxes of unused ones had been stolen from the foreign ministry) and other documents. I could hardly take a step without sending shell casings clattering or treading on somebody's cherished collection of family photographs, rejected as worthless by the looters— who, incidentally, emerged from the ranks of all of the factions. Jimmy, for example, a 27-year-old Libero-Lebanese, was at home when the frontline moved past his house. Ethnic Krahn fighters swarmed in, put one gun to his head, another to his belly and told him: "We're gonna steal everything and then we're gonna kill you." They were halfway done with the first part of their promise when the frontline changed again and the Krahns swarmed back out to do battle, giving Jimmy a chance to flee to the building next door...the Mamba Point Hotel. From the balcony, Jimmy had a clear view of so-called government forces (in reality fighters loyal to Charles Taylor and Alhaji Kromah, but what's important is they were fighting the Krahns) taking over from where the others had left off. By the time they were through, Jimmy's house looked like it had been derelict for years.

####

The only vehicles that moved were ECOMOG's armored personnel carriers, looted aid agency 4x4's, and windowless and often doorless jalopies, spilling over with heavily armed youths, their factional allegiance displayed in messy graffiti. One group had installed an antiaircraft gun in the well of a stolen pickup truck.

When fighting broke out in early April, thousands of civilians fled the city center for makeshift camps for the displaced, such as the Greystone compound, a 27-acre site once housing just seven U.S. diplomats and their families. It quickly became the temporary home to 20,000 Monrovians. As if the threat of cholera and other diseases were not enough, Greystone's residents had to put up with a daily diet of gunfire and explosions as factions battled just outside the compound's walls. Stray bullets ended their trajectories in tragedy on several occasions.

####

At least the kids with the guns had a good time of it, even when doing their utmost to kill each other. Perhaps it was fortunate that this was an activity carried out with staggering incompetence. Most of those involved in direct combat were very young teenagers already veterans of a war that by 1993 had claimed the lives of 150,000, mainly civilian, Liberians. Only commanders were beyond their twenties. They had adopted a bizarre variety of *noms de guerre*. Among the "senior officers" I met were Generals No Mother No Father, Housebreaker, Fuck Me Quick and Butt Naked.

Those without guns, a good half, made do with what they could find to justify sticking with the gang. Waterpistols, broomsticks, garden rakes, rolling pins, air filters, Coke bottles and powerless power drills were among the makeshift weapons at hand. Those with guns often had no idea of how to use them. On the first day I dared to leave the relative safety of the hotel, I found myself chatting with a group of fighters. Suddenly there was a loud explosion and a blast of hot air rushed up my leg. I looked down to see a small crater in the tarmac and the teenaged gunmen next to me looking sheepishly guilty. He had fired his rifle accidentally, almost with tragic consequences for my left foot. The gun's magazine, like many in the city, was held together by adhesive tape printed with the logo of the aid agency Save the Children Fund.

Much of the fighting itself was also chaotic, a tragic parody of cowboys and Indians, cops and robbers —with real bullets. From our ringside seats on the hotel balcony we watched battles conducted with Kalashnikovs held high above the heads of the young warriors, who screamed obscenities in Liberian English at their enemies. A favorite war-cry was "Yo ma pussy-oh," a genital insult also daubed on many of Monrovia's walls.

It was not uncommon to see boys of nine or ten on the frontlines, the bravest or most brainwashed of them all. Looking into the eyes of these boys, self-assured arrogant eyes, long-robbed of anything resembling childhood innocence, was a chilling experience. One morning such a child got into an argument with a comrade fighter some ten years his senior. They shouted at each other at the gates of the Mamba Point Hotel, neither willing to back down in front of the rest of the gang. The older boy calmly removed a rifle from his shoulder, passed it to a friend and squared up to the child, whose nose reached no higher than the gunman's chest. Undaunted by the other's size, the child continued to remonstrate and the argument grew more heated. The child then fished in the pocket of his shorts and pulled out a hand-grenade, held it to the face of his adversary, fingering the pin. I was no more than a couple of yards away.

"Shut up, man, or I'll pull it! I tell you man, you don't shut up I'll fucking pull the pin!"

Despite my presence and my appeals to wait until I had made myself scarce, I believe that pin would have been pulled had the gang's leader not intervened.

Ray Benedict, a lanky, befreckled twentysomething (he was unsure of his age) with implausibly ginger hair, was not a typical Liberian fighter in that he was adept at using his weapon, a cherished rocket propelled grenade launcher. Recruited into Charles Taylor's National Patriotic Front of Liberia at the age of 14 to "defend his country," Ray had become something of a hero among both his comrades and his foes, even the media. Although it had rendered him near-deaf, Ray was at his happiest when firing his rockets, and never more downhearted than when his daily allowance was used up. In the ecstatic moments following each explosion, he wore the triumphant expression of an Olympic sprinter about to break the tape. One photographer had captured such a moment, Ray almost in silhouette running towards the camera from a large cloud of smoke produced just

LIBERIA

seconds earlier by his RPG. The picture appeared on the cover of a special supplement on Liberia published in a Madrid newspaper, brought to Monrovia by a Spanish journalist. Ray probably doesn't receive gifts very often, and I'm sure this testimony to his unsolicited international fame is now among his most treasured possessions.

He hadn't spent much time analyzing his role in the war: "The people I killed, I killed 'cause they wanted to take Monrovia. The people I killed, plenty-oh."

Out of this modern conflict conducted with medium-tech weapons emerged much older aspects of Africa: magic, nudity, mutilation, even cannibalism. Fighters wore a variety of "protective" talismans such as cowrie shells and strips of animal skin. Since the beginning of the civil conflict, Liberia's warlords had taken advantage of the widespread faith in such bullet-proofing trinkets to encourage children as young as eight into the frontline. The Butt Naked Brigade, whose leader elicited cheers when seen in public, regularly disrobed in the face of enemy fire as a sign of defiance and invincibility. Other men went into battle decked out in women's dresses, wigs and floral hats. Some said this practice was rooted in the inability of young recruits in the bush to distinguish between female and male attire when attacking the first town in which they had ever set foot.

Juju gear and cross-dressers notwithstanding, there was little to distinguish battle-dress from ordinary street clothes. Combat boots and camouflage fatigues were rare. Charity-donated tee-shirts (Malcolm X was a favorite design), cutoff jeans and flip-flops were more the order of the day.

The prisoner's ordeal was a vicious one. Having been stripped, punched and kicked, his arms would be tied at the elbow behind his back—"to stop him flying away" one captor explained. Not only is this position excruciatingly painful (just try it), it also leads to slow suffocation. But there is rarely time for that process to take its deadly effect.

Looking at the victims, it wasn't always clear whether it was the machete cuts or the bullet to the head that finished the job, but it was often evident that vital organs had been removed before the moment of death. The eating of enemies' innards was a common, if discreet, practice said to imbue the consumer with the strength of the consumed.

"Hey, man, you want some meat?" one fighter asked me at a checkpoint. He held out his hand to reveal half a fresh heart. I couldn't swear it was human, but then again I hadn't seen many pigs around the city. I wondered where the other half was.

Decapitation was also prevalent and dozens of heads in various states of decomposition littered the streets. Fresher ones were prominently displayed at battlefronts, while others were left to rot away in gutters. When fighters from opposed factions called a temporary truce one day in mid-May, they put down their weapons and decided to play soccer. Since no football was available, they kicked around a fleshless skull found nearby.

At least the media had a good time of it. The Mamba Point Hotel was among the very few establishments still functioning in Monrovia. Thanks to some judicious palm-greasing, it had barely been looted. The world's press enjoyed intermittent electricity, fine wines and excellent food prepared by Ming, a Chinese chef who, when asked, as we took cover under a table during a shootout, why he was still in town, said "No money go home."

Among the regulars at the bar were our armed factional protectors, eager to see themselves on CNN.

We felt safe there, even when battles raged just yards away, occasionally sending bullets into the hotel. One of these projectiles entered the owner's bedroom, passing through a closet containing his wife's dresses and leaving a coin-sized souvenir hole in the left shoulder of each.

Of the dozens of journalists who came to Monrovia during the seven weeks of fighting, only one, a French photographer, was injured. A rocket-propelled grenade exploded twenty yards away and its shrapnel broke his leg.

Most of the fighters treated the media with respect and often offered advice as to the safety of crossing roads or venturing down alleys. War-zone veterans said it was the only conflict they had covered where they could cross frontlines in a matter of minutes, often by staying in the same place.

In retrospect it seems foolish to have refused armed demands for money or cigarettes, but at the time, lies such as "I'm broke" or "I don't smoke" came easy. A joke was always enough to defuse tense situations. Of course it took a while to get used to the liberties one could take. A radio correspondent, on his first day out, eagerly handed over his watch to an appreciative militiaman.

"Yeah, that looks good, man," said the young fighter, admiring his new acquisition. "But tell me, man, what time does it say?"

—**Anthony Morland**

Mexico
★★

Run for the Border

It's hard to take Mexico seriously. Its currency is about as useful as a moist tow-elette. Drug dealers ring its borders like souvenir stands. Separatist insurgents in the south threaten to topple Ernesto Zedillo's government with toy guns and ski masks. Church groups raise money for real guns. Tourists are attacked by Volk-swagen Bugs in Mexico City. The president's son is the victim of a carjacking at-tempt—by a policeman. A pizza vendor is robbed 23 times in a single year. The country's most violent rebels, the EPR, hold press conferences from their head-quarters in the jungle near (where else?) Acapulco.

Mexico's woes are either so laughable or so pitiable, the Barcelona, Spain-based Clowns Without Borders sent a fearless volunteer into Chiapas dressed up like Bozo to entertain villages victimized by clashes between Mexico's ruling Institu-tional Revolutionary Party and supporters of the Zapatista National Liberation Army. This is one NGO that seems to be perfectly at home here.

Imagine a bunch of armed Texans in ski masks in 100° heat rallying around a statue of Sam Houston and declaring the state an "autonomous region." On sec-

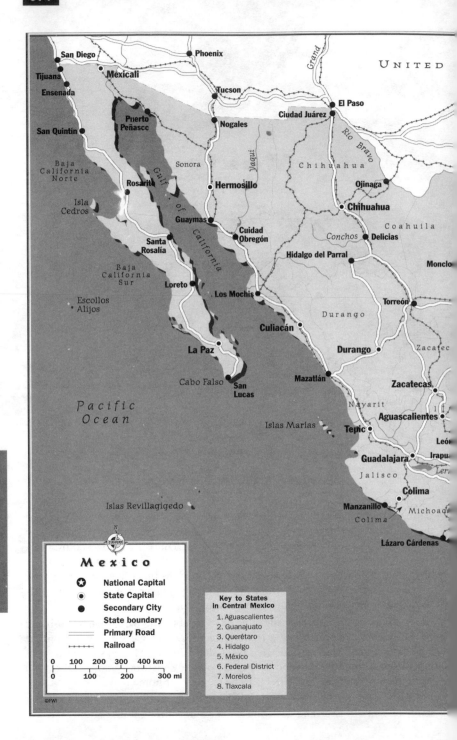

MEXICO

UNITED

San Diego
Phoenix
Tijuana
Mexicali
Ensenada
Tucson
El Paso
Ciudad Juárez
Puerto
Peñasco
Nogales
San Quintín
Baja
California
Norte
Sonora
Chihuahua
Ojinaga
Gulf of California
Rosarito
Hermosillo
Chihuahua
Isla
Cedros
Coahuila
Guaymas
Cuidad
Obregón
Conchos
Delicias
Santa
Rosalía
Hidalgo del Parral
Monclo
Baja
California
Sur
Loreto
Los Mochis
Torreón
Escollos
Alijos
Durango
Culiacán
La Paz
Durango
Zacatec
Cabo Falso
San
Lucas
Mazatlán
Zacatecas
Pacific
Ocean
Nayarit
Aguascalientes
Islas Marías
Tepic
Leó
Guadalajara
Irapu
Jalisco
Colima
Islas Revillagigedo
Manzanillo
Michoac
Colima
Lázaro Cárdenas

Rio Bravo

Grand

Yaqui

Mexico

⊛ National Capital
⊙ State Capital
● Secondary City
State boundary
Primary Road
Railroad

0 100 200 300 400 km
0   100   200   300 mi

**Key to States
in Central Mexico**

1. Aguascalientes
2. Guanajuato
3. Querétaro
4. Hidalgo
5. México
6. Federal District
7. Morelos
8. Tlaxcala

©FWI

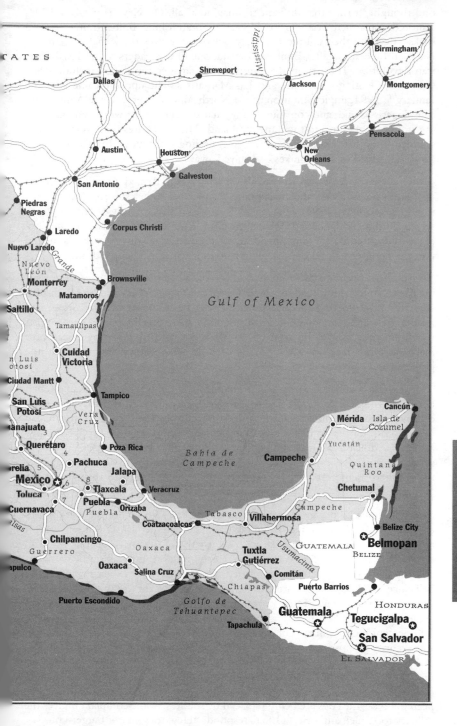

ond thought, it isn't that difficult to imagine at all. On New Year's Day 1994, hundreds of armed peasants in ski masks—brandishing bolt-action rifles and sticks—declared their autonomy. They called themselves the Zapatista Army of National Liberation, after Emiliano Zapata, one of the leaders of the 1910 Mexican Revolution. They stormed a number of Chiapas communities, including San Cristobal, Ocosingo, Altamira and Las Margaritas. The uprising came with the January 1, 1994, implementation of the North American Free Trade Agreement. The Zapatistas said, and continue to say, that the agreement will essentially strip the *indigenes* of claims to their ancestral land. The tour buses that previously descended upon San Cristobal and the surrounding indigenous Indian villages in droves slammed on their brakes and stayed away.

After a lengthy cease-fire, the rascals were back at it. Armed Zapatista rebels set up countless roadblocks and checkpoints across Chiapas in a surprise "military action" in December 1994. They virtually doubled the amount of territory they seized during the January 1994 insurrection. But, as with the last occupation, once confronted by the superior forces of the Mexican army, the rebels melted into the rainforest ahead of advancing troops, leaving 145 people dead.

Adventure nuts, daredevil tourists and bleeding heart Eurokids have been visiting the town of La Realidad in Chiapas since February 1994, including high-profile visits in 1996 to Subcommander Marcos by filmmaker Oliver Stone and former French President Francois Mitterand's jetsetting PC wife. Zapatourists who want to follow in the footsteps of MTV and graying left wingers can now make the pilgrimage down the muddy path to the Zapatista camps deep in the jungle near Toluca.

Mexico has been faced with a triple-whammy. Not only have the Chiapas rebels been a thorn in the country's side, and the EPR threatening the discos at Acapulco, but, while the central bank wasn't looking, the peso crashed. Investors began makin' a run for the border in droves in January 1995. The peso dropped so low against the dollar that Mexicans stopped robbing other Mexicans. With armed insurgent highlanders brandishing black flags emblazoned with a red star stalking the southern rainforests, it's a wonder so many still venture to this part of the world.

It's thought that if a mere five percent of Mexico's 96 million people took to the streets, Mexico's criminal-laden government would collapse. But why isn't it happening? Namely because folks are too busy trying to survive. As one Mexican activist commented: "Mexico is a culture of survival." About half of the working-age population in Mexico is unemployed. Families have seen their savings cut in half since 1982. Crime is soaring. There was a 35-percent rise in crime in 1995. Organized crime up was 16 percent the same year. Homicides in Mexico City average three daily. And you might consider walking to work. There has been a 100-percent increase in violent car thefts in the capital. Vigilante groups and private security groups are doing what the cops won't: offing the bad guys. The Federal District's 741 security firms employ 37,000 people, 10,000 more than the number of cops on the district's streets. Drug dealers and runners and other shadowy types have gone missing in the hundreds. They are called the "narco-disappeared." Now the cops are being replaced by soldiers. Some complain it gives the military too much authority. Others respond, "Hey, they've got bigger guns."

For the traveler, Mexico is filled with extremes. Whether you want the coke-dusted lifestyle of the rich and famous on the Mexican Riviera, or like to shop for .45 caliber ammo behind the saloon in Sonora, Mexico has a little danger for everyone.

What can you say about a country that's rapidly becoming one of Mercedes-Benz's biggest markets where a full quarter of the population lives in extreme poverty? Mexico is where the Third World runs smack into the First World—like putting Mogadishu next to Santa Barbara. Tell any red-blooded American he's gotta stay here for more than a week, and he'll be scrambling over the chain-link fence and dashing for the promised land. Even in the far south where Mexico blends seamlessly into Guatemala there is turmoil. Although the contrast between these two countries is obvious, Mexico itself is a land of contrasts and turmoil.

That's a Lot of Moneygrams...

Mexicans living in the U.S. sent US$4.2 billion home to their families in 1996, a 15-percent increase over the US$3.7 billion sent over the border in 1995, according to Mexico's central bank, Bank of Mexico. Mexico residents had more than US$10.3 billion stashed in U.S. banks at the end of 1996.

Popular Revolutionary Army (EPR, PRA, PROCUP-PDLP)

When you're number two you try harder. Or kill faster. Unlike the laid-back, amiable, college-educated and Internet-savvy ranks of the Zapatistas, the EPR are some mean dudes. Marxist/Leninist/Maoist-mean, like the Shining Path and the PKK.

The EPR first showed up on June 28, 1996, when 80 masked men with automatic rifles announced their presence at a political rally in Guerrero state. They say they are made up of 14 organizations. Their 45-point wish list includes canceling foreign debt and nation-alizing any U.S-held interests. They did not discuss back end points and credit type size on movie deals. The government wrote them off as one shots, the press scrambled (unsuccessfully) for witticisms and some people thought they were army stooges sent in to provide an excuse to send in government troops. Meanwhile, the tourists on the beach in Acapulco and shopping for silver in Oaxaca thought they might be in 1950s Cuba, but Club Med in Huatulco is a lot further than 90 miles to safety.

In September of '96, the EPR officially started a second uprising in Mexico by launching coordinated attacks in five of Mexico's 31 states. When it was over, 16 people were dead and the army got to use all the nice new U.S. issue military toys. The EPR was officially formed and took up arms in June 1996. By mid-1997, it had killed more than 30 people. For now the EPR attacks government, military and police installations, and although their attacks take place in heavily touristed areas, they do not focus on attacking foreign travelers; they just want to scare off the turistas. Enterprising journalists, beware; the EPR did kill two security guards at a newspaper that refused to run their press release.

Popular Revolutionary Army Web Site

http://www.xs4all.nl/insurg

Rafael Sebastin Guillen Vicente (a.k.a. Subcommander Marcos)

(Starring in *Che for a Day*, or *The Adventures of Subcomedian Marcos*)

Although the image of the intellectual revolutionary is an appealing one in Latin America, there are few Latinos who are willing to lead a heroic group. Che Guevara did, and now it seems like the son of a furniture store owner in Tampico is going for it. Rafael Guillen, er, sorry, Marcos, is a former college professor (with a degree in sociology) from a well-off family in the state of Tamaulipas.

Alas, his revolution will never match Uncle Fidel's nor Chairman Mao's nor even that of his real idol, Sandino. Vicente was born on June 19, 1957, and educated at the National Autonomous University of Mexico. He left in 1980 with a degree in sociology, earned a graduate degree, and became an associate professor at Xochimilco south of Mexico City.

In 1984 he left for Managua, where he taught and learned about revolution. He returned to Mexico in the late '80s to start up the Zapatista National Liberation Army. Its acro-nym—EZLN—sounds like the call letters of a soft pop radio station.

The pipe-smoking, balaclava-wearing "Marcos" appeared on January 1, 1994, when the rebels suddenly said they were mad as hell and not going to take it anymore. What attracted the world's press was the '60s aura of a group of peasants led by a charming, wisecracking mystery man who never appeared without his trademark disguise, shotgun bandoleer, pistol and pipe. He communicated with the press via video press release, sat-ellite phone, fax machine and word processor. Adventurous types, including filmmaker Oliver Stone, beat a path to his "secret" jungle hideaway for a high-profile rebel audience. He was long on rhetoric and short on results. His methodology was to "capture" a town with his ragtag army (some armed with sticks carved to look like rifles), then hightail back into the bush before the troops arrived. Most of the victims were innocent villagers killed by bombs or wild crossfire when the rebels didn't move fast enough. He is now making the transition to political respectability.

EZLN Web Sites

http://www.peak.org/~justin/ezln/ezln.html
http://www.ezln.org

Zapatista or Blast-ta-Piece-a-s? The *DP* guide to Revolutionaries.

Before you run off to La Realidad to hang with the latest poster boys of the revolution you should know the difference between the EZLN (who don't kidnap, torture and kill people) and the EPR (who do)

The EPR are hard-core terrorists and criminals. Although they wear cute green camouflage and wear brown face masks for the press, the EPR usually operates in 12-man cells in urban areas in plainclothes. If in uniform, the EPR have red and green arm patches and assault rifles. They are very heavily armed, politically indoctrinated and will go out of their way to protect their identity if stumbled upon.

They have bombed U.S and Japanese corporate offices, robbed dozens of banks and kidnapped prominent businessmen in Mexico. Tourists are not specifically targeted but the EPR uses plenty of ammo in their attacks. A tourist was hit by the crossfire at Huatulco Club Med.

Their training bases are deep in the Sierra Madre mountains. They practice hit and run raids and shoot to kill. They are closer to terrorists, have little grass roots support and are in the DP dictionary under "bad guys."

The Zapatistas is a 10-year-old homegrown Indian group led by poorly trained but laid-back commanders. Most cell are village-based with no real distinction between the military arm and the political arm. There was only one actual clash in January of '94. They wear a yellow and red star patch and favor balaclavas. Chances are some will be carrying sticks and their guns will be rusty. The Zapatistas welcome foreigners as insurance policy against military excesses and the government does turn back people at checkpoints in the area. In August 1996, over 2000 people visited five Chiapas villages in a weeklong convention (called the Intercontinental Encounter for Humanity Against Neo-Liberalism) to hear Marcos crack a few jokes and tell a few stories. By the way, trivia fans, Oliver Stone is a DP reader and Marcos turned down his chance to star in his own feature-length movie. Stay tuned for Revolutionary Land coming to Orlando soon.

President Ernesto Zedillo

Accused of being weak and indecisive and smarting from his recent trashing of the peso, Zedillo ordered the Boris Yeltsin manual, "How to Stamp Out Insurrections." He initially bombed the hell out of Chiapas and ended up with truckloads of dead peasants. He then adopted a conciliatory stance, and, after the peso was lower than a cucaracha's belly button, he sent the troops in again. This time, the stock market went up and the white ruling class applauded, while the working class protested. The bottom line is that Zedillo has the tanks, men and helicopters; Marcos doesn't.

Above the Law. Waaay Above

Blood tests of the staff of the Attorney General's office of Mexico found 424 employees (241 of them cops) testing positive for illegal drugs.

Juan García Abrego (El Muñeco) and the Gulf Cartel

As the reputed supplier of a third of the cocaine that reaches the United States, Abrego ("The Doll") was the first international drug trafficker to get his name pasted to post office walls as an elite member of the FBI's Ten Most Wanted list. He joked to his captors after he was busted by the FBI in January 1996 that "I never thought you'd get me." And he probably had a good reason to think they wouldn't. You see, "The Doll" was cozy with former Mexican President Carlos Salinas de Gortari's brother Raúl. In fact, Raúl used to party regularly with the boys of the cartel, one of Mexico's big four, and stashed some $84 million into frozen Swiss bank accounts. The stinger was Raúl Salinas de Gortari's alleged trip to Colombia to pick up $10 million from the Cali drug cartel, which he then tried to use to fund Luis Donaldo Colosio's bid for the presidency. When Colosio turned down the contribution, he was wasted by the Gulf cartel in March 1994. Raúl is now in prison for plotting the September 1994 murder of one of Mexico's top politicians. One thing for sure, while Carlos Salinas de Gortari was in office, the Gulf cartel rose to the top rank among Mexico's drug syndicates. Now this conglomerate of traffickers is on the downslide; 70 of its members have already been convicted in three U.S. states.

Amado Carrillo Fuentes ("Lord of the Heavens") and the Juárez Cartel

With the capture of Abrego and other gold-chained fat dudes of the Gulf cartel, the Juárez cartel emerged as Mexico's strongest dope alliance. Cartel kingpin Amado Carrillo Fuentes, who died mysteriously in July 1997, was the most powerful drug lord in Mexico and was chummy with the Cali cartel. He was accused of facilitating huge jet loads of dope into Mexico from Colombia, thus his moniker. From Ciudad Juárez, the coke moves to American cities like Los Angeles, Dallas, Houston and New York. Until his death, Fuentes managed to elude one of the most extensive dragnets by drug agents on both sides of the border.

Miguel Caro Quintero and the Sonora Cartel

Quintero's northwest Mexico-based gang mostly runs ganja into Nogales, Arizona, and other western states but also dabbles in the white stuff. Quintero, 32, assumed the helm of the cartel after his brother Rafael was busted for the murder of DEA agent Enrique "Kiki" Camarena. The softspoken Quintero is under indictment in Denver and Tucson.

The Arellano Felix Brothers and the Tijuana Cartel

Ruthless and territorial, Benjamin Arellano Felix is supposedly running the most violent dope syndicate in Mexico (his brother is wasting away in a Mexican jail cell). The cartel is behind the massive quantities of methamphetamine that have been flooding into San Diego, L.A. and points east. Arellano Felix's enforcers are thought to have been the trigger men in the 1993 assassination in Guadalajara of Catholic Cardinal Juan Jesus Posadas-Ocampo. This Tijuana-based cartel has already penetrated the Mexican military—which has taken over Mexico's anti-narcotics efforts—perhaps all the way up to the president's bodyguards. Graduates of Mexico's most prestigious military academy are known to serve as security advisers to the Arellano clan, and the gang has employed former army officers as assassins to whack any potential witnesses against it. In Tijuana and Mexico City, at least seven federal prosecutors and a state attorney have been murdered in slayings connected to the cartel.

The DEA and the FBI

The DEA and the FBI have considered each other deadbeat Princeton flatfoots for years. The DEA guys think they're cool because they're above politics and can meddle in the sovereignty of every banana and bongo junta with MFN status on the globe, not to mention MFN wannabes, centuries' old monarchies, Mother Russia and Uncle Sam. The fibbies are making a run at catching the splinters of the disintegrating CIA's turf, having never been content with hanging out in step vans and tapping phones in cheap motels. The two have kissed and made up for the purpose of nailing Mexican narco-monarchs and *contrabandistas* who, for decades, have been ponying guns, liquor, flake, smack and blue jeans across the Rio Grande. Together, they scored a coup with the García Abrego bust. Maybe a bigger one than they think. García Abrego may know enough mud in the Mexican government to cause the country's greatest crisis since the 1910 revolution.

All U.S. citizens visiting Mexico for tourism or study for up to 180 days need a tourist card to enter and leave the country. The tourist card is free and may be obtained from Mexican consulates, Mexican tourism offices, Mexican border crossing points and from most airlines serving Mexico. If you fly to Mexico, you must obtain your tourist card before boarding your flight; it cannot be obtained upon arrival at an airport in Mexico. The tourist card is issued upon presentation of proof of citizenship such as a U.S. passport or a U.S. birth certificate, plus a photo I.D. such as a driver's license. Tourist cards are issued for up to 90 days with a single entry, or if you present proof of sufficient funds, for 180 days with multiple entries. Upon entering Mexico, retain and safeguard the pink copy of your tourist card so that you may surrender it to Mexican immigration when you depart. You must leave Mexico before your tourist card expires, or you are subject to a fine. A tourist card for less than 180 days may be revalidated in Mexico by the Mexican immigration service.

If you wish to stay longer than 180 days, or if you wish to do business or perform religious work in Mexico, contact the Mexican embassy or the nearest Mexican consulate to obtain a visa or permit. Persons performing religious work on a tourist card are subject to deportation. U.S. citizens visiting Mexico for no more than 72 hours and remaining within 20 kilometers of the border do not need a permit to enter. Those transiting Mexico to another country need a transit visa that costs a nominal fee and is valid for up to 30 days.

Embassy of Mexico

1911 Pennsylvania Ave., N.W.
Washington, D.C. 20006
☎ *(202) 728-1600*

Mexico has an extensive road, rail and air system. Travelers in the remote areas should be very careful at night or when stopped outside of town. Robbery is common in these areas. Roads may seem well paved but huge potholes, animals, people and large objects can be found around blind corners.

During heavy seasonal rains (January–March), road conditions become difficult and travelers can become stranded. For current Mexican road conditions between Ensenada and El Rosario, travelers can contact the nearest Mexican consulate or tourism office or the U.S. consulate general in Tijuana.

Between 4 and 6 million U.S. citizens visit Mexico each year, while more than 300,000 Americans reside there. Although Mexico is "just across the border," it cannot be compared to Canada in terms of safety, health and crime threats. Remember that you are entering a country struggling to leave its Third World status. All tourists (both Mexican and American) are best targets for criminal acts simply because they routinely carry cash and expensive goods. Expect to be viewed as an easy mark for robbery whenever you travel to major cities and tourist areas in Mexico. There are an average of 35 homicides yearly in Baja, 40 percent of which are connected to the drug trade. Most of the murders are in Tijuana and most of these executions occur in daylight.

Chiapas

Travel throughout Chiapas, Mexico's southernmost state, may be delayed due to security checks. Chances of meeting a rebel roadblock are reduced after the recent military crackdown. Sometimes you may run into a roadblock put up by locals. Roadblocks in the Chiapas region can be as simple as a piece of string held up across the road. Many times rebels or locals will ask for articles of clothing. Journalists are also restricted in their movements. Interviews with Subcommander Marcos, although fairly easy to obtain, frequently involve long waits (up to a week or more) and a late-night rendezvous in a remote location.

The town of San Cristobal in the state of Chiapas is relatively quiet. The situation could become unstable in areas of Chiapas state outside of San Cristobal. Locals claim that law and order has ceased to exist in Chiapas, despite the presence of government troops. The army rarely intercedes in local disputes, even when they turn deadly.

The Mexican government is highly suspicious of foreigners traveling in the Chiapas region. In May 1997, 12 foreigners—including Spanish, Dutch, German, French and Italian nationals—were deported for participating in a protest march by Chol indians demanding the release of political prisoners.

Highways 15, 40 and 1

Beware of Highway 15 in the state of Sinaloa and of Highway 40 between the city of Durango and the Pacific coast areas. These are particularly dangerous and are where a number of criminal assaults have occurred. Avoid express Highway 1 (limited access) in Sinaloa altogether—even in daytime—because it is remote and subject to bandits.

Never sleep in vehicles along the road. If your vehicle breaks down, stay with it and wait for the police or the "Green Angels." Do not, under any circumstances, pick up hitchhikers; not only do they pose a threat to your physical safety, but they also put you in danger of being arrested for unwittingly transporting narcotics or narcotics traffickers in your vehicle. There are checkpoints and temporary roadblocks where vehicles are examined.

Tijuana

What you have thought or read about Mexican border towns is true. Tequila-happy gringos looking to break every rule in the book, señoritas with hearts of gold, hardened and impoverished immigrants all controlled by a police force that makes the Keystone Kops look like the Delta Force. Don't blame the cops for all the raucous bloodletting and bad times. Just in the last two years, 19 Tijuana cops have been gunned down, so forgive them if they are a little trigger-happy or looking for a handout. Cops in Tijuana must not only supply their own uniforms, but they drive beat-up cop cars that Americans dumped years ago. They even have to buy their own bullets, and they do all this on a salary of about US$179 a month. So give them a break; in the first four months of 1997, 67 folks were gunned down dead by firearms. During the same time period, cops seized 175 pistols, rifles and shotguns. By the middle of May, there had been 102 murders in the city.

Jalisco State

Jalisco possesses the highest crime rate in Mexico. In 1996, there were 15,899 car thefts, 5935 muggings and 5926 store robberies. Today, there is an average of six truck hijackings per day. During the first four months of 1997, 18 banks were robbed and there were nine armored truck hijackings. Two-thirds of the crimes were committed by first-time offenders. Helluva retirement place.

Mexico City

If you wanna get jacked around, Mexico City is a good place to start. Crime against foreigners rose 39 percent during the first eight months of 1996. Most of the activity has been street crime. Pickpocketing, armed robbery and purse-snatching are common. Using ATMs is a kiss of death. Thugs and other nasties hang in the shadows. Use only highly visible ATMs inside commercial establishments and only in daylight. Thieves have been known to beat up victims for their PIN codes and then abduct them overnight so as to use the machine the next day. An average of 443 criminal suspects are nabbed each day in Mexico City. More than 650 crimes are reported each day in the capital. Murder has become one of the 10 leading causes of death in Mexico. More than 15,000 people are murdered each year. Forty percent of the victims are between the ages of 15–29. In Guerrero state, 50 of every 100,000 people suffer a violent death. The figure is nearly 20 for every 100,000 in Mexico City. A Mexico City hotline took more than 8500 calls on robberies through the first nine months of 1996. The kidnapping of non-Mexicans is skyrocketing. The number of reported kidnappings in Mexico rose to 2000 in 1995, double the figure of 1994. Most kidnappings involve Mexicans popping other Mexicans. Typical ransoms are in the US$4000–$5000 range. However, the 1996 abduction of a Japanese senior executive with Sanyo netted the kidnappers a cool US$2 million. The U.S. consulate in Guadalajara says that only half of Guadalajara's kidnappings are reported. Most kidnapping victims' relatives won't involve authorities with abductions due to the high rate of botched rescue operations, leaving the victims killed.

Street Kids

There are more than 13,000 homeless kids living on the streets of Mexico City, a number that has doubled over the last three years. More than 75 percent of the street kids are boys, and nearly two-thirds of all the street kids have criminal records. Handing out candy may not be such a good idea.

Protests

There are an average of 7.7 protests a day in Mexico City. Between January and May 1997 there were a total of 1164 marches and demonstrations in the capital involving some 520,000 people. The leftist Democratic Revolutionary Party (PRD) led the tally with 295 marches, mandating a carbo-load diet for its supporters.

Driving

Poor roads, infrequent repairs and lack of repair stations make motoring in Mexico a true adventure. It is not uncommon to be driving for 50 miles along a newly paved highway only to find a four-foot-wide chasm marked by a single branch. You have more to fear from cows than rattlesnakes, since livestock like to sleep on the warm asphalt at night. Many routes have heavy truck and bus traffic, some have poor or nonexistent shoulders, and many have animals on the loose. Also, some of the newer roads have very few restaurants, motels, gas stations or auto repair shops. If you have an accident, you will be assumed to be guilty, and, since you are a "wealthy foreigner," all efforts will be made to detain you until you until you are a little less wealthy.

In Mexico, a blinking left-turn signal on the vehicle in front of you could mean that it is clear ahead and you may pass, or it could mean the driver is making a left turn. An outstretched left arm may mean an invitation for you to pass. When in doubt, do not pass. An oncoming vehicle flashing its headlights is a warning for you to slow down or pull over because you are both approaching a narrow bridge or place in the road. The custom is that the first vehicle to flash has the right of way and the other must yield.

Sport-utility vehicles are in demand by Mexican thieves. Some even display California license plates long after they are pinched. About 10 percent of the stolen vehicles in San Diego County end up in Mexico. The recovery rate for sport-utilities is only 20 percent compared to 82 percent for stolen cars. Ideal for the rough roads of Tijuana and the Baja peninsula, the sturdy, swiped vehicles are also the favorites of Mexican officials, who keep the trucks once they are recovered from *aspirinas*, or paid enforcers, who control the theft rings in California.

Drugs

Sentences for possession of drugs in Mexico can be as long as 25 years plus fines. Just as in the U.S., purchase of controlled medication requires a doctor's prescription. The Mexican list of controlled medication differs from the U.S. list, and Mexican public health laws concerning controlled medication are unclear. Possession of excessive amounts of psychotropic drugs such as Valium can result in arrest if the authorities suspect abuse.

Drugs are a major part of Mexican life. Some areas are considered to be run by narcotics dealers. Drug dealers can be spotted by their love for Chevy Suburbans and Jeep Cherokees, Ray-Bans and AK-47s hidden behind the seats.

Because Mexican authorities need to show Uncle Sam they are cracking down on drugs, the government rigorously prosecutes drug cases where the defendant can't cough up enough money to get out of it. Under Mexican law, possession of and trafficking in illegal drugs are federal offenses. For drug trafficking, bail does not exist. Mexican law does not differentiate between types of narcotics: Heroin, marijuana and amphetamines, for example, are treated the same. Offenders found guilty of possessing more than a token amount of any narcotic substance are subject to a minimum sentence of seven years, and it is not uncommon for persons charged with drug offenses to be detained for up to a year before a verdict is reached.

Emergencies

It's best if you avoid them, because it may take awhile to be assisted. (If you think 911 is a sports car, welcome to Mexico.) In Mexico, "rapid response" is simply your reaction to the gravity of your predicament. During the first six months of 1996, there were 72,548 emergency calls received in Mexico City. In more than four percent of those requiring emergency police, fire or ambulance assistance, no one bothered to show up. In many other instances, it took more than an hour for a response. The situation is so bad, the city has contracted with a private "08" service to help handle the flood of calls. The catch? You have to be a paid subscriber. Sort of like cable for hypochondriacs.

Firearms

Do not bring firearms or ammunition of any kind into Mexico, unless you have first obtained a consular firearms certificate from a Mexican consulate. To hunt in Mexico, you must obtain a hunting permit, also available from the consulate. Travelers carrying guns or ammunition into Mexico without a Mexican certificate have been arrested, detained and sentenced to stiff fines and lengthy prison terms. The sentence for clandestine importation of firearms is from six months to six years. If the weapon is greater than .38-caliber, it is considered of military type, and the sentence is from five to 30 years. In some areas of Mexico, it is not wise to carry anything that might be construed as a weapon. Some cities, such as Nuevo Laredo, have ordinances prohibiting the possession of knives and similar weapons. Tourists have even been arrested for possessing souvenir knives. Most arrests for knife possession occur in connection with some other infraction, such as drunk and disorderly behavior. Strangely enough, Mexicans are allowed to bring in to the United States three weapons and a whopping 1000 rounds of ammo.

Mexican Jails

The Mexican judicial system is based on Roman and Napoleonic law and presumes a person accused of a crime to be guilty until proven innocent. There is no trial by jury nor writ of *habeas corpus* in the Anglo-American sense. Trial under the Mexican system is a prolonged process based largely on documents examined on a fixed date in court by prosecution and defense counsel. Sentencing usually takes six to 10 months. Bail can be granted after sentencing if the sentence is less than five years. Pretrial bail exists but is never granted when the possible sentence upon conviction is greater than five years.

Mexico has the highest number of arrests of Americans abroad—over 2000 per year—and the highest prison population of U.S. citizens outside of the United States—about 425 at any one time. If you get busted in Mexico, contact a consular officer at the U.S. embassy or the nearest U.S. consulate for assistance. U.S. consular officers cannot serve as attorneys or give legal assistance. They can, however, provide lists of local attorneys and advise you of your rights under Mexican law.

Phony Cops

Be aware of persons representing themselves as Mexican police or other local officials. Some Americans have been the victims of harassment, mistreatment and extortion by criminals masquerading as officials. You must have the officer's name, badge number and patrol car number to pursue a complaint. Make a note of this information if you are ever involved with police or other officials. Do not be surprised if you encounter several types of police in Mexico. The Preventive Police, the Transit Police and the Federal Highway Police all wear uniforms. The Judicial Police who work for the public prosecutor are not uniformed.

Real Cops

For a $125 payoff to their commanding officers, a cop in Mexico City can get assigned to a busy intersection in the capital, netting him a cache of extortion money at the end of a day's work. The cops charge six bucks to overlook a parking violation, $12.50 for running a stop sign and $30 to back off from calling a tow truck. Mexico can boast the world's most corrupt police forces; so corrupt are they, in fact, that the Zedillo government is replacing a huge chunk of Mexico City's forces with soldiers.

Volcanos

Popocatepetl volcano, (or "Popo" as it is called) about 40 miles south of Mexico City, has been active. Villages in the area were evacuated in December 1994, and travelers in the region should avoid areas near the mountain's base. Popocatepetl, which means "Smoking Mountain" in the local Nahuatl language, had its last major eruption in 1921. Mexico City is not considered to be in danger, although ash has fallen on the city as recently as July 1997 due to minor eruptions.

VW Beetle Taxis

Don't even think about hailing Volkswagen Bug taxis on the street. The incidents of violent crimes against foreigners in these vehicles is escalating. Tourists are not only robbed, but beaten silly. Drivers often work as cohorts of other thieves, who stop the cars at knife- or gunpoint. Use taxis only from authorized taxi stands (CTO or *sitio* stands). In Mexico City, beat feet from the taxis parked outside the Bellas Artes Theater, as well as those parked in front of discos, nightclubs and other venues tourists frequent. The safer Mexico City radio taxis can be reached at ☎ *271-9146, 271-9058, 272-6125, 516-6020* and *655-0077.*

Good medical care can be found in all major cities, and many U.S. prescription drugs are available over the counter. Most major hotels have a doctor on call who can treat everything from venereal diseases to broken bones. Health facilities in Mexico City are excellent, and are generally quite good in the major tourist and expat cities, including Cancun, Acapulco, Puerto Vallarta, Mazatlan, Merida, Manzanillo and Guadalajara. Care in more remote areas is limited.

In some places, particularly at resorts, medical costs can be as high as or higher than in the United States. If your health insurance policy does not cover you in Mexico, it is strongly recommended that you purchase a policy that does. There are short-term health policies designed specifically to cover travel.

Immunizations are recommended against diphtheria, tetanus, polio, typhoid, and hepatitis A. For visitors coming directly from the United States, no vaccinations are required to enter Mexico. If you are traveling from an area known to be infected with yellow fever, a vaccination certificate is required. Malaria is found in some rural areas of Mexico, particularly those near the southwest coast. Travelers to malarial areas should consult their physician or the U.S. Public Health Service and take the recommended dosage of chloroquine. Although chloroquine is not considered necessary for travelers to the major resort areas on the Pacific and Gulf coasts, travelers to those areas should use insect repellent and take other personal protection measures to reduce contact with mosquitoes, particularly from dusk to dawn when malaria transmission is most likely.

Montezuma's revenge is as sure as hangovers from cheap tequila. Drink only bottled water or water that has been boiled for 20 minutes. Avoid ice cubes. A good rule of thumb is, if you can't peel it or cook it, don't eat it. If symptoms of diarrhea present themselves and persist, seek medical attention, because diarrhea is potentially dangerous. Air pollution in Mexico City is severe. It is most dangerous during thermal inversions, which occur most frequently from December to May. Air pollution plus Mexico City's high altitude are a particular health risk for the elderly and persons with high blood pressure, anemia, or respiratory or cardiac problems.

Mexico has a population of 95,800,000 with Mexico City being the largest population center with 9,800,000. Mexico's climate varies from arid desert in the north to tropical in the south. About 97 percent of Mexicans are Roman Catholic; the remaining three percent are Protestant. The official language is Spanish. English is understood in highly touristed areas, but not in the countryside.

Telephone and fax service is good in the major cities and direct-dial calls to the U.S. can be made from the tourist centers and major cities. In the boonies, if you can find a phone, an international operator may be required to make an international call. Almost every town in Mexico has a post office. Most are open from 9 a.m.–5 p.m. Mexican businesses are also open during the same hours, most taking a one-hour break for lunch (some close for 2 hours). The electrical current is 110V/60C. Mexico's currency is the peso (7.5 pesos=US$1).

In an emergency, call ☎ [91] (5) 250-0123, the 24-hour hotline of the Mexican Ministry of Tourism. The hotline is for immediate assistance, but it can give you general, nonemergency guidance as well. In Mexico City, dial ☎ 06 for police assistance.

If you have problems filling out a police report or in filing a report, you can call the Silver Angels. This group helps tourists who are victims of crime file a police report.

If you have an emergency while driving, call the Ministry of Tourism's hotline to obtain help from the Green Angels, a fleet of radio-dispatched trucks with bilingual crews that operate daily. Services include protection, medical first aid, mechanical aid for your car and basic supplies. You will not be charged for services, only for parts, gas and oil. The Green Angels patrol daily, from dawn until sunset. If you are unable to call them, pull well off the road and lift the hood of your car; chances are good that they will find you.

Embassy and Consulate Locations

American Embassy

Paseo de la Reforma 305
Mexico 06500, D.F.
☎ [52] (5) 211-0042
FAX [52] (5) 511-9980

U.S. Export Development Office/
U.S. Trade Center

31 Liverpool
Mexico 06600, D.F.
☎ [52] (5) 591-0155

American Consulate

Circunvalacion No. 120 Centro
Mazatlan, Sinaloa
☎ [52] (678) 5-22-05
FAX [52] (678) 2-1775

American Consulate

Paseo Montejo 453
Merida, Yucatan
☎ [52] (99) 25-5011
After Hours (emergencies) ☎ [52] (99) 25-5409
FAX [52] (99) 25-6219

American Consulate General

Avenue Lopez Mateos 924-N
Ciudad Juarez, Chihuahua
☎ [52] (16) 134-048
After Hours (emergencies) ☎ (915) 525-6066
FAX [52] (161) 34048 ext. 210 or [52] (161) 34050 ext. 210

American Consulate General

Avenida Constitucion 411 Poniente
Monterrey, Nuevo Leon
☎ [52] (83) 45-2120
FAX [52] (83) 42-0177

American Consulate General

Progreso 175

Guadalajara, Jalisco
☎ [52] (36) 25-2998, [52] (36) 25-2700
FAX [52] (36) 26-6549

American Consulate

Avenida Allende 3330, Col. Jardin
Nuevo Laredo, Tamaulipas
☎ [52] (871) 4-0696 or [52] (871) 4-9616
After Hours (emergencies) ☎ (512) 727-9661
FAX [52] (871) 4-0696 ext. 128

American Consulate

Calle Monterrey 141, Poniente
Hermosillo, Sonora
☎ [52] (621) 723-75
After Hours (emergencies) ☎ [52] (621) 725-85
FAX [52] (62) 172375 ext. 49

American Consulate General

Tapachula 96
Tijuana, Baja California
☎ [52] (66) 81-7400 or (706) 681-7400
After Hours (emergencies) ☎ (619) 585-2000
FAX [52] (66) 81-8016

American Consulate

Avenue Primera No. 2002
Matamoros, Tamaulipas
☎ [52] (891) 2-52-50 or [52] (891) 2-52-51
FAX [52] (89) 138048

Embassy of Mexico

1911 Pennsylvania Avenue N.W.
Washington, D.C. 20006
☎ (202) 728-1600

06/07/1997	The ruling Institutional Revolutionary Party suffers biggest electoral setback in its 69 years in power in Mexico.
03/23/1994	Leading presidential candidate Luis Donaldo Colosio is assassinated.
01/01/1994	Chiapas uprising begins.

05/05/1867	Archduke Maximilian of Austria, who was established as emperor of Mexico in 1864 by Napoleon III of France, was deposed by Benito Juarez and executed in 1867.
12/06/1822	Establishment of the Republic.
09/16/1810	Independence from Spain was declared by Father Miguel Hidalgo. The war for independence continued until 1822, when the Mexican Republic was established.

MEXICO

Yangon

Myanmar

Politically Incorrect

Watching tourism surge and hard currency flow into its former Third World neighbors such as Thailand, Malaysia, Vietnam and Indonesia, the generals of SLORC (the State Law and Order Restoration Council) figured that their own ancient temples, smiling people and steaming jungles were ripe for the picking—so they bulldozed villages, press-ganged the citizenry into slave labor and started razing the rainforest. Oh, isn't that how you attract tourists?

The generals' bizarre version of tourism, human rights and overall heavy-handedness has made Burma (whoops, Myanmar) the most politically incorrect destination on earth. While its buddies along the Pacific Rim sponsor tourism and award lucrative contracts to companies to build up the infrastructure and create tourist attractions, Myanmar saves a few bucks by having its general population do it—at gunpoint.

A few tourists showed up for the heavily promoted Visit Myanmar Year 1996 (which actually ran until the end of 1997 so the numbers would look good), but had to duck out of the way of occasional student demonstrations, mobs of SLORC Youth skinheads and truckloads of pissed-off Buddhist monks firebombing Muslim mosques. Yes, there's been a flood of foreign investment here over the last couple of years, mostly by ASEAN countries tucked behind the bombastic banner of "constructive engagement." And, yes, new hotels are springing into the Rangoon (Yangon) skyline like mushrooms after a May shower. But the high-tech and electonics industries are a little more hesitant. You see, unauthorized possession of a fax machine, modem and even a walkie-talkie is punishable by several years imprisonment. Sort of limits the market.

Then there are the drug lords. Notorious Khun Sa, who once supplied the U.S. with more than half of its heroin, "surrendered" to SLORC in January 1996. His brutal punishment? A cushy villa in Yangon, 10 personal aides, four cars, a military escort, a personal Taiwanese doctor, a hotel and real estate empire, twice-weekly golf outings with the generals and the concession to run Yangon's bus system. He supplements his income with a line of ladies' shoes that fetch 20 grand a pair. That's what we call doing time.

To keep the "Prince of Death" (as Khun Sa translates into) in retirement funds, the generals look the other way while he runs a chain of methamphetamine factories ringing the Thai and Laos borders that rivals the number of Iowa's Pizza Huts. *Yaa baa*, as the Thais call it, has become all the rage in Thailand, where everyone from school kids to truck drivers gobble the stuff down like breath mints. It has killed hundreds. To get more of the youngsters hooked, Mr. K's freedom-fighters-turned-jungle-chemists coat the little devils with chocolate. Yummy.

There's also the ugly boil on SLORC's smiling face; the insurgent Karen National Union (KNU) has been slugging it out in a jungle rumble with various Yangon regimes since 1948 for a defined homeland, making its efforts the longest running rebellion in Southeast Asia. SLORC, trying to rake the leaves in its back yard as it enters ASEAN, has pushed more than 100,000 Karen refugees into camps in Thailand over the last few years. An early 1997 dry season offensive—which all but wiped out the KNU—sent some 20,000 people streaming across the border alone, many recounting horrific tales of rape and torture at the hands of the libido-savaged Burmese regulars along with their doped-out DKBA stooges—former freedom fighters who sold out to SLORC for a crate of AKs and some syringes.

Between SLORC, the KNU and Aung San Suu Kyi—the Nobel prize–winning activist who was officially released after six years of house arrest but may as well still be under it—Myanmar makes for a bad soap opera. But let's go back a bit.

In keeping with the trend among developing and newly independent states to throw off the stigma of their colonial past, Burma became Myanmar in 1989 in a Joe Mobutu-like attempt to instantly decolonize the country. (Burma has always been called "Myanma"—that's right, no 'r'—in the Burmese language.) Somerset Maugham turned in his grave when Rangoon became Yangon and the Irrawaddy became Ayeyarwady.

SLORCies and their fans will point out that Myanmar has been a nation of bellicose rulers and brutal suppression since 2500 B.C., when the Yunnan enslaved the Pyus along the upper Ayeyarwady River. Throughout its various occupations by the Mons, the Arakanese, the British and the Japanese, there have been tales of ruthless excess and exotic splendor. Unlike the nepotistic concept of royal hierar-

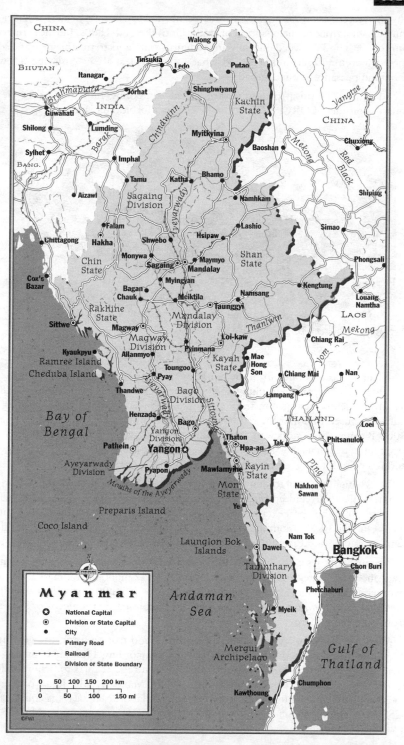

Myanmar

- ✪ National Capital
- ◉ Division or State Capital
- • City
- Primary Road
- +++ Railroad
- --- Division or State Boundary

| 0 | 50 | 100 | 150 | 200 km |
| 0 | 50 | 100 | 150 mi |

©FWI

chy in Western countries, it was considered normal for Burmese rulers to exterminate heirs, rivals or the offspring of rivals. Until the mid-1800s, Burmese rulers burned, beat and drowned not only any potential claimants to the throne but also their children and servants. Hey, so what's the big deal about enslaving a few thousand peasants to build a road?

Today, the despotism continues. It's called something right out of a "Get Smart" episode: SLORC. A foreboding name in a forbidding land.

Myanmar was cocooned from the world by General Ne Win, who seized power in 1962. His 26-year reign plunged Myanmar backwards. He ruled until 1988, when pro-democracy demonstrators won and Ne Win stepped down. But the military refused to honor the results of an election it itself organized. More than 3000 Burmese protestors were killed when SLORC wrested control of the government in a military crackdown. The 80-something Ne Win lives in the shadows and is a close friend of current intelligence chief Major-General Khin Nyunt.

The 21-member military junta of General Than Shwe continues to violently suppress dissidents and uprisings, and has firmly consolidated its vise on the nation by coming to "peace terms" with 15 of the 16 active rebel factions in Myanmar. Only the KNU continues to snipe at Burmese troops in remote jungle hamlets in the southeast of the country, but to date can claim no town as its base.

The current boy's club government has started to lure a steady stream of politically incorrect, eager investors, but the bulk of the 42 million Myanmars are condemned to exist on an average per-capita income of US$200. Even the normally idealistic causes of insurgent groups have been replaced by the need for profits from opium production.

In getting ready for Visit Myanmar Year 1996, and true to form, the government—to prepare for the jumbo jet–loads of camcording Honshu islanders—chain-ganged not only criminals and dissidents, but regular folks to help rebuild monuments, palaces, temples and attractions. In Mandalay, the junta ordered each family to contribute at least three days of free labor. Mandalayans could pay US$6 a month to be exempted from this drudgery. The average wage is about $6 a week in Mandalay.

There are an estimated 26,000 insurgents in and around Myanmar fighting for various causes at any one time, though most of them have at least temporarily laid down their arms through various peace (and drug profit sharing) agreements with SLORC. But figuring out who's fighting who is like getting an urchin out of a gill net. The military regularly abducts villagers in rural areas to serve as porters in its war against the insurgents, and to build roads to get there. Porters also come in handy after razing and pillaging refugee camps inside Thailand; their wives make suitable disposable lovers.

The forbidden zones and the Golden Triangle may lure adventurers, but there is little to see or do in these mostly rural and deforested areas. As the government creates an uneasy but profitable peace with rebel groups, more and more areas will open up to tour bus–bottomed "adventurers." In many places, you will be expected to have an MTT guide, who's very disinterested in anything adventurous.

Rangoon (whoops, Yangon) has the feel of 1938 Berlin. To hell with a cop on every corner, this place has got a loaded troop carrier on every corner. If it isn't NLD college kids out for a Sunday stroll en masse, truckloads of pissed Buddhist monks (or "external stooges" dressed up like monks, according to SLORC) are hurling Molotov cocktails at Muslim mosques. There are so many plainclothes spooks on the street, SLORC might consider eschewing a uniform budget altogether. Myanmar lucked out and hopped onto the ASEAN hay ride in July 1997 along with Laos and Cambodia. The only one that really deserved it was Laos. Meanwhile, Unocal is forging ahead with its $1 billion natural gas pipeline, Aung San Suu Kyi remains as accessible as Carlos the Jackal, and the last remaining insurgency, the KNU's struggle, is getting smoked in the south. Myanmar is the very definition of "hard line."

Aside from politics, there's also news to upset eco-types: Myanmar grows about 75 percent of the tropical teak left in the world. The government, the Karens and the Shans, along with about 20 Thai logging companies, are rapidly sawing everything down before the political winds shift direction. According to some estimates, in 10 to 15 years, there won't be enough teak left to put together a decent deck chair.

Everyone

In Myanmar, you can't tell the bit players without a program. Even *DP* dares not dive too deeply into the various military, political, narco, ethnic, regional and ideological groups that want a piece of Myanmar for themselves. There are estimated to be at least 35 insurgency groups fighting or operating inside Myanmar (19 of them under the leadership of Karen leader Bo Mya), although most of them have made a precarious peace with Yangon. Depending on who's counting, they range in size from a handful of overeducated hotheads living in refugee camps, bad-ass shoot-to-kill drug smugglers, archaic political parties, regional warlords, and well-meaning but poorly equipped tribes to large, well-equipped armies of over 25,000 soldiers, complete with armored divisions. There are four major ethnic divisions, with 67 recognized tribal groups, with the majority Burmese living along the fertile center. Keep in mind as you travel around the country that most border and northern areas have some sort of grudge match going on at any one time. The Karen Nationals have been fighting for independence since 1948. The various groups fighting the SLORC are united under the name Democratic Alliance of Burma, but virtually all factions have made peace with Yangon over the last two years.

SLORC and the Generals

With a 400,000-man army, the 21-member junta comprised of the ruling families and selected investors holds all of the marbles here, at least in the majority of the country. These guys are mostly seen in public and the media petting goats, kissing babies, inspecting chickens, being deified by famous monks and passing out numbers to queues of foreign businessmen.

People's Desire

- Oppose those relying on external elements, acting as stooges, holding negative views.

- Oppose those trying to jeopardize stability of the State and progress of the nation.

- Oppose foreign nations interfering in internal affairs of the State.

- Crush all internal and external destructive elements as the common enemy.

—Daily announcement appearing in the 'New Light of Myanmar.'

These folks have zero tolerance for dissent—in any form over any issue. Aung San Suu Kyi remains in isolation, most of her key supporters are in jail after dissident round-ups in May 1996 and May 1997. And the KNU has been all but crushed.

Monks

Ethnic groups and freedom fighters aside, even Buddhist monks aren't immune from a little stormtrooping to keep them in line. After an alleged incident in March 1997 involving the rape of a young Buddhist girl by a Muslim businessman, monks in Mandalay decided to have a little tea party at the area's Muslim mosques. SLORC troops killed one of the rampaging monks and then slam-dunked Mandalay with a dusk-to-dawn curfew. The violence spread south to Yangon before it was quickly squashed.

Drugs

Recent announcements of peace between insurgents and the government are assumed to be "live and let live" agreements, which allow the Wa and Shan people to concentrate on the more lucrative business of opium rather than vying for political power. Consequently, for the first time since World War II, it appears the Yangon government has control over its entire 1600-km border with Thailand. Myanmar is the largest producer of opium in the world.

Wood

Although some parcels of Myanmar are controlled by insurgent groups, there exist tacit agreements between SLORC generals and Thai logging companies permitting rebel factions to smuggle hardwood and gems out of the country into Thailand. In turn, the logging roads created by this lucrative trade provide the government an expedient route to send in troops during the dry season to pressure-play the insurgents.

Karen National Liberation Army (KNLA)

The largest insurgent group is the Karen National Liberation Army of the Karen National Union (KNU), headed by 70-year-old Saw Bo Mya and based in Manerplaw before the brutal SLORC crusher offensives of the mid-1990s which dispersed the remaining rebels to the jungle. Converted to Christianity by missionaries at the turn of the century and allied with the British during WWII, they have been fighting for their own independence since Burma was granted its independence without provision for a Karen homeland. The Karen battle for sovereignty has been ongoing since 1948, one of the longest struggles for freedom in Asia. They are funded through their control of the smuggling routes between Myanmar and Thailand. About 100,000 government troops, supported by ethnic Wa militia and the Buddhist DKBA (Democratic Karen Buddhist Army), are squeezing the life out of the Karen rebels. By reaching at least temporary peace agreements with most of the other factions battling Yangon, SLORC can now direct its full attention to the KNU.

The Karens are divided by religion, with Buddhist and Christian factions. The Buddhist faction (DKBA) has aligned itself with the Myanmar government and has been brutalizing and razing KNU refugee camps inside the Thai border. Meanwhile, aging and soon-to-retire Bo Mya continues to direct strikes against Burmese troops from a mobile base camp inside Myanmar. The rebels' strength, however, has been decimated to fewer than 2500 fighters.

The Thais, Refugees & Natural Gas

For more than 20 years Thailand has provided safe haven for Burma's Karen refugees, which number more than 100,000. The Thais have built and maintained the numerous border camps and even footed the bill without appealing to the international community for help. Noble by any standards, save for those of Thai companies looking to make a killing off Myanmar's abundant natural resources. With more of Thailand's investment abroad ending up in the generals' coffers, Thailand appears to have shifted its policy on refugees. For the first time, there were reports in early 1997 of the Thai army forcibly repatriating Karen refugees. With a US$1 billion gas pipeline aimed at Thailand's front yard at stake, a little cooperation between Bangkok and Yangon isn't surprising. The Petroleum Authority of Thailand (PTT), with a 25-percent stake, is expected to be the big winner with the Yadana field pipeline. As some companies are pulling out of Myanmar, PTT is plunging in head-first. It has acquired a big stake in a second gas pipeline project, which would connect the Yetagun field with Bangkok. The company's gas purchase is estimated to generate US$200 million for Yangon and the developing consortium. This is on top of the US$400 million a year that PTT will be paying the generals for Yadana gas. But if Thailand's refugee policy has indeed changed, it marks an about-face of Bangkok's longtime course to permit ethnic guerrilla groups to find refuge along its border with Myanmar, which will, in turn, provide the Thais a buffer between themselves and their longtime bitter enemy—but now ASEAN neighbor—the Burmese. Regardless, for PTT and other Thai concerns in Myanmar, life's a gas.

The Kachin Independent Organization

This is a seriously dwindled group of rebels—formerly 5000 strong—also known as the Kachin Independence Army (KIA). The Kachins are animists and Christians of Tibeto-Burman descent who originally migrated from China. Found in northern Myanmar, they are funded in part through the mining of rich jade deposits in the area. The jade is then sold to China. At one time this group was the primary organizer of opium transportation to the Thai border. Although the KIA has been mostly KIA'ed (killed in action) since several recent SLORC blitzes against its strongholds in Kachin state, Putao remains off limits to visitors, suggesting the mopping up isn't entirely completed.

The National League for Democracy

The National League for Democracy is the opposition party which won the May 1990 general elections by a landslide, capturing 82 percent of the vote—and whose rarely seen dissidents have mostly all hidden in the jungle since then, when the Myanmar military suppressed a nationwide uprising for democracy. They've come out of the closet recently with the 1995 release from house arrest of NLD leader Aung San Suu Kyi, but may have to step back into it after walking out on SLORC's late-1995 constitution convention and the subsequent government suppression of Ms. Suu Kyi's activities and movements.

Aung San Suu Kyi

The charismatic and brave figurehead of the NLD. She stood in front of SLORC's rifles during the student riots of '88, was busted by the evil generals and received a Nobel prize for her efforts. Placed under house arrest in 1989, she wasn't heard from until her release in the summer of 1995. She's chosen not to leave Myanmar, but instead to engage in "constructive dialogue" with SLORC and to consult with her NLD colleagues to find a way of bruising the SLORC bullies without winding back in the slammer. SLORC sees her as more of a nuisance (albeit a major one) than a threat, as Euro and ASEAN conglomo-cash is beginning to flow into Myanmar, ensuring the generals a lasting reign. But the foreign investment well may dry up suddenly if they lock Suu Kyi inside again. After her release from house arrest as many as 10,000 people jammed the street in front of her lakeside compound to hear her weekly addresses. But roads leading to her home have been blocked now for months and she's no longer allowed to speak in public. She and some supporters have been rousted by Khin Nyunt's Ray-Ban cops a number of times, leading to an estimated 1000 arrests. Some 260 NLD members were busted shortly before a party congress in May 1996, and another 50 or more ahead of a party meeting in May 1997 to mark the seventh anniversary of the May 27, 1990, elections that would have swept the NDL to power if recognized by the jealous generals. With Myanmar joining ASEAN it seems the road's going to be even tougher for the Iron Lady.

You can try getting to Suu Kyi's house. During our last trip, we were stopped by soldiers a couple of hundred yeards away. University Avenue in Yangon is barricaded off near her house. Her address is 5456 Tekkhtho Yeiktha Avenue in Yangon. Her home phone number is ☎ 530365.

SLORC Bullies Hurl Tomatoes in Bid to Get Drafted into the Majors

Former Los Angeles Dodger manager Tommy Lasorda has found pitchers everywhere from the desert of Mexico to the base of Mount Fuji. He may want to start sending some scouts to Yangon for a new generation of hurlers. SLORC figures if they start gunning down NLDers like they did in 1988 with real bullets, the world will back out of oil and pipeline deals and half-finished hotels. So, through sheer political genius, they've resorted to hiring thugs to lob tomatoes at Suu Kyi and her supporters. The generals figure a few tomatoes and a few messed-up hairdos won't make the pages of the New York Times. So they've enlisted the services of the Union Solidarity and Development Association (USDA)–ostensibly a government-sponsored social welfare association, but in reality a gang of shock troops and a Cleveland Indians farm team–to practice their pitching skills at NLD demonstrations. In one instance, in February 1996, as Suu Kyi was speaking at a memorial ceremony for former Burmese Prime Minister U Nu, a Toyota pickup filled with crates of tomatoes rolled up; the tomatoes were intended to be lobbed at the participants by USDA fledgling Florida Marlins. They refused to fire the tomatoes at the crowd, thinking that crates of jackfruit (a much larger fruit) were to be supplied instead.

The Khun Sa Gang (formerly the Shan United Army, or Mong Tai)

The Mong Tai army was the private play-toy of ruthless drug-lord-turned-hotel-mogul Chang Chi Fu, also known by the thespian title Khun Sa (the Prince of Death; see below). It broke up into factions in June 1995, charging their leader with spending too much time tinkering with his dope business and not enough fighting for freedom. (Khun Sa theatrically claimed the defections occurred because he is half Chinese.) And government troops seized the drug warlord's mountain stronghold at Ho Mong in January 1996. The cagey guerrilla commander cut a deal with SLORC in which he turned over his territory and what was left of his army to the government in exchange for amnesty. Problem is, it seems he didn't tell his guerrillas. One Mong Tai army officer who made it into Thailand shortly before SLORC took the base said, "We were told our commanders were negotiating with SLORC for a cease-fire—but it turned out they were allowing the Burmese troops to take over our bases." Oh, well. Khun Sa has maintained all along that he was never an opium trader but a freedom fighter, and that he taxed drug runners moving through his territory to help fund the Shan liberation cause. An unknown number of the former soldiers remain loyal to Khun Sa and have been tasked with building and operating at least a dozen methamphetamine factories in the jungle along Myanmar's borders with Thailand and Laos.

Khun Sa's Boy Soldiers

Khun Sa had hundreds of kids with guns whacking SLORC troops and rival drug armies, most of them between 10 and 14 years old. With the drug warlord's army now defunct, at least 500 of the kids don't have a home. SLORC's policy? They've asked that local families adopt the kids as farm laborers. Most won't take the kids in. Who knows, they may become the next rage in the States, like pet rocks and Vietnamese pygmy pigs. Want to adopt one of Khun Sa's boy guerrillas? Check with the Myanmar embassy in Bangkok or Washington, D.C. (see addresses and phone numbers on following page).

Khun Sa

Khun Sa (a.k.a. The Prince of Death or Mr. K), wanted by the U.S. government for heroin trafficking, was the world's largest single supplier of heroin until he "surrendered" to SLORC in January 1996. The U.S. government credits Khun Sa with providing a full two-thirds of the world's heroin supply when he was in business. Rather than rotting and languishing in some Third-World piss-stained jail cell, "Mr. K," as he's referred to by his close associates, instead lives opulently with the generals in Yangon. He has a number of hotel interests and runs the capital's bus system. It's golf twice a week with the generals and a military escort when he leaves home. His choice of restaurants doesn't need to be marred by how busy they might be. Soldiers simply clear the place out. Mr. K and his 10 aides—who followed him from his Ho Mong headquarters—can then dine in peace before taking Khun's four cars back to the compound for some afternoon pitch-and-putt in the back yard. Then, after a little nap, it's time to get that annoying diabetes checked out by his very own live-in Taiwanese doctor. Nonetheless, his best buddies say that Mr. K is both bored and stressed by Yangon and yearns for the mountains of Shan State and his former glory as a ruthless drug warlord. Not that he's left them entirely; his Khun Sa gang runs a network of methamphetamine factories where his poppies used to grow. Much of the dope ends up in Thai high schools and the glove boxes of long-distance truckers.

Can I get a dictionary?

A partial listing of Myanmar's insurgent groups, illegal political parties and rebels.

All Burma Students Democratic Front (ABSDF)

Burmese Communist Party (BCP)

Chin National Front (CNF)

Democratic Alliance of Burma (DAB)

Karenni Liberation Army (KLA)

Karenni Peoples United Liberation Front (KPULF)

Kayah New Land Revolution Council (KNLRC)

Kuomintang (KMT)

Ma Ha Faction of the Wa Army

Mon Liberation Front (MLF)

National Democratic Front (NDF)

National Coalition Government of the Union of Burma (NCGUB)

Pa-O Shan State Independence Party (PSSIP)

Palaung State Liberation Organization (PSLO)

Tai National Army (TNA)

Shan United Revolutionary Army (SURA)

Shan United Army (SUA)

United Pa-O Organization (UPO)

Visas are required of all travelers to Myanmar, ages 7 years and over, for a stay of up to 30 days (formerly, you couldn't stay in the country for more than two weeks). From Bangkok, visas now only take about two to three days to be processed and cost 800 Thai baht (US$32). Tourists can travel independently in Myanmar, but aren't permitted to stray from the "approved" tourist sites. Tourist visas are not extendable except in rare circumstances (i.e., you want to become a monk). Once inside Myanmar, a business visitor may possibly apply for an extended visa with the invitation and recommendation of a state enterprise. For a tourist visa, you'll need three passport-sized photographs.

Check with: or

Myanmar Embassy
132 Sathon Neua Road
Bangkok, Thailand
☎ 66-2-233-2237

Myanmar Embassy
2300 S St., N.W.
Washington, D.C. 20008
☎ 202-332-9044

Sneaking into Myanmar can be easily done by hiking over land or along logging roads into the country from Thailand. Troubles you encounter won't be with the government but with the various ethnic and rebel groups, who will have no qualms about shooting you and leaving you to rot. You can try contacting the various groups through expat sympathizers; however, don't try this from inside the country. Another alternative is having a couple of 13-year-old schoolkids-turned-commandos sneak you across the border near Mae Hong Son in Thailand for a nominal fee.

Entry by air into Myanmar is via Yangon International Airport, the country's only international gateway besides Mandalay (which is serviced from Chiang Mai, Thailand). Daily flights take less than an hour between Bangkok and Yangon. Myanmar Airways (MAI) has recently purchased new aircraft (Boeing 737-400s) for use on its routes to Singapore, Bangkok and Jakarta and has upgraded its safety agenda far enough to get off of the FAA's ☆#% list. Thai International offers slightly better service than Myanmar Airways between the two capitals but only three times a week. There are also direct flights available from Singapore, Calcutta, Kathmandu, Dacca, Moscow and Beijing on a variety of Third World airlines.

MAI flies twice a week to Singapore and Jakarta. Jakarta has become the seventh foreign city that MAI flies to, in addition to Bangkok, Hong Kong, Singapore, Kuala Lumpur, Dhaka and Kunming. The MAI international fleet consists of three Boeing 737-400s. Flights to and from Bangkok have been increased from twice daily to three times daily. MAI flies to Singapore once a day.

Yangon International Airport is situated about 19 kilometers northwest of Yangon, and there may or may not be a BAC bus to transport passengers into the major hotels. If you are traveling on a package tour, transfers are definitely provided. Expect to pay about US$6 if using local taxis (and don't forget to bargain a little).

Departure tax (US$6) is included in tour package prices. Or pay it yourself at the airport if traveling independently.

Getting there by sea was formerly an option by cruise boat. You can't get into the country by sea today, but check for the current regulations, as they change constantly. In February 1997, a group of foreign tourists visited the Mergui archipelago off Myanmar's southern coast aboard the 51-foot ketch rig trimaran *Gaea*. Operated by Southeast Asia Liveaboards, the boat made the run, with official permission from SLORC, from Thailand's coastal city of Ranong. There's every reason to believe the company will continue making regular cruises to the Merguis in the future. For the time being, voyagers aboard the *Gaea* can expect some degree of intrigue, like being stopped by Myanmar navy coastal patrols, which haven't yet gotten word the cruises (which are restricted to the inner islands only due to an ongoing fishing rights dispute in the outer islands between the Burmese and the Thais) are kosher with the generals in Yangon. For more information, contact Thailand-based **Southeast Asia Liveaboards** at ☎ 66-76-340406; FAX: 66-76-340586; or e-mail seadiver@loxinfo.co.th.

Yangon is the country's major port, and it lies at the mouth of the Ayeyarwady River. Visitors are welcome to travel upriver on private cargo ships or conveyances owned by the government-run Inland Water Transport Corporation to either Mandalay or Nyaung-U (for Bagan).

The journey is hot, picturesque and overly time-consuming, but still popular now that you can get a 30-day visa.

Cruise ships in the Far East area often schedule calls at Yangon, but thus far, no company has been successful in arranging regular visits.

The overland route between Thailand and Myanmar, where visitors could travel from Mae Sai, Thailand, to Kengtung, Myanmar—an eight-hour trip by road each way—was closed at press time. Travelers using this route had been limited to a three-day/two-night trip (East-Quest and others offer tours). At press time, groups could no longer enter Myanmar by land from Tachilek, Three Pagodas Pass and Kawthaung in Thailand. The opening of a China overland route, from Kunming in Yunnan province, which was under consideration for independent travelers, has been shelved for the time being. Tour groups have made the crossing in the past. Things change all the time regarding land crossings. Check regarding all land crossings beforehand. There have been numerous instances of fighting along the border with Thailand, particularly opposite Tak, Kanchanaburi, Ratchaburi and Chumphon provinces in Thailand.

Transit, at least the mechanized means, in Myanmar has gotten better in the last few years. Now one can comfortably get around via minibus, train, modern aircraft and new, comfortable bus coaches. In Bagan, it is possible to find a guide with a Jeep or Land Rover.

Taxis have red license plates and can usually be found outside major hotels, but agree on the fare before setting off. Private cars with drivers go for about $50 a day, and motorcycles and bikes can be rented for $25 and pennies a day, respectively.

City buses are overly crowded and not recommended for Westerners, who tend to take up too much room and cause a terrible commotion if they don't understand something. MTT and perhaps a dozen other private companies operate buses from Yangon up-country. Buses to Mandalay take about 13 hours. Regular bus services today connect Yangon and Mandalay, Mandalay and Bagan, Bagan and Taunggyi, and Taunggyi and Mandalay. For a better description of the bus services, see the "Directory" in the Yangon chapter.

The rail network in Myanmar is growing quickly (some say with the help of slave labor). The Yangon-Mandalay line is the trunk route in the country, with a number branches. Special counters to help tourists have been opened at the stations in Yangon, Thazi and Mandalay. At present, there are about 2739 miles of railway spreading across the country. About 1000 additional miles are being constructed in states and divisions which were formerly under the control of rebel insurgents and dope traffickers.

The train station for overland destinations is between Sule Pagoda Road and Upper Pansodan Street across from Aung San Stadium in Yangon. Here, there are regular long-distance train connections with Mandalay, Prome, Thazi and Pegu. Regular express trains running daily between Yangon and Mandalay take about 12–14 hours. Visitors to Bangan and Inle Lake have to get off at the Thazi station and take a bus from there. To Bagan the bus trip takes about four hours, and from Thazi to Shwe Nyaung (Inle Lake) about five hours.

In addition to Myanmar Airways, two other air carriers serve Myanmar's domestic routes: Air Mandalay and Yangon Airways. As both are relative upstarts, it's difficult to appraise their safety levels. Myanmar Airways has rocketed their safety standards over the last few years and it's safe to assume that Air Mandalay and Yangon Airways subscribe to the same levels as the national carrier. The last crash of a Myanmar carrier was a Myanmar Airways F-27 which crash-landed at Myeik airport in July 1996. Domestic flights offered by the three carriers connect Yangon with the following cities: Bagan, Heho, Kawthoung, Mandalay, Myitkyina, Myeik and Tachilek.

Myanmar possesses hundreds of navigable rivers and streams and a huge deltaic region in the south below Yangon. Inland Water Transport operates a large network of waterways transportation plans. Most tourists to Myanmar take a cruise down the Ayeyarwady River, a day-long trip from Mandalay to Bagan/Nyaung Oo. The journey takes 12 hours. In the Ayeyarwady Delta, travelers can take a boat to Pathein (Bassein). The trip from Yangon takes 1 day (16-20 hours). Other delta destinations are also possible, such as Labooda and Hpayapon. Boats depart from Lan Thit Street Jetty in Yangon

Up the Lazy River

Myanmar not only has about 50 steam engines still in service; they still operate hundreds of ancient riverboats that go back as far as the 1880s. These paddle wheelers (now converted to diesel) chug up the 8000 km of navigable rivers in Myanmar, carrying passengers and freight. Many are used as ferryboats. There are now newer luxury versions, but the hard core can still read their Rudyard Kipling poems on the deck of a slow-moving 19th-century paddle boat.

You might need permits to travel outside the standard tourist rut (Yangon, Mandalay, Bagan, Inle Lake, Taunggyi). Permits are letters generated from MTT and approved by the military. MTT or Yangon-based travel agencies will arrange for these. You will need to have a guide or driver and a pretty clear idea of where you want to go. You will not know which areas are specifically out of bounds until you apply to go to them. You can try to travel without a permit (many do) but be prepared to be turned back at any one of the military checkpoints throughout the county. Soldiers at checkpoints in partially controlled zones, like the Chin, Mon, Kayin or Shan states, will rarely bend the rules. You can, however, enter from Thailand illegally and take your chances with the insurgent checkpoints. You can fly into some areas much easier than by road. In many cases, the roads are controlled by insurgent armies. The need for permits and the areas that are considered dangerous or hot change regularly, so check with the local embassy or the MTT in Yangon.

You can fly in from Chiang Mai to Mandalay and Bagan. Pwin Ol Lwin, or Maymyo as it was formerly known, is an old British hill station that still has 153 horse-drawn carriages left over from colonial times. The Burma Road in the Shan hills is the major trade route with Yunnan in China.

The Golden Triangle area in Myanmar can be reached by train from Mandalay. You can also make the arduous 160-km trip from Kengtung to Tachileik. Additionally, travelers have been able to get from Kengtung to Mai Sai in Thailand's Chiang Rai province. But the border is shut, and you'd probably get popped anyway.

Lashio is a mecca for adventurers, for this is where the Burma Road begins its long, winding path into China. Mogok is 115 km from Mandalay and is the site of jade and ruby mines controlled by rebels on odd days, and the government on even days. You can see (and purchase) the fruits of their labors by posing as a buyer at the annual gem auction each February in Yangon.

Good maps are not available. Bartholomew, Nelles and Hildebrand are the best brands for maps of the country. The local MTT office in Athenian and Mandalay can provide street maps.

DP likes to group Myanmar in a group of countries that includes Turkey, Egypt, Cambodia, Russia, the Philippines, Israel and Colombia—countries that aggressively seek tourists even though they are, uh, well, kind of having a few problems in the hinterlands. Like Cambodia, if you stay on your leash and visit all the nice monuments, you will be fine. But if you head into the boonies, you are guaranteed to meet a lot of pissed-off folks. Those won't be rolled up election posters they're pointing at you.

Shan State (The Far North and Southeast)

So, where do you stay away from (or run to, depending on your taste in travel)? Well, start with any hilly, northern area bordering Thailand, China and Laos. This is where drugs are grown, sold and refined. (See "Drugs" for more than you ever wanted to know about the opium trade.) Shan state is home to the Shan, Kachin, Karen, Wa and other ethnic groups, all of whom have armies and control movement inside and across the borders. The mountainous areas are ideal for growing opium poppies. This region is headed by a narco government run by warlords with large armies.

Mon State (Southern Area)

The Mon and the Karen insurgents hide out in this strip of land that parallels the Thai border. Although there was a cease-fire in 1995 between the government and the Mon National Liberation Front, the Mon still duke it out with the Karen over control of the smuggling checkpoints into Thailand. Banditry along the highways by armed groups is prevalent in daylight.

Chin State

The ethnic Chin want their own remote mountainous country, and guess what they want to call it? Yep, Chinland. These folks need a little better feel for Marketing 101. The Chin are Tibeto-Burmese who are primarily animists. Of course, where there are happy animists, there are Christian missionaries handing out faded Ninja Turtle shirts and Adidas shorts. The government has also sent in Buddhist missionaries to tug their souls in another direction.

There are many people with Indian or Bengali ties, so the government is also actively persecuting the Muslims, forcing many to flee to neighboring India or Bangladesh.

Rahkine State

Rahkine state is stirred up by the activities of the Arakan Rohingya Islamic Front and the Rohingya Solidarity Organization, extra-agitated folks from among the quarter of a million Muslim refugees who live across the border (not by choice) in scenic, affluent Bangladesh.

Travel Restrictions

Traveling in Myanmar these days, although far less restrictive than in the past, is still like a bumper car ride. Just when you get out of first gear, you smack into a nasty little ethnic insurrection, a warlord state or a general's poppy field and have to double back to find some way around it. And just to add a little more confusion to the situation, package groups are permitted in some places where independent travelers are prohibited.

SLORC has a name for the indies: Foreign Independent Travelers (FIT). For everything naughty you can say about the government, you will indeed give them fits. They come up with some pretty cute acronyms, and this one is an accurate one.

Forget what you've read elsewhere; this is where you can and cannot go inside Myanmar— and how you can and cannot get there.

Kachin State

1) Both package tours and FIT are permitted to travel to Myitkyina either by plane or train.

2) Both package tours and FIT are allowed to Hopin, Mohnyin, Mogaung and Indawgyi by train. Prior permission is required to travel to these regions by car. Do not attempt to head out to these places by car unless you have written permission from the MTT or Ministry of Hotels & Tourism.

3) Package tours and FIT are allowed to travel to Jinghkrang, Myitsone, Waingmaw and Washaung in Myitkyina.

4) Package tours and FIT are no longer permitted (at press time) to go to Putao due to a pesky little secessionist war. Package tours could formerly get in by plane, with FIT having to sign up on a tour to get there. Putao should open up again after the body count. The problem here is with the Kachin Independent Army (KIA), a dwindling band of about 5000 or so fighters. You'd want your own country, too, if you had mountainloads of jade in your back yard. Today, though, the KIA lives up to Myanmar's uncanny propensity for choosing for itself appropriate acronyms—it's mostly Killed in Action. But these folks remain infestive, nonetheless. Check with the MTT to see if the restriction has been lifted.

5) If Putao opens up, package tours visiting Manse, Mu Daung, Noi Nan, Machambaw, Hun Nan, Mulashidi, Ho Pa and Ko Pa can only do so through an authorized MTT tour supervised and guided by either on staff officer or an assistant manager of the Ministry of Hotels & Tourism. A detailed itinerary to the Putao area has to be submitted to MHT in advance.

6) Package tours and FIT are allowed to Bamaw by plane or by boat.

Northern Shan State

Package tours and FIT are permitted to Lashio through the inland route by planes, trains and automobiles.

Southern Shan State

1) Package tours and FIT are permitted to travel to Taunggyi, Inlay, Pindaya, Kalaw and Yatsauk through the inland route by planes, trains and automobiles.

2) Package tours and FIT are permitted to travel to Kyaing Tong, Tachilek by plane only.

Kayah State

Foreigners, either on a package tour or traveling independently, cannot travel to any area within Kayah State.

Rakhine State

1) Package tours and FIT are allowed through the inland route to Sittway, Mrauk U, Ngapali, Thandwe, Gwa and Taungkoke by plane, train or automobile. Travel is not permitted to Ahm and Kyauktaw.

2) Package tours and FIT are permitted by car to Kantharyar via Ngathaing Kyaung-Gwa Road, and to Ngapal via Pyay-Taungkoke Road.

Kayin State

Package tours and FIT are permitted to Tharmin Nya, Pa-an, Hlaingbwe either by train or car.

Mon State

Package tours and FIT are no longer allowed to Kyaik Htiyo, Kyaik Hto, Thaton, Kyaik Maraw, Mawlamyaing, Balukyun, Thanbyuzayat and Kyaik Kami by either train or by car. The Christian Karens of KNU down there have been been getting their butts hammered by both SLORC troops and fighters of the government-backed Democratic Karen Buddhist Army (DKBA), a splinter group of Karen National Union (KNU) which has been beating up on its Karen brothers with SLORC arms for the last couple of years. Recent fighting in early 1997 sent more than 90,000 refugees streaming across the border into Thailand's Tak Province. There are perhaps 11,000 KNU rebels sluging it out with about 17,000 SLORC troops in the region.

Tanintharyi Division

1) Package tours and FIT are allowed to Myeik, Dawei, Maungmagan, Kawthaung and Lanpi Kyun by either plane or boat.

2) Foreigners are not permitted to travel to Zadetgyi Kyun, either independently or as part of a tour package.

Yangon Division, Mandalay Division, Bago Division,
Magway Division and Ayeyarwaddy Division

Package tours and FIT are permitted without any restrictions to travel by boat or car within these divisions.

Sagaing Division

1) Package tours and FIT are allowed by car to Alaungdaw Kathapa, Po Win Taung, Monywa, Twin Taung, Butalin, Kyauk Ka, Yinmar Pin and Yeshantwin.

2) Package tours and FIT are allowed to Khamti by either plane or boat. Travel to any area outside Khamti is prohibited.

3) Package tours and FIT are allowed to Homalin by boat. Travel to any area outside Homalin is not permitted.

4) Package tours and FIT are allowed to Kale by plane. However, travel outside a four-mile radius of the town is prohibited.

Chin State

Foreign tourists, both tour groups and FIT, are prohibited from traveling anywhere in Chin State due to another annoying separatist blood feud, this time between SLORC and the Chin people of northwestern Myanmar. The Chin are of Tibeto-Burmese stock, and are primarily animists with ties to Bangladesh and India.

The Ayeyarwaddy River

Package tours and FIT are permitted to cruise along the Ayeyarwaddy River on the following routes: Mandalay/Bamaw/Mandalay; Mandalay/Bagan/Nyaung U/Mandalay; Yangon/Mandalay/Yangon; the delta regions and Mawlamyaing/Pa-an/Mawlamyaing.

Other Restrictions

Mogoke

Authorized travel and tour companies arranging package tours to Mogoke are required to make booking arrangements through the Union of Myanmar Economic Holdings Ltd. However, MTT—a division of the Ministry of Hotels & Tourism—can make its own arrangements for package tours to Mogoke. Tours here can only be arranged by car, and travel to Hpakant is prohibited.

Border Crossings

At the time of this writing, independent travelers were not allowed to enter or leave Myanmar through any land border. The border at Tachilek is intermittently open to foreigners traveling to and from Thailand, but visitors are not permitted outside Tachilek and must return the way they came into the country. Package tourists have more options:

Northern Shan State

1) Visitors coming from China with a valid border pass are allowed to enter Myanmar through Muse, Namkhan, Kyu Koke and Kun-Lone checkpoints provided they are part of a package tour organized by authorized travel and tour companies. It is then possible to proceed by car up to Lashio.

2) Visitors entering Myanmar through the Lwe-je checkpoint with a valid border pass are permitted to continue on to Bamaw Township if they are members of a package tour organized by an authorized travel and tour company.

Southern Shan State

1) Visitors entering from Thailand with a valid border pass can enter Myanmar at Tachilek, but are resricted in their movements once there. Travel by road or plane to other parts of the country is prohibited.

2) Visitors entering through Wun Pone with a valid border pass are allowed only as far as Tachilek.

3) Visitors entering through Mai Lar are not permitted to visit Kyaing Tong. The government said it will give consideration to this restriction in the future.

Legal Border Pass Destinations

Foreign travelers on tour packages with valid visas and border passes entering Myanmar through a border checkpoint listed below are permitted to the areas mentioned here:

Muse, Namkhan, Kyu Koke and Kun Lone checkpoints

1) Package tours arranged by authorized travel and tour companies are allowed to enter through Muse, Namkhan, Kyu Koke and Kun Lone checkpoints and proceed on to Mandalay and Yangon via Lashio by plane, train or automobile.

Lwe-je

2) Package tours arranged by authorized travel and tour companies are allowed to enter through Lwe-je and proceed on to Mandalay and Yangon via Bamaw either by plane or boat.

The Name Game

Despite all the PC babble about Myanmar being the bad guys' name for Burma, don't believe it. Myanmar is the name of the country and Burmese (or Myanmars) the name of the people. Burmese is the language found around the capital city of Yangon and is spoken by ethnic Burmese. The region has been called Myanmar even as far back as the 13th century, by Marco Polo, no less. It makes more sense to call the country a name other than just one of the many ethnic groups. Imagine if America were called India, after what was its largest ethnic group. All the generals were doing was a little colonial house cleaning when they renamed the country and many of its cities.

Myanmar experiences the typically Southeast Asian tropical monsoon climate, with hot, humid lowlands and cool highlands. The wet monsoon season is from June through September, the cool dry season from November to April.

The official language of Myanmar is Burmese; a number of ethnic languages are also spoken. Burmese is a completely indecipherable script for most casual visitors. English signs have been removed so bring a phrase book if you want to do anything more than eat or sleep. It is helpful to know that Burmese have one given name between one to three syllables, usually preceded with a form of address. In Burmese, use Oo (uncle) for adult males, Ko (elder brother) for males of the same age, Bo for leader, Ma (sister) for young girls, Daw (aunt) for older women, and Saya (master) for teachers or employers. Other ethnic groups use variations on this theme.

Buddhists comprise 85 percent of the population, while animists, Muslims, Christians and other indigenous religion followers comprise the rest. Sixty-eight percent of Myanmar's population is Burmese; however, there are five major ethnic groups (Shan, 11 percent; Karen, 7 percent; Kachin, 6 percent; Arakanese, 4 percent; and Chin, 2 percent.). The Shan are found in the northeast. The Karen straddle northern Thailand and eastern Burma and pay little attention to the border between the two countries. The Mon populate the same fertile area as the Karen and are ethnically related to both the Khmers and the Burmese. The Burmese live primarily in the central plains along the Ayeyarwady River and were the builders of the great monuments at Bagan.

The literacy rate stands at 81 percent. The monetary unit is the kyat. The free market exchange rate at press time was nearly 300 kyat to the U.S. dollar, but should should settle down again to about 167 kyats to the dollar. The free market rate is now legal, replacing the ridiculously artificial rate of 6 kyats to the buck.

Big Brother

The military rulers of Myanmar keep a very close watch on their own people and particularly hnakaung shays or long noses. That probably means you. Do not converse freely with strangers. It can be safely assumed that anyone who loiters near you or reappears often in your travels is a paid intelligence operative.

Telephone calls can be made from hotels and the Central Telegraph office in Yangon. International calls go through operators (watch what you say and who you call). There is no guarantee of a phone line being available or even usable. Telexes can be sent from major hotels as well as the telegraph office.

It costs six kyats to post an airmail letter, but don't count on it getting there anytime soon. Buy the stamps and mail your postcards or letters from Bangkok. MTT, *77-79 Sule Pagoda Road*, is the main source for travel info in Yangon. There are also offices in Mandalay, Bagan and Taunggyi.

Voltage is 220/50 cycles when it works.

Note: February and March are bad times to visit due to the influx of gem buyers into Yangon for the annual auction.

Embassies/Consulates

American Embassy
581 Merchant Street
Box B
Yangon
☎ *[95] (1) 282055/6 or 282059*

Australian Embassy
88 Strand Rd.
Yangon
☎ *[95] (1) 280711*

United Kingdom Embassy
80 Strand Rd.
Yangon
☎ *[95] (1) 281700, 281702*

Permanent Mission of Myanmar to the U.N.
10 East 77th Street
New York, NY 10021
☎ *(212) 535-1311/0/1716*
FAX (212) 737-2421

Embassy of the Union of Myanmar (USA)
2300 S Street, N.W.
Washington, D.C. 20008
☎ *(202) 332-9044-5*

Money Hassles

The currency of Myanmar is the **kyat** (pronounced "chat"), which is divided into 100 *pyas*. Notes are used in denominations of 1, 5, 10, 15, 20, 45, 50, 90, 100, 200, 500 and 1000; make sure markings are in both Burmese and Arabic numerals. SLORC seems to have a sense of humor, after all; without warning, it has had a tendency of arbitrarily banning certain denominations, as it has done with the K100 note. Coins are available in denominations of 1 kyat and 1, 5, 10, 25 and 50 pyas. Coins are difficult to decipher because they are marked only in Burmese numerals.

INSIDER TIP: NO 50s, NO 100s

You may find yourself in a situation where the change offered consists of either K50 or K100 notes marked "Union of Burma Bank." Do not accept them. They are no longer legal tender. Myanmar people possessing large amounts of these notes became impoverished after the government banned the circulation of them. The worthless notes have been known to be passed on to naive foreign tourists.

Unlimited amounts of foreign currency, whether in cash or traveler's checks, may be brought into the country. But remember that what is declared upon entry must be accounted for upon departure. There are plenty of taxi drivers and tourist guides eager to offer a "better than official rate" for your dollars, so proceed at your own risk (see "Burma's Bogus Buck System" below). Keep the currency conversion form with you at all times, and present it to the customs officials upon exit. Loss of this document can be very troublesome. It's likely you won't be asked for the document when you leave, as it's easy to bribe your way out of the mandatory changing of US$300 into Foreign Exchange Certificates (FECs) in the first place—and the Customs officers know it. Unless your entire tour has been prepaid in U.S. dollars outside the country, your hotel may demand payment in foreign currency or by credit card. Keep the receipt as an extra precaution.

Unspent kyats cannot be reconverted to U.S. dollars at the time of your departure. If you are unfortunate enough to possess enough kyat near your departure time that makes reconversion necessary, hope that you have a friend in Yangon. You'll have to do it on the black market. But a word of caution: there are far fewer folks around who change kyat into dollars than who change dollars into kyat. Ask only those you trust where to find someone to make this transaction for you. If the friend is a good one you can expect to pay the black marketeer 1 kyat for each 160 kyats or FEC$1 you want to reconvert into U.S. dollars.

Foreign Exchange Certificates (FECs)

Myanmar, quite simply, is the most tourist-unfriendly country in the world to exchange money. FECs come in the same denominations as U.S. dollars and when used as such, they possess an equal value. They can be used for payment anywhere U.S. dollars are accepted, such as hotels and upscale restaurants. They cannot legally be converted into U.S. dollars, however. So if you play by the rules, you'll have to spend at least US$300 during your stay in Myanmar—even if you're a businessman only in town for an afternoon meeting.

If you don't play by the rules, there are a couple of ways around this. Simply ask the exchange clerk if there is any possible way you can avoid having to change the $300 into FECs. More than likely he or she will respond that, for a gift, of course there is a way. In all likelihood, for a "gift" of US$10, the clerk will require you only to exchange US$100. This is really only marginally worth it if you're going to be in-country for only a few days (marginally because it saves you the headache of finding a black marketeer who will exchange dollars for your FECs; see below). If you're going to stay in Myanmar for the duration of your visa, this isn't a deal, as you'll spend the 300 bucks anyway.

Although the government says any amount of currency you exchange over US$300 can be redeemed in U.S. dollars, don't count on it. Most, if not all, banks that cash traveler's checks will only do it with FECs, even if you show evidence that you've already exchanged US$300 into FECs. You are again forced to deal with the prospect of leaving the country with useless currency. Cashing a traveler's check is a two-step process if you want dollars. First it must be cashed into FECs at a bank, then into dollars on the black market or an FEC exchange center, with each middleman taking his own chunk out of it. Expect to lose US$4 or more for each US$100 you want exchanged into U.S. dollars.

Derring-Do & Burma's Bogus Buck System

In the tradition of the country's propensity for generating uncannily appropriate acronyms for its various factions and functions–i.e., SLORC, KIA (Kachin Independence Army, or "Killed in Action") and FITS (Foreign Independent Travelers, who give the government plenty)–has been born FECS, or Foreign Exchange Certificates. (I'll leave the pronunciation of the acronym to the reader's imagination).

Derring-Do & Burma's Bogus Buck System

For a negotiated "gift" of US$10 to the FEC exchange clerk at Yangon airport, you in all proba-bility will be permitted to only exchange US$100 instead of the required US$300. At this point you and the bureaucrat exchanger will share a perceived covert camaraderie, as if you've both just stuck one to SLORC, a similar feeling shared by a couple of college kids who've just scrawled a "Free Suu Kyi!" slogan at the base of Shwedagon Pagoda and then ducked into a toilet. To fur-ther inflate your newly-found sense of subversive self importance is the fact that your new friend is wearing a SLORC uniform. How exciting!

Then the final reinforcement: the clerk leans and whispers to you that you can stick it further up SLORC's backside by exchanging your FECs on the black market at a rate of 150 kyats to the U.S. dollar. A deft smile crosses her lips, as if she's just given you the key to smuggling a trunk-load of Jews out of 1939 Hamburg. My, the good fight feels good, despite the clerk handing you an official government receipt saying you exchanged only US$100, even signing it–the same receipt you are theoretically required to show Customs when you depart the country–proving that you exchanged US$300.

With the formula for revolution memorized, you accept the offer of your taxi driver (also, it turns out, a freedom-lover and co-conspirator! And a real, live demonstrator, to boot!) to exchange your FECs into kyats on the black market at a rate of 150 kyats to the dollar. He seems overly in a hurry to perform this service for you, as if your FECs were stamped with an expira-tion date, like milk, and he senses a sour effluvium was emanating from your wallet. You take him up on the offer as he pulls down a dark alley and instructs you to wait in the car–there could be guys in Ray-Bans and Hawaiian shirts hanging around.

It isn't until you check into your hotel, after the driver has squealed his tires, that you discover from the receptionist that the black market rate is actually 167 kyats to the dollar, that the hotel will be quite happy to do that for you, or that you can visit a clearly-marked FEC exchange office downtown on Thein Byu Road that will be equally delighted to perform the same service. And you'll find out that the black market rate is no longer the black market rate. It's the official rate.

So much for the revolution.

Internet Sites

http://www.freeburma.org
http://danenet.wicip.org/fbc

Two places to find information on Aung San Suu Kyi and contact other people interested in a democratic Burma (calling the country Myanmar is *tres outre* for these folks). There is also an electronic service called BurmaNet which will distribute information on the goings on inside Myanmar. You might want to let all your boycott tuna, save the whales and Body Shop pals join in what is the '90s most "in" protest. To be politically correct, you're not supposed to visit Myanmar so that your dollars don't fall into the evil hands of the Generals. *DP* takes no sides but you might actually want to visit Myanmar and form your own opinion.

The Barking Dogs

Another dog-hot day came to a close at the dusty Wanka (Huaykalok) Karen refugee camp near Mae Sot and the Moei River—the silty ribbon of lazy backwater which meanders between northern Thailand and the free-fire zone of eastern Burma. It was the kind of day that moved at the pace of a snapshot—nothing unusual for the thousands of ethnic Karens who call Wanka a temporary home, stowaways from the protracted fighting between the KNU and SLORC.

That night, though, life at Wanka would be turned upside down.

Camp Leader Mary On had heard the "barking dogs" before, a reference to the DKBA, or "SLORC stooges," who were always making threats at the Demoractic Korean Buddhist Army (DKBA). But the 6800 Karen refugees here at Wanka hadn't expected so much so suddenly.

It started with chirping on the walkie talkies. As they, and the rest of the camp, were preparing for sleep. On and a couple of aides listened to the voices. The language was Burmese, not Karen—an ominous sound along this part of the Moei River.

"The words were 'act swiftly and methodically,'" On says. Before On had time to make sense of what she was hearing, flames began spitting skyward from the roof of the camp's primitive clinic.

Then the raiders came for Mary. She dashed for the brush. There were the shouts and cries of women and children in the disconnected orange darkness, and the staccato reports of AK-47s being discharged. The soldiers reached On's spartan hut and set it aflame   and then swiftly and methodically razed hundreds of homes in the camp during the next 75 minutes of terror.

At 11 p.m., Wanka was engulfed in flames, but the job was only half-finished, the marauders heard sirens in the distance. Mistaking the sounds for an approaching company of Thai soldiers, the 137 Burmese and DKBA soldiers slipped from the Karen camp—along with 50 porters, charged with hauling anything that could be found in Wanka of value—across the Moei River into the blackness of the Burmese jungle.

At least 20,000 ethnic Karen had spilled into Thailand during this final bloody overture in early 1997 by SLORC in its race to "reconcile" the country in time to join the Association of Southeast Asian Nations by July. Of course, this ascent into legitimacy would necessitate silencing the KNU, the longest single running-insurgency in Asia and the only faction of the 16 separate groups fighting the Yangon regime that had not made peace with SLORC. In all, some 100,000 Karen refugees were forced into camps inside Thailand by March 1997.

The KNU has been fighting various Rangoon/Yangon governments since 1948 in its bid for independence. The current regime, considered the most brutal since Burma forged its own independence from Britain the same year, has made crushing the remaining pockets of KNU guerrillas—scattered along the Thai border near the provinces of Tak, Ratchburi, Kanchanaburi and Chumpon—its main priority in 1997.

SLORC deployed more than 100,000 troops in 1997 to mop up the remaining 3000 or so KNU fighters still active in the jungle, guerrilla forces still fiercely loyal to KNU President Gen. Bo Mya and the four platforms of Karen patriarch Saw Ba Oo Gyi: "Surrender is out of the question; we will retain our arms; the Karen state must be realized; we will decide our political destiny."

Shortly after the raid on Wanka near Mae Sot, both refugees and fighting spilled over into Thailand at Umphang, about 200 km south of Mae Sot. Burmese regulars with their butterfly nets set on automatic were chasing Karens through the forest—in this case, Thai forest—and the Thais began firing back. Flashpoints dotted the Thai-Burma map: Umphang, Songklaburi, Kanchanaburi, Ratchaburi—even as far south as Chumpon. Refugees began streaming across the border in Kanchanaburi; some were being turned back. Generals both from SLORC and the Thai army met at Tachilek to smooth feathers and get their photos taken in starched uniforms.

Mae Sot enjoys many of the benefits of Thai prosperity; modern, clean banks, service stations and hotels flank well-paved roads. Souvenir markets spill into the street at the unfinished Friendship Bridge on the Moei River. A smattering of Western tourists apply sunscreen and point camcorders toward forbidden Myanmar on the far side of the brown river. Unshaven Burmese men dressed in *longyis* lurk in the shadows of the gem stalls hawking hidden cartons of Marlboro; their mastery of English vocabulary is limited to the word "Marlboro." When this one-word sales pitch is combined with a smoking gesture of two fingers to the lips, it appears as if a Marlboro is what the salesman seeks rather than what he is offering. Naively believing the former, I hand one such black market vendor a cigarette from my own pack of Marlboros. Bemused, he lights it anyway.

The Wanka refugee camp is pitched in a giant, rolling field of parched grasses and brush. It is a brown, dusty and desolate moonscape that seems to have been selected by a freshman at refugee camp design school—or an A student. Every available twig and crusted banana leaf has been utilized to shelter this rickety, unsturdy city of 6831. The little vegetation here has been scorched to the color of old tobacco. Smoke lofts lazily in the midday heat from lean-tos and small hootches.

A procession of rail-thin, *longyi*-clad men and women stoically accompany a tiny coffin down a rutted path past their sun-skewered thatched homes to the camp's Christian cemetery. They pass a spirited volleyball match between Wanka's more fit being contested beneath "The Dome," a canopy of corrugated, oxidized aluminum sheets perched atop makeshift bamboo scaffolding to shade the players from the searing sun. It is Wanka's version of a national stadium.

But what is most noticeable is the destruction of what little is here to begin with. Squares of scorched earth stick out in the landscape like a bad effort at Game Boy. What were trees are now charred stumps. Three of the bare, blackened trunks rise together like the crosses Christ and the two thieves were executed on.

Mary On is walking on a narrow dirt path sluicing through a gauntlet of charred frames and ash-covered foundations that had been homes before the SLORC raid. A small child sifts through the soot at the base of one gutted dwelling, panning the ash like a gold prospector in search of anything that might be of value. At first, it is not apparent that Mary On is a woman at all. She is diminutive and brushes her short wavy hair from a wide left part, like a schoolboy whose mother fusses with his trusses for him. She is also smoking a pipe and wearing golf trousers with a white belt.

On is the camp leader at Wanka; she is also the vice chairman of the Karen Refugee Committee and has been the KNU's matriarch since firing her first machine gun at Yangon troops in the early 1960s. On was born in 1934 in Yangon, the daughter of strict Baptists. Her father was active in the Karen rebel movement early on. By the time she was serving on the front lines with KNU guerrillas in the Pegu Mountains, there was little doubt where her loyalties were, and equally as little doubt she was prepared to die for them: the KNU's Four Principles. Throughout the 1970s On smuggled guns to the Karen guerrillas operating in the Delta and, in the 1980s, fought Yangon troops from the KNU base at Wanka. When that was finally overrun in 1984, she was asked to oversee the refugees at Huaykalok.

And On runs a tight ship. The lives of the camp's inhabitants are regimented; the children are remarkably disciplined and well-behaved. Wanka is meticulously clean, despite having been almost entirely razed by the SLORC and DKBA raiders. There was a school here with an American teacher. He left after the attack. The camp has yet to rebuild its clinic, as well as the makeshift churches that were destroyed in the fires. Despite the destruction, perhaps because of it, there is serenity here, a lack of urgency and despair. The rutted, dusty road that snakes through Wanka is flanked by the flimsy shacks still left standing; many serve as stores, selling sundries, food and "household" items. The camp's water is drawn from artesian wells. NGOs such as the American Refugee Committee help feed the population and aid the sick.

"The most important thing is to be clean," On says, her English flawless. "Most of the men are off fighting the SLORC, so I have to implore the camp's women about cleanliness. Cleanliness is the way to survive under these conditions." The words of a headmistress, but also the words of someone who is as comfortable with an M-16 as with a kitchen spoon. On is part Mother Teresa, part Joan of Arc. More part Joan of Arc.

"The KNU will fight to the end, to the single last person," she says. "The SLORC and the barking dogs know this. Stooges, all of them—like a Mickey Mouse under the table of the SLORC. The SLORC acts with their name. There are seven million Karen people in Irrawaddy Division. We will not be defeated. All we want is peace. And if we get peace, we would go back tonight. We wouldn't wait until tomorrow."

The KNU held four rounds of negotiations with SLORC between December 1995 and November 1996, and was seeking a fifth round of peace talks when Yangon launched a massive dry season offensive against the Karens in January 1997. Although the Yangon-backed DKBA, a KNU spin-off that sold out to SLORC, is blamed for most of the attacks on Karen refugees living inside Thai territory, thereby sparing SLORC from accusations of direct military involvement on foreign soil, On knows better.

"These aren't DKBA who crossed into Thai territory and burned our camp," she says. "This is what the SLORC wants you to believe. The men that night were mostly SLORC regulars. There were 107 SLORC soldiers, 30 DKBA barking dogs and 50 porters to carry all of our belongings and food away. What they couldn't carry away they burned. Their leaders were SLORC commanders. They ordered everyone from their homes. Their commands to the villagers were in Burmese, not in Karen.

"The soldiers demanded that we return to Burma. The villagers asked them: 'Are you going to put us in forced labor? Are you going to throw us in prison?' (The commander) said he couldn't guarantee it. 'Then of course we will not go,' the villagers said. It is better to stay in Thailand as a refugee than go back to Burma as a slave."

There had been some forewarning of the raid. A few days earlier, On had received a letter from the "barking dogs," signed by Chit Thu, demanding that the refugees return to Burma or face violent consequences. But On had received such threats before, and thought this latest note to be merely another SLORC wolf cry.

"We were totally unprepared for the attack," she says. After setting fire to the clinic, the soldiers set off for On's home about 200 meters away. On was hiding. "I never sleep in the same place. I am always moving."

The soldiers set fire to On's home first, then began randomly torching the camp's 1360 flimsy homes. When they had finished, 690 had burned to the ground. Porters with bamboo baskets were ordered to strip the houses and small stores clean before they were set afire. Women screamed and tried to salvage their belongings. Soldiers shouted that they would be killed and fired into the air. The raiders next burned two Baptist churches, a Pentecostal church and ransacked the camp's Catholic church, according to On. They spared the camp's Buddhist monastery.

Finally, at 11 p.m., came the sirens. The SLORC and DKBA attackers, along with their porters, fled Wanka across the Moei River. The sirens were not those of the Thai army, but of a Mae Sot firefighting detachment. "We didn't get any help at all," On says.

On is not quick to bite the hand that feeds it, however. Since 1984, Thailand, with little help from the rest of the world, has welcomed and provided food and shelter for hundreds of thousands of refugees and ethnic insurgents battling the Yangon regime. "We owe the Thai people a lot. The Thais have given us peace for 13 years," On admits.

Thailand's generosity is borne of two reasons: out of mercy for those displaced by war, and the strategic advantage anti-Yangon groups ringing Thailand's border give Bangkok in the form of a buffer between two traditionally hostile nations.

But it is Thai strategy that worries On. News that at least 900 Karens, fleeing into Kanchanaburi province to escape the early 1997 fighting, were forced back into Myanmar is foreboding to Thailand's displaced Karens. Thailand, in recent years, has raced to do business with SLORC's generals, to capitalize on Myanmar's opening economy. And it doesn't inspire Thailand's humanitarian concerns that Karen guerrillas are the only remaining obstacle to Myanmar's $1 billion natural gas pipeline—being built by French oil company Total and U.S. fuel giant

Unocal through Myanmar's Tenasserim region—which will ensure Thailand of much of its energy needs.

Meanwhile, On and the Karens at Wanka patiently wait for the day they can walk the few meters back into Myanmar as free people. On's assertions that ultimately, somehow, the U.N. and the U.S. will mediate the Karen crisis to a favorable resolution sound hollow, however, but indeed reflect a different reality: the Karens are simply outgunned, and that vested interest in their struggle is waning. This suggests, of course, that vested interest is the only interest outsiders have ever had in the KNU, and that as the last of Myanmar's 16 ethnic insurgencies to still do battle with SLORC, it will become the 16th footnote in the legacy of SLORC's internationally sanctioned dictatorship.

"If you've come to see the Karen, you will see the Karen in a museum," On says. "This is the policy of the SLORC."

For the KNU, the barking dogs are also biting. For the first time since World War II, Myanmar's entire 1600-km border with Thailand is thought to be under government control. But despite losing its bases of operation, Gen. Bo Mya's fighters continue to pick and peck at Myanmar troops in the jungle. It's the mischievous gleam in On's eyes that reminds a visitor that the Karens are to Myanmar what Vietnam was to the U.S., what Afghanistan was to Russia—and have been for 50 years. On is part of the reason Yangon might postpone its hunt for a curator.

—**Wink Dulles**

Monks Going Ape

Yangon has a slightly cosmopolitan feel. The sidewalks are packed with a mishmash of races in the colorful garb denoting their ethnic blueprints: Indian, Burmese, Bangladeshi, Chinese, Shan. They stroll past the washed-out aqua, yellow and pink pastels of apartment buidings and businesses and the restored, grand buildings of British colonial days.

During rush hours, Yangon's streets rival those of any other Southeast Asian capital; traffic crawls at the pace of democratic reforms here. But not at the pace of hotel construction; five-star caravansaries are shooting skyward in all parts of the city like a seismograph in Riverside County, California.

Shwedagon Pagoda, a Buddhist version of Disneyland—which still dominates the city's skyline and can be seen 30 kilometers away—is packed with pilgrims and tourists alike. Minibuses from the city's more than 250 tour operators jam the parking lot.

The streets of Yangon are clean, curbs freshly painted in red and white stripes. Lawns, parks and even road medians are meticulously manicured and landscaped. There are few beggars. People dress remarkably well, if not particularly stylishly. North of Shwedagon, magnificent Western-style mansions flank U Wisara Road—the homes of SLORC generals and druglords for whom the generals have provided haven. Comparisons with Singapore come to mind. In fact, a visitor here is struck with an indelible sense of Yangon being a prosperous city-state rather than a Third World capital.

Unless one is accustomed to hanging around dictatorships, the casual visitor won't get it. "What's all the fuss about?" a tipsy Western businessman tells me between slurps of a double martini at the Strand Hotel's bar. "Hell—people dress well, drive nice cars, attend beautiful churches and pagodas and run successful private businesses. Sure, there are a lot of cops around and trucks packed with soldiers. But motorists still ignore the cops. That's freedom, baby! This place is about as commie as Fort Davis, Texas. Hell with Clinton; if I had the bucks, I'd build a natural gas pipeline, too!"

But dig a little deeper and the observer will be shocked at how little the "cosmopolitan" Yangonese know of the outside world, their own country, even their own city. Satellite dishes are prohibited (only hotels catering to foreigners can give guests their CNN fix); the internet is prohibited; foreign newspapers and magazines are prohibited. The few that are available—again, to foreign visitors—have been clipped of any story even mentioning Burma. Domestic journals are so thoroughly censored they are little more than brochures.

The English-language *New Light of Myanmar*, after first mandating each morning that its readers "crush all stooges and external elements" seeking to destabilize the country, then delves into such meaty topics on the front page as SLORC generals touring chicken farms, manure processing plants and future golf course sites, and overseeing university graduation ceremonies (not recently, however, as universities themselves are prohibited). Programs on the capital's one television station are regularly interrupted by generals giving speeches at chicken farms, manure processing plants and future golf course sites. Or, rather, the speeches are rarely interrupted by the station's regular programming.

Yangon is like a library. You go about your business quietly and don't talk to anyone. Queries are hushed. Talk about the weather or your wife's hangnail and you're okay. Mention politics and you'll clear a room no less quickly than had you passed wind. Even the capital's taxi drivers, unlike those found anywhere else in the world, keep their mouths shut. It is not from a lack of curiosity. Ask a shopkeeper in Yangon why barbed-wire barricades have been set up on the street in front of his establishment and he'll answer "to slow traffic." Ask what kind of traffic and you'll be asked to leave. If you happen to mutter "Suu Kyi" it had better be in a Japanese restaurant.

Nighttime is best for observing the viscera of Yangon. The streets clear by 10 p.m. There are a couple of reasons for this: there is about as much nightlife in Yangon as in Attica prison, and try to get to what little there is and you'll be arrested, or your driver's license plate number will be jotted down—and be arrested the following day. The streets are taken over by soldiers.

I picked a delightful March evening for a stroll through the capital. The stars were bright, the breeze cool and, up north, Mandalay had just been put under a dusk-to-dawn curfew. Apparently, a Muslim or more had raped a young Buddhist girl there and local monks had taken to the streets, burning and pillaging mosques. One monk had been killed by soldiers in the brawling. The rioting had spread south to Yangon. Monks had been raiding Yangon mosques for two nights running, stoning and fire-bombing the buildings from the beds of speeding pickups.

I chose a large mosque on Thein Byu Road to stake out. I first dined on curried roadkill down the street. A group of nearby students who had been engaging me in an animated political discussion announced they had to leave; it was 9 p.m. and they'd be arrested if they stayed long enough for dessert.

A troop transport truck rolled up to the corner; a half-dozen rifle-toting soldiers jumped to the street and made themselves conspicuous. The rest of the patronage paid their bills. I did so as well and headed in the direction of the mosque, where three other troop transport trucks, packed to the stakes with soldiers, had set up shop for the night. I walked past; the soldiers all wore the same expression—like the way the Green Beret guy with the bloody hands stares at Martin Sheen when he arrives at Col. Kurtz's kingdom in "Apocalypse Now."

I passed the mosque and went over the railroad bridge. On the other side there were a lot of shadows, and they afforded a good view of the mosque. No soldiers. I buried myself in the darkness and waited. Thirty minutes later a troop carrier pulled up directly in front of me. About 20 soldiers leaped from the truck and positioned themselves on each side of the road, some posturing themselves in a spread-eagle combat position at the base of some bougainvillaea bushes. Others took tarps from the truck and laid them out on the grass, bivouacking for the night.

Although just a few meters from some of the soldiers, I hadn't been spotted. A few minutes later two more trucks pulled up. Same routine. By the time these soldiers had finished deploying, Thein Byu Road by the mosque was a gauntlet. From the shadow of the overpass, I noticed a man dressed in a traditional *longyii* nervously pacing on the road beside one of the troop carriers. He had a mobile phone and decided to use it. A moment later, a sedan pulled up to the trucks. Out of it came four other men dressed in civilian Burmese clothes. They looked in my direction, eyes sweeping past me. Although I was in the darkness, I wasn't technically hiding. If these folks didn't expect someone in their immediate vicinity, I wouldn't be seen. However, if someone decided to actually look around…

A sixth man appeared with a hand phone, a single street lamp casting a long shadow of the man's gait. Big and burly with a thick black moustache, he was the only one of the men dressed in pants—the others were clad in *longyiis*. The new man—of Indian, or perhaps Bangladeshi descent—was obviously in charge. The others talked with him excitedly. Then, comically, all six men started pacing in front of the troop carrier, five of them following their leader in circles like baby ducks.

Finally, a solution to whatever their problem was appeared to have been selected. The men started in my direction and it became clear that I was at the root of their anxiety. The big man spoke perfect English.

"How long have you been here?" he said, quite politely. I stepped up from the shadow of the overpass.

"I just had dinner down the street. I stopped here for a smoke."

"You could not have just had dinner down the street nor just stopped here for a smoke."

"I was looking at the trains," I said.

"Or sending someone a signal."

"Are you with these guys?"

"You might say that," he said. "You're not supposed to be here. My guess is that you probably know that."

"Oops," I said.

"Not 'oops,'" he said. "You have made a diplomatic blunder."

"I'm not a diplomat; I'm a tourist," I said.

"A tourist is a diplomat. Would you like an escort to your hotel?"

"No, thank you, it's just down the street," I said.

"Then good night to you."

I got an escort just the same, though I wasn't supposed to know it. As I said—if folks don't expect someone in their immediate vicinity, you won't be seen. However, if someone decides to actually look around...

—**Wink Dulles**

Lagos

Nigeria
★★★
Formula 419

Four-one-nine. That's Nigeria's code for criminal fraud. Travelers know that a trip to corrupt, impoverished Nigeria can make even the hardened adventurer swear off travel to Africa entirely. For nearly two-thirds of its 37-year history, Africa's most populated country has been bullied by military despots who promise elections and then spend more time shopping at Harrods than running the country.

So it is not surprising that, despite current leader General Sani Abacha's promise to set up a democratically elected government, the current scenario in Nigeria seems like a precursor to another coup or civil war. In the meantime, what do the enterprising Nigerians do to bolster their economy? In keeping with its tainted image as one of the most corrupt nations in Africa, there are a number of quasi-sanctioned, clever scams that sucker in dozens of unsuspecting foreigners every year (see below).

Nigeria's biggest export is oil (with Uncle Sam slurping up about half). Yet that darn oil money keeps getting lost. Former President (and, of course, Army General) Babangida managed to misplace US$12.2 billion dollars worth. A black hole if there ever was one.

Shell Oil Co. has sucked about US$30 billion worth of Nigerian oil since its discovery in 1958, yet the Ogoni tribe still lives in poverty in the swamps. When they tested the trickle-down theory, their leaders (including Ken Saro-Wiwa) were hanged in November 1995, and the Ogonis chased into the swamps. Another black hole.

As one would expect, even though the Christian south is where the oil riches are coffered, the government has always been from the Muslim north.

Grow Hair, Pick Up Chicks and
Make Big Money in Nigerian Oil Deals!

Nigerians have finally figured out how to bring corruption and misery straight to you without you having to leave the comfort of your office. Nigerian business scams are confidence schemes, designed to exploit the trust you develop in your Nigerian partner and to bilk you of goods, services or money. The scams are flexible, and operators adapt them to take the greatest advantage of the target—you.

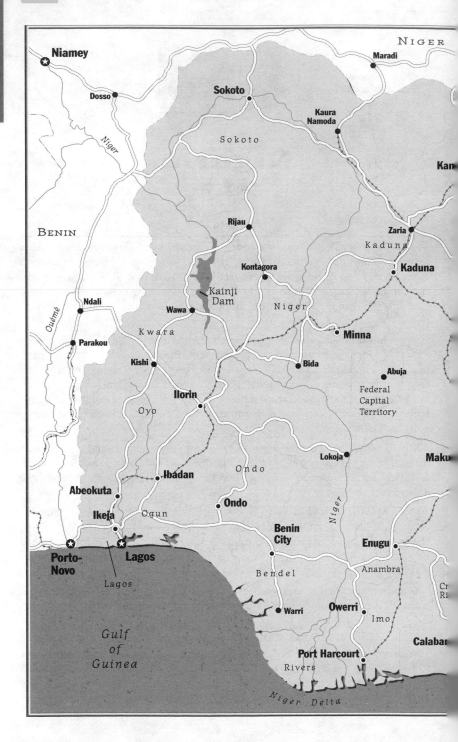

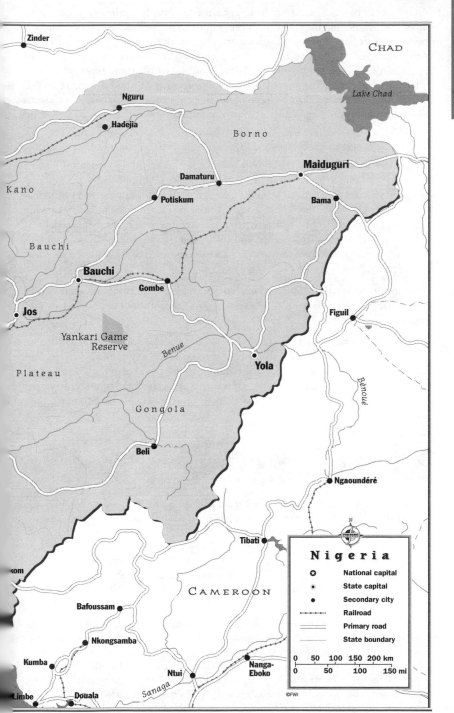

Zinder

CHAD

Lake Chad

Nguru

Hadejia

Borno

K a n o

Damaturu

Maiduguri

Potiskum

Bama

B a u c h i

Bauchi

Figuil

Gombe

Jos

Yankari Game
Reserve

Benue

Bénoué

Yola

P l a t e a u

G o n g o l a

Beli

Ngaoundéré

Tibati

Bafoussam

C A M E R O O N

Nkongsamba

Kumba

Nanga-
Eboko

Ntui

Sanaga

Limbe

Douala

Nigeria

⊛ National capital
⊙ State capital
● Secondary city
╫─╫ Railroad
─── Primary road
─── State boundary

0   50   100 150 200 km
0   50   100   150 mi

©FWI

Every week, the U.S. embassy in Lagos tries to console victims of these scams where businesspeople have lost sums ranging from a few thousand to upwards of one million dollars. Patsies who have traveled all the way to Nigeria to clinch these "lucrative" deals have been threatened, assaulted or even killed. Local police couldn't care less, and Nigerian officials find the whole thing funny. The U.S. embassy can't do much more than lend you a toothbrush and a quarter to call your mother for airfare. Some Nigerian immigration officials have begun to warn folks upon arrival at Lagos airport, but the lemmings keep arriving to pick up their pot of gold.

Scams range from attempts to engage American businesspeople in fictitious money-transfer schemes to fraudulent solicitations to supply goods in fulfillment of nonexistent Nigerian government contracts. Most scam operators are sophisticated and may take victims to staged meetings, often held in borrowed offices at Nigerian government ministries. They do their research and can often provide plausible, but nonexistent, orders written on seemingly genuine Ministerial stationery, replete with official stamps and seals. Nigerian business scams are not always easy to recognize, and any unsolicited business proposal should be carefully scrutinized.

It is not possible to describe how each of several hundred different scams works in Nigeria, but they all center on greed (yours), gullibility (yours) and money (yours).

This scam stuff is so much fun that we won't even dwell on the conflict (Muslim north versus Christian south) that ripped the country apart during the Biafran war, the billions of oil dollars that go straight into the pockets of the select few, or the overall poverty and population growth that plague this large country. For now, we just keep seeing how many suckers will travel here looking to make their fortune.

As OPEC's fourth-largest oil producer, Nigeria is oil rich and human-rights poor, the scam capital of the world, a boot camp for fatigue-clad banana dictators, and the Bermuda Triangle of currency. For all but nine of its 37 years of independence, Nigeria has been ruled by the military. The current bunch of boys chomping on stogies behind Ray-Bans work for General Sani Abacha. He and his cronies siphon off the country's multi-billion dollar annual oil earnings, returning hardly a trickle to Nigeria's oil-producing regions. In another report from the cookie jar, Nigeria Airways said in February 1996 that the US$100 million paid by the government in 1992 to create an international airline had vanished without a trace. Another black hole.

Unlike other African dictatorships, there is no government-in-waiting in Nigeria—nor in exile elsewhere—ready to play the white-knight role when Nigeria finally implodes. Starting in February 1996, there was a renewed crackdown on the few dissidents with the nuts even to make a soupy verbal challenge to Sani Abacha's supremacy. Nine political activists were executed for their anti-government views in November 1995. Meanwhile, the government continues its grabbing of the Ogonis' land for oil. Although Abacha has said free elections will be held sometime in 1998, a series of bomb attacks that have been blasting Lagos in 1997 may give the strongman an excuse to call off the elections.

More than 250 ethnic groups in Nigeria's population of 100 million have been manhandled by seven different military rulers since 1960. And the situation looks only bleaker. Nigeria's civilian politicians are extremely weak and divided like an Arizona chasm. The general keeps them in his coop with enough hush money for hookers and Johnny Walker's. The government recently admitted that fully two-thirds of the 55,000 people in Nigerian jails have never had a trial.

The Nigerians have been trying to get a little good PR in recent months. After the democratically elected Sierra Leone government of Ahmed Kabbah was toppled in a coup in May 1997, Nigeria, in a move at least tacitly applauded by the West, sent troops to restore Kabbah to power. Nigerian soldiers took Freetown's airport but got bogged down after that. However, Freetown's airport is about as strategic a trophy as the Florida Everglades.

When You Gotta Go, You Gotta Go

A group of chanting, dancing and shouting youths were seen parading down the streets of Kano with an unusual object on the end of a long stick. It was the head of Gideon Akaluka, an automotive spare parts dealer who had been accused of using the Koran for toilet paper. He was originally arrested and detained for the charges, but a group of Islamic youths broke into the jail, beheaded him and presented his head to their traditional leader, the Emir of Kano. The Emir sent a messenger to tell the crowd that they had acted in a barbaric manner and that he was shocked. The crowd reacted by caning the courier with 100 strokes. There was never any proof of the victim's guilt brought forward.

General Sani Abacha

As Nigeria's seventh military dictator, Sani Abacha takes destitution, murder, repression, corruption and greed to a new stratosphere. This guy makes Idi Amin look like a bona-fide Berkeley philanthropist. The fat man is unscrupulous, power-mad and paranoid. He rarely leaves Nigeria (who the hell would have him over for a state dinner anyhow?) and was involved in the last three coup attempts before finally taking the government's reigns on November 17, 1993. His first act was to abolish all democratic institutions, including the senate, national assembly and state councils. As well, he banned all political parties. He swept in military rule and purged the government of all civilians and the army of officers loyal to former President Major General Ibrahim Babangida, who himself seized power through a coup in August 1985. Without any political or ideological agenda at all, Abacha busies himself these days stuffing his pockets with embezzled cash—and lining those of the brown-nosing northern primroses—and executing dissidents.

General Sani Abacha
Chairman, Provisional Ruling Council
State House
Abuja, Federal Capital Territory, Nigeria
FAX: [234] (9) 523-2138

Shell Oil Company

Oil accounts for 90 percent of Nigeria's foreign exchange and most of it is getting pumped out by Royal Dutch Shell. Shell's been catching a lot of flak from bleeding hearts groups—from human rights lobbies to environmentalists. Some of it's deserved, some isn't. Nigeria sits atop a confirmed 20 billion barrels of oil. Shell (Nigeria Shell) accounts for half of the government's income. So what's the big deal about the unexplained loss of a few billion dollars here or there? On the other hand, the oil giant has started a US$3.6

billion liquefied natural gas project that's gotten a clean slate from the green crowd and can only be for the welfare of all Nigerians. Militant activities, including ethnic strife between Ijaw and Itsekiri tribesmen, have been on the increase in the oil-producing Niger River Delta, forcing Shell to reduce its output.

The Ogonis

The Ogoni people are a small minority in Nigeria—perhaps numbering 500,000—but Abacha has been systematically raping their oil-rich land, and, of course, the Ogonis have nothing to show for it. So when Ken Saro-Wiwa decided to champion the group's rights, he and eight of his buddies were promptly executed by the government. Nigeria was suspended from the Commonwealth (which is like getting a bimonthly bye in the weekly bridge club), and Britain—in protest—recalled its ambassador, who was back in his Lagos digs by the middle of January 1996, only a couple of months after Saro-Wiwa was hanged and Abacha had his wrists slapped by the West. Now, it's back to the business of pumping for petro-bucks. Hey, life goes on.

National Democratic Coalition (NADECO)

NADECO is a coalition of pro-democracy and human rights groups which has been accused of a rash of bombings in 1997. All the bombings have fit the same profile: the targeting of an army transport vehicle using a remote-controlled device. Fifteen suspected members of NADECO, including Nobel Prize winning writer Wole Soyinka, were charged in March 1997 with conspiring to wage war on the nation and the detonation of bombs. Of the 15 busted, 11 were already in jail and the remaining four out of the country, including Soyinka. To date, the government hasn't identified any of the attackers in the dozen or so blasts since December 1996.

United Front for Nigeria's Liberation (UFNL)

This previously unknown faction (in Nigeria, all rebel factions are unknown) claimed responsibility for the plane crash on January 19, 1996, that killed the son of military dictator Abacha. The UFNL then blasted a bomb at the airport where the plane had taken off. Given the West's aloofness in supporting an overt democracy movement in Nigeria, something scary is happening: a murderous African terrorist group endorsed by Middle America.

The United Democratic Front of Nigeria

Composed of 13 exiled democracy groups, the UDFN was formed on April 1, 1996. This fledgling body is more identifiable than UFNL, which the government claims doesn't even exist.

A passport and visa are required. Visas, at no charge, are valid for one entry within 12 months of issue. You'll need one photo, a yellow fever vaccination, proof of onward/return transportation, and for a tourist visa, a letter of invitation. Business visas require a letter from counterparts in Nigeria and a letter of introduction from a U.S. company. For further information, contact the following:

Embassy of the Republic of Nigeria

2201 M Street, N.W.
Washington, D.C. 20037
☎ *(202) 822-1500 or 1522*

Consulate General (in New York)

☎ *(212) 715-7200*

If you think you are going to save money by flying Nigeria Airlines from Europe, think again. Remember, NA flights are banned from entering the U.S., and one of its new Airbus A310s was nabbed by the Belgians for nonpayment of debt. Another NA plane had to make an emergency landing in Algiers and has been sitting there for months waiting for spare parts. Many flights are canceled because politicians borrow the planes to go shopping in Europe or just feel like visiting their money in Saudi Arabia.

Nigeria is primarily dependent on road transportation. During the oil boom in the mid-1970s, a number of long-distance roads were built—but arteries have become dilapidated in recent years due to the civil war and shrinking government revenues. And the accident rate in Nigeria is nearly the worst in the world. There is a nominal railway system, but even this has fallen into disrepair.

Lagos

The capital is a free-for-all, plagued by acute crime. Violent crime committed in broad daylight is the norm, and foreigners are particularly targeted and sometimes murdered for no reason. Shakedowns, muggings, carjackings, robberies, assaults, armed break-ins and even murders are frequently committed by uniformed police and soldiers in the capital. The Nigerian government has not heeded urgent U.S. embassy requests for the perpetrators to be disciplined. Unlike other coconut coalitions in the Third World, Nigeria possesses a capital city that is every bit as dangerous as the countryside.

The Rest of the Country

Factional fighting continues in Nigeria. Areas of noted danger include the border region in the northeast near Lake Chad—where outbursts of communal violence are common—usually involving clashes between Muslim fundamentalists and Christian proselytizers, southern Nigeria along the Niger River and regions in and outside Lagos in the southwest. Armed break-ins, muggings and carjackings are especially prevalent in the north.

There has been an increase in the number of unauthorized automobile checkpoints. These checkpoints are operated by bands of police, soldiers, or bandits posing as or operating with police or soldiers, whose personnel should be considered armed and dangerous. Many incidents, including murder, illustrate the increasing risks of road travel in Nigeria. Reports of threats against firms and foreign workers in the petroleum sector recur from time to time. Chadian troop incursions have reportedly occurred at the border area in the far northeast, near Lake Chad.

Bakassi Peninsula

Nigeria and Cameroon have been duking it out in the disputed Bakassi Peninsula, where the two nations have long been at odds. Since February 1994, the armed forces of the two nations have frequently clashed in the peninsula, a series of impoverished islands in the oil-rich Gulf of Guinea, which each claims to be its territory. Elf-Sarepca, the Cameroonian unit of France's Elf-Aquitaine and several other oil firms are exploring for crude oil there and just south of the islands.

Politics

Chief K. O. Abiola won the 1993 democratic elections fair and square. When he was imprisoned and charged with treason by Abacha for declaring himself president, it sent a clear message that politics is not a healthy career choice in Nigeria. Former President General Olusegun Obasanjo is cooling his heels in the clink for his two coup attempts against Abacha, and there are an estimated 43 dissidents sharing his cell. On March 16, 1996, Nigeria held elections for 593 local councils, but the government prohibited members of the Movement for the Survival of the Ogoni Peoples—the anti-government group Ken Saro-Wiwa championed—from running. On March 21, 1996, Abacha signed a law permitting the military junta to dismiss any local councilman without cause.

Crime

Nigeria has one of the highest crime rates in the world. There are 94 murders for every 100,000 people and 1256 thefts. Murder often accompanies even the simplest burglary.

Organized Crime

In April 1996, German police uncovered a Nigerian organized crime ring that was operating throughout Europe, who were allegedly involved in counterfeiting, drug running, and credit card fraud. Over the past few years, German police investigations of these crimes have inevitably led them to Nigeria. Since 1990, the Nigerians have worked the following fraudulent trick: Offers were made to private individuals and medium-sized companies via letters or fax that they should help with the transfer of millions of dollars from Nigeria to Germany. In return, between 30 and 40 percent of the amounts were promised. In reality, however, the gangsters were interested in collecting high amounts for alleged charges in Nigeria from those whom they were cheating. By investigating these scams, the Germans were able to uncover that the Nigerians suspected of the crimes obviously were part of well-organized, internationally active groups.

Nigeria's organized crime enterprises are active in at least 60 countries. And the U.S. provides Nigerian scam artists a barrelful of suckers. The U.S. Secret Service estimates that Nigerian advance fee fraud letter scams cost Americans US$250 million a year. But back to basics; the South African government says Nigerian criminal operations have penetrated the entire southern African region, with enterprises in heroin and cocaine trafficking, alien smuggling, document fraud, car theft and gang activities.

Fuel Shortages

Nigeria possesses four major oil refineries and produces two million barrels of oil a day but can't even gas up its own cars. Nigeria's gas crisis of 1997 has brought traffic to a standstill. Thousands of commuters in Lagos have nowhere to go and no way of getting there. Queues of cars outside empty fuel pumps make the U.S. gas lines of the 1970s look like the turnstiles at a Chicago Cubs game. It remains to be seen how the farmers are going to get crops to market.

"New Breed" Churches

These instant churches promise to their followers wealth, jobs and other miracles. Thousands of Nigerians now take part in religious money-making rituals, which can occasionally get out of hand. In one instance in Imo state, outraged crowds burned down the houses of suspected "new breed" church members after the discovery of the head of a missing child, two tongues, skulls and other human remains on the grounds of the Overcomers Church. These churches have sprung up all over Nigeria. The only folks getting rich, though, are their owners/pastors, who trot the globe in private jets and show up for sermons in luxury imported cars.

Uniforms

Many petty and violent crimes committed against foreigners are performed by bandits dressed in police or military uniforms. Bandits regularly murder foreigners without provocation. As well, foreigners are frequently robbed, assaulted and/or killed by legitimate police officers and soldiers, and never reprimanded or punished by the government. Pickpockets and confidence artists, some posing as local immigration and other government officials, are especially common at Murtala Muhammad Airport. In addition to harassment and shakedowns of American citizens by officials at airports and throughout Nigeria, there have been reports of violent attacks by purported government officials on Americans and other foreigners.

Going to University

According to the AP, university life is never dull. It seems over 500 kids have been expelled from Nigeria's 39 universities for indulging in a little organized mayhem. Over 20 people have died in two years, and their deaths have been attributed to secret societies with colorful names like the Pirates, Black Ax, the Buccaneers and the Green Berets. It seems that after the government banned student unions with political agendas, the groups quickly grew from their origins in the '80s on the University of Jos in the North. The groups were created to correct the ills of Nigerian society. I guess they would get an "F" so far.

Road Travel

Road travel is extremely dangerous throughout Nigeria, but particularly in the south and the northeastern border near Lake Chad. Unauthorized automobile checkpoints are set up regularly in rural areas and manned by armed bandits or police/military personnel with the sole purpose of hijacking, assaulting and/or robbing motorists. Foreigners are targets for carjackings, robberies and violence. Most of Nigeria's roads are pothole-ridden and nearly impassable.

Azikiwe's Long Road to Salvation

The funeral of Nigeria's first president, Nnamdi Azikiwe, who died in May 1996, had to be delayed until November to allow government road crews time to repair the roads to his home town of Onitsha. Think it was tough for the road workers? How 'bout for the driver of Azikiwe's hearse?

Flying

The U.S. FAA has prohibited aircraft from Nigerian Airlines from landing in the U.S. due to the unsafe upkeep of the airline's fleet. Additionally, the quality of fuel used in the airliners doesn't meet international minimum requirements—it's low-grade, often dirty and spiked with other ingredients that don't help planes stay off the ground.

GETTING SICK

You don't want to get sick in Nigeria. In recent times, more than 2000 of Nigeria's doctors have fled to the United States, with another 2000 opting for Saudi Arabia, the Gulf States, Canada and Britain. Health services are generally limited to the cities, and only affordable for wealthy Nigerians. Modern medicine is nonexistent in rural areas. Public health has crashed with the government's pilfering of anything of value sent into the country. Yellow fever, chloroquine-resistant malaria, trachoma and yaws are the biggest medical threats in Nigeria. Malaria is found in all parts of the country, including all urban areas, and the risk is present all year. There is a 17 percent risk of malaria exposure. Dracunculiasis, meningitis, lassa fever, leishmaniasis (both cutaneous and visceral), rabies, relapsing fever, African sleeping sickness and typhus (endemic flea-borne, epidemic louse-borne and scrub) are prevalent. Muslim northern Nigeria is the area worst affected by the meningitis scourge that has killed thousands of people in the Sahal belt of West Africa. Nigeria is also receptive to dengue fever, and schistosomiasis may be found throughout the country. There is one doctor for every 6134 people in Nigeria.

Outbreaks of meningitis, cholera, measles and gastroenteritis swept across the arid areas of West Africa in March and April 1996, particularly in Nigeria. Around 70,000 people in 17 African countries have been afflicted by meningitis alone, and nearly 9000 have died, more than half of them in Nigeria. The health problem is seen as so grave by Saudi Arabia that it banned all Nigerians from entering the Kingdom to perform the annual pilgrimage, or Haj, to the Islamic world's two holiest shrines. Meningitis is inflammation of the brain and spinal cord. If treated in time, its victims can be saved, although complications can bring deafness or loss of the fingers.

The Federal Republic of Nigeria is a tropical country (356,668 square miles, or 923,770 square kilometers) with two different climatic zones. The south is hot, rainy and humid for much of the year, while the north is equally hot but dry from October through April.

Nigeria is a federation of 30 states under the control of a military dictatorship and marred by corruption and instability. Muslims comprise 50 percent of the population, while Christians make up 40 percent. The Hausa-Fulani, Yoruba and Ibo ethnic groups total 65 percent of the population, and the estimated 250 ethnic groups comprise the other 35 percent. The official language of Nigeria's 100 million people is English.

There are more than 20 English-language newspapers in the country, but they are heavily monitored and supervised by the military junta. Foreign journalists are routinely expelled for citing corruption in the government.

The literacy rate is 51 percent. Less than 20 percent of the population graduates from secondary school. The official currency is the naira, divided into 100 kobo.

03/1996	Nigeria moved troops into Cameroon.
03/21/1996	Abacha signed a law permitting the military junta to dismiss any local councilman without cause.
01/19/1996	UFNL claimed responsibility for a plane crash that killed the son of military dictator Abacha.
11/10/1995	Writer and Ogoni rights champion Ken Saro-Wiwa and eight colleagues were executed by the Abacha government.
11/17/1993	General Sani Abacha's coup made him Nigeria's seventh military ruler.
06/23/1993	General Ibrahim Babangida annulled elections; military remained in power.

06/18/1993	It was leaked that Moshood Abiola won the presidential elections comfortably over Bashir Tofa.
05/1992	Two hundred people were killed in ethnic clashes.
07/03/1986	Former President Shehu Shagari and former Vice President Alex Ekwueme were released after spending 30 months in detention.
05/23/1986	Fifteen students were killed in clash with police.
08/27/1985	Major General Ibrahim Babangida takes over the government in a military coup.
01/15/1966	A group of army majors (mainly Ibo) failed in Nigeria's first coup attempt.
10/01/1960	Independence declared.

Pyongyang

North Korea

Il or Illin?

At Pyongyang's Mansudae Hill, a line of street cleaners who look more like housewives (which, of course, they actually double as), armed with straw brooms, march stooped over like a bad ensemble at Pasadena's DooDah Parade. Like a 17th-century Zamboni machine, they clear what little soil has accumulated on the walkway in front of the Korean Revolution Museum before a giant bronze statue of the late North Korean leader Kim Il Sung. Kim's massive right arm is eternally locked forward in a handshake with the clouds, which was about all he was able to shake hands with during his neurotically xenophobic, despotic and frequently brutal 46 years of rule of a country that may as well be on Mars.

Shaking hands with nothing. The image lingers with you, even after reading the romantic, campy description in the city's official guidebook: "The statue of Kim portrays his sublime figure looking far ahead, with his left hand akimbo and his right raised to indicate the road for the people to advance."

The road to the 38th parallel, no doubt.

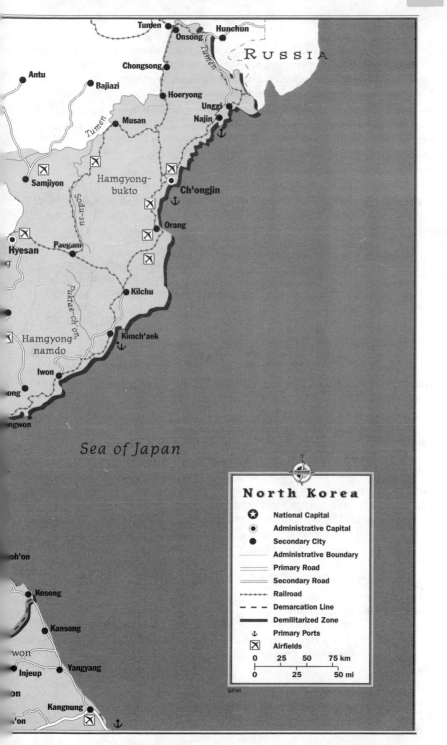

The Great Leader departed for the Great Unknown on July 18, 1994, succumbing to illness that he tried vainly to thwart with a combination of meteorology and herbs. Millions of North Koreans have made pilgrimages to the statue and other shrines, openly weeping for a man who they were taught since birth created the dawn of each new day. Literally. It must have come as quite a shock when the sun rose the morning after Kim headed for that great *juche* in the sky.

Myth and legend shrouded Kim Il Sung. His legendary heroics against the Japanese during World War II, by all historical accounts, never occurred. His greatest victory was a stalemate in the Korean War, at the cost of a half million North Korean lives. He might also claim a victory of sorts in the arrest of more than 20 million people.

North Koreans are taught that Kim was the inventor of everything from centuries-old scientific and physics theories to such modern conveniences as the automobile and the toaster. Some believe he's walked on the moon. By law, every North Korean household must possess at least two portraits of the Great One. Not Gretsky, but of Kim. That's overachievement.

Certainly not overachieving is Kim's son, 55-year-old Kim Jong Il—the Great Leader's heir apparent and a Jenny Craig "before" model—who is just beginning his duties as president and leader of the Communist Party after an extended grieving for his dead dad. Tagged the Supreme Leader (or Dear Leader), it's likely that some of the military boys had put a rifle to Jong's head and ordered him to grieve for a while. Cry, baby, cry.

And they may have had a good reason. Reclusive, cognac-guzzling Kim Jong Il is both a reported lush and an alleged terrorist. He's been implicated as the mastermind behind a number of terrorist attacks, including a Korean Air jetliner explosion that took 115 lives in 1987. He is believed responsible for North Korea's nuclear program (the bomb part, anyway), as well as the foiled assassination attempt on the South Korean president in Myanmar that instead blew away 17 high-level South Korean officials.

It is also thought that North Korea's recent binge in amphetamine and opium trafficking to kickstart its moribund economy is being personally directed by The Chubby One. In April 1997, a cache of 154 pounds of amphetamines with a street value of US$95 million was found on a North Korean freighter in port at Hiroshima, Japan. Dope is grown or manufactured in the DPRK (Democratic People's Republic of Korea) and then smuggled through diplomatic channels to Pyongyang's embassies abroad, where it is then sold to domestic dealers, or by North Korean diplomats themselves on the street level. It's believed that huge quantities of opium go through Russia via North Korean workers commuting to timber projects there.

But the mythmaking continues. Kim Jong Il was actually born in Siberia, but because most North Koreans have never heard of Siberia, Jong Il was reborn near North Korea's famed Mount Paektu. He is reputed to have written hundreds of books, all epic masterpieces. He can stop rain and predict the discovery of natural resources.

However, the Dear Leader isn't a been-there, done-that type of fellow. He's reportedly been abroad only once, to neighboring China—and that was probably by mistake. No backpacks in this dude's closet. In all likelihood, he's met only a couple of Westerners in his entire life. Trying to get hip in time for his formal ascension to power during the summer of 1997, Jong practiced his English (and probably his Korean, too) to Star Trek reruns and the Larry King Show.

His face fills the television screens every night, at all times and on every channel. The man who claims "socialism is not administrative and commanding" may have a different relationship with communism and alcohol. He is reported to spend nearly three-quarters of a million dollars a year on Hennessy cognac, specifically the Paradis line. That's commanding. Yet, he remains the subject of adulation. Normally bright, responsible scholars and educators from North Korea and abroad reduce themselves to writing driveling, soppy odes to this inglorious, silver-spooned papa's boy. Sample this, written by a doctor at Delhi University in India:

> *Dear leader Kim Jong Il*
> *Friend of masses, savior of*
> *humanity*
> *Increased efforts of yours inspired*
> *the masses*
> *You have awakened them*
> *To build modern DPRK*
> *Brick by brick*
> *Made them independent and masters*
> *of their own destiny*
> *Dear leader Kim Jong Il*
> *A rising star on the horizon*
> *Shown the path of salvation*
> *Of realism*
> *Removed flunkeyism in the face of*
> *Severe odds*
> *Dear leader Kim Jong Il*
> *A versatile personality*
> *I salute you*

Removed flunkeyism? Whoa.

The "My Automatic Rifle" Dance

In North Korea, propaganda has become an art form. Perhaps the most entertaining reading we've come across at *DP* is the "consumer" magazine that comes out of Pyongyang—*Korea Today*, of the DPRK. There are magnificent book reviews, all on Kim Jong Il's hundreds of books. No room for anything else. And no comments such as "The plot is frayed; the characters develop like a fungus. The author has talent, but should have restricted it to flyer writing for the PTA." Nope, nothing like that. You'd end up in the gulag for a few centuries.

The harshest criticism we spotted was surprisingly scathing, though: "Many of the world's people call Kim Jong Il the giant of our times. This means that he is unique and distinguished in all aspects—wisdom, leadership, ability, personality and achievements." (*Korea Today*, No. 3, 1992.) The writer was anonymous, fearing for his life if his byline were to be published. There's coverage of some great plays and performing arts shows. One particularly caught our attention, a tear-jerking rendition of the "My Automatic Rifle Dance," performed by two voluptuous actresses prancing about the stage with their AKs.

Korea Today publishes cutting-edge, bohemian poetry that mainstream periodicals wouldn't have the balls to print:

> *My song, echo all the way home from the trenches.*
> *When I smash the American robbers of happiness,*
> *And I return home with glittering medals on my chest,*
> *All my beloved family will be in my arms.*

Cool stuff. Want to subscribe? Write: The Foreign Language Magazines, Pyongyang, DPRK.

For more laughs, write The Korean People's Army Publishing House (Pyongyang, DPRK) for a copy of their enormously popular *Panmunjom*, a chronicle of North Korea's innumerable military accomplishments. There are some great combat shots, with captions like "U.S. imperialist troops of aggression training South Korean puppet soldiers to become cannon fodder in their aggressive war against the northern half of Korea." Another innocuous shot of a group of soldiers is depicted as, "A U.S. military advisor and the South Korean stooges are on the spot to organize the armed invasion of the northern half of Korea." Another photo shows a 1953 armistice meeting between North Korean and U.N. officials breaking up, and is appropriately captioned: "The U.S. imperialist troops of aggression hastily leave after their crimes have been exposed at a meeting held at the scene of the crime."

But the *DP* runner-up in the book goes to a 1976 shot of an American soldier using a chain saw to cut down a tree. The caption: "The U.S. imperialist troops of aggression committed a grave provocation, cutting down a tree."

And the winner? A fuzzy shot of a letter from Secretary of State John Foster Dulles to a South Korean colonel, dated June 20, 1950. The caption reads: "Secret messages exchanged between the south Korean puppets and the U.S. imperialists to invade the north, and Dulles' secret letter instigating the puppets to start a war." It took a magnifying glass, but we read the letter:

> *The dinner which you gave in our honor last night was something I shall always remember. The setting was really glorious, the company distinguished, the entertainment most interesting to us and last, but not least, the food was delicious. The antique vase (you gave us) will grace Mrs. Dulles' living room in New York and always keep fresh the memory of our visit with you.*

For even more knee-slaps, check out the Korean Central News Agency's new web site. Although graphically as creative as a pancake, you're sure to howl at the copy, which continually adulates Kim Jong Il as having "perfectly controlled the complicated situation of the world." Of course, don't expect much on the mess the leader has perfectly controlled in his own back yard, namely two consecutive years of famine that one UN official said could turn into "one of the biggest humanitarian disasters of our lifetime."

Korean Central News Agency
http://www.kcna.co.jp

No one's quite sure. North Korea is perhaps the most closed society on the globe. It is also perhaps the most lobotomized. Obtaining information from abroad is illegal, as is picking up hitchhikers (who might reveal contaminating Western secrets, such as John Travolta actually is a decent actor). North Koreans can't even visit many areas in their own country. Talking to a foreigner is grounds for arrest.

For sure, the pawns of Pyongyang have nuke capabilities, scaring the hell out of the U.S. puppet imperialists to the south and, of course, Japan. So much so, that Uncle Sam has gone to the brink of (dread!) normalizing relations with Pyongyang.

The Chubby One has been stung by two years of famine—caused by floods and maladroit mismanagement of farmland—and a string of defections, including the high-profile bailing from the North of Hwang Jang Yop in February 1997. Hwang was number six (or 26 depending on who you talk to) in the pecking order and the architect of Pyongyang's *juche* ideology of self-reliance. How well that concept has worked is evidenced by Pyongyang's willingness to store Taiwan's nuclear waste if the renegade Chinese island-state will also send along as a lucky-strike-extra US$200 million worth of rice. That's self-reliance.

North Korea's a damn difficult place to get around. Number one, there aren't any cars (bicycles were even illegal in many areas until the early 1990s). Western tourists can only visit selected areas of the country and only under the chaperoned and watchful eye of a government guide.

Kim Il Sung

Yeah, he's dead. But long live the Kim. The effects of playing God for 46 years don't go away overnight. The North Koreans still show, and will continue to show for years, blinding adoration of their beloved pinko deity, except for, perhaps, the estimated 20,000 political prisoners held in the country. But, remember, in North Korea, you're a political prisoner if you don't turn on your television in the morning.

Kim Jong Il

The Dear Leader isn't seen around a lot. Rumor has it he's in ill health, excuse the pun. But more likely he's at a Blockbuster somewhere in L.A., either stocking up on copies of *Rambo*, *Godzilla*, and *Goodfellas* or abducting waitress/actresses. Jong's a movie freak; he owns perhaps 20,000 videotapes. It's also widely believed that Jong once kidnapped a South Korean actress and director and held them captive for nearly a decade while he played Dino de Laurentis. He shot a series of anti-Japanese films that make Crichton's *Rising Sun* look like the Meiji Constitution.

Kim Pyong Il

Half-brother of Kim Jong Il. A January 1995 shoot-out occurred in the streets of Pyongyang between followers of Kim Jong Il and Kim Pyong Il, suggesting a power struggle between the two. Jong's response? He banished his half-brother to one place on earth more miserable to live in than North Korea. He made him ambassador to Finland.

Jimmy Carter

Jimmy goes where no Bill dares. Carter was instrumental in brokering the October 1994 nuclear agreement between Pyongyang and Washington. Carter was born to be an ex-president. Enjoying the now popular and strong credentials of having been weak in office, this ex has been globe trotting to the nastiest places on earth, meeting face-to-face with bullies, warlords, pranksters and gangsters and washing his hands later. For the most part, it's worked.

The Military

North Korea has approximately 1.2 million troops, most of them massed along the border with South Korea. The balance are starving and roaming the streets of famine-struck cities and rural areas with their AKs hitting the "people" up at gunpoint for food and money. Fortunately, for the time being, Jong has their support. The biggest reason is that the Dear Leader apparently has no plans to socialize the military, whose elite members enjoy such Western luxuries as Mercedes, Marlboros and mint-flavored Crest.

Passport and visa are required. Visas must be arranged prior to arrival in Pyongyang, usually through a tour packager. The best places to procure North Korean visas are in Bangkok and Macau. You must pay for your entire trip before you depart, as you will be part of a government-organized tour. The North Korean Visa Office is a better bet than the North Korean embassy in Beijing. Perhaps even a better bet is through M.K. Ways in Bangkok *(57/11 Wireless Road, Bangkok 10330; ☎ [66] (2) 254-4765, 255-3390, 254-7770, 255-2892)*. The company specializes in tour packages to Indochina, but has introduced packages to North Korea in an exclusive agreement with the government.

Tours of North Korea vary in length, but most are for 14 days. You'll need three passport photos and approximately US$15 for the visa. If asked if you are a journalist, it would help facilitate the process to say no. Inside the country, you may be able to extend your visa, but, again, you'll have to pay in advance for accommodations and guide services. Your guide should be able to make the necessary arrangements.

By air, you can get to Pyongyang via Beijing on Air China or Korean Airways. By train, you can enter North Korea from Beijing via Tianjin, Tangshan, Dandong and Shinuiju. You'll be met at the Pyongyang station by your guide. By boat, you may want to try the ship that runs from Nagasaki, Japan, to Wonsan on North Korea's east coast.

It would be foolish to try and enter North Korea illegally. You won't get back out.

You won't have much choice in the matter. Most likely, you'll be with a government guide in a government vehicle and you'll go where the government wants you to go. U.S. citizens may spend money in North Korea only to purchase ordinary travel necessities such as hotel accommodations, meals and goods for immediate personal consumption in North Korea. There is no longer any per-diem restriction on these expenses, and the use of credit cards for these transactions is also authorized. Because the sanctions system prohibits business dealings with North Korea, unless licensed by the U.S. Treasury Department, purchases of goods or services unrelated to travel are prohibited. There exists only the skeleton of a public transit system in North Korea: very few buses, virtually no cars and no domestic flights. Travel by train is your best bet if you're not traveling by car. Again, you'll have no say. But trains are usually used to visit some of the more popular tourist sites (which sites aren't?).

The Entire Country

The entire country if you are an American: The North Koreans think all Westerners who visit the country are spies. North Korea is host to few foreign tourists, and those who do get in will only see areas of the country targeted by the government for them to see. All visitors are accompanied by a government guide. You will be subjected to intense propaganda wherever you go. And you will never be permitted to stray off the beaten path unattended, although you might be occasionally permitted an unattended evening stroll around Pyongyang. Crime is not a problem in North Korea. There is wide speculation that thieves and criminals get the death penalty. In this regard, no area of North Korea can be catgorized as unsafe. There is no U.S. embassy in North Korea.

South Korea's Beaches

If it's the sun, the sand, the surfing or the babes you're after, you're in the wrong country, but North Korean submarines have a propensity for basking in South Korea's surf. In one such incident in 1996, a North Korean sub hit some rocks and dropped off more than a dozen guys on a South Korean beach with binoculars, night vision equipment and other surveillance goodies. (Those who escaped were subsequently hunted down and shot by the South Koreans.) We have to assume they come looking for babes.

Insulting the Great Leader, or the Dear Leader

Want to end up in the slammer fast? Here's how: Tell your guide that Kim Jong Il wears Kim Jong Suk's (his mother) army boots. Or, perhaps, mention you believe that the U.S. would kick North Korea's ass in soccer or in a ground war. Or mutter your suspicion that Kim Il Sung was gay. You get the point.

Giving Gifts

Never give North Koreans gifts of any nature, especially Western items, foreign currency or any currency. Although the individual might gracefully accept your generosity (most won't), you're setting that person up for trouble. Remember, you're a spy. Anyone you come into contact with will be assumed to be collaborating with your efforts to pass information and gather intelligence. Silly, but true.

Touching a North Korean Woman

Regardless of how she might come on to you (she won't, by the way), never touch a North Korean woman. Do not even shake hands. This will be construed as an immoral act and will undoubtedly get you both in trouble.

Famine

By mid-1997, grain rations were down to 3.5 ounces a day per person, the result of two years of flooding and bureaucratic mismanagement of agricultural lands. In North Korea, 4.82 million tons of grain are needed as food for the country's 24 million people every year. In 1996, grain output dropped to 2.5 million tons in unhulled state. And most of that had been cut with grass and tree bark. In 1995–96, the famine affected at least 5.2 million people, left 500,000 homeless and ruined 359,936 hectares of arable land. In 1997, food rations dropped to a level four times lower than normally considered essential for a healthy population. The country, at press time, has only half the grain it needs to feed its people. Yet, to celebrate his 55th birthday on February 16, 1997, Kim Jong Il had 10,000 young Koreans take part in a gymnastics festival in Pyongyang—to burn calories. *Juche*!

North Korea has a shortage of medical supplies, facilities and doctors. Western medicines and remedies are even more rare. On the plus side, the water is potable, and the hygiene and sanitation very good. Also, you won't find the food stalls that are seen throughout the rest of Asia. North Korea is squeaky clean.

After the Japanese surrender of 1945, Korea was divided into two directorates: The U.S.S.R. occupied the north, while the U.S. controlled the south below the 38th parallel. In 1948, the division between the two zones was made permanent. Trade was cut off between the two zones at the advent of the Cold War in the late 1940s.

The Democratic Peoples Republic of Korea (DPRK) is very much a communist nation. Before the demise of the Soviet Union, the DPRK imported nearly three-quarters of a million tons of oil from the U.S.S.R. per year. These supplies have been essentially cut off. North Korea is nearly US$6 billion in debt.

The country is covered almost entirely by north-south mountain ranges and is about the size of Pennsylvania.

The language in North Korea is Korean, with indigenous elements in the vocabulary. Religions in North Korea include Buddhism and Confucianism. However, religious activities within the country basically don't exist. There is no public worshiping of deities in the DPRK. The currency is the won. The won=100 jon. Per-capita income is US$1000.

The time in North Korea is GMT plus nine hours. Electricity is 220 V/60 Hz. Overseas phone calls can be made from the major hotels, and IDD is available in certain establishments. Mail can be received at some hotels and the Korea International Tourist Bureau. But it will be read by the government. Fax services are readily available.

The climate in North Korea is cold and dry in the winter with warm summers. More than 60 percent of the annual rainfall occurs from June through September.

The capital of North Korea is Pyongyang.

02/12/1997	Leading party ideologue Hwang Jang Yop defects to the South Korean embassy in Beijing.
11/12/1994	An American army helicopter was shot down in North Korean airspace. One pilot died in the crash, and the other repatriated more than two weeks later.

07/18/1994	The death of the Great Leader, Kim Il Sung.
07/27/1953	The armistice ending the Korean War was signed.
09/15/1950	U.N. Commander General Douglas MacArthur made an amphibious landing at Inchon, behind North Korean lines, and routed the North Korean army.
06/27/1950	U.S. President Harry Truman ordered U.S. combat units into action to enforce the U.N. condemnation of North Korea's invasion of South Korea.
06/27/1950	The United Nations condemned North Korea's attack of South Korea and decreed a withdrawal of the invading forces.
06/25/1950	North Korea mounted a surprise invasion of South Korea.
05/01/1948	The establishment of the Democratic Peoples Republic of Korea.

Pakistan
★★★★

Dodge City with Skiing

The North and South of Pakistan, like its neighbor Afghanistan, have been surprisingly effective in resisting the influences of the outside world. Even though planeloads of trekkers, hippies, and hard-core mountain climbers travel here to explore some of the world's most rugged scenery, there are still many wild and dangerous areas. British adventurers, such as writer Rudyard Kipling and explorer Sir Richard Burton, maintained a healthy respect for the "wily Pathans," who have always controlled the remote mountainous regions of northwest and the arid south west of Pakistan.

The North West tribal areas of Pakistan have never really felt the presence of any government, let alone tourists. Here Pashto-speaking tribes and warlike clans maintain their own social, political and military structures, free from politics, taxes and MTV. Many of the more entrepreneurial tribes still view travelers and visitors as walking CARE packages. Today, Pakistan is a crude welding together of four semiautonomous provinces—Punjab, Sind, North-West Frontier Province (NWFP) and Baluchistan. It also encompasses federally administered tribal

641

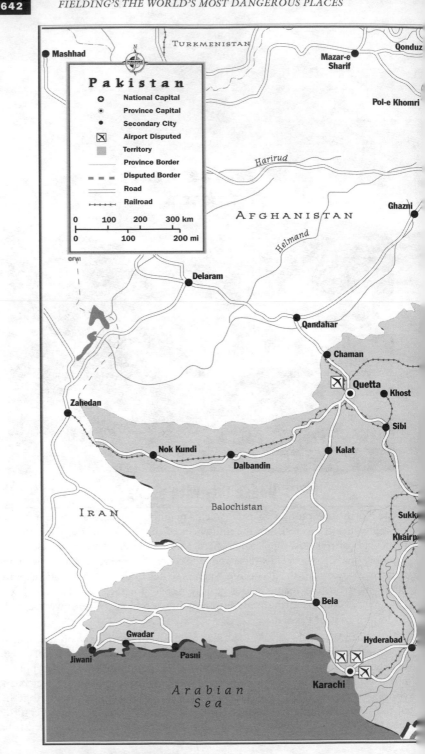

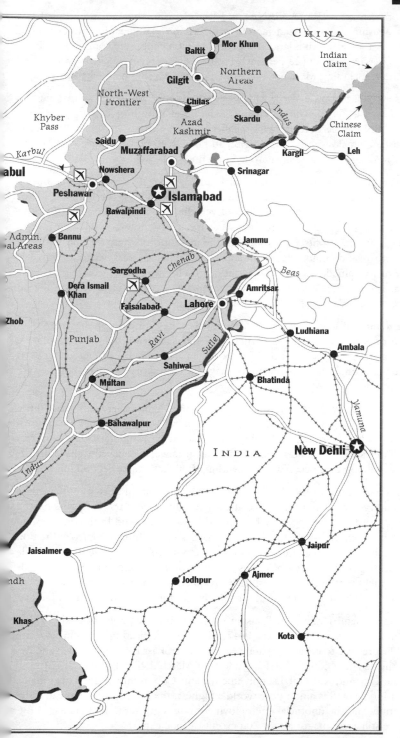

and northern areas (FATA/FANA) and lays claim to the Indian-occupied but mostly Muslim states of Azad Jammu and Kashmir. The teeming population of Pakistan is as diverse as it is large. Its 115.59 million people are comprised of Punjabi (56 percent), Sindi (23 percent), Pashtun (13 percent), Baluchi (5 percent) and others, including Mohajirs, or Urdu-speaking Muslim emigres from India.

Pakistan is dirt-poor, even by African standards. The per-capita annual income in 1992 was US$410. Thirty percent of the population lives below the poverty line, and only 35 percent of the population can read and write. Only 20 percent of Pakistani females can read and write, and barely 40 percent of children of primary school age were actually enrolled in schools.

Pakistan was the first country created as an Islamic state. By law, the country's president must be a Muslim. The legal system follows both the Islamic code of justice, or *Sharia*, and old British laws. Even the banking system must abide by Koran dictates that say it is improper to charge or pay interest. Bank customers actually share the profits and losses with the institutions where they do business. However, fiscal common sense still supercedes religious zeal, when, every year, just prior to Ramadan, customers withdraw their entire bank accounts to avoid the Zakat tax, a 2.5 percent levy on certain bank accounts charged annually on the eve of Ramadan.

Even a minor discussion with a Pakistani will evoke a long devotional treatise on the joys of Islam and the power of Allah. Pakistanis may not be entirely supportive of their government (I heard the phrase, "Benazir is a bitch," numerous times to describe the contempt many Pakistanis have for their female leader), but they are certainly wild about Allah.

And just to throw a little more mayhem into the picture, there's this nasty little nuclear arms race going on with India. Being on each other's borders means both nations don't require the technology to blast intercontinental ballistic rockets 10,000 miles able to strike a dime. India, for instance, is believed to have the capability of lobbing a nuclear warhead within 1000 feet of a target 150 miles away.

In this part of the world, that's close enough. India and Pakistan, in their relatively embryonic relationship, have already fought three wars. Firefights on the disputed border occur regularly between the two sides. And both countries aid separatist extremists—Pakistan funds the nasties in the Indian-controlled region of Kashmir, while India fans the flames of hatred in Pakistan's Sind area. While the world ignores the global consequences of this seemingly Hatfield-and-McCoy stick-fight in the boonies, the CIA quietly announced recently that Pakistan and India are two of the planet's top choices for potential serious instability.

Pakistan (Islami Jamhuria-e-Pakistan, or the Islamic Republic of Pakistan) became independent on August 15, 1947, when Britain sliced up India in response to public pressure to create a separate Muslim state. East Pakistan seceded and became the separate country of Bangladesh in March 1971. Pakistan aligns itself with the U.S. and was a vital supply line for anti-Communist Afghan insurgents. Population growth is among the world's highest, the literacy rate is low and deteriorating, and the unofficial unemployment rate is greater than 25 percent. Agriculture still accounts for about 70 percent of total exports.

Good For What Ails You

Travelers to Muslim countries are used to getting goofy on too sweet tea and whooping it up on watery yogurt. Ingesters of the fermented liquid form of the hop, grape and grain will be happy to learn that alcohol in Pakistan can be prescribed for medicinal purposes. Although alcohol is banned in Pakistan under Islamic law, you can order hard liquor and beer by the bottle through room service at the swank hotels in the large cities. You must fill out a form (for non-Muslims only), pay a small fee (about a dollar), and then sit in the quiet solitude of your room feeling like a junkie on methadone treatment. Malt beverages (beer without alcohol) are commonly available, and some remote areas feature homemade brews.

Pakistan is still the classic adventurer's paradise, a wild mountainous region (to the north) and an arid wasteland (to the south), inhabited by fierce warring tribes and squabbling minorities. The isolation and poverty are positively biblical in the smaller towns. The big cities make *Bladerunner* look like a Caribbean resort. Sensory-numbing amounts of noise, dirt, poverty, temperature extremes, crime and general mayhem send most travelers fleeing to New York seeking peace and quiet. But as many Pakistanis point out, don't forget India is worse. Pakistan offers natural, archaeological and historical sites, as well as a wealth of interesting backwaters. Amazingly, amongst this Third World developmental disaster, the Pakistani people are some of the most handsome, generous and engaging to be met on this planet...despite their constant warfare and banditry.

There have been major ethnic tensions in Pakistan since the country became independent. Pakistan has been pushed closer to the edge by the massive influx of weapons and refugees caused by wars in Afghanistan and conflict with India. There are a lot of guns in Pakistan with a lot of people who use them on a regular basis. Tourists are kidnapped for ransom but have not been harmed or executed.(Though a Swede was killed in 1991 in a messy government rescue attempt.) Your health is definitely at risk; everything from cobras to dengue-carrying mosquitoes can end it all rather suddenly. Mountainous highways and insane drivers make Pakistan's roads a killing ground. Much of the country is not under the control of the government but ruled by tribes. Professional bandits prey on poor and rich alike. What better place for a stroll through the countryside?

The Army/Government

You have to give Pakistan an A for effort when it comes to defending their Muslim state. Even though Pakistan has lost every war they have started, they still love to rattle their rusty colonial-era sabers at the huge Indian army to their east and watch their backs as Afghanistan descends into the apocalypse. Warring tribes in Baluchistan, Sind, the North West Frontier and the tribal areas keep the army's bullets from corroding in their clips, while criminals and ethnic terrorists in Karachi, Quetta and Hyderabad make soldiers sleep with one eye open. Having China as a neighbor to the north and Iran to the west does not make flower power high on the political agenda either.

The government, bolstered by total armed forces of 580,000 (513,000 reservists), is actively stirring up revolt in what they consider to be occupied (by India) Jammu and Kashmir. In June 1990, the Pakistan army had a total strength of over 500,000 soldiers. The navy has a total force of 20,000 men (including naval air personnel). The Pakistan air force (PAF) has 30,000 servicemen. Pakistan supplies much of the Middle East's cheap labor and is the world's prime low-cost supplier of military troops. About 30,000 military contract personnel from Pakistan were serving with the U.N. in Saudi Arabia, Libya, Oman, the United Arab Emirates and Kuwait in mid-1989, mainly in an advisory capacity. There have been complaints that the government actually makes money by renting out its poorly paid troops to serve in U.N. peacekeeping missions. The U.N. compensates Pakistan at a higher rate of pay, and the government allegedly pockets the difference. The government of Benazir Bhutto is consistently criticized for the plight of the poor Pakistanis, but considering that Ali Bhutto was strung up—his son was killed mysteriously in France, and General Zia Ul-Haq died in a mysterious plane crash—it's a wonder anybody wants to run this country. If you'd like to, it's a fax away.

Prime Minister Benazir Bhutto

Office of the Prime Minister
Islamabad, Pakistan
FAX: (+92)-51 821 835 (with remark: please forward to Prime Minister)
Telex: 082 5742; telegrams: Prime Minister Bhutto, Islamabad, Pakistan
Or:

Foreign Minister Assef Ahmad Ali

Office of the Foreign Minister
Islamabad, Pakistan
FAX: (+92)-51 821 835 (with remark: please forward to Foreign Minister)
Telex: 082 5742; telegrams: Foreign Minister Assef Ahmad Ali, Islamabad, Pakistan

The "Afghans"

There are 3 million "Afghan" refugees in Pakistan, most of them live in squalid mud-walled refugee camps outside of Peshawar and Quetta. Many others live in UNHR tents in small mountainous villages and deserts. There is little chance for education or economic future, but most prefer Pakistan to returning to war-wasted Afghanistan. There are also hundreds of "Afghans" from Libya, Egypt, Yemen, Jordan, Palestine, Algeria and Tunisia based, recruited and trained in Peshawar, and the border regions between Pakistan and Afghanistan.

The inner circle of the "Afghans" consists of 300 Egyptians. The "Afghan" branch of the Islamic Jihad is directed by Mohammed Shawky Islambuli, brother of the assassin of President Anar el-Sadat. Some 30 Egyptian "Afghans" work directly with the Iranian Pasdarans. Eight of these Egyptians constitute the central command of the Islamic Legion, a terrorist and political group active in Egypt, Eritrea, Kenya, Tanzania, Sudan, Algeria, Libya and Lebanon.

Some of the "Afghan" leaders have fled to Jalalabad from Peshawar. The Arab "Afghans" have ties with fundamentalist Muslims in the United States. Ramzi Ahmed Yussef, a suspect in the bombing of the World Trade Center in New York, is an "Afghan." Yussef was trained from 1987 to 1990 in Peshawar camps in the ranks of the Islamic Jihad groups under the orders of Dr. Ayman al-Zawahiri.

The Mohajirs

As of the beginning of 1995, the Mohajirs are the principal disturbers in the Karachi area. The Mohajirs are Urdu-speaking Muslim immigrants who came here from India after the partition between Pakistan and India in 1947. Their political/military group, the Mohajir National Movement (MQM), is directly battling police and strongarming locals. There are six major political and religious groups in Karachi. In total, they have 1000 armed guerrillas and snipers operating at any one time.

A passport and visa are required. The visa must be obtained from a Pakistani embassy or consulate before arrival at the point of entry. Information on entry requirements can be obtained from the embassy of Pakistan or the Pakistani consulate general. There is a $20 fee for the visa and a $10 fee for rush delivery. Business visitors and tourists are required to carry a valid Pakistan visa in their passports that must be obtained prior to entry. Pakistani requirements to legally cross the country's borders are different for each nationality. U.S. citizens must have a visa issued by a Pakistani consulate as well as a valid U.S. passport. Make sure you apply for your visa in the country of your residence, since you will be told that only the embassy in your home city or country can issue visas.

Embassy of Pakistan

2315 Massachusetts Avenue, N.W.
Washington, D.C. 20008
☎ *(202) 939-6200*

Pakistani Consulate General

12 East 65th Street
New York, New York 10021
☎ *(212) 879-5800*

Do not bring in alcohol; it will be confiscated and given back to you upon your departure. Crossing from Afghanistan officially is forbidden for foreigners, although many of the remote tribal areas do not observe any immigration formalities. Currently, the Afghanistan-Pakistan border is closed, but it is easy to streak across. Only U.N. personnel and locals are allowed to cross the border officially. The Iranian border can be crossed using weekly train service (Zahedan–Quetta), or by a painfully slow 22-hour bus trip (Taftan–Quetta). Folks who like avoiding those messy passport stamps can expect to be arrested and tried in court, which can result in deportation, fines and/or imprisonment.

You can enter from China via the efficient, but weather-sensitive Karakoram Highway. The road is open from May 1–November 30 if Mother Nature obliges. The route continues to the famous trading town of Kashgar, but the bus ride will test the stamina and intestines of any traveler. Coming in from India is via train (Lahore–Wagh) or a four-hour bus ride (Lahore–Amritsar) but subject to closure due to Sikh attacks. Check with the government or the embassy for exact restrictions and closures. The only land border crossing with India is Amritsar.

Safe travel inside Pakistan is subject to weather, regional idiosyncrasies and plain luck. Bandits prey on buses and trains; the roads are makeshift, and if the robbers don't get you, the dilapidated buses might. Pakistan is a patchwork of tribal- and government-controlled areas, sprinkled liberally with bandits who couldn't care less who "rules" the area. Most travelers have a great time, despite the chaos.

Substantial areas within North-West Frontier Province are designated tribal areas, outside the normal jurisdiction of government law enforcement authorities. Travel within these areas is particularly hazardous. Tribal feuds or conflicts between smuggling factions may incidentally involve foreigners. Even in the settled areas, ethnic, political or sectarian violence may target foreigners. Car hijackings and the abduction of foreigners are occasionally reported from the tribal areas. If visitors must enter the tribal areas, a permit must be obtained from the Home Department, which may require that an armed escort accompany the visitor. *DP* was in the market in Peshawar when a man was shot dead trying to take off with a stolen car. Three bullets in the neck. They did not ask for ID before they shot.

Driving

Today, Pakistan is busy spending the millions appropriated to it by the World Bank to upgrade its highways. Unfortunately, no one has been taught to drive. The white lines on those freshly made highways are an old colonial anachronism. Drivers weave, honk, squeeze, yell, wave, swerve and do everything except brake when faced with an oncoming car.

Considering the Pakistanis' creative use of their roadways, it is not surprising that, despite all the press about *dacoits* (local bandits) and civil unrest, the greatest potential for injury while traveling through Pakistan is the chance of being involved in a crash or being smacked like a cricket ball when crossing the street. To give pedestrians and other drivers a chance, Pakistanis decorate their vehicles with as many bright and shiny objects as possible

The aging Bedfords, three-wheeled rickshaws and "Suzukis" are adorned with loud horns, extensive murals, miniature disco systems, tassels and other bric-a-brac. Prayers to Allah, bucolic scenes, dingleberries, doodads and mascots glued like African fetishes are just some of the advanced safety techniques designed to ensure the longevity of the driver (but not necessarily the passengers). The decorations are supposed to ward off danger but, apparently, are ineffective in stopping the carnage.

Of a total 35,258 miles of roads in Pakistan, 24,952 (a generous 70 percent) are paved. The torturous terrain requires major engineering feats to put in roads. Most of the country can only be traversed via pack-trails and footpaths. The main highway is the Grand Trunk Road between Karachi and Peshawar.The multi-lane highway linking Karachi with Hyderabad is also a major route, permitting crazed drivers to get more out of their sheet-metal buckets than Isaac Newton would ever advise. The Indus Highway, the other north-south artery, is being improved, and there will eventually be a highway connecting Peshawar with Karachi, via Islamabad and Lahore.

The most impressive highway is the 1200-km Karakoram Highway, built over a 20-year period to link the remote Chinese market town of Kashgar with Peshawar to the south. The road is a mind-blower for its mountainous scenery and is frequently closed due to landslides, snowstorms, floods and other topographical afflictions. Various adventure groups offer bicyling tours for the eco-adventurous. Obviously, the hundreds of ever smiling drivers would think nothing of adding one more shiny decoration to the side of their overloaded trucks.

On paper, Pakistan borrows the British rule of driving on the left. In reality, driving is a death-defying blend of the German habit of operating motor vehicles with the pedal to the floor, the Italian habit of talking with their hands, and the Asian custom of ignoring mirrors, or side and rear windows. The fact that most Pakistani roads are designed for Alexander's (the Great) camels keeps it interesting. If you want less control over your destiny, you might want to hire your own talkative driver and deathtrap car from the Pakistan Tourism folks. A 4WD jeep is preferable for more rugged trips in the north. Suzukis and Jeeps are popular. You will need a large security deposit and will be dinged about eight rupees per km and 200 rupees per day. Or, you can negotiate a fixed rate if you know your itinerary.

In the cities, yellow taxis are cheap and should be hired round-trip, since they tend to gravitate to hotels and are hard to find elsewhere. Wildly decorated buses are cheaper, but remember they expect you to jump on (and off) while they are moving. Don't forget the seats by the driver are for women and don't be shy about yelling before your stop.

The taxi fare from the airport to the centers of both Islamabad and Karachi is approximately 150 rupees. Peshawar is about 50 to 80 rupees. As you exit the terminal you will be mobbed by hundreds of official and nonofficial cabdrivers. It doesn't matter who you choose. Negotiate the fare with at least three drivers, since foreigners have traditionally been charged what the market will bear (about twice to three times the correct rate). Serious cheapskates will walk out past the airport and catch the sardine-can-like rickshaws who will ding you about 20 to 30 rupees. If you want to see the country by bus, stick to the more comfortable "Flying Coach" buses rather than the brightly decorated but deadly local buses. For brief amusement but not long-distance touring, try the horse-drawn *tonga* carriages and cheap three-wheeled motorized rickshaws. Big Westerners may not fit in the back of a rickshaw.

By Rail

As with many other former British colonies, Pakistan was built around its aging railway system. The country is linked by the north-south railway between the southern port of Karachi and the city of Peshawar in the North-West Frontier Province. The line runs through most major population centers.

Pakistan Railways offers 8775 km of track, 907 stations, 78 train stops, 714 locomotives, 2926 passenger coaches and 32,440 freight wagons. Sixty percent of Pakistan's track and 30 percent of its rolling stock are supposed to be scrapped, but are in use every day. Express trains have been held up by *dacoits* on the link between Karachi port and Lahore. You'll have a choice between 2nd, Economy, 1st, and Air-Conditioned classes. Go for the Air-Con class, since rail travel is cheap, slow and nostalgic in this class. The other classes are just torture. Bedding, toilet paper, soap and towels are not supplied on first-class couchettes but can be rented from the reservations office. The train between the Afghan border and Peshawar is the most interesting, as two steam trains (one at each end of the train) labors up and back down the Khyber Pass every Friday. Currently, Westerners are not allowed on this train, since it goes through the locked-down Khyber area.

By Air

Air travel is the recommended means of transportation between the major cities in Pakistan. Air travel, particularly to the northern areas, is often disrupted due to weather conditions. Regional airlines in the north have to fly *below* some of the world's tallest mountaintops.

Islamabad/Rawalpindi International Airport is five miles northwest of Islamabad and a 20-minute drive by taxi. State-run Pakistan International Airlines (PIA) maintains tardy but vital service to 41 international and 33 domestic destinations. There are 112 airfields, of which 104 are usable, 75 have a permanent surface. There are 31 runways over 8000 feet. Domestic tickets are cheaper when bought inside Pakistan. Pakistanis pay about half what you will pay. Airfares are laughably cheap (about US$10–$80 for any internal leg). You must pay in rupees. International flights to Karachi or Islamabad should be bought in major European or Asian bucket shops. Security is very tight. On nearly every flight, I had to go through X-ray, metal detector, tag, stamp tag, punch tag, rip tag, claim luggage and scrotum-squeezing personal searches. My film and luggage were X-rayed so much I am sure they glow in the dark.

Pakistan International Airways has the dubious task of flying very used equipment around the world's most hostile flying environments. Soaring mountains, dust, high winds, turbulence, down- and updrafts and the extra maintenance required to keep planes airborne may be the reasons why the landing announcement is a Muslim prayer: "Ladies and Gentlemen, *Inshallah* (God willing), we will be shortly landing." The feeling of flying heavily loaded turboprops well below many of the world's highest mountains is, quite frankly, a thrill. The turboprops can be very bumpy, and don't be surprised to find passengers praying fervently on rough flights. Despite the white-knuckle flights, air travel is still the recommended means of transportation between major cities in Pakistan. Keep in mind that many flights are overbooked, but seats on these flights can be bought by sweet-talking (and, of course, bribing) an airport porter.

Insider Tip

Pakistan is a land of frustrating red tape but there are many ways to cut through it. For example, you can be told that a flight is overbooked, only to find out that a flight with one connection to the same destination is available. You can be stopped from entering a region by an emphatic border guard, only to walk 20 yards further along the border and walk right through. There is little that cannot be bought, solved, rented or fixed in Pakistan for a moderate fee. In fact, getting around problems is a major source of income for enterprising Pakistanis and "Afghans." There was little DP could not do or make happen in Pakistan with a little financial lubrication. So, when in doubt, whip it out (your rupees). A case in point.

A newly made friend asked me if I could get him a visa to America. I said, "It's not like Pakistan, you can't just pay people off."

"Surely you can pay the police 2000–3000 rupees (about US$100) to get me in? I could be your gardener."

"Sorry, no way."

"What kind of country is that?" he said in disgust.

Trekking

Since many of the major historical sites have been pounded to rubble by invading armies, and the vast deserts to the south do not inspire too many nature photographers, Pakistan realizes that most of the tourism is related to its spectacular northern mountain scenery. You will find this area of Pakistani tourism well run and efficient. In a country where you would have a hard time finding a decent motor-coach tour, you can climb a major mountain with great ease (or at least make the preparations). To facilitate understanding and access, tourism officials have divided the country into open, restricted, and closed zones for trekkers. Open zones go up to only 6000 meters. Travel above that point is classified as mountaineering and requires a separate permit. The best source for information and permits is through the various trekking packagers well in advance of your trip (permits can take months). Good sources for information, permits, guides and porters are the following:

Pakistan Tours
Flashman's Hotel
The Mall
Rawalpindi
☎ 64811

Adventure Pakistan
10 Kahayaban-e-Suharawardy
Aapara Market
Islamabad
☎ 28324

A *DP* money-saver tip: There are literally hundreds of expensive European hiking boots for sale in the bazaars of Pakistan. These $100–$300 leather mountaineering boots can be bought for $4 to $7. Where do they come from? Simple! They are stolen from trekkers in hotels and shipped to Karachi.

Climbing

Although Everest is number one on the list of climbers, K2 (8611 m, 28,251 ft.) really is the tougher climb. It is also one of the world's most dangerous climbs. Only 119 people have made it to the top of K2, compared to the 600 that have planted a flag on Mt. Everest. What makes K2 the most dangerous mountain in the world is its annual death toll. When *DP* was in northern Pakistan, there was a reward to find the bodies of two climbers who had disappeared in an avalanche. Seven died in 1995 and 13 were killed in 1986. Everest is on the border with Nepal and Tibet and costs a staggering $50,000 for six climbing permits. K2 is a bargain at $10,000 for six climbers. These are just the climbing fees, and with supplies, porters and excess baggage fees, climbing the big peaks is a sport for not only the brave—but also the rich.

You will need an exit visa to leave the country. Although you may adhere to the paper chain faithfully, expect to get a quizzical look if the immigration official notes certain "irregularities" and requires additional funds to let you catch your plane out. If you are carrying anything that can be interpreted as being an antiquity, you are in trouble again. You'll need an export permit for rugs, and don't think for a moment that nifty pen-gun you bought in Darra Adam Khel is not going to be spotted and confiscated. If you're bringing some smoking green back with you, expect it to be discovered by sniffer dogs at Karachi and Lahore airports. Also, you will get dinged for the carpet export license scam. Every carpet must have an export permit, and every rug dealer claims you don't need one. Regardless of the value of the carpet, demand an export receipt. Please note that although hashish and heroin are as easy to buy in Peshawar as Snickers bars in Pacoima, there is much money to be made (5000 rupees last we checked) turning frugal hippies in to police. The naive stoners will then have to pay up to 5000 US *dollars* to the concerned but financially adept police to save their skin.

Remember, you will need to keep your exchange receipts to change your grubby rupees into more stable currencies. Most people take care of exchanging their money in the bazaar (watch out for bogus US 100 bills printed in Syria, Iran and Lebanon before 1989). Remember to keep enough for your taxi, something to eat at the airport, 200 rupees for your departure tax. Everything else can be paid for in dollars. Some banks only cash traveler's checks and do not take foreign cash. The border with Afghanistan is technically closed, but *DP* found plenty of folks who will take you by camel, truck, foot or private car. This is illegal, of course. You can exit using the Karakoram Highway north into China, but you will need the correct paperwork before you get there. The only land crossing to India is from Lahore to Amritsar. If you have *cojones* and strong legs, you could walk across the Hindu bush through Afghanistan into Tajikistan. Iran requires a visa that is double-checked in Teheran. The best place to get creative about your country of exit is in your home country with a double-check with the embassies in Islamabad.

Karachi

Some consider Karachi to be the most dangerous city in the world. About five to 10 people die every day as a result of political violence in Karachi. Karachi is a dirty, bustling port town, with a population of more than 5 million people. Robbery and kidnapping are often carried out with the distinct intention of creating terror and instability among the populace. Bombings have occurred at Pakistan government facilities and public utility sites. Vehicular hijacking and theft by armed individuals are common occurrences. Persons resisting have very often been shot and killed. Overly detailed and gory reports of murders, bombings, robberies and assassinations fill the papers every day.

If you get bored waiting around to be shot or kidnapped, you can spend a few hours crabbing or rent a camel on the beach.

The North-West Frontier Province

An area created in 1901 by the British who could never figure how to "civilize" the many tribes and clans, the NWFP is still the land of *badal*, or revenge. It is the oldest continuously lawless area in the world. Home to the "wily Pathans," this rugged land of green valleys and snowcapped valleys has never been fully conquered by Alexander, Moghuls, Sikhs, Brits or even the Russians. The North-West Frontier Province has an affinity with Afghanistan in the west and is known for its well-armed populace. Weapons are carried and sold openly on the streets. Peshawar, the largest city and capital of the province, could be accurately described as Dodge City without Wyatt Earp. Peshawar is the home of over 1 million Afghan refugees who live in three large mud cities. Western travelers and well-heeled residents are frequently kidnapped to bring attention to their causes and to get some quick folding money. Expect to pay about $20,000 to $35,000 if you know someone in Peshawar or a lot more if you are working for a Western company in Peshawar.

Khyber Pass

It would be an understatement to say that it is dangerous to travel overland through the tribal areas along the Khyber Pass from Peshawar to Kabul. The North-West Frontier areas are ruled by the Afridi tribes and are not under the control of the Pakistani government or police. Many, if not most, make money smuggling hashish, heroin and contraband into Pakistan. If you can get past the checkpoint at the smuggler's market (just walk through the gate in the north market square into the Afridi bodyguard complex) expect eight more Pakistani army checkpoints until you reach Afghanistan. Once you are in Afghanistan, you are on your own. There are many deadly tribal feuds over things as important as stolen goats or errant wives, so lightening some dumb foreigner of his vehicle or belongings does not even appear on their list of "things not to do." Car-hijackings and the abduction of foreigners are occasionally reported from the tribal areas. If visitors must enter the tribal areas, a permit must be obtained from the Home Department, which may require that an armed escort accompany the visitor.

Sind Province

Hundreds of years ago, travelers called Sind the "Unhappy Valley," because of its burning deserts, freezing mountain peaks, dust, lack of water and general fear of the predatory tribes. Today in rural Sind Province, neither the weather nor the emotional tone have improved, and the security situation is still hazardous, especially for overland travelers. Foreigners have occasionally been kidnapped. Drug smugglers and *dacoits* (local bandits) make the rural areas unsafe for travel. Smugglers use the local beaches of Karachi to move drugs and contraband at night. Sinds, Pathans and Mohajirs are jostling for political supremacy in the region. The result is frequent assassinations, firefights, bomb attacks, murders and overall mayhem. Travel outside of Karachi into the Sind interior must have prior approval of the government of Pakistan and usually requires an armed guard or convoy.

Dacoits are well armed and will attack travelers even with your trusty police escort. They have been known to stop entire trains or vehicle caravans, often kidnapping and killing passengers. Anyone contemplating travel into the Sind interior should first contact the American Consulate (*8 Abdullah Haroon Road, Karachi,* ☎ *515081)* for advisability.

Gunmen can be hired from travel groups or on the street (not advised) for about 4000 rupees a day. You will have to pay for your bodyguards' room and board.Sind province still has a fairly healthy kidnappings-for-ransom business.

Hyderabad

In Hyderabad, there have been recurring outbreaks of ethnic and sectarian violence which have been characterized by random bombings, shootings and mass demonstrations. Recent incidents have resulted in several deaths and the unofficial imposition of curfews. There have also been numerous incidents of kidnapping for ransom.

Islamabad and Rawalpindi

Welcome to the Twin Cities: Dirty Rawalpindi and squeaky-clean Islamabad, the capital of Pakistan, are only 10 kilometers and two worlds apart. Islamabad is the showcase city for the embassy folks, and Rawalpindi is where all the real people live. The crime rate in Islamabad is lower than in many parts of Pakistan, but it is on the rise. In the recent past, Americans have been the victim of armed robberies and assaults, although these types of incidents are not frequent. Thefts from the massive walled residences are common. As usual, they are typically inside jobs. Most incidents experienced by the American community are committed by servants employed in the household. Rawalpindi has experienced some bombings in public areas, such as markets, cinemas and parks.

Lahore/Punjab Province

The Punjab Province has been the site of numerous bomb blasts occurring at cinemas, marketplaces and other public areas. A professional criminal element exists in the Punjab (operating mainly in the interior), with kidnapping for ransom, robbery and burglaries all being carried out by gangs of professional criminals. There are frequent armed clashes between Pakistani and Indian army groups along the border area and in east Punjab and particularly in the disputed territory of Kashmir. Lahore is placid but famous for rip-offs of tourists in cheap hotels, bogus traveler's checks and other tourist crime.

Kashmir

In 1947 the princes who ran the "princely states" cut a quick deal with mainly Hindu India instead and screwed their predominately Muslim subjects. The Kashmir dispute, which caused the 1948 and 1965 wars with India (Pakistan was whipped both times), remains unresolved. Kashmir has turned into a war zone with both sides owning large chunks of land. The Simla Agreement after the 1971 Bangladesh war adjusted the boundary between the Indian state of Jammu and Kashmir and the Pakistani state of Azad and Kashmir. The Muslims in the Indian state of Jammu and Kashmir demand, greater autonomy from Hindu and somewhat colonial India.

The separatist elements within Jammu and Kashmir, particularly the Jammu and Kashmir Liberation Front (JKLF), and the Shura-e-Jihad (a Kashmiri based organization that is made of seven separatist groups) openly receive training and military equipment from Pakistan.

Baluchistan/Quetta

The province of Baluchistan that borders both Iran and Afghanistan is notorious for cross-border smuggling operations. It should really be in our "Forbidden Places," since few if any permits are given and you must have the permission of the local tribal chief to move in relative safety. Why anyone would want to travel to Quetta, southern Afghanistan, eastern Iran or the bleak Pakistani coast is a good question. We say relative safety, because kidnapping for money is as popular here as it is in the tribal regions up north. Any student of geography will quickly figure out that the fastest way from landlocked Afghanistan is through remote Baluchistan. The major drug smugglers (actually smuggling may be too ludicrous a term to apply here) run large truck and even camel caravans from Afghanistan to the coast.

This region also has a high occurrence of armed robberies, probably because just about everybody carries a gun. Terrorist bombings have occurred frequently in the region, primarily concentrated among those districts along the Afghanistan border. There is limited to no provincial police. Those hardy persons considering travel into the interior should first notify the province's home secretary, travel in a group and limit travel to daylight hours and see a psychiatrist. Although the Pakistani government tells *DP* that permission from the provincial authorities is required for travel into some interior locations, I couldn't help but wonder which government folks would be around to check.

Bogus Boogie

When the International Federation of the Phonographic Industry, the global cop for pirate CDs, comes to town, music store owners will want to run for the hills. Over 92 percent of all CD and tape sales in Pakistan were bootlegged copies.

Crime

Pakistan is a special place when it comes to crime. There are three levels of crime. The first is the friendly constant pressure to relieve the unwitting of their possessions. Just as the wind and rain can erode granite mountains, the traveler to Pakistan will find his money slowly slipping from him. Perhaps this is not a crime, since the victim is consensual, but it nevertheless is not an honest transfer of funds.

The second level is petty crime, the fingers rummaging through your baggage, the wallet that leaves your pocket or the camera that disappears from the chair next to you. Everyone will caution you on petty theft. Here, theft is an art, almost a learned skill. These crimes happen to the unwary and unprepared. Lock your zippers, do not leave anything of value in your hotel room, and do not tell people your schedule. The luggage of most airline and bus passengers looks like a Houdini act with locks, rope, sewn-up sacks, and even steel boxes used to keep out curious fingers. Mail must be sent in a sewn-up sack to prevent theft. Naturally, thieves love the many zippered, unlocked backpacks of foreign trekkers. The best solution is to put your luggage in a canvas or vinyl duffel bag, and keep all valuables on your person. Do not carry any money in pockets, and use money belts as well as decoy wallets when traveling. (Decoy wallets are cheap wallets with old credit cards, pictures and addresses of your worst enemy, and Iraqi dinars.)

The third level is where Pakistan outshines many other areas: The cold calculated art of kidnapping, extortion and robbery. There is little any traveler can do to prevent this crime in certain areas. People who have regular schedules and who travel to crowded markets, along well-known paths, or do not have good security are at risk. Check State Department reports and contact the local embassy for the latest horror stories. All large cities have Security agencies that can provide advice, drivers and bodyguards for reasonable daily rates.

Dacoits

Possibly the most lucrative night job in Pakistan. Many *dacoits* are professional bandits aligned along tribal lines who hold normal day jobs and then head out into the country for a little extra cash at night. Unlike the greasy thugs of Russia or the gold-toothed banditos of Mexico, *dacoits* are usually bad guys for hire led by educated or civil service level young men. They cannot find employment, so they use their organizing and planning skills to support political parties, back up rebel units, raise operating funds and expand operations areas. Despite the genteel background of the leaders, the actions of their members are bloody and crude. *Dacoits* will stop buses and trains, rob, rape and murder, and generally create a bloody mess. They also use kidnapping as a way to generate funds and "flip the bird" to the local government. Expect to be a well-treated but powerless pawn, as the *dacoits* negotiate with the strapped local government (not your fat, rich, home government) for payment for your release. Your biggest problem may be a heavy-handed (but fiscally efficient) rescue attempt staged by the government on your behalf. Stay out of remote tribal areas or areas known for *dacoitry*.

Ethnic Clashes

Pakistan is the botched result of seven weeks of planning by Sir Cyril Radcliffe in 1947 in an effort to separate warring Muslims from the Hindus. The hastily created border caused instant riots and violence, sending 6 million people from each region fleeing across the new border. It is estimated that up to a million people were killed. Today, with 60 million Muslims in India and more than 10 million Hindus in Pakistan, there is little hope for peace. Demonstrations often get ugly in Karachi and Hyderabad, where Sindhis and immigrant groups in Karachi and Hyderabad duke it out. Between January 1990 and October 1992, Pakistan-trained militants killed 1585 men and women, including 981 Muslims, 218 Hindus, 23 Sikhs, and 363 security men. In three years, over 7000 Kalashnikov rifles, 400 machine guns, 400 rocket launchers, 1000 rockets, 7000 grenades, 2000 pistols and revolvers, and thousands of mines were seized. One of the keys to staying alive in heavily armed areas is to not bring a knife to a gunfight. If you visit Pakistan, you might want to bring your own army. (See "Cheap Guns.")

Cheap Guns

The border regions of Pakistan are (and traditionally have been) a Wild West region with most tribal, ethnic and criminal groups being well armed with cheap weapons brought in from Afghanistan or manufactured on demand. There are few tribes that don't possess large arsenals and have fierce rivalries against one another. Most urban residents employ *chowkidaars*, or private guards, for protection. If you are not caught in the middle of a firefight, you may be worse off at a wedding or party. In the tribal areas, Pathans have a bad habit of celebrating weddings using their AK-47s as firecrackers and shoot bursts into the air, ignorant of Newtonian physics.

The Pathans (Pahktuns)

Pakistan's Pathan community still wants to unite with the Pathans in Afghanistan to create Pahktunistan. No major shooting or activities yet but remember that the taliban are mostly Pathan and have displaced a Tajik government.

There are good medical facilities in all major towns in Pakistan. You may need it after your first fly blown kabobfest. Pakistan may not be the dirtiest place in the world, but it is enough to make some Siberian mining towns look positively pristine. Expect to get the runs, unless you have a PVC gastrointestinal tract. Some folks go gaga over the spicy food, and other folks end up crouched over a grubby pit toilet learning the hard way that fiery spices and peppers burn as bad going out as they do going down. Take the normal precautions you would take in any Third World country, and carry medicine for diarrhea.

You need proof of a cholera vaccination if arriving from infected areas. You should get a typhoid shot and take malaria prophylaxis. Yellow fever vaccination and certificate are required if you have visited a country in the endemic zone recently.

Inoculations against yellow fever and cholera are required for visitors arriving in Pakistan within five days after leaving or transiting infected areas. In addition, immunizations against typhoid, polio and meningitis are recommended, as are prophylactic antimalarial drugs. Malaria is present throughout Pakistan at altitudes below 2000 meters. Remember, even if you are heading straight for the mountains, you can still get bitten in the airport waiting lounge in Karachi. Hepatitis and tetanus are further health risks in Pakistan, as are amoebic dysentery and worms. Bilharzia (schistosomiasis) and elephantiasis (filariasis) are also endemic diseases, although not widespread. Follow the usual precautions for countries with poor sanitation. Military hospitals, frequently open to fee-paying local civilians and foreigners, often provide the best facilities.

Pakistan is a land of hard extremes. The climate is generally arid and very hot (very, very hot), except in the northern mountains, where the summers are hot and winters are very cold (very, very, cold). The best time to visit Pakistan is between October and April. Karachi and Lahore are pleasant; Islamabad can get cool. The average annual temperatures in the southern city of Karachi are between 55° F and 93° F. Summer brings the monsoon season, but rainfall is negligible at other times of the year. After April, the temperatures climb from mid-July through September during the monsoon season, which can dump up to 16 cm of rain. North of Islamabad is mountainous, with a temperate climate. Summers are cool, winters cold, and the average annual rainfall is 120 cm.

The currency is the rupee; about 32 rupees to the U.S.dollar. You can only bring up to 100 rupees into Pakistan but who would? The rupee is best purchased at a bank, not at your hotel. Many money changers will try to foist off the faded dirty notes, but don't take them. They will be tough to exchange back. You will need to carry around the paperwork you get when you swap dollars for rupees. Most folks change their money at the market. Credit cards are worthless outside the major cities, but good old AMEX has offices in Islamabad, Rawalpindi, Lahore and Karachi. Don't expect much help from Amex, other than cashing a personal check up to $500 or replacing your card. The best exchange rates are on the black market. Merchants will give you a slightly better exchange rate if you pay in U.S. dollars. You will not get a receipt for the transaction, since the transaction is illegal.

Baksheesh is the Pakistani version of tipping. When people help you, it's normal and expected that you will drop a few rupees (about 10 percent) in their palm. Don't forget to haggle, haggle, haggle. Having a local guide do your haggling (shopping, bus, hotel, air fares, taxis, bribes, souvenirs) for you can easily save you his fee. You can bring in as much foreign currency as you want, but it must be declared upon arrival.

Electricity is 220V/50Hz. The electrical system can only be described as deadly, and shorts and blowouts are common. Be careful plugging in appliances around wet areas. Many water heaters are electric. Do not turn lights or appliances off with bare feet or in the shower.

If you hate crowds and crave danger, Pakistan provides excellent opportunities for winter sports, including mountaineering and hiking in the Himalayan hill stations. Folks who like to ski will be glad to know that there are absolutely no downhill ski facilities in this mountainous paradise. Pakistan features the longest continuous drops on the planet (heli-boarding anyone?) as well as breathtaking scenery. The AK-47s, pistols and 50-caliber machine guns are dirt-cheap in Peshawar but a bitch to bring home as hand luggage. Down below, where the Indus River makes the Punjab and Sind fertile, temperatures are more moderate, with an average of 60° F in January to an average of 95° F in the summer. Baluchistan consists of deserts and low bare hills. Here and in northern Sind, temperatures can climb over 120° F in the summer.

Normal office hours from Saturday to Wednesday are from 9 a.m. to 2 p.m., with at least one hour for lunch. Offices close earlier on Thursdays, usually at lunchtime. Friday is the weekly Muslim holiday. Banks are open from 9 a.m. to 1:30 p.m. from Saturday to Wednesday, and until 11 a.m. on Thursday. Urdu (the national language) and English are the official languages of Pakistan. Punjabi, Sindi, Pashtu, Baluchi, Seraiki and other languages and dialects are also spoken. Most children and older adults speak English.

Many people confuse Pakistani cuisine with Indian food. Kebabs, *tikkas* (spiced grilled meats) and curries are the staples; they're served with *naan* (flat bread). The most popular drinks are tea (black or green), *lassi* (a milk drink) and Western-style soft drinks, which are widely available.

Polo

One of Pakistan's most famous exports (besides drugs and terrorists) is polo. Afghans and Pakistanis love polo, a violent spirited game that is as close to horse-mounted warfare as one can get. The British picked it up while stationed here, and it quickly became the upper-class macho sport of Britain. You can still see polo games played by soldiers, cops and just regular folks in Chitral and Gilgit. Today, the best polo players in the world are from Argentina. The Argentinian gaucho put back a lot of the violence and death-defying elements of the game. Before polo, the Argentinians played puto, *a tamer form of the Afghan game of* buzkashi, *instead of a headless goat being manhandled around a huge field, the Argentinians would whack a duck with sticks. The most violent form of polo in Argentina is the Creole style. Ponies are ridden hard, bones are broken, and each seven-minute* chukka, *or period, is guaranteed to be full of action.*

Useful Addresses

Associated Press of Pakistan (APP)
House 1, Street 56
F 6/3 POB 1258, Istanbul
☎ *[51] (8) 26158, FAX: [51] (8) 13225*

Canadian Embassy in Pakistan
Diplomatic Enclave, Sector G-5
P.O. Box 1042
Islamabad
☎ *[92] (51) 211101*

Pakistani Embassy in Canada
151 Slater Street, Suite 608
Ottawa, ONT. K1P 5H3
☎ *(613) 238-7881, FAX: (613) 238-7296*

Pakistan International Airlines Corp. (PIA)
Head Office Building, Quaid-i-Azam
International Airport
Karachi
☎ *(21) 4572011, FAX: (21) 4572754*

Pakistani Embassy in United States
2315 Massachusetts Avenue, N.W.
Washington, D.C. 20008
☎ *(202) 939-6200, FAX: (202) 387-0484*

Pakistan Tourism Development Corp. Ltd.
House No. 2, Street 61, F-7/4
Islamabad
☎ *811001*

UK Embassy
Diplomatic Enclave, Ramna 5
P.O. Box 1122
Islamabad
☎ *822131, FAX: 823439*

U.S. Embassy in Pakistan
Diplomatic Enclave, Ramna 5
P.O. Box 1048
Islamabad
☎ *[92] (51) 826161,*
FAX: [92] (51) 214222

Embassy Location

The Consular Section
Located separately in the USAID building
18 Sixth Avenue, Ramna 5

The Consulate General
8 Abdullah Haroon Road
Karachi
☎ *568-5170*

The U.S. Consulate General
Sharah-E-Abdul Hamid Bin Badees
50 Empress Road
New Simla Hills
Lahore
☎ *636-5530*

The U.S. Consulate
11 Hospital Road
Peshawar Cantonment
Peshawar
☎ *279-801, 279-802, 279-803*

The U.S. Embassy
Diplomatic Enclave, Ramna 5
Islamabad
☎ *826 161*

04/07/1991	Shia Muslims mark the death of Hazrat Ali, fourth caliph of Islam.
08/05/1988	Arif Hussain al-Hussaini, a leading Shiite religious and political leader in Pakistan, was shot to death in Peshawar.
07/17/1988	An airplane carrying President Zia Ul-Haq and U.S. Ambassador Arnold Raphel crashed, killing everyone aboard.
09/05/1986	Twenty-one persons, including two Americans, were killed in an abortive hijacking of Pan Am flight 73 by four Arab gunmen.
04/10/1986	The daughter of former President Bhutto, Benazir Bhutto, returned from exile in Europe.
07/18/1985	Shahnawaz Bhutto, son of executed President Zulfikar Bhutto and older brother of Pakistani People's Party Leader Benazir Bhutto, died under mysterious circumstances in France.
07/14/1985	Bombing of Pan Am office.
11/22/1979	The U.S. embassy in Islamabad was attacked and burned by Islamic militants, following rumors that the U.S. was involved in the violent takeover of the Grand Mosque in Mecca, Saudi Arabia.
04/04/1979	Former president of Pakistan Zulfikar 'Ali Bhutto was executed by the Pakistani government under President Zia. The terrorist group al-Zulfikar, founded by his two sons, is named after him.
07/05/1977	Army Chief of Staff Mohammad Zia led an army coup to seize power and became chief martial law administrator.
06/08/1962	Martial law, which was imposed in 1958, was lifted and the national assembly convened.
03/23/1962	A new constitution was promulgated by President Ayub Khan.
10/07/1958	President Iskander Mirza, supported by senior military officers, seized power and imposed martial law.
09/06/1957	Defense of Pakistan Day.
03/23/1956	The national assembly adopted a new constitution that rejected Pakistan's status as a dominion and became an "Islamic Republic" within the commonwealth. Also known as "Pakistan Day."
08/14/1947	Independence Day. Pakistan became a self-governing dominion within the British commonwealth.

PAKISTAN

Pakistan: Along the Northwest Frontier

The Northwest Frontier of Pakistan is adventure defined. Men in turbans and robes stroll hand in hand down dusty streets carrying machine guns. *Mujahedin*, spy, separatist and smuggler are considered normal occupations in this high risk border area. Shootouts, bombings, kidnapping and violence are common. This is also the land of the Pakhtun (or Pathan) who live by the code of Pakhtunwali, an unwritten code of revenge against your enemies, hospitality to strangers and refuge to friends (*badal, melmastia* and *nanwatu*). The trick is knowing whether you are friend, stranger or enemy. I will travel to Peshawar, in Northwest Pakistan, then travel onward to Afghanistan to meet with the *talihan* army.

I arrive at Green's Hotel in Peshawar. Not upscale, but definitely Western. Walking down the streets of Peshawar it becomes quite apparent that I am the only pigeon in town. I smile and wave, and within 20 minutes shopkeepers, touts, gawking loiterers and an entourage of kids know me as Mr. Robert. Peshawar is an interesting city for those looking for adventure. For years this was the gateway to Afghanistan through the Khyber Pass by train, road or air. Now the war in Afghanistan between the *taliban* and the government of Rabbiani has closed the pass. Although not reported in most Western papers, there are kidnappings, murders, robberies and other violent acts as life goes on in this dusty, bustling border town.

Any Westerner in Peshawar is automatically affiliated with aid organizations, journalism, arms, drugs or spying. Most yuppies head straight to the mountains and hippies head straight to the drug markets. The heat has been turned up a little too high for itinerant adventurers because of the kidnappings and robberies.

Since I do not speak Arabic or Pahktun (Pathan or Pashto depending on your translation) I will need a guide. Since I naively assume I will have to travel over the Khyber Pass into Kabul, I will need a member of the Afridi clan. The wily Pathans are actually three main groups: the Sarbanni, the Bitanni and the Ghurghush. The Afridi tribe is a member of the last—the typical stereotype of the "wily Pathan" proud, noble as well as treacherous and cruel. The Afridis look like throwbacks to the old testament with their long flowing robes, turbans and long magnificent beards. They are the same men that bedeviled conquerors from Alexander to the Russians along the Khyber pass.

If I am to enter Afghanistan I will also need to find someone who works with another Afridi. Yaqub Afridi is "the man" around here—the largest drug and gun smuggler in Northern Pakistan. His people control all the illicit trade between Kabul, Jallalabad and Peshawar.

Jawing with Jabba

After a few discreet inquiries, I am directed to ascend a rickety spiral staircase above a dusty tourist shop. Here I wait for my host who ascends after I am uncomfortably seated cross legged on a dirt-filled rug and given sweet tea in a dirty glass. My host, who shall remain nameless, reminds me immediately of Jabba the Hut—the rotund, grubby alien of *Star Wars* fame. When my host smiles he reveals a set of black and brown teeth and breath that forces me to sit back a few more inches.

I make it clear why I am here but he is determined to unload some of his faded trinkets before granting my wish. He instructs his sons to bring out Russian bayonets, Russian uniforms, Russian money, Russian field glasses, and then with a conspiratorial wink, a Russian AK-47.

Nope, not interested.

Then a parade of ancient coins, ethnic bric-a-brac, tattered rugs and rusty knives follow.

Nope, don't need it.

Then my host leans toward me and looks around as if the crowd of grubby cross-eyed children blocking the stairs have never heard the word and whispers "hashish?"

His breath is painful, but I wheeze back. Nope.

He sits back and scratches his scrotum under his dirty white shalwar. Frustrated and pensive, he picks his rotten teeth and then burps while he figures out how he will make a little money from me. He puts on a squeaky Tom Waits tape in a stolen Walkman to make me feel at home.

Temporarily freed from reviewing the piles of war surplus and cheap clothing, I restate that my need is only for a trustworthy guide who can take me into the Afghan camps and around the Khyber Pass beyond. Trying to figure how much to gouge me, he probes my intentions (or backers). He asks me if I am a journalist and smiles conspiratorially. Nope. Are you a diplomat? Nope. A spy? I think that this guy has been watching too many Sidney Greenstreet movies. I tell him that I want to meet the *taliban* and he gives me a pained look. "This can be difficult."

He says something to one of his sons who scuttles down the staircase and out into the street. The other sons continue to stare as if they paid admission and want to get their money's worth.

Finally eyeing me after a pregnant pause and flicking something off his toothpick, he says, "I have the man but it will cost you 100 rupees. He will not make trouble for you if you do not make trouble for him."

Not agreeing or disagreeing, I thank him and then figure I should loosen up a little cash so that he will have a vested interest in keeping me alive for further plucking. I tell him that I am traveling, but I will come back to buy souvenirs of my trip. Invigorated he pushes the pile of rusty weapons, smelly caps and trinkets towards me again. I ask him at what generous price would he sell me these fine ancient coins. We haggle for about 20 minutes until what looks like a bearded gopher sticks its head up the stairwell and introduces himself as Papa. He is introduced to me by Jabba the Hut as "my man." I quickly pay him an outrageous sum of $50 for the counterfeit Greek coins and Russian rubles and push my way down the stairs with my new guide in tow.

A well fed but sprightly man of about 60, Papa is wearing the white Chitrali cap and white robes of the region. He is a Pahktun and he speaks perfect but imprecise English. He worked at the U.S. base in Pakistan and learned his English while being the house *wallah*. He has forgotten much of his English but I promise him I will teach it back to him. Papa struggles to keep up with my stride. He has a long white beard, glasses, a pot belly and a nervous, happy personality that reminds me of one of the Seven Dwarfs. Then I decide it's not a Disney character he reminds me of, Papa looks exactly like the R. Crumb character who keeps on trucking. So we set off down the street with Papa hustling to keep up with me. Papa tugs at my sleeve:

"We have made a bargain, my friend?"

Puzzled as to why he is starting the negotiations anew I ask him what he means

"I have been sent to you to guide you, yes? There are many things I can show you."

"Like?"

He rattles off the list of bazaars and tourist sights and I stop him midsentence.

"I am not here for these things. I am interested in meeting the *taliban*."

After a brief silence and a cinematic look around to see who is listening, he says: "There are many things to see in Pakistan, my friend."

Sensing that my aims are not strictly touristic, he launches into another hushed spiel. "I can take you to a place where we can find hashish, heroin, marijuana."

"Papa, I am here to meet with the *taliban*."

Finally I figure out why he doesn't understand me. *Taliban* means religious student here. It is not directly associated with the Afghan group called the *taliban*.

"You want guns? I can take you to where we can fire many guns, even rockets, many, many rockets. Hand grenades, anti-aircraft, boom boom."

"No Papa."

I wait for the women or young boys pitch but it doesn't come. Papa, who I find out later is devoutly religious, sticks to clean stuff; drugs and weapons. It dawns on me that there will be much to discuss in the days ahead.

We get back to his original topic of discussion, his rate. He explains that he must pay his friend for the referral and asks to borrow 10 rupees to pay his commission. He runs back and conspiratorially mentions that our deal is now between us and that I should not mention anything to our friend if he asks what we did. The impression is that Papa was to continue the *baksheeh* until we are through.

He asks me what I would like to do. Thinking that I had already failed in explaining exactly what I wanted to do, I say, "Let's go to the Afghan refugee camps." At least Papa would come in handy as an interpreter. He explains that we can go to the market, but that I cannot go into the camps because I would be kidnapped. There are three camps outside of town. Actually small cities complete with mud huts, phone, electricity and a smattering of services. There are about 3 million Afghan refugees who live in Pakistan in camps like these and they are here to stay, something the financially beleaguered Pakistanis don't like. The Afghans handle all the transportation in Peshawar. They also evoke the wild west feel of men strolling around with machine guns. Shootouts enforce *badal* or revenge, and a host of entrepreneurial efforts include kidnapping people for ransom.

We jump on a bus to the market and Papa is very nervous. Although the people are cheerful and glad to see me, there is a dark curious look in many of the men's faces. We push past the money changers and kabob houses to the depths of the market. We stop in a simple *chai* house for tea and cakes. Not much to look at. Just a large tent with three wide carpeted tables running the full length. Men sit and sleep on the tables in the midday heat. None are particularly thrilled to see us. I finally figure out what I am looking at. We are surrounded by out of work *mujahedin*. Tough 30 and 40 something men with hard gaunt faces, many of them scarred or limping. They all stare directly and impassively at us. Papa is nervous. I ask Papa who these men are. He replies these are the fighters. I ask them if I can take their pictures. He says no. I acknowledge some of the men. Some nod back, others continue to stare. Papa and I talk about the fighters. He tells me that many men came during the war with Russia for money, but now there is not much work.

After our tea I ask him to take me to the Smugglers Bazaar. Once it was in Landi Kotal at the end of the rail line. Now it has moved to the outskirts of Peshawar. I can tell that Papa is not entirely thrilled with my choice of tourist spots. He asks me if I want to see where they paint the buses. Once again I tell him my purpose. He, once again, is suddenly hard of hearing.

The Walking Dead

We jump off the bus, just before a military checkpoint and end up in a carpet of trash in an area of shade trees. Among the trash are what look like piles of dirty rags. Upon closer inspection they are people. Bearded and blackened with the hard core soot of derelicts, it is hard to tell if they are dead or alive. Since they are not bloated I assume they are alive. Other men with frizzed hair and beards stagger in slow motion. Papa warns me away. These are the walking dead—heroin addicts left to wander and then die in the boulevard facing the market. A sobering sight and not one inclined to induce anyone to buy drugs here, one of the largest drug markets in the world.

It would be unfair to characterize this place as all seedy and depressing. Here shoppers can also buy gold Rolexes, Panasonic radios, and cameras. The fact that you can also buy heroin, hashish, machine guns and rocket launchers is more a result of an enthusiastic retail strategy than anything sinister. At one shop, I intimate that maybe his Rolex watches are the same ones found on the streets of New York—tinny, Chinese made with $5 workings. Insulted, he pulls out an entire tray of solid gold GMT Masters and Datemasters. I shut up. He even offers to buy my battered and faded 25-year-old steel GMT master for US$800. Not a bad deal, but I decline. I give him a Mr. DP sticker for his door and we are friends again.

I mention to Papa that I wish to travel on to Afghanistan and meet with the *taliban* army. He smiles and says "Come with me." We go to the far end of the bazaar and Papa cautions me to walk quickly and not get lost. He also stops and tells me that when we cross into the other side he cannot help me if I am kidnapped or killed. I ask him how much it would cost to pay my ransom. Without pausing he tells me US$35,000.

Through the Door

Papa drops his guard and takes me into a quiet corner. He looks me straight in the eye and asks me: "Are you CIA?" I say no. He asks me: Are you a journalist? I say no, but I write a travel guide to dangerous places. He then asks me if I will make trouble for him. I say no.

Papa satisfied for now says "Come with me."

We wait until the soldiers at the military checkpoint are occupied with a heavily laden truck than we walk quickly but purposely into a compound of shops. Papa smiles conspiratorially and points at the large red on white sign "No Foreigners Past this Point." After a couple of lefts and rights through the shops we walk through a large gate in the high wall. Thinking that this has been far too easy, we turn the corner and run smack into a group of armed men pointing machine guns at us.

Having been asked many times what was my most dangerous moment, I always answer that I really have no idea of when I am in danger or not. But considering that I am surrounded by unsmiling machine gun-carrying Afghans and escorted by a total stranger who for some strange reason, seems to know exactly what kidnapped foreigners are worth, the first few seconds of this experience would rank up there.

Papa pauses briefly and then makes the introductions. It turns out that these are some of Afridi's men. A group of about 10 out of 100 heavily armed men who make about 2000 rupees a month to make sure the drug and contraband business runs nice and smooth. And who should be their long lost friend (or best customer) but Papa. I don't know why, but it seems in this part of the world you always get kissed (twice) by men who were pointing machine guns at you a few moments before.

Welcomed into their simple barracks I am introduced to my brigand friends. Not only are the men carrying well-used SKSs and AK-47s but there are machine guns and ammunition cases lying around the wire cots. They thrust weapons into my hands and urge Papa to take pictures of me. They pose with me and bring me tea.

They chat in Pashto while I smile and hand out *DP* stickers. I run out of stickers as they paste them on their rifle butts. They ask me if I would like to fire the gun. I decline thinking of the armed police not more than 200 yards away behind the sandbagged checkpoint.

We talk about getting into Afghanistan and Kabul. Everyone is coming out of Kabul. Kabul is under siege. No one is going in. They will definitely not let foreigners in. The *taliban* is camped above the hills waiting to attack. I ask if can go in disguise. They laugh and tell me "You can take the bus right from here for only 50 rupees but there are eight checkpoints from here to Jalalabad and one of them is sure to find you." Another development is that Afridi has been asked to get out of Pakistan because of the heat the U.S. government is putting on him. He graciously has moved out of his mansion to another one high in the hills of Jalalabad. He is not about to get into more trouble by inviting some foreigner for dinner and a ride into Kabul. Although his bodyguards are eager, they know I'll be arrested and turned back. They also explain that the *taliban* execute drug dealers and it might not be wise for me to arrive under their protection. It looks like the Khyber is not the way to go.

Papa shows me around the market where piles of sickly looking hashish and heroin are on display. There are piles of well-used weapons and even lethal pen guns that fire one bullet. The merchants watch me with some remorse as I jot down the going rates. Two kilos of hash goes for 5000 rupees, 10 grams is 80 rupees, one gram of injection heroin for 100 rupees and one gram of smoking heroin is 50 rupees. In this market weapons are to drugs as shovels are to farming. I can pick up a slightly used rocket launcher for 30,000 rupees (Rockets are 400 rupees each) hand grenades are 100 rupees, Russian AKs go for 6000, a beat up AK-47 goes for 8000, a "short" Chinese-made assault version of the Kalashnikov is 30,000, 30 bullets go for 300 rupees. A helpful salesman reminds me that the barrel of the Chinese AK doesn't get as hot as the home-made versions.

Thinking of the wasted humans outside on the boulevard, I pass on buying anything, even after Papa explains the profits to be made once we cross back inside the gate. Papa excuses himself to do a little shopping while we wander through stacks of hashish and marijuana.

On the way back to town, Papa loosens up. He says he does a little bit of this and that to make ends meet. Besides drugs, (he prefers to buy his drugs directly in Afghanistan, in the region of Mazar-i-Sharif, he also buys stamps for stamp col-

lectors, takes the occasional tourist around Peshawar, but mostly he directs foreigners to where they can buy drugs. He warms to the fact that I have no interest
in drugs and seem to be comfortable around his well-armed friends. I tell him
that I would like to look around the border areas until I can figure out how to get
into Afghanistan. It seems getting to Afghanistan through Peshawar is a bust.
There is a Red Cross plane that flies into Kabul now and then but I am told it is
always full with supplies. I figure it might be worth trying the more scenic and
wild northern borders. I ask him if he wants to go visit the remote mountain areas
of Gilgit and the Kalash valley and he agrees.

The North West Frontier

The next day Papa shows up with just a single blanket and a plastic shopping
bag with his toiletries. I thought I traveled light, but Papa puts me to shame. We
take the postal bus north to Mingora. He mentions in an offhand way that the
bodyguards we met yesterday were asked by the Pakistani police to help show the
U.S. that they were cracking down on drugs, so Afridi's bodyguards offered Papa
10,000 rupees to bring them people to turn over to the police. I ask if he would
have set me up. He smiles in a hurt way and says, "But you are my friend."

It is important to remember that the Afghans are a complex result of their code
of honor. They are hospitable to strangers, will invite you into their house, and if
you become their friend they will deny you nothing. In fact Pathans hate haggling or coyness and are much happier when you simply state your purpose no
matter how far from the legal path it strays. You just never want to be on the
wrong side of a Pathan because they will kill you even for the slightest wrong.

Along the way we talk about many things. Papa is amazed at the strange places I
have been, and I am equally intrigued with his stories about his home in Afghanistan. He grew up in a small town along the Khyber Pass in a fortresslike house
where the only profession was smuggling. Every member of the family must post
guard duty in the tower and every house is heavily armed. The tower has peep-
holes to allow the defenders to shoot back when attacked and the thick mud and
stone walls make it cool in the summer and warm in the winter. They fight over
goats, women, past wrongs and anything else they find worth killing for. Many
villages and clans have been warring for years simply because every new generation must carry on the revenge or *badal* for the continuing seesaw of bloodshed.
Papa looks into my eyes and says dramatically: "Mr. Robert, if you kill someone,
you come to my village, I will give you house, bodyguard, no problem." I keep
that in mind.

As we come out of the hot arid valley we head up the Grand Trunk line into the
rugged mountains. We pass the old British forts and wind up and down the tortuous passes. Papa tells me stories of how one Australian named Keith came to his
village to make a hollowed out Samsonite briefcase so he could smuggle hashish
back home. The trick worked once and the second time he was caught. Keith's
girlfriend flew in to get him out of jail and lived with Papa in his house helping
him cook and even posting guard duty. An Afghan chief from another town took
a fancy to her and one day gave her a black Afghan horse worth about $30,000
rupees. Meanwhile Keith liked it in jail because he got to smoke cheap hash with
the other inmates. Finally the girlfriend saved up enough money (Papa wouldn't
tell me how she made it) and she bribed his way out of jail and flew back to Australia.

Papa sees the pictures of my twin daughters and exclaims; "I must have these for the chief of the Kyhber's son." He is a fine man and his father feeds 50 people a day! I don't know how I will break the news to my daughters that they have both been betrothed to one of the world's largest drug smugglers.

I Read the News Today... Oh Boy

The Northwest Frontier is a land with bad endings. The Peshawar paper has a story about a young Afghan couple, each from a different village, who were spotted kissing by one of the boy's relatives. The father of the boy kidnaps the girl and a cousin ties them up and pumps 75 bullets into them. Just yesterday in the Smugglers Bazaar a man was shot in the neck three times as he tried to run the checkpoint we had so deftly sidestepped. He was trying to take a stolen car into Afghanistan. The newspaper fills up five pages of murders, shootings and crime. Just another day in Pakistan.

I ask Papa how old he is. He tells me that only rich people pay attention to paper and since he cannot write he has no idea how old he is.

####

We are back on the road in the back of a battered Toyota pickup truck I hired. We talk to pass the time. I tell him I like to cook. He tells me that is women's work. He has no idea how to cook. I joke and tell him that he would starve if he did not have a woman to cook for him. "I cook tea" he replies indignantly. Papa's main interest for coming with me seems to be the disparity between the prices of weapons in the north versus Peshawar. In his village in Afghanistan he can get AK-47s for around 6000–8000 rupees. He figures he can unload them in the northern town of Dir for 12,000–15,000 rupees each. All he needs to do is find a buyer on this trip and he'll be back in a week.

We arrive at Dir that night. The evening air is frigid. I check into a room for 300 rupees. Papa takes the cheap one for 200. I get a straight razor shave for 5 rupees. That night I have a warm shower by plugging in a heating element directly into a bucket of cold water. The lights in the hotel dim and I wonder how may people are electrocuted like this. I shiver all night. Dir is a dirty frontier town. Severed goat heads neatly laid out in rows and all business from tailoring to tinkering is conducted while you wait. Overly decorated and loaded trucks blast through town. The blasting of their air horns and jangling of the steel chains that decorate the bumpers are the only things that interest me.

At breakfast the next day we sit next to a stubbly old man with a pure white beard. Both he and Papa extol the virtues of Allah and the Koran as they drink their tea. They are shocked when they find out that I have read the Koran and drag me into the conversation. Proselytized to the point of pain, I try to change the subject and mention that the short man has a nice beard. He blushes deeply. Papa tells me that with Allah all things are possible and that it will only be a matter of time before I am converted.

He warns me about the tough going ahead, the cold, the lack of food and even the danger of traveling in this area. I reassure him that I enjoy wild mountainous places and that bathing in an ice cold stream by moonlight is one of my favorite things. I realize that it is Papa who doesn't like the cold and the mountains.

It is October and as we climb higher and higher into the mountains we are getting cold. Papa is shivering and I give him my black Goretex jacket newly bought in Frankfurt. He praises Allah for creating such a marvelous garment. Knowing full well that it is a custom to give something that is so lavishly praised as a gift, I say "No Papa, you can't have it." We climb to the summit of the pass at 10,500 feet. Far down below we can see the overloaded diesel trucks that grind and groan up the switchbacks at less than five miles an hour. It is actually faster walking than taking one these trucks. They will continue northward into China along the Karakoram pass loaded with everything from rice to brake pads. Heading down the other side of the pass is unsettling. We descend across 45 switchbacks down to the river below. An armed policeman appears out of nowhere and flags us down. No, we are not in trouble. It seems the government has just put in electricity and the minister will be coming along the other direction. Could we please tell the policemen stationed along the road not to smoke or drink tea? Pakistan is a polite place.

On the truck is a man from the village of Bahrain. He invites us to stay at his home. Although there are a number of new and reasonable hotels in Bahrain we take him up on his offer. His house is a 20' by 20' room with large security bars on the doors. He has a spectacular view of the valley and rushing river that carves through the town. We buy food and fruit and he is embarrassed. He invites his relatives from around the valley to meet me. We eat a large but simple dinner. While his son entertains us by reading out of a primary school English book he confesses that he is a Pahktun separatist and is eager to fight for a separate homeland for the Pahktuns. After seeing the difference between the dark-skinned leather jacketed Punjabi tourists from Lahore and the light haired Afghans it is understandable.

That night something hit me like a train. Lying shivering I had to go to the bathroom, and fast. Maybe it was the fly covered kebab I had in Mingora or the dinner that night but I jumped up and realized I was in a pitch black room with no windows and no idea how to get out. I frantically searched for the heavy bolts that sealed the top and bottom of the doors. Rushing outside the night was brilliant with stars. I couldn't get my pants down in time and for the first time in my life felt like a three-year-old who wasn't diaper-trained.

The panic over, I took my clothes off in the freezing night air and decided to clean myself in a stream or river. As I walked through the orchids along the side of the hill, I punctured my feet with the sharp thorns from the trees. Finally I found an ice cold stream tumbling down the mountain. I began the painful process of washing myself and my clothes. As I shiver and shake under the stars I can't help thinking how funny this is. Papa and my guest find me and they are frantic. I tell them relax, I just came out for a bath. Papa points to me in my nakedness and says "I didn't believe when you told me you like to bathe in mountain streams but now I see that you are made of steel. Allah be praised." My host is less poetic. He tells me that the villagers shoot anyone found walking around at night. And that if I had gone down to the river I would have been killed.

In the morning I tell Papa the real reason I went for a walk in the middle of the night. He doesn't believe me and thinks I am being modest. My host apologizes thinking it is food that has caused it and I feel like an idiot. I don't eat for the next four days.

The Valley of Swat

Shivering from the high altitude we pull into the valley of the Kalash. The Kalash (which means black because of the black garments they wear) are an animist tribe who live in a region sometimes called Kafiristan. The Kalash are considered to be descendants of Alexander's army but have no recorded history. They are known for their colorful festivals, the fact that they leave their dead in exposed coffins and they are in an anthropological timewarp.

It is hard to imagine such a beautiful place in the middle of such desolation. The valleys are lush and green and the people who live in this valley are either touted as the lost tribe of Israel or descendants of Alexander the Great. In any case they are mentioned in many guidebooks as a lost race of peoples rarely seen or visited. Yeah sure.

We make the tortuous trip into the valley along a road that is smashed out of a sheer rock cliff. Coming down from the valleys and mountains beyond are Indian Jeeps with a single 2–3 foot diameter log tied like a battering ram over the cab and hood of the truck. Places where the road has caved in are patched with rubble. Even Papa exclaims "hacha!" as we veer out over the edge of the cliff.

Naturally when we pull up to the main junction there is no primitive scene but instead a huge billboard with all the rules that tourists must follow when taking pictures of the Kalash. Just like a low budget amusement park there is a fee for everything. It seems that the Punjabis come up here in the summer to escape the heat and gawk at the diminutive white-skinned Kalash. Not only do we pay an admission fee to get in, we pay to bring in my camera. Hard to believe that this valley was just opened up to road traffic in the '70s.

Once inside there are tiny hotels with names like the "Hayatt Hotel" and restaurants that serve "meshed potatoes" or even spaghetti. Here we are just a few yards from the Afghan border. As we finally meet the famed Kalash, an old lady not only tells us how much we must pay for their photos (20 rupees), but adds up the fee for every time she hears the shutter click. I assign them to the other Kodak cultures who make their living wearing "authentic garments" and pose for tourists wearing Tilley hats. The dark-haired Kalash look like ethnic Greeks, Macedonians or even Armenians. Now they have the cultural relevance of a cigar store Indian. There is one Punjabi group in the valley who direct the Kalash to perform for their massive VHS recorders. They look like they are having a day at the zoo. Papa mentions that we could take a six hour trip to Afghanistan from here on mules for 80–150 rupees but there are no mules for rent. I see the heavy snow cover in upper valley and remember how cold it was coming over the pass in our thin clothes. I say no thanks, let's try somewhere else. As a bizarre footnote there is a solar eclipse and I can't help but think of Kipling's *The Man Who Would be King*. The only difference now is this time, the Kafirs or kalash do not fall down and worship me, they just want more money because I am using a "big" lens to take their picture.

The Foothills of the Hindu Kush

We head into the mountain town of Gilgit, beneath the snow-capped mountains of the Hindu Kush. Within a 60 mile radius there are 20 peaks that rise above 20,000 feet. Nearby K2 is the most dangerous mountain in the world. The 28,250-ft. high peak has killed an average of every second person who attempts its summit. It is very cold and usually by now the snow in the high passes has cut off Gilgit from the rest of the world. Fokkers can fly out of the 4000 foot high valley by just scraping the tops of the passes but bad weather can lock people in for weeks and once the runway is snowed in you are in for the duration. Gilgit is a one horse town with the spectacular backdrop of Tirich Mir towering above its main street. In the simple hotel there is a Pakistani quiz show on the United Nations.

We walk around the town. In one stall I watch a tailor patiently work on fixing a torn button hole for 20 minutes. He charged his customer 2 rupees or eight-tenths of a penny.

Hobnobbing with the Nawab

Gilgit is the home of two things. One is polo, the other is the Sultan of Swat. Not Babe Ruth but a dynasty that has ruled this remote kingdom for centuries. Technically the Sultan or Nawaab was removed from his position of authority in 1969.

I check out the red brick British fort by the river. Despite the "Do Not Enter" signs, I poke around over the protestations of Papa. The fort looks as if it was abandoned by the British last week with coal fireplaces, rose gardens and hunting trophies of antelope, snow leopard and mountain sheep adorning the balcony. British cannons from 1898 and 1913 still point across the river. Earthquakes have destroyed some parts yet other parts are definitely nostalgic. Turning a corner I am caught trespassing by security guards. I find myself in the presence of a small dapper man in an Eddie Bauer blazer with a small cocker spaniel. It seems I am in the presence of Saif ul Mulk Nasir the Nawab or Mehthar of Swat.

Instead of chastising me, the Nawab (or Nabob in its English form) is pleased to find a Westerner here. He invites me to have coffee at his former home, now a hotel. As we sit on the lawn with bodyguards and aides, he tells me his story.

The kingdom of Gilgit used to control the trade along the ancient Silk Road. It has been overrun and occupied by everyone from the Chinese to the British. The Nawab says his family has ruled the valley since the 15th century. In 1969 Pakistan declared the sultanate dissolved. His father was the last to hold official power and his job is strictly ceremonial. (20 percent of the people in the valley are direct descendants of his dynasty.) His father was one of 16 children. His oldest brother was killed in a plane crash, so it is now his turn to be the Wali.

The hotel is run by a bearded lanky German and I can't help but comment on it. The Wali mentions that his manager was a truck driver from Germany who had studied hotel management. He stayed in Pakistan and has now become a Pakistani national and runs his hotel. He slyly comments that he found out that his trusted hotel manager has local interests of the smoking kind. I noted on the path into the hotel grounds that marijuana plants grew wild along the road.

We spoke of many things. The Nawab likes to hunt and with some sadness pointed to his hunting lodge high up on the mountain behind us. He set up a game preserve to protect the wildlife and now the government wardens can be bribed for US$10 and use .22 caliber rifles to hunt deer (which only wounds them).

He is trying to breed cocker spaniels to be bird dogs but is not having much luck. I comment on the fact that the fort looks good in its coat of red paint. He says he painted it that color because it was the cheapest paint he could find.

Things will change—the Nawab travels every year to San Francisco to the University of California for medical treatment and he has four daughters. When he goes the dynasty will end.

Polo, With or Without Headless Goats

Since I am in Gilgit I can't skip the polo game. I hang out in the fields by the river with the Afghans who have come to play *buzkashi*. Although polo has been played here for 400 years, *buzkashi* is the real thing. Buzkashi is a very violent game played with a headless goat. It is rough and it is violent and it packs the spectators in. Naturally there were none when I was there but during the summer people fly in from the South to watch both *buzkashi* and polo being played.

An Afghan tribe has set up camp and welcomes me. The horses have the skin rubbed down to the muscle in some places and there are scabby bull mastiffs tied to trees. It seems the Afghans get paid the equivalent of 1000 rupees for each game they play. The dog fights are a way of entertaining themselves and making some extra money. The chief offers to let me ride a horse all day for 200 rupees. As we hang around the camp of 20 people I watch the men take the horses out in the field. They ride fearlessly through trees, over broken ground and over brush. They treat their horses brutally yet they never make a false move. Even when the horse rears up in fear they keep pushing it to ride faster.

We talk to the Afghans. They ask us if we want to see a dog fight between their massive Kochi dogs (traveling dogs). They are from Mazar-i-Shariff and will gladly take us to Kabul.

We can hire pack horses for 300 rupees a day and walk across the pass. We say we want to leave now, but they say we are too late. It will be too cold, the snow will be too deep and the horses will starve or freeze. Why not wait until spring they ask? I don't bother to explain my Western impatience.

Later that day we watch the polo matches. Polo is from 2 p.m. to 6 p.m., timed more by the narrow band of light that the mountains allow into the valley than by a clock. The long field slopes downward and is bordered on the long sides by six foot cement walls. The spectators squat and sit along the wall cheering and yelling. When the horses and riders crash into the wall, mallets flailing, the spectators are ejected like ducks in a shooting gallery. The only thing I could compare it to was the sight of an Indy car going into the railing flicking off spectators in a long ragged rooster tail. When a team charges the open ends of the fields to score a goal, the crowd simply gets run over by the stampeding horses. Finally, a sport that is as dangerous for the spectators as the participants.

The long nose Chitralis are not only good at polo, but they play each game like it is the world championship. Few wear protective gear and many are limping or bleeding afterwards. The ones that do wear gear wear plastic construction helmets tied with string, others wear just the padded Chitrali wool cap. A band plays exotic whiney music to keep the spectators pumped up. When I climb up on the wall to take a picture of the band they suddenly stop. I motion with two fingers towards my mouth to communicate that I want the band to play again. The audience explodes with laughter and the flute player laughs so hard he can't play for five minutes. I had used the symbol for "give me a blow job" to indicate I wanted him to play his horn. So much for cultural literacy.

The game is full of chills and spills. One player hits the goal post so hard it falls over. Horses limp off the field and players are knocked unconscious. Mallets fly and hit both horses and riders. The white wooden ball bounced off the heads of more than a few myopic spectators. Horses were crushed against the rough stone walls and after a while it becomes painful to watch.

Stymied with any attempt to get to Afghanistan, we decide to avoid the tortuous trip back to Peshawar and fly out. We join the crush at the PIA ticket counter. In Pakistan all flights are full but then magically have seats. I pay 650 rupees for myself and 300 for Papa on the exact same flight. It is actually cheaper to fly in Pakistan than drive. Waiting at the airport I gather two oddly striped stones from the river as souvenirs. As he waits for the plane Papa is nervous. I find out it will be the second time he has ever flown.

As the twin engine plane strains to get off the ground I notice that we never actually clear the mountain tops. We are flying in between the peaks. Down below I recognize the long winding mountain passes, ridged fields and small villages that took so long to drive through. Despite the spectacular scenery outside, Papa stares straight ahead and prays for the entire flight.

Back in Peshawar

Back in Peshawar, Papa asks to go home to see his daughter and I set out to find the *taliban*. I visit the local newspaper to ask the editor where I can find the *taliban*. He says they have a headquarters in the Afghan market. Stunned by this simple truth I realize I have come full circle. Peshawar, along with Damascus and Beirut is a major center for revolutionary Islamic groups. There was even a university for terrorists here until three months ago. The *New Yorker* had featured them much to the displeasure of the U.S. government who politely asked the Pakistanis to shut it down. The editor rummages through his Rolodex and gives me a local number. He says there should be somebody there who speaks English. Good Luck.

I call the number and ask if anyone can speak English. There is a pause as the person at the other end yells out something in Pashto.

"Hello," an educated voice answers.

"Is this the *taliban*? I ask.

"Who is this?"

I explained who I was and asked if I could ask them some questions to better understand what their goals are.

"Are you a journalist?"

"No. I came here to meet you because no one else in the world seems to know who you are.

"We are in the Afghan market. Just ask anybody and they will bring you to us," he says.

####

Pleased with my detective work, I go back to the hotel to get Papa to act as translator. Papa is not pleased. It seems that he heard me just fine when I asked him about the *taliban* before.

Papa was dead serious. "You understand that we are going to a place where they can kill you?"

"Yes, but I don't think they will."

"Do you realize we are going to a place where they may kill me?"

"Then don't go."

"I cannot let you go alone because then they will kill you and I will be to blame."

"Then come and we will visit the fighters."

We get on a bus and I grab my cameras. I am elated. Papa is quiet.

As I stride through the market past the money changers we ask where the office of the *taliban* is. The men point in a general direction but do not take us there.

As we come across the tracks of the train that goes into Afghanistan, the muezzin calls the people to prayer. "It is time for me to pray," Papa says. "Please wait here."

As I plunk myself down in the shade, I notice two sun-browned men with black turbans sitting eating in the open. Black turbans with long tails and white stripes—the symbol of the religious student. I couldn't believe how blind I'd been—this was the uniform of the feared *taliban*. I nodded in their direction and they just stared back grimly.

Papa comes from washing up and praying and nods towards the fighters. "*Taliban*." I wave as I walk by and ask if should take their picture. Papa says "Please, no." I notice that besides praying, Papa has fortified himself with hashish.

A young boy directs us to a nondescript house with heavy green metal gates. Outside two men with machine guns sit in the shade. I walk past the men and push through the lower half of the green gates. I startle a man behind the gate. I am staring into the face from the first century. The man is dressed in white robes with a white turban. His eyes are piercing and ringed with black eyeliner, a custom rural Afghanis have to keep evil souls from entering their eyes. He just stares. Behind him are a group of men with vicious wounds, some with missing legs others with gashes and bandages. They sit on a pile of dirty blankets 3–4 feet high. Papa is about 8 feet behind me and I motion him forward to make the introductions.

In the courtyard we walk past a battered ambulance and the *taliban's* troop carrier of choice, a well-used white Toyota pickup truck. Black headdresses are hung up to dry. They are over 20 feet long and look like odd mourning flags hanging horizontally in the sun. The men in the courtyard just stare as we walk up the dusty steps. There are wounded men lining the staircase. At the head of the stairs are piles of cheap plastic sandals. My hiking boots look odd among the piles of dirty brown sandals. I am met by a young man named Abdul Ghafoor Afghani. He is 23 and when asked for his title calls himself the "information person." We are taken into a dingy green room to wait. We sit on the scabby yellow and red plastic mat and take in our surroundings. A ceiling fan is motionless. There is no electricity but the light switches are grubby from many hands.

In various other rooms are badly dressed turbaned men in shalwars who huddle in deep discussions. They do not have the hard look of killers but rather of unwashed country bumpkins. By the hard brown look of their hands and faces many of the men look like farmers not like soldiers. Our host invites us into the main room in to chat with the leader. He is wearing a fully packed bandolier containing an ancient revolver, the white turban of the mullah, and he looks a little pissed at us for interrupting his meetings. He asks our host to apologize for the pistol but the market is a stronghold of Hekmatyar and somebody tried to assassinate him yesterday. So he is wearing it just in case they try it again. They also apologize for the armed men outside the door, saying they were put there by the government to make sure nothing got out of hand.

They tell me that this is a staging area for volunteers and bringing out wounded for treatment in the hospitals of Peshawar. Recruits are gathered from the religious schools and the wounded are dropped off at the Chinese hospital. The recruits are sent via 3rd class mini bus to Quetta and then onward to the front by pickup truck. The Pakistanis do not stop the recruits or ask for papers. When the volunteers get to the front they will be given a weapon, ammunition and food supplies. In the double talk of killing, our host explains that there is no recruiting, the men come for *jihad*. This is definitely a low budget war. The dirty faded blankets outside are testament to the fact that the refugees donated their own blankets so that the men would not freeze this winter. He said that during the haj people donated the sales of animal skins slaughtered in the festival and raised 8000 rupees (about US$250) and that even the dingy office we were in was donated by local businessman at 7000 rupees a month. Occasionally they would get 100,000 and 200,000 rupee donations from businessmen to the cause.

He apologized for having no "propaganda" to give me, but he said that the *tal-iban* was in its formative stages and only a year old.

####

"We the *taliban* wish to rid Afghanistan of robbers, rapists, killers and militia and to create a new Islamic country." He tells stories of how the movement start-ed in October of 1994. In Kandahar there was a brutal warlord who stopped ev-eryone at roadblocks (most of these people would be robbed). But when he began stopping men, having them put makeup on, sodomizing them and killing them, it infuriated the people. The religious students at the mosque got the people together and hung the leader and the gunmen from the barrels of their tanks. From that point on, the revolution was in motion. They now have a radio and television station in Kandahar, but it cannot broadcast very far. So far, they have sent in a BBC crew and an independent TV crew but that is it. I am the first person from North America they have met.

I ask him if I can journey to Kandahar and the front lines or send in film crew to interview the leaders and cover the war. He would like that and I ask him again to make sure he is not just being polite. There is one catch—the leaders of the *taliban* do not allow their photographs to be taken because of the Koran. I explain very carefully that only cowards do not show their faces and that in my culture a man who does not wish to be seen cannot be trusted. He said this is not his decision but I can discuss it with them.

I ask him if they are supported by the Pakistani Secret Police. He looks puzzled. A man from the back of the room booms back in an educated English public school voice.

"Do you see any foreign backing in this room?"

He is an orthopedic surgeon trained in Britain and volunteering his time to repair the damage of mine blasts. He is mildly pissed since it is obvious even to the blind that the *taliban* are running this operation with one Panasonic phone and little else.

Throughout our conversation my host is painstakingly polite and takes great pains to give full details to my questions. When I ask him how many men they have or other sensitive questions he replies with an embarrassed look. "That is a secret. I cannot tell you or our enemies might find out."

He goes on to tell me that they have no designs on neighboring countries and that "after they win the war, they have expressed their desire to communicate with all peace loving countries of the world." As for foreign policy, economics and other items, they will get to that after they win the war. I ask him where all those shiny new tanks and weapons come from if they are just simple students. He smiles and says that when they captured Herat from Hekmatyar they found enough new weapons, vehicles and ammunition to fight Rabbiani for 25 years. I did not get into the fact that all those shiny new toys were actually courtesy of Uncle Sam vs. the Russians via Pakistan. When asked about training he said they have enough people who were trained during the war with Russia. Many were trained by Pakistan with U.S. help. He complained that Rabbiani now has planes and pilots from India and ammunition and weapons from Russia and military advisors from Iran. He said his backers were Saudi and Pakistani businessmen.

There is no trace of artifice, no haranguing, no pat answers. When I ask him to show me what parts of the country the *taliban* control, he pulls out the only reference book in the room. The six inch stack of reports turns out to be copies of the same document. (A well-thumbed 1991 UN report on Kandahar with maps and statistics.) During our conversation, there is a constant coming and going of men who wait patiently outside. The bandoliered mullah excuses himself, goes out and then rejoins us. We drink tea while along the back of the wall about 20 men watch us in silence as we talk. The phone rings throughout our conversation and my host apologizes every time. It seems they are arranging for a Danish Red Cross shipment and are trying to figure out how much to charge them. They are waiting for a fax with the bill of lading which must be sent to a copy shop down the street. The field commanders use a wireless radio to keep in touch.

He invites me to share lunch and, as we eat red beans and flat bread, I am amazed at being in a place where a group of rag tag students are taking over a country. As we share lunch, it is obvious that he is hoping to convince me that they are sincere in their goal. He does not understand why I ask some of the questions. I tell him that it helps me understand the world better and hopefully I can help other people understand as well.

He and some fighters that have joined us insist that I finish the last of the watery broth as a courtesy. It is a humbling experience. After lunch he shows me around the compound and says I cannot take pictures of the men upstairs but that maybe the men downstairs won't mind. He explains they had trouble before with the Russians using pictures to identify and kill people. The men are lounging on the blankets recovering from various wounds. As I lift my camera a man with a deep face wound begins swearing at me. He says that Allah does not like photographs and that I should get a better job than being a thief. I click away while my host and Papa get nervous. Trying to ease the tension, I ask my host to take my picture. He holds my camera up backwards with the lens facing his nose.

The haranguing continues as I tour the compound. I point to the black clothing and ask him if this is the uniform of the *taliban*. He laughs and points to all the men and says "He is *taliban*, he is *taliban* and he is *taliban*. We do not have a uniform."

He excuses himself and I thank him for his time. I remind him that I will be sending in a film crew. That night in the hotel I will call Coskun in Istanbul and tell him that we can have the world's first filmed interview of the *taliban* leaders. They will pass a special fatwah for us to allow us to film them. I tell Coskun of the route I have set up and give him my contact's name. He thinks I'm crazy but he says he will be here as soon as he can.

Out in the bright light of the market, people stare at me. I have my picture taken by an old man with an ancient wooden camera. A crowd of Afghans press around him and never take their eyes off me during the long process. Someone plunks an Afghan chitrali cap on my head. He uses the lens cap as a shutter and then develops the paper negative inside the camera. He then photographs the negative to give me a blurred 2" paper portrait. He hands me the crude, orthochromatic picture. I am a pale eyed Afghan from the 18th century. I am in a time machine and I am holding the proof in my hand.

I sit in the shade while Papa goes to pray in the simple mosque across the tracks. A fighter comes up to me to practice his English. We watch a young boy walking around with a white plastic garbage bag and a handful of wooden splinters and sticks. My new friend sees me looking at the young boy and says, "He does this every day. He will take these things and make a beautiful kite." As I look around at the dirty ancient scene peopled with the hard-faced, turbaned *mujahedin* all I see is the result of centuries of warfare.

My new friend pauses and then says proudly, "He will fly this beautiful kite very high."

—RYP

Peru

★

Shadow and Light

When Francisco Pizarro and the Spaniards "discovered" Peru in 1531, the Incan empire was already past its zenith. The Incas were licking the wounds of a nasty civil war and were easily thumped by their uninvited guests.

The Spanish weren't the first or the last conquerors to impose a military dictatorship on Peru. But the nation's destiny was reflected in a historical strobe light as it vacillated between despotism and democracy, continuing to this day, nearly 500 years later.

After almost 300 years of Spanish rule, it took more outsiders—Jose de San Martin of Argentina and Simon Bolivar of Venezuela—to finally break Spain's grip on the country. Peru announced its independence in 1821, but it took a few more years to purge the Spanish. In December 1824, General Antonio Jose de Sucre defeated the Spanish troops at Ayacucho, ending Spanish rule in South America. Spain recognized Peru's independence in 1879 after yet another war with Peru between 1864 and 1866.

Today, the ruling class is a tossed salad of predominantly white-bread landed gentry hailing from families of global origins, with a sizable garnishing of East Asians. It's quite the norm in Peru to have a surname of German, Spanish, English, Japanese or French lineage. But that hasn't enhanced the "civility" of Peru. Modern Peru is the world's leading producer of coca and perhaps its largest concealer of citizens killed, tortured or abducted. In 1993, a Peruvian human rights group estimated that 28,809 people had been killed in 12 years of political violence. The government fessed up to only 53 of the deaths (leaving at least 2660 people unaccounted for). The Maoist rebel group Shining Path (SL) seems proud to admit that nearly half the body count came at their hands.

In 1992, 3101 people were killed in violent actions; 60 percent died in battles, 30 percent were murdered. Two hundred and eighty-six people were abducted in the same year; 178 weren't heard from again. The balance were summarily executed. Torture is the favored method, and a routine, mode of interrogation employed by Peru's armed forces, and used even during investigations of petty crime.

The U.N., the Red Cross and the U.S. Department of State all agree that, in Peru, human rights are human wrongs. Executions by the military, the disappearance and murder of students and the torture of arrested persons and missing people are simply everyday life in Peru. The only good news is that deaths by terrorism were down in 1993 and 1994—almost by half. Only 1692 people died in guerrilla wars in 1993, compared to 3101 in 1992. Things are getting better.

The country has been under emergency rule permitting President Alberto Fujimori to put some heavy-duty dents into terrorist itineraries. And, he did some serious name-dropping. Literally, the names dropped. Victor Polay Campos, head of the Tupac Amaru Revolutionary Movement (MRTA), was recaptured (he had escaped from custody in 1990) after he was recognized in a Lima bar. Peter Cardenas Shulze, MRTA's second-in-command, was busted in a raid by security forces on a safe house in Lima. Government forces snatched Abimael Guzman Reynoso, the SL founder, along with seven other SL members. His personal diary and plans for an upcoming SL offensive were also found.

Now that Fujimori has Guzman and Campos wearing stripes and is singing for peace like a lonely finch (with a little prodding from the head of the secret police), you'd think he could relax. Fujimori also brags that he has convicted more than 1000 terrorists, reformed another 1500 and captured thousands. The fact that he thinks he's David Copperfield by making students, political opponents and journalists disappear doesn't seem to bother hardworking Peruvians, who are sick and tired of the terrorist actions.

Well, dictators can never relax.

Fujimori fled his Lima palace the night of November 13, 1992, after being tipped-off about a coup attempt. Not to a television station did he dash to plead for calm or reassure a frightened nation, nor to a military base to bravely lead his troops on a counterassault. Instead, Fujimori high-tailed it to the Japanese embassy to save his own butt. Safe, sound and sushi-satiated, he then directed his crush against the insurrection by calling coup leader General Jaime Salinas from his cellular phone. Finally, after a predawn shoot-out with Salinas' rogues, the coup was put down; thank Vladimiro Montesinos for saving his bacon. Montesinos is the man who runs the military; he's got direct connections to the CIA and

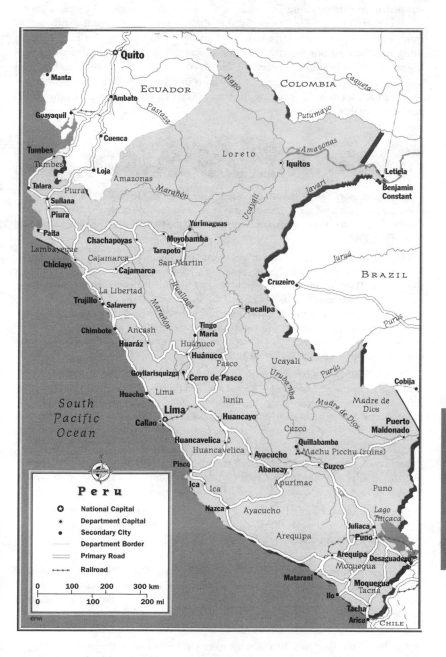

the drug mafia. Montesinos is allegedly the man who directs death squads, bullies the military with his secret files and put Fujimori into power. He apparently intends to keep him there. Fujimoro seemed to be taking care of business. Inflation was down from an amazing 7650 percent in 1990 to a modest 12 percent. Investors were attracted by Peru's new fiscal health, and the government continued to annihilate terrorists with impunity. In January 1995 fighting broke out again along the disputed border with Ecuador, claiming nine lives. Peru declared a unilateral cease fire in mid-February. In the April elections that followed, Fujimori was reelected president. So far, his efforts to improve the economy and control Shining Path seem to be working, but there is still a great disparity in the distribution of wealth.

Among the more than 6 million dispossessed, homeless and impoverished souls in Lima hides, arguably, the most apocalyptic group of terrorists on earth. The squalid, nameless shantytowns dotted across the Peruvian landscape are where the Shining Path (Sendero Luminoso) recruits its legions.

With the exception of certain tourist areas (Arequipa, Cuzco, Ica, Iquitos, Paracas, Puerto Maldonado, Puno and Trujillo), many regions of the country are designated as "emergency zone" areas. These are areas under terrorist threat and governed under martial law by well-armed soldiers who rip off a couple of clips on full automatic first and ask questions later. Despite the arrest of key leaders in 1992, two insurgent organizations—the Shining Path (SL) and the Tupac Amaru Revolutionary Movement (MRTA)—continue to carry out bombings and other terrorist attacks against a range of targets in Peru, principally Peruvian nationals, government installations, banks and foreign interests.

The unofficial headquarters of terrorism is the city of Lima, a designated "emergency zone." Bombings and terrorist incidents have been frequent in the city, and violent crime is common. There are power outages during the day, due to the drought conditions affecting the hydroelectric plants. This is important to know when choosing a high-rise hotel. Ask if the hotel has its own generator. Hotel rooms are favorite targets of burglars. The lack of tourists means that you will be particularly conspicuous.

Banks do not normally cash traveler's checks, but money changers will come to your room to exchange soles into U.S. dollars. Credit cards are accepted. There is a black market in soles, but don't be scammed by trading U.S. dollars for old notes.

Police augment their meager paychecks by setting up checkpoints on Thursday and Friday evenings to finance their weekends. Use air transportation when possible, and don't trust reports claiming that certain areas are safe.

Junkyard locos, like the Shining Path, have deliberately killed governors, mayors, tourists, schoolteachers, civil servants, hundreds of campesinos, entire villages, journalists, elderly people, children, presidential candidates, British ornithologists, Mormon missionaries, an agronomist, nuns and priests from various countries, mine workers and their wives, American helicopter crew members and a helluva lot more. They have bombed embassies, power lines, police vans, police stations, even public parks.

The Tupac folks have gone back into the more low key but profitable business of kidnapping. If you get nabbed expect to have to cough up around $30,000. Consider yourself lucky that's about 1/10 what FARC asks for in Colombia.

If, by some miracle, you don't run into the military or terrorists, there are always the hard-working farmers who live off the land. The fruits of their labor generate about US$1 billion in sales. What is the favorite cash crop of Peru? Why coca, of course.

Alberto Fujimori

The current ruler is President Alberto Fujimori. Fujimori is Peruvian of Japanese descent. In two years, he managed to dissolve parliament and assume the role of dictator. His stated goal was to deal with political corruption, and he bestowed upon himself absolute, unimpeachable authority in destroying the terrorist elements within Peru. Fujimori deftly constructed a new congress completely under his control, albeit behind a facade of democracy.

A tough-talking leader who is criticized for his abuses of human rights, Fujimori was elected in July of 1990 and took absolute power in an *auto-golpe*, or self-coup, in April 1992. He was reelected democratically in April, 1995. He is also applauded by the ruling classes for his success against the two main terrorist groups, the MRTA and the SL, but despised by others for his brutality toward opposition groups and elimination of human rights and the democratic process. The first acts of Fujimori's new government were to have the army spend two days and nights destroying over 10,000 judicial files on active cases in the Palace of Justice. Not only did the most incriminating evidence disappear on all legal files on Fujimori and his family; those of his trusted confidant Vladimiro Montesinos magically disappeared, as well. This act took place the same day Fujimori dissolved parliament and became a dictator. He was in his element after the hostage situation last year was resolved at the Japanese embassy wearing his bulletproof vest and looking tough. *DP* and folks in the know will tell you that the real tough guy behind the photogenic Fuji baby is the seldom seen Vladimiro Montesinos.

Vladimiro Montesinos

Vlad did not get to his position behind the throne with kisses and cocktail parties. There is a reason why every single MRTA terror-teen ended up cold and slippery. That reason is Vladimiro Montesinos. Presidential advisor and unofficial director of the National Intelligence Service, Montesinos has had ill-defined connections with the drug kingpins, Peruvian military, intelligence community and, since 1990, the direct support of the CIA. Called Rasputin by one local paper, Montesinos is the power behind Fujimori. Born in Arequipa, the same neighborhood as the SL's Guzman, he has had a rocky and convoluted climb to the top. A former court-martialed soldier, fugitive and legal fixer for the corrupt members of the Peruvian military, Montesinos is considered instrumental in helping Fujimori climb to his position of power. Montesinos is accused of directing death squads and being responsible for ordering various massacres and disappearances. He is also in charge of the eradication of drugs in Peru, using Peruvians trained and equipped by the CIA. Much like similar programs in Haiti, their efforts were diverted from drug eradication into private activities that helped overthrow the democratic leadership.

In August of '96, one of Peru's top drug runners testified that he paid Montesinos $50,000 a month for protection of drug flights into Colombia. When the MRTA took over the Japanese embassy, Montesinos was the man who planned the raid, but he made sure he was backstage when the curtain came down while only Fujimoro took the bows.

Coca

Coca is at the root of most of the killings—it's the base for the "white stuff," nose candy, rails, speedballs and crack. The Upper Huallaga Valley near the provincial city of Tingo

Maria is one of the world's biggest coca-producing centers. In May 1991, Peru was the producer of 60 percent of the world's supply of raw coca leaf. One irate but naive web surfer to *DP's* DangerFinder says that coca is good for Peru because it makes them work harder. So do whips and chains.

The Military

Emergency legislation has permitted the military special autonomous powers in fighting terrorist and politically subversive elements. The military administers and tightly controls emergency zones comprising over one-quarter of the country's territory. People arrested by the military are subject to the dreaded military courts. Many are not seen again afterwards.

The military appreciates its new power, but continues to be antagonistic toward the government. Fujimori still does a lot of personal promoting of buddies and demoting of fast-trackers. Any soldier opposed to his policies is relieved of duty, sometimes of bodily functions as well.

In 1992, 286 people were reported abducted, 178 of whom were subsequently reported missing. Responsibility for almost 90 percent of missing detainees was believed attributable to the armed forces. The same year, there were 114 extrajudicial executions, including 50 people who were captured by security forces and later found dead.

Since 1983, Peru has managed to win the grand prize or at least the runner-up trophy for the "Country with the Highest Number of Missing Detainees," a dubious and oft-sought distinction awarded by the United Nations work group on missing people. In 1992, the Red Cross counted 3330 arbitrary arrests; the State Department counted 654 bodies attributed to the Sendero Luminoso and 95 as the work of the government, the result of victims being executed without trial. In that same year, 30 students disappeared, 11 of whom turned up dead.

Armed forces personnel number about 80,000 conscripts in the army, 25,000 in the navy and 22,000 in the air force.

At least 300 military men have been investigated and charged with drug connections since 1990.

Sendero Luminoso (Shining Path, or SL)

Oscar Ramirez Durand (or Comrade Feliciano) has taken over leadership from the jailed Abimael Guzman (#1509) also known as Presidente Gonzalo and is working hard to keep the group's reputation for badness and cruelty they once possessed. The name came from Jose Carlos Mariategui, the founder of the first communist party in Peru, who called Marxism "a shining path to the future." The group was led by Manuel Ruben Abimael Guzman Reynoso, a pudgy, Ray-Banned, bearded ex-philosophy professor, who now will spend the rest of his life in San Lorenzo naval base on an island just off Callao. Guzman follows the teaching of Mao and was a student in the Chinese Communist Party's cadre school. The Shining Path began its armed struggle in 1980 and has been responsible for numerous bombings and assassinations. It has vowed to pursue "total war" until the government is overthrown. The group hopes to create a peasant-worker state along Maoist lines. The group's ideology is a strange hybrid of Maoism, Marxist-Leninism and the religious beliefs of the highland Quechua Indians of Peru. What began as a rural following in the remote highlands around Ayacucho spread along the mountainous rural areas toward the south and the east, until the Shining Path included rural revolutionaries, urban terrorists and the coca-growing farmers of Upper Huallaga Valley.

The Shining Path became famous for its Viet Cong tactics of intimidation of villagers. Villagers would be tried, the victims publicly tortured, mutilated, executed and left on display.

In urban areas, car bombs have been another successful terror weapon. Using a simple mixture of ammonium nitrate, diesel and dynamite, these car bombs had the strength of hundreds of pounds of explosives.

Most of the SL leaders are college-educated, middle-class Peruvians from Lima, who command Indian peasant armies. The approximately 10,000 attacks since 1980 against the government and innocent villagers have killed 30,000 people and cost the country more than US$24 billion. The SL likes to bomb symbols of bourgeois power: banks, police stations, political party headquarters and factories in Lima. Before the arrest of their leaders, the SL was estimated to comprise 5000 to 10,000 armed members. Now their numbers are dwindling to about 1000.

Shining Path leader Guzman has issued a number of government-sponsored communiques from prison that call for an end to the guerrilla war, alienating about half its membership in the year following his bust. Prior to Guzman's arrest, the SL controlled an impressive 40 percent of Peru's territory.

The group is self-sustaining, with some fund-raising done in Europe. It gets cash from the lucrative drug trade, which it uses to procure weapons and supplies. The group controls large portions of the Upper Huallaga Valley, the center of Peru's coca plantations, and taxes drug traffickers near their base in the southern highlands around Ayacucho.

Movimiento Revolucionario Nuevo Peru
(New Peru Revolutionary Movement)

These boys don't like holidays. The movement is a new, hard-line group of radicals once part of the Shining Path and based in the highland provinces of Huancavelica and Puno. The group has carried out attacks in the highlands and detonated bombs in the capital over holiday weekends, including an attack on an army post late one Christmas day that wounded eight people in Lima's impoverished El Agustino section. The group apparently split from Shining Path after its jailed leader, Abimael Guzman, called for peace. The leader is Oscar Ramirez, or "Comrade Feliciano." Comrade Feliciano says those who support any peace process with Fujimori's government are servants of Yankee imperialism and terms such pacts as "revisionist bitches' excrement." The man's got a way with words.

Tupac Amaru Revolutionary Movement (MRTA)

The current MRTA groups are the ragged remnants of a traditional Marxist-Leninist revolutionary movement formed in 1983 in Peru. The MRTA, led by Nestor Serpa and Victor Polay—now in prison—maintains that its objective is to rid Peru of its imperialist influence and establish a Marxist regime. Their chances are slim at this point, but, in their heyday, they were responsible for more anti-U.S. attacks than any other group in Latin America. Originally 1000 to 2000 combatants strong, it has dwindled to less than a hundred, which have split into unorganized criminal bands. But they aren't simple thugs. Most have received training in Cuba. And, at one time, the MRTA enjoyed close ties to Libya but now gets its only support from Cuba.

If you are detained by MRTA cadres, remember that most are former college students who may have lived in Russia or Cuba in the 1970s who like to kick Yankees' asses. So you may get a lecture and a whipping and be told to go on your way. If you are stopped by a xenophobic Maoist of the SL, bend over and kiss it adios.

The MRTA is not as violent or unpredictable as the Shining Path. Founded in 1984 and based in Lima, the MRTA has links to Colombia's M-19 guerrillas, Ecuador's Alfaro Vive and the Cuban government. Using publicity as its major weapon, the MRTA likes to attack the news media and U.S.-related businesses.

The MRTA tried to wrest control of the coca traffic from the SL but lost. And their battles with the government ended with the capture of their leader. With most of their leaders behind bars (Victor Polay Campos studied in France and Spain in the 1970s, was captured in 1989, escaped and then was recaptured in 1992), the MRTA has broken down into small bands of criminals with little or no coordinated political agenda. They continue their financially (if not politically) successful M.O. of kidnapping and extortion.

The Alianza Popular Revolucionaria Americana
(APRA–American Popular Revolutionary Alliance)

A democratic left-wing, middle-class party with strong worker support and led by former President Alan Garcia Perez, the APRA did not get along with the military during the party's rule of Peru.

The Frente Democratico (FREDEMO–Democratic Front)

A right-of-center coalition with three main partners: the liberal, pro-U.S. Accion Popular (AP–Popular Action); the Partido Liberal (Liberal Party), a right-wing group led by former presidential candidate Mario Vargas Lhosa; and the conservative Partido Popular Cristiano (PPC– Christian Popular Party).

Izquierda Unida (IU–United Left)

A mishmash of left-wing groups including the Partido Comunista Peruano (PCP–Peruvian Communist Party), the Frente Obrero, Campesino, Estudantil y Popular (FOCEP–PopularFront of Workers, Peasants and Students), the Partido Comunista Revolucionario (PCR –Revolutionary Communist Party), the Partido Integracion Nacional (PADIN–National Integration Party), the Partido Socialista Revolucionario (PSR–Revolutionary Socialist Party), and the Partido Unificado Mariatequista (PUM–Unified Marietaguista Party).

The Izquierda Socialista (IS–Socialist Left)

Way, way left. Toward the dateline. A coalition of left-wing groups that broke away from the IU before the April 1990 elections.

A passport is required. For U.S. citizens, a visa is not required for tourist stays up to 90 days, extendable after arrival. Tourists may need an onward/return ticket. For official or diplomatic passport and other travel, visas are required and must be obtained in advance. A business visa requires a company letter stating purpose of trip and US$27 fee. For current information concerning entry and customs requirements for Peru, travelers can contact the following:

Embassy of Peru

1700 Massachusetts Avenue, N.W.
Washington, D.C. 20036
☎ *(202) 833-9860*

For further information, contact the embassy of Peru or nearest consulate:

Los Angeles, California
☎ *(213) 383-9896/5*

New York, New York
☎ *(212) 481-7410*

San Francisco, California
☎ *(415) 362-5185 or 7136/2716*

San Juan, Puerto Rico
☎ *(809) 250-0391*

Miami, Florida
☎ *(305) 374-1407*

Houston, Texas
☎ *(713) 781-6145/5000*

Chicago, Illinois
☎ *(312) 853-6173*

U.S. Embassy

*Corner Avenidas Inca Garcilaso de la Vega
and Espana
Box 1995, Lima 1*
☎ *(51) (14) 33-8000*

Consular Section

*Grimaldo del Solar 346
Miraflores, Lima 18*
☎ *[51] (14) 44-3621 or 44-312*

Peru is a tough place to get around via land. Internal air services link a number of cities that are difficult to get to by land. A number of new airlines have sprung up in recent years, causing domestic prices to go down somewhat. The four principal carriers are AeroPerú, Cia de Aviacion Faucett, Aero Continente and Americana. The two most dangerous airlines are Expreso Aéreo, which connects with some of the isolated burgs in the jungles and the mountains, and Aero Tumi, which hauls a few passengers aboard its cargo routes. Schedule changes and delays are frequent. Cancellations are common during the rainy season. The main airport is Jorge Chavez International, about 10 miles northwest of Lima, about 35 minutes by cab. A trip between the center of Lima and the airport costs about US$5.

Arrange to be met at the airport by someone you can identify. Hire only taxis from inside the airport. Unlicensed taxi drivers have been known to drive victims into the barrios and rob them.

The streets are not safe at night, despite vehicle curfews. Inside major hotels, there is a generally decent level of security. Hotels are usually empty so don't be shy about negotiating a good rate.

Very few roads in Peru are paved, the major routes of the Pan-American and Central Highways being the exceptions. The roads connecting Pacasmayo with Cajamarca and Pativilca with Caraz and Huaraz are also paved. The road to Bolivia from Puno-Desaguadero has been completed. There are also numerous toll roads in Peru. Outside the cities, travel can be a mess. Roads are dusty when they're dry and impassable when they're wet. The roads have been falling apart since 1985, when the government stopped maintaining them. Some work has begun rebuilding the south section of the Pan-American Highway. The South American Explorers Club is a good source for maps, as well as the Touring y Automóvil Club del Peru (Av César Vallejo 699, Lince, Lima; ☎ *403270; FAX: 419652*). As throughout most of the world, green and red are merely pretty colors, hardly incentives to brake or accelerate. Be wary of drivers everywhere in Peru.

Trains are more comfortable than buses, although many routes are cut back or even cancelled in the rainy season. Trains link virtually all the major cities in Peru. There are two major rail lines. One runs inland from the capital, Lima, and reaches the highest point of any standard gauge railway in the world at 4780 meters. The other major line runs inland from the port of Matarani in the south, linking the Altiplano to the sea. This line stretches in the Altiplano from Puno on Lake Titicaca to Cuzco, and extends from Cuzco to the Quillabamba on the Urubamba River, the main waterway to the jungle region. It passes the Inca city of Machu Picchu, Peru's most famous tourist attraction. The Cuzco–Machu Picchu route accounts for about 30 percent of all rail traffic.

Bus service is generally good, but exceedingly uncomfortable. Avoid bus travel at night. Bandits prey on tourists dozing on nighttime bus rides.

Taxis, identified by a small red-and-white windshield sticker, are plentiful and cheap. Taxis have no meters and fares are negotiated in advance. A map is useful, as few drivers know specific streets in the sprawling suburbs where many businesses and ministries are located.

Huallage Valley

Sort of a Napa Valley for cokeheads and dealers. Tingo Maria in the Northwest of Peru is the capital of coke and of course home base for the Shining Path. If you are hitchhiking around here (as one female *DP* reader did) expect to be stopped by the SL on the Hemilio Valdsan highway. They won't shoot you, but they will give a lecture on the benefits of communism and then demand a $4 contribution to their cause. Seems like they have something mixed up here. Next time *DP* readers should try to convince the young men and women with the bandannas to give *you* the $4 and then lecture them on the basic concepts of communism. Last time we checked, the SL weren't giving away all that coco or guarding it for free.

Military areas, or "Emergency Zones"

More than 25 percent of Peru's land and 50 percent of its population are situated in "emergency zones;" areas where terrorist groups still control large parts of the country. Here, the "military-political commander," usually an army general, is the supreme authority. Elected civilian representatives have little or no real roles in local affairs. The military has also acquired wide powers in the administration of justice. Leading terrorists charged with "treason to the fatherland" are tried by secret military courts. They regularly receive summary life prison sentences from what critics describe as "faceless" judges. Travel to, and within, emergency zones outside Lima subjects one to extraordinary risk. These zones are extremely dangerous regions where both terrorism and violent crime are common. Overland travel to, or through, the emergency zones outside the capital city of Lima is particularly dangerous.

The following departments have been designated as "emergency zones" by the Peruvian government: Apurimac, Ayacucho, Huanacavelica, Huanuco, Junin, Lima (except the city of Lima). Also the areas of Pasco, San Martin, Ucayali (except for air travel to the city of Pucallpa), as well as La Convencion and Calco Provinces within Cuzco Ucayali and Alto Amazonas Provinces within Loreto Department. The military has started arming peasants in an effort to make the SL's job of intimidation a little more risky. This, in turn, prompts the SL to execute entire villages as punishment for bearing arms. Guerrillas can expect speedy and one-sided military trials, and there are plenty of stool pigeons fluttering about to put away their former cohorts. Villagers can look forward to a few more centuries of oppression and brutality.

Cuzco and Iquitos

Pickpocketing and armed robbery in or near hotels is common. Foreigners, unarmed and cash rich, are sitting ducks for thieves. The police are too busy sniffing out terrorists, so don't expect a team of detectives to be put on the trail of your missing camera case or AMEX card.

Police or Military Facilities

If you haven't guessed by now that the Peruvian zanies have a thing for bombs and government facilities, hang around and find out for yourself.

Lima

Despite the setbacks suffered by Sendero Luminoso during 1993, the terrorism that occurred in the capital in 1994 helped certify Lima as one of the most violent cities in the hemisphere. While the number of attacks and deaths in Lima during 1993 were down significantly compared to 1992, nearly 60 percent of the total number of attacks nationwide were carried out in the capital in 1994, comprising 20 percent of the total number of deaths. According to statistics issued by a political violence monitoring group, at least 153 persons were killed in some 639 terrorist-related incidents in Lima's metropolitan area in 1994. Lima's central district (where the U.S. embassy is located) accounted for some 25 percent of all incidents and close to 40 percent of related deaths in Lima, making it decidedly the most dangerous part of the city. (Incidents in the outlying shantytowns are sometimes underreported.)

The western districts, including Lima's port city of Callao and the international airport sector, were the next most dangerous areas, with some 16 percent of Lima's terrorist incidents and deaths reported in these areas. Residential districts accounted for only 12 percent of the incidents and 5 percent of the deaths, but were the target of 13 of Sendero's 33 car bombs in 1993. At least 12 bystanders were killed by car bombs in 1993, a brutal example of being in the wrong place at the wrong time. The 33 Lima car bombs in 1995, however, do not include at least eight other car bombs (three in residential districts) that were defused or did not explode. For a brief comparison, there were 62 car bombs in Lima during 1992, with 19 in the residential districts. While the overall number of car bombs dropped by almost half in 1993 (33 versus 62), it is important to note that the number of car bombs in the residential districts remained almost the same (13 in 1993 versus 19 in 1992).

The city of Lima is located in Lima department, a designated emergency zone. Bombings and terrorist incidents have been frequent in the city, and violent crime is common. Most acts of terrorism occur in Lima. The targets are police stations, banks and commercial areas. Terrorist activities are shifting from the rural areas (which require money to support) to urban areas (which make money). Although many of the threats are for extortion, some robberies result in goods being confiscated and then distributed in the shantytowns. The SL continues to murder villagers and assassinate high-level government and military officials.

The group known as "Los Destructores" are knocking off banks and armored cars with continued success. There are problems with petty theft of auto parts taken from parked cars. Lima's airport and American Airlines have been the targets of terrorist attacks. On January 22, 1993, an AA flight from Miami was hit by three bullets while taxiing shortly after landing. The shots were assumed to have come from the Villa El Salvador shantytowns bordering the airport. No one was hurt. Four days later, a small bomb went off in the duty-free shop. Again, no injuries were reported.

If you need police assistance in Lima (don't hold your breath), contact the following:

Policia de Turismo (Tourism Police)
Avenida Salavarry 1158
Jesus Maria
☎ *71-4313 or 71- 4579*

American Businesses
The SL continues to target high-profile American businesses, such as IBM, Coca-Cola and American Airlines, and to bomb the U.S. embassy. Japanese interests have also been targeted.

The Border with Ecuador
Why these people fight over their northern border is a mystery to most civilized folks. Dense jungle, monkeys and mud are the spoils that will go the victor. Ecuador and Peru fought a war over this 1000-mile-long swamp in the Amazon basin back in 1941. In 1942, the Protocol of Rio de Janeiro was signed and Peru ended up gaining 77,220 square miles. Because the border was defined as "the river flowing into the Santiago

River," it didn't take long for Ecuador to figure out there were two rivers flowing into the Santiago and they changed course every rainy season. So they fought again in 1981 and called each other nasty names in 1991.

Now they are squabbling over a 50-mile stretch in the lush, jungle-covered mountains of Cordillera del Condor, which would give Equador access to the Amazon and Maranon rivers, an area that is supposedly rich in gold. Naturally, any heavily armed visitors posing as ecotourists with metal detectors are highly suspect.

Drugs

In January 1995, three tons of pure cocaine and 500 kg of cocaine paste were seized and 20 traffickers were busted in northern Peru in what was to date the greatest amount of hydrochloride confiscated in the 1990s. Among those arrested were the leaders of the notorious Los Nortenos cartel. The cocaine empire covers one-fifth of Peru's territory and affects the lives and activities of 1.2 million people inhabiting 60 percent of the Peruvian Amazon. The "empire" handles nearly 300 tons of cocaine per year and receives US$1 billion annually. Additionally, the cartel controls 241 clandestine airstrips.

Money Changers

Tourists have been ripped off while changing money with street money exchangers called *cambistas*. Counterfeit U.S. dollars are exchanged or slipped in during the transaction. These counterfeit bills are of very high quality, and most people do not realize they are counterfeit until they try to pass them, or compare them to real bills in bright sunlight.

Power Outages

When the towns go black, the crooks grow hair on their palms and howl at the moon. Get inside a hotel or business during a power outage. Ahooooooo!

Medical care does not meet U.S. standards. Cholera is present in Peru. However, visitors who follow proper precautions about food and drink are not generally at risk. U.S. medical insurance is not always valid outside the United States. In some instances, supplemental medical insurance with specific overseas coverage has proved useful. Malaria and yellow fever are present in Peru.

The official language is Spanish, the mother tongue of around 70 percent of the population. Quechua and Aymara are also official in some regions. Numerous other languages are spoken by Indian tribes in the Amazon basin.

Peru's three distinct geographic regions present significant difficulties for economic development. Offshore and coastal areas in the northwest contain oil deposits, but the width of the arid Pacific coast that runs the length of the country averages less than 160 kilometers, and rivers flowing from the Andes irrigate only a few valleys. Major traditional exports include fish products, cotton and fruit grown on the coast, and coffee grown in the Andean foothills.

The Andean highlands rise sharply from the coast to a height of more than 4000 meters, and much of the country's mineral wealth comes from mines in the Andes. Coffee and coca are the major cash crops of the foothills of the east Andes. The real agricultural export is coca, the United States being the biggest customer with more than US$1 billion generated in coca sales. Half the country lies in tropical lowlands. The northern jungle is a wealthy oil-producing area that used to cause friction with Peru's neighbors.

The coastal population is primarily mestizo, with a small percentage of whites of European descent. The Quechuan highlanders are direct descendants of the Incas, and the Amerinds are related to the jungle tribes of the Amazon.

The currency is the Nuevo Sol, which fetches about 2.1 to the U.S. dollar. Electricity is 220V/60Hz. Any time of the year is best to visit Lima, since it's dry with temperatures ranging from an average high of 82° F in January to lows of 66° F in August. Lima is arid with an annual rainfall around 48 mm; the marine layer is a common factor, with long periods of overcast skies, *garua* between June and September. Higher up in the Andes and the Amazon, the rainy season is from December to March. Remember, the summer and winter are reversed. There are also fertile valleys, such as those of Cuzco and Cajamarca. Lake Titicaca in the south, at an altitude of 3815 meters, is the highest navigable lake in the world. About 60 percent of Peru's area is covered by the triple-canopy rain forest in the Amazon basin. The Andes, of course, with some peaks as high as 7000 meters, can get quite frigid.

The informal "*tu*" form is commonly used with younger Spanish-speaking business visitors. While Peruvians are sometimes inclined to be late for appointments, visitors are expected to be punctual. Phone calls are very expensive from the hotels in Lima.

Useful Addresses and Phone Numbers

Aeroperu

Avda Jose Pardo 601
Miraflores, Lima 18
☎ [51] (14) 322995

Aeropuerto Internacional Jorge Chavez

Avda Elmer Faucett
Lima
☎ [51] (14) 529570

Empresa Nacional de Ferrocarriles, del Peru

Ancash 207
Apdo 1379, Lima
☎ [51] (14) 289440

Foptur (Tourist Promotion)

Jiron de la Union 1066
Belen, Lima
☎ [51] (14) 323559
FAX [51] (14) 429280

Ministry of Industry, Commerce, Tourism and Integration

Calle 1 Oeste, Corpac
San Isidro, Lima 27
☎ [51] (14) 407120

UK Embassy

Edif El Pacifico Washington
Piso 12, Plaza Washington
Esq Avda Arequipa
Casilla 854, Lima 100
☎ [51] (14) 334738
FAX [51] (14) 334735

U.S. Embassy

Avda Garcilaso de la Vega 1400
Apdo 1995, Lima 100
☎ [51] (14) 338000
FAX [51] (14) 316682

Embassy Location/Registration

Upon arrival, U.S. citizens are requested to register with the consular section of the U.S. embassy in Lima to obtain the latest travel and security information within Peru.

U.S. Embassy, Consular Section

Grimaldo del Solar 346
Miraflores
☎ [51] (14) 44-3621 or 44-3121

PERU

10/07/1992	Abimael Guzman, the founder and leader of Sendero Luminoso, was sentenced to life imprisonment by a military court.
04/05/1992	President Alberto Fujimori, with military cooperation, closed the congress and courts and set aside portions of the constitution in an action that concentrated extraordinary powers in his hands. The Organization of American States (OAS) demanded that Fujimori restore the constitution. Opposition parties and leftist insurgents oppose Fujimori's takeover.
06/18/1986	Security forces killed more than 200 jailed members of the Sendero Luminoso (SL) guerrilla organization during a riot at Lima's Canto Grande prison. The event is marked by the guerrillas as "Heroes Day."
07/28/1985	President Alan Garcia Perez succeeded Fernando Belaunde Terry as president, the first transfer of power from one democratically elected Peruvian president to another in forty years.
11/04/1982	MRTA founded the Tupac Amaru Revolutionary Movement (MRTA), a Cuban-inspired Marxist guerrilla organization.
05/18/1980	The Maoist Sendero Luminoso (Shining Path) guerrilla organization began its armed struggle with an attack on a rural polling station; it has since grown into the largest and most active insurgent group in the country.
12/03/1934	Birthday of Abimael Guzman, also known as "President Gonzalo," the founder and leader of the Sendero Luminoso guerrilla organization. Guzman's followers often "celebrate" his birthday by carrying out attacks or murdering soldiers, public servants and municipal authorities.
12/26/1893	The birthday of Chinese communist leader Mao Zedong has been "celebrated" by the Sendero Luminoso (SL) guerrilla organization reveling in terrorist attacks.
07/28/1821	Independence Day.
10/07	Communist Party founded.
02/21	Birthday of Haya de la Torre Victor, the founder of the American Popular Revolutionary Alliance (APRA), the former ruling party of Peru. Date is also celebrated in Peru as the "Day of Fraternity."

PERU

Manila

The Philippines
★ ★

The Crescent and the Cross

The Philippines seems to get bypassed on most travelers' Southeast Asia itineraries. Idyllic, yes, but earthquakes and volcanoes pound the islands when Muslim guerrillas aren't. Most tourists to the Philippines these days seem to be horny Australians on sex junkets, despite an Australian government ban on sex tourism amid the specter of AIDS.

In the 1950s, the Philippines had the strongest economy in Southeast Asia, if not all of Asia, surpassing even those of South Korea, Japan, Thailand and Malaysia. Today, however, nearly half of all Filipinos live on the poverty line.

But it's not only the rudimentary infrastructure that's keeping the charter jets away. See, there's a nasty little problem with imported terrorism. All that money from Saudi Arabia and the United States that was funneled into Afghanistan to stave off the Soviets has found its way not only to the World Trade Center in New York but to a brutal and strengthening Muslim insurgency on the island of Mindanao.

691

The Muslim separatists of Mindanao have been around for a while. Their quest for autonomy from the Roman Catholic Philippines isn't one of those Johnny-come-lately bus bombings or rocket attack parties. The Spanish tried for 300 years to extinguish the flame of Allah; they couldn't. Neither could the Americans during their 50-year rule of the islands; nor could the Japanese during their occupation of the country during World War II. Although various Philippine governments have negotiated with the principal Muslim extremist group, the Moro National Liberation Front (MNLF)—with varying degrees of success—an even nastier, deadlier faction has come on the scene, the Moro Islamic Liberation Front (MILF). Not to be confused with moderate Moros (who signed a peace agreement with the government in September 1996) or morons, these Hezbollah-backed fundamentalists have been quietly proliferating and arming themselves, while Manila busies itself hosing down the Libyan-brokered autonomy agreement with the MNLF reached in Tripoli in 1976.

The government claims the MILF is only about 60,000 poorly trained guerrillas yet it deploys nearly two-thirds of its 70,000-soldier army on Mindanao to contain the separatists. The MILF itself claims 120,000 troops, but Western analysts believe the group numbers about 40,000 combatants, only about a third of whom are on "active duty" at any given time. Even at that number, the MILF is far stronger than the communist New People's Army of the mid-1980s. And just to give the movement a little international flavor and foreign intrigue, as many as 1000 MILF members were sent to fight in Afghanistan in the 1980s. The current Muslim uprising in the Philippines has been going on for a quarter of a century and has killed more than 120,000 people.

And, unlike the MNLF, the MILF is unlikely to cave in. Whereas a number of MNLF leaders have been co-opted into the mainstream Philippine social and business fabric since the diluted and still unimplemented 1976 autonomy plan, the MILF is hard-core Islamic fundamentalism at its nastiest, a downright jihad, Southeast Asian style. As a case in point, the MILF has received at least 29 arms shipments from Hezbollah and other extremist groups in the Middle East since 1994. They're packing Russian-made AKs and rocket-propelled grenade launchers, the same equipment with which their jihad buddies in real wars are blasting each other. And, historically, they haven't had a lot of opposition, as they've been largely ignored by Manila since their inception in 1978, due to the government's preoccupation with the communist threat. Not any longer.

Manila had its reasons for ignoring the Muslim threat. First of all, Muslims comprise only about 5 percent of the Philippine population, and they are even greatly outnumbered by government supporters on Mindanao itself. Secondly, since the 1987 constitution was ratified, any successional or autonomy move must be approved by a plebiscite, and both Moro groups would lose handily on Mindanao.

So, for now, the Muslim insurgents are content to be left alone in the mountains of the central Philippines, occasionally terrorizing towns and villages. They lie in waiting. The MILF couldn't win a head-to-head war with the Philippine army, and the group admits as much. But they'd make it a bloody enough battle to be marginally victorious at the negotiating table. Instead, the Front is waiting for the collapse of the Philippine government, as did the fundamentalists in Iran under the shah.

THE PHILIPPINES

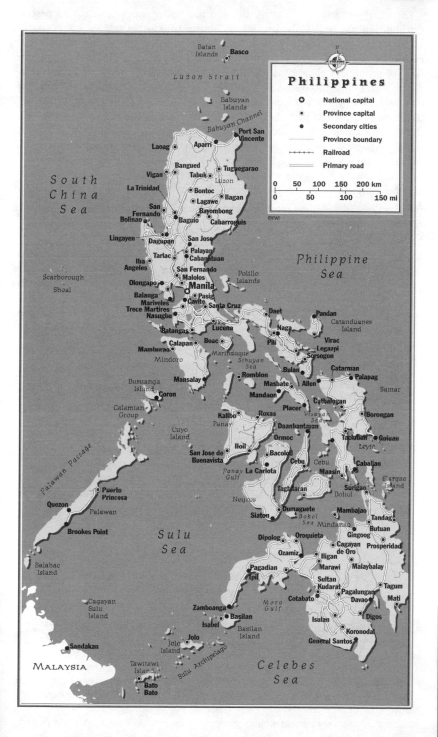

Philippines

- ⊕ National capital
- ⊙ Province capital
- ● Secondary cities
- —— Province boundary
- ++++ Railroad
- === Primary road

| 0 | 50 | 100 | 150 | 200 km |
| 0 | 50 | | 100 | 150 mi |

©FWI

Batan Islands
Basco

Luzon Strait

Babuyan Islands

Babuyan Channel

Port San Vincente

Laoag · **Aparri**

Bangued · **Tuguegarao**

Vigan · **Tabuk**

La Trinidad · **Bontoc** · **Ilagan**

Luzon

San Fernando · **Lagawe**

Bolinao · **Baguio** · **Bayombong** · **Cabarroguis**

Lingayen · **Dagupan** · **San Jose**

South China Sea

Iba · **Tarlac** · **Palayan** · **Cabanatuan**

Angeles

San Fernando

Olongapo · **Malolos**

Balanga · **Manila**

Mariveles · **Pasig**

Trece Martires · **Cavite** · **Santa Cruz**

Nasugbu

Scarborough Shoal

Batangas · **Lucena**

Calapan · **Boac**

Mamburao

Mindoro

Marinduque

Philippine Sea

Polillo Islands

Daet · **Pandan**

Catanduanes Island

Naga

Pili

Virac

Legazpi

Sorsogon

Bulan

Catarman

Sibuyan Sea

Romblon · **Masbate** · **Allen** · **Palapag**

Samar

Mansalay

Mandaon · **Catbalogan**

Busuanga Island

Coron

Calamian Group

Cuyo Island

Kalibo · **Roxas** · **Placer** · **Borongan**

Panay *Visayan Sea*

Daanbantayan

Ormoc · **Taclodan** · **Guiuan**

San Jose de Buenavista · **Iloil** · **Bacolod** · **Cebu** *Leyte*

Palawan Passage

Panay Gulf · **La Carlota** · **Cebu** · **Cabalian**

Tagbilaran · **Maasin** · **Surigao**

Negros *Bohol*

Elargao Island

Puerto Princesa · **Dumaguete** · **Mambajao** · **Tandag**

Quezon · **Siaton** *Bohol Sea* · **Butuan**

Palawan · **Gingoog** · **Prosperidad**

Brookes Point · **Dipolog** · **Oroquieta** · **Cagayan de Oro**

Sulu Sea · **Ozamiz** · **Iligan** · **Malaybalay**

Pagadian · **Marawi**

Ipil · **Sultan Kudarat** · **Pagalungan** · **Tagum**

Balabac Island

Cotabato · **Davao** · **Mati**

Cagayan Sulu Island · **Zamboanga** · **Isulan** · **Digos**

Basilan *Moro Gulf* · **Koronadal**

Isabela · **General Santos**

Basilan Island

Sandakan

MALAYSIA

Jolo **Jolo**

Tawitawi Island *Sulu Archipelago*

Celebes Sea

Bato Bato

Mindanao

There are perhaps 4 million Muslims in the Philippines—which is 83 percent Catholic and the only Christian state in Southeast Asia. Mindanao has become a virtual battlefield, as MILF guerrillas and government troops shoot bullets at each other and trade camps. Farther south still and nearly 1000 kilometers from Manila—yet only a short boat ride from the mainly Muslim Malaysian and Indonesian island of Borneo—secessionists on the two principal islands in the Sulu Archipelago, Basilan and Jolo, continue to fight for their independence, a fight that's lasted the better part of 300 years. Many of the Muslim people who inhabit the Sulu Archipelago have been split by modern national borders and, as a result, travel frequently and freely between neighboring countries. Numerous radical Muslim groups have emerged from the poor fishing villages scattered across the islands, but most have evaporated over the years, taking a more conciliatory path or becoming entangled with more radical factions. As the Mindanao-based Moros (the Moro National Liberation Front, or MNLF) have worked out a peace agreement with the Philippine government, a new, more radical group has emerged, the MILF.

The southern Philippines always was predominantly Muslim but immigration from the north has increased the Christians to a majority. That's why the Muslim groups will not agree to a plebiscite to determine who should rule the south. It is estimated that communist guerillas in the northern Philippines have dwindled from a high of 25,000 in 1987 to about 5000 now. The communist New People's Army is a spent force which sporadically makes the headlines these days with an assassination or kidnapping or two.

The Hours Suck
But Think of The Accrued Holidays

Hiro Onada makes the Energizer Bunny look like a piker. Second Lieutenant Onada fought World War II for 30 years. The fact that nobody bothered to tell him that Japan surrendered in 1945 didn't stop him from hanging on until 1974. The 73-year-old Onada hid out on the island of Lubang in the Philippines, living off wild animals and plants. A Japanese journalist found Onada in 1952, but Onada thought he was a U.S. spy. In a way you can't blame him since he could see the activity at Subic Bay and the constant U.S. military activity made him believe that the war raged on. His orders were to stay in Lubang if the Americans captured it and to wage a guerrilla campaign. His only companion, Private Kinshinchi Kozuka, was shot by Philippine police after 19 years on the island.

He was finally convinced to give up his fight when Norio Suzuki, a Japanese adventurer, conveyed a direct order by his commander to surrender. He now teaches at an outdoor survival school in the Fukushima prefecture of Japan.

Muslim and communist separatists have been battling various Manila governments for nearly 30 years, resulting in more than 10,000 firefights between insurgents and government troops during that time. More than 120,000 people have been killed. The government kept a relative lid on the extremist problem—in the interests of promoting tourism—until the recent terrorist plot to kill the Pope and blow up numerous airliners simultaneously. Meanwhile, army rebels are busy plotting the next coup of the month. In all, the mayhem keeps the hotel rates down.

The Big Blast

Project Bojinka, or "the Explosion," was supposed to be the biggest terrorist attack in history. The idea was to blow up eleven U.S. airliners over the Pacific on the same day. Five Muslim terrorists would plant bombs aboard 747 aircraft. The plotters, Pakistani nationals Ramzi Ahmed Yousef and Abdul Hakim Murad, were arrested. Both men were also accused of trying to assassinate the Pope in January of "96. The plot was discovered when the men were mixing up chemicals to make explosives in their sixth-floor apartment's sink. The mixture began smoking and the firemen were called. The men hid out in a karaoke bar down the street, and, when Murad was sent back to get the incriminating evidence, he was nabbed by the cops. The smoking gun? Their computer's hard drive had been erased but when restored, contained complete details of the plot.

The scary part is that the two men successfully carried out a dry run when they placed a small bomb under the seat of Tokyo-bound Philippines Airlines Flight 434 on December 11, 1994. The bomb killed a Japanese tourist and wounded 10 others. Yousef had placed the bomb under the seat when he flew the same airliner. The difference is, he got off at Cebu and then the ill-fated flight continued on to Tokyo.

Yousef actually made the bomb in the toilet of the airliner from liquid nitroglycerine and other inert chemicals. He hid the clear nitroglycerin in a bottle of contact lens wetting fluid.

Moor Firepower

Philippine Muslims have been called Moros since Spanish colonial times. The word "Moro" means Moor, or Muslim in Spanish. The U.S. Army's 1911 Colt .45-caliber pistol was actually developed because smaller-caliber bullets just couldn't knock down drug-crazed Moors.

Hashim Salamat & the Moro Islamic Liberation Front (MILF)

An offshoot of the MNLF that sprang up in 1978 in the wake of the Tripoli-brokered autonomy agreement between Manila and the Moros, the MILF has no word for "compromise" in its Islamic dictionary. MILF troop strength is estimated at between 20,000 and 40,000 by independent analysts, but no one seems to know for sure. The MILF itself claims a force of 120,000 members, 80,000 of them armed in 13 major camps in seven provinces—while the Philippine government says the group numbers no more than 8000. The military guesstimates 60,000. More than 1000 Filipino Muslims in its ranks fought against the Soviets during the war in Afghanistan, although Philippine military intelligence says no more than 300 did. When *DP* paid a visit, we found the MILF to be highly disciplined and equally as radical. The MILF doesn't simply seek autonomy (as the more moderate MNLF has sought) but complete secession of Mindanao from the Philippines and the creation of a fundamentalist Islamic state—and will settle for no less. The Front's military commander, Al-haj Murad, boasts of possessing six full divisions of soldiers; however, it seems to be a rotating army, with only two divisions on duty at any given time. This may explain the massive gap in estimates of the group's strength. MILF leader Hashim Salamat is a tough guy to get hold of—military commanders and many of the Front's other bellwethers have never set eyes on him—but does give regular religious sermons on radio broadcasts in Mindanao. *DP* had no problem setting a chin wag and a guided tour at his base camp. Salamat received his religious training in Egypt and Pakistan in the 1960s (he was heavily influenced by Syed Abul Ala Mau'dudi of Pakistan's Jamaat i Islami Party and Syed Outh of Egypt's Muslim Brotherhood) and formed the Moro National Liberation Front in 1970. His training in the Middle East made him a lot of bearded buddies with bombs, so he had no problem arming his spin-off gangsters when he founded the MILF. These days, the MILF is busy funding itself through the kidnapping of Taiwanese diplomats and Chinese-Filipino businessmen and by attacking Philippine military detachments and burning schools. They also like to bring along high-tech video cameras on their raids (a la Hezbollah) so they can pop the footage off to TV stations in time for the 11 o'clock news.

The Abu Sayyaf Group (ASG)

The Abu Sayyaf Group (ASG) is an Islamic fundamentalist faction with zero tolerance for the Christian government. It first appeared in August 1991. The ASG began as Tabligh (Spread the Word), an organization founded in 1972 by Iranian missionaries who came to the Philippines to spread the doctrines of Ayatollah Ruhollah Khomeini. The ASG figured the poor Muslim communities of the Philippines were a good place to wage a secessionist jihad.

Tabligh's military arm became known as the Mujahedin Commando Freedom Fighters (MCFF), and later tagged as the Abu Sayyaf Group—named after charismatic leader Abdurajak Janjalani Abubakar, who goes by the handle of Abu Sayyaf (Father of the Sword). Abubakar is a Filipino trained in Libya and fluent in Arabic. He was reported killed in combat with government troops on January 13, 1996, but *DP* has heard that he is still very much alive. The ASG is at least partially financed by Iran and Pakistan. The group is based in Darayan, Patikul and Sulu and can muster only about 120 armed combatants. But these boys are fierce, namely because they can afford to be. They're supported by Libya and Iran and generate their own income by kidnapping businesspeople. Since August 1992, the rebels have been targeting members of the Roman Catholic Church. They kidnap priests, missionaries and nuns, usually releasing them after a lengthy captivity. The MCFF also provides protection for the numerous smugglers and pirates who prowl the Sulu Sea. There have been reports of *mujahedin* veterans from the Afghan war providing training to MCFF members in guerrilla tactics and explosives.

The Moro National Liberation Front (MNLF)

A formidable and brutal Muslim insurgency group for a quarter-century, The MNLF signed a peace agreement with the Ramos government on September 2, 1996. Today, the MNLF is a mainstream political entity. Some 7500 former guerrillas are now being trained and paid to fight alongside government troops to battle the even nastier MILF and Abu Sayyaf group. The former guerillas get $170 and a monthly allowance of $30. The MNLF chairman, Nur Misuari is now in charge of a four province Autonomous Region in Muslim Mindanao.

The New People's Army (NPA)

The communist NPA is an outgrowth of the Maoist Communist Party of the Philippines founded in 1968. In 1969 they created an armed group called the New People's Army. the most powerful insurgent group in the Philippines. At their peak in 1988 there were 26,000 guerillas and supporters but government fighting, assassinations, amnesties and defections have whittled them down. Once figured to be an anachronism, a recent government study found that the NPA have increased the number of guerillas to 6700, up 10 percent from 1996. One of President Fidel Ramos' principal objectives was to pursue peace with the NPA, which has been largely accomplished. José María "Joma" Sison, is now in exile in the Netherlands. Ramos scored a success when he was able to persuade another NPA leader, Leopoldo Mabilangan, to leave the group. Mabilangan was later assassinated by NPA operatives. The NPA occasionally lets people know it's still around, though. In March 1997, the group ambushed five police officers and two civilians who were on their way to a crime scene in Zambales province, north of Manila. All seven were killed. The same month it also kidnapped and executed a Filipino businessman. Today they operate in small groups called "sparrows" to assassinate people and extort money.

The Alex Boncayao Brigade (ABB)

The ABB is a lethal leftist death squad led by Sergio Romero that has taken scores of lives in its 10-year history. These guys are the assassin branch of the Communist Party of the Philippines. Most recently, the group has been offing Chinese businessmen in sort of an ethnic cleansing of the ranks of the Philippines' industrialists. In December 1995, President Fidel Ramos "declared war" on the group which Romero responded with an announcement that the death squad would expand its arenas of operation beyond Manila to throughout the country. The government has drawn up a list of more than 160 ABB members targeted for arrest.

Sniffing Out Terrorists

Most white-bread folks think it's easy to spot a terrorist. It's the guy with dark skin, a big nose, a scraggly beard with a towel wrapped around his head. Problem is that less than .01 percent of all guys who look like this are terrorists. And Timmy McVeigh fit this profile about as well as Roseanne fits into Pamela Anderson Lee's swimsuit. The Philippines think they have a better formula for sniffing out terrorists. The Immigration Bureau's Civil Security Unit (CSU) advises immigration officers to detect the following when assessing if an arrival might be a terrorist: foul foot odor and calloused skin. That's right. Passport stampers are advised to eyeball guys carrying only one bag, whose eyes are darting around the room. This qualifies the might-be nasty for a strip search, according to the CSU. Strip searchers should then be on the lookout for calloused elbows and hands, marks on the stomach and chest, and athlete's foot—all of which suggest the potential perpetrator has undergone rigid military training. In 1996, immigration inspectors turned away some 200 arrivals as suspected terrorists because of smelly feet. Probably half of them were gardeners from Brunei on vacation.

Wanna Buy Baby Gang (WBBG)

Yeah, you read it right. Philippine security forces are hunting a gang that snatches babies and children and sells them to childless Filipino and foreign couples. The group, called Wanna Buy Baby Gang, preys on babies and children aged eight months to two years. The going price per child is US$20,000 if the buyer is a foreigner and 20,000 pesos (US$785) if the client is a Filipino. The chief of the anti-kidnapping unit of the National Bureau of Investigation (NBI) said the existence of the gang was reported by parents who had been victimized. Women gang members carry out the abductions by applying to work as maids. After gaining the trust of their employers, they disappear with the babies. The gang has reportedly taken over 30 babies and small children in recent years. (We couldn't make this stuff up if we tried).

The Pirates of Zamboanga

Zamboanga is a colorful, dangerous place and home to pirates, smugglers, terrorists and the most charming people *DP* has met. The name Zamboanga is derived from the Samal word *samboangan*, meaning "anchorage." The Samals live in stilt houses built over the shallow waters. The children play in the "front yards," just like children play on grass, but in the water. They travel to market and to visit neighbors in tiny dugout canoes. They find it quite exciting when foreigners visit; they wave and hold up their children for a picture when strangers are in town.

Zamboanga is a city of half a million people and is the center for the export of copra timber and other natural products. The population is 75 percent Christian and 25 percent Muslim. Originally a Christian outpost surrounded by Muslims, the city was occupied by American troops in 1899. They believe that Sabah, the oil- and timber-rich state of Malaysia, should be part of the Philippines. They base their claim on the historic rights, going back to the 16th century, belonging to the Sultanate of Sulu. One of the sultans leased Sabah to a private firm, the British North Borneo Company, in 1878, even though the boundaries were ill-defined and disputed by other rulers in the region.

In 1946, the company handed Sabah over to the British government, which, in turn, ceded it to Malaysia in 1963. But Manila claims that the Sultan of Sulu had already transferred his rights to the Philippines in 1962. The ancient 16th-century document is considered a gimmick by Manila, similar to selling a tourist the Brooklyn Bridge, as both the Sultan of Sulu (or Sooloo) and the Sultan of Brunei grandly claimed all the islands in the region, even though they had little idea of just how large Borneo really was.

Even now, the Philippines has never renounced its formal claims to Sabah, principally because the Philippines congress would have to ratify such a step.

The Muslims living in southwestern Mindanao and on the Sulu islands have been trading for centuries with their fellow Muslims in Sabah to the west and Sulawesi (Indonesia) to the south without considering that anyone would create a demarcation line between them. There are between 300,000 and 700,000 illegal immigrants from the southern Philippines living in Sabah, as well as Timorese from the Indonesian island of Timor. They work cheaply, but are a growing concern for the Sabahans because the Sabahans are outnumbered.

Zamboanga is a historic trading center, where luxury goods from Indonesia, Malaysia, Singapore and China are as plentiful as the raw materials from the sea and jungles that surround the city. The goods are brought in on *tora-toras*, flat-bottom boats, that are usually loaded to the gunnels with cheap TVs, beer, cigarettes and other prized items.

The "pirate" ships are an assortment of rusting freighters, aging ferries, modern speedboats, *basligs*—the large boats with outriggers to avoid capsizing in the heavy seas—and speedy canoelike *vintas* with their colorful sails.

The amount of trade in high-ticket items from duty-free ports, such as Labuan in Brunei, make legitimate traders easy targets for pirates who employ everything from *parangs* (machetes) to machine guns to kill their victims.

A passport and onward/return ticket as required. For entry by Manila International Airport, a visa is not required for a transit/tourist stay up to 21 days. Visas are required for longer stays; the maximum is 59 days. You'll need to fill out an application and provide one photo, at no charge. Company letter needed for business visa. AIDS test required for permanent residency; a U.S. test is accepted. For more information contact the following:

Embassy of the Philippines

1600 Massachusetts Avenue, N.W.
Washington, D.C. 20036
☎ *(202) 467-9300*

Or nearest consulate general at:

Hawaii, ☎ *(808) 595-6316*

New York, ☎ *(212) 764-1330*

Illinois, ☎ *(312) 332-6458*

Texas, ☎ *(713) 621-8609*

California, ☎ *(213) 387-5321 and (415) 133 6666*

Washington, ☎ *(206) 441-1640*

Arrival into the Philippines from abroad is primarily through Manila's Ninoy Aquino International Airport, a modern facility with 14 jetways. Located in nearby Pasay City, the airport is less than 30 minutes away by car to any major hotel and services an average of 170 international flights weekly. Manila is just over an hour by air from Hong Kong, three hours from Singapore, five from Tokyo, 17 hours from San Francisco and 22 hours from New York.

Several Southeast Asian regional carriers have direct flights into Zamboanga, Mindanao, and proposed international airports are due for Cebu City and Zamboanga.

PTICs are located at Ninoy Aquino International Airport (☎ *828-4791/828-1511*), Nayong Pilipino Complex, Airport Road (☎ *828-2219*) and on the ground floor, Philippine Ministry of Tourism (Ermita) building near Rizal Park in Metro Manila (☎ *501-703, 501-928*). Field offices are situated in Pampanga, Baguio, Legazpi, La Union, Bacolod, Cebu, Iloilo, Tacloban, Cagayan de Oro City Davao, Marawi and Zamboanga. The Department of Tourism hotline is ☎ *501-660/728*.

In North America, the Philippine Tourist Office has the following locations:

Philippine Center

556 Fifth Avenue
New York, NY 10036
☎ *(212) 575-7915*

Suite 1212, 3460 Wilshire Boulevard
Los Angeles, CA 90010
☎ *(213) 487-4525*

Suite 1111, 30 North Michigan Avenue
Chicago, IL 60602
☎ *(312) 782-1707*

The Philippines might be the world's second most popular sex tourist destination after Thailand. Although the U.S. squids have packed up and shipped out, horny foreigners keep the hookers gainfully employed in places like Angeles, Sabang and Subic City. If this is your thing, get hold of Asia File and subscribe to their newsletter, which handles the particulars of these places pretty thoroughly:

Asia File

P.O. Box 278537
Sacramento, CA 95827-8537
FAX: (916) 361-2364
e-mail: asiafile@earthlink.net

Accommodations, food and travel in the Philippines offer some of the best bargains found in Asia. The National Railway serves the island of Luzon, from Lagaspi in the south to San Fernando, La Union, in the north. Car rentals are available in the major cities, with or without a driver. Jeepneys are cheap and plentiful in Manila and other large towns. Domestic flights connect Manila daily with about 50 other towns, cities and rural areas. Where scheduled flights do not serve, there are aircraft for charter. Local service is bare-bones basic, with nothing offered but plastic cups of water. Allow plenty of time before departure for security inspection.

THE PHILIPPINES

Around the archipelago there are inter-island sea vessels with first-class accommodations that sail between several different ports daily.

If you find yourself in a pinch, or need quick transport out of the Philippines, you can charter a boat from Sitangkai for the 40-km trip to Semporna in the Malaysian state of Sabah. This, of course, is completely illegal. However, there are a slew of boats that make the trip from the Philippines to the busy market in Semporna. Keep in mind that Sabah has its own customs and immigration requirements, so you'll need a separate stamp when you move back and forth from Sabah to peninsular Malaysia. These waters are also home to Sulu pirates, actually a combination of minor smugglers and armed thugs who prey on large commercial vessels. Pirates have also been known to rob banks and terrorize entire towns in coastal Sabah. Just inquire at any fishing village or dockside hangout in Sitangkai. Usually, you'll have to cross at night, and don't be surprised to pay two to three times the normal rate of P$150. Going the other way is also easy; there are boatmen who can hook you up with the many speedboats that are for rent in Semporna. Be careful dealing with the Ray-Banned entrepreneurs you meet along the docks. They might turn you in for the reward money and simply pocket the sizable fee you paid them to get you across.

Leaving from Ninoy Aquino International or Domestic Airport can be a drag due to the tight security inspections. The airport taxes are P$500 for international flights and P$25 for domestic flights.

![Dangerous Places]

Mindanao

More than 10,000 firefights between government soldiers and rebel separatists as well as countless bombings and other politically motivated slayings have left 50,000 people dead over the last 30 years in the Philippines, most of them on the island of Mindanao. Sultan Kudarat is particularly dangerous. Government soldiers are regularly attacked by MILF guerrillas in this area, and surrounding parcels of land change hands regularly. Dangerous as well is Zamboanga, where a wave of bombing attacks by ASG terrorists rattled the city for six days in March 1996.

Basilan

This island, just southeast of Mindanao in the Moro Gulf, has been the scene of separatist activity for decades, if not centuries. Muslim separatists here prefer blowing up schools— as there is little else here to watch go kaboom.

Crime

Crime is high throughout the Philippines, particularly in urban areas. Many stores employ armed guards. There are 30 murders and three rapes per 100,000 people. There are 72 thefts for every 100,000 people.

Kidnapping

If you're a Chinese businessman living and/or working in the Philippines, consider wearing a mask or seeing a plastic surgeon, as you're the favorite target of kidnappers. Kidnappers like snatching Chinese guys for ransom, because their companies/embassies/families invariably will pay up. Filipino body snatchers aren't stupid. Kidnappers realize that if they take a Westerner, they'll have to feed the poor SOB for a couple of months, only then to get stormed by police commandos. In 1995, more than 160 people were abducted in the Philippines—many of them belonging to rich ethnic Chinese families—hauling in more than a US$3.6 million booty for the kidnappers. That's positive cash flow. Through the first eight weeks of 1997, kidnap gangs had seized 42 victims—most of them ethnic Chinese—making the Philippines the kidnapping capital of Asia. The kidnap rate in the Philippines, by mid-1997, reached one person a day. (Most anti-crime groups say the figure is much higher; about 1000 people are kidnapped every year in the Philippines, they say.). There are an estimated 40 different kidnapping syndicates in Manila alone.

Kidnapping by the Numbers

Kidnapping has become such a way of life in the Philippines that gangs now accept checks to cover their ransom demands. At least three Filipino-Chinese businessmen were quickly freed by kidnappers after they issued checks ranging from US$11,500 to US$38,000. One anticrime watch official stated that he doubts "if they gave stop payment instructions because the kidnappers would certainly have gotten back to them."

YEAR	NO. OF KIDNAPPINGS	RANSOMS PAID
1992	123	51
1993	104	28
1994	205	41
1995	199	N/A
1996	241	N/A
1997	370*	N/A

Source: Pinkerton (Asia) Limited
* estimated from DP sources

Being a Journalist

Investigative journalists in the Philippines may want to consider forwarding their CVs to "Hard Copy," or just simply getting the hell out of the Philippines. On June 3, 1997, Danny Hernandez, news editor of the *People's Journal Tonight*—the country's most popular tabloid daily—was shot dead in a taxi cab. He is believed to have been assassinated for his anti-crime reporting. Another anti-crime journalist, Albert Berbon of radio station DZMM, was assassinated outside his home in December 1996. A leading anti-crime group then stated: "If a radio reporter of the caliber of Bert Berbon could be killed in Mafia fashion, then it would not be difficult to comprehend that an ordinary Filipino citizen could be killed any time by people who wish them harm."

Shots for smallpox and cholera are not required for entry, but cholera shots are suggested when the Philippines appears on a weekly summary of areas infected (according to the World

Health Organization). Yellow fever vaccinations are required of all travelers arriving from infected areas. There is one doctor for every 6413 people in the Philippines. Medical care in the Philippines outside of Manila can be below Western standards, with some shortages of basic medical supplies. Access to the quality facilities that exist in major cities sometimes requires cash dollar payment upon admission. Most of the general hospitals are run privately. Malaria, once a big problem in the Philippines, has been eradicated in all but the most rural regions. Tuberculosis, respiratory and diarrheal diseases pose the biggest threats to travelers. The U.S. embassy and consulates maintain lists of health facilities and of English-speaking doctors. Drinking only boiled or bottled water will help to guard against cholera, which has been reported, as well as other diseases. More complete and updated information on health matters can be obtained from the Centers for Disease Control's international travelers' hotline, ☎ *(404) 332-4559*.

The world's second-largest archipelago after Indonesia, the Republic of the Philippines comprises 300,000 square kilometers (777,001 square miles) on 7107 islands in the South China Sea between Borneo to the southwest and Taiwan to the north; only 4600 are named and a mere 1000 are inhabited. The islands are in three main groups: the Luzon group, the Mindanao group and the Sulu and Visayan group. The country's 65.2 million inhabitants speak Tagalog and English. Roman Catholics comprise 83 percent of the population, Protestants, 9 percent, Muslim, 5 percent; and Buddhists, 3 percent. There are more than 100 ethnic groups in the country.

The Philippines has one of the developing world's highest literacy rates. Nearly every child in the country finishes primary school and nearly three-quarters of the population completes secondary school. The education system is based on the U.S. model. Although relatively highly educated, about 50 percent of Filipinos live at or below the poverty line, namely because economic expansion falls short of the country's population growth rate. The official currency is the Philippine peso. Approximately 26 pesos equal US$1. Hard foreign currency and traveler's checks are easily exchanged at banks, hotels and authorized money changers throughout the country. Credit cards are also now widely accepted.

Local time in the Philippines is GMT plus eight hours, i.e., exactly 13 hours ahead of Eastern Standard Time. Manila is in the same time zone as Beijing, Taipei, Macau, Kuala Lumpur, Singapore and Hong Kong, but one hour ahead of Seoul and Tokyo. It is one hour ahead of Bangkok, Jakarta, and 1-1/2 hours ahead of Yangon.

The local water is generally potable, except in remote rural areas. Hours of business in the Philippines are from 8 a.m. to 5 p.m. Monday through Friday, with most offices closed from noon to 1 p.m. or so. Banks open from 9 a.m. to 4 p.m. Monday through Friday. Shops in major tourist centers open at 9 or 10 a.m. until at least 7 p.m. daily.

Telephone, telex and fax services in the Philippines are surprisingly poor, and communication with the outside world is slower than you'll find in other parts of the Far East. Overseas calls take from 30 minutes to an hour to put through and are expensive, although IDD has arrived at the better hotels.

The local current is 220 volts/50 cycles—when there is power. One of the biggest infrastructural problems in the Philippines is electricity. The country experiences frequent and lengthy power outages on 258 out of the 297 working days each year.

Although the Philippines exports copper and is the world's largest supplier of refractory chrome, perhaps 90 percent of the country's natural resources have yet to be tapped, as the Philippines hasn't been largely surveyed.

Embassy Locations

United States Embassy

Roxas Boulevard, near the Manila Hotel
Manila
☎ *598-011.*

The Canadian Consulate

4th floor, Philippine Air Lines Building
Ayala Avenue
Makati
☎ *876-536.*

DANGEROUS DAYS

09/1996	Moro National Liberation Front agrees to a peace plane with the government.
02/25/1986	Marcos flees into exile in the U.S.
08/21/1983	Opposition leader Benigno Aquino shot to death by military police as he arrives in Manila after returning from self-exile.
01/17/1981	President Ferdinand Marcos ends eight years of martial law.
07/04/1946	Philippines gains independence.
12/08/1941	Japan invades the Philippines.

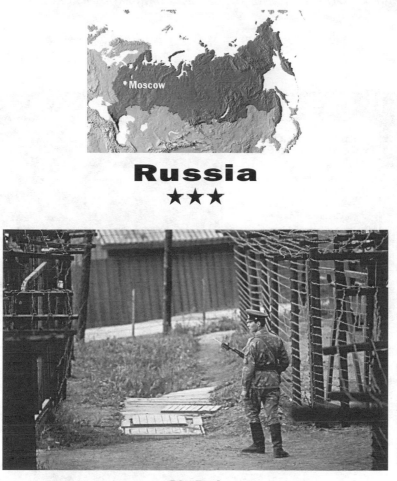

Moscow

Russia
★ ★ ★

Big Red

Russia is a mere six years into its experiment with democracy, but if its people are any richer than they were under the hammer and sickle (they're not), they're certainly not living any longer. War, disease, drugs, unemployment, crime, poverty and all those other frills of freedom are taking their toll on the erstwhile resilient Russians with a vengeance.

Male life expectancy has fallen a staggering seven years, to 58, since the flag of freedom was hoisted over the Kremlin. Men in Russia today live 15–17 fewer years than their counterparts in the U.S. and Western Europe. Russian men were more likely to reach 60 a century ago than they are today. Russia is being ravaged by a disease. It is CIS-positive, malignant with the growing pains of liberty, which Russians are abusing like a chemically dependent pharmacist. Russian men are 20 times more likely to be murdered than Western European males. In 1996, Russian men committed suicide and boozed themselves to death twice as much as they did in 1990. The war in Chechnya took the lives of some 4300 Russian soldiers. Tobacco causes nearly 300,000 deaths every year. Nuclear reactor leaks, en-

Commonwealth of Independent States

1. Adygea
2. Karachay-Cherkessia
3. Kabardino-Balkaria
4. North Ossetia
5. Checheno-Ingushetia

| 0 | 400 km |
| 0 | 400 mi |

©FWI

Svalbard (Norway)
Arkhangel'sk

Barents Sea

Baltic Sea
Finland
Karelia
Murmansk
White Sea
Kara Sea
Arkhangel'sk
Pechorskoye More
Kaliningrad
Estonia
Latvia
Lithuania
Pskov
St. Petersburg
Leningrad Oblast
Novgorod
Arkhangel'sk
Nenetsia AOk
Belarus
Vologda
Tver'
Komi
Smolensk
Yaroslavl'
Moscow
Kaluga
Ivanovo Kostroma
Moscow
Yamalia AOk
Bryansk
Vladimir
Orel
Tula
Nizhniy-Novgorod
Ryazan'
Kirov
Permyakia AOk
Ukraine
Kursk
Lipetsk
Mordovi
Mari El
Chuvashia
Perm'
Khantia Mansia AOk
Belgorod
Tambov
Penza
Ul'yanovsk
Tatarstan
Udmurtia
Voronezh
Sverdlovsk Oblast
Saratov
Samara
Bashkortostan
Rostov
Volgograd
Orenburg
Chelyabinsk
Tyumen'
Tomsk
Krasnodar Kray
Kalmy
Kurgan
Omsk
Novosibirsk
Kemerovo
Stavropol' Kray
Astrakhan'
Georgia
Dagestan
Altay Kray
Khaka
Armenia
Azerbaijan
Aral Sea
Kazakhstan
Gorno-Altay
Caspian Sea
Iran
Turkmenistan
Uzbekistan
Lake Balkhash
China

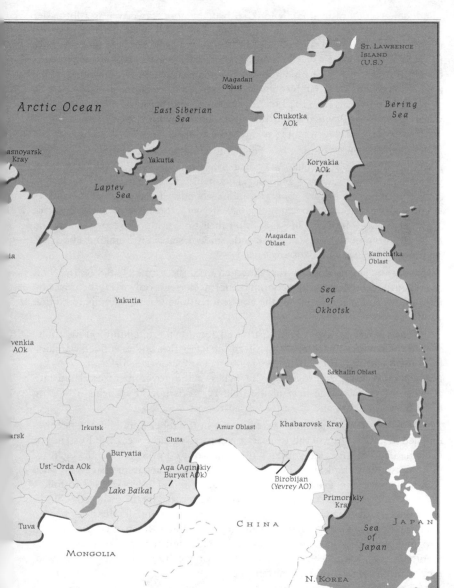

Arctic Ocean

East Siberian Sea

Krasnoyarsk Kray

Yakutia

Laptev Sea

ia

venkia AOk

arsk

Irkutsk

Ust'-Orda AOk

Tuva

MONGOLIA

Buryatia

Lake Baikal

Magadan Oblast

Chukotka AOk

ST. LAWRENCE ISLAND (U.S.)

Bering Sea

Koryakia AOk

Magadan Oblast

Kamchatka Oblast

Yakutia

Sea of Okhotsk

Sakhalin Oblast

Chita

Aga (Aginskiy Buryat AOk)

Amur Oblast

Khabarovsk Kray

Birobijan (Yevrey AO)

CHINA

Primorskiy Kray

Sea of Japan

JAPAN

N. KOREA

vironmental hazards—pollution and toxins in the soil—vodka, crime, civil war and a border with Caucasus that becomes more shredded each day with Islamic insurgencies spreading like lymphatic cancer are the ingredients of weeping Mother Russia today.

Suddenly communism doesn't look so bad anymore. Poverty was a lot easier when you could blame it on the U.S. imperialist aggressors. The only reason fewer people are feeling the pangs of indigence in Russia today is that there are fewer Russians around to feel anything. There have been a million more deaths than births each year in Russia since the days of the crowds at Lenin's tomb. If the population continues to fall by a million a year, in a half-century Russia won't be much more populous than the Los Angeles basin—but without the palm trees. A victory of sorts for Planned Parenthood, but a bad day for baby formula makers.

In December 1991, the Cold War ended when the Soviet Union collapsed. The high-flying Russian revolution had finally run out of gas and crashed. The jagged pieces totalled 12: Armenia, Azerbaijan, Belarus, Georgia, Kazakhstan, Kyrgyzstan, Moldova, Russia, Tajikistan, Turkmenistan, Ukraine and Uzbekistan. And most of these states are going through a secondary breakup, as ethnic and religious factions fight for sovereignty, usually with the help or antagonism of "Mother Russia," Iran or gangsters. After their brief taste of independence (and financial insolvency), many of these independent states are thinking about realigning themselves with Moscow.

Russia is the largest country that emerged from the former U.S.S.R. In 1992, Russia introduced an array of economic reforms that not only freed the prices on most goods and services, but set the course for a downward economic spiral that continues today.

Although President Boris Yeltsin survived a national referendum on his ability to lead the country in 1993, he dissolved the legislative bodies still left dangling from the Soviet era and signed a peace treaty. On October 3, 1993, tensions between the executive and legislative branches of the government escalated into armed conflict. With the help of the military, Boris got to keep his whopping $21,000 a year salary and free Moscow apartment.

A December 1994 attempt to take Grozny in the rebel Republic of Chechnya revealed in a rebel rout of the Russian forces precisely how weak the Russian war machine had become, and subsequent events showed even greater disorganization. Yeltsin may think he is in charge, but it became apparent that when push comes to shove, the army will decide. Renegade commanders refused to follow orders or never received them. Russian soldiers captured by the insurgent Chechens revealed that they were without food and maps—essentially that they had no direction nor any idea of what the hell they were doing. Russian corpses littered Grozny like dead worms after a heavy rain. Although the vastly superior forces eventually took the Chechen capital in 1995 only to retreat in August of 1996, they've faced a repeat of Afghanistan since.

However, crime may be Russia's biggest export in the next decade. The brutal control of a central government has been reborn in the form of Russian Mafias. In Russia, there are an average of 84 murders a day; many are contract killings, according to the Ministry of the Interior. In 1996, at least 200 Russian business executives were whacked by the Chechen Mafia in Moscow alone. Compare the rate of 16 murders per 100,000 in Russia to the U.S. rate of nine per 100,000, and you can see why even trigger-happy Americans look like Buddhist monks next to the Russians. Someone is murdered in Russia every 18 minutes. Sixty percent of the murders are for material gain, and 20 percent are thought to be murders of gangsters by rival gangs. In fact, there are more gangsters than there are police in Russia. Less than half of all perpetrators are ever brought to justice.

There is more afoot than just thuggery in Russia. Tired of polishing their ICBMs and rotating their nuclear weapons, some army units have decided to strip them down into more economically attractive components and, by doing so, generate a little cash. In 1993, there were 6430 reports of stolen weapons, ranging from assault rifles to tanks. To date, there have been more than 700 reports of nuclear material being sold to various buyers outside and inside Russia. On the black market, a kilo of chromium-50 can go for $25,000, cesium-137 for $1 million and lithium-6 for $10 million. Prospective customers for these goodies are Iran, North Korea, Libya and other nations looking for a big bang for their money.

Russia's myriad woes defy being capsulized. Chechnya is giving Colombia and the Philippines a run for their ransoms as the kidnap capitals of the world. Five Russian TV journos snatched earlier in 1997 are still missing. A police crackdown has netted dozens of hostage-takers. The Russian military remains in shambles. More than 10 Russian soldiers die each day from non-combat causes—including suicide and malnourishment. The Chechens should have just waited for the Russkies to off themselves. (The Russian population decreases by 1.2 million people a year.) To boost dismal morale and put more potatoes on the officers' plates, Boris has started peddling anti-aircraft missiles to Cyprus, despite threats of force from Turkey, which would assuredly kick Boris' behind in a full-auto pistol polo match. Now that Yeltsin has been invited into the Boys Club of the Eight, he gets his mug on CNN more, but still has to deal with Russia's nemesis supreme: Afghanistan. Afghanistan has been a burr between Moscow's buns for two decades—hastening the collapse of the USSR—and the *taliban* doesn't bode well for Mother Vodka. Once again, Moscow is faced with possible military intervention (a Russian oxymoron), as Afghanistan has become a staging ground for Islamic insurgents seeking to topple the Russian-backed government in Tajikistan. Drinking games aside, Boris fears a domino effect if the *taliban* gets a foothold in Tajikistan. Turkmenistan and Uzbekistan would surely be next. Russia's military can hardly afford another ass-kicking.

It's amazing enough that Boris' button-pushers even possess this information at all. Kremlin intelligence (another Russian oxymoron) has been as ravaged as the army. The dreaded KGB has been replaced by the threaded FSB (Shit For Brains), who are so hard up for good spies and information other than Iditarod scores that they've set up a telephone hot-line to bring Russian agents spying for foreign intelligence services back into the fold. That's right! Turncoat agents can now call a special number and turn themselves in! Callers are immune from prosecution and can continue to collect CIA, MI6 and Mossad paychecks, but are asked in return to provide those spook agencies with bogus information. Wow. In Russia, a mole is a birthmark with a bunch of hairs growing out of it.

Russia has reverted back to a 19th-century society of potato farmers. But potato farmers with nukes. The middle class, a key to a successful democracy, is dissolving like cheap dentures in an acid bath. The rank-and-file of the army hasn't been paid in months. Russia will never be the West. Look for a military coup and a scenario that makes the Cold War look like a hockey game.

It Doesn't Get Much Worse...

Boris Yeltsin has decreed that government officials will have to exchange their Mercedes and other luxury imported cars for domestic Volga sedans. The luxury cars will be sold by the government at open auctions. This comes at a time when millions of Russians haven't seen a paycheck for months. Some bureaucrats have put in a request for two Volgas to replace a single Mercedes because Volgas "break down so much," said one.

The Russian Mafia (*Organizatsiya* or Mafyia)

The Russian Interior Ministry says that in 1993, police uncovered 5700 organized crime groups and brought charges against 11,400 people. One-sixth of these groups were working in more than one region, while 300 were operating outside Russia's borders. The report also claimed that 150 major criminal societies controlled 35,000 enterprises. Most crime in Russia is controlled by eight "families," such as the Chechens, the most powerful group and descendants of a centuries-old tribe who still control the Caucasus Mountains. The Chechens specialize in bank fraud and extortion. Some $12 billion gets flushed out of Russia each year into accounts in Switzerland and Cyprus, according to a February 1997 report. The Russian Mafia has about $10 billion in Swiss bank accounts. Half of Russia's banks and 80 percent of the joint ventures involving foreign capital have connections with organized crime.

The Government

What government?

Show Me The Money

The average Russian makes $1700 a year. An army lieutenant makes $1000 a year and a senior civil servant makes a $2000 a year salary. The Russian prime minister makes righteous bucks: $8000 per year. Even Boris isn't in the 28-percent tax bracket. The Russian president makes a mere $21,000 a year, about the same as an experienced sandwich-maker at Subway.

The Army

The army is slowly building back its power base in Russia and the CIS but is still as disheveled as a Moscow drunk. In Chechnya alone, Russia lost 4300 soldiers. Another 703 were MIA, and 705 deserted. The army finds itself the target of organized criminals. In some areas, army commanders rent out weapons and men are hired out as mercenaries to the highest bidder. It's not a very tight ship. More than 6000 crimes involving corruption and embezzlement were committed in the Russian armed forces in 1996, double the figure of three years ago. More than 20 generals were being investigated as of mid-1997, many in housing schemes. An estimated 110,000 troops lack proper housing, and 428 soldiers committed suicide in 1996. In the spring of that year, Yeltsin announced that conscription would end in Russia by 2000, causing Moscow's Generation Xers to party in the streets. It was an empty campaign pledge. Russia cannot afford an all-volunteer army until 2005 at the earliest, Boris' defense minister has said. Bummer. Induced by a chronic food shortage, many soldiers have resorted to begging. And thousands of soldiers died in 1996 from acts of torture and ill treatment by other soldiers. The Kremlin's army has shrunk to a measly 1.7 million soldiers. Russia's version of web-surfing is draft-dodging.

A reason for the army's decline is quite simple, really; Russia took over 85 percent of the Soviet Union's armed forces and only 65 percent of its economic potential.

Perestrelka

No, not *perestroika*, a word used by Mikhail Gorbachev to symbolize reforms. *Perestrelka* means "shoot-out" in Russian and is a better description of what is going on in Russia today.

The military vacuum in Russia has allowed the rise of the *vory v zzakone*, or thieves in law. A class of thugs created before the revolution and toughened in Soviet gulags, these gangsters are enamored with pomp and circumstance and even possess private jets. The government estimates that there are 289 "thieves in law" operating in Russia and 28 other countries around the world. Below these very wealthy and powerful Mafia figures are the gangs. There are about 20 criminal brigades, or gangs, that control Moscow with L.A.-style monikers for their neighborhoods. There are estimated to be 5800 gang members in Russia. The gangs aren't quick or smart enough to control the country, so it's left to the *vory v zzakone* to reap the profits of absolute control.

There are four levels of Mafia in Russia. The lowest stratum consists of shopkeepers who sell goods at inflated prices to afford protection money. The enforcers are burly, loud men with a fancy for imported cars (usually stolen). They'll also double as pimps, gunrunners and drug dealers. The businessmen are unfettered capitalists who steer most of the lucrative deals the Mafia's way.

Finally, at the top of the food chain, is the "state Mafia." They are the controllers of a large percentage of the money earned by the lesser Mafia. These politicians/gangsters allow the lower echelons to operate in peace and without fear of prosecution. They have driven away a lot of Western investment and businessmen who find themselves forced to retain a local "partner" in their enterprises.

A passport and Russian visa are required for all U.S. citizens traveling to or transiting through Russia by any means of transportation, including train, car or airplane. While under certain circumstances travelers who hold valid visas to some countries of the former Soviet Union may not need a visa to transit Russia, such exceptions are inconsistently applied. Travelers who arrive without an entry visa may be subject to large fines, days of processing requirements by Russian officials and/or immediate departure by route of entry (at the traveler's expense). Carrying a photocopy of passports and visas will facilitate replacement should either be stolen.

All Russian visas, except transit visas, are issued on the basis of support from a Russian individual or organization, known as the sponsor. It is important to know who your sponsor is and how they can be contacted, as Russian law requires that your sponsor apply on your behalf for replacement and extension of or changes to your visa. The U.S. embassy cannot act as your sponsor. Tourists should contact their tour company or hotel in advance for information on visa sponsorship.

For current information on visa requirements, U.S. citizens can contact the Russian consulates in New York, San Francisco or Seattle or the embassy:

Russian Embassy

Consular Division
1825 Phelps Place, N.W.
Washington, D.C. 20008
☎ *(202) 939-8918, 939-8907, or 939-8913*

All foreigners must have an exit visa in order to depart Russia. For short stays, the exit visa is issued together with the entry visa; for longer stays, the exit visa must be obtained by the sponsor after the traveler's arrival. Russian law requires that all travelers who spend more than three days in Russia register their visas through their hotel or sponsor. Visitors who stay in Russia for a period of weeks may be prevented from leaving if they have not registered their visas. Errors in the dates or other information on the visa can occur, and it is helpful to have someone who reads Russian check the visa before you depart the United States.

Many areas along Russia's southern borders are not manned, and checkpoints are only on main roads. Russian soldiers can be bribed due to their low pay and acceptance of side income.

Internal travel, especially by air, can be erratic and may be disrupted by fuel shortages, overcrowding of flights and various other problems. Travelers may need to cross great distances, especially in Siberia and the Far East, to obtain services from Russian government organizations or from the U.S. embassy or its consulates. Russia stretches over 6000 miles east to west and 2500 miles north to south. Winter can last a long time.

Unlike the old days, you can go just about anywhere you want these days. You don't even need to use Intourist to get around. The cheapest way into Moscow from Cheremkhovo airport is via the regular bus. You can use rubles. Taxis usually require long waits and one *DP* reader suggests having your sponsor pick you up at the airport. You can also pick up a private car from one of the many people who will try to offer you one. Expect to pay $50 in real money (not rubles) or the equivalent amount in cigarettes. You run the risk of getting waylaid or robbed if you take the wrong car. For about the same price, you can arrange a car in the arrivals section. You must use a credit card. In Moscow, most taxis demand U.S. dollars, or one to three packs of cigarettes, or R10 to R20.

About half the roads in Russia are paved. The worst time to traverse Russian roads is during the spring, when the rural roads become muddy rivers. About 20 percent of the roads are simple tracks. The railways are the major means of transport, with most routes spreading out from Moscow on 11 major trunk lines. There are 32 railway subsystems within the former Soviet Union. The main route is the passenger artery through Russia along the Trans-Siberian Railway, which travels east from Moscow across Siberia to the Pacific and China, Mongolia and Korea.

Traveling by sea is also an efficient way to get around Russia, particularly in the Baltic. Twenty-seven former Soviet passenger ships form the largest such fleet in the world.

Russian airlines service 3600 population centers inside Russia. Airlines are viewed as busses with wings so don't expect much. The severe winters can affect schedules and flights into places like Tajikistan are subject to fuel shortages. The telecommunications infrastructure remains underdeveloped. Only 30 percent of urban and 9 percent of rural families have telephones. More than 17 million customers have ordered telephones, but are still waiting (sometimes for years) to have them installed.

All items which may appear to have historical or cultural value—icons, art, rugs, antiques, etc.—may be taken out of Russia only with prior written approval of the Ministry of Culture and payment of a 100 percent duty. Goods that are purchased from street vendors can be problematic and expensive to export. Russian customs laws state that any item for export valued at more than 300,000 rubles (value is established by customs officials at the time of export—for example, just prior to a traveler's departing flight) is subject to a 600 percent export tax. Items purchased from government-licensed shops, where prices are openly marked in hard currency, are not subject to the tax. Request a receipt when making any purchase.Caviar may only be taken out of Russia with a receipt indicating it was bought in a store licensed to sell to foreigners. Failure to follow the customs regulations may result in temporary or permanent confiscation of the property in question.

Embassy and Consulate Locations and Phone Numbers

Moscow

Novinskiy Bulvar 19/23
☎ *[7] (095) 252-2451.*
After-hours duty officer: ☎ *[7] (095) 230-2001/2601.*

U.S. Consulate General in St. Petersburg

Ulitsa Furshtadskaya 15
☎ *[7] (812) 275-1701.*
After-hours duty officer: ☎ *[7] (812) 274-8692.*

U.S. Consulate General in Vladivostok

12 Mordovtseva
☎ *[7] (4232) 268-458/554 or 266-820.*

Consulate General in Yekaterinburg

☎ *[7] (3432) 601-143*
FAX [7] (3432) 601-181
Provides emergency services for American citizens.

The situation remains unsettled in Russia's north Caucasus area, which is located in southern Russia along its border with Georgia. Travel to this area is considered dangerous. The regions of the Chechen Republic, the Ingush Republic and the North Ossetian Republic have experienced continued armed violence and have a state of emergency and curfew in effect.

The Caucasus

In Nagorno-Karabakh, Armenians have been fighting for independence from Azerbaijan since 1988. More than 3000 people have died, according to a count in 1992. Things are quiet now, but *DP* wouldn't recommend buying any real estate any time soon.

Georgia

In Georgia, fighting in the south Ossetia region and the Mingrelia area has killed hundreds since 1989. In May of 1991, Zvaid Gamsakhurdia was elected president of Georgia with an overwhelming majority of the popular vote (86.5 percent). Not content with popular support, Zvaid began to conceive and implement very undemocratic statutes, such as "making fun of the president gets you six years in the slammer." He also put his money on the wrong ponies when he backed the coup plotters who failed to overthrow Yeltsin. He cracked down on the southern Muslim state of Ossetia, which instigated a revolt effective enough to force him to flee on January 6, 1992. The opposition, which consisted of his prime minister and foreign minister (who had backed Yeltsin), invited Eduard Shevardnadze, the former Soviet foreign minister and first secretary of the Georgian Communist Party, to be chairman of the state council.

The return of old hard-line communist hacks did not satisfy the Muslim Abkhazian separatists, who, feeling their oats, had taken over the Abkhazian region along the Black Sea.

The Russians meddled and brokered a cease-fire, which was quickly broken on September 16, 1993. Despite a pistol-waving Shevardnadze, the rebels took over the strategic Black Sea port of Sukhumi. The bizarre twist is that Shevardnadze blames the Russians for setting him up by brokering a phony cease-fire and then letting the rebels take over the country. The fact that the "rebels" were using Russian-supplied weapons and equipment confirmed the perception that the Russians were backing the Abkhazians.

Additionally, there is the continual threat of Zvaid Gamsakhurdia and his efforts to set up his own republic in Mingrelia.

(See "Georgia")

Moscow

In Moscow alone, in 1993, there were 5000 murders and 20,000 incidents of violent crime. The local population easily recognizes U.S. tourists and business travelers as foreigners because of their clothing, accessories and behavior. American visitors tend to experience a relatively high incidence of certain types of crime, such as physical assaults and pickpocketing of wallets, traveler's checks, passports and cameras on the street, in hotels, in restaurants and in high-density tourist areas.

St. Petersburg

St. Petersburg has a crime rate 30 percent higher than Moscow's. The area around Gostiniy Dvor and the underground passage on Nevsky Prospekt, as well as train stations, the food markets, the flea markets and the so-called "art park" are frequent stages for street crime against foreigners. It is estimated that 20 percent of the foreign businesses are controlled by the Russian Mafia. Most groups who try to set up businesses in the city find they are hit up for a $10,000 fee to arrange the "necessary contacts." If you are edgy, bodyguards can be hired for about $600 a month (U.S. dollars only). Not bad, when you figure that the average monthly wage is about $20. Most crimes are committed in broad daylight, since the police will do little, if anything, to help or track down your assailants. If you are staying in one of the better hotels in St. Petersburg, have them send a car for you at the airport. If not, you can take a taxi into town for about $30. If you want a car for the entire day, figure on spending about double that.

Emergency Numbers

Fire	**Hard Currency Taxi**
☎ *01*	☎ *298-6804, 298-3648*
Police	**Western-Style Medical Care**
☎ *02*	☎ *310-9611*
Ambulance	**American Express**
☎ *03*	☎ *311-5215*
U.S. Consulate	**Delta Airlines**
☎ *274-8692*	☎ *311-5819/20/22*
Taxi	
☎ *312-0022*	

Chechnya and the "Chechens"

A remote Trans-Caucasian region just north of Georgia, the Republic of Chechnya is home to Russia's largest and most powerful crime families. In fact, they have a friendly neighborhood branch in what may be your own hometown (Boston, Philadelphia, Chicago, Los Angeles and New York). The Chechens told Yeltsin to get stuffed during the winter of 1991, and Boris must have thought they meant snuffed. Boris turned his eyes away for a while, but then launched one of the most bloody military attacks in Russian history that has so far killed more than 80,000 people.

There were, at last report, about 1500 Chechens living in Moscow. Many came back to Chechnya after the outbreak of hostilities to fight Yeltsin's army. The "Chechens" in Moscow are really an old-line crime family originally from Chechnya or Chechestan, one extremely difficult to infiltrate or join, unless you are a member of the family.

The Chechens are split into three main criminal factions. The most powerful is the "Central," followed by the "Ostankinsky" and the "Automobile." Finding these groups used to be easy, as they operated from plush Moscow hotels until the war. The Centrals could be found in the Hotel Belgrade, the Golden Ring and the Russia Hotel. Here, they controlled drugs, prostitution, restaurants, Moscow markets and the retail trade. The Ostankinsky takes its name from the Ostankinsky Hotel. The group is also headquartered in the Voskhod and Baikal hotels. Their specialty is the transfer and shipment of all types of goods (including drugs) between Moscow and their home base of Chechnya. The "Automobile" group brings in cars from Western Europe and looks after seven gas stations.

The transport and sale of drugs are a major source of income for the Chechens. They also employ the time-honored method of extortion to supplement their income. Everyone from street vendors to major international corporations have to cough up about 10 percent of their gross or face the music. The Chechens are linked to the three main Italian Mafia families as well as members of the former Soviet government, the KGB and former Soviet Communist Party members. See "Chechnya."

Tajikistan

Afghanistan-based Tajik guerrillas continue their attacks against Russian border posts and inside the country. Russian planes have been bombing rebel positions inside Afghanistan. The Russians have tracked dozens of Arab mercenaries on their way to aid the insurgents, armed with Stinger missiles and mines. See "Tajikistan."

Train and Metro Stations

Many attacks against tourists take place on trains (both city and national) and in the subways. The Trans-Siberian Railway is a common target of organized gangs of criminals who rob, rape and murder passengers. Russian businesses have stopped sending any valuable commodities through Chechnya.

Airlines

Airline passengers are more likely to be killed in Russia than anywhere else in the world. The number of fatalities per million passengers has risen from one in 1990 to 5.5 in 1993. The breakup of Aeroflot into hundreds of regional carriers that cannot afford to properly maintain their planes has a lot to do with it. Pilots, who make an average of $21 a month, have even spoken out.

Shari'a Law & Russian Jails

If living in Chechnya, it pays to be a Russian and not a Muslim. Shari'a law in Chechnya dictates that convicted murderers have their throats slit, while non-Muslims committing the same offense can expect a cozy, lifelong stay in the slammer. However, not all lifers are smelling the roses in Russia. In a recent survey among Russian prisoners whose death sentences had been commuted to life terms in prison, 20 percent said they preferred death. Lifers are sent to brutal, hard-labor prison camps in Siberia. Many are confined to tiny cells for 23 hours a day.

Nuclear Plants

The Russians handle plutonium like a strainer does water. And it seems Chernobyl did little to motivate nuclear engineers to screw the bolts in a little tighter. An April 1997 toxic leak (cadmium dimethyl) at Nizhny Novgorod's nuclear power plant sent 43 people to the hospital. The environmental group Greenpeace said that toxic discharges from nuclear and chemical plants, factories and burning trash dumps are poisoning almost three-quarters of Russia. God knows what would happen should these folks try to launch an ICBM.

The Water

Fully 70 percent of Russia's tap water is not safe for human consumption.

Cannibals

The Russians' propensity for eating each other makes Jeffrey Dahmer look like a Napa Valley wine taster. Reports of cannibalism fail to make headlines in a country where most are scrounging for their next crumb of bread. Sasha Spesivtsev is awaiting trial on 19 counts of murder, whose victims he shared with his mother at the dining room table. In the southern town of Krasnodar, another guy was caught munching on human flesh after stir-frying it over the stove. A day earlier, a Kemerovo man was busted for killing a man and cooking him to eat with his drinking buddies. A prisoner in the Siberian town of Barnaul was given the death sentence for chowing down his cell mate. Cannibals in Russia have plenty of time to fatten up, as well. Police rarely look for murder victims during the winter. There's too much snow.

Bogus Vodka

Talk about a hangover; in Russia, one of every six bottles of Russian-made vodka is hazardous for human consumption. Some 340,000 cases of counterfeit vodka that were brought to Moscow in June 1997 aboard 70 railroad cars were sent to a chemical plant for reprocessing into car windshield cleanser and brake fluid. Perhaps because these concoctions are more palate-friendly.

Crime

In a place where hiring a hit man to kill someone costs only $200, you had better watch your step. Foreigners are targets of crime in Russia, especially in major cities. Pickpocketing and muggings occur both day and night. Street crimes are most frequent in train stations, airports and open markets; on the Moscow-St. Petersburg overnight train; and when hailing taxis or traveling by the Metro late at night. Groups of children who beg for money sometimes pickpocket and assault tourists. Foreigners' hotel rooms and residences have also been targeted. Some victims have been seriously assaulted during robberies. If you receive a replacement for your lost or stolen U.S. passport from the U.S. embassy or a consulate in Russia, your exit visa must also be replaced, with assistance from your sponsor, so that the passport number written on the visa matches your new passport. This normally requires a Russian police report.

Older people are also targets of crime in Russia. In addition, there has been a sharp rise in the number of taxi drivers killed while on duty. Policemen have been killed at their posts. And, to make matters worse, Russian jails are becoming overcrowded. An expected 40,000 prisoners in Russian jails have been, or are expected to be, released earlier than scheduled, much earlier. The government has been calling it amnesty. Keep up your guard.

Even more so if you decide to hire a guard. There are 9800 private security firms registered in Russia. And of the 5000 firms inspected by the Interior Ministry in 1996, 10 percent had criminal connections.

Extortion

Apart from the street muggings, which are the most dangerous thing in Russia, extortion is number two. If you're lucky, you'll get mugged and hit up for a bribe. Russians say that 70 to 80 percent of businesses pay extortion demands to criminal groups. Only about 10 to 15 foreigners file extortion charges each year.

Kidnapping

Foreigners are routinely kidnapped because they bring higher ransoms than locals. In Chechnya, the problem is particularly bad. In the first four months of 1997, a special unit of the Chechen police busted nearly three-dozen hostage-takers.

Drinking, Eating and Smoking

If murder doesn't take out most Russians, vodka will. Russian deaths as a result of disease caused by toxins such as alcohol and nicotine are rising at an alarming rate. There was a 20 percent increase in alcohol poisoning between 1993 and 1994, and a 17.9 percent increase in infectious disease in the same period. Russians are famous for their love of vodka, heavy, greasy foods and smoking. Stress, leading to cardiovascular disease, is another big killer. One disease not commonly reported as a cause of death is cancer. Russia produces 75 million tons of toxic waste each year. It also does not have a single toxic waste treatment center.

Kids

Crimes by kids pose a unique threat to the population. Adolescents, often unemployed, travel and operate criminally in groups. One may also find younger boys of ages 10 to 12 operating in small groups or as individuals. The groups may have an adult ringleader for whom the kids work. If you're a victim of youth crime in Russia, especially in the cities, contact the police and fill out a report. In many instances, youths strike in the same place, employing similar methods, making them easier to catch. Some foreigners have also reported successes in catching thieves by advertising on local TV stations.

Overnight Trains

Thieves routinely rob the sleeping berths in overnight trains throughout Russia. The problem is most acute along the Moscow-St. Petersburg route. The common M.O. is for the thief to drug victims before robbing them.

Police

An alarming trend in Russia is the growing police involvement in crimes against fellow Russians and foreigners. This is particularly worrisome in Moscow and St. Petersburg. In other instances, the police may not come to the aid of a crime victim, even if the crime is being committed in their presence.

Some Helpful Hints from the Locals

A booklet titled *How Not to Become a Crime Victim/Advice of Professionals*, published by the Leningrad Association of Workers, offers advice to citizens on avoiding crime. Here's an excerpt:

- **Make purchases at reputable outlets.**

- **Count your change carefully before leaving the cashier or the seller. Recount your change if the seller has recounted it a second time because of a problem, to make sure you have not been tricked during the recounting.**

- **Check to make sure that the article you believe you have purchased is the one that is packed for you.**

- **Do not invite people you do not know well into your living quarters or drink alcohol with them, to avoid the possibility of being drugged.**

- **Do not open the door to your quarters to unknown individuals.**

- **If you feel you are being followed, apply to the police for help.**

- **Do not get into an elevator alone with a stranger.**

- **If you are in trouble, yell *pozhar* (fire) to attract attention for aid.**

- **Be constantly aware and on the alert.**

St. Petersburg security office recommendations:

- Dress down and do not flash cash or jewelry.

- Do not tell strangers where you are staying or your travel plans.

- Avoid crowds. Although this is difficult to do, do not let your curiosity get the better of you. Leave the area as soon as you can.

- When deciding when and where to make your purchases or to change money, do not place convenience over your personal security. Street vendors are certainly more convenient, but dealing with them necessitates that you subject yourself to the scrutiny of bystanders who will make note of the location of your passport, money and other valuables. In many instances shortly after making a purchase, the customer falls victim to street thieves.

- Do not purchase drinks from already-opened bottles; i.e., in bars.

- When out on the town, leave hard-to-replace, nonessential items, such as passports, credit cards, driver's licenses and family pictures, with the hotel security office or at home. Disperse your money throughout your garments. Remember the amounts in each location and when making purchases retrieve only the amount of money needed for that purchase. Never display large sums of money.

- Do not believe that you are getting a bargain. When you believe this, watch out; chances are that you are being set up. Thieves understand and utilize human emotions such as greed and lust. Situations in which these emotions are most commonly played upon include dealings with vendors of so-called "antiquities," with prostitutes and in currency exchanges.

- Never patronize unmarked taxis or enter any taxi carrying unfamiliar passengers. Agree upon the price and destination prior to entering the vehicle.

- If you have a car with you, do not leave any items inside the vehicle when it is parked. These items will be attractive to thieves and will encourage break-ins. Also, remove windshield wiper blades when parked. Do not park in dark and isolated places.

- Never drink alcoholic beverages without having a trusted friend along who has agreed to remain sober. Even slight intoxication is noted by professional thieves.

- When a victim of a crime, be it a violent act or general trickery, do not let your vanity or apathy prevent you from immediately making a report to the police and U.S. embassy or consulate. Others will benefit. In addition, stolen items are routinely retrieved.

GETTING SICK

Medical care in Russia is usually far below Western standards, with severe shortages of basic medical supplies. Access to the few quality facilities that exist in major cities usually requires payment in dollars at Western rates upon admission. The U.S. embassy and consulates have a list of good facilities and of English-speaking doctors. Many expats travel outside of Russia for most of their medical needs. Travelers may wish to check their insurance coverage and consider supplemental coverage for medical evacuation.

An outbreak of diphtheria continues in Moscow, St. Petersburg, and other parts of Russia. Although only a small number of cases have been reported, up-to-date diphtheria immunizations are recommended. Typhoid can be a concern for those who plan to travel extensively in Russia. Drinking only boiled or bottled water will help to guard against cholera, which has been reported, as well as other diseases. More complete and updated information on health matters can be obtained from the Centers for Disease Control's international travelers' hotline, ☎ *(404) 332-4559.*

The Russian Federation is the largest republic of the CIS; it's almost twice the size of the United States. Moscow, with nearly 9 million residents, is the largest city.

The Russian Federation officially came into existence in December 1991. Russia is a presidential republic, containing 22 autonomous republics that maintain an uneasy balance between the Russian president and the Congress of People's Deputies (parliament). In practice, the power base is much more complex. Russia's vast size (10.5 million square km) and population (148 million) could make the region ripe for exploitation by Western investors; the corrupt infrastructure, however, makes business profits unlikely for years to come.

Russian is the official language, although there are many local ethnic tongues. English is widely read but not yet fluently spoken. Translators, of varying abilities, will be found in all sizable organizations. The country boasts a nearly 100 percent literacy rate.

Business hours are from 9 a.m. to 1 p.m., with a break for the typical heavy Russian lunch between 1 and 2 p.m. Some stores close from 2 to 3 p.m. Banks are open from 9:30 a.m. to 12:30 p.m., with currency exchanges open longer. You can change money at Sheremetyevo II International Airport in Moscow 24 hours a day. Also, the American Express office in Moscow can cash your Amex traveler's checks into dollars.

Russia is $80 billion in debt but still manages to keep finding major oil fields, such as the Tenghiz field in Kazakhstan. The field is estimated to contain between 7 and 25 billion barrels of oil. The Azeri oil field in the Caspian Sea and the Timan Pechora basin in the north Russian Archangels province will help to pay off that debt. The former U.S.S.R. had about 6.4 percent of the world's oil reserves and was the world's largest producer and exporter of natural gas. However, poor management has led to annual decreases each year since the 1980s.

Gas comes from western Siberia; the largest areas are Urengoi and Yamburg. New fields on the Yamal peninsula are waiting for development. The former U.S.S.R. was the world's third-largest coal producer in 1990 (after China and the United States). Russia possesses the world's largest explored reserves of copper, lead, zinc, nickel, mercury and tungsten. It also has about 40 percent of the world's reserves of iron ore and manganese. Figures released in September 1990 show confirmed iron reserves of 33.1 billion tons. The world's largest gold deposits at the Sukhoi Log reserves are estimated at more than 1000 tons, much of which is smuggled out of Russia through the Baltic States. Russia is also trying to retain more control over its diamond reserves. The government created the Federal Diamond Centre, granting parliament more control over the industry. The intent is to weaken control over Russia's diamonds by DeBeers, which has operated a supply cartel and maintained Russia's output at 7,500,000 carats per year.

Russia will be a net food importer for some time to come. In 1990, though, there were record harvests, but despite this wealth, a shortage of labor caused the crops to rot in the fields.

Arms sales continue to be an important part of Russia's exports, although there is worldwide concern that a lot of high-tech systems are getting into the wrong hands. In 1992, Russia sold more than $2 billion worth of weapons through contracts with China, India, Iran and Syria.

Useful Addresses and Phone Numbers

British-Russian Chamber of Commerce

60a Pembroke Road
London W8 6NX
☎ *[44] (71) 602-7692*
Services for members: (Moscow office)
group visits to Russia, seminars in conjunction with Oxford University scholars
and others.

Department of Trade and Industry,
Russia Desk

Overseas Trade Division
1 Victoria Street
London SW1 0ET
☎ *[44] (71) 215-5265/4268*
FAX [44] (71) 222-2531/2629

Consulate of Russia

Kensington Palace Gardens
London W8 4QS
☎ *[44] (71) 229-3215/6*

EETC GUS-Russia Trade
and Economic Council

805 Third Avenue
New York, New York 10022
☎ *(212) 644 4550*

The official currency is the ruble; it's pointless to post its rate against the U.S. dollar, since it changes as frequently as most people change their underwear. But at press time, 5000 rubles=US$1. There are 100 kopeks to the ruble. Electricity is 220V/50Hz.

Money Hassles

Traveler's checks and credit cards are not widely accepted in Russia; in many cities, credit cards are only accepted at establishments catering to Westerners. Old, or very worn, dollar bills are often not accepted, even at banks. Major hotels or the American Express offices in Moscow or St. Petersburg may be able to suggest locations for cashing traveler's checks or obtaining cash advances on credit cards. Western Union has agents in Moscow, St. Petersburg and some other large cities that can disburse money wired from the United States.

Better Living Through Chemistry

Russia's drug addicts number 1.5 million (or 1 percent of the entire population), and the figure keeps growing. Illegal hemp fields in Russia cover an area exceeding 40 million hectares. During a recent eight-month period, Russian law enforcement bodies made arrests in connection with 40,000 drug-related crimes, seizing 13.3 tons of various drugs. Police have busted 3300 gangs engaged in drug trafficking and sale. From 30 to 35 percent of the drugs are imported. In Moscow and St. Petersburg, however, the figure reaches 80 to 90 percent.

The price of one gram of cocaine in Moscow is from 400 to 900 percent higher than in New York, for which reason the Russian drug market looks very attractive to the international Mafia. The drug trade in Russia is a $100 million-a-year business. The police force fighting drug dealers today numbers as few as 3500. Police are especially concerned that a new synthetic drug–trinisilsyntholin–is being produced in Russia. It formerly had only been produced in the U.S. The substance is so strong that one gram of it is enough to make 10 liters of narcotics more powerful than heroin or cocaine. Imported drugs, such as heroin and cocaine, are now sold everywhere in this country. In Moscow, for instance, the price of one gram of heroin ranges from $200 to $300.

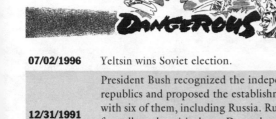

07/02/1996	Yeltsin wins Soviet election.
12/31/1991	President Bush recognized the independence of all 12 former Soviet republics and proposed the establishment of full diplomatic relations with six of them, including Russia. Russian President Yeltsin responded formally and positively on December 31, 1991, the date officially considered to be when the U.S. established formal diplomatic relations with Russia.
12/25/1991	Mikhail Gorbachev resigned as president of the Soviet Union and transferred control of the Soviet nuclear arsenal to Russian President Boris Yeltsin. A few hours later, the United States recognized Russia as the successor state to the Soviet Union. These actions marked the end of the Soviet Union, 74 years after the Bolshevik revolution.
12/21/1991	Russia joined with 10 other former republics of the Soviet Union (which ceased to exist on December 25, 1991) in establishing the Commonwealth of Independent States. The Commonwealth was expected to have military and economic coordinating functions and would be headquartered in Minsk, Belarus.
08/19/1991	Failed coup attempt that symbolized the end of communism in Russia and the breakup of the Soviet Union. Violent demonstrations occurred in Moscow in August 1992, resulting in several deaths.
05/02/1945	Berlin fell to the Soviets.
02/01/1943	Germany's 6th Army surrendered to Soviet forces in Stalingrad.
06/22/1941	German invasion of U.S.S.R.
11/07/1917	Revolution Day, considered the most sacred day by Russian communists.

Rwanda
★★

Tutsi Pop

Maps don't often show Merama Hill, but it's the border post on the main road from Uganda to Kigali. The land (scrub, candelabra trees), what game you can see (fine impala) and the longhorn cattle look much the same on both sides. But the minute you're in Rwanda, you know things are getting treacherous.

Traffic, for one, is running on the right, not the left, as it does in Uganda, and if it takes more profound dangers to unsettle you, there's the genocide that seems to have stopped at a million, but may merely have paused. In three months of 1994, the Hutu hard-liners killed as many people as the Khmer Rouge did in Cambodia in three years.

Here is where you'll find the tumbling Kagera River, a.k.a., the Alexander Nile, rushing on to Lake Victoria, from where its waters will spill into the Albert Nile, from where they will find the Mediterranean. It tumbles fast, there are whitecaps, and you can almost see the bodies of children rushing with the river down to Tanzania, to which their killers have fled in fear of retribution.

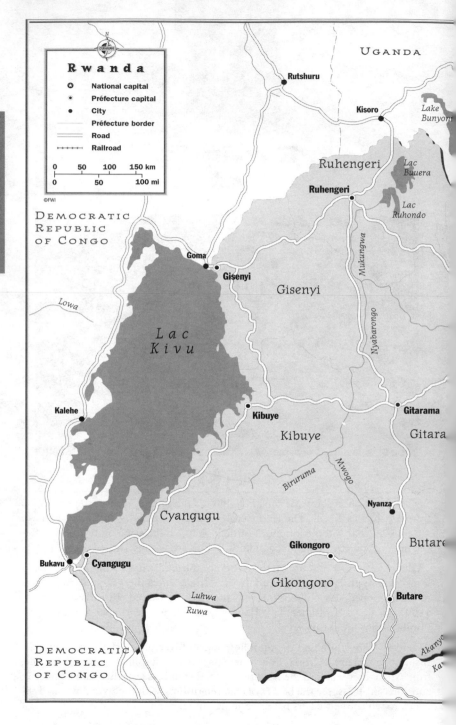

Across the border, Ruhengeri is charming as only a mountain town anchored by a grass air strip can be. But what haunts Ruhengeri are fully developed ghosts, in particular a group of about 100 Tutsi mothers caught in the Christmas season pogroms of 1962–63. On a road just out of town, they found themselves trapped between two mobs of Bahutu. Beneath them flowed the Nywarungu River, alive with crocodiles. They threw their children in, then jumped in after them.

This was not an isolated incident. It echoed from the past, it echoed again in 1994, and, even as those women jumped, it was echoing throughout Rwanda. Another 100 Tutsi women in the town of Shgira jumped into the river after their husbands were rounded up and they knew they'd never see them again. Children were skewered alive and left to die, buried alive, thrown into rivers, heads tied to knees. Tutsi men were left to bleed to death after having had their legs cut off at the knees. After 10,000 Watutsi were killed near Gikongoro, a thousand women and children there gathered and committed collective suicide.

There's a third way into Rwanda from Uganda. Halfway between Merama Hill in the east and Kisoro in the west is the road from the Ugandan town of Kabale to Biumba, just over the border, and here the story turns from genocide to war.

On the Horns of a Dilemma

Paul Kagame, head of a force of 5000 mostly Tutsi insurgents, was watching a soccer video in a tent near Biumba when a runner came with the news that a burst of shellfire had brought down the president's plane as it took off from Kigali airport, killing the president, the chief of staff of the armed forces, plus Burundi's president. This confronted him with a dilemma. He could concentrate his forces, as sound doctrine dictates for outnumbered forces, or he could split his men up in an attempt to stop the genocide, which was now beginning in earnest. Hutu hard-liners blamed the Watutsi for the attack, and the Hutu Radio Des Milles Collines explicitly incited the population to slaughter Watutsi. But this was only one aspect of his bind.

Under the cease-fire that preceded the outburst, he was permitted to barrack 600 troops in Kigali; now they were stranded and under heavy attack. More fundamental was the strategic position of his main force in the north. As the press put it, his forces "controlled" this corner of Rwanda. It would be accurate to say that the heavily armed, French-trained, 25,000-man Rwandan Army, backed by Guarde Nationale troops everywhere, had him cornered here. When the news of the crash came, he was in a tent near Biumba, not in the town. Based in Biumba were seven battalions of the Rwandan Army, backed up with heavy weapons, armored personnel carriers, paratroops, and helicopter gunships. Kagame's troops, with no such weaponry, were scattered out of harm's way, entirely afoot, carrying all their materiel on their backs. Now that was something of a blessing. He immediately sent orders for them to gather at preplanned assembly points, but it would take them a little time, which gave him a chance to think what to do with them when they got there.

Reporters didn't write much about the war itself. It was not easily accessible, and at that point, the French-Canadian officers running the United Nations contingent in Rwanda had little to say about what little they knew. Off the record, there was speculation aplenty. All agreed that whatever Kagame's numbers, he must take the offensive, and to be successful in any way, he must concentrate his limited forces for a focused attack. But beyond that, they split into two camps.

Camp one kept it simple: Find a weak spot, concentrate forces, attack it for a doable big victory in one battle, certainly no more than a few, then use the Hutu pogroms to call for a cease-fire that the United Nations might actually enforce, then negotiate.

Camp two said negotiations with the less extreme government of the late president were barely working. Negotiations with the extremists who killed him just weren't really promising. Concentrate, yes, they said, but in a bold strike at Kigali.

Camp one said impossible, since a major force was defending the capital. Assuming he could get around the major force cornering him in Biumba, Kagame's small, ill-equipped force would be ground up in a frontal assault on Kigali, even if it won. Meantime, on its rear would be the heavily armed Biumba force it had earlier bypassed. There would be virtually no Watutsi left to negotiate anything.

Kagame knew camp one was right. Both the force cornering him in the northwest and the force defending Kigali were too strong to attack frontally. Meantime, all over the country, Watutsi were being slaughtered, a powerful inducement to split up his forces rather than concentrate them to win a significant battle. For years, he had planned for this moment, but now that it was at hand, and his forces were assembling, he didn't know what to do.

Reporters strive for economy, but digging into the making of this fight, and the danger that hangs over Central Africa, a quick telling of the Watutsi's swift victory over the Bahutu can make what must have been a monumentally difficult and dangerous undertaking seem downright easy. Kagame's strategy pivoted on mobility. Without vehicles, that meant moving at night—fast. If you caught a glimpse of them, it would be in those same hours that Africa's great predators are about, amid the fog and smoke of dusk and dawn. Maybe it's them, maybe it isn't.

To this day, there are a few of the pygmoid Batwa living amidst the smoke and mist of the forests around Lake Kivu west of Biumba, but mostly the country to the west is heavily cultivated and thick with Bahutu. In fact, in early '94 it was a stronghold of hard-line Bahutu, and with Kagame unlikely to strike in this inhospitable direction, the strong blocking force of the Hutu based in Biumba was positioned to keep him from slipping to the east in an attempt to bypass the blocking force and strike at Kigali, due south.

Not long after the president's plane crashed, the Presidential Guard assassinated Prime Minister Agathe Uwilingiyimana; Kagame struck, and every observer who knew about the assassination (no news reports) was nonplussed. First surprise: He struck west into that inhospitable country thick with Bahutu, which caused some terror, even though he had no designs here at all. The strike to the west finessed the Hutu force deployed mostly to block an attempt to bypass them on the east. Having passed them on the west, he moved south toward Kigali. That surprise, however, seemed almost natural in retrospect. The second surprise didn't. Having bypassed the blocking force in Biumba, Kagame split his forces in two, sending one in a wide sweeping arc to the savannas of the east, and sending barely half his men, now doubly vulnerable, to strike at Kigali.

The Importance of Focus

Afoot, Kagame's Kigali-bound force cut through 40 miles of enemy held turf in four days in April. As they approached the city, U.N. staffers in town were reporting widespread slaughter of noncombatant Watutsi by the Army and the Guarde Nationale, both of which often fired large volumes of ammunition wildly. But Kagame didn't attack. The city was defended all around by heavily armed Hutu forces with ambushes prepared along street after street.

Instead, Kagame focused on three more modest objectives. First, he organized an advance to link up with his force of 600 men in Kigali as they tried to break out of their compound that was under heavy attack. The Bahutu were intent on those 600, and many showed exceptional courage attacking the compound. But the Watutsi inside were at least as intent; they broke out, joined up with Kagame's Kigali force, and Hutu morale was hit hard.

Then, as the Hutu generals redeployed to defend a city Kagame had no intention of taking at that point, the Tutsi leader wheeled his strengthened Kigali force on his second objective, the airport. By mid-April, his mortar fire had shut it down, and hard fighting for limited targets filled the next month, with no sign of a concerted attack on the city whose streets were seeing the slaughter of more and more Watutsi civilians. Then, on May 22, these tactics paid off. Both the airport and Kagame's third limited objective, the Rwandan Army's Kanombe barracks, fell to the Watutsi.

Reporters and the Hutu population were stunned. But military observers knew Kagame had still not won a major pitched battle with a heavily armed Hutu force. His enemy in Kigali was still more numerous and better armed, and his force was split, with half of it off somewhere to the east. But those were just military observations. Everyone else expected Kagame to join a battle for Kigali, and as days passed without an attack, reporters wondered in print why he was taking so long, as Watutsi in Kigali were butchered. Kagame answered, "We have to do this methodically; we can't rush in."

What reporters didn't know—but the Hutu military did—was that even as Kagame was explaining why he was proceeding so slowly, his Kigali force was wheeling rapidly away from Kigali and toward a new target: the heartland of the hardline Bahutu in the hills to the west. Their core constituency threatened, the Hutu generals moved reinforcements to defend this heartland.

What they didn't know is that Kagame had no intention of seeing his troops chewed up in this Hutu heartland, where the largely untouched Biumba force was still based. Instead, he turned again, all the way around to the east, again ignoring Kigali, even though some of its defenders had been drawn off for the defense of the western heartland. He left just enough forces to keep the Hutu generals pinned down and wondering, and linked up with the eastern spearhead he had launched at the beginning of April. Now, at last, his forces were rejoined and concentrated, as they swept around Kigali from the north to the south and then to the west, nearly enveloping the capital, but carefully leaving the government one avenue of escape, and an attractive one at that: west to the Hutu heartland.

Panicked, the Hutu leadership took the bait and quit the capital for the town of Gisenyi. At the time, it sounded much more like a retreat to the bush, with a government representing the vast majority fighting with its people from the countryside. But Gisenyi is a resort on Lake Kivu, a lighthearted place where steep lawns sweep in extravagant expanse around equally extravagant villas. Nonetheless, it was surrounded by heavily Hutu country, and now the Hutu armed forces, still unhurt by any major defeat in battle, were deployed to defend a much more compact area, backed by a friendly border with Zaire. When Kagame's force first invaded in 1990, Zairois troops had joined the French and Belgians to fight the Watutsi. In an arc from Biumba to Ruhengeri to Gisenyi, strong points were set up. On high ground dominating all three key towns, paratroops, regular army troops and militiamen from the Guarde Nationale manned armored personnel carriers, heavy artillery, and an array of other weapons Kagame didn't have.

A Face-off with the Bahutu

Thanks to a U.N. weapons boycott, the Hutu forces were running low on ammunition, lower than that of the Watutsi, who had greater fire discipline. But the Bahutu still had heavy weapons, armor and aircraft, none of which Kagame had, and its forces still had not lost a major pitched battle. The way the elusive Watutsi had fought, there had been no major pitched battles. But now, at last, that day was at hand, and the Hutu hard-liners had the weapons.

Come the end of the day, who would be the victor? That was the question, as Kagame's force headed from southeast to northwest. But it was never really answered. The rulers of Hutu Rwanda's rump government in carefree Gisenyi took one look at the Watutsi headed their way, and they were out of there.

The French Connection

As France publicly deliberated putting together a force to rescue civilian Watutsi from slaughter, belligerent members of Kagame's front charged that France was actually planning to join the war on behalf of the Bahutu. True, the Bahutu were still French clients, and true, the French had fought against the Watutsi. But it was clear this time that with the slaughter of the Watutsi so horrible, no French government could survive actually going to war for the Bahutu against the Watutsi. This was surely clear to Kagame, as well. But that was just his dilemma. With the French public aware that the government would not possibly fly in to fight the Watutsi, the government could comfortably fly in to rescue civilian Watutsi, and in so doing, secure strategic ground for their Hutu clients. In short, unless Kagame played this dangerous game just right, the French could again defeat the Watutsi, this time without firing a shot.

Specifically, the French could fly in to the uncaptured south of Rwanda in order to stop the slaughter there, and, not incidentally, to keep the south out of Kagame's hands. And that's pretty much how it developed. With the world calling for an end to the butchery, French President Francois Mitterand announced Operation Turquoise, a short-term rescue mission to demilitarize the south and southwest. On July 3, as the world heard of Kagame's troops moving into a largely deserted Kigali, France choppered paratroops and naval commandos to a lower profile, political prize— Rwanda's second-largest city, Butare, far to the south on the Burundi border, a city bursting with Bahutu who had chosen French protection in the south to protection by their own army in the north. France would not battle Kagame for turf. Having proclaimed neutrality, they couldn't. But they would occupy turf like Butare in the far south that he had not yet reached. What they didn't realize as they flew in was how fast Kagame's foot soldiers were moving, and now there were nearly 25,000 of them.

What the French found as they landed in far southern Butare on July 4 was Kagame's army just 500 yards from the city line. They pulled out, and Bahutu driving everything from Peugeots to backhoes followed them. Their license plates were from all over Rwanda, not just the "CB" plates of Butare, but "ABs" from Kigali, and even "IBs" and "HBs" from Ruhengeri and Biumba.

The French had to make a deal, and after the hot words of his cohorts, Kagame proposed one that was very tough for them to refuse. Essentially, it was a deal that would make certain that the French "rescue mission" was indeed just that, terms confining the French to a small refuge they would briefly protect on Zaire's border.

On paper—and in the papers—this looked like no big deal; basically, it was just getting the French to affirm their benign intent. But a big deal it was. France's deputy commander in Rwanda, Colonel Jacques Rosier, frankly acknowledged that the agreement amounted to a retreat. "This is not what we thought two days ago," he said as he pulled his force back, virtually *hors de combat*, to positions along the edge of the Nyungwa Forest (a primeval place where the forest elephant, with its small, hard tusks, has long dwelled, and where six of them may yet dwell).

As the Bahutu in Gisenyi watched the French pull back, they knew the French wouldn't be choppering here and there as a "humanitarian" blocking force between them and the Watutsi. Meantime, Kagame could ignore the far southwest, temporarily secured for him by his French friends, and drive his entire concentrated, strengthened force to a foregone conclusion in Gisenyi.

When Elephants Fight

One of Africa's oldest proverbs—"When elephants fight, the grass gets trampled"— couldn't be better suited for the slaughter of Central Africa. How can one of the tiniest, lushest countries in Africa become one of the largest killing fields in the world?

Tribalism.

Rwanda, like neighboring Burundi, is a rather simple (for most African states) hybrid of two tribes: the Hutus and the Tutsis. A four-year uprising made minor headlines every time Tutsi guerrillas would infringe on the territory of Rwanda's famous silverback gorilla families. When full-scale war broke out after the death of Burundi's and Rwanda's leaders in a plane crash, the majority Hutu tribe blamed the minority Tutsis and began indiscriminately slaughtering them. But the surprise success of the ragtag Tutsi rebels transformed them from freedom fighters into outright butchers. The Hutu-controlled government has been replaced by Tutsi rebels, and the wholesale massacre started being directed at the Hutus.

Now waves of refugees have been making tentative explorations homeward from eastern Congo (at least those who have not been slaughtered by Congo president Laurent Kabila's mostly Tutsi forces) under the auspices of the U.N. Estimates put the Tutsi fatality toll at more than a million in the last few decades, and the number of refugees at more than twice that figure. The genocide in this decade has topped 1 million dead. Almost half of Rwanda's population of 8 million fled during the hostilities in April 1993; 10,000 per minute at its peak crossed the borders.

Rwandan leader Major-General Paul Kagame is trying to bring the refugees back, particularly the Hutus, who fled the country en masse after Kagame's Tutsi Rwandan Patriotic Front (RPF) came to power in 1994. Kagame has ordered the execution of any soldier who kills a civilian. That he's serious was evidenced by the 1116 Tutsi soldiers jailed by Kagame in 1996. Eighty of them were officers—most facing murder charges. There are 90,000 people in prison in Rwanda awaiting trial in connection with slaughter.

For refugees returning from eastern Congo, though, there is no guarantee of safety. Former neighbors have turned hostile. Some returnees are ostracized, some accepted, some murdered. Returning Hutus are being shot as war criminals.

In 1959, a faction intent on maintaining Tutsi privilege in Rwanda assassinated several Hutu leaders. Hutu rage slaughtered 100,000 Rwandan Watutsi, and the carnage was on—a 22-year genocide that, in 1994 alone, would wipe out half a million Watutsi in Rwanda. Today, Rwanda is a state paralyzed with fear. Kagame and Uganda leader Museveni's have a firm grip on a Tutsi power bloc. But a new Hutu insurgency is brewing in northwest Rwanda. Some 6000 Hutu extremists are hiding in the dense jungle, waiting for their comrades—participants in the 1994 genocide—who joined innocent refugees in their flight to Zaire (now Congo) and fought the new Rwanda government from their refugee camp bases in eastern Zaire. Now they're returning to Rwanda—sneaking in from Congo over the Virunga chain of extinct volcanoes and, ironically, aboard U.N. aircraft.

Paul Kagame and the Rwandan Patriotic Front (RPF)

The man is a Rwandan Tutsi, born in Rwanda, and residing there today. He is the most powerful man in the Tutsi homelands of Rwanda and Burundi and probably the most powerful man that either of those two precarious states have known since they both became independent in 1962. But most of his life he lived in Uganda, during that country's most wretched years—and there's the twist. The very wretchedness of that period helped bring the Watutsi and their son Kagame back to Rwanda.

The Uganda in which Kagame matured was a nether world, a place of attenuated pain, both psychological and physical. This, the Watutsi shared with their Ugandan hosts and helped them bear, first the nightmare of Amin, then two more nightmares. With little more outside help than refugee Watutsi could provide, the people of Uganda finally ended those nightmare years, and when they did, the Watutsi were not without influence.

First among these influentials was young Paul Kagame, Rwandan refugee, intelligence chief for all of Uganda...and a key organizer of the RPF. The Tutsi front was formed by the guerrilla years its leadership had spent with Yoweri Museveni's National Resistance Army, which drew its strength from popular support. This meant, above all, discipline. Rape was punishable by death, and a summary execution for just such an offense was meted out to a Tutsi fighter in the midst of 1994's 14-week war for Rwanda. The front demanded no privileges for the Watutsi, though there was little rhetorical nonsense, either: It was clear that majority rule would be balanced by minority rights. And there was clearly a danger that with meager resources, it could not control the climate of terror.

As a member of Uganda's military, Kagame was able to apply for a course in tactics given by the U.S. Army Command and General Staff College at Fort Leavenworth, Kansas. In fact (and reflecting in part Tutsi chutzpah), Kagame was in Kansas in October 1990, the very month he and a close comrade-in-arms, Fred Rwigyema, had planned to invade Rwanda. The invasion went ahead anyway, and it went well, until France put together a combined force of French troops, Zairois troops, Belgian troops and French-trained Hutu paras. In 1991, his movement launched its last frustrated invasion. Again, it went well, but with the prospect of intervention again hanging on the horizon, he stopped short in the north and agreed to talks. These were to drag on for two years in the Tanzanian town of Arusha at the foot of Mt. Kilimanjaro. At last, late in 1993, Rwanda's hardline president agreed in priniciple to terms that called for a moderate Hutu to be installed as president and another as prime minister. The hard-line president signed a formal ceasefire, Rwanda's even harder-line military was enraged, and a large question began to loom as to whether Rwanda's government would or could fulfill the terms to which it had agreed. As he watched from his camps along the Biumba road, this was the chessboard upon which Kagame had to focus all his strategic faculties: French armor in Hutu hands, French heavy weapons, a Hutu military for which France and Belgium had successfully bought time for a huge buildup—Hutu airborne troops and 30,000 regulars, all trained by the French. Against this, he had no armor and no heavy weapons, just mortars and rocket-propelled grenades that Uganda had to pretend it didn't supply. As for training, it's basically the homegrown discipline of Museveni's children's crusade, plus Kagame's course, which was in tactics, not strategy, as American reporters were wont to boast.

Mwalimu Julius Nyerere

A great teacher of lessons, not all of which should be taught. Tanzania's soft-spoken leader, now retired, is influential still: For Africans, he remains *mwalimu*, the teacher. In fact, without portfolio, he is more influential than most African heads of state. His power has declined distinctly, but this has little to do with his retirement. What he retired from, the presidency of backward, resource-poor Tanzania, was never the prime source of his influence. The decline is due almost entirely to the failure of his most ambitious ideas. He is known, will long be known, for a magnificent idea that has failed magnificently. Nyerere tried to craft, from the Swahili word for family, *ujamaa*, something between a voluntary Israeli kibbutz and a compulsory Chinese commune. It rarely worked. It cost millions. Whole villages were uprooted. Labor was forced. It never came close to paying its way. Today, the effort is largely abandoned. Regardless, he is a man of integrity, remains a powerful teacher of integrity, and many believe Africa needs more leaders like him.

Congo President Laurent Kabila

Kabila was born by Rwandan politics whether he admits it or not. The success of his rebellion against Mobutu Sese Seko was due to the support of U.S. connections and Paul Kagame. Now Kabila's holding the marbles in Kinshasa and has his own massacre to cover up. He'll have to think quick to account for some 250,000 Rwandan Hutu refugees missing in his reborn Congo. Kabila let a U.N. team into Congo to check the allegations out. But getting around to inspect the dozens of alleged massacre sites may be as difficult for this team as it was for Boutros-Ghali's boys to inspect Saddam's chemical weapons sites.

The U.N. International Criminal Tribunal for Rwanda (ICTR)

An understaffed, unqualified, mismanaged, overpaid and bumbling U.N. International Criminal Tribunal for Rwanda (ICTR) is overseeing the genocide trials of a handful of Rwanda's slaughterhouse curators. The ICTR has only managed to indict 21 people. And only 12 of these suspects are in detention in Arusha, Tanzania, where the trials are taking place. Only in a little league atmosphere like this could any credibility be given to the defense arguments that the killing of 800,000 Tutsis and moderate Hutus was not genocide but "mass killings in a state of war where everyone is killing his enemies," as was stated by defense lawyer De Temmerman in his defense of notorious Hutu *interahamwe* warlord Georges Rutaganda. The Hutus claim that the massacres were a spontaneous uprising which they tried to prevent. Laughable, but similar arguments have won the release of *interahamwe* officers and continuances for monsters like Jean-Paul Akayesu, who is suspected of ordering the wholesale slaughter of Tutsis and encouraging Hutus to murder their own grandchildren, nephews, nieces and in-laws.

A U.N. report concluded the ICTR is dysfunctional "in every administrative area." The tribunal has a cash fund of US$600,000 but no written rules for disbursing it. The financing head doesn't have a degree in financing, accounting or administration. The procurement head has never bought anything for the U.N. in his life. Some personnel don't get paid for months while others receive duplicate paychecks. The prosecutors have decided the court makes a good forum for arguing among themselves. How bad is it for the boys in sky blue? U.N. Office for Internal Oversight chief Karl Paschke admitted in an understatement: "Justice (in Rwanda) has been delayed."

NGOs

There are some 4600 Western-based NGOs working in the Third World. When 2 million Rwandans, mainly Hutus, fled the country in mid-1994, more than 200 aid organizations were on the scene instantly. These "refugee cities" soon became headquarters for extremist Hutu former government militias plotting their next civil war in Rwanda, the same folks responsible for the slaughter of some 800,000 Tutsis and moderate Hutus earlier in 1994. NGOs spent more than $1 billion between 1994 and 1996 supplying food, water and shelter to Rwandan refugees. The refugee camps in eastern Congo today have been feeding and clothing Hutu nasties who have apparently started feeling nourished enough to head back to Rwanda to stir up trouble. The U.N. estimates that 25 percent of its food is stolen.

Diplomatic ties have been restored between the United States and Rwanda. Passport and visa are required. Multiple-entry visa (extendable) for a stay of up to 1 month requires a US$30 fee (cash, check or money order), two application forms, two photos and immunization for yellow fever. Exact date of entry into Rwanda is required with application. Include prepaid envelope or $1.50 postage for return of passport by certified mail.

At the height of the hostilities, when *DP* asked about entry permission, a spokesperson replied, "We know nothing." Later, after things had calmed down, it seemed the embassy staff had developed a sense of bureaucratic humor. When we asked if there were any Americans in jail in Rwanda, we were told, "We have none; they have been behaving so far." You should know the first of the 12 conditions for entry and stay in Rwanda is that "proper attire and conduct are required of persons staying in Rwanda." The embassy maintains that it is safe to travel in Rwanda.

Embassy Locations

U.S. Embassy in Rwanda
Boulevard de la Revolution
BP 28, Kigali
☎ *[250] (7) 5601/2/3*
FAX [250] (7) 2128

Embassy of the Republic of Rwanda
1714 New Hampshire Avenue, N.W.
Washington, D.C. 20009
☎ *(202) 232-2882*

Canadian Embassy in Rwanda
Rue Akagera, BP 1177
Kigali
☎ *73210, FAX: 72719*

Rwandan Embassy in Canada
121 Sherwood Drive
Ottawa, Ontario, Canada K1Y 3V1
☎ *(613) 722-5835/722-7921*
FAX (613) 729-3291

Permanent Mission of Rwanda to the U.N.

124 East 39th Street
New York, NY 10016
☎ *(212) 696-0644/46*

Consulate General in Chicago
☎ *(708) 205-1188*

Consulate General in Denver
☎ *(303) 321-2400*

Rwanda has a total road length of 3036 miles; a mere 286 of them are paved. There are neither railways nor ports. There are eight airfields in the country, three of them with a permanent surface.

Air Rwanda flies internally from Kigali to Gisenyi and Kamembe. Occasionally, you can fly between Gisenyi and Kamembe. Due to the amount of foreign aid into the country, Rwanda's road system isn't too bad. As in neighboring Burundi, the roadways are served by a fleet of relatively late-model Japanese minibuses. The buses leave most towns when they are full. Larger government buses also traverse Rwanda's roads, although they are fewer and farther between. They cost less than the minibuses, but take longer to get to their destinations.

The Entire Country

The entire country of Rwanda can be considered unsafe. Travelers are regularly the victims of theft, petty crime and murder. Sporadic violence is a problem in Kigali as well as in the interior. Fighting caused thousands of refugees to flee into neighboring Burundi as well as other countries in the region. In 1996, Paul Kagame ensured the safety of returning refugees and a trickle began returning to Rwanda, many to find their land and dwellings seized by squatters. The northwest has recently swelled with extremist Hutus, many returning from refugee camps in Zaire. This area is becoming a hotbed for insurgent activity. Travelers should use extreme caution everywhere in Rwanda. Do not travel into the troubled areas of Kigali or anywhere in or near Gisenyi. Do not travel after dark.

The Lakes

There are very large man-eating crocodiles and an abundance of germs to be found in all lakes and large rivers in Rwanda.

Land Mines

Land mines are especially prevalent in Byumba, Cyangugu, Kigali and Kigali rural prefectures. Avoid unpaved roads and don't tip-toe through the tulips in uncultivated fields.

Medical facilities, doctors and supplies are dangerously scarce in Rwanda. There is one doctor for every 33,170 people under normal conditions and 15 hospital beds for every 10,000 people in the country. There are 34 hospitals and 188 health centers in this tiny country, so the traveler has some access to treatment. Cholera and yellow fever inoculations are required. Tetanus, polio, typhoid and gamma globulin vaccines are advised, as are antimalarial prophylaxes: DPT, measles and mumps vaccines are recommended for children. Tap water is not potable.

About the size of Vermont and located in east central Africa, Rwanda (the capital is Kigali) is a landlocked country just south of the Equator bordering Uganda to the north, Burundi to the south, Tanzania to the east, and Zaire to the west. There were estimated to be over 8 million people in Rwanda before the holocaust. They live packed at 789 people per square mile: 85 percent are Hutu, 14 percent Tutsi. Almost half of the Tutsis were murdered during the genocide.

Rwanda is home to rare mountain gorillas and the bizarre topography and plant life of its forests found in Parc National des Volcans. The gorillas of the park have been mainly unharmed in the nation's unrest due to its remoteness and that most Rwandan park guards have remained on duty. At last count, there were only 650 mountain gorillas left on the planet, of which 320 live in the 125-sq.-kilometer Parc National des Volcans in Rwanda's northern mountains.

The currency is the Rwanda franc (RFr). There are 100 centimes to the RFr. There are 222 RFr to the U.S. dollar. Local time is two hours later than GMT, seven hours later than U.S. EST. Electricity is 220V/50Hz. Hutu comprise 85 percent of the population; the Tutsi account for 14 percent. Sixty-five percent of the population is Roman Catholic. Protestants make up 9 percent, Muslim 1 percent and indigenous beliefs 25 percent.

Kinyarwanda and French are the official languages, and Kiswahili is used commercially. Illiteracy stands at 50 percent. Rwanda has a tropical climate that varies slightly with altitude. The major rainy seasons are February through May and November through December, with an average annual rainfall of 31 inches.

06/1997	Perhaps 250,000 Hutu Rwandan refugees are feared dead in a slaughter by Congo President Laurent Kabila's rebel troops in eastern Congo.
06/18/1997	Two U.N. World Food Program employees are killed by gunmen.
04/28/1997	Rebels murder 17 schoolgirls and a Belgian nun.
11/1996	Rwanda war crimes trial resumes in Arusha, Tanzania.
08/12/1994	Thousands of Rwandan refugees begin moving toward Zaire from southwest Rwanda.
07/19/1994	Pasteur Bizimungu is sworn in as president at a ceremony at the parliament building in the capital of Kigali. Rebel commander Major General Paul Kagame is named vice president and defense minister.
07/18/1994	The rebel Rwandan Patriotic Front (RPF) claims it has won Rwanda's civil war.
07/15/1994	A tidal wave of Rwandan refugees pours into neighboring Zaire.

07/04/1994	Rwandan rebels capture the capital of Kigali and the last major government-held southern town of Butare.
04/06/1994	President Juvenal Habyarimana is killed in a plane crash, sparking nationwide fighting.
01/28	Democracy Day.
07/01	Anniversary of Independence.
07/05	National Peace and Unity Day.
10/26	Armed Forces Day.

RWANDA

Rwanda, 1994: The Slaughter

The apocalypse in Rwanda is too dark and compelling to ignore. In the 20th century, an entire nation is being murdered, while the world sits by and refuses to believe it. If any story needs to be captured, it is this one. We fly to Nairobi. On our arrival, we discover that the jeep we have reserved is not available. It is the height of safari season, and they have rented out four-wheel-drive vehicles for the $250 to $500 a day they can get.

For $20 a head, we take a five-hour minibus ride to Arusha just south of Nairobi. Seeing our massive professional camera, the locals just assume we are tourists. For $5, we can take still photos and, for $20, all the video we want. We pass. We find a 4x4 and driver that will take us on the 13-hour trip to Nyanza, a major staging area for the relief effort in Rwanda. The price is $100, but we have to squeeze in all the locals who want to go along as well. We go through some of the more dramatic scenery of East Africa, but the rough road and long trip make it an ordeal.

We treat ourselves to a three-star hotel when we arrive in Nyanza. There is a U.N. crew, and, wherever there are U.N. people, there are usually pilots around. Naturally, we go straight to the hotel bar to find them. Strangely, not a pilot to be found. The next day we find the pilots eating breakfast. I go to the oldest and ask him if he will fly us to the Ngara refugee camp. The answer is a definite no. We work on them until finally they agree to take us on. When we let people know that our footage and coverage will support the relief effort, they have a greater desire to help us. As we climb into the Spanish-built *CASA*, we make ourselves comfortable among the crates of medicine and food destined for the refugees.

The 90-minute flight is uneventful, except for the trip over Lake Victoria. From our altitude, I can see tiny islands floating in the turquoise water—they are clumps of bloated bodies. We land on the dusty runway surrounded by a tent city that seems to stretch for miles. A fleet of Land Rovers arrives to collect the supplies and takes us to the U.N. headquarters for the camp. There is a veritable United Nations of relief organizations here—the U.N., the Red Cross, MSF, CARE and the Red Crescent. All of them tell us that they have no room for us. The Tanzanian branch of the Red Cross gives us some simple mats to sleep on and a hot meal.

There are endless lines of Hutus and Tutsi waiting for their daily handout of milk, flour and rice. We shoot some photos and interview the people. There are clusters of children, newly orphaned and wandering around with blank expressions on their faces. There is not much to capture here, other than a sea of gaunt faces. We find a Tutsi chauffeur who, for $100, will take us as far as the headquarters of the "Rwandese Patriotic Front" about 10–15 km inside the border. We don't bother with a visa, since we doubt there is much of a government left. It takes us an hour to get as far as the Tanzanian border post on the eastern shore of the Kagera River. It should only take 15 minutes, but we are like salmon swimming upstream as we try to make our way through the river of refugees streaming out of Rwanda. The people are carrying the last of their possessions; even the children carry bundles. Old men carry firewood, now a valuable commodity. At this rate, it will take us all day just to get to the headquarters in Rwanda where there are no basic commodities and terror reigns at night.

We decide to try to cross the border the next morning. Our hunch is right. All the refugees are sleeping by the side of the road and the going is easy. We are waved across the Tanzanian border with little fuss. Our exit visas are simply gifts of pens and Camel Trophy stickers, strangely powerful international currency. As we cross the bridge high above the Kagera River, we can see bodies floating downstream. It is strange how their dark skin turns white. One cadaver is caught between two rocks and bobs up and down in the fast-moving water.

At the other side, there is no one manning the border posts. Our relief is short-lived. About 50 meters past the bridge, we are stopped by armed members of the RPF. They ask for ID, question our purpose here, and treat us like celebrities when they see our press cards.

Our Tutsi driver does not fare as well. The guards treat him as a deserter and question his ownership of the vehicle. They take him away to a nearby building, despite our desperate protests. We never see him again. Distraught, we come across two old friends—fellow journalists Luc Delahey and James Natchway. We hug each other and exchange information. They have come from Kigali to report on the recently discovered massacre in the village of Nyarubuye 115 km away. They never got there, having all the tires on their vehicles blown when they ran over sabotage spikes laid across the road. They had spent two days trying to find a way out. They had flown in from Uganda, and then were stuck in Kigali by the fierce fighting. They had seen our vehicle and are disappointed that it is no longer here.

We hang around the bridge pondering our situation. When a truck crosses the border, we flag it down and cut a deal on the spot. For $400, we now have wheels. A guard from the RPF rides shotgun in the front with Jim Natchway. Our first dramatic sight is thousands and thousands of rusty, bloodstained machetes confiscated by the RPF from captured Hutus. I immediately think of the piles of glasses, shoes and clothing photographed in the concentration camps in WW II. We drive through burned-out villages and by rows of bodies—most killed with machetes. Among the bodies are stunned survivors searching for relatives. I am struck by the look in these people's eyes. I have seen many, many wars but never one that created so much fear and horror.

The 115 km of horror brings us to Nyarubuye, site of a dark tale we had heard from the refugees inside Tanzania. They told us of hundreds of men, women and children herded into a church and slaughtered like pigs. We smell the heavy stench of rotting flesh long before we come upon the scene. We try to inhale the scent of the eucalyptus trees, but all we can smell is the revolting odor of decay. There are pieces of humans strewn everywhere. Wild dogs had probably been feasting on the corpses. None of us has ever seen anything like this before. Even Luc, Jim and I, who have seen so much, cannot comprehend the horror that we behold. The monastery is surrounded by a brick wall. Inside the wall is a flower-filled garden. Among the flowers are the rotting bodies of hundreds of women and children. The building is a low brick structure built during the Belgian colonial period. There is a simple church adjoining the monastery.

We had all emptied our stomachs when the stench first hit us a natural and healthy reaction to human decay—but I continue to wretch as nausea comes over me in waves. The people had fled to the church afraid for their lives. They had been taught that the church was the place of last refuge. They were wrong. Men armed with machetes ordered them into the garden and began to slash and cut them. Some tried to escape. One man's upper torso is halfway up the metal ladder on the church steeple. His lower torso and legs hang half a meter below.

Inside the church, a man lies hacked to death at the altar. Piles of bodies lie among the pews. I stare at the dead bodies in the bushes, probably dragged there by the dogs, at the strange grimacing expressions of the contorted faces, as they putrefy.

We return the way we came, knowing that we have captured mankind at its most base. The perverse irony of this sin being committed in a church makes it even more tragic and surreal.

—Coskun Aral

Rwanda: Split Milk

I well remember our friend, Gupta, as we sat in this gray light, sipping piping-hot tea from chipped enamelware cups on the Tanzania side of the Kagera. Peering into the mists, he would wonder not just about the identity of the shifting shadows they shrouded, but at the nature of the shroud itself: fog, mist, smoke from a cooking fire, from a land-clearing fire, from a dry-season fire set by lightning, from fire set by poachers to flush game.

This is Karagwe country; it had been a long day, we'd had a decent meal, and, as we pass the plastic Listerine bottle full of *waraki* among us, we feel the spell of the old empires hereabouts. Karagwe, Ankole, Tutsi, have Gupta conjuring punch-drunkenly, straining to glimpse Lord knows what through the mists, as he tells us that an ancient Iron Age city has recently been excavated on the flanks of the Ngorongoro crater on the Serengeti Plain, a highly developed place whose people and whose collapse remains a mystery. He says they had buildings made of brick, which required firing in kilns, which in turn required charcoal. "That mist over there," he says, gesturing toward a cloud that looks like fog to me, "I'm reckoning it's a charcoal mound. What they're doing, you see, is they're digging a pit, lining the bottom with damp leaves and hot coals, filling it with timber, then covering it with dirt, and you're walking about and you're seeing this mound of earth with smoke rising from it, as if the earth itself were smoldering. Well, soon enough they're coming along and uncovering it all, and there you have your charcoal."

He tells us it was also done that way in an ancient empire on the Indian subcontinent called Mohenjo-Davo, and apropos of nothing charcoal, he tells us one of the primal legends of the Watutsi. "As Rwanda's first king lay dying, he summoned his sons, Gatwa, Gahutu and Gatusi. Here's a jug of milk for each of you, he told them. Guard it all night. But Gatwa drank all his, and Gahutu fell asleep, spilling half his jug as he rolled over. Only Gatusi sat up the night, presenting his father with the full jug, and thus Watutsi came to rule the land, Bahutu became serfs, and Batwa were driven from mankind to live in the forests."

—Jack Kramer

Freetown

Sierra Leone

★★★★★

RUF & Ready

The trail of coups and corpses continues in Sierra Leone. The names change but the game stays the same. For now, the peacekeeping forces of ECOMOG are busy shelling the markets in Freetown in a bid to oust the current mid level soldier who has grabbed the top political spot by force. Politics in this tiny West African nation is like an after-school match of king of the hill—a bunch of muddy kids pulling at each other's trouser cuffs. In Sierra Leone anyone with a gun seems assured of a term in office, and their fifteen minutes in the sun—but rarely a few moments past that.

On May 27, 1997, an obscure army major with the name of a Brooklyn rapper, Johnny Paul Koroma, deposed democratically elected President Ahmed Tejan Kabbah in Sierra Leone's third military coup in five years. Koroma accused Kabbah of being "nurtured on tribal and sectional conflict," and cited the government's failure to end a rebel uprising and low pay as reasons for scizing Kabbah's office. The U.S. ambassador to Sierra Leone, John Leigh, was probably closer to the mark when he remarked the coup's organizers were simply "out to line their own pockets."

Kabbah was Sierra Leone's first elected president in five years, and is credited with negotiating a November 1996 peace treaty designed to end the government's five-year civil war against rebels of the Revolutionary United Front (RUF). In fact, things seemed to be going pretty well for the respected Kabbah before his ouster, so well the Nigerians waited only long enough for U.S. Marines to evacuate foreigners out of the capital before pummeling it with shells from offshore in an effort to reinstate the Sierra Leone leader, who fled safely to Guinea during the coup. The latest is just another episode in Sierra Leone's sorry legacy of chaos, killing and corruption.

The former British colony of Sierra Leone gets its sustenance from diamonds. It also yanks enough bauxite, gold and iron ore out of the ground to keep it mildly solvent. But diamonds are the lifeblood of this sweaty little backwater.

Sierra Leone hasn't had it easy. In 1787, Sierra Leone (Lion Mountain) became an experimental community for freed slaves after British do-gooders bought a swath of 52 square kilometers and called it Province of Freedom. Within three years, 90 percent of the former slaves and white settlers in the territory had died of tropical diseases. Of the 1200 freed slaves who fought for King George during the American Revolution and were brought to Province of Freedom shortly afterward, 800 were dead in two years. Some 50,000 freed slaves were dumped into this sweaty hell-hole between 1807 and 1864.

Britain ceded independence to Sierra Leone in 1961, and the country formed a republic in 1971. In 1992, the people overwhelmingly voted to have democratic elections, which was a cue to the folks who were draining the diamond coffers that it was time for a coup. In April 1992, Captain Valentine Strasser seized control of the government and ruled whichever pieces of the pie he could govern.

The problem with the word "democratic" in Africa is that it is an antonym of the word "tribal." In Sierra Leone, where 52 percent of the population are animists, 39 percent are Muslim and 8 percent are Christian, it doesn't make for a recipe for democracy. Soon after Strasser's coup, a rebel group of Muslim blacks were formed by a former army photographer, Foday Sankoh. Libya trained the motley, human flesh-eating RUF as best it could, and mayhem has served as Sierra Leone's constitution ever since.

The rebels were at the doorstep of the capital Freetown until Strasser rented a group of mercenaries under the command of well-known American merc Bob MacKenzie. MacKenzie had fought in Vietnam, with the SAS in Rhodesia, and in El Salvador, and he had trained HVO (Croat-Bosnian Defence Force) troops for Colonel Zeljko "Nick" Glasnovic 1st Guards' Brigade at Capaljina in Bosnia. The British government (unofficially, of course) asked him to head a group of Ghurkas from Nepal to safeguard the diamond mines in Sierra Leone and push back the rebels. When MacKenzie was killed two months later (some say shot by his own troops and then later cannibalized by the rebels), the Ghurkas flew home. Pretoria, South Africa–based Executive Outcomes saw an opportunity and put together a small army of 200 South African mercenaries, complete with an air force and supply jets. They began training the Sierra Leone army and got to work liberating the diamond fields. The army was pumped up to about 14,000 men (and children).

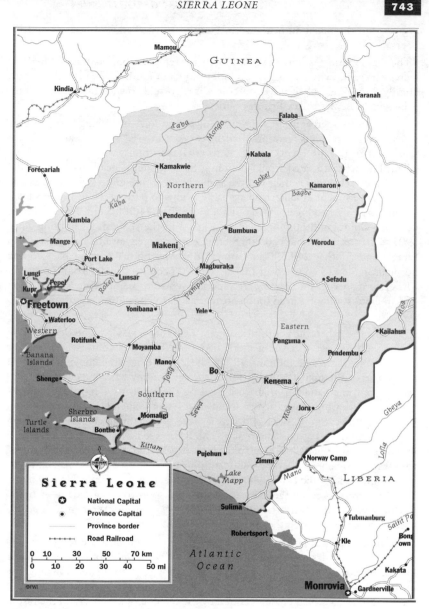

Sierra Leone

- ✪ National Capital
- • Province Capital
- — Province border
- ┼┼┼ Road Railroad

| 0 | 10 | 30 | 50 | 70 km |
| 0 | 10 | 20 | 30 | 40 | 50 mi |

©FWI

Battles mainly consisted of brief encounters, with both sides discharging only a single clip before running like hell in the opposite direction. Both the army and the RUF rebels were whacked out of their brains on ganja and booze, which made for low casualties. Executive Outcomes carved disciplined killers out of the government army ranks, and the face of the war changed. The body count started rising (thanks in part to EO's very own Russian Hind Mi-24 helicopter gunship air force flown by Russian mercenary pilots), and the rebels went into retreat. Sierra Leone soldiers stopped selling their weapons and uniforms to the RUF rogues, and the diamond fields were returned to the hands of Strasser and De Beers.

The diamond mines were the first targets for repossession, as Strasser hired the mercs on credit, with a promise of US$500,000 a month payment in diamonds. Hardly surprising, as Executive Outcomes is reportedly owned by a mining company with close ties to key British politicians.

The rebels took great pleasure in not only killing folks but taking Western hostages. Seven foreigners were grabbed in two days by RUF rebels and then released. Then the insurgents snatched seven Italian nuns, who were summarily killed, but at least spared from becoming Sunday night meatloaf. Because the drug-crazed rebels enjoy their victims as meals, most foreigners split Sierra Leone and the government mobilized all available troops to prevent the insurgents from getting any closer to Freetown. To date, more than 24,000 Sierra Leonians have fled into Guinea and 50,000 have been killed in the six years of fighting since 1991. There are still some 120,000 Sierra Leone refugees awaiting repatriation in Liberia and another 240,000 in Guinea. But why bother coming back? Some hospitals in Sierra Leone report that up to 100 people a day die from starvation. The eastern areas of the country are especially volatile. Sierra Leone's population of 4 million is suffering from food shortages and a general disintegration of society.

It seems that when the youthful Captain Valentine Strasser—who doesn't look old enough to have received a merit badge in the Cub Scouts—seized power from General Joseph Momoh in 1992 he didn't quite have the undying loyalty of the people or the military. Only four of the seven army battalions were loyal to Strasser, and the battalions that were fighting the rebels were mostly kids pressganged into slowing down the rebels' advances. Consequently, mercenaries from Britain, America, South Africa and Russia were busy fighting alongside Nigerian and Guinean troops against the rebels. The RUF is led by Foday Sankoh, whose first demand was that all foreign soldiers be expelled from the country. Strasser, who was personally guarded by Guinean soldiers, didn't see a good reason for it. Apparently, neither did Sankoh himself when the cards were dealt. He and his irregulars were backed by Liberian guerrilla—and soon-to-be president—Charles Taylor, who invaded Sierra Leone in April of 1991 because West African peacekeeping forces were using the country as a base for fighter planes.

The rebels had gotten their asses kicked deep enough into the jungle by EO that the mercenaries left Sierra Leone in early 1997—with both of their Mi-24 Hinds, despite the $75,000 in diamonds offered by RUF to anyone downing one of them. For now Johnny has elevated RUF to full fledged political status (even though Foday Sankoh is being detained by the Nigerians in Abuja) and the rest of West Africa is trying to blast and blockade them out. Most of the people he elected to his government had no idea (or desire) to be politicians in his government.

Sierra Leone is a tin-pot dictatorship with a rotating list of guest star small time military dictators (with the odd elected president once in a while). When peaceful, the country lives off the largesse of outside mining companies since it has the world's second-largest producer of titanium oxide (an ingredient for paint pigment) and a major source of diamonds. For now, it's a nasty place run by heavily armed, Ray-Banned army punks who zoom around the capital and countryside in pick up trucks. These guys make mercenaries look like Mother Teresa's helpers.

President Ahmad Tejan Kabbah was overthrown in an unpopular coup in May 1997 by army major Johnny Paul Koroma. Koroma, like a kid a little too young for his new toys, swore himself in on June 17, invited 6000 RUF rebels to the party and made RUF's Foday Sankoh Deputy AFRC Chairman and second-in-charge in Sierra Leone. Koroma's coup pissed off the Nigerians, who are now poised to take out Johnny with the help of ECOWAS now that they've finished their business in Liberia and can turn their full attention to the mess Koroma's making. More than 10,000 people have been slaughtered in Sierra Leone's civil war since 1991, and 380,000 displaced.

Voodoo Ju-Ju Boom-Boom

Pubescents, beware. In Sierra Leone, the Jombobla secret society is striking terror into the hearts of anyone tuffed at the groin. The group has launched a campaign of sexual violence in the south and east of the country. Jombobla (which translates from the Mende language as "remover of pubic hair") has terrified even its most staunch skeptics with its alleged supernatural powers. In a two-week period in 1997, the group raped at least 10 women in and around the town of Bo. Group members attack women wearing ju-ju charms and a fetish around the neck. After doing the dirty deed, they pluck the pubic hairs from their victims to make empowering fetishes or talismans. Ouch.

Johnny Paul Koroma and the Armed Forces Revolutionary Council (AFRC)

This totally unknown army major seized power in May 1997 and charted Sierra Leone toward more squalor. He had just gotten out of jail for a previous coup attempt. He invited RUF leader Foday Sankoh into his cabinet and declared the army would be running the government until 2001. The fact that they killed 40 civilians and 24 Nigerian soldiers, looted stores and banks and stole dozens of UN vehicles set the tone for his regime. That didn't sit well with the Nigerians who have been contemplating invading SL in earnest. Peace talks in Abidjan were quashed in August 1997 after Koroma's announcement of "four more years" for the soldier-boys, and his government began to implode. With ECOWAS now finished in Liberia with the election of Charles Taylor as president, it can turn its might toward Liberia and the unfinished business there.

The Mercenaries (Executive Outcomes, GSG, et al)

The Sierra Leone government made no pretenses about using mercenaries to fight against the Libyan-trained and Liberian-backed RUF. The government army was an anemic 1000 men back in 1991 but is now estimated at 10,000–14,000 troops, consisting mainly of press-ganged youths with about a week of training. Colonel Bob MacKenzie, a well-known mercenary (and former 101st Airborne with a Purple Heart earned in Vietnam) was killed and eaten by rebels in Sierra Leone in 1995. The government of Sierra Leone maintained that all the foreigners in the country were being utilized as "advisors," but it wasn't so. The old guard white mercenary stereotype was fading; the 150–200 Executive Outcomes (EO)-hired mercenaries were predominantly black (about an 8:1 ratio of black to white) and were recruited from the ranks of former ethnic Angolan ex UNITA fighters with extensive spec ops/bush warfare experience in South Africa, Namibia and Angola.

Drug and alcohol abuse are considered to be a major obstacle to training Sierra Leone government soldiers. EO is no fly-by-night merc group. For US$500,000 a month, they supplied the Freetown government 150 men (who earned about US$2000 a month), a 20-chopper-strong air force (all Russian Mi-24s and Mi-17s), nationwide radio communications, a full-time doctor and two evacuation aircraft on 24-hour standby (one based in Freetown and another in Luanda). EO also chartered two Boeing 727s to run supplies in and out of the country to South Africa. The EO training camp in Sierra Leone was at Waterloo, about 32 km east of the capital of Freetown. Troops went through a three-week boot camp.

In Sierra Leone, EO fought for diamonds in payment but EO sister companies also mine for gold in Uganda and drill boreholes in Ethiopia. In all, EO is part of a family of 32 companies, ranging from adult education firms to computer software interests, in countries such as Angola, South Africa, Zambia, Botswana and Lesotho. In September of '96, President Kabbah managed to get a discount on the $18.5 million they owed to EO for their security work. *DP* wonders if EO could foreclose? EO left Sierra Leone in February 1997, ahead of schedule, leaving the accountants to settle the bills—but may be back. In July 1997, Kabbah's government-in-exile and fugitive Indian banker Rakesh Saxena (on the run in a Thailand bank fraud case) were talking with Sandline International (i.e. EO), and paid Sandline CEO Tim Spicer (of Papua New Guinea fame) $70,000 to come up with a plan to punt Johnny Paul. Saxena has a bauxite concession in West Africa while Sandline chairman Tony Buckingham is a major shareholder in a Vancouver diamond mining company with six mining properties in SL.

EO has more than 1000 employees, three-quarters of whom are black. Most got their hard knocks in the elite tiers of the former South African Defense Force. For now EO is out of Sierra Leone but standing by, waiting for the phone to ring.

Executive Outcomes

Recruitment Officer
PVT. BAG X-105
Hennopsmeer 0046
South Africa
☎ *[27] (12) 666-8429/7005*

Ahmad Tejan Kabbah

Sierra Leone's first civilian president in five years promised to make peace with the RUF rebels and nearly succeeded. On April 23, 1996, Tejan Kabbah and rebel leader Foday Sankoh met in the Ivory Coast and announced a truce in order to detail peace and disarmament accords. Later that year, a peace accord was signed, ending the five-year civil war. But the peace didn't last long. At the end of February 1997, the government claimed to have intercepted a radio message delivered by Sankoh calling for his troops to begin a major offensive against the government. Fighting between RUF and government troops began anew. Kabbah was overthrown in yet another coup in May 1997. But look for him to return. He's been playing Let's Make a Diamond Deal with Executive Outcomes.

The Nigerian Army

The Nigerians weren't happy with Johnny Paul Koroma seizing the government. They began lobbing shells into Freetown as soon as all the foreigners had been evacuated, and Nigerian ground troops quickly took control of Freetown's airport, but have been getting trounced since. But with the backing of ECOWAS, they may be knocking on Johnny's front door soon. For now they are fighting a sloppy war with RUF rebels, the coup boys and innocent civilians in their on again, off again attacks.

Ahmed Foday Sankoh

Sankoh, RUF's leader, is a former army corporal and photographer. A member of the Jemme tribe, he joined the Royal West African Forces in 1956 and was trained as a wireless operator by the British. In 1961, Sankoh was put in jail for taking part in an attempted coup against Joseph Momoh. Pardoned in 1980, he traveled to the U.S. to meet with black Muslim groups. Returning to Sierra Leone, he put together a cadre of like-minded revolutionaries and knocked on Qaddafi's door for some bullets and bucks. While there, he was introduced to Charles Taylor, the chief instigator of Liberia's misery. Taylor used the border areas of Sierra Leone for his bases, and Sankoh received guns and support from Taylor during the late '80s and early '90s. In April 1992, a group of peach-fuzz army officers calling themselves the National Provisional Ruling Council (NPRC) overthrew the new government of Momoh, and 28-year-old Valentine Strasser took over, only to be bounced by another soldier who then set up democratic elections. All of this transpired without Sankoh even being invited to the inauguration or getting to threaten the boss. Strasser did bring in Executive Outcomes, who pushed Sankoh's 300 tattered Revolutionary United Front rebels even further into the bush and obscurity. Sankoh was arrested during an early 1997 trip to Nigeria but emerged as Johnny's No. 1 man after the coup. He's now Deputy AFRC Chairman and second-in-charge in Sierra Leone. When it was discovered that Foday had become the Vice Chairman of Sierra Leone, the Nigerians hustled him from his five star suite at the Abuja Sheraton to house arrest in a neighborhood said to also be the upscale holding pen for Moshood Abiola the democratically elected but jailed president of Nigeria.

The Rebels: Revolutionary United Front (RUF)

The 3000-man Revolutionary United Front is predominantly Muslim and consists mainly of ragtag adolescents and villagers forced into fighting. It began its civil war against the government in 1991. The group has an office near the Liberian border and a press office in Abidjan (run by RUF leader Alfred Foday Sankoh's brother, Alimany Sankoh) on the Ivory Coast. RUF offers a US$2000 reward to anyone who can capture a mercenary alive.

RUF rebels were known to commit atrocities on a regular basis. The eating of victims is not uncommon. The most favored entrées are the liver and heart. Another nasty trick the guerrillas employ on captives is the slashing of ankle tendons and neck muscles.

The guerrillas forced into service are under the constant threat of torture and execution, as are their family members. Beside the rebels getting support from Charles Taylor, there is also backing from the Ivory Coast and Guinea. Libya is a major supplier of arms and money to RUF. The rebels continued their battle against government troops despite a peace accord signed in November 1996. They renewed the civil war in earnest with a May 1997 attack on Kalangba. Red Cross workers reported the rebels sporting flashy new uniforms and automatic rifles. New duds and guns must've made it quite tempting to break a peace agreement.

The Army

Apparently, the soldiers in the 12,000-man Sierra Leonean army would rather make love than war on their two bags of rice a month and 15 leo.

The Kamajors

These obscure, traditional hunters from the south and east of Sierra Leone have been thrown into the conflict, as well. But no one can quite figure out which side they're on. The hunters, originally hired by local chieftains to protect their villages from RUF attacks and considered a militia of the government army, have been throwing sticks and stones at both sides using crude, homemade rifles. But there's no doubt about it; these are nasty folks to deal with. They're making a reputation for themselves through summary execution of RUF rebels they capture and by kidnapping aid workers for ransom. They accuse government troops of pillaging and plundering civilian property and blaming it on the rebels. They promised to leave their farms and whack Johnny Boy, but Kabbah pleaded with them to stay home—to no avail. For now the Kamajors are controlling large parts of the outlying jungles and would like nothing more than to march into town for a little bloodletting.

Sierra Leone's borders are as lax and corrupt as you can imagine. Most visitors are Lebanese diamond traders who zip in and out with small amounts of stones. Someone who enters with a backpack and a ponytail might provoke a few minutes of respectful silence before being relieved of all his possessions. Visas can be had for a stay of 30–90 days and can be obtained at Sierra Leone embassies and consulates. The country maintains embassies in the U.S., Great Britain, Germany, Belgium, Sweden, the Netherlands, Egypt, Austria, Switzerland, Spain and Italy—to mention the major sources of visas. In countries where Sierra Leone does not maintain an embassy, it may be possible to obtain a visa through the British High Commission. The Sierra Leone embassy in the U.S.:

Sierra Leone Embassy

1701 19th Street N.W.
Washington, D.C. 20009
☎ *202-939-9261*

If you are a U.S. citizen applying for a visa through the Washington embassy, you will most likely be required to provide a letter from both your employer, stating that you've indeed got a job to which you must return, and your bank, stating that you have enough funds to motivate you to return. Officials at the embassy may require you to first send a self-addressed stamped envelope for a list of visa requirements. A 90-day single-entry visa costs US$20. You'll need two passport-sized photos and quite possibly proof of your round-trip airline ticket. Allow two weeks for processing.

Although entry permits for Sierra Leone can be obtained in West African states, visas and entry permits cannot be had at the border.

The single 52-mile (84-km) railroad line was abandoned in 1971. Most roads are hellish; the airlines bring in the odd supplies and whisk the wealthy away for shopping sprees in Paris or London. Freetown is perpetually under siege; the countryside is slowly being upgraded from absolutely deadly to very dangerous. It will be a long time yet before travelers can wander through the rainforests in Sierra Leone looking for rare orchids.

Illegal Diamond Mining

Diamond mines are considered off-limits to all outsiders, and, if bumbling travelers happen to stumble upon them, they will be extremely lucky if they are merely detained and lectured on their stupidity. If you come across diamond smugglers, you'll likely end up in a shallow, hastily dug grave.

Being a Journalist

Journalists are routinely rounded up, arrested and beaten by government thugs. The French-based reporters' rights group, Reporters Sans Frontieres, occasionally sends in lawyers from Brussels to Freetown to bail out and defend busted reporters. They, too, are usually beaten up and busted.

Malaria in the severe falciparum (malignant) form occurs throughout the country and is chloroquine-resistant. Tungiasis is widespread. Many viral diseases, some causing severe hemorrhagic fevers, are transmitted by ticks, fleas, mosquitoes, sandflies, etc. Relapsing fever and tick-, louse- and flea-borne typhus occur. Sleeping sickness (human trypanosomiasis) is regularly reported. Foodborne and waterborne diseases are highly endemic. Bilharziasis is present and widespread throughout the country, as are alimentary helminthic infections, the dysenteries and diarrheal diseases, including cholera, giardiasis, typhoid fever, and hepatitis A and E. Hepatitis B is hyperendemic; poliomyelitis is endemic, and trachoma widespread. Frequently fatal are navirus hemorrhagic fevers which have attained notoriety. Rats pose a special hazard; lassa fever has a virus reservoir in the commonly found multimammate rat. Use all precautions to avoid rat-contaminated food and food containers. Ebola and Marburg hemorrhagic fevers are present but reported infrequently. Epidemics of meningococcal meningitis can occur. Echinococcosis (hydatrid disease) is widespread in animal breeding areas. One atlas of the world lists even childbirth as a communicable disease in Sierra Leone. So be careful—there is only one doctor for every 13,153 people in the country. Witch doctors provide the only "health care" available outside the capital.

Sierra Leone was founded in the late 18th century by the British as a settlement for Africans freed from slavery. The country's nasty brother to the south, Liberia, was established by the Americans for the same purpose. In retrospect, even the snowiest of doves has conceded this was a bad idea. So, for now, the British content themselves with relieving the country of its natural resources (mainly diamonds and bauxite) and meddling into the questionable affairs of a questionable government.

Sierra Leone is the classic West African hell hole. The country can proudly boast the lowest life expectancy of any country in the world (41.5 years). It also has the second-highest infant mortality rate on the globe, and leads the human race in overall destitution and despair in other key categories as well. Zany and paranoid, the government executed 26 people in December 1992 for plotting to topple the regime—while most were in jail at the time!

Sierra Leonians bathe in rain water, and they have plenty of opportunities for showers. It rains about 195 inches a year in Freetown and on the coast, making the country the steamiest and wettest in coastal West Africa. During the *harmattan* season from November to April, it can be hot and dry. Most of Sierra Leone is fetid lowlands with scenic mountains in the northeast.

The currency is the *Leone*, which is worth nothing (SL823=US$1 at press time), perhaps due to the country's 81 percent inflation rate. Unemployment is endemic and Sierra Leonians make an average of US$145 a year, making it the sixth most impoverished nation on Earth. The official language is English. Electricity is 220V/50Hz.

Embassy Location

The U.S. Embassy is located in the capital of Freetown

Corner Walpole and Siaka Stevens Street
Freetown
☎ *26481*

07/30/1997	Kabbah announces that the military will run the government until 2001.
05/27/1997	Maj. Johnny Paul Koroma overthrows Kabbah as president.
05/10/1997	Fighting between RUF rebels and government forces resumes in earnest.
11/30/1996	President Tejan Kabbah and RUF leader Foday Sankoh sign peace agreement to end the civil war.
01/16/1996	Captain Valentine Strasser is deposed in a military coup.
9/1992	Liberian-backed RUF rebels began offensive against the NPRC.
6/20/1992	Three British mercenaries are arrested and accused of plotting to overthrow the government.
5/29/1992	President Joseph Momoh is deposed by Captain Valentine Strasser.
1991	ULIMO rebels from Liberia set up camp in Sierra Leone.

Sierra Leonabonics: Local Words of Wisdom

If you wonder why Sierra Leone politics are so convoluted, a good place to start might be looking at what passes for words of wisdom. Sierra Leonean proverbs would challenge the deepest clearest thinker but could provide some good hooks for the latest rap songs.

KRIO (English Pidgin) SAYING:	TRANSLATION:
Kakroch noh de go na makit, boht i de it pamai.	The cockroach doesn't go to market, but it eats palm oil.
We yu go na kohntri, if yu mit pipul dehn de dans wit wan fut, yusehf foh dans wit wan fut. boht if yu dans wit tu fut, dehn go koht di ohda wan ohnda yu.	When you go to a country where the people dance on one foot, you should dance on one foot as well. If you dance on two feet, they'll cut one of them from under you.
Sehn kakroch foh go kohl fohl.	Send a cockroach to go call a chicken.
Trohki wan bohks, boht in han shoht (boht i noh geht han).	The turtle wants to box, but its arms are too short (but it has no arms).
Nohbohdi noh de was wata.	Nobody washes water.

Sierra Leonabonics:
Local Words of Wisdom

If kakroch se i de dans, kohl kak, leh i kam nak sangba foh-ram.	If the cockroach says he will dance, call the cock, have him come and beat the drum for him.
Mblama! Mblama! luk motoka tinap!	Mblama! Mblama! There's the vehicle!
Sira-man dohn fohdohn wit in motoka.	The Lebanese has had a car accident.
We fohl wet, i wet.	When a chicken is white, it's white.
If yu tek tehm kil anch (maskita) yu go si in goht.	If you kill an ant (mosquito) carefully, you will see its guts.
If yu yams wet, kohba-ram.	If your yam is white, cover it.
Wan fingga noh go ebul opin baksai.	One finger can't open up an anus.
Yu wan kaka, boht yu noh wan it.	You want to shit, but you don't want to eat. You want the reward, but you don't want to work to get it.
Yu noh jehntri, yu se yu noh de it dohg.	You're not rich, you say you won't eat dog. "Beggars can't be choosers."
Mohnki nohba [noh go] lehf in blak han.	A monkey will never be rid of its black hands. A bad person, especially a thief, will never give up his bad ways. "A leopard won't change his spots."

Source: Sierra Leone website that carries krio proverbs and stories.

Sierra Leone 1996: RUFing It with the Guerrillas

SIERRA LEONE

The taxi driver wanted $40 for the journey. From Gueckedou, the largest and closest Guinean town to Sierra Leone, to the border was a tricky road, he explained. There are military checkpoints all along the road, not to mention that the road is likely to ruin his precious car with its vast and numerous potholes. I cave in, reflecting as we cruise past the numerous refugee camps en route, that it's a small price to pay if it gets me to my destination without any hassles. The Doma refugee camp is right on the border with Sierra Leone and that's where I'm heading to join guerrillas of the Revolutionary United Front (RUF) in one of the nastiest low-intensity wars around.

The checkpoints are a breeze, until the dreaded question comes. "Do you have a permit to be in the area?" a soldier asks. I try to dodge the issue of permits by telling the driver to say that we're just going to a village up the road and will be back in a couple of hours. That and about $5 seems to satisfy the soldier and we move off, eventually reaching the sprawling mass of mud huts and thatched roofs that the Doma refugee camp consists of. Now is the moment of truth. According to my briefing by RUF officials, barely 48 hours earlier in the Ivory Coast, I will be approached in the camp by the RUF contact man who will arrange my passage across the border.

For some time, the only people who surround me are a group of curious, raggedly clad children, who find seeing a white man something of an exotic spectacle. They are soon joined by adults of the camp. Just as my faith in the RUF organizational ability begins to fade completely, I am approached by a young man named Christopher. "Welcome to my Moa," he says, which are the words I have been waiting to hear from my contact since my arrival. In his hut, we discuss how I will cross the border. He speaks in barely comprehensible pidgin English and I struggle to understand his words. He explains that we will leave the camp in the early morning, but before we can cross the border, I will have to give some money to the Guinean border guards. They supposedly have the key to a small boat that will take me across the river to Sierra Leone.

Even reaching the border poses problems. Some of the villages are inhabited by Guineans, Christopher explains, and if they see us, the alarm will be raised, dashing any hopes of crossing the border. The next hour, is chaotic as we run through villages only to find that even at this late hour there are people colliding with each other in the darkness in their attempts to backtrack and hide before the oncoming invasion. It's like a scene out of The Keystone Kops and would be comical except that I am overdosing on adrenaline.

Finally we reach the compound housing the border guards, and by flashlight I count out the equivalent of $100 for the captain, who after a cursory examination of my bag, allows us to proceed to the riverbank. It is dark and moonless as my boat sets out from the Guinean side of the border. At the rear of the dug-out tree that serves as our canoe, a Guinean soldier paddles us across the river Moa, which separates Guinea from Sierra Leone. This part of Sierra Leone is currently under control of guerrillas of the RUF, who have waged a five-year war against successive governments, and they are the guerrillas I am clandestinely crossing the border to meet.

There is something surreal about the presence of the Guinean soldier. Just across the border, his compatriots are doing their incompetent best to help the Sierra Leone government defeat the rebels, but he appears indifferent to the contradiction of ferrying a journalist into rebel territory. He gratefully takes the $5 I offer him in local currency. From the far riverbank, a flashlight suddenly flashes three times and I reply with two short dashes from my own flashlight.

Three teenage guerrillas are waiting for me on the riverbank. They are dressed in what I will come to recognize as the standard guerrilla uniform of jeans, T-shirts and plastic flip-flops on their feet. Additionally, of course, there are three AK-47s slung casually over the shoulders. It is an hour walk through the jungle before we arrive at the first village. The cacophony of noise the jungle emits is alternately hypnotic and disconcerting. Except for the handful of guerrillas billeted there, the village is deserted. In one of the houses a group of guerrillas listens to raucous reggae music. A bowl of cold, unappetizing rice is provided for me to eat. Wagging his head from side to side to the beat of the music, a guerrilla shouts, "Power to the people!" A little inappropriate, perhaps, as all the locals seem to have taken a rather permanent vacation.

At dawn, I stroll around the village with the commander, Lt. Stanley. The guerrillas, like almost all their ilk, are eager for me to take their photographs, as they hope for a fleeting moment of fame on the inside cover of a magazine. The village is smeared with graffiti: crude drawings of AK-47s grace the walls as well as the usual misspelled slogans, such as "RUF is fighting for [sic] di people." Another building has "Agriculture Committes Office–Dia" written on the wall, but the office is an empty wreck and has probably never been anything other than a few words on the wall.

The following day I receive word that the RUF leader, Foday Sankoh, wants to see me at his headquarters. It will take several days to walk through the bush to reach the leader's camp, says Lt. Marba, into whose care I am entrusted. The daily

30-kilometer trek is exhausting, the breaks infrequent and the fear of government troops constant. During a break, as we sit eating oranges in one of the innumerable burned-out villages, a guerrilla, under the *nom de guerre* of "Rebel 245," rolls up a cigarette with a page from the Bible. I ask if he can read the paper he is using. "Small, small," he says with a contrite grin. "When I smoke through the Bible I become very strong...all the words go up to my head and I become invincible," he boasts. "The Bible is very good."

Others apparently prefer more traditional methods of increasing their strength, or making sure their insurance premium stays at a reasonable level. Noticing that another guerrilla has a series of rectangular cuts on his upper arm, I inquire about their significance. "Bulletproof" comes the slightly embarrassed reply, as if he is fearful (quite rightly) that I won't believe a word of it. "They (the cuts) protect me from bullets," he says, jabbing at his chest with his fingers, then flinging his arms away in imitation of the imaginary bullets bouncing off his body. My suggestion that a proper bulletproof jacket would probably be more effective is met with horrified denials. "No, no, it's African culture...very powerful," he says emphatically. I suspect he means African magic or voodoo, but he can't find the right words. Despite such protestations of faith, however, he churlishly refuses to let me put the power of his protection to the test.

As I join the march again, the lieutenant hands me lunch, which proves to be lumpy, cold lamb. Gesturing to the jungle path, which has already consumed most of the column, and between mouthfuls of lamb, he asks if I know about antipersonnel mines. With a sinking heart, I admit some knowledge. "Well, then," he says, "the whole of this area is mined and you must make sure you follow exactly in the footsteps of the man in front of you." Amazingly, after two days of jungle trekking, we reach the first of the base camps without incident. The camp is constructed almost entirely from roofing zinc, and now I begin to realize why so many of the deserted villages that we have passed through have no roofs.

The camp mascot is Strasser, a dog irreverently named for the former military ruler of Sierra Leone, Captain Valentine Strasser, who had recently been deposed by his second in command, Brigadier Julius Maada Bio. Like almost every rebel camp I visit, it resounds to the sound of reggae music as guerrillas relax, confident that the previous day's declaration of a cease-fire will spare them shelling. The strains of Bob Marley and "Buffalo Soldier" emanate from ghetto blasters attached to looted car batteries that have been recharged courtesy of equally looted British Petroleum solar panels.

A guerrilla turns up the music and begins to dance. He is no older than 9 or 10, but he handles the Kalasnikov hanging from his shoulder with the confidence of a veteran. In his hand he is holding a book, "Elementary English for Beginners." It is the kind of surreal contradiction that has become all too familiar in Africa— children whose only real schooling in life are lessons in dispensing death. He is joined on the earthy "dance floor" by a woman who loosely holds a Russian-made Tokarov pistol in her hand as she sways, rather fittingly, to the rhythm of Marley's composition, "I Shot the Sheriff."

Some days later I set off again to the headquarters in the southeast of the country. By now Foday Sankoh has left the bush for negotiations with the government of newly elected President Ahmad Tejan Kabbah. As we enter one of the many camps en route to the headquarters, I notice a human skull impaled on a stick rising above a cluster of undergrowth. "Enemy's head," says Corporal Chinese Pepper by way of explanation, with a grin. Corpses and skeletons become a gruesome but common sight among the shattered remnants of the rural villages. The body of a semi-decomposed man, huddled on a pathway, still clad in what looks like a sports jacket, is ignored as we pass by. It is only as I move downwind and the stench of death catches up with me that I, like the guerrillas escorting me, move faster.

In the early evening we arrive at a village where we are met by a platoon that will take me on the final leg of the journey to the headquarters. The senior NCO is decked out in camouflage and white Adidas sneakers—he seems to be the equivalent of a richer cousin to his colleagues from the north. A party is dispatched to find food, a euphemism, I later learn, for raiding a village. If they are unsuccessful, we will eat the standard bush meal of raw boiled bananas and snails. In the meantime, the two platoons relax and chatter in the ruins of the village. Dried tobacco leaves are torn up, and with a piece of paper from notebook, rolled into cigarettes that are passed around. A fire is quickly lit and wet clothes are hung around the flames to dry.

Some hours later, flushed with success, the food team returns carrying large quantities of rice and fried fish. Their leader, improbably named High Firing, confirms that they paid a social call to one of the local villages. They told the villagers that running away is bad form, gave them a lecture about the war and convinced them that the RUF is fighting on their behalf. In turn, the villagers donated food, cigarettes and money to them. It's amazing what an AK-47 does for good PR and mutual understanding.

In the morning we set off again. Trooping through open swamps, we can hear the sound of throbbing in the distance. It is almost certainly a helicopter, but the crucial question is what kind. A guerrilla column caught in the open by one of the newly acquired Mi-24 Hind gunships might, despite the cease-fire, prove too tempting a target for the gunners, and it was with an added urgency in his voice that the commander told us to head quickly for cover. Running toward the closest dense bush, I can hear the click-clacks of weapons cocking, and by the time we reach the bush, the sound of the helicopter is deafening. The density of the foliage around us means that we cannot see the helicopter flying over, and more importantly neither can it see us. Eventually the sound fades into the distance.

On arrival at the Zagoda headquarters I am greeted by the commander in Sankoh's absence, Lt. Col. Mohammed Tarrawally. He is resplendent in a pair of American military jungle boots, combat trousers and Nike-emblazoned sweatshirt. The green beret worn jauntily on his head, courtesy of the Sierra Leonean army, is as good an indicator of his status as anything else. Soft-spoken and small, he is the replica of a little Napoleon as he escorts me to my new quarters. In comparison to the other camps, my accommodation is five star—even including the rare luxury of Lipton's teabags, which, like cigarettes, are regularly smuggled in from Guinea.

But even here, far from the front line, the war is never far away. The sound of a jet fighter through the roof of the forest canopy galvanizes guerrillas into frantic action. While they rush to turn over the solar panels that might give away the exact position of the camp, others forlornly seek cover as the jet screams overhead leaving sound waves in its wake, but thankfully, no bombs. "It's just their means of letting us know that they're still around," says Lieutenant Colonel Tarrawally, with a smile, as the camp returns to normal. "The war is not over yet."

—**Roddy Scott**

Sierra Leone: Diamonds Are a Guerrilla's Best Friend

It's amazing the number of wars I've covered in Africa where there just happens to be diamonds. Of course, the side that's dressed in rags and running around in the bush with guns invariably has an earnest Columbia graduate doing the Washington cocktail circuit telling any dimwit prepared to listen that his side is only fighting for democracy and the rights of the common man. What he doesn't mention is that there happens to be oodles of diamonds where he comes from. Or that his side would really like to get their hands on those babies. Not to mention the gold deposits. And the...well, you get the picture.

Speaking of pictures, if there is ever one made about Sierra Leone it will be a surefire hit. Imagine the opening scene as a 4x4 filled with black and white soldiers and one journalist (that's me, played by Robert Redford for the *gravitas*) noses into the shabby African village. Cut to: close-ups of narrowed eyes following its progress along the potholed streets. Above the buzz of flies, whispers of "South Africans" ripple ahead. The jeep bumps into the market square and the gathered throng freezes, then approaches timidly, surrounding the car in silence. One woman suddenly shrieks, "South A-fri-ca!" the words becoming a mantra picked up by the others. Children dart in to touch their heroes, racing away in giggling triumph. A woman grabs my arm. "They saved us. They are saints!" These special forces veterans of the Namibian and Angolan wars, case-hardened tools of the old apartheid regime, cast shy looks at the dancers, then at me. "This happens every time we come here," mumbles the driver. He ducks his head in embarrassment as the wails gather strength. "They really like us."

Now as a serious war tourist you might be thinking, "So far, so good. Might be fun, but how the hell do I go about getting there?" Okay, imagine it's the middle of the night and your KLM or Sabena flight has just landed in Sierra Leone after a six-hour flight from Amsterdam or Brussels. The good thing is, even if you're at the back of the line, you won't wait long to get through immigration. Not many people get off in Sierra Leone.

Immigration may be a breeze, but customs can be a little tricky. Before the officer tells you about his ailing mother and crippled children and asks for a small contribution, say that you're here to interview the Prez and what is the nice customs officer's name so you can mention it to the Big Fella. This will get you a quick and remarkably obsequious "Welcome to Sierra Leone, sir."

Be aware that Lungi airport is separated from Freetown by 10 very dark miles of potholes punctuated by kerosene-lit check points, followed by a rust bucket ferry ride, then another 10 miles to your hotel. Outside the terminal, about two dozen shouting taxi drivers will dive for your luggage. Once someone grabs it, you're not getting it back until you're at the hotel and he's demanding 100 bucks, so keep a grip. Your few fellow travelers will be heading in the same direction, so suggest sharing a taxi. Sharing or solo, however, the bone-jarring ride will carry a tariff of at least $50, plus another tenner each for the rust bucket. The best thing about the ferry is the open upper deck and the opportunity to rehydrate yourself with cold beer. Take the opportunity. The flight from Europe may have spanned 1500 miles and six hours, but the 25-mile journey from Lungi to your hotel is likely to take three more.

If you're on an expense account, the only place to stay is the Cape Sierra. The rooms are air-conditioned and, critically important for a hack, there is a well-appointed bar. In the event you're moved to actually file a story, the telephones do work. If your editor is prepared to spring for a C-note a night, you're laughing. If you're a freelancer and can't convince any of your editors to cough up ("We'll be happy to take a look at what you've got when you get back."), then it's down the road to the charmingly named Mammy Yoko. Just across the road from a stunning beach, the rooms were cleanish when I was there, there wasn't too much fungus in the showers, and the air-conditioning worked— sometimes. Although I negotiated down to $50 a night, Mammy Yoko's recently undertook a major refurbishment and may now be less inclined to accommodate journos on a budget.

If you're hoping to be snapping bang-bang photos from your beachside balcony, by the way, you're out of luck; the war's in the interior and you're going to have to get over to army headquarters for an introduction to the South Africans of Executive Outcomes. Bribing your way in isn't desperately difficult, but it may take a while, in which case hire a taxi to wait for you. You should be able to negotiate a daily rate of about $30.

Bribes are definitely part of Sierra Leone's cultural fabric. The aforementioned customs officer, for example, could have been bought off for a couple of dollars. There may well be other instances where the demand will be substantially inflated. An acquaintance found himself under arrest for taking photos of Freetown's landmark baobab tree. For a mere 100,000 Leones ($100), however, the police were prepared to overlook this open and shut case of espionage. After much haggling, they meekly accepted five dollars. Bribe money should be carried in bills of $1 and $5 denominations. (But never in one wad.)

So what's all the palaver about Sierra Leone, anyway? Unless you picked up this book because you thought it was about public toilets in Brooklyn, you'll already have guessed they have one of those dinky little wars going on. And guess what? It's all about diamonds. Mountains of diamonds. Not to mention the biggest rutile (titanium ore) mine in the world, serious bauxite and gold deposits, and a good chance of platinum and oil. But it's the same old story: there are a few folks who have it all, and few folks who'd like to have it all. Naturally. The screwy thing is that since independence the haves have turned Sierra Leone into the world's sixth-poorest country. Officially. And they were about to lose the whole shebang to the have-nots, until they dialed 911 for outside help.

At the South Africans' base overlooking the Koidu diamond fields a Mi-24 gunship settles noisily. I snap a few photos and fall in with the Belarussian crew, offering to send copies to their families in Minsk. Volodya and Valerii, grizzled veterans of Afghanistan, growl an unmistakable "Nyet!" Valerii slaps a mosquito. "Look, our wives think we're flying cargo here. If they knew what we're really doing, they'd kill us." He stops alongside Colonel Rudolph van Heerden, the South African commander for the Kono District, and takes the offered beer. "But you can send them to Rudolph and he'll make sure we get them," he says as the former mortal enemies turn to discuss tomorrow's joint operation against the rebels.

The side without the goodies are the rebels of the Revolutionary United Front. Their idea of a good time is a bit of ritual cannibalism in between lopping parts off innocent bystanders. Their head dude is Alfred Foday Sankoh, a 62-year-old former corporal, who a couple of decades ago ended up in the slammer for trying to overthrow the government. Eventually granted amnesty, but still sore at everyone, he headed to Libya for some counseling. A pal at Qaddafi's college for aspiring revolutionaries was warlord Charles Taylor from Liberia, which happens to be right next door to Sierra Leone. Taylor went on to overthrow Liberian President Samuel Doe. Between capturing Doe and putting him out of his misery, Taylor sliced off poor Sam's ears, then sauteed and fed them back to him. One of those cultural things, I guess. I mean, who are we to judge? (Besides, Sam ate his predecessor's liver and inherited his vote at the U.N.) Anyway, when Al Sankoh's time came, Charlie gave him a start with a few guns and thugs to keep the standards up. Oh, and they're fighting for democracy and the rights of the common man. I almost forgot to mention that.

Until recently, the side that did have the goodies was led by Captain Valentine Strasser and his four best chums. Back in 1992 the Boyz From the Barracks, all grumpy lieutenants and captains, marched up to the presidential mansion one day to complain about not being paid for months. Seeing them coming, President Joseph Momoh, ever mindful of his neighbor Mr. Doe's fate, was out the back door like a flash and making tracks for the airport. When the last of the lads' "Hellos?" echoed through the empty mansion, they propped their boots on Momoh's desk and discussed the latest in job opportunities. After flipping coins, 25-year-old Strasser ended up as chairman of the new National Provisional Ruling Council. The others gave themselves the inspired, if not actually prescient, titles of S.O.S., for Secretary of State, it's said, and P.L.O., for permanent liaison officer, then shot craps for S.O.S. for Mines, S.O.S. for Treasury, for Defense, for Tourism, Fisheries, Trade and Industry... you name it, they divvied up all the P.L.O. positions. It was tough, but they knew where their duty lay and accepted the heavy burdens of responsibility.

Back in the jungle, the rebel attacks were low key at first: a village for food, a clinic for medical supplies, an everyone-asleep-at-the-wheel army convoy for more guns and ammunition. All straight out of Al's favorite course at Goofy Qaddafi's University, How to Get Your Start in Revolutionary Warfare 101. But with a twist: instead of being nice to the people to get them onside, which every guerrilla leader since Mao has preached, Al Sankoh preferred chopping off arms and legs and heads. This, according to a RUF defector, was Uncle Al's way of suggesting the survivors join up. As recruiting programs go, it was said to be rather persuasive.

As the rebel attacks moved closer to Freetown, a stressed out Strasser & Co. began grabbing kids off the streets, giving them guns, uniforms and a few words on their sacred duty to Sierra Leone, then shoving them into the jungle. The intermittent salaries of $20 and two bags of rice a month, coupled with the prospect of the RUF pouncing on them, convinced a fair number to do a bit of looting, murdering and amputeeing themselves.

There was a certain ebb and flow to the business until Sankoh's Neanderthals grabbed the mines. Suddenly there were no millions flowing into the treasury. Almost as bad was that the diamond smugglers, who paid certain folks good money not to have their bags examined too closely at the airport, had nothing to pay anyone not to look for. And to top it all, the pesky rebels were threatening Freetown itself. It was a vexing moment. Were the boys about to do a Momoh and hightail it for the tall and uncut, or bring in some muscle?

In April 1995, Pretoria-based Executive Outcomes, a private security company staffed by black and white former special forces soldiers, signed a contract to sort things out. To the astonished relief of the Boyz, it took less than a week to eliminate the RUF threat around the capital. Before the even more astonished rebels could ask, "Who was that masked man?" EO roared off to recover the diamond fields. That two-day operation barely worked up a sweat. As soon as rumors of this reached London, I wangled an invitation, got myself a visa and sprinted for the airport.

Hours after arriving I was sitting on the tailgate of an Mi-17 surrounded by black and white South Africans in all their feathers and warpaint as we skimmed the trees. At Koidu they dragged me off on a jolly op to mortar the bejeezus out of the bad guys. Our nights were spent either under monsoon rains or running back and forth to escape columns of enormous army ants. Two choppers eventually picked us up, then dropped down to a town just captured. Dripping with cameras, I was out the door and down on one knee in my best Hollywood pose, looking for action. I blinked at the sight of the wheel struts lengthening on my helicopter. That means it's taking off, I choked. This is not good. Deafened by the whop-shriek of blades and turbines, I next saw the gunner frantically motioning me to return. Are the bad guys coming? Is someone shooting at us? When the wheels actually left the ground, the determined expression of the professional poser dissolved into near—well, total, actually—panic at the prospect of being left to the mercies of the RUF. (You won't say anything about this to Bob Redford, will you?) This was followed by a leap that left me clinging catlike to the bottom of the door. Hands grabbed my wrists and hauled me inside 100 feet above the jungle. "That'll teach you to get out of my helicopter without telling me," the South African pilot said over a few beers that night. "If you had just stayed there, you silly twit, I'd have come back for you."

Back at Executive Outcomes' headquarters, I leap aside as a shiny 4x4 skids to a stop. Two Sierra Leonean soldiers stagger out under the weight of chromed pistols, shotguns, Bowie knives and hand grenades. One also carries a machine gun and about 50 yards of ammunition belt wrapped around him. The mere weight of it all has this metallic mummy pop-eyed and sweating buckets. The ear protectors perched atop his head are a particularly fetching touch. They are followed by their boss, Colonel Tom Nyuma, universally loved as one of the five coup d'etat-ers back in '92. To the everlasting joy of all Sierra Leoneans, he was recently promoted from captain to colonel, skipping the tiresome ranks in between, and added S.O.S. of Defense of the NPRC of Sierra Leone to his other S.O.S.s. He held on to all his P.L.O.s for old time's sake. It's rumored that the main requirements for holding the high octane titles are being able to say them without a crib sheet or taking a breath. You probably think I'm joking.

Colonel Tom struts past his bodyguards, the patches on his vest proclaiming him "Ranger," "Airborne," and "Special Forces." Tom is not known to have attended any such courses anywhere in the world. Ever. His clear favorite is a skull and crossbones with the warning, "Mess With the Best, Die with the Rest." Tom, who went from being an impecunious captain with an attitude to a senior government minister with property in England and monthly trips to the U.S., is said to have purchased the patches through *Soldier of Fortune* magazine. Tom is 26 years old. The reader will sleep better knowing he is also in charge of the war.

Inside the operations room Colonel Renier Hugo, EO's operations officer, is briefing the Belarussian gunship pilots and Colonel Tom on another attack. Next to Tom is a Sierra Leonean major whose men have been guarding the diamond fields for Tom since the South Africans chased out the rebels. It should be stated here and now that even though he's keeping a very close eye on the diamond fields, it has nothing to do with him being tight with Tom's sister, or that Tom might have one or two ideas about what to do with those diamonds.

Hugo's pointer taps the map, his tone crisp and professional: The infantry company will advance to this point, another company will be landed here by helicopter, support elements will be placed there, the gunship will orbit over here until.... The pilots listen intently, making notes on their own maps. The major, whose men are integral to the operation, is content with the plan; so content that he's snoring gently. A blinding flash fills the room. Duck! It's Tom's official photographer. Tom sidles up to the map to explain how the attack should be conducted. Volodya and Valerii's eyebrows lift, then meet in bewilderment. The South Africans smile fixedly. Two more flashes for the Freetown newspapers and Tom takes his seat. Hugo carries on as if nothing has happened.

The attack was successful. Of course, Tom and his sister's boyfriend really didn't think it important enough to be at the sharp end with their troops. It was too small an operation for them to be involved, they told me hastily when reports of six wounded were radioed from the advancing soldiers. Consummate professionals, they spent their time studying tactics as revealed in their complete collection of Rambo videos. And no, I'm really not joking this time. But if there ever is a film made, by God you'll split your sides laughing.

—Jim Hooper

Somalia

★★★★★

Clan Bake

It's tough running a country financed by locals selling camels, bananas, frankincense, spiny lobster tails and shark fins. Tax revenue also comes from roadblocks, license plates, port duties and whatever spare change is left in the sand. Up north in breakaway Somaliland things are much calmer. The eastern half of this tiny area is called Sanaag and is controlled by a clan that does not agree with Mohammed Ibrahim Egal's presidential ambitions. Self-elected Egal has put the lid on half of his new country. The country of Somaliland (not to be confused with Somalia or Disneyland) prints its own money in Britain, has a funky homemade flag (it may humor our readers to know that the Somali flag is actually based on the blue UN flag) and is protected by a ragtag army of about 15,000 kids and unemployed men. The main airport is closed (so what?), and its ill-defined border with Ethiopia to the south is a free-fire zone ruled by rejects from a Mad Max movie. Heavily armed clans dodge land mines in the rocky wastelands in their technicals, rusty tanks and camels. Its main exports are goats, sheep and camels to Saudi Arabia and the Gulf States. Oh, I suppose we should mention that Somalia's 1700-mile coast has great beaches.

Somalia (like most to blown to hell countries) was actually a pretty cool place about 1000 years ago. Known as Punt (an appropriate political strategy these days), it was the home of the Queen of Sheba, spices, traded with China, yadda yadda, yadda. Today Somalia is an arid, high speed cross between Leone's *Once Upon A Time in the West* and a '60s Drugs n' Biker movie, or maybe more like Lucas's wasted brown planet of Tatooine without the colorful bar scene. If you like looking on the sunny side, there is a web site titled "Visit the Somali Republic, the Jewel of the Indian Ocean. The Cross Roads of Africa...The Gum of the Sea Ways, The real Paradise for the Hunter, The country of Peace, Culture and Stability." The site lures the tourist with phrases like "Mogadiscio, with its stable climate is a paradise for the tourist." A quick peek at the airlines, however, lists a subsidiary of BOAC, an airline name that has been defunct for abut 20 years. Oh well, maybe you should postpone your trip for the next century when they have the annual clan get-togethers on the streets of Mog.

The syrupy home-spun web hype forgets to mention that Somalia's clans have been drilling holes in each other ever since the first Somalis decided to marry someone other than their sister. How long will this clan-banging go on? Well, until they run out of bullets and somebody ties down every rock in this parched, godforsaken country. Recently, the clans have cloaked themselves with high falu-tin political names so that it sounds more like a church gathering than a street fight. Names such as the Somali Salvation Democratic Front or the Somalia National Alliance may conjure up visions of crew-cutted, white-shirted, apple-cheeked kids riding around tree-lined neighborhoods with Korans, but that is far from accurate. These clans are more likely to be scrawny, bug-eyed (from chewing khat), flip-flopped kids who charge around the shattered 100 degree plus streets in smashed up Toyota pickup trucks featuring welded together 50 calibre or anti-tank guns stolen from Uncle Sam's finest. Since a good living in Somalia is $3 a day, we figure the kids are allowed to roar around drunk or stoned and shoot off a few armor-piecing rounds at each other. To be fair, some Somali sources describe the young drug-whacked kids as militiamen, "unpaid volunteers who fight, not on orders but out of desire to defend their communities." They conclude by saying, "A well organized civilian militia, protected by the right to keep and bear arms is still the most effective protection for the security of a free state." Uh, yeah, and I'll take that shiny new watch you're wearing in the name of freedom and security.

But before we dive into the players, you must know that there are really three but equally lawless Somalias.

The dodgy Republic of Somaliland in the northwest with the capital of Hargeisa; Somali, the land that makes up the long southern coastal section and the home of the Digila and more agrarian Rahanweyne clans; and the northeast with Bosaso as its hub. The capital of the south is the hotly contested city of Mogadishu. To further complicate the divisions, Djibouti is actually half-Somali. Beirut was easy to figure out compared to Somalia. The breakaway republics are not recognized by any international body, although perhaps they should be.

Only the southern part makes the news—that section of Siad Barre's defunct Somali Republic which was formerly Italian Somaliland. The south is simply lawless territory inhabited by nomadic Somalis and ruled by clans. The northern part, formerly British Somaliland, misses the headlines and is sometimes portrayed as

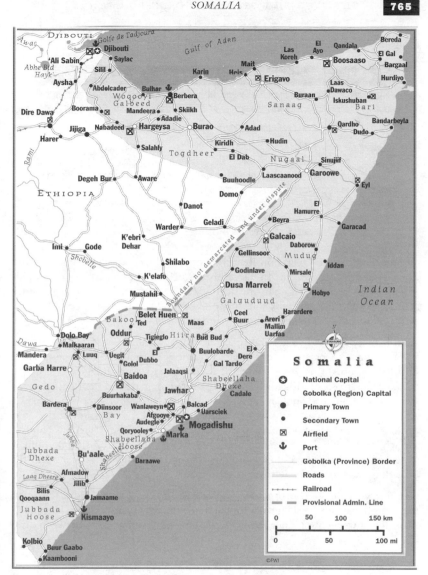

considerably more peaceful. Unlike the south, the north has had something of a government—the government of Somaliland—since the fall of Barre's republic, and even, at times, a head-of-state.

Yet overall, it's been an orgy of blood feuds in Somalia. After the rebel United Somali Congress (USC) captured Mogadishu during the last week of 1990 and toppled Barre's despotic regime (although it at least was a regime), Somalia watched its last government—or anything resembling it—go down the drain. Siad fled and the USC installed Ali Mahdi Mohamed as temporary president. But the USC was marred by internal bickering and bloodshed within its ranks, and from them rose General Mohamed Farah Aidid. Aidid and Ali Mahdi signed a U.N.-bullied peace agreement in March 1992, but it broke down as perhaps a million Somalis fled the country's famine and clan warfare. Soldiers looted U.N. food supplies the world body was unable to protect.

Somali Warranty

As you approach the compound's high white walls, a teenager's eyes challenge, demand and insult all at once. A rifle slips from his shoulder, then slips back.

Nowhere in the world have I felt the predatory menace you feel on these streets.

On paper, the property in the particular neighborhood I was visiting belonged to a once-privileged clan, the Murusade. By the terms of force majeure, it belongs to a heavily bandoleered clan named the Habr Gedir. A couple of weeks before I approached the compound on this street, a gunman had slipped in the gate, pulled a mechanic out from under the Land Cruiser on which he was working, and shot the man in the head, then calmly walked out. Now a visitor must bang on the heavy steel plate of the gate to enter. A peephole slides open, and you slip through a small gate within the gate. Such is Somalia.

Enter the U.S. and Operation Restore Hope. Eighteen hundred American marines landed in Mogadishu on December 9, 1992, the first of nearly 30,000 troops to arrive here with the mission of restoring some semblance of order. (Hussein Aidid, the general's son, was one of the U.S. Marines. See "The Players.") Aidid and Ali Mahdi grudgingly shook hands.

On January 11, 1993, a general cease-fire was agreed to. But it, like the dozens before it, hadn't a prayer. After Somalis became accustomed to the strange aliens called Americans, they decided to off a couple and even dragged one corpse through the streets of Mogadishu. CNN got it all on tape and the Pentagon, not wanting any more bad publicity and angry mothers, brought the boys home. U.S. efforts to bring Aidid down were like a Philadelphia SWAT team attack: they kept turning the wrong house into Swiss cheese. So Uncle Sammy washed his hands of the whole Somali affair in November 1993. With the Americans gone, Somalis were again permitted to resume killing, raping and maiming each other. Only this time they had more U.N. leftover toys to play with.

The only bright spot was the May '97 peace accord between Aidid (currently the self-proclaimed president of Somalia) and his chief rival, Ossan Hassan Ali Ato's Rahanweyne Resistance Army (RRA). Fighting still goes on between other clans.

Elvis is Alive!

At least the Somalis think so. The Islamic Court in north Mogadishu, the closest thing resembling an administrative body since the overthrow of Mohamed Siad Barre in 1991, has warned that clean-shaven men had better grow beards—in the Islamic tradition—or suffer the consequences. The court's leader, Sheikh Ali Sheikh Mohamed, brought a clean-shaven youngster before a gathering of faithful and ordered the crowd to boo at the kid. "Those who shave like Elvis Presley, Sylvester Stallone and the U.S. Marines will not go unpunished," Ali Sheikh proclaimed.

The youngster was decidedly sans Elvis' sideburns, being barely old enough to sport a tuft of pubic hair, much less a cascade of ZZ Top whiskers. But, prepubescent teenagers and secular governments aside, it's Gillette and Schick that have to be worried the most about the rise of Islamic fundamentalism.

The 26 factions of the National Salvation Council (NSC) are trying to get a central government together in the south but have been stymied by Hussein Farah Aidid—an ex-U.S. Marine with a disdain of idle rifles—whose trumped-up charges of "foreign intervention" have served as an excuse to keep the bullets whistling. As many as 50,000 Somalis have been killed since 1991—300,000 have died due to war-induced starvation. There has been no central government since 1991. Some semblance of order has returned to north Mogadishu, if only because folks there want to hang on to their limbs. The Islamic *shari'a* courts are the law here (you know, the folks who cut off hands for stealing)—the Jenny Craig of criminal justice. You, too, can lose weight fast.

The Clans & Everybody Else

In this clan war, if your mama's from a different family tree than Aidid's, you are the enemy. There are more than 500 clans and 20 political groups in Somalia. The Lisan sub-clan clashes with Aidid as do the forces of Ali Atto and Ali Mahdi. The Yaalahow militia controls the Mecca and Medina districts of Mogadishu, depending on what day it is. Break out those phonebooks and history books if you want to figure this one out. If you can figure out the backgrounds and shifting alliances between the Habr Gedir, Marehan, Abgal, Majertein, Murusades drop us a line.

Hussein Mohammed Aidid

"Aidid" means "rejector of insults." In Hussein's case, it also means "AWOL." Ironically, Somalia's newest warlord, Hussein Mohammed Aidid, is a corporal in the United States Marine Reserve who served as a translator for the Marines in Somalia in 1992–93, and who has been conspicuously absent from his Pico Rivera, California, artillery unit since 1995. Hussein Aidid is the son of the slain General Mohammed Farah Aidid, and once worked as a $9-an-hour municipal clerk for the city of West Covina, California, and graduated from high school there. He joined the Marine Corps Reserves in 1987, last reporting for duty in July 1995. He moved back to Somalia shortly afterwards. Aidid was first brought to the United States as a teenager by his mother, Asli Dhubat, Gen. Aidid's first wife. Recently interviewed by the Associated Press in Somalia, Aidid said he valued his Marine experience: "I'm proud of my background and military discipline," he said. "Once a Marine, always a Marine." His CO isn't in complete agreement, however. Aidid's top foreign policy advisor also spent time in the U.S.; he was a Washington cab driver for three years—making him overly qualified in this "regime." When *DP's* Rob Krott hired about 100 U.S. resident Somalis for a Dept. of the Army project about 10 percent were Washington area cab drivers. If you want to shoot the breeze on your next trip you can find Aidid in his headquarters in Southern Mogadishu.

Mohamed Farah Aidid and the Somalia National Alliance

"President" Mohamed Farah Aidid was killed in factional fighting in late July 1996. According to his enemies, he died "while killing people." An understatement, we say. Aidid led troops that killed 18 U.S. soldiers in 1993. That action resulted in the U.S. withdrawing its forces and blocking the U.N. effort to reconstruct the country. His Somalia National Alliance had been duking it out with Ali Mahdi's Somali Salvation Alliance. In reality, the chance of either side actually controlling all of Somalia is nonexistent. Aidid collected taxes from—or shot—anyone who crossed his "green line." His son has now taken on the mantle of being self-proclaimed president.

Mohamed Siad Barre, the ex-president of the Somali Republic, whose excesses finally undid him, was cozy with Egypt and a buddy of Boutros-Ghali's when Boutros-Ghali was with Egypt's Foreign Ministry. When Barre's man Aidid became Barre's enemy Aidid, Boutros-Ghali, understanding the exercise of power, targeted Aidid. He worked against him before the U.N. intervention, and it was during his tenure as secretary general, with his men ensconced in Mogadishu, that he allowed the U.S. functionaries to get so worked up over Aidid that they shifted the focus of the U.N. mission there. As Boutros Ghali looked on, the U.S. went after Aidid.

The U.N. Security Council issued an arrest warrant for Aidid but he managed to elude both U.N. forces and U.S. troops. The U.S. never got Aidid. (Strangely enough while all this was going on *DP* saw Aidid attending a rubber chicken dinner in Nairobi on the front page of the local newspaper.) Despite the price on his head and the number of spooks who we assume can read a newspaper, nothing ever happened and the military continued its search-and-destroy mission at great cost in both money and, later on, lives. Between 6000–10,000 Somalis were killed and 18 U.S. soldiers died.

Aidid was weakened by the defection of his sugar daddy, the wealthy Osman Ali Atto. Atto stepped on a land mine, and he lost most of his left foot. His dissatisfaction with Aidid split the Haber Gedirs.

Ali Mahdi Mohamed

Ali Mahdi Mohamed controls the relatively sedate northern area of Mogadishu. He is allied with Osman Ali Atto, who formerly bankrolled Aidid's fight for power. Atto and Aidid battled it out in the south, with casualties per day between 60–100 people killed and 10 times as many wounded. Ali Mahdi, the other "president" of Somalia, is backed by the Somali Salvation Alliance and supported by the Saad and Abgal clans. Ali Mahdi presents himself as a moderate and is in favor of alignment with the West. His brand of Islamic justice has led to amputations, stonings and floggings in the northern Mogadishu areas he controls. In the last year, the SSA has judged at least 500 cases and ordered five executions, 21 amputations and 421 floggings. In one case, a court of 12 religious leaders sentenced a man to stoning for rape. He was shackled to the ground and stoned to death with cinder blocks hurled by an enthusiastic crowd. Naturally, the media was invited to film the festivities.

The Habr Gedir Clan

Mohamed Farah Aidid's Habr Gedir clan (actually a subclan of the Hawiye) comes from the Mudug region. The hot, dry and destitute condition of the Mudug region ensures that only the strong survive. Aidid's driving ambition was to forge a Somali state. When his U.S. pursuers boasted of getting so close to catching him that his bed was still warm, reporters invited into that "still warm" sanctum found a book on Thomas Jefferson on the bedside table. But this was not merely a man who, as head of the Habr Gedir clan, was unable to accommodate other clans. Within his own Habr Gedir, vicious infighting has erupted between extended families.

Ethiopia

The Ethiopians are getting a little tired of the "Kids from Hell" next door. They killed 232 "terrorists" last year.

Al Hahad

The Saudis are backing a small group of Islamic fundamentalists based along the Juba River on the Ethiopia border. They have also been attacking Ethiopia which simply sends in troops to the lawless area of Somalia and kills as many as they can (see "Ethiopia").

Visas are not available at either the airport in Mogadishu nor at any of the border crossings. From the U.S., unless you're an aid worker or have been specifically invited by whomever's in charge at the time, forget it. However, it may be possible to obtain a visa from Somalia's embassies maintained in Kenya, Egypt, Djibouti and Tanzania. In Nairobi, try the International House (Mama Ngina Street). For a three-month visa, you'll need three photographs and a letter of introduction, preferably from your embassy. You should be able to pick up your visa the next day. In Cairo, try the Somali mission on Dokki Street. Here, you'll definitely need a letter from your embassy stating the purpose of your journey, as well as proof of onward travel by air. There are no land crossing visas issued. Here, you'll also need three photos. Processing takes a day. In Tanzania, Somali visas are issued at the Italian embassy:

Italian Embassy
   Lugalo Road

P.O. Box 2106
   ☎ *46352/4*

Somalia has a consulate in Djibouti and this may be the easiest place to get a Somali visa:

Somalia Consulate
   Boulevard del Republique
   BP 549
   ☎ *353521*

U.K.: Embassy of the Somali Democratic Republic,
   60 Portland Place,
   London, England, W1N 3DG,

☎ *[171] 580-7148.*

U.S.: Somali Permanent Mission to the United Nations,
   425 East 61st Street, Suite 703,
   New York, NY 10021,
   ☎ *(212) 688-9410, FAX: (212) 759-0651.*

The road network in Somalia is thoroughly dilapidated. About a tenth of the 27,000 miles are paved. There are surfaced roads between Mogadishu, Kisimayo and Baidoa in the south, and between Hargeisa, Berbera and Burao in the north. There is the skeleton of a bus network in the south and no public transportation in the north. Fifty percent of the Somali people are nomads, and the camel is the principal form of transportation in the country. The IDA agreed to repair the road network in Somalia but has yet to get started on the work, for obvious reasons. It seems the Somalis like to steal every AID vehicle they can get, chop the roof and slap a stolen.50 caliber machine gun on the back. The only way to get around, at present, is to hitch a ride with one of the few aid agencies remaining in the country. In the past, lifts have been available with United Nations High Commission for Refugees vehicles in Mogadishu and other areas. In Mogadishu, you can try hiring a cab or motorbike driver, but you'll probably be abducted or shot, or both. The twice-weekly Somali Airlines flights between Mogadishu and Berbera and the weekly flights to Hargeisa and Kisimayo from Mogadishu have been suspended.

If you do attempt to travel by road, make sure you bring along some friends. Technicals (ideally, with 50-caliber guns) come in very handy at the many roadblocks, which are just a way for the locals to make money. A show of force or a short burst above their heads will force them to ponder the relative value of dying for a few dollars. There are no fixed prices for renting a technical with *mooryaan*, or teenage gunmen, but there will be plenty of offers. It is estimated by the U.N. that there are 2 million assault rifles in Mogadishu alone.

There is supposed to be a $20 departure tax when the airport opens, but you should keep in mind that when the UN left, they needed heavy armor and hundreds of marines. The UN probably promised to mail in their $20 when Somalia gets a postal service to deliver it, a bank to cash it and a government to spend it.

The South

The guerrilla force that overthrew Siad Barre in Mogadishu—the Somali National Movement—got its start in the north, and having seen to Barre's overthrow, it has long since gone back to the north. The problem in the north is that the victorious guerrillas turned the government over to an interim president—Abdirahman Tour—who at worst was bent on destroying his own government because he wanted to see a reunited Somali Republic (he has ties to the old Barre regime and to Egypt, which supported Barre) and at best was simply unable to contain clan warfare. In fact, clan warfare began in the north when the president sent armed men from his own clan, the Habre Younis, to seize Berbera, the north's chief port and the turf of the Issa Musa. Already ensconced in the capital at Hargeisa, it now appeared as if he were set. At least for a few months.

Along came an old man now commonly acknowledged to be brilliant, Ibrahim Dhega Weyne. Under his direction, the Issa regrouped and took Berbera back. With that, the two clans repaired to a mountain village, where for 17 days they argued fiercely.

The Green Line

Nope, this ain't a Los Angeles rapid transit line, but the front line in Somalia's civil war. It runs in Mogadishu on a southeast axis down Afgoye Road with Atto controlling the area around the former U.S. embassy and Somali National University and Aidid controlling the south and the port of Merca. Atto's area borders on the Medina district, where he is backed up by Mussa Sudi, an ally of Mahdi.

The North

In October 1994, fighting broke out between President Mohamed Ibrahim Egal, who is supported by the Habir Awal, Gadabursi and Saad Musi clans, and the Idegale militia, who are aligned with the Habir Younis. Normally, a peaceful area, the fighting quickly sent 150,000 refugees fleeing from the capital of Hargeisa. The Idegale make a little folding money by controlling the airport and charging a tax on all who use it. The government muscled in, and that's when the fighting started.

The Habir Younis (now remember, they support the Idegale Militia) appealed to Aidid and were sent a plane full of rifles and ammo. Egal (the guy who runs the country) called Ali Mahdi Mohamed (Aidid's enemy in the south) and received a nice letter in return but no guns. So Egal hit up his buddies the North Koreans, and then got busy fighting. The fighting spread to the Garhadjis (a subclan of the Idegale and Egal in Burca, Sheikh and Burao). The government forces didn't do so well, so now the Garhadji militias have most of the government weapons in their possession. To make things more complicated, Egal does not have support from the majority of people but is pushing for an independent

Somaliland. His opponents want to join up with Somalia. His predecessor, President Abdurahman Tur of the Habir Younis clan, was voted out and is now hanging out in Mogadishu under the protection of Aidid.

Even though Egal has done a good job of whipping Somaliland (not Somalia) into fiscal and governmental shape, not one Western country will recognize its sovereignty. Go figure. OK, now who's ready for a pop quiz on Somalia politics?

SomalilandNet

http://www.compmore.net/~hersi/index.html

The Somaliland Page

http://www.users.interport.net/~mmaren/somlandarc.html"

Bandits and Clans

Most of the factions are simply extended families engaged in blood feuds. They take no prisoners, and, if you stumble onto anybody's turf, expect to be treated accordingly—i.e., shot or macheted. Where clans don't rule, bandits do. Bandits control large rural areas and snipe around in the cities, as well. Police forces are present in some cities, but are essentially impotent and refuse to stand up to the clans and bands of thugs. They have few resources and are as likely to be targeted for death as anyone else. Muslim *sharia* law, which has replaced any form of institutional legal system in Somalia, is enforced in a non-cohesive fashion by clan elders.

Kidnapping

Kidnapping of whatever foreign-aid workers are left is on the rise. The good news here is that hostages are rarely harmed and often released quickly. The bad news is that more of them are being taken, as they make convenient political bargaining chips. On December 18, 1995, Italian aid worker Marco Lorenzetti was taken hostage by a gang loyal to Aidid. On December 26, Aidid ordered the man turned over to his own custody, after which he "arrested" and "deported" the Italian for entering Somalia without a valid visa issued by the "legitimate" government (Aidid's). By releasing the hostage, Aidid was seeking to be seen in a good light by the Italians. On March 23, 1996, an American aid worker was kidnapped but released the next day. On March 21, five U.N. workers were abducted from Balidogle airport by gunmen and rescued on the 22nd by a Somali militia that recognized them on a BBC broadcast.

Khat

Although technically not dangerous by itself, most of the gunmen cruising around the country have that tweaky, faraway look that sends chills down the spine of visitors. Khat is also one of the underpinnings of the economy here resulting in the occasional shootout over territory or delivery routes. Those who don't fight battles or raise camels grow khat, an amphetamine-like stimulant that, when chewed, provides a mild high. Khat is preferred fresh, and Federal Express would be green with envy to watch the bundles of khat being airfreighted out of Mogadishu to Yemen and the Gulf States. Khat can also be used as a form of currency.

Technicals

Every American teenage kid's fantasy is to drop a big 454 into an old Chevy Nova and terrorize the neighborhood. Here every Somali's fantasy is to drop an anti-aircraft gun onto the back of a Toyota pickup truck and terrorize the country. Actually, a technical might be a great way to get through the morning commute. Technicals are essentially anything with wheels to which Somalis can bolt a belt-fed machine gun. Homemade technicals were invented in Lebanon in the '80s when warring groups wanted to hit and run (and make a lot of noise). Technicals became the ride of choice when the locals found out that the U.N. workers would hire them as security. Needless to say, it was harder to find a Toyota Land Cruiser with a roof after that. Thank goodness it only rains bullets here.

Journalists

No need for nasty letters to the editor here. The Somali warlords are a well-read bunch, and if they take issue with something you've written, they send a *mooryaan* to knock on your door and deliver their response. Four Somali journalists were executed by followers of Aidid for offending him in an article they wrote in a U.N.-sponsored paper. An Italian journalist was executed after being mistaken for an executive of an Italian banana exporter. Most journalists do not sign their name on local articles for fear of reprisals.

Bananas

In October of '95 Ali Mahdi's men fired at banana boats trying to dock in the ports of Mog. You see Aidid is Ali Mahdi's mortal enemy and Aidid controls the banana trade. Now we don't know what happens if you are carrying a banana through customs but we should warn *DP* readers that a customs inspector might say, "Is that a banana in your pocket or are you just showing your support for Aidid?"

Killing People

With all these guns and hair-trigger tempers, it doesn't take more than a few minutes for a clan fight to break out and people to get killed. The only consolation we can offer you if you are convicted of killing someone is that the *sharia*, or Islamic law, mandates that you must pay 100 camels. If you are a woman, the penalty is 50 camels.

The state-run medical system has collapsed in Somalia, and only rudimentary care is available through NGOs. Statistically there is supposed to be one doctor for every 4640 people in Somalia. Good Luck. Diarrhea, communicable and parasitic diseases are rampant in the country. Chloroquine-resistant malaria is present in all parts of the country. Larium should be used for chemical prophylaxis. Cholera, dracunculiasis (Guinea worm), cutaneous and visceral leishmaniasis, rabies, relapsing fever and typhus (endemic flea-borne, epidemic louse-borne and scrub) are prevalent. Somalia is also receptive to dengue fever, as there have been intermittent epidemics in the past. Meningitis is a risk during the dry season in the savanna portion of the country, from December through March. Schistosomiasis may also be found in the country and contracted through contact with contaminated freshwater lakes, streams or ponds. A yellow fever vaccination certificate is required for all travelers coming from infected areas.

There's also a pesky little problem with Tumbu Fly, a local maggot that burrows into human skin, munching on flesh all the way. The larvae grows big enough to rip out flesh before it turns into a fly. You don't see a lot of horror movies in Somalia because real life beats David Cronenberg every time. The best place to be evacuated to is Riyadh, Saudi Arabia.

Somalia is flat hot place wrapped around Ethiopia like a bandage. The north has hills 3000–7000 ft/900–2100 m. The rest is a wasteland of dirt. Located in the Horn of Africa, British Somaliland and Italian Somaliland formed independent Somalia in 1960. The population is 9.3

million with a 12-percent mortality rate. Somalia covers 637,655 square kilometers (246,199 square miles). Best time to go? Well the term hot as hell would be the phrase of choice describing the climate most of the year. June–September is hot with cool evenings. October–May hot enough to give cockroach heatstroke. If you like your heat wet, head to Mog where the humidity is a constant 80 percent with the occasional breeze.

Somalia is not really set up to be the next big tourist attrition in Africa. Its long coastline has some of the nicest sand beaches on the continent, but the waters are infested with sharks and there is little shade. Believe it or not there is a tourist office in Mogadishu. Let the phone ring a long time (if you can get through).

Somalia National Agency for Tourism

Box 533,
Mogadishu, Somalia,
☎ *3850 or 3479.*

March to June and September through December are the rainy seasons. Nomadic grazing is the name of the game here, with temperatures hot and landscape arid. The country is 100 percent Sunni Muslim; the entire population is ethnic Somali. English is widely spoken, and Italian is popular in the south. Somali is a difficult language and uses the Roman alphabet. Somali has been a written language only since 1972 so understandably just 24 percent of the country is literate. Things like telephones (country code 252) electricity (220), gas or food are in short supply, so look for a hotel with a roof and a generator.

Money is the Somali shilling broken down into 100 centesimi. The money is surprisingly stable since there is no government to print more. Oh, did we forget to tell you that there is no government? Hotels run about 45 shillings a day. Depending on which region you are in most of the city folk speak Arabic, Italian or English

Somalis like to be called by their nicknames. The slender Somali frame creates a lot of nick names like *Ato*, or thin, or *Dheere* which means tall.

Contacts:

For more information contact:

Australia (represented by its embassy in Kenya)

P.O. Box 39341,
Riverside Drive (just off Chiromo Road),
Nairobi, Kenya
☎ *[254] (2) 445-034, FAX: [254] (2) 444-617.*

Canada (represented by its high commission in Kenya)

Comcraft House,
Haile Selassie Avenue, Box 30481,
Nairobi, Kenya
☎ *[254] 221-4804, FAX 254-226-987.*

British Embassy

Waddada Xasan Geedd Abtoow 7/8,
P.O. Box 1036, Mogadishu,Somalia

☎ *20288.*

U.S. (represented in Kenya)

U.S. Liaison Office for Somalia,
U.S. Embassy, Moi and Haile Selassie Avenues,
Nairobi, Kenya,
☎ *[254] (2) 334141, FAX: (2) 340838.*
Mailing address:
P.O. Box 30137, Nairobi, or Unit 64100,
APO AE 09831.

Somalia News Update

Department of Cultural Anthropology
Uppsala University
Tradgardsgatan 18
S-753 09 Uppsala, Sweden
e-mail: Bernhard.Helander@antro.uu.se

Web Resources:

There is absolutely nothing that is up-to-date on Somali and even less that is accurate. The web is a good starting point for recent news reports. Most of these sites all link back to the same places.

Greater Horn Information Exchange (USAID)

http://198.76.84.1/HORN

SOMALIA

Somalia (CIDA)

http://www.synapse.net/~acdi03/index-afr/externe/eastcent/country/somalia.htm"

Somalia (CIA)

http://www.odci.gov/cia/publications/nsolo/factbook/so.htm"

Somalia Page (University of Pennsylvania)

http://www.sas.upenn.edu/African_Studies/Country_Specific/Somalia.html

Somalia Page (University of Indiana)

http://www.cs.indiana.edu/hyplan/dmulholl/somalia/somalia.html

Somalia gopher (University of Missouri)

gopher://umslvma.umsl.edu:70/11/LIBRARY/GOVDOCS/ARMYAHBS/AAHB3

Somalia (MLAS)

http://192.203.180.62/mlas/somalia.html"

City.Net Somalia<

http://www.city.net/countries/somalia/

Somalia Country Profile (GHIE)

http://198.76.84.1/HORN/somalia/somalia.html

Somalia's WWW Sites

http://www.liii.com/~hajeri/somalia.html"

Somalia Archive

http://www.users.interport.net/~mmaren/somarchive.html

Somalia ≠ Law

http://lawlib.wuacc.edu/forint/africa/somalia.html

Abdirazak: Somali Music Online

http://www.iuma.com/IUMA/band_html/Abdirazak.html"

Ethnologue Database: Somalia</a> </dt>

http://www-ala.doc.ic.ac.uk:80/~rap/Ethnologue/eth.cgi/Somalia/

Horn of Africa Bulletin<

http://www.sas.upenn.edu/African_Studies/Newsletters/menu_HAF_Main.html"

Somalia (Eye on Africa)

http://www.webperfect.com/afrinet/somalia/news.htm

Somalia news

http://www.staff.uiuc.edu/~akagan/News/so.html"

Somalia News Update (gopher)

gopher://gopher.etext.org:70/11/Politics/Somalia.News.Update/

INFOHUB Somalia Page

http://www.infohub.com/TRAVEL/TRAVELLER/AFRICA/somalia.html

DANGEROUS DAYS

03/21/1996	Five U.N. aid workers were taken hostage at the Balidogie airport.
09/95	Aidid and 600 men seize Baidoa in the south
6/95	Osman Hassan Ali Atto is elected as Chairman of the Somali National Alliance
03/95	UN forces withdraw from Somali
06/05/1993	Twenty-six Pakistani peacekeepers and 50 Somalis were killed in a battle with Aidid's men.
03/93	Aidid and the four tribes of NW Somalia adopt the Somali constitution called Xeer (pronounced "hair") two more clans join on June 4
12/09/1992	In Mogadishu, 1800 U.S. marines arrived prior to 28,000 other American troops—for the start of Operation Restore Hope.
03/03/1992	Under U.N. pressure, Ali Mahdi and Aidid signed a cease-fire.
01/25-31/ 1992	United Somali Congress rebels captured Mogadishu.

1991–1992	Massive famine. Seventy-five percent of the country's 6 million people were at risk from starvation.
06/91	Aidid elected chairman of United Somali Congress
10/31/1980	President Siad Barre declared a state of emergency.
10/21/1969	Bloodless coup brought Siad Barre to power.
07/1960	British Somaliland and Italian Somaliland united to become independent Somalia.

SOMALIA

Colombo

Sri Lanka
★★

Body Count

Perhaps in no other insurgency in the world are the foes so anal about body counts as in Sri Lanka's bitter 14-year civil war. Each day brings not only bombings, suicide attacks and jungle battles to the headlines of Sri Lanka's newspapers, but also the number of folks who were whacked in the attacks. Daily, the numbers rack up like a basketball score—300 rebels dead, 500 injured; 25 government troops dead, 73 injured, and so on. Rather than fighting, the insurgent Liberation Tigers of Tamil Eelam (LTTE) spend most of their time—thanks to their London PR office—in a media battle with the Colombo government disputing the body count. Both sides in the conflict steadfastly refuse to let DP help with the math. Journalists aren't allowed to cover this little civil war. Coskun went in only to cool his heels watching fire-walking performances for tourists. However, no matter whose calculator is on the blink, one thing is for sure: some 50,000 Sri Lankans have been killed in this inglorious ethnic conflict since 1983. The LTTE says it has lost only 9000 soldiers in 14 years. As usual it is civilians that make up the bulk of the casualty list.

The bitter conflict in Sri Lanka hasn't only claimed the lives of combatants and innocent civilians. It can also chalk up a president, the Navy commander, the government's opposition leader and the husband of new President Chandrika Kumaratunga, not to mention India's Prime Minister, Rajiv Gandhi.

Just when things seem to be going the government's way, the pesky Tigers blow a few Sri Lankan navy ships out of the water and lay siege to major army bases. Or, of course, they revert to their time-tested tradition of car-bombing Colombo skyscrapers into tiny glass shards, shredding a couple of hundred innocents in the process. These guys make Northern Ireland's IRA look like a bunch of schoolkids with scraped knees pounding caps with a rock.

Perhaps even more ingrained into our memories than tattered duchesses staggering half-naked and bloodied out of Harrods—than body parts twitching on the street in front of a blown-out Sarajevo supermarket—are scenes of downtown Colombo, ripe with screaming Sinhalese, fresh from amputations they hadn't paid for. The glass is falling like a hard rain, unheard by the hundreds whose eardrums have exploded like an aerosol can tossed into a fire.

Although the Sinhalese and Tamils have been at odds with each other for more than 2000 years, much of the tension and fighting that has gripped the island has occurred only in recent years. The fighting began in earnest after a Tamil Tiger ambush of an army patrol in the Jaffna area in 1983. Sinhalese all over the island then went on a rampage for the next three days, murdering and looting Tamils and burning down their villages. Perhaps 2000 Tamils were killed in the uprising.

The north and the east of the island have been war zones for the better part of 12 years. Although areas in the south are still relatively safe, nowhere on the island are things 100 percent secure. The former Tiger "capital" of Jaffna was taken by government troops on December 5, 1995. The entire Jaffna peninsula was wrested by the army in May 1996. But the rebellion continues. Even visiting the ruins at Anuradhapura and Polonnaruwa is risky. The Batticaloa region remains the Tamil Tigers' principal area for staging operations in the south.

President Kumaratunga, during her election campaign in 1994, promised to find a peaceful means of ending the war, and the government offered a proposal

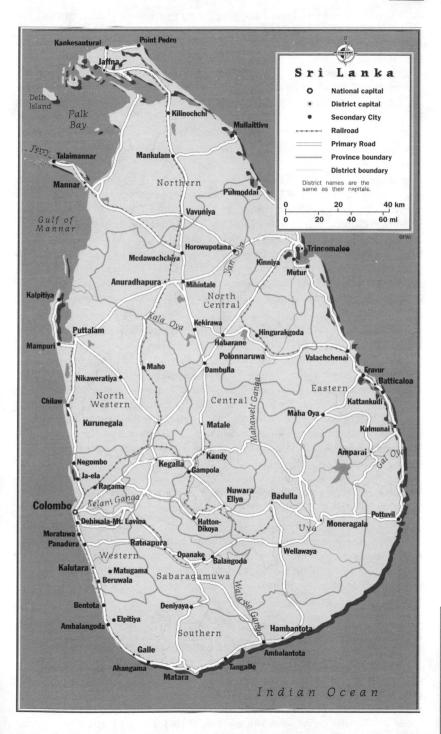

Sri Lanka

✪ National capital
● District capital
● Secondary City
✛✛✛ Railroad
═══ Primary Road
─── Province boundary
─── District boundary

District names are the same as their capitals.

| 0 | | 20 | | 40 km |
| 0 | 20 | 40 | | 60 mi |

©FWI

Kankesanturai
Point Pedro
Jaffna
Delft Island
Palk Bay
Kilinochchi
Mullaittivu
Ferry
Talaimannar
Mankulam
Northern
Pulmoddai
Mannar
Vavuniya
Gulf of Mannar
Horowupotana
Medawachchiya
Jan Oya
Trincomalee
Kinniya
Mutur
Anuradhapura
Mihintale
North Central
Kalpitiya
Kekirawa
Hingurakgoda
Puttalam
Kala Oya
Habarane
Mampuri
Maho
Polonnaruwa
Valachchenai
Dambulla
Eravur
Nikaweratiya
Batticaloa
Central
Mahaweli Ganga
Kattankudi
Chilaw
North Western
Matale
Maha Oya
Kurunegala
Kalmunai
Negombo
Kandy
Amparai
Ja-ela
Kegalla
Gampola
Gal Oya
Ragama
Nuwara Eliya
Badulla
Colombo
Kelani Ganga
Dehiwala-Mt. Lavinia
Moratuwa
Hatton-Dikoya
Uva
Pottuvil
Panadura
Ratnapura
Moneragala
Western
Opanake
Kalutara
Balangoda
Wellawaya
Matugama
Beruwala
Sabaragamuwa
Bentota
Walawe Ganga
Deniyaya
Elpitiya
Hambantota
Ambalangoda
Southern
Galle
Ambalantota
Ahangama
Tangalle
Matara

Indian Ocean

for "devolution" to the Tigers, granting Tamil provinces in the north and east nearly complete autonomy. The government move was lauded both internationally, by moderate Tamils, and by Sri Lanka's imposing and Tiger-backing neighbor, India. But a restless military persuaded Kumaratunga, whose ruling coalition party had a majority of only one vote, to launch an attack on Jaffna and the north on October 17, 1995. Government forces were spectacularly successful in capturing Jaffna in December, but took heavy losses. According to the government, 500 soldiers died while nearly 2000 Tigers were killed. The guerrillas, of course, claimed the reverse figures in their continuing war of the body count.

By 1988, the entire country was in turmoil and the economy was crippled. Government forces tripled in size to 126,000 from 1983 to 1997 in order to fight the Liberation Tigers of Tamil Eelam (Tamil Tigers, or LTTE). More than 50,000 people have died since 1983. The Tigers have been pushed back into the jungle where leader Velupillai Prabhakaran vows to continue their fight. President Kumaratunga claimed in January 1996 that the war would be won in 12 months. In 1995, more than 6 percent of Sri Lanka's gross domestic product was shoveled into the 14-year-old civil war. In May 1996, government forces took the Jaffna peninsula. But it has hardly declawed the Tigers. On January 31, 1996, LTTE guerrillas crashed a truck packed with explosives into Sri Lanka's central bank in Colombo. The blast killed nearly 100 people and wounded more than 1400.

And the Tigers didn't lick their wounds simply by trashing a few buildings in the capital. They've continued to be a formidable military force in the field. In July 1996, LTTE forces besieged the key northern military base of Mullaittivu about 170 miles north of Colombo. They took the base on July 22 after a five-day siege. Although the government claimed the base was still in government hands, Tamil Tiger spokeswoman Helen Whitehead told *DP* in London a rather different story, one in which the results were the loss of 1208 government soldiers and 241 guerrillas (including 68 women fighters). "We have taken the base at Mullaittivu," Whitehead said. Sri Lanka claimed its forces killed 400 rebels, while suffering only 300 casualties of its own. A couple of days later, government forces retook Mullaittivu, finding alive only 11 of the 1200 troops stationed there. The siege marked the bloodiest fighting of the 14-year-old conflict. And just to keep Colombo on its toes, two LTTE bombs aboard a commuter train in the capital killed nearly 70 innocents on July 24. Obviously, Sri Lanka is partying on.

In this battle of the body count, where the number of stiffs is so high both sides are considering hiring outside auditing firms, getting a realistic figure is downright problematic. You see, journalists are not allowed in the war zone. So we must rely on the babbling mouthpieces of both sides, who count the enemy dead and multiply by three—and their own and divide by two. Ace of spades, we say.

The Sinhalese Buddhists and the minority Tamils (18 percent of Sri Lanks' population) have been massacring each other since 1983. The conflict has been going poorly for the Tamils since the government blew them out of Jaffna in 1995. They are now squeezed into the remote NW jungle. Their main support comes from Tamil Nadu in SE India and it is one of the few insurgencies that is fought on the ocean with gunboats. The major danger to travelers is when the

Black Tigers get dressed up in C-4 and dynamite and head into town to join a political rally. Don't ever offer to pull a thread on someone's clothing in Sri Lanka.

Velupillai Prabhakaran and The Liberation Tigers of Tamil Eelam (LTTE)

The LTTE began in 1976, and today it is the largest Tamil separatist guerrilla group. They began the military fight with the Sri Lankan government in 1983. The Tigers have maintained their hard-line position on separatism and conducted numerous military and terrorist acts to further their cause. They are most famous for their suicide attacks on prominent politicians. These attacks not only snuff their intended victims, but, because of the type of bomb employed (usually a very powerful explosive unleashing a volley of shrapnel or metal pellets), they usually take out a couple of dozen innocents as well. It is believed that LTTE members were responsible for the 1993 assassination of President Ranasinghe Premadasa.

Led by Velupillai Prabhakaran, the LTTE maintains its own navy, called the Sea Tigers. Operating now in waters off the northeastern coastal city of Mullaittivu, each light boat carries five or six guerrillas who attack Indian Navy ships or make landings to attack Sri Lankan army units. Sea Tigers also are suicide frogmen who blow up navy ships with self-detonated explosives.

Bombs are the favored method of Tamil suicide guerrillas. Suicide bombers are revered among the Tamils. Their pictures are defiantly and proudly displayed along the road and in the houses of their families. Their families are accorded a distinction equal to the mothers of saints. How do you spot a suicide bomber or Black Tiger? Despite the fact that an average Tamil lives until he is over 70, most suicide bombers are young, in their early 20s; they wear a pendant around their necks with a cyanide capsule dangling from the end. The cyanide will kill within 5 minutes when bitten.

The LTTE lost its "capital" of Jaffna in December 1995 and is on the run from a major offensive by the government. The Tamils have retaliated by slaughtering innocent villagers to slow the government offensive. Prabhakaran, widely believed responsible for the 1991 assassination of Indian Prime Minister Rajiv Gandhi and the 1993 snuffing of Sri Lankan President Ranasinghe Premadasa as well as a wave of other suicide bombings, is hiding out in the Vanni forests in the north west plotting his next target.

The 3000 lasses who help make up the Tamil Tigresses don't seem to mind taking a bullet or two, either. Some 68 female LTTE guerrillas were whacked during the siege of Mullaittivu. And on July 4, 1996, a female suicide bomber adorned in designer explosive devices crashed into a Jaffna motorcade on her scooter trying to assassinate the minister of construction. He survived, but 23 people were killed and 60 others were injured by the blast. Tamil Tiger strength is estimated to be between 6000 and 10,000. They claim to have lost 9000 fighters killed in the 14 years of warfare. If you want to talk to some of the Tamil Tigers and get the scoop for yourself, you can—but you better have a good reason. They talked to *DP*, but only after "checking us out." The Tamils do not target tourists since it would dramatically affect their off shore fund-raising. The U.S. government believes that the LTTE is involved in smuggling drugs and Tamils have acted as couriers of narcotics to Europe.

Liberation Tigers of Tamil Eelam

211 Katherine Rd.
London E6 1BU
United Kingdom

☎/FAX 011-44-181-470-8593
Other groups to contact are World Tamil Association (WTA), World Tamil Movement (WTM, Federation of Associations of Canadian Tamils (FACT) and the Ellalan Source.

The Government

The current president and daughter of two former Sri Lankan prime ministers, Chandrika Kumaratunga, 51, didn't let the assassination of her husband by the LTTE get in the way of the peace process. In November 1994, she sent delegates to begin discussions on ending the 14-year-old civil war. The protracted talks ended up with the government's proposed offer of autonomy for Tamil provinces in the north and east. Since that effort failed, she's pounding the LTTE and everyone unlucky enough to be in the vicinity with everything she's got.

The army under Deputy Defense Minister Anuruddha Ratwatte took the Jaffna peninsula from rebel forces in May 1996 but not until he had fired his top field commander and replaced him with. The army sent in 30,000 troops for 50 days and after the smoke cleared 2500 people had died. Jaffna had been the financial, military and medical base for the Tigers and now they must fight a jungle insurgency. The army is now fighting to clear the 45 mile road to Jaffna. So far 1700 have been killed in this operation.

May 1997 offensive sent thousands of innocents fleeing into the jungle, leaving hundreds of government soldiers and Tamil rebels dead.

A passport, onward/return ticket and proof of sufficient funds (US$15 per day) are required. A tourist visa can be granted at the time of entry into Sri Lanka, and may be valid for a maximum period of 90 days. For business travel or travel on an official or diplomatic passport, visas are required and must be obtained in advance.

Business visas are valid for one month and require an application form, two photos, a company letter, a letter from a sponsoring agency in Sri Lanka, a copy of an onward/return ticket, and a US$5 fee. Include US$6 postage for return of your passport by registered mail.

Yellow fever and cholera immunizations are needed if arriving from an infected area.

For further information, contact the following:

Embassy of the Democratic Socialist Republic of Sri Lanka

2148 Wyoming Ave., N.W.
Washington, D.C. 20008
☎ *(202) 483-4025*
or nearest consulate:

California	**New Jersey**
☎ *(805) 873-7224*	☎ *(201) 627-7855*
Hawaii	**New York**
☎ *(808) 735-1622*	☎ *(212) 986-7040*

About a third of Sri Lanka's 47,070 miles of road are paved. There are 1210 miles of heavily traveled railroad and 14 airfields; the only major airport is in Colombo. There aren't any internal flights in Sri Lanka, so the traveler is limited to buses and trains. Trains are arguably more comfortable than buses, but are slower and don't service as many areas of the island as do buses. The train stations, although dilapidated, aren't nearly as crowded as those in India, where rail travel is the lifeblood of Indians. However, don't fall asleep on the trains. You'll more than likely get ripped off by a thief.

There is a long-standing armed conflict between the Sri Lankan government and the Tamil extremist group, the Liberation Tigers of Tamil Eelam (LTTE). Fighting between government security forces and the LTTE continues in northern and eastern areas of the island. Sri Lankan defense regulations forbid travel in much of the island's northern area. Journalists are, as of mid-1997, prohibited from war zones.

National Parks

Remote forested areas, such as Wilpattu and Galoya national parks, are considered especially unsafe. Rebels like the peace and quiet and may take exception to your need to explore and save their rainforest. They're doing just fine beneath their blanket of triple-canopy forest hidden in deep bunkers—excellent cover from air force helicopter and bomb attacks.

Jaffna

In retreating from their stronghold at Jaffna in November 1995, LTTE Tigers booby-trapped virtually the entire city with trip-wired antitank and antipersonnel mines. Anything that could be picked up—from books to cooking utensils to clothes on the floor—were booby-trapped by the fleeing rebels. The city's population plummeted from 120,000 to a mere 6000 in just a few short weeks. Like Paris in August—with land mines.

Vavuniya to Kilinochchi

This is a 55-mile stretch of roadway under LTTE control that would link Colombo with the Jaffna peninsula if the government forces could just get their hands on it. For now, government troops on the Jaffna peninsula can be reinforced and resupplied only by air and sea. A fierce government offensive to seize control of the Vavuniya-Kilinochchi road began in May 1997. It involved some 20,000 Sri Lankan soldiers, supported by warplanes, chopper gunships, tanks and artillery.

North and East

Currently, fighting between the government forces and the LTTE continues in much of the north and east. Although the situation appears to be contained in these regions, security checkpoints have become the norm along major crossroads in and around Colombo, as a result of the March 1991 bombing assassination of Deputy Defense Minister Ranjan Wijertaine, the June 1991 bombing of the Ministry of Defense's Joint Operations Command and the January 1996 bombing of the Central Bank of Sri Lanka in Colombo—just a few hundred yards from President Chandrika Kumaratunga's office. (The LTTE is believed to be responsible for all three incidents.) Travelers should be alert to the continuing threat of bombings in Colombo.

Colombo

The LTTE bombings here are just plain scary. On January 31, 1996, a blast took nearly 100 lives and wounded 1400 others. On July 24, 1996, the Tigers blew up a train leaving Dehiwala, a southern suburb of Colombo. This detonation killed 57 people and injured 500 others. However, other than the blood splattered by the LTTE, the level of criminal activity in Colombo is moderate in relation to other cities of the world. Violent crimes such as armed robberies are rare, particularly among the expatriot and tourist population. The Sri Lankan police, though limited in resources, generally make every effort to provide assistance to foreign visitors. This is particularly so within the confines of Colombo. Police coverage tends to be less reliable outside of the city. Important police emergency telephone numbers for the greater Colombo area:

Police Emergency (24 hours daily)
    ☎ *433333*

Cinnamon Gardens Police Station
    ☎ *693377*

Colpetty Police Station
    ☎ *20131*

Bambalapitiya Police Station
    ☎ *593208*

DANGEROUS THINGS

Political Rallies

The Black Tigers, or suicide bombers, cast their votes and reduce the pool of voters by blowing themselves and anyone else in a 50-yard radius into small fleshy pieces. Using massive explosives packed around ball bearings, pellets and other homemade shrapnel, they can kill up to 60 people at a time. Prominent national leaders and senior military personnel have been targets and/or victims of terrorist violence, which, of course, makes anyone else in the neighborhood a target, as well.

Roadblocks

Travelers who encounter roadblocks staffed by security personnel are wise to listen closely and heed any instructions given.

Dudes with Amulets Around Their Necks in Colombo

At least 60 LTTE suicide bombers are combing the streets of Colombo searching for somebody important to blow up. Because security is so tight around President Kumaratunga and other high-ranking government officials, the bombers have started stalking anyone with a title or who's gotten his or her name in a newspaper—even leaders of the opposition. Assisted suicide has never been easier.

Sea Tiger Gunboats

The Sea Tigers (the marine version of the LTTE) operate small gunboats to conduct naval- and marine-style raids. Each boat usually carries five or six guerrillas. When *DP* used these boats in the Jaffna Lagoon to visit the Tigers, the boat in front of us was blown from the water by a naval shell. Usually, though, the high-speed boats manage to outrun the slower naval gunners. About 40 of these mini-warships are based on an island just off the coast of the rebel-held town of Mullaittivu.

Air Tiger Warplanes

The LTTE has added a miniature air force to complement its miniature navy. The Tigers have started employing microlight aircraft to attack government targets. There is speculation that the LTTE might begin using airborne suicide bombers to attack Temple Trees, President Chandrika Kumaratunga's official residence in Colombo.

GETTING SICK

Medical facilities are limited—you'll find one doctor and 27 hospital beds for every 10,000 people. Doctors and hospitals often expect immediate cash payment for health services. Malaria is prevalent in many areas outside of Colombo. Visitors must take precautions against malaria, hepatitis and yellow fever prior to arriving in Sri Lanka. Rabies is common in many animals in

Sri Lanka; take some comfort that the painful injections against rabies can be obtained locally. Tap water is laced with everything from amoebas to horses and should not be ingested unless boiled for a couple of decades, strained through an offset press and carpet-bombed with iodine.

Sri Lanka was once known as Serendib in ancient times and then as Ceylon under the Brits. The emerald isle is made up of a teardrop-shaped main island and groups of smaller islands 50 miles off the southern coast of India. Sri Lanka, with its lush jungles and dramatic interior, has been called one of the most beautiful islands in the world. Thirty-one percent of the island is mountainous jungle nestling ancient cities such as Polonnaruwa and Anuradhapura. The 833 miles of coastline are primarily pristine, coral-fringed beaches.

The major ethnic group is the Sinhalese (74 percent) followed by the Tamils (18 percent) and Moors (7 percent). Burghers, Malays and Veddhas comprise the last 1 percent. The Sinhalese are predominantly Buddhist and the Tamils are Hindu. Christians and Muslims make up only about 8 percent of the religious pie.

English is widely spoken in this former British colony. Sinhala is the official language, but Tamil is recognized as a national language. As one would expect in the Indian Ocean, the heat and humidity can wring you out like a wet sponge in a boxing match. Since the British were fond of colonizing tropical destinations with cooler hill stations, you can expect cool, moist weather up high. The average temperature along the coast is 80° F with little change all year. There are two cooling monsoon seasons, the southwest and the northeast monsoons, which dump about 100 inches of rain every year.

The Sri Lankan currency is the rupee (58.6 rupees=US$1). Electricity is 230-240V/50Hz.

Embassy Location and Registration

Updated information on travel and security within Sri Lanka is available at the U.S. embassy:

U.S. Embassy
P.O. Box 106
210 Galle Road

Colombo
☎ *[94] (1) 448007*
FAX [94] (1) 437345

U.S. citizens are encouraged to register at the U.S. embassy upon arrival in Sri Lanka.

Embassy Locations

Canadian Embassy in Sri Lanka
6 Gregory's Road
Cinnamon Gardens
Colombo 7
☎ *[94] (1) 695841*
Postal address:
P.O. Box 1006
Colombo, Sri Lanka

Sri Lankan Embassy in Canada
85 Range Road, Suites 102–104
Ottawa, Ontario, Canada K1N 8J6
☎ *(613) 233-8440/8449*
FAX (613) 238-8448

05/13/1997	Government offensive begins to establish land link with Jaffna.
01/31/1996	Colombo blast kills nearly 100 people, injures 1400. LTTE believed responsible.
12/05/1995	Jaffna falls to government forces.

10/17/1995	Government offensive of the north begins.
05/01/1993	Assassination of President Ranasinghe Premadasa.
09/04/1992	Dasain (Hindu) Festival.
06/13/1990	The Liberation Tigers of Tamil Eelam (LTTE) launch a renewed offensive against Sri Lankan government forces by storming at least 24 police stations in northern and eastern Sri Lanka. Several hundred police officers are taken hostage and a number of them later killed.
08/18/1987	Grenade attack on Sri Lankan parliament. One legislator is killed.
07/29/1987	Indo-Sri Lankan peace accords.
07/20/1986	Sinhalese rioting.
05/14/1985	Tamil separatists kill more than 150 people in an attack on a Buddhist shrine at Anuradhapura.
07/23/1983	The killing of 13 Sri Lankan soldiers in an ambush by Tamil militants touches off widespread anti-Tamil violence that leaves as many as 2000 Tamils dead and 100,000 homeless.
05/22/1972	Republic Day. Also known as National Heroes' Day.
11/24/1954	LTTE founder's birthday. Prabhakaran birthday is marked by the LTTE as "Heroes Week," which also commemorates LTTE members who have died in battle.
02/04/1948	Independence Day.
05/24/ 563 B.C.	Birth of Buddha.
01/14	Tamil Thai Pongal Day.

Sudan
★★★

Black Tide Rising

There is the north, a dry arid, Islamic land; and there is the south, a lush, Christian land of black skinned Nilotes. But the black tide of southern rebels is slowly making its way up north. With the help of the CIA, the SPLA (Sudan's People's Liberation Army) is flowing around and over the northern garrisons like a black wave. There is also another tide that has not begun to rise. It is estimated that Sudan has oil reserves equal to Saudi Arabia.

Sudan is cursed not only by poverty (a per-capita income of only US$330), its size (it is the largest country in Africa) and a history of fundamentalist leaders who declare Holy War on the West, but it is also crippled by its dubious distinction of straddling the uneasy and unmarked border between the arid Islamic Arab north and the lush, animistic black south. These two cultures have never dwelled in harmony, and, in Sudan, they never will. The two tribes continue to battle, as the north persists in imposing its political will on the tribal south.

Sudan is 70 percent Muslim, 20 percent animist and 5 percent Christian—a bad mix on any continent. Ethnically, it's an even nastier brew: Sudan is 52 percent black, 39 percent Arab and 6 percent Beja. The hatred between the north and south has killed more than 500,000 people and driven 4.5 million others from their homes. One million have starved to death.

Even the rebel factions are known for their intolerance of each other. They wage warfare against each other, using starvation and terror as weapons of war. The SPLA (Sudan People's Liberation Army) rebel factions have been known to murder international aid workers and will not even guarantee safe passage for relief aircraft in case they may be providing food or medicine for enemy factions.

Since Iran has 21 years left on its leases of bases in Port Sudan and Suakin, there are thousands of Iranian soldiers stationed and training in Sudan. There is also an Iranian-funded radio station based in Port Sudan that broadcasts Islamic and Iranian propaganda to Egypt and other Arab countries. Sudan's strategic position and its holy alliance with Iran give it a powerful presence in the Red Sea and the Horn of Africa. Iran's recent meddling, and the resultant civil war in nearby Yemen, might provide a good reason to dust off the domino theory formerly applied to Southeast Asia.

Iran pays its new friend with oil and military supplies, while it receives strategic real estate and full cooperation from Sudan. Sudan also has new lethal exports to pay its militant friend: murder and mayhem.

Some side effects of this new export business include the terrorist attack on the World Trade Center in New York, the murders of more than 210 of the Algerian defense forces by Algerian fundamentalist groups and the continuing attacks on tourists and officials in Egypt. Although a Muslim country, Egypt is considered too soft on Israel and becoming too Westernized.

Since Sudan's independence in 1954, there has been a succession of military leaders and little relief from overwhelming poverty. In 1972, the Addis Ababa accord gave the south limited autonomy (an oxymoron) that ended the war against the Anyana guerrilla movement. But in the early 1980s, the SPLA came into being to fight the same battle. In 1984, Islamic law was introduced and the SPLA began fighting in earnest. The SPLA was supported by Cuba, Ethiopia, Libya and, strangely, by Israel. In 1985 Nimeiri's regime was overthrown in a coup and democratic elections were held. "Democracy" lasted until yet another coup in 1989 brought in the current ruler, General Omar Hassan Ahmad al-Bashir, in June of that year.

The Ethiopians have had their hands in the pie since November of 1987. Khartoum has also sought the assistance of Iran and Libya, including MiG-25s flown by Libyans. Even Iraq and the PLO (Palestine Liberation Organization) lent a hand by flying bombing missions over the south.

Ethiopia hasn't meddled in Sudan's affairs since the ouster of Mengistu, allowing the SPLA to go on a roll. They almost took the city of Juba in the spring of 1989, when a factional group led by Garang's second in command, Riek Machar, created SPLA/United. The two southern factions began to battle each other. In 1993, the two southern SPLA groups called a truce after killing thousands of each other's members. The CIA is busy working to get the two sides to kiss and make up.

The Islamic fundamentalist military government of al-Bashir finally launched its long-awaited offensive against the rebel Sudan People's Liberation Army in Feb-

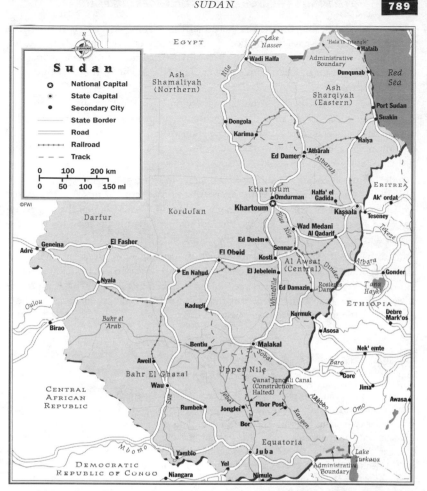

ruary 1994 in an effort to end the 25-year civil war. Tens of thousands of refugees have fled to the Ugandan border.

Today, southern Sudan south of Malakal is controlled by the SPLA, with the exception of the city of Juba and a half-dozen Sudanese army strongholds. But the government positions are isolated and have been cut off from Khartoum. Under the constant psychological pressure of imminent attack, they man their trenches and watch their food and medical supplies shrink by the day. By containing the Sudanese army units with relatively small numbers of men, SPLA leader John Garang can marshall his forces and supplies for the eventual assaults on the strategic garrisons of Juba and Wau. He is in no rush to do so; the longer he waits, the weaker his for becomes.

Garang's chunk of real estate in the south is rich in gold, hardwood, cotton, tea, coffee and tobacco. The fertility of the soil is such that even during the height of the war, farmers sympathetic to the SPLA were able to feed the guerrillas with surpluses of rice, corn, sorghum, goats and cattle.

Meanwhile, in the northeast, the National Democratic Alliance is threatening the crucial road and rail links to Port Sudan. In Sudan's central-eastern region, the NDA is within striking distance of the hydroelectric dam at Damazine, the source of 80 percent of Khartoum's power. The NIF has not publicly admitted to losing any ground.

Sudan was formerly perhaps the largest recipient of Western aid, but most of that was cut off in 1991, after the government supported Saddam Hussein's efforts in the Gulf War. The Sudanese people now only receive emergency aid from outside relief agencies. Aid workers experience delays regarding travel permits and visas, and sometimes are arrested.

Only Islamic agencies are allowed to operate in government-occupied areas of the south, since the government claims many Western groups are fronts for Christian missionary work or intelligence-gathering. Dawa Islamia, the largest Islamic aid agency, with close links to the government, withholds food from Christian and animist Southerners unless they convert to Islam.

Sudan has been expelled from the World Bank, suspended from the IMF (and likely to become the first country to be thrown out of the International Monetary Fund entirely since the fund was created) and kicked out of both the Arab Monetary Fund and Arab Fund for Economic and Social Development. Sudanese experience 100 percent inflation per year.

Sudan is a big, bad, ugly place with a belligerent, extreme Islamic government hell-bent on choking the entire country under Islam's shroud. Khartoum is Terrorist Central. The country is one massive training camp for suicide bombers, hijackers, assassins, car bombers, grenade chuckers and synagogue saboteurs. Three guys who were involved in the plot to assassinate Egyptian President Mubarak are in Sudan getting their hair cut and nails done and watching the V Channel, despite an OAU call for the government to hand over the thugs. In all, there are an estimated 15,000 militants living or training in Sudan. This Allah's hornet nest hasn't gone unnoticed by the UN, though, who slapped diplomatic and travel sanctions on Khartoum in April 1997.

The Khartoum government has had its work cut out for it keeping the lid on the insurgent SPLA, whose numbers have swelled while chalking up battlefield wins in the south and east of Sudan in 1997 with CIA assistance. The mainly-Christian SPLA, through the efforts of the American covert intelligence community, has gotten an overhaul in recent months. Its warlord-style commanders have been diced from the ranks. Egypt, Eritrea, Uganda and Ethiopia have also boosted the SPLA's capacity to out-muscle Sudanese troops. The SPLA has teamed up with another rebel group, the National Democratic Alliance (NDA)—which includes the Beja Congress Armed Forces—and their joint offensives have overrun army garrisons in a drive westward from Ethiopia and Eritrea. These joint operations have posed the greatest threat to the Khartoum regime to date.

The NDA—based in Asmara, Eritrea—is moving to cut off Khartoum's access to the Red Sea. They've captured some towns in the east and pose a threat to hydro-electric projects in both Roseires and Kassala. A number of Sudanese opposition groups, with CIA support, are training their forces at camps in Eritrea. It is expected all of the camps will soon be united under the command of the NDA's leader, General Fathi Ahmed Ali. Eritrea makes no secret of its support for the rebels. Asmara cut ties with Khartoum in December 1994. To rub it in

Sudan leader Omar al-Bashir's face, Eritrea gave the former Sudanese embassy to Sudanese rebels for use as a headquarters.

As he has done in other of the world's nastiest places, ex-prez Jimmy Carter has been brokering broken knuckles between Sudan's bullies. He doctored a brief cease-fire in 1995 and got four insurgent groups to bite his carrot in April 1997. The four southern groups—fresh with a surprisingly decent 501K package, including limited autonomy, rights to a secession referendum and permission to keep their guns—then formed an alliance, the Southern Sudan Defense Forces (SSDF), to help off the SPLA. We're not sure what kind of wrist-slapping Carter got by the CIA when he got home.

Dr. Hassan Abdullah al-Turabi

This is the man pulling the strings. Intelligent, well-educated and determined to be the first guy on his block to have his own fundamentalist state. He has described himself as being the symbol of a new movement that will change the history of humanity. His goal is to unify the billion or so Muslims under one guiding theocratic government. He was educated in London and earned his doctorate at Sorbonne in 1964. Five years later, he became leader of what was then a small and fanatical group of religious nuts. Turabi became the head of the Muslim Brotherhood, only to be banished from Sudan less than a month later, when General Nimeiri's Marxist coup made Turabi's style of religion out of style. Saudi Arabia took him in and the Brotherhood took hold among the 350,000 professional Sudanese working in oil-rich but skills-poor Saudia Arabia. They provided a source of funds, which Turabi used to send the brightest Sudanese to Western universities to get their Ph.D.s. The Brotherhood was busy turning out doctors, lawyers, writers and teachers, who would then take the message of Islam back to other Muslim countries. They created the Islamic African Relief Fund (now the Islamic Relief Association) to help with the millions of African refugees in sub-Saharan Africa. In the mid-1970s, they created Faisal Islamic Bank to handle the deposits of expat workers in the Gulf States. Islamic banks charge no interest, pay no interest and share profits with their depositors. The bank made loans to small businessmen, taxi drivers and shopkeepers.

After building a strong financial and political base from Saudi Arabia, Turabi returned to Sudan in 1977 as attorney general under Nimeiri's program of national reconciliation with former enemies. In 1983, Nimeiri declared *Sharia*, or Islamic law, after a particularly vivid dream. Turabi was not the force behind the change. Although Turabi is extreme in his long-term plans, he is a moderate in affecting change.

The dramatic changeover did not affect the political climate as much as it influenced the financial health of Sudan. Nimeiri instituted the 354-day year, and taxes were abolished and replaced with voluntary tithing. Interest was abolished, and the resultant loss of revenue and fiscal chaos plunged Sudan into bankruptcy. Sudan was US$8 billion in the hole and sinking fast. When the government couldn't cut a check for US$250 million, they went into default with the IMF. By March of 1985, Nimeiri blamed the country's slide into debt on the Islamic laws now ostensibly enforced by Turabi. Leaders of the Muslim Brotherhood were removed from political office, and Turabi was put in jail. Three months later, Nimeiri was ousted in a coup, and the first thing General Siwar el-Dahab did was dispatch a plane to fly Turabi back from prison to Khartoum. By then, Turabi was head of the National Islamic Front, originally an opposition party. But Turabi, once again, became attorney general. The Muslim Brotherhood was welcomed back into politics.

Lieutenant General Omar Hassan Ahmad al-Bashir

Al-Bashir was reelected as president in a fraud-tainted, "supervised" election March 23, 1996. He is the leader of the 15-member National Salvation Revolutionary Council, a junta comprised entirely of military officers. Reigning in a state of emergency and with a suspending constitution, al-Bashir has brought Sudan into the swelling ranks of despot-ruled countries in Africa. There have been only three periods of civilian rule since 1955. He continues to appoint National Islamic Front (NIF) loyalists, though more for their religious zeal than political skills. The NIF leader Dr. Hassan Abdullah al-Turabi was the minister of justice and attorney general under Maj. Gen. Gaafar Mohamed Nimeiri and was the architect of both the 1983 and 1991 versions of *Shari'a* (or Islamic law). Before the new federal structure was introduced, *Shari'a* only applied to administrative and civil cases and not to criminal cases. The first victim of the new *Shari'a* was a Christian southern Sudanese petty thief, whose punishment was the "cross-amputation" of his right hand and left foot. Nimeiri was said to have fainted while attending his first amputation. Al-Bashir is not so squeamish about carrying out the wishes of al-Turabi's NIF. He is busy battling the 55,000 or so armed Southerners with his 68,000 soldiers. Iran's largesse in providing arms to al-Bashir is considerable, and there is circumstantial evidence that Iranian *mujahedin* in the guise of volunteers are serving with the Sudanese army. Iraq has also sent arms and technicians. China, with large oil concessions in the south, is also providing Khartoum with guns ate bargain-basement prices. Drop al-Bashir a line at:

Lt. General Omar Hassan al-Bashir
People's Palace
P.O. Box 281
Khartoum, Sudan

Sudanese People's Liberation Army (SPLA)

Like the Shilluk and the Nuer, the Dinka are Nilotes, perhaps the tallest, blackest people in the world. For centuries, the Muslim north raided them for slaves, concubines, wives. For decades, they have been so ravaged by venereal disease that many clans are almost totally barren. When we drove overland from Malakal to the heart of the Sudd at Bor, warriors from a barren Nuer village raided a Shilluk village, carrying off several girls.

The minimum demands of the SPLA are for the abolition of Islamic shari'a law, introduced by Bashir, and the creation of a new constitution. The breakaway faction of the SPLA is calling for the complete independence of southern Sudan. The SPLA is headed by Dr. John Garang de Mabior, a former Sudanese army colonel. He is a graduate of the Infantry Officers Advanced Course at Fort Benning, Georgia, and has a Ph.D. earned while Stateside. Some see him as the next president of Sudan.

Garang's original job was to fight the rebels, but he ended up joining them instead. He worked his way to the top of the SPLA, mostly because he was on very close terms with Ethiopia's Lieutenant General Haile Mengistu Mariam. He feels that the simplistic principle of Muslim against Christian and black against Arab is too Western in concept. It is simply a matter of discrimination, which gets in the way of economic development and political power—a *raison d'etre* echoed by German mercenary Rolf Steiner, who helped the Anya in the 1970s and was tortured, tried and imprisoned for his troubles. The current war is about life for the south not about death for the north. Iran is pushing Sudan relentlessly to create a fundamentalist Islamic state. The fact that the black Africans of the south predate the Muslims of the north is immaterial. The SPLA armed forces are estimated to number 55,000. Support, even clandestine training in the bush, has come from Israel and Ethiopia. Garang is chummy with Ugandan president Museveni, who has allowed SPLA movement on the Ugandan side of the border.

Sudan may have petroleum reserves nearing those of Saudi Arabia. Western concessionaires who previously flipped the SPLA the bird when it warned against collaboration with

Khartoum, are now deeply worried about losing their investments, while those previously uninvolved are actively wooing Garang.

The SPLA currently controls five regions in the south where it maintains civil authority. They get weapons and support from Ethiopia and Eritrea. Sudanese rebels train in Eritrea. Following massive gains by the SPLA in 1997, southern Sudanese refugees in neighboring Kenya, Uganda, Congo and Central African Republic are returning to their homes en masse. Journalists or travelers need travel permits from the SPLA if they want to travel in the southern areas.

A peace accord was signed with the Lam Akol, SPLA-United Faction in April of '97 six other groups signed a peace agreement with the government. Akol's group is small group comprised on of Shuluk tribesmen and their homeland is sitting on giant oil reserves.

The SPLA led by Garang is the last hold out.

The SPLA maintains offices in London, Washington, Asmara and Addis Ababa. You, too, can get the scoop but don't count on a well planned trip to front:

SPLA London

☎ 0171-209-5859
Spokesman Stephen Back

SPLA Asmara

☎ 29-11-181114
The press officer for the SPLA here is Yasir Kharman. The office occupies the former Sudanese embassy.

SPLA Addis Ababa

☎ 201394
Press officer Arop Deng Majok.

National Democratic Alliance (NDA)

The NDA is an awkward coalition between the SPLA and nine Muslim-based parties: the DUP, Umma, Legitimate Command, the Beja Congress, Alliance of Trade Unions, Alliance of Forces, the Federal Party and the Communist Party, all of which not only supported the imposition of shari'a on the south, but also opposed southern autonomy or secession prior to the 1989 coup. For the Muslim members, many of whom were jailed or exiled by the NIF, the alliance gives them military muscle. Given that the Prophet Mohamed forbade Muslims fighting Muslims, the alliance provides the SPLA with a crucial shield against the involvement of most Muslim countries—Iran and Iraq being the exceptions—on the side of Khartoum in its declared jihad against the infidel southerners. The SPLA's stunning military success in 1997 also prompted mass defections of Muslim Popular Defence Force units to John Garang. Inasmuch as the SPLA (under the banner of the "New Sudan Brigade") provides over 95 percent of the NDA combatants, Garang heads the Joint Military Command of the NDA. His growing popularity and military might saw him named at a recent NDA conference in Asmara as the possible next president of all Sudan.

Nuba Mountains Central Committee of the SPLA (NMCC/SPLA)

Another splinter group of the southern Dinka dominated SPLA formed in June of 1996. Only three out of the 58 senior SPLA positions were filled by Dinka. The NMCC/SPLA is led by chairman Mohamed Haroun Kafi Aburas.

Southern Sudan Independence Movement of Riek Machar (SSIM)

A spin-off of the SPLA is fighting the SPLA and has captured Akobo and Nyandit. Some say it is a front for the northern government and signed a peace treaty in April of '96. The group is led by Kerubino Kwanyin Bol who was imprisoned by Garang from 1987 to 1992.

South Sudan Independence Movement (SSIM)

The SSIM is a small splinter group of the SPLA, which has been wreaking havoc. However, the government accepted a cease-fire offer by the SSIM in March 1996, which led the larger SPLA to accuse the SSIM of complicity with the government.

Nafi Osman Nafeh

The powerful intelligence chief of the National Islamic Front (NIF), directed by Hassan al-Turabi. He was trained in intelligence in Pakistan and the United States after becoming a member of the fundamentalist movement in the 1960s. Using Saudi money, he created a clandestine fundamentalist intelligence network inside the Sudanese army. He was one of the brains behind the June 1989 military coup that brought al-Bashir to power.

General al-Fateh Orawa

Security advisor to the Sudanese president, Orawa is a member of the powerful Orawa clan. Trained in the United States, Turkey and Pakistan, he worked closely with the CIA in 1985 during the Nimeiri regime to organize the transfer of Falashas from Ethiopia to Israel via Sudan.

General Hachim Abu Said

The director of Sudan's foreign intelligence service. CIA-trained, Abu Said served as a senior Sudanese intelligence officer during the regime of Gaafar Nimeiri. He was later employed by Saudi intelligence, before taking up service with the new fundamentalist government of Sudan.

The Iqhwan

The Muslim Brothers, the Iqhwan, in conversation simply *aqhi*, "brothers," the Arab world's oldest Islamic party, was founded in Egypt in 1928 and today is a force in Syria, Jordan, the Sudan. Trying to use his riveting personality to transform Egypt, Nasser banned them as reactionary. Under fire from the Nasserite left, Sadat brought it back to legal life as a counterweight. Today, Hosni Mubarak uses them as a foil to parry the Islamic radicals bearing down on his regime; he pressures them to renounce terror, and he makes sure the favors due Islam either go their way or the way they favor.

Spies

The Horn of Africa is buzzing with spies from the French DGSE, the American Defense Intelligence Agency (DIA) and the British MI6. Regardless of the latest political makeover of this war, there is no denying that a war for liberation between the south and the north has been fought since 1956, when Sudan gained its independence. The SPLA is the latest name under which the south has been fighting. It has undergone a power struggle, and the north is content to let the two subfactions try to kill each other.

The government of the north has little jurisdiction in the south. The provinces of Upper Nile, Equatoria and Bahr el Ghazal are controlled by the SPLA.

Sudan is trying to distance itself from Iran. With the recent serving up of Carlos and the flurry of media interviews that al-Turabi has given, things may be changing.

Charles Pasqua and the Deuzieme Bureau in the Horn of Africa

This back-slapping Corsican has made good use of his aggressive cultivation of contacts in the Arab and African world. Even before nabbing Carlos, Pasqua was riding a wave of popularity for ordering nightly ID checks of the immigrants surging into France from dangerous places throughout the community, and especially from Algeria. There was even talk of him succeeding Francois Mitterrand as president, and even if that was a long shot for a one-time salesman for the Marseille pastis, Ricard, it was clear he was boosting the presidential stock of his boss, Premier Edouard Balladur.

Pasqua is most famous for nabbing Carlos. The press hinted that this was a swap—the Jackal for the passage of northern armored units to the south. Drawing on deep French influence in two of the most corrupt states in Africa, Zaire and the Central African Republic (where de Gaulle's "noble idiot" practiced cannibalism in the Presidential Palace), Pasqua persuaded these governments to permit the Sudanese Army to cross into their territory with entirely mechanized brigades.

The move permitted the Sudanese to deploy for a climactic push on the beleaguered Southerners, and it promised to internationalize the war even beyond Zaire and the Central African Republic. Squeezed from these two directions, many of the Southerners would be cornered in the Nimule theatre at the Sudan's far southern extremity, thus making a player of a man who didn't need the headache, but to whom France was glad to give it.

The French have a charming capacity to be as frank about politics as they are about sex. We find it hard to believe that in the post–Cold War world, something as craven and pointless as the grab for Africa is on again. Who needs the Sudan? *Beau geste* imperialists out of French West Africa once faced-off against Edwardian Brits down from Cairo over these badlands that neither could ever control, bring peace to, or make any decent use of. Are we still that nuts?

In a dictated memoir published late in the winter of 1995, Pasqua confirmed everyone's worst fears about the French in Africa: Indeed, when Felix Mumie, a leader of the opposition in Cameroon, was assassinated in Geneva, it was on French orders. Indeed, many French ambassadors to many a state in France's African sphere have a hotline to the head of state's bedroom. Yes, many such heads of state have signed blank communiques authorizing French intervention. Yes, Omar Bongo, president of Gabon, literally had to audition for the job before he got it; in fact, Foccart conducted the interview. Yes, America is as much a predator in Africa as the leopard. Indeed, France installed Jean-Bedel Bokassa as dictator of the Central African Republic. Indeed, Bokassa called Charles de Gaulle, "papa." Yes, de Gaulle called Bokassa, "a noble idiot."

Is Foccart the last of his kind? Is that sort of thinking gone from the French Foreign Office? From the Deuzieme Bureau? Have the French spent all these years cultivating that Gallic shrug for nothing? But to be fair, this cynicism is not totally unrelieved. Sometimes they even insist they value common decency, and to demonstrate theirs, they participate when they feel we're doing something right.

The Non-Players

The tall and muscular Nuba people of Sudan used to number nearly 1.5 million. The latest and best estimates say only 200,000 remain. Is it because of disease and pestilence? Hardly. Rather they've been banished to "peace camps" by the government to keep them fighting in support of the separatists in the south—and evidently from propagating, as well.

A passport and a visa are required to enter Sudan. Both a standard and business visa cost U.S. citizens US$50 and allow for a stay of up to three months. The approval process takes three to four weeks, sometimes longer, as applicants must be approved by Khartoum. Travel is not permitted in the southern area of the country under SPLA control. However, according to a Sudan embassy spokeswoman, travel is permitted overland to Eritrea in the east. The Sudanese government recommends that malarial suppressants be taken and that yellow fever, cholera and meningitis vaccinations be administered. Visas are not issued to those who have previously traveled to Israel. Business visas require a letter from a sponsoring company in Sudan with full details on length of stay, financial responsibility and references in Sudan. All borders are open, but questionable people who enter in the South may experience problems.

Journalists have been known to enter Sudan from the village of Periang, 500 miles northwest of the Kenyan border. From there, it is about 100 miles into the Nuba Mountains and SPLA-controlled territory.

Others enter from Uganda to interview pro-SPLA groups and leaders without a passport or visa. There is a minor catch you need travel permits from an SPLA representative to enter the "New Sudan".

Accessing Sudan from the south is dependent on aid organizations willing to provide transportation from Lokichogio in Kenya, or Adjumani, Moyo, Koboko in Uganda, something they are unlikely to do without seeing a letter of laissez passer from the SPLA. Bring cigarettes and small gifts, and be prepared to meet starvation and disease head-on. There is little to help you tell the difference between freedom fighters and bandits. Both may happily shoot you for your boots or supplies. Accessing the south from Khartoum is impossible, especially using a letter from the SPLA. you will be arrested, tried under every Islamic law known and jailed forever in the deepest, darkest dungeon in Islamdom.

The trip to the center of Khartoum from the airport is about 4 km. Negotiate and write down the agreed-upon taxi fare on a piece of paper before you get into the cab. There is a surcharge after 10 p.m. Remember, before you use our taxi tip, that 73 percent of the population is illiterate, according to the World Bank. Those travelers who enter illegally will be prosecuted under Sudanese laws. Contact the Sudanese embassy for more information:

Embassy of the Republic of the Sudan

2210 Massachusetts Avenue N.W.
Washington, D.C. 20008
☎ *(202) 338-8565*

Unforeseen circumstances, such as sandstorms (April and September) and electrical outages, may cause flight delays. The Khartoum Airport arrival and departure procedures are lengthy. Passengers should allow three hours for predeparture security and other processing procedures at the airport.

Only 994 of Sudan's 12,428 miles of roads are paved. The main paved routes are from Port Sudan through Kassala to Shavak, and from Khartoum through Sennar to Malakal. Most rural roads are simple tracks. In the northern part of the country, most of the roads are impassable during the July to September rainy season. There is an ancient rail system (with only 40 out of 150 locomotives working) with 3418 miles of track. The rail system links Khartoum with Port Sudan, Kassala, Wau, Nyala, and Wadi Halfa. The Sudan Railways Corporation operates a three-class service, including air-conditioned cars as well as sleeping and dining cars. There are 66 airfields, eight with permanent surfaces and four runways over 8000 feet. The main international airport is Khartoum International Airport.

Major airlines flying to Khartoum include Aeroflot, Air France, British Airways, Egypt Air, Ethiopian Airways, Gulf Air, KLM, Kuwait Airways, Lufthansa, and Saudia. Other less attractive carriers include Iraqi Airways, Libyan Arab Airlines, Kenya Airways, Middle East Airlines, Tunis Air and Yemenia. The national airline is Sudan Airways.

In the north, the major attractions are ancient temples and pyramids, and the ruins at Shendi and Karima.

Travel in all parts of Sudan is considered hazardous.

The South

Civil war persists in southern Sudan in the three provinces of Upper Nile, Bahr El Ghazal and Equatoria. The most recent phase of the civil war has killed 259,000 people and driven 3 million from their homes. In 1988, 250,000 died and over 4 million fled their homes. Sudan is anti-Christian and Zionophobic to the point of psychosis. Iran and Sudan have joined together in declaring Jihad on the Great Satan, so consider yourself Satan's Fuller Brush salesman.

The West

Banditry and incursions by southern Sudanese rebels are common in western Sudan, particularly in Darfur province along the Chadian and Libyan borders, and in southern Kordofan province.

Khartoum

Western interests in Khartoum have been the target of terrorist acts several times in recent years.

Iraqi Military Sites

Iraqi missiles and fighter planes were positioned in Sudan to threaten the Saudi Arabian Port of Jeddah and Egypt's Aswan High Dam.

Fighting

Renewed fighting between Sudanese and rebel forces in southern Sudan is sending 500 refugees a day into Uganda. The bombing and firefights between the Sudanese forces and members of the SPLA can be heard well into northern Uganda.

Terrorist Training Camps

Sudan is considered very dangerous for Western travelers because of the large number of terrorist training bases here. There are Islamic fundamentalist and terrorist training camps outside Khartoum, along the coast and in other nameless places.

Curfews

The government of Sudan has ordered a curfew that is strictly enforced. Persons who are outside during curfew hours without authorization are subject to arrest. Curfew hours change frequently.

Dinner Parties

It is against the law in Sudan to have a gathering of more than four people at one time, making pick-up basketball games and AA meetings a real problem here.

Hassles with Local Police

Travelers are required to register with police headquarters within three days of arrival. Travelers must obtain police permission before moving to another location in Sudan and register with police within 24 hours of arrival at the new location. These regulations are strictly enforced. Even with proper documentation, travelers in Sudan have been subjected to delays and detentions by Sudan's security forces, especially when traveling outside Khartoum. Authorities expect roadblocks to be heeded.

Medical facilities are as scarce as literate Sudanese outside Khartoum. In 1981, the country had 158 hospitals with a total capacity of 17,205 beds. There were 220 health centers, 887 dispensaries, 1619 dressing stations and 1095 primary health care units. Although there were 2122 physicians and 12,871 nurses working in the country, you can expect less than one doctor and nine hospital beds per 10,000 people. Don't expect squat in the rebel-held south. Some health care is provided free of charge, but your best bet is to have repatriation insurance should you get truly ill. Visitors traveling to the south of the country will need a valid certificate of vaccination against yellow fever. Travelers entering Egypt from Sudan will need to produce either a certificate of vaccination against yellow fever or a location certificate showing that they have not been in a yellow fever area. A valid cholera certificate is required of travelers arriving from infected areas.

Malaria, typhoid, rabies and polio are endemic. Bilharzia is also present, and visitors should stay out of slow-moving freshwater. Other prominent diseases include amoebic and bacterial dysentery, cerebral malaria, giardiasis (a hemorrhagic fever similar to Ebola) and guinea worm. The latter affliction is quite nasty. The eggs of the worm are ingested through river water. After hatching, the larvae cruise the blood system until finding a suitable home, where they mature and proceed to eat their way out of the body.

The arid north of Sudan is mainly desert with greener, agricultural areas on the banks of the Nile. Crops can only be grown during the rainy season (July to September). The south is mainly swamp and tropical jungle. The most important features are the White and the Blue Nile. The Blue Nile is prone to severe flooding. Mid-April to the end of June is the hot, dry season with temperatures above 110°F.

The official language is Arabic, but English is widely understood. The government is trying to eradicate the use of colonial-tainted English as part of its Islamification. Ta Bedawie and Nubian are also spoken, as are dialects of the Nilotic, Nilo-Hamitic and Sudanic languages. Evening meals are served around 10 p.m. The staple diet is *fool* (beans, or *dura*) eaten with vegetables.

Disruptions of water and electricity are frequent. Telecommunications are slow and often impossible.

Banks are open from 8:30 a.m. to noon Sunday to Thursday. Businesses are open 8:30 a.m. until 2.30 p.m. Government offices are open in Khartoum 8 a.m. to 2 p.m. Sunday to Thursday, and other centers are open 6:30 a.m. to 2 p.m. with a break for breakfast. Shops are open 8:30 a.m. to 1:30 p.m., then 5:30 p.m. to 8 p.m. Saturday through Thursday. Note: Government offices and businesses have been closing on Sundays since 1991 in an effort to conserve energy.

The strict Islamic code (the Sharia) has been in force since 1991. There is no gambling or alcohol allowed in the north. Individuals who exchange money anywhere other than an authorized banking institution risk arrest and loss of funds through unscrupulous black marketeers. The dinar is the official currency. The new dinar (introduced May 18, 1992) is equal to 10 Sudanese pounds.

Photography Restrictions

A permit must be obtained before taking photographs anywhere in Khartoum, as well as in the interior of the country. Photographing military areas, bridges, drainage stations, broadcast stations, public utilities, slum areas and beggars is prohibited. Sudanese are reluctant to be photographed without their permission.

Registration

U.S. citizens who visit or remain in Sudan, despite the warning, cannot, at press time, register at the U.S. embassy to obtain updated information on travel and security, as the embassy was closed in 1996.

Embassy Locations

The U.S. Embassy is located at *Sharia Ali Abdul Latif* in the capital city of Khartoum. The mailing address is *P.O. Box 699, or APO AE 09829.* ☎ *74700* and *74611.* The work week is Sunday through Thursday. However, at press time, the embassy was closed due to the continuing turmoil.

U.S. Embassy in Sudan (temporarily closed)
P.O. Box 699
Sharia Ali Abdul Latif
Khartoum
☎ *[249] (11) 74700/74611*

UK Embassy
St 10, off Baladia Street
P.O. Box 801
Khartoum
☎ *[249] (11) 70760*
FAX 873-1445 605 ext. 239

Sudanese Embassy in Canada
85 Range Road, Suite 407
Ottawa, Ontario, Canada K1N 8J6
☎ *(613) 235-4000*
FAX (613) 235 6880

Embassy of the Republic of Sudan
2210 Massachusetts Avenue, N.W.
Washington, D.C. 20008
☎ *(202) 338-8565/6/7/8*

Other Addresses

Bank of Sudan
Gamaa Avenue
P.O. Box 313
Khartoum
☎ *[249] (11) 78064*

Sudan Airways Co. Ltd.
SDC Building Complex, Amarat Street 19
P.O. Box 253
Khartoum
☎ *[249] (11) 47953*

Ministry of Trade, Cooperation and Finance
Khartoum
☎ *[249] (11) 730030*

Sudan Chamber of Commerce
P.O. Box 81
Khartoum

The following days are good days to stay inside, due to the proclivity of terrorist groups to generate lethal publicity on media spin days (i.e., anniversary dates).

06/30/1989	A group of officers led by general Omar al-Bashir overthrew the government of Sadiq Mahdi.
04/15/1986	A U.S. embassy communicator was shot and wounded while riding home from the embassy in Khartoum. The shooting was believed to be in retaliation for U.S. air raids on Libya earlier in the day.

SUDAN

05/16/1983	Founding of the SPLM/SPLA (The Sudanese People's Liberation Movement/Army).
03/01/1973	U.S. Ambassador Cleo Noel and Deputy Chief of Mission George Moore were assassinated in Khartoum during the seizure of the Saudi embassy.
03/03/1972	Anniversary of the Addis Ababa accords that ended the insurgency against the central government and granted southern Sudan wide regional autonomy on internal matters.
07/22/1971	Anti-Communist military elements loyal to Gaafar Nimeiri led a successful countercoup and brought him to power several days after a coup by the Sudan Communist Party.
06/09/1969	The south declared independence.
05/25/1963	The Organization of African Unity was founded on May 25, 1963. The day is celebrated as Africa Freedom Day. The OAU is organized to promote unity and cooperation among African states.
01/01/1956	Independence Day.

Victory in Sudan

Koranic verses on the dashboard and plastic flowers round the windshield are legacies of a former driver, but two bullet holes suggest the recent change of ownership has not been amicable. "We are smashing the enemy!" the young rebel officer shouts over the blat of unmuffled engine as the captured truck lurches sideways and two tires drop into a rock-hard rain gully. With a horrible grinding, the new driver finds first gear and puts his weight into the wheel. In the back, half a dozen guerrillas bounce atop tons of mortar and artillery shells abandoned by the fleeing Sudanese army. "Near Yei, we made a big ambush!" the officer yells exuberantly. The truck climbs resentfully out of the gully and immediately pitches the other way on a dirt track that hasn't seen a grader in fourteen years of war. "You will see. It is a very smelly place!"

Barely 72 hours have passed since I returned from a Bosnia update and listened to the telephone message. The Sudan People's Liberation Army has launched a massive offensive against government forces and have already captured Yei, the second-largest town in the south. Do I want to cover it? I swore silently. Just six weeks earlier I'd been in southern Sudan, gambling that, with the end of the rainy season, the SPLA would open a third front against the Sudanese army. In the previous five months the National Democratic Alliance, an unlikely coalition between the SPLA and Muslim parties ousted by Fundamentalists in 1989, had advanced in the eastern part of the country, and were threatening Port Sudan in the north. A desperate National Islamic Front government in Khartoum had declared a jihad and begun drafting high school students to throw pell-mell against the seasoned rebels. With the Sudanese army badly overstretched, military logic dictated that a southern offensive had to be imminent. And indeed my visit had revealed a snorting, bullish SPLA pawing the earth in preparation for a headlong charge. Thousands of new recruits, fresh from months of intensive training, were engaged in large scale infantry and armor exercises; food, ammunition and diesel were being stockpiled; and morale—from senior commanders down to the newest recruit—was stratospheric. It was clear that the biggest donnybrook of the war was gathering force, but my pleas of "When?" received innocent replies of "What offensive?" and I came home in a funk. My editor at *Jane's* was sympathetic and promised a page for my tenuous predictions, but the SPLA had been saying for years that they were on a roll and we can't really justify using much space on maybes, can we? Now it had happened. I picked up the phone.

War comes in different ways, in disparate climates and terrain, at the hands of a rainbow of colors wielding weapons from a rainbow of sources, but its immediate and irreducible end is death. And for those who earn a precarious crust reporting the world's conflicts, each war has a defining image distinct from those past or yet to come.

The road, hemmed by teak forest, straightens and smooths. Through the cracked windshield I see the first burned-out Toyota Landcruiser. Beyond it clusters of scorched trucks and abandoned equipment stretch a mile into the distance.

The engine bellows painfully as the driver down-shifts and we pass the first body. "Now you will see," my escort says. "Under just one tree more than twenty enemy." We grind to a halt in a cacophony of hissing air brakes, shaking bodywork and the thud of an ammunition crate against the back of the cab. Here is the "smelly place." Tying a bandanna across my mouth and nose, I step down and glutted ravens fly heavily into the sky. Then the stench penetrates and my stomach rebels as the smaller, darker objects come into focus wherever my eye settles—on the road, the shoulders, deeper into the undergrowth. Bodies, hundreds, lie where they fell ten days earlier, their own eyes long since taken by the birds. Most had died alone, but under a large tree to my left, I see twenty bodies rotted under a blanket of maggots, gunned down as they sought safety in numbers. The gorge rises, I gag and somehow hold it down. Then I shoot them—this time with my camera—and step over an unexploded mortar shell. Just beyond the tree a dry streambed disappears under the road. Two more people, feet and legs protruding from the culvert, had died scrambling desperately for cover. A third lay full length just behind. Click. A few paces more and I see a shriveled form—a white skull and black scalp resting against the warhead of a rocket-propelled-grenade. Pause and...click. I keep walking. Now a fifty-foot swathe of saplings scythed down with another dozen men. I cut around a heavy tree limb chain-sawed off by automatic weapons fire and jerk to a stop, one foot in the air, before stepping back and detouring past three who fell with it. Then I spot a desiccated body, rigidly straight, reclined at right angles to the road, its head broken loose and resting at the ankles. Scattered between and around all of them are piles of small arms ammunition, heavy machine gun belts, mortar and artillery shells—and thousands of Korans. I stoop and pocket an amulet of some sort lying next to a bullet-holed copy. Here and there a page turns idly in the nauseating breeze, but as I lower the camera, the only sounds come from the ravens scolding us for the interruption.

Eight months in the planning, Operation Thunderbolt was a three-pronged attack against government forces along the road between the Ugandan border and Yei. Launched on March 9, 1997, the southern axis took less than an hour to rout the Sudanese brigade headquarters at the border town of Kaya, then began driving towards Yei, 56 miles to the north. The next eight Sudanese army positions, complete with heavy weapons and bulging ammunition bunkers, were taken without a shot, tales of rebel strength having convinced the defenders to grab what they could carry and join the retreat. By now the SPLA's central axis had cut the road twelve miles below Yei, while the northern axis had already struck four miles north of the provincial town. Four days later Yei, a strategic target since the war began in 1983, was in rebel hands. In what would be an incredible stroke of luck for the SPLA, the panicking defenders failed to send a single message that they were abandoning the position. Its impact on the other side would prove catastrophic, for at that moment a column of almost 6000 demoralized Sudanese army and 4000 West Nile Bank Front combatants—a Ugandan Muslim terrorist group armed and funded by Khartoum—was struggling towards the presumed safety of the garrison. Forewarned of its approach, the SPLA commander sent the Yei victors south to join the central axis, which lay directly in the path of the approaching enemy. Outnumbered by almost 2:1, the rebel force would have to rely on surprise and the shock of massed firepower if it were to survive. Tanks and heavy concentrations of anti-aircraft and anti-armor weapons were moved into the forest and hastily camouflaged by newly-blooded infantry, who then filled the gaps and settled silently in their positions. Thirty minutes later the Sudanese and Ugandan column reached the edge of the ambush. Not until the bulk of it had entered the killing zone was the order given to open fire. When it finally stopped, close to 2000 lay dead and more than 1000 had surrendered, the balance abandoning tanks and vehicles and fleeing into the dense forests.

The truck groans to a stop in Yei. The immediate news from Chief of the General Staff Salva Kiir Mayardit is of an attempted government counterattack smashed that very morning 40 miles from the southern capital of Juba. Three enemy battalions had been thrown back with heavy losses. There was now one less obstacle in the way of capturing Juba, the fall of which would be the final step before total victory. My camera trigger finger begins itching. How far from here? Sixty miles. Can I go there? At the moment it is too dangerous. The enemy have been attacking with gunships and MiGs to cover the withdrawal of their ground forces. Perhaps in a day or two. Okay, then I'll start with the prisoners.

Outside the POW officers' block a depressed Sudanese army colonel accepts a cigarette. Colonel El Tayep El Hussain, who had arrived at Kaya only five weeks before the base fell to the SPLA, speaks passable English, having once attended a U.S. Army munitions course in Savannah, Georgia. Why, I ask, had the NIF closed all churches in the south? "It is government policy to introduce Islam to the southern people," he replies. And the arming of West Nile Bank Front Muslims to murder and mutilate Sudanese refugees in Uganda? El Tayep twists uncomfortably in his chair. "It is government policy," he repeats. What can be done to end the war? "The government must recognize the religious and political rights of the people." The SPLA officers nearby stare stonily at the horizon. They've heard it all before.

Much farther down the scale of prisoners is 18-year-old Yasir Sheik Idris Agib, one of the few surviving members of a self-styled Sudanese *mujahedin* unit. Visibly frightened at being singled out for my questioning, he describes being kidnapped from his high school in Khartoum, given two weeks training and sent to the southern front. What did the instructors teach him? To assemble, load and fire an AK-47. What else? Agib shakes his head. "Only to assemble, load and fire," he mumbles. At the end of the two weeks his class of new holy warriors was addressed by a member of the National Islamic Front, who described the "perfumes of heaven" that would greet those so fortunate as to be martyred in the jihad, whereupon they were each presented with a *hejab*, a tightly folded page of Koranic verses wrapped in cotton, and a key. The first was to protect them from infidel bullets, the second to unlock the gates of heaven should the first fail. I show him what I picked up at the ambush and he nods: "Yes, that is what they have been given." Hopefully the key was working better than the hejab, for less than half of Agib's classmates had survived. "After they took me from school my parents were never told," he tells me, blinking back tears. "They don't know where I am."

One tire climbs a rock and the Toyota pickup leans precariously on its way down the riverbank. "They managed to destroy the bridge here three days ago," Commander George Athor says as we lurch up the other side, "but didn't get any farther." A decomposing body stripped to its underwear lies near the road. "That was the Sudanese battalion commander, a lieutenant colonel," he says grimly. We stop and Athor leads me along the bottom of a ridgeline to where half a dozen bodies sprawl in hastily prepared positions. Athor points to one. "He was too light-skinned to be Sudanese. We're sure he was Iranian or Iraqi." But after three days the bloated corpse has blackened beyond recognition; only the straight hair suggests a Middle Eastern origin. "We captured a Farsi speaker, probably an Iranian, at Mile 40," Athor continues matter-of-factly back in the pickup. "He'd been badly wounded and we tried to save him, but he died. Too bad. He would have been proof that the government is using mujahedin from other countries to fight their jihad."

Ten minutes later we're looking at three burnt-out tanks squatting in earth plowed by explosions and gunfire. Thomas Cirillo, another of the SPLA's young, fighting generals, sweeps his arm across the front line battlefield. "They tried an end play here. Two battalions with armor were sent beyond our right flank as a diversion, then turned west to surprise us. Our tanks were waiting for them. When the enemy passed, we crossed their tracks and hit them from behind." Cirillo hitches his AK sling a little higher on his shoulder as my camera focuses on a turret-less tank and half of a body. Beyond it, dozens more lie motionless under a fine drizzle that has just started. "It was a massacre," he says with professional pride.

Story and photos tucked safely away, I wait next to the 4x4 that will carry me south from Yei to the border. My hosts, ebony giants in battle fatigues, crowd around to wish me safe journey. "You must return when we take Juba," they insist. Looking over my shoulder to wave good-bye, I remember my last question to Colonel El Tayep: Could the Sudanese army hold Juba? A truck carrying cheering rebels towards the front captured his attention and he squinted after it for a long moment, then sighed and shook his head. "I don't think so."

—Jim Hooper, 1997

Dushanbe

Tajikistan
★★★★

Tragikistan

Tajikistan is one of those "stan" places (like Afghanistan, Pakistan, etc.) we skip over in geography lessons. The word stan means two things. First, it means Muslim homeland. Second, it is named after the tribe or people (Afghan, Turkmeni, Kazak, Uzbek etc.) who claim it as their homeland. The problem here is that one man's home can be another man's...well, home—the crisp clean lines on a map don't necessarily translate as borders after the Russians were through rearranging them.

Its kissing cousin is Afghanistan (another Stan-fabrication of a colonial power) and Tajikistan (along with the Russian border guards and Dostum's Uzbek army) acts as a lifeline to the beleaguered Afghan government under Rabbiani and Shah Ahmad Massoud (see "Afghanistan").

To say there is a civil war would assume that there are two clearly defined sides in a conflict. The truth is that in Tajikistan there is no solid definition—only that if a warlord doesn't like what the Russian backed stooge of the week says, he fights back. You can always tell if a peace agreement is about to be signed by the number of bombs that go off in Dushanbe.

This mountainous, sparsely populated country is hard, ugly, deadly and controlled by tribes and clans. If space dictates simplification it could be said that the western third is lowland plain with most of the infrastructure and civilization while the country ascends in height and descends in civilized amenities towards the east. The borders are not marked because only Afghan drug smugglers brave the narrow mountainous passes into its rough and tumble neighbors of Kyrgyzstan, Uzbekistan, Pakistan, China and Afghanistan.

The main geographical feature of Tajikistan is the Pamir, an almost impassable range of mountains that act as a physical barrier between southern Asia and Russia. Here is where the radiating Asian mountain ranges were twisted into a huge knot to create a vast wasteland of stark beauty. It is also the new buffer zone between the Russians and the Muslim "barbarians." Remote border posts manned by bored and brutal veterans of Afghanistan have become high speed distribution centers for the ancient but rapidly-expanding Afghan drug trade. In between buying drugs, they also fight skirmishes with Tajik separatists, rogue warlords and each other.

But if you thought the Russians just started killing Tajiks (or vice versa as is more often the case) in the last few years, you need to brush up on your history. China, Russia and Afghanistan have been using the area called Tajikistan as a battleground ever since the Mongols under Tamerlane came cruising through. Tamerlane's habit of making mountains of skulls make today's terrorist seem like Jimmy Carter. In 1717, an entire Russian army that came to explore Tajikistan was killed. Even in 1917, there was a group of terrorists called the *basmachis* who fought the Bolsheviks for an independent Muslim homeland. They were defeated after four years and fled to Northern Afghanistan creating the nucleus of the current Tajik rebellion.

When the area was known more appropriately as Central Asia, Stalin (a Georgian mountain boy) decided to chop his Southern real estate into five quasi ethnic clumps. His artificial boundaries were designed to lump together and divide minorities. The Russians created a Tajikistan to be an autonomous satellite of Uzbekistan in 1924 and then changed to a full union republic in 1929. In the Russian tradition of totally screwing up ethnic and indigenous history, they left 475,000 Tajiks in Uzbekistan and every important government position was usually run by a round-faced, hard drinking Soviet from the north. Things were relatively calm (or undocumented) under the iron fist of Mother Russia. In the '80s a fundamentalist group called the Islamic Resistance Party began pushing for Tajik nationalism and started to raise hell. They really didn't come into their own until 1990 when the Russians threatened to resettle Christian Armenians in Muslim Dushanbe.

In 1991, when the rest of post-Soviet central Asia declared independence, Tajikistan's lack of national wherewithal and importance as a buffer zone for Russia, delegated it to its current status as an independent republic. The population magically voted in a corrupt communist government. This didn't sit well with some locals, who decided to take over the presidential palace to install a coalition government run by Akbarshah Iskandarov. Other factions also realized that the gun was much more efficient than the ballot box and began to use bullets instead of stern memos to get their point across. The lines broke down as the Moscow - friendly old liners from the North battled the Kulyabis from the south.

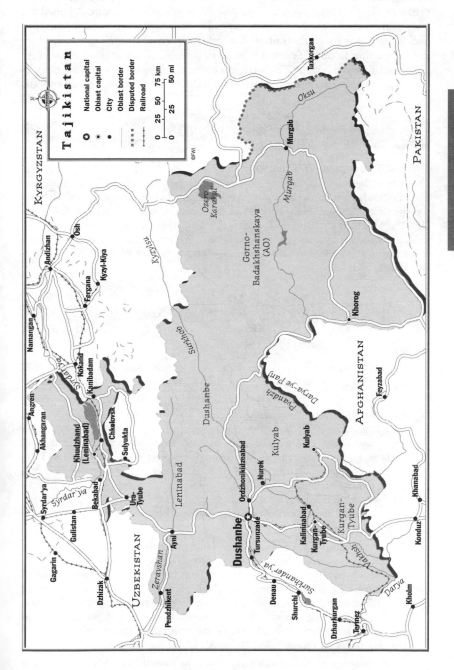

The civil war erupted in a very nasty shootout until 1993. Over 40,000 people lost their lives in this flare-up and not too many folks in the west even heard of the massacre. The ethnic cleansing and precarious political structures opened the door to the Russian army who then stepped in to babysit their puppet ruler Imamali Rakhmanov (from the Kulyab district) and then proceeded to spank all the various warring factions. Seemingly blind to the history lesson dealt them in Afghanistan, Russia still views Tajikistan as a buffer zone and does not want nasty Islamic fundamentalists sneaking in to mess up their nice Moscow neighborhoods.

Tajikistan is a poor country where 90 percent of food and all fuel is donated by aid groups. The average wage is $5 a day and that's if you can find a job. Tajikistan is a low budget wasteland where downsized Russian army can still afford to play the Great Game. Russia's army has also provided a high speed pipeline for heroin and hashish straight to Moscow via Spetnaz 'R Us overnight military cargo service. The ruling clan is simply government de jour but the Russians call the shots and pay a lot of bills here. For now the only tourist attractions are a ring of armed border forts manned by 25,000 Russian soldiers, weekly firefights with Afghan smugglers and Tajik rebels.

The Tajiks

It would be charitable to say that the Tajik Islamic Movement led by Sayid Abdullo Nuri represents the Tajiks in Tajikistan, but that would be overstating his importance. They want 40 percent control of the government, but they don't really represent all Tajiks.

His 2000 or so rebels have been pounding away for 6 years (since the Soviet meltdown) at the Russian forts along the Afghanistan/Tajikistan border, and once in a while they lob a grenade in downtown Dushanbe, so the reporters don't have to travel so far to report the news. For now they are trying to make good on a peace treaty signed in May of '97. An attractive option after President Rakhmanov survived an assassination attempt a month earlier. Nuri finally came to Dushanbe in September to kiss and make up. It seems his photo op was delayed by a wave of bombings. A peace agreement with Sayid Abdullo Nuri was signed after 5 years of exile. He will have about 560 fighters to make sure he stays alive in Dushanbe.

The often Shia (some are Sunni) Muslim Tajiks are Persians originally from northern Afghanistan. They are Persians and consider themselves a superior race and have a millennium of cultural achievements to back it up. Their capital was Bukhara where some of Islam's brightest stars held court. Poets, philosophers, artists and calligraphers spread their skills throughout the Muslim world from here. There are about 5000 Tajik fighters based in Northern Afghanistan. *DP's* pal Ahmed Shah Massoud uses Tajikistan as a supply line, and is a hero to these folks, and will more than likely come to visit if the *taliban* push him out of the Panshir valley. This could start the war going the other way.

The Tajiks appear similar to South Europeans due to Alexander's randy army and political agenda. Tajiks are primarily Sunni Muslims with the Pamirs being Shia's. You can also find Tajiks in Uzbekistan (860,000), Kazakhstan (100,000) and the Xiajang region of

China (30,000). For now, the Tajiks fight in four major groups that include The Democratic Front, The National Front and the following major groups.

Islamic Revival Party

About 2000 fighters based in Kunduz, Afghanistan, Taloquan and Jalalabad. The IRP are supported and trained by Gulf state businessmen, Pakistani and Afghan fundamentalists, Libya and Iran. Many trainers and support personnel are connected to Gulbuddin Hekmatyar's Jamaat-e-Islami and Pakistan's ISI. The IRP has a political office in Moscow.

L'ali Badakhshan Party

The "Ruby" of Badakhshan is a Pamiri based group in Eastern Tajikistan with bases in Taloquan and support from Iran. They effectively control the rugged Pamir region and seek autonomy under a caretaker government.

The Russians

The Russians must have forgotten their history lessons and decided that Tajikistan is a lot easier to defend as a border than Afghanistan. (The first time the Russians came to Tajikistan in 1717, their entire army was massacred.) Maybe they didn't notice the mountains, nasty weather, hardened fighters and silly puppet government make for deadly politicians. The Russians spend about 3 billion rubles a year to keep 50 border posts open along a 900 km border with Afghanistan. The 25,000 troops include a number of Afghan veterans including OMON and Spetznatz commandos. The same folks who showed the Afghans how to get drugs into Europe without using camels. The Russians have about 200 T-72 battle tanks, 420 hard shell combat vehicles and artillery against a third as many rebels using cheap running shoes and beat up AKs. Considering the Russians draftees are offered $60 a month and three year contracts, it is not surprising that they are having a hard time finding grenade fodder to man the frozen border with Afghanistan. Local boys who volunteer can serve for only 6 months. If you have combat experience, you can be a contract soldier and serve 18 months for a lot more money. It is assumed that many Afghan vets (all the way to General level) actually choose Tajikistan because they can supplement their income with drug deals. There are about 150 contacts a year with rebels with a third ending up in firefights. The kill ratio is about 10 to one for the Russians with much of the activity occurring along the Pyandzh river at night. The towns of Pyandzh and the Kulyab region are the hottest.

When not selling weapons to Massoud the border guards like to shoot the rare Marco Polo sheep for food. (It'll cost you $20,000 for a hunting license if you want to bag one.)

The Pamiris (Ismailis)

The Pamiris barely survive in the high altitude valleys between the imposing peaks. Most have a hard time communicating with each other. The people are poor and in many cases destitute. Ninety percent of food is supplied by aid organizations and all fuel is brought in. Seems like just the place for a former playboy who was born in Switzerland and jet sets around the world to be a religious leader. The Pamiris are Ismailists who believe in a sect of Shia Islam, a religion that has no house of worship, icons, holy men or even holidays. Their leader is the Aga Khan, a direct descendant of Mohammed who keeps the Pamiris alive by the generosity of his Swiss based charity foundation. He is considered a living deity and his photograph is hung in every home. There are some 210,000 people with 45,000 arable acres, but little hope of any future improvement.

The Clans

Forget the Hatfields and McCoys, here you have the Pamiris from the Gorno-Badakhshan, the Leninabaders from the north, Kulyabis from the south, the Kurgan-Tyube, Garmis from east, Afghan drug smugglers, Tajik rebels from across the border and doped up Russian soldiers supplementing their paychecks. Some warlords are happy just to knock off a profitable business like the aluminum smelter such as Kadyr Abdullayev did in Tursunzode (west of Dushanbe). To make matters worse, the nearby Russian commander and his 200 soldiers, angered at Abdullayev's men stealing weapons from his garrison and tired of feuding warlords, disobeyed the President and shot their way into the town and wrested control away from Abdullayev and his rival.

Some, like Bakhram Sadirov (based in Kalainav, 52 miles east of Dushanbe), just snatch up 23 people (UN workers monitoring the cease fire, a government minister sent to negotiate a settlement and journalists covering the event) to help them in various negotiations; in this case to release his brother who was kidnapped by another warlord allied to the government. In short the political situation in Tajikistan is like having every NHL hockey team playing on the ice at the same time…using rocket launchers.

Although Tajikistan is officially part of Russia, you need specific permission on your visa to enter. These days travelers are allowed in, but it is still more of a journo spot. In the U.S., visas for Tajikistan are issued by the Russian Embassy, Consular Division, *1825 Phelps Place N.W., Washington, D.C. 20008,* ☎ *(202) 939-8907,* or the Russian Consulates in New York, San Francisco or Seattle. For information about the country, you might also try the Tajik Mission to the UN, *East 67th Street, New York, New York 10021;* ☎ *(212) 472-7645, FAX (212) 628-0252.* Tajik visas granted by these offices are valid for a stay of five days. These visas are also valid in other Commonwealth of Independent States for five days, except in Uzbekistan, where they are valid for three days only for transiting to another country. Visas are required when you check in at a hotel. If travelers plan a longer stay, they may apply at the Ministry of Foreign Affairs for a longer visa. If you want to stay longer than 90 days you will need an AIDS test or supply a medical certificate. The Gorno-Badakhshan border requires a special advance permission. You can apply for a longer stay once in country. If you are bouncing back and forth between Uzbekistan, remember to get a double or multiple entrance Russian visa.

Also, you will need an exit visa to leave Tajikistan so whatever you said (or paid) to the nice immigration person may come back to haunt you on your way out. Worst case, there is the OVIR (immigration) office in Dushanbe that can try to iron things out. Road rats can try getting a visa at the Tajik embassy in Almaty in Kazakstan at *Ulista Emeleva 70,* ☎ *[7] (3272) 611760, FAX 610225.*

When airlines are going into Dushanbe you can take the six hour flight directly from London to Dushanbe via Tajikistan Airlines *(TIA, 154 Horn Lane, London, W3 6PG* ☎ *(0181) 993-8885, FAX: 993-7504)* on Sunday and from Moscow about every second day. There is also a 1.5 hour flight to Delhi. You can also go once a week on the two hour Karachi-Dushanbe flight. If you find yourself in one of these places, sit back and enjoy the retro feeling of a creaky '60s era Boeing 707 maintained by post Soviet-era mechanics. Aeroflot won't guarantee it, but they list a four hour flight from Moscow for about $300 one way. Because of frequent aid flights there are a variety of charter flights from Dushanbe with outbound space. Just head to the airport and beg or haggle. There is also a crime ridden but more reliable train from Moscow and a daily bus from Samarkand. Internal flights are often cancelled or delayed by lack of fuel, passengers or whatever.

Due to a lack of fuel, there are not many taxis. Taxis can be called in Dushanbe by dialing ☎ *24-66-29* or catching one at the Hotel Tajikistan. Negotiate and agree to a fare first. Take the bus into and around town. There are private buses that cruise Dushanbe. *DP* recommends hiring a private driver and car for about $30–$50 a day. A *DP* reader in Belgium tells us that he used a Kyrgz visa and used the "72 hour rule" which gives you 72 hours to get a visa for the FSR you are entering. Make sure you get clearance from the police in Osh to cross at Sary Tash.

Tajikistan is not a country designed for leisurely touring. Ninety three percent of the country is mountainous. Only 10 percent can be cultivated. Some tourist itineraries provide a three-day tour of which two and half days are getting in and out of Dushanbe with a half day sprint from the hotel and back to see the Gissar fortress before it gets dark. Not much a draw for bus tours. The eastern mountains make most of the country an adventure, the civil war makes the driving interesting, and the general lack of infrastructure means you come in or you go out, but you don't cruise around. There are daily train 22-hour connections to Tashkent, Uzbekistan, but sit with your back to the engine to avoid most of the rocks thrown through the windows by guerilla wannabes thinking that Russians are on board. There are three rail lines inside Tajikistan, but check to see if the track has been blown up and, of course, look out for thieves while on board.

You can try to hitch rides with the aid of convoys and truck drivers going through the northern mountains into Kyrgyzstan and Uzbekistan. The alpine scenery along the Pamir Highway into or from Kyrgyzstan is worth the life-shortening ride, bad food and lack of accommodations. The embattled M41 highway along the border with Afghanistan is used only by Russian military vehicles. The high passes are snowed in from October to March. The M41 road between Osh, Kyrgyzstan and Khorog is kept open year round and is the most scenic, but once past Khorog, it becomes one of the most dangerous as it hugs the border between Afghanistan and Tajikistan.

There are supposed to be regular flights via Tajik Air to Khojand, Khorog and most major towns in Tajikistan, but once again weather, crashed planes and the availability of Stinger air to ground missiles dictate the flight schedules here. Reservations are not taken until 3–7 days before the flight. You have to buy your tickets at the airport since the locals get to pay a lot less at the airline offices. You can get the latest from **Tajik Intourist** ☎ *7 (3772) 21-68-92* or Russia's Intourist *630 Fifth Avenue, Suite 868, New York, New York 10111* ☎ *(212) 757-3884, FAX: (212) 459-0031* and good luck getting a straight answer.

You must be very specific about which cities you wish to visit and make sure they are clearly written in. There are a lot of checkpoints if you travel by road. Soldiers will shoot if you do not stop. When you do stop they will shake you down for a bribe. Smile and act stupid and they may give up on you. If you do not have the proper paperwork you will be sent back. You could also be detained and fined. For in country security reports contact the UN Military Observers Team at Shevchenko Street in Dushanbe ☎ *[7] (3272) 21-01-47* Travel anywhere within 15 miles of the Afghan border is very dangerous and controlled by Russian soldiers.

You can't take any antiques out of the country. That, of course, is the least of your worries. Antiques could be anything from the phone system to the political philosophy of the current rulers. You are also not allowed to take any local currency out. Again, this won't be too much of a problem since there is not much call for Tajik rubles in the cafes of Paris. The only place you might run into a customs person would be at the border with Kyrgyzstan. Needless to say, the border with Afghanistan is more concerned about folks trying to sneak in at night with rocket launchers and trucks full of opium. The only thing you should concern yourself with is how to get out of this godforsaken place with Afghan fighters to the south, mountains to the north and a whole lot of Central Asia to the north and west. Tajikistan is a long way from any-where. The only thing your credit cards will be good for is scraping the ice off the dilapidated truck's windshield and your travelers checks will make good kindling on those nights in the mountain passes.

If you hire a driver to take you to Uzbekistan, remember that you may have to change cars at the border since the Uzbeks often do not let Tajik tagged cars in.

The M41 Highway

There is a road that heads east from Dushanbe and then winds south along the Afghan border that is off limits to even locals. You will be turned back at any one of the military checkpoints or even find yourself front and center at a Tajik attack on your Russian bor-der stop. Many sections of the road are mined every evening by rebels. The rebels steal the mines the Russians lay down and then put them back in places where the Russians sus-pect least. Some people take the daily flight from Dushanbe to Khorog ($60) and then take a bus through the mountains into Osh, but don't count on regular departures or the weather being compliant.

Bus Stops

Bus stops are Tajik rebels' favorite place to shoot or roll grenades at Americans, Russians or people that look like Russians or Americans. If you have a death wish, wear your uni-form (complete with U.S. or Soviet flag) and hang around Dushanbe for a while.

Dushanbe

The capital city of Dushanbe (Tajik for Monday, the day of the weekly market) is a dan-gerous place due to street crime and violence after dark. It's only three hours by tank from the Afghan border. Westerners are targeted not only in public, but in their hotel rooms. Even armed soldiers stay off the streets at night. UN vehicles have been hijacked in daylight. Bombings are frequent within the city. Call the U.S. embassy in Dushanbe for the latest ☎ *[7] (3772) 21-03-56.*

Flying

When there is air service, the chances of crashing are good in Tajikistan. The Russians pay their pilots an additional sum to make the 45 minute flight between Dushanbe and Khorog—white knuckle flying at its finest. The high altitude prevents the aircraft from passing gracefully over some of the highest mountains in Russia. So the pilots simply fly in around, and by the peaks. You should know that you are flying over (or rather through) an active war zone, and one unlucky flight was downed by Tajik rebels using a surface to air missile. You can call the London office of Tajikistan International Airlines (we're pretty sure they're not that busy) at ☎ *(0181) 993-8885, FAX: 993-7504*).

Opium

The border with Afghanistan and the presence of the Russian OMON means that the opium poppy is growing in great abundance in the valley areas and transported in large quantities. Although the farmers don't have any axe to grind with foreigners, you may find yourself in an area controlled by smugglers.

Journalism

Over 40 journalists have been murdered in Tajikistan since 1992. Most of the killings are at the hands of the rebel groups who haven't quite learned how to send pithy and scathing "letters to the editor." There is no censorship of media in the 13 TV stations, 3 radio stations along with 202 newspapers and magazines, there just seems to be a very violent readership.

Russians

Ethnic Russians, politicians and military men are popped off by wild eyed Tajiks rebels. So if you're an American with a potato nose, cauliflower ears and gold teeth, you might want to visit Brighton Beach or Istanbul instead.

The Alma

There have been over 500 eyewitness accounts of the *alma* or the *almasty* in Tajikistan. The *almasty* is Tajikistan's version of the yeti (or "that thing") and is said to be about 6 ft. 6 in., weigh in at about 500 lbs. and walk on two legs. The man/animal has reddish-brown fur and can move along the ground at up to 40 m.p.h. They root for berries, amphibians and rodents. They are seen at night and run away when spotted. *Alma* youngsters look just like human babies except smaller.

Some scientists say they are Neanderthals driven into the wilderness by our ancestors, the Cro Magnons. Others say they are a result of active imaginations. But somewhere on the "Roof of the World" exists a large hairy creature. Is it dangerous? Not really. It is said that it will attack pack animals. There are ancient stories of similar creatures from Oregon to Chechnya to Mongolia to Borneo. So why not be the first one on your block to have a pet *Alma*?

Money Hassles

Tajikistan started printing its own version of the ruble in 1995. Remember that the lowly Tajik ruble is only worth 100 Russian rubles. You get about 400 rubles for a U.S. dollar. Needless to say, napkins and coasters might retain their value longer than this creative solution to insolvency. You can't take money out of the country. Credit cards are useless. Banks have no idea what a traveler's check is. Needless to say, the almighty dollar is good as gold here, but you will need Tajik rubles to buy airline tickets in country. Don't take or accept 100 dollar bills before 1990 because of the high amount of bogus Iranian printed C notes. Worst case is that money changers will discount your ragged greenbacks for up to 25 percent of their value. The locals pay a much lower price for just about everything, and if you get caught hiring a local to buy your tickets, you will get dunned for the difference or a bribe.

Tajikistan has malaria in the southern and lower regions. The water supply is not potable and bottled water should be your only source. Hepatitis A is a risk. Ticks are found in higher elevations in grassy and wooded areas. Rabies is a significant risk from local dogs, many of which are trained to attack strangers. Add meningitis, tuberculosis, schistosomiasis and typhoid (Dushanbe and south) to your disease list.

There has been a significant deterioration in the medical infrastructure in Tajikistan with many trained personnel having fled the country after the recent kidnappings. Tajikistan has a general scarcity of medical equipment and medicines. The potential exists for significant disease outbreaks, because of massive population displacement and a partial breakdown in immunization activities.

Electricity is 220v/50 hz of the two-pin European type. The language is officially Tajik written in the Arabic script, Uzbek, and about a third of the people speak Russian. The moola is the Tajik ruble (100 kopeks to the ruble and about 400 rubles to the U.S. dollar). You can leave home without your American Express because Tajikistan is a cash-only economy. International banking services are not available and if there was a decent bank it would be knocked off within five minutes of opening. The phones are funky (the country code is 7 and Dushanbe is 3772) and the general infrastructure non-existent outside the major cities. The tajik ruble is good for toilet paper, blowing your nose or souvenirs when you leave the country. The average income of Tajiks is around $2.50 a month so they don't see any rubles or dollars.

The best times for masochists to visit would be between October and May to experience the blizzards or between June and October to be sandblasted in the heat by the dust storms. Well at least there's a breeze. Since most of Tajikistan is above 3000 meters, Tajikistan is frigid in the winter and hot and arid in the summer. March and May bring the most rain, the heat in June to August will fuse your Airwalks to the pavement with temperatures reaching well over 100 degrees. Only 7 percent of the land is arable and the rest is comprised of alpine hidey holes for gun toting mountainfolk. For what it matters, American soap operas and trash TV are big during those long winter nights. Number one is *Santa Barbara*, a show with a plot about as convoluted and strange as the political situation in Tajikistan. The hotels usually don't serve food, you can stay in funky dachas or the upscale (for Tajikistan) tourist hotels along with the embassy staff and pilots. The only other major town is Khorog where you can risk your life to see the town's one tourist attraction: a bunch of faded, badly stuffed animals and a collection of Lenin photos.

Tajikistan is dangerous, mountainous, earthquake-prone and an ideal place to start *DP's* pick for the new Central Asian extreme sport: Helicopter gunship skiing, where contestants try to ski past machine-gunning Russian border guards and Hind-D gunships carrying five keys of opium gum on their back. Too whacko? Well how about Yeti hunting?

Embassy Locations

The U.S. embassy in Dushanbe is providing only emergency consular services. The Canadian embassy is in Moscow and Almaty, Kazakstan. ☎ *[7] (3272) 50-11-51, FAX: 581-1493.*

U.S. Embassy (Dushanbe)
   Oktyabrskaya Hotel (October Hotel)
   105A Pospekt Rudaki
   Dushanbe, 734001, Tajikistan
   ☎ *[7] (3712) 21-03-56, no fax*

Russian Embassy (US)
   Consular Division
   1825 Phelps Plaza NW
   Washington, DC. 20008
   ☎ *(202) 939-8918*
   There are Russian consulates in New York, San Francisco and Seattle.

Russian Embassy (CANADA)
   285 Charlotte Street
   Ottawa, Ontario K1M 8L8
   ☎ *(613) 235-4341, FAX: (613) 236-6342*

WEB/e-mail
   The Embassy of the USA
   irage@usis.td.silk.glas.apc.org

http://www.wtgonline.com/country/tj/gen.html

http://reenic.utexas.edu/reenic/Countries/Tadjikistan/tadjikistan.html

http://yellow.ccs.uky.edu/~rakhim/turkistan.html

http://www.nsrc.org/ASIA/TJ/country.html

http://www.west.net/~wwmr/fsu.htm
   News from the former Soviet Bloc</A>

http://www.securities.com/

http://solar.rtd.utk.edu/friends/science/ecostan/ecostan.index.html

http://ukanaix.cc.ukans.edu/ex-ussr/ex-ussr_main.html

http://kuhttp.cc.ukans.edu/ex-ussr/whoswho-tajikistan.html

http://www.spb.su/ryh/tadjvisa.html

3/8/97	Rebels and government sign a pact to create a peace agreement.
4/97	President Emomali Rakhmanov survived a grenade attack in Khudjand by a 21-year-old Tajik.
2/8/97	Nine UN workers, Russian journalists and Tajikistan's security minister are kidnapped by warlord Bakhram Sadirov. They are later released with the help of Ahmad Shah Massoud.
09/10/1992	Declaration of Independence.
09/07/1992	President Rakhmon Nabiyev resigned after Islamic rebels forcefully took control of the government. The Islamic Party was overturned in a bloody coup late in October 1992. September 10 is recognized as the date of Tajikistan's declaration of independence. Islamic rebels have continued fighting since early September 1992.
12/25/1991	President Bush formally recognized Tajikistan and 11 other former Soviet republics. On that occasion, he also stated that formal diplomatic relations would be established with six of the republics as soon as possible and that diplomatic relations would be established with the other six (Tajikistan was one of them) when they met certain political conditions.
12/21/1991	Tajikistan joined with 10 other former republics of the Soviet Union (which ceased to exist on December 25, 1991) in establishing the Commonwealth of Independent States.
02/12/1990	Twenty-five persons died as Interior Ministry troops fired on demonstrators massed outside the Tajikistan Communist Party headquarters in Dushanbe, the capital of Tajikistan. February 12 now is celebrated as "Memory Day," and an obelisk was unveiled on February 12, 1992, to commemorate the persons who died in February, 1990.

Ankara

Turkey
★★★

Muddle East

Here is where East meets West. A place that can be as cosmopolitan as Paris and as depressingly medieval as Iran. Most Americans think of the movie *Midnight Express*, the harrowing story of a young American arrested for drugs and tortured by his Turkish captors. Others think of temples, beaches and happy people. To others, Turkey is simply some godforsaken, giant landing strip for American black birds, a convenient place for allowing us to periodically blow the hell out of Baghdad and spy on Russia. It's a country where, within 100 miles of each other, you can find stealth fighters and people who live in caves.

Although Turkey is as civilized as Paris, France, it can get as wild as Paris, Texas. In Southeastern Turkey everybody is off the street by sundown because Turkey is waging an all-out war against the terrorist Kurdistan Workers Party (PKK), the stated representatives of the ethnic Kurds and the unstated representatives of the grim reaper. Turkey's Marxist guerrillas of the PKK have declared war on the country and attack tourist targets as well as teachers, government workers and other innocent bystanders. They believe that by destroying the infrastructure and hard currency earners of Turkey, they will be ceded their own homeland. The PKK operates primarily in Turkey and Western Europe. Its targets also include civilians and government forces in the eastern portion of the country. For some variety, they began taking Western hostages in 1991. Nothing nasty but a nagging reminder that tourism to Turkey has its adventurous side.

Perhaps Turkey's biggest problem has been its long denial of even the existence of the Kurds. The Kurds' demands as recently as the 1970s had been limited to the government's recognition of their language in culture, but rising Kurdish pride and a recognition of their resources turned into vehement nationalism and moves toward independence. Although the Kurdish political parties that formed in the late '70s were illegal, they nonetheless brought huge parcels of Kurdistan under their own control, until another period of assimilation began after the Turkish military coup of 1980. Enter the PKK, which, in 1984, not only forced the government to open its eyes to the Kurdish problem, but also the eyes of innocent people who began finding themselves staring down the barrels of AKs.

The next time you stare at those romantic tourist posters remember that they need your bucks. The war against the Kurds costs the Turkish government about $7 billion a year and keeps about 75 percent of its 500,000-man army busy. On the other side, the PKK has a fairly backwoods army of between 8000 and 15,000 soldiers recruited from the refugee camps and trained in Syria, Northern Iraq and eastern Turkey. Many of the PKK's fighters are women.

In the nine-year period between 1987 and March of '96 the government figures that it knocked off about 10,663 terrorists while they only lost 3400. Oh yeah, about 3938 civilians got aced in the cross-fire and about 1200 villages (give or take a few) have been razed to the ground by the Turkish army. The 12 to 15 million Kurds make up about 15–20 percent of Turkey's 62 million population. More than 80 Turkish journalists, academics and writers have been imprisoned for speaking out on the Kurdish issue.

What is Syria's beef with Turkey? Well, it doesn't like Turkey siphoning off water from the Tigris and Euphrates Rivers. So it continues to support the PKK and its leader, Abdullah Ocalan, who shuttles between Northern Iraq, Damascus and the Bekaa Valley. Despite the 17,500 number offered by the government, other sources estimate that well over 30,000 people have been killed since 1984—many more in northern Iraq.

The PKK likes to target tourist sites and tourist-oriented facilities in western and Aegean Turkey in an effort to scare away tourists. Back in 1993, there were seven attacks against tourist facilities by the PKK, injuring 27 tourists. The PKK also kidnapped 19 foreigners (one American) in southeast and eastern Turkey. That same summer a series of bomb attacks in Antalya wounded 26 persons; in Istanbul, a grenade was thrown under a tour bus, injuring eight persons, and a bomb was thrown at a group of tourists as they were sightseeing around the city walls, resulting in six injuries. A hand grenade was found buried on a beach southeast of Izmir, and there were reports of similar incidents in other areas along the west coast. In 1994, the attacks continued, PKK bomb attacks were conducted on some of Istanbul's most popular tourist attractions, including St. Sophia and the Covered Bazaar, resulting in the deaths of two foreign tourists. Intermittent terrorist bombings have also occurred elsewhere, including Ankara, the state capital, causing damage to property and loss of life. After the Turkish Army invaded the

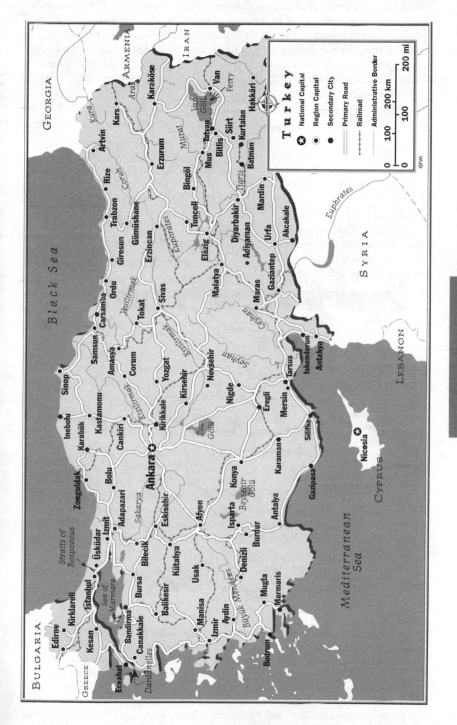

PKK's main base at Zap, Ocalan held press conferences from the Bekaa valley ranting that "every Kurd will be a living bomb". He also has decided to pick on German tourists this time. Time will tell whether he will carry out this threat. Just to even things out the Turkish government reminded "Apo" that he better show up for his mandatory military reserve service or they will revoke his citizenship. Maybe the government thought they could make some headway if they fielded college professor Ocalan against his own Pesh Mergas.

In addition, the Dev Sol has been up to its old nasty ways. Early in 1996, the leftist guerrillas executed two prominent Turkish businessmen and a secretary in their offices on the 25th floor of the swanky Sabanci Center in downtown Istanbul. Each was killed with a single bullet to the head—a left-wing flag was left behind as a calling card. The attack was to avenge the deaths of three prison inmates at Istanbul's Umraniye prison, when security forces brutally quelled a riot there. The inmates' deaths ignited five days of riots in 10 different Turkish prisons, which ended only after the government suspended two top officials at the Umraniye facility. Under pressure from the leftist member of Turkey's ruling coalition government, new Prime Minister Yilmaz extended emergency rule for four months, beginning at the end of March 1996, and promised he would lighten up the government's stand on the PKK.

Incest?

An enraged mob of 200 Alawite demonstrators attacked the Istanbul headquarters of a private Turkish television channel, Interstar, with stones, sticks and shovels after a game show host had suggested that Alawites—an esoteric branch of Islam—practiced incest regularly. The host later apologized and admitted his allegation was merely an uneducated guess.

Although you will hear about "terrorist" activity in Turkey, it would be more accurate to say that—with over 30,000 people killed since 1984 in violent encounters with the PKK and the Dev Sol—the situation is better summed up as an ongoing civil war. The group with the most bucks and bullet is the PKK (Kurdistan Workers Party) who despite the leftist leanings make some decent change babysitting drugs coming from the East and have a Smack R'Us franchise in Europe. They have a big enough allowance to afford a satellite lease and a TV station so the their business must be good. (Also see the "Kurdistan" chapter.)

The Military

Turkey has been, will be and continues to be run by the military. Despite a revolving cast of democratically elected politicians, the army steps in when things get too silly for their tastes. That is not to say there are not democratic freedoms, it just means only the people who play ball get to have them. The Kurds are considered no different than any other minority in Turkey and logically they are entitled to all the benefits and responsibilities all Turkish citizens have. It is only when you drive east of Diyarbakir that you see why the east is so impoverished and poor. Turkey does not want to invest too much money in case

Russia, Armenia, Iraq, Iran or Syria comes in and gobbles it up. It is essentially a buffer zone of poor nomadic peoples (the Kurds) who resent the flashy, Mercedes-Benz lifestyle of the ethnic Turks in the West. The government feels it has a lid on the PKK problem and has an annual spring outing to their headquarters in Zap just to piss them off.

The man with the job of fighting the PKK is General Cetin Dogan who is the Turkish Chief of Operations. He has been chasing the PKK since 1984. The other man who wants the PKK to be a bad memory is Necati Bilican, Supreme Governor of the nine SE Turkish provinces that have been under emergency rule since 1987. The most recent foray into Northern Iraq (in which *DP's* Roddy Scott was in the wrong place at the right time and ended up being deported from Kurdistan) left a death toll of 3009 PKK guerillas and 113 Turkish soldiers—a number the PKK vehemently deny. The military is far more concerned about the rise of fundamentalism which could strike them in the Ankara and Istanbul. Journos who want to poke around should contact:

Prime Ministers Office

General Directorate of Press and Information
56 Konur Sokak
Ankara Turkey
TEL 312 417 6311

Kurdistan Workers Party (PKK)

The largest, best-organized and most active Kurdish group in Turkey is the PKK. Founded in 1978, the PKK is a Marxist group led by Abdullah Ocalan, a former law student from the University of Ankara, fled when the PKK was outlawed in 1980 and now lives in Damascus. Things got military in 1984. He is supported by Assad of Syria because its gives Syria a bargaining chip when the issue of water is discussed. Turkey is busy damming the Euphrates in three places, cutting off Syria's much needed supply.

Unlike the PUK or the KDP, the PKK wants to represent or rule all 20 million Kurds in the Middle East, being the best-known and most violent advocate of Kurdish independence. Towards that end the PKK has not only declared war on Turkey, but they have aimed their sights on tourists since it feels that income from tourism (US$7 billion a year) funds the Turkish government's war against the Kurds. The 20 or so tourists that have been kidnapped have all been released unharmed. Why? Because frightened tourists make for better interviews on CNN than dead ones.

The PKK is most active in southeast Turkey, setting up roadblocks, placing land mines (the Turks apparently have lost the maps for all the mine fields they have planted along the Syrian border) and blasting away at villages protected by "loyalists." The army has assigned about 7000 locals who are paid $200 a month. The army provides them with a gun and then hope that too many of them won't be made an example of by the PKK. About one village guard is killed for every two soldiers. The Army likes to point out that their kill ratio is about 10;1 in favor of the loyalists and soldiers against the PKK. Others say the government is just creating bandits and terrorists-in-training by handing out guns and ammo to Kurds.

The PKK has a lot of support amongst expat Kurds. In Germany alone, there are more than 450,000 Kurds, about a quarter of the total Turkish population in Germany. The PKK, along with 35 other organizations, was banned by the German government in November 1993. The PKK uses this offshore group to extort money from Turkish businesses and professionals in Europe. They threaten to kill those who do not contribute "taxes" to their cause. The PKK makes big money from its fees for safeguarding drug shipments from Lebanon into Afghanistan, Iran and Russia and from its retailing of hard drugs in Europe.

There are estimated to be about 8000 armed PKK members, with about 3000 of them in mountainous Tunceli province and about 5000 inside Iraq.

There is a US$94,000 reward for information leading to the arrest of "Fingerless Zeki," whose real name is Semdin Sakik. Zeki is a rebel commander who is in charge of the PKK troops in eastern Turkey. (*DP* will give you a head start: He can be found in Tunceli province.) If you want to collect, give Prime Minister Mesut Yilmaz a call.

The PKK doesn't maintain any high profile press or media offices nor does it have any graphic heavy college project web sites ("That would be pretty stupid, don't you think?" Estella Schmidt of the Kurdistan Solidarity Committee told *DP*.) The PKK have created a number of Kurdish "political action organizations" (i.e., front groups) in London as conduits for disseminating information. These activist cells are semi-legal in Great Britain and often used by the PKK for entirely illegal activities. Many of their members are kicked out of the country and deported to Germany, which will then send the nastiest of the lot back to Turkey. The one with the closest ties to the PKK is the London-based Kurdistan Information Centre. London also seems to be a safe house for these other nasties' front operations. *DP* has also met with Ocalan in the Bekaa Valley in his efforts to stir up more spin on his anti-Turkish, anti-German goals. The basic gist is that he wants to spin the Turkish army's spring visits to his camps as minor setbacks and he often likes threatening everyone.

American Kurdish Information Network

2623 Connecticut Avenue NW #1
Washington, D.C. 20008 1522
TEL (202) 483-6444 FAX (202) 483-6476
http://www.kurdistan.org
e-mail: akin☆kurdish.org

Kurdistan Information Centre

10 Glasshouse Yard
London EC1A4JN
United Kingdom
☎ 011-44-171-250-1315
Att: Mizgin Sen

Kurdistan Solidarity Committee

☎ 011-44-171-586-5892
Att: Estella Schmidt

MED-TV

The Linen Hall, 162-168 Regent
Street, London W1R 5AT
(44) (0) 171-4942523
FAX (44) (0)171-494-2528
http://www.med-tv.be
e-mail: med☆med-tv.be

Kurdistan Workers Association

☎ 011-44-181-809-0743

PKK (Kurdish Workers Party)

Mekte-Bi Amele-1 Kurdistan
Barelias-Chotura
West Bekaa, Lebanon

Patriotic Union of Kurdistan

☎ 011-44-181-642-4518
Att: Latif Rashid

Dev Sol (Devrimci Sol, or Revolutionary Left)

This isn't a retro surf reverb rock group out of California, but a splinter faction of the Turkish People's Liberation Party/Front formed in 1978. They espouse a Marxist ideology and are intensely xenophobic, virulently anti-U.S. and anti-NATO. Dev Sol seeks to unify the proletariat to stage a national revolution. The group finances its activities largely through armed robberies and extortion. Their symbol is a yellow star with hammer and sickle against a red background.

Dev Sol has conducted attacks against U.S., Turkish and NATO targets but was weakened by massive arrests from 1981–'83. In the early 1990s, the group killed several foreigners, including two Americans. Five members, including one of its leaders, were shot and killed in Istanbul on March 6, 1993. Dev Sol is down to several hundred hard-core radicals with several dozen armed militants. Its support comes from Lebanon, with training and logistical support from Palestinian radicals.

While other groups have concentrated their actions in Adana in recent years, only Dev Sol has attacked Americans. In February 1991, the group assassinated an American employee of a Department of Defense contractor outside his home in downtown Adana. The same year, the group bombed the American consulate and other U.S.-affiliated organizations.

Early in 1996, Dev Sol guerrillas murdered two prominent Turkish businessmen and a secretary in their offices in downtown Istanbul, to avenge the deaths of three prison inmates at Istanbul's Umraniye prison. Local state banks are a favorite target and have been bombed numerous times. Dev Sol is led by Karatas.

IBDA-C/IKK (Islamic Great East Raiders-Front/ Islamic Retaliation Detachments)

This is the Iranian-backed fundamentalist group that attacks the PKK as well as the Turkish establishment. Their goal is to create a more rigid Islamic state.

Hezbollah

This is where things get complicated. Iranian-supported Hezbollah (based in the Bekaa Valley in southern Lebanon) has unleashed a scourge on the Marxist PKK. Imagine a terrorist group that preys on another terrorist group. You would think the Turkish government would be ecstatic, but Hezbollah is gunning down Islamic fundamentalists as fast as the Marxist rebels. Thirty-five Hezbollah are on trial in a state security court in the southeast on charges ranging from supporting separatism to killing 25 people and wounding 32 others in 39 attacks in recent years around Diyarbakir and Batman. The Hezbollah calls on its followers to kill PKK members on sight and is believed to be behind many street murders in the southeast. For a more complete description, see "The Players" section in the Lebanon chapter.

Turkish Workers Peasants Liberation Party (TIKKO)

A small group with a fetish for blowing up automatic teller machines (everyone's enemy) and banks in major cities. What fun.

Kawa

Kawa is a legendary folk hero among the Kurds. The Kawa group was established in 1976 after breaking away from the Revolutionary Culture Association (DDKD), a pro-Soviet Kurdish group advocating uniting all the Kurdish people under the Marxist banner. Kawa's anti-Soviet stance was the reason for the break with the DDKD. Kawa also fell victim to dissension within its own ranks over the teachings of Mao Zedong.

Alawites

The Alawites are a Muslim minority who live in Turkey but are unrelated to both the Shiites, who consider Ali to the be successor to Mohammed, or to the Syrian ruling faction, which is also called Alawite. They adhere to a moderate branch of Islam started in the 13th century by philosopher Bektas Veli. Occasionally, there are violent demonstrations and riots in the Istanbul and Ankara areas. In March 1995, 16 people were killed in two days of riots.

The Army

Turkish military forces control the southeastern region. Special ops units under the control of the local governor conduct raids against the PKK and are known for their brutality and treatment of villagers and Kurdish journalists. (In plain language, they beat the shit out of you, like they did to Sedat Aral.) Their utilization of the latest American military hardware (i.e., Cobra helicopter gunships) against the PKK's guerrilla tactics and small arms (AK-47 rifles) gives the conflict a neo-Vietnam aura. They were invited into Northern Iraq by the Kurdish Democratic Party (KDP) to help clean up the PKK and the KUP. Complicated? Read the Kurdistan chapter for more info.

A passport is required. A visa is not required for tourist or business visits of up to three months. For information on entry requirements to Turkey, travelers can contact the nearest Turkish Consulate in Chicago, Houston, Los Angeles or New York, or the embassy in Washington, D.C.:

Embassy of the Republic of Turkey

1714 Massachusetts Avenue, N.W.
Washington, D.C. 20036
☎ *(202) 659-8200*

When you get off the plane in Istanbul, you need to proceed to the line to the left of the longer lines. You'll know what we're talking about.

If you wish to travel to eastern Turkey, your request may be refused. There are numerous police, militia and army roadblocks with numerous police and special ops operations taking place. Do not believe any tourism hype about a minor problem with rebels. Certain areas and roads around southeast Turkey are under the control of the PKK.

The authors have traveled extensively in eastern Turkey, both alone and with an armed military escort consisting of armored personnel carriers and commandos using Land Rovers. We consider traveling with a military escort to be the most dangerous way to travel, since the PKK regularly ambushes the military. Travel by road after dark is hazardous throughout Turkey. There are currently four groups fighting at night, and any one of them will shoot you dead without asking a question. When we were staying in a small village, we were told about a man who set out to fetch his cow on a recent evening. Hearing noises in the dark, the entire town militia began firing their AK-47s and G3s into the dark on full automatic. Luckily, the man was only injured. Road and driving conditions off the main highways and in remote areas are particularly dangerous. A curfew exists from dusk to dawn, so plan your itinerary accordingly. Turkish drivers drive fast but are generally considerate. Buses are common but are subject to lengthy searches at all checkpoints. Turkish authorities expect travelers to cooperate with travel restrictions and other security measures imposed in the east—which means you should get plenty of permission and paperwork before you go.

Ataturk Airport, near Istanbul, is the main international entry and exit point. Istanbul is an excellent link between the east and the west. The kind of airlines that would be arrested if they landed in the U.S. fly regularly from Turkey. You can also get plenty of cheap tickets and just about everyone speaks English. Turkish air carriers are modern and safe. Ankara's airport is the hub for domestic flights and about 20 miles from downtown.

Istanbul Ataturk Airport
☎ *(212) 663-64-60*

Ankara Airport
☎ *(312) 398-00-00*

Izmir Airport
☎ *(232) 274-24-05*

The East

With the exception of the Mediterranean and Black Sea coasts, travel in Turkey can be hazardous—particularly eastern Turkey. Terrorist acts by the PKK continue throughout the eastern provinces. These attacks are not only against Turkish police and military installations, but also against civilian targets, including public ground transportation. While most attacks have been at night, daytime attacks are increasingly frequent. Over the past 10 years, several thousand Turkish civilians and security personnel have been killed in terrorist attacks. In 1991, the PKK began kidnapping foreigners in eastern Turkey to generate media attention for their separatist cause. Over the past three years, a number of foreigners, including Americans, have been held by the PKK and eventually released. On October 9, 1993, an American tourist was abducted by the PKK while traveling by bus on the main highway between Erzurum and Erzincan. Due to the tense security situation, the climbing of Mt. Ararat in eastern Turkey is extremely dangerous, even with the required Turkish government permits. In light of these dangerous security conditions for travelers in eastern Turkey, the U.S. military has advised its personnel to avoid all tourist travel to this region. U.S. embassy and consulate personnel travel to eastern Turkey only for essential U.S. government business, and only with prior approval. In instances where travel to cities in eastern Turkey is essential, air travel is considered safer than other forms of public transportation. As stated above, travel to this part of Turkey should not be undertaken without first consulting the American embassy in Ankara, ☎ *[90] (312) 468-6110*, or the American consulate in Adana, ☎ *[90] (322) 454-3774*.

The Hills Are Alive with the Sound of Gunships

Travel to east Turkey is most dangerous in the spring and summer. That's when the government offensives get going. In other countries, like Cambodia, the dry seasons herald the sound of rockets and mortars. Keep this in mind when making your travel plans.

Western Turkey/Mediterranean and Aegean Areas

Visitors should stay aware of recent incident reports. Terrorist activity has died down but there is always a risk of it starting up again. During the summer of 1994, the PKK conducted a series of hand grenade attacks against establishments frequented by tourists in Antalya and planted at least six hand grenades in beaches around Izmir and Kusdasi. The Antalya attacks injured both Turkish nationals and tourists, as well as causing extensive property damage. The good news is that crime against Americans is rare in western Turkey other than the usual pickpocketing and petty theft.

Crime, Muggings and Bar Brawls

There is the usual petty crime against tourists, including pickpocketing, purse snatching and mugging. In Istanbul, incidents have been reported of tourists who have been drugged and robbed in nightclubs and bars, usually by other foreigners who speak English and French. Americans have been involved in fights at discos, and bar scams involving girls ordering drinks at inflated costs have been reported.

Pavions

There is a certain style of clipjoint in Istanbul and Ankara called a glitter bar, or *pavion*. Many are found around Taksim Square in Istanbul. The pretty ladies you meet will order enough drinks to melt your VISA card. Even if you drink yourself into a coma without the help of a local lass, your eyeballs will roll back in your head when you see the bill. Owners of pavions do not take kindly to debt restructuring or threats of recrimination. Many patrons have been robbed of watches or rings to meet payment with little sympathy from the local cops.

Antiques

Unauthorized purchase or removal from Turkey of antiquities or other important cultural artifacts is strictly forbidden. Violation of this law may result in imprisonment. At the time of departure, travelers who purchase such items may be asked to present a receipt from the seller as well as the official museum export certificate required by law.

Newspaper Publishing

Don't publish anything advocating separatism or the Kurds in Turkey. Turkish police seized two days' editions of the pro-Kurdish journal *Ozgur Ulke* and accused it of publishing separatist propaganda. On orders from an antiterrorism court, police seized about 13,000 copies of the daily. Turkey maintains strict laws against advocating separatism.

Drugs

In Turkey, the penalties for possession, use, and dealing in illegal drugs are extremely strict, and convicted offenders can expect lengthy jail sentences and fines. Turkey is subject to smuggling of drugs due to its proximity to Syria and activity in the eastern states. Do not get involved.

The U.S. embassy security office can be reached at ☎ *[90] (312) 426-5470, extension 354* and the Air Force Office of Special Investigations at ☎ *[90] (312) 287-9957.*

Medical facilities are good in the West, few in the East. In the southeastern city of Diyarbakir, there are recurring outbreaks of dysentery, typhoid fever, meningitis and other contagious diseases. Typically Turkey is a healthy place to travel.

The local currency is the Turkish lira, a limp currency that makes you an instant millionaire each time you exchange about 15 bucks. Turkey has high plateaus and Mediterranean coastal areas. The plateau areas in the east get very cold in the winter and very hot in the summer. The fall and spring are quite pleasant. Istanbul has moderate temperatures year-round, with summer temps in the 80s (F) and winter lows in the mid 40s (F). Istanbul gets about four inches of rain a month in the winter.

The bulk of tourists in Turkey are Russians, attracted by the proximity, beaches and cheap goods. Germans comprise the second-largest block, followed by tourists from England, Romania and Israel.

The world's first town was Catalhoywk in central Anatoylia; it was founded in 6500 B.C.

Embassy and Consulate Locations

U.S. Embassy in Ankara

> 110 Ataturk Boulevard
> ☎ [90] (312) 468-6110

U.S. Consulate in Istanbul

> 104–108 Mesrutiyet Caddesi
> Tepebasl
> ☎ [90] (212) 251-3602

U.S. Consulate in Adana

> At the corner of Vali Yolu and AtaTurk Caddesi
> ☎ [90] (322) 453-9106

Adana local police emergency number
> ☎ (322) 435-3195

Americans who are victims of crimes may also call the consulate
> ☎ (322) 454-2145

04/17/1992	Turkish police killed 11 suspected Kurdish guerrillas in a series of raids in Istanbul. Kurds undertook several terrorist attacks in 1992 in Germany and Turkey citing this date.
08/30/1991	August 30, 1991, was celebrated as Victory Day and made an official Turkish holiday.
05/27/1991	May 27, 1991, was celebrated as Constitution Day and made an official Turkish holiday.
04/25/1988	Hagop Hagopian, leader of the Armenian Secret Army for the Liberation of Armenia (ASALA)—aka the Orly group, 3rd October Organization—was shot dead in his home in Athens by two gunmen. No group claimed responsibility for his murder.
09/06/1986	Twenty-one Jewish worshippers were killed in Istanbul during an attack on a synagogue by an Abu Nidal terrorist team.
08/15/1986	Turkish troops raided Kurdish rebel camps in Iraq.
08/15/1984	The day that Kurdish Workers Party (PKK) elements first launched an attack against Turkish government installations.
08/27/1982	The Turkish military attache in Canada was assassinated by Armenian extremists.

08/07/1982	Nine people, including one American, were killed, and more than 70 were wounded in an attack on the Ankara airport by the Armenian Secret Army for the Liberation of Armenia.
01/28/1982	The Turkish consul general to the U.S. was assassinated in Los Angeles by members of a group calling itself the Justice Commandos for the Armenian Genocide.
03/10/1979	The death of Kurdish leader Mullah Mustafa Barzani (Kurdish regions only).
11/27/1978	Considered to be the date on which the Kurdish Workers Party (PKK) was founded. PKK guerrillas may engage in terrorist attacks in connection with this date.
05/01/1977	More than 30 leftists were killed during clashes with security forces in Istanbul.
10/24/1975	The Turkish ambassador to France and his driver were shot and killed in Paris by members of the Armenian Secret Army for the Liberation of Armenia (ASALA).
01/22/1946	Kurdish Republic Day.
11/10/1938	Death of Kemal Ataturk.
10/29/1923	Turkish National Day. The date commemorates the declaration of Turkey as a republic by Mustafa Kemal Ataturk and his inauguration as its first president.
03/16/1921	Signing of the Soviet-Turkish border treaty that ended Armenian hopes of establishing an independent state.
04/24/1915	Armenians observe this date as the anniversary of the alleged 1915 Turkish genocide of Armenians.
03/12/1880	Birthday of Kemal Ataturk, founder of the modern Turkish state.
06/16	June 16 is the anniversary date of the founding of the Turkish leftist terrorist group, 16 June. Until 1987, the group acted under the name Partisan Yolu. Since 1987, the group has claimed responsibility for numerous acts of terrorism, including the December 1989 firebombing in Istanbul of the Hiawatha, a U.S. Government–owned yacht.
03/21	Kurdish New Year.

TURKEY

East Turkey: Rocking the Cradle of Civilization

The road is full of vehicles—tractors, horse carts, sawed-off buses with sagging rear ends, yellow taxis, overloaded motorcycles with sidecars—some carrying entire families with their goats. Everything is square and grey. The road and sidewalks are broken, dirty and patched. Unlike the deathly grey of the towns, the hills beyond are a rich chocolate-brown. The water is a sickly green-blue-black. The sky is the color of slate, with one enormous white cloud stretching off toward the hills in the distance. Acres of cheap boxlike housing sprout from the plains.

DP has come to the cradle of civilization, the uppermost tip of the fertile crescent, now torn apart by ethnic, political, tribal and religious strife. We are determined to get at the heart of this land, in order to understand why so much of the world is a dangerous place.

We stop to buy gas at a new petrol station. The attendant is baffled by our credit card. I run the card and sign the bill for him.

We drive past scattered groves of figs and pistachios. Trucks carry giant pomegranates. We are following the Iraqi pipeline on a highway originally built by the U.S., formally known as the "Silk Road."

Cheap Iraqi diesel, or *masot,* sells for 10,000 TL (Turkish lira or lire) a liter. It is brought from Iraq by trucks fitted with crude, rusty tanks.

As we go east, the fertile soil becomes fields of boulders and sharp rocks. The hills are ribbed and worn by the constant foraging of goats. Not much has changed here in 1000 years.

At Play in the Fields of the Warlords

We drive through the nameless streets of Sevirek, a small town that serves as the center of the Bucak fiefdom. In this age of enlightenment, there are still dark corners in the world where ancient traditions persist. We are in the domain of the Bucaks, an age-old feudal area in war-torn southeastern Turkey.

As we drive along the cobblestones, we notice that there are no doors or windows in the stone houses, only steel shutters and gates. We ask the way to the warlord's house. Men pause and then point vaguely in the general direction.

We pull up to the Turkish version of a pizza joint. From inside, two men in white smocks eye us apprehensively. The fat one recognizes Coskun and walks out to our car when we call out for directions.

We drive up a narrow cobblestone alleyway just wide enough for a car to pass. There's a Renault blocking the way. Getting out of the car, we notice for the first time that there is a man behind a wall of sandbags pointing an AK-47 in our direction. The large house was built 200 years ago and is lost in the maze of medieval streets and stone walls.

We politely explain who we are and why we have come. We had telephoned earlier and were told that no one was at home—an appropriate response for someone who has survived frequent assassination attempts from terrorists, bandits and the army.

Out from a side door comes a large man with a pistol stuffed into his ammunition-heavy utility vest. He flicks his head at me and looks at Coskun inquisitively. He hears our story. He recognizes Coskun from a year ago, when the photojournalist stayed with the warlord for three days. He smiles and gives Coskun the double-buss kiss, the traditional greeting for men in Turkey. He then grabs me by the shoulders, does the same, and then welcomes us inside. We walk up one flight of stairs and find ourselves in an outside courtyard. We are joined by two more bodyguards. They're older, more grooved, hard looking. Most of one man's chin has been blown off his face; it tells us that we should probably just sit and smile until we get to know each other a little better. We sit on the typical tiny wooden stools men use in Turkey. These have the letters DYP branded into them, the name of the political party with which the warlord has aligned himself.

The bodyguards stare into our eyes, say nothing and watch our hands when we reach for a cigarette. It seems that Sedat Bucak, the clan leader, is out in the fields, but his brother Ali is here. We are offered *chai,* or tea, and cigarettes. The bodyguards do not drink tea, or move, but they light cigarettes. One of the bodyguards sucks on his cigarette as if to suffocate it.

When Ali finally emerges, he is not at all what one would expect a warlord to look like. The men rise and bow. Ali is dressed in shiny black loafers, blue slacks, a plum-colored striped shirt and a dapper windbreaker. He looks like an Iranian USC grad. That he and his brother are the absolute rulers of 100,000 people and in control of an army of 10,000 very tough men is hard to imagine.

A Drive in the Country

Not quite sure why we're here, he offers to show us a gazelle that he was given as a gift by one of his villages. The gazelle is kept in a stone enclosure and flies around the pen, leaping through doors and windows. We ask if we can visit with Sedat. Ali says, "Sure," and repeats that he is out in the fields.

Realizing they would be embarking outside of their compound, they bring out an arsenal of automatic weapons from another room. Ali and his bodyguards get in the Renault and drive down the streets with the barrels of their guns sticking out the windows. Strangely, nobody seems to mind or notice. Even the soldiers and police wave as they drive by.

Following close behind, we are brought to their fortress, an imposing black stone compound that dominates the countryside. It is a simple square structure, each wall about 100 feet long. A central house rises to about 40 feet. The walls are made from *kaaba*, or black stone and are hand-chiseled from the surrounding boulders into squares, filled with special cement to make them bulletproof. One wall is over 20 feet tall.

The men appear nervous when I photograph the compound. This building is intended for combat. For now, it serves as a simple storage place for tractors and grain. From the top, one feels like a king overlooking his land and his subjects, which is exactly what the Bucaks do when they are up here. From this point, we can only see 50 miles to the mountains in the north, but we cannot see the rest of their 200 miles of land to the south and west of us.

We continue our caravan along a dusty road past simple villages and houses. The people here are dirt-poor. They subsist off the arid land. The children run out into the road to wave at us as we drive by.

Ali stops near a field where men, women and children are picking cotton. Cotton needs water, and there's plenty of it. It also needs cheap labor, another commodity of which the Bucaks have plenty.

The people stand still, as we get out of our cars. Ali tells them to continue working, while we take pictures. They resume picking, but their eyes never leave us.

The men decide this would be an opportune time to show off the capability of their arsenal. For one nauseating moment, I have the impression they intend to gun down this entire village. Yet it is target practice that Ali has in mind. Boys will be boys. So we then start plinking away at rocks, using all sorts of automatic weapons. We aim for a pile of rocks about 400 yards away. We are only aware of little puffs of smoke, as we hear the sound of ricochets as the bullets hit the black boulders. Ali is more interested in our video camera, so he plays with that while we play with his weapons.

When boredom sets in, we continue our journey in search of Sedat. We finally locate him about three miles away. We know it's him because of the small army that surrounds the man. His bodyguards are not happy at all to see us. We are instantly engulfed by his men poised in combat stances. Ali introduces us, but we still have to state our case. Sedat recognizes Coskun, but instead of the kiss, we get a Western-style handshake. We introduce ourselves to his dozen or so bodyguards. They do not come forward, so we reach for their hands and shake them. It's awkward, unnerving. They never let their eyes stray from ours.

Ahmed, a chiseled sunburned man who wears green camouflage fatigues, seems to be the chief bodyguard. He appears to like us the least. He wanders over to our car and starts rummaging through the luggage and junk on the backseat. I deliberately put my stuff there so that it would be easy to confirm that I am a writer. He picks up a Fielding catalog and starts flipping through the pages. When he sees my picture next to one of my books, he points and then looks at me.

The Feudal Lord

We chat with Sedat. He is eager to present a positive image to the outside world. We have brought a copy of an interview he had just done with a Turkish magazine. In it, he proposes linking up with the right-wing nationalist party and, together he says, they could end the Kurdish problem. Coskun suggests that such a comment could be taken as a bid for civil war. Sedat says, "Hey, it's only an interview. But I'm still learning." We suggest getting some shots of him driving his tractor. He is happy driving his tractor. But out here there are few other farmers who drive a tractor with an AK-47-armed bodyguard riding behind on the spreader.

Turkey has been at war with the PKK, or Kurdish Workers Party, since 1984. The Kurds want a separate homeland within Turkey, but Turkey insists they possess all the rights they need for now. The Turkish government is correct, but it doesn't stop the PKK from killing, maiming, executing and torturing their own people. The Bucaks are Kurds and the sworn enemies of the PKK, who are also Kurds. The difference is that the Bucaks have essentially carved out their own kingdom and even managed to integrate themselves into the political process in an effective, albeit primitive, way. They use votes rather than bullets to curry favor. They are also left alone by the government. They pay no taxes and have complete control over what goes on in their ancestral lands.

The Bucak family has been in Sevirek for more than 400 years. They are Kurds, but more specifically, they're from the Zaza as opposed to the Commagene branch of the Kurds. They also speak a different language from the Commagene. They have always controlled a large part of southeastern Turkey by force and eminent domain. Their subjects give them 25 percent of the crops they grow, and, in return, they receive services and are protected by a private army of about 10,000 men. Many other groups have tried unsuccessfully to force them off their land. In times of all-out warfare, all the subjects are expected to chip in and grab their rifles. The Bucaks have wisely aligned themselves with the current ruling political party, the DYP. Realizing that the Bucaks can deliver 100,000 votes goes a long way toward successful lobbying and handshaking in Ankara, the capital of Turkey. Sedat Bucak is head of the clan, at the age of 40. A warrior and farmer by trade, he is now a sharp and shrewd politician. If he's killed, his younger brother Ali will take the helm. Ali is only 24.

Sevirek has long been a battleground. The city was completely closed to all outsiders, including the army, between 1970 and 1980. During this period, there was intense street-to-street fighting between the Bucaks and the PKK. Thousands of people were killed; the PKK moved on to choose easier victims. The Bucaks cannot stray eastward into PKK held territory without facing instant death.

The countryside the Bucaks rule consists of rolling plains, similar to Montana or Alberta. This is to the benefit of the Ataturk dam project, the fifth-largest dam project in the world.

Sedat can never travel without his bodyguards; neither can Ali. The bodyguards match the personalities of the brothers. Sedat's bodyguards are cold, ruthless killers. They're picked for the bravery and ferocity they showed in the last 10 years of warfare. Ali's bodyguards are younger, friendlier, but just as lethal.

They pack automatic weapons: German G-3s, M-16s and AK-47s. They each also carry at least one handgun as well as four to six clips for the machine guns and three to four clips for their pistols. Ali and Sedat also carry weapons at all times. Their choice of weapons also reflects their personalities. Ali packs a decorative stainless steel 9mm Ruger, and Sedat carries a drab businesslike Glock 17.

Some of the bodyguards, such as Nouri, wear the traditional Kurdish garb of checkered headpiece and baggy wool pants. The *salvars* appear to be too hot to wear on the sunburned plains. One of the guards explains that they work like a bellows and pump air when you walk, an example of something that works. Others wear cheap suits. Some wear golf shirts; still others wear military apparel.

While we are taking pictures of Sedat on his Massey Ferguson, the guards bring out the *gnass*, or sniper rifle (*gnass* is Arabic for sniper). It is an old Russian Dragunaov designed to kill men at 400–800 meters. When I walk down to take pictures, Ahmed, the cagey one, slides the rifle into the car and shakes his head. He knows that a sniper rifle is not for self-defense but is used for one thing only, as they explain to us, "With this rifle, you can kill a man before he knows he is dead."

Many of the men have a Turkish flag on the butts of their clips. One bodyguard offers me a rolled cigarette from an old silver tin. It tastes of the sweet, mild tobacco from Ferat. We both have a smoke. I open my khaki shirt and show him my Black Dog T-shirt, a picture of a dog doing his thing. He laughs: Seems as if we're finally warming up this crowd.

The younger brother of Ali's bodyguard asks me if I am licensed to use guns. He likes the way I shoot. I try to explain that, in America, you need a permit to own a gun and that people are trained or licensed. He looks at me quizzically. It's no use. I doubt they would understand a society that lets you own a gun without knowing how to use it.

We blast off some more rounds. Ali's bodyguards are having fun. We then bring out the handguns. We are all bad shots. Trying to hit a Pepsi can, no one comes close. Then one of the bodyguards marches up to the can and "executes" it with a smile. It is a chilling scene, and I'm glad it's only an aluminum can.

While Ali's bodyguards clown around with us, Sedat's bodyguards never move, or even take their hands off their guns. Nouri has his AK-47 tucked so perfectly into the crook of his arm, it is hard to imagine him not sleeping with it.

After chatting with Sedat and nervously entertaining his bodyguards, we head back into town. There, we're taken to lunch at Ali Bucaks restaurant and gas station. We eat in Ali's office. The bodyguards act as waiters, serving us shepherd's salads and kabobs with yogurt to drink. They serve us quietly and respectfully. They eat with one hand on their guns. The SSB radio crackles nonstop, as various people check in. We talk to Ali about life in general. Can he go anywhere without his guards? No. What about when he goes to Ankara on the plane? They have to put their guns in plastic bags and pick them up when they land. What about in Ankara? They change cars a lot. Does he like his role? He doesn't have a choice. Does he like feudalism? No, but he doesn't have a choice. The government does not provide services or protect their people, so they must do it themselves. Who would take the sick to the hospitals? Who would take care of the widows? Since power is passed along family lines, it is his duty.

As we eat, a storm comes in from Iraq. Lightning flashes and thunder cracks. We talk about politics, baseball cards and America. They are all familiar with America because every Turkish home and business has a television blaring most of the day and night. The number-one show is the soap, "The Young and the Restless," which comes on at 6:15 every night.

Sedat is a soft-spoken man—about 5 feet 6 inches tall, sunburned and suffering from a mild thyroid condition. He wears a faded green camouflage baseball hat, Levis and running shoes, as your neighbor might. He also carries a Glock 17 in a hand-rubbed leather holster. It is unsnapped for a quicker draw. Maybe not quite like your neighbor! He is never more than 15 feet from his bodyguards. Men drawn from his army as personal bodyguards have the lean, sunburned look of cowboys. He comes from an immediate family of 500 Bucaks. They make their money by growing cotton and other crops they sell in Adana.

It is hard to believe that this gentle, slightly nervous man and his forces are the only ones in Turkey who here been able to beat the PKK at their own game.

For now, everything is well in the kingdom. The dam will bring water for crops; the PKK is now concentrating on other areas; the people are happy, and Sedat is now a big-wheel politician. There is much to be said for feudalism. I offer to send him some of my books so that he can read about the rest of the world. He thinks this is a great idea. But he doesn't speak or read English.

DP Fashion Tip

Mekap is the brand of sneakers preferred by the PKK. They can be identified by the red star on a yellow badge. If you ask at a shoe store for Mekaps, you will get a very strange reaction; the merchant will assume you're from the police and testing him.

We drive from Sevirek to Diyarbakir. The city of Diyarbakir is built on a great basalt plain and has 5.5-km long walls made from this ominous looking black stone. The triple walls and functional look betrays its origins as an ancient military outpost. Today, the 16 keeps and 5 gates have barbed wire, sand bags and machine gun nests. We will pass from a feudal kingdom to a large, bustling city that is the flashpoint for much of the violence that grips Turkey. We realize as we drive down the lonely roads that we are leaving the protection of the Bucaks and will soon be in PKK territory. If we were to be caught with Ali's address, we'd be killed. If the PKK had any knowledge of our contact with the Bucaks, we'd be instant enemies.

The PKK control the countryside and, it is said, the whole of eastern Turkey at night. It is not a particularly large group, perhaps some 8000 soldiers trained in small camps, but they're armed with small weapons—AK-47s and RPGs and a few grenade launchers. They travel in groups of 12 men and can muster a sizable force of about 200 soldiers for major ambushes. Their leader lives in the Bekáa Valley in southern Lebanon, under the protection of the Syrian government. He calls for an independent Kurdistan, which Saddam Hussein has given him by default in northern Iraq. But he wants more. He wants a sizable chunk of Iran and Turkey as well.

Despite the numerous checkpoints and military presence in the area, there has been little success in defeating the PKK. The Turkish Army has set up large special ops teams and commando units that specialize in ambushes, foot patrols and other harassment activities. But once you see the topography of eastern Turkey, you realize that you could hide an army 1000 times the size of the PKK. The terrain is riddled with caves, redoubt-shaped cliffs, boulders, canyons and every conceivable type of nook and cranny. It is easy terrain to move in, with few natural or man-made obstructions.

The PKK go into the villages at night to demand cooperation. If villagers do not cooperate, they are shot. In some cases, entire families, including babies, are executed. The PKK follow a Marxist-Leninist doctrine and play out their guerrilla tactics similar to the former Viet Cong or the Khmer Rouge. The PKK also likes to kidnap foreigners for money and publicity, and they like to execute schoolteachers and government officials. Special ops teams report to the civil authorities and to the military. Turkey considers the PKK as criminals and is reluctant to use civil law and superficial civilian forces against it.

Turkey has been in a state of war for 10 years now—that being the war the military is waging within its own borders.

The Test Pilot

We decide to spend an evening with a former leader and trainer of special ops teams. Hakan is now Turkey's only test pilot. In Turkey, this doesn't mean flying new prototype planes; it means flying out to helicopters downed by the rebels, making repairs and then flying or sling-loading them out.

Hakan lives in a high-rise building, guarded by three soldiers, barbed wire and fortifications against attack. His apartment is modern and well furnished. There are no traditional rugs, just black lacquer furniture complete with a fully stocked bar. Except for the barbed wire, we could be in Florida, which is where he trained as a Sikorsky Blackhawk pilot.

He has a two-month-old baby and is looking forward to being transferred back to western Turkey. His contempt for the PKK is obvious, having killed many of its members and having many PKK rounds aimed at him. He feels that the PKK is winning in this part of the country, but there will be no victory. The PKK problem cannot be solved militarily. It must be solved economically, by making the Kurds the beneficiaries of government help and giving them a stronger political voice. Killing terrorists is merely his job. He can't wait to get transferred out of Dyabakir. His wife plays with their baby on the floor. The baby never stops smiling and laughing. I think of the barbed wire and nervous soldiers downstairs. He can offer no political insights: PKK are people who he is paid to fight. When he is in Ankara, he will occupy himself with other things.

Eastern Turkey is the poorest and least developed part of the nation. Most educated people come from western Turkey. Most of the soldiers, politicians and professional classes are from western Turkey. The government sends these people to eastern Turkey for a minimum of two years of service. Most can't wait to get back to Istanbul or Ankara. Eastern Turkey has much closer affiliations with Armenia, Iran, Iraq, Azerbaijan, Syria and Georgia. Western Turkey has the ocean as a border. Eastern Turkey is rife with dissension and must deal with its warlike and poor neighbors. Iraqi, Iranian, Armenian and Syrian terrorists actively fight the government and each other. Hezbollah, the Iranian-backed fundamentalist group, hates the PKK. The PKK hates the government. The militia hates all rebel agitators, and the army and police clean up the messes left behind.

The Governor

I decide that we need another point of view. We go to Siirt about 40 km from the Syrian border and directly in the heart of PKK territory. Siirt was once a great city during the Abbasid Caliphate with the remnants of 12th and 13th century mosques. We are definitely in harm's way, since the PKK travel from Syria into the mountains behind us. Just down the road is the military outpost of Erub, designed to control a critical mountain road that leads down toward the Syrian border. There is another reason why we have chosen this tiny town. Coskun was born and raised in Siirt. I suggest that we go and chat up the governor and get his point of view.

Coskun is somewhat hesitant about meeting with the governor of Siirt province because he has a natural (and well-founded) aversion to politicians. But since we will be traveling directly into and through the war zone, we want to be sure that when we get stopped by the military we can drop names, flash the governor's card and ensure at least a moment of hesitation before we are shot as spies or terrorists.

As we pass the heavy security of the Siirt administration building, it seems that the governor is in. His bodyguards are quite perturbed that these strangers have walked right in and asked for an audience. They quietly talk into their walkie-talkies and stand between us and the soundproof door that leads into the governor's office. The governor takes his time to put on his game face and finally invites us in. It is kisses all around, chocolates, tea and cigarettes. We thank him and tell him our business. We are here to see what is going on in Turkey. He is proud to have us in his region. Two of his aids sit politely on the couch. The governor speaks in long, melodious, booming soliloquies that, when translated into English, come out as "We are maligned by the press" or "There is no danger here." Finally, they ask me what I have seen and what I think of their country. I tell them the truth. The people here are extraordinary in their friendship and warmth, but we are in a war zone. He launches into a response that boils down to "It's safe here, and we want you to tell your readers to come to Turkey and Siirt province." He then tells us of the attractions that await the lucky traveler: canyons as deep as the Grand Canyon, white-water rafting, hiking, culture, history, etc. We say great, give us a helicopter and we'll go for a spin tomorrow.

He goes one further. He invites us to dinner that night so that he can spend more time with us. Coskun wants to kick me, as I accept. Later that night we go to the government building for dinner. Joining us will be the head of police, the head of the military, three subgovernors and a couple of aides.

We pass through security and are ushered into the dining room. Sitting uncomfortably, we make small talk while a television blares away against the wall. As we sit down to dinner, we indicate that we are curious and ask the military commander just what is going on. Everyone is dressed in a suit and tie or uniform. Coskun and I do the best we can with our dusty khakis. Either because the room is hot or they are just being polite, they take their jackets off for dinner. The governor carries a silver 45 tucked into his waistband. His formal gun? As the men sit down to dinner, something strikes me as funny. Coskun and I are the only ones not packing a gun for dinner.

The dinner is excellent: course after course of shish kebob, salads and other delicacies washed down with *raki* (a strong anisette liquor) and water. The taste of the *raki* brings back memories of the hard crisp taste of Cristal aquadiente, the preferred drink of the Colombian drug trade. Throughout dinner, the head of police is interrupted by a walkie-talkie-carrying messenger who hands him a piece of paper. He makes a few comments to the side, and the man disappears. Every five to 10 minutes the man returns, the police chief makes a quiet comment, and he goes away.

Meanwhile, the governor continues to extol the beauty of his country—nonstop. He is the center of attention, simply because no one else is speaking. The others nod, smile or laugh. Most of their attention is on the television blaring in the corner. Suddenly, the red phone next to the television begins ringing. The call is answered by the attendant. It is for the colonel. The colonel excuses the interruption and speaks in low tones. The police chief puts his walkie-talkie on the table. It becomes apparent that the base is under attack by a group of PKK of unknown size. Throughout dinner, the conversation steers toward politics as it must. Like many countries, there are two parallel worlds here: the world of administrators, occupiers and government, then the world of the dispossessed—the people who till the soil, who build their houses with their own hands, who bury their dead in the same ground that yields them their crops. Tonight and every night, that world is ruled by the PKK, Dev Sol, Armenian terrorists, Hezbollah and bandits. At dusk, the world is plunged into fear, ruled by armed bands of men that are neither chosen nor wanted by the ordinary people. At dawn, the country is back in the hands of the government, the people and the light. During our conversation, there is no right and no wrong, only an affirmation that each side believes it is in the right.

The red phone continues to ring, and the little pieces of paper continue to be brought up to the police chief. The police chief is now speaking directly into his walkie-talkie. Meanwhile, the governor continues to regale us with stories about Siirt. As we eat course after course, I am offered cigarettes by at least three to four people at a time. Doing my best to accommodate my hosts, I eat, smoke and drink the sharp *raki*, all the time keeping one ear on the governor's conversation and the constant mumbled conversations being carried out on the phone and the walkie-talkie.

The governor is very proud of the tie he wore especially for me—a pattern of Coca-Cola bottles. He brings in his young daughters to meet me. They are shy, pretty and very proud of their English. We chat about life in Siirt, and I realize that they are virtually prisoners in the governor's compound. The governor tells us of a road we should take to enjoy the scenery, a winding scenic road to Lice via Kocakoy. Finally, the colonel is spending so much time on the phone that he excuses himself. The police chief is visibly agitated but is now speaking nonstop on the walkie-talkie. Messages continue to arrive.

The television is now featuring swimsuit-clad lovelies and has captured the attention of the governor's aides and his subgovernors. As the dinner winds down, we retire outside to have coffee. I am presented with a soft wool blanket woven in Siirt. We have a brief exchange of speeches, and I notice that the colonel and police chief have now joined us. I ask them what all the commotion was about, and they mention that it was a minor incident that has been handled. The governor reminds us to tell people of the beauty of this place, the friendliness of the Turkish people and the people of Siirt.

As we prepare to go, they wrap my blanket in today's newspaper. Smack dead center is a full-color photograph of a blood-soaked corpse of a man who has been executed by the Dev Sol terrorist group for being an informer.

The next day, there is no helicopter waiting for us. When we inquire as to its whereabouts, we are told that it was needed to do a body count from the attack the night before. We ask the blue-berated special ops soldier what the best way is to see the countryside. He assumes that we must be important, and, instead of telling us to get lost, he carefully reviews our options. As for the road we want to take into the mountains, he informs us that it is heavily mined and would have to be cleared before we could attempt a crossing. In any case, we would need an armored car and an escort of soldiers and probably a tank. We ask about the helicopter, which would be safer, but we will need to wait until he can get a gunship to accompany us.

A Place in Time

We figure the only sightseeing we are going to do today is on foot. Coskun reminisces with his first employer, a gentle man who puts out a tiny newspaper with a 19th-century offset press and block type. He has broken his arm, so he apologizes on the back page for the paper being so small. Everyday he laboriously pecks out the local news with one finger using an old Remington typewriter; he then reads his copy, marks it up, and hands it to the eager teenagers who sort through the dirty trays of lead type. He has a choice between two photo-engraved pictures that sit in a worn old tray. One is the governor, the other is the president of Turkey. When the type is hand-set, they laboriously run off a couple of hundred copies for the dwindling number of loyal readers. I leave Coskun with his old friend.

Siirt is a dusty, poor Kurdish town, with a history of being occupied by everyone from Alexander to the Seljuks to the Ottomans. Some of the people are fair-skinned, blonde and blue-eyed. Others have the hard Arabic look of the south; while still others have the round heads and bald spots of the Turks. Siirt is a happy town, with the children contentedly playing in the muddy streets. As I walk around the town, the children begin to tag along with me. All are eager to try out their words of English. I urge them to teach me Kurdish. They point at houses, dogs, people, and chatter away, "Where come you from?" and "Hello mister, what eeze your name?" I wonder where I would ever need to use Kurdish. Some visitors say Siirt looks like a poorly costumed bible story. Here and there along the broken streets are ancient houses with tapered walls; many people still use the streets as sewers. Goats, cows and chickens wander the streets. Near the mosque, the less fortunate goats are sold and then slaughtered on the spot. Donkeys sit patiently. Men physically pull me over to where they are sitting and demand that we have tea. I realize it would take me years if I stopped and had tea with everyone who wanted to chat. I begin to respect the delicate but strong social web that holds this country together. Soldiers, fighters, rebels, farmers, politicians, police all offer us hospitality, tea and a cigarette. The tiny parcels of information and face-to-face encounters transmit and build an understanding of what is going on, who is going where and why.

In every shop a television blares. Western programs and news shows constantly bombard these people with images that do not fit into their current world. At 6:10 "The Young and the Restless," dubbed in Turkish, captures the entire population. It is typically Turkish that they would treat the TV like a visitor, never shutting it up and quietly waiting for their turn to speak. I can only imagine that the blatant American and Western European images are as familiar and comforting to the older generation as MTV's "The Grind" is to us. As with all small rural towns around the world, the young people are moving to the big cities. The future is colliding with the past.

They're Your Modern Stone Age Family

We decide not to hang around and wait for the helicopter and the helicopter gunship to be arranged. Instead, we decide to drive into the countryside, where the army has little control. Along the way, we stop in a little-known troglodyte village called Hassankeyf. This was once the 12th century capital of the Artukids, but today, it is a little visited curiosity. Here, Coskun knows an old lady who lives in a cave. This historic area will be underwater when the massive hydroelectric dam is completed. Hassankeyf could be a set from "The Flintstones." The winding canyon is full of caves that go up either side, creating a cave-dwellers high-rise development. Far up in the highest cave is the last resident of this area. The lady claims to be 110-years old. My guess is that she is closer to 80. But it probably doesn't matter, since in this land, she could be older than Methuselah and have seen nothing change. We climb up to chat with her, while down below the golden rays of the sun illuminate the Sassouk mosque. Across the canyon are the ruins of a Roman-era monastery. This was once a remote outpost for the Romans.

She doesn't seem pleased to see us. In a grouchy manner, she invites us into her cave. The lady lives alone with a cat and her donkey. The donkey has his own cave carved cleanly and laboriously out of the soft limestone.

The cave where the old woman lives leads back into a rear cave, where she makes her bed on straw and carpets. The roof is covered with a thick greasy layer of soot from the small fire she uses for cooking. She says she is ill and needs medicine. We have brought her a bar of chocolate but we do not have any medicine with us. We give her some money but realize she is days away from any drugstore and her only method of transport is her donkey or a ride from one of the villagers.

People from across the steep valley yell and wave at us. They do not get many visitors. We take pictures of the lady. She seems happy to have someone to talk to, and, after her initial grumpiness, she offers us some flat bread. It crunches with the dirt and gravel baked into it. We smile and say it is good.

As the sun sets further, the ancient ambience is broken by the loud thumping and hoarse whistling scream of a Cobra gunship returning to Siirt. This was probably our escort, but we are glad to be sitting here in the cool golden dusk in a cave, in a place that will soon be erased off the map.

We have to leave. Travel at night is not safe. The PKK control this area and the military will fire at anything that moves on the roads at night. We must make it to the Christian town of Mardil, or as the locals call it Asyriac, before it gets completely dark. The old lady wishes us well. The Christians who live in the town of Mardil speak the language of Jesus: Aramaic. Strange that we are also in the land of the Yezidi, the religion that prays to Satan. We are told the PKK do not attack Asyriac because of their ties to Assad. Here, we will spend the night with some people who hold the honor of having the most dangerous profession in east Turkey: schoolteachers.

The Most Dangerous Job

Schoolteachers are part of the colonial oppression against which the PKK is fighting. Kurdish children are not allowed to speak the native tongue in school.

Teachers in Turkey are assigned to work for four years in East Turkey before they can work in the more lucrative eastern cities of Istanbul and Ankara. Here, they are paid 8 million Turkish lira a month, about US$220 and about 30 percent more than they would usually make. About 30 percent never do their time in east Turkey and buy their way out of the dangerous assignment. By comparison, soldiers get paid 35–40 million Turkish lira a month.

The teachers live in simple stone houses—one room for living and one room for sleeping. There is no plumbing; the bathroom is an outhouse about 20 yards from the house. But these conditions are not what make this job dangerous. Over the last three years, 75 schoolteachers have been executed by the PKK. Schoolteachers in east Turkey are not raving political stooges of the government who spread torment and hate. They are bright college-educated people who teach reading, writing and math. Many are just starting families and enjoy the work they do. The few who are dragged out of their houses at night, sentenced, and shot in the chest probably wonder what they did to deserve such a cold and uncelebrated death.

We spend the evening with two young teachers, a husband and wife, and their two young girls. They share their simple food and are good company. There is little to do here once the sun goes down. The inside of the simple stone house reminds me of a bomb shelter: whitewashed, cold and damp. The house is lit with a single bare lightbulb hanging down from the ceiling. After dinner, we walk to the homes of the other teachers in this small village. Each family of teachers is happy to meet outsiders. There are two young female teachers who bring us cookies and tea, and there are two married couples, each with a small child. We gather together in their simple homes and talk about life in the war zone. Three days ago, three teachers just northwest of here were rounded up, tied hand and foot, and shot the same way you would kill an old dog.

Many people feel that the teachers were shot because they had weapons in their houses. After the shootings, the teachers from this village traveled to town to talk to the region's military commander and protest the arming of teachers as militia. The colonel instead greeted them as the protectors of the village. Taken aback, they explained that they thought he was the protector of the village. "No," he smiled and said, "it is much too dangerous to have troops out there at night." The colonel offered them rifles and ammunition to give them peace of mind. "After all," he said, "I am surrounded by hundreds of soldiers, barbed wire and fortifications as well as over a hundred trained antiterrorist commandos for backup." He offered the teachers one of each: a "big gun" (a German G-3) for the men and a little gun (AK-47s) for the women. Not knowing how to react, the teachers abandoned their first line of attack and glumly accepted the weapons and boxes of ammunition. They admitted to us they had no idea how to use them and were terrified that the children would find the rifles under their beds. So they kept them unloaded.

As I walked back under a brilliant star-filled sky, I marveled at the ridiculousness of it all. Here we were with eager, youthful young men and women—educated, enthusiastically discussing life and politics, sharing what little they have and trying to make sense of it all, while a few miles down the road sat the PKK training base of Eruh and the Syrian border only 50 km away. The town has been the scene of heavy fighting between the PKK and the Turkish special forces. No one dares go out of the village at night for fear of being shot as a terrorist by the nervous militia.

The people are thankful for their stone houses, as they cower below windows during the heaviest shooting. Here, there is no doctor, no store, no transportation, no facilities of any kind. To think that a beautiful night like this could be interrupted by sudden death is unimaginable.

Tearing Down the Silk Road

Despite our token flirtation with death, we spend a sunny morning playing with the children and then continue on our way to the Iraqi border. I am curious. Just before we leave the village, we are stopped by a group of people. They point to a stinking swamp in the center of the village. They complain that the government came in to build a pond and now it is a sewer. They seem to think that we have some way to restore it. We listen, shrug our shoulders and sadly drive off.

Winding our way down to the main road, we inhale the clean mountain air and stop to take pictures of the sparkling brooks and lush scenery. This can't be a war zone. Down on the main road, the military checkpoints begin. At the first checkpoint 14 km from Cizre, we are quite bluntly asked, "What the hell are you doing here?" The appropriate answer seems to be the most absurd: "Just looking around." Cooling our heels and drinking tea in the commander's bunker, we are given our passports back and smugly told that we have been scooped. A television news crew from "32 GUN" (a Turkish news show) had already made it into Iraq. The commander assumes that we are journalists trying to cover Saddam's big military push to the south. Apparently, the television crew got special permission from the Iraqi embassy in Ankara and is the only news crew in Iraq. Not too bothered by this revelation, we share a cigarette with the sergeant, and more tea is brought out. It appears that our time with the governor and the military commander of Siirt province has paid off. We ask the officer in charge if he could radio ahead and let the trigger-happy soldiers know we are coming.

We should be in the cradle of civilization, between the fertile thighs of the Tigris and the Euphrates. Instead, we are in a hair-trigger war zone, where every man is a potential killer and every move might be your last.

We take a few Polaroids for the officer and we hit the road again. At each blown bridge and sandbagged checkpoint, we stop and chat with the soldiers. Up ahead of us is Mount Kadur, where the Koran says the ark of Noah rests: It sits like a forbidden beacon 3500 meters high. We drive along the Syrian border clearly defined by eight-foot high barbed wire and 30 foot guard towers every 500 meters. We are on a beautiful piece of smooth two-lane blacktop built right smack on top of the "Silk Road." We are not traveling by camel today. I keep the Fiat's gas pedal pressed to the floor, the speedometer spinning like a slot machine. The only time we have to slow down is at a checkpoint or when a bridge has been blown up. The heavy trucks labor toward the west, as we pass burned-out hulks of gas stations. We stop in Silapi, the last Turkish town before the Iraqi border, to get something to eat. Silapi is one of the dirtiest, drabbest holes I have ever visited. Row after row of truck repair shops, dusty streets, and grease-smeared people watching as we drive by.

We pick a restaurant where the secret police eat. You can tell the secret police by their bull necks, gold chains and walkie-talkies. The hotel next door is decorated with stickers from the world's press and relief agencies. The food is good. Outside our restaurant, a retarded man with no legs sits on his stumps. Using blocks to get around, he is black from the soot and grime of the street. He uses an old inner tube to prevent the hot road from burning his stumps. He watches us eat. The people pass him by as he grimaces and grunts, his hand extended. I marvel that this man is still alive in this godforsaken outpost. I go outside and give him some lira. He begins to cry and tug at my leg, thanking me in his tortured way. When I leave him, children begin to crowd around and start to beat him for his money. I go back outside, and another man chases the children away. We tuck the money away, since his spastic hands keep flailing around. When I go back into the restaurant, one of the men at a table next to ours tells us that the beggar will probably be dead tonight, killed for the money he now has. I feel very sad and want to leave this place.

As we blast down the road toward the Iraqi border, I notice that the big guns in the Turkish bunkers are not facing south across the road to Syria, but toward Turkey to the north and the rebel-held hills beyond.

The Angels

Much later, back in Istanbul, I stand in front of the massive Hagia Sophia Mosque. Inside, it is quiet. Two men make their prayers in the serious, hurried style of Islam. The worn carpets and the vast ceiling absorb the whispering and rustling like a sponge.

Outside, it is dark and the rain is cold and heavy, pushed by the sharp wind. The brilliant floodlights cut tunnels of light upward into the low clouds above the softly sculpted building. It is as if the prayers of centuries power this energy, sending the shafts of pure blue light through the clouds and to the stars. High above, I think I see angels. A mysterious low chorus seems to pervade the atmosphere. But alas, the angels are just seagulls and the chorus is a distinct ship horn. And the prayers of a thousand years are lost and rubbed to dust in the aging carpets inside the mosque.

For a brief moment, it was calm and peaceful. The angels had come to answer those prayers. Instead, I know that out in the rolling fields of the east, there will be more death under the Turkish stars tonight.

Postscript

On Sunday, November 12, 1996, there was a car accident in Susurluk, about 90 miles south of Istanbul. A black Mercedes slammed into a tractor trailer truck killing three of the four passengers aboard. This would not be unusual for a Sunday on the deadly highways of Turkey except the only surviving passenger was *DP's* buddy Sedat Bucak. Although Bucak is colorful in his own right, his now deceased friends are more interesting.

One of the four on board was Abdullah Catli, an accused hit man for the Turkish military, convicted drug smuggler, former member of the extreme nationalist group the Grey Wolves and blamed for a number of arson attacks in the Greek Islands and assassinations in Athens in 1988. He was also accused of selling drugs in Switzerland. In July of '96 he escaped from Swiss prison. Catli was accused of murdering casino operator Omer Lufi Topal. Three policemen were also implicated. These policemen then became part of Sedat's bodyguard. Bucak was accused of trying to grab Topal's assets and to be behind his execution. A search of Catli's body found a false ID card, a badge showing him to be a police officer and a green Turkish passport that only senior civil servants have to avoid visas when traveling.

In the trunk were seven pistols, silencers and ammunition. The registration plates were bogus and it took a while for the government and press to understand exactly what had happened

Mr. Catli's companion in the car was Gonca Us, a former Miss Cinema in Turkey. She was accused of being a Mafia hitwoman under the watchful eye of Catli. He isn't exactly on every girl's crush list. He began his notoriety on March 9, 1978 when he personally strangled seven university students for being members of the Turkish Labor Party. He was wanted by Interpol and was on their "Most Wanted" list.

Catli was also famous for being the man who supplied the gun to the Bulgarian who shot the Turk, Mehmet Ali Agca, who shot Pope John Paul II in 1981.

Sedat Bucak, True Path MP, the head of Bucak clan and leader of a tough anti-PKK army of 10,000 men is still the undisputed lord of the Sevirek valley between Dyabakir and Urfa. Although some say his army is only 2000 men, others estimated 8000, he is paid over $1 million a month to fight the PKK. That brands him as a mercenary in the eyes of the PKK. He is also accused of using these men as death squads, smuggling drugs and weapons. They are considered by Turkish politicians as being "out of control."

The fourth passenger was one that started an uproar in the press and government. He was the president of the Erog Police Academy in Istanbul. Although it sounds like a comedy role, Huseyin Kocadag is one of the creators of the Special Teams—groups of civilians who execute suspected terrorists and sympathizers. They too are accused of competing with the PKK to smuggle heroin, launder political donations, sell arms and carry out personal vendettas.

The truck driver who slammed into the car was given a "most respected citizen honor" from a minor leftist party. Around 1000 pro PKK civilians have disappeared in Bucaks region along with 100 people who have disappeared while in police custody. About 23,000 people have been killed in Turkey since 1984 as a result of the conflict with the PKK and the army.

Bucak was seriously injured, and yanked out of the car by his bodyguards who were following behind in a second car. They left the others to die, crushed and bleeding in the wreck. Bucak has recuperated with the assistance of his bodyguards who guarded him 24 hours a day.

The parliament finally confirmed the connection between organized crime and the security establishment and some politicians. Unfortunately the generals that really run Turkey are more concerned about the rise of Islamic fundamentalism, a greater threat to the west than the war in the east.

—RYP

Kampala

Uganda
★★★
Where Danger Still Hangs Out

Until Rwanda became the new symbol of man's descent into his dark soul, Uganda typified our stereotype of fear. But that was 10 years ago, and seventy-something Idi Amin is now retired (sort of) in Saudi Arabia; Obote is gone, and the 13 main ethnic groups are supposed to be working in harmony to restore this beautiful land. Return to Central Africa after four or five years and you court disorientation. This place, once decent, is deadly again.

Back in January 1971, correspondents came out of State Department backgrounders in more than one capital, reporting, "This new guy Amin might be okay." ("Establishment military," authoritative sources had said; "we've dealt with him.") They were wrong.

Alas, when Yoweri Museveni's outlaw army began showing up on a distant bush horizon 15 years later, it wasn't so easy to get the scoop. He just wasn't the State Department's type. All we could tell was that authoritative sources were uneasy. So we were uneasy, too.

We speculated about Museveni, the radical, about reports he'd been with FRE-LIMO in Mozambique, among Maoist Chinese on the Tanzanian island of Pemba. We heard reports that this renegade off in the shadows of the bush was even sending children into battle...and, hey, the reports checked out. He was. Now he runs the place.

We pictured a gang of bush-hardened cultural revolutionaries, armed with AKs and simple-minded slogans, about to drag Uganda right back into chaos, just as new and moderate leaders were at last in place to nurse that sorry realm back to life.

During his long march on Kampala through a shell-shattered free-fire zone in Buganda known as the Lowery Triangle (shattered largely by the government's North Korean shells), Museveni had slipped out to London. In fact, he was there during a period when any practical leader (and he is a practical man) could see his cause was lost. He had virtually no financial resources, no trained military resources. The triangle was hamburger, it was over, and guile with reporters was pointless.

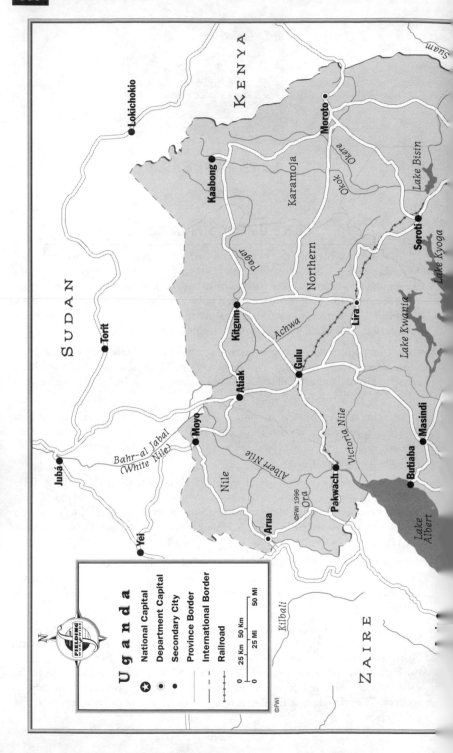

UGANDA

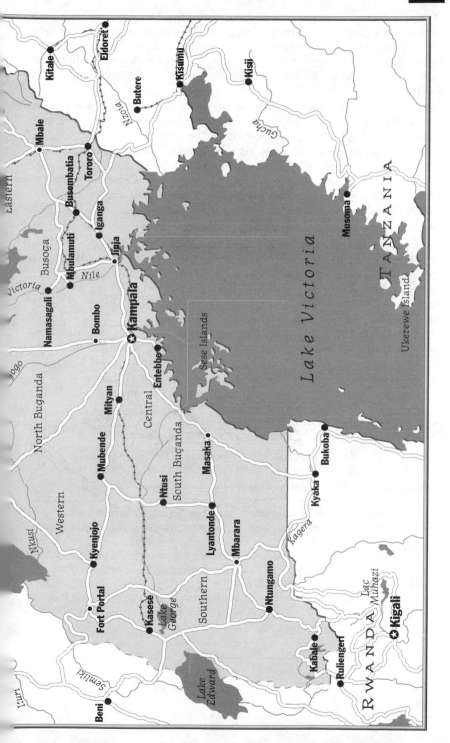

We paid slight attention to him then, just as we failed fully to appreciate until too late that Uganda's "moderates" were crooks who killed more Ugandans than Amin. A little more attention to quiet voices and we might not have evoked such foolish dismay as we relayed third-hand reports about a bullet-riddled beast (so rudely subhuman in its ability to live after such punishment), slouching toward Kampala.

This beast, as we now know, was an army of some 20,000 adolescents and kids in their 20s—those the despairing Museveni had left behind. On their own, they had hung on, and at last, slowly, pushed on. Less dependent on authoritative sources, we might even have provided some modest inspiration in dispatches about a true children's crusade, about orphans left with no choice but combat, their families and their lands having been trashed first by Amin, then by the undisciplined, unpaid and rapaciously angry soldiers of Tanzania, and then again by Amin's old military, now led by corrupt "moderates."

We didn't deliver that story until Museveni's kids were on the cusp of victory in mid-1985. To this day, many are surprised to learn that Julius Nyerere's protégé, the school teacher Apollo Milton Obote, killed more Ugandans than Amin.

All this matters now because all of Central Africa is dangerous. Museveni had almost succeeded in removing most of Uganda from the world's most dangerous places. The State Department reports that snatch and grabs from cars stalled in Kampala traffic are common, but security in Kampala and Entebbe is by no stretch frightful. Uganda's frontier with Rwanda is notably less dangerous than the refugee-ridden frontiers that Tanzania, Burundi and Zaire share with Rwanda. But throughout East and Central Africa, you hear that we ignore Uganda at the risk of getting taken by surprise yet again…and not just in Uganda.

President Yoweri Museveni is actually making some parts of Uganda a decent place to make a living without the threat of getting whacked by crazed rebels or government troops on a binge for some beer money. Uganda's eight percent annual growth rate is the largest in sub-Saharan Africa. However, most of the prosperity is being felt in the south, where Museveni is from, while the northern half of the country continues to be bogged down in butchery, debauchery, bribes and beggary. Northerners feel the government has neglected them and left them exposed to attack. The land is fertile. But the ongoing insurgencies of the Lord's Resistance Army and the Allied Democratic Forces are forcing farmers to flee into Uganda's larger towns and across the border into Congo. As fighting between the government and now well-trained and Sudanese-armed rebels spreads to central and western Uganda, there seems little hope for any peacemaking. Khartoum is pissed at Museveni for supporting Sudan's insurgency in the south, and Museveni isn't going to talk peace with a northern rebel backed by Sudan. It makes for a good, old-fashioned bush war.

President Yoweri Museveni

The new president of Uganda is former guerrilla chief Yoweri Museveni. He was born in 1944, raises about 1500 head of cattle and became a guerrilla fighter in 1971. With the help of Tanzanian troops, he ousted Idi Amin in 1979. He married Janet Kataha in 1973 and has four children.

When word of Museveni and his guerrillas began popping up in the mid-1980s, they were the most obscure of players. In Kampala, moderates of various stripes had been at work trying to pull Uganda from the pit into which Amin had shoved it.

Uganda is still struggling to recover. Large portions remain insecure. Its military (Uganda's National Resistance Army [NRA], now with a political wing, the National Resistance Movement) is poorly armed and underpaid (they make about US$30–160 per month). But Museveni, without seeking the role, has become the most powerful man in Central and East Africa today.

Uncle Sam

As part of Clinton's Recolonization of Africa (see Sudan, Congo chapters) U.S. Special Forces are in Uganda training and supervising the annihilation of all Sudanese backed rabble rousers.

Lord's Resistance Army

The LRA is an armed faction, led by a former altar boy, that's been pouring freshly trained and armed guerrillas into Uganda from Sudan in recent months. It is—get this—a Christian fundamentalist group. Their agenda is to create a theocratic state based on the 10 Commandments. There are daily occurrences of looting of convoys and hit-and-run firefights with the army, usually leaving scores of government soldiers and civilians dead. Joseph Kony leads this savage group—armed and uniformed by Sudan—whose members believe their bodies will deflect bullets when smeared with tree oils. In June 1997, Kony ordered his men to avoid killing civilians and to await reinforcements from Sudan. In the first six months of 1997, the LRA was responsible for 400 deaths in the northern third of Uganda and the displacing of some 200,000 farmers. The LRA specializes in abducting children, whom they train and enroll in their ranks. Some 3000 schoolchildren were abducted in 1995 and 1996 by rebels targeting them as recruits.

The strength of the LRA has been estimated by the government at 600 men, but ganja-inspired Kony says he has 6500 men in three brigades that operate in groups of 30 or less. They have warned villagers that anyone within six miles of a road, riding a bicycle or motorcycle, and anyone keeping ducks or sheep will be killed. The LRA considers ducks and sheep to be unclean animals.

The LRA has experienced a number of setbacks at the hands of Clabe Akandwanaho, the brother of Museveni.

Around 5000 children have been kidnapped and escaped from the LRA but another 5000 are still being held in rebel bases in the Southern Sudan according to Amnesty International.

Allied Democratic Forces (ADF)

These guys are Sudan backed Muslim nasties, the West Nile Bank Front (WNBF) and what's left of the old National Army for the Liberation of Uganda (ANLU). They operate out of the cool green mountains in Western Uganda and they are trying to carve a niche for themselves along the Congo border. Most of the clashes between the ADF and government forces have been occurring in and around the town of Bundibugyo. And, true to form, most of the casualties have been civilians. One June 1997, attack killed 40 innocents. Meanwhile, between 5000 and 10,000 Ugandan villagers have fled across the border in the former Zaire to escape the fighting.

West Nile Bank Front (WNBF)

Former aide to Idi Amin Dada, Juma Oris, leads about 2000 WNBF rebels against the Ugandan government. Based in Sudan (who isn't these days?), they make sporadic attacks on the Ugandan army in the Arua area along the Ugandan-Sudanese border. They began their insurgency in May of 1995. The rebels are loyal to former dictator Idi Amin and were supported by the former Zaire when Mobutu was at the helm. Sudanese troops even provide covering artillery fire for the WNBF incursions into Uganda. Amin, living in relative luxury in Saudi Arabia and now over 70 years old, was bounced by the Tanzanians and current president Museveni in 1979, after causing the deaths of over half a million of his own people. Oris was reported killed in a clash with government troops in March 1997, which may mean the end of the WNBF. Oris has been reportedly killed a few times but he keeps coming back to life.

Ronald Mutebi and the Kingdom of Buganda

A king named Ronald? Yes, Buganda's back and Ronald is king. The ancient kingdom of Buganda was symbolically restored in July of 1993, and the tourists still stay away.

Hezbollah

No, this isn't a misprint; even Hezbollah is a player here. In the middle of January 1996, the Lebanon-based, Iran-backed terrorist group threatened to overthrow the Ugandan government. Did they get off at the wrong airport, perhaps?

A passport is required. Visas are not required of U.S. citizens. Visas can be had at border checkpoints, usually for a cost of US$20. Immunization certificates for yellow fever and cholera are required (typhoid and malaria suppressants recommended). For a business visa and other information, contact the following:

Embassy of the Republic of Uganda

5909 16th Street N.W.
Washington, D.C. 20011
☎ *(202) 726-7100-02*

Permanent Mission to the U.N.

☎ *(212) 949-0110.*

From the U.S., the best connections by air are made through Europe, Nairobi and Johannesburg. Sabena flies from Brussels to Entebbe, while British Airways flies to Kampala from Gatwick. Air France flies direct from Paris. Uganda Airways is the national carrier. By rail, there is twice-weekly service to Kampala from Nairobi and Mombasa. Ugandan Railway Corporation (URC) has in the past operated a ferry to Port Bell from Mwanza in Tanzania, but the service was suspended at press time. By road, border crossings are open at Malaba, Busia Mutuku, Kisoro, Arua and Lwakhakha. Drivers will need an international license and proof of insurance. There will be a fee for a temporary Uganda road license.

There is something to be said for the third-class train. There is a branch line to Gulu, and if it is running, it could be a reasonably safe way to get to Gulu and see the country. Driving to Gulu is discouraged; there have been numerous incidents. Hitchhiking is even less advisable, but you may end up hitching if you decide to drive. URC operates passenger service between Kampala and the towns of Jinja, Toroco, Mbale, Soroti, Lira, Pakwach and Gulu. There are also services to Kasese in western Uganda and a weekly service to Nairobi.

There are more than 2000 km of paved roads in Uganda and 6000 km of murram (dirt) feeder routes. Four-wheel-drive vehicles are preferable for both surfaces. The only fuel stations are along the major routes. Drivers should inquire with locals about the distances and times between towns and villages. International car rental companies are based in Kampala and Entebbe. Taxis can be found at the airports and in the main towns. Fares are negotiable and should be determined before you set out. In Kampala, long-distance buses depart from the station near the stadium. Ferries run to the Ssese Islands from Port Bell and Bukakata when they're operating.

There is an eerie quiet in this once bustling country—akin to the sound of waiting for another boot to drop. Uganda can be seen as an inherently civilized country surrounded by nasty neighbors: Sudan to the north, Zaire to the west, Rwanda to the south. The white minority in Kenya to the east is betting on prosperity as a ravaged economy begs for outside investment. There are only about 85,000 or so visitors every year compared to Kenya's 800,000, but it is growing at about 10 percent each year.

Crime is common in Uganda, with violent crime being more common than not. Roadblocks around the country are just as likely to be manned by thugs. Taking pictures of the military is considered a crime. Border areas are not safe. The north is dangerous for any kind of travel. We can only vouch for two towns, Gulu and Moroto, and one outpost, the National Resistance Army Camp on the Kidepo River frontier with the Sudan. Moroto is a lovely place in this sere wilderness. There are even some decaying colonial structures surrounded by green, and a huge green mountain rises due east of the town. But as far as we know, this has always been the sort of African town where you sleep on the floor of the police post.

Gulu, on the road to the Sudanese frontier town of Nimule to the north, and the rail line to Pakwach on the Albert Nile to the west, offers considerably more, but outside of town, this country is just as dangerous. There are the proper, if faded, Acholi Inn (a reminder that this is the country of the Acholi, many of whom were killed en masse by Amin) and, a notch down, the Luxor Lodge (a reminder, perhaps, that the Khedive, through his agents in the Sudan, once claimed all Uganda as Egyptian territory). These days it's unlikely that either of these hotels would require reservations, but even if they do, it's not a police-post town: Both the Church of Uganda and the Red Cross Society are said to offer accommodations.

Mbarara and Ankole Country

The maxim for most dangerous places is, don't go unless you have to. That's not what you hear about the town of Mbarara and Ankole country just north of Rwanda and Tanzania, where you still find, after years of the white man's devastating rinderpest, longhorn

UGANDA

Ankole cattle. Not unlike Tutsi cattle, they are owned by a tall, dark aristocracy, descended like the Watutsi from northern invaders who seized a Bantu-speaking kingdom. Here, the serfs are the Hima people, the aristocrats, the Ankole.

This is the region through which Henry Morton Stanley (the explorer who presumed to discover Dr. Livingstone) passed in 1875 on his way to meet Mutesa, king of Buganda, and what you hear about it is don't let the danger keep you away.

For one, it's beautiful, often the spare, dry beauty of the savanna rather than the ever-lush beauty of Buganda just to the north. (Buganda's deep green light filtering through banana groves colors the Uganda of our imagination.) For another, there is both the human and animal population. Mbarara is not an unusual African town, but then you begin to realize how combat tore the place up, and how other towns, similarly battered, still languish in a decrepit state. It's bracing to experience the resilience of this much patched place. Gusty *jambos* in a town with cheap hotels sporting names like The Super Tip Top Lodge Bar & Restaurant; this is Africa? Wildlife is devastated, but just when you think it is utterly gone, there it is, and seeing it in such circumstances, the sudden appearance of a bull eland brings a melancholy rush.

Gulu and the North

Kampala, Entebbe, the Uganda of repute, is a place of enveloping warmth, lush-green, coffee-rich, a jacaranda breeze. The far north of Uganda is nothing like this. The country north of the Victoria Nile and Lake Kyoga is drier than the savanna in the far south—wide open land, often trackless, which even before the days of Idi Amin, travelers were warned to enter with no less than two four-wheel-drive vehicles. Today, you're warned to shun it altogether, unless you can rent a light plane to get in and out of secure redoubts like the army base on the Kidepo River frontier with the Sudan, a region whose land, people and animals are so close to the Pleistocene, and so palpably distant from the rest of the world, that you find yourself hypnotized.

This is Nilote country. Amin came from the Nilotic tribes that populate this harsh country; likewise, Obote. Meantime, Museveni's crusade came from the green south and west, the heartland of the old Bantu kingdoms.

The far north has always been a rough place, a place where men can still be seen with chest scars toting their kills (left breast for women, right for men), and cattle rustling has long been both a routine way of life and a routine way of death. Today, it's especially dangerous. Remnants of Amin's army are about, along with the Lord's Resistance, as well as outright *shiftas*. In this territory, the term *shifta*, meaning bandit, is likely to be used honestly, and not as a euphemism for guerrillas.

Travel Outside Kampala

Kampala is relatively safe, but outside the capital is a war zone. LRA guerrillas control the roads north of Kampala at night, and bandits those to the southwest. Teams of LRA rebels regularly ambush convoys to the north and have even tried to take the key northern city of Gulu. A convoy of 140 vehicles, complete with armed escort, was ambushed by LRA zanies on April 6, 1996. The guerrillas like to burn dwellings in their hasty retreats as a calling card.

Safaris

In the best of times, driving into the country north of the Victoria Nile has entailed the sense of entering country so open and vacant that once you're off the track and in trouble, it could be weeks before you're found. Kampala safari operators maintain radio contact with safaris. Should things get hot, they'd likely get their clients out fast; there's a chance they could get you out aboard a light plane with an extra seat. A minor problem is that you might have to kiss your gear good-bye. Depending on distance and danger, count on paying anywhere from US$750 to $10,000. If there is anyone flying out of Entebbe or any other field, the best way to find out would be through Wilson Airport (not Embakazi, out of which the commercial airlines fly) north of Nairobi. **Z. Boskovic Air Charters** (☎ *501210*) is one possibility; **Air Kenya Aviation** (☎ *501421*) is another. Whether or not they are flying, they are in as good a position as anyone to know who might be. If you can't get through, and even if you can, you should either have a car and driver available or be looking for one. The best bet is a group of two or three who hire a four-wheel-drive vehicle and a driver. Self-drive rental cars are not easily available in Kampala.

Cattle Rustlers

Cattle rustlers from Kenya are making life miserable for ranchers in the east. In one attack in May 1997, rustlers from Kenya killed 76 Ugandan villagers, including 50 children, as they made off with 300 head of cattle.

Bicycles

The hospital in Lachor has started receiving children with their feet hacked off by rebels of the LRA. They have been losing their limbs as punishment for riding bicycles, which the rebels claim can be used to ferry information to the Ugandan army.

You're on your own, friend. Any number of Western embassies in Kampala can, of course, advise where to get competent medical attention in Kampala, but Kampala isn't a dangerous place, nor for that matter are the actual towns of Gulu and Moroto, where there are also adequate (and, of course, inadequate) medical facilities. Yet, when a country has an average of one doctor for every 22,291 people, your chances of getting one are slim to none. AIDS is a big killer here, along with the usual Central African lineup of malaria, intestinal bugs, respiratory ailments and other tropical killers. Malaria is present throughout the country and chloroquine-resistant. Louse-borne typhus is especially prevalent where groups of people congregate together.

Uganda has a population of about 21 million people. The capital is Kampala, with a population of 800,000. The climate is tropical with hot lowland areas and cooler temperatures in the mountains.

The official language is English, but you'll also hear a lot of Swahili spoken. There are another 30 indigenous languages, the most common is Luganda. About two-thirds of the Ugandan people are Christians, while Islam makes up about 16 percent of the population.

The Ugandan currency is the Ugandan shilling (UGs1000=US$1). Credit cards are accepted at the major hotels but not in the boonies. Banking hours are 8:30 a.m.–2 p.m. Business hours are 8:30 a.m.–12:30 p.m. and 2–5 p.m. Telephone and fax services are available in the main towns. The IDD code for Uganda is +256. Uganda is on GMT+3. Electrical supply is generally 220V/50C.

Ugandans drive on the left hand side of the road (where they should!). As a rule, photos shouldn't be taken of people unless you have their permission. But who follows rules? Nor should they be taken of religious ceremonies and strategic buildings. Professional photogs should check in with the Ministry of Information.

05/1996	Museveni wins elections with 72 percent of the vote.
01/29/1986	Museveni declared president after NRA seizes Kampala.
07/27/1985	Milton Obote is ousted as president for the second time in a military coup.
05/27/1981	Obote returned as president after nine years in exile.
04/10/1979	Tanzanian and UNLF forces enter Kampala after driving out Idi Amin's forces.
10/1978	Idi Amin's forces invade Tanzania.
06/1976	Israel launches commando raid on Entebbe airport.
01/25/1971	Idi Amin becomes president.

Washington D.C.

The United States
★

How the West Was Stunned

Land of the free and home of the brave. And you'd better be damned brave here, because people are free to do pretty much anything they like. Behind white picket fences and two-car garages, husbands clobber their wives silly while their kids make crack deals over the phone with *Scarface* on the tube.

In Los Angeles, a couple of guys who may have been consultants to the movie *Heat* pop a bank armed to the teeth and in full body armor, turning the streets of North Hollywood into a battlefield. The cops are so outgunned they raid a gun shop for an arsenal usually reserved for beach landings.

This is a land where doctors kiss their wives good-bye and later lose their lives outside burning abortion clinics in Massachusetts, Virginia, Florida, Oregon, Ohio, Minnesota and California—the victims of preachers, former altar boys, and women who look more like manicurists than terrorists.

In Idaho, Montana, Alabama, Louisiana, Georgia, Texas and Utah, young white-trash punks, parading as "Freemen" under the lofty and pontifical banner

859

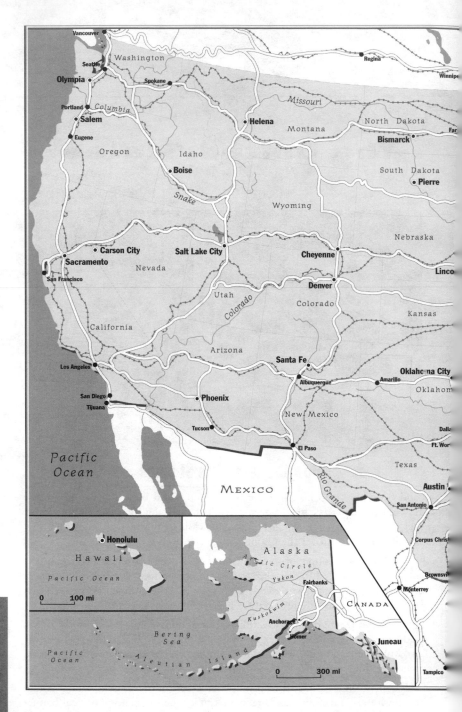

CANADA

Lake Winnipeg

Lake Superior

Duluth

Minnesota

Minneapolis

St. Paul

Wisconsin

Michigan

Lake Michigan

Lake Huron

Sudbury

Toronto

Ottawa

Montreal

Quebec

Maine

Augusta

Montpelier

Vt.

N.H.

Concord

Boston

Mass.

Providence

R.I.

Iowa

Madison

Milwaukee

Lansing

Chicago

Detroit

Lake Erie

Cleveland

Lake Ontario

New York

Albany

Hartford

Conn.

New York

Des Moines

Indiana

Ohio

Pittsburgh

Pennsylvania

Harrisburg

Philadelphia

Md.

Trenton

New Jersey

maha

Illinois

Columbus

Indianapolis

Washington D.C.

Dover

Delaware

Springfield

West Virginia

Annapolis

Kansas City

St. Louis

Ohio

Charleston

Frankfort

Richmond

Norfolk

eka

Jefferson City

Kentucky

Virginia

Missouri

Nashville

Tennessee

North Carolina

Raleigh

Arkansas

Memphis

Mississippi

South Carolina

Columbia

Little Rock

Atlanta

Charleston

Birmingham

Georgia

Atlantic Ocean

Louisiana

Jackson

Montgomery

Alabama

Mississippi

Tallahassee

Jacksonville

Baton Rouge

New Orleans

Florida

Tampa

Miami

Gulf of Mexico

Key West

THE BAHAMAS

Havana

CUBA

U.S. Naval Base

United States

⊛ National capital

⊙ State capital

● Secondary city

┼┼┼ Primary road

＋＋＋ Railroad

State border

0   800 km

0   500 mi

©FWI

of white supremacy, stash a couple of years' worth of Spam into a cave in the hills, run around in the forest with paint guns, and plot the demise of every "nigger" and "kike" west of Bethesda. Fear not, because in this land of equality and free speech, the JDL and Nation of Islam do their part to keep the hate at a scalding pitch.

In L.A., inner-city toddlers catch stray bullets from drive-by shooters, while, in New York, Islamic whackos use a rented van full of fertilizer makings to blow up the World Trade Center. In San Diego, a despondent plumber hot-wires a tank, flattens some cars, and is shot to death after high-centering on a freeway divider. Rival rapsters in New York and L.A. gun down each other in a war of the coasts. What would Ozzie and Harriet Nelson say?

In Miami, a renowned fashion designer out to fetch his morning paper—whose only crime is penning groin-high hemlines—is blown away by a young, bar-hopping trendie from West L.A. who looks disturbingly like another young, bar-hopping trendie from West L.A., only this one is allegedly hacked up by a famous football and movie star.

In Wisconsin and Illinois, deranged cannibals lure teenage gay hookers into their homes, decapitate and disembowel them, boil their heads and consume their viscera for dinner. In jail, they get beaten to death by nasties who can't live with a guy who's munched on some dead dude's brains.

A recent Gallup poll discovered that 40 percent of the American people think that "the federal government has become so large and powerful that it poses an immediate threat to rights and freedoms of ordinary citizens."

In Oklahoma City, the Alfred P. Murrah Building is blown up. The nondescript building has no significance other than being the headquarters for the DEA, Secret Service and the ATF. The aftermath is a nine story-hole, a crater 30 feet wide by 8 feet deep, and 168 innocent people killed. The methodology is very similar to that used in the World Trade Center bombing: a 1000 to 1200-pound fertilizer- and diesel-based bomb packed into a rented Ryder truck and detonated by remote control or timer. Different folks, same strokes.

Farther south, some 300 miles away in Waco, Texas, the site of the Branch Davidian compound has become a popular local tourist attraction. The bomb blast in Oklahoma City occurred two years to the day after the attack by the ATF on the cult's compound. During the ATF raid, a brainwashed prophet with an arms cache the size of the Serbs' had his followers blow their brains out as he torched his compound—and their children.

The 1996 Olympic Summer Games bring American terrorism to international headlines when a pipe bomb explodes during a concert resulting in two deaths and hundreds injured.

And across the South, African American churches are being destroyed by fire—apparently the result of racially motivated arson. More than 30 churches had been hit within an 18 month period.

Not to be slighted, however, Muslim extremists continue to remind us of their nastiness. Mir Aimai Kansi, a Pakistani, takes target practice with an AK-47 on CIA employees headed for work in Langley, Virginia. It takes four years to catch him. Hani Abdel Rahim Hussein al-Sayegh thought he'd have a better chance of wasting Americans and getting away with it if he did his dirty deeds on foreign soil. He blows away 19 American servicemen in Dhahran, Saudi Arabia. He's nabbed, though, a year later. Then, a despondent Palestinian, Ali Abu Kamal, ascends to the 86th floor of the Empire State Building with a .380 semi-automatic Beretta and guns down seven people; one is killed. But Kansi has no such delusions of escape; he shoots himself in the head. Different stokes, same folks.

Mayhem, Tabloid Style

We used to chuckle at the tabloids, as we bought them with our groceries. Now we can't figure out if it's the news we're watching or promos for the latest B movies.

In all 50 states, plumbers, carpenters, politicians, real estate agents, movie moguls and cops get into their cars after a fifth of gin at their local Sam's Bar and later plow into and kill a family on the interstate.

In Nowherevilles across the country, 12-year-old kids playing on the railroad tracks stumble across one of their classmates—who was sodomized and strangled to death...a month ago.

In California, fires ravage the hills of Berkeley and Malibu. Tremors, measuring 7.1 on the Richter scale, rattle hills that later disappear entirely—along with the houses on them—after 10 inches of rain fall in a 14-hour period.

And the corpses of Central American would-be illegal immigrants float like logs down the Rio Grande. Those who make it to the other side of the river are looted, beaten and raped by sinister "coyotes."

Criminals as Superstars

Hard times breed strange heroes. The hardscrabble days of early America bred the outlaws of the Wild West. Jesse James and Billy the Kid were popularized in East Coast dime novels. The Great Depression gave us Dillinger and Al Capone. Today, in down-on-its-luck L.A., we are hatching a new breed of famous ne'er do wells. In Los Angeles, the land of "three strikes you're out" has become "do a crime, do the prime time." Here, random violence and thoughtless pain take on plot, character and movie deals, as two rich kids splatter their parents' brains against a wall with a 12-gauge for a couple of Rolexes. In Los Angeles, a former football hero and movie star is accused of nearly severing his ex-wife's head and brutally stabbing to death her acquaintance. Meanwhile, during his "getaway," traffic on plagued L.A. freeways comes to a halt; motorists emerge from their cars waving banners urging, "Go O.J.!" and "Save the Juice!" After the most publicized trial in history, the jury lets him go free.

Here, crime needs a subplot and linkage. A mother tosses her kids off a bridge and jumps herself afterward. The news media immediately connects it to a woman in the South who rolled her two kids to their watery end—a woman who played the media like a fiddle in her search for her "kidnapped" children.

Crime also needs a surprise ending, a payback. Rodney King gets the crap beaten out of him, sues and gets millions. Reginald Denny gets the crap beaten out of him and hugs and kisses the mother of one of his attackers. The Unabomber's big demand is that he have his anti-technology manifesto published. We Americans like our crime. Just keep it fresh, surprising and very brutal.

Hey, America... what time is it?

Every 2 seconds	a criminal offense
Every 12 seconds	a burglary
Every 17 seconds	a violent crime
Every 20 seconds	a vehicle is stolen
Every 51 seconds	a robbery
Every 5 minutes	a rape
Every 29 minutes	a murder
Every 28 seconds	an aggravated assault
Every 30 minutes	news, sports and weather

Sources: F.B.I. Uniform Crime Report, DP

Some samplings from *The Army of God* (U.S. version) manual:

- If terminally ill, use your final months to torch clinics; by the time the authorities identify you, you will have gone to your reward.

- Use a high-powered rifle to fire bullets into the engine block of a doctor's car.

- Never make a bomb threat from anywhere but a pay phone.

- Hot-wire a bulldozer at a construction site, drive it to a clinic, jump off and let the bulldozer crash through the clinic wall.

- Drop butyric acid into dumpsters or boxes of trash when people are in the building.

- Put holes through clinic windows. The problem with .22-caliber weapons is the noise—the Fourth of July and New Year's Eve are great times for gunshots.

- Why get out of the way of an abortionist's car? The current lawsuit-crazy attitude can be used against baby-killers, and many awards have been received.

- Look up magazines such as *Soldier of Fortune* or *Survivalist.* Guaranteed that you'll be amazed, if not shocked, by the materials available.

You can find out about the goings on of the Army of God on the Abortion Rights Activist web site. Check out:

Abortion Rights Activist

http://www.cais.com/agm/main/aog.htm

We live in the land of the free, the home of the brave, where everyone has a right to do something, to speak his mind, to 15 minutes of fame, to a guest appearance on the "Ricki Lake Show." What is wrong with this picture? It seems that Americans are punctuating their angry sentences with bullets. The beat goes on.

As Not Seen on TV

In 1965, 91 percent of homicides were solved. Today, only 65.5 percent become untangled. The majority of murders are committed by family members and acquaintances against each other. The chances that you will get killed by a stranger are only two out of 10, that is, if you take into account just the solved murders. When unsolved murders are tallied, the FBI estimates that 53 percent of all homicides are being committed by strangers, and that only 12 percent of homicides take place within families. Eighty percent of crimes are committed by same-race perpetrators. Robbery is committed by strangers 75 percent of the time, and aggravated assault is committed by a stranger 58 percent of the time. Eighty-seven percent of all violent crimes are committed against whites and Hispanics. Lone white offenders select white victims 96 percent of the time, and lone black offenders select white victims 62 percent of the time. White rapists select white victims 97 percent of the time, and black rapists select white victims 48 percent of the time.

Although 51 percent of prison inmates are black, the balance is out of whack, since African Americans make up about 12.3 percent of the U.S. population. The number of black males in prison between the ages of 25 and 29 is 7210 per 100,000. According to the Department of Justice, the homicide rate for whites is 5.2 per 100,000 and for blacks about 44.7 per 100,000. Urban killers tend to be male (90 percent) and young (15–29). Something is very wrong.

In 1960, 12 percent of the population reported owning one or more handguns. In 1976, 21 percent owned a handgun. Today there are well over 200 million handguns, with 4 million new guns being manufactured each year. Professor Gary Kleck of Florida State University estimates that 1500 citizens used guns to kill criminals in 1980. Police only kill about 500 criminals each year.

U.S. Incarceration Rate (per 100,000 people)	
States with Highest Incarceration Rate	
Texas	659
Louisiana	573
Oklahoma	536
Arizona	473
States with Lowest Incarceration Rate	
Vermont	135
W. Virginia	134
Maine	112
Minnesota	103
North Dakota	90

In America one in every 175 people is in jail. Prison populations have doubled in the last 15 years. But, wait. Major crime was down 17.5 percent in New York. The decrease in violent crimes in the nine U.S. cities with populations of more than one million was down 8 percent. Hallelujah, the streets are safe, or are they? Those figures were 1994 numbers. What they didn't tell you was that the '95 and '96 numbers put violent crime right back on track again. The major reason for the drop was the reduction of kids in the crime-prone ages of 15–19. The bad news is that the next wave of kids is meaner, badder and more prone to kill.

Top-10 Talk Show Subjects	
Parent-child relations	48%
Dating	36%
Marital relations	35%
Sexual activity	34%
Reconciliations	25%
Physical health	24%
Abuse	23%
Alienation	23%
Physical appearance	23%
Criminal acts	22%

Entertainment is no family affair. A cable industry–sponsored report says that 57 percent of shows feature violence. In 1995, the three major networks ran 2574 stories on crime, four times the number they ran in 1991.

Bang Bang Boogie

Rocky Mountain Media Watch estimates that crime disaster and war coverage make up an average of 42 percent of all newscasts. UCLA researchers say that even though murders make up 2 percent of all felonies in Los Angeles, the news devotes 27 percent of its coverage to them. In the same study, it was disclosed that 50 percent of crimes committed by blacks in L.A. are violent and that 47 percent of crimes committed by whites are violent. There were about 30 percent more stories on black crimes involving violence than white crimes.

Two Hundred Grand, Free Housing and All the Bullets You Can Dodge

In Washington, D.C., a convicted crack freak is re-elected mayor. In Louisiana, an admitted KKK leader and affirmed racist nearly gets elected to the U.S. Senate. In South Carolina, an already elected and longtime U.S. senator warns the president of the United States that he had better have a lot of bodyguards if he's going to visit a military base in that state. America is the land of the tough guy, people who don't take any crap, and will gun you down if you give them any lip. In New York, Bernard Goetz gets slammed in a $41 million lawsuit for gunning down thugs (while Bronson makes millions in movies doing the same thing). Meanwhile, on the other coast, prosecutors won't file murder charges against a white man who guns down Latino taggers. Go figure.

Being the boss man of the land of the free is no picnic. In America, four presidents have been assassinated. Two others have been shot. There have been nearly successful assassination attempts on three others. Three serious contenders for the presidency have been critically shot, two dead.

The White House should consider opening up a shooting range to give irate voters an outlet for their violent tendencies. The venerable building has been riddled with the bullets of drive-by shootings, bad snipers, even a crashed airplane. America is not a Pepsi commercial or the "Brady Bunch." America is a dangerous place.

President Bill Clinton has called crime "the great crisis of the spirit that is gripping America today." The number of crimes recorded by police in the U.S. has risen by more than 60 percent since 1973. Violent crime, by the most conservative estimates, has risen by nearly 25 percent during that same period. The Statue of Liberty may well want to pull her arm down and take in the welcoming mat. In the U.S. nearly 10 of every 100,000 people are the victims of a homicide. In 1900, only one person in every 100,000 could expect to become a murder victim.

The United States is a large modern country with devolving inner cities. There are more than 200 million guns in the possession of Americans. Most violent acts in the States are the result of robberies, domestic disputes and drug-related violence. Terrorist acts, ranging from the killing of abortionist doctors to the bombing of the World Trade Center, are highly publicized but not considered a real threat to travelers. The threat of robbery or violent crime in inner cities and some tourist areas is real and should be taken seriously. Travel in America is considered safe, and danger is confined to random violence and inner cities. Those seeking adventure can find it in a New Orleans bar at five in the morning or strolling through South Central L.A. after midnight.

Whackos

In most dangerous places, the players have a sense of purpose—through lineage or frustrated political or theological ambition. Here in America, we possess a bunch of whackos whose motivations make the "Pee Wee Herman Show" look intellectual. And most of these folks wouldn't know what to do with this country even if we gave it to them. Even Ross Perot looks like a puppet with a bad haircut when he takes on presidential trappings. Bottom line is, there are no more Ben Franklins or George Washingtons vying for political power.

Aryan Nation, the KKK and Hate Groups

These are right-wing belligerent groups that specialize in pipe bombs and the intimidation of blacks, Jews and immigrants. Although not considered a threat to the social structure, they constitute a growing menace. On July 30, 1994, two skinhead thugs of the white supremacist group Aryan Nations Brotherhood were busted on charges that they offered to kill a federal drug agent in exchange for $120,000 in cash, weapons and cocaine. One of the men allegedly said he would kill a Drug Enforcement Agency (DEA) agent by bombing his home. On July 29, 1994, two zanies from Washington—members of the white supremacist group known as the American Front—who were in possession of three metal pipe bombs, four rifles, military-type clothing, wigs and white supremacist literature, were busted by the FBI in Salinas, California. The men were allegedly behind a pipe bomb explosion on July 20, 1994, at the Tacoma chapter of the National Association for the Advancement of Colored People (NAACP).

Another terrorist goon squad to hit the scene in 1996 was the Aryan Republican Army. On April 2, 1996, a pipe bomb tore through the offices of a Spokane, Washington, newspaper, followed by two men who ripped the paper off for $50,000, who then set off another explosion. They left a letter behind announcing the end of "Babylon," a popular buzz term white supremacists use to call the federal government. These guys get off using the names of federal agents when they rent getaway cars.

Bring on the Port-o-Johns

In June 1996, The Ku Klux Clan adopted a half-mile stretch of Interstate 55 running through the south of St. Louis through Missouri's "Adopt-A-Highway" program. Backed by a court ruling protecting free speech, hooded and robed Klansmen took to the stretch of road with plastic garbage bags and rakes. Irate locals began using the section of highway as a dumpster.

Rights Groups

Activities by rights groups are centered around the abortion issue, but certainly aren't confined to it. Animal rights activists have been out doing dirty deeds, but their acts go largely unnoticed. The Animal Liberation Front (ALF), an underground animal rights group, claimed responsibility for a number of fires that caused damage in downtown Chicago department stores. Five of eight incendiary devices ignited, causing fires in Marshall Field's, Carson Pirie Scott and Saks Fifth Avenue stores. While death is not an objective in the actions of most rights groups—as it undermines their causes—each possesses its crazies, as terror and death serve as their tools.

Islamic Terrorists

Despite the seriousness given Islamic terrorists by American journalists, they tend to resemble the gang that couldn't shoot straight. True, Islamic terrorists were behind the February 26, 1993, bombing of the New York World Trade Center (WTC), which killed six and wounded more than 1000 others. The FBI and local authorities busted nine suspected Islamic terrorists associated with the bombing as well as other plots to bomb targets in New York, including the U.N. building and the Lincoln and Holland tunnels beneath the Hudson River. They also are alleged to have put plans together to assassinate both prominent American and Egyptian politicians. FBI agents and immigration authorities nabbed a blind Egyptian cleric named Sheikh Omar Abdel-Rahman (famous for allegedly issuing the *fatwa* that led to the assassination of Egyptian President Anwar Sadat in 1981) on felony charges in connection with the WTC bombing and the other proposed terrorist activities. Rahman and his nine followers were convicted in October 1995 of seditious conspiracy and will be guests of Uncle Sam (using your tax dollars, of course) for a long time.

However, on closer inspection, it seems that the sheik's bodyguard, Emad Salem, a former Egyptian army colonel, was an FBI informant who supplied 150 hours of audio- and videotapes of the entire plot. The videotapes even include shots of the men mixing their homemade fertilizer bombs. Many experts agree that it was a miracle that any of the crudely made bombs could go off at all. Some defendants turned the table on Salem, accusing him of selecting the bombing targets, renting the safe house and having the only key to the garage that held the explosives. Salem stands to make almost a million dollars for his work in turning in the one-hit wonders, who will now never make anything more complicated than licence plates.

Additionally, the indictment named El Sayyid Nosair as aiding in the planning of the bombings. Nosair, a close associate of Abdel-Rahman, had been in prison on a weapons possession conviction at the time and an assault rap in connection with the killing of Rabbi Meir Kahane in New York City in 1990. The charges also accused the group of planning to bomb bridges and U.S. military facilities.

The Rugged Mountain Folk of Montana

This remote, rugged and mountainous state breeds individualism, for sure, but it also produces a disproportionate share of mental cases and whackos. Some of these folks have just been in the woods too long and eaten too many squirrels. Montana is the home of the suspected Unabomber, Theodore Kaczynski, who was busted by the feds April 3, 1996, in his remote Montana cabin. The Unabomber killed three people and injured 23 during a 17-year mail bombing spree. Montana is also the home of extremist militiaman John Trochmann (see "Militia of Montana" below), as well as Terry Nichols of Oklahoma City blast fame. And the state is the base for a bunch of zanies who go by the handle "Freemen" (they're not free any longer). These guys, devout white supremacist Christians who reject government authority, refuse to pay taxes and like to write bad checks. On March 25, 1996, a standoff began in Jordan, Montana, between 20 armed Freemen and more than 100 FBI agents after two of the Freemen's leaders were jailed over a $1.8 million fraudulent check scheme, the theft of television equipment and for threatening a federal judge. Even former Green Beret and borderline fascist James "Bo" Gritz couldn't negotiate this wolfpack's surrender. Toss in another chunk of meat.

Office Workers

There's an alarming trend of murder in the workplace. More than 1000 Americans are murdered on the job every year. The U.S. Postal Service has had 34 employees gunned down since 1986.

Gangs

America's willingness to absorb large masses of refugees resulted in the importing of some of the nastiest and hardest groups of street gangs in any Western country. In New York, rival gangs of Puerto Ricans, Irish or blacks don't actually break out into spontaneous choreography when they want to settle a dispute. *West Side Story* has become *Apocalypse Now*. In L.A., fast cars and even faster weapons have elevated gangs into small armies. The weapons of choice are full-automatic weapons with semiautomatics reserved for rookies. Assault weapons, like the AK-47, Tec 9, MAC, UZI or shotguns are preferred. Most gangs are created along ethnic and neighborhood lines. Bloods and Crips are the new Hatfields and McCoys. The *gangsta* look has become big business now. Baggy pants, work shirts, short hair, and that unique gangsta *lean* have all been adopted by freckle-faced kids from Iowa. Gangsta music has towheaded kids reciting tales of inner-city woes, just as their parents were able to recite *Ittsy Bittsy Teeny Weenie Yellow Polka Dot Bikini*. The new proponents of this violent/hip culture seem to live life a little too close to their lyrics. Rappers Tupac Shakur and Snoop Doggy Dog both probably wish they were singing Barney's theme of *I love you, you love me*. In Los Angeles, there are over 800 gangs with 30,000 members. There are at least 1000 homicides every year and well over 1000 drive-by shootings. According to figures presented to the White House, there are 500,000 gang members in 16,000 gangs in the U.S. Eight hundred American cities are home to these gangs, compared to 100 in 1970. Fifty-seven percent of towns with over 25,000 residents have reported gang-related incidents.

But gangsterism in America is not black, white and Hispanic. Gang members come in all flavors. The most dangerous gangs in America are the new Asian gangs, groups of Cambodian, Vietnamese, Laotian and Filipino youths whose families came from the refugee camps, killing fields and dung heaps of Southeast Asia. Chinese-American gang members are being blamed for the February 25, 1996 murder of Cambodian actor Dr. Haing Ngor, a former refugee of the Khmer Rouge and the star of the 1984 movie *The Killing Fields*. After enduring four years of savage brutality under the Khmer Rouge during the guerrilla group's reign of terror between 1975 and 1979, the Academy Award-winning doctor was ironically slain in the land of the free, for a Buddhist amulet.

Your Next Door Neighbor

Four out of 10 violent crimes in the U.S. are committed by relations or acquaintances of the victims.

Militias

Militias were once social centers for good 'ole boys with a strong sense of gun love. Ignored by the mainstream press until the Oklahoma bombing, they were free to dress in army surplus gear and shoot off guns in the swamps of Florida or the mountains of Colorado. The Branch Davidians created a dangerous mix of Jesus, gunpowder and news attention and became targets for their insolence.

Now militias are in the spotlight, and they don't quite know what to do with their political notoriety. Given a few more longnecks and a couple of pinches of Skoal, it won't be long before they come up with a coherent political agenda.

The Southern Poverty Law Center has identified 440 self-proclaimed antigovernment militias. And they've infested every state in the union. The government calls them "Internet commandos," but is taking them quite seriously (see "The Babylonians"). Currently, there are 24 states where the higher-profile militias are in operation. California, Arizona, Nevada and Colorado make up the South/Western area while the Southeastern area includes Florida, Alabama, Georgia, Tennessee, Arkansas, Missouri, North Carolina and Virginia. There is also a Northeastern area that is composed of New York, New Hampshire, Ohio, Pennsylvania, Indiana and Wisconsin.

It is interesting to note that many of the militia groups are growing in popularity, thanks to Janet Reno and the massive television coverage of the immolation of the Branch Davidians. The most well-known militias in the good 'ole U.S.A. are the following:

Florida State Militia

A right-wing Christian group with about 500 members led by Robert Pummer.

Guardians of American Liberties (GOAL)

This Colorado-based group wants to be the mouthpiece for militias everywhere (probably in direct competition with the Unorganized Militia based in Indianapolis).

Lone Star Militia

Leader Robert Spence (who bills himself as an Imperial Wizard of the True Knights of the Ku Klux Klan) says he heads up 11,000 militia members. Most of them are finding some place to fart at chili cook-offs.

The Republic of Texas Militia

A hundred and fifty years ago these guys would have gotten some respect. In fact, Sam Houston would have been at the helm. But it's the late 1990s, so, instead, we get a demento named Richard McLaren, who refers to himself as the Ambassador of the Republic of Texas. The RTM emerged in 1995 with the agenda seceding Texas from the union, claiming the state was annexed illegally in 1845. The "ambassador" took a couple of hostages in April 1997 to grab some PR, but now is without portfolio in some Texas dungeon.

Militia of Montana (MOM)

John Trochman heads a little family-run militia in the wide-open, "Negro free" lands of Montana. This white supremacy group is reported to be working closely with the Aryan Nations Church in Hayden Lake, Idaho.

Northern Michigan Militia

It's cold in Michigan, so cold that it can freeze the rational parts of most folks' brains. Considering the inclement weather and "band together or freeze" syndrome, it seems that joining a militia is the next favorite activity after ice fishing. Commander Norm Olsen manages to combine his skills as minister, gun store owner and former air force officer to lead his flock of 12,000 NMMS (Numbs?).

Police Against the New World Order

Although we couldn't find a *Yellow Pages* listing for the New World Order (we couldn't figure out if it was a Chinese restaurant or a church), apparently this group thinks "it's" out there. Probably the most famous and visible of the groups, PANWO is captained by former Phoenix police officer Jack McLamb. McLamb was last seen nationally doing some expostulating and mugging for the camera with Bo Gritz at the ill-fated Waco compound.

Texas Constitutional Militia

Once headed by Jon Roland, the group claims 1500 members in 30 separate groups.

Unorganized Militia of the United States

Created by Linda Thompson, a lawyer from Indianapolis whose specialty seems to be suing the Federal government. The only nationally organized militia with far, far less members than the 3 million their PR claims.

The Babylonians

President Bill Clinton

The current rash of domestic terrorism—not seen since the bombings by radical students in the 1960s and early 1970s—must be driving the man nuts. Responding to what Clinton termed "a wave of crime and violence" in America, the Senate passed a modified version of the President's crime bill in September 1994. It's difficult to say whether politicians are echoing public anger over crime or fueling it. Although most Americans believe the levels of crime have increased in recent years, some statistics say that they have indeed dropped. Whereas police statistics show that violent crime affects more than 180 Americans for every 100,000—up from 100 people in 1973—a recent National Crime Victimization Survey has shown the actual level to be slightly lower than 100 people per every 100,000.

Executive Working Group on Domestic Terrorism

This secret task force meets at the Justice Department every couple of weeks and plots strategy against the burgeoning number of boy scouts-turned-Abu Nidals. How much damage they're doing isn't certain, but since its inception in late 1995, the number of FBI investigations into militias around the country has increased 300 percent. The group is privately being called instrumental in stopping a Texas terrorist from blowing up Austin's IRS office in 1995.

The Mob

The Russians

The Russians started coming in the late 1970s and early 1980s—300,000 in all—when the Soviet government temporarily lifted immigration barriers allowing persecuted Soviet Jews to emigrate. Included in this batch was what the FBI terms as "second-echelon" criminals, who settled in Brighton Beach in Brooklyn. They basically beat up on each other, and the Feds stayed out of it. The second wave arrived after the collapse of the Soviet Union, when Russia upped the number of visas to the U.S. from 3000 a year to nearly 33,000—a more than 10-fold increase. Savage and unrepentant, the Russian mob counts on fear to scare its enemies—and doesn't think twice about wasting cops. In 1994, the FBI—with the help of the Russian Ministry of Internal Affairs (MVD)—got a tip on a top Moscow crime boss, Vyacheslav Ivankov, who was coming to New York to oversee the gang's U.S. operations. Ivankov was under surveillance once he got to the States and then made the mistake of extorting a couple of Russian emigrés who owned a Wall Street investment consulting firm. To show he was serious, Ivankov had one of the targets' father show up dead in a Moscow train station. Ivankov was later busted and ended up spitting at and kicking reporters after he was fingerprinted. The Feds have a lot more to learn about the Russian gangsters, who one MVD official categorized as "very tough, very smart, very educated and very violent." (See "Dangerous Things")

The Triads and Tongs

The FBI knows quite a bit more about the Chinese *triads*, *tongs* and street gangs than they do about the Russians. The Chinese population in the U.S. has been spiraling for decades and have provided a far more penetrable profile for the Feds. They're well aware of the three tiers: the Hong Kong–based *triads*, the secretive criminal families that were on the scene well before the Sicilian mafia; the *tongs*, which are ostensibly Chinese-American business associations, but in reality crafty overseers of devious doings; and the Chinese-American street gangs brought in as enforcers. The *triads* and *tongs* do their biggest business bringing Chinese white heroin into the U.S., but also dabble in the smuggling of Chinese illegal aliens. The *triads* get them to Mexico, or somewhere else knockin' on Uncle Sam's door, where the *tongs* take over and put the illegals to work at slave wages in sweat shops and whorehouses. For their freedom, they have to pay off the *tongs* from US$30,000–$50,000.

Cosa Nostra

See "In a Dangerous Place: New York City."

Right Wing Groups

There is a movement afoot in America, distrust of big government and a need to push back. There are two dispossessed groups in America. The first is the large groups of racial minorities who live in the inner cities; the other is the much larger group of whites who for whatever reason cannot avail themselves of the American Dream. Most of these folks are content to listen to Rush Limbaugh and throw empty beer cans at Bill Clinton on TV. Others gather together and create groups that commiserate and plot. Few ever do anything meaningful, but they do exist.

Luckily, none of the right wing whacko groups are under the players sections. Although the names sound interesting, even a brief review of their political agenda or beliefs will convince you that many of these folks aren't firing on all cylinders. Most groups are poorly financed, loosely organized, like guns, think small, have few members, drink a lot of beer, live in the woods and usually have a pot-bellied leader who likes to go by a goofy name as exalted something or grand poobah.

The guys who do decide to get violent practice a pattern of violence similar to the "calendar terrorism" we saw executed by the leftist groups of the 1970s, when attacks coincided with specific historical events. Their MO is mostly bomb attacks. Explosives-related arrests accounted for 22 percent of criminal incidents involving extremists in a two-year period ending in December 1996. The bombmakers rely heavily on the Anarchist's Cookbook (*http://www.murzik.com/book*) for their lethal recipes. None have graduated to building nuclear devices (*http://www.pal.xgw.fi/hew*).

The 1997 number of incidents of political violence is expected to eclipse the previous high of 44 in 1995.

Klu Klux Klan

The Klan is probably the most well known hate group in the U.S. Known for decorating the south with flaming crosses, they now are more of a parody of the old guard right wing in America. Some people jokingly estimate that most remaining Klan members are actually FBI plants. (It could also be those dorky bed sheets they have to wear.) The Klan in North America has some proponents like Louis Beam (leader of the Fifth Era Klan) of Texas and Dennis Mahon (who leans more towards Tom Metzger's WAR movement) of Oklahoma who demand revolutionary violence. There are Klan-lite groups like the one led by Arkansas-based Thomas Robb who portray the Klan as the white man's nonviolent NAACP. For now they are targets of the FBI and left wing groups who prosecute the group on behalf of its victims for any hate crime.

White Aryan Resistance (WAR)

WAR is a group led by Tom Metzger, a television repairman who lives in rural Fallbrook California. He lost everything he had in a landmark lawsuit which determined that he and the activities of his group were responsible for the beating and death of a man in the Pacific Northwest.

Christian Identity Groups

It's hard to believe that you could get enough people for a cocktail party under the premise that the most egregious "theft of culture" in human history was perpetrated by Satan and the Jews to dispossess the Anglo-Saxon and kindred peoples of their birthright but there are Christian Identity groups that use this basic pretext at their core. These folks also believe that the world is heading into an apocalypse soon. These folks blame the Jews for making them live in trailer parks and shanties and say that it will be payback time when the millennium rolls around.

National Alliance

The National Alliance is a Neo-Nazi group begun after leader William Pierce wrote a book called the *Turner Diaries* (under the pen name of Andrew McDonald). The radical right wing adopted the book about a Neo-Nazi underground group that kills Jews, blacks, and those whites guilty of "racemixing," as part of an effort to overthrow a Jewish-dominated government. The *Turner Diaries* is one of Timothy McVeigh's favorite books.

Odinism

Odinism is a Christian-based type religion that also includes ritual magic, anti-Semitism, and a desire to get back to the good old days when the Aryan race (Nordic/Germanic) was cool. Fellowship, Wiccan witchcraft, and a supremacist bent make this religion popular with white groups. Odinism has followers in Scandinavia, Germany, South Africa and America. Asatru is a belief much like Odinism, except for the racist part.

Mountain Kirk

The Mountain Kirk is Robert Miles' take on a medieval French sect called the Cathari. Miles passed on in 1992.

The Order

Robert Mathews' group known as the Order is a scrambled omelette made up of skinheads and National Socialists who are also Odinists.

Church of the Creator

Church of the Creator was created by a charismatic and highly authoritarian leader Ben Klausen who ministers via mail order. The COC centers on the belief that all religions are false since Christianity was built on a Jewish fable. Reverend Ben (he called himself "Pontifex Maximus") said that "creativity" is the thing, a blend of militant atheism, health faddism and racism is where it's at. The problem is that Ben offed himself, and his followers can still be found primarily in Europe and the U.S.

Posse Comitatus

Posse Comitatus founded by William Potter Gale fights the idea of income tax.

The Army of God

Not to be confused with Hezbollah (meaning "Army of God"), this group has taken responsibility for a series of early-1997 bomb attacks on gay discos and abortion clinics in Atlanta. The group has known sympathies with the Branch Davidian sect which got burnt to a crisp by federal authorities in April 1993. A gay disco bombed by the group was characterized in one press release as a "sodomite bar."

Revolution 2000

A shadowy group (or single individual) which is currently threatening a number of U.S. military institutions with attack. So far, the faction's actions have been bombast only.

Phineas Priesthood

The PP is ultra-right group known for its attacks on cops and gays. The PP has been characterized as "one of the most violent ideologies in the extremist movement today."

Skinheads

The Anti-Defamation League estimates that there are a minimum of 3500 skinheads in the U.S. *DP* does not know how many of them are actually prematurely bald men.

Passport required. The United States has over 20 different types of visas indicating different reasons for travel. Visa type and length varies by country. Travelers from selected countries can stay for up to 90 days without a visa. New Zealand and Australian nationals need visas, not necessary for British citizens. Contact the nearest U.S. embassy or consulate to obtain visa information and requirements.

However you want. The United States possesses perhaps the most modern and comprehensive transportation systems in the world, both private and public. As public transportation in the U.S. is not nationalized, you can expect different levels of service in different areas. Whereas New York City possesses an intricate public transit infrastructure, public transit in Los Angeles is still in the development stage. However, intercity and interstate transportation links in the U.S. are considered excellent. Problem areas are principally inner-city areas at night. Avoid late-night trips in these areas due to the increased probability of crime.

Nevada

According to crime statistics, Nevada is the most dangerous state in the country, and has been since 1996. It is followed by Florida, Louisiana, Maryland, California, Arizona, New Mexico, Illinois, Tennessee and Alaska.

Miami

Florida has the second highest crime rate of all 50 states and Miami is America's second most dangerous city. In 1995, 41.3 million tourists flowed through Florida, so it may not seem like a big deal when one or two of them are offed. A Dutch tourist couple on their way to a shopping center in west Dade was robbed and murdered on February 23, 1995. After a brief respite of two years, it seems that the tourist death toll is beginning to climb again. The Dutch tourists were lost in the seedy area of Liberty City in Dade County in the mid-morning. Many tourists are victims of bump-and-rob scams in which the perpetrator rear-ends the victims on the highway and then robs them as they pull over to exchange info. Miami is home to thieves who like to create confusion by spilling food, asking directions or bumping into you while their accomplice grabs your belongings. These folks tend to be from South America. In July 1997, fashion designer Gianni Versace was gunned down by a homosexual serial killer in Miami's trendy South Beach. Haitian seamen have been dropping like flies on freighters at Miami's docks. A July 1997 massacre aboard one freighter left six Haitian crewmen dead in an ongoing series of assaults on cargo ships by bad guys looking for drugs to steal. And speaking of drugs, the DEA's Miami office confiscated 16,465 pounds of cocaine during the first nine months of fiscal 1996. That was more than five times the amount seized in Houston and four times the amount nabbed in L.A. during the same period. In 1996, the U.S. Customs Service seized 70,000 pounds of cocaine, an increase of more than 50 percent over 1995. The Cali cartel makes Miami its North American home, and the DEA says South Florida is home to more cocaine traffickers than it was a decade ago. Sonny Crockett, where the hell are you?

Atlanta

This southern city has the dubious distinction of possessing one of the highest crime rates in North America. The FBI headed a counterterrorism network to neutralize any terrorist threats at the 1996 Olympic Summer Games in Atlanta. Then a pipe bomb allegedly planted by a "good ole boy" killed two innocent people and injured nearly 200 other attendees (the suspect was later deemed innocent). The Army of God was busy in Atlanta in 1997, bombing an abortion clinic and a gay disco. In January and February of 1996, there were 29 bomb threats in Atlanta. During the same two months of 1997, there were a whopping 112.

Los Angeles

The men (and women) in blue that patrol the home of gangsta' rap are proud to announce that crime is actually down in L.A. Whether it is our videotaped beating of traffic offenders, turning thugs into music stars or putting on top-rated trials of former football heroes, L.A. must be doing something right. Total crime fell from 312,415 to 278,352 during a recent two-year period. Murders were down from 1076 to 846. It would appear that no one has notified the 1140 street gangs that rule the night in L.A.'s poor neighborhoods. There are an estimated 142,000 gang members in L.A.'s South

Central—10,000 make their livings simply by selling crack—and the strip that connects downtown to the harbor like a digestive tract is still the most dangerous place in L.A. Apart from the 230 black and Latino gangs identified by the L.A.P.D., there are some 80 Asian gangs that specialize in burglary and carjackings. The L.A.P.D. has started issuing shotguns to its motorcycle officers to meet "the firepower carried by many criminals."

Nonetheless, there are nearly 2000 willful homicides annually in the county, a place where folks can get away with murder. Only half of all homicide investigations result in arrests and charges. There's a conviction in only a third of the cases. In the early 1990s, murders involving gang members accounted for 38 percent of the cases. The figure is up to 45 percent today.

L.A. is also the bank robbery capital of the world. There were 1126 of them in 1996, though down from 2641 in 1992. Eighty percent of the heists are drug-related. Although the number has dropped, the ferocity in their execution hasn't. North Hollywood was turned into a war zone on February 28, 1997 when two gunmen in full III-A body armor, and packing AK-47s and an HK91A3 converted to full auto, took a Bank of America and then took on the L.A.P.D. The crooks sprayed the cops with nearly 100 rounds in the Bank of America parking lot. Civilians and cops dropped like flies. Thoroughly outgunned, some of the officers sped off to a local gun shop to level the playing field. When it was all over the bad guys were dead, but not before they wounded 11 police officers and six civilians. Just to the south of L.A., in Orange County, so-called "takeover" robberies, where gunmen take customers and tellers hostage, jumped 140 percent between 1994 and 1996.

New Orleans

It's not the bad guys here that make "The Big Easy" so damned uneasy. It's the cops. The 1285-member New Orleans Police Department can be considered the most corrupt and brutal major city force in the U.S., according to an FBI investigation into police abuses of civil liberties and overall corruption. Since 1993, more than 50 NOPD officers have been arrested on felony charges, including murder and rape. A few years ago, the week before Rodney King was clobbered by the cops in L.A., one *DP* writer was arrested and beaten by the police in New Orleans—he was hauled in on drug trafficking and prostitution charges after he had been seen giving an impoverished black guy (he's white) a few dollars for directing him to an ATM in the French Quarter. But the good-ole-boy attorney network in N.O. went to work for him. His attorney played golf with a prominent judge a few days later and got the charges dropped—and it only cost the writer five grand. During a subsequent attempt to sue the department and the city, he was informed that the highest damages he would receive would total no more than $3000, that the city was bankrupt and that any damage award would be paid over 18 years.

Although the murder rate dropped 14 percent in New Orleans in 1995, the city still possesses highest homicide rate of any major city in the country: 75 murders for every 100,000 residents. In the city's public housing developments, the murder rate is about 18 times higher than the nation's. In the French Quarter, it is best to stay south of North Rampart Street and keep to the center of the street. Do not stop if someone asks you for the time. The housing projects are rife with crime—Desire, Florida and B.W. Cooper are the worst. Do not visit the cemeteries after dark.

Anchorage, Alaska

Yes, Anchorage, though we hate to say it. This city of 260,000 has finally caught up to the 20th century. There are drive-bys, crack houses, handguns and Uzis—in the hands of teenagers. There were more than 25 homicides in Anchorage in 1995, tying a record. The Crips and the Bloods are here. Even the Mexican and Asian gangs have arrived, all wearing colors. And the legal climate in Alaska offers a warm welcome to young criminals and thugs, if the weather doesn't. Under Alaskan law, first- and second-time juvenile offenders are typically punished with a letter that is sent to their parents from authorities. "We still have laws from the 'Leave it to Beaver' era," Alaska Governor Tony Knowles said, "for thugs from the 'Terminator' age."

Still Murder Central

City	Total	Rate per 100,000
Washington	397	73
New Orleans	351	72
Richmond, Virginia	112	55
Atlanta	196	47
Baltimore	328	46
St. Louis	166	44
Detroit	428	43
Birmingham	113	42
Newark, New Jersey	92	35
Jackson, Mississippi	67	34
USA Average	19.224	7

Source: USA Today, FBI Uniform Crime Reports

Schools

School used to be a simple red building with a bell on top and belle inside. Today, some high schools use metal detectors and armed security guards to keep the peace. Recently in Los Angeles, a five-year study proved once and for all that schools are safer than the neighborhoods around them. For example, gun use was down from 391 reported incidents in 1990–91 to 291 in 1994. Assaults were down to a paltry 99, battery almost disappeared at 686, and assault with a deadly weapon was a nonevent with only 291 incidents of students, teachers or school employees being attacked or threatened with knives, pipes and guns. Child molestation and rape was edging up to 477 incidents, and robbery (to buy more guns?) was up at 461. Incidents of marijuana usage at school were exploding from 185 in 1990–91 to 729, and burglaries were almost nonexistent at 946. If you want to know which age group was responsible for all this raping, shooting, burning, stealing, beating and doping, it was 14-year olds. Remember these are the crime statistics just for L.A. *schools.*

Fast Food Joints

Food service ranks fourth among the world's most dangerous occupations, behind cab drivers, liquor store employees and police officers. How frequently are fast food chain employees whacked? Of the 52 U.S. murders which occur each day, food service employees are the victims in two of them.

The South

The southern states lead the U.S. in per-capita murder rates. Seven of the 10 states with the highest murder rates are in the South. The U.S. is the most murder-prone country in the developed world.

The Golden Gate Bridge

San Francisco's Golden Gate Bridge has the dubious distinction of being the most popular bridge for death. The Golden Gate Bridge District is finally getting around to considering a US$3 million steel wire fence to erected across the bridge's span as a suicide barrier. More than 1000 people have leapt to their deaths from the bridge since 1937, the year it opened.

Minnesota During the Winter

A Minnesota home is the most dangerous place in the state to be when it comes to fire. There were 40 residential fire deaths in the state in 1994. By November 1995, that year's death toll had swelled to 62—still early in the home heating season. The most dangerous time of the year? The week between Christmas and New Year's Day, when winter heating, decorative lights, holiday cooking and too much booze make Minnesota such a kinetic kettle of embers that the state fathers are considering flying in B-17s from California and placing Red Adair on 24-hour call at the Wisconsin border. Ouch.

Minneapolis

While murders are going down in some major U.S. cities, the rate is soaring in Minneapolis (pop. 368,383)—approaching even those found in New York and Washington, D.C. By the middle of August 1995, Minneapolis had already topped its yearly record for homicides; there were 67 killings by mid-August, four more than the total for all of 1991, previously the city's deadliest year. Nearly three-quarters of the victims were black, although blacks make up only 13 percent of the population.

The Most Dangerous Cities in the U.S.

Although Uniform Crime Report (UCR) statistics released by the FBI show a slight decrease in overall crime, the report found that minorities remain in the grasp of a major crime wave. Black teens between 16 and 19 years are becoming victims of serious crimes at nearly seven times the national rate. Blacks in America are three times more likely than whites to be victims of violent crimes. Cities with the highest populations do not necessarily possess the highest crime rates.

	Most Dangerous	Safest
1.	Newark, NJ	Amherst, NY
2.	Atlanta, GA	Thousand Oaks, CA
3.	St. Louis, MO	Irvine, CA
4.	New Orleans, LA	Simi Valley, CA
5.	Detroit, MI	Sunnyvale, CA
6.	Baltimore, MD	Virginia Beach, VA
7.	Miami, FL	Livonia, MI
8.	Washington, D.C.	Madison, WI
9.	Flint, MI	Lancaster, PA
10.	Birmingham, AL	Mesquite, TX

Source: F.B.I. and city crime statistics, Morgan Quinto

Murder

About 52 people are murdered each day in the U.S. In 1996, 19,224 people were whacked (compared with 21,600 in 1995). The U.S. homicide rate is 17 times greater than Japan's, and 10 times the rate in Germany, France and Greece. Louisiana has the highest homicide rate in the country, with 18.5 murders per every 100,000 people. Anywhere in the South is dangerous; the southern states possess the highest rates in the country. But the place where you're most likely to be snuffed is in the nation's capital; a whopping 66.5 people are murdered in Washington, D.C., for every 100,000 people. Males between the ages 15 and 24 are most likely to commit murder. Men commit 91 percent of the murders in the U.S.

For those of you currently contemplating committing a murder (automatically pegging it as Murder One!), you might want to consider your venue. Texas leads the nation—big time—in the number of executions since 1976 at 119, followed by Virginia and Florida at 39 each. Of the death penalty states—present and past—Idaho has capped the fewest guys: only one. Fifty-six murderers were put to death in 1995 in the U.S., nearly twice as many as the year before. It was the largest number in four decades.

Being Black

African-Americans make up about half of the murder victims in the U.S. Young African-Americans are more likely to be killed than any other segment in the country.

Being an Immigrant in California

Immigrants are more likely to be wasted than people born in the United States. Between 1970 and 1972, immigrants were the victims in about 23 percent of the homicides in California, even though they represented only 17 percent of the population. Non-Latino white immigrants, most of whom emigrate from European countries, are more than twice as likely to be the victim of a homicide than U.S.-born whites.

AIDS

According to the U.S. Centers for Disease Control, in 1993, AIDS surpassed accidents as the leading cause of death for Americans between 24 and 44 years old. For every 100,000 people, about 35 die of AIDS, about 32 die in accidents. There are 275,000 adults living with HIV in the U.S. There are 4500 children under 13 with the virus.

"Redfellas"

The Russian mafia has moved into town. You knew it would only be a matter of time. In the former Soviet Union itself, there are some 5600 organized crime groups with 100,000 active members. Of the 300 crime groups that have moved abroad, 24 of them have turned up in American cities. Russian mafia in Miami reached a US$5.5 million agreement in early 1997 to purchase a Russian submarine, complete with a 62-man crew, which would be used to shuttle South American cocaine up the west coast of the U.S. to San Francisco. Although the plot was busted up by the DEA, even such intentions make the Russian "redfellas" a clear and present danger

America's Most Dangerous Highways (Fatalities per 100 Million Miles Traveled)		
1.	I-90 (Silver Bow, Montana)	6.206
2.	I-70 (Emery, Utah)	4.136
3.	I-15 (Beaverhead, Montana)	4.031

America's Most Dangerous Highways (Fatalities per 100 Million Miles Traveled)		
4.	I-25 (San Miguel, New Mexico)	3.749
5.	I-10 (Crockett, Texas)	3.511
6.	I-59 (Lamar, Mississippi)	3.342
7.	I-15 (Millard, Utah)	3.250
8.	I-27 (Lubbock, Texas)	3.233
9.	I-80 (Churchill, Nevada)	3.197
10.	I-20 (Ector, Texas)	3.108
U.S. Average		0.645

Diplomatic Immunity? Tops in Tickets

It can be assumed the foreign diplomatic in the U.S. gets away–in the name of "diplomatic immunity"–with a lot of stuff that would send the average Joe to jail for life, such as smuggling state secrets, jet fighter blueprints, Cuban cigars and Afghan heroin. But like everyone else in the greatest democracy on earth, diplomats have to pay parking tickets. These nations' diplomatic corps received the most tickets in New York City in 1996. Having the largest fleet, Russia led the way. But the DP Cheapskate Award goes to the boys from Pyongyang, with most tickets per vehicle. We don't imagine the parking change these guys figured they'd save went toward feeding its starving population. More likely Cuban cigars.

MOST TICKETS IN 1996		
RANK	COUNTRY	NUMBER
1	Russia	31,388
2	Indonesia	5706
3	Bulgaria	5527
4	Egypt	5074
5	Nigeria	3551
AVERAGE PER VEHICLE (PER MONTH)		
1	North Korea	38
2	Bulgaria	20
3	Kyrgyzstan	16
4	Russia	15
5	Kazakhstan	13

Source: Los Angeles Times

Big Rigs

While large trucks make up only three percent of all registered vehicles in the U.S., they account for 21 percent of all deaths in crashes involving two or more vehicles. In 1995, accidents involving heavy trucks killed 4903 people and injured 116,000. That makes for an average of 13 deaths every day in truck crashes. Twelve of the 13 victims are occupants of passenger cars.

Handguns and Rifles

Americans own more than 6.7 million handguns (200 million of all types of guns), and aren't afraid to use them. About one-quarter of all American adults own a firearm. On a typical day, one million adults in the U.S. are packing heat and another two million have a gun in their car. Firearms send almost 40,000 Americans to their graves each year. The deaths and injuries from shootings aren't all borne of malice. In the last year, an Indiana woman fired a .410-gauge shotgun at her foot to remove a callus. A Kentucky man shot himself in the chest "to see what it felt like," he told paramedics. An Oklahoma man got hit with the ricochet after convincing a buddy the best way to kill a millipede crossing a sidewalk is with a .22-caliber rifle. Meanwhile, in Wyoming, a House committee approved a bill that would lower the minimum age for big-game hunters to 12.

Being a Kid

Who says it's great being a kid? American youngsters are 12 times more likely to die by gunfire than their counterparts in other industrialized nations. And American children are five times more likely to be killed by any other means than their industrialized counterparts. In the U.S., the homicide rate for children under 15 is 2.57 of every 100,000, compared to 0.51 per 100,000 in other industrialized countries. U.S. kids are also twice as likely to commit suicide. The U.S. rate is 0.55 for every 100,000 children. In the rest of the industrialized world, the rate is 0.27 per 100,000. Tricks are for kids.

Being a Cop

More than 160 police officers were killed in the line of duty in 1995. California was the deadliest state, with 18 police fatalities. Florida and New Jersey had nine deaths each. Kids are mostly to blame. Between 1984 and 1993, 94 cop killers were under the age of 18. Each year, more than 66,000 police officers are assaulted and 24,000 are injured.

Sidewalks

Ft. Lauderdale, FL, is the most dangerous city in the country for pedestrians, based on fatalities relative to population and the number of people who walk to work in U.S. cities. Some 60 pedestrians die each year in this Florida city. The highest number of average annual pedestrian fatalities, however, belongs to New York City. About 310 pedestrians die on its mean streets every year. L.A. is a close second, with an average of 299 killed. Pedestrians account for 14 percent of all motor vehicle-related deaths in the U.S. each year. About 6000 pedestrians are killed each year in the U.S. and another 110,000 injured. So much for getting healthy.

Mortality

Car accident deaths among young people are most highly concentrated in the southeast. Prostate cancer deaths are highest among black men along the south Atlantic coast, and for white men along the northern perimeter of the U.S. The southeast has the highest rate of death from heart disease. Lung cancer deaths among white women is highest along the Pacific coast and the desert southwest. Most strokes occur along a belt from North Carolina to Mississippi. Call it different strokes for different folks.

Appearing on "America's Most Wanted"

During its nine years on the air, the television show "America's Most Wanted" has been directly responsible for the capture of 433 robbers, killers and kidnappers, meaning, of course, ratings for the reruns won't motivate advertisers.

Excellent health care is available throughout the U.S. Medical facilities and supplies, including medicines, are in abundance. The level of medical training of U.S. doctors is considered excellent. Foreign visitors without medical insurance will be expected to pay in cash or by credit card where accepted. No special precautions are required.

Hassles with the Police

The U.S. features one of the most disciplined and honest police structures in the world. However, there are bad apples. Prejudiced detainment of travelers is frequent. Use of excessive force, particularly in the inner cities, occurs frequently. False arrest occurs less frequently but is also common in the inner cities. Police response time in most areas of the U.S. is considered excellent. Police in rural areas are known to stop speeders and demand immediate payment for traffic violations. Refusal to pay will result in free room and board.

03/25/1996	Standoff began in Jordan, Montana, between 20 armed "Freemen" and more than 100 FBI agents after two of the Freemen's leaders were jailed over a $1.8 million fraudulent check scheme.
04/19/1995	Bombing of the Alfred P. Murrah Federal Building in Oklahoma City, which killed 167 and injured more than 400.
03/04/1994	Four convicted in the bombing of the World Trade Center.
03/01/1993	Law agents besieged Texas Davidian religious cult, after six were killed in raid at Waco.
02/26/1993	New York's World Trade Center was bombed by Islamic extremists.
06/05/1968	Robert F. Kennedy assassinated.
04/05/1968	Martin Luther King assassinated.
11/22/1963	President John F. Kennedy assassinated.
09/06/1901	President William McKinley assassinated.
07/02/1881	President James A. Garfield assassinated.
04/14/1865	President Abraham Lincoln assassinated.

Los Angeles: Having a Riot

Above Los Angeles, aboard a Delta jetliner that's been forced to deviate from its approach due to zero visibility, the result of thick black plumes of smoke billowing into the sky, the captain announces to the passenger cabin: "Ladies and gentlemen, the city of Los Angeles is in a state of civil unrest. We will be landing; however, we must urge you in no uncertain terms to use extreme caution in reaching your final destination. Lawlessness and violence exist in many areas of the metropolitan region. A Delta representative will be at the gate to advise you about which sections of the city should not be traveled through under any circumstances."

A petite dental hygienist in 26B turns and says to a long-haired record store manager from Van Nuys in 26A: "So? What else is new?"

The scene here is pure Beirut. Pillars of thick black smoke rise straight up in the hot windless afternoon. Looking down from the hill where I live, I see dozens (I counted at least 120) of puffy dark columns rising up from Long Beach in the south to the Valley to the north. Down there, people are looting, burning, killing, maiming and beating each other up. In the air over 20 helicopters circle and swoop like hawks. Onboard are video cameras with new image stabilizers that make your living room feel like the cockpit of a Huey going into a hot LZ. The cameras are in tight. Kids look up and make victory signs as they hustle six-packs, clothes, backyard toys, 19-inch televisions and even mattresses out of shattered storefront windows. Ostensibly, the black community is angered at the "not guilty" verdict in the Rodney King trial. King, a known criminal, was stopped, detained and beaten into submission. Had a neighbor not captured the scene on videotape, Rodney would have been just like any one of L.A.'s petty hoodlums. Today, he is a lucky man. His violated civil rights have elevated him to the level of celebrity.

Because the television viewers can see the expressions of joy on the faces of the looters, we know this is shopping time. These folks are tired of paying retail for the American Dream, and they are going straight for that Friday night Smith & Wesson discount. This isn't necessarily about race nor is it necessarily about anger; it's about maximizing the one benefit of being forced to live in the foul, wasted bowels of one of America's wealthiest cities. It's payback time. Poverty means not being able to buy all the things they advertise incessantly on TV. Well, now every looter in South Central L.A. is rich.

Normally, the merchants of the inner city have iron bars, security guards, video cameras, buzzers, 911 autodialers, shotguns taped under counters and fast-draw waist holsters to enforce compliance with their usurious prices. Anyone who attempts a five-finger discount (a stickup) is either gunned down, picked up, or chased down with police helicopters, dogs and car patrols. This day, the balance is out of whack, big time.

Although the police try to put a lid on the initial drunken violence, they are quickly outnumbered. Fearing for their safety, the police try using its cars to scare off the first malcontents. When the spectators start throwing beer cans and rocks at the cop cars, they beat a hasty retreat. The police are reigned in by politics and not being able to fight fire with fire. They are prisoners in their stations. When the word goes out over the news that the police are not going in, all hell breaks loose. For the first time since the '60s, America looks straight into the face of its dispossessed and blinks.

Business stops; people dash to their cars and head home. Along with most residents of L.A., the police watch the mayhem live on television and wonder how it will end.

On the street, looters are methodically knocking off liquor stores, then the big chain stores. The Koreans, the only people tough enough to run the inner-city's five-and-dimes, waited a long time for this day. They finally have a chance to use all that German and American firepower they have been oiling for years.

Any visitor to L.A.'s shooting ranges can't help but notice the Asian shooters with their black Cordura bags full of expensive and well-oiled weapons. They range from shotguns to 9mm handguns to MAC 10s and AKs, many with full-automatic capability.

As the riot rages, the Koreans luckily never get to use all their ammo and weapons. The looters think twice and focus on the national chain electronics and camera stores.

The 911 lines are jammed with terrified people who have spotted cars full of "black" men or "Hispanics" in their white neighborhoods. The police inform the people that they are responsible for the safety of their neighborhood, not for the safety of individuals or their private property. Suddenly, people start rummaging in the attic for their old WWII-era Garands, hunting rifles, even BB guns. Gun stores quickly sell out of ammunition, and the city works fast to ban gun sales as they hit record highs. People now sit in their Barca Loungers, watching the news, waiting for the first sign of looters heading into their neighborhood.

As in *War of the Worlds*, people sit glued to their television screens and radios tracking the spread of the violence. Reports come in from Beverly Hills, Santa Ana and Huntington Beach—some false, all inflated, but ominous just the same. The rioters move to the north like locusts. Along the way, some business owners, tired of living out a miserable existence, clean out their cash registers and torch their own businesses.

Coskun calls me from Istanbul. Always the photographer, he asks, "What's it like, are you getting pictures?" The world has learned that L.A is in flames and its ethnic population has risen up. I tell him that years of hard knocks have taught me that driving my nice new car into a Maelstrom of fire, smoke, bullets, looters and thugs is probably not a wise idea.

Into the night, coverage from helicopters gives us all the amazing sights of hundreds of glowing fires over the Los Angeles Basin.

Once the drinking lets up and the National Guard rolls in, the riots subside. Many proud new owners of ironing boards, car stereos and toasters can't wait to try them out. Driving through the worst hit area is no different from visiting Groxny, Beirut or any other burned-out war zone, except there are no bodies on the street and the curious splatter marks from RPGs and 50-caliber bullets are absent. In the aftermath, the civic leaders pledge to rebuild L.A. and a committee is formed to do absolutely nothing. Most inner-city business owners decide that the snow in Iowa looks a lot more inviting than the white soot that gently falls on their burned-out lot.

When it was all over, there were 52 people dead, 2383 injured, 10,000 arrested, 4500 buildings or homes destroyed and $735 million in property damage.

New York: A Night in the Life of Midtown South

Midtown South at 357 West 35th Street, near Eighth Avenue, is the largest precinct house in New York City. For officers Gene Giogio and Charlie Edmond, on the four to midnight shift, the routine this summer night starts with a swing right up Eighth. Both are young and trim, Edmond with light hair, Giorgio, dark.

Some heavy real estate money is pouring into Eighth Avenue and the entire Times Square area, which, in fits and starts, is improving. Forty-second street has drifted upward from total decrepitude marked by child pornography, to moderate decrepitude, marked by sex shops that provide shopping carts for men in suits to push through aisles marked "Tickling," "Shoes," "Spanking," "Slaves"...

Eighth Avenue has never been pretty, but beneath its grime there's always been real life and still is. As Giorgio and Edmond cruise north, they pass an Italian pork store with a 62-cent-a-pound special on pig's toes, a kosher meat market featuring the world's best pastrami, a halal meat market featuring the world's best *basterma* (which not only sounds but tastes like a distant cousin of pastrami), and further up, some totally different meat markets: lounges with three-gold-chain minimums where wise guys from the union go to pick up broads.

At 44th and Eighth is Smith's Restaurant, one of those long-established operations that's open 24 hours for a neighborhood that works 24 hours: a takeout counter, a bar the length of a bowling alley, booths, the kind of place where you can get your pleasure at 4 a.m., breakfast or a tumbler of Irish whiskey and a steak. They get a lot of trade from Midtown South.

"You see those prostitutes over there," says Charlie Edmond to me, looking over his shoulder from the driver's seat.

"Men," says Giorgio. "Over here on Eighth, most of the prostitutes are men."

The Seventh and Eighth Avenues corridor is not the most dangerous in New York, but it is periodically plagued, and will be so in the weeks ahead. Rapper Tupac Shakur will be shot in a lobby on Seventh (this is before he was fatally shot in Las Vegas in 1997), and as summer fades to autumn, a rash of knifings will overtake Eighth Avenue. A victim will be knifed, a few hours later a uniform just coming on duty will scan the report, look into space a second, then inform himself out loud: "I think we got a prior aggrieved party." Finally in October, a rookie cop, Timothy Torres, will make a collar.

As they cruise slowly past what might be a nascent game of three-card monte, an order, diluted with indecipherable static, breaks over the radio and suddenly we're shooting east across town on 42nd Street a lot faster than I'm used to. The siren wails on, and I look around to see where it's coming from.

"Mugging," says Edmond. "Grand Central. Right in front." By then, we're there. Another squad car had squealed up even earlier, and a large, muscular man, so dirty you can't tell what color he is, wearing hardly any clothes, is lying face-down on the sidewalk, handcuffed. The cops from the other car had just finished stringing their yellow tape, outside of which a crowd is gathering and inside of which there are just "the perp," the other two cops, and two college kids in shorts, looking like they're on the wrong side of the yellow tape. But nobody's asking them to leave.

The victim, an elderly woman who spoke only Spanish, has just been taken away, shivering, they say, in the heat.

The kids look mildly stunned. The front of Grand Central Station, just after dark on a pleasant summer evening, right on Park Avenue, should not be among New York's most dangerous places.

Just like that, it is over, the street is returning to normal, and, as we are getting back into the squad car, through the New York cacophony of honks, shouts and distant sirens, I catch snatches of a conversation a black man in a smartly tailored business suit is having with a liveried black doorman. *"Le probleme aujourd'hui est…"* Haitien, I think to myself, then wonder why this incidental detail in a brutal picture has stood out and induced me to jump to a conclusion. To impress on myself that this is New York? Haitians are in the news, and Haitian refugees are everywhere. But here, these men could be from Martinique, Senegal, the Ivory Coast...

Thus mulling as the lights twinkle by, there's a sudden lurch and I realize we're violating the speed limit again. Back to the West Side. A silent alarm on an office building in one of the side streets between Eighth and Seventh.

"This time of day over there, or I should better put it, this time of night over there, it's real closed up. Dark." It's the driver, Edmond, talking, as we shoot toward the intersection of 42nd Street and Sixth Avenue; the light's red ahead, and I'm hoping that at this time of night up there, drivers pay attention to sirens. "Not long ago, we're just driving around, checking things out, and up ahead we see bales of dresses getting thrown out of a window, maybe six, seven stories up, must have been thousands of 'em. Later we hear it's been going on. Perps ran, but two weeks later, they're collared."

"Thing is, you never know what you're going to run into there," says Giorgio. By now, we're coming up on the block and the siren goes off; we roll down the narrow, deserted side street. In a city where a parking place is a valued commodity, there are more dumpsters strewn along the curb than parked cars. Way ahead, a homeless guy is rooting through one of them. We pull to a stop. One light is on in the lobby, but that's it. We get out. I make a point to stay out of the way (or if you prefer, harm's way.) "Generally, it's a false alarm," says Giorgio, "and, generally, perps in this line of business don't give you trouble."

"Unless sometimes. When they get surprised," says Edmond. It comes back to me: This was a silent alarm.

"Problem building," says Giorgio.

They already have keys. They draw their.38s. After the first floor, the building is dark. At a control panel, they snap on lights, push the elevator button. From above, there's a noise. Floor to floor, along the corridor walls—if there's no one there, it's faintly ridiculous, but then how do you know when it's for real?

False alarm. No actual danger. Just the daily drumbeat of tension.

There are homeless wherever we go, not in great droves, but they're here, thanks to a byzantine system of aid that parks some of New York's poorest people on some of New York's most expensive real estate. In the theater district, they come because the pickings are good. Virtually next door to the Algonquin Hotel where the legendary round table once regularly held forth, a 300-pound woman with an amputated foot now regularly holds forth with her sweet eight-year-old son who lives there with her. They've got an address at the distant end of some subway line, but it's clearly not much, it's hard for her to get around, and this is where the money is. The conversation with Edmond and Giorgio is professional. They're just checking. She knows they can't move her. They know they can't either.

One of the homeless of Midtown South, Carlos Sam, by name, is a computer repairman. Not a former computer repairman fallen on hard times, but a computer repairman now, on the street, with no prior training beyond electronics picked up in an uncle's TV repair shop. He's illiterate, periodically delusional, crippled. He owns a jealously guarded tool box and three canvas mail carts. From discarded computer parts rummaged out of dumpsters, he's taught himself computer repair. Nowadays, he's not only a repairman, but he's in the business. For $15 to

$45, you can get a repaired monitor or keyboard. His shop is on the 43rd Street sidewalk between Seventh and Eighth.

By this hour, Carlos Sam is off the street, but this is when the porn shops, now run largely by Indians and Pakistanis, bring in their biggest bucks. "Stuff they sell isn't as rank as it used to be, and on top of that, they're mostly cheap copies, but these guys rake it in," Giorgio informs me.

The porn store is, above all, a business struggle. Landlords who rent to porn shops between 40th and 53rd get $90 to $125 a square foot. If it isn't porn, it only commands $60 to $90. Meantime other landlords are trying to light a fire under the redevelopment that slowly proceeds, anticipating a boom that may already be getting underway...if they can finally get rid of the porn. Disney is spending $34 million to renovate the extravagant, dilapidated New Amsterdam Theatre on 42nd, a 92-year-old landmark that was home to the Ziegfeld Follies. But still there are those rental rates the porn shops generate. They say one group of landlords actually went to the rabbi of a wavering colleague to help him resist.

There are other ways in which this midtown corridor is less impersonal than it seems. Timothy Torres, the Midtown South cop who collared the Eighth Avenue stabber a couple of months after our cruise through the precinct, was a college dropout, on the force barely two years, wearing the same badge, No. 4049, that his dad, Cesar, had worn as a New York cop before he resigned. Young Torres was on foot patrol the October night he saw the suspect racing up Eighth Avenue on a bike, knife in hand. He jumped the guy, and came out of it bloodied, but with considerable pride for father and son.

Another rapid-fire set of directions over the radio, again indecipherable to me.

"A heavy bleeder," Giorgio translates. "Group therapy session at this hotel, a welfare hotel, a welfare hotel for guys with AIDS actually. Terminal cases. Looks like the group therapy got out of hand, and we got a heavy bleeder."

The dispatcher's voice cracks over the radio again: "All units. Stay off the air unless you have priority. All units."

We brake to a stop, with squad cars from every direction. Cops are all over the place. They're up there for 15 minutes, a half hour. Gaunt, unshaven men in stocking caps stand about in the grim light; beefy young men in stocking caps, also unshaven, come out, an undercover team. There's tension, but when Giorgio and Edmond return, they don't make a big deal out of it.

"If it was serious, they would have had a sergeant over here."

A few minutes later, cruising up Seventh Avenue, we're flagged by a cabbie, Indian or Pakistani. His fare won't pay. Fare is out of the cab by now, a little stocky, substantial, middle-aged guy in a suit, maybe a little tight but not obviously drunk, and meantime he's quiet, even sort of fatherly with the cops, who ask him what the trouble is. He doesn't have the money? Come on, he says. A wad is discreetly flashed. He's getting a little more fatherly. So what's the trouble, sir? Again, fatherly, but no direct answer.

It was going nowhere, except from fatherly to patronizing to abusive. Once they got him to pay, they let it be, but of everything that happened—the mugging, the silent alarm, the 300-pound amputee living on the street with her eight-year-old son, the heavy bleeder at the AIDS hotel—this seemed to get under their skin the most. Perhaps because of its lack of uniqueness—and that it was so unnecessary.

Across the country, about 300 cops killed themselves in 1994; that's more than twice as many as the 137 who died in the line of duty. Over the past decade in New York City, more than 20 cops have been killed in the line of duty; 64 killed themselves.

Columbia University released a study in '94 that showed NYPD officers killing themselves at a rate of 29 for every 100,000. Among the general population the rate is 12. The cops are almost always young, with clean records. The study notes that a virtually standard feature of every suicide is a statement from the department or the family or both that the suicide was personal, the job had nothing to do with it.

Christmas Eve, Timothy Torres, who had brought down the stabber in October and wore his father's badge, pulled the midnight to eight in the morning shift at Midtown South, foot patrol. A little after midnight, he responded to a call on West 43rd, where a man was distraught and raving in the lobby. Torres got him to Bellevue for treatment.

At four, he met up with another cop on foot patrol, and they went to Smith's, the landmark on Eighth Avenue, for breakfast. It was now Christmas Day. Torres shot himself in the head in a booth.

"My understanding was that he went through a divorce six months ago," said a police spokesman.

On the same street that Torres responded to the call about the man raving in a lobby, Carlos Sam is still doing business. He melts plastic spoons to solder the innards of keyboards and monitors. If you want to know if he's really fixed the thing, he uses the swivel chair, which is among his few possessions, to squeak over to a light pole, at the base of which is an electrical outlet. In fact, every light pole in New York City has an outlet at its base, usually sealed. Carlos Sam swears he only uses the ones that are already open.

—**Jack Kramer**

Coming Attractions

Over the last 10 years, there have been more than 100 wars with 20 million fatalities. So it would take a moronically optimistic person to assume that the next millennium will bring love, peace and happiness to this planet. This is the first year we sent down some star attractions to the minor leagues. Among them are Angola, Armenia, Georgia, Bosnia, Bolivia and other places we just got too damn tired waiting for something major to happen in. It would seem that most of the Coming Attractions are like '80s sitcoms—they just never go away, but then they never get big again either.

So with some trepidation and a roll of the dice, we open ourselves to possible ridicule as we present our low-budget trailer of things to come in the next *The World's Most Dangerous Places.*

Angola

Crystal Green Persuasion

Poor Angola has been downgraded from a full chapter in last year's *DP* to a coming attraction. The only pissed off rebels left are FLEC (Frente Liberacion de Enclave Cabinda) running around the oil fields in the north. Jonas Savimbi and his UNITA forces are doing a better job holding on to its oil and diamond fields in the north. Savimbi pockets $500 million a year and used to rely on Mobutu to watch his back in the former Zaire. No more. Kabila supports the current government and is eyeing the diamond fields greedily. Since Savimbi used to use the ports in Zaire to ship his booty to Europe, he is having a hard time trying to keep up the flow. When UNITA was first formed in 1966, he also had South Africa and the CIA watching his bottom and wallet. No more. For now UNITA is officially part of the MPLA (the official party in power since 1975), but it does not let the government wander into its diamond fields or the 70 percent of the country it controls. It remains to be seen how the government can coax Savimbi and his army out of the diamond fields. Currently, they are shipping troop convoys and supplies into the northeast to expand the current fighting. So what's it going to be Jonas? Green backs or bullets?

Bangladesh

Head for the Hills

The Shanti Bahani, and Shantu Larma and Chakma are fighting for tribal rights against a sea of immigrants. They and the government of Bangladesh are working under the 24th extension of the 1992 ceasefire. The rebels have been fighting for control of a 5500 sq ft. area in the Hill Tracts. They want 300,000 Bengalis expelled from the region. Since 1973, 3500 people have been killed as a result of the uprising. The government said they cannot give the Shanti Bahini self rule or expel the settlers.

The Basque Country

There's No Place Like Home

Straddling the border of France and Spain, the seven provinces of the Basque Country (or *Euskal Herria* in the Basque language of Euskaria)—three on the French side, four in Espana—stretch across both sides of the Pyrenees mountain chain all the way over to the Atlantic Coast and the Bay of Biscay. They have boundaries that harbor ethereal mists, snowcapped peaks, ancient monasteries, world-class surf spots, and semi-naked-Beautiful People resorts. And you can also toss in an abundance of ambrosia-like food and wine. Ah, but even Shangri-La was merely an illusion, and Euskadi also exudes some tricky shadow play.

The fiercely independent Basques—about 2.5 million of them—have for decades been trying to gain autonomy from both Spain and France. Simply, they'd like to establish their own homeland, an exclusive turf on which to preserve their much-older-than-the-hills traditions and language of Euskaria. And, just as simply, both the Spanish and French governments would as soon see those feisty and troublesome Basques either shut the hell up or disappear off the face of *their* respective lands. The result? The usual unpleasant loop of rebel/underdog strategies versus powerful-government-and-police tactics—i.e., terrorism.

The players have been at each other's throats and other body parts in earnest since the 1960s. Franco and his not-famous-for-humanitarianism regime had sought to crush the Basque political presence (if not the entire population) back in 1937. The Generalissimo and His Boys may have quashed the movement for the short-term but—come the '60s—the Basques' big itch for freedom reared up with a vengeance. Vengeance at least for the ETA (*Euskadi Ta Askatasuna*, or "Basque Homeland and Freedom"), the *muy* energetic militant extremist movement with a commitment to violence. The ETA advocated armed struggle for the independence of Euskadi, and its inaugural pranks included bombings, grenade attacks, and an all-out ferocious war—aimed mainly at the Spanish government down in Madrid, its power mongers and henchmen. The ETA's blockbuster wake-up call was the 1973 assassination of Francoist Prime Minister Luis Carrero Blanco. Spain, obviously, could forget about *this* unwanted bunch just disappearing into the paella.

In a seemingly good-faith attempt to appease the ETA, Euskadi was granted semi-autonomy in 1979, four years after Franco's death. Basically this translated to permitting signs in the native Euskal language to be erected along roadsides and on public buildings, along with the usual lip service about "official talks" and "future concessions." Meanwhile—lest the peasants became a little too impatient or semiautonomous, the Spanish government immediately installed its own particular brand of "safeguards" in the region, i.e., a sizable "special" police force and a veritable military occupation—plus all the predictable perks: blatant abuses of power, unfounded arrests, police brutality, and, everybody's favorite antiguer rilla cure—death squads.

Prime Minister Felipe Gonzalez, who in the 1980s claimed to be oh-so-sensitive to the Basques' plight and desire for home rule, is alleged to have had knowledge of the death squads (G.A.L.) which were in full swing at the same time of his heartfelt outpourings. Another finger is pointed at Julian Sancristobal, Spain's former Director of State Security and head of the antiterrorist unit in one of the Basque provinces—directly linking him to G.A.L. snuffing of suspected Basque separatists.

But, hey, the ETA wasn't falling for all that semi-autonomy fluff-stuff anyway. No G.A.L. death squads were going to make them run for the hills. They simply went elsewhere for support—purportedly Libya, Iran, Syria, and the Irish Republican Army—collecting explosives, arms, and post-Rambo training. Anyway, the ETA wants full autonomy. Consequently, the past two-and-a-half decades have added up to one miserable cycle of attack and retaliation. And while tourists to the Basque Country come to "take the waters"—for some of the locals and their enemies, the big soak has been one long blood bath.

What makes the Basques so damned special? They profess to be the oldest people—with the oldest language—in all of Europe. And no one can refute the claim that their origins are a mystery, their language a linguistic oddity. Scholars refer to them as "Europe's mystery people."

Long isolated in the Pyrenees border region, they are so secretive that many of their accomplishments have either been overlooked or credited to others. The Basques claim—and evidence agrees—that their fishers and whalers cruised to the New World at least a century before Columbus and his *Nina*, *Pinta*, and *Santa Maria menage a trois* ever hit the shores. Historians believe the early Basques were far more sophisticated than even the rich and shapely sunbathers over at Biarritz. Among the findings are intricate navigational aids, a fanatical precision in recording topography, a base-seven numerical system, and a whole lot of Stonehenge-era fancies.

The contemporary Basques are jovial, spirited, fun-loving and strong. Very few are members of the ETA and most deplore the violence—however, the death squads and military presence quickly turned a lot of the "can't-be-bothereds" into sympathizers (albeit silent ones). They continue to practice their culture no matter what any government entity decrees, going about their business in the mountain villages—dancing, singing, producing crafts, drinking local wine and cooking hearty meals. Most of the men play a mean game of *pelota* (a sport they invented) as well as the unique "Basque lifting"—weight-lifting with 200-kilogram-plus stones. They love contests of strength—tossing poles, dragging boulders and oxen. To prepare their famous "mountain oyster stew," specially trained shepherds simply gnaw off a sheep's testicles with one deft bite.

Originally, ETA attacks were launched on the Spanish side of the border, after which the guerrillas would head over to the French side for refuge. (The Basques refer to themselves as *Zaspiakbat*, or "the seven make only one"—united without regard to any "artificial" borders.) Since 1992, however, the French police have stepped up their crackdown on suspected terrorists—encored by France's right-wing government breathing down their necks. The ETA, to its credit, has tried to keep innocent bystanders out of its scope, predominately targeting politicians, industrialists, and civil guardsmen. Some of the larger railway stations and banks, however, have been sporadically hit by bombs. Cars with French license plates are also red-flagged. As for the police and military in the region—anyone can qualify for their brand of fun and games.

You're about as safe in the Basque Country as in most other places in Western Europe. Beach resorts, ski areas, spas, and the Tour de France route are visitor-friendly. Searches at border crossings are occasional inconveniences—and it's probably best not to linger around any railway stations or public buildings.

Bosnia Herzegovina

It is assumed that the Balkans will explode again in order to get back to its God given right to be the Balkans. For now there is a knife edge tension as U.S. troops pretend to be blind with war criminals. The good news is that over 7 million people are visiting neighboring Croatia after they spent $167 million to repair the war damage. So could Sarajevo be the next vacation hot spot?

Central African Republic

CAR Cesspool

We'd like to warn you that it is getting more dangerous, but then it never has been safe in this pocket-sized cesspool. The only thing that keeps it from turning into Liberia or Zaire is the French Paratroopers that baby-sit the potentate for a day. There are about 2500 French citizens in the country.

In May of '96 the streets were slippery with blood as the French put down another weeklong mutiny attempt. The French use CAR as a staging ground to defend Chad against Libya.

The Caucasus Region

Hatfields and Mcozkis

You know Chechnya, but you could care less about Dagestan, Georgia, Abkhazia, Ingush-Ossetia and those other unpronounceable forgettable Russian wastelands. This region is mountainous, full of warring ethnic tribes and clans and was totally messed up by Stalin in the '40s and '50s. So it's natural that pretty much every clan member, criminal, nationalist, government and military group hates, mistrusts and attacks every other group. For now, the region is full of drugs, insurgencies, mafias, criminals, corrupt politicians, corrupt Russian military and police units all trying to make a living and hoping that the pipelines from Baku into Russia will make live wonderful again. It takes more space than its worth to try to make heads or tails until things get really nasty. For now, being kidnapped or blown up should be your major concern.

Ceuta and Melilla

It's a Small War After All

DP can never be accused of painting the world with too broad a brushstroke. In these two minuscule Spanish enclaves on the north coast of Africa, it seems they have enough room for an insurgency group. The two areas were kept by Spain when they handed over Morocco in the 16th century. It has taken this long for a coalition called the "August 21" group, led by Moslem activist Mohamed Abdou, to threaten Spain with further armed attacks. The August 21 group claimed responsibility for two car-bomb attacks in April of 1995; no one was hurt. In a recent visit by the Spanish prime minister with the king of Morocco, they forgot to bring up the issue. It appears Spain shut Morocco up back in 1974, when they handed them their colony of Spanish Sahara. The August 21 group sent a threatening fax and asserted that their cause was "as holy and noble... as other nationalist groups."

China

Breaking Up is Hard To Do

China has its problems. In the next five years it is estimated that the current 100 million people who have migrated to the city to find work will swell to 200 million. Beijing has over 3 million who cannot find steady work. Forty million are unemployed. Inflation runs about 25 percent. One hundred million people are unemployed. Half of the 100,000 state owned business lose money and will be shut down or sold off. Eight hundred million peasants live a subsistence life and resent the new city based economic growth. There are serious doubts that China will be able to feed itself without importing massive amounts of food. After Xiaoping's death, things are relatively calm in China, but for how long.

If all of China's 1.2 billion people were to do anything at once, let alone jump off a wall, it would paralyze the country.

This isn't good news for tourists and even worse news for the government because tourism to China has been surging in recent years. About 1.74 million foreign tourists visited Beijing alone in 1992, compared with less than 300,000 in 1978. In the first six months of 1993, 882,600 foreigners visited the capital city, up 13 percent over the corresponding period the preceding year. Throughout China, tourism brought in a whopping US$1.69 billion in the first five months of 1993, up 22.2 percent over the same period in 1992. That figure is a record.

China possesses no known terrorist groups (that is if you ignore the entire populations of East Turkmenistan and Tibet) , but a ride on one of their domestic airliners may make you wish they did—so the plane could be hijacked to a country with decent air traffic control. Unlike in other parts of the world, hijackers in China aren't trying to draw world attention to a cause (they wouldn't get it, anyway). They're not likely to make ransom demands. And it's not done for the love of God. They're simply trying to get the hell out. Taiwan is the favored destination. There are about 10 hijackings to Taipei a year and about a dozen that are foiled.

The good news is that 4367 Chinese criminals were executed last year. About a couple more thousand were sentenced to death but for some reason they couldn't find time for the quick pop to the back of the head and a trip to the morgue to have their organs ripped out. Why good news? Well, it seems between 2000–3000 kidneys and corneas are available each year for transplant in China. Human Rights Watch has even accused China of keeping condemned prisoners alive until the organs are needed. Crimes are generally nonviolent; thefts form the bulk of them. Despite the executions, major crime incidents have risen by nearly 20 percent annually in the past four years.

If you don't want people in pieces you can also get them whole. China also has gangs that kidnap teenage women for sex trades and young boys for families that seem to plop out girls.

The Chinese Public Security Ministry has admitted the country does not have the resources to protect tourists from the rising rate of crime across the mainland. The Qiandao Lake incident may be a precursor of what's to come. There have been numerous recent incidents where tourists have been robbed, beaten and even murdered. However, in considering whether to report a crime in a country where residents can be executed for stealing a ball point pen or for hooliganism, the normal traveler is more likely to let that disposable camera go instead of making a federal case.

Dangerous Places

China loves a revolution except when other folks want to revolt. Like most dictatorships, freedom means enslaving and forcibly occupying other people's countries.

Tibet

China invaded Tibet in 1950, and, in the process, killed 1.2 million people, a tenth of the Tibetan population. China has destroyed 6,241 monasteries. There are only 13 left.

East Turkmenistan

The muslim turks don't want to be Chinese, so groups based in neighboring countries keep the revolution at a simmer.

Getting In

Passports and visas are required. Most tourist visas are valid for only one entry. Travelers are required to obtain new visas for additional entries into China. Those who arrive without a visa will be fined a minimum of $400 at the port of entry and might not be allowed to enter China (or get out!). A transit visa is required for any stop (even if one does not exit the plane or train) in China. Specific information is available through the Embassy of the People's Republic of China or from one of the consulates general in Chicago, Houston, Los Angeles, New York or San Francisco.

Chinese Embassy in the U.S.

2300 Connecticut Avenue, NW
Washington, DC 20008
☎ *(202) 328-2500.*

U.S. Embassy in China

Xiu Shui Dong Jie 3
Beijing -100600
☎ *[86] (1) 532-3831*

The Comoros

Backwater Bungle

These fragrant islands in the Indian Ocean don't seem big enough for prob lems, but things never seem to cool down (see the *Mercenaries* chapter). In August of '97 residents of Anjouan Island (under seccessionist leader "president" Abdullah Ibrahim) decided to break away–back to French colonial rule. They may be on to something since sister isle Mayotte was doing much better economically under French control. France said thanks, but no thanks.

Machete sales soared, and when the main island sent in troops, they were forced to retreat with 105 captured, 40 dead and 30 wounded. Thinking this retro independence thing was a good idea, the smallest island of Moheli decided to declare its independence from the Comoroan Federation and elected an army officer to be "president."

Corsica

The Tourist War

Petru Pogglii, born in 1940, is the leader of the Corsican Nationalist Alliance. The CNA is an offshoot of the Corsican National Liberation Front/Front Liberation National Corsican (NLNC) founded in 1976. Their headquarters is in Carbuccia.

There are about a 1000 separatist rebels in a number of small gangs, most of whom are aligned with a liberation front. The gangs spend as much time fighting among each other as they do the French. Over the last 20 years, there have been 8400 terrorist attacks and 100 deaths. A poll in 1996 showed that 86 percent of Corsicans are against independence. On July 2, a car bomb exploded in daylight in the middle of Ajaccio, killing one of leaders of the Corsican FLNC and injuring another leader seriously. About 2 million tourists visit the island each year.

Cyprus

U (N) Can Never Go Home Again

The oldest U.N. mission in the world is living testament to the fact that you can keep the kids from squabbling, but you will never make them kiss and make up. It's the Greeks versus the Turks. Both sides will tell you horror stories of what will happen once you cross the U.N. border. As usual, both sides are comprised of charming, hospitable people. There are 198,000 Turks (double compared to 1960) and 650,000 Greek Cypriots. Meanwhile, gangsters from Eastern Europe fight amongst each other for control of nightclubs and entertainers.

Ecuador

Rumble in the Jungle

What do you get when you have a border that no one can see and changes like a baking loaf of bread? And with hot heads baking it? Why, Equador and Peru, of course. Ecuador and Peru fought a war over this 1000-mile-long swamp in the Amazon basin back in 1941 and they haven't forgotten about it. In fact, they duked it out again in 1981 and almost came to blows yet another time in 1991. There was even a bullet pinball game in early 1994.

This time it's over a 50-mile stretch in the lush, jungle-covered mountains of Cordillera del Condor that would give Equador access to the Amazon and Maranon rivers—if they had it. Although no one seems to be able to prove it, the area is supposedly rich in gold deposits. Just the rumor alone is apparently enough to raise rifles.

The Protocol of Rio de Janeiro was signed in 1942 to end that first war, but Ecuador later said "screw you" after getting their hands on one of the world's first portable calculators and realizing the ramifications of losing half their territory—nearly 77,220 square miles, to Peru. The problem with the Rio Pact was that it defined part of the border between the two countries as "the river flowing into the Santiago River." Well, there are two rivers flowing into the Santiago River. Sprinkle some gold between the two and you've got a good fight. Even though Pope John Paul II has issued a call to both countries to stop the fighting, no one's listening.

Equatorial Guinea

Dictator of the Week

Coups could become a weekly event replacing soccer in this forgotten armpit of Africa. Back in 1969, Macias Nguema took over this oversized cocoa plantation and began systematically killing all his fellow politicians. By the time he was done, he had killed 50,000 of his own people, including every senior politician and civil servant, and 100,000 people, a third of the population, had fled.

When he was finally tried and executed in 1979, he had managed to spend the entire $105 million treasury. Since then, the remaining residents have been playing dictator for a week. One coup in 1986 only took 30 people to overthrow the government. Why not invite your church choir, and you too could be dictator for a day. The one good outcome is that there have been so few tourists that there technically is no tourist crime.

Greece

November 17; a Good Day to Die

The November 17 group is the most feared terrorist group in Greece and perhaps the most ruthless in Europe. The terrorist ring got its start with the December 1975 assassination of Athens CIA station chief Richard Welch while he was on his way home from a Christmas party, zapping him with what would become its signature grim reaper: a.45-caliber pistol.

Since then a.45 has been used in six more of its subsequent 20 executions, including four Americans, 13 Greeks and couple of Turkish diplomats. It doesn't sound like a particularly huge body count in these days of *Hezbollah*, GAI and Chechen whackos, but considering that not a single member of this shadowy group has been identified—much less arrested—it is. And the group has also conducted at least 35 other attacks on multi-national companies and Greek tax offices, employing bombs that suggest their construction techniques were learned in the Middle East in the early 1970s.

Of all of Europe's homegrown radical assassins, only the November 17 group remains entirely an enigma. Italy's Red Brigades and the German arm of the Red Army Faction have been snuffed. Rebel Basque, Irish and Corsican separatists have been picked off like flies by INTERPOL. Action Direct in France was similarly destroyed. But November 17's 10–25 members continue to allude all attempts to expose and drain them.

The terrorists named themselves for the day in 1973 when a student uprising at Athens Polytechnic University was crushed by soldiers and tanks sent in by the ruling military junta. These guys don't work on a single agenda. When the U.S. was supporting the military junta in Greece during the first decade of the terrorists' existence, the group blew away Americans. When Turkey occupied Cyprus in 1974, Turkish diplomats became the targets. For sure, November 17 is a Marxist outfit, professing hatred for both the U.S. and NATO, as well as the European Union. It's thought that its founding members belonged to a resistance group created by Socialist Premier Andreas Papandreou during the 1965–1975 military dictatorship. And there has been some indication that Papandreou knows who they are. But he's not talking.

The former East German police are believed to have been chummy with November 17, however attempts to retrieve information from their files have been futile. In the meantime, suspicions of connections with Middle East terror clans continue—as do .45 slugs to the head.

Indonesia

Timor Bomb

Indonesia is an archipelago of more than 13,000 islands, the largest of which are Kalimantan (Indonesian Borneo), Sumatra, Irian Jaya (West Irian), Sulawesi and Java. Nearly two-thirds of the population lives on Java, one of the most densely populated areas in the world. Sumatra contains 25 percent of Indonesia's land area and 20 percent of its population.

But it's on the far flung island of Timor where a lingering insurgency festers since the Indonesian invasion in 1975 (and annexation in 1976). The Timorese are not fond of their Indonesian rulers and continue to battle for their independence. More than 100,000 people are believed to have died in the Indonesian invasion of east Timor in 1975. About 200–450 rebels whack away at the soldiers while their leader and former poet; Jose "Xanana" Gusmao rots in Jakarta's Cipinang jail serving a 20 year sentence. Jose Ramos-Horta runs a slow steady PR campaign to keep East Timor in the limelight. The funny thing is the real ruler (according to the UN) is Portugal, not exactly known as a tread-lightly colonizer.

The Players

Ray Rala Jose "Xanana" Gusmao

Gusmao was born in the East Timorese town of Mana Luto on June 20, 1946. He studied at a Jesuit seminary and went to Dili High School. After compulsory service in the colonial forces he moved to Australia after winning East Timor's poetry prize in 1974. He became involved with the FRETILIN independence group and returned to East Timor in November 1975, a week before the invasion by Indonesia.

He became the leader of FRETILIN's military wing in 1978 and was a romantic symbol of liberation among the people. He negotiated a three month cease fire in 1978 and was captured and sentenced to life in prison in 1992. It was reduced to 20 years in 1993. His wife, Emilia, and his two children live in Melbourne.

Jose Ramos-Horta

The Nobel Peace Prize winner is Timor's biggest spokesperson and works closely with UN special envoy to Timor, Jamsheed Marker.

On the other end of the archipelago, the rebels of Aceh, on the northern tip of Sumatra, have all but ceded their war of independence.

Free Papua Movement/Organasi Papua Merdaki (OPM)

Timor isn't the only place in the archipelago with guerrillas in the midst. Often, entirely forgotten are the ragtag rebels of the Free Papua Movement (OPM), who have been fighting the Indonesian government for the independence of Irian Jaya (High Victory) with sticks, stones and rusty flintlocks for the last 30 years. Irian Jaya was supposed to gain their independence in 1965, but Indonesia decided to not leave. These guys don't get into the news that much and are often called the "T-shirt" army because they're about as trained and equipped as a Connecticut cub scout den. For now, the Indonesian government gets a third of its oil exports from Irian Jaya.

But for a group of seven unlucky foreigners, the rebels may as well be the charge of the Light Brigade. In January 1996, two Dutch researchers, four British students and a German stumbled into a solitary OPM unit, probably out gathering nuts and berries; the guerrillas found the juicy, plump, white-skinned Westerners a godsend. Just think, real live hostages—frightened Anglo pussycats—just like the kind we pick up on our satellite dish! The world, and CNN, had discovered the OPM.

Now known by the outside world, they and their supporters have taken to the streets. On March 18, 1996, thousands rioted in the Irian Jaya provincial capital of Jayapura, torching vehicles, shops and other buildings. Three demonstrators were shot dead, one a policeman who joined the rioters and was blown away by a shopowner protecting his investment. Since 150,000 people have died in this conflict and many more will. Don't expect a Visit Irian Jaya Year anytime soon.

President Suharto

Istana Negara, Jalan Veteran
Jakarta, Indonesia
Fax: (+62) 2136 0517, (+62) 2136 7781, (+62) 2136 7782 (all via Ministry of Foreign Affairs)
Suharto is the man in Indonesia. He and his family control most of country's wealth along with ethnic Chinese businessmen. His aggressive philosophy of "Mapalindo" has created wars in Borneo, East Timor, Irian Jaya.

Kenya

A Rift in the Valley

Tourism to Africa's most "civilized" country has declined due to attacks in game parks, lawlessness in the major cities and continuing tribal clashes in areas such as the Rift Valley. Tourism revenue plummeted from US$400 million in 1991 to US$295 million in 1992. The Gulf War and Somalia were a couple of good reasons. Somali bandits crossed the border and attacked U.N. relief workers in Wajir province. At least 35 security officers and 50 civilians have been killed in Wajir, Garissa and Mandera provinces. The Red Cross has suspended selected relief operations in the northern provinces due to bandit attacks and the theft of materials.

In Nairobi, armed robbers ambush expensive vehicles as they drive in exclusive neighborhoods: Mercedes Gelandwagons, Land Rover Defenders, Discoveries, Range Rovers, Toyota Land Cruisers and Isuzu Troopers are their favorite targets. In Nairobi, 1224 cars were stolen in the first six months of 1992. Twenty-five were stolen from the U.N. High Commission for Refugees alone. The M.O.: Carjackers cut off the intended victim, occasionally utilizing an accomplice to prevent a rear escape. Most carjackings take place after 7 p.m., but there have been incidents during daylight hours in populated places.

With more than half of the population of Kenya under the age of 15 and unemployment at over 60 percent, there is ample motivation for criminal behavior. Average per-capita income in Kenya is below US$450 a year. Add to the soup bloodthirsty cops and more than 330,000 refugees and thousands of automatic weapons from Somalia, and the continent becomes darker indeed. Displaced by the war in Somalia, rugged hardy bands of desperate Somali men go south in search of anything of value. Just hope you don't have what they want.

Kenyan police enjoy bragging that they've killed (not apprehended) 70 percent of the bandits operating in the game park regions. But that's little solace. There's no guarantee you won't run into elements of the other 30 percent.

No unraveling republic would be complete without a little religious clan violence. Although religion-based political parties are banned in Kenya, there are outlaws who love to whoop it up. The Mombasa-based Islamic Party of Kenya gets involved in frequent clashes with the pro-government United Muslims of Africa party. In the Rift Valley, it's everyone for themselves, as Daniel Arap Moi's Kalenjin tribe battles with the dominant Kikuyu tribe in the valley. More than 1000 people have been killed in such violence since 1991.

Laos

Bombies and Zombies

From 1964 until 1973, U.S. planes averaged one sortie every eight minutes over this unfortunate slice of Spam wedged between Vietnam and Cambodia. More than 285 million bombs were dropped over Indochina during the Vietnam War, a good number of them over Laos; a good number of those remain unexploded.

Many payloads were jettisoned by B-52s, which had to get back to their bases in Thailand in a hurry; other warplanes used Laos for target practice. But mainly, Laos was pounded into oblivion to prevent Pathet Lao guerrillas from advancing from their jungle bases in the northeast toward the capital of Vientiane, as well as to wreak havoc on North Vietnamese forces shuttling up and down the Ho Chi Minh Trail, which cuts a narrow swath through the mountains of Laos.

The Laotians call the unexploded ordinance "bombies," a cute term for the cluster bombs that today take scores of Laotian lives every month. And because farmers cannot take advantage of valuable agricultural land due to the "buried treasure," thousands more Laotians face malnourishment and starvation seemingly with zombielike indifference. In heavily carpet-bombed Xieng Khouang province northeast of Vientiane, hundreds of families subsist on virtually no food at all for three to four months of every year due to the "bombies" in the fields. These "bombies" are actually small bomblets (or cluster bombs)—but very lethal—that spill from large casings as they're dropped from aircraft. The bomblets, about the size of a tennis ball, number about 650 to the case. Covered in bright yellow plastic, they make a particular curiosity to children, who comprise 44 percent of all bomb accidents in Laos. Half these accidents result in death. You don't want to see what the other half look like. Thirty-one percent of all bomb accidents occur while children are playing, giving a new meaning to Romper Room.

There aren't many soccer fields in Laos.

Northern Ireland

McPieces in our Time

The IRA and Sinn Fien waffle back and forth between peace and bombing. For now it's peace talks. It would be very hard to foresee any peaceful solution to clear away centuries of anger and hate.

Morocco

Beach Blanket Bingo

The government of Morocco informs us that there are currently 30 foreign-backed Islamic fundamentalists working to advance its causes. Gee, do you think it might have something to do with the fact that the Moroccan military grabbed 102,675 square miles of desert without asking? The war began in 1975 when Spain pulled out and Morocco moved in. Polisario Front was created in 1973.

Quite a windfall, when you consider all the heat Israel gets for grabbing only a cactus or two from its neighbors. Technically, the 17-year war with the Polisario Front was wrapped up in 1991, but the peace talk invitations probably didn't get delivered at every camel stop. For now, the Moroccans are doing a tidy business cultivating and exporting ganja (about US$2 billion a year), and are crossing their fingers that nobody asks them where they got all that extra beachfront property to the south. Give 'em a shout.

Sa Majeste Roi Hassan II (His Majesty King Hassan II)

Bureau de sa Majeste le Roi, Palais Royal
Rabat, Maroc (Morocco)
Telex: 0407 31744, 0407 32908,
Telegrams: sa majeste le roi, Rabat, Maroc (French or English)

Panama

Down in Noriegaville

Panama is a mean, dirty poor little place. Bombs continue to go off in public places and there's still a holdout group left that just can't get over the days when their nostrils were packed with speedballs. The M-20 Group (or 20th December National Liberation Group, named after the date the U.S. invaded Panama) is made up of Manuel Noriega's old drinking buddies. These former Panamanian Defense Force folks don't have much of an agenda or even a good press agent. Their goal is to oust the occupiers of Panama and bring the current political administration to justice as traitors. Most of the 600–900 murders committed each year are by people under the age of 18.

Senegal

Lovelorn

Sengal's southern Casamance Province has been home to the Movement of Democratic Forces of Casamance (MFDC) since 1982. They are fighting for autonomy from the central government citing neglect. They continue to indulge in shoot-outs, looting, and throat slitting incidents. Four French tourists never returned from one deadly region in April of 1995, and locals are occasionally found slaughtered like sheep. Although the government will tell you everything is hunky dory, 50 rebels attacked a military camp in August.

South Africa

Tied Apart

A British Consumers Association survey has claimed that South Africa is one of the world's most dangerous places for tourists. It estimates that 5 percent of all tourists that visit are attacked or robbed. South Africa has the dubious distinction of having the highest crime rate of any country not at war. With about 61.1 murders per 100,000 people, South Africa has the dubious distinction of being the rape capital of the world with 119.5 per 100,000 people. The government thinks only one in 20 rapes is reported. Some sources only 20 percent of commercial crimes are reported and only half of regular crimes are brought to the police's attention. The good news? The average murder victim is killed with a knife or a broken bottle by an acquaintance with whom he had got into a drunken weekend brawl, according to Reuters. So make sure you order your beer in paper cups. Crime is on a downward trend.

Most of the crime is in Joburg, and though Mandela has instituted some tough new laws, the average case load for a cop is 47 crimes. So it's no surprise that about half go unsolved. Residents actually considered a plan by prison boss Khulekani Sitlole to put violent criminals in mine shafts.

What do politicians do when things get tough? Why, give themselves a raise of course. Mandela's predecessor, F.W. de Clerk, pulled down US$73,817 a year as well as US$6000 for expenses. He also received a US$77,770 car allowance every four years. And he didn't drive to the U.N. once. Mandela, on the other hand, decided he was going to make up for what he had been missing all those years in prison and he bumped his compensation to US$191,660 a year. The average annual wage in South Africa for whites is about US$4000; blacks in the townships make considerably less. Members of parliament aren't complaining though they jacked their salaries from US$34,160 up to US$44,720.

More good news? An ominous force that has arisen to counter crime is PAGAD (People Against Gangsterism and Drugs). PAGAD is a Muslim anti-drug group out of Cape Town who began in 1996 by executing a local drug heavy in the Cape Town suburbs. They seem to be effective since for the first time anywhere, about 2000 gangster and drug dealers actually protested in front of Parliament seeking protection from the police. One gang leader was shot 72 times and set on fire by a PAGAD member. The bad news? It seems that PAGAD is alleged to have direct ties with Hezbollah and Hamas.

President Nelson Mandela
☎ *(012) 21-2222; FAX (012) 323-3114*

Beemmer the Redeemer

In response to the public impression in South Africa that BMWs are thieves' and carjackers' most sought-after automobiles, the German luxury car manufacturer–to protect its market share–has taken the unusual step of including anti-theft and hijacking insurance in the price of a new BMW model. In 1994, vehicle thefts rose nearly 30 percent over 1993 in South Africa to 110,000. The figure in 1995 was expected to be higher. During the first 11 months of 1995, 9400 vehicles were seized by armed groups and 43 drivers murdered in Gauteng province alone (which includes Johannesburg and Pretoria).

But the biggest problem for BMW is the public misconception that BMWs are more often targeted than other makes, prompting soaring insurance premiums on BMWs that often climb as high as 25 percent of the vehicle's retail value (from a typical rate of 5–10 percent). BMW's eminence as the Holy Grail of hoodlums and hooligans is fodder for the cocktail party circuit, but indeed isn't data-based. In fact, the police and insurance companies rarely release a breakdown of statistics showing which makes of cars are favored by crooks and cods. But South Africa's National Crime Information Center did mistakenly leak numbers revealing that BMW wasn't any more prone to theft than other makes–that, in truth, the cars are stolen in numbers commensurate with or below the percentage of the automaker's market share in South Africa (6.19 percent of all vehicles stolen or hijacked; 7.59 percent market share). Toyotas are most often ripped off.

BMW is taking the fight even closer to the Bimmer-busters; the company is providing police, free of charge, with 100 of its most powerful models to chase down carnappers and other culprits.

The Spratlys

Makin' Mischief

These flyspeck islands are custom-made for an international dispute. This group of islands just north of Borneo is floating on oil close to nowhere. China, Brunei, the Philippines, Vietnam and anybody else in the neighborhood who has a half-assed reason to lay claim to these isles is talking tough and showing off military hardware like gangs in a schoolyard. China has occupied the aptly named Mischief reef. The Philippines sent its entire fighter airforce (nine planes) to sit nearby and look tough. The other countries have gone running to the world court to mediate. Meanwhile, China has built ramshackle fishing-boat shelters to get squatters rights. Looks like the court may have to separate the kids in this messy divorce.

Taiwan

The Seed of World War III

Chinese Premier Li Peng is not happy with Taiwanese President Lee Teng-hui, who's considering taking the lethal gamble of declaring Taiwan's independence from Mother China. The scarlet latter considers Taiwan a renegade province and will not tolerate such tomfoolery. China has been doing military "exercises" in the Taiwan Strait, lobbing missiles to within a few hundred meters of the Taiwanese coast, just to let the islanders considering independence know the next volley will fall on their heads. The U.S. Navy, in March 1996, sent two carrier groups close to the Strait in a show of force as the Chinese continued to splatter rockets into the waters off Taiwanese beaches. Sunbathers beware. If China decides to take the island by force, they've got a billion or so people who can help them out in the operation. Will Uncle Sam let it happen? Probably. Hell, it's confusing enough with two Congos, why do we need two Chinas? Will Beijing back off at American threats? Doubtful. The skies again could be gill-netted by MiGs and F-16s, duking it out over Formosa. This wouldn't be any Cold War, folks. China invading Taiwan would be the real thing.

MR. DP'S
LITTLE BLACK BOOK

Save the People

I always get a little nervous when I see the amount of money and time that goes into helping the cause of animals—whether it's celebrities demonstrating on camera or an auction to help an endangered species. The images of small children dying of starvation and disease seem to have less impact on the general public than the image of a baby seal having its brains bashed in.

Civilization is a machine that does not offer an instruction manual. Humans are constantly learning cause and effect the hard way. Cut down trees to grow crops, and the dirt washes away. Start a war over oil, and an entire nation is plunged into the Middle Ages. Pocket aid money from Western governments and use it to go shopping in Paris, and entire populations starve. We don't see the cause a lot of times, but we do see the effect.

These days, the hides of Americans are thicker than that of the endangered rhino. Reality TV shows spawn like flies from maggots, and people watch the pain and suffering of total strangers interrupted every eight minutes by commercials selling toothpaste and new cars. The 4 o'clock, 6 o'clock, 7 o'clock, 8 o'clock, 9 o'clock and 10 o'clock news cut together the world's woes and wars into 15 minutes, complete with snazzy graphics, logos and maps. Designed to stop channel surfers and fire freaks, television zooms in with nice clean images of blood, explosions, screaming and "you are there" action. The trouble is, you aren't there, and even if you are, television makes it seem more distant and less painful. Anything too disturbing can be cast away with a simple click of the remote control.

People helping people can make a difference. Whether it be teaching kids a song or working for 10 years for their indigenous rights, every time you do something for someone, you change his or her life. Dangerous places need people who can help push back the danger. You don't need to be a bomb disposal expert or a facial reconstruction doctor to make a difference; by simply picking up a shovel you can do wonders.

Those seeking a productive outlet for their urges to make the world a better place should look into the variety of groups that strive for global peace. Many of the groups are bad hangovers from the Cold War era. Some engage in endless discussion to provide solutions, while other groups get their hands dirty, and clean up the mess. We would advise you to investigate the results of a group's efforts rather than its intentions. Don't waste your time polluting the world with more hot air.

The more people who look for solutions and actively carry out the remedies, the better off the world will be. There are groups that can provide an outlet for your need to make the world a better place. Some require major commitments of time; others can take your money and put it toward projects that do good. There is no way we could list every charitable organization that seeks to elevate the position of people in the world, but here is a start:

Life Enhancers

American Field Service Intercultural Programs

220 East 42nd Street, Third Floor
New York, New York 10017
☎ *(212) 949-4242, (800) 876-2377,*
FAX (212) 949-9379
Since 1947 AFS has been a global leader in promoting intercultural understanding through high school student exchanges. AFS offers U.S. students more than 100 programs in 46 countries around the world. Students live and study abroad for a year or a semester of high school. Or they can take time out between high school and college to do valuable community service work in another country. AFS also offers opportunities for families and high schools in the United States to host selected students from 50 countries who come to live and study in America for a semester or a year.

Amnesty International USA

322 Eighth Avenue
New York, New York 10001
☎ *(212) 807-8400*
Amnesty International likes to shine light in dark places. When the London-based organization organizes the dissemination of thousands of letters, they tend to send jailors and governments scattering like cockroaches scurrying for cover. By showing these governments that they are aware, they hope to embarrass or pressure governments into better treatment of political prisoners. Their method is simple and easy to effect. They coordinate the writing and mailing of letters to the captors of prisoners of conscience. Their methods have been proven successful and the international group was awarded the Nobel Peace Prize in 1977 for their efforts to promote observance of the U.N. Universal Declaration of Human Rights.

The membership is over 500,000 people in over 150 countries. Together, they can create an avalanche of mail and global protest over the mistreatment of prisoners. Amnesty International has groups that focus on health needs, legal support, human rights awareness and education and even a writers group that writes three prisoner appeals each month to government authorities. There is an Urgent Action network which will step up the pressure to aid prisoners who are in immediate danger of execution or torture.

Amnesty International began in London in 1961 and so far claims they have come to the rescue of 43,000 prisoners. Today, the staff of 200 monitors news and information and communications from around the world to seek out cases of mistreatment. Their goal is to pressure governments to end torture, executions, political killings and disappearances, to ensure speedy trials for all political prisoners and to effect the release of prisoners of conscience provided they have neither used nor advocated violence. Many countries with political prisoners (don't be so smug, the U.S. is on their list) insist that they are just meddlers. They are the only global organization that can really apply enough pressure to save the health and life of many political prisoners.

As a member, you can provide letter writing assistance, organizing skills or financial support. Memberships run $25 a year ($15 for students), and you are urged to participate in as many programs and networks as you would like. Freedom writers are sent sample letters which are then written and mailed by the member. Lawyers can contribute research and defense skills. Doctors can work to dissuade medical practitioners from participating in torture and executions. Students can join a 2000-school-wide student network that works in groups of five to 100 people to write letters, educate peers and gather signatures for petitions. Regular Joes can get writer's cramp sending letters to prisoners identified in the *Amnesty Action* newsletter. Amnesty International has local chapters in 47 states as well as four regional offices and their national office in Washington, ☎ *(202) 544-0200*. If you want to attend the monthly orientation session held in New York leave a message on Randy Paul's machine, ☎ *(212) 873-1073*.

A Few Tips on Writing Letters to Governments

AI encourages members to write letters, but telegrams are more effective in gaining the attention of the reader. State the purpose of your letter in the first sentence and make sure you end it with your request. If you are writing about a specific person, clearly state his name. The letters should be short. Be polite and state your concern as simply and honestly as possible. Always assume that the person you are writing to is a reasonable person. Tell the reader what you do for a living and what country you are from. Do not bring up politics, religion or opinions. Use the proper title of the addressee, write in English, write it by hand and sign the letter "Yours respectfully."

CARE

Worldwide Headquarters
151 Ellis Street
Atlanta, Georgia 30303
☎ *(404) 681-2552, FAX: (404) 577-4515*
CARE was founded when 22 American organizations joined to help European survivors of World War II. It is the world's largest private, nonprofit, nonsectarian relief and development organization. In 1994, CARE provided $367 million in goods and services to more than 30 million people in developing countries. There are programs for disaster relief, food distribution, primary health care, agriculture and natural resource management, population, girls' education, family planning and small-business support. Ongoing self-help projects are in place in 61 of the least developed countries of Africa, Asia and Latin America, and programs are in progress for the emerging economies of Eastern Europe and the former Soviet Union. CARE responds to disasters overseas and has sent emergency aid to victims of famine and war in Rwanda, Haiti and the former Yugoslavia.

CARE Austria

11 Invalidenstrasse
Vienna, Austria 1030
☎ *[43] 171-50-715*
CARE Austria provides mobile gynecological and women's clinics in Bosnia and Croatia. They also offer care to ex-Yugoslavia's refugees. To help out, contact them at the number above or in Croatia at *Poljickih Knezova 15, Stroxanac, 58312 Podstrana, Croatia.*

The Carter Center

One Copenhill
Atlanta, Georgia 30307
☎ *(404) 331-3900, FAX: (404) 331 0283*
Jimmy Carter has been busy since he left office. His peace negotiations in North Korea, Haiti and Bosnia have been effective in achieving short-term results as well as angering many hard-liners by his friendly approach to our enemies. Carter shows that a mild-mannered, ever smiling good ol' boy from the South can play the perfect good cop to the U.S. military's bad cop. Jimmy Carter seems to be working overtime for the Nobel Peace Prize. Not because he needs more stuff to hang on his wall, but because he really believes that all people have good in them and he has a responsibility to make the world a better place.

Jimmy and Rosalynn's "keep busy and do good" organization is the Carter Center. Eternally miffed by Reagan's skunk job on the Iran hostages, Jimmy is in the good guy business in a big way. He works out of a 100,000-square-foot complex, complete with chapel, library, conference facilities and museum. Seeded by $28 million in donations, the center works to fight disease, hunger, poverty, conflict and oppression in 30 countries. The center is linked to Emory University and operated by the Federal government. Jimmy Carter has been busy acting as a force for good and justice everywhere, from doing Bill's dirty work in Haiti and North Korea to monitoring elections in Africa. It could be argued that Carter has done better out of office than in. Some programs could be considered downright useless (preparing for democratic elections in Liberia and teaching CIS TV journalists how to cover elections), to down-home practical (like eradicating the Guinea worm and immunizing kids). The center is always happy to receive donations and resumés of motivated individuals who want to volunteer their time. With Jimmy's upstaging of fellow Southerner Clinton, you might just be making it to the Soviet Union, northern Ireland and elsewhere.

Cultural Survival Inc.

215 First Street
Cambridge, Massachusetts 02142
☎ *(617) 495-2562, FAX: (617) 621-3814*
There is much talk that there is more work being done to save the rain forest than the people who live in it. Nomadic forest dwellers have no money, own no land and in many cases do not integrate into societies who are pushing them out of their homeland. Having seen the havoc wreaked on our own native Indians and Inuit, it is difficult to come up with viable alternatives to their eventual extinction.

This is an organization of anthropologists and researchers whose goal is to help indigenous peoples (like tropical forest dwellers) develop at their own pace and with their own cultures intact. Cultural Survival's weapon is the almighty dollar, and they put it in the hands of the groups they help. Working with indigenous peoples and ethnic minorities, they import sustainably harvested, nontimber forest products. What are those, you ask? Well, handicrafts, cashew and Brazil nuts, babassu oil, rubber, bananas, even beeswax. The end result is that indigenous peoples gain lands, develop cash crops and don't have to live in shantytowns or timber camps to support themselves.

Founded in 1972, the group has a variety of methods of achieving its goals: education programs, importing and selling products, providing expertise to larger aid groups and providing technical assistance to local groups seeking economic viability.

The organization has projects in Brazil, Guinea-Bissau, Guatemala, Ecuador, the Philippines and Zambia. Membership ($45) gets you a subscription to the *CSE Matters* and the quarterly journal *Cultural Survival Manual*. Ask for a free catalog of products. By purchasing the products for sale, you directly support the peoples who gather and manufacture them, something very rare in this world of markups and middlemen.

If you would like to work as an intern, they are looking for people to help crank out the newsletter, raise funds, handle the office work and expand the network of indigenous groups and supporters. To receive an application, contact Pia Maybury-Lewis, Director of Interns, Cultural Survival, *46 Brattle Street, Cambridge, Massachusetts 02138,* ☎ *(617) 441-5400,* or fax your resume and a letter that explains your personal interests to *(617) 441-5417.*

The Eisenhower Exchange Fellowships Inc.

256 South 16th Street
Philadelphia, Pennsylvania 19102
☎ *(215) 546-1738, FAX: (215) 546-4567*
You don't have to be a pimply-faced student to do good in the world. Captains

of industry, artists, farmers and educators can do their bit too. Based on the premise that the best leadership is by example, the Eisenhower Exchange Fellowship (EEF) is looking for prime examples of successful people from education, business and government. The organization allows you to submit your own ideas on what needs to be done and how you intend to do it. In other cases host countries ask for specific expertise and they try to fill the need. Either way, you will find the opportunity offered by the EEF rewarding and stimulating. You can reach out and touch someone, and EEF will pick up the bill.

If you have a few years, a little knowledge and a yen for travel, but don't have too much money, you might want to apply for an Eisenhower Exchange Fellowship. They offer two shades of the same color, the USA-EEF program and the USA Emerging Democracies Program. The former is a one-month gig in October that will take you and your spouse to a selected foreign country (this year's choices are Argentina, Taiwan and Turkey), where you'll speak on topics like journalism, international relations and human rights. The EEF will take care of all the arrangements (and the basic bills) on this short but intense trip.

The Emerging Democracies will require three months of your life and will usually plunk winning candidates in places like the Czech Republic or Romania, talking on topics like information technology, arts management and helping extend the growing season in Romania. Candidates should be "mid-career professionals who have demonstrated outstanding achievements in their professions." You will compete with other overachievers, but once selected, expect the foundation to pick up airfare, domestic travel, housing and meals for you and a spouse (yours, of course). Leave the kids at home. You will conduct workshops, attend numerous meetings, get one on one and, it is

hoped, inspire and enlighten your hosts. You must be an American citizen and have some experience in leadership and participation in organizations outside of your regular place of work. The bowling league won't cut it.

The Eisenhower Exchange Fellowship was founded in 1953 to honor and emulate then President Eisenhower. Their goal is to promote the exchange of ideas, information and perspectives throughout the world.

Human Rights Watch

1522 K Street, N.W.
Suite 910
Washington, D.C. 20005
☎ *(202) 371-6592*
This organization promotes and monitors human rights worldwide. Human Rights Watch serves as an umbrella organization to Africa Watch, Asia Watch, Americas Watch, Middle East Watch, Helsinki Watch and the Fund for Free Expression.

International League for Human Rights

432 Park Avenue South
New York, New York 10016
☎ *(212) 684-1221*
ILHR is a nongovernmental organization with a history of human rights advocacy since 1942. Originally a voice for those fleeing Nazi-occupied Europe, the League became a force for the promotion and protection of human rights throughout the world. With the Universal Declaration of Human Rights as its platform, the League addresses a full range of international human rights issues and holds consultative status with the United Nations, UNESCO, the ILO and the Council of Europe. The Children of War project aims to improve state protection of human rights for children. The Religious Freedom project attempts to improve the protection of persecuted religious groups. The Eastern European Gender Discrimination project strives to achieve more equal treatment of women in Eastern European countries. The Human Rights and Business project works with transnational business for the promotion and

protection of human rights around the world. ILHR conducts briefing sessions with U.N. delegates regarding human rights issues and offers a number of publications, including *Mission Reports*, *Critiques*, and the ILHR *Human Rights Bulletin*.

National Charities Information Bureau (NCIB)
☎ *(212) 929-6300*
NCIB regularly publishes listings and reports on charities, monitoring which groups meet their standards. Ask for a copy of their *Wise Giving Guide*. Individual contributions of $25 or more and corporations and foundations contributing $100 or more will be sent the *Wise Giving Guide* for one year. NCIB also publishes detailed evaluations about organizations. As many as three reports at a time are available without charge.

Overseas Development Network
333 Valencia Street, Suite 330
San Francisco, California 94103
☎ *(415) 431-4204, FAX (415) 431-5953*
The ODN is primarily for students who want to work overseas in an intern (read no pay) position.This is also called "alternative tourism" in the San Francisco area. The benefit is that you get to get in there and do something about hunger, poverty and social injustice. The 12-year-old organization has placed over 200 interns overseas and in the Appalachian area of the States (yes, Third World standards do still exist in America). If you want to do your good deeds even closer to home, ODN membership ($15 Student, $25 for a regular member) will introduce you to other like-minded students. There are also positions with ODN requiring about 12–20 hours a week. You can gain experience organizing, promoting, writing and marketing and get a good "foot in the door" position if you want to get serious in global affairs. All positions are unpaid and require a minimum commitment of three months and eight hours a week. You can take part in a local ODN chapter, work to build sustainable locally initiated development programs within your local community or just

contribute to the ODN's ongoing programs.

Peace Corps
1990 Street, N.W.
Room 9320
Washington, D.C. 20526
☎ *(800) 424-8580*
When most people in the '60s and '70s thought about how they could change the world, the Peace Corps came to mind. It may surprise you to know that the Vietnam-era hearts and minds division of the U.S. Government is still hard at work making the world a better place without killing or maiming.

The Peace Corps is pure American do-goodism from its Woodstock-style logo (the Peace Corps was formed in 1961) to its Puritan slogan "The Toughest Job You'll Ever Love" and goes straight to the soul of every Midwestern farm boy. The Corps appeals to the American love of doing good things in bad places. In the 30 years of the Peace Corps' existence, 140,000 Americans have heeded the call and the world has truly benefited by an outpouring of American know-how. Last year there were about 6500 volunteers spread out over 90 countries. What do you get? Well, the answer is better stated as what do you give. Successful applicants go through two to three months of language, technical and cultural training for each "tour." You will get a small allowance for housing, food and clothing, airfare to and from your posting and 24 days of vacation a year.

While in-country, you will work with a local counterpart and may be completely on your own in a small rural village or major city. The payoff is that you can actually make things happen, understand a different culture and say that you did something about the world. Does the reality meet the fantasy? Apparently it does. The average length of time spent in the Peace Corps is six years with nine months of training. That works out to three two-year tours with the minimum training. All ex-Peace Corps volunteers we talked to said it was among the most rewarding years of their lives.

Getting in is not that easy, but once in, you join a club that can benefit you greatly in your career. Being an ex-Peace Corps member says that you are about giving and hard work and a little more worldly than most.

You must be a U.S. citizen and at least 18 years old and healthy. Most successful applicants have a bachelor's degree. You must also have a minimum 2.5 grade point average for educational assignments or experience in the field you want to enter. Although there is no limit on age, the Peace Corps is typically a young person's game and considered to be an excellent way to get a leg up in government and private sector employment. The government will give you $5400 when you get out, find you a job in the government on a noncompetitive basis and even help you apply for the over 50 special scholarships available for ex-Peace Corps members.

The emphasis is on training and education in the agricultural, construction and educational areas. There are not too many fine arts requirements, although they do have a category for art teacher. Couples with dependents are a no no, and couples are strongly discouraged. It helps if you know a foreign language, have overseas experience and have a teaching/tutoring background.

The Peace Corps does not mess around in countries that are overtly hostile or dangerous to Americans, like Peru, Colombia, Angola, Algeria and Iran. Also, you will not be posted to Monaco or Paris. You can be posted to Fiji, Thailand, Central Africa or most countries in the CIS. If you are curious, the Peace Corps recruiters hold two-hour evening seminars at their regional offices. Don't be put off by the slightly '80s banner of "Globalize Your Resume." You can meet with returning volunteers and ask all the questions you want.

Philanthropic Advisory Service (PAS) of the Council of Better Business Bureau (CBBB)

☎ *(703) 276-0100*

The Council and its Philanthropic Advisory Service (PAS) promote ethical standards of business practices and protect consumers through voluntary self-regulation and monitoring activities. They publish a bimonthly list of philanthropic organizations that meet the Council of Better Business Bureau's (CBBB) Standards for Charitable Solicitations. The standards include Public Accountability, Use of Funds, Solicitations and Informational Materials, Fund-Raising Practices and Governance. Ask for a copy of *Give But Give Wisely* ($1.00). Many of the groups have e-mail addresses, databases and on-line services.

Peace Brigades International

5 Caledonian Road
London, England N1 9DX
☎ *[44] (171) 713-0392, FAX: [44] (171) 837-2290*
http://www.igc.apc.org/pbi/index.htm
The Peace Brigades try to prevent human rights violations by escorting individuals at threat, carrying a camera, holding all night vigils and other non violent actions.

Refugee Relief International

P.O. Box 693
Boulder, Colorado 80306
Founded in 1982 to provide medical supplies and other aid for refugees and war victims. There are no salaried staff and volunteers pay their own expenses. All administrative offices are donated. RRI has assisted people in Afghanistan, Myanmar, the Balkans, Thailand and Cambodia

Reporters Sans Frontieres

International Secretariat
5, rue Geoffroy-Marie
Paris, France
☎ *[33] 144-838-484*
RSF was founded in 1985 and has offices in Belgium, Canada, France, Germany, Italy, Spain and Switzerland with members in 71 countries. Their job is to defend imprisoned journalists and press around the world. Their annual report offers tips for journalists on 152

countries, including the ones where journalists have been harassed, threatened and murdered. The annual report is available for US$20.

They will send protest letters and provide lawyers (if possible) and other forms of assistance to reporters in jail. If you want to convert to journalism after you are jailed, these folks can't help you.

Save the Children

50 Wilton Road
Westport, Connecticut 06880
☎ *(203) 221-4245, (800) 243-5075,*
FAX (203) 222-9176
SCF is a nonprofit, nonsectarian organization, founded in 1932, to make positive and lasting differences in the lives of disadvantaged children both in the United States and abroad. SCF has more than 60 years of experience in 59 countries and throughout the United States providing emergency relief and community development assistance. The group targets four key sectors: (1) health/population/nutrition, (2) education, (3) economic opportunities and (4) commodity-assisted development/emergency response.

UNICEF

338 East 38th Street
New York, New York 10016
☎ *(212) 686-5522, (800) FOR-KIDS*
UNICEF is the leading advocate for children throughout the world, providing vaccines, clean water, medicine, nutrition, emergency relief and basic education for children in more than 140 nations. Children in Rwanda and the former Yugoslavia have been recent recipients of emergency relief. UNICEF is an integral but semiautonomous agency of the United Nations with its own executive board. Financial support for its work comes entirely from voluntary contributions. UNICEF's budget is not part of the dues paid by the member governments of the United Nations. An extensive network of volunteers work for UNICEF throughout the world, and local volunteers are always needed.

UNHCR

P.O. Box 2500
1211 Geneva 2, Depot, Switzerland
☎ *[41] 22-739-8502*
The United Nations High Commission for Refugees works to prevent refugees from being forcibly returned to countries where they could face death or imprisonment. It also assists with food, shelter and medical care. *Refugees Magazine* focuses on a different refugee movement each month. The U.N. defines a refugee as anyone who flees his home country in fear of loss of life or liberty.

U.S. Committee For Refugees

1717 Massachusetts Avenue, N.W., Suite 701
Washington, D.C. 20036
USCR In Review compiles statistics and reports from more than 100 field workers. The U.S. Committee documents and defends the rights of refugees worldwide, regardless of their nationality, race or religion.

World Learning Inc.

Kipling Road, P.O. Box 676
Brattleboro, Vermont 05302-0676
☎ *(802) 257-7751, (802) 258-3248*
This organization offers a school for international training in teaching languages, intercultural management and world issues as well as college semester abroad programs in 30 countries. Citizen exchange and language programs include summer abroad programs for students and seniors, corporate language projects and youth adventure camps. Au pair arrangements and exchange programs are also offered. Projects in international development and training strive to improve economic and social conditions around the world through development management, human resource development and development training.

Youth Exchange Service (YES)

4675 MacArthur Court, Suite 830
Newport Beach, California 92660
☎ *(800) 848-2121, (714) 955-2030*
An international teenage exchange-student program dedicated to world peace. If you are interested in hosting an international teenage "ambassador," contact this group.

Web Resources

Volunteer Groups

Doctors of the World

375 West Broadway, Fourth Floor
New York, New York 10012
☎ *(212) 226-9890, FAX: (212) 226-7026*
e-mail: Dow@igc.apc.org
http://www.interaction.org:80/ia/mb/
dow.html

Doctors Without Borders

Medecins Sans Frontieres USA (Doctors
Without Borders USA)
11 East 26th Street, 19th Floor, New York,
NY 10010
☎ *(212) 679-6800; FAX: (212) 679-7016*
http://www.interaction.org:80/ia/voln-
teer.html

InterAction's Guide to Volunteer Opportunities

gopher://gopher.igc.apc.org:7050/00/
alli/volopp.car

The Alliance of European Voluntary Service Organizations

http://www.astro.rug.nl/~grijs/
aevso.html

Amigos de las Americas

http://www.amigoslink.org/

The Council on International Educational Exchange

http://www.ciee.org/ciee.htm

Cross Cultural Solutions' Project India

http://www.Opus1.com/emol/project-
india/index.html

Emory University's Page Dedicated to International Volunteer Opps

http://www.cc.emory.edu/OIA/
Volunteer_Opp.html

Global Service Corps

http://www.earthisland.org/ci/gsc/
gschome.html

Global Volunteers

http://www.globalvlntrs.org/home.htm

Impact Online directory

http://www.impactol.org/iol/volun-
teer/international.html

Peace Corps

http://www.clark.net/pub/peace/
PeaceCorps.html

Service and Internship Opportunities in the Developing World and Eastern Europe

http://www.isp.acad.umn.edu/istc/
Work/VolServDevW.html

United Nation's Volunteer Programme

http://suna.unv.ch/

Volunteers Exchange International

http://userwww.sfsu.edu/~jopam/

Volunteers for Peace

http://www.vermontel.com/~vfp/
home.htm

The Council on International Educational Exchange (CIEE)

International Volunteer Projects
205 East 42nd Street
New York, NY 10017
☎ *(888) COUNCIL*
e-mail: info@ciee.org
Offering more than 600 projects in 30
countries, CIEE gives volunteers the
option to work in archaeology, nature
conservation, construction and renova-
tion, or social service. The directory
costs $15, a charge that CIEE will
deduct from the $295 project registra-
tion fee. For a directory or more information, write to:

Operation Crossroads Africa

475 Riverside Drive, Suite #831
New York, NY 10115-0050
☎ *(212) 870-2106, FAX: (212) 870-2055*
E-mail: crw@loop.com (for brochure and
an application)
E-mail: oca@igc.apc.org (for summer pro-
gram: Africa/Brazil)
Operation Crossroads Africa has volunteer opportunities in several African
countries as well as in Brazil. Since
1957, 10,000 Crossroads participants
representing 500 universities, colleges,
organizations, etc. have come together
to work for a better world. Being a
Crossroads volunteer is an intense living, working, and learning experience at
the grassroots level.

Cross-Cultural Solutions

965 Stunt Road
Calabasas, CA 91302
☎ *(818) 222-8300, FAX: (818) 222-8315*
EMAIL: ccsmailbox@aol.com
Project India Cross-Cultural Solutions
has established Project India, a volunteer program that allows participants to
hold short-term positions in India.

VOCA-California at:

1008 S Street, Suite B
Sacramento, CA 95814
☎ *(916) 556-1620, FAX: (916) 556-1630*
EMAIL: voca-california@voca.org

Friendship Force

57 Forsyth Street, NW, Suite 900
Atlanta, GA 30303 USA
☎ *(404) 522-9490, FAX: (404) 688-*
6148
EMAIL: 254-9295@mcimail.com
The Friendship Force is a private, non-profit organization whose purpose is to create an environment where personal friendships can be established across the international barriers that separate people.

Peacework

gopher://gopher.bev.net/00/commu-nity/peacework
EMAIL: 75352.261@compuserv.com
Sponsors short-term international volunteer projects in developing communities around the world.

Partnership for Service Learning

EMAIL: pslny@aol.com.
Offers programs which combine structures academic studies with volunteer community service for summer, January term, semester or year

Findhorn

http://www.tiac.net/biz.fcie

EMAIL: college@findhorn.org.
Findhorn College in Scotland is a global college offering semester and year-long programs in human ecology and environmental studies.

Volunteers Exchange International

e-mail: LEIDS@ICYEUS.IGC.APC.ORG
The US committee of an international network of volunteers: the Federation of the International Christian Youth Exchange (ICYE).

The Overseas Development Network

EMAIL: odn@igc.Org.
Offers summer volunteer internships in Mexico.

Alliance for a Global Community

InterAction Suite 801
1717 Massachusetts Avenue, NW
Washington, DC 20036
☎ *(202) 667-8227, FAX: (202) 483-7624*
EMAIL: alliance@interaction.org
A coalition of more than 150 organizations working together to educate Americans about the developing world and the global issues that will shape the future.

Peace Groups

These are comprised of mostly university-funded think-tanks on developing peaceful solutions to conflict.

The Albert Einstein Institution

http://hdc-www.harvard.edu/cfia/pnscs/aei.htm"

The Carter Center

http://www.emory.edu/CARTER_CENTER/

The Center for Defense Information

http://www.cdi.org/

The Commission on Global Governance

http://www.cgg.ch/"

The Conflict Resolution Consortium

http://www.colorado.edu/conflict

Consortium on Peace Research, Education, & Development

http://www.igc.apc.org/copred

The Cyprus Peace Center

http://www.isr.umd.edu/~pzaphiri/peace_center/index.html

Fellowship of Reconciliation

http://www.netaxs.com/~nvweb/for/

The Foundation for Prevention & Early Resolution of Conflict

http://www.conflictresolution.org/

Harvard University: The Program on Nonviolent Sanctions and Cultural Survival

http://hdc-www.harvard.edu/cfia/pnscs/homepage.htm

Initiative on Conflict Resolution and Ethnicity

http://www.incore.ulst.ac.uk/

Institute for Conflict Resolution Studies (ICRS)

http://www.vvaf.org/icrs

Institute for Global Communications: PeaceNet, EcoNet, etc.

http://www.igc.apc.org/

International Peace Research Association

http://www.antioch.edu/~peace//ipra/IPRA.html

International Peace Research Institute, Oslo

gopher://csf.Colorado.EDU:70/11/peace/orgs/prio

National Conference on Peace & Conflict Resolution

http://web.gmu.edu/departments/NCPCR/

Peace Brigades International

http://www.igc.apc.org/pbi/index.htm

Relief Web, a project of the UNDHA
> http://www.reliefweb.intl

Stockholm International Peace Research Institute
> http://www.sipri.se/new_location.html

Tampere Peace Research Institute, University of Tampere [Finland]
> http://www.uta.fi/laitokset/tapri

United Nations homepage
> http://www.un.org

U.S. Institute of Peace
> http://www.usip.org

University of California: Institute on Global Conflict & Cooperation
> http://www-igcc.ucsd.edu/IGCC2/igcc-menu.htm

WarChild
> http://www.warchild.org

UNICEF
> gopher://hqfaus01.unicef.org:70/00.cef-data/.emerctyprof95/

Human Rights Watch
> http://www.hrw.org/research/afghani-stan.html

The Disaster Response Unit of Interaction (The American Council for Voluntary International Action)
> http://www.interaction.org/ia/sitrep/afgan.html

United Nations High Commissioner for Refugees (UNHCR)
> http://www.unhcr.ch

U.S. State Department Human Rights Report
> http://www.usis.usemb.se/human/

World Disasters Report (IFRC)
> http://www.ifrc.org/pubs/wdr/95/

Medical Aid Groups

There are angels in Rwanda, Somalia, Angola, Afghanistan and Iraq. They are not there to convert souls or play harps. They are not soldiers or politicians but white-coated volunteers who sew back limbs, pull out shrapnel from babies' heads and minister to the sick and dying. They are the men and women who try to ease the suffering caused by violent actions. Natural disasters also tax the resources and stamina of aid workers to the limit. If you don't mind stacking bodies like firewood or can live with the ever-present stench of too many sick people in one place, you will do just fine.

The world needs people who are capable of cleaning up the mess caused by governments. If there is a disaster, chances are you will see these folks in there long before the journalists and the politicians. These are nondenominational groups that are found in the world's most dangerous places. If you have medical skills and want to save more lives in a day than a tentful of TV evangelists in a lifetime, this is the place to be. Conditions are beyond primitive, usually makeshift refugee camps on the edges of emerging conflicts. Many groups will walk or helicopter in to war-torn regions to assist in treating victims. Many aid workers have been targeted for death because of their policy of helping both sides. There is constant danger from rocket attacks, land mines, communicable diseases and riots. These people are not ashamed to stagger out of a tent after being up 48 hours straight, have a good cry and then get back to work saving more lives. It hurts, but it feels good. Contact the following organizations for more information:

American Red Cross
> *National Headquarters*
> *17th and D Street, N.W.*
> *Washington, D.C. 20006*
> ☎ *(202) 737-8300*

For 115 years, whenever there has been a disaster or war, these folks have been on the scene knee-deep in bandages, blood and cots, helping the injured and consoling those who have just lost everything. They always have a need for volunteers, particularly people with medical and technical skills. If you can't

volunteer your time or skills, blood donors are desperately needed.

AmeriCares
> *161 Cherry Street*
> *New Canaan, Connecticut 06840*
> ☎ *(203) 966-5195, (800) 486-4357*

AmeriCares is a private, nonprofit disaster relief and humanitarian aid organization that provides immediate response to emergency medical needs and supports long-term health care programs for people around the world, irrespective of race, color, creed or political persuasion. Since 1982 AmeriCare has delivered more than $1.4 billion worth of medical and disaster aid around the world. AmeriCare works with corporate America to secure large donations of supplies and materials. Cash contributions are used primarily for logistical costs. For every $1 donated, AmeriCare is able to deliver $22 worth of relief supplies.

Doctors Without Borders (Medecins Sans Frontieres)

11 East 26 Street, Suite 1904l
New York, New York 10010
☎ *(212) 679-6800, FAX: (212) 679-7016, France:* ☎ *[72] 73-04-14*
http://www.interaction.org:80/ia/volnteer.html
Doctors Without Borders, founded a quarter of a century ago, is the largest international emergency medical organization in the world. Every year around 3000 volunteers leave for three to six months of service in more than 70 countries around the world. Many of the countries are in a state of war. Sixty percent of the volunteers are medically trained and come from 45 countries around the world. Most are 25–35 years old. The organization assists victims of natural disasters and health crises like Ebola, and ministers to refugees and war victims. To deploy people as quickly as possible (within 24 hours when possible), special emergency kits were created with strict operational and medical procedures. Today, these kits and manuals are used by other international organizations around the world.

Doctors of the World

375 West Broadway, Fourth Floor
New York, New York 10012
☎ *(212) 226-9890, FAX: (212) 226-7026*
http://www.interaction.org:80/ia/mb/dow.html
e-mail: Dow@igc.apc.org

International Medical Corps

12233 West Olympic Boulevard, Suite 280
Los Angeles, CA 90064-1052
☎ *(310) 826-7800; FAX: (310) 442-6622*
e-mail: IMC@IGC.APC.ORG
IMC is a private, non-sectarian, non-political, non- profit organization established by US physicians and nurses to provide emergency medical relief and health care training to devastated regions worldwide

Medecins Sans Frontieres USA (Doctors Without Borders USA)

International Medical Corps
12233 West Olympic Boulevard, Suite 280
Los Angeles, CA 90064-1052
☎ *(310) 826-7800, FAX: (310) 442-6622*
e-mail: IMC@IGC.APC.ORG
IMC is a private, non-sectarian, non-political, non- profit organization established by U.S. physicians and nurses to provide emergency medical relief and health care training to devastated regions worldwide where few organizations operate

Northwest Medical Teams, International

Portland Oregon
The International Red Cross
http://www.icrc.org

Physicians For Peace

229 West Bute Street, Suite 820
Norfolk, VA 23510
☎ *(757) 625-7569, FAX: (757) 625-7680*
PFP is an apolitical non-profit organization that helps to foster international peace and cooperation by improving health care.

Save the Planet

Save the Rain Forest

The statistics fly around on deforestation like curses at a barroom brawl. Typically, like the curses, the numbers are half-right, half-wrong, but rooted in truth. Rain forests comprise only 2 percent of the planet's surface, yet they contain half the world's species. Half of the world's rain forests have disappeared since World War II, which is understandable when you consider the value of the timber and the need for emerging countries to develop their wilderness into towns, factories and grazing land.

Many conservation groups paint a Disneyesque picture of sunny glades populated with singing birds, bright flowers, romping animals and happy native peoples. The reality is much darker. Triple-canopy tropical forests have one of the lowest biomasses of mammals and birds. They are typically dark, dank, still and oppressively hot—ideal incubators for plant life. The native people live in isolation, sometimes culling each other in violent tribal conflicts, a natural thinning process that is also accelerated by disease and early death. When cleared, the land is barren and provides at most two years of scanty crops. Forest dwellers are forced to use swidden, or slash-and-burn cultivation, a method whereby trees are cleared, the ground burned, crops are planted for one or two years, and then the area is left to regenerate for up to 10 years before any nutrients are put back in the soil.

The term "rain forest" pertains to a variety of environments. There is no single way to saving the montane moss forests and the mangrove swamps, since they are in jeopardy from a variety of sources. The major enemies of the Asian forests are logging companies that pull out first-generation hardwood using crude and inefficient methods. Because of the low cost of this wood, tropical hardwoods are turned into everything from concrete construction forms to coffee table veneers. Decline is also accelerated by repopulation programs that clear large areas for cultivation and grazing. The country itself has the most to lose, but there are few options. Many countries, like Malaysia, point to our denuded forests and first World prosperity, then ask us why we think we have the right to tell them not to develop the same resources to achieve the same success.

The West's view of the rain forests seems to be as a potential location for tourism (if they ever get there) and as the lungs of the world. The East's view of the rain forests are that they provide short-term jobs and income. They still view the forests as the wilderness and as a symbol that they are not fully developed like the West. Both sides seem to agree that the rain forests are a resource, but the two hemispheres don't see eye to eye on how they should be used. We say to cut at sustainable yields, and they say they need the money now. The hitch is that the valuable timber in those triple-canopy forests is well over a hundred years old; unlike our fast-growing softwoods, they will not be back in our lifetime. There are answers and there are groups that are coming up with solutions and programs. The major thrust seems to be toward finding higher returns on the same resources. For example, over 70 percent of plant species that may help in the fight against cancer come from the rain forest, yet only one percent of the species has been tested for this property. Many foods, such as rice, potatoes, chocolate, tomatoes, oranges and cinnamon, have come from the tropical forests.

Although experts on both sides duke it out over how much rain forest is lost every minute, there is no denying that a lot more forest is being cut down than is being planted. Does it matter? Of course. Can you stop it? Of course not. Can you slow it down? Absolutely.

If you want to save the rain forest, or any forest for that matter, there are groups that make a difference. Joining any one of the following groups supports their activities as well as introduces you to other like-minded people. The variety of programs is bewildering, but then the answers required for solid preservation and management are even more complex.

Start by asking for information and attending some meetings. You can communicate with many of these people via computer. Many groups have needs for active volunteers as well as members. If you are looking for more active pursuits, as was the case of Bruno Manser, a Swiss national who helped the Punan organize against the timber companies in Sarawak, they can introduce you to sponsors, legal funds, mentors, and so forth.

You may just be happy to receive the ever-present newsletter and know that your money is supporting a good cause.

The top projects worth looking into are the Bakun dam in Borneo, which will remove 27 cubic meters of forest and flood 200,000 acres of what was triple canopy rainforest. The Hidrova project will threaten the Pantanal in Brazil. In China, the Three Gorges project will destroy thousands of miles of land and displace over a million Chinese.

American Forests

Post Office Box 2000
Washington, D.C. 20013
☎ *(800) 873-5323*

OK, so everyone wants to save the rain forests, but when was the last time you visited Washington, Alaska or Hawaii? It seems we like to cut our rain forests as fast as our Third World cousins do. The American Forestry Association is about cutting down trees and about growing trees, but mostly about the need to grow trees. I worked on both sides of the fence, both for the Forest Service (basically counting trees) and as a logger (cutting them down). I, like most people, prefer walking through virgin forests to cutting them down. I just don't know whose forests we are going to cut down if we don't rebuild and manage ours.

Both sides of the fray (loggers and environmentalists) agree that we need to preserve trees. They just don't agree about how. Loggers say grow 'em as fast as you cut 'em down, and conservationists say don't cut 'em. Loggers like to ask who is going to supply the timber to build the house you return to after your hike in the woods. The fact is we still consume them a lot faster that we replace them. Joining American Forests puts your money toward replanting trees. Whether you shell out $30 to plant 10 trees or $1000 to plant an entire acre of trees (500), your money gets right to the heart of the matter. The 120-year-old organization is the creator of the Global ReLeaf program and works to make the country and the city a more livable place by planting more trees. It should be known that this group views trees as a renewable resource and not as sacred plants, so the more strident preservationists may want to spend their money with the Sierra Club or other "preservation-only" groups. For now, as long as we continue to use wood as a resource, management is the first step to better logging practices. The group also offers trips to forested places like New Zealand and even has a magazine on urban forests.

American Forestry Association (AFA)
☎ (202) 667-3300
To donate $5.00 for Global ReLeaf,
☎ (900) 420-4545
To plant trees, contact their Global ReLeaf Campaign.

Better World Society
☎ (202) 331-3770
Become a BWS video advocate and obtain *Profits from Poison*, a documentary about the dangerous misuse of pesticides in developing countries.

Conservation International
1015 18th Street, N.W.
Suite 1000
Washington, D.C. 20036
☎ (202) 429-5660, FAX: (202) 887-5188
CI tries to integrate people into its conservation efforts. Their major focus is the rain forest in 24 countries in Latin America, Africa and Asia. They strive to integrate economics, community development and scientific solutions. Being down to earth, they tell you exactly what your donation can provide. Whether it is a $100 donation that buys a grinding wheel for making handicrafts from sustainable rain-forest products in Ecuador, or $1000 that provides one thousand tree seedlings and planting equipment in Costa Rica, they do a good job of putting your money to work. Their idea

of being able to create economic benefit seems a refreshing alternative to the eco-Nazis who demand natural preservation at the cost of local development.

Earth Island Institute
300 Broadway, Suite 28
San Francisco, California 94133
☎ (415) 788-3666, FAX: (415) 788-7324
EII is somewhat of an incubator for conservation, preservation and restoration projects. In 1982 David Brower, the founder of Friends of the Earth and first executive director of the Sierra Club, set up an institute to support creative solutions to the world's problems. Projects that have sprung from the institute include films, conferences and a variety of organizations. The Rain Forest Action Network, International Rivers Network and the International Marine Mammal Project all went on to become self-sustaining separate organizations. Earth Island Institute supports numerous projects around the world, from protecting mangrove forests to educating Australian aborigines about uranium waste disposal. Annual membership is $25 and gets you a subscription to the quarterly *Earth Island Journal.*

Greenpeace
1436 U. Street, N.W.
Washington, D.C. 20009
☎ (202) 462-1177
Their Toxics Campaign seeks to solve the toxic pollution problem through waste prevention. Greenpeace takes direct action against the polluters, fighting to cut off toxic substances at their source. Ask for a copy of *Toxics: Stepping Lightly on the Earth, Everyone's Guide to Toxics in the Home* (free).

National Audubon Society
700 Broadway
New York, New York 1003-9501
☎ (212) 979-3000
Ask for a copy of "The Audubon Activist Carbon Dioxide Diet," a worksheet that explains how to reduce your household's production of carbon dioxide, CFCs and trash ($2.00).

Rainforest Action Network (RAN)

450 Sansome Street
Suite 700
San Francisco, California 94111
☎ *(415)398-4404, FAX: (415) 398-2732*

RAN is a feisty little group (13 full-time employees) formed in 1985 that yaps around the heels of big business. Their Darth Vader of the rain forest is Mitsubishi, "the worst corporate destroyer of rain forests in the world." They have also targeted oil companies like Texaco and Unocal and anybody who destroys rain forests or endangers indigenous peoples. They use public pressure, direct action and the coordinated actions of hundreds of like-minded groups around the world to force change and conservation.

They claim to have forced Burger King to stop importing beef from Central America—beef raised on land formerly occupied by rain forests. Their boycott caused a 12 percent drop in income and BK now no longer makes Whoppers out of Third World cows.

Their biggest weapon is a group of 150 independent Rain Forest Action Groups (RAG), which raise funds, educate their community and conduct campaigns to save the rain forest. RAN is proud of the fact that at least 82 percent of donations go directly toward rain-forest preservation. Their most effective program is the Protect-an-Acre program. RAN uses funds to help forest peoples secure communal land titles and helps them develop livelihoods and long-term protection programs. To date, they have secured more than 2.5 million acres of land title.

They offer a variety of publications including the monthly *Action Alert* and the quarterly *World Rainforest Report*, and produce numerous fact sheets and brochures targeting specific rain-forest issues. There are directories of over 250 groups that are working to save the rain forest in the Amazon and 250 groups in Southeast Asia.

If you would like to get involved, you can start your own RAG, join one, support the group with funds or work as an unpaid intern in their San Francisco headquarters. You must put in 12 hours a week for three months.

Sierra Club

739 Polk Street
San Francisco, California 94109
☎ *(415) 776-2211, (202) 547-1141 (D.C.)*

The granddaddy of ecoclubs, with 102 years under its belt and 600,000 members. The Sierra Club was founded in 1892 by John Muir with the idea that the natural areas of America needed to be saved from the industrialists who were ravaging the West.

Backed up by a staff of 350 paid volunteers, 20 regional field offices, 32 chapter offices and a rapidly growing membership roster, the Sierra Club is by far the most effective voice for conservation in America. They track the environmental profiles and voting history on environmental issues of members of the U.S. Senate and House of Representatives. They support their activities by publishing an impressive array of books, calendars, licensed products and *Sierra* magazine. They also lead about 300 trips every year and fight a number of legal battles from their six Legal Defense Fund Offices in San Francisco, Denver, Juneau, Honolulu and Washington, D.C.

You don't have to be a reformed lumberjack to help out. You can join as a member, or you can apply for a paid (or unpaid) job in their head office in San Francisco or in one of the regional offices. The Sierra Club is looking for low-paid, hardworking staff to work on books and their magazine. They need human resources, financial, data-entry, management, public affairs, travel, conservation and campaign workers. Their Washington office needs lobbyists, support people, media reps and issues specialists. If you are hoping to be paid to hike around the parks and take those amazing photographs in *Sierra* magazine or their books, sorry, its all on spec or freelance. They welcome submissions though, so keep trying if you get turned down the first time. The Sierra Club can give you a reduced fee on one of their outings in exchange for some trail clearing and maintenance work. Twenty lucky interns can work for nothing throughout the organization with the hopes of getting a full-time job later. If you do get a job, expect full dental, medical and life insurance programs, a pension plan and generous vacation accrual (that means you will work plenty of OT) and discounts on calendars, out-ings, etc. If you are interested, contact the Human Resources Department at ☎ *(415) 923-5581.*

Worldwatch Institute

*1776 Massachusetts Avenue NW
Washington, D.C. 20036*
☎ *202-452-1999*
A global environmental research organization. Ask for publications such as *Clearing the Air: A Global Agenda, Air Pollution, Acid Rain, and The Future of Forests,* and *The Bicycle: Vehicle for a Small Planet.*

Save the Animals

Animal rights activists are not always bulimic models and washed-up celebrities. There are plenty of square-jawed park rangers who hunt down and kill poachers on a nightly basis. I spent three days badgering the Tanzanian game wardens in Selous park to take us man hunting with them at night. I found out why they didn't want me along; it seems they left their remote little hut, drove about half a mile away and slept. Oh, well. In any case, you can make a difference, whether you are on the ground or in your living room. Your meager contribution is a spit in the ocean and is guaranteed not to save an animal species from extinction, but a lot of people chipping in a few bucks and a few hours will go a long way to doing something concrete.

If you just can't stand by and watch another elephant get chain-sawed for his tusks, then there are active outlets for you. One of the best ways to visit dangerous places is to do good. The image of the great white hunter as adventurer has been replaced by the great white conservationist as adventurer. If you have dreams of getting sunburnt, dusty and wrinkled while bouncing around Africa in an old Land Rover 88, your best bet is to look into the many conservation groups that need volunteers and support. Those who preferred *Indiana Jones* to *Born Free* can also check into the many archaeological digs that need helping hands. If you just want to read about and keep one more white rhino on the planet, then by all means tuck in your love gift and get warm fuzzies (and usually a colorful newsletter).

African Elephant Conservation Coordinating Group

*c/o Dr. David Weston
Wildlife Conservation Intl.
P.O. Box 62844
Nairobi, Kenya*
☎ *[254] 2245-6922-1699, FAX: [254] 2159-6922-1699*
This group works with other wildlife protection groups to help protect elephants and ensure that they do not fall victim to poachers.

African Wildlife Foundation

*1717 Massachusetts Avenue, N.W.
Washington, D.C. 20036*
☎ *(202) 265-8393*
Founded in 1961 with the belief that only Africans can save African wildlife, the AWF operates two colleges of wildlife management. Their colleges have trained hundreds of game wardens and rangers for parks all over Africa. AWF is unique in that it works with Africans within Africa to manage African wildlife. They also educate children on conservation, help local communities benefit from wildlife preservation and show them ways to make more efficient use of land.

The AWF developed programs and trained staff in Rwanda's Parc des Volcans to protect the remaining 650 mountain gorillas. They have continued their support of the rangers throughout the recent bloodshed and report that no gorillas were harmed. They also run the longest continuous study of elephants in Africa in Kenya. They have been tracking the 790 elephants in Amboseli National Park to understand elephant behavior and social patterns. There are a field office in Nairobi and a fund-raising center in Washington. Supporters receive a thrice yearly newsletter *Wildlife News*, and contributions are tax-deductible.

Convention on International Trade in Endangered Species (CITES)

c/o UNEP
DC2-0803 United Nations
New York, NY 10017
☎ *(212) 963-8093*
The United Nations Environment Program (UNEP) was created in 1972 as a result of the Stockholm Conference on the Human Environment. Its original purpose was to raise environmental awareness and promote action at all levels of society worldwide. UNEP monitors and assesses the state of the world environment, develops policies, and provides a forum for global environmental concerns. UNEP is the guardian of international environmental law. At the 1992 U.N. Earth Summit in Brazil, UNEP's role was reconfirmed and strengthened by its ambitious Agenda 21 plan. Endorsed by world leaders, this document provides a plan of action for dealing with ongoing problems including the depletion of the ozone layer, biological diversity, hazardous wastes and droughts.

The Cousteau Society

Membership Center
870 Greenbriar Circle
Suite 402
Chesapeake, Virginia
☎ *(800) 441-4395, or (804) 523-9335*
This worldwide organization, started in 1973, serves to protect the oceans, marine animals and ultimately humans from pollution and abuse. Their noble but somewhat ambitious goal is to "provide a centralized facility for continuing studies of man and his world." They also strive to "protect and improve the quality of life for present and future generations," another goal that I am sure would be difficult to oppose. They freely admit that their job is to "bridge the gap between specialists and the public," meaning doing cool things with a scientist as baby-sitter. Their methodology might be overly dramatic and the late Inspector Clouseau/Captain Cousteau's voiceover horribly mangled and poetic, but many of my generation can't imagine going diving without saying at least once: "Luuk at zee leetle feeshes adrrrift in zeee vaaast ocheoon."

Well anyway, join the club and let me know. In the meantime, if you like diving as I do you have to give Jacques-Yves his due for being the coinventor of the aqualung and making diving such a popular sport.

If you join up, you'll get a free bimonthly mag called *The Calypso Log* and the *Dolphin Log* for kids. The money goes toward supporting the activities of the Cousteau Society and publicizing their ongoing activities, which consist primarily of creating films on various regions of the world and acting as PR agents for whales and other wet things. The Society is currently on his rediscovery of the world, which means they have pretty much blown through it once before. His shows are bankrolled by Ted Turner and continue to be the best aquatic filmmaking out there. On the downside, it seems to keep discovering places that people have lived in for thousands of years. Simplification and a somewhat lopsided view of the world (ocean) make for great entertainment but sometimes provide only sketchy scientific content. Oh hell! I admit I love bumper stickers that say things like "Nuke the gray whales for Jesus" and "I do eat fish." Can you actually do anything or come along for the ride? No. But you can watch their television specials, buy the books and join the society. Membership is $20 for an individual and $28 for families.

National Wildlife Federation

1400 16th Street, N.W.
Washington, D.C. 20036
☎ *(202) 797-6800, FAX: (703) 790-4040*
The National Wildlife Federation was founded in 1936 as a nationwide network of grass-roots conservationists. Its mission is to educate, inspire and assist individuals and organizations of diverse cultures to conserve wildlife and other natural resources and to protect the Earth's environment in order to achieve a peaceful, equitable and sustainable future. Representatives of 45 state and territorial affiliates meet annually to establish NWF's conservation policy. The National Conservation Office based in Washington, D.C., campaigns in Congress, federal agencies and the courts for these priority issues: endangered species, clean water, wetlands, farm policy, public lands reform, environmental justice and environmental quality. The International Affairs Department works to assure environmental considerations are incorporated into U.S. trade agreements, to assure citizen access to environmental decision-making, and to encourage economic, cultural, human welfare and population initiatives.

The Nature Conservancy

1815 North Lynn Street
Arlington, Virginia 22209
☎ *(800) 628-6860, (703) 841-5300,*
FAX: (703) 841-4880
The Nature Conservancy seeks out, develops and works to create conservation areas around the world. Its goals are to assist in the development of local conservation institutions, provide on-the-ground protection assistance, create sustainable conservation financing and generate improved conservation information. The group sets up Conservation Data Centers for developers trying to avoid vulnerable species and for conservationists designing preserves. It is active in the Caribbean and Latin Amer-

ica with programs in Mexico, Panama, Costa Rica, Ecuador and Brazil. It also is working to build and protect parks in the South Pacific.

The Student Conservation Association, Inc.

Post Office Box 550
Charlestown, New Hampshire 03603
☎ *(603) 826-4301, FAX: (603) 826-7755*
The SCA offers 12-week positions assisting in the management and protection of U.S. national Parks, forests and other conservation areas. You might be maintaining trails, educating visitors, helping archaeology surveys and telling people to turn their ghetto blasters down in campsites. You will get to work in the great outdoors, have food and housing supplied, as well as have your travel expenses covered in the U.S.

The year-round program is open to those over 18, and it helps if you have academic qualifications. The list of positions available is published every July and December and is available by contacting the recruitment director.

Wilderness Conservancy

1224 Roberto Lane
Los Angeles, CA 90077
☎ *(310) 472-2593, FAX: (310) 476-7527*
This nonprofit conservation organization, headed by Dr. Robert Cleaves, provided four anti-poaching aircraft for governments in Zimbabwe and Kwazulu, supplies for game scouts in Zambia and funds for a preschool in Zimbabwe. They are now raising funds for four more aircraft for Southern Africa. If you are interested in getting involved in the real world of conservation and the effort to prevent the extinction of black rhinos, elephants, cheetahs and other species, give them a call.

Wildlife Conservation International

☎ *(212) 220-5155*
Their Tropical Forest Campaign supports field researchers and conservation action plans at work in 37 tropical forests around the globe.

World Wildlife Fund

1250 24th Street, N.W.
Washington, D.C. 20037
☎ *(202) 293-4800*

For more than 30 years, World Wildlife Fund (WWF) has worked to save endangered wildlife. Their activities include halting global trade in endangered animals and plants, training and equipping anti-poaching teams, undertaking research on wildlife behavior and habitat needs, and mounting international campaigns to save flagship species like tigers, rhinos and giant pandas. WWF has helped to create and preserve hundreds of parks and other protected areas around the world. WWF also works with local leaders, grass-roots groups, governments, and international funding institutions to improve living standards and to integrate conservation into public and private-sector development programs.

Save Yourself

How to Stay Alive and Well (for At Least Four Weeks)

I guess just about any type of school can be called a survival school (translating Homeric poems from the original Greek version could help you survive British boys school reunions). Knowledge is power and power creates self-confidence. America offers little in the normal school curriculum that would help us survive in either urban or rural environments. In fact, most high school kids don't even know how to open a bank account, let alone trap, skin and cook a rabbit.

There are three types of survival schools. The first is sport- or location-specific (mountain, diving, jungle, jumping); the next deals with bush lore, and the last type is the southern "be a mercenary" school that does little but promote the sales of black T-shirts with skulls, and cheap beer. Having never received any formal military training, I learned my survival skills from a variety of eclectic sources: guides, boatmen, headhunters, Indians, trappers, botanists and others.

The first tool for survival is knowledge, the second is self-confidence, and the third is ingenuity. I would like to say that luck is by far the most important element of survival, but let's put that aside for now.

Armies have long known that training can replace thinking in men. If someone is exposed to rote learning, common experience and instinctive reaction, they will often do the unthinkable. In the trenches of WWI, thousands of men crawled out of relative safety to follow their dead comrades into withering machine-gun fire. Intensive training can suppress our natural instinct to run away, cower in fear or scream at the top of our lungs.

What does that have to do with survival training? First of all, most people have never been in a life-threatening situation. Or more correctly, most people don't know how to deal with life-threatening situations. Second, most urban people left in remote places don't have the foggiest idea about how to build a fire, construct shelter and find food.

Most adventurers eagerly look forward to the serendipity of being thrust into unforeseen or harsh circumstances. Many of them have a smattering of training and good sense, but few are honest-to-god bushmen, so if you want the odds stacked in your favor, try spending some time at one of the training spots listed in this section.

The best sources for survival training are the special forces or commando sections of the British, American, Australian and French military. Most require a minimum of four to five years and will consume the flower of your youth. You may find yourself with skills that lead you to a life of hard-core adventure, since the first place security and mercenary recruiters go is to the bars that the SAS and French Foreign Legion frequent. If you wish to sidestep the endless years of boredom spent on military bases and go straight for the good stuff, you can look into these schools, many taught by the cream of the SAS or American special forces vets. Don't be shy about setting up a one-on-one itinerary if you have special educational needs.

If you gravitate toward the more earthbound, then be prepared to learn survival the politically correct way: no killing, no field stripping of weapons and a definite slant toward New Age thinking. Will these skills save your life when you have to E&E Khmer Rouge terrorists? Maybe. Will they make you more comfortable and secure in the wild? Yes.

Adventure/Recreation Schools

OK we should say schools for dangerous people, or schools that will make your adventures less dangerous; Oh hell, it sounds better our way. Herein you can find a list of institutions, events and resources that will help the curious and adventurous add to their survival skills.

Bremex

Expedition Leadership Training Scheme
London Information Center
18 Westbourne Park Villas
London, England W2 5EA
☎ *[44] (71) 229-9251*
Bremex operates a school in expedition planning, leadership and survival skills. The briefings and lectures are on Tuesday evenings, with weekend training wilderness expeditions in the winter. All courses are London-based and vary from "Weekend Taster" courses to nine-month qualifying courses for expedition leaders. Training includes first aid, survival skills, mountain rescue, leadership studies, canoeing, snow and ice climbing, navigation and orienteering.

Fees are about $50 a month, with transportation provided to weekend moor and mountain locations.

National Outdoor Leadership School

Post Office Box AA
Lander, Wyoming 82520
☎ *(307) 332-6973, FAX: (307) 332-3031*
This school gets past the superficial imagery of some survival schools and right down to business. People who want to make money in the outdoor adventure business come here to learn

not only survival aspects, but the nuts and bolts of adventure travel outfitting. You can also take the 34-day, $2100 NOLS instructor's class once you have passed a basic wilderness class. The emphasis here is on safety, since your future charges will be less than amused if they end up living off the land because you forgot to pack their favorite pudding. Choose from sea kayaking, winter camping, telemark skiing, backpacking or mountaineering. Some courses qualify for college credit.

Entry-level classes are in reality great adventure vacations depending on your area of interest. Mountaineering classes are taught in Alaska, British Columbia and even Kenya. Expect to spend two weeks to three months on location learning the specialized skills you will need to lead other groups. If you want to cram in a class on your vacation, then opt for their selection of two-week courses on horsepacking, winter skiing, rock climbing or canoeing. If you flunk, well you had a good time on a well-organized adventure tour.

School for Field Studies
16 Broadway
Beverly, Massachusetts 01915
☎ *(508) 927 5127*
A nonprofit group that runs 40 month-long and semester-length programs that allow students to gain field research experience. Targeted to high school and college students, the college credit courses are run all around the world. There is a wide choice of topics, from coral reef studies (the Caribbean), marine mammals (Baja, Mexico), tropical rain forests (Australia) and wildlife management (Kenya). Scholarships and interest-free loans are available.

SOLO (Stonehearth Open Learning Opportunity)
Rural Federal District 1
Box 163
Conway, New Hampshire 03818
☎ *(603) 447-6711, FAX: (603) 447-2310*
A school for professionals, SOLO is designed to teach wilderness guides what to do in an emergency. They offer a four-week, $1200 Emergency Wilderness Training Certification course that will get you on the preferred list of just about any expedition. Shorter two-day seminars are taught around the country for $100. The areas of specialization are wilderness emergencies (such as frostbite, hypothermia, bites and altitude sickness), climbing rescue, and emergency medicine (wounds, broken limbs, shock and allergy). Participants are expected to have a basic grounding in climbing and outdoor skills.

Adventure Experience Organizations

British Schools Exploring Society
Royal Geographical Society
1 Kensington Gore
London, England SW7 2AR
☎ *[44] (71) 584-0710, FAX: [44] (71) 581-7995*
BSES sets up an expedition for young people (16-1/2 to 20 years old) every year. The six-week expeditions are usually to the arctic regions of Europe (Canada to Russia) and are during the summer holidays. They have been sneaking in expeditions to tropical climes and offer four- to six-month expeditions to Botswanna, Greenland, Alaska and Svalbard.

Over 3000 people have taken part since 1932, and interviews take place in London in November. Participants pay a fee to cover costs; membership to BSES is by election after the successful completion of a BSES expedition.

Castle Rock Center for Environmental Adventures
412 County Road 6NS
Cody, Wyoming 82414
☎ *(800) 533-3066, (307) 527-6650, FAX: (307) 527-7196*
Here's a place that is about halfway between the Boy Scouts and Outward Bound, targeted directly to bored teens. Called "Man and His Land Expeditions," they allow you to choose from

fishing, ice climbing, white-water rafting, horse packing, mountain biking and llama trekking, or you can do all of them. The eight-week Full West program will pack more rootin' tootin' Western adventure than a year of *National Geographic* TV specials. How about a seven-day backpack trip in the Rockies; then you're off to the Grand Canyon; then you zip over to the Green River for a little white-water rafting, and zoom, you blast up to Mount Rainier for mountain climbing and rescue training. Still not totally bagged? More thrills and spills await, as you tour the rain forests of the Olympic Peninsula and then more river running, then in one last eco-adventure blast in the Absaroka Range in Wyoming, you spend the next week mountain biking, llama trekking, horse packing and camping. If there are any survivors, the final week is spent climbing mountains in the Tetons as part of the Exum school of Mountaineering. And all you thought there was for teenagers to do in the summer was play video games and listen to heavy metal.

Earth Skills

570 Shepard Street
San Pedro, CA 90731
☎ *(310) 833-4249*
There is a school where you can learn tracking, survival, plant uses and general bush lore. The Earth Skills school was founded in 1987 by Jim Lowery to introduce people to the great outdoors in a very practical way. Most of the classes are over a three-day weekend and run between $50 to $160. The wilderness skill course is a three-day class that will teach you how to trap, identify edible plants, weave baskets, build shelters, start a fire with an Indian bow, make primitive weapons, purify water and generally learn how to survive more than 50 miles from a 7-Eleven.

The one-day classes, usually held on a weekend, teach tracking skills or plant uses. Once you have graduated from tracking or wilderness, you can move up to the advanced levels where you can learn Earth Philosophy. Using the methodology and philosophy of aboriginal peoples, Lowery will show you how to apply your inner vision to communicate with the animals. If this is a little too California for some folks, you can skip Earth Philosophy and go into Advanced Tracking and Awareness. This class is taught in the Los Padres mountains at an elevation of 8000 feet in the summer or in Joshua Tree in the winter. Both are spectacular sites.

Ready for graduate work? Once you have completed the above, you are ready for the Track-Reading workshop, a one-day class that teaches you foot movement and biomechanics so that you will essentially be reading the animals' mind and actions as you follow the tracks of wild animals. If that is not enough, there is a whole weekend of tracking in Nipomo dunes near Pismo Beach. Here, you will track coyote, bobcat, raccoons, opossums and other small animals.

The school has had about 3000 graduates who have spent serious "dirt time" with Jim. He recommends his class for nature center leaders, biologists, Scout leaders and anyone who wants to understand our world a little better. He offers a quarterly newsletter called *Dirt Time* for $10 a year.

Four Corners School of Outdoor Education

East Route
Monticello, Utah 845535
☎ *(800) 525-4456*
Four Corners provides outdoor skills, natural sciences and land stewardship in the Colorado Plateau. The activities include rafting, jeeping, hiking and backpacking. Costs are between $375 to $2495, with courses given between February and November.

The Hardt School of Wilderness Living and Survival

Post Office Box 231-A
Salisbury Vermont 05769
Ron Hardt and those rugged Vermonters must specialize in the lighter side of survival. Here you can spend six days doing all the things the Indians did without being banished to the wilder

ness to prove your self-sufficiency. Better yet, you can look forward to a cozy cabin and three robust meals a day, while you learn how to skin rabbits and make tepees. The summertime classes cost $525, with a weekend program for about $200.

International Journeys Inc.

☎ *(800) 622-6525*
Travel up the Amazon on a research vessel ($1695 from Miami); extensions to Macchu Pichu and Cuzco are available.

Outward Bound

384 Field Point Road
Greenwich, Connecticut 06830
☎ *(800) 243-8520, (203) 661-0797*
Colorado School: ☎ *(800) 477-2627*
Pacific Crest School: ☎ *(800) 547-3312*
Do you want to develop that calm, steely-eyed approach, that strong warmth that exudes from those '40s male movie stars with an unshakable faith in your abilities and courage? All right, how about just being able to sleep without your Mickey Mouse nightlight on? Outward Bound starts with the mind, and the body follows. The program has been used with the handicapped, the criminal and the infirm, and it creates magical transformations in all. What is the secret? Well, like the tiny train that said, "I think I can, I think I can," OB teaches you to motivate yourself, trust your companions and step past your self-imposed limits. What emerges is self-confidence and a greater understanding of your fellow man.

The idea for the school was developed in 1941. Today, there are 31 Outward Bound schools around the world, with seven in North America: Colorado, Maine, New York, North Carolina, Oregon, Minnesota and Toronto. The instructors are not strutting, barking ex-marines but warm, caring individuals who hold safety and understanding above pushing limits. So now that you're sold, what actually happens to effect this magical change in people? Well, first you must put aside about two grand for the two-day-long programs; shorter programs cost about half that.

You can choose from hiking, rafting, winter camping, climbing, trekking, canoeing and ski mountaineering. Each program is broken into four phases (I sense a heroic structure through these schools.) First, students are instructed in the sport-specific skills they need. Phase two is the journey. Small groups of eight to 12 people tackle a specific journey via their chosen mode of travel. Phase three is the Challenge, where students now must go into the wilderness (their instructors check in on them daily) and be self-sufficient, meditate and reflect on their general state of affairs (40 days and 40 nights is probably too extreme, so the usual length of time is one to three days). Phase four lets the students break into smaller groups without the benefit of instructors and complete their own mini-expedition. At the end of the course, the students are reunited and they participate in one last activity. Whew! After all that, most students rave about the change in their self-confidence, their lust for life and their re-centering (a California word that means they are on the right track).

If you find this process stimulating and rewarding, Outward Bound has leadership courses to prepare you for positions as a guide or just to help you teach other people to expand their self-confidence and awareness.

Outward Bound has expanded to include executive training courses, but the results are not as glorious as anticipated. In one recent session, instructors in England divided executives into two groups and told them to rescue two injured people on the side of a mountain. One group then proceeded to steal the other's stretcher, brought their "victim" to safety, then stood and cheered while the other victim lay stranded on the mountain. Oh, well. Maybe learning to survive the urban jungle makes men tougher than we thought.

John Ridgeway Adventure School

Ardmore, Rhiconich
By Lairg, Sutherland, Scotland IV27 4RB

☎ [44] (97) 182-229
The Ridgeway School is an established (since 1969) place for young people to learn outdoor skills. For those young people jaded by the choices offered by the Wild West, John Ridgeway can put them on a 57-foot sailing ketch, teach them how to sail a dinghy and provide a different angle on survival training, backpacking, canoeing, rock-climbing and interpersonal skills. Open to 12- to 15-year olds and 15- to 18-year olds, these two-week summer courses run about $800. An interesting alternative if you are spending the summer in Europe and are looking for something to occupy the teens.

U.S. Space Camp

Huntsville, Alabama
☎ *(800) 63-SPACE*
All right, this one is not quite a life-and-death experience, but for the young it is a great way to understand why astronauts need the right stuff. It might be the beginning of a life of adventure for the next generation.

This commercial enterprise (no pun intended) strives to deliver a youthful replica of the space program and will really turn on science geeks and flight nuts. During the weeklong experience students will perform water survival training, and eventually earn Space Academy wings.

If you can cough up an additional $75 or $225, trainees can either fly as an observer, or get behind the controls of a *Tampico Club* training aircraft when instructors from the University of North Dakota's aerospace department fly Space Academy and Aviation Challenge trainees in single-engine planes.

More than 183,000 trainees have graduated from U.S. Space Camp programs in Alabama and Florida in the past 12 years, more than enough to supply the next few generation of astronauts. Campuses also are located in Japan and Belgium, with Space Camp Canada scheduled to open soon.

Survival Training

Boulder Outdoor Survival School

Post Office Box 3226
Flagstaff, Arizona 86003
Summer: ☎ *(801) 335-7404*
Winter: ☎ *(208) 356-7446*
If you want to live like a native (no, they do not offer casino management courses), check out the BOSS progam. The big one is the 27-day course in Utah, where you will go through four phases. For openers, you will spend five days traveling without food or water. The second phase is 12 days, with the group learning and practicing your survival skills. The third phase has you spending three to four days on a solo survival quest with minimal tools (no credit cards or Walkmans), living off the land until you finally make the grade by spending five days in the wild traveling a substantial distance. Graduation ceremonies are somewhat informal and muddy. For this, you pay about $1300. Naturally, food, accommodations and

transportation are not included. One added benefit is that most participants lose about 5 to 8 percent of their body weight after taking the month long course.

For those who don't have a month to spend on a forced weight-loss system, or can't miss reruns of "McGyver," there are one- to three-week courses that range from basic earth skills and aboriginal knowledge for $550, to winter survival courses that include making snowshoes, mushing dog sleds and cold weather first aid for $565. The one that appeals to me is the seven-day desert and marine (as in water) survival course held in the Kino bay area of Sonora, Mexico. This course teaches you how to find your food underwater and on land, finding water, what there is to eat in arid lands and general desert survival knowledge. BOSS is consistently held above the others as the toughest and most rewarding survival school.

Green Mountain Wilderness Survival School

Post Office Box 125
Waitsfield, Vermont 05673
☎ *(802) 496-5300*
Green Mountain offers a softer and lower-cost approach than BOSS to survival training, and, in the process, the owner, Mike Casper, has more takers. He runs 10-day courses in the summer in Vermont State Parks and wilderness areas. Students will learn how to gather food via tracking, trapping, hunting or fishing. Edible plant identification, cooking without the aid of pots or pans and finding and purifying water round out the culinary aspect of this $950 course. You don't need to be Hawkeye to join, and you might actually have some fun.

International Adventure

7 Melbourne Street
Royston, Hertfordshire, England SG8 7BP
☎ *[44] (763) 242-867*
This British school will send you off to train under Preben Mortensen, a survival instructor who also provides military survival training to the armed forces. The course is held in the Varmland area of Southern Sweden during the winter and the summer. There is little Indian lore or men barking at the moon—just how to stay alive in wilderness conditions. Expect to pay about a grand for 10 days.

Scotti School of Defensive Driving

10 High Street
Suite 15
Medford Massachusetts 02155
☎ *(617) 395-0046, FAX: (617) 391-8252*
http://www.ssdd.com
For two decades this school has been teaching evasive and survival driving to personnel in 600 corporations in 28 companies.

Executive Security International

0234 Seneca Drive
Silt, Colorado 81652
☎ *(800) 874-0888*
http://www.esi-lifeforce.com
Training school (est 1980) for body guarding, self defence, marine security and driving skills.

S.O.S Temps

Eastern Michigan University
122 Sill Hall
Ypsilanti, MIchigan 48197
☎ *(313) 487-1161, FAX: (313) 487-8755*
Richard Marcinko's version of a temp agency. Medical, edged weapons, SWAT, maritime assault special weapons and other courses are taught in conjunction with EMU.

Explo-Tec, Inc.

P.O. Box 1687
Eglin AFB, Florida 32542
☎ *(800) 535-6428, FAX: (904) 678-3515*
e-mail: explotec@counterrorism.com
Four day mine awareness and explosive handling courses start at $825.

ETI Wilderness Survival Training Program

Enviro-Tech International
P.O. Box 2135
Montrose,Colorado 81402
☎ *(970) 249-7590*
www.montrose.net/eti/surv.htm
Courses in Arctic, desert and plain old survival.

Hisradut

www. hisradut.com
Courses in unarmed self defense, shooting, adventure racing and home defense.

RTC Water Survival

www. ntcpao.com/swim

Hoods Woods Survival School

www.av.qnet.com/~diogenes/

Survival Training

www.kiruna.se/turism/doc0060.htm

Voyageurs Survival Training

www.mu.edu/dept/reslife/html/program/voyage/documnts/survival/html

Survival School for Reporters

Most reporters brag about trial by fire or the red badge of courage. The reality is that very, very few war correspondents have any military or survival training. Much like the effect of those Drivers Ed. movies in high school, hours of watching mangled bodies and gimpy people might make them think twice about journalistic heroics.

It is safe to say that the 125 journalists who were killed in 1994 and 1995 didn't deliberately get up in the morning and decide to lay down their lives in hopes of gaining eternal fame. They just screwed up. The wrong place at the wrong time, an over-enthusiastic sniper, a leftover land mine, ricochets, booby traps—you name it.

There is an interesting course designed to at least lower the odds of violent death for journalists. The four-day Battlefield First Aid Training Course run by the British Army has certified more than 500 journalists since 1992. Journalists are taught how to stay alive: avoiding snipers, identifying and understanding mines and booby-traps, and the effects and damage of weapons of various calibers, as well as first aid and basic training rules. Some tips gleaned from the course:

- Learn to estimate the source and direction of shooting.
- Understand the various calibers and weapons used.
- Seek cover and stay low (most people shoot high).
- Stay off rooftops.
- Wear dark colors but do not wear green.
- Do not carry military equipment, including military food rations.
- Stay alert.
- Watch all openings for snipers or combatants.
- When entering buildings, push windows or doors slowly in case of booby traps.

A watered-down version of hand-to-hand combat is taught along with first-aid techniques. The first-aid classes teach more than just how to administer for shock and bleeding as a result of gunshot wounds. The students are shown and then asked to use hypodermic needles on themselves in case they need to inject morphine. To minimize the need for first aid, attendees are educated on the amazing variety and types of land mines and booby traps.

For information on course dates and fees, contact the following:

British Army Medical Services Training Center
☎ *[44] 125-234-0237*

Government Travel Advisory Services

Most governments provide information for travelers in an effort to give a general sense of what dangers or problems exist in certain countries. Advisories are updated sporadically and may be so generic as to be useless. Don't be surprised to find a general disagreement on why and which countries are deemed to be dangerous. The single most useful tool for us are the Country Information Sheets and the Daily Incident Reports supplied by the U.S. State Department. For those who still use the venerated telephone the State Department can be reached at ☎ *(202) 647-5225*, or call from a fax machine phone to get info on ☎ *(202) 647-3000* or use your funky old modem at ☎ *(202) 647-9225*.

Fielding's DangerFinder®

http://www.fieldingtravel.com
The searchable database version of this book. When our own U.S. military calls it "the best source of unclassified intelligence in the world" then maybe it should be your first stop before you head into harm's way. You can also hang out at Fielding's BlackFlag® Café, leave messages or send us questions. If we are in town we try to give a semi intelligent answer. You can also order books using Fielding's Bookfinder®

United States Travel Advisories (Overseas Security Advisory Council)

http://travel.state.gov/osac.html
Provides a searchable database of incident reports (usually criminal and terrorist acts from local news services), crime reports that are written for expats and government workers posted overseas, terrorist profiles that are so old and vague they seem like they are written in the '80s and embassy contact numbers. Some reports are in depth, revealing and helpful most are bureaucratic blather. If

you want the government to come to you send an e-mail to travel-advisories-request☆stolaf.edu and put the word "subscribe" in the message. Then the old State Department server at St. Olaf College in Northfield, Minnesota will send you the latest advisories.

Other government advisory services:

United States Travel Warnings and Consular Information Sheets

http://travel.state.gov/travel_warnings.html

United Kingdom Travel advisories

http://www.fco.gov.uk/reference/travel_advice/frames_index.html

Canadian Government Travel Advisories

http://dfait-naeci.gc.ca/english/mcnu.htm
Pretty much follows the line of U.S. and U.K. advisories.

Australia Travel Advisories

http://www.dfat.gov.au/consular/advice/advices_mnu.html
It's strange how the former colonies can't agree on what is dangerous.

Nongovernmental Information

Committe to Protect Journalists

http://www.cpj.org/
330 Seventh Avenue
New York, New York 10001
☎ *(212) 465-1004, FAX: (212) 465-9568*
e-mail: info@cpj.org
Not an advisory organization per se, but a good place to check out the political climate. A nonpartisan, nonprofit organization founded in 1981 to monitor and protest abuses against working journalists and their news organizations, regardless of their ideology or nationality. Excellent site of interest to travelers.

Amnesty International

http://www.io.org/amnesty/
Information on human rights and what you can do to defend other people's rights.

ArabNet

http://www.arab.net/welcome.html
Saudi Research and Marketing Group
PO Box 17507
Jeddah 21494
Saudi Arabia
☎ *[966] (2) 642-0647, FAX: [966] (2) 642-9809*
e-mail: sprc1@srpc.geis.com
Almost 2000 pages of content and links. An excellent online resource for 22 countries in the Middle East and North Africa.

Stockholm International Peace Research Institute

http://www.sipri.se/
Frösunda
S-169 70 Solna, Sweden
☎ *[46] (8) 655 97 00, FAX: [46] (8) 655 97 33*
e-mail: sipri@sipri.se
Background on global conflict

The Center for African Studies

http://wsi.cso.uiuc.edu/CAS/
University of Illinois at Urbana-Champaign
210 International Studies Building
910 South Fifth Street
Champaign, IL 61820
☎ *(217) 333-6335, FAX: (217) 244-2429*
e-mail: akagan@uiuc.edu.
Background on African countries

NATO Handbook

gopher://marvin.stc.nato.int/11/nato-data/HANDBOOK

Lonely Planet

http://www.lonelyplanet.com.au/
Good country background excerpted from their major guides

City.Net by Excite

http://www.city.net/
A link resource for international professionals and other frequent travelers with links to Fielding's DangerFinder®, government agencies and information sources specific to each country.

CIA World Factbook

http://www.odci.gov/cia/publications/nsolo/wfb-all.htm
Rather dry statistical information on every country in the world updated annually. Don't bother using it to get info on fourth world countries because the information is ancient or missing.

Foreign Services Posts

http://www.state.gov/www/about_state/contacts/index.html
Contact information on U.S. embassy personnel overseas

International Relations and Security Network

http://www.isn.ethz.ch/

A daily updated electronic clearinghouse for resources in the field of security and defense studies, peace and conflict research, and international relations. Supported by the Swiss Government. Good links to papers, books and information

Center for Security Studies and Conflict Research:
http://www.fsk.ethz.ch/

Swiss Foreign and Security Policy home page
http://www.fsk.ethz.ch/swiss/

ENCOP - Environment and Conflicts Project:
http://www.fsk.ethz.ch/encop/

American Foreign and Security Policy Home Page
http://www.fsk.ethz.ch/usa/usa_hom.htm

Aussenpolitik, German Foreign Affairs Review
http://www.isn.ethz.ch/au_pol/

Bundesinstitut für ostwissenschaftliche und internationale Studien:
http://www.uni-koeln.de/extern/biost/

Danish Institute of International Affairs (DUPI)
http://www.dupi.dk

European Information Network on International Relations and Area Studies (EINIRAS)
http://www.isn.ethz.ch/einiras/

Health

There are hundreds of health related sites. Start with the CDC for information and then link to more specialized sites for clinic addresses for prevention and treatment options

Center for Disease Control
http://www.cdc.gov/travel/travel.html

Travel Health Advisories
http://www.leland.standford.edu/~naked/stms.html

The Reference Desk
http://www-sci.lib.uci.edu/HSG/RefHealth.html#INTW

Disabilities Access
http://www.healthworks.co.uk

Good Health Web
http://www.social.com/health/index.html

Mayo Clinic
http://www.mayo.edu

Natural Medicine and Alternative Therapies
http://www.amrta.org/~amrta

Virtual Hospital
http://vh.radiology.uiowa.edu

Air France Travel Health Information
http://www.airfrance.fr/prod/medaf/Medpax.html

Executive Registry
http://www.med.cornell.edu/nyhexr/exr5.html

High Altitude Acclimatization Illnesses
http://www.princeton.edu/~rcurtis/altitude.html

International Travel Medicine Clinic
http://www.hsc.unt.edu/clinics/itmc/travel.htm

International Travel and Health
http://jupiter.who.ch/programmes/emc/yellowbook/yb_home.htm

MCW International Travelers Clinic
http://www.intmed.mcw.edu/travel.html

Travel First Aid Kit
http://regina.ism.ca/trakker/Medical/TravMedK.htm

Travel Health Information
http://www.intmed.mcw.edu/ITC/Health.html

Travel Health Information and Referral Service
http://travelhealth.com/
Information on staying healthy when you travel: general guidelines, by country, by disease. Forum and interesting cases.

Travel Health Online
http://www.tripprep.com/

Traveler's Diarrhea
http://regina.ism.ca/trakker/Medical/TravDiar.htm

Travelers Medical Immunization Services
http://www.tmis.com

Safe Traveler's Online Catalog
http://www.safetravel.com

Emergency/Rescue

If you become seriously ill or injured abroad, a U. S. consular officer can provide assistance in finding medical services and informing your next-of-kin, family or friends. A consular officer can also assist in the transfer of funds from the United States, but payment of hospital and other expenses is your responsibility.

It is wise to learn what medical services your health insurance will cover overseas before you leave on your trip. If you do have applicable insurance, don't forget to carry both your insurance policy identity card as proof of such insurance, and a claim form. Many health insurance companies will pay customary and reasonable hospital costs abroad, but most require a rider for a Medivac flight back to the States. This is usually done via private plane or by removing airline seats. You will be accompanied by a nurse or medical assistant who will also fly back to the country of origin. Medivacs can burn money as fast the *Lear Jet* you charter, so plan on spending a minimum of five grand and up to $30,000. If you are really banged up, you may need more medical technicians, special equipment and a higher level of care during your flight. The Social Security Medicare program does not provide for payment of hospital or medical services outside the U.S.A.

If you're getting toward the back end of your adventuring career, the American Association of Retired Persons (AARP) offers foreign medical care coverage at no extra charge with its Medicare supplement plans. This coverage is restricted to treatments considered eligible under Medicare. In general, it covers 80 percent of the customary and reasonable charges, subject to a $50 deductible for the covered care during the first 60 days. There is a ceiling of $25,000 per trip. This is a reimbursement plan so you must pay the bills first and obtain receipts for submission to the plan. Keep in mind that many insurance policies may not cover you if you were injured in a war zone.

To facilitate identification in case of an accident, complete the information page on the inside of your passport, providing the name, address and telephone number of someone to be contacted in an emergency. The name given should not be the same as your traveling companions, in case the entire party is involved in the same accident. Travelers going abroad with any preexisting medical problems should carry a letter from their attending physician. The letter should describe their condition and cover information on any prescription medications, including the generic name of any prescribed drugs that they need to take.

Any medications being carried overseas should be left in their original containers and be clearly labeled. Travelers should check with the foreign embassy of the country they are visiting to make sure any required medications are not considered to be illegal narcotics.

Access America, Inc.
Post Office Box 90310
Richmond, Virginia 23230
☎ *(800) 284-8300*

Air Ambulance Services:

Air Ambulance Inc.
Hayward, California, ☎ *(800) 982-5806, (510) 786-1592*

Aero Ambulance International
Ft. Lauderdale, Florida, ☎ *(800) 443-8042, (305) 776-6800*

Air Ambulance Network
Miami, Florida, ☎ *(300) 327-1966, (305) 387-1708*

Air-Evac International
8665 Gibbs Drive, Suite 202

San Diego, California 92123
☎ *(800) 854-2569*

Air Medic - Air Ambulance of America
Washington, Pennsylvania, ☎ *(800) 321-4444, (412) 228-8000*

Care Flight - Air Critical Care Intl.
Clearwater, Florida, ☎ *(800) 282-6878, (813) 530-7972*

National Air Ambulance
Ft. Lauderdale, Florida, ☎ *(800) 327-3710, (305) 525-5538*

International Medivac Transport
Phoenix, Arizona, ☎ *(800) 468-1911, (602) 678-4444*

International SOS Assistance
Philadelphia, Pennsylvania, ☎ *(800) 523-8930, (215) 244-1500*

Mercy Medical Airlift

Manassas, Virginia, ☎ *(800) 296-1217, (703) 361-1191*
(Service area: Caribbean and Canada only. If necessary, will meet commercial incoming patients at JFK, Miami and other airports.)

AIRescue

7435 Valjean Avenue
Van Nuys, CA 91406
☎ *(800) 922-4911, (818) 994-0911, FAX: (818) 994-0180*
(This number can be called collect by patients and customers from anywhere in the world.)
AIRescue is a company whose services you hope you never need. AIRescue was started in 1991 by former UCLA MED-STAR physician Francine Vogler, with the primary goal of providing emergency aeromedically trained physician/nurse teams along with chartered aircraft to get your butt back in the U.S.A. Naturally, they assume you're sick and that your insurance company won't faint when they see the bill. The cost for getting you home can run up to $100,000. In some cases, a small commercial jet can be chartered or normal airliners can be used. In the case of using regularly scheduled airlines, you will be dinned for four to 12 seats to accommodate the stretcher, equipment and staff required. The majority of emergency flights are national, but they can come and get you just about anywhere you can call them.

Keep in mind that many insurance policies do not cover repatriation costs, yet the extra coverage is minimal. (Don't tell them you're off to liberate Angola under "Reason for travel.") You can and should buy this coverage if you know you are heading out of town. The older you get and the farther you travel should make the coverage that much more compelling. Don't think the coverage is only for the wild and dangerous. You'll be surprised to see what a rancid taco in Mexico or a burst appendix in Aruba can do to your body.

American Red Cross

National Headquarters
17th and D Street, N.W.
Washington, D.C. 20006
☎ *(202) 737-8300*
For 115 years, whenever there has been a disaster or war, these folks have been on the scene knee-deep in bandages, blood and cots, helping the injured and consoling those who have just lost everything in a disaster. They always have a need for volunteers, particularly people with medical and technical skills. If you can't volunteer your time or skills, blood donors are always needed.

Anca De Jica

Worldwide Operations Manager
International SOS Assistance
15 Rue Lombard,
1205 Geneva, Switzerland
☎ *[22] 347-6161*
FAX: [22] 347-6172

Médecin Sans Frontière

Amsterdam
FAX: [20] 205-170
Equilibre Association L01 1901
France
☎ *[72] (73) 04-14*
This medical-aid assistance organization goes into countries where no one else will dare. They provide essential medical services to war victims and countries in transition for whom medical care would be nonexistent without their services. Emergency kits are provided in large part through donations from large corporations. Doctors and medical technicians are recruited from all over the world.

Medico International

Frankfurt, Germany
☎ *[49] (69) 94-43-80*

Healthcare Abroad

243 Church Street, N.W., Suite 100-D
Vienna, Virginia 22180
☎ *(800) 237-6615, (703) 281-9500*

Political and World Affairs

CIA World Factbook

An accurate if frumpy look at 250-odd countries of the world. Covers government statistics and economics. Order from U.S. Government Information Office.

Superintendent of Documents

P.O. Box 371954
Pittsburgh, Pennsylvania 15250-7954
☎ *(202) 512-1800, FAX: (202) 512-2250*

État des Drogues, Drogue des États

Hachette ISBN 2 01 2/8701 0
A 322-page, annually updated guide to the world of illegal drugs from the Geopolitical Observatory of Drugs in Paris.

This unique guide breaks down the world of illicit drugs into three levels of intensity. It provides a country-by-country analysis of the global drug trade. With 63 sections on individual countries. Identifies "narco states" such as Myanmar, states under the influence like Colombia, and "fragile states" like Italy where corruption as a result of drug trafficking is a problem.

Pinkerton Risk Assessment Services

200 N. Glebe Road, Suite 1011
Arlington, Virginia 22203-3728
☎ *(703) 525-6111, FAX: (703) 525-2454*
Pinkerton provides risk assessments of over 200 countries on-line or in person. Some are in-depth, and some are simply rehashes of outdated State Department info. They offer access to a database of over 55,000 terrorists' actions and daily updated reports on security threats. The non-techie can order printed publications that range from daily risk-assessment briefings to a monthly newsletter. Their services are not cheap, but then again, how much is your life worth? Annual subscription to the on-line service starts at about $7000, and you can order various risk and advisory reports that run from $200–$700 each. Pinkerton's can still get down and dirty with counterterrorism programs, hostage negotiators, crisis management and Travel Security seminars.

The service is designed for companies who send their employees overseas or need to know what is going on. Some reports are mildly macabre, with their annual report-like graphs of maimings, killings, assaults and assassinations. Others are downright enlightening. In any case, Pinkerton does an excellent job of bringing together the world's most unpleasant information and providing it to you in concise, intelligent packages.

Reporters Sans Frontières Annual Report

John Libbey & Co. Ltd.
13 Smiths Yard
Summerley Street
London SW18 4HR
☎ *[44] (181) 947 2777, FAX: [44] (181) 947 2664*
This fact-filled book covers the state of freedom of the press in every country in the world and tells you the scoop on what to expect in the way of murders and disappearances, arrest, imprisonment and torture, threats and harassment, administrative, legal or economic pressure and obstacles to the international free flow of information. It is an exhaustive, informative and obviously self-serving reference book that should be required reading for every traveling journalist.

I.B. Tauris

c/o St. Martins Press
257 Park Avenue South, 18th Floor
New York, New York 10010
☎ *(212) 982-3900, FAX: (212) 777-6359*
I.B. Tauris is an English publisher who specializes in political and nontraditional books on world affairs. Their coverage of the Middle East, Balkan region and the religion of Islam is excellent. Titles like *A Modern History of the Kurds, The Making of the Arab-Israeli Conflict* and *Violence and Diplomacy in Lebanon* are useful reference guides. They also publish books on Yemen, Turkey, Jordan, Algeria, Pakistan, Iran, Syria and Albania. Books on assassins, gypsies, mythology, politics, war and Africa are a great addition to the politically astute reader's library.

Understanding Global Issues

FREEPOST GL496
The Runnings
Cheltenham, England GL51 9BR
☎ *[44] (242) 245252, FAX: [44] (242) 224137*
UGI publishes 10 mini-briefings (18–22 pages) that range from *The Kurds, Caught Between Two Nations* to *The Rubbish Mountain, Tackling Europe's Waste.* The almost monthly mailings are well illustrated, somewhat simplistic

(which, in this case, is good), politically unaligned and an ideal overview of the world's global issues. Although it is published by a German schoolbook company, the teenage-level presentation, complete with charts, graphs, maps and photos, does provide an easy entry point into complex social issues.

An annual subscription (10 issues) is £22.50; back issues are £2.50. You can order your binder for £4.95.

The World Bank

1818 H Street, N.W.
Washington, D.C. 20433
☎ *(202) 473-2941*
The World Bank can provide you with some interesting information on world population projections, saving the rain forest, health care, literacy and general information on global financial topics. Although this agency has been blamed for many of the world's woes by financing large mining, development and dam projects, it would be best to understand why they are so busy developing the

world while some ecologists are busy trying to undevelop it.

The World's Statistics on CD-ROM

DSI Data Service & Information
CD-ROM Department
Post Office Box 1127
D-47476 Rheinberg, Germany
☎ *[49] (28) 43 3220, FAX: [49] (28) 43*
3230
or
American Overseas Book Company
550 Walnut Street
Norwood, New Jersey 07648
☎ *(201) 767-7600*
Number crunchers can pig out with statistics from the United Nations and Europe, even census information from a variety of countries. The information is very expensive but worth it for those who make their living by knowing the right numbers. Relevant titles would be *International Statistical Yearbook* (DM 5000), *World Climate Disc* (DM 2300), *United Nations* (on CD-ROM contains over one million entries for all countries and regions of the world) and the CD *Atlas of France* (DM 2600).

Organizations

Committee To Protect Journalists (CPJ)

333 Seventh Avenue, 12th Floor
New York, New York 10001
☎ *(212) 465-1004*
This group defends the rights of journalists worldwide. Their mission is to promote freedom of the press throughout the world by defending the right of journalists to report the news without fear of reprisal. CPJ's professional staff based in New York City includes an area specialist for each region of the world. These specialists track press conditions through independent research, reports from the field and fact-finding missions. The Committee's activities are directed by a board of prominent U.S. journalists. The committee's activities are funded entirely by donations from journalists, news organizations and foundations. CPJ also publishes a database of local journalist contacts around the world as well as practical safety guides offering advice to journalists on danger-

ous assignments. Membership is $35 per year.

Control Risks Group

8200 Greensboro Drive
Suite 1010
McLean, Virginia 22102
☎ *(703) 893-0083, FAX: (703) 893-8611*
http://www.crg.com

Employment Conditions Abroad

Anchor House, 15 Britten Street
London SW3 3TY
☎ *[44] (71) 351-7151, FAX: [44] (71)*
351-9396

Organization Resources Counselors

Rockefeller Center
1211 Avenue of the Americas
New York, New York 10036
☎ *(212) 719-3400, FAX: (212) 398-1358*

Reporters Sans Frontieres

5 rue Geoffroy-Marie
Paris, France
☎ *[33] 144-838-484*
RSF was founded in 1985 and has offices in Belgium, Canada, France, Germany, Italy, Spain and Switzerland with members in 71 countries. Their job is to defend imprisoned journalists and

press around the world. Their annual report, available for $US20, covers 152 countries and offers tips for journalists working in dangerous countries. They will send protest letters and provide lawyers (if possible) and other forms of assistance to reporters in jail.

Travel Assistance International
1133 15th Street, N.W., Suite 400

Washington, DC 20005
☎ *(800) 821-2828, (202) 331-1609*

Travmed
Post Office Box 10623
Baltimore, Maryland 21285
☎ *(800) 732-5309*

World Care Travel Assistance
1150 South Olive Street, Suite T-2233
Los Angeles, California 90015
☎ *(800) 253-1877*

Security/Hostage Negotiations

Pinkerton Risk Assessment Services
1600 Wilson Boulevard, Suite 901
Arlington, Virginia 22209
☎ *(703) 525-6111*
FAX: (703) 525-2454
Once on the trail of bank robbers in the Wild West, Pinkerton has gone global and high-tech. Today, you can get risk assessments of over 200 countries online or in person. They offer access to a database of over 55,000 terrorists' actions and daily updated reports on security threats. The non-techie can order printed publications that range from daily risk-assessment briefings to a monthly newsletter. Their services are not cheap, but then again, how much is your life worth? Annual subscription to the on-line service starts at about $7000, and you can order various risk and advisory reports that run from $200–$700 each. Pinkerton's can still get down and dirty with counterterrorism programs, hostage negotiators, crisis management and travel security seminars.

The service is designed for companies that send their employees overseas or need to know what is going on. Some reports are mildly macabre, with their annual report–like graphs of maimings, killings assaults and assassinations. Others are downright enlightening. In any case, Pinkerton does an excellent job of bringing together the world's most unpleasant information and providing it to you in concise, intelligent packages.

Kroll Associates
900 Third Avenue, 7th Floor,
New York, New York 10022

☎ *(800) 824-7502, (212) 833-3206,*
FAX: (212) 750-8112
www.krollassociates.com
Kroll has a travel service that provides warnings about crime, medical concerns and even such hazards as missing manhole covers (stolen by the thousands in Beijing to be sold as scrap metal). The reports are compiled from about 270 cities in 89 countries (including the United States). The Travel Watch is produced and distributed by Kroll Associates, a firm offering security and "riskassessment" to corporate clients. The reports fill one 8-by-11-inch page and are delivered to the computers of about 29,000 travel-agency clients of SABRE, one of the industry's principal electronic reservation systems. Within the first two weeks of offering the reports in June, Kroll Travel Watch reported about 10,000 requests. The reports are free through travel agency requests. For more information or a Travel Watch for your destination, contact your travel agent or purchase the reports from Kroll directly.

Political Risk Services
6320 Fly Road
P.O. Box 248
East Syracuse, New York 13057
☎ *(315) 431-0511, FAX: (315) 431-0200*
Providing international, political, economic and business risk assessments, this company offers forecasts for 148 countries. They claim to be politically and economically nonplussed and employ a network of 250 experts on various countries who provide input for the reports. The series of reports are designed to provide many levels of

information, including political stability, investment and trade restrictions, and economic forecasts, and are also available on CD-ROM. A 50-page printed report on one country costs US$325. Two or more reports are $250 each. CD-ROM are available by region for $2000, or you may purchase a CD with condensed reports on hundreds of countries. A monthly 14-page newsletter summary of the latest forecasts is available for $435 per year. A 450-page bound volume, published twice each year, summarizes the current forecasts for 100 countries from all country reports and executive reports. Extensive tables compare and analyze global and regional rankings. Rates are $350 for one volume or $545 for a one-year, two-issue subscription.

Seitlin & Company Insurance

2001 N.W. 107th Avenue, Suite 200
Miami Florida 33172
☎ *(305) 591-0090, FAX: (305) 593-6993*
Providers of insurance for Kidnaping, Recovery and Prevention

Security Paraphernalia

Counter Spy Shop of Mayfair London

360 Madison Avenue, 6th Floor
New York, New York 10022
☎ *(212) 557-3040, FAX: (212) 983-1278*
The ideal upscale store for the paranoid. When we visited their Washington store we were rudely told that they "are not allowed to talk about their new catalog." Oooh. Now that's really secret. Counter Spy sells a variety of gizmos that are supposed to put you back in control of your life. Start by securing your phone lines from tapping, bullet-proofing your car and body from terrorist attacks, and even use a voice stress analyzer to see if your spouse is really working late. Most of the gizmos they sell seem to be designed to be used in domestic quarrels or corporate spooking.

Executive Protection Products Inc.

1325 Imola Avenue West, #504S
Napa, California 94559
☎ *(707) 253-7142, FAX: (707) 253-7149*
Need another source for spy and surveillance gizmos at discount prices? How about a pinhole video camera system for only $2500?

Fuji Safety

P.O. Box 190430
San Francisco, California 94119
☎ *(415) 677-5140*
The place to go for a Fuji escape mask guaranteed to provide helpful protection from smoke and harmful fumes.

International Medcom

7497 Kennedy Road
Sebastopol, California 95472
☎ *(707)823-0336*
The Radalert Nuclear Reaction Monitor contains a beeper that sounds when radiation reaches "alert" level ($290).

Magellan Systems

960 Overland Court
San Dimas, California 91773
☎ *(909) 394-5000*
The Trailblazer Satellite Navigator ($400) picks up signals from 21 satellites. The global positioning system can pinpoint your location anywhere in the world. A mere $8000 will get you a communications system the size of a portable computer that will enable you to send faxes, e-mail or voice messages via Inmarsat-M satellites.

Quark Research Group

537 Third Avenue
New York, New York 10016
☎ *(212) 889-1809*
Budding spies and undercover types will find bulletproof umbrellas ($2500), Kiss of Death lipsticks ($39 and a blade pops up instead of lip color) and other James Bond–inspired paraphernalia here.

Romero Close, CAFOD

Stockwell Road
London, SW9 9TY
☎ *[44] 171-733-900*
Run For Your Life is a board game for those who want to experience the life of a refugee. The object of the game is to get from your village to the refugee camp while dodging obstacles along the way, such as land mines and artillery attacks. Send US$12.50 to the address above or call for more information.

Spy Supply, Inc.

1212 Boylston Street
#120 Chestnut Hill, Massachusetts 02167
☎ *(305) 340-0579, (617) 327-7272*
Specialists in phone systems. They can also program two phones to one number.

Tele-Adapt

☎ *(408) 370-5105, FAX: (408) 370-5110*
UK [44] (0) 81-421-4444
Adaptors for U.S. phone plugs to foreign plugs.

Port Inc.

66 Point Street
Norwalk, Connecticut 06855
☎ *(203) 852-1102, FAX: (203) 866-0221*
http://www.port.com
Port sells handy adaptor kits for modems and telephone adaptors. They also sell a cradle phone modem adaptor for funky countries or old phone booths.

Road Warrior

(800) 274-4277
www.warrior.com
Sells adaptors to link to foreign lines, digital systems and other gizmos for computers users on the road.

Bullet Proof Vests

Federal Body Armor
150 West 30th Street, 9th Floor
New York, New York 10001
☎ *(212) 279-0234, FAX: (212) 279-0237*
In a land where there are over 200 million hand guns, it makes sense that bullet proof vests are a big item. Annual sales in the States are estimated to be around $200 million a year with about $10 million being to civilians. About 64 percent of all law enforcement officers wear bullet-proof vests on the job. Federal Body Armor in New York City sells a bunch of PR grabbing items like bullet-proof bras, jockstraps, mink coats. They say they cater to "executives" but we can't think of too many executives who need bullet-proof jock straps. Although the press likes to goof on this trend, bullet-proof vests are registered and most of the business is with law enforcement, doctors, lawyers and other people who feel the need for protection against robbery or assassination.

Owner Paul Anton told *DP* that his best selling product is the simple concealable vest that goes under a business shirt ($700–$800). He also sells Flak Jackets ($1 400) but mostly to Russia, the Dominican Republic and other bad places. Despite the press hype about bullet-proof mink coats, he only makes the goofy stuff on special order and if he thinks "you are from the streets," you better shop somewhere else. He thinks that the new Goldflex is better than Dupont's Kevlar. He has plenty of vests in stock.

Health and Safety

Adventure Link, Inc.

Post Office Box 510434
Melbourne Beach, Florida 32951
☎ *(407) 724-5368*
Oceanese waterproof reference cards provide medical information on how to treat injuries from marine animals. They also have illustrations of animals for easy identification and avoidance. The information is sparse but could save your life. There is one card for the Atlantic and another for the Pacific; they run $4.95 each.

American Society of Tropical Medicine and Hygiene

6436 31st St. N.W.
Washington, D.C. 20015-2342
☎ *(301) 496-6721*
Ask for *Health Hints for the Tropics.*

Centers for Disease Control and Prevention

1600 Clifton Road, N.E.
Atlanta, Georgia 30333
☎ *(404) 639-3311*
The Centers for Disease Control in Atlanta maintains the international travelers hotline at ☎ *(404) 332-4559.*

Citizens Emergency Center

☎ *(202) 647-5225*
U.S. State Department Consular Information Sheets and Travel Warnings may be heard anytime by dialing the Citizens Emergency Center using a touch tone phone, or by contacting any of the 13 regional passport agencies, field offices

of the U.S. Department of Commerce and U.S. embassies and consulates abroad, or by writing and sending a self-addressed, stamped envelope to the Bureau of Consular Affairs.

The Citizens Emergency Center maintains a travel notice on HIV/AIDS entry requirements. Call to obtain these requirements. A number of countries require foreign visitors to be tested for the AIDS virus as a requirement for entry. This applies mostly to those planning to reside overseas. Before traveling, check the latest entry requirements with the foreign embassy of the country to be visited.

Directory of Medical Specialists

The authoritative reference is published for the American Board of Medical Specialists and its 22 certifying member boards; it contains detailed information on physicians abroad. This publication should be available in your local library. If abroad, a list of hospitals and physicians can be obtained from the nearest American embassy or consulate.

Emergency Medical Payment/ Information Services

Available through American Express:

1) A directory of *U.S. Certified Doctors Abroad* (price: $3.00).

2) A health insurance plan is available through the Firemens Fund Life Insurance Company, *1600 Los Gamos Road, San Raphael, California 94911.* Attention: American Express Card Service.

Health Information for International Travelers

By the Centers for Disease Control;
☎ *(404) 639-3311.*
Publication No. HHS-CDC 90-8280 ($6.00 each) is an annual global rundown of disease and immunization advice and other health guidance, including risks in particular countries; may also be obtained from the Government Printing Office.

IAMAT International Association for Medical Assistance to Travelers

736 Center Street
Lewiston, New York 14092
☎ *(716) 754-4883*
A medical directory, clinical record and a malaria-risk chart are sent without charge; however, a contribution is requested for World Climate Charts.

Immunization Alert

P.O. Box 406
Storrs, Connecticut 06268
☎ *(203) 487-0611*
For $25, a traveler is provided with an up-to-date, detailed and personalized health report on up to six countries to be visited. It will tell you what diseases are prevalent and what precautions are recommended or advisable.

The following are vendors that can supply non-FDA-approved drugs. Remember, it is best to use Federal Express to ship drugs.

Medical Sea Pak Company

1880 Ridge Road East
Suite 4
Rochester, New York 14622
☎ *(800) 832-6054*
Most first-aid kits are great for homes and construction sites, but what about for divers? How about Sea Paks, a selection of four different kits for divers? The largest is the $900, 30-pound Trans Ocean Pak and the smallest is the Day Pak, a seven-pound, 15" x 6" x 3" day pack with instruction booklet.

U.S. Assist

Two Democracy Center, Suite 800
6903 Rockledge Drive
Bethesda, Maryland 20817

☎ *(301) 214-8200, FAX: (301) 214-8205*
Since 1988, U.S. Assist has been the American headquarters of the SFA Group, a world leader in assistance services based in Paris, France. A network of 14 operating centers includes Washington, D.C., Paris, Hong Kong, Mexico City, Buenos Aires, Sao Paulo, Milan, Barcelona, Lisbon, Munich, Cardiff, Brussels, Stockholm and Taipei. The company assists travelers with a variety of medical, financial and legal services. It offers 24-hour service every day of the year and is accessible worldwide. A network of 54,000 agents and correspondents cover more than 210

countries. The multilingual staff speak 40 languages. The company's newest product for travelers is a MedData card, a wallet-sized card with a microfiche of an individual's medical history. It can easily be read with a magnifying glass. Other products available include medical kits, vaccination recommendations, site surveys, predeparture packages and city profiles.

Travel Medicine
351 Pleasant Street, Suite 312
North Hampton, MA 01060
☎ *(800) 872-8633, (413) 584-0381*
An annually updated guide that is much more comprehensive and far more useful than the government info. It is 456 pages, updated annually and costs $25.95. *DP's* favorite pick for health advice.

National Safety Council
Accident Facts
Customer Service
1121 Spring Lake Drive
Itasca, Illinois 60143
☎ *(708) 285-1121*
Every year the National Safety Council adds up all the dead bodies, severed limbs, infections, etc., and puts together a 115-page guide to what's dangerous in America. It is good reading for people who worry about bacon causing cancer or just how dangerous flying is.

Books

There are thousands of books on health safety and travel. Here are a few:

Pocket Doctor by Dr. S. Bezruchka
(Mountaineers)

Passport to World Band Radio
(IBC)

Hosteling International
(IYHF)
Language Schools Athabasca University,
Box 10,000 Athabasca AB T06 Canada

International Health and Travel
(World Health Organization)

Travel by Cargo Ship
(Cadogan)

Ford's Freighter Guide
(Ford's)

Peterson's Learning Adventures
(Peterson's)

Work, Study, Travel Abroad
(St.Martins)

Volunteer Vacations
(Chicago Review Press)

Staying Healthy in Asia etc.
(Moon)

Work Your Way Around the World
(Peterson's)

Do's and Taboo's Around the World by Roger Axtell
(John Wiley)

World Stompers by Brad Olsen
☎ *(415) 552-3628*

Guide to Cheap Airfares by Michael McCall

Courier Flights
The Intrepid Traveler
P.O. Box 438 New York, New York 10034
Guide to courier flights worldwide.

International Travel Health Guide
Travel Medicine Inc.
351 Pleasant Street, Suite 312
Northampton, Massachusetts 01060
☎ *(800) 872-8633*
Annually updated guide to vaccinations and medical health around the world

Specialty Travel Index
305 San Anselmo Ave.
San Anselmo, California 94960
☎ *(415) 459-4900, FAX: (415) 459-4974*
www.spectrav.com
Magazine style directory of adventure and specialty tours.

Insurance

The following companies provide international travel insurance to travelers who live in the U.S. (Because of varying insurance regulations, Canadian policies differ.)

Access America Intl
☎ *(800) 284-8300*

American Express
☎ *(800) 756-2639*

Berkeley Carefree
   ☎ *(800) 323-3149*

CSA
   ☎ *(800) 348-9505*

Global Emergency Medical Services
   ☎ *(800) 249-2533*

Health Care Abroad
   ☎ *(800) 237-6615, (540) 687-3166*

International SOS Assistance
   ☎ *(800) 523-8930*

Travel Guard
   ☎ *(800) 826-1300*

Travel Insurance Service
   ☎ *(800) 937-1387*

The Travelers
   ☎ *(800) 243-3174*

Worldwide Assistance
   ☎ *(800) 821-2828*

The Web

The Web has become the best single place to obtain hard-to-get news and information. You need an account with an Internet provider, like AT&T WorldNet or NetCom, a net browser like Netscape, a fast modem (28,800) and a computer. Cruising the Web is like browsing through the world's largest magazine newsstand except you don't have to pay for most of the info out there. For now there is a wealth of information available to anyone who can stand the phone bill and has the patience to watch funky little graphics download. More importantly, it is the only way you are going to keep up on the local news in Peshawar or Port Moresby on a real time basis and be able to communicate with people around the world.

A few tips from *DP* on using the Web for info.

Believe it or not, I did a stint as a spokesperson for AT&T as their resident expert on how to use the web. Little did I realize that the biggest question most people had was still, "How do I get on the internet?" That's the easy part, just call AT&T, Net-Com, Microsoft, or any one of the dozens of net providers and get a monthly "all you can use account." Usually people use Netscape although Microsoft is slowly gaining ground with Explorer. It really doesn't matter what you use as long as you have the fastest modem you can afford.

- Start with a major web searcher that searches content. We always start with excite (http://www.excite.com) to search for keywords. Try to pick a word or phrase that is unique to the source you are looking for. Just using "travel" or "dangerous" will get you millions of useless web sites.

- Use your bookmark function to build a library of other indexers and esoteric sites.

- Don't be surprised if you get dumped back in the same old web sites. For example just about every web site likes to link you back to the CIA World Factbook.

- Send e-mail and ask. I am surprised how many responses you can get if you ask a succinct answerable question such as "Do you have a list of web sites for Afghanistan?" as opposed to "What is your opinion on the recent tri-party political structure in Kabul?"

- Send good links to your favorite links. This way everyone benefits.

- Remember that the beauty of the web is also its biggest danger. You can say or post anything you want. Also you never know when something was written. Always double check and contact people directly.

What to Pack

You know the drill: Travel light, keep clean, dress casually and buy what you need when you get there. That's why every travel writer then proceeds to give you a list of crap that would give a pachyderm a hernia.

I have traveled with nothing (after all my luggage was stolen) and lots (on assignment, complete with tripod, tape recorders, video cameras and camera), and having nothing is the way to go. Most travelers travel with less and less as they gain experience or as they get mugged and pick-pocketed. You choose: lose it now or later. The only exception would be specialized expeditions, where you are expected to come back with footage or samples of your discoveries. Even if you consider porters for your gear, maintain your credo of traveling light.

This is just a rambling list of tips and ideas. Please don't pack everything we mention.

Luggage

I prefer a frameless backpack and a fanny pack. Avoid outside pockets, or fill them with your dirty laundry. Locks and twist ties from garbage bags are good to slow down thieves. Put everything inside large heavy-duty Ziploc freezer bags, and then put those inside large garbage bags. Bring some spares of both types of bags. Some people like to use thick rubber "rafting" sacks, but in my experience they are useless, being neither waterproof nor durable. Inside my pack, I like to put a small Pelican case with the delicates and expensives. I also carry a second fanny pack for toiletries and personal stuff. I use clear Tupperware containers to store first aid, medicines, and other assorted small objects. Don't scrimp on your pack but remember it will come back foul smelling, ripped and covered in dirt.

Tent

Do you really need a tent? Consider a hammock, a bug net or even a simple plastic tarp. You can substitute a groundsheet with rope for warmer climes or a jungle hammock for swamps. Or you can get extra friendly and crash with the locals. After your first night on the ground in the jungle, you will realize why the apes sleep in the trees. Your first night in the desert will teach you that tents are strictly for yuppies. L.L. Bean, *Freeport, ME 04033*, ☎ *(800) 221-4221*, makes a great jungle hammock (make sure that where you are going there are at least two trees or Land Rovers from which to hang it).

Sleeping Bag

Get a light cotton-lined sleeping bag that has anything but down stuffing. Down does not insulate when wet. Get a sleeping bag, small enough so that it can be washed (it will get funky!).

Toiletry Kit

Combination comb/brush, toothbrush, toothpaste, floss, deodorant, toilet paper, tampons, condoms, small Swiss Army knife with scissors and nail file, shaver, shampoo, liquid soap.

Compass

Even if you don't know how to use a compass, you should have one. If you take along the manual you'll easily learn how to use your compass to tell time, measure maps, navigate by the stars, signal airplanes, and, God forbid, even plot your course if you get lost. The best compasses are made by Silva, *P.O. Box 966, Binghampton, NY 13902, ☎ (607) 779-2200*, and are available at just about any sporting goods store.

Flashlight

There are only two kinds you should consider buying—a small Tekna waterproof flashlight (get a yellow one so that you can find it when you drop it); better yet, get two or three because they make great gifts for your guides. The other kind is a Petzl or REI waterproof head-mounted flashlight. You will use both. Try putting up a tent with a handheld flashlight. Maglites are great but are a bitch to hold on to in the mud. Get lots of AA Duracell batteries.

Mosquito Netting

REI sells a nifty mosquito tent. Mosquitoes like to start feeding as soon as you drift off to sleep, so this light tentlike mesh will keep your head and arms safe. It can also be used to catch fish, strain chunks out of water and strain gasoline. Bring bug repellent with the highest DEET content. Wash it though, because it may cause some nasty rashes if not washed off. In hotel rooms, mosquito coils can make life bearable. They do not scare off large rats.

Clothing

Cotton is about the only fabric worth wearing, and don't get carried away with too many changes. After one week, everything you own will be stinky, damp and wrinkled, so it's best to rotate three shirts, three T-shirts, two pants, one shorts, three socks, three underwear, a hat, poncho, one pair of sneakers, hiking boots and flip-flops. And that's it.

Pants: The plain khaki army fatigues made in Korea are your best bet. You will find them in any surplus or Army Navy store. Cabellas is also an excellent source. Banana Republic used to be the place for adventurers, but the only thing they make that is worthwhile now is their correspondent's vest, which has to be special-ordered.

Light cotton T-shirts: Preferably with the name of where you are from or a *DP* shirt (use as gifts later).

Wool socks: Take three pairs—one to wear, one to wash and another to wear because you forgot to wash the first pair. Do not get the high-tech synthetic socks, just the funky rag type.

Underwear: Loose cotton boxers; get groovy-looking ones so that they can double as swim trunks.

Shirt: long-sleeved cotton, not too butch so you can wear it to dinner.

Poncho: cheap plastic to protect pack and camera gear and to sleep on.

Hat: wide-brimmed canvas hat. Tilleys are the best, but who wants to look like a geriatric on safari? Another choice is to pick up a cheap straw hat when you get there. Natty and disposable.

Hiking boots: Lightweight mesh and canvas or leather, no foam padding if possible.

Sneakers: I use Chuck Taylor's Converse in beige. Get 'em one size larger 'cause your feet will swell up. The world's greatest (and cheapest) jungle boots.

Cooking

I bring a standard stainless-steel cooking set that doubles as an eating set: a knife, fork and spoon with a hole in the handle so that they can be carried on a belt ring. (That way, I am always ready to eat.) Other people just bring the old military mess tin and one spoon. I notice that the more I travel and the friendlier I get, the less I use my own mess kit and end up eating at other people's homes.

If you are on an expedition, you need a cooking stove that burns not just stove fuel but diesel and every grade of automotive gasoline. (You haven't lived until you have tasted a dinner cooked over diesel fuel.) Bring a multifuel stove and a small fuel bottle. They work best with white gas, since car fuels clog up the stove and require frequent cleaning (so bring the kit and a spare O-ring). When it comes to freeze-dried food, don't be swayed by those high-end organic meals. You won't hear many complaints when you serve up those trailer trash cheese-and-potato meals they sell at regular supermarkets (at about a tenth of the price). Remember to bring fruits and treats. I can live off peanut butter, beef jerky and warm beer, but no normal human can live on those low fat, high fiber, monkey shit meals they sell in those yuppie outfitting stores. (By the way, some African termites and caterpillars have between 600 to 700 calories per 100 grams. Insect fatty acids are low in cholesterol. The food value of ants, grubs and caterpillars is about the same as liver or sausage.) Power Bars and freeze dried foods can be life savers but taste like hell and will constipate you rather dramatically. So don't be shy about trying the local tucker.

First Aid Kit

A prescription from your doctor or a letter describing the drugs you are carrying can help. Pack wads of antidiarrheals, electrolyte powder, antibiotics, insect-sting kit, antacids, anti-histamines (for itching and colds), antibiotic ointment, iodine, water purifier, foot powder, antifungal ointment and a syringe or two.Single sides razor blades, a lighter, condoms, rubber gloves, IV drip (needle and bag) and small first aid kid are good to have.

Camera

If you are a total idiot, bring an auto-everything camera and find out when you return how it turns on and what batteries you should have packed. If you are an idiot-in-training, bring a brand-new outfit with too many lenses and never use it. Pros bring two or more bodies, a 300mm 2.8, a zoom to cover the middle and then a 20mm. The new autofocus lenses suck in moisture and dust. Try to stick to the old manual metal mount lenses. I shoot with a Leica range finder and R system. Nikon, Canon and Zeiss systems are just as good.

Video

I love the now discontinued Sony TR-200, Hi-8 system and consider it a must-have on any trip. It's light, tiny (even with all the accessories) and easy to shoot.

Binoculars

Don't bring binoculars. You can always bum somebody else's, unless you are going to Africa or want to avoid gunships—then they are a must. Leica and Zeiss roof prisms are the only ones to consider.

Survival Kit

Survival kits are like an African fetish. We hope that just having these items around means we will never have to use them. Remember to keep this kit separate from your main pack, ideally in a belt mounted bag. Your entire pack should consist of first-aid kit, two space blankets, Bic lighters, Swiss Army knife (get the one with the saw), a whistle, Power Bars (get one of each flavor), string, extra money, your photocopied ID, fishing line with hooks (not too helpful in the desert), candle butts, Stop Trot or any other electrolyte replacement product and headache pills. Also bring a sewing kit, and buy a surgical needle shaped like a fishhook. You will need this to sew up your skin (sterilized with a lighter first) if you suffer a severe gash. Baby wipes are handy for many uses. Hydrogen peroxide is a nasty but useful disinfectant. Reader Trond M. Vågen from Norway also suggests tampons (for wounds), a small magnet (for a makeshift compass with needles or razor-blades), magnesium fire starting kit (hell why not bring C-4 explosives?) and to cap it off, a Lapplander knife. Thanks for the tips, Trond.

You may also want to bring steel wool (it burns as tinder) aluminum foil, plastic bags and a small flare gun.

Water Bottle

Bring a metal water bottle that can double as a spare fuel bottle (use a large silver one for your water and a small red one for fuel). Condoms or rubber gloves can hold water in a pinch.

Essentials

Your passport, airline tickets, money, credit cards, traveler's checks, drivers license, malaria pills, sunscreen, lip salve, spare contacts, glasses, sunglasses. Make two copies of all documents Including credit cards. Leave one at home, take one with you in a place other than the originals.

Letters of Recommendation

If you get in a jam or need special dispensations, it doesn't hurt to have plenty of glowing letters about you on fancy stationery. Lots of official stamps help too. Money is better.

Gifts

Most of the Third World views you as a rich capitalist pig. Because you think you are a *poor* capitalist pig doesn't let you off the hook when it comes to giving gifts. Keep it simple and memorable and have plenty to go around. Mirrors, beads and shiny paper were big in Columbus' time, but you are expected to do better than that today. Here are a few suggestions to make you the hit of the village:

Pens

Call an advertising specialty company to get cheap pens printed with your name and message on them. They will still be as cheap as drugstore Bics and a lot cooler as gifts.

Stickers

Buy a bag of them from party stores; if you can't resist a little self-promotion, have your own stickers printed up on foil and give 'em out to the eager hordes.

Cigarettes

I know it is not cool to smoke, but passing around smokes is a successful way to initiate male-bonding in the rest of the world. In the Muslim world, where men don't drink, they smoke enough to make up for it. Even if you don't smoke, carry a couple of packs of cigarettes as gifts and icebreakers. I know for a fact that peoples' intentions to shoot me have been altered by the speed with which I have offered up the smokes.

Balloons

Kids love the farting sound they make, and they will play with the balloons until they mysteriously pop—at which point, they will head straight back to you asking you to repair it. So carry lots.

Holograms

I carry stacks of cheap hologram stickers. They will amaze, confuse and delight your hosts.

Weird Stuff No Adventurer Should Be Without

Everyone tells you to pack light (including me), so here are all the little items that can make your day or night in the bush:

Travel Clock Calculator

I can never find the kind I like, so I buy them in the duty-free shops. The Sharp EL 470 acts as an international timepiece, alarm clock, calculator, currency converter and business card holder. Some of the new personal assistants put this tiny thing to shame, but think about packing one along.

Adventurer Watch

A number of companies make waterproof watches with all sorts of gee whiz features including alarms, compasses and dual dials for different time zones. Divers will want a watch made for specific underwater depths.

Utility Vest

Not the kind that holds grenades or ammunition clips, but the fishing, cruising or photo vests they sell in various adventure stores. They make great organizers hung over the back of your seat or hanging in the tent. Don't wear the damn thing; you might be mistaken for a tourist.

Books

Buy them by thickness. My faves are *Information Please Almanac*, the *Book of Lists*, Penguin compendiums of classic stories and fat chunky adventure novels like *Three Musketeers* or *Les Miserables*. The Bible or the Koran will do in a pinch, and I have been known to write a book out of boredom. Trade 'em or give them away as gifts along the way. We hope the first thing you pack is a Fielding guidebook. Also think about phrase books, survival manuals, and even poetry if you know all is lost. Address books are useful too.

Maps

Good maps are very difficult to get in Third World countries. Especially in war zones. Spraying them with a spray fixative available at any art store will help to waterproof them.

Business or Calling Cards

If you are the sociable type, have a bunch of cheap cards with plasticized ink made up (be sure moisture doesn't make the ink run). Look in the phone book for a translator if you would like them in two languages. Leave enough room for your new friends to write their name and address on them. Make sure you also bring plenty of extra passport photos.

Shortwave Radio

Now that Sony makes those teensy-weensy shortwave receivers, you need never spend a 10-hour bus ride without entertainment.

A Notebook and Pens

For the nontechnical, a notebook is an indispensable part of the travel experience. You will have plenty of time to wax poetic and capture your thoughts.

Caribiners

Use them to snap your pack to a bus rail or bike frame, hold items on your belt, hang things from trees, rescue people and use as a belt when you lose weight.

Yellow and Black Danger Zone Tape

I use the heavy striped tape to mark my luggage, tape rips, pack boxes and even fix my runners.

Syringes

Just visit a Third World hospital.

Razor Blades

Boils, slivers, infected cuts—all may require a little field surgery.

Hydrogen Peroxide

Cleans out cuts, hurts like hell, stops major infections.

Ziploc Freezer Bags

Organizes, holds anything, waterproofs everything from passports to cameras. Use it for everything but food. The plastic transmits an icky plastic taste to food when kept in hot climates.

Trash Bags

Heavy-duty garbage bags make great waterproofers. They also double as ponchos, groundcovers, umbrellas, water catchers, spare windows, sails and even garbage bags.

Tupperware

It organizes and waterproofs, and you can eat out of it and give it away as gifts. Get the clear stuff and size it to the pockets or corners in your luggage.

Bubblegum

Get the kind that Amerol makes in the tape form. It's sold in a plastic snuff tin. Get the dayglo pink stuff; it drives the natives crazy to watch you blow those bubbles.

Empty Film Cannisters

The clear kind that Fuji film comes in. Take the top off, squeeze them and they act like suction cups. Squeeze them with the tops and they are like tiny popguns. You can amuse the little ones for hours.

Polaroid Camera

I could create peace in the world and brotherly love if I just had enough Polaroid film to take pictures of every headhunter, mercenary, tribal warrior, soldier and politician. They love it, and smiles break out all around. Think about it: How many times does somebody take your picture where you work and actually give you a copy?

If any of our rabid readers have more gizmos or tips send them in or fax them ☎ *(310) 376-8064* or email fielding@fieldingtravel.com.

Those Hard to Find Items

Camouflage Passports

International Company Services
1591 East Atlantic Avenue, Suite 200
Pompano Beach, Florida
☎ *(954) 943-1498, FAX (954) 943-1499*

Scope International
P.O. Box 2286 Forestside House
Rowlands Castle, Hants, P09 6EE
☎ *(01705) 631-751, FAX: (01705) 631-322*

A phone passport, ID cards, and drivers licenses that look real but aren't. The passports are for defunct countries like British Honduras, Rhodesia and other former Brit colonies. Let's hope those terrorists aren't up on their geography. For those that know that real terrorist studied geography and history you can also buy citizenship (and get a bona fide passport) from Grenada, Dominica,

Antigua and Barbuda for as little as $13,000. Remember that a U.S. citizen cannot "swear loyalty to any other prince or potentate" other than Uncle Sam. So you could be breaking the law even though it is a fairly common occurrence for immigrants to keep their old passports going.

Pith Helmet

Brigade Quartermaster
☎ *(800) 338-4327, (770) 428-1248*
www.actiongear.com
For those colonial daydreamers you can get a pith helmet (made with cork instead of tree pith) for $79.99.

Camelbak

☎ *(800) 767-8725*
www.camelbak.com

Carry up to 100 ounces of water for bikers, desert hikers and fish.

Suunto Compasses

Carlsbad, California 92009
☎ *(800) 543-9124*
www.bpbasecamp.com/encly/
map_compass/
Compass manufacturer.

Silva

Egham Surrey
TW20 8SA
☎ *(01874) 471721, FAX: (01784)*
471097
Suppliers of altimeters, compasses and GPS equipment.

GPS Equipment

Positioning Resources
☎ *[44] (01224) 581-502, FAX: [44]*
(01224) 574-354
email sales@posres.com
Supplier of GPS equipment and satellite phones.

Snowsled

Market Place Mews
off The Green
Tetbury, Gloucestershire GL8 8DN
☎ *[44] (01666) 504-002, FAX: [44]*
(01666) 502-731
English suppliers and custom manufacturers of equipment for Polar expeditions.

MSR

Miniature stoves that burn on all types of fuel.

Leatherman

P.O. Box 20595 Portland Oregon 97294
☎ *(800) 762-3611*
www.leatherman.com
Pocket sized American made tool kit that is slowly replacing the Swiss Army knife for ruggedness and usefulness.

Katadyn

3019 North
Scottsdale, Arizona 85251
☎ *(800) 950-0808*
www.sportsite.com/katadyn
Water purifiers that use ceramic filters to remove bacteria like e. Coli. giardia and other water borne bugs.

MPS

1441 West John Street
Matthews, North Carolina 28106
☎ *(704) 847-8793, FAX (704) 847-4447*
Suppliers of bulletproof vests

Nomad Travellers Store and Medical Center

3-4 Wellington Terrace
Turnpike Lane
London N8
☎ *(0181) 889-7014*
Suppliers of equipment and supplies for travelers.

Mantec Services

Unit 1
The Green
Hartshill
nr Nuneaton
Warwicks, CV10 0FW
☎ */FAX: [44] (1203) 395368*
Manufacturers and suppliers of four wheel drive equipment. Also provide training, advice for expeditions and vehicle purchase advice.

Adventure Equipment Suppliers

Brigade Quartermaster

☎ *(800) 338-4327, (770) 428-1248*
www.actiongear.com
Lots of military surplus, hunting and camping gizmos.

WHAT TO PACK

INDEX